S.R.O.

S.R.O.

THE MOST SUCCESSFUL PLAYS IN THE HISTORY OF THE AMERICAN STAGE

COMPILED BY BENNETT CERF

and

VAN H. CARTMELL

Introduction by John Chapman

Garden City Publishing Co., Inc.

GARDEN CITY, NEW YORK

GARDEN CITY PUBLISHING CO. Reprint Edition 1946, by special arrangement with DOUBLEDAY & COMPANY, INC.

PRINTED IN THE UNITED STATES
AT
THE COUNTRY LIFE PRESS, GARDEN CITY, N. Y.

ACKNOWLEDGMENTS

FOR PERMISSION to include the following plays, acknowledgment is here made to the authors of the plays and the publishers under whose imprint they were originally issued:

Uncle Tom's Cabin: A Dramatic Version, by A. E. Thomas, reprinted by permission of D. Appleton-Century Company, Inc.

The Old Homestead, by Denman Thompson, and *Rip Van Winkle,* as played by Joseph Jefferson, reprinted by permission of Walter H. Baker Company.

The Two Orphans, by Adolphe d'Ennery and Eugene Cormon, reprinted by permission of Dramatists Play Service, Inc.

Tobacco Road, by Erskine Caldwell, reprinted by permission of Duell, Sloan & Pearce, Inc.

The Bat, by Mary Roberts Rinehart and Avery Hopwood, reprinted by permis sion of Farrar & Rinehart, Inc.

Abie's Irish Rose, by Anne Nichols, *Peg O' My Heart,* by J. Hartley Manners, and *Lightnin',* by Winchell Smith and Frank Bacon, reprinted by permission of Samuel French.

Life with Father, reprinted from Clarence Day's *Life with Father,* made into a play by Howard Lindsay and Russel Crouse, by permission of and special arrangement with Alfred A. Knopf, Inc., authorized publishers.

Arsenic and Old Lace, by Joseph Kesselring, copyright, 1941, by Random House, Inc. Copyright, 1941, in Canada by Random House, Inc.; and *Oklahoma,* by Richard Rodgers and Oscar Hammerstein II, copyright, 1944, by Oscar Hammerstein II. Reprinted by permission of Random House, Inc.

The Man from Home, by Booth Tarkington and Harry Leon Wilson, reprinted by permission of Booth Tarkington and the Estate of Harry Leon Wilson.

ACKNOWLEDGMENTS

The [illegible] wishes to acknowledge the following plays appearing in this book with thanks to the authors of the plays and the publishers (and others) whose reprint permission is specially noted:

Hazel Kirke [illegible], reprinted by permission of D. Appleton-Century Company, Inc.

The Old Homestead, by Denman Thompson and George W. Ryer, [illegible] reprinted by permission of Walter H. Baker Company.

[illegible], by [illegible], reprinted by permission of Dramatists Play Service, Inc.

[illegible], reprinted by permission of [illegible].

[illegible], reprinted by permission of [illegible].

[illegible], by [illegible] and [illegible], reprinted by permission of [illegible].

Life with Father, reproduced from Clarence Day's Life with Father made into a play by Howard Lindsay and Russel Crouse, by permission of and special arrangement with Alfred A. Knopf, Inc., authorized publishers.

Arsenic and Old Lace, by Joseph Kesselring, copyright 1941 by Random House, Inc. Copyright 1941, [illegible] and Oklahoma! by Richard Rodgers and Oscar Hammerstein II, copyright [illegible] by [illegible] Oscar Hammerstein II. Reprinted by permission of Random House.

The Man from Home, by Booth Tarkington and Harry Leon Wilson, reprinted by permission of Booth Tarkington and the Estate of Harry Leon Wilson.

FOREWORD

THERE have been many drama anthologies before this one, but all of them consisted of plays the editors believed people *ought* to like. This one includes the plays people really *did* like. They are the "golden fourteen" that have rung up the biggest grosses at the country's box offices, and as that great philosopher, Lee Shubert, once remarked, "The box office never lies."

It is fashionable to poke fun at the public taste, and to hold that no really good play can be a financial success. The record, spread out on the following pages, does not wholly support such a theory. True, there's nothing here by Eugene O'Neill, or Clifford Odets, or the self-confessed genius Saroyan, but, on the other hand, the smash hits of the last decade at least represent sound dramaturgy and good taste. *Life with Father* is a first-rate comedy by any standard, and priceless Americana as well. *Oklahoma* is as delightful a musical play as has ever reached the boards. For every *Abie's Irish Rose* that hits the jackpot, a dozen really fine plays ring almost as lusty a tune on the box-office cash registers.

The editors will leave to John Chapman, erudite pundit of the New York *News,* the privilege of holding forth on the individual merits of the fourteen plays in the collection. This time it was the American public, and not the editors, who made the selection, so for once we cannot be blamed for it. The variety of the plays proves anew that there is no sure-fire formula for success in the theater. The pendulum of public favor seems in general to have swung from lurid melodrama to folklore and comedy, but for every play in the magic circle there were a hundred cut in the same pattern that lacked the certain something that spelled nationwide success. It is not always possible to detect just what that something is. *Abie's Irish Rose* and *Tobacco Road,* for instance, were marked down as unqualified failures the day after they opened by every important drama critic in New York.

This is the fifth drama anthology in a series that already includes the best American, English, and European plays, and a collection of thirty one-act pieces. Obviously, it was easier to compile than its predecessors: we went by the records. Our task was confined to securing the necessary texts and permissions (for which many thanks) and contributing a foreword and biographical notes. Some of the old scripts were harder to come by than we had anticipated. One play, *Way Down East,* which certainly merited inclusion, we were forced by legal complications to omit.

Although a few of the early plays are not too easy reading today they will have a nostalgic appeal to many, and, on the whole, we believe you will find the reading of these super-successes amusing, instructive, and, in many instances, thoroughly engrossing. Remember that for one reason or another they won the hearts of millions from one end of the country to the other. They have been played in perfectly equipped city theaters, in YMCA auditoriums, in country barns. They have been acted by brilliant stars and fourth-rate hams. Regardless of the circumstances and surroundings, these are the plays above all others that lured the crowds and caused deliriously happy managers to dust off that magic sign, "STANDING ROOM ONLY."

A few years ago Max Gordon produced a film version of *Abraham Lincoln,* and took the first print to the White House at the express request of President Roosevelt. At the conclusion of the picture, the President was enthusiastic. "It's a splendid job," he exclaimed. "Dignified, authentic, and restrained. Everybody concerned in its making has good cause to be proud."

"That's all very well, Mr. President," said the practical Mr. Gordon, "but you haven't answered the really important question. *Will it make a quarter?"* The fourteen plays that follow made a quarter, all right—a quarter of a billion. Exactly why they did is beside the point. That the success of a few of them is, at the first reading, incomprehensible, should make a study of their technique and subject matter all the more rewarding. That the final three are, from any viewpoint, the soundest and most thoroughly representative of their type, is an encouraging augury to lovers of the theater. American playwrights and American audiences can face the future with high hopes and light hearts.

BENNETT CERF AND VAN CARTMELL

New York, June 1944.

CONTENTS

INTRODUCTION

By John Chapman

From this compendium of fourteen most successful plays in the history of the American theater one can evolve no formula for success. Hokum, tears, social significance, worm-turning, shudders, corny gags, extravagant humor, sticky sweetness, black villainy, accurate observation of the human being, and admirable artistry are to be found here—in one place or another, but never all together. There are "vehicles" which lived as long as their stars did, but no longer; and there are actor-proof plays whose leading roles have been portrayed by many players with equally happy returns at the box office. There is only one certain rule for success in the theater: Give the public what it likes.

I prefer to think that taste has improved; that *Life with Father* and *Oklahoma!* are better works of art than *The Old Homestead* or *Lightnin'*, or even *The Bat* and *Abie's Irish Rose*. This, however, may merely be the self-satisfaction the human being has always had with his own time. There is vigor in each of the fourteen works which follow, and I should like to see thirteen of them played straight any time. The exception, Denman Thompson's *The Old Homestead,* seems now to be such a grab basket of corn that not even an overplayed burlesque of it could be very funny.

Omitted here are the commercial melodramas of the late nineteenth and early twentieth centuries, which, according to Garrett H. Leverton, came closer to reaching a universal audience than any other theater in all history. In a volume edited by Leverton, *The Great Diamond Robbery and Other Plays,* one will find, for instance, Theodore Kremer's *The Fatal Wedding,* which opened in Brooklyn in 1901 and was still a great stock success in 1910. Another is Clarence Bennett's *A Royal Slave,* which was written some time in the eighties and was still being played in 1915.

An insurance man, Colonel Edward M. Alfriend, and a drama critic, A. C. Wheeler (Nym Crinkle of the *World,* the *Sun,* the *Star,* and the *Dramatic Mirror*), wrote *The Great Diamond Robbery* in 1895 and it lasted ten years. Walter Woods's *Billy the Kid* spanned a dozen years, up to World War I. Lillian Mortimer, an actress, wrote a piece for herself called *No Mother to Guide Her,* and it kept her occupied from 1905 to 1913.

These souvenirs of Leverton's were, of course, ten-twent-thirt thrillers and tear-jerkers making little concession to reality. Popular though they were, it can be argued that their success was not so sound, either artistically or financially, as that of the plays here offered. One of them, though, provided the debut of an actress who later made the all-time Hit Parade. In

1903 Charles A. Taylor wrote a wow called *From Rags to Riches,* and in it was one Laurette Cooney. Nine years later this young lady, who had married the playwright and was known as Laurette Taylor, appeared in J. Hartley Manners' *Peg o' My Heart.* Mr. Manners was her second husband.

"Peg" was a sure-fire combination of Irish sentimentality, American democracy, and British snobbery. As in many another play in this volume, a simple soul with a true heart triumphed over such trying obstacles as greed and false superiority. The comedy made its appearance in Los Angeles May 26, 1912, and ran there for 101 performances. Moving to the Cort Theatre in New York the following December, it ran until May 30, 1914, totaling 604 performances. Then followed a year's run in London—for, although Peg made fools of phony aristocrats, she did manage to capture the heart of a fine, upstanding lord who represented all that was good in the true Briton. (The untrue, or silly-ass, character was, incidentally, played by Hassard Short, now noted as the director of such musical extravaganzas as *As Thousands Cheer* and *Carmen Jones.*)

Miss Taylor played *Peg o' My Heart* 1,099 times, but it was not a one-girl show. During the 1914–15 season eight companies were touring in it, and by 1918 it had amassed a record of 5,987 performances.

Despite the fact that this volume contains the most socially significant drama in the nation's history, *Uncle Tom's Cabin,* social significance is not exactly rife within its covers. One will find no Eugene O'Neill, no latter-day Robert E. Sherwood, no Elmer Rice, no Maxwell Anderson. One does, it is true, discover Erskine Caldwell, whose *Tobacco Road* is a document. But the public which has made *Tobacco Road* a phenomenon of the stage does not regard this play as a shocking exposure of life among the lowly in the South, but rather as a roughly funny, satisfactorily dirty comedy which contains one of the fruitiest of all roles.

Joseph Jefferson was a bum in *Rip Van Winkle;* Frank Bacon was a bum in *Lightnin'*—but they were Fauntleroys as compared to Henry Hull, James Barton, or Taylor Holmes in *Tobacco Road.*

When Jack Kirkland's dramatization of Caldwell's novel appeared at the Masque Theatre December 5, 1933, it was looked upon with considerable horror by the critics. Robert Garland said "Life is just a bowl of hookworms marching Sherman-like through Georgia." Brooks Atkinson allowed there were moments, but called the play clumsy and rudderless and shabbily directed. Richard Lockridge labeled it callow and unpleasant, and Burns Mantle declared "It isn't the sort of entertainment folks buy in the theater." John Mason Brown thought the play was as feeble as it was unpleasant, and only the late Percy Hammond saw hope for it. Said Percy, "It is a vividly authentic, minor, and squalid tragedy, lighted in the right spots with glowing and honest humor."

However, the reviewers were in enthusiastic agreement about the performance of Henry Hull as Jeeter Lester. "If I have ever seen a completer impersonation," said Hammond, "I have forgotten it." Mantle called it a perfect study, amazingly detailed, and Atkinson said it was a character portrait as mordant and brilliant as you could imagine.

As so happily often occurs, the critics were wrong. *Tobacco Road* caught on, and Mr. Hull doubtless could be spending the rest of his life being Jeeter, perfectly in the tradition of Joe Jefferson and Denman Thompson.

But in time he wearied of the part and now came the test: Was *Tobacco Road* a one-passenger vehicle, or could someone else climb aboard? James Barton, vaudevillian and song-and-dance man, became Jeeter with such astonishing success that many persons believe that he, and not Henry Hull, created the part. Jim's uncle John took on the part, and still tours in it. Mild and dapper Taylor Holmes even transformed himself into what Percy Hammond called the moth-eaten old jungle Georgian. Jeeter is actor-proof. No bad actor could play him, of course, but apparently any good actor can.

The greatest of all American successes, *Uncle Tom's Cabin,* has been played by so many companies and has had so many versions that its detailed history would make a book the size of this one. The dramatization chosen here is the one which A. E. Thomas made from an earlier one by George L. Aiken, which The Players used for its scintillating revival in 1933, with the late Otis Skinner as Uncle Tom. Thomas eliminated the visit of Ophelia and Topsy to Vermont, and made from a few short moments into a big scene the auction at which Ophelia buys Topsy.

Somebody always was tinkering with *Uncle Tom,* and quite often the adapters forgot to mention the author they were stealing from, Harriet Beecher Stowe, in their programs. The first *Tom* show appeared at the Troy, New York, Museum early in 1853 and ran 100 performances. On July 18, 1853, it was produced at New York's National Theatre with G. C. Germon as Tom, G. C. Howard as St. Claire, Mrs. Howard as Topsy (or Topsey, as it frequently was spelled), the fabulous George L. Fox as Phineas Fletcher, and Cordelia Howard as Eva.

The Evas were usually billed as Little Somebody. The National Theatre production (which played 330 times and was called "a crude and aggravated affair" by the *Herald*) had Little Cordelia. Other Evas were Little Annie Slavin, Little Gracie Wade, Baby Beatrice, and Little Minnie Maddern.

Only a notable basic work such as the Stowe novel could survive the monkey business which was done to it on the stage. There have been *Tom* shows without Evas, without Topsys, without St. Claires (or St. Clairs), without visits to Vermont, without auctions. In 1897 Harkins and Barbour "streamlined" it, omitting bloodhounds, ice, the slave market, and the ascension to heaven on the part of some wire-hung Little Somebody.

In 1863 or 1864 another adaptation of the work of a female novelist appeared upon the stage—*East Lynne,* by Mrs. Henry Wood. This one mixed sex, high fashion, humble worthiness, and quarts of tears, so that it ran practically forever. Lucille Western was its most notable practitioner in this country as Lady Isabel. According to John Parker, British theatrical historian, the first version of *East Lynne* was produced in 1864 under the title of *The Marriage Bells; or The Cottage on the Cliff*. But that was in England, and American historians have Miss Western playing *East Lynne* here in 1863.

The drama, like *Uncle Tom's Cabin,* has had many adapters. But always it has had such vitamin-rich lines as Richard Hare's "Even now the lynx-eyed officers of the law may be on my track." It has the strength to survive, and wouldn't be bad right now.

Most of us may remember *The Two Orphans* as D. W. Griffith's movie, *Orphans of the Storm,* starring Lillian and Dorothy Gish. It had come to us much earlier than that, by way of Paris and London. Here again was a mixture of high life and low, of virtue and dastardy, of tears without laughter. Adolphe d'Ennery and Eugene Cormon wrote it and it opened at the Porte St. Martin, Paris, in January 1874. Nine months later it hit London, and by the end of the year A. M. Palmer had put it on at his Union Square Theatre, New York, where the initial run was 180 performances.

The star of Palmer's production was Kate Claxton, who played the blind orphan. Ultimately Claxton bought Palmer's interest and played the role of Louise for twenty years.

The Old Homestead, unlike *Tobacco Road* or *Life with Father,* was a one actor job. Denman Thompson wrote it for himself as a short sketch, *Joshua Whitcomb,* and appeared in it at Harry Martin's Varieties, Pittsburgh, in February 1875. *Josh Whitcomb* provided for Thompson from that time until the actor's death in 1911. Three years after the sketch appeared Thompson made it into a full-length play and appeared in it at the New York Lyceum. Eight years later a new version, titled *The Old Homestead,* was devised by Thompson and George W. Ryer and presented in Boston. In 1877 it came to the Fourteenth Street Theatre, New York.

The Old Homestead is as Yankee as a radio philosopher, as full of corn as a hillbilly still. The simple virtues of Josh Whitcomb shine steadily, fancy life in New York is put in its place, songs such as " 'Lawn Tennis,' or other lively selection," are dropped in at will, and the gags are still being used in wireless soap operas. A comedy slavey, Rickety Ann, helps, just as did May Vokes in *The Bat* in practically modern times.

One of the most durable of all characters is Washington Irving's Rip Van Winkle, and right now I should like to see a David O. Selznick film production of the play with W. C. Fields as Rip. I never saw Joe Jefferson in *Rip Van Winkle,* of course, for he died in 1905—a time when I was absorbed in Buster Brown and Tige; but at The Players are some portraits of the actor which are so immensely, humorously alive that I rather wish I'd been born earlier and could have seen the sitter.

Washington Irving's story appeared in 1819. In 1828 an anonymous thief wrote a dramatization of it and Thomas Flynn acted it in Albany, New York, not far from the Troy which later saw the first *Uncle Tom.* In 1829 John Kerr, an English actor, appeared as Rip in Philadelphia, having brought his version from London. The Kerr version is the beginning of Jefferson's, for in 1850 Charles Burke, Jefferson's half brother, revised the Kerr work and played it in Philadelphia. Supporting Burke was Jefferson in the minor role of Seth Slough, the landlord.

Nine years later, in the Pennsylvania Poconos on a holiday, Joseph Jefferson was reading the *Life and Letters of Washington Irving,* and this put him in mind of doing a new *Rip.* First he worked out a costume; then, apparently, he tinkered a bit with the Burke play and took it to Washington, D.C. It was a disappointment, but Jefferson wouldn't give up. In 1865 he commissioned Dion Boucicault to do a carpenter job, and the resultant *Rip Van Winkle*—now the standard—was produced in London in the fall of 1865. *Rip* served Jefferson off and on, but mostly on, until 1904, when he retired to Palm Beach to die in 1905. Six months after his death, Jefferson's son, Thomas, played Rip for two weeks at Wallack's in New York.

The Man from Home, like *Peg, The Old Homestead,* and *Lightnin',* praises the virtues of the simple American. Booth Tarkington and Harry

Leon Wilson wrote it, according to Burns Mantle, for David Warfield, but before it was finished Warfield was lined up for *A Grand Army Man* and George Tyler bought the comedy for William Hodge. It was the jackpot for Hodge, and the play had a career of nearly six years.

Here again we have a piece which puts a "typical" American in foreign surroundings, to the detriment of the foreign surroundings. Daniel Voorhees Pike goes to Sorrento to reclaim his Indiana-born ward, who has become an expatriate, hyphenated her name, and set out to buy herself the usual silly-ass titled Britisher for $750,000.

According to the Burns Mantle-Garrison Sherwood *Best Plays of 1899–1909*, Tarkington now claims that he and Wilson had written their jingo American ironically, and what made the play a hit was the fact that audiences took Pike straight. Says Tarkington: "They burst with loud patriotic applause when he said, 'I wouldn't trade our State Insane Asylum for the worst ruined ruin in Europe.' "

Well, perhaps I am dumb, but a reading of the comedy forces me to take Pike straight too. I can detect practically no irony in it; certainly not the kind of irony which George Kaufman, Marc Connelly, Ring Lardner, and others were to write later, in which you laughed at a character instead of with him. Perhaps Tarkington now likes to believe that he and Wilson, inveterate travelers who indulged in practical jokes all over Europe in company with Julian Street, were more sophisticated than they actually were at the time they wrote *The Man from Home.*

Practically everybody was happy when, August 26, 1918, Frank Bacon appeared in *Lightnin',* which Bacon and Winchell Smith had written; for Bacon was an unusually lovable man and people rejoiced in his success of a lifetime. The comedy ran 1,291 performances on Broadway, and endured afterward as long as Bacon did. The actor died in 1922.

Lightnin' Bill Jones, being a shiftless lover of liquor, is not unlike Rip Van Winkle, and one might even say that Bacon's comedy was a modern rewrite of Jefferson's, just as Jefferson's was a rewrite of Kerr's and Burke's. As in so many of our lifetime hits, simple virtue and a true heart win out over greed and deceit. What makes *Lightnin'* hold up so well now is that there is plenty of plot involving several well-drawn characters. The Nevada-California border setting, besides making the play a pleasant Western, minus cowboys, miners, or shooting, is interesting even now for its divorce-plot possibilities.

The comedy shows a trend toward realism—toward making a character an understandable human being and not just a tool in the hands of a story manipulator—which culminates in the completely human classic, *Life with Father.*

Just who is the most successful man on Broadway is something that only the Department of Internal Revenue knows. It might be Lee Shubert. Or George S. Kaufman, a successful playwright and wise investor. Or one of a dozen others. But certainly the most successful team, for the time they have been operating, are Howard Lindsay and Russel Crouse. They wrote one of the hits in this volume, and one of them has been acting in it; and they pro duced another.

Certainly the stage phenomenon of our time is *Life with Father,* which opened November 8, 1939, at the Empire Theatre, and has shown no signs of departing. Each year touring companies take it through the country and it is always welcomed on a return visit. Here, again, is an actor-proof play. When Lindsay and Crouse so lovingly and cleverly adapted it from Clarence Day's superbly funny sketches, they figured on Lindsay and his wife, Dorothy Stickney, playing Father and Mother Day. In it the Lindsays were perfect; yet time has proved the comedy itself is the star and not any one actor. The creators of the main roles have become accustomed, come summer, to drop out of the Broadway cast and allow others to take over, and this has no adverse effect at the box office. Touring companies have had innumerable leading players, and the list of those who have played Father and Mother with great success includes Louis Calhern, Percy Waram, Dorothy Gish, Margalo Gillmore, Nydia Westman and Arthur Margetson.

Such is the fame of the team of Lindsay and Crouse that one sometimes forgets that Joseph Kesselring wrote *Arsenic and Old Lace* and the team merely produced it. *Arsenic* was indeed a phenomenon, for no other piece of nonsense has been so durable. The comedy, about two nice old ladies who love to poison people, opened in New York January 10, 1941, and closed on June 17, 1944. During its 1,440 performances it played to more than $2,000,000, and in that period touring companies garnered almost as much. At the time of writing, the London company was in its eighteenth month and two other troupes were touring the British provinces.

Judging from its first venture, *Oklahoma!* the new team of Oscar Hammerstein, II, and Richard Rodgers may be as successful a combination as Crouse and Lindsay. Any guess as to how long this operetta will last would be futile, for there have been no unsold seats for either the New York or Chicago performances.

Some people say that *Oklahoma!* is the best musical since *Show Boat* (which Hammerstein wrote with Jerome Kern); others come right out and say it is the best musical play of all time. Comparisons are futile, for the moods of the two shows are different; so all one really should say is that each is perfect.

Besides being perfect, *Oklahoma!* is as thoroughly American as a buffalo nickel. Its book, from Lynn Riggs's intelligently American folk play, *Green Grow the Lilacs,* is a work of art, for there is neither too much of it nor too little. The quality of the song numbers, both in lyrics and melody, must now be known to every American over the age of four who can hear, thanks to broadcasting and the phonograph. And the manner in which the song numbers fit into and carry along the plot is an example for all show-makers to follow henceforth.

All the credit for *Oklahoma!* cannot go to Rodgers and Hammerstein, for here is a perfectly blended production. Lemuel Ayres's backgrounds have the simple, spacious feeling of the work of Grant Wood or Thomas Benton, and are completely in the mood of the play. Agnes de Mille's dances are more than merely excellent ballet numbers: like the songs, they advance the plot. Costumes and Rouben Mamoulian's direction contribute just what they should, and the main characters are so vividly and cannily outlined that numberless good actors can play them.

Lee Shubert, an expert in business affairs if there ever was one, once had a guess at the total success of the Theatre Guild's operetta. He told me he thought it would net, counting movie sale, $2,000,000. He may be wrong, for even the producer of *The Voice of the Turtle* has been asking $3,000,000 for his property. But a net of $2,000,000 would be fiscally fabulous—for *Oklahoma!* cost only $80,000.

The power of dramatic critics is always much less than people believe. Critics go crazy about plays and the plays promptly fail; they hate them and the plays ultimately succeed. Not one of the pieces in this volume got unanimous, unreserved praise—not even *Oklahoma!* and *Life with Father.* Most notable of the pieces which survived the critics was Anne Nichols' *Abie's Irish Rose,* which made Miss Nichols something like $3,000,000.

Abie, a corny collection of all the Irish-Jewish and Jewish-Irish gags extant, tried out in Stamford, Connecticut, and came to the Fulton Theatre, New York, May 23, 1922. The critics fell on it with all the dead weight of a yak attacking an opponent, and *Abie* languished for a while. Languished so badly, in fact, that Miss Nichols had to scout around for some new financing to keep it going. She found, possibly among others, one man who had seen the play and loved it; loved it so much that he was willing to gamble $5,000 on its future. He was the late Arnold Rothstein, the gambler, whose colorful rubbing out is still a Sunday-supplement mystery.

Abie's Irish Rose played continuously at New York's Fulton and Republic theatres—having moved from the one to the other—until 1927, totting up 2,532 performances. Meanwhile, many other companies hit the road, and at one time there were seven busy *Abie* troupes. In Erie, Pennsylvania, normally a bad one-night stand, the comedy remained three weeks, with the result that when it hit Chicago it was billed as "The Original Erie, Pennsylvania, Company."

In 1942 the play was revived as a radio serial, and such was its power that the comedy itself was dug out of the corn silo and was quite successful in Detroit, Pittsburgh, and Chicago.

The editors of this volume, ignoring *The Great Diamond Robbery, Rags to Riches,* and other early melodramas, still feel that no such omnibus as this would be complete without an out-and-out chiller. With good reason they have chosen a more modern version of high blood-pressure theater, *The Bat.*

The Bat, written by Mary Roberts Rinehart and Avery Hopwood, was produced August 23, 1920, and ran on Broadway for 867 performances. It also had a substantial career on the road and is still to be found here and there in stock. Involving murders, hidden money, and secret chambers, it also had a perfect comedy maid part, played perfectly in New York by May Vokes. Miss Vokes, in fact, is about all that most of us remember about *The Bat,* for she was indeed a terror-struck wench.

Murder novels set the style for murder plays, and both novels and plays have gone a long way beyond the simple horrors of *The Bat.* Such fiction writers as Dashiell Hammett, S. S. Van Dine, Erle Stanley Gardner, and Raymond Chandler have made the murder-detective yarn a thing of photographic reality. They have turned up their shirt cuffs and have hidden nothing behind sliding panels or revolving bookcases. The result is that the public—although it still goes for the fantastic and unbelievable chills of Hollywood's B thrillers—will devote itself to more reasonable suspense drama. It will now support so clever, so theater-wise an endeavor as Patrick Hamilton's *Angel Street.* Perhaps the editors will put *Angel Street* in their next collection of fifteen hits.

Uncle Tom's Cabin

Revised version by

A. E. THOMAS

Based upon the dramatization by
GEORGE L. AIKEN *of the novel*
by HARRIET BEECHER STOWE

WARNING

This play is for reading purposes only. The fact that you have purchased it does not give you permission to produce it, unless you have received permission to do so from the owner of copyright in the play. Directions are given concerning the names and address of the owner of copyright.

This play is fully protected in all countries by the copyright law, all requirements of which have been complied with. No performance, professional or amateur, no public reading, no radio broadcast, may be given without permission of the publishers, D. Appleton-Century Company, Inc., 35 West 32nd Street, New York City, or D. Appleton-Century Company, Inc., 34 Bedford Street, Covent Garden, London, England.

Performances of this play are subject to royalty. Any one presenting this play without the consent of the owner of the copyright will be liable to the penalties provided by law:

> "Section 4966:—Any person publicly performing or representing any dramatic or musical composition for which copyright has been obtained, without the consent of the proprietor of said dramatic or musical composition, or his heirs and assigns, shall be liable for damages thereof, such damages, in all cases, to be assessed at such sum, not less than one hundred dollars for the first and fifty dollars for every subsequent performance, as to the court shall appear to be just. If the unlawful performance and presentation be willful and for profit, such person or persons shall be imprisoned for a period not exceeding one year."—U.S. Revised Statutes: Title 60, Chap. 3.

THE CAST

As produced by THE PLAYERS *at the Alvin Theatre, New York, May 29, 1933, under the direction of Earle Booth*

Uncle Tom	Otis Skinner
Simon Legree	Thomas Chalmers
George Harris	Pedro de Cordoba
St. Clair	Ernest Glendinning
Marks	John Daly Murphy
Phineas Fletcher	Edward MacNamara
Shelby	Malcolm Duncan
Haley	Lyster Chambers
Tom Loker	John C. King
Waiter	W. B. Taylor
Gumption Cute	Gene Lockhart
Mr. Wilson	George Christie
Harry	Roy Le May
George Shelby, Jr.	George Gaul
Major Mann	Wright Kramer
George Fisk	Frank Wilcox
Adolph	John Knight
Caesar	Burford Hampden
Skeggs, the auctioneer	Harold Gould
First Bidder	Francis H. Day
Second Bidder	Edward T. Emery
Third Bidder	Harold McGee
Clerk	John Kramer
Sambo	Ben Lackland
Quimbo	Harry Gresham
Overseer	Earl Mitchell
Eliza	Elizabeth Risdon
Aunt Chloe	Cecelia Loftus
Marie	Sylvia Field
Eva	Lois Shore
Aunt Ophelia	Minnie Dupree
Topsy	Fay Bainter
Nurse	Eleanor Goodrich
Emmeline	Joanna Roos
Aunt Hagar	Kate Mayhew
Cassy	Mary Nash

LADIES, SLAVES, ETC.: *Alice MacKenzie, Florence Short, Kathleen Lockhart, Essie Emery, Katherine Doyle, Amy Groesbeck, Janice O'Connell, Elizabeth Dewing, Nancy Levering, Mrs. Edward D. Dunn, Patricia O'Connell (Soloist)*

PLANTERS, OVERSEERS, ETC.: *Oswald Hering, Grenville Vernon, Owen Culbertson, George Riddell, Richard Hoffman, Harold Stanton, Edward Delaney Dunn, William Fisher, Oswald Marshall, Russel Crouse*

SINGERS: *James Stanley, Paul Parks, Frederick Jagel, T. H. Montgomery, Joseph Cummings Chase, Harry Gilbert (Leader), Raymond Thayer, Samuel Merwin, John Barnes Wells*

STAGE MANAGER — *Walter F. Scott*

ASSISTANT STAGE MANAGER — *S. Asher Smith*

THE SCENES

ACT ONE

Scene I: Shelby's Dining Room
Scene II: Exterior of Uncle Tom's Cabin
Scene III: The Tavern by the River
Scene IV: The Road to the River
Scene V: Ohio River (Liza Crossing the Ice)
Scene VI: St. Clair's Parlor
Scene VII: St. Clair's Garden
Scene VIII: The Tavern by the River

ACT TWO

Scene I: Eva's Bedroom
Scene II: A Quaker Kitchen in Ohio
Scene III: A Rocky Pass in the Hills
Scene IV: St. Clair's Study
Scene V: St. Clair's Garden
Scene VI: Eva's Bedroom
Scene VII: St. Clair's Parlor
Scene VIII: Slave Market

ACT THREE

Scene I: A Street in New Orleans
Scene II: Legree's Cabin
Scene III: An Old Roofless Shed
Scene IV: Legree's Cabin
Scene V: A Street in New Orleans
Scene VI: An Old Roofless Shed
Scene VII: Apotheosis

UNCLE TOM'S CABIN

ACT ONE

SCENE I

Shelby's dining room. Table and two chairs. One chair to the right of the audience. Bowl of fruit on table, oranges and raisins.

Liza enters and puts tray with decanter and glasses on table. GEORGE HARRIS enters.

ELIZA. Ah! George! (*Goes to him*). I am so glad you've come! What's the matter? (*George regards her mournfully.*) Why don't you smile and ask after little Harry?

GEORGE (*bitterly*). I wish the boy had never been born! I wish I'd never been born myself!

ELIZA (*sinking her head upon his breast and weeping*). Oh, George!

GEORGE. I wish you had never seen me—you, at least, might have been happy!

ELIZA. George! How can you talk so? What dreadful thing has happened? We've always been happy.

GEORGE. So we have, dear. But oh! I wish I'd never seen you, nor you me!

ELIZA. Oh, George! How can you?

GEORGE. Yes, Eliza, it's all misery, misery! The very life is burning out of me! (*Crosses and sinks onto a chair beside table; puts hat on table.*) I shall only drag you down with me! What's the use of our trying to do anything—know anything—be anything? I wish I was dead!

ELIZA. Oh! George, that is wicked! I know how you feel about losing your place in the factory, and you have a hard master—but pray be patient.

GEORGE. Patient! Haven't I been patient? Did I say a word when he came and took me away—for no earthly reason—from the place where everybody was kind to me? I'd paid him every cent of my earnings, and they all say I worked well.

ELIZA. After all, he is your master, you know!

GEORGE. My master! Just because I've a few drops of Negro blood in my veins! And Mr. Shelby, he's *your* master, and for the same reason—no other reason in the world! (*Rises.*) Look at us! Who could tell us from white people! Hear us speak! Who could tell the difference? They sent us to school down there! They gave us education! What for? Just to make us more valuable property!

ELIZA. Darling! (*Follows him.*) You mustn't go on like this—you really——

GEORGE. Who made this man my master? What right has he to make a dray-horse of me?—to take me from things I can do better than he can, and put me to work that any horse can do?

ELIZA. Oh, George, George! You frighten me! Why, I never heard you talk so! I'm afraid you'll do something dreadful. I don't wonder at your feelings; but oh! do be careful —for my sake and Harry's.

GEORGE. I have been careful, and I have been patient, but it's growing worse and worse—he takes every chance he can to insult and torment me. He says I've got the devil in me, and he means to bring it out. And one of these days he will bring it out, in a way that he won't like!

ELIZA. Well, I always thought that I must obey my master and mistress, or I couldn't be a Christian.

GEORGE. There is some sense in it in your case. You've been decently treated, but I have been kicked and cuffed and sworn at, and I've paid for all my keeping a hundred times over; so they have no claim on me. Master will find out that whipping won't tame me.

ELIZA. Oh! George, don't do anything wicked; trust in heaven and try to do right!

GEORGE. I can't trust in heaven! Why does it let these things happen to me?

ELIZA. Oh, George! Mistress says we must all have faith.

GEORGE. That's easy for people like her; but let them be where I am—you don't know what's going to happen to me!

ELIZA (*alarmed*). What do you mean?

GEORGE (ELIZA *backs away in astonishment*). Well, lately my master has been saying that he was a fool to let me marry off the place—and he says he won't let me come here any more, and that I must take a wife and settle down on his place.

ELIZA (*goes to him impulsively*). But you were married to *me* by the minister, as much as if you had been a white man.

GEORGE. Don't you know I can't hold you for my wife if he chooses to part us? That is why I wish I'd never seen you—it would have been better for us both—it would have been better for our poor child, if he had never been born.

ELIZA. But my master is so kind.

GEORGE. Yes, but who knows?—He may die and then Harry may be sold to nobody knows who. (ELIZA *moves away.*) What good is it that he is so handsome and smart? It will make him worth too much for you to keep.

ELIZA. Heaven forbid!

GEORGE (*picks up hat from table*). So, Eliza, I must say good-by now. (*Kisses her.*) For I'm going away!

ELIZA. Where are you going, George?

GEORGE. To Canada; and when I'm there I'll buy you—and the boy.

ELIZA. Oh, George! For my sake, do be careful! But go, if you must, and pray heaven to help you!

GEORGE. Well, then, Eliza, hear my plan. (*Crosses to* ELIZA; *looks off stage.*) I've got some preparations made, and there's them that will help me; and in the course of a few days I shall be among the missing.

ELIZA. But if you should be taken?

GEORGE. I won't be taken, Eliza—I'll *die* first! I'll be free, or I'll die! (*Both exit.* SHELBY *and* HALEY *enter.*)

SHELBY. That is the way I should arrange the matter.

HALEY. I can't trade that way—Mr. Shelby, an' I'm in a hurry!

SHELBY. You must have a drink before you go!

HALEY. Thank you, I will! (*Sits*). (SHELBY *pours drinks.*)

SHELBY. The fact is, Haley, Tom is an uncommon fellow! He is certainly worth that sum anywhere. He's capable, he's honest and runs my plantation like a clock.

HALEY. You mean honest as niggers go! (*Drinks.*)

SHELBY. No; I mean, really. Tom got religion at a camp-meeting, four years ago, and I believe he really *did* get it. I've trusted him since then, with everything I have . . . and I always found him true and square in everything!

HALEY. Some folks don't believe there is pious niggers, Shelby, but I *do.* I had a fellow now, in this yer last lot I took to N'Orleans, 'twas as good as a meetin' now, really, to hear that critter pray; and he was quite gentle and quiet-like. He fetched me a good sum too, for I bought him cheap of a man that was 'bliged to sell out, so I realized six hundred on him. Yes, I consider religion a valeyable thing in a nigger, when it's the genuine article and no mistake.

SHELBY. Well, Tom's got the genuine article, if ever a fellow had. Why, last fall I let him go to Cincinnati alone, to do business for me and bring home five hundred dollars. "Tom," says I to him, "I trust you, because I think you are a Christian —I know you wouldn't cheat." He come back, just as I knew he would. Some fellows said to him, "Tom, why don't you make tracks for Canada?" He said: "I couldn't do that. Master trusted me." I'll be sorry to part with Tom. You ought to let him cover the whole balance of my debt to you and you would, Haley, if you had any conscience.

HALEY. Well, I've got just as much conscience as any man in business can afford to have, just as little, you know, to swear by; and then I'm ready to do anything in reason to 'blige friends, but this yer, you see, is a leetle too hard on a fellow—a leetle too hard! (*Fills glass again.*)

SHELBY. Well, then, Haley, how *will* you trade?

HALEY. Well, ain't you got a boy or a girl that you could throw in with Tom?

SHELBY. Hum! None that I could well spare. To tell the truth, I don't like parting with any of my hands. Nothing but stern necessity would drive me to it. (HARRY *enters.*) Hulloa! Jim Crow. (*Throws a bunch of raisins toward him. He catches them.*) There you are!

HALEY. Hulloa, little 'un! (*Throws an orange, which* HARRY *catches. He sings and dances around the stage.*) Hey, young 'un! (*He stops.*) Tell you what, Shelby! Fling in that chap, and I'll settle the business.

(ELIZA *enters. Starts, on beholding* HALEY, *and gazes fearfully at* HARRY *who runs and clings to her dress, showing the orange, etc.*)

SHELBY. Well, Eliza?

ELIZA. I was just looking for Harry, please, sir!

SHELBY. Well, take him away then!

(ELIZA *grasps the child eagerly in her arms and casting another glance of apprehension at* HALEY, *exits hastily.*)

HALEY (*rises*). By Jupiter! There's an article, now! You might get something handsome for that ar gal in Orleans any day. I've seen over a thousand, in my day, paid down for gals not a bit handsomer.

SHELBY. No, sir, I'd rather not talk about her. Another glass o' wine? (*Fills the glasses.*)

HALEY (*drinks and smacks his lips, sits again by table*). That's good wine. Come, how will you trade about the gal? What shall I say for her? What'll you take?

SHELBY. Mr. Haley, she is not for sale—my wife wouldn't part with her for her weight in gold.

HALEY. Ay! Ay! Women always say such things. Just show 'em how many trunkets a body's weight in gold would buy, and that alters the case, I reckon.

SHELBY. I tell you, Haley, there's no use talking about it—I say no, and I mean no.

HALEY. Well, then, you'll let me have the boy.

SHELBY. What on earth can you want with the child?

HALEY. Why, I've got a friend that's going into this yer branch of the business—wants to buy up likely boys to raise for the market. Well, what do you say?

SHELBY. I'll have to talk with my wife.

HALEY. Oh, certainly, by all means! (*Rises.*) But I'm in a devil of a hurry to get down river and shall want to know as soon as possible what I may depend on. (*Puts on his overcoat, which hangs on a chair, takes hat and whip.*)

SHELBY (*Rises to* HALEY). Well, send round this evening, between six and seven, and you shall have my answer.

HALEY. All right. Take care of yourself. (*They shake hands. Exit* HALEY.)

SHELBY. If anybody had ever told me that I should sell Tom to those rascally traders, I should never have believed it. (*Crosses to table. Puts stopper in decanter.*) And Eliza's child too. But, I'm afraid it must be done!

BLACK-OUT

SCENE II

Exterior of UNCLE TOM'S *cabin. Snow on roof. Practicable door and window. Dark stage. Music.*

Enter ELIZA *hastily with* HARRY *in her arms.* ELIZA *goes to cabin and taps on the window.* AUNT CHLOE *appears at the window.*

CHLOE (*inside*). Good Lawd! What's that? My sakes alive, if it ain't Lizy! (*Enters through the door.*) What you doing here, Lizy? (*Calls to* TOM.) Get on your clothes, ole man, quick! I gwine to open the door!

(*The door opens and* UNCLE TOM *enters in his shirt sleeves holding a tallow candle.*)

TOM (*holding the light toward* ELIZA). Lawdy, Lawdy, what brung you, Lizy? I'm skeered to look at ye, chile, you look just like a ghost. What's come over ye, child?

ELIZA. I'm running away, Uncle Tom, carrying off my child! Master sold him!

TOM AND CHLOE. Sold him!

TOM. What? Sold him? (*Chloe takes hold of* TOM'S *arm.*)

ELIZA. Yes, sold him! I crept into the closet by mistress' door to-night and heard master tell mistress that he had sold my Harry and you, too, Uncle Tom, both to a trader, and that the man was to take possession tomorrow.

CHLOE. The good Lawd have pity on us! What has he done that master should sell *him!*

ELIZA. He hasn't done anything—it isn't for that. Master don't want to sell, and Mistress—she's always good. I heard her plead and beg for us, but he told her 'twas no use—that he was in this man's debt, and he had got the power over him, and that if he did not pay him off clear, it would end in his having to sell the place and all the people and move off.

CHLOE. Well, Tom, why don't you run away, too? Will you wait to be toted down the river, where they kill niggers with hard work and starving? I'd a heap rather die than go there, any day! There's time for ye to be off with Lizy—you've got a pass to come and go any time. Come, bustle up, and I'll get your things together.

TOM. No, sir! No, sir! Not me! You all kin go, Lizy, I'm gwine stay.

CHLOE. Stay? Is you crazy, Tom?

TOM. Mebbe I is. But I'm gwine stay. You hyar what dat gal say? Marse Shelby go to rack an' ruin—ever'body git sold down de ribber if dey don't sell me. Well, sir, I s'pose I can stan' it like ever'body else. I gwine stay.

CHLOE. Tom! ELIZA. Uncle Tom!

TOM. Massa Shelby alluz fin' me when he want me an' he alluz will.

I ain't never broke mah trus' nor use mah pass contrairy to mah word an' I ain't gwine do it now. You all t'ink I can see dis place broke up—ever'-body put in a misery. I jus' gwine alone.

CHLOE. No, you ain't. You cain't.

TOM. Don' you fret now, Chloe. Massa Shelby take keer o' you.

ELIZA (*starts to go, turns*). Then it's good-by, Uncle Tom?

TOM. Ah reckon it is. You jus' trus' de Lawd, Lizy. He's your bes' friend. He ain't never gwine fail you.

ELIZA. For the last time, Uncle Tom—come with me!

TOM. No, no, chile. Time war when I would, but de Lawd's give me a work 'mong mah people. He say to me—"Tom, you 'mong dem people jus' like Moses down in Egypt. You hyer me, Tom?" An' I says: "Yes, Lawd," an' I pass mah word to Him dat I sticks to de end. (ELIZA *moves toward him.*) You all's diffunt, Lizy. Your burden's mighty big. You go while you kin.

ELIZA. I will. Good-by. (*Exit.*)

TOM. Amen! The Lawd stay by ye and save ye from de quicksand.

CHLOE. What goin' to become o' you, ole man?

TOM. Him dat save Daniel in de den o' Lions an' brung de Chillun outer de fiery furnace—Him dat walk on de sea an' tell dem winds dey got to be still—He's alive!

CHLOE. I reckon you're right, ole man!

TOM. You come along, ole woman, you go back to your bed an' tell your troubles to de Lawd. (CHLOE *enters door, then turns.*) He ain't deaf.

CHLOE. No, sir! He hear me sure enough! (*Enters cabin.* TOM *turns, looks off stage.*)

CURTAIN

SCENE III

The tavern by the river. A large window in flat, through which the river is seen filled with floating ice in the moonlight. A table and three chairs are on the stage.

Enter PHINEAS.

PHINEAS. Chaw me up into tobaccy ends! How in the name of all that's onpossible am I to get across that yer pesky river? It's a reg'lar blockade of ice! I promised Ruth to meet her tonight, and she'll be into my har if I don't come! (*Goes to window.*) What in creation's to be done? That thar river looks like a permiscuous ice-cream shop come to an awful state of friz. If I war on the adjacent bank, I wouldn't care a teetotal atom. Rile up, you old varmint, and shake the ice off your back! (*Exit.*)

(*Enter* ELIZA *and* HARRY.)

ELIZA. Thank God—we have reached the river. Let it but roll between us and our pursuers, and we are safe! (PHINEAS *re-enters. Goes to window.*) Gracious! The river is choked with ice!

PHINEAS. Hulloa, gal! What's the matter? You look kind of streaked.

ELIZA. Is there any ferry or boat that takes people over now?

PHINEAS. Well, I guess not; the boats have stopped running.

ELIZA (*in dismay*). Stopped running?

PHINEAS. Maybe you're wanting to get over—anybody sick? Ye seem mighty anxious.

ELIZA. I—I—I've got another child that's very sick over there. I never heard of it till last night, and I've walked quite a distance today in hopes to get to the ferry.

PHINEAS. Well, now, that's onlucky; I'm re'lly consarned for ye. Thar's a man, a piece down here, that's going over with some truck this evening, if he duss to; he'll be in here to supper tonight, so you'd better set down and wait. That's a smart little chap. Say, Young Un, have a chaw tobaccy? (*Takes out a large plug and a bowie-knife.*)

ELIZA. No, no!

PHINEAS. Oh! He don't use it, eh? Hain't come to it yet? Well, I have. (*Cuts off a large piece, and returns the plug and knife to pocket.*) What's the matter with the Young Un? He looks kinda white in the gills!

ELIZA. Poor child! He is not used to walking, and I've hurried him on so.

PHINEAS. Tuckered, eh? Well, there's a little room in there, with a fire in it. Take the babby in there, make yourself comfortable till that thar ferryman shows his countenance—I'll stand the damage.

ELIZA. How shall I thank you for such kindness to a stranger?

PHINEAS. Well, if you don't know how, why, don't try; that's the teetotal. Come, vamoose! (*Exit* ELIZA *and* HARRY.) Chaw me into sassage meat, if that ain't a perpendicular fine gal! She's a reg'lar A No. 1 sort of female! How'n thunder am I to get across this refrigerated stream of water? I can't wait for that ferryman. (*Enter* MARKS.) Hulloa! What sort of a critter's this? (*Advances.*) Say, stranger, will you have something to drink?

MARKS. You are excessively kind; I don't care if I do.

PHINEAS. Ah! He's a human. Hulloa, thar! Bring us a jug of whiskey instantaneously, or expect to be teetotally chawed up! Squat yourself, stranger, and go in for enjoyment. (MARKS *and* PHINEAS *sit at table.*) Who are you, and what's your name?

MARKS. I am a lawyer and my name is Marks. Have a card?

PHINEAS. A land shark, eh? Well, I don't think no worse on you for that. The law is a kind of necessary evil; and it breeds lawyers just like an old stump does toadstools. Ah! here's the whiskey. (*Enter* WAITER *with jug and tumblers. Places them on table.*) Here, you—take that shin-plaster. (*Gives bill.*) I don't want any change—thar's a gal stopping in that room—the balance will pay for her—d'ye hear?

WAITER. Yaas, sir!

PHINEAS. Vamoose! (*Exit* WAITER.) Take hold, neighbor Marks. (MARKS *fills glasses.*) Don't shirk the critter. Here's hoping your path of true love may never have an ice-choked river to cross! (*They drink.*)

MARKS. Want to cross the river, eh?

PHINEAS. Well, I do, stranger. Fact is, I'm in love with the teetotalist pretty girl, over on the Ohio side, that ever wore a Quaker bonnet. Take another swig, neighbor. (*Fills glasses, and they drink.*)

MARKS. A Quaker, eh?

PHINEAS. Yes—kind of strange, ain't it? The way of it was this: I used to own a grist of niggers—had 'em to work on my plantation, just below here. Well, stranger, do you know I fell in love with that gal—of course I was considerably smashed—knocked into a pretty conglomerated heap—and I told her so. She said she wouldn't hear a word from me so long as I owned a nigger!

MARKS. You sold them!

PHINEAS. You're teetotally wrong, neighbor. I give 'em all their freedom, and told 'em to vamoose!

MARKS. Ah! Yes—very noble, I daresay, but rather expensive, but it won you your lady-love!

PHINEAS. You're off the track again, neighbor. She felt kind of pleased about it and smiled and all that; but she said she could never be mine unless I turned Quaker! Thunder and earth! What do you think of that? You're a lawyer, come, now, what's your opinion? Don't you call it a knotty point?

MARKS. Most decidedly. Of course you refused.

PHINEAS. Teetotally; but she told me to think better of it, and come tonight and give her my final conclusion. Chaw me into mince-meat, if I haven't made up my mind to do it!

MARKS. You astonish me!

PHINEAS. Well, you see, I can't get along without that gal—she's sort of fixed my flint, and I'm sure to hang fire without her. I reckon I shall make a queer sort of Quaker, because you see, neighbor, I ain't precisely the kind of material to make a Quaker out of!

MARKS. No, not exactly!

PHINEAS (*rises*). Well, I can't stop no longer. (*Goes up to window.*) I must try to get across that candaverous river some way. It's getting late—take care of yourself, neighbor lawyer. I'm a teetotal victim to a pair of black eyes. Chaw me up to feed hogs, if I'm not in a ruinatious state! (*Exit.*)

(MARKS *pours himself another drink.*)

MARKS. Queer genius, that, very. (*Enter* TOM LOKER.) Well, Tom Loker, so you've come at last!

LOKER. Hello, Marks! How are you?

MARKS. Tolable! Tolable! Have a drink?

LOKER. Don't care if I do! (*Looks into jug.*) Empty! Waiter! More whiskey!

(WAITER *enters R. with jug and takes the empty one and exits. Enter* HALEY.)

HALEY. By the land! If this yer ain't the nearest, now, to what I've heard people call Providence! Why, Loker, how are ye?

LOKER. The devil! (*Crosses to him at the window.*) What brought you here, Haley?

HALEY. I say, Tom, this yer's the luckiest thing in the world. I'm in a devil of a hobble, and you must help me out!

LOKER. Ugh! Like enough! A body may be pretty sure of that when you're glad to see 'em, or can make something off of 'em. What's the blow now?

HALEY. You've got a friend here—partner, perhaps?

LOKER. Yes, I have. Here, Marks—here's that ar fellow that I was with in Natchez.

MARKS (*rises, grasping* HALEY'S *hand*). Shall be pleased with his acquaintance. Mr. Haley, I believe?

HALEY (*foot on chair*). The same, sir.

MARKS. I'm a lawyer and my name is Marks, have a card!

HALEY. The fact is, gentlemen, this morning I bought a young 'un of Shelby up above here. His mother got wind of it, and what does she do but cut her lucky with him; and I'm afraid by this time that she has crossed the river (*goes up to the window*) for I tracked her to this very place!

MARKS. So, then, ye're fairly sewed up, ain't ye? He, he, he! It's neatly done, too!

HALEY. This young 'un business makes lots of trouble in the trade.

MARKS. Now, Mr. Haley, what is it? Do you want us to undertake to catch this gal?

HALEY. The gal's no matter of mine—she's Shelby's—it's only the boy. I was a fool for buying the monkey.

LOKER. You're generally a fool!

MARKS. Come now, Loker, none of your huffs; you see, Mr. Haley's a-puttin' us in a way of a good job! Leave it to me, I'm a lawyer and I know my business! This yer gal, Mr. Haley—— (*He comes down a step.*) How is she? What is she like?

HALEY. She's almost white and damned handsome—well brought up. I'd have given Shelby eight hundred or a thousand—and then made well on her. (*Goes to window.*)

MARKS. White and handsome—well brought up! Look here now, Loker, a beautiful opening. We'll do a business here on our own account. We does the catchin'; the boy, of course, goes to Mr. Haley. (HALEY *beside table.*) We take the gal to Orleans—sells her and I takes the proceeds.

LOKER. What!

MARKS. Of course you gets your share! Ain't it beautiful? (*They confer together.*)

(ELIZA *appears outside the window.*)

MARKS. Well, Tom Loker, what do you say?

LOKER. It'll do! (*Strikes his hand violently on the table.* ELIZA *screams. They all start to their feet,* ELIZA *disappears. Music chord.*)

HALEY. By the land, there she is now! (*They all rush to the window.*)

MARKS. She's making for the river!

LOKER. Let's after her!

(*Music. They all leap through the window.*)

CURTAIN

SCENE IV

Road to river. Snow landscape. Music.

Enter ELIZA *and* HARRY *hurriedly. It is snowing. Wind effect, etc.*

ELIZA. They press upon my footsteps—the river is my only hope. Heaven grant me strength to reach it, ere they overtake me! My child, we will be free—or perish!

(*Rushes off. Music continues. Two men enter with hounds on leash. As they exit the others follow.*)
(*Enter* HALEY, LOKER *and* MARKS.)

HALEY. We'll catch her yet; the river will stop her!

MARKS. No, it won't! Look! She has jumped upon the ice! By the Lord! She's a brave gal, anyhow!

LOKER. She'll be drowned.

HALEY. Curse that young 'un! I shall lose him, after all!

LOKER. Come on, Marks, to the ferry! (*Exits, followed by* MARKS.)

HALEY. Aye, to the ferry! A hundred dollars for a boat! (*Exits . . . Music.*)

CURTAIN

SCENE V

River. The entire depth of stage representing the Ohio River filled with floating ice.

ELIZA *appears with* HARRY *on a cake of ice and floats slowly across the scene. Hounds chase after her.*

HALEY, LOKER *and* MARKS *follow across after the hounds.*

CURTAIN

SCENE VI

ST. CLAIR'S *parlor.* MARIE *discovered reclining on ottoman C.*

NURSE (*looking at a note*). But, Madame, what can possibly detain Mr. St. Clair? According to this note he should have been here a fortnight ago. Is it possible . . . (*Noise of horses' hoofs.*) Oh, I do believe he has come at last.

MARIE. Let's hope so! He's been gone long enough to make six journeys to Vermont.
(NURSE *exits.* EVA *runs in.*)

EVA. Oh, Mama! Mama! (*Throws her arms around* MARIE'S *neck and kisses her.*)

MARIE. That will do—take care, child—don't you make my head ache. (*Kisses her languidly.*)

(*Enter* ST. CLAIR *with* OPHELIA, *nicely dressed.*)

ST. CLAIR. Well, my dear Marie, here we are at last! The wanderers have arrived. Oh! Allow me to present my Yankee cousin, Miss Ophelia. As I wrote you, she has consented to be our housekeeper. (OPHELIA *crosses to* MARIE *and sits beside her.*)

MARIE (*rising to a sitting posture*). Oh, that will be splendid!

EVA (*running to* OPHELIA). My own home! Isn't it beautiful?

OPHELIA (*patronizingly*). Very nice—very nice, I'm sure!

ST. CLAIR. And, Marie, I've bought you a new coachman. (EVA *crosses to* ST. CLAIR.)

MARIE. Bought him?

ST. CLAIR. And a pretty price, too! Fourteen hundred dollars! The fellow was on the steamboat and this little minx (*pinching* EVA'S *cheek*) gave me no rest till I had paid down my good cash for him.

MARIE. I hope he'll turn out well.

OPHELIA. Probably he'll get drunk!

ST. CLAIR. Never fear. His pedigree's sound—guaranteed safe, healthy, pious and well worth the money.

EVA. And oh, Mama, you'll never guess. Something terrible happened.

MARIE. Don't tell me! My nerves, my nerves!

ST. CLAIR. Oh, it turned out all right. But we had a fearful few moments. Somebody got excited at the gangplank when we landed. There was a fearful jam and little Eva was pushed off into the river.

MARIE. Gracious heavens!

ST. CLAIR. But she no more than struck the water before a man leaped over the rail and as she rose to the surface, grasped her in his arms.

MARIE. Oh! Oh! I can't bear it. (*Buries her face in her hands.*)

EVA (*crosses to her*). But I'm all right now, Mama. Look at me, I'm all right!

ST. CLAIR. Got pretty wet, didn't you, puss? And scared, too! Now tell your mother—Eva—who was that man?

EVA (*running to the door and throwing it open*). Uncle Tom!

ST. CLAIR. Come in here, you rascal, and hear your praises sung. (*Enter* TOM.)

EVA. Uncle Tom!

(*Throws herself into his arms and kisses him.* OPHELIA *rises.*)

TOM. Bless you, Miss Eva.

ST. CLAIR. You see, Marie, he's her favorite already!

OPHELIA (*turning up her nose*). Really! Now, really!

ST. CLAIR. What's the matter, Ophelia?

OPHELIA. Well, I'm sure, it's not my business, but as to that child kissing——

ST. CLAIR. Niggers? Oh, bless you, you'll get used to that!

OPHELIA. I beg leave to doubt it!

ST. CLAIR (*to* TOM). Now, you old angel of mercy, say how d'you do to your mistress!

TOM (*bobbing*). I'm painful glad to see you, Miss St. Clair.

ST. CLAIR. Of course you are, and everyone's going to be glad to see you, too, after all that's happened.

TOM. Please, massa, there ain't no call to say nothin' 'bout me. I'll git along.

ST. CLAIR. You see, Marie, Eva took a fancy to him the moment she saw him on the boat, long before she fell overboard!

MARIE. She's an odd child!

EVA. Papa, may I show Uncle Tom the house?

ST. CLAIR. If you like.

EVA (*pulling him by the hand*). Come along, Uncle Tom!

TOM. Kin I go, massa?

ST. CLAIR. Of course!

(EVA *starts to exit.*)

MARIE. Don't exert yourself too much, Eva!

EVA. No, Mama. Come along, Uncle Tom!

ST. CLAIR. Yes, and remember, Tom, from now on she's your little mistress. Her word is your law.

TOM. Yassa, yassa, looks like it's gwine to be a very nice kind of a law!

EVA (*stamps her foot impatiently*). Uncle Tom!

ST. CLAIR. The voice of the law, Tom!

EVA (*stamping her foot*). Uncle Tom!!!

TOM. I'm comin', missy, I'm comin'! (*They exit.*)

CURTAIN

SCENE VII

ST. CLAIR'S *garden. Tom discovered seated on a bank with* EVA. TOM *sings "Let My People Go!" His buttonholes are filled with flowers. And* EVA *is hanging a wreath around his neck. Music at opening of scene.*

EVA (*at end of song*). No—no. Keep your eyes shut. Don't you peek. (*Arranges flowers, business, ad lib.*)

TOM (*eyes closed*). What all is you doin' to me, Miss Eva? I feel like a Christmas tree!

EVA. I'm making you beautiful!

TOM. Dat need a heap o' doin', I reckon. (EVA *hums "Here Jerusalem" as she decorates him.*) What you t'ink you papa say. (*Starts to open eyes. She laughs.*)

EVA. No—no—wait till I say "when." (*Closes* TOM'S *eyes with her fingers.*)

TOM. Seems like I cain't rightly keep 'em shut, Miss Eva.

EVA (*completes task by putting daisy wreath on his head*). Now—*when!*

TOM (*opens his eyes*). My! My! I'se like de ox de Good Book say "dressed for de sacrifice." I reckon I's de decorationest nigger ever was.

EVA (*kneels before him; picks up dandelion from bench, holds it up for Tom to blow off petals*). Now blow! (TOM *blows.*) You've got your wish! You've got your wish! (*She sits on floor, leans against* TOM'S *knees.*)

EVA. Tell me a story, Uncle Tom?

TOM. What kind of a story, Miss Eva?

EVA. Bible story!

TOM. Want to know about the burning bush?

EVA. Oh, please!

TOM. Well, missy—you know Moses man? Uh huh?

EVA. Uh huh!

TOM. Well, Moses he don't know much about dem chillun of Israel down in Egypt, so de Lawd he come to him in a burning bush and it didn't scorch the Lawd's clothes one little bit and he says, "Moses, you Moses," and Moses he says, "Here I is, Lawd." Den the Lawd say take off them shoes, Moses, cause de place where you stand is Holy ground. "I sure will, Lawd," say Moses and Moses took them off and de Lawd send him down to Egypt to set dem people free . . .

EVA. Did he go all the way without any shoes, Uncle Tom?

TOM. I don't know, Miss Eva; if he did I reckon he don' get mighty sore feet!

(*Enter* ST. CLAIR.)

EVA (*seeing* ST. CLAIR). Oh, Papa! Uncle Tom got his wish!

ST. CLAIR. Bravo!

TOM (*rises*). Yassa! Yassa! Only I done forgot to make any wish!

ST. CLAIR. Well, you're certainly a picture!

TOM (*takes off some of the decorations*). Foolish kinder picter, I 'spect, Massa St. Clair.

ST. CLAIR. Well, now, Eva, which do you like best—to live in your Uncle's house way up in Vermont or down here?

EVA. Oh, down here, Papa!

ST. CLAIR. And why?

EVA. Why . . . why . . . because . . .

ST. CLAIR. Lot more people here, perhaps, eh?

EVA. Yes—there's so many more around you to love.

ST. CLAIR. And I suppose you've been pretty busy doing just that, eh, puss?

EVA. I've been hearing Uncle Tom sing.

ST. CLAIR (*with mock ferocity*). Indeed! And what have you been singing, Tom?

TOM. Oh, nothin' much, sir. Jes' 'bout de New Jerusalem, an' de Lan' o' Canaan.

EVA. And he's going to teach them to me.

ST. CLAIR. Singing lessons, hey? You are coming on.

(*Enter* OPHELIA.)

EVA. Yes, he sings for me, and I *read* to him in my Bible, and he explains what it means!

TOM. Yassa, when I *knows* what it means!

EVA. Come along, Uncle Tom! (*She takes his hand, and they exit.*)

OPHELIA. How shiftless! How can you let her?

ST. CLAIR. Why not?

OPHELIA. Why, I don't know; it seems so dreadful!

ST. CLAIR. You would think no harm in a child's caressing a big dog, but a black creature that can think, reason and feel, you shudder at. Confess it, Cousin! You shrink from him as you would from a toad; yet you are indignant at his wrongs.

OPHELIA (*sits on bench*). Well, Cousin, there may be some truth in what you say!

ST. CLAIR. Tom, now, is a hero to Eva. His stories are wonders in her eyes; his songs and hymns are better than an opera, and the traps and little bits of trash in his pockets a mine of jewels, and he the most wonderful Tom that ever wore a black skin and look here——(*Sees* TOPSY *off stage . . . Calls.*) Hey, Topsy, come here!

OPHELIA. What's that?

ST. CLAIR. A purchase I made for your department.

(TOPSY *runs on.*)

TOPSY. Yas sir, here I is!

OPHELIA. Good gracious! What a heathenish, shiftless looking object. St. Clair, what in the world have you brought that thing here for?

ST. CLAIR. For you to educate, to be sure; and train in the way she should go. Here, Topsy, give us a dance. (TOPSY *dances a breakdown.*)

OPHELIA (*at end of dance, paralyzed*). Well, of all things! If I ever saw the like!

ST. CLAIR (*smothering a laugh*). Topsy, this is your new mistress—I'm going to give you to her. See now that you behave yourself!

TOPSY. Yas, massa.

ST. CLAIR. You're going to be good, Topsy, you understand?

TOPSY. Oh, yas, massa.

OPHELIA (*rises*). Now, St. Clair, what on earth is this for? Your house is so full of these plagues now, that a body can't set down their foot without treading on 'em! What on earth did you want to bring this one for?

ST. CLAIR. For you to educate. You're always preaching about educating. Here's a fresh caught specimen. Try your hand on her and bring her up in the way she should go!

OPHELIA. Well, it might be a real missionary work. I'll do what I can!

(*Advances to* TOPSY.) She's dreadfully dirty! How old are you, Topsy?

TOPSY. Dunno, missis!

OPHELIA. Don't know how old you are? Didn't anybody ever tell you? Who was your mother?

TOPSY (*grinning*). Never had none.

OPHELIA. Never had any mother? What do you mean? Where were you born?

TOPSY. Never was born!

OPHELIA. You mustn't answer me in that way. Tell me where you were born, and who your father and mother were?

TOPSY. Never was born, tell you; never had no father, nor mother, nor nothin'. I was raised by a speculator. (OPHELIA *turns to* ST. CLAIR.) Old Aunt Sue used to take car' on us!

ST. CLAIR. She speaks the truth, cousin. Speculators buy them up cheap, when they are little, and get them raised for the market.

OPHELIA. How long have you lived with your master and mistress?

TOPSY. Dunno, missis.

OPHELIA. How shiftless! Is it a year or more, or less?

TOPSY. Dunno, missis.

ST. CLAIR. She does not know what a year is, she don't even know her own age.

OPHELIA. Have you ever heard anything about heaven, Topsy? (TOPSY *looks bewildered and grins.*) Do you know who made you?

TOPSY. Nobody as I knows on, he-he-he! I 'spect I just growed.

OPHELIA. The shiftless little heathen! What can you do? What did you do for your master and mistress?

TOPSY. Fetch water—and wash dishes —and rub knives and wait on folks and dance breakdowns.

OPHELIA (*backs away*). I shall break down, I'm afraid, in trying to make anything of you, you shiftless mortal!

ST. CLAIR. You find virgin soil there, plant your own ideas—you won't find many to pull up. (*Exit laughing.* OPHELIA *starts to follow* ST. CLAIR, *stops, turns back.*)

OPHELIA (*takes out her handkerchief; a pair of gloves falls.* TOPSY *picks them up slowly, and puts them in her sleeve*). Follow me, you benighted innocent! (*She starts to exit.*)

TOPSY. Yes, missis.

(*As* OPHELIA *turns her back to her,* TOPSY *seizes the end of the ribbon she wears around her waist and twitches it off.* OPHELIA *turns and sees her, as she is putting it in her other sleeve.* OPHELIA *takes the ribbon from her.*)

OPHELIA (*pulls ribbon slowly out of* TOPSY'S *sleeve*). What's this? My ribbon! You naughty, wicked girl, you've been stealing this?

TOPSY. Laws! Why that ar's missis' ribbon, ain't it? How could it got caught in my sleeve?

OPHELIA. Topsy, you naughty girl, don't you tell a lie! You stole that ribbon!

TOPSY. Missis, I declare for't, I didn't —never seed it till dis yer blessed minnit!

OPHELIA. Topsy, don't you know it's wicked to tell lies?

TOPSY. I never tell no lies, missis; it's just de truth I been telling now and nothing else.

OPHELIA. Topsy, I shall have to whip you, if you tell lies so!

TOPSY. Laws, missis, if you's to whip all day couldn't say no other way. I never seed dat ar—it must a got caught in my sleeve. (*Blubbers.*)

OPHELIA (*seizes her by the shoulders*). Don't you tell me that again, you barefaced fibber! (*Shakes her. The gloves fall on stage.*) There you, my gloves too—you outrageous young heathen! (*Picks them up.*) Will you tell me now, you didn't steal the ribbon?

TOPSY. No, missis; stole de gloves, but didn't steal de ribbon. It was permiskus.

OPHELIA. Why, you young reprobate!

TOPSY. Yes—I's knows I's wicked!

OPHELIA. Then you know you ought to be punished! (*Boxes her ears.*) What do you think of that?

TOPSY. He-he-he! De Lawd, missis, dat wouldn't kill a skeeter! I's been whipped by those as *knows how!!* (*Runs off laughing.*)

CURTAIN

SCENE VIII

The tavern by the river. Table and chairs. Jug and glasses on table. On flat is a printed placard, headed: "Four hundred dollars' Reward—Runaway—George Harris!"
PHINEAS *is discovered seated at table.*

PHINEAS. So yer I am; and a pretty business I've undertook to do. Find the husband of the gal that crossed the river from here on the ice two or three days ago. Ruth said I must do it, and I'll be teetotally chawed up if I don't. (*Turns in his chair, looks at placard.*) I see they've offered a reward for him; dead or alive. How in creation am I to find the varmint? He ain't likely to go round looking natural, with a full description of his hide and figure staring him in the face. (*Enter* MR. WILSON.) I say, stranger, how are ye?

WILSON. Well, I reckon.

PHINEAS. Any news? (*Takes out plug and knife.*)

WILSON. Not that I know of.

PHINEAS (*cutting a piece of tobacco and offering it*). Chaw?

WILSON. No, thank ye, tobacco don't agree with me.

PHINEAS. Don't, eh? (*Putting it in his own mouth.*) I never felt any the worse for it!

WILSON (*sees placard*). What's that?

PHINEAS (*rises*). Nigger advertised. (*Advances towards it and spits on it.*) There's my mind upon that!

WILSON. Why, now, stranger, what's that for?

PHINEAS. I'd do it all the same to the writer of that ar paper, if he was here. Any man that owns a boy like that, and can't find any better way of treating him than branding him on the hand with the letter H, as that paper states, *deserves* to lose him. Such papers as this are a shame to old Kaintuck!

WILSON. Well, now, sir, that's a fact!

PHINEAS. Yes, sir, I used to own a gang of boys, sir—that was before I fell in love—and I just told 'em: "Boys," says I, "run now, dig! Put! Jest when you want to! I never shall come to look after you!" That's the way I kept mine. Let 'em know they are free to run any time, and it jest stops their wanting to. It stands to reason it should. Treat 'em like men, and you'll have men's work!

WILSON. I think you are altogether right, friend, and this man described here is a fine fellow—no mistake about that! He worked for me some half dozen years in my bagging factory; and he was my best hand, sir. He is an ingenious fellow, too; he invented a machine for the cleaning of hemp—a really valuable affair; it's gone into use in several factories. His master holds the patent on it.

PHINEAS. I'll warrant ye; holds it, and makes money out of it, too, and then turns round and brands the boy in his right hand! If I had a fair chance, I'd mark him, I reckon, so that he'd carry it *one* while!

(*Enter* GEORGE HARRIS, *disguised.*)

GEORGE (*speaking as he enters*). Jim, see to the trunks. (*Sees* WILSON.) Ah! Mr. Wilson!

WILSON. Bless my soul, can it be?

GEORGE (*advances and grasps his hand*). Mr. Wilson, I see you remember me, Mr. Butler, of Oaklands, Shelby County.

WILSON (*recognizes him.*) Er—ye-yes—yes, sir.

PHINEAS. Hulloa! You seem to be struck into a pretty considerable heap of astonishment. May I be teetotally chawed up! If I don't believe that's the identical man I'm arter. (*Crosses to George.*) How are ye, George Harris?

GEORGE (*starting back and thrusting his hands into his breast*). I think you've made a mistake, sir.

PHINEAS. Ha, ha, ha! I rather conclude I ain't, but don't get riled, I ain't a bloodhound in disguise.

GEORGE. How did you discover me?

PHINEAS. By a teetotal smart guess. You're the very man I want to see. Do you know I was sent after you?

GEORGE. Ah! By my master?

PHINEAS. No; by your wife.

GEORGE. My wife! Where is she?

PHINEAS. She's stopping with a Quaker family over on the Ohio side.

GEORGE. Then, thank God, she is safe.

PHINEAS. Teetotally!

GEORGE. Take me to her, please—please!

PHINEAS. Just wait a brace of shakes and I'll do it! I've got to go and get the boat ready! Chaw me up! But this is what I call doing things in short order! (*Exit.*)

WILSON. George?

GEORGE. Yes!

WILSON. I couldn't have thought it!

GEORGE. I am pretty well disguised.

WILSON. George, this is a dangerous game you are playing. You can't hope to carry it out; if you're captured they'll abuse you. And half kill you and sell you down the river!

GEORGE. I know all that—I do run a risk—but there—(*Shows pistol.*) I'm ready for them down South. I will never go—if it comes to that I can at least earn myself six feet of free soil, the first and last I shall ever own in ole Kentucky!

WILSON. You're setting yourself in opposition to the laws of your country.

GEORGE. *My* country! What country have *I*? Sir, I haven't any country any more than I have any father. I don't want anything of *your* country, except to be left alone—to go peaceably out of it; but if any man tries to stop me, I'll fight for my liberty, to the last breath.

WILSON. Why, George, something has brought you out. You hold up your head, and move and speak like another man.

GEORGE (*proudly*). Because I'm a *free man!* Yes, sir! I've said "master" for the last time, *I'm free!*

WILSON. Take care! You may be taken!

GEORGE. All men are free and equal *in the grave,* if it comes to that, Mr. Wilson!

(*Enter* PHINEAS.)

PHINEAS. Them's my sentiments, to a teetotal atom, and I don't care who knows it! Neighbor, the boat is ready, and the sooner we make tracks the better. I've seen some mysterious strangers lurking about these diggings, so we'd better put.

GEORGE. Good-by, Mr. Wilson.

WILSON (*grasping his hand*). You're a brave fellow, George. I wish in my heart you were safe through.

PHINEAS. And ain't I the man of all creation to put him through, stranger? Chaw me up if I don't take him to his dear little wife; in the smallest possible quantity of time. Come, neighbor, let's vamoose!

GEORGE. Farewell, Mr. Wilson!

WILSON. My best wishes, George! (*Exit.*)

PHINEAS. You're a trump, old Slow-and-Easy.

GEORGE (*looking off stage*). Look! Look! They're after me!

PHINEAS. What! Are you sartain?

GEORGE. Yes—yes—I know them all!

PHINEAS. Consarn their picters, here they come! We can't get out of the house without their seeing us! We're teetotally treed!

GEORGE. Let us fight our way through them!

PHINEAS. No, that won't do; there are too many of 'em for us. We should be chawed up in no time! (*Looks round and sees trap door.*) Hulloa! Here's something. Just you step down here a few minutes, while I chin with 'em! (*Lifts the trap.* GEORGE *goes down trap.* PHINEAS *closes trap and stands on it.*) Here they are!

(*Enter* HALEY, MARKS, LOKER *and three men.*)

HALEY. Say, stranger, you haven't seen a runaway darky about these parts, eh?

PHINEAS. What kind of a darky?

HALEY. A mulatto chap, almost as light-complexioned as a white man.

PHINEAS. Was he a pretty good-looking chap?

HALEY. Yes.

PHINEAS. Kind of tall?

HALEY. Yes.

PHINEAS. With brown hair?

HALEY. Yes.

PHINEAS. And dark eyes?

HALEY. Yes.

PHINEAS. Scar in his right hand?

HALEY. Yes, yes.

PHINEAS. Well, I ain't seen him!

HALEY. Oh, bother! Come, boys, let's search the house. (*Exeunt.*)

PHINEAS (*raises trap*). Now then, George. . . . (GEORGE *enters up trap.*) Now's the time to cut your lucky—

GEORGE. Follow me, Phineas! (*Exit.*)

PHINEAS. In a brace of shakes! (*Is closing trap as* HALEY, MARKS, LOKER, *etc., re-enter.*)

HALEY. Ah! He's down the cellar! Follow me, boys! (*Thrusts* PHINEAS *aside and rushes down trap, followed by the others.* PHINEAS *closes trap and stands on it.*)

PHINEAS. Chaw me up! But I've got 'em all! (*Knocking below.*) Be quiet, you varmints! (*Knocking.*) They're getting mighty oneasy! (*Knocking.*) Will you be quiet, you savagerous critters! (*The trap is forced open.* HALEY *and* MARKS *appear.* PHINEAS *seizes a chair and stands over trap—picture.*) Back into your cage you pesky varmints, or I'll smash you into apple-fritters!

(*Tableau. Closed in.*)

CURTAIN

ACT TWO

SCENE I

EVA's *bedroom.*

TOPSY (*without*). You go 'long. No more nigger dan you be! (*Enters—shouts and laughter without—looks off stage.*) You talk like you's white folks. You ain't nerry one—black *nor* white . . . I'd like to be one or tutter. Law! (*Looking off stage.*) You niggers, does you know yu's all sinners? Well, you is—everybody is. White folks is sinners too—Miss Feely—say so—but I 'spects niggers is the biggest ones. But Lor'! Ye ain't any on ye up to me. I's so awful wicked there can't nobody do nothin' with me. I used to keep old missis a-swearin' at me half de time. I 'spects I's de wickedest critter in de world.

(EVA *enters.*)

EVA. Oh, Topsy! Topsy! You have been very bad again.

TOPSY (*still sitting on floor, playing with doll*). Well, I 'spects I have!

EVA. What makes you do so?

TOPSY. I dunno; I 'spects it's 'cause I's so wicked.

EVA. *Why* did you spoil Jane's earrings?

TOPSY. 'Cause she's so proud. She call me little black imp, and turn up her nose at me 'cause she is whiter than me. I was gwine by her room, and I seed her coral earrings lying on de table, so I threw dem on de floor, and put my foot on 'em, and scrunched 'em all to little bits, he-he-he! Golly, I's wicked!

EVA. Don't you know that was very *wrong*?

TOPSY. I don't car'! I 'spise dem what sets up for fine ladies, when dey ain't nothing but cream-colored niggers! Dere's dat Rosa—she gives me lots of 'pertinent remarks. T'other night she was gwine to ball. She put on a beau'ful dress dat missis give her—wid her hair curled, all nice and pretty. She hab to go down de back stairs—dey is dark—and I puts a pail of hot water on dem, and she put her foot into it, and den she go tumbling to de bottom of de stairs, and de water go all ober her, and spile her dress, and scald her dreadful bad! He! He! He! Golly, I's wicked!

EVA. Oh, how could you!

TOPSY. Don't dey 'spise me 'cause I don't know nothing? Don't dey laugh at me 'cause I'm black and *dey* ain't?

EVA. But you shouldn't mind them!

TOPSY. Well, I don't mind dem; but when dey're passin' under my winder, I trows dirty water on 'em! And dat spoils their complexion. (*Rises.*)

EVA. What does make you so bad, Topsy? Why won't you try to be good? Don't you *love* anybody, Topsy?

TOPSY. Can't recommember.

EVA. But you love your father and mother?

TOPSY. Never had none, ye know. I telled ye that, Miss Eva.

EVA. Oh! I know; but hadn't you any brother or sister or aunt or—

TOPSY (*climbs over bed, sits on foot of it*). No, none of 'em—never had nothing nor nobody. I's brack—no one loves me!

EVA (*standing by bed*). Oh! I love you, Topsy! (*Laying her hand on* TOPSY'S *shoulder.*) I love you because you haven't any father or mother, or friends. I love you, and I want you to be good. I wish you would try to be good for my sake. (TOPSY *looks astonished for a moment and then bursts into tears.*) Oh, Topsy—only think of it—you can be one of those "*spirits* bright" Uncle Tom sings about!

TOPSY. Oh! Miss Eva—Miss Eva! I will try—I will try. I never did care nothin' about it befor'.

EVA. If you try, you will succeed! (*Takes* TOPSY'S *hand.*)

TOPSY. Oh, Ah'll try; but den Ah dunno, I's so wicked!

BLACK-OUT—CURTAIN

SCENE II

A Quaker kitchen in Ohio. Enter GEORGE. ELIZA *and* HARRY *discovered, seated.* ELIZA *rises, crosses to* GEORGE.

GEORGE. Thank God, Eliza, after many wanderings, we are together again. My brave girl! You deserve your freedom—you have richly earned it!

ELIZA. And when we get to Canada I can help you to work, and between us we can find something to live on.

GEORGE. Yes, Eliza, so long as we

have each other, and our boy, the rest will follow.

ELIZA. But we are not quite out of danger; we are not in Canada yet!

GEORGE. True; but it seems as if I smelt the free air, and it makes me strong!

(*Enter* PHINEAS, *dressed as a Quaker.*)

PHINEAS (*with a sniffle*). Verily, friends, how is it with thee?—Hum!

GEORGE. Why, Phineas, why do you talk like that?

PHINEAS. I've become a Quaker! That's the meaning on't!

GEORGE. What—you?

PHINEAS. Teetotally! I was driven to it by a strong argument, composed of a pair of sparkling eyes, rosy cheeks, and pouting lips. Them lips would persuade a man to assassinate his grandmother! (*Crosses to* GEORGE, *assumes the Quaker tone again.*) Verily, George, I have discovered something of importance to the interests of thee and thy party, and it were well for thee to hear it!

GEORGE. What is it?

PHINEAS. Well, after I left you on the road, I stopped at a little, lone tavern, just below here. Well, I was tired with hard driving, and after my supper I stretched myself down on a pile of bags in the corner, and pulled a buffalo hide over me—and what do I do but go fast asleep!

GEORGE. With one ear open, Phineas?

PHINEAS. No, I slept ears and all for an hour or two! For I was pretty well tired; but when I came to myself a little, I found that there were some men in the room, sitting round a table, drinking and talking. So I kept quiet, and heard them lay off all their plans. They've got a right notion of the track we are going tonight, and they'll be down after us, six or eight strong. So, now, what's to be done?

ELIZA. What *shall* we do, George?

GEORGE. I know what I shall do! (*Takes out pistols.*)

PHINEAS. Ay—ay, thou seest, Eliza, how it will work, pistols—phitz—poppers!

ELIZA. But I pray it doesn't come to that!

GEORGE. I don't want to involve anyone else. I will drive alone to the next stand.

PHINEAS. Ah! Well, friend, but thee'll need a driver for all that. Thee's quite welcome to do all the fighting thee knows; but I know a thing or two about the road that thee doesn't.

GEORGE. But I don't want to involve you.

PHINEAS. Involve me! Why, chaw me—that is to say—when thee does involve me, please to let me know!

ELIZA. Phineas is a wise and skillful man. You will do well to abide by his judgment. And, oh, George, don't be hasty with these—(*laying her hand on pistols*).

GEORGE. I will attack no man. All I ask of this country is to be left alone, and I will go out peaceably. But I'll fight to the last breath before they shall take from me my wife and son! Would not you, sir, do the same, in my place?

PHINEAS. Yes, well, of course! Before I got to be a Quaker. Still, I pray that I be not tried; the flesh is weak —but I think my flesh would be pretty tolerably strong in such a case. I ain't sure, friend George, that I shouldn't hold a fellow for thee, if thee had any account to settle with him.

ELIZA. Heaven grant we be not tempted!

PHINEAS. But if we are tempted too much, why, consarn 'em! Let them look out, that's all!

GEORGE. It's quite plain you were not born for a Quaker. The old Adam has its way in you pretty strong yet.

PHINEAS. Well, I reckon you are pretty teetotally right!

GEORGE. Had we not better hasten our flight?

PHINEAS. Well, I rather conclude we had; we're full two hours ahead of them, if they start at the time they planned; so let's vamoose. An' lookee here. If you see me forgettin' that I'm a Quaker; why, you jest remind me!

(*Exeunt.*)

CURTAIN

SCENE III

A rocky pass. Music. Large set rock and platform occupy a large part of the stage.

PHINEAS (*without*). Out with you in a twinkling, every one, and up into these rocks with me! *Run* now if you ever did run! (*Music.* PHINEAS *enters with* HARRY *in his arms,* GEORGE *supporting* ELIZA.) Come up here; this is one of our old hunting dens. Come up . . . (*They ascend the rock.*) Well, here we are! Let 'em get us if they can! Whoever comes here has to walk single file in fair range of your pistols—d'ye see?

GEORGE. I do see. And now, as this affair is mine, let me take the risk, and do all the fighting!

PHINEAS. Thee's quite welcome to do the fighting, George. But, see these fellows are kind of debating down there, and looking up, like hens when they are going to fly up onto the roost. Hadn't thee better give 'em a word of advice, before they come up, jest to tell 'em handsomely they'll be shot if they do!

(LOKER, MARKS *enter.*)

MARKS. Well, Tom, your coons are fairly treed.

LOKER. Yes, I see 'em go right here, and here's a path—I'm for going right up. It won't take long to ferret 'em out!

MARKS. But, Tom, they might fire at us from behind the rocks.

LOKER. Ugh! No danger, niggers are too plaguey scared! Always for saving your skin, Marks!

MARKS. I don't know why I shouldn't save my skin, it's the only skin I've got!

GEORGE (*rising on the rock*). Gentlemen, who are you down there, and what do you want?

LOKER. We want a party of runaway niggers. One George and Eliza Harris, and their son. We've got the officers here, and a warrant to take 'em too. D'ye hear? Ain't you George Harris, that belonged to Mr. Harris, of Shelby County, Kentucky?

GEORGE. I am George Harris. A Mr. Harris of Kentucky did call me his property, but now I'm a free man. My wife and child I claim as mine! Come up if you like, but the first one that comes up that pass is a dead man!

MARKS. Oh, come, come, young man, this ain't no kind of talk for you. We're officers of justice. We've got the law on our side; so you'd better give up peaceably!

GEORGE. I know very well that you've got the law on your side; but you haven't got us. We are standing here as free as you are; and we'll fight for our liberty till we die! (*During this,* MARKS *draws a pistol, and when he concludes, fires at him.* ELIZA *screams.*) It's all right, Eliza; I am unhurt.

PHINEAS (*drawing George down*). Thee'd better keep out of sight with thy speechifying; they're teetotal mean scamps.

LOKER (*to Marks*). What did you do that for, Marks?

MARKS. Why not? In Kentucky a dead nigger is worth just as much as a live one!

GEORGE. Now, Phineas, the first man that advances I fire at; you take the second, and so on. It won't do to waste two shots on one man!

PHINEAS. Creation! Chaw me up if there ain't stuff in you!

MARKS. I think I must have hit some of 'em! I heard a squeal!

LOKER. I'm going right up for one. I never been afraid of niggers—yet, and I ain't agoing to be now! Come on!

(*Music.* LOKER *dashes up the rock.* GEORGE *fires. He staggers for a moment, then springs to the top.* PHINEAS *seizes him. A struggle.*)

PHINEAS. Friend, thee is not wanted here! (*Throws* LOKER *over the rock.*)

(*Music.* MARKS *and party run off.* GEORGE *and* ELIZA *kneel in an attitude of thanksgiving with the child between them.* PHINEAS *stands over them exulting. Tableau.*)

CURTAIN

SCENE IV

ST. CLAIR'S *study.* ST. CLAIR *discovered seated, with* TOM *standing beside him. He is in riding clothes.* .

ST. CLAIR (*giving money and papers to Tom*). There, Tom, are the bills and the money to pay them.

TOM. Yes, Massa.

ST. CLAIR. Well, Tom, what are you waiting for? Isn't all right there?

TOM. I'm a-feared not, Massa.

ST. CLAIR. Why, Tom, what's the matter? You look as solemn as a coffin.

TOM. I feel very bad, massa. I always have thought that massa would be good to everybody.

ST. CLAIR. Come, now, what do you want? There's something you haven't got, I suppose, and this is the preface.

TOM. Massa allays been good to me. I ain't got nothing to complain of on that head; but there is one person that massa ain't good to.

ST. CLAIR. Why, Tom, what's got into you? Speak out—what do you mean?

TOM. Ah mean, massa ain't very good to *hisself*.

ST. CLAIR. Ah, I see! You allude to the state in which I came home last night. Well, to tell the truth, I *was* slightly elevated. A little more champagne on board than I could comfortably carry. That's all, isn't it?

TOM. Mebbe you don't 'member the Good Book whar it says: "At last I biteth like a snake and stingeth like an adder."

ST. CLAIR. You poor old fool! I'm not worth worrying over.

TOM. Oh, massa! Please, please don't do it no more.

ST. CLAIR. Well, I won't go to any more of their cursed parties, Tom, on my honor, I won't! (*Exclamation from* TOM.) I don't know why I haven't stopped long ago; I've always despised myself for it. So now, Tom, wipe your eyes and go about your errands.

TOM. Bless you, massa . . . that make me feel powerful good! You tuk a load offum my ole black heart! Lawd bless you fer dat!

ST. CLAIR. Come, come, no blessings; I'm not so wonderfully good yet, but there, I'll pledge my honor. (*Rises.*) Tom, you don't see me like that again. Off with you now!

TOM. Yes, massa! (*Exits.*)

ST. CLAIR. I'll keep my faith with him too!

OPHELIA (*without*). Come along, you shiftless mortal!

ST. CLAIR. What new witchcraft has Topsy been brewing? That commotion is of her raising, I'll be bound!

(*Enter* OPHELIA, *dragging in* TOPSY.)

OPHELIA. Come here now, while I tell your master!

ST. CLAIR (*rises*). What's the matter now?

OPHELIA. The matter is that I cannot be plagued with this girl any longer, it's past all bearing; flesh and blood cannot endure it. Here I locked her up and gave her a hymn to study; and what does she do, but spy out where I put my key; and has gone to my bureau, and got a bonnet-trimming and cut it all to pieces to make dolls' jackets! (TOPSY *laughs.*) I never saw anything like it in my life!

ST. CLAIR. What have you done to her?

OPHELIA. What have I done? What haven't I done? Your wife says I ought to have her whipped till she couldn't stand!

ST. CLAIR. I don't doubt it!

OPHELIA. I am sure, St. Clair, I don't know what to do. I've taught her and taught—I've talked till I'm tired; I've whipped her; I've punished her in every way I could think of; and still she's just what she was at first!

ST. CLAIR. Come here, Tops, you monkey! (TOPSY *crosses to* ST. CLAIR *grinning.*) What makes you behave so?

TOPSY. 'Spects it's my wicked heart—Miss Feely says so!

ST. CLAIR. Miss Ophelia's done all she could for you.

TOPSY. Lor' yes, massa, old missis used to say so too! She whipped me a heap harder and used to pull my ha'r and knock my head agin the door; but it didn't do me no good. I 'spects if they's to pull every spear of h'ar out o' my head, it wouldn't do no good neither—I's so wicked! Laws! I's nothin' but a nigger, no ways!

OPHELIA. Well, I shall have to give her up; I can't be bothered any longer!

ST. CLAIR. Ophelia, I'd like to ask you one question.

OPHELIA. What is it?

ST. CLAIR. Why, if your doctrine is not strong enough to save one heathen child that you can have at home here, all to yourself, what's the use of sending one or two poor missionaries off with it among thousands of heathen? I suppose this girl is a fair sample of what your heathen foreign are . . .

OPHELIA (*sits*). I'm sure I don't know; I never saw such a girl as this!

ST. CLAIR. What makes you so bad, Tops? Why won't you try and be good? Don't you love anyone, Topsy?

TOPSY. Dunno nothing 'bout love; I loves candy and sich, that's all.

OPHELIA. But, Topsy, you could be good if you'd only try.

TOPSY. Couldn't never be nothing but a nigger! (OPHELIA *sits.*) If I was ever so good. If I could be skinned and come white, then I'd try.

ST. CLAIR. People can love you, if you *are* black, Topsy. Miss Ophelia would love you, if you were good. (TOPSY *laughs.*) Don't you think so?

TOPSY. No, she can't b'ar me, 'cause I'm a nigger—she'd's soon have a toad touch her. There can't nobody love niggers, and niggers can't do nothin'! I don't car'! (*Whistles.*)

ST. CLAIR. Stop it! Stop! you incorrigible imp, and get out of here! Begone!

TOPSY. He! He! He! Didn't get much out of dis chile! (*Exits.*)

BLACK-OUT

SCENE V

ST. CLAIR'S *garden. The flat represents the lake. The rays of the setting sun tinge the waters with gold.* EVA *and* TOM *are seated side by side, on bench.* EVA *has a Bible open on her lap. Music.*

TOM. What's dat, Miss Eva? 'Bout de "sea of glass"? You read me dat once more, please?

EVA (*reading, points out each word to* TOM). "And I saw a sea of glass mingled with fire." (*Suddenly pointing off.*) Tom! There it is. (*Hands Bible to* TOM.) There's a sea of glass mingled with fire!

TOM (*after a pause*). It sure is, Miss Eva!

(TOM *sings softly as they both gaze into the sunlight.*)

O had I de wings of de mornin'
I'd fly away to Canaan's shore!
Bright angels dey conveys me home
To the New Jerusalem.

EVA (*turns, looks at him.*) Where is that, Uncle Tom?

TOM. Where what, Miss Eva?

EVA. The New Jerusalem.

TOM. Oh, up dere!

EVA. Up high?

TOM. Pow'ful high!

EVA. High as a mountain?

TOM. So high you cain't see it, standin' all alone up in de air!

EVA (*looking off stage*). Oh, but I *can* see it! Those aren't clouds, Tom, they're big gates of pearl! And you can see something else far, far off—it's all gold!

TOM. My! My! So 'tis, all gold, ain't it!

EVA (*turns to* TOM). Are there beautiful houses in New Jerusalem?

TOM. Yas'm, dat's dem wot you see, gold houses!

EVA (*looking off stage again*). And diamonds?

TOM. An' diamonds!

EVA (*turns to* TOM). And dogs?

TOM. Yes! Huh? Well, I don't rightly recon' 'bout dogs, Miss Eva!!

EVA (*looks off stage*). And trees?

TOM. Yas'm, tree of fire an' tree of life.

EVA. And flowers?

TOM. An' flowers.

EVA. And plantations?

TOM. An' plantations.

EVA (*turns to* TOM). But, Tom, what do they stand on?

TOM. What do *what* stan' on, Miss Eva?

EVA (*eagerly*). Houses? If they're up in the air why don't they fall down?

TOM. Dey stan' on somethin' firm as a rock, Miss Eva. Dey stan' on faith, an' you fly dere on wings.

EVA (*amused*). They'd have to be pretty big wings for *you* to fly away with, I think!

TOM. Wings of de mornin'? Yas'm, big black wings!

(EVA *breaks into a merry laugh.* TOM *joins in vastly pleased.*)

EVA. Wouldn't you be funny? Just like a buzzard! . . .

TOM. Yas—big, black buzzard!

EVA (*stops laughing, snuggles close to* TOM). Now you've got to sing me. . . .

TOM. Sing? Once more?

EVA. Yes. About the "spirits bright."

TOM'S SONG:

I see a band of spirits bright
That tastes the glory there.
They are all robed in spotless white,
And conquering palms they bear!

EVA. Uncle Tom! (*Pause.*) I've seen them! They come to me in my sleep sometimes. "They are all robed in spotless white, And conquering palms they bear." *I'm* going there, Uncle Tom; to the spirits bright!

TOM. You don't have to go, Miss Eva. Dey done come—come to you—you is one of the family. . . .

EVA (*dreamily*). No, I'm going, I'm going pretty soon, I think, Uncle Tom. (*Rises, going toward sunset glow.*) "A sea of glass mingled with fire." (*Pause.*)

TOM (*looking after her, still sitting*). She sure got de Lord's mark on her forehead, dat chile! Somethin's down deep in her eyes. It's jest no use tryin' to keep her here. She ain't never like a child dat's gwine to live.

(*Enter* ST. CLAIR. TOM *rises.*)

ST. CLAIR. Ah! My little pussy, come here to me! Let me look at you! You are better nowadays, aren't you?

EVA. Papa, I've had things I wanted to say to you for a long time—I want to say them now, while I can!

ST. CLAIR. No, no! Eva, you know you grow stronger every day!

EVA. Papa, isn't there a way to have slaves made free? If I should die, won't you think of me, and do it for my sake?

ST. CLAIR. Oh, child, don't talk to me so! You are all I have on earth!

EVA. Papa, those poor creatures love their children as much as you do me. (*Looks at* TOM.) Tom loves *his* children! (*To* ST. CLAIR.) Oh, do something for them!

ST. CLAIR. There, there, darling; only don't distress yourself, and I will do everything you wish.

EVA (*looks at* TOM). Then promise me that Uncle Tom shall have his freedom as soon as . . . (*hesitating*) I am . . .

ST. CLAIR. My darling, I will do anything in the world—anything you could ask me to.

EVA (*turns to* ST. CLAIR *delighted*). Oh, Papa! I knew you would! I knew you—— (*She grows faint and sways.*)

ST. CLAIR (*catching her;* TOM *hurries up*). Eva! What's the matter?

EVA (*rallies and smiles*). It—it's all right, Papa . . . I . . . I just felt a little dizzy!

ST. CLAIR. Here, Tom—take her to her room. This air is too cold for her. All right now, puss?

EVA. Oh, yes, Papa—all right now!

(TOM *takes her in his arms and carries her off toward L.* TOM *sings* "Swing low, sweet chariot.")

SLOW CURTAIN

SCENE VI

EVA's *bedroom. Slow curtain up.*

EVA *lies asleep in her bed. The* NURSE *sits near.*

Enter L.1.E. OPHELIA, *carrying a candle. She glances at the bed. (Light cue for candle.)*

OPHELIA (*pause*). How is the child?

NURSE (*rises*). No change. She's sleeping quietly.

OPHELIA. Has the doctor been here?

NURSE. Yes, he's just gone!

(OPHELIA *looks into the hall, having kept the door open.*)

OPHELIA. Come in, Tom. (*Enter* UNCLE TOM). Now, why on earth do I find you hanging about outside this room?

TOM. Well, Miss Feely, you know dere must be somebody waitin' an' watchin' for the bridegroom.

OPHELIA. What!

TOM. You know it say in de Scripture how at midnight dere was a great cry made: "Behol' de bridegroom cometh" . . . Dat's what Ah'm spectin' ebbery night now.

OPHELIA. Why do you feel like that, Tom?

TOM. Well, Miss Eva, she tell me, an' she *know,* an' when the time come I just gotta be here, cause when that blessed li'l chile go into de Kingdom dey gwine open de do' so wide we all gets a look in at de Glory!

OPHELIA. Did she say she felt worse today?

TOM. No, Miss Feely! But she telled me it was comin' nearer. Dar's dem what tells dat child, yas, Miss Feely. It's de angels of de Lawd, Miss Feely!!

(*Enter* ST. CLAIR.)

ST. CLAIR (*sotto voce*). How is she, Nurse?

NURSE. She's sleeping!

ST. CLAIR. What did the doctor say?

NURSE. He saw little change!

ST. CLAIR. No hope!

(*The* NURSE *shrugs her shoulders.* EVA *stirs and opens her eyes.*)

NURSE. She's awake!

(*The group surround the couch. Enter* MARIE.)

ST. CLAIR. Marie, come here, come here!

(MARIE *joins the group.*)

MARIE. My dearest! (*Kneels by the bed.*)

ST. CLAIR. Do you know me, darling?

EVA. Dear, dear Papa! Mama, please kiss me! (MARIE *does so.*) Uncle Tom, now, I'm happy! (*She sighs.*)

ST. CLAIR. Marie, she's dying! . . .

TOM. Look! Look! Massa, she can see things we can't see!

(TOM *kneels reverently.*)

EVA (*staring before her and smiling*). I see . . . I see . . . the crystal gates, wide—wide open—Love—joy—peace——

(*Her head falls to one side, her eyes close. The* NURSE *puts her finger on the pulse. All look at her. She lays* EVA'S *wrist down.*)

NURSE. It is over!

ST. CLAIR. Eva! My darling!!

SLOW CURTAIN

SCENE VII

ST. CLAIR'S *parlor.*

ST. CLAIR *discovered on ottoman in dressing gown. He is deep in thought.* TOM *is standing solicitously by.*

TOM. Is anything mo' I kin do fo' you, Massa St. Clair?

ST. CLAIR. Nothing. Oh, Tom, my boy, the whole world is as empty as an eggshell!

TOM. Yes, Massa, I knows dat, but if you-all could look up to where Miss Eva is . . .

ST. CLAIR. I do look up, Tom. I look up and I see *nothing*. I wish to God I could! It seems to be given to poor, honest fellows like you, to see what we cannot!

TOM. I reckon you kin, Marse St. Clair, if you pray to de Lawd! "Lawd, I believe, help Thou my unbelief!"

ST. CLAIR. No, Tom, I want to believe, but I cannot. I see nothing but doubt. Who knows anything about anything? Was all that beautiful love and faith but a shifting phase of feeling passing with a breath? And there is no more Eva—nothing!

TOM. Oh, yes, Massa St. Clair, there is. I knows it!

ST. CLAIR. How do you know there is? You never *saw* the Lord!

TOM. Well, Massa, you can't see pain, kin you? But you kin feel it—jes' so Ah feel de Lawd, in my soul, Massa St. Clair. When I was sold away from mah ole woman an' mah children I was jus' mos' broke up.

I says they ain't nothin' left—nothin' at all. Then the Lawd He stood by me and He say: "You cheer up, Tom, they ain't nothin' to be 'fraid of!" An' wot He done do fo' me, He do for Massa St. Clair!

ST. CLAIR. Tom, I believe you're fond of me!

TOM. Ah's willin' to lay down mah life fo' you, Massa St. Clair!

ST. CLAIR. You poor, foolish fellow!

TOM. An' dere's mo' dan me done love you—— (*Points up.*) De blessed Saviour, He love you, too!

ST. CLAIR. Singular! That the story of a man who lived and died eighteen hundred years ago can affect people still! I bet He was no mere man! (*Rises.*) But I'm forgetting why I sent for you. Tom, go pack your trunk and get ready to start for Kentucky. As I promised Eva, I'm going to make a free man of you!

TOM (*joyously*). Oh!!! Bless de Lawd! Bless de Lawd!

ST. CLAIR. Well, you needn't be in such a rapture about it! You haven't had such a hard time. You never could earn as a free man such clothes and such a living as I have given you.

TOM. Youse ben too good to me, Massa St. Clair, an' dis ole darky mighty grateful, but I'd ruther have poor clothes, poor house, poor everything an' have 'em *mine,* dan have de bes' ef dey b'long to somebody else.

ST. CLAIR. I suppose so, Tom. Ah well! I shall have your papers drawn up at once and then *you'll* be off! (*Sits again.*)

TOM. Not while Massa's in trouble!

ST. CLAIR. And when do you think my trouble will be over?

TOM. When you is a believer!

ST. CLAIR (*smiling*). No, Tom, I won't keep you till *that* day! Well! Go home, to your wife and children and good luck to you!

TOM. Dat day gwine come, Massa St. Clair, de Lawd got a heap o' work for massa to do!

ST. CLAIR. You seem to think the Lord needs a *great deal* done for Him!

TOM. Pow'ful lot, Massa St. Clair. We does fo' Him when we does fo' His critters.

ST. CLAIR. Tom, you've cheered me up! Now run along to the stable, and tell Jim to fetch my horse!

(*Exit* TOM.)

OPHELIA (*outside*). What are you doing there, you limb of Satan! You've been stealing something! (OPHELIA *drags in* TOPSY.)

TOPSY. You go 'long, Miss Feely, 'tain't none o' your business!

ST. CLAIR (*rises*). Heyday! What is all this commotion?

OPHELIA. She's been stealing again!

TOPSY (*sobbing*). I hain't neither!

OPHELIA. What have you got in your dress?

TOPSY. I've got my hand dar.

OPHELIA. But what have you got in your hand?

TOPSY. Nuffin'.

OPHELIA. That's a fib, Topsy.

TOPSY. Well, I 'spects it is!

OPHELIA. Well, give it to me!

TOPSY. It's mine, I hope I may die this bressed minute, if it don't b'long to me!

OPHELIA. Topsy, hold out your hand! (TOPSY *reluctantly takes the foot of an old stocking from her bosom and hands it to* OPHELIA.) Sakes alive! What is all this? (*Takes from it a lock of hair and a small book, with a bit of crape twisted around it.*)

TOPSY. Dat's a lock of ha'r dat Miss Eva gave me. She cut it from her own beau'ful head herself!

ST. CLAIR (*takes book*). Why did you wrap *this*—(*pointing to crape*) around the book?

TOPSY. 'Cause—'cause—'cause 'twas Miss Eva's. Oh! Don't take 'em away please! (*Sits down on stage and putting her apron over her head, begins to sob vehemently.*)

OPHELIA. Come, come, don't cry! you shall have them.

(ST. CLAIR *gives book back to* TOPSY.)

TOPSY (*jumps up joyfully and takes them*). I wants to keep 'em, 'cause dey makes me good; I ain't half so wicked as I used to was. (*Runs off R.1.E.*)

OPHELIA. The little imp has improved. I begin to have hopes of her.

ST. CLAIR. You see, my dear, there's something of our darling Eva left with us still. . . .

OPHELIA. Shakespeare wasn't always right . . . sometimes the good that folks do lives after them.

ST. CLAIR. Well, you may have the little devil! She's yours as soon as I can have my lawyer draw up the papers.

OPHELIA. You give me Topsy!

ST. CLAIR. If you'll take her!

OPHELIA. Well, I never got such a present as that in all my life!

ST. CLAIR. Well, what do you say?

OPHELIA. Well, I guess I might as well.

ST. CLAIR. Splendid!

OPHELIA. She seems to be hung around my neck anyhow, so I might as well go the whole hog. . . .

ST. CLAIR. Ha, ha, ha! Well, then she's yours and I wish you joy of her! (*Goes off laughing.*)

OPHELIA (*rises, thinks it over, is a little frightened of the bargain but makes up her mind to swing it; and goes to the door, sees* TOPSY *off and calls her*). Topsy, you come right here now. (*Enter* TOPSY.) Sit down! Topsy, I've got something very particular to say to you! (TOPSY *sits*.) Now!

TOPSY. Does you want me to say de Catechism?

OPHELIA. No, not now!

TOPSY (*aside*). Golly, dat's one comfort!

OPHELIA. Now, Topsy, I want you to try and understand what I am going to say to you.

TOPSY. Yes, missis, I'll open my ears dreffful wide.

OPHELIA. Mr. St. Clair has given you to me.

TOPSY. Den I b'longs to you; now don't I? (*Pause*.) Golly!

OPHELIA. I have the authority to call you my property.

TOPSY. I's your property, is I? Well, if you say so, I 'spects I am!

OPHELIA (*sits next her*). Topsy, I can give you your liberty.

TOPSY. My liberty?

OPHELIA. Yes, Topsy!

TOPSY. Have you got it with you?

OPHELIA. I have!

TOPSY. Is it clothes or wittles?

OPHELIA. How shiftless! Don't you know what your liberty is, Topsy?

TOPSY. I never seed it!

OPHELIA. Topsy, I am going to leave this place; I am going many miles away to my own home in Vermont!

TOPSY. What's going to happen to my liberty?

OPHELIA. I will take you with me, if you wish to go! How do you like that?

TOPSY. Miss Feely, does dey hab any oberseers in Varmount?

OPHELIA. No, Topsy!

TOPSY. Nor cotton plantations, nor sugar factories, nor darkies nor whippin' nor nothing?

OPHELIA. No, Topsy!

TOPSY (*rises*). By golly, de quicker we is gwine de better!

OPHELIA (*rises*). But you must try to be good!

TOPSY. Miss Feely, I tell you de truif, dere's somepin' de matter wid me!

OPHELIA. Are you sick?

TOPSY. I reckon so, 'cause I ain't done hardly anythin' wicked since Miss Eva done go way. I gits betterer an' betterer ebbery day. I 'spects when I'm daid I'm goin' to be turn into a . . . li'l brack angel!

BLACK-OUT

SCENE VIII

The auction mart. Auction stand—eight soap boxes across the stage. Bales of cotton standing about. A couple of barrels, etc.

At rise TOM, EMMELINE, OLD WOMAN, ADOLPH, TOPSY *and various other darkies are discovered sitting about or standing on the boxes singing various plantation songs. Enter* SKEGGS, *the auctioneer.*

SKEGGS. Hey, stop this infernal howling! Don't you know you're all going to be sold? Shut up; and look cheerful! I'll try and get you some good masters. (*He shouts off.*) Hey, gentlemen, come right along, come right along! . . . The sale is about to begin; we've some very fine property to offer you this morning. (*A number of white men stroll casually on and examine the Negroes as they pass by.*) That's right, gentlemen, look 'em over, look 'em over, there'll be no deception about any of 'em as long as I am auctioneer. Got all their pedigrees right in this yere book. (*He taps the big book under his arm.*)

(*Enter* MARKS.)

MARKS. Why, hello, Skeggs!

SKEGGS. Hello, Mr. Marks!

MARKS. Well, well, what have you got goin' on here today!

SKEGGS. Why, it's a sale of slaves, belonging to Mr. St. Clair.

MARKS. St. Clair, hey, what happened to him?

SKEGGS. Didn't you hear?

MARKS. Not a word.

SKEGGS. He got killed, interfering in a fight.

MARKS. You don't say so!

SKEGGS. I do say so. He had it all fixed up to set some of these slaves free, but he died before he had the papers made out. His estate was in bad shape, and they have got to be sold to settle it up.

MARKS. Well, Skeggs, you'll find I'll be running up your principal bidders!

SKEGGS. Look 'em over, Marks, look 'em over. You'll find some damn good niggers in the lot.

LEGREE (*heard outside*). Hey, boys, hold my horse! (*He enters and bumps rudely into* MARKS, *without paying any attention to him shakes hands with* SKEGGS). Hello, Skeggs, what's on the books today?

SKEGGS. Well, look 'em over yourself, they belonged to St. Clair.

LEGREE. And a damn lazy lot he always had.

SKEGGS. Oh no, you'll find some very good niggers there. Look 'em over!

By the way—allow me to introduce to you my old friend. This is Mr. Legree——

MARKS. I'm a lawyer and my name is Marks! Have a card!!

(LEGREE *shakes hands.*)

LEGREE. I'm pleased to meet you, Mr. Marks.

MARKS (*Wincing*). Hold on, hold on, hold on!

LEGREE. That's what I am doing.

MARKS. When I say hold on, I mean let go.

LEGREE. Well, why don't you say what you mean! (*Swings* MARKS *to Stage C.*)

MARKS. My, my, that's a hard hand you've got.

LEGREE. Do you know how that hand became hard?

MARKS. No, how did it?

LEGREE. By knocking down niggers.

MARKS. Well, I'm no nigger.

LEGREE. There's nothing soft about me.

MARKS (*Laughing*). Oh, yes, there is!

LEGREE (*Laughs*). Perhaps you mean my heart.

MARKS. No, I mean your head.

LEGREE (*in a rage*). What! (*Raises his whip to strike* MARKS, *who cowers away.*)

SKEGGS. Come, come, gentlemen . . . none of that if you please! Now if you're ready we'll get on with the sale. The first item I have to offer is the boy Adolph who was valet to the late Mr. St. Clair. Adolph, take the stand! (ADOLPH *does so.*) Now look him over, gentlemen, look him over!

(LEGREE, MARKS *and several other bidders go up to the block and look the boy over.*)

LEGREE. A nigger with his boots blacked! Bah! (*Spits on his shoe.*)

MARKS. Well, Adolph, you're a fine-looking fellow. How old are you?

ADOLPH. Eighteen, sir!

SKEGGS. Well, gentlemen, now you've examined this property, how much am I offered?

LEGREE. One hundred.

FIRST BIDDER (KRAMER). Thirty-five.

MARKS. Seventy-five.

SECOND BIDDER. Two hundred.

MARKS. Seventy-five.

THIRD BIDDER (MR. STUART). Three hundred.

MARKS. Seventy-five.

SKEGGS. Three hundred and seventy-five—three hundred and seventy-five—— Any more bids, gentlemen, any more bids? Going, going—if that's all—— Gone! Sold to Mr. Marks, the lawyer!

MARKS. Now, Adolph, you belong to me! All you got to do is work. (*Points right.*) Now you go right down there and I'll come along presently, if not sooner.

SKEGGS. Well now, Mr. Marks. . . . (*Holds out his hand for the money.*)

MARKS. What can I do for you?

SKEGGS. Come . . . come . . . haven't you forgotten something?

MARKS. Yes, siree, I've forgotten more than you ever knew!

SKEGGS. I mean the pay for that boy.

MARKS. Oh yes, of course. You want the money! Here you are. (*Takes dollar bill from his pocketbook and gives it to* SKEGGS.) Twenty-five cents change please.

SKEGGS (*looking at the bill*). What's this . . . What's this?

MARKS. Oh, did I give you a two-dollar bill!

SKEGGS. No, sir, this is a one-dollar bill!

MARKS. That's right! Twenty-five cents change.

SKEGGS. Look here. . . . What do you think you bid for that boy?

MARKS. I never bid anything but seventy-five.

SKEGGS. Seventy-five what?

MARKS. Seventy-five cents, of course!

SKEGGS. Say, do you think I'm standing here knocking down full-grown boys for seventy-five cents?

MARKS. Well, I ain't very particular. Have you got any little boys for twenty-five cents?

SKEGGS (*pulling out a gun*). Why you . . . get out of here! (MARKS *runs out.*) He's your nigger for three hundred dollars, Mr. Stuart.

(ADOLPH *gets off block.*)

SKEGGS. The next on the list is the boy Caesar. (*Waves his mallet at the boy.*) On the block, Caesar, on the block. (*The boy starts to go on the block when an old Negro woman clings to him.*)

OLD WOMAN (*anxiously*). Dis chile ain't goin' to be sold without me! We goes in de lot togedder! I ain't so old an' I's real strong. I can do lots o' work yet.

LEGREE (*laughing*). That's likely.

SKEGGS. Gentlemen, I would like to sell these two together.

LEGREE. Bah! That old hag o' bran ain't worth her salt!

SKEGGS. Well, it's a pity, her heart's sot on that boy, she'll go cheap!

LEGREE. Wouldn't take her for a gift!

SKEGGS (*looks at* MANN). How about you, Major?

MANN. Couldn't hardly use her, Skeggs.

OLD WOMAN (*patting boy's shoulder*). You keep close to your ole mammy. They'll put us up togedder, they've got to. I jes' can't live no-how ef dey don't.

SKEGGS (*rapping on his desk*). Come, Caesar, jump up on the block, show your springs.

OLD WOMAN (*clinging to the boy*). Put us up togedder . . . Oh, please, massa, don't . . . (SKEGGS *pushes her back, drags the boy away, drives him up onto the block.*)

OLD WOMAN. Oh, please, please, leave me dis one, old Massa always said I could have dis one, dis one lamb. . . . (*She subsides, whimpering.*)

SKEGGS (*rapping on desk*). Well, gentlemen, what do I hear for this boy?

LEGREE. Two hundred and fifty.

FIRST BIDDER. Two hundred and seventy-five.

LEGREE. Three hundred and fifty.

FIRST BIDDER. Three hundred and seventy-five.

SKEGGS. Three hundred and seventy-five, I have, three hundred and seventy-five . . . three hundred and seventy-five . . . do I hear four hundred? Four hundred? Who says four hundred? Come, come, gentlemen . . . this is no price for this young, healthy boy . . . let me hear four hundred! No! Going at three hundred and seventy-five . . . going . . . going. . . .

LEGREE. Four hundred.

FIRST BIDDER. Four hundred and fifty!

SKEGGS. Four hundred and fifty! Four hundred and fifty! Do I hear any more . . . are you all done? Once more, are you all done! Going. . . .

MAJOR MANN. Five hundred dollars!

SKEGGS. Thank you, Major! Any more? Sold to Major Mann for five hundred dollars!

OLD WOMAN (*pleadingly to* MAJOR MANN). Buy me, too, massa, for de Lord sake, buy me! I'm goin' to die if you don't, please, massa.

(MANN *shakes his head and turns away.*)

OLD WOMAN. Oh, my baby, he's my last baby! My last little man!

SKEGGS (*kindly*). Now, Aunt Hagar, pull yourself together!

OLD WOMAN. Ah can't, Ah can't. I've lost my baby! Ole massa always said I could keep him.

SKEGGS. Come, come, Aunty, get on the block, let 'em see how smart you are. (*He whispers to her.*) Maybe the Major will take you after all!

OLD WOMAN (*eagerly*). Do you think so, massa?

SKEGGS (*nods encouragingly;* OLD WOMAN *tries to brace up and walks smartly to block; she limps a little, but tries to disguise it*). Now, gentlemen, you see Aunt Hagar isn't so feeble. She's just a little bit lame!

OLD WOMAN. Lame . . . lame . . . dat's no lame, no sir, dat's a bunion dat is!

SKEGGS. All right, all right, now, gentlemen, what do you offer?

LEGREE. Fifty cents!

OLD WOMAN. Fifty cents! Oh de good Lawd! (*She looks at* LEGREE. *She looks pleadingly at* MANN.)

MANN. Skeggs, will you take fifty dollars for her?

SKEGGS (*quickly*). Major, you bought her!

OLD WOMAN. Rest de good Lawd! Rest de good Lawd!

MANN. That's all right, mammy, you just stand back there awhile. (OLD WOMAN *gets down from block with some effort, crosses to* LEGREE *and as she passes him speaks.*)

OLD WOMAN. Fifty cents for a nigger.

SKEGGS. Come, come, mammy, get up back!

OLD WOMAN. Yassa, sir, I's goin'. (*Goes up, repeating over shoulder:*) Fifty cents for a nigger!

SKEGGS. Now, gentlemen, the next is a very useful gal either for the house or in the field. . . . Step up here, Emmeline. . . . (EMMELINE *takes the block.*) Now, gentlemen, look her over; and tell me if you ever saw a better one. (*Bidders crowd around.*)

LEGREE. Well, you're a smart lookin' gal, Emmeline. How old are you? (*At this point* MARKS *sticks head in at right.*)

MARKS. Seventy-five. (*They chase him out.*)

LEGREE. How old are you, I say! (*Squeezes her arm.*)

EMMELINE. Please . . . please don't, you hurt me!

LEGREE. Oh, I hurt you, did I? That's just too bad!

SKEGGS. Come, gentlemen, what do I hear now . . . what do I hear?

LEGREE. Four hundred!

FIRST BIDDER. Twenty-five.

SECOND BIDDER. Thirty-five.

FIRST BIDDER. Fifty.

LEGREE. Five hundred.

MARKS (*entering*). Seventy-five.

SKEGGS. Will you get out of here or shall I throw you out?

EVERYBODY. Throw him out!

MARKS. Just a moment, gentlemen! I'm a free-born American citizen, and I have a right to bid at any auction sales. (*To* SKEGGS.) I insist on my right to bid!

SKEGGS (*drawing gun*). Well, what do you *bid?*

MARKS (*with his eye on the gun*). I bid you good day! (*He exits.*)

SKEGGS. Well, gentlemen, I have five hundred bid, who'll . . . ?

FIRST BIDDER. Six hundred!

MANN. Seven hundred!

SKEGGS. Seven hundred I have, seven hundred dollars . . . Gentlemen, a beautiful gal for seven hundred dollars, do I hear any more?

LEGREE (*to crowd*). Eight hundred dollars!

SKEGGS. Eight hundred I hear! Come, come, gentlemen, the last call, positively the last call for this beautiful gal . . . going . . . going . . . sold! To Simon Legree for eight hundred dollars!

(LEGREE takes EMMELINE *roughly by the arm and drags her off the block. Puts metal tag on string around her neck.*)

SKEGGS. Now, gentlemen, we have here a real, ripe article! Topsy, take the stand!

TOPSY. What's that, massa?

SKEGGS. I said take the stand!

TOPSY. I am standin' right now, ain't I?

SKEGGS (*exasperated*). Come, and stand here up on this block! Do you hear me? (TOPSY *goes on block.*) This yere gal, gentlemen, this yere gal has got talents!

LEGREE. You don't say so!

SKEGGS. I do say so!

LEGREE. Well, what the hell are they?

SKEGGS. They tell me she's a right smart dancer!

FISK. A dancer, is she?

SKEGGS. Well, well, George Fisk? How are you, and how's the showboat business?

FISK. Pretty fair to middlin', thank you!

SKEGGS. Well, well, Mr. Fisk, here is somethin' right in your line!

FISK. How's that?

SKEGGS. Wait till you see! Topsy, show him what you do!

TOPSY. What I do?

SKEGGS. You heard me!

TOPSY. I do a lot of things.

LEGREE. Including stealing, I reckon!

SKEGGS. Not at all, not at all! Her record's first class. Come on, Topsy, shake your feet now!

TOPSY. My feet don't feel very shaky, boss!

SKEGGS. Well, they better!

TOPSY. I'm powerful sorry, boss, but I don't reckon they do!

SKEGGS. All right, then we'll sell you for a field hand, how will you like that?

TOPSY. Does you mean work?

SKEGGS. That's it!

TOPSY. Diggin' in de dirt?

SKEGGS. That's it!

TOPSY. Sweatin' in de sun?

SKEGGS. That's it!

TOPSY. Reckon I's goin' to dance, boss!

SKEGGS. All right, then, go ahead and dance. . . . (TOPSY *does a dance.*) There you are, gentlemen, come now, what am I offered?

FIRST BIDDER. Fifty dollars!

SKEGGS. That's plumb ridiculous! Fifty dollars for this young gal!!

SECOND BIDDER. One hundred dollars!

FISK. One hundred and fifty dollars!

(*At this point* OPHELIA *comes on at the back of the crowd, watching bidding.*)

SKEGGS. Well, gentlemen, do you hear that now? Mr. Fisk offers one hundred and fifty dollars . . . and . . . he knows dancing . . . one hundred and fifty dollars! Do I hear two hundred? Mr. Fisk . . . is getting a bargain . . . going . . . going. . . . Won't anybody give two hundred dollars?

OPHELIA (*stepping forward*). Two hundred dollars!

(*Everybody looks at* OPHELIA.)

SKEGGS. Another county heard from! Ma'am, I thank you . . . two hundred dollars. . . . Do I hear any more? Mr. Fisk, do I hear two hundred and fifty? I'll take two hundred and twenty-five. (FISK *shakes his head.*) No? Going at two hundred dollars! . . . Going . . . going . . . sold, for two hundred dollars! Madam, you've bought a very cheap nigger. . . .

(OPHELIA *suddenly overwhelmed with dismay.*)

TOPSY (*descending from block and going to* OPHELIA). My Lord, Miss Feely, I's yo' property after all!

OPHELIA (*crosses to* SKEGGS *and pays two hundred dollars*). Good heavens yes, and what will people up in Vermont say when they find out I've bought a slave! You come with me, Topsy!!

(*She goes out.* TOPSY *follows but manages to pass close to* LEGREE *and thumbs her nose at him as she goes out.* RIDDELL *exits after them.*)

SKEGGS. Now, gentlemen, my next item is a rare one. . . . His late master, St. Clair, would not have parted with him for his weight in gold, and I'm right sorry, gentlemen, he must go! Uncle Tom, come in here! (UNCLE TOM *who has been sitting at the very outskirts on a bale of cotton now turns around.*) Look him over, gentlemen! (*Bidders swarm around him.*)

LEGREE. Let's see your teeth, old man! (*Crosses to* TOM, *grabs him by jaw and opens mouth.*) Now bend your back. (TOM *does so.*) Um! Hold up your arm till I feel your muscle! You're still pretty strong. Where was you raised?

UNCLE TOM. In Ole Kentucky, massa!

LEGREE. What did you do there?

TOM. Had charge of massa's plantation.

LEGREE. Whose plantation?

TOM. Massa St. Clair.

LEGREE. Ha, that's a damn lie!

SKEGGS. It's quite true, Mr. Legree, I have it all here in black and white. Take the block, Uncle Tom. (*Pats book.* TOM *does so.*) Well, gentlemen, how much am I bid?

LEGREE. Eight hundred dollars!

FIRST BIDDER. Eight hundred and fifty!

SKEGGS. I have eight hundred and fifty dollars . . . eight hundred and fifty! Eight hundred and fifty! . . . What's the matter, gentlemen; why, this is one of the finest articles I've ever put up for sale, gentlemen, this nigger is a well-qualified manager of a plantation. He's handled scores of farm hands, thousands of his master's money, and never a penny missing. Why, gentlemen, this is the finest bargain in the world, and I hear only eight hundred and fifty dollars!!

LEGREE. Nine hundred!

SECOND BIDDER. One thousand dollars!

SKEGGS. One thousand dollars, that's a little more like it. Gentlemen, you've never had such an opportunity, one thousand—one thousand—do I hear fifteen hundred?

LEGREE. Twelve hundred!

SKEGGS. Twelve hundred dollars . . . twelve hundred, twelve hundred, twelve hundred, do I hear any more? Last call, gentlemen, going at twelve hundred dollars . . . last call twelve hundred, going, going. . . . And sold for twelve hundred dollars to Simon Legree. . . .

LEGREE (*takes out wallet and pays* SKEGGS; *taking hold of* TOM). Now you belong to me! (*Puts slave tag around his neck.*) And you too, nigger, come along!! (EMMELINE *crosses to* TOM. LEGREE *crosses to entrance.*)

TOM. May heaven have mercy on us both!

LEGREE. Mercy, hey? Ha, ha! I'll give you mercy! (*Cracks whip. Starts off with them through arch.*) Come along!

SKEGGS. Next article on the list, gentlemen, this here yellow gal. . . . (*Points her out.*) Recommended highly for lady's maid or house servant. Excellent record all in the book. . . . Look her over, gentlemen, and make your offer. . . . How much am I bid, how much am I bid?

CURTAIN

ACT THREE

SCENE I

Street in New Orleans. Enter GEORGE SHELBY.

GEORGE SHELBY. At last my mission of mercy is nearly finished; I have reached my journey's end. I have now but to find the house of Mr. St. Clair, repurchase Old Uncle Tom, and take him back to his wife and children, in old Kentucky. Someone approaches; he may be able to give me the information I require. (*Enter* MARKS *on his donkey.*) Pray, sir, can you tell me where Mr. St. Clair dwells?

MARKS. Where I don't think you'll be in a hurry to seek him.

GEORGE SHELBY. And where is that?

MARKS. In the grave!

GEORGE SHELBY. Wait a moment! You may be able to give me some information concerning Mr. St. Clair . . . Mr. . . .

MARKS. I am a lawyer; my name is Marks. Have a card! As a lawyer I never *give* anything!

GEORGE SHELBY. But you would have no objections to selling it?

MARKS. Not the slightest.

GEORGE SHELBY. What do you value it at?

MARKS. Well, say ten dollars (*pause*) . . . five dollars. . . .

GEORGE SHELBY. Here you are! (*Gives money.*) Now tell me. I've been abroad and have had no news. What happened to Mr. St. Clair's slaves?

MARKS. All sold.

GEORGE SHELBY. How were they sold?

MARKS. At auction—dirt cheap, too!

GEORGE SHELBY. How were they bought—all in one lot?

MARKS. No, they went to different bidders.

GEORGE SHELBY. Did you bid at the sale?

MARKS. Did I bid at the sale? I was the runner-up for the biggest bidders!

GEORGE SHELBY. Do you remember seeing a Negro among them called Tom?

MARKS. What—Uncle Tom?

GEORGE SHELBY. Yes, that's the one! Who bought him?

MARKS. A Mr. Legree.

GEORGE SHELBY. Where is his plantation?

MARKS. He lives in Louisiana, on the Red River; but a man never could find it unless he had been there before!

GEORGE SHELBY. Who could I get to direct me there?

MARKS. Well, stranger, I don't know of any one better than myself could find it for you; it's such an out-of-the-way sort of hole, and if you are a mind to come down handsomely. . . .

GEORGE SHELBY. The reward shall be ample.

MARKS. Where you stoppin', sir?

GEORGE SHELBY. At the St. Charles Hotel.

MARKS. Why, I stop there too!

GEORGE SHELBY. Why, I don't remember seeing you!

MARKS. Well, you see, I stop on the outside. Have you had your dinner yet?

GEORGE SHELBY. Not yet.

MARKS. Well, sir, you shall be allowed to dine with me at the St. Charles Hotel, and you may pay for the dinner!

(*They go out.*)

CURTAIN

SCENE II

LEGREE'S *cabin. Lighted candle on table.*
TOM *is discovered in old clothes, seated on a stool beside table. He holds in his hand a paper containing a curl of* EVA'S *hair.*
The scene opens to the symphony of "Old Folks at Home."

TOM. I come to de dark places; I's going through de vale of shadows. My heart feels just like a big lump of lead! 'Pears like I ain't going to be smart no more; just ole scarecrow, that's what you is. They take everything away from me, everything except this here lock of Miss Eva's ha'r. Massa Legree don't get you, no sir! You'se my comfort, you is! And these yere shiny dollar Little Massa George give me when I was sold away. Massa George—I wonder what become of Massa George. He must be grown man by now.

(*Tom sings "Old Folks at Home." Enter* LEGREE, EMMELINE, SAMBO *and* QUIMBO.)

LEGREE (*as he enters*). Stop that damn yowling, you black dog! (*Turns to* EMMELINE.) Now, gal, you're home! (EMMELINE *shrinks from him. He takes hold of her ear.*) Never wore earrings, did you?

EMMELINE (*trembling*). No, massa.

LEGREE. Well, I'll give you a pair, if you're a good girl. You needn't be so frightened; I don't mean to make you work very hard. You'll live like a lady with me; only you've got to be a good girl.

EMMELINE. I'll try to, massa!

LEGREE (*to* EMMELINE). Come, gal, you go in here with me! (*Takes* EMMELINE's *hand and leads her toward exit.*)

EMMELINE (*Withdrawing her hand and shrinking back*). No, no, let me work in the fields; I don't want to be a lady!

LEGREE. Oh! You're going to be contrary, are you? I'll soon take all that out of you!

EMMELINE. Please! Please!!

LEGREE. Tom, take that gal out and flog her! (TOM *stands aghast.*) I told you I didn't buy you jest for common work, I mean to promote you and make a driver of you. Ye may jest as well begin to get yer hand in. Take her out and flog her, do you hear?

TOM. I hopes massa won't set me at that. It's what I ain't used to—never did!

LEGREE. Never did, eh? Well, you'll do a lot of things ye never did before I've done with ye. (*Strikes* TOM *with whip three blows. Music chord each blow.*) There! Now will ye tell me ye can't do it?

TOM. Yes, Massa! I'm willing to work night and day, while there's life and breath in my body; but this yere thing 'tain't right to do!

LEGREE. What! Ye black beast! Tell *me* ye don't think it right to do what I tell ye! What have any of you cussed cattle to do with thinking what's right? What do ye think ye are? A gentleman, to be telling me what's right and what ain't! So you think it's wrong to flog the gal, Master Tom!

TOM. Yes, Massa! If you mean to kill me, kill me; but dis yere I can't do it —I'll die first!

LEGREE. Well, here's a pious dog—let down among us sinners—didn't you never read out of your Bible, "Servants, obey your masters"? Ain't I your master? Didn't I pay twelve hundred dollars for all there is inside your cussed old black hide? Ain't you mine, body and soul?

TOM. No, no, Massa, my body belongs to you, but my soul belongs to de Lawd, an' you never can buy that!!

LEGREE. I can't? We'll see, we'll see! Here, Sambo, Quimbo! Take this dog up to the whippin' post, an' give him such a floggin' he'll remember it till the day he dies! (*They take* TOM *out.*)

TOM (*going*). Oh Lawd, help me!

LEGREE. Well, now, let's see if He will! (*Starts to embrace* EMMELINE.)

CURTAIN

SCENE III

An old, roofless shed. Night. Pallet of straw, lantern. TOM *discovered lying on some old cotton bagging.* CASSY *kneels by his side, holding a cup to his lips.*

CASSY. Drink a little more, take all you want! (TOM *drinks again.*) It ain't the first time I've been out in the night carrying water to such as you!

TOM. Dat's pow'ful good. Thank you, missis!

CASSY. Don't call me missis. I'm a miserable slave like yourself, lower than *you* can ever be. It's no use, Tom—this you're trying to do. You're in the Devil's hands. He's the strongest and you may as well give up!

TOM. How can I give up, Miss Cassy?

CASSY. You don't know anything about it—I do! Here you are on a lone plantation, ten miles away in the swamps. If you were burned alive, there's no law here that can do any good! And this man? You think there's any use in resisting? 'Twould make your flesh crawl if I told you what I've seen. Did I *want* to live with him? Wasn't I a woman gently reared by my white father? And Simon Legree! God in heaven! What *is* he? I've lived with him five years, and night and day I've cursed every moment of my life!

TOM. Oh, sweet Lawd Jesus! Has you done forgot us poor critters?

CASSY. And what are these miserable low dogs you work with that you should suffer on their account? Every one of them would turn on you the first time they get a chance. They're all of them vile and cruel! There's no use your suffering for *them!*

TOM. What made 'em cruel? Ef I give out I gwine get used to it, and den I be jus' lak dem. No, no, missis, I done lost ever'thing—mah wife, mah childun, mah home. I lost ever'-thing in dis worl', an' now I ain't gwine lose heaven, too!

CASSY. But it cain't be that He'll lay sin to our account when we're forced to it! He'll charge it to them that drove us to it! Can I do anything more? Do you want some more water?

TOM. Oh, Miss Cassy, why don't you go to Him what can give you livin' water?

CASSY. Go to Him! Who is He? *Where* is He?

TOM. He up dere, Miss Cassy, yo' Heavenly Father!

CASSY. I saw a picture of Him once! When I was a girl, over the altar, with the white flowers and the bright candles shining around Him. But He ain't here! There's nothing here but just Hell!

TOM. But, Miss Cassy . . .

CASSY. There, there . . . don't talk any more! Try to sleep if you can! (*Rises.*) I must go back or they'll suspect. Think of me when I'm gone, Uncle Tom. (*Picks up lantern.*) And pray for me some time!

TOM. Yes, Miss Cassy, I done gwine pray!

(*Exit* CASSY.)

CURTAIN

SCENE IV

LEGREE'S *cabin. A rough chamber. Enter* LEGREE. *Sits.*

LEGREE. Damn that Sambo, to kick up this yere row between me and the new hands! (CASSY *steals on stage and stands behind him.*) The rascal won't be fit to work for a week now, right in the press of the season!

CASSY. Yes, just like you!

(*Bottle whisky, tumbler.*)

LEGREE (*turns*). Hah! You she-devil! You've come back, have you!

CASSY (*crosses to him*). Yes, I have; come to have my own way too!

LEGREE (*sits by table*). You lie, you jade! I'll keep my word. Either behave yourself, or stay down in the quarters and fare and work with the rest!

CASSY. I'd rather ten thousand times live in the dirtiest hole at the quarters than under your roof!

LEGREE. But you are under my roof, for all that! So sit down here and listen to reason! (*Grasps her wrist.*)

CASSY (*dominates him*). Simon Legree, take care! You're afraid of me, Simon, and you've reason to be. . . . Simon, I've got Satan in me! (*He lets his hold go.*)

LEGREE. Come, come, Cassy, why can't we be friends as we used to be?

CASSY (*bitterly*). Used to be!

LEGREE. Why can't you behave yourself decently!

CASSY. *You* talk about behaving decently! And what have you been doing? You haven't even sense enough to keep from spoiling one of your best hands, right in your busiest season, all for your devil's temper!

LEGREE. I was a fool, to let any such wrangle come up, but when Tom set up his will against mine, he had to be broke in!

CASSY. You'll never break *him* in.

LEGREE. Won't I? (*Drinks.*) If I don't, he'll be the first nigger that ever come it around me! I'll break every bone in his body but he's got to give up! (*Enter* SAMBO *with a paper in his hands; stands bowing.*) What's *that,* you dog?

SAMBO. A witch thing, massa.

LEGREE. A what?

SAMBO. A witch thing. Something that niggers gits from witches. Keep 'em from feelin' when they's flogged. He had it tied round his neck with a black string. (LEGREE *takes the paper and opens it; a silver dollar drops on the stage, and a long curl of light hair twines around his finger.*)

LEGREE. A lock of hair! (*Rises.*) Damnation! (*Stamping and writhing, as if the hair burned him.*) Where did this come from? Take it away! Burn it up! Burn it up! (*Throws the curl away.*) What did you bring it to me for?

SAMBO (*trembling*). I's sorry, massa; thought you would like to see um.

LEGREE. Don't you bring me any more of your devilish things! (*Shakes his fist at* SAMBO *who runs off stage.* LEGREE *kicks the dollar after him.*) Damn it! Where did he get that? If it didn't look just like—! I thought I'd forgot that. Curse me if I think there's any such thing as forgetting anything, anyhow. (*Sits by table, drinks.*)

CASSY. What is the matter with you, Legree? What is there in a little curl of golden hair to frighten a man like you?

LEGREE. Cassy, tonight the past has been recalled to me—the past that I tried to forget.

CASSY. Is there anything on this earth that can soften a soul like yours?

LEGREE. Yes, for hard as I now seem, there has been a time when I have been rocked on the bosom of a mother, cradled with prayers and pious hymns.

CASSY (*aside*). And can't these memories of your childhood soften your heart of iron?

LEGREE. In my childhood my mother used to lead me, at the sound of Sabbath bells, to worship and to pray. But I followed in the footsteps of my father, wild and tyrannical. I despised all *her* counsel, and broke from her, to seek my fortunes on the sea. I never came home but once after that and then my mother, with the yearning of a heart that must love something and had nothing else to love, clung to me; and sought with prayers and entreaties to win me from a life of sin.

CASSY. That was your day of grace, Legree; then the good angels called you, and mercy held you by the hand.

LEGREE. My heart nearly relented; there was a conflict, but sin got the victory; and I set all the force of my nature against the conviction of my conscience. I was wilder and more brutal than ever. And one night, when my mother, in the last agony of her despair, knelt at my feet, I threw her from me—left her senseless on the floor and fled from her life forever! (*Leans his head on arms on table.*)

CASSY. Then the devil took you for his own!

(LEGREE *drinks.*)

LEGREE. The next I heard of my mother was one night while I was carousing and drinking, a letter was put in my hands. I opened it, and a lock of curling hair fell from it and twined about my fingers, even as that lock twined but now. The letter told me that my mother was dead, and that dying she blessed and forgave me! (*Buries his face in his hands.*)

CASSY. That was a sign to you, Legree. Why didn't you give up your evil ways *then?*

LEGREE. It was too late. I burned the letter and the lock of hair, and when I saw them hissing and crackling in the flame, I thought of everlasting fires! In the deep night, I have seen that pale mother rising by my bedside and felt the soft twining of that hair around my fingers, till the cold sweat would roll down my face. (*Rises, crosses to C. in horror.*) Christ! What the hell ails me? I believe I am bewitched! (*Crosses to table, takes a drink.*) I'll have Sambo and Quimbo up here to sing and dance and drive away these blue devils! Here, Sambo! Quimbo! (*Crosses to C.*)

CASSY. Simon Legree, that lock of hair *was* charmed! Each hair bore a spell of terror to conjure you! (LEGREE *moves toward her.*) Look out, Legree!! Your end is near!

LEGREE. You she-devil!

CURTAIN

SCENE V

A street in New Orleans. Enter MARKS *on a donkey, singing "Listen to the Mocking Bird." Enter* CUTE, *very breezy.*

CUTE. Well, well, well. Two of a kind if ever I seen 'em. Hello, Stranger, ain't we met up before somewhere?

MARKS. I wouldn't be surprised—I meet a lot of queer folks. My name is Marks. I'm a lawyer. Have a card.

CUTE. Howdy, Mr. Marks. My name is Gumption Cute. I'm a card but I haven't got one.

MARKS. Oh, I remember you. Ain't you the feller who ran the shell game on the *Robert E. Lee?*

CUTE. Maybe I am and maybe I ain't.

MARKS. Come, come. You can tell me. I'm a lawyer.

CUTE. I know that—but are you *my* lawyer?

MARKS. Well, say I am.

CUTE. If you are my lawyer I could tell you I done a murder, and you couldn't tell the police, could you?

MARKS. That's right. No violation of a client's confidence.

CUTE. Then are you my lawyer, or ain't you?

MARKS. Well—say I am your lawyer.

CUTE. All right. I am the feller who ran the shell game on the *Robert E. Lee*. What of it?

MARKS. I thought so. What are you doing just now?

CUTE. The best I can. Ever since I got chased off the river boats I've had a hard time making a dishonest living.

MARKS. Ever try making an honest one?

CUTE. Once. But everyone was alluz wantin' me to work. Now you wouldn't like that yourself.

MARKS. Well, maybe I can suggest something.

CUTE. Go ahead and suggest.

MARKS. Do you know Simon Legree?

CUTE (*startled*). Simon Legree!

MARKS. Yes. I've agreed to guide a young feller named Shelby to his plantation. Do you know where it is?

CUTE. Yes—but I can't go there.

MARKS. Why not?

CUTE. I saw the fight when Legree stabbed Mr. St. Clair. I was the only witness.

MARKS. You were? Then I tell you what we'll do. We'll get a warrant for the arrest of Legree. Then we go to him and I'll say, "Look here, Legree, here's a warrant for your arrest for murder. My friend Cute and myself are the only witnesses."

CUTE. But you didn't see the fight.

MARKS. I'm telling you what I'm going to say to Legree.

CUTE. Oh!

MARKS. Then I'll say, "Now you give us a thousand dollars and we'll keep quiet. If not . . ." See?

CUTE. Then Legree forks over the thousand dollars, and your friend Cute takes five hundred of it. Is that the calculation?

MARKS. That's it. And then we go and tell the police.

CUTE. About the thousand dollars?

MARKS. Good God, no! About the murder.

CUTE. I breathe again. . . . Mr. Marks, I'm your man.

MARKS. Shake on it.

CUTE. Right. (*They do so.*)

MARKS. But suppose this Legree shows fight?

CUTE. Fight! Do you know what will happen to him if he does? He'll find himself lying on the ground—bound hand and foot—and both his eyes gouged out.

MARKS. Would you do that?

CUTE. No, but I'd find somebody who would.

MARKS. All right then, suppose the two of us go somewhere and talk it over.

CUTE. No, the three of us will talk it over. (*Starts to leave.*) Come on, Jenny.

MARKS. No, no, no. Not Jenny—Willie.

CUTE. My mistake. (*They exit.*)

CURTAIN

SCENE VI

An old roofless shed.
Enter LEGREE *followed by* SAMBO.

LEGREE. Go and send Cassy to me!

SAMBO (*hesitatingly*). Well, you see, Massa . . . !

LEGREE. Off with you! (SAMBO *goes to door.*) Curse the woman! She's got the devil's own temper! I'll grind her to bits, one of these days! (SAMBO *creeps back in, frightened.*) What's the matter with you, black scoundrel!

SAMBO. S'help me, massa, she ain't no place! I's been all over de house, every room except the haunted garret, and they sure don't go in there . . . can't find nothing of her nor Emmeline neider.

LEGREE. Bolted! Call out the dogs! Saddle my horse! Stop! By the Lord, I have it! Sambo, go and walk that Tom in here. *Quick!* (*Exit* SAMBO *L.U.E.*) This black toad is at the bottom of this, and I'll have it out of his infernal black hide, and ain't he *mine!* Can't I do what I like with him? Who's to hinder? (TOM *is dragged on by* SAMBO *and* QUIMBO *and thrown to the floor,* LEGREE *grimly confronting* TOM.) I've made up my mind to *kill* you, Tom!

TOM. It's very likely, massa.

LEGREE. I'm going to do *just—that thing.* Tell me what do you know about these yer gals? (TOM *is silent. He grabs* TOM, *lifts him to his feet.*) D'ye hear, speak!

TOM. I hain't got nothin' to tell, massa. (LEGREE *gives him a toss.*)

LEGREE. You black bastard, you dare tell me you don't know where those gals have gone?

TOM. I know, but I can't tell nothin'.

LEGREE. Yes—you can and you will! You've always stood out agin me; now, I'll *conquer ye or kill ye!* I'll count every drop of blood there is in you; and take 'em one by one, till ye give up!

TOM. Massa, if you was sick, or dying, I'd give every drop of blood in this old body to save your soul from hell. Do your worst, Massa Legree, my troubles will be over soon; but if you don't repent, yours won't never end! (LEGREE *in a rage strikes* TOM *down with the butt of his whip.*)

LEGREE. God damn you!

SAMBO (*crosses to him, lifts him to reclining position; bending over him*). He's most gone, massa.

TOM (*rises feebly on his hands*). There ain't no more you can do. I forgive you with all my soul!

LEGREE. Take that thing away!

(TOM *sinks back and is carried off by* SAMBO *and* QUIMBO.)

LEGREE. His mouth is shut at last! Damn him! (*Enter* GEORGE SHELBY *with* MARKS *and* CUTE.) Well, what do you want?

GEORGE SHELBY. I understand that you bought in New Orleans a Negro named Tom?

LEGREE. Yes, and a devil of a bargain I had of it too! I believe he's trying to die on me, but I don't know as he'll make it out.

GEORGE. Where is he? Let me see him.

SAMBO. Dere he is!

(*Points to* TOM.)

LEGREE. Shut your black mouth and get out!

(*Drives* SAMBO *and* QUIMBO *off stage.* GEORGE *exits.* CASSY *enters.*)

CUTE. Now's the time!

MARKS (*as* CASSY *stands behind* LEGREE'S *back*). How are you, Mr. Legree?

LEGREE. What the devil brought you here?

MARKS. This little bit of paper. It's a warrant for your arrest for the murder of Mr. St. Clair. What do you say to that?

LEGREE. I say this! (*Makes a blow at* MARKS *who dodges and* CUTE *receives the blow. He cries out and runs off.*)

(MARKS *tries to run but stumbles,* LEGREE *pounces upon him and starts in to strangle him when* CASSY *produces a knife and stabs* LEGREE *who falls dead. A moment's silence.*)

CASSY (*after inspecting* LEGREE'S *body*). Lord Jesus, his time has come. I waited . . . waited . . . till my heart was sick. He wrung the life blood out of me! I was called on. They all called on me to avenge them!

GEORGE. Oh, Uncle Tom, dear Uncle Tom! Don't you know me? I'm your little Master George!

TOM (*opening his eyes*). Massa George! Bress de Lawd! Dey ain't forgot me, now I can die an' be happy!

GEORGE. Die! No! Don't talk like that! I'm going to buy you and take you home, back to old Kentucky!

TOM. You're too late, Massa George, de Lawd *He's* going to take me home.

GEORGE. Oh, Tom, you mustn't die! . . . You mustn't, oh you poor old fellow!

TOM. Massa George, dat's all pas' an' gone now. I's right at de doh, goin' into de glory . . . oh, Massa George . . . look . . . look . . . Dere's Massa St. Clair an' li'l Eva . . . I's comin', I's comin'. . . . (*He dies.*)

GEORGE. He's gone!

GEORGE (*continues*). Dear Old Uncle Tom, your body shall rest beneath the blue grass of your beloved old Kentucky, till the Judgment Day!

CURTAIN

SCENE VII

APOTHEOSIS

East Lynne

A PLAY

In Five Acts

ADAPTED FROM THE NOVEL OF THAT NAME

BY MRS. HENRY WOOD

East Lynne was first performed in this country at the Brooklyn Academy of Music, January 26, 1862, with the following principals:

Sir Francis Levison	Lawrence Barrett
Archibald Carlyle	Charles Barron
Lord Mount Severn	J. B. Studley
Justice Hare	T. E. Morris
Richard Hare	John Ferris
Captain Thorne	George E. Andrews
Lady Isabel / Madam Vine	Lucille Western
Barbara Hare	Kate Denin
Miss Carlyle	Mrs. G. C. Garmon
Susanne	Jennie Lacy

EAST LYNNE

ACT ONE

SCENE I

A chamber.
Enter MISS CORNELIA *and* DILL.

DILL. And so, Miss Corney, Mr. Carlyle will be here today, and bring home his bride.

MISS C. His bride, indeed! A pretty bride for him to take, an earl's daughter! And I've no doubt she'll prove as idle and extravagant as her worthless father. She'll waste his means and bring him to beggary.

DILL. I trust not, Miss Corney. But do you know I had a notion when Mr. Carlyle left home he went to be married?

MISS C. You did, eh? And Archibald never to tell me! I, who have been like a mother to him! But I always thought he loved that girl a great deal better than he should; for when he first took possession of East Lynne, she left some goldfish in his care, and when they died he made such a fuss about them—oh, I was so disgusted with such silly nonsense! However, I am glad that silly Barbara Hare has not got him—after all the years she has been fishing for him. A woman has no business to be always running after a man—it ain't decent. But I've made up my mind to make East Lynne my home for the future. There's no use of keeping up the expense of two establishments. Besides, here I can watch over his interests, for I know she'll bring him to beggary.

DILL. Well, I must go now, and prepare myself to meet Mr. Carlyle and his lovely bride. (*Exit.*)

MISS C. Lovely, indeed! Beauty is but skin deep. Here—Joyce—Joyce! (*Enter* JOYCE.) Joyce, is everything prepared in Mr. Carlyle's apartment?

JOYCE. Yes, ma'am, we've made everything look as tidy and as cheerful as possible.

MISS C. Cheerful, indeed! and for her! Well, there—do get along about your business, for I expect them here every minute now. I'm sure I'd as soon see Archibald hanged as married. (*Enter* DILL.) What an old fool! Why, what on earth has taken you? Why, you are decked out like a young buck!

DILL. I hope I'm not too fine, Miss Corney?

MISS C. Fine! I don't know what you call it, but I wouldn't make such a spectacle of myself for untold gold. Why, all the boys in the street will be taking you for the bridegroom.

DILL. Well, now, really, Miss Corney, I thought this coat quite plain.

MISS C. Plain! and what would you have it I should like to know! Perhaps you'd like a wreath of embroidery around it—gold leaves and scarlet flowers, and a swan's down collar. Pray do you know your age?

DILL. I do; and I'm just turned sixty.

MISS C. You just one! And do you consider it decent for an old man of sixty to be decked out as you are now? Take care the boys don't tie a tin kettle to your coat-tails.

DILL. Well, now, Miss Corney, pray don't get excited about the matter. I'll go and change it to please you. Hush! I hear the carriage wheels now. (*Goes up stage and looks off stage.*) And here comes Mr. Carlyle and his bride.

MISS C. Well, I know one thing certain, I never will forgive *him* or tolerate *her*.

(*Gets in corner. Enter* ARCHIBALD CARLYLE *and* LADY ISABEL.)

ARCH. Welcome to East Lynne—to your childhood's home, Isabel! (*To* DILL.) Ah! Dill, my old friend, I hope you are well. (*Shakes hands with him, and crosses to* MISS CORNEY.) Ah! Cornelia, my dear sister, this is kind in you to meet me here. (*Shakes hands with her and returns.*) This is my wife—the Lady Isabel. Isabel, this is my sister, Cornelia. (ISABEL *bows.*)

MISS C. (*snappishly*). I hope you are well, madam.

ARCH. This is my old friend and confidential clerk, Mr. John Dill.

ISABEL. I hope I see you well, sir.

MISS C. Would you like to go upstairs and take off your things before supper?

ISABEL. I will go to my room, if you please, but Archibald and I have dined. I don't require anything, thank you.

ARCH. Isabel, I have some private matters to talk over with Dill. I'm sure you will excuse me for a little time.

ISABEL. Oh, yes; to be sure I will. I will remain here and talk to your sister.

ARCH. Do so, then, if you like. I'll not be long absent. Come, Dill. (*Exit with* DILL.)

MISS C. What would you like to take?

ISABEL. I would like some tea, if you please. I am very thirsty.

MISS C. Tea! so late as this? You'd never sleep a wink all night.

ISABEL. Oh, well, then don't trouble yourself. I don't think I want anything. I'll just stay and talk to you about Archibald. He has often spoken to me about you, and I feel certain I shall like you.

MISS C. I hope you will be contented at East Lynne.

ISABEL. Contented! why, of course I shall. The dear old place! I was very happy here when a child; and it was here that poor Papa died, too. And then Archibald came, and bought the place, and he was very kind to me, too. I do believe it was that which first made me learn to love him.

MISS C. Archibald has a very kind and generous nature.

ISABEL. He has indeed; and I shall try and be a good wife to him, and under him as happy as possible; and so, you know, I've been thinking how I can be of service to him, and I mean to try and persuade him to let me ride to town with him every morning, and assist him in his business affairs, and be his confidential clerk. Don't you think he will let me?

MISS C. He'd be a fool if he would.

ISABEL. And then we'd all be so happy together; and you'll let me love you too—won't you, Miss Corney? Oh, do let me love you a little! (*Goes and puts her arms around* CORNELIA, *and kisses her.*)

MISS C. (*pushes her off*). She's really a most extraordinary girl. (*Exit.*)

ISABEL. Why, she acts very strangely. I hope I haven't done anything wrong. (*Re-enter* ARCHIBALD.) O Archibald, I'm so glad you've come! I am quite at a loss to know how to act. I think your sister is a very queer person. Do you know, I kissed her just now, and she seemed quite frightened. I don't believe she was ever kissed before.

ARCH. My sister is not over-pleasant in her manner, but she is a very upright and just person. You'll like her better when you come to know her. Now, Isabel, if you like, I'll walk with you through the grounds. (*Exeunt.*)

SCENE II

Landscape.
Enter RICHARD HARE, *disguised in a plowman's suit, with heavy black whiskers, carrying a large whip in one hand.*

RICH. Here I am at length, after my absence of nearly two years, once more in sight of the dear old home. But, alas! I dare not enter even for a moment. I am a fugitive from justice, and even now the lynx-eyed officers of the law may be on my track, and discover me in spite of my disguise. Would I could see my dear mother, if only for a moment! (*Goes to R.*) Ah! the garden gate is open, and I see my sister Barbara standing in the door. I'll venture to speak and call her out. Hist, Barbara! Barbara, come out! Don't you know me?—it is I, Richard!

(*Enter* BARBARA.)

BARB. O Richard! my dear brother—it is indeed you! What brings you here? How could you run such a risk? If you are discovered, it is certain death upon—you know.

RICHARD. Upon the gibbet—I *do* know, Barbara.

BARB. Then why risk it by coming here? Should Mamma see you, it would kill her outright.

RICHARD. I can't live as I am living. I have been working in London ever since.

BARB. In London, Richard? How are you working—what at?

RICH. In a stable yard.

BARB. In a stable! O Richard, you——

RICH. Did you expect it would be as a merchant or as a banker, or that I was a gentleman living at large on my fortune? I get 12s a week, Barbara, and that has to find me in everything.

BARB. O Richard! my poor brother!

RICH. I could do no better. I was brought up to no kind of labor, and I did understand about horses. Besides, a man that the police-runners were after would be more safe in such obscurity than if he were a gentleman in fine clothes.

BARB. Poor Richard! what a miserable night that was for you, and for all of us! Our only comfort is, Richard, that you must have committed the deed in madness.

RICH. I did not commit the deed at all, Barbara. I swear to you that I am innocent of the crime. I was not even in the cottage at the time of the murder. The man who really did the deed was Thorn.

BARB. Thorn! Who was Thorn?

RICH. I don't know. I wish I did. I wish I could unearth him. He was a friend of Afy's.

BARB. Richard, you forget yourself when you mention her name in my presence.

RICH. Well, it was not to discuss such topics as these that I have put my life in jeopardy by coming here tonight; and to assert my innocence can do no good. It cannot set aside the coroner's verdict of willful murder against Richard Hare, the younger. If I had not fled like a coward, I might have stood some chance; but that flight, you know, looked like guilt. Is my father as bitter as ever against me?

BARB. Quite; he never mentions your name, or even suffers it to be spoken by the servants in his presence. After the delivery of the verdict, he took an oath in the justice's room, in the presence of his brother magistrates, that if he could find you, though it might not be for ten years, he would deliver you up to justice. You know his disposition; therefore you may be sure he will keep his word.

RICH. I know he never treated me as he ought. Had my home been happier for me, I should not have sought the society I did elsewhere. Barbara, I must be allowed an interview with my mother.

BARB. It is impossible to think of that tonight. Papa has only gone of an errand, and may return at any moment. I don't see how it can be managed.

RICH. Why can she not come out to me as you have done?

BARB. Because she is ill, and has retired for the night. This separation from you has nearly killed her.

RICH. It is hard, after so long an absence, to go back without seeing her. What I want, Barbara, is a hundred pounds; and I think she can let me have it. If I can get that sum I have an opportunity for doing better for myself than I have done. That was what I came to ask for. Do you think she can let me have it?

BARB. You must be here tomorrow night again. The money can no doubt be yours. But if, as you say, you *are* innocent, why not try and prove it?

RICH. Who is to prove it? The evidence was strong against me; besides, no one at West Lynne knew anything about Thorn but myself. He only came over on certain nights to see Afy, and he took precious good care to keep out of the way in the daytime.

BARB. Richard, why not tell the whole truth to Archibald Carlyle? If any one can help you, or take measures to establish your innocence, he can; and you know he is true as steel.

RICH. Well, perhaps you are right. He is the only person who ought to be entrusted with the secret of my being here. Where is it generally supposed that I am?

BARB. Some think that you are dead; others that you are in America or Australia. This very uncertainty has very nearly killed Mamma. But come again tomorrow night, at this same hour, and meanwhile I'll see what can be done about the money.

JUSTICE HARE (*outside, R.*). Barbara! Barbara!

BARB. Hark! there's Papa returned. I dare not remain another instant. You must go now, Richard. Good night.

RICH. (*going L.*). Barbara, you did not seem to believe my assertion of innocence, but we are standing here alone in the still night, with Him above us, and as truly as that I must one day meet Him face to face, I have told you the truth. It was not I who committed the murder. I swear it—there——(*Points to heaven.*) Good night, sister. (*Exit.*)

(*Enter* JUSTICE HARE.)

JUSTICE H. (*speaking as entering*). Barbara! Barbara! I say—halloo! young lady, what brings you here this time of night?

BARB. I went down to the gate to meet you, and had strolled over the side path, and so I suppose that was how I missed you.

JUSTICE H. Come into the house then. You ought to have been in bed an hour ago. (*Both exeunt.*)

SCENE III

Same as Scene I.

Enter JOYCE, *meeting* WILSON.

WILSON. O Joyce, did you see who is come? A whole carriage-load of visitors, and she among them. I watched her get out.

(*Enter* ISABEL . . . *listens.*)

JOYCE. Watched *her*? who?

WILSON. Why, Miss Barbara Hare to be sure. Only fancy her coming to pay a wedding visit here! My lady had better take care she don't get a bowl of poison mixed for her. Master's out, or else I'd have given a shilling to have seen the interview between them.

JOYCE. Wilson, you had better take care what you say here. Go and attend to the company. (*Exit* WILSON.)

ISABEL (*advancing*). Joyce, what was that I overheard you and Wilson gossiping about just now?—about Miss Hare giving me a bowl of poison? Something in the dramatic line, I should fancy. Please tell her to keep her whispers to herself in future.

JOYCE. It was merely a bit of nonsense, my lady. These stupid, ignorant servants will talk; and every one in West Lynne knew that Miss Barbara was in love with Mr. Carlyle; but I do not think she was the one to make him happy with all her love.

ISABEL. Joyce, how would you like the situation of lady's maid? that is if Miss Carlyle will consent to the transfer.

JOYCE. O my lady, you were very kind! I should so like it, and I would serve you faithfully to the best of my ability.

ISABEL. Well, then, if Miss Carlyle consents, you shall have it. I'll speak to her about it today. Now leave me, Joyce. (*Exit* JOYCE.) Who is this Barbara Hare of whom I hear so much, and whom East and West Lynne are busy associating with the name of my husband? Oh, I remember now; I noticed her at the church door the first day we came to East Lynne; and Mr. Carlyle said, as he pointed her out, "That is Miss Barbara Hare. Don't you think her a very pretty girl?" Perhaps he has loved her; perhaps he loves her still, and only married me out of sympathy. Oh! if I only thought that, it would drive me frantic! But no—no—no! I will not harbor a thought so foolish as that. Mr. Carlyle is an honorable man; he loves me truly—he has told me so, and he would not deceive me.

(*Enter* MISS CORNEY.)

MISS C. Lady Isabel, they are waiting for an order for dinner.

ISABEL. Order a dinner, Miss Corney? (*Aside.*) What shall I say? I never ordered a dinner in all my life. I must say something. She's evidently waiting for an answer. Well, then, Miss Corney, you may tell them we'll have something to roast and something to boil.

MISS C. Something to roast and something to boil! Are you aware that such an order would puzzle the butcher to know whether you desired a few pounds of meat or a whole cow?

ISABEL. A whole cow! Oh, bless me, Miss Corney, we never would eat a whole cow. (*Aside.*) I've evidently made a mistake this time. I'll try again. What shall I say? I wish I dared to ask her; but she looks so cross and severe, and she would despise me for my ignorance. I'll venture again. Well, then, Miss Corney, order as much meat as you think Archibald and yourself will require. I don't want any.

MISS C. Lady Isabel, if you desire it, I will give the necessary orders myself.

ISABEL. Oh! do, if you please, Miss Corney. I wanted to ask you to do it all the while, but I didn't want to trouble you. I don't think I know much about housekeeping.

MISS C. I don't think you do. Poor Archibald! so much for marrying against my will. (*Exit.*)

ISABEL. I wish Archibald would come. The time hangs heavily when he is from my side.

(*Enter* LORD MOUNT SEVERN, *advances, and bows stiffly.*)

LORD M. What is the meaning of this, Isabel? You are married, it seems.

ISABEL. Yes; some days ago.

LORD M. And to Mr. Carlyle, the lawyer. How did this come about? And why was I kept in ignorance of the affair?

ISABEL. I did not know that you were kept in ignorance of it. Mr. Carlyle wrote to you at the time, as did also Lady Mount Severn.

LORD M. I suppose this comes of your father having allowed him to visit daily at East Lynne, and so you fell in love with him.

ISABEL. Oh, no, indeed! I never thought of such a thing as falling in love with Mr. Carlyle; but he came to Castle Marling at Easter; he proposed to me, and I accepted him. I like him very well, he is so good to me.

LORD M. How comes it you are so nice in your distinctions between liking and loving? It cannot be that you love any one else. Who has been staying at Castle Marling during my absence?

ISABEL (*confused*). Only Francis Levison.

LORD M. Francis Levison! You surely have not been foolish enough to fall in love with him! Isabel, Francis Levison is not a good man. If ever you are inclined to think him one, dispossess your mind of that idea, drop his acquaintance, encourage no intimacy.

ISABEL. I have dropped it already, sir. But Lady Mount Severn must think well of him, or she would not have him there so often.

LORD M. (*surprised*). She thinks none too well of him. None can of Francis Levison.

(*Enter* ARCHIBALD. *Offers his hand to* LORD MOUNT SEVERN, *who refuses it.*)

LORD M. Isabel, I am sorry to turn you out of the room, but I must say a few words to Mr. Carlyle.

ISABEL. Oh, certainly, sir, I'll retire. (*Exit door.*)

LORD M. (*severely*). Mr. Carlyle sir, do you possess so little honor that, taking advantage of my absence, you must intrude yourself upon my family and clandestinely espouse Lady Isabel Vane, my ward?

ARCH. Sir, there has been nothing clandestine in my conduct toward Lady Isabel Vane, nor shall there be anything but honor in my conduct toward Lady Isabel Carlyle, my wife. Your lordship has been misinformed.

LORD M. I have not been informed at all. I was allowed to learn this through the public journal—*I*, the *only* relative of Lady Isabel!

ARCH. My first action after Isabel accepted me was to write to your lordship asking your consent.

LORD M. And pray, sir, where did you direct your letter?

ARCH. Lady Mount Severn could not give me your address, as you were then traveling; but she said if I would entrust my letter to her care, she would forward it to you with others she was then writing. I did so, and in a few days received a message from her ladyship, that, as you had returned no answer, you of course approved of the match.

LORD M. Mr. Carlyle, is that a fact?

ARCH. My lord, whatever may be my defects in your eyes, I am at least a man of truth. Until this moment the thought that you were ignorant of this transaction never occurred to me.

LORD M. So far then, I ask your pardon. But how came the ceremony to be hurried on in this unseemly fashion? You made the offer at Easter, and were married three weeks after.

ARCH. Business took me to Castle Marling on Good Friday. I called at your house. I found Lady Isabel ill-treated and miserable, far from enjoying a home in your house.

LORD M. What, sir? Ill-treated and miserable?

ARCH. Ill-treated even to blows, my lord. I learned all this through the chattering revelations of your little son. Isabel, of course, would not have told me; but when he had spoken she could not deny it. In short, she was too completely bowed down in spirit to deny it. It aroused all my feelings of indignation; it excited in me an irresistible desire to release her from the thraldom that this cruel life had thrown around her, and take her where she would find affection, and, I hope, happiness. There was only one way in which I could do so.

I risked all and asked her to become my wife, and return with me to East Lynne.

LORD M. Then I am to understand that when you called at my house you had no intention of proposing to Isabel.

ARCH. Not any. It was an impromptu step, the circumstances under which I found her calling it forth.

LORD M. May I inquire if you love her, sir?

ARCH. I do love her passionately and sincerely. I learned to love her at East Lynne, but I could have carried my love silently within me to the end of my life, and never have betrayed it; and probably should have done so, had it not been for that unexpected visit to Castle Marling. If the idea of making her my wife had even previously entered my mind, the reason why I did not urge my suit was that I deemed her rank incompatible with my own.

LORD M. And so it was.

ARCH. Country solicitors have married peers' daughters before today. I only add another to the list.

LORD M. But you cannot keep her as a peer's daughter, I presume.

ARCH. East Lynne will be our home. Our establishment will be small and quiet to what it was in her father's time. I explained all this to Isabel at the first, so that she might have retracted had she chosen to have done so. Your lordship now perceives, I hope, that there was nothing clandestine in my conduct toward Lady Isabel.

LORD M. Sir, I refused you my hand when you came in; perhaps you will refuse me yours now, though I should be proud to take it. When I find myself in the wrong I'm not above acknowledging my fault, and I must say that, in my opinion, you have acted most kindly and honorably. (*They shake hands.*) Of course, I cannot be ignorant that in speaking of Isabel's ill-treatment you allude to my wife. Has this transpired beyond yourselves?

ARCH. Sir, you may be sure that neither Isabel nor myself will ever mention it. Let it be as though you never heard it; it is past and gone.

(*Re-enter* ISABEL.)

LORD M. Isabel, I came here today almost prepared to strike your husband. I go away honoring him. Be a good, faithful wife to him, for he deserves it.

ISABEL. Oh, of course I shall, never fear.

LORD M. And now with your permission I'll take a look about the grounds.

ISABEL. We will accompany you. (*All exeunt.*)

(*Enter* MISS CORNEY *and* BARBARA HARE.)

BARB. Papa was out on business; Mamma was too ill to come; so I have ventured here alone.

MISS C. I am glad you have come. I thought perhaps you would not be pleased with Archibald's selection of a wife.

BARB. Not pleased, Miss Corney? Why, what have I to do with his choice of a wife?

MISS C. Oh, nothing; only there are so many ladies in East and West Lynne that seemed to take such an interest in Archibald's welfare, that I thought they might be disappointed in his marriage—that's all.

BARB. On the contrary, I wish him all the happiness possible. He has ever treated me most kindly, and I sincerely hope he has found a wife worthy of him.

MISS C. Well, I like her better than I thought I should. I expected to find her full of airs and graces, but I must say she is perfectly free from them, and she seems quite wrapped up in Archibald; she watches for his coming as a cat would watch for a mouse.

BARB. That is quite natural, I suppose.

MISS C. I suppose it is very absurd. I give them very little of my company; they go strolling out together, or she sings to him, while he hangs over her as if she were made of gold. Oh, dear! I have no patience with such silly nonsense.

BARB. You must make some allowance for the fervor of youth.

MISS C. Fervor of fiddlesticks! Shall I tell you what I saw last night? Well, Archibald had a severe headache after dinner, and went into the next room and lay upon the sofa. She took him in a cup of tea, and never came back again, leaving her own until it was perfectly cold. I went to say so to her, and there was my lady's fine cambric handkerchief soaked in cologne lying on his face, and she kneeling beside him. Now, Miss Barbara, don't you regard that as the height of nonsense?

BARB. I must say that I cannot agree with you in that respect.

MISS C. Well, I know this much. If he had a headache before he was married, I gave him a good dose of senna and salts, and sent him to bed to sleep the pain off. (*Exit.*)

BARB. And she is happy with him—the only man I ever loved, or ever can love. Why did he pass me by for a baby-faced girl like that? It cannot be that she is capable of loving him with the deep affection I might have bestowed on him. Ah! they are coming this way. I'll retire into the conservatory. I could not endure a meeting now. (*Retires.*)

(*Re-enter* ARCHIBALD *and* ISABEL.)

ARCH. You are fatigued, are you not?

ISABEL. Oh, no, not in the least! You say you have been intimate with this Hare family for a long time.

ARCH. Quite so. Cornelia, my half-sister, is related to them.

ISABEL. Don't you think Miss Barbara is very pretty?

ARCH. Yes, very pretty.

ISABEL. Then, intimate as you are, I wonder you never fell in love with her. Did you, Archibald,—oh! did you?

ARCH. Did I what, Isabel?

ISABEL. You never loved Barbara Hare, did you?

ARCH. Loved her? Why, Isabel, what is your mind running on? I never loved but *one*—and *that one* I have made my own, my cherished wife.

ISABEL. Oh! I believe you, my dear husband.

ARCH. Well, now you must sing to me, and then I'll pay you with a kiss.

ISABEL. With all my heart. What shall it be?

ARCH. Oh, you know my favorite song.

ISABEL. Yes. Alas! that was poor papa's favorite too. (*She sings song, "You'll Remember Me."* ARCHIBALD *gets chair, taking one hand in his, leans tenderly over her. At end of song, kisses her on the forehead. Barbara at back listening. Picture.*)

CURTAIN

ACT TWO

SCENE I

Chamber. As in Act I. Books on table, vases, etc., etc.

(*Enter* LADY ISABEL *and* LEVISON.)

LEVISON. Do you remember the evening, Lady Isabel, such a one as this, we all passed at Richmond—your father, Mrs. Vane, you, I, and the others?

ISABEL. Yes, I remember it well. We passed a very pleasant day. The two Miss Challoners were with us. You drove Mrs. Vane home, and I went with poor Papa. You drove recklessly, I recollect, and Mrs. Vane declared you should never drive her again.

LEVISON. Which meant, not till next time. Of all capricious, vain, exacting women, Emma Vane was the worst. She was a systematic flirt, nothing better. I drove her recklessly on purpose to put her in a fright and pay her off.

ISABEL. Pay her off! Why, what has she done?

LEVISON. Put me in a rage; saddled herself on me when she knew I desired another companion.

ISABEL. Oh, yes! I know—Blanche Challoner.

LEVISON. Blanche Challoner! What did I care for her? No, Lady Isabel, it was not Blanche; you might have made a better guess at that time.

ISABEL. I do not understand you, sir.

LEVISON. The past is gone, and cannot be recalled. We have both played our cards like simpletons. If ever two beings were formed to love each other, you and I were. I sometimes thought you read my feelings.

ISABEL. Francis Levison—sir!

LEVISON. I must speak, Lady Isabel; but a few words, and then I am silent forever. I would have declared myself then; but my debts, my uncertain position, my inability to keep a wife, as your taste and style demanded, crushed my hopes, and so I suffered you to escape me.

ISABEL. I will not listen to this language, sir!

LEVISON. One single moment yet, I pray you. I have long wished you to know why I lost you—a loss that tells upon me yet; but I knew not how passionately I loved you until you became the wife of another. Isabel, I love you still.

ISABEL. How dare you presume to address me thus?

LEVISON. What I have said can do no harm now; the time has gone by. We have each chosen our parts in life and must abide by them. The gulf between us is impassable, but the fault was mine. I ought to have avowed my affection for you, and not to have suffered you to throw yourself away on Mr. Carlyle.

ISABEL. Do I hear aright? Throw myself away on Mr. Carlyle, my husband—beloved, honored and esteemed by all who know him! Why, I married him of my own choice, and have never since regretted it. Look at his manly bearing, his noble mind, his generous nature! What are you in comparison? You forget yourself, Francis Levison.

LEVISON. No, I do not. I pray you forget and forgive what has escaped me, and suffer me to be as heretofore, the kind friend, the anxious brother, endeavoring to be of service to you in the absence of Mr. Carlyle.

ISABEL. It is what I have suffered you to be, looking upon you in the light of a friend—I might say relative; not otherwise would I have permitted your incessant companionship; and thus it is you have repaid me. My husband, whom you would depreciate in my eyes, has sheltered you and screened you from the law. He has thanked you for your attention to me. Could he have read what was in your false heart, he would have offered you thanks of a different sort, I fancy.

LEVISON. I ask your pardon, Lady Isabel. I have acknowledged my fault; I can do no more. I shall not offend you again. But there are moments when our heart's dearest feelings break through the conventionalities of life, and betray themselves in spite of our sober judgment. But I see that I must leave you now; so adieu—not adieu, but *au revoir*. (*Exits.*)

ISABEL. Oh, how can I ever tell my husband that this man, whom he has befriended and sheltered from the law, has thus dared to speak to me of love! Heaven only knows what the consequences would be—a duel, perhaps. No, no, I cannot tell him; yet, I feel I ought to tell him all. I will seek him instantly, my kind, my good, my noble husband. (*Exit.*)

(*Enter* JOYCE, *meeting* WILSON.)

WILSON. I say, Joyce, don't you think she looks very ill?—my lady, I mean. She looks just as if she'd never get over it. My goodness! wouldn't somebody's hopes be raised again if anything was to happen?

(*Re-enter* ISABEL. *She listens.*)

JOYCE. Oh, nonsense! what stuff!

WILSON. You may cry out nonsense as much as you like, but they would; she'd snap him up to a dead certainty; she'd never let him escape her a second time. She is just as much in love with him as ever.

JOYCE. That's all rubbish—all talk and fancy! Mr. Carlyle never cared for her, at all events.

WILSON. That's more than you know. I've seen him *kiss* her; and he gave her that locket and chain which she wears about her neck; she hardly lets it off, either; and I do believe she sleeps with it.

JOYCE. How thoroughly stupid she must be!

WILSON. And that's not all. I saw them one evening, many months ago, when I lived at Miss Hare's house. She always steals out to the gate when she thinks it is about time for Mr. Carlyle to pass on his way from his office, on purpose to have a sly chat with him. Well, this evening I crept down behind the hedges, and then I heard all they were saying; she was crying bitterly, and then I heard Mr. Carlyle tell her that in future he could only be a dear brother to her; and then I saw him kiss her.

JOYCE. Then she's a downright fool to go on crying for a man that never cared for her.

WILSON. But she does do it yet; and so I say if anything was to happen now, Miss Barbara, as sure as faith, would step into her shoes. I mean if Mr. Carlyle should ever get tired of my lady.

JOYCE. Wilson, have the goodness to recollect yourself.

WILSON. Well, what have I said now? Nothing but the truth. Men are shamefully fickle; husbands are worse than sweethearts, too, and if anything was to happen now——

JOYCE. I tell you what it is, Wilson, if you think to pursue this sort of topic at East Lynne, I shall inform my lady that you are not fit for the situation.

WILSON. Oh, you were always one of the straight laced sort; but I've had my say, and now I'm satisfied. (*Exit* WILSON *and* JOYCE.)

ISABEL. Oh, misery, misery! Oh, how palpable to all eyes must be that woman's love for my husband! Palpable indeed, when all East and West Lynne are talking of it; and even my servants daily gossip over it, and extend their pity to me. Oh! I cannot bear it—the thought will drive me frantic! (*Sees* ARCHIBALD *entering C.; rushes to him and in a frantic manner.*) Oh, Archibald, do not marry her! I could not rest in my grave if you did. She would draw your love from our children and from my memory. Archibald, you must not marry her.

ARCH. Why, Isabel! you must be speaking under the influence of some terrible dream, and you are not awake. Be still awhile, and recollection will return to you. There, love, rest on me. (*Folds her to his breast.*)

ISABEL. Oh, no; I know perfectly well what I am saying. To think of her as your wife brings pain enough to kill me. Promise me you will not marry her.

ARCH. I will promise anything in reason, my dear wife. But I do not know what you mean. There is no possibility of my marrying any one. You are my wife, are you not?

ISABEL. I know I am now, but I might die. Indeed, I think I shall die. Oh, do not let her usurp my place!

ARCH. Why, Isabel, what is your mind running on? Who is it that is thus troubling you? Of whom are you speaking?

ISABEL. Of Barbara Hare.

ARCH. Isabel, what notion you can possibly have picked up concerning Barbara Hare and myself, I am unable to conceive. I never loved her either before marriage or since.

ISABEL. But she loved you.

ARCH. If this was so, she was more weak, reprehensibly foolish, than I could have thought her. I had given her credit for having better sense. A woman may almost as well love herself as suffer herself to love unsought. If, however, she did give her love to me, I can only say that I was entirely unconscious of it. Believe me, Isabel, you have as much cause to be jealous of my sister Cornelia as of Barbara Hare.

ISABEL. Oh, I will believe you, Archibald; it is only a foolish thought. I will banish it forever from my mind. (*Aside.*) I cannot tell him I was foolish enough to listen to the gossip of my servants; he would despise me for it. (*Aloud.*) I will leave you now. I am fatigued; I will retire to my own room. Yes, I will trust him; if not, in whom can I trust? (*Exit.*)

ARCH. What can have put this bygone nonsense into my wife's head?

(*Enter* MISS CORNEY.)

MISS C. Archibald, I wish to speak to you in regard to that Francis Levison. I don't like either his appearance or his manners.

ARCH. Cornelia, he is my guest, and as such must be treated with respect.

MISS C. With respect indeed! He's a good-for-nothing villain if I'm any judge of character, and I don't care how soon you tell him so. (*Exit.*)

ARCH. Poor Cornelia! she's hard to please; she's evidently annoyed at some trifling matter.

(*Enter* BARBARA.)

Ah! good morning, Barbara. I am glad to see you at my house. Did you come by yourself?

BARB. Yes, Archibald. You must pardon my intrusion at this hour, and regard me as a client. I came on some business for Mamma, but it's of a private nature. Mamma was too ill to come out herself, so she has sent me. Can we converse without being overheard?

ARCH. Be at ease, Barbara, this room is free from the intrusion of strangers. (*Gets chairs.*) Pray be seated, Barbara. Come, what state secrets have you to disclose?

BARB. Richard is here.

ARCH. Richard at East Lynne!

BARB. He appeared near the house last night, and made signs to me from the grove. You may imagine my surprise on finding it to be Richard in disguise. He has been in London all this time, working, half starving. I am almost ashamed to tell you, but working in a stableyard; and oh, Archibald, he declares he is innocent. He says he was not even in the cottage at the time the murder was committed, but the man who really did the deed was a person by the name of Thorn.

ARCH. Thorn? What Thorn can it be?

BARB. I don't know; some friend of Afy's, who used to ride over to the cottage in secret visits to her. Archibald, he swears to me in the most solemn manner; and I believe him as truly as that I am now speaking to you. I want you to see him yourself. He is coming to the grove again to-night. He will tell you all the circumstances of the terrible night, and perhaps you can find out a way in which his innocence can be made manifest. You are so clever, you can do anything.

ARCH. Not quite everything, Barbara. But was this the purport of Richard's visit—to tell you this?

BARB. Oh, no; he thinks it would be of no use to assert his innocence, for nobody would believe him against the evidence already given. He came to ask for a hundred pounds. He says if he can get that sum he has an opportunity of doing better for himself than he has hitherto done. So Mamma has sent me to you. She has not that sum by her at present, and as it is for Richard, she dare not ask Papa for it. She says if you can oblige her with the money, she will arrange it with you about the repayment.

ARCH. Do you want it now? If so, I must send Dill to the office. I have not that sum by me in the house.

BARB. Can you not bring it with you, and see Richard at the same time?

ARCH. It is hazardous—for him I mean. Still, as he is to be in the grove, I may as well see him. What disguise is he in?

BARB. That of a farm laborer—the best he could adopt in these parts; also a heavy pair of black whiskers. He is to be there at ten precisely.

ARCH. Well, then, I think I can come; but in order to do so I must disappoint a supper party to which we have been invited. However, my wife won't mind that when I tell her the business is so urgent. Yes, you can tell your mother I'll come.

BARB. Oh, Archibald, you are very kind to us! You have ever treated me like a dear sister, and Mamma is grateful to you for all your attentions to her. I fear we can never repay you sufficiently. (*Rises to go.*)

ARCH (*rising*). I have only done what I felt to be my duty in the matter. Let me escort you to the gate.

(*Exit with* BARBARA, *arm-in-arm; at the same time enter* LADY ISABEL *and* LEVISON, *in time to see them off.*)

ISABEL (*R., looking after them*). That woman here—in privacy with my husband—under my very roof, too! Ah! then it is too true. My husband no longer loves me. (*Turns and sees* LEVISON.) You here, sir? (*Sits at table.*)

LEVISON. Who the deuce is that Barbara Hare? She's a devilish pretty girl. She seems to have a very good understanding with your husband. Several times I've encountered them together on the lawn, enjoying moonlight walks and private confab.

ISABEL (*coldly*). What did you say, sir?

LEVISON. Nothing; I only spoke of Monsieur, your husband. I meant not to offend.

(*Enter* JOYCE.)

JOYCE. If you please, my lady, little Isabel wishes to retire for the night, and she wants you to kiss her before going to sleep.

ISABEL (*angrily*). Tell the nurse to put the child to bed, and leave me.

JOYCE (*aside*). What! put the child to bed without even saying good night! There's something strange going on here. (*Exit.*)

LEVISON. By the bye, Lady Isabel, don't you think that Barbara Hare a devilish pretty girl?

(*Enter* MISS CORNEY, *L.; looks sharply at* LEVISON. *He crosses by her, bowing and exits.*)

MISS C. Lady Isabel, I have taken the liberty of countermanding the order for little Isabel's new frock. I think she has quite enough already.

ISABEL (*still at table*). Countermanding my orders, Miss Carlyle, is a liberty you have taken a great deal too often. Allow me to tell you that I am the most competent judge of what is best for my own children, and that for the future I will be mistress in my own house.

(*Enter* ARCHIBALD.)

MISS C. Archibald, what did Barbara Hare want with you just now?

ARCH. Why, Cornelia, she merely wished to see me on some business, that's all.

MISS C. Why don't you say right out what she wanted, without making any mystery about it? She seems to be always wanting you now. Can it be that old affair is to be raked up again?

ARCH. Cornelia, you will oblige me by never referring to that old affair again.

MISS C. Oh, indeed! Very well, very well; but I trust they will listen to me when they are brought to ruin through Lady Isabel's extravagance. Poor Archibald! he works like a horse now, and can hardly keep expenses down. (*Exit.*)

ISABEL (*coming forward*). Archibald, what *did* that woman, that Barbara Hare, want here?

ARCH. It is a private business, Isabel. She brings me messages from her mother.

ISABEL. Must the business be kept secret from me?

ARCH. It would not make you happier to know it, Isabel. There is a dark secret hanging over the Hare family; it is connected with that. I am summoned away on some urgent business this evening, therefore I cannot attend you to the supper party. You can use the carriage and go by yourself. I will endeavor to be there in time to escort you home. I am already late, and as I have to go to my office first, I must away at once. Good evening, and a pleasant party to you. (*Exit.*)

ISABEL. What mystery can they have between them that he dares not reveal to me, his wife! Ah! he is deceiving me—I am certain of it. Oh! I am wretched, jealous, mad!

(*Sits at table. Enter* LEVISON.)

LEVISON (*aside*). I wonder what the deuce that Hare girl can want with Carlyle. I followed them down to the gate and overheard them plan a meeting in the grove for this evening. Perhaps Lady Isabel would like to be present also. (*Aloud.*) Ah! still alone, I see, Lady Isabel. I expected to find you so. I suspect that Mr. Carlyle is more agreeably engaged.

ISABEL. Engaged! in what manner, sir?

LEVISON. As I came up the lawn, a few minutes since, I saw a lady and gentleman enjoying a tête-à-tête by moonlight. I followed them to the gate, and overstepped the bounds of good manners so far as to listen to a part of their conversation. I heard them arrange a meeting in the grove for this evening, and unless I was very much mistaken, the favored individual was Mr. Carlyle.

ISABEL (*rising*). My husband! Oh, sir, you cannot mean that! Oh, if I thought him capable of such a falsehood to me, I would leave his roof at once!

LEVISON. That's right; be avenged on the false hound. He never was worthy of your love. Leave your home of misery and come to one of happiness. Come, let me prove his perfidy to you.

ISABEL. Only prove this and I will quit his house forever!

LEVISON. With me, Isabel?

ISABEL. Ay, with you. I care not who shall be the instrument of my vengeance. (*Exeunt.*)

SCENE II

Landscape as in Act I.

(*Enter* RICHARD *and* BARBARA.)

BARBARA. Richard, we must not stand so near the house; Papa is at home, you see, of all the nights in the world. You must wait till tomorrow night, and then perhaps you can see Mamma.

RICH. I don't like waiting another night. Barbara, there's danger in every inch of ground this neighborhood contains.

BARB. You must wait, Richard, for other reasons. The man who caused all the mischief is at West Lynne; at least there is a man staying there by the name of Thorn; so Bethel just told Mr. Carlyle as we stood by his gate, and Mr. Carlyle wishes you to see him. Should it prove to be the same, perhaps nothing can be done immediately toward discharging you, but it will be a great point ascertained. Are you sure that you should know him again?

RICH. Sure that I should know him? Should I know my own father? Should I know you? Is he not engraven on my brain in letters of blood? But how or when am I to see him?

BARB. I cannot tell you more till Mr. Carlyle comes. Poor Richard! I hope the time will soon come when you can walk forth in open day.

(*Enter* ARCHIBALD.)

Oh, Archibald, I am so glad that you have come. Our suspicion with regard to the man Thorn can now be set at rest. It seems to me that Providence has directed his steps here at this very time. You must contrive that Richard shall see him.

ARCH. (*crossing to* RICHARD). Richard, your sister tells me that you wish to disclose to me the true history of that lamentable night. There is an old saying, and it is a sound advice, "Tell the whole truth to your doctor and your lawyer." If I am to judge whether anything can be attempted for you, you must tell me the whole truth without reserve; otherwise I would rather hear nothing. It shall be a sacred trust.

RICH. Well, if I must make a clean breast of it, I did love the girl Afy, and would have made her my wife in time; but I could not do so then in the very face of my father's opposition. I went to the house on the evening in question to take my gun—Hallijohn had requested the loan of it; he was out at the time, so I handed it to Afy, who met me at the door. She would not allow me to go inside of it as usual. I was mad with jealousy, for I felt sure that Thorn was in the cottage with her, although she strongly denied it; so I determined to wait and convince myself. I secreted myself in the shrubbery in the garden, where I could see all that passed within the cottage. Presently I saw Hallijohn come up the path by me, and go into the house. Not long after, perhaps twenty minutes, I heard the gun fired, and at the same time saw Thorn leap from the cottage window and run wildly down the path, directly by me, to where his horse had been tied, jump in the saddle, and gallop off.

ARCH. Did you know where this Thorn lived?

RICH. I could never ascertain. Afy said he lived away ten miles distant. He used to ride over once or twice a week to see her. I always thought he came there under a false name. He appeared to be an aristocrat, though of very bad taste. He made a great display of jewelry, expensive too—such as diamonds.

ARCH. But you were afterward seen with the gun in your hand coming from the cottage.

RICH. I went there to upbraid Afy for having deceived me. Mad with jealousy, I hardly knew what I did; but I had no idea that a murder had been committed. As I entered the door, the first thing I stumbled over was Hallijohn's lifeless body. I saw my gun lying beside him. Some vague idea flashed across my mind that my gun ought not to be found there; so I seized it and rushed out just as the people began to collect, and to my horror I was taken for the murderer; so I threw down my gun and fled.

ARCH. And that act alone condemned you. You acted like a guilty man, and that line of conduct often entails as much trouble as real guilt.

BARB. And you do not believe him guilty?

ARCH. I do not. I have little doubt of the guilt of Thorn; but I do not think, from your description of the man, that it is the same person who is now in the neighborhood. There is the money, Richard. (*Hands him notes.*) You had better depart now, for fear of spies; but be here again tomorrow night at this hour, and, in the meantime, I'll decide what course you are to adopt, and how I can best serve you.

RICH. Good night, my more than friend; good night, my dear sister. (*Exit.*)

ARCH. And now, Barbara, I'll see you to your gate.

BARB. Never mind, Archibald, it is only a few steps; I can go by myself.

ARCH. Nonsense, Barbara! Allow you to go by yourself along the high-road at this hour? Take my arm. (*Exeunt.*)

(*Enter* LADY ISABEL *and* LEVISON *in time to see them off.*)

LEVISON. There, Lady Isabel, I told you what you might see—there is the proof.

ISABEL. Take me away from this accursed place, Francis Levison. I am faint—ill—wretched—mad! (*Exeunt.*)

SCENE III

Chamber, as in Scene I.

(*Enter* ARCHIBALD. *Goes to table and rings bell. Enter* JOYCE.)

ARCH. Joyce, where is your mistress?

JOYCE. Is she not in her chamber, sir?

ARCH. I have been looking everywhere. She is not in the house.

JOYCE. Oh, heavens! I see it all now; her wild words to me—her strange looks. Oh, master, she has destroyed herself, and she's been driven to it!

ARCH. Destroyed herself! What do you mean?

JOYCE. Master, she has destroyed herself as sure as we two are living. But a short time ago she called me to her—her face was like death—and exacted of me a solemn promise to stay here at East Lynne with the children if anything happened to take her away from them. I asked her if she was ill, and she said, "Yes, Joyce, ill and wretched!" Oh, sir, may heaven support you in this dreadful trial!

(*Enter* MISS CORNEY.)

MISS C. What's all this? whatever's up? where's my lady?

JOYCE. She has gone and taken the life that was not hers to take, and I say she has been driven to it by *you.* You've curbed her, you've snapped at her, and reproached her with extravagance—you know it, ma'am. All these years she's been crossed and put upon by you, and she's borne it all in silence like a patient angel. We all loved her, we all felt for her, and master's heart would have bled for her, had he only known what she had to put up with from you, day after day, year after year. Many and many's the time I've seen her coming from your reproaches with quivering lip and moistened eye, and her hands clasped meekly across her breast as though life was too heavy to bear. (*Goes up to table.*)

ARCH. (*crosses to* CORNELIA). Cornelia, if this be true, may Heaven forgive you for it!

JOYCE (*finding letter on table*). Oh, master—see! Here's a letter she has left; it is my lady's handwriting; read it, master. (ARCHIBALD *takes the letter; opens it, reads it, and staggers to chair by table.*)

JOYCE. Oh! what does she say? is she dead?

ARCH. Worse than that!—worse than that!

MISS C. Why, Archibald! what do you mean?

ARCH. She has eloped with Francis Levison!

MISS C. Oh! the disgraceful, unworthy——

ARCH. Hush, Cornelia! not one word against her—no—not one! (ARCHIBALD *in chair, overcome by deep grief.* JOYCE, *appealing to Heaven.* MISS CORNEY *bending over* ARCHIBALD. *Picture.*)

CURTAIN

ACT THREE

SCENE I

Chamber. As in Act I.

(*Enter* ARCHIBALD, *reading a letter.*)

ARCH. (*reading*). "*When years go on, and my children ask where their mother is, and why she left them, tell them that you, their father, goaded her to it. If they inquire what she is, tell them also, if you will, but tell them at the same time that you outraged and betrayed her, driving her to the depths of desperation ere she quitted them in her despair.*" Oh, Isabel! I forgive you the injustice these words do my heart! May they never cause you the pangs of misery they have inflicted on me.

(*Enter* MISS CORNEY.)

MISS C. Archibald, what's the time, I wonder?

ARCH. Just nine, Cornelia.

MISS C. Well, then I think I'll go to bed, and after I'm in it, I'll have a basin of arrow-root or gruel, or some slop of that sort. I'm sure I've been free enough all my life of wanting any such sick stuff.

ARCH. Well, do so, if you think it will do you any good.

MISS C. Well, there's one thing I know of that's excellent for a cold in the head, and that is to take your red flannel petticoat and tie it on crosswise over your night-cap. I'll try it too. (*Sneezes.*) (*Exit.*)

ARCH. I'm uncommonly gloomy to-night; it's a bitter night out, too. I wonder if it's snowing yet. (*Goes to window in flat.*)

(RICHARD HARE *speaks outside.*)

RICH. Oh, Mr. Carlyle! for the love of Heaven, let me come in. I'm nearly frozen; it is I, Richard! (ARCHIBALD *opens door.*)

(*Enter* RICHARD HARE.)

ARCH. Richard, I'm thunderstruck! I fear you have done wrong in coming here.

RICH. What could I do better? The Bow Street officers were after me, set on by that wretch Thorn. I had to leave London at a moment's notice, without a thing belonging to me. Even now the officers may be in pursuit. I have walked all the way from London here. I had no money to pay for a lodging or even to buy food. I waited outside the window till I saw you were alone; so I thought I would ask your advice.

ARCH. Have you then discovered this man Thorn?

RICH. Yes; about a week ago, for the first time, I got a glimpse of him as he was passing by in a carriage. I tried to follow him then, but they drove too fast for me; but last evening I saw him again, standing in front of one of the theaters. I went up and stood close at his elbow; he saw and in a moment recognized me, for he turned deadly pale. "What do you want, fellow?" said he in an angry tone. "I want to know who you are," I replied. Then he flew into a fierce passion, and swore that if he ever caught me near him again he would hand me over to the nearest officer; "and remember," yelled he as he walked away, "people are not given into custody for merely watching people!" That convinced me beyond all doubt that it was he. I tried to follow, but the great crowd of people in the street at that time kept me partially out of sight. At length he called a carriage, and as he rode away he pointed me out to an officer who had been standing near; but I managed to get among the crowd again, and fled as fast as possible. After that I knew I was no longer safe in London. Oh, Mr. Carlyle, is this life to go on with me forever?

ARCH. I am deeply sorry for you, Richard. I wish I could remedy it.

MISS C. (*outside*). Archibald, whom have you got in that room?

ARCH. It's some person to see me on business, Cornelia. You cannot come in now. It's only my sister, Richard. Be a man and shake off this fear. No harm shall come to you in my house. But you had better retire till I have spoken to my sister. (*Puts him off stage.*)

MISS C. (*outside*). Not come, indeed! Open the door, I say! (ARCHIBALD *opens door and* CORNELIA *enters with a red petticoat tied on her head; looks round stage.*)

MISS C. Where is she, I say? Oh! you ought to be ashamed of yourself—you, a married man with children in the house, too! Oh! I'd rather believe anything wicked of myself than of you, Archibald.

ARCH. Why, what do you mean? Are you crazy, Cornelia? There has been no woman here, but a man who fears the police are on his track; you ought to be able to guess his name.

MISS C. What! not Richard Hare? Let me see him.

ARCH. Why, surely you would not present yourself to him in that guise.

MISS C. What? not show myself to Richard Hare in this guise? He whom I have whipped ten times a day when he was a boy, and he deserves it now for getting into such a scrape. He looks no better than I do, I dare say. Where is he? (ARCHIBALD *brings him out.*) Why, Richard, what on earth has brought you here? You must have been crazy.

RICH. The Bow Street officers were after me, and I had to cut away from London at a moment's notice. I had no money to pay for a lodging or to buy me food; so I came to Mr. Carlyle to befriend me.

MISS C. It just serves you right. You would go hunting after that brazen hussy, Afy Hallijohn.

ARCH. Cornelia, this is no time for upbraidings. Do you go and prepare him some food, while I see after his lodgings. (*Crosses and exits.*)

MISS C. Well, come along, Richard; I'll see what can be done for you; but you know you always were the greatest natural born fool that was ever let loose out of leading strings. (*Exeunt.*)

SCENE II

Chamber. LADY ISABEL *discovered seated at a table near fireplace, wrapped in a large shawl—very pale and very ill.*

ISABEL. Alas! What is to be the end of my sufferings? How much longer can I bear this torture of mind, this never-dying anguish of soul? From what a dream have I awakened! O lady, wife, mother! whatever trials may be the lot of your married life, though they may magnify themselves to your crushed spirit as beyond the nature, the endurance of woman to bear, yet resolve to bear them. Fall down on your knees and pray for patience; pray for strength to resist that demon who would tempt you to accept them. Bear them unto death rather than forget your good name and your good conscience. Oh! I have sacrificed husband, home, children, friends and all that make life of value to woman—and for what? To be forever an outcast from society, to never again know a moment's peace. Oh! that I could die, and end my suffering and my misery. (*Sinks her head on table. Enter* LEVISON. *She sees him and speaks coldly.*)

ISABEL. You here, sir? Why did you come now?

LEVISON. Why did I come? Are these all the thanks a fellow gets for traveling in this inclement weather? I thought, at least, that you would be glad to welcome me.

ISABEL. I am glad, for one reason, to welcome you—that we may come to an understanding with each other. Let there be plain truth in this interview, if there never was before.

LEVISON. With all my heart. It is you who have thrown out the challenge, mind. (*Sits by table.*)

ISABEL. When you left me in July, you gave me your solemn promise to be back in time for our marriage. You well know what I mean when I say *in time.*

LEVISON. Oh, of course I meant to do so. I gave you the promise; but no sooner had I set foot in London than I found myself completely overwhelmed with business from which I could not extricate myself.

ISABEL. You are breaking faith with me already; your words are not words of truth, but of deceit. You did not intend to be back in time for our marriage; otherwise you would have caused it to take place ere you went away.

LEVISON. Well, Isabel, you must be aware that it is an awful sacrifice for a man in my position to marry a divorced woman.

ISABEL. When I wished or expected the sacrifice it was not for my own sake. I told you so then. It was for the sake of my child. But it is too late now, and his inheritance must be that of sin and shame.

LEVISON. Isabel, I am now the representative of an ancient and respected baronetcy, and to make you my wife would offend my family.

ISABEL (*rising. At table*). Stay, sir! You need not trouble yourself to find new excuses now. Had you taken this journey on purpose to make me your wife, nay, were the clergyman standing by to perform the ceremony, I tell you, Francis Levison, I would not have you! I can imagine any fate in life better than being compelled to pass it with you. (*Sinks in seat exhausted.*)

LEVISON. Indeed! You made commotion enough once about my making you reparation.

ISABEL. I know I did; but that time is over now. All the reparation in your power to make, all the reparation the whole world could invent, could not undo my sin; it and its effects must be upon me forever.

LEVISON (*laughing sarcastically*). O sin! you ladies should think of that beforehand.

ISABEL. I pray heaven they may! May Heaven help all so to do, who may be tempted as I was!

LEVISON. If you mean that as a reproach to me, it's rather out of place. The temptation to sin lay not in my persuasion half so much as in your ridiculous, jealous anger against your husband.

ISABEL. Quite true! Quite true!

LEVISON. With regard to your husband and that Hare girl, you were blindly, outrageously jealous. For my part, I don't believe Carlyle ever thought of the girl in the way you imagine he did. There was some disreputable secret connected with the Hare family, and Carlyle was acting in it *under the rose* for Mrs. Hare. She was too ill to attend to the matter herself, so she sent the young lady.

ISABEL. You told me a very different tale then, sir.

LEVISON. I know I did. That was merely my stratagem. All stratagems are fair in love and war. By the bye, what have you named the young article there? (*Points to cradle.*)

ISABEL. The name which ought to have been his by inheritance—Francis Levison.

LEVISON. What does he look like? Is he anything like my handsome self?

ISABEL. If he did, if he were like you in thought, or in spirit, I would pray to heaven that he might die before he ever spoke.

LEVISON. Anything else? I would advise you to be careful how you deal out your small change, Lady Isabel. You may get it back with interest. Is my room prepared?

ISABEL. You have no room here, sir. These apartments are rented to me in my own name, now; they can no longer afford you shelter. I received these from you one month ago. (*Takes package of bank notes from box on table.*) Forty pounds—count them. Is it all right? because I wish to return them to you. I wish all to end between us.

LEVISON. If it be your wish that all relation between us should cease, why, so be it. Remember, though, it is your own doing, not mine. But you cannot suppose I will allow you to starve; a sum shall be placed at your banker's to your credit half-yearly.

ISABEL. I beg you to cease. What do you take me for?

LEVISON. Take you for? Why, how can you live? You have no fortune—you must receive assistance from some one.

ISABEL. But not from you; no, not from you. If the whole world denied me, if I could receive no help from strangers or means of earning a livelihood, I'd go and ask my *husband* for bread, sooner than accept one farthing from you.

LEVISON. Bless us, how bitter! Oh, yes, I know, your husband—a very generous man. It's a pity you left him, though. Well, Isabel, since you will accept nothing for yourself, you must for the child. He, at any rate, falls to my share. I'll give you a few hundreds a year for him.

ISABEL. Not a farthing now. Or even, sir, were you to send it, I would throw it into the nearest river. Whom do you take me for? If you have put me beyond the pale of the world, I am still Lord Mount Severn's daughter.

LEVISON. Well, Isabel, if you will still persist in this perverse resolution, of course I cannot amend it. In a little while, however, you may wish to recall it; if so, a line addressed to me at my banker's will always reach me.

ISABEL. It will not be needed, sir. Your clothes which you left here when you went to England, you will have the goodness to order Pierre to take away this afternoon. And now, it is my wish that we part.

LEVISON. To remain as mortal enemies forever?

ISABEL. To be as strangers, sir.

LEVISON (*rising—offering her his hand*). And will you not even shake hands at parting?

ISABEL. I should prefer not, sir.

LEVISON. Oh! very well; just as you please. Da-da—ta-ta! (*Exit.*)

ISABEL. And what is left me now but the deepest, blackest despair! I am bowed down by the weight of my own sin and shame. Why did I ever leave my home and my dear husband? Oh, would I could wake and find it all a terrible dream; that I could find myself once more at East Lynne with my husband and children about me, a happy, contented mother. But no—no—it cannot be! and I must bear the consequences of my sin forever! (*Sinks her head on table.* LORD MOUNT SEVERN *enters. She sees him and covers her head with the shawl.*) Oh, go away, Lord Mount Severn, I beg! Why did you seek me out? I am not worth it. I have brought disgrace enough upon your name.

LORD M. And upon your husband and your children. Nevertheless, it is incumbent on me, as your nearest blood relative, to look after you and see that you do not fall lower. You were one of the last I should have feared to trust. If ever a woman had a good husband in every sense of the word, you had one in Mr. Carlyle. How could you so requite him?

ISABEL (*at table*). I believed that his love was no longer mine. I thought that he had deserted me for another.

LORD M. I had given you credit for having better sense, Isabel. But was that enough to hurl you on to the step you took? Surely not; you must have yielded to the persuasions of that bold, wicked man.

ISABEL. It is all over now.

LORD M. Where do you intend to fix your future home?

ISABEL. Wherever Heaven directs. I shall leave this place as soon as I am strong enough to travel.

LORD M. You were *here* with *him*—were you not?

ISABEL. Yes; they think I am his wife.

LORD M. It is well. How many servants have you?

ISABEL. Two; a maid, and a—a—nurse.

LORD M. A nurse! Isabel, is there then a *child*? Coward—sneak! may all good men shun him henceforth! O Isabel, you, an earl's daughter! How utterly you have lost yourself!

ISABEL. Oh, spare me—I beseech you! You have been rending my heart ever since you came here. I am too weak to bear it.

LORD M. How do you propose to live?

ISABEL. I have some money left.

LORD M. His money, Isabel?

ISABEL. No, not his money. I am selling my trinkets one by one. Before they are all gone I shall look out for some means of earning a livelihood; by teaching, most probably.

LORD M. What sum will it take for you to live upon?

ISABEL. I cannot accept anything from you.

LORD M. Absurd, Isabel. Do not add romantic folly to your other faults. Your father is gone, but I stand in his place.

ISABEL. No—no—I do not desire it. I have forfeited all claim to assistance.

LORD M. But not to mine. I look upon this as a duty, an imperative one too. On my return to England I will settle four hundred a year upon you, and you can draw it quarterly, and so, Isabel, I bid you farewell. May your future life be peaceful, for happy it can never be. (*Taking her hand kindly.*) Farewell, Isabel. (*Exit.*)

ISABEL (*rises and crosses to left of table*). And now I am alone forever! Why don't I die!—why don't I die! (*Falls in chair—bows head on table, sobbing bitterly.*)

CURTAIN

ACT FOUR

SCENE I

As in preceding scene.

(*Enter* ARCHIBALD *and* DILL.)

DILL. Mr. Carlyle, who do you think has had the audacity to come to West Lynne, and set himself up as a candidate in opposition to you?

ARCH. A second man? Let him come on; we shall have the satisfaction of knowing who wins in the end. Well, who is this formidable opponent?

DILL. Mr. Francis Levison. But you won't let that beast frighten you from the contest, will you?

(*Enter* BARBARA HARE, *now* MRS. CARLYLE.)

BARB. Archibald, you will not suffer this insolent man's doings to deter you from your plans? You will not withdraw?

ARCH. Certainly not, Barbara. He has thrust himself offensively upon me in this measure, and I think my better plan will be to take no more notice of him than if he were the dirt under my feet.

BARB. Quite right, quite right, my husband.

(*Enter* MISS CORNEY.)

MISS C. Archibald, have you heard this disgraceful news?

ARCH. I have heard it, Cornelia, and had I not, the very walls would have enlightened me.

MISS C. You will carry on the contest now? I was averse to it before; but now I withdraw all my objections. You will be no brother of mine if you yield the field to him.

ARCH. I do not intend to yield it.

MISS C. Good! You will bear on upon your course, and let him crawl on his.

Take no more notice of him than if he were a viper. Archibald, you must canvass now.

ARCH. No, I shall be elected without canvassing. You'll see, Cornelia.

MISS C. I'll give you a thousand pounds myself for all the electors.

ARCH. Keep your money, sister, it will not be needed.

MISS C. Well, I've heard of a Lady Somebody that kissed a blacksmith to ensure her husband's election. Now, I'm sure I'd kiss every man in East and West Lynne, blacksmiths included, to ensure your election. (*Exits.*)

DILL. And I'm sure I'd kiss every woman. (*Exits.*)

BARB. Archibald, I wish to say something to you. I fear I've done a foolish thing.

ARCH. I fear we all do sometimes. Well, what is it?

BARB. It is something that I've had on my mind for months. You remember that night three years ago that Richard came to us in the grove. I mean that—that night that Lady Isabel quitted East Lynne. Richard came back to me again after he had left us in the grove. I was standing at the open window. He saw me, and motioned me out to him. He declared to me that he had just met the real Thorn in the lane. He described a peculiar motion of the hand as he constantly threw back the hair from his brow, and also spoke of the diamond ring, how it glittered in the moonbeams. Since that time I have had a firm belief that Thorn and Levison are one and the same person.

ARCH. Indeed! Why did you not mention this before?

BARB. I did not like to remind you of that night before; but today I saw Sir Francis Levison in the street, addressing a crowd of people who had assembled to hear him speak, and there was the old action of the hand that my brother had before described. I have therefore written to Richard to steal down here, and try, if possible, to discover his identity. The letter has gone.

ARCH. Well, we must shelter him as best we can. I, myself, feel convinced that Thorn and Levison are one.

BARB. Indeed! How long have you thought so?

ARCH. Not until today. I never suspected it before; but from many circumstances that I can now call to mind I am almost certain of it.

BARB. Archibald, dear husband, what can be done to clear him?

ARCH. Being Levison, I cannot act.

BARB. Not act?—not act for Richard?

ARCH. My dearest, how can I? You had not considered, Barbara,—any one in the world but Levison. It would seem like my own revenge.

BARB. Forgive me. I did not think of it in that light. You are right, my husband, as you always are. Let us wait till Richard comes.

ARCH. Spoken like my own wife. Now, Barbara, you must sing to me. (*She sings song,* "You'll remember me." ARCHIBALD *in same situation with* BARBARA *as with* ISABEL, *at end of Act One.*)

(*Enter* LADY ISABEL, *as* MADAM VINE, *during song. At end of song she sighs deeply.* ARCHIBALD *and* BARBARA *turn and see her.*)

BARB. Ah! This is Madame Vine, I believe, our new governess. Please to step this way, Madame Vine. I hope you are not overfatigued with your journey. Why, how pale you look! You are ill, are you not?

MAD. V. No, not ill, madam, only a little fatigued.

ARCH. Barbara, you had better ring for a glass of wine and some lunch. I am sure Madame Vine must require some refreshment after her tiresome journey. And now I'll leave you to arrange matters between yourselves. (*Looks closely at* MADAME VINE *as he goes out.*) I've seen those features before, I'm certain of it; but where can it have been? (*Exits slowly, as if in deep study.*)

BARB. Madame Vine, will you allow me to ring for some wine and lunch?

MAD. V. Oh, no, madam, don't trouble yourself. I can't take anything just now.

BARB. You looked so pale I feared you might be ill.

MAD. V. I am generally pale, sometimes remarkably so, but my health is good.

BARB. Mrs. Latimer wrote us that you were a very estimable and worthy person, and that you would be sure to suit us. I hope you may, and that you will find your residence here agreeable. Have you lived much in England?

MAD. V. In the early portion of my life.

BARB. And you have lost your husband and your children. I think Mrs. Latimer mentioned children.

MAD. V. Madam, I've lost all—all!

BARB. Oh! it must be a terrible grief when our little ones die. I could not lose my babe for the world; it would kill me to part with him.

MAD. V. Terrible grief indeed, and hard to bear; but it does not always kill.

BARB. You are no doubt aware that these children you will have charge of are not mine; they are the children of Mr. Carlyle's first wife.

MAD. V. And Mr. Carlyle's; yes, madam, I have heard so. She is dead, is she not?

BARB. Yes, she was killed by a railway accident in France some two years ago. She was the only daughter of the late Lord Mount Severn. She was very attractive and beautiful; but I do not think she cared much for her husband. Be that as it may, she ran away with Sir Francis Levison.

MAD. V. I have heard so, madam; it is very sad.

BARB. Sad; it was very wicked,—it was infamous. Of all husbands in the world, of all men living, Mr. Carlyle least deserved such a requital; but the affair was a mystery throughout. Sir Francis Levison had been staying some time at East Lynne, but no one had ever detected any undue intimacy between them, not even Mr. Carlyle. To him, as to others, the cause must remain a mystery. But of course the disgrace is inflicted on the children, and always will be—the shame of having a divorced mother.

MAD. V. But you say she is dead, madam.

BARB. Yes, true; they will not be the less pointed at; the little girl especially. They allude to their mother now and then in conversation, Joyce tells me; but I would recommend you not to encourage them in that. They had better to forget her altogether, if possible. Mr. Carlyle would naturally wish them to do so. I trust you may be able to instill such principles into the mind of the little girl as shall keep her from a like fate.

MAD. V. I will, madam. But do they enjoy good health?

BARB. Quite so, all except the oldest boy, William. He has a slight cough, and the doctors think his lungs are affected. Mr. Carlyle also fears that he is not long for this world.

MAD. V. And how does Mr. Carlyle bear the thought of parting with him?

BARB. Bravely, madam. Mr. Carlyle is not the man to betray emotion, whatever his feelings may be. Even when Lady Isabel left him he made no outward sign of grief, although it must have wrung his very heart strings.

MAD. V. Ay, madam, because he did not love her truly; his best love was given to another.

BARB. You are mistaken. She was his heart's sole idol. Mr. Carlyle is a man who always speaks the truth, and he told me, in his confidence, that he never would have married again during Lady Isabel's lifetime.

MAD. V. But is it sure that she is dead?

BARB. Oh, yes, beyond all doubt. She was journeying with her nurse and infant child at the time of the shocking accident. Her uncle, the present Lord Mount Severn, wrote to the authorities of the little town where it happened, and they sent him word that the nurse and child were killed on the spot, and that the two ladies occupying the same compartment of the carriage had since died of their injuries, and that one of them was certainly the mother of the child. Besides, Lord Mount Severn had placed an annuity in the bank, to be drawn by her quarterly, that has never been touched; so that proves, beyond all doubt, that she no longer lives.

MAD. V. Quite true, madam.

BARB. It was a shocking affair all through. Poor Lady Isabel! Could she have foreseen her fate, she never would have taken such a rash step; or had she known what a villain Levison was. He was not only a bad man in principle, but he was a murderer!

MAD. V. Oh, no—no; not a murderer, a bad man, a very bad man; but not a murderer.

BARB. Oh! did you know him, then?

MAD. V. Oh, no; I did not know him, madam; but I have heard the story.

BARB. It has not been proved; but I feel confident, in my own mind, that it soon will be.

(*Enter* WILLIAM, *followed by* JOYCE. JOYCE *goes up to the table.*)

BARB. This is the little sick boy I spoke of, Madam Vine,—little William.

MAD. V. (*rushes to him and clasps him in her arms*). Oh! my boy, my boy! Are you ill, my darling? *Are* you sick, William? (*To* BARBARA.) I beg your pardon, madam; but I have lately lost a little boy of his age, and when we have lost children of our own, we are apt to love fondly all we come near.

WILLIAM (*with* MADAM V.) Mamma, may I ride to town with you today?

BARB. My dear, I shall not go to town today; besides, you are not yet strong enough; you did wrong to leave the nursery today; this air is too chilly for you. Take him in, Joyce.

JOYCE (*gives* BARBARA *letter*). My lady, here's a letter the postman has just brought; I forgot it till now. Come, William.

BARB. Madam Vine, this is Joyce, who has had charge of the children ever since their mother left them.

(JOYCE *goes to take* WILLIAM *from* MADAM VINE; *recognizes her as* LADY ISABEL; *makes a movement of surprise as if to scream.* ISABEL *puts a finger on her lips as a signal to be silent and not betray her;* JOYCE *takes* WILLIAM *and exits slowly.* BARBARA *is busy reading the letter, and does not see this action.*)

BARB (*aside*). Ah! this is from my brother Richard, to inform me of his coming. I must go and see my husband at once. (*To* MADAM V.) Madam Vine, I must beg you to excuse me for the present. I am called away by some important duties. Make yourself perfectly at home in my absence. East Lynne is small, and I've no doubt you'll soon become familiar with it. (*Exit.*)

MAD. V. Familiar with East Lynne! Did she but know how familiar East Lynne is to me! What will be my trials now! to see him, my husband once, caress the woman I hate; to be compelled to witness the thousand little proofs of affection that were once bestowed upon me; to see his love for her child, while I must teach my own children to forget my memory. Oh! why did I come here? why place myself in such daily torments? O Isabel! patience—patience! Is it thus you bear your cross in life? (*Retires up stage as closed in.*)

SCENE II

Landscape. As in Act I, Scene II.

(*Enter* SIR FRANCIS LEVISON, *walking hurriedly about.*)

LEVISON. What a confounded fool I was to think of trying it on at East Lynne! Carlyle has, no doubt, double the friends I have; but since I've entered the lists against him, I'll not back out. I'm determined to stand my ground.

(*Enter* MISS CORNEY. *She meets* LEVISON *face to face. He lifts his hat and bows.*)

MISS C. Did you intend that insult for me, Francis Levison?

LEVISON. That all depends upon how you are pleased to take it.

MISS C. You dare lift your hat to me? Have you forgotten that I am Miss Carlyle?

LEVISON. It would be a hard matter to forget the face, having once seen it.

MISS C. You contemptible worm, I despise you! Do you think I am to be insulted with impunity? Out upon you for a bold, bad man.

(*Enter* OFFICER. *Taps* LEVISON *on the shoulder.*)

OFFICER. Francis Levison, I arrest you,—you are my prisoner.

LEVISON (*pushing* OFFICER'S *hand off him*). Hands off, vermin! You are too familiar on short acquaintance. Of what crime am I accused?

OFFICER. That you will soon learn. You must come with me at once. (*Handcuffs* LEVISON.)

LEVISON. Oh, certainly, sir, if you desire it. This is some ridiculous mistake,—it will be set right in the morning. Good day, angelic Miss Carlyle, loveliest of your sex. I'm sorry this agreeable little confab was cut so short. I'll come back and renew it in the morning. Take care of your precious self, and look out for the naughty, naughty men,—ta-ta—ta-ta. (*Exit, followed by* OFFICER.)

MISS C. (*calls after them*). Here, Officer! Officer! Be sure you get his photograph taken. It will be an excellent picture for the rogues' gallery! Oh, dear, he's put me in such a fluster, that I must get home as fast as possible, and get some juniper-berry tea to settle my nerves. (*Exit.*)

SCENE III

Chamber.

WILLIAM *discovered lying on couch.* MADAM VINE *seated behind at head, bending over him.*

WILLIAM. Madam Vine, how long will it be before I die?

MAD. V. What makes you think you will die, William?

WILLIAM. I am certain of it, Madam Vine; but it is nothing to die when our Savior loves us; but why do you grieve so for me? I am not your child.

MAD. V. I know you are not my child, but I lost a little boy like you.

WILLIAM. It will be so pleasant to go up there, and never be tired or ill any more.

MAD. V. Pleasant? Ay, William, would that time were come.

WILLIAM. Madam Vine, do you think Mamma will be there? I mean my own mamma that was.

MAD. V. Ay, child, ere long, I trust.

WILLIAM. But how can I be sure that she will be there? You know she was not quite good to Papa or to us, and I sometimes think she did not grow good and ask Heaven to forgive her.

MAD. V. Oh William! her whole life after she left you was one long scene of repentance,—of seeking forgiveness; but her sorrow was greater than she could bear, and her heart broke in its yearning for you.

WILLIAM. What makes you think so?

MAD. V. Child, I know it—I know it.

WILLIAM. Did you ever see her, Madam Vine? Did you know her abroad?

MAD. V. Yes, child, I knew her abroad.

WILLIAM. Why did you not tell us before? What did she say to you?

MAD. V. That she was parted from her children here, but that she should meet them again in heaven, and be with them forever; there, where the awful pain and sadness, all the guilt of this world will be washed out, and He will wipe our tears.

WILLIAM. How shall I know her there? You see I have nearly forgotten what she was like.

MAD. V. You will know her when you see her there, never fear, William.

(*Enter* ARCHIBALD. *Sits on foot of couch.*)

ARCH. Well, Madam Vine, how is your little patient this evening?

MAD. V. He appears worse,—more weak.

ARCH. My little son, Madam Vine is an untiring nurse to you, is she not?

WILLIAM. Papa, I want to see my sister Lucy, and Joyce too.

ARCH. Very well, my little son. I'll send them to you presently. Madam Vine, do you not perceive a change in his countenance?

MAD. V. Yes, he has looked like that since a strange fit of trembling that came over him this afternoon.

ARCH. Oh! it is hard to lose him thus.

MAD. V. He will be better off. We can bear death; it is not the worst parting the earth knows. He will be quit of this cruel world and sheltered in heaven. It would be well for all of us if we could go there as pure as he is.

ARCH. There, William, keep yourself quiet. I'll go and bring your sister Lucy and your mamma to see you. I'll not be gone many minutes. (*Exit.*)

MAD. V. (*rising*). O Heaven! my punishment is more than I can bear. He has gone to bring that woman here that she may mingle her shallow sympathy with his deep grief. Oh, if ever retribution came to woman, it has come to me now. I can no longer bear it. I shall lose my senses. O William! in this last, dying hour try to think I am your mother.

WILLIAM. Papa has gone for her now.

MAD. V. No, not that woman there, not that woman. (*Throws off cap and spectacles.*) Look at me, William, I am your mother! (*Catches him in her arms. He says* "Mother" *faintly, and falls back dead in her arms.*) Oh, he is dead!—he is dead! O William! wake and call me mother once again! My child is dead—my child is dead!

(*Enter* JOYCE.)

JOYCE (*at foot of couch*). O my lady, let me lead you from this room, they will discover you.

MAD. V. O Joyce! leave me to my grief. See here—my child is dead! and never knew that I was his mother. I don't care what I've been, I am his mother still. Oh my child—my child—my heart will break! my heart will break! (*Falls and sobs convulsively.*)

CURTAIN

ACT FIVE

SCENE I

Landscape, as before.

(*Enter* BARBARA *and* JOYCE, *R.*)

JOYCE. But, my lady, will not Madam Vine's illness prevent you from making your usual trip to the seaside?

BARB. Oh, no. Miss Corney will look after the house in my absence, and Dill will be here to assist her. Richard's trial will be over today, and, if he is cleared, I shall prevail upon him to accompany me. I shall start on Monday; this, you know, is Friday; so you will have ample time to get everything in readiness.

JOYCE. Very well, my lady. I'll attend to it. (*Exits.*)

BARB. My poor brother! If he were only *free,* my happiness would be complete. (*Shouts.*) Hark! what mean those shouts?

(*Enter* MISS CORNEY.)

MISS CORNEY. Well, it's all settled at last. Richard's free at all events. I heard the news as I came along, and the very people who have been abusing him for the last seven years are the very ones who are cheering him. I saw that Afy Hallijohn as I came along,—not that I'd condescend to notice such a creature, but she *was* decked out. She had on a green and white silk, flounced up to the waist, extended over a crinoline that would reach from here over yonder; a fancy bonnet stuck on the back part of her head, with a wreath and veil; delicate kid gloves, and swinging a handkerchief highly perfumed with musk. Oh, it was perfectly disgusting. (*Retires.*)

(*Enter* RICHARD HARE; *crosses to* BARBARA.)

RICH. Barbara, my dear sister, I am free at last. Once more I can walk abroad without fear.

BARB. I thank Heaven my dear brother is restored to me at last.

RICH. Yes, the trial is over. Sir Francis Levison has been proved guilty, and has just received his sentence.

MISS C. What was it?

RICH. Transportation for life, for the murder of John Hallijohn.

MISS C. Only for life?

BARB. O Miss Corney, you may depend upon it his punishment is quite sufficient. The lingering torture of mind he will have to endure in the galleys is a thousand times worse than death. But see, Richard, here comes Papa to welcome you.

(*Enter* JUSTICE HARE; *crosses to* RICHARD.)

JUSTICE H. O Richard, my dear boy, I am now proud to own you. This is the happiest day of my life. (*Shouts and groans, L.*) Hark! what's that uproar and confusion? Oh, I see; it's that villain Levison; they are taking him to prison, and the mob are after him. They are coming this way, too; let's be off. I'm so happy that I don't want to encounter that villain, for fear the sight of him would put me in a passion again. Come, my children. (*All exit, except* MISS CORNEY.)

MISS C. Well, *they* may all go; but I shall remain to have the pleasure of wishing Sir Francis Levison a pleasant journey to prison.

(*Enter* LEVISON *followed by an* OFFICER.)

LEVISON. Thank fortune, I have escaped the mob at last! They are on the wrong track, and I can now proceed in quietness. (*Turns and sees* MISS CORNEY.) Oh! that hag there?

MISS C. Good day, *Sir* Francis Levison; those bracelets become you exceedingly well.

LEVISON. Yes, as you say, they are of a very choice pattern. The workmanship about them is very elaborate—truly fine. I'm sorry they've got such an affectionate hold on me, else I'd transfer them to you with the greatest pleasure. By the bye, Miss Corney, give my regards to your brother, the pettifogging lawyer at East Lynne, and tell him that, should he want a lock of his first wife's hair, I have one, which I will give him, free gratis.

MISS C. Sir Francis Levison, you are utterly devoid of feeling or honor. But times are changed since last we met. What will you do for your diamonds, your kid gloves, your perfumed handkerchiefs, in the hulks?

LEVISON. Do? why I suppose I shall have to do without them as many a man has done before me. There's one thing I shall have to console me though,—I shan't be bored with your ugly mug there. (OFFICER *taps him on shoulder and points off.*) Yes, I know, directly, sir. Don't interrupt me when you see I'm talking to a lady. (*To* MISS CORNEY.) I hate to be severe upon you, *angelic* Miss Corney. Don't forget my advice about the naughty, naughty men; and take good care of yourself—your precious self; and also of your red flannel petticoat—ta, la—ta, la!

(*Exit with* OFFICER.)

MISS C. Well, I do declare he's an out-and-out villain, and I do believe he'd try to practice his arts on me, if he thought there was any chance of his succeeding. (*Exit.*)

SCENE II

Chamber, as before.

(*Enter* ARCHIBALD, *meeting* JOYCE *from R.*)

ARCH. Well, Joyce, how is Madam Vine today?—no worse, I hope.

JOYCE. Oh, sir, I fear she is dying.

ARCH. Dying! I'll see her myself. (*Attempts to exit.*)

JOYCE (*stopping him*). Oh! no, no, sir, do not go to her room please, sir; don't think of going to her room.

ARCH. What! let a lady die in my house and not look after her.

(*Enter* MISS CORNEY.)

Cornelia, Joyce tells me that she thinks Madam Vine is dying.

MISS C. Dying! I can't think what has come over Joyce. Lately she acts more like a simpleton than anything else. Move out of the way, girl. (*Going toward door.*)

JOYCE. Oh! no, no, ma'am; you must not enter her room.

MISS C. Well, I declare! What will you do next, I wonder? Archibald, do you go for a physician directly. (*Exits* ARCHIBALD.) Joyce, I think your brain must be softening—move out of the way. (*Throws* JOYCE *round and exits.*)

JOYCE. O my poor lady! What will become of you now? They will discover all. (*Exit.*)

SCENE III

Chamber, as before.
ISABEL *discovered in bed.*

ISABEL. Oh! I am dying—dying alone! and with no one to soothe and comfort me. Oh! if I could but see Archibald and ask his forgiveness, I should die in peace.

(*Enter* MISS CORNEY.)

MISS C. Well, now, if that Joyce was a drinking woman, I should certainly say she was frightfully boozy. (*Recognizing* ISABEL.) Mercy be good! How came *you here?*

ISABEL. Oh! do not reproach me, Miss Corney. I am on my way to heaven, to answer for all my sins and all my sorrows.

MISS C. (*at side of couch*). No, poor child! I'll not reproach you.

ISABEL. I am glad to go. Our Savior did not come, you know, to save the good like you, but for the sake of guilty wretches like me. I have tried to take up my cross as he bade me, and bear it bravely for his sake, but its weight has killed me.

MISS C. Had I anything to do with sending you from East Lynne?

ISABEL. No, I was not happy here with you; but that was not the cause of my going away. Forgive me, Miss Carlyle, but I want to see Archibald and ask him to forgive me before I die. I have prayed to Joyce to bring him to me; but she said it could not be. O Miss Carlyle, do let me see him, only for one little minute, and I will die blessing you.

MISS C. Poor child! You shall see him. (*Goes to door and calls.*) Here, Joyce, Joyce!

(*Enter* JOYCE.)

Go and request your master to come up to me.

JOYCE. O ma'am, do you think it will do—I mean, would it be well?

MISS C. Go and do as I bid you. Are you the mistress here, or am I? Go! (*Exit* JOYCE.) Now, poor child, I will leave you. You shall see Archibald alone.

ISABEL. Oh, bless you, Miss Corney; you have taken a load from my soul, you are too kind. (MISS C. *kisses her.*) And you have kissed me *too*, and I thank you for that.

MISS C. Well, I believe I did kiss her; but it was all the fault of that Joyce, she has flustered me so. (*Exit*)

ISABEL. And I shall see my dear husband once more,—ask him to forgive me,—and then I shall have done with life.

(*Enter* ARCHIBALD.)

ARCH. I am deeply grieved, Madam Vine—— (*Recognizes* ISABEL.) Great heavens! Isabel—here!

ISABEL. Archibald, I could not die till I had your forgiveness. Oh, do not turn away from me,—bear with me one little minute,—only say that you will forgive me, and I can rest in peace.

ARCH. Why did you come here?

ISABEL. I could not stay away from you and my children. The longing for the sight of them was killing me. I never knew one moment's peace after the mad act I was guilty of—in quitting you. Not an hour had I departed ere repentance set in. Even then I would have come back, but I did not know how. My sin was great, and my punishment has been greater; it has been one long scene of mental agony.

ARCH. Why did you go away?

ISABEL. Did you not know why?

ARCH. No; it was always a mystery to me.

ISABEL. I went out of love for you. Oh, do not look at me in that reproachful way! I loved you dearly, and I grew suspicious of you. I thought you false and deceitful to me; that your love was given to her who is now your wife, and, in my sore jealousy, I listened to the temptings of that bold, bad man, who whispered of revenge. But it was not so, was it, Archibald?

ARCH. Can you ask me that, knowing me as you did then, and as you must have known me since? I never was false to you in word, in thought, or in deed.

ISABEL. I know it now, but I was mad. I never could have committed the act in anything but madness. Oh, say that you will forget all and forgive me!

ARCH. I cannot *forget*—I have forgiven already.

ISABEL. Think what it has been for me to live in the same house with her who is now your wife, to watch the envied caresses which once were mine, to see your great love for her; think what it was for me to watch by the death-bed of my own child, to see his decaying strength, to be alone with him in his dying hour, and not be able to tell him *I* was his mother. And then, to see you soothe her petty grief, and I, his *mother,* standing by. Oh, it has been to me as the bitterness of death!

ARCH. You were wrong to come back.

ISABEL. I know it was all wrong; but you were *my* husband once. Oh, that the fearful past could be blotted out, that I could wake and find this all a hideous dream! Archibald, let your thoughts go back to the time when you first knew me, when I was a happy girl here, and my dear old father's petted child; and after, in the happy days when I was your wife, and our little ones were about us. Do you not wish that all this dark fact had never been? Do you not wish it, Archibald?

ARCH. Yes, Isabel, for your sake I wish it.

ISABEL. I am going to William, but my other children will be left with you. Do not, in your love for your late children, do not lose your love for *them.*

ARCH. Isabel, *they* are as dear to me as *you* once were.

ISABEL. As I once was, and might have been now. Archibald, I am now on the very threshold of the other world; will you not say one word of love to me before I pass it? Let what I am be blotted for the moment from your memory. Will you not bless me? Only a word of love—my heart is breaking for it.

ARCH. You nearly broke mine when you left me, Isabel. (*Goes to her and takes her hand.*) May He so deal with you, as I fully and freely forgive you. May He bless you and take you to his rest in heaven!

ISABEL. To His rest in heaven! Archibald, you are leaving me.

ARCH. (*gets back at head of couch*). You are growing faint, Isabel. Let me call assistance. (*Takes her head in his arms.*)

ISABEL. No, do not stir—it is not faintness—it is—death! Oh, but it is hard to part so! Farewell, my once dear husband, until—eternity! (*Soft music.*)

ARCH. Until eternity.

(*She falls back in his arms and dies. He lays her gently down and stands in attitude of deep grief, as if invoking the blessing of Heaven for her soul.*)

CURTAIN

The Two Orphans

Romantic Play in Three Acts

BY ADOLPHE D'ENNERY AND EUGENE CORMON

Adapted from the French by N. Hart Jackson

NOTE

This text is as revised and edited by Glenn Hughes for a 1939 production at the Showboat Theatre, University of Washington, Seattle.

The Two Orphans was first presented in this country at the Union Square Theatre in New York City, December 21, 1874, with the following principals:

Chevalier Maurice de Vaudrey	Jack R. Mero
Count de Linieres, *Minister of Police*	W. D. Lucas
Picard, *Valet to the Chevalier*	Brice Howard
Jacques Frochard, *an Outlaw*	Claude James Carlson
Pierre Frochard, *the Cripple, his Brother*	Gershon Marans
Marquis de Presles	Leslie Houde
Lafleur, *in the service of the Marquis de Presles*	Ellis Thorlakson
Doctor *of the Hospitals St. Louis and La Salpétrière*	Gerard Appy
Martin, *Citizen of Paris*	Charles D. Stover
Officer of the Guard	Jim Merritt
Chief Clerk in the Ministry of Police	Paul O'Brien
De Mailly	Gerard Appy
D'Estrees	Bill Bowles
Antoine	David Maurier
Footman	Bill Bowles
Tumbler	Warn Toms
Countess Diane de Linieres	Marcia Hopper
Henriette } *The Two Orphans*	Ruth Byrne Lockwood
Louise } *The Two Orphans*	Helen Emmons
La Frochard, *Mother of Pierre and Jacques*	Lucille Fuller
Marianne, *an Outcast*	Adele Hull
Sister Genevieve	Frances Robison
Julie	Irma Roald
Florette	Florence Tustin
Marie	Marjory Sapp
Sister Therese	Lovella Lackey
Cora	Genevieve H. Johnson
Singer	Lorene J. Nicolai
Nun	Jean Houlahan
Parisians	Jeraldine Kluck Margie Ivey Kathryn Cameron
Guards	Bill Bush, Paul O'Brien
Abductors	Charles D. Stover, David Maurier

Dramatic Direction by Michael Ferrall
Art Direction by John Ashby Conway
Technical Direction by James Hicken

THE SCENES

ACT ONE

Scene I: An open place on the banks of the Seine, Paris, near the Pont Neuf. An early evening in September, 1784.

Scene II: The Château du Bel-Air in the outskirts of Paris. Later that night.

ACT TWO

Scene I: Private office of the Minister of Police. Forenoon of the day before Christmas.

Scene II: The square in front of the Church of St. Sulpice. Noon of the same day.

Scene III: Henriette's room. A few minutes later.

ACT THREE

Scene I: Courtyard of the Prison La Salpétrière. Two days later.

Scene II: La Frochard's hovel on the banks of the Seine. That night.

THE TWO ORPHANS

ACT ONE

SCENE I

The stage represents an open place on the banks of the Seine, Paris, near the Pont Neuf. The river and the opposite bank with the city are seen in the distance. A beautiful warm sunset lights up the scene. In the distance are to be seen the towers of Notre Dame. Across the back of stage in front a stone wall or quay overlooking the river, which should be seen below. At the right a building with the office of the Normandy coach, which has a bench in front of it. There is, to the left, a drinking shop, open in front to the audience, with tables and glasses. Nearby are booths of itinerant merchants. The curtain rises on a moving, animated crowd of people going and coming; chair-bearers cross the stage; merchants cry their wares; a singer is mounted on a bench, having just finished his song; crowd is applauding.

VARIOUS CRIES. Sprats! fresh sprats! just fried! sausages! hot sausages! rag babies! wooden shoes! who'll buy? who'll buy? here they are! the very best! old hats made new! who'll buy? who'll buy?

LA FROCHARD (*addresses passers-by*). Charity, good friends, charity, if you please, for the love of Heaven—help a poor infirm old woman that can't work and has seven blessed little ones at home to feed. (*A child comes out of the crowd and gives her a coin.*) Ah, the dear little angel—may the good Lord return it to you. Amen.

(*Enter* LAFLEUR *and* ANTOINE *hastily.*)

LAFLEUR (*as he enters he speaks hastily*). Now, Master Antoine, I have a delicate commission to execute for our master, the Marquis de Presles, and I am going to test your discretion and ability to serve him.

ANTOINE. You are very kind, Monsieur Lafleur.

LAFLEUR. You are aware that the marquis returned today from a visit to Normandy. On the road his carriage passed the coach, in which he discovered a treasure he is resolved to possess.

ANTOINE. A treasure? No robbery, I hope?

LAFLEUR. No, stupid! Listen to me and don't interrupt. The treasure is a young girl, whose acquaintance he made at a station when the passengers had alighted for refreshment. He learned that she was coming to Paris in company with her sister, where they have no relations, but are recommended to the care of an old fellow whom they expect to meet them on this spot. (MARTIN *enters, looks around inquiringly.*) All I want you to do is to keep him out of my way. I will contrive to get him into that cabaret, and you must detain him. (*As he looks toward cabaret he discovers* MARTIN.) Pardieu! this may be the very man. Go into the cabaret and wait for me.

(*Exit* ANTOINE *into cabaret.*)

MARTIN (*looking at watch*). Six o'clock. I am a little early.

LAFLEUR (*approaching* MARTIN). Ah! good day, sir. Waiting for the Normandy coach like me, I suppose?

MARTIN (*to bench by coach house*). Yes, monsieur, I expect the arrival of two young girls, orphans, whom I have never seen.

LAFLEUR. Indeed! That's very odd. I also am looking for some one I have never seen.

MARTIN. They are recommended to me by my wife's brother, who has written, begging us to look after them.

LAFLEUR. Your wife's brother was very kind.

MARTIN. Yes, for they will be company for us, for me particularly because I live alone; that is, alone with my wife.

LAFLEUR. Which is not particularly amusing, eh?

MARTIN (*taking snuff*). No, no; that is, not generally.

LAFLEUR. Well, my dear sir, we have two hours to wait; the coach will not arrive today until eight o'clock, instead of six as usual. A gentleman just arrived by post, who passed it on the road, says it has been delayed by an accident, and will certainly not be here for two hours yet.

MARTIN. How very provoking. What shall I do with myself for two hours?

LAFLEUR. What do you say to a game of picquet to pass the time?

MARTIN. Picquet, my dear sir; I love picquet and my wife hates it. Sir, I shall be delighted to play picquet.

LAFLEUR. Let's step into this café and play for the price of a glass of wine. The waiter will tell us when the coach comes in sight.

MARTIN. Yes, yes, that's important; I would not miss it for the world.

LAFLEUR. No, no, certainly not. I expect a lovely young person, too, and must not miss it either.

MARTIN. Ah! you young fellows are so gay. I love young people, they are so different from my wife.

LAFLEUR. I imagine so.

MARTIN. An excellent woman, but so aggravating.

LAFLEUR (*takes* MARTIN'S *arm and goes toward cabaret*). Yes, wives usually are.

(LA FROCHARD *enters and meets them.*)

LA FROCHARD. Good gentlemen, charity, if you please, for a poor old woman.

LAFLEUR. You bothersome old woman, will you clear out?

(LAFLEUR *and* MARTIN *exeunt into cabaret.* PIERRE *enters at back, with scissors-grinding wheel, which he puts down.*)

PIERRE. Knives to mend—scissors to grind—knives to mend. (*Sees* LA FROCHARD.) Why, Mother, is that you?

LA FROCHARD. Yes, it's me. You lazy good-for-nothing.

PIERRE. Lazy? Why, Mother, I do all the work I can!

LA FROCHARD. Work? You call *that* work? Bah! Why did Heaven bless you with such a beautiful deformity? Why, to earn your living by, you puny, limping cripple—and you work when all you need to do is to sit here, hold out your hand, and make your fortune.

PIERRE. Mother, I cannot beg, it is not possible.

LA FROCHARD. Eh? Not possible—why not?

PIERRE. Mother, when I was an infant you carried me through the streets and taught me to repeat begging-prayers I did not understand. They put money in your pocket and I knew no shame. But now it is different. You drove me out and bade me come here to beg. When I knelt and held out my hand to ask alms in the name of the misfortunes with which Heaven has chastised me, shame choked me, and I was overcome by anger at my own humiliation. When a passer-by looked on me with pity and put a coin in my hand, a great lump came in my throat, and my eyes filled with tears. No, Mother, I cannot beg—I cannot!

LA FROCHARD. You undutiful son—you would rather leave your poor brother and me to starve.

PIERRE. My brother need not starve. He has health and strength, and you support him in idleness.

LA FROCHARD. Why should my beautiful Jacques work? My handsome boy, the very image of his poor dead father, that those scoundrels of the law robbed me of.

PIERRE. He suffered death for a murder of which they found him guilty.

LA FROCHARD. And can I look to you to avenge him? No, no; my handsome Jacques will do that one of these days. He's no milksop, nothing frightens him.

PIERRE. No! Not even the sight of blood.

LA FROCHARD. Shut up; you are good for nothing but to be honest. I hate honest people; scum that imposes on the poor. (*Couple enter from cabaret and cross stage.* LA FROCHARD *approaches them.*) Good people, charity for the love of Heaven!

PIERRE. Perhaps she is right, I *am* good for nothing except to be honest. (*Sadly.*) Alas! I have never had any one to teach me. (*Returns to his wheel, starts away with it, stops as he hears noise in the cabaret.*) Ah!

(*Laughter heard in the cabaret. When it is over* JACQUES *comes out, followed by crowd who look over his shoulders.)*

JACQUES. Hello! Here is the old woman and her precious abortion of a son. (*To* LA FROCHARD.) Has Marianne come yet?

LA FROCHARD. Not yet, my son.

JACQUES. Never mind, she'll come in time. (*To crowd.*) You can order everything you want, wine, brandy, anything, I'll stand it.

(*Crowd returns to the cabaret.*)

LA FROCHARD. My son, are you going to pay? Have you found a purse?

JACQUES. No, but Marianne has. I have ordered her to bring me some money, and she will do it. (*To* PIERRE.) Come here.

LA FROCHARD (*admiringly*). Isn't he in a good humor?

JACQUES. Look ye! Good children always give an account of their earnings to their parents. Isn't that so, Mother?

LA FROCHARD. Certainly, my lamb—you have excellent principles.

PIERRE. And when I give an account you pocket all.

JACQUES. Well, what if I do?

PIERRE. It is unjust—it is——

JACQUES (*threateningly*). That's enough. None of your fine speeches. I want your money. How much have you got?

PIERRE (*hands the money to* LA FROCHARD). Twenty-two livres, seven sous, six deniers.

JACQUES (*taking money from* PIERRE'S *hand*). And all this fuss about that! Why, what have you been doing for a whole week with those spindle legs and arms?

PIERRE. I have walked the streets from morning until night, with my wheel upon my back. I have lived on bread and water. I could do no more.

JACQUES. Well, your trade don't pay. I must find you something better.

PIERRE. Something better? You? No! no! (*Returns to his wheel.*)

LA FROCHARD. I have saved three livres, eighteen sous—put them with Pierre's, that makes——

JACQUES. Oh, never mind how much it makes, I don't want it particularly, but I'll take it on principle. (*Takes money from* LA FROCHARD.) Come, cripple, let's drink.

PIERRE. No; I don't like to drink.

JACQUES. Why, who would think we are brothers? You have the blood of a sheep in your veins—you're a disgrace to the family. I boast the blood of a Frochard, the Frochards who have been outlaws for one hundred and fifty years.

LA FROCHARD. Ah, what a man! I love him—he's so like his father.

JACQUES (*takes* LA FROCHARD *by the arm*). Come along, then, if you love me. I'm thirsty. (*To* PIERRE.) Are you coming with us?

PIERRE. No, no, there's the Normandy coach has just arrived. I'll run and see if there's not a chance to earn a few sous.

(*Coach horn and clatter of horses' hoofs off stage.* LA FROCHARD *and* JACQUES *exeunt into cabaret; exit* PIERRE *through arch.* LAFLEUR *comes out of cabaret. Crowd of travellers and porters come on carrying baggage, etc. Some go into the office. Scene becomes animated. People going and coming. Enter* DE PRESLES.)

DE PRESLES (*seeing* LAFLEUR). Ah, Lafleur, there you are.

LAFLEUR. Marquis, I thought it was time for you to be here.

DE PRESLES. Are the arrangements made?

LAFLEUR. Yes, my lord. I've provided for Monsieur Martin: he's in there, drunk as a lord and quarreling with Antoine over the virtues of his wife.

DE PRESLES. Good. . . . You'll take this note to the Chevalier de Vaudrey. I desire his presence at my fête at Bel-Air this evening, in honor of the capture I expect to make. (*Aside.*) His presence will check any awkward inquiry. (*Aloud.*) Are you all ready?

LAFLEUR. All ready, my lord—but to know the lady!

(DE PRESLES *and* LAFLEUR *look off stage.*)

DE PRESLES (*pointing*). There, that is she just alighted from the coach now, helping her sister down. Do you see, the taller of the two—look at her well!

LAFLEUR. Yes, my lord—she is charming enough to remember!

DE PRESLES. Use every means at your command, and this evening at my villa of Bel-Air—you understand me?

LAFLEUR. Certainly. I am going to find my men!

(LAFLEUR *and* DE PRESLES *exit.*)

HENRIETTE (*outside*). Come, Louise, come this way! (*Enter* HENRIETTE, *leading* LOUISE. *The stage gradually becomes empty during following scene.* HENRIETTE *comes to the center of the stage, looks around and sees bench.*) Here, Louise, sit here!

(LOUISE *sits on bench in front of office.*)

LOUISE (*sitting*). I am surprised that Monsieur Martin is not here to meet us!

HENRIETTE. Oh, he'll come soon! Ah, Louise, Paris is beautiful! My poor sister, if you could only see its wonders!

LOUISE. Tell me what you see! Where are we?

HENRIETTE. In an open square on the bank of a river and there's a beautiful bridge further down, which has a magnificent statue in the middle.

LOUISE. That's the Pont Neuf—Papa used to speak of it!

HENRIETTE. And on this side I can see two great towers—it must be Notre Dame Cathedral.

LOUISE. Notre Dame. (*Sadly.*) How I wish I could see it. It was on that spot I, a helpless infant, was left to perish. There your dear father found me! But for him I should have died of cold and hunger—perhaps, perhaps that would have been better!

HENRIETTE. My darling sister, why do you say so?

LOUISE. I should not have lived to become blind and unhappy!

HENRIETTE. Louise, do not speak thus—our dear parents loved us both alike—you were their consolation and happiness, and it was their first grief when Heaven deprived you of your sight.

LOUISE. Misfortune pursues me, sister—scarcely had this affliction befallen me when we were left orphans without help or friends.

HENRIETTE. No, no, dear Louise! Not without friends I hope! I have turned all we possessed into money and have come to this great Paris, where there are skillful doctors who will soon restore my poor Louise's eyes to their old time brightness!

LOUISE. Heaven grant that your hopes may be realized! But where can Monsieur Martin be? Why doesn't he come for us?

HENRIETTE. Perhaps he is waiting now in the office—I'll go in and see! (*Enters the office, leaving* LOUISE *seated on the bench.*)

(*The voices of* JACQUES *and others are heard laughing boisterously in the cabaret.* MARIANNE *enters at back, pale and staggering.*)

MARIANNE (*listens for a moment*). Yes, it is his voice, singing and laughing. Aye, drink and carouse; forget her whose heart you have broken. Enjoy yourself while the victim of your brutality seeks the only refuge left to her—the river! One plunge and it will all be over. (*She goes up to the quay. Re-enter* HENRIETTE *from the office.*) No, it is not yet dark enough. I might be seen and perhaps saved.

HENRIETTE (*to* LOUISE). He is not in the office!

LOUISE. And you do not see him here?

HENRIETTE (*anxiously looking round*). No, not yet. But what can be the matter with that woman? (MARIANNE *falls.*) She has fallen; she must be ill.

LOUISE. Go to her; speak to her, Henriette; go, go, sister.

(HENRIETTE *goes up to* MARIANNE.)

HENRIETTE (*to* MARIANNE). Pardon me, madame; can I do anything for you?

MARIANNE. Nothing.

HENRIETTE. You seem exhausted; are you suffering?

MARIANNE. Yes, yes; I am suffering.

LOUISE (*to* HENRIETTE). She said that with a voice full of misery and despair. Help her, sister.

HENRIETTE. Madame, have confidence in us. We are not rich, but if we can help you——

MARIANNE. I have already told you I want nothing. There are griefs that cannot be consoled; sufferings that cannot be alleviated. I only wish to—to——

LOUISE (*rising and joining them*). You wish to die.

MARIANNE (*rises*). Who told you so? How do you know I want to die?

LOUISE. I feel it while I listen to you. Do you not know that we who are blind can listen with our whole being?

HENRIETTE. Tell us your troubles. Perhaps we can relieve them.

MARIANNE (*softening, and taking their hands*). You do not know me; have never seen me before, and yet you pity me. No, no; there is no help for me. Leave me; leave me, and do not attempt to save me. (*Rises, as if to move away.*)

HENRIETTE (*retaining her*). Stay.

LOUISE. For the love of Heaven, stay.

MARIANNE. I am pursued by the officers of the law. I have no strength to fly further; they will arrest me.

HENRIETTE. What have you done?

MARIANNE. I have stolen! (HENRIETTE *and* LOUISE *recoil a moment.*) Stolen money confided to my care. All the meager savings of a poor workwoman. I stole it for *him*, for a wretch whom I despise; but whom, alas, I love!

(*Loud voices heard in the cabaret—laughter.*)

JACQUES (*in the cabaret*). Good—good; a capital joke.

MARIANNE. Listen; that is his voice. He is there, wasting in debauchery the money purchased by my crime. When I am away from him my reason returns, and I only feel the hate his baseness inspires. Alas! when he speaks to me my hate disappears. I cower and tremble before him, and am his slave. I have stolen for him, and I believe I would *kill* at his bidding. No, no; it is better I should die.

HENRIETTE. You cannot atone for a fault by committing a crime.

MARIANNE. If I am found they will arrest, imprison me.

LOUISE. When you have left the prison you will have paid the debt you owe to man.

HENRIETTE. And repentance will pay the debt you owe to Heaven.

MARIANNE. Heaven! Do you believe there is a Heaven?

HENRIETTE (*energetically*). Do I believe there is a Heaven?

MARIANNE. I cannot believe that that there is a Heaven for outcasts like me.

LOUISE. Oh, unhappy woman!

HENRIETTE (*pointing to the river*). See where such a belief would lead you. Listen and believe us. You can redeem your past and your future will be happier. (*Slips money into her hand.*) Take this!

MARIANNE (*refusing*). No, no!

LOUISE. Do not refuse, I implore you.

MARIANNE (*weeping*). Ah! You are right. There must be a Heaven, for has it not sent two angels to succor and to save me? (*She takes their hands and weeps over them.*)

HENRIETTE. Courage, courage!

MARIANNE. Yes, yes, I will have courage. I'll fly from Paris, from him. Have I the strength? I do not know. I only know I wish I could give my life for you. (JACQUES *appears at the door of cabaret.*) May Heaven bless you! Farewell. (*Exits*).

JACQUES (*calling after her*). Marianne?

(MARIANNE *stops suddenly, does not turn.*)

LOUISE (*to* HENRIETTE). What is she doing?

HENRIETTE (*to* LOUISE). Alas! She stops!

JACQUES. Where are you going?

MARIANNE (*with averted head*). Away from you, whom I hope never to see again.

JACQUES (*coming out and going up to her*). Bah! You don't want to see me. (*Takes her hand.*) Then why did you stop when I called? What makes your hand tremble?

MARIANNE. It does not tremble. I have found strength to resist you. I'm ashamed of the life I lead, and of the infamy into which you have plunged me.

JACQUES. Pooh! pooh! Put all that stuff out of your head and follow me.

MARIANNE (*disengaging her hand*). I will not!

JACQUES. You must. Come! Do you hear?

MARIANNE (*hesitates*). I—I—— (*Looks at the girls and gains courage.*) Yes, I hear and I refuse, I will not obey you.

JACQUES. You want me to persuade you in the usual way, eh, do you?

MARIANNE. You shall not. Never again.

JACQUES (*threateningly*). We'll see! (*Rushing upon her.*)

(*At the same moment the watch enter, an officer at their head.* MARIANNE, *looking round her for some means of escape, sees the guard.*)

MARIANNE. Ah, you *shall* see! (*To* OFFICER.) Monsieur, arrest me. I am a thief!

OFFICER. Arrest you? Who are you?

MARIANNE. My name is Marianne Vauthier. Officers are in search of me. I escaped from them an hour ago. Now I wish to deliver myself to justice.

JACQUES (*goes up to hide himself*). She has gone crazy.

(OFFICER *takes paper from his belt and looks at it.*)

OFFICER. Marianne Vauthier. Yes; accused of theft.

MARIANNE (*looking at* JACQUES). Of which I am guilty.

OFFICER. Well, if you confess it I must take you to La Salpétrière.

MARIANNE (*to* OFFICER). Come! (*They place her in the midst of the guard and march her off. As she passes* JACQUES *she stops.*) I said I would escape you this time. You see I keep my word!

OFFICER. Forward, march!

(*Exeunt* OFFICER, GUARDS *and* MARIANNE.)

JACQUES. To Salpétrière. She is a fool. Humph! (JACQUES *exits into cabaret, when the singing and noise continue.*)

(PIERRE *enters. Exits.*)

LOUISE. Henriette.

HENRIETTE. You are frightened, sister.

LOUISE. Yes, yes. I am, indeed.

HENRIETTE. And night is falling fast.

LOUISE. Why doesn't Monsieur Martin come?

LAFLEUR (*entering*). Here I am, mademoiselle.

HENRIETTE (*with joy*). Ah!

LOUISE. At last.

HENRIETTE. We began to be very anxious.

LAFLEUR. You must excuse me, for I live at a great distance from here.

HENRIETTE (*astonished*). A great distance?

LOUISE. Why, we were told your house was but a few steps from the bridge.

LAFLEUR (*aside*). A mistake. (*Aloud.*) Yes, yes; indeed it was—that is, I did live but a short distance from here; but, you see, I have moved. Come, come, let us go, mademoiselle!

HENRIETTE (*shrinking from him, in doubt*). You have moved?

LAFLEUR. Yes, yes; only yesterday.

LOUISE. And you said nothing of it in your letter to——

LAFLEUR (*quickly*). To my brother-in-law. No. Of course it was my brother-in-law who sent you to my care. No, no. I did not write it to him because—because, in short, I did not know I was going to move; but if you doubt me, here are some neighbors of mine—good, honest citizens, who will vouch for me.

(LAFLEUR *goes up, makes a sign, and two men come on.* HENRIETTE *crosses and looks at them.*)

HENRIETTE. Honest citizens?

LOUISE (*extending her hands*). Henriette, do not leave me.

(*The men seize* HENRIETTE, *place handkerchief to her mouth and carry her off, followed by* LAFLEUR.)

HENRIETTE (*as she is carried off*). No, no! Help, help!

LOUISE (*alone*). I hear nothing. Henriette, where are you? Sister, why do you not answer me? (*With terror.*) Henriette, Henriette! Speak to me. Speak one word. Answer me. Henriette! (*With despair.*) No answer?

HENRIETTE (*heard in the distance with stifled voice*). Louise?

LOUISE (*screaming*). Henriette, Henriette! Ah! 'Tis she. They have dragged her away from me. Oh! what shall I do? Alone! alone! Abandoned. What will become of me? Alone in this great city; helpless and blind? (*She breaks down weeping, after a pause. She gropes her way up the stage and reaches the stone coping of the quay over the river, and, just as she does so, stumbles as though about to fall into the river.*)

(PIERRE, *entering, catches her in his arms just in time to save her.*)

PIERRE (*brings her back to the center of the scene*). Great heavens! What were you going to do?

LOUISE (*trembling with fright*). Nothing, nothing; what was it?

PIERRE. Another step and you would have fallen into the river.

LOUISE. Oh, save me! Save me!

(*Enter* LA FROCHARD *from the cabaret.*)

LA FROCHARD. Why, what is the matter? What are you doing there, Pierre? (*To* LOUISE.) Young woman, did you fall?

LOUISE. Ah, madame, do not leave me, I beg, I entreat you, do not leave me here all alone.

PIERRE. Calm yourself, mademoiselle, there's no danger now.

LA FROCHARD. What is it? Have you lost your head?

LOUISE. Yes, yes. I believe I shall go mad. Alas! madame, a few minutes ago my sister was here with me and they have stolen her away from me.

PIERRE. Stolen her?

LA FROCHARD. Well, you must let your parents know.

LOUISE. Our parents? Alas, madame, we are orphans!

PIERRE. You have acquaintances—friends——

LOUISE. We have only just arrived in Paris and I know no one here.

LA FROCHARD. No one; no one at all?

PIERRE. Were the people who took your sister away gentlemen or common people?

LOUISE. How can I tell?

LA FROCHARD. You could see their clothes.

LOUISE. Alas! madame, I am blind!

PIERRE. You are blind?

LA FROCHARD. Blind, without relations, friends or acquaintances in Paris. (*Looks at her.*) And young and pretty.

PIERRE (*aside and low*). It is true, young and pretty.

LA FROCHARD. (*To* PIERRE.) Go! Leave me alone with her; I'll take care of her.

PIERRE. Yes, Mother. We must help her to find her sister.

LA FROCHARD. That's all right. I know what to do. You clear out.

(PIERRE *crosses to wheel.*)

LOUISE (*uneasily*). You will not leave me, madame?

LA FROCHARD. Never fear, my dear, I'll not leave you.

PIERRE (*goes up and takes his wheel*). Blind! So young and so pretty. (*Laughing sadly to himself.*) Pretty! What is that to you, wretched cripple? (*Exits.*)

LA FROCHARD. Come, come, my pretty child, don't be downcast.

LOUISE. Alas! to whom shall I go for help?

LA FROCHARD. To me. I am an honest woman, mother of a family. I'll give you a home until you find your sister.

LOUISE. Ah! madame—you are very good to have pity on me. But we will find her, won't we?

LA FROCHARD. Oh yes, certainly, in time. Come, then, come along with me.

LOUISE. I trust myself to you, madame.

LA FROCHARD. You couldn't do better—you have fallen into good hands. Come! (*As she leads her off.*)

CURTAIN FALLS

SCENE II

The Château du Bel-Air. Illuminated terrace and garden. DE PRESLES, DE MAILLY, D'ESTREES, JULIE, CORA, FLORETTE *and other guests discovered seated in groups. Others dancing. Music at rise, but stops shortly. Laughter, applause.*

DE PRESLES. Well, what do you think of my retreat from the whirl and bustle of Paris? Is Bel-Air equal to its reputation?

JULIE. My dear marquis, I am delighted; it is a satisfaction to find a gentleman who maintains the customs of his rank.

DE MAILLY. And yet there are fools who wish to change them.

DE PRESLES. You are right, fools, fools. But come, some champagne, wine, wine!

FLORETTE. Yes, yes; champagne!

(*They turn up to take glasses, all fill, come down.*)

D'ESTREES. Yes, yes, some wine. (*Holds up glass.*) To the health of our noble host.

JULIE. To your health, marquis!

(*They all drink.*)

DE PRESLES. To yours, my pet!

JULIE. You are too affectionate, marquis. By the way, have you heard the news?

CORA. The news? No! What is it?

JULIE. They say that the new minister of police is as hard as stone and as cold as a fish. He is going to put a stop to all our amusements; in short, marquis, this may be the last entertainment you will give at Bel-Air.

DE PRESLES. Nonsense! I'd like to see the minister of police who would dare to interfere with the pleasures of a French nobleman. Who is this Puritan?

JULIE. He is from Touraine, is called the Count de Linieres, and is the uncle of the Chevalier Maurice de Vaudrey.

FLORETTE. Where is the chevalier? You promised I should see him!

DE PRESLES. So I did, and I expect him. Also another guest. And I warn you, ladies, a rival to you all.

JULIE. I fear no rivals, if they will leave us your delightful entertainments, marquis. Who is your other guest?

DE PRESLES. A young lady, sweet sixteen, beautiful as a rose, innocent as an angel.

FLORETTE. Where did you find such a pearl?

DE PRESLES. In Normandy.

JULIE, CORA and FLORETTE. In Normandy? (*All laugh.*)

JULIE. Yes, I know these Normandy beauties, with caps six feet high.

FLORETTE. In wooden shoes.

CORA. And hair plaited down her back.

DE PRESLES. Laugh away, ladies. You shall see a Norman beauty in a high cap, wooden shoes and all, and see how jealous you will all become at sight of her.

VOICE (*outside*). You can't pass here.

(*Noise of struggling heard without and the voice of* PICARD.)

PICARD (*outside*). I tell you I must go in and I will. I must speak to your master.

DE PRESLES (*goes up*). What is it? Who must speak to me?

PICARD (*outside*). Picard, valet to the Chevalier de Vaudrey!

DE PRESLES. Let him come in. (*Enter* PICARD.) Well, what is it?

PICARD. Most excellent marquis and most beautiful ladies, I am very sorry, but my master asks you to excuse him.

FLORETTE (*pettishly*). Excuse him? But he promised!

PICARD. I did the promising. He said he did not know whether he could come or not; but thinking I could persuade him, I promised for him.

DE PRESLES. Then you took a great liberty. He ought to punish you for it.

PICARD. Certainly he ought. I wish he would, but, alas! My master is not like other masters. In fact, he is no master at all.

D'ESTREES. Indeed!

PICARD. Positively. He spends his nights in pleasure as a young nobleman ought to do, but his days—what do you suppose he does with his days?

DE PRESLES. Sleeps, of course.

PICARD (*takes the men down and speaks confidentially*). Hush, gentlemen! He works—actually works. He sits down and reads and writes—just as though he were a lawyer's clerk.

D'ESTREES. Bah! You don't expect us to believe that.

PICARD. Yes and more too. Why, how do you suppose he acts to the common people who want to see him? Creditors, for instance?

DE PRESLES. Why, if they are importunate he beats them, I suppose.

PICARD. Yes, he beats them—he pays them. Gentlemen, he pays his tradespeople.

GENTLEMEN. Oh! oh! oh!

DE PRESLES. Oh! the poor fellow is lost!

PICARD. Completely; all owing to the bad company he keeps; he won't be guided by me.

DE PRESLES. Perhaps he is right in that. But where is the attraction elsewhere tonight?

(*Enter* MAURICE DE VAUDREY.)

DE VAUDREY. I will tell you, gentlemen.

(*All turn.*)

ALL. Why, here he is. The chevalier himself!

DE PRESLES. What is all this that Picard has been telling us, that you were not coming?

DE VAUDREY. I did not expect to come, so sent him with my regrets.

PICARD. And now he brings them himself!

JULIE. Oh, we much prefer your last messenger. Where have you been?

DE VAUDREY. At the theatre, to see Beaumarchais' new piece.

DE PRESLES. Ah! yes. Some seditious stuff which the police had forbidden.

DE VAUDREY. Seditious or loyal, it matters little. The people took sides with the author, and the king was compelled to yield.

DE PRESLES. The king compelled to yield? If that is true, royalty has lowered its dignity.

DE VAUDREY. No, marquis. It is the people who are asserting theirs.

DE PRESLES. Why, if this goes on they will not be satisfied until they suppress our titles and privileges.

DE VAUDREY. That would not at all surprise me.

(*All laugh,* PICARD *the loudest and longest.*)

PICARD. Oh, oh! That's too good.

DE VAUDREY. Why, Picard, that seems to amuse you.

PICARD. Excuse me, sir; but that is as ridiculous as though you were to say that one of these days the Parisians would rise and demolish the Bastile!

DE VAUDREY. Who knows?

PICARD. What! The Bastile? (*Laughs.*) Well, when that time comes everything will be upside down. They won't even respect a nobleman's valet.

DE VAUDREY. Nor a nobleman either.

PICARD. If that is the case I'll go home and set my house in order. (*Exit, bumping into two or three guests in his haste.*)

DE PRESLES. Really, my dear De Vaudrey, you are a riddle. Sometimes you are the *nobleman,* and sometimes you assume——

DE VAUDREY. The plebeian—well.

DE PRESLES. Where will all this end? What are you trying to do?

DE VAUDREY. Trying to do? To take advantage of the few quiet days that may be left for such as we are. Have you not eyes to see, and ears to hear? Look around you. The fatal irresistible tide is hourly advancing, and every wave is red with blood.

DE PRESLES. Fancies, my dear chevalier, fancies. Picard was right: you associate with a lot of dreaming theorists and philosophers, who fill you with their levelling ideas. Let us enjoy ourselves while we can. Come. Wine, more wine and a song! (*They fill their glasses.* JULIE *stands on sofa and sings. All join in chorus.* LAFLEUR *enters hurriedly and crosses to* DE PRESLES.) Ah! here you are at last! Well?

LAFLEUR. Marquis, your orders are executed.

DE PRESLES. Good! And the girl?

LAFLEUR (*pointing off stage*). Is there!

DE PRESLES. Let her be brought here at once. (*Exit* LAFLEUR. DE PRESLES *turns to others.*) Ladies, here is my other guest! Look!

(HENRIETTE *is carried in by two abductors, preceded by* LAFLEUR, *who place her on a sofa. All the people gather around at back and end of it, except* DE VAUDREY, *who comes down* R. *with a glass of wine in his hand.*)

FLORETTE. Ah, this is our threatened rival!

DE VAUDREY. A young girl! I see the sport has been good.

CORA. Why, she has fainted.

JULIE. Sleeping, my dear; it's much more becoming.

DE VAUDREY. I'll wager that her eyes are but half closed, and that she is laughing to herself at all the trouble you are taking.

DE PRESLES (*to them around sofa*). What do you think of my treasure?

FLORETTE. Very ordinary face.

JULIE. Exceedingly common person, big feet! (*Laugh.*)

CORA. Arms and hands like a washerwoman! (*Laugh.*)

DE MAILLY (*to* DE VAUDREY). Chevalier, your opinion.

DE VAUDREY (*without looking*). Lovely face; distinguished air; with the feet and hands of a duchess.

DE PRESLES. But you have not seen——

DE VAUDREY. No, but I have heard those young ladies.

JULIE. Isn't she going to wake up?

LAFLEUR (*gives* DE PRESLES *a small vial*). A few drops of this on your handkerchief will be sufficient to revive her.

DE PRESLES. Excellent! (*Takes vial.*) I am well satisfied with you. (*Gives him purse.*) You can go.

LAFLEUR. And I am well satisfied also. (*Shaking purse as he exits.*)

DE PRESLES. What will she say when she comes to her senses?

DE VAUDREY. What will she say? As though we did not know by heart the everlasting phrases of these willingly abducted maidens. When the proper moment arrives she will awake and go through it all. "Where am I?" "Why have you brought me here?" "Where am I?" "What is it you wish?" "Great Heavens!" "Oh, my mother!" (*Laughs.*) Then by slow degrees this profound and virtuous despair, which commenced in a torrent of tears, will be drowned in—a flood of champagne!

JULIE. We will see. Let me wake her, marquis. (DE PRESLES *gives* JULIE *the vial, she puts a few drops on her handkerchief, and applies it to* HENRIETTE'S *mouth.*) Look, her eyes open.

(HENRIETTE *comes to very gradually, raises herself, looking around confusedly from one to the other until her eye rests on* DE PRESLES.)

HENRIETTE. Am I mad? Do I dream? (*Recognizes* DE PRESLES.) Ah!

FLORETTE (*aside to* DE VAUDREY). That is not exactly the old way.

DE VAUDREY. No, that is singular. Something of an improvement.

HENRIETTE (*rises and goes to the* MARQUIS *and speaks in a decisive tone of voice*). Monsieur, has this outrage been committed by your orders? Is this your house?

DE PRESLES. Ah! mademoiselle, I see you do me the honor to recognize me. It was I who——

HENRIETTE. Not another word, sir. I wish to return this very instant to the place where my sister awaits me. Come, sir, at once give your servants orders to take me back. You must—do you hear me, sir? You must, you shall!

DE PRESLES (*taking her hand*). Mademoiselle, after all the trouble we have taken to bring you here, you can scarcely suppose we will let you go so soon?

HENRIETTE (*jerking free from him*). Listen, sir! I see the horrible trap you have laid for me. But you, vile as you are, can scarcely understand the extent of your own villainy. You have separated me from a poor child whose only help in life I am, whose misfortunes command the respect of criminals even worse than yourself. She is dependent on me alone; without me she cannot take a single step, for she is blind!

ALL. Blind?

HENRIETTE. Yes, blind, and alone! Alone in Paris, without money, without help, wandering through the streets, sightless, homeless, wild with despair. What will become of her? She is blind! Gentlemen, do you hear me? She is blind!

JULIE. Poor child!

DE VAUDREY (*aside*). Oh! this is too horrible!

DE PRESLES. Oh! well, compose yourself, mademoiselle. I will give orders to have search made for her; my people will find her and bring her here.

HENRIETTE. Bring her here? To this house—no, no, never! Is this the only answer you have to my prayer? Is there no one here who dares to raise a voice against you? (*Turning.*) Is there not amongst all these men one gentleman?

DE PRESLES. You are mistaken, mademoiselle. We are all noblemen and gentlemen!

(DE VAUDREY *breaks his glass angrily.*)

HENRIETTE. Then, amongst all these noblemen and gentlemen, there is not one man of honor?

DE VAUDREY. You are mistaken again, mademoiselle. (*Crosses to her.*) Take my hand, we will leave this place.

HENRIETTE. Oh! thank you, monsieur!

DE PRESLES (*quickly bars the way*). Excuse me, chevalier, this is my house, and I do not permit——

DE VAUDREY (*coldly*). Give me room, sir.

DE PRESLES. Pardon me, I will brook no interference! (*Clock strikes sharply and quickly twelve.*) Do you hear? Midnight. After twelve o'clock no one ever leaves this house.

DE VAUDREY. Then we shall be the first to do so. Stand aside, sir!

DE PRESLES. Do you know, chevalier, that you speak to me as though I were your lackey?

DE VAUDREY. I would not speak to a lackey who acted as you do. *I would cane him!*

DE PRESLES (*drawing his sword*). Enough, monsieur; you are more than insolent. Attempt to pass me and . . .

DE VAUDREY (*draws*). I certainly shall, and this young lady with me!

LADIES, DE MAILLY and D'ESTREES. Chevalier, marquis, no! no! We cannot allow this!

DE PRESLES. Stand back, gentlemen. After such an insult not a word. On guard, sir!

(*They fight. The* MARQUIS *staggers back wounded, falls in the arms of* DE MAILLY *and* D'ESTREES *with a cry, as* DE VAUDREY *quickly takes* HENRIETTE'S *hand.*)

DE VAUDREY. Come, mademoiselle. Come! (*Goes up rapidly as*)

CURTAIN FALLS

ACT TWO

SCENE I

The private office of the Minister of Police. COUNT DE LINIERES *discovered seated at a table, which is covered with papers which he is in the act of signing, hastily reading them over.* CHIEF CLERK *is at the table, standing in a respectful attitude.*

DE LINIERES. I regret that my recent accession to the position of minister of police compels me to occupy so much of your time.

CLERK. I am entirely at your service, my lord.

DE LINIERES. I desire that there should be no relaxation in the severity of the police towards gambling dens, low drinking places and other haunts of crime. Professional beggars, too, must be driven from the streets.

CLERK. Their number increases daily.

DE LINIERES. The king is desirous that a stop should be put to the scandals which disgraced the administration of the police during the preceding reign. Night-brawls went unpunished, and abductions, bringing shame and disgrace upon many honest families, were of common occurrence. And, apropos of that subject. (*Taking up a paper and rising.*) I have here a report which needs an explanation. How is it possible that a young girl could be abducted in the open street at eight o'clock in the evening, and there should be no one to oppose such an outrage?

CLERK. There are scoundrels in Paris audacious and dexterous enough to do anything.

DE LINIERES. Where were the police?

CLERK. They have discovered the accomplices of the chief actor and compelled them to confess.

DE LINIERES. Three months have elapsed since this most daring outrage, and the really guilty ones, the instigators of the crime, have not been punished.

CLERK (*in a very meaning tone*). That is due, my lord, to certain circumstances.

DE LINIERES. What circumstances? To whom does this Château du Bel-Air belong?

CLERK. To the Marquis de Presles.

DE LINIERES. De Presles! An ancient and illustrious family, whose last scion would not hesitate to stake all its glories on the cast of a die, or the thrust of a sword in a drunken brawl. But the girl—after the duel—what became of her?

CLERK. She was carried off—by—by—the antagonist of the marquis.

DE LINIERES. His name—speak, sir.

CLERK (*after a pause*). The Chevalier de Vaudrey.

DE LINIERES (*astonished*). My nephew! H—m. I appreciate the sentiment that caused you to hesitate, but for the future, sir, remember that justice is no respecter of persons. Humph! The Chevalier de Vaudrey—are you sure?

CLERK. Quite sure. We have a list of all who were present—both gentlemen and ladies.

DE LINIERES. These gentlemen must be made to understand that such orgies will be tolerated no longer. It is not enough to bear a noble name—it must be borne worthily. And these *ladies* must choose between Salpêtrière and exile.

CLERK. Do you wish, my lord, that this affair should be entered in the secret archives of the police?

DE LINIERES. The secret archives of the police? Do such records really exist?

CLERK. Certainly, my lord. The secret and complete history of every noble family in France may be found there. You have but to mention a name and in five minutes the desired volumes will be in your hands.

DE LINIERES. Very well, then. If the history of the house of De Vaudrey is there, let that history be complete!

CLERK. I shall obey you, my lord! (*He salutes and exits at the same moment as* PICARD *enters.*)

DE LINIERES (*seated*). Ah, Picard! I am glad to see you. I wish to speak to you of your master! How is he behaving himself?

PICARD. With all respect, my lord, his conduct is scandalous, perfectly scandalous and unbecoming a nobleman of his rank! Formerly he had a few gentlemanly associates, with whom he occasionally amused himself and saw life, and thereby gave me some opportunities. Alas! It is different now. For the last three months he has changed entirely. Indeed, my lord, my life has become so monotonous, that a man of spirit like myself can stand it no longer!

DE LINIERES. Am I to understand you wish to leave his service?

PICARD. Yes, my lord! The chevalier, your nephew, has principles which I can no longer accept—they clash with all my opinions, and although the chevalier thinks proper to compromise his nobility, I cannot compromise my livery!

DE LINIERES. Very well, I will take you back into my service!

PICARD (*joyfully*). You will! Ah, my lord, you have relieved me, and I resume my personal dignity!

DE LINIERES. On one condition. I wish you to remain for a time with my nephew. It is important that I should know his movements; I could employ the police, but I have already learned too much from them, and through you, who are attached to him, I desire to know the rest.

PICARD. The rest? What has he been doing? You frighten me. What do the police know?

DE LINIERES. They know that after the duel——

PICARD. The duel! What duel?

DE LINIERES. Do you pretend not to know that he dangerously wounded the Marquis de Presles in a duel about a woman?

PICARD. He fought a duel and dangerously wounded his antagonist, and about a woman? Oh, the sly dog, and I wanted to leave him!

DE LINIERES. No, no, not yet. I desire that you remain with him and discover where he hides himself.

PICARD. Of course I will! I thought he would not disgrace the blood of a French nobleman. Certainly I'll find out this saucy little beauty for whom he neglects all his friends. Of course she must be little, and saucy, with a jaunty, piquant air. That's the style I like!

DE LINIERES. Oh, indeed!

PICARD. Doubtless he has done everything in good style—has taken some elegant quiet little house, rooms hung with velvet, and furnished in silk and laces, all that sort of thing.

DE LINIERES. Why, at that rate you will ruin your master.

PICARD (*assuming the airs of a gentleman*). Bah! If she is worth the trouble, where is the harm in a little ruin?

DE LINIERES. There, that will do for today! (COUNTESS *appears at back.*) Go, and do not forget my orders!

PICARD. I will obey them, my lord! (*Salutes the* COUNTESS *as he exits.*)

COUNTESS. Monsieur, I am informed you wished to speak with me.

DE LINIERES. I was about to come to you, but you have anticipated me. I desire to speak with you on the subject of your nephew, the Chevalier de Vaudrey, and to ask you to prepare him for the marriage which the king——

COUNTESS (*sadly*). Wishes to impose upon him. (*Sits.*)

DE LINIERES. Impose on him? A magnificent alliance which will complete the measure of the distinguished honors with which his majesty deigns to favor us.

COUNTESS. Do these honors give you happiness?

DE LINIERES. I try to find happiness in the discharge of the duties I have assumed.

COUNTESS. What miracle has worked this change in you? You whose life passed so quietly and so happily at our dear home in Dauphine, far from the bustle of the city and the intrigues of a court. (*Looking him steadily in the face.*) You have become ambitious. Of what?

DE LINIERES. Yes; I am ambitious.

COUNTESS (*sadly*). I cannot believe it!

DE LINIERES. What do you mean?

COUNTESS. I mean that it is for me, and for my sake alone, that you have accepted these great honors.

DE LINIERES. You read my heart aright. It is for you that I seek the distraction and occupation of high place. Diane, my wife, I have vainly sought every means in my power to dispel the melancholy which has never left you since the first days of our marriage. Share with me the glorious task I have undertaken. Is it not a noble privilege to have the power to seek out and console those that weep, to assist the suffering, to relieve the misery of the unfortunate, to be able to say to the unhappy "Here is help"? Can you not share my ambition with me to do good?

COUNTESS (*shrinkingly*). Ah! I did not think of the limitless power placed in your hands—a power before which all doors are opened, a power that can penetrate all secrets, search here, there and everywhere, to the lowest depths where crime and misery hide themselves—a power which can accomplish everything which would be impossible to another, and which will, perhaps, enable you to discover——

DE LINIERES (*astonished*). Discover? What?

COUNTESS (*recovering herself*). The extent, as you say, of the misery in this great city. (*Enter servant at back, and announces the* CHEVALIER DE VAUDREY. *Servant retires and* DE VAUDREY *enters.*) Ah, Maurice!

DE VAUDREY. My dear aunt!

DE LINIERES. Chevalier! I am glad to see you. The countess and myself have an important communication to make to you.

DE VAUDREY. I regret that I should have been detained.

DE LINIERES. My dear Maurice, the king did me the honor to receive me yesterday, and he spoke of you.

DE VAUDREY. Of me?

DE LINIERES. He takes a great interest in your welfare. He wishes you to accept a position at the court, and desires at the same time that you should marry.

DE VAUDREY. Marry?

COUNTESS. My dear nephew, I see that this news surprises you. Yet there is no fear that the king's choice will do violence to your feelings. The lady whom he has chosen has youth, beauty, and fortune.

DE LINIERES. In proof of which I have only to tell you that his choice is Mademoiselle——

DE VAUDREY. Do not name her.

DE LINIERES. Why not?

DE VAUDREY. I refuse to marry.

DE LINIERES. Before committing yourself irrevocably, Chevalier de Vaudrey, reflect. I know the weakness of youth and the temptations to which it is exposed; I know that within certain limits, it is well to close the eyes to faults, provided they are not serious. This marriage is an honor which his majesty desires to confer upon you, and when the king has spoken——

DE VAUDREY. I will go to the king. I will thank him for his goodness, I will place my services at his disposal; my devotion, my life are his, but my affections are my own, and I wish to remain—free.

DE LINIERES. Free! Free to lead a life of dissipation which you may not always be able to hide from the world.

DE VAUDREY. There is nothing in my life to hide, nothing for which I have reason to blush.

DE LINIERES (*severely*). Are you sure of that, chevalier?

DE VAUDREY. Monsieur!

COUNTESS (*rising anxiously and interfering*). Maurice! (*To the* COUNT.) My husband! Defer this for the present—permit me——

DE LINIERES. Very well. We will return to this another time. You must remember that, as head of the family, its honor is confided to my care, and I will not suffer any one to sully it with a stain. (DE VAUDREY *attempts to answer him*—COUNTESS *makes a mute appeal to him and he refrains.*) I leave you with the countess, and I hope that your respect and affection for her will lend more weight to her counsels than you are disposed to give to mine. (*Exits.*)

COUNTESS (*crossing to* DE VAUDREY). Who is this woman you love? What obstacle prevents the avowal of your affection? If it is only a matter of fortune, take mine. It is all at your disposal. I will give it to you cheerfully.

DE VAUDREY. Ah! Where shall I find a heart like yours? You have divined my secret. I love a young girl, as charming as she is pure. I love her, yet my lips have never sought hers. I adore her, yet I have never dared to whisper my passion.

COUNTESS. Her name—her family?

DE VAUDREY. She was born of the people. She is an orphan and lives by the labor of her hands.

COUNTESS. And you would make such a one your wife?

DE VAUDREY. Do not judge her until you have seen her. Consent to see her, then advise me.

COUNTESS. In such a marriage there can be no happiness for you, and for her only misery. Believe me, I know the result of these unequal unions. You must renounce her—you owe obedience to your family and to your king.

DE VAUDREY (*with force*). Can *you* tell me that? You who have suffered so much, you who have been the victim of a blind obedience which has sacrificed your life and made you miserable.

COUNTESS (*uttering a cry*). Ah! How do you know that? Who could have revealed to you the anguish I have suffered for sixteen long years?

DE VAUDREY (*holding her hand*). There was but one soul in all this world tender and noble enough to appreciate and sustain your own in its trials. Your dearly beloved sister! My mother! In her last moments she exacted from me the promise to devote myself to you, should misfortune ever come, and I gladly gave my word.

COUNTESS. And she told you of my sufferings, my despair. Yes, yes, you speak the truth, my life has been one long sacrifice to duty. I was young and mad, I loved and was loved without knowing wrong. I consented to a secret marriage with a man beneath me in rank. Our secret was soon discovered, they thought him my lover and killed him almost under my very eyes, and I was a mother. The family honor demanded that my child should disappear, because my hand was promised to the Count de Linieres. The family honor demanded that I should deceive an honorable man or sacrifice the life of my child. I bowed to the inflexible will of my father. I prayed that God would have pity on the life of the little creature whom I had scarce embraced when they cruelly tore it from me. I consoled myself with the hope that perhaps I should see it again some day. Alas! The days have passed into months, the months into years, and all my prayers are in vain.

DE VAUDREY. My poor aunt. They were indeed cruel!

COUNTESS. So cruel that I often ask myself, if it would not have been better had they killed me too. Yes, yes, far more merciful than to have inflicted the punishment I have suffered for so many years. I dare not think she lives; if she does, into what abyss may not my criminal abandonment have plunged her? And the horrible thought that, if living, she may accuse me of her misery, perhaps of her shame! May she not cry out from the depths of her despair, "Accursed be my unnatural mother!" Ah! I hear that frightful curse now ringing in my ears, it pursues me in my prayers, torments me in my dreams. I hear it always, always!

(COUNT *enters at back and stands unobserved.*)

DE VAUDREY. Then do you, who have suffered so much, who suffer still, counsel me to obey? Would you have me chain my life to one woman, while my heart is filled with the image of another; will you advise me to this?

COUNTESS (*very emphatically*). No, no, never! (*Turns and sees the* COUNT, *then speaks to him.*) Ah! Monsieur, have pity on him, do not ask him to stifle the cry of his conscience. His heart revolts against the sacrifice you ask. Do not imitate those parents whose pride condemns their children to lives of falsehood and despair.

DE VAUDREY (*unobserved by the* COUNT *and in a low voice*). Take care!

(*The* COUNTESS *checks herself and stands in dejected attitude before her husband.*)

DE LINIERES (*severely*). Madame! Pride! Falsehood! Despair! To whom do you refer? Of what are you speaking?

COUNTESS (*trembling*). I meant—I spoke of——

DE VAUDREY. Monsieur, the words of the countess are but the echo of those she just heard me utter; they are the irrevocable revolt of my heart against the marriage and the suffering you would impose upon me.

DE LINIERES (*coldly*). Indeed, madame; had your words no other meaning?

COUNTESS. No, no. I am agitated—faint—you see, monsieur, I am ill.

DE LINIERES. That is evident. Chevalier, conduct the countess to her room. (DE VAUDREY *bows to the* COUNT, *offers his hand to the* COUNTESS *and both exit, followed by the gaze of the* COUNT; *when they reach the exit the* COUNT *speaks.*) And return immediately. I desire to speak with you. (*Exeunt* COUNTESS *and* DE VAUDREY. *The* COUNT *goes to his desk, writes on a paper, and rings a bell.* CHIEF CLERK *appears.*) Take this to the keeper of the secret records, and return with what he gives you. (DE VAUDREY *re-enters.* CLERK *salutes and exits.*) Chevalier, you can readily understand that propriety and considerations for my own dignity induced me to accept the explanation made by you on behalf of the countess.

DE VAUDREY. Monsieur!

DE LINIERES. You also understand that that explanation did not satisfy me.

DE VAUDREY. Well, sir, what are you pleased to think?

DE LINIERES. I think, sir, that the countess wept not for you but for herself. You spoke of her own griefs, of her early life, which is shrouded in some dark secret, perhaps a guilty one, which weighs upon her conscience, and is the torment of her life and mine. Speak, chevalier, what is it?

DE VAUDREY. Monsieur de Linieres?

DE LINIERES. I command you to speak.

DE VAUDREY. I know nothing, monsieur.

DE LINIERES. Very well, sir; you choose to forget all you owe to me. Twice today you have refused obedience to my wishes, nay, to my commands. Nevertheless, I will know the secret which you refuse to disclose.

DE VAUDREY. I am ignorant of the secret to which you refer.

(CLERK *returns with a large folio in his hand, which he gives to the* COUNT, *salutes and exits.*)

DE LINIERES. Then we will learn it together.

DE VAUDREY. What are you going to do?

DE LINIERES. Here, here in the archives of the police are entered the secrets of every noble family in France, and here will I learn the secret of Diane de Vaudrey, Countess de Linieres.

DE VAUDREY (*while* DE LINIERES *is turning over the leaves*). Why, that would be shameful! Infamous!

DE LINIERES. H-m—yes, here it is. House of de Vaudrey, and each member has a page. Ah! Diane Eleanor, daughter of the Count François de Vaudrey.

DE VAUDREY (*crosses rapidly toward the table and places his open hand on the page*). Monsieur, that you must not read.

DE LINIERES (*starting up*). What do you mean!

DE VAUDREY. I mean that the act you are about to commit is unworthy of you; unworthy of a gentleman. You must not, shall not.

DE LINIERES. Who will prevent it?

DE VAUDREY. Your own honor, which will revolt against such treason. And, sir, if your own honor does not speak loud enough, I will!

DE LINIERES. You?

(DE VAUDREY *crumples up the page under his hand, tears it from the book and puts it in his bosom. Puts his hand to his sword.*)

DE VAUDREY. I warn you, sir, that you can only wrest this paper from me with my life. You shall kill me before I part with it. Remember, sir, that it is not alone her secret I have saved you from violating, 'tis your own dignity and self-respect. I defend your honor against yourself! (*The* COUNT *bows his head as*)

CURTAIN FALLS

SCENE II

The open square in front of the Church of St. Sulpice. Ground is lightly covered with snow. Church portico and steps at R. PIERRE *discovered, seated on a stool.*

PIERRE. Nearly twelve o'clock; they will soon be here. (JACQUES *enters at back.*) Ah! there is Jacques already.

JACQUES (*to* PIERRE). The women have not come yet?

PIERRE. No, not yet. Mother and Mamzelle Louise are busy elsewhere, no doubt.

JACQUES. They ought to be here. The service will soon be over and they will miss the charitable idiots.

PIERRE. Ah! You need not worry about them. They will be here in good time.

JACQUES. None too soon.

PIERRE (*rising*). Jacques! I have a favor to ask of you.

JACQUES. If it is money, I haven't got any!

PIERRE. No, no, it is not money; but look you, Jacques, when you are angry with me, curse me, beat me, if you want to, but do not call me cripple—not—not when Louise is present.

JACQUES (*surprised*). Ah! ah! indeed. We must speak to monsieur respectfully, take off our hats I suppose! Why, we will dress you up in silk and velvet. You would like to wear gloves and carry a sword I suppose. Ha! ha! ha!

PIERRE (*supplicatingly*). Jacques!

JACQUES. So it hurts your feelings to be called cripple, does it? Well, look at yourself. What are you?

PIERRE. I am a poor deformed cripple, and whom do I owe it to? Who, when I was but an infant, beat me and broke and twisted my limbs. Who but you, Jacques, because I refused to steal a coat for you.

JACQUES. You lie, it was a cloak!

PIERRE. Ah! That is always your way; to make some one else steal for you. That was what forced poor Marianne——

JACQUES (*angrily and threatening to strike him*). Marianne! Don't you mention that ungrateful fool's name to me again; a heartless jade, who would rather go to prison than give me her money.

PIERRE. She saved you from punishment.

JACQUES. That is enough; I don't want to hear anything more about her. I have found another, better looking and more useful. And as to you, as you don't want to be called cripple any more——

PIERRE. Well?

JACQUES. I'll rechristen you, Cupid.

PIERRE (*discouraged*). Do as you like!

JACQUES. Now I come to think of it, though, it is only when Louise is about that you object to being called cripple; perhaps—— (*Laughing.*) Ha! ha! ha! Oh! That would be too good!

PIERRE. What do you mean?

JACQUES. You are not so stupid after all; she is blind and does not know the difference between a handsome man like me and a miserable abortion like you. Oh! ha! You're in love, in love with the blind girl. Ha! ha!

PIERRE. I? I? In love!

JACQUES. Why, then, are you ashamed of being called cripple before her? Afraid she'll find out your beautiful shape, eh?

PIERRE. Yes, yes, it is so. I want to think there is one in the world who does not regard me with disgust. If she thought I was made like others, she might have some feeling of friendship for me. But in love, in love with her, she who is beautiful enough, good enough to be an angel!

JACQUES. How the devil did you find out all that? I don't know or care anything about her goodness. Bosh for all that—and as to her beauty, I know that her eyes are more use to her now than if she could see with them.

PIERRE (*to himself*). Yes, yes, she is blind, but her face is so sweet that it would move a stone to pity. And her great beautiful eyes seem to look at me so truthfully that I almost fear she can see me.

JACQUES. There, there, what are you muttering about? Come along with me. I want you, Cupid. Come.

PIERRE (*rousing himself*). No, no. I won't. You shan't.

JACQUES. Eh? Hello! What's this? Rebellion, eh? Now do as I order you or look out for a beating.

PIERRE. Jacques, you are older than me, you're straight and strong, I must submit to you, but when I see the use you make of your strength I am satisfied with my ugly shape and my miserable weakness.

(JACQUES *shrugs his shoulders contemptuously, and at the same moment* LOUISE *is heard singing outside.*)

JACQUES. Ah! here they are at last. (LOUISE'S *song continues approaching.*) That voice ought to be worth a louis a day at least.

(*Enter* LOUISE, *led by* LA FROCHARD. LOUISE *is miserably dressed in rags and bits of clothing, is pale and wan, and walks with faltering steps, continuing her song. Crowd gather around to hear her song.* LA FROCHARD *goes round to people on stage.*)

LA FROCHARD. Pity a poor, unhappy, blind child. Charity, if you please.

PIERRE. How she suffers! (*Sits on steps.*)

JACQUES. Good; that's part of the business. Look out, Master Cupid, no getting soft, I tell you.

(*As* LA FROCHARD *approaches each person in the crowd, asking alms, they go off by ones and twos. She returns to* LOUISE *with a few coins she has obtained.*)

LA FROCHARD. Ah! There's nothing to be got from these miserable common people. They will stop and listen quick enough, but when you ask them for a sou they clear out.

JACQUES. It will be better when the church is out.

LA FROCHARD. We'll come back then. (*Takes* LOUISE *by the arm.*) Come, come, let us be moving.

LOUISE. I am very tired, madame.

LA FROCHARD. You can sleep tonight.

LOUISE. Oh, madame, I am so very tired, I can scarcely stand, we have walked so much today.

LA FROCHARD. Well, didn't you want to walk? Didn't you say you wanted to look for your sister?

LOUISE. Yes, but you always walk in the same part of the city.

LA FROCHARD. Bah! How do you know? You can't see.

LOUISE. I know that, madame, but when you found me you promised——

LA FROCHARD. I promised to help you to find your sister. Ain't I doing it? I ain't rich, you must earn your bread. You must sing and I'll do the begging.

LOUISE (*weeping*). I'll sing, madame, if you wish it.

LA FROCHARD. Yes, but how do you sing? Like a mourner at a funeral.

LOUISE (*weeping*). I sing as well as I can. I cannot help it. I cannot—indeed I cannot. When I think of what I am—of what I am doing—I—I—— (*Breaks down entirely—sobs.*) I am so unhappy—so miserably unhappy.

PIERRE (*starts forward*). Louise!

JACQUES (*pushing him*). Hello, what are you up to, Master Cupid?

PIERRE. Nothing, nothing. (*Aside.*) I am so helpless.

JACQUES (*looking at* LOUISE). She is pretty when she cries.

LA FROCHARD (*to* LOUISE). Come, come. Enough of that. Let us be moving.

LOUISE (*tries to wipe her eyes*). Very well, madame. I will.

LA FROCHARD (*stops her*). Don't do that. What! Wipe away real tears. Why, that is the very thing to catch your soft-hearted fools. (*A man crosses the stage, sees* LOUISE, *stops a moment, and slips a coin in her hand. Exits into church.* LA FROCHARD *takes the money.* Ah! there. What did I tell you? Go on singing. Have pity on a poor blind child. Charity, good people, if you please.

(*They exeunt.* JACQUES *and* PIERRE *exit. Organ commences to play. People come on and go into church. Sedan chair is brought on with the* COUNTESS DE LINIERES. *It is set down.* DOCTOR *enters.*)

DOCTOR (*stopping*). I ought to know that livery. Certainly it is the Countess de Linieres. (*He goes up to the chair, and offers his arm to the* COUNTESS, *who comes out.*)

COUNTESS. Ah! Doctor, I am glad to meet you.

DOCTOR. Because it is not a professional visit, I suppose?

COUNTESS. No, doctor. I am always happy to receive you as a friend.

DOCTOR. And not as a physician. I understand, countess. Will you then permit me, as a friend, to advise you?

COUNTESS. Doctor, I assure you I am not ill. You are mistaken.

DOCTOR. Very well then, madame, I will concede that you are in perfect health. Yet perfect health is scarcely consistent with the expression of fixed sadness imprinted upon your countenance. Pardon me for speaking thus plainly to you, but I have already been consulted by——

COUNTESS (*startled*). My husband?

DOCTOR. The Count de Linieres has imparted to me the great anxiety he feels on your account.

COUNTESS. What did he say? What does he fear?

DOCTOR. That you are wearing yourself out with a secret grief.

COUNTESS. Alas! Yes. What am I to do?

DOCTOR. Address yourself to the Great Physician. (*Pointing to the church.*) There you will find consolation and cure for your wounded heart, and learn that the heaviest burden is easier borne when shared by him who has the right to know your inmost thoughts.

COUNTESS. You mean my husband. Impossible!

DOCTOR. No, no! Not impossible. A generous heart like his will appreciate your confidence. Seek strength here, madame! (*Leads her to the church.*)

COUNTESS. I thank you, doctor; a thousand times I thank you. Ah! If one such friend as you had been given me years ago, I might have been spared this anguish. (*Exits into church.*)

DOCTOR. Ah! What a strange thing is human nature. Well, well, we doctors see odd things now and then. (*Looks at his watch.*) So late, indeed; it is time for my visit to the hospital, and then to La Salpétrière.

(LA FROCHARD *and* LOUISE *appear.*)

LA FROCHARD (*stopping in his way*). Please, my good sir.

DOCTOR. Oh, clear out!

LA FROCHARD. Pity for a poor blind child, if you please, charity.

DOCTOR. Blind? Who? This young girl? (*Coming forward.*)

LA FROCHARD. Alas! Yes, my good sir, pity.

DOCTOR. Poor unhappy child, at your age. Let me look at your eyes.

LA FROCHARD (*harshly interposing*). What for?

DOCTOR. Come here, my child. Let me see your eyes. I am a doctor!

LOUISE (*joyfully*). A doctor?

LA FROCHARD (*to* LOUISE). Come along. (*To* DOCTOR.) They can't be cured; it is no use. (*To* LOUISE.) Come along, my dear. (*Going R.*)

DOCTOR. But I insist. You are impostors, and I will hand you over to the police.

LA FROCHARD. Well, then, see for yourself if she is not blind. (*Passing* LOUISE *across. Aside.*) Curse him, I know him; he is that good whining doctor at the hospital.

LOUISE (*as* DOCTOR *comes to her*). Oh! sir, if you are a doctor——

LA FROCHARD (*comes alongside of her and takes her wrist*). Well, do you see? She's blind, ain't she?

DOCTOR (*after examining her eyes*). You have not always been blind, my child, have you?

LOUISE. No, monsieur. I was fourteen years old when this misfortune befell me.

DOCTOR. Fourteen? And you have had no treatment?

LOUISE (*quickly*). Monsieur.

LA FROCHARD (*interrupting*). We are so poor, good doctor, we have not the money to——

LOUISE. Oh, monsieur, for mercy sake, if you have any pity, speak to me, tell me is there any hope for me; oh, if you knew from what misery your words would save me.

LA FROCHARD. Yes, yes, indeed there can't be any worse misery than to be blind. If she could see, she could work and would not have to beg. Isn't that so, my dear?

LOUISE (*in great agitation and fear*). Yes, yes, I would work—I would—I—I would.

DOCTOR. Calm yourself, my child, calm yourself. (*He takes* LA FROCHARD *aside.*) Come here!

LA FROCHARD (*pushing* LOUISE *back and crossing to* DOCTOR). What is it, doctor?

DOCTOR. Listen, you must not excite her, you must not tell her too suddenly what I hope; bring her to me at the hospital St. Louis.

LA FROCHARD. Yes, yes, I know, I have been there often.

DOCTOR. I thought I recognized you. Let me see, you are called Mother ——

LA FROCHARD (*indignantly*). Widow Frochard, monsieur.

DOCTOR. Yes, I remember. Well, when she is calmer, you can tell her gently that I think there is hope for her, and then, when she is more accustomed to the idea, bring her to me.

LA FROCHARD. Yes, yes, I will. I'll tell her gently. Trust me, doctor, for that. You can depend on me.

DOCTOR (*crosses to* LOUISE). Here, my poor child. (*Giving her a piece of money.*) Courage, my dear, I will see you again. (*Exits.*)

LA FROCHARD (*following him to exit*). May Heaven bless you, good doctor. Heaven bless you. (*After his exit.*) Curses on you for an intermeddling fool! (*Returns to* LOUISE.)

LOUISE. What did he tell you, madame?

LA FROCHARD. He said it was not worth the trouble. There is no hope for you.

LOUISE. No hope! No hope! Alas! What am I to do? What will become of me?

LA FROCHARD (*aside*). If I bring her here every day he will see her again. No, no; that won't do. (*Aloud to* LOUISE.) Look you, child, I am a good woman; you have been complaining that I always take you to the same places; now tomorrow we will look for your sister in some other part of the city.

LOUISE. Oh, madame, I thank you. I have now but one hope left, to find my dear sister, my dear Henriette.

(JACQUES *re-enters, followed by* PIERRE.)

JACQUES. Well, Mother, how is business?

LA FROCHARD. Yes, yes; what did the doctor give you?

LOUISE. Here it is, madame.

(*As* LA FROCHARD *goes to take it* JACQUES *steps in and takes it out of* LOUISE'*s hand.*)

JACQUES. Tut, tut; gold! What thieves these doctors must be. Gold! (*Pockets coin.*)

LA FROCHARD. But that is mine!

JACQUES. Eh? Never mind, Mother. I'll treat you to some brandy.

LA FROCHARD. With my own money, brigand! (*To* LOUISE.) Look you, they will be coming out of the church soon; now sing out loud. No laziness, mind you; I'll be watching you.

LOUISE. Yes, madame.

LA FROCHARD. Pierre! Where is that lazy scamp? Here! (PIERRE *comes down.*) Put her on the church steps.

PIERRE. Yes, Mother.

JACQUES (*pushes him aside*). Never mind, Cupid; I'll take care of her. (*He leads* LOUISE *to the church steps, looking at her fixedly all the time.*) Yes, yes; she is devilish good-looking, considering she is blind.

LA FROCHARD. (*To* PIERRE.) You stay here and look out that no one speaks to her.

PIERRE. I will watch her. (*Crosses to* LOUISE.)

JACQUES (*ironically*). Oh! There's no danger that he'll let any one run away with her. Is there, Cupid?

(JACQUES *and* LA FROCHARD *exeunt.*)

LOUISE (*sitting on steps and trying to cover herself with her rags*). I am so cold. (PIERRE *takes off his coat. Snow commences to fall.*) I am so very cold. (PIERRE *puts his coat on her shoulders.*) Ah! Is that you, Pierre?

PIERRE. Yes, mamzelle.

LOUISE. Yes, it must be you, Pierre; you are the only one who is kind to me. (*Touches his coat.*) But this is your coat. What will you do without it, Pierre?

PIERRE. Oh! I'll do very well, indeed, mamzelle. I have my jacket, and my woolen waistcoat, and my—oh, that is only my overcoat. Besides, I am warm; very warm, indeed! (PIERRE *shivers.*)

LOUISE. Pierre, without you I should die; without your help I shouldn't have strength to endure my sufferings.

PIERRE (*seating himself beside her*). I know they make you wretched; my heart bleeds at the sufferings they inflict on you; but I am helpless, helpless. I can do nothing, nothing!

LOUISE. Is your sympathy, your compassion, nothing? Even now—(*she touches the coat on her shoulders*)

—I have to thank you. Yes, your pity, your kindness alone sustains me. (*She gives her hand to him, which he grasps eagerly; she touches his shoulder with the other hand and discovers that he is in his shirt sleeves.*) Oh, how selfish I am! (*She takes off the coat and offers it to him.*)

PIERRE. No, no!

LOUISE. Pierre, do, do, my dear Pierre, for my sake. (*He takes the coat and kisses her hand.*) I am not cold now, and if I were, am I not accustomed to suffering? Did they not leave me in the cold garret to starve because I refused to beg? But alas, I must beg or die and lose all hope of seeing my dear sister Henriette once more.

PIERRE (*looking around*). Have you never thought of escaping? I can help you. Let me inform the police and they will protect you.

LOUISE. No, no, you must not. I have thought of it, but that would deprive me of the only chance of finding my sister. They would shut me up in an asylum for the blind, and then I would be lost to her forever. Besides, I have an idea which sustains me and is my last hope. If they take me from one quarter of the city to the other, perhaps some day my voice may reach my sister's ears. I will sing the songs we learned together and when I finish I will cry out, "Henriette! 'Tis I, your sister Louise. Do you not hear me, Henriette, sister?"

(*Organ heard playing softly.*)

PIERRE. Hush! They will hear you. The service is over, and Mother will be coming back to watch you. (*Rises and helps* LOUISE *up.*)

LOUISE (*rising*). If she does not hear me singing, she will beat me.

PIERRE. I'll not be far away. (*Exits.*)

(LOUISE *sings same ballad as before. The footman of the* COUNTESS *orders the chair to be brought C. and holds the door open. The* COUNTESS *comes out of the church and stands on the steps.*)

COUNTESS. I have prayed to Heaven to restore to me my child. Will my prayer be answered? (LOUISE *sings.* COUNTESS *goes toward the chair, and is arrested by the sound of* LOUISE*'s voice.*) What a voice! How tender, how sad! (*Approaches* LOUISE.) It awakens a pity akin to pain! (*Coming down to* LOUISE. *Aloud to* LOUISE.) My child, can you not see me?

(*Enter* LA FROCHARD *quickly. Stops and looks on.*)

LOUISE. No, madame!

COUNTESS. Poor child!

LOUISE. Do you pity me, madame?

COUNTESS. Pity you; indeed I do, my child!

LOUISE. You pity me because I am blind. Alas! madame, *that* is not my *greatest* misfortune.

COUNTESS. What do you mean? Speak, child. I am rich, perhaps I can——

LOUISE. Ah! If I dare——

LA FROCHARD (*goes between them*). Eh, eh? What is it?

COUNTESS. You have relations—a mother?

LOUISE. Mother!

LA FROCHARD (*goes between them and seizes* LOUISE *by the wrist*). Yes, my beautiful lady; she has a good mother, if I *do* say so.

COUNTESS. Is this your daughter?

LA FROCHARD. The youngest of seven that Heaven has blessed me with, my lady. That is what the darling was going to tell you, isn't it, deary? (*Twists* LOUISE'S *arm.*)

LOUISE. I—I——

LA FROCHARD (*tightens her grip threateningly on* LOUISE, *who bows her head*). Certainly. Isn't it so, my dear?

COUNTESS. She seems to be ill and suffering.

LA FROCHARD. Ah! Good charitable souls, like you, my lady, have pity on her. She has a nice, good home. Haven't you, my darling? (*Aside, threateningly.*) Speak out! (*Twists her arm harder.*)

LOUISE (*with great effort*). Yes, yes.

COUNTESS (*gives her money*). Give this to your mother and pray for me.

LOUISE. I will, madame.

(COUNTESS *enters her chair.*)

FOOTMAN (*as he closes the door*). Does madame wish to go home?

COUNTESS. No, I promised the chevalier I would visit that young girl. (*Giving card to* FOOTMAN.) To this address! (*Enters chair.*)

FOOTMAN (*to the* CARRIERS). Faubourg St. Honoré! (*Closes door.*)

(*Chair containing* COUNTESS *is carried off.*)

LA FROCHARD (*seizes* LOUISE'S *hand and snatches the money which the* COUNTESS *had given her*). Ah! A louis, another gold piece, a good day after all. Come on and sing out, sing. (*She leads* LOUISE *upstage.*)

(LOUISE *commences to sing as she walks off.* PIERRE *enters and starts across, is about to follow them when* JACQUES, *entering, follows him and strikes him heavily on the shoulder.* PIERRE *turns.*)

JACQUES. Stop. I have a word to say to you.

PIERRE. What is it?

JACQUES. I forbid you to follow Louise.

PIERRE. What? You forbid?

JACQUES. Yes, and I forbid you to even think of her.

PIERRE. Jacques, I cannot help it. You would not be so cruel. No, no, Jacques. Why are you so cruel?

JACQUES. Never mind why, I forbid you, that is enough, and if you disobey me, I'll break those misshapen legs over again, Cupid! (*As he speaks he places both hands on* PIERRE'S *shoulders and forces him to the ground on his knees.)*

PIERRE. Ah! Kill me, kill me, if you will, Jacques. (*Aside.*) But I love her and you cannot forbid that!

CURTAIN FALLS

SCENE III

A plainly furnished chamber; in an alcove is a bed hung with plain curtains, a small work-table, covered with sewing materials, etc. Plain chairs, a fireplace and candles on chimney. HENRIETTE *discovered seated at table, sewing.*

HENRIETTE. Three long months since the dreadful day that robbed me of my darling sister. The Chevalier de Vaudrey promised he would come today and tell me if he had learned anything. Ah! How I try to cheat myself into the belief that my anxiety to see him arises solely from the hope that he may bring me news of Louise. I cannot doubt that he loves me, and I madly indulge in dreams of happiness, while my poor Louise is wandering helpless in the streets of this great, heartless city. (*A knock is heard at the door.*) Come in.

(*She runs hastily and opens the door. Enter* CHEVALIER DE VAUDREY.)

DE VAUDREY. Henriette! (*He takes her hand, looks at her steadily a moment; they come down; she is agitated.*) Have you heard anything? You seem agitated.

HENRIETTE. I was expecting you. (*Recovering herself.*) I mean I thought, perhaps, you would bring me news of Louise.

DE VAUDREY. No, I have heard nothing. Yet you know I have occupied myself unceasingly for the past three months in vain endeavors to ascertain her fate. But, today, Henriette, I wish to speak to you of something else—of myself.

HENRIETTE. I know, monsieur, all that you would say to me. I know that you rescued me at the risk of your own life from a frightful peril, and, believe me, I am not ungrateful.

DE VAUDREY. Henriette, do you feel no other sentiment than gratitude? Do you not understand my heart? Until yesterday I was bound in honor to impose silence on my lips; circumstances have released me, and today I can and dare avow with pride—I love you! (*She grasps the back of the chair to support herself.*) Henriette, mine is not a trifling, frivolous love. I loved you from the moment I first saw you.

HENRIETTE. Oh! This is wrong—wrong. I have known all that your heart was striving to hide from me, and I have been guilty in allowing it to distract me from the only duty I have in life. You should not compel me to confess my weakness.

DE VAUDREY. Henriette!

HENRIETTE. When Louise is restored to my arms, I shall have earned the right to be happy. Then tell me you love me, and I will listen.

DE VAUDREY. Henriette! dear Henriette! (*She gives him her hand, he kisses it warmly.*)

(*The door opens suddenly and* PICARD *enters.*)

PICARD. Don't disturb yourselves.

HENRIETTE (*with a cry*). Ah! (*Goes to table.*)

DE VAUDREY. Picard?

PICARD. Yes, monsieur. Picard—only Picard.

DE VAUDREY. What do you want? What brings you here? (*Crosses to* HENRIETTE, *who is at table folding her work.*) The fellow is my valet!

PICARD. Yes, mamzelle, Picard. I am Picard the discreet (*aside*). This must be the chambermaid, and he is in her room. Oh, he is doing well.

DE VAUDREY (*sharply*). What brings you here?

PICARD (*mysteriously*). A communication for you, sir, of the utmost importance.

DE VAUDREY. What do you mean?

HENRIETTE. I must take my work downstairs, they are waiting for it. (*She goes toward the door.*)

DE VAUDREY (*following her to door*). You will return?

HENRIETTE. Oh, yes, in a few minutes. (*Business before she exits.*)

PICARD (*aside*). She will return; well, that is good. Mistress below stairs and a pretty chambermaid up here. This is the young man who is studying philosophy!

DE VAUDREY. Well, sir, we are alone now. What brings you here?

PICARD. I took the liberty of following you, monsieur.

DE VAUDREY. Following me, you scoundrel!

PICARD (*delighted and aside*). Scoundrel is good, very good. Now he is something like a master.

DE VAUDREY. What do you say?

PICARD. I was saying, monsieur, that scoundrel is not half strong enough, particularly when I come to find out that after all——

DE VAUDREY. After all? What?

PICARD (*aside*). Good, go on. He will kick me in a minute. (*Aloud.*) You must know, monsieur, that I had become so disgusted with your good conduct that I begged your uncle to relieve me of the duty of serving you any longer, and if he had not insisted on my remaining and watching you——

DE VAUDREY. So you have become a spy, Master Picard, have you?

PICARD. Yes sir, a spy on you. (*Aside.*) Now he will kick me. (*Turns and waits.*) No! (*Aloud.*) Why, monsieur, if I had not, how should I have found out that you were a gallant and a roué?

DE VAUDREY. Gallant? Roué? (*Laughs.*) Ha! ha! Well, how did you find that out?

PICARD. By obeying the instructions of your uncle. I follow you to the house of your inamorata, and instead of finding you with that much honored lady, I discover you enjoying the society of her chambermaid!

DE VAUDREY (*angrily*). Chambermaid?

PICARD. Oh! You have the fairest of excuses; she is as pretty as——

DE VAUDREY (*interrupting quickly*). Look you, Master Picard, another word and I throw you out of that window.

PICARD (*crossing to window and looking out*). Oh! That is going further than I bargained for. Thrown out of a sixth-story window.

DE VAUDREY. Listen to me, sir.

PICARD. I am all ears, monsieur, but please to remember that we are very high up.

DE VAUDREY. Return at once to the Count de Linieres, and tell him that, after having dogged my footsteps day by day, you have at last found me in the presence of the woman I love.

PICARD. You mean of the chambermaid of the woman you love. Same thing!

DE VAUDREY. Silence, sir. I tell you that you have seen the woman I love, and you may inform the count that she is to be my wife.

PICARD (*astounded*). Eh, your wife? (*Aside.*) Oh! oh! This is—this is disgraceful; he is no gallant after all.

DE VAUDREY. Silence! Ah, Henriette!

(*Enter* HENRIETTE *hurriedly and weeping—throws herself upon a chair, at table.*)

HENRIETTE (*weeping*). Shame! shame! I am sure I do not deserve to be so insulted!

DE VAUDREY. Who has insulted you?

HENRIETTE. I am ordered to leave the house!

DE VAUDREY. Ordered to leave the house! Why?

HENRIETTE. Alas! Monsieur, they tell me that a young girl living alone has not the right to receive the visits of gentlemen such as you.

DE VAUDREY. Such as I—I who have always treated you with the respect due to a sister!

PICARD (*aside*). Just now she was his wife—now she is his sister! Oh, it's all right!

HENRIETTE. The mistress of the house, who until now has been so kind to me, says she cannot permit me to remain, for she has a good name to protect, which my conduct scandalizes. What could I say? She has ordered me to leave at once!

PICARD. Poor thing! Monsieur, I say this is unjust, this is—is——

DE VAUDREY. Shameful!

PICARD (*to* HENRIETTE). Certainly, it is shameful! Ma'amselle, I will go to that woman myself! I'll tell her you are not yet——(HENRIETTE *looks up at him astonished; he becomes abashed and stammers.*) That is—I mean that you—that he—that I—I don't know what I do mean!

DE VAUDREY (*coming down*). Henriette, dry your tears! You shall leave this house to enter mine!

PICARD (*aside*). That is pretty cool!

DE VAUDREY. Not mine alone, Henriette, but yours as well, for you shall enter it on the arm of your husband!

PICARD (*aside*). There he goes again! Husband—wife!

HENRIETTE. Your wife! No! no! That is impossible!

PICARD. I agree with you perfectly!

HENRIETTE. Think of the immeasurable distance which separates us! Believe that I appreciate the generosity which inspires you, yet my duty compels me to refuse!

DE VAUDREY. Refuse!

PICARD (*admiringly*). Spoken like a sensible girl!

HENRIETTE. How can I defy the will of your family? They are rich and powerful—a marriage with me would entail their enmity, even their persecution.

DE VAUDREY. If my family will not *give* their consent, I will find means to compel them!

PICARD (*very energetically*). Certainly—we'll compel them!

DE VAUDREY. Picard, my hat, we must go!

(PICARD *gets hat and hands it to him.*)

PICARD. Yes, monsieur, we must go. (*Aside.*) I shall want to marry her myself in a few minutes!

DE VAUDREY. Henriette, I go to find the means of assuring our happiness!

HENRIETTE. Farewell, monsieur, farewell!

DE VAUDREY. No, Henriette, I will not say farewell, I cannot part with all my hopes! I need them to give me courage—au revoir!

HENRIETTE (*gives him her hand and forces herself to smile*). Au revoir. (*Exit* DE VAUDREY. HENRIETTE *throws herself on a chair.*) No; I will not see him again. I have not the strength to continue this conflict between love and duty. He loves me. Oh! Is it not a beautiful dream? Ah! It is but a dream, and the awakening has come to remind me of my guilty neglect. I am justly punished. Insulted, driven from this house. I must go where I shall never see him again! (*During the last lines she rises and commences to search for her things as though preparing to go. Knock is heard and the door opens.*)

(*Enter* COUNTESS DE LINIERES.)

COUNTESS. Mademoiselle Henriette Gerard, I believe.

HENRIETTE (*surprised*). That is my name, madame.

COUNTESS. You have been warmly recommended to me, mademoiselle.

HENRIETTE. Recommended to you, madame?

COUNTESS. I am one of a society of charitable persons who, if the good report I have heard of you is true, can assist you.

HENRIETTE. I have no need, madame. (*Changing tone.*) Alas! I do not mean that, I mean that I am not in want. I can work.

COUNTESS. Can I do nothing for you?

HENRIETTE. Nothing. What do I say? Yes, madame, I accept your aid; nay, I implore it.

COUNTESS (*sits*). Speak.

HENRIETTE. Madame, I do not need money, I only ask for some shelter where I can live and work, far from falsehood and calumny and away from him.

COUNTESS. From him? You wish to escape from the persecutions of some one?

HENRIETTE. From one who wishes to make me his wife.

COUNTESS. His wife?

HENRIETTE. I have refused that title, and yet I distrust my courage to resist his entreaties.

COUNTESS. You have done well, mademoiselle, and it is my duty to speak frankly to you. I am a near relative of the Chevalier de Vaudrey. I have known for some time the attachment which exists between you, and I have defended him against the wrath of his uncle, my husband. But reflection has shown me my duty to both of you. The opposition of his family renders this marriage impossible.

HENRIETTE. Madame, I had determined on my course before seeing you. The path of sacrifice and duty.

COUNTESS. I shall not prove ungrateful. I am rich and powerful.

HENRIETTE (*looking up interested*). Powerful?

COUNTESS. And if at any time I can show my appreciation of your noble and disinterested conduct——

HENRIETTE. Madame, you can; now, at this very instant, you can.

COUNTESS. How?

HENRIETTE. Use your power to find the poor child who has been torn from my protection, restore her to me and you can ask no sacrifice I will not make. I will tear my love from my heart and disappear with her where you and yours shall never see us more. Do I ask too much?

COUNTESS. No, no. I promise you not alone my aid but that of the greatest power in Paris. Give me her name, her age, and description.

HENRIETTE. A description, alas, madame, too easily given; she is but sixteen and blind!

COUNTESS. Blind?

HENRIETTE. Her name is Louise.

COUNTESS (*with feeling*). Louise! That name is very dear to me; be comforted, my child, we will find your sister.

HENRIETTE. She is not my sister, madame.

COUNTESS. Not your sister?

HENRIETTE. No, madame, but I owe her the love and tenderness of a mother and sister combined, for she saved us all from misery and want; my father, my mother, and myself.

COUNTESS. How could a poor blind child do that?

HENRIETTE. My father found her on the steps of the church——

COUNTESS (*quickly*). On the steps of a church! Tell me when and where. You say she saved you all from misery. How?

HENRIETTE. From poverty so terrible that my father had not even bread to give us. Anxious to save at least the life of his child, he took me, while my mother slept, and set out toward Notre Dame. Snow covered the steps of the church, and my father stood weeping and irresolute, when suddenly he heard a plaintive cry; he approached and saw a little babe already half buried under the snow. He took her to his breast to warm her benumbed and frozen limbs, when the thought came to him that, as this child would have died had he not arrived in time to save it, so his own might die before help could reach her. "I will leave neither of them," he said, and he returned carrying both infants in his arms.

COUNTESS. Oh! Go on, mademoiselle. Go on.

HENRIETTE. Entering his home, he said to my mother, "We had only one child, Heaven has sent us another." And he was right. Heaven did reward his generous action, for on opening the clothing of the child a roll of gold was found, with these words written on a scrap of paper, "Her name is Louise, save her."

COUNTESS (*struggling with herself*). Ah!

HENRIETTE (*astonished*). Are you ill, madame?

COUNTESS (*trying to be calm*). No! no! I—it is nothing; your sad story has moved me greatly. Then the infant fell among good and worthy people?

HENRIETTE. Ah, madame, I cannot tell you how we loved her.

COUNTESS. Now I know why Maurice loves you. I will love you too.

HENRIETTE. Then you will help me to find her?

COUNTESS (*with force*). Help you? (*Rises.*) All Paris shall be searched from end to end. But, gracious Heaven, she is blind! How is that? And how did you lose her? Tell me all—all.

(*The voice of* LOUISE *is heard very faintly at a great distance, gradually approaching; as* HENRIETTE *speaks she grows more abstracted, listening to the voice.*)

HENRIETTE. Yes, madame—it—was—one evening——

COUNTESS. Go on—my child——

HENRIETTE (*listening*). About—about two years ago.

COUNTESS. Two years ago. Well?

HENRIETTE. Yes, two years ago. Louise was then——

COUNTESS (*astonished at the abstraction of* HENRIETTE). Go on.

HENRIETTE. Louise was then—fourteen. (*Voice approaches nearer.*) We were playing together one evening, when—— (*Voice is now quite close under the window; screams.*) Ah!

COUNTESS. What is it?

HENRIETTE. Hush—sh, listen!

COUNTESS. I think I remember that voice.

HENRIETTE. It is she, madame, it is she! (*Rushes to the window.*)

COUNTESS. She? The poor little beggar whom I just left on the steps of the church.

LOUISE (*outside, after finishing her song*). Henriette! Henriette! Do you hear me?

HENRIETTE. Louise! I am coming. I am coming.

LOUISE (*outside*). It is I; Louise, your sister. (*Then cries out as though she had been checked.*) Ah!

HENRIETTE (*frightened*). Ah! What is that?

COUNTESS. Come, come! (*As they reach the door it is violently thrown open and the* COUNT *enters, followed by an officer and guard.* COUNTESS *stops suddenly.*) My husband!

HENRIETTE. Gentlemen, gentlemen, do not stop me!

DE LINIERES. (*To officer.*) Do your duty!

(*Officer signals to men and two of them seize her.*)

HENRIETTE. In the name of Heaven let me go! Take pity; let me go or I shall lose her again.

DE LINIERES. Take this girl to Salpêtrière!

HENRIETTE (*screams*). Ah! No, no!

COUNTESS (*tries to go out*). At least let me go. I must go!

DE LINIERES (*takes her by the arm*). You will remain where you are, madame. You have not yet told me what brought you here.

COUNTESS. Later, monsieur, I will tell you everything. But now let me go before she——

COUNT. Of whom are you speaking, madame?

COUNTESS. Of whom? Why—of—of—my—— (*The* COUNT *looks at her sternly and threateningly. She screams and faints.*) Ah!

(*The voice of* LOUISE *is heard faintly in the distance as*)

CURTAIN FALLS

ACT THREE

SCENE I

The courtyard of the prison of La Salpétrière, surrounded by leafless trees. At the back a wall over which can be seen the dome of a church. Grated gate in wall. At the right is a door leading to dormitory. At the left is a door leading to hospital.

MARIANNE, CORA, JULIE, FLORETTE *and other prisoners discovered. Some of the prisoners at back walking, dressed in prison uniform, some are seated at work sewing, others on benches, weeping.* SISTER THERESE *seated as Portress at gate.*

MARIANNE (*on bench, to* FLORETTE). Do not grieve so, mademoiselle.

FLORETTE (*weeping*). Oh! I can never live such a life as this.

MARIANNE. Try to work, it will make you forget your troubles.

FLORETTE. I can't work, I don't know how. I have never had any harder work to do than to amuse myself.

JULIE. That would be precious hard work in this place.

MARIANNE. Our paths in life have been very different. I was compelled to work for a man who beat me and forced me to become a thief.

FLORETTE. Scores of admirers crowded around me, willing to ruin themselves for my amusement.

JULIE. And it all comes to a prison, and eating gruel with a wooden spoon.

MARIANNE. You will get accustomed to that.

JULIE. But it does not end there; some day we shall be treated as those poor creatures were yesterday, hurried off with a guard of soldiers to see us safe on our way into exile.

FLORETTE. And a jeering crowd insulting and maltreating us.

MARIANNE (*to* JULIE). Does the idea of exile frighten you?

JULIE. Who would not be frightened at the idea of a two months voyage in the vilest company, and at the end of it to be landed in a desert filled with serpents and tigers. Ugh! I who am scared to death at the sight of a mouse.

CORA (*coming forward to* MARIANNE). What will you do if they send you away?

MARIANNE. I shall try to be resigned, perhaps I shall find some satisfaction in being sent away out of the reach of temptation. There is work to be had there.

JULIE. They say that women are scarce out there in Cayenne; maybe I shall find a husband and revenge myself that way.

MARIANNE. You may not be sent into exile—show yourself repentant and the Sister Superior will interest herself in your behalf.

(SISTER GENEVIEVE *appears at the door of the hospital.*)

FLORETTE. The superior!

MARIANNE. She has been tending the sick, now she comes here to console the afflicted.

(CORA *goes up to the back.* SISTER GENEVIEVE *goes to some women at back who are weeping and talks with them.*)

JULIE. Well, for so good a woman, she is the meekest I ever saw.

MARIANNE. What do I not owe her? Her gentle words first awakened feelings in my heart I thought long since dead. Hope for the present and faith in the future! (*Pointing to the* SISTERS.) When I see these pure and humble women, who have nothing but virtues to confess, daily kneeling in prayer, what mercy can I expect—I who am so guilty?

FLORETTE (*weeping*). And I too.

MARIANNE. But they have taught me that I can atone for the past, that every good deed will efface a fault committed.

JULIE. I am afraid I could not live long enough to balance the account. (*Goes up.*)

(*The gate opens and the* DOCTOR *enters.*)

SISTER THERESE. Madame, it is the doctor.

SISTER GENEVIEVE. Ah! Doctor, I have been waiting impatiently for you.

DOCTOR (*looking at his watch*). I am not late, I believe.

SISTER GENEVIEVE. No, but you led me to hope that when you came today you would bring me——

DOCTOR. Good news? Yes. Well, I have done everything in my power. I have spoken of the interest you take in this unfortunate woman, of her sincere repentance, and I even went so far as to add a few good qualities on my own account.

SISTER GENEVIEVE. You did wrong, Doctor. There is no cause sacred enough to justify the violation of the truth.

DOCTOR. You will thank me nevertheless, sister.

SISTER GENEVIEVE. Then you have succeeded?

DOCTOR. Completely!

SISTER GENEVIEVE. Ah! Heaven be praised. (*Calling.*) Marianne, come here, my child! (MARIANNE *comes down.*) Here is our good doctor, who will tell you what he has done for you.

MARIANNE. For me?

DOCTOR. You must thank Sister Genevieve, not me; touched by your repentance, she has solicited and obtained your pardon and release. (DOCTOR *hands two official papers to* SISTER GENEVIEVE.)

MARIANNE. My benefactress! My mother!

SISTER GENEVIEVE. No, no. It was he who obtained it for you.

DOCTOR. No, your release is granted to the good Sister Genevieve. To that good and noble woman, who, born within the walls of La Salpétrière, has never consented to cross its threshold; who has made this prison her country and its unfortunate inmates her family; who brings to you all her daily blessing of consolation and prayer, so that even the vilest here respect and love her. (*They gather round* SISTER GENEVIEVE; *some of them kiss her hands.*) I did not intend to make you weep, nor you either, my poor Marianne; nor you, nor you. (*Looking at the others.*) Come, come, I shall be crying too in a minute.

(*Bell is heard striking.*)

SISTER GENEVIEVE. It is time to go in. Come, my child; this evening you will be free. (*Gives her one of the documents which the* DOCTOR *brought.*) Do not forget that I am responsible for you. Society sent me a guilty woman; I return it a repentant one, I hope, Marianne!

MARIANNE. I hope so, sister.

(*Exeunt* FLORETTE, CORA, JULIE *and all prisoners. Loud noise is heard outside in the hospital.*)

HENRIETTE (*outside*). Leave me, leave me! Let me go!

SISTER GENEVIEVE (*going toward door*). What is the meaning of those cries?

DOCTOR. Some refractory patient, no doubt!

SISTER THERESE. Doctor, it is that young girl who was brought here two days ago, who has been delirious ever since.

(HENRIETTE *appears at door, held by two nurses, with whom she is struggling.*)

HENRIETTE. You shall not keep me. I must go; I tell you I must.

MARIANNE (*looking at her*). Good heavens! (*Goes up.*)

HENRIETTE (*runs to* SISTER GENEVIEVE). Oh, madame! If you are mistress here, have pity on me; order them to set me free. I ask you on my knees.

SISTER GENEVIEVE (*gently*). Be calm, my child; you are ill.

DOCTOR. Certainly you are. Why have you left your bed without my permission?

HENRIETTE (*crossing to* DOCTOR). Ah, monsieur! Have you attended me in my illness?

DOCTOR. Yes, yes. And I cannot permit you to act in this way.

HENRIETTE. But, monsieur, I am well now. Now that you see I am quite well, you will tell them to let me go, will you not?

DOCTOR. That is impossible. To release you from this place requires a far greater power than mine.

HENRIETTE. This place? Why, what is it? Is it not a hospital?

DOCTOR. A hospital and a prison.

HENRIETTE. A prison! Ah, I remember. Yes, I remember the soldiers who dragged me hither, and he who commanded them. "To the Hospital of La Salpétrière!" he said, the prison for—(*looking round her*)—unfortunate women. Oh! My God! (*Goes up to bench at back, sits and weeps.*)

DOCTOR (*to* SISTER GENEVIEVE). Sister, this is not a case for my care. You must be the physician here. (*Crosses and exits into hospital.*)

SISTER GENEVIEVE. I have seen many guilty women, but this one——

MARIANNE. Is not guilty, sister.

SISTER GENEVIEVE. Do you know her?

MARIANNE. When I came here I told you that on that very day, overwhelmed with despair, I had attempted to destroy myself.

SISTER GENEVIEVE. Yes, I remember.

MARIANNE. And how I had been prevented from adding that crime to my many sins by two young girls, angels of virtue and goodness. This is one of them.

SISTER GENEVIEVE. How is it possible that she should be here?

MARIANNE. Misfortunes may have overtaken her, but I am sure that vice has never sullied her life.

(PICARD *appears at the gate, speaks with* SISTER THERESE, *and shows her a paper. After a few words he is admitted.* SISTER GENEVIEVE *and* MARIANNE *go to* HENRIETTE *and bring her forward.*)

SISTER GENEVIEVE. Courage, my child. Look up.

MARIANNE. Look at me, mademoiselle. Do you not know me? Do you not remember the woman who wished to drown herself?

HENRIETTE (*looking up slowly*). You—you? Ah, yes! I remember you too well. (*Despairingly.*) Alas! We were together then. That was before they dragged me away from her. You saw her, my poor sister.

MARIANNE. I told madame that you were as pure as an angel.

(PICARD *is admitted.*)

HENRIETTE (*to* SISTER GENEVIEVE). Yes, madame, I am innocent. I call Heaven to witness. I swear——

SISTER GENEVIEVE. I believe you. You would not be guilty of the shameful sin of falsehood.

HENRIETTE. No, no.

SISTER GENEVIEVE. But why? By whose orders were you sent here?

PICARD. By order of the Count de Linieres, madame.

SISTER GENEVIEVE. Who are you, sir?

PICARD (*with importance*). First valet de chambre to his excellency the minister of police!

SISTER GENEVIEVE. Then it is by his order that this poor child is——

PICARD. Alas! Madame, the honor of an illustrious house must be protected.

HENRIETTE. You are a witness that I refused the hand of the Chevalier de Vaudrey.

SISTER GENEVIEVE. Is that so, monsieur?

PICARD. That is true, I am compelled to admit it.

MARIANNE (*coming forward*). Madame, I told you she was innocent.

PICARD. If madame the superior will allow me to inform the young lady of the further wishes of his excellency the minister of police, I think I can make her understand.

SISTER GENEVIEVE. You may do so. (*To* HENRIETTE.) Have courage, my child, and trust in Heaven. (*Kisses* HENRIETTE *on forehead, crosses and exits.*)

MARIANNE. Courage—courage, mademoiselle!

(*They exit into hospital. As they go* PICARD *salutes the* SUPERIOR. *Is about to salute* MARIANNE, *and recognizes her prison uniform. Recovers himself.*)

HENRIETTE. We are alone. What new misery do you bring me? You, whom I thought devoted to your master, and yet come here to betray him?

PICARD. Come, come, mademoiselle, that is too bad, to have you reproach me, too. Because the master I deceive is the minister of police.

HENRIETTE. But Monsieur de Vaudrey, what of him?

PICARD. He refused to obey his uncle; and—and yesterday he was sent to the Bastile.

HENRIETTE. He, too, is a prisoner, then?

PICARD. Yes, in the Bastile. He made me swear to come to this prison and tell you that if, at the worst, they decided to send you into exile to Cayenne . . .

HENRIETTE. Exile! Cayenne! Why, that would be death!

PICARD (*in an undertone*). Wait a little, ma'amselle. If my pretended master comes to that decision, he will release my real master from the Bastile, and once he gets out of there—why, off he goes, followed by your humble servant; we overtake the guard having you in charge; with the gold with which we will take care to be provided, my real master will bribe the servants of my other master, and if they should be incorruptible, that is, if we have not money enough with us to buy them, why, then, we will share your exile, and we will be happy in spite of the treachery of my other master.

HENRIETTE. You speak to me of happiness? But Louise, my darling, my sister, who will search for her?

PICARD. Where am I? Do I count for nothing? Do you suppose that a member of the secret police of his excellency the minister is going to fold his arms quietly? No, indeed. Come, come, mademoiselle; don't worry yourself. I will arrange everything. Then, if they want my head, they can come and take it. I am ready!

(OFFICER, *with guards, appears at the gate.* SISTER THERESE *opens gate.*)

HENRIETTE (*pointing to guards*). Good heavens! Look there!

PICARD. Good gracious! Have they taken me at my word?

(*Gate is opened and* OFFICER *with guard enters.* OFFICER *arranges his men across the stage, as* SISTER GENEVIEVE, DOCTOR *and* MARIANNE *enter from hospital.*)

OFFICER. Sister Superior, I have the honor to hand you this list of prisoners, who are condemned to exile. If you will permit me to order the prisoners to be assembled here we can then proceed to identify them. (OFFICER *hands paper to* SISTER GENEVIEVE.)

SISTER GENEVIEVE. You may do so, monsieur. I will follow you. (OFFICER *salutes and exits.*) The list! I dread to look at it. (*She opens the paper hesitatingly, and reads. Looks at* HENRIETTE, *and cries out.*) Ah!

HENRIETTE. Madame, why do you look at me so? Answer me, for pity sake! Have mercy!

SISTER GENEVIEVE. Ah, my poor child!

HENRIETTE. I see it. Alas! I am condemned. I am lost, lost!

PICARD (*aside to* SISTER GENEVIEVE). Madame, is this true?

SISTER GENEVIEVE (*showing the list*). Henriette Gerard.

HENRIETTE. Ah! (*Screams and falls weeping into the arms of the* DOCTOR *and* MARIANNE, *who lead her to a bench.* SISTER GENEVIEVE *stops and looks at her pityingly for a moment and exits.*)

PICARD. They are going to send her off immediately. Today! I will go to the Bastile, inform the chevalier, my master, that my other master has villainously deceived me. That he has had the indelicacy to actually suspect my fidelity. Ah! He shall pay for that!

(*During* PICARD'S *speech* HENRIETTE *has recovered.*)

HENRIETTE (*to* MARIANNE, *coming forward*). Ah! Now I understand why one may wish to die!

MARIANNE. Do not speak so, mademoiselle. Remember the words of hope you spoke to me.

DOCTOR. If you have a family think of them.

PICARD (*coming down*). Think of my master, the chevalier!

HENRIETTE (*to* DOCTOR). Ah! Monsieur, exile has no terrors for me. I do not weep for my own misfortunes.

MARIANNE. She has a sister of whom she was the sole support. A sister who is blind.

HENRIETTE. I had found her at the moment when they arrested me. I heard her voice. I saw her. She was covered with rags, and her beautiful golden hair fell in disorder on her shoulders. She was being dragged along by a horrible old woman, who I know ill-treats her—beats her, perhaps—and they would not let me go to her. Now I have lost her forever—forever! (*She sobs.*)

DOCTOR (*trying to recall*). Wait a minute, my child; I believe I have met that very young girl.

HENRIETTE. You, monsieur?

DOCTOR. Yes, yes; a young girl led by an old woman who called her Louise.

HENRIETTE. Yes, yes; that's her name.

DOCTOR. I know the old woman, too; she is called La Frochard.

PICARD. La Frochard? An old hag who goes about whining for alms in the name of Heaven and seven poor children. Where does she live?

MARIANNE (*aside*). Jacques' mother! She must be saved from their vile hands. (*Aloud.*) She lives in a hovel by the river side; it was formerly used as a boathouse, but has long been occupied by thieves and the worst criminals. There is a secret entrance from the Rue Noir, but it is difficult to find, and is always carefully guarded.

PICARD. Never mind that. The police of Paris can find their secret entrances. If not, we'll capture the main one. To the Bastile first, release my master, and then for the boathouse. (*Exits through gate.*)

HENRIETTE. You are sure she lives there? Then we will go at once. I have found her again! (*Recollects herself, utters a cry.*) Ah! I am to be sent away, away far from her.

MARIANNE. No, no, mademoiselle, you need not, you shall not be sent away.

DOCTOR. What do you mean?

HENRIETTE (*in despair*). But these guards who have been sent to take me, who wait for me. Oh! Louise, my sister, my poor darling!

MARIANNE. I tell you that you need not go!

HENRIETTE. What do you mean?

(*The prisoners enter, followed by the* OFFICER. *Two of them are placed under charge of the guard; the others, with* FLORETTE, JULIE *and* CORA, *are grouped on stage.*)

MARIANNE. Silence. (*Aside to* DOCTOR.) Doctor, have pity on her and consent to help me.

(DOCTOR *goes up a little.*)

OFFICER. I need another prisoner to complete the list, Henriette Gerard.

MARIANNE (*advances very quickly*). Here, monsieur.

HENRIETTE (*low*). Ah!

DOCTOR (*seizes her arm*). Silence!

MARIANNE (*to* OFFICER). Permit me, monsieur, to bid her a last farewell!

(OFFICER *makes gesture of consent, exits. She crosses to* HENRIETTE.)

HENRIETTE. No! no! I cannot, I will not consent!

MARIANNE. Hush! It is not you whom I save, Henriette, it is myself. If I remain, Jacques will find me again, and once in his power I should be lost. You will remain, you will find Louise, and you will both be saved!

HENRIETTE. Louise?

MARIANNE. Here, take this. (*Gives* HENRIETTE *the paper which* SISTER GENEVIEVE *has given her.* HENRIETTE *hesitates and looks at* DOCTOR.)

DOCTOR (*behind* HENRIETTE). Take it; your sister's fate depends upon it. (HENRIETTE *takes the paper and embraces* MARIANNE, *weeping. Enter* SISTER GENEVIEVE *and* OFFICER.) The Sister Superior!

MARIANNE (*low*). Ah!

OFFICER. Madame, will you please verify this list and identify the prisoners who are intended for exile?

SISTER GENEVIEVE. I am ready, monsieur!

OFFICER (*reading from list*). Marie Morand?

SISTER GENEVIEVE (*looking at prisoner*). Yes.

OFFICER (*same business*). Jeanne Raymond?

SISTER GENEVIEVE (*same business*). Yes.

OFFICER (*turning to* MARIANNE). Henriette Gerard?

MARIANNE. Here, Mother! (*Crossing to* SISTER GENEVIEVE *and kneeling.*)

SISTER GENEVIEVE. You?

(DOCTOR *points to* HENRIETTE *with an appealing gesture.* SISTER GENEVIEVE *looks from one to the other and seems greatly agitated.*)

MARIANNE. Mother! Mother! Have pity. Bless me and let me go, for this exile will purify a guilty soul and save an innocent one.

OFFICER. Well, sister?

(SISTER GENEVIEVE *takes* MARIANNE'S *head in her hands, stoops and kisses her forehead, and then, with firm voice and eyes uplifted to heaven.*)

SISTER GENEVIEVE. Yes. (*Aside.*) Ah! Doctor—my first falsehood.

DOCTOR. It will be recorded to your credit—there! (*Points to heaven.*)

CURTAIN FALLS

SCENE II

The hut of LA FROCHARD. *The stage represents an old and dilapidated boathouse; at back are two large and heavy doors opening down, which are closed with a bar across, resting in heavy socket and secured by padlock and staples. At right is a staircase leading up to a garret with door opening down. Door has lock and bolt. Under the staircase, which is masked in, is a door flush with the masking. Lock on door, which also opens down; at left is a rude bed. A table and a knife-grinding machine are on the stage. Beyond the doors, when they are forced open, are discovered steps leading down to the river, and across the river a view of Paris by starlight, partially illuminated. At the rise of curtain* LOUISE *and* PIERRE *are discovered,* LOUISE *asleep upon a miserable straw bed, and* PIERRE *seated on stool at foot of the bed.*

PIERRE. Poor child! So young, so weak, so lovely, and yet condemned to so hard a fate. Ah, me! I can do nothing. Jacques suspects and watches me. If I were to gain courage enough to make one step toward her release, he would discover it and kill me. Then what would become of her? I shudder to think of it. (*He rises and looks at her.*) She shivers in her sleep, her breath comes short and quick. She must be ill!

LOUISE (*half-rising*). Who is there?

PIERRE. It is I—ma'amselle, Pierre!

LOUISE. Ah, Pierre! I am glad it is you. I may sleep a little longer, may I not?

PIERRE. Sleep, ma'amselle, sleep—don't be frightened, I will not leave you.

LOUISE. Oh! I am so tired—thank you, Pierre, thank you. (*She lies down.*)

PIERRE (*looking at her*). Yes, sleep, poor child, and forget your misery. (*Pauses.*) She seems calmer now. Perhaps she is dreaming of happier days, of those she loves and who love and weep for her now. (*Comes down.*) Jacques has forbidden me to think of her, but I can defy him there; I will think of her, aye, and save her, too, even if it costs me my life; yes, yes, that would be better. Die for her, if I can save her. I can weaken these bolts, and Jacques will not discover it. (*He goes to his wheel, takes a screw-driver and works at screws in heavy bolt across the door.*) What am I doing? Alas! I shall have to pay for this with my life. No, no; I cannot!

LOUISE (*sighs in her sleep*). Henriette! Sister Henriette!

PIERRE (*runs to her side*). She is dreaming of her sister—a smile lights up her pallid face. She never smiles when she is awake. (*Thoughtfully.*) Ah! If I help her to escape and her happy dream were to become a reality, she would remember me with pity, perhaps with love. (*Goes up.*) I have begun my work and I will finish it.

(*Returns to doors at back and is about to commence work when* LA FROCHARD *enters from door under staircase.*)

LA FROCHARD (*brings in carrot and turnip with her, which she puts on table and scrapes through dialogue which follows*). Hello, master knife-grinder! What brings you home so early; no work outside, eh?

PIERRE. It is growing dark. I have brought my work home with me.

LA FROCHARD. So as to be near to Ma'amselle Louise. Oh, oh! I have my eye on you.

PIERRE. It would be better to have your eye on Jacques. But you never find fault with him.

LA FROCHARD. Why should I? He is the oldest, and master here.

PIERRE. Where is he now?

LA FROCHARD. At his work, to be sure. He has worked two days this week. Think of that; isn't it a shame that a handsome fellow like him should have to work?

PIERRE. Don't I work every day in the week?

LA FROCHARD. What else are you fit for?

(*Enter* JACQUES *by door under staircase.*)

JACQUES. There, that will do for today. (*Takes off apron and throws it aside.*) No more work for me, I am tired of it. (*Sits on stool.*)

LA FROCHARD. It is tiresome, isn't it, my son?

JACQUES. Ugh! Disgusting. (*Sees* PIERRE.) Hello, Master Cupid. Go sharpen my cutlass. You'll find it at the wine shop in the back street.

PIERRE. Very well.

JACQUES (*looking at* LOUISE). What is this? Asleep. Why isn't she at work?

LA FROCHARD. That is what I want to know, sleeping instead of working for her living.

JACQUES (*looking at* LOUISE). Why, she is so used to it, that she cries when she is asleep.

PIERRE (*making a movement toward* LOUISE). Is she crying?

JACQUES (*stops him*). What's that to you?

LA FROCHARD. She is an obstinate, lazy hypocrite. This morning I had to push her along to make her walk at all, and as to singing, she has no more voice than a crow.

JACQUES (*sitting*). I will make her sing, if I try!

PIERRE. You will kill her. Can't you see she is ill?

LA FROCHARD. Nonsense—she is shamming—I know her tricks.

JACQUES. What is the matter with her now?

LA FROCHARD. She has got some new notion in her head—I can't tell what.

PIERRE. I can. You remember the night of the snowstorm; after finishing her song she cried out at the top of her voice, "Henriette, Henriette, my sister!"

LA FROCHARD. Yes, and I stopped her mouth pretty quick, too.

PIERRE. Yes, yes; you twisted her arm until you nearly broke it.

LA FROCHARD. Well, why didn't she mind me?

PIERRE. You're killing her.

LA FROCHARD. I can't afford to support her in idleness. She must work, and if she won't——

JACQUES (*sitting on stool*). I'll find the way to make her——

PIERRE. You? What would you do?

JACQUES (*crossing to* PIERRE). That is my business.

LA FROCHARD (*goes to* LOUISE). Come, get up, my fine lady. No more airs! You must go out and make your living. (*She makes* LOUISE *rise.*) Give me that shawl. (*Throws shawl on bed.*) Take off this scarf, it keeps you too warm. (*Takes off scarf and puts it on her own neck.*) You'll shiver more comfortably without it.

LOUISE. I don't wish to go out, madame.

LA FROCHARD (*to* JACQUES). Eh? eh? What next? You hear that? She don't wish to go out.

JACQUES. We'll see about that. (*Crosses to* LOUISE *and goes to take her hand.*) Come here, my little beauty.

LOUISE (*recoils from his touch*). I forbid *you* to touch me.

JACQUES. Oh, ho! Then we're no longer friends?

LOUISE. Friends! You? You're cruel wretches. Both of you!

JACQUES. Yet you were glad enough to share our home when we picked you up in the streets.

LOUISE. Yes; I was grateful to you then, because you offered me a shelter. Alas! I learned too soon it was not pity for my misfortunes that moved you. No, no; you wanted to make use of my affliction. You have starved, tortured, *beaten* me; but now, weak as I am, my will shall be stronger than your violence! (*Straightening herself up.*) I will beg no more!

PIERRE (*terrified*). Louise.

JACQUES. Ah! When her blood is up she is superb!

LA FROCHARD. Oh, well, well, that is all mighty fine; but where is the bread and butter to come from?

LOUISE. I care not!

PIERRE (*crossing to* LA FROCHARD). Do you hear? Do you know what she means? She will starve rather than beg.

LA FROCHARD. Nonsense. She will get tired of that soon enough.

LOUISE. Never!

LA FROCHARD. Well, we'll see if locking you up in that garret won't bring you to your senses.

LOUISE. If I enter that place I will never leave it alive.

JACQUES. Why, she is magnificent. I'd never have believed she had so much spirit. (*Advancing toward her.*) Why, I love you! (*Seizes* LOUISE *and attempts to kiss her.*)

LOUISE. Ah! (*She screams and escapes from him.*)

PIERRE (*angrily*). Jacques! (*Loudly.*)

JACQUES. Well, what is it? You don't like it, I suppose, Master Cupid? Well, forbid it, why don't you?

PIERRE (*angrily*). I do. (*Looks at* JACQUES, *who eyes him sternly and he cowers upstage.*) Oh, miserable, cowardly wretch that I am! (*Breaks down sobbingly, goes to wheel.*)

LA FROCHARD (*crosses to* LOUISE). Come; come along. You're strong enough when you want to be. Up into the garret with you. (*She leads* LOUISE *to the foot of the stairs;* LOUISE *falls on steps.*)

JACQUES. Yes, that is right, Mother; take her up there out of the way. Ah! oh! Here, I want to speak to you.

(LA FROCHARD *crosses to* JACQUES; *they whisper.*)

PIERRE (*goes to* LOUISE, *who is at the foot of the staircase, L., and speaks in low tone very rapidly*). You can escape. I have unscrewed the lock; the key to the door to the street is under your mattress. Trust to Heaven to guide you. Nothing worse can happen than threatens you here.

JACQUES (*aloud to* LA FROCHARD). Lock her up securely. I have my reasons for distrusting Master Cupid there!

LA FROCHARD. Yes, yes; I understand.

JACQUES. My innocent, hard-working brother, come with me; I want you——

PIERRE. I have work here. (*Going toward wheel.*)

JACQUES. And I have work for you elsewhere. I told you to sharpen my cutlass. Come with me and keep your whining for this blind beauty till another time. Come along, I say!

PIERRE (*aside as they exit*). Ah! If I had anything but water in my veins, I'd do something more than whine.

JACQUES (*shoves him out of door*). By-by, Mother!

(*Exit* PIERRE, *and* JACQUES *follows.*)

LA FROCHARD (*sitting.*) Ah! What a splendid fellow he is. The very image of his dear father. There was a man for you. They cut off his head. Ah! It makes me sick when I think of it. I must take something to strengthen me. (*Turns to* LOUISE.) Yes, yes, young woman; I'll attend to you in a minute. (*She takes out bottle from her pocket from which she drinks.*) Ah! That warms my heart! (*To* LOUISE.) We'll see how you'll enjoy a couple of days' starvation. Yes, Jacques is right; we must break your obstinate spirit. (*Drinks again.*) Then, when you come out, you won't refuse to help your friends make an honest living. (LOUISE *has sunk down on the steps.* LA FROCHARD *goes up to her.*) Ah! Shamming again. Get up and come with me! (LA FROCHARD *forces her to rise and they go up the stairs.*)

LOUISE. Oh, madame, have you no soul, no pity? Do not kill me!

LA FROCHARD. I don't intend to. You're too valuable. There, get in with you. I'll see you safe inside.

(LA FROCHARD *and* LOUISE *exit into garret, and* LA FROCHARD *closes the door. After a moment's pause the door under the stairs is opened briskly and* PICARD *enters.*)

PICARD. Ah! At last I've found a door that leads to something and somewhere. (*Looks about him.*) There's nobody at home! (*Sees brandy bottle, takes it up.*) Hello! What's this? Brandy! (*Smells it.*) Bad brandy; very bad brandy! Pooh! Any one who would drink that would have the stomach to imprison a whole blind family. What is my best course? Let me see. (*Examines doors.*) These doors must open on the river. Good. That is the point for the police. Now to return through the half-mile of dark passages to the Rue Noir where I left Ma'amselle Henriette; then to the chevalier, who has been liberated by his uncle from the Bastile on the supposition that Mlle. Henriette has been sent to Cayenne. And now, if I have not earned my promotion, my name is not Picard! (*Exit under stairs, slamming door.*)

(LA FROCHARD *opens door of garret.*)

LA FROCHARD. Hmm! Eh, what's that? (*Comes down the stairs quickly.*) I thought I heard some one. Jacques, is that you? No, there is no one here! I'm an old fool to be so easily frightened. I always am scared when I hear any one. It's my nerves. (*Drinks.*) Oh! Oh! What a wicked, obstinate creature that girl is—and Jacques is in love with her too. She's bewitched him. I am sure of it. A blind girl, but that is nothing; that doctor said he could cure her; that would never do though; if she could see—good-by to business. (*Knock at the door.*) Who's that? (*She listens and knock is heard again.*) Who can have found their way here? (*She hides the bottle and then goes to the door.*) Who is there? What do you want?

HENRIETTE (*outside*). I am looking for some one—for Madame Frochard.

LA FROCHARD. What do you want of her?

HENRIETTE (*outside*). I must speak with her.

LA FROCHARD. Are you alone?

HENRIETTE. Yes, I am alone.

LA FROCHARD (*cautiously opens the door and looks behind* HENRIETTE). Well, if you are alone you may come in.

(*Enter* HENRIETTE, *looking around her with affright.* LA FROCHARD *closes the door.*)

HENRIETTE. How imprudent I was to leave the spot where Picard left me. I have lost him and wandered here by accident. Great Heaven! Can this be the place?

LA FROCHARD. Well, well, young woman, you want to see Madame Frochard; what have you got to say to her? Do you expect to find any one here?

HENRIETTE (*looking around searchingly*). Yes, yes, I am looking for the person that lives here with you.

LA FROCHARD. What person?

HENRIETTE. A young girl.

LA FROCHARD. I don't know anything about any young girl.

HENRIETTE (*astonished*). You don't know her?

LA FROCHARD. No!

HENRIETTE. Am I mistaken? This house answers the description, and your name is Frochard, is it not?

LA FROCHARD. Euphemie Frochard—what then?

HENRIETTE. You beg in the streets with a young girl who sings, do you not?

LA FROCHARD. Me beg in the streets—what for? Haven't I two sons who work for me? One of them is a knife-grinder; look, there is his wheel, and the other one—— (*Aside.*) Ah! If he were only here now.

HENRIETTE (*doubtfully*). Yet the doctor told me that he knew you. (*Looks around her and sees* LOUISE's *shawl on the bed.*) Ah! (*Utters a loud cry.*)

LA FROCHARD. What is the matter?

HENRIETTE (*seizes the shawl*). This shawl! I know it—it is hers, it is hers, I tell you!

LA FROCHARD. Not a bit of it. It is mine. (*Attempts to recover the shawl.*)

HENRIETTE. And this scarf around your neck?

LA FROCHARD. Well, what of it?

HENRIETTE. It was made for her by my own hands. (*Tears the scarf from* LA FROCHARD's *neck.*) Ah! Wretch, you have lied to me.

LA FROCHARD. Well, well, if you must know the truth I'll tell you. When you came in you were so excited and frightened that I didn't dare to tell you all——

HENRIETTE. What? Speak quickly!

LA FROCHARD. One evening, about three months ago, I met the girl you are looking for wandering about the streets. I had pity on her and brought her home with me, where I took good care of her.

HENRIETTE. Go on, for Heaven's sake, go on!

LA FROCHARD. Well, she knew I was poor and could not afford to keep her for nothing, so she sang sometimes in the streets, just to help me—and she sang like a little bird.

HENRIETTE. And then? What then?

LA FROCHARD. And then—why, you see the poor child wasn't very strong, and what with the life we lead and the sorrow she felt, she could not stand it; the little bird broke down entirely, she said she couldn't sing any more, and that was the end of it. For two days she has been dumb—she'll sing no more—no more!

HENRIETTE. Dead! Louise—dead! (*She faints.*)

LA FROCHARD. Ah! ha! fainted. What am I to do with her? Oh, if Jacques were only here! I must go for him. But if she were to come to and see the other one. No, no; I'll fix that. (*She goes up the stairs—locks the garret door, and takes the key with her.*) There, there is nothing to fear now; I'll go and call Jacques. (*She exits at door L. and is heard to lock the door on the other side after her; as soon as she is off the door of the garret is seen to move, at first gently, then with more force, finally the lock tumbles off, the door opens and* LOUISE *appears.*)

LOUISE. They are all gone. Pierre told me the truth, the lock would not hold. (*She comes down.*) If I can find my way to the street, through that long passage, I will ask the first passer-by to take me to that good doctor at the Hospital St. Louis. (*She gropes around and passes very close to* HENRIETTE.) Where is the door? Ah! here! (*She tries the door L.*) Locked, locked; what shall I do? Ah! I remember—Pierre told me he had made another key for it. (*She gropes her way rapidly to the bed, feels under the mattress and finds the key.*) Ah! Good, brave Pierre, now I will go at once. (*She crosses the stage with rapid steps and stumbles against* HENRIETTE. *She recoils, frightened, then advances and stoops, feeling with her hands.*) A woman! (*She touches* HENRIETTE'S *hand.*) She is cold, she is dead! Oh Heaven! They have committed some terrible crime and fled. (*She raises* HENRIETTE'S *head to her knees and puts her hand on her heart.*) She is not dead; madame, madame, speak, speak to me. She does not hear me. What shall I do? I cannot leave her thus!

(*The door is heard to unlock and* LA FROCHARD *and* JACQUES *enter quickly.*)

LA FROCHARD. How is this? Together!

JACQUES. Separate them at once—quick!

LA FROCHARD (*drags* LOUISE *away from* HENRIETTE). What are you doing here? How did you get out?

LOUISE. I—madame—I!

JACQUES (*seeing* HENRIETTE *recovering*). Quick, get her out of the way

—quick, I tell you, the other one is coming to.

(PIERRE *appears at the door.*)

LOUISE. But this woman who is lying here!

PIERRE (*aside*). A woman!

LA FROCHARD (*pushing her up the stairs*). That is our business, and none of yours. Get along with you!

(*They reach the top of the staircase.* LA FROCHARD *opens the door; at that moment* HENRIETTE *opens her eyes and sees* LOUISE.)

HENRIETTE (*screams*). Ah, Louise! Louise!

(JACQUES *puts his hand over her mouth.*)

LOUISE (*stops*). That voice? I know it!

LA FROCHARD. Go in—I tell you, get in with you!

HENRIETTE (*pushes* JACQUES' *hand away*). Louise! Sister!

LOUISE (*with an effort pushes* LA FROCHARD *aside—runs down the staircase.* HENRIETTE *disengages herself from* JACQUES, *and they meet C. Embrace—pause*). Henriette! Henriette! Is it you!

HENRIETTE. Louise! Louise! My sister!

PIERRE (*joyfully*). Her sister!

HENRIETTE. Oh, my Louise, my poor Louise! How you must have suffered here among these miserable wretches! Yes, miserable wretches that you are! I will have you punished. (JACQUES *goes to door.*) Let us go at once! Let us go!

JACQUES (*barring the passage*). No, you shall not go!

HENRIETTE. What! Would you dare prevent us?

PIERRE (*to* LA FROCHARD). Better warn him against violence!

LA FROCHARD (*on stairs*). Pooh, we must, or they will escape and denounce us!

JACQUES. You cannot leave here!

HENRIETTE. I will cry out—I will call for help!

JACQUES (*backing them*). Try it, and see what good it will do! Besides, I warn you we come of a family who kill. (*Seizes* LOUISE.) She is mine and I will keep her!

LOUISE (*screams*). Ah!

PIERRE. Oh, this is infamous! (*He rushes in between* LOUISE *and* JACQUES, *forcing* JACQUES *to release* LOUISE, *and he faces* JACQUES.)

JACQUES. Do you dare to interfere against me?

PIERRE. I dare!

JACQUES. Against me!

PIERRE. Against you! I have acted the coward long enough. I thought, because you were big and strong, that you were brave—but you are not! You fight with women—you are a coward! In their defense my courage will be more than a match for your strength!

LOUISE. Brave Pierre!

PIERRE. Depend on me, mademoiselle!

JACQUES (*advancing to him*). What do you want?

PIERRE. Let these two women go!

JACQUES. Indeed! Suppose I refuse, what then?

PIERRE. What then? What then? Well, you have said it. We come of a family who kill.

LA FROCHARD (*on stairs*). Pierre!

PIERRE. Dare to lay a hand on either of them (*runs to his wheel and takes up knife*) and I plunge this knife into your heart.

(JACQUES *recoils as though in spite of himself.*)

JACQUES. Your life shall pay for this!

PIERRE. Or yours.

LA FROCHARD. Remember you are brothers.

PIERRE (*bitterly*). Yes, brothers, as of old—the sons of Adam—only this time the parts are changed, and Abel will kill Cain!

JACQUES. Very well, if you will have it! (*They fight and* JACQUES *wounds* PIERRE *in the shoulder.*)

HENRIETTE. He is wounded!

PIERRE. No!

JACQUES. Isn't that enough, cripple?

PIERRE. No; cut again, for while she is in danger you may slash my flesh into ribbons. I shall feel nothing.

(*They fight again.*)

HENRIETTE (*screams*). Help! help!

(LA FROCHARD *threatens* HENRIETTE. JACQUES *presses* PIERRE *down, immediately opposite the door, and is just in the act of stabbing him when the door is thrust violently open; the* CHEVALIER *enters, with drawn sword in his hand, beats up* JACQUES' *weapon and stands. Tableau.*)

DE VAUDREY. What is this? A ruffian attacking a cripple? Down with your weapon, or by Heaven I'll beat it out of your hand, and spit you as I would a dog.

JACQUES. What right have you to interfere? You shall pay for this!

(PIERRE *is released from the fight.* HENRIETTE *and* LOUISE *are menaced by* LA FROCHARD, *and* PIERRE *interposes between them.*)

DE VAUDREY (*to* JACQUES). Now, villain, down with your weapon I say, and permit these ladies to leave this place, before you compel me to punish you as you deserve.

JACQUES. Ha! ha! You punish me! So, you are the lover of the other one. Well, take her and go; leave the little one to me.

DE VAUDREY. Scoundrel! (DE VAUDREY *beats down* JACQUES' *weapon, and a noise is heard at back beyond the door in C., and the voice of* PICARD *above the din.)*

PICARD (*outside*). Open, open in the king's name!

(PIERRE *attempts to go to door as though to unbar it, and* LA FROCHARD *prevents him.)*

PICARD (*outside*). Then, in the king's name, I will open it for you! (*The noise of a battering ram is heard against the door, and after a few strokes the bar falls, and discovers armed men; view of the city across the river beyond. The men headed by* PICARD, *who wears a white scarf, embroidered with fleur-de-lis, and has sword in hand, pour up the steps. At the same moment that the door is opened, the* CHEVALIER *disarms* JACQUES *and holds him at the point of the sword.*) Ah! Master, you found your way along that passage before me and mademoiselle, too.

DE VAUDREY. Yes, and in good time, Picard. Here, some of you bind this ruffian! (*Two or three of the soldiers advance and bind* JACQUES, *who at first resists, then sullenly submits.* HENRIETTE *comes down.* DE VAUDREY *to* HENRIETTE.) Henriette, my love!

HENRIETTE. A second time I owe my life to you!

DE VAUDREY. No, not to me. Thank Picard there, whose selfish bravery left me to defend the end of a passage where there were no foes, while he stormed the front of the castle. Your cries for help guided me to the rescue.

HENRIETTE (*brings* LOUISE *down*). Louise, darling sister, thank your preserver!

LOUISE. Ah! Monsieur, you do not know from what a frightful fate you have saved us.

(*During the preceding* LA FROCHARD *has crept down to L. and endeavors to escape by the door.* PICARD *sees her.*)

PICARD. Oh! No you don't, old lady; you must not run away from your dutiful son because he is in a little trouble. He'll need your motherly care now more than ever.

LA FROCHARD (*resumes her whining, begging tone*). I'm only a poor old woman. I don't know anything about their evil doings.

DE VAUDREY. Picard, take charge of this worthy couple, mother and son. My uncle, the count, will see to their punishment. Off with them!

(*Soldiers take* LA FROCHARD *up, and she is placed under guard with* JACQUES.)

LA FROCHARD (*as they are going*). Please, good gentlemen, I am only a poor old woman!

JACQUES. Stop your whining. Remember you are a Frochard.

PIERRE. Jacques, Mother, one word before you go.

JACQUES. Not one. Go to your fine friends and remember that you sent your brother to the scaffold. (*Rushes at* PIERRE *as though to strike him. Soldiers interfere and drag him off with* LA FROCHARD.)

DE VAUDREY. Now, *monsieur le capitaine,* how are we to get away from this hole of a place?

PICARD. Monsieur le Chevalier, I have provided for everything. The minister of police promised to follow me here, with your aunt, the countess, as soon as possible.

HENRIETTE. The minister of police coming here? Let me go with my poor Louise at once.

DE VAUDREY. Stay, Henriette! I have restored your sister to your arms, to replace your care by the endearing protection of a mother.

(*The* COUNT, COUNTESS *and* DOCTOR *enter up the steps.*)

HENRIETTE (*Bewildered*). A mother?

LOUISE (*joyfully*). My mother!

(COUNT, COUNTESS *and* DOCTOR *enter. The* CHEVALIER *meets the* COUNTESS *and brings her down.*)

DE VAUDREY. Your mother, the Countess de Linieres.

COUNTESS (*embracing her*). My child; my Louise!

HENRIETTE (*sadly*). I have found her, only to lose her again!

COUNT. Not so, mademoiselle. It is only within the past hour that I have learned the truth. The countess has confessed the secret which has clouded our married life!

DE VAUDREY. Picard, you may unpack my trunks. I shall not go to Cayenne.

PICARD. No necessity for it, monsieur. We found our Cayenne in Paris, and for a few minutes as hot as we wanted it.

(*The* COUNTESS *comes down with* LOUISE *and* HENRIETTE.)

LOUISE. Monsieur, we are all so happy, yet you must not forget poor Pierre. Noble, brave Pierre! Pierre—Pierre; where is he?

PIERRE (*comes down to* LOUISE). I remained, mademoiselle, to ask the privilege of saying farewell. Your good heart will not forget the poor cripple?

LOUISE. Never, never, Pierre.

COUNTESS. A mother thanks you with more than words.

DE VAUDREY (*to* HENRIETTE). Let his reward be my care. Henriette, is my reward to be delayed?

HENRIETTE. To be near Louise, my sister, and to be your wife, seems too great a joy.

LOUISE (*to* COUNTESS). Oh! Mother, if I could only see you!

DOCTOR. Ah! That is my affair.

COUNTESS. And do you think you can restore her sight, doctor?

DOCTOR. I can be the instrument; the rest is in the hands of Heaven!

CURTAIN

The Old Homestead

A Play in Four Acts

BY DENMAN THOMPSON

THE OLD HOMESTEAD

All Rights Reserved

The first production of the Denman Thompson version of this play took place at the Fourteenth Street Theatre, New York City, January 10, 1887, with the following cast of principals:

Joshua Whitcomb	Denman Thompson
Cy Prime	George A. Beane
Happy Jack	Walter Gale
Frank Hopkins	Alfred Schwartz
Eb Ganzey	J. L. Morgan
John Freeman	Frank Thompson
Henry Hopkins	Walter Lennox
Judge Patterson	Gus Kammerlee
Reuben Whitcomb	T. D. Frawley
Len Holbrook	C. M. Richardson
Pat Clancey	Frank Mara
Francois Fogarty	Frank Martin
Aunt Matilda Whitcomb	Louisa Morse
Rickety Ann	Annie Thompson
Miss Annie Hopkins	Virginia Marlowe
Miss Nelli Freeman	Lillian Stone
Maggie O'Flaherty	Minnie Luckstone
Mrs. Henry Hopkins	Venie Thompson
Mrs. Murdock	Mrs. Owen Marlowe
Miss Nellie Patterson	Leonore Willard

SYNOPSIS

Act One: Homestead farm of the Whitcombs'.
Act Two: Interior of the Hopkins mansion.
Act Three: Grace Church at night.
Act Four: Kitchen in the Old Homestead.

THE OLD HOMESTEAD

ACT ONE

SCENE—*Homestead farm of the* WHITCOMBS. *The back scene, or drop, depicts undulating farm lands and in the foreground a typical stone wall is seen. A cosy farmhouse with, or without, flowered porch appears to the left of the audience. Entrance to house is made by step through screened door. A curtained window above door and one facing audience. Beneath upper window, a common bench with milk pans and pails. At the corner of the house, a rain spout and rain barrel parallel to footlights. By the barrel—below window, facing audience—a low wash bench with bar of common soap. A common chair stands beside rain barrel—at corner of house. To the right of the audience is a barn or granary. There is a square, old-fashioned well with windlass, bucket and dipper, with a small bench in front and a common chair beside it. Near well is a wood-saw, saw-horse, wood-block, split kindling wood and chips. Grass mats and farming implements can give further atmosphere to typify the farm yard and homestead.*

(*At rise of curtain mixed quartette sing "Lawn Tennis," or other lively selection, off stage.* AUNT MATILDA *and* RICKETY ANN *discovered listening.* MATILDA *is sitting on bench in front of well and* RICKETY *is standing up stage looking off at singers.*)

MATILDA. Our visitors are enjoying themselves. Well, I like to see it. Shows they are happy. Sent word to Joshua by the Bennets boy to come up to the house. He's down in the meadow helping the hired men—wish he'd come. Suppose he wants to get all his hay mowed up in case it should rain before morning. (*Crosses to* RICKETY.) What's that they are playin' over there, Rickety Ann? Some new kind of a ball game, ain't it?

RICKETY. Guess it 'tis, Aunt Tildy—never seed one like afore. Come near breaking a window a while ago, too.

MATILDA. Did they? Well, now, that's dreadful careless. You tell them, Rickety Ann, that they must be careful. (*Goes down to steps of porch.*)

RICKETY. Yes'm. (*Calling off to singers.*) Say, you folks, Aunt Tildy says if you break a window she'll make you pay for it.

FRANK H. (*outside—off stage*). You don't say so.

MATILDA. Why, Rickety Ann, I didn't say nothin' o' the sort.

RICKETY. Well, if you didn't you thought it.

(*Comes down beside* MATILDA.)

MATILDA. Never mind what I think—you do what I say.

RICKETY. All right, Aunt Tildy; but I didn't mean nothin'.

MATILDA (*mounting porch*). All right then, bring in the wood and we'll finish getting the supper. Come! (*Exits into house.*)

RICKETY (*crosses going to wood-block* L.—*kneeling and picking up split kindling wood and chips, piling it up on one arm, speaking as she does*). Well, that new hired girl don't know enough to blow hot soup. Put the ice in the well the other day to cool the water. (*Laughs.*) She don't know nothin'.

MATILDA (*inside of house*). Rickety Ann!

RICKETY. Yes'm, I'm comin'. (*Cross to house* R. *with wood. Enter* FRANK *and* ANNIE HOPKINS *followed by* JOHN *and* NELLIE FREEMAN. *They variously group about* C. *and point at* RICKETY—*all laughing.*) What are you laughing at? Is there anything on me? (*Turning around.*)

FRANK H. Quite a wild flower, isn't it?

JOHN F. A daisy I should say. (*All laugh.*)

RICKETY. Now what you laughing at me for?

FRANK H. Oh, nothing in particular, but we must have something to laugh at. (*All laugh*).

RICKETY. Think they're smart. I bet they don't know beans when the bag's untied.—(*Exits into house.*)

FRANK H. Well, we are doing very well. Only been here two hours, lawn tennis up, trunks in our rooms and by Jove! I'm hungry as a hunter

ANNIE H. (*comes down beside well*). So am I.

JOHN F. (*has taken position at well*). If supper isn't ready pretty soon I am going to ask for a piece of bread and butter.

NELLIE (*has taken position by* JOHN). Well, if I have to wait much longer I shall faint.

FRANK H. (*going to door of house*). Come over here and get a whiff of this. (*Before door of house.*)

ALL. What is it? (*All going to house.*)

FRANK H. Fried pork.

ALL. Oh, doesn't it smell good!

FRANK H. Yes, and I never could bear it at home.

ALL. Nor I.

(*Enter* RICKETY *from behind house.*)

RICKETY (*shouting*). Look out for snakes.

(*Runs to back of well, laughing. The girls scream.* ANNIE *runs across stage and jumps on chair near lower corner of house, near* FRANK. *Simultaneously* NELLIE *leaps on bench in front of well with* JOHN *beside her.*)

JOSH (*running on, hat in hand. Enter* MATILDA *from house—same business of jumping as* JOSH *stands*). Hello! Hello! Hello! What's all this hollerin' about?

ALL. Snakes!

JOSH. Snakes? (*Jumps around and looks on ground.*) Git out! I don't see any snakes!

FRANK H. Well, that sunflower over there said there was. (*Pointing to* RICKETY.)

RICKETY. Oh, I didn't nuther! I said look out for snakes.

FRANK H. (*helping* ANNIE *down from chair and same business for* JOHN *and* NELLIE). What did you say that for?

RICKETY. Well, I got to have something to laugh at, hain't I?

(*All laugh but* JOSH *and* MATILDA. *Exit* RICKETY, *back of barn*).

JOSH. Want to know if you're Henry Hopkins' boy!

FRANK H. Yes, Mr. Whitcomb.

JOSH. How de-do? (*Shakes hands with* FRANK H.) Knowed your father first rate; he and I used to go to school together.

MATILDA. Looks a little mite like Henry used to, don't you think so, Joshua?

JOSH. Yes, a little mite, his hair ain't quite so red. (JOHN *is quietly communicating his delight.* JOSH *turns to* ANNIE.) I want to know if you are Henry's daughter?

ANNIE H. Yes, Mr. Whitcomb. (*Crosses to* JOSH *and shakes hands.*)

JOSH. Well, it beats all natur imazingly how these youngsters do grow.

MATILDA. She favors the Richardsons.

JOSH. So she does.

MATILDA. I can see it, she looks like her mother. Knowed your mother first rate when she was a gal.

JOSH (ANNIE *explains the use of the racket which she holds in her hand*). So did I, too!

FRANK H. Mr. Whitcomb, this is Mr. Freeman and his sister.

(JOSH *shakes hands with* NELLIE *and* JOHN *in front of well.*)

JOSH (*shaking hands with* NELLIE *and* JOHN). How de-do, sir? (*Same business with* NELLIE.) How de-do, Miss? Glad to see yer.

FRANK H. They were on their way to the White Mountains and I took the liberty of asking them to stop over a day or two.

JOSH. That's right! That's right! We'll stow 'em away somewhere. Now I want to call you all to order on one p'int.

ALL. What is it?

JOSH. Call me uncle and Matilda aunt, then we'll get acquainted quicker.

ALL. Why, certainly!

JOSH. Gosh! You are all dressed up like a circus, ain't you?

FRANK H. These are lawn tennis suits.

JOSH. Little too slick to hay in. You'll have to get on your old clothes tomorrow.

FRANK H. But we're all going fishing in the morning.

JOSH. Gosh! I thought so, I see yer net stuck up to dry over on the grass there. (*Pointing off stage.*) Now what do you expect to catch in a scoop like that? (*Pointing to tennis racket in* FRANK'S *hand.*)

FRANK H. (*pointing off stage*). What you see over there is a lawn tennis net and this is a racket.

JOSH. Want to know.

FRANK H. A new one on you, isn't it?

JOSH. Shouldn't wonder a mite.

(*Enter* MAGGIE O'FLAHERTY *from house.*)

MAGGIE. If ye plaze, mum, shall I peel the potatoes or bile them with their jackets on? (*Exits into house.*)

MATILDA. That girl will be the death of me. (*Exits into house.*)

JOSH. Bile the potatoes with their jackets on? It wouldn't surprise me if she biled them with their overcoats on—not a mite.

(*Enter* RICKETY.)

RICKETY (*speaks mysteriously to visitors.*) Hush, don't say a word, but if any on you have got any gold watches, you'd better hide 'em for I jest seed the awfullest looking tramp running around one of the haystacks that I ever seed in all my life.

ANNIE H. A tramp? Why, we'll all be robbed. Come, Nellie and John.

(*Exit into house followed by* NELLIE *and* JOHN *quickly—back of well.* RICKETY *crosses back of* JOSH.)

JOSH. Here! Here! Here! There ain't no danger, not a mite! (*Turns to* RICKETY.) What's the matter with ye, want ter scare everybody to death?

RICKETY (*crosses stage to doorstep*). Well, if he ain't a robber, I jest bet he's a wild man escaped out of a menagerie.

(FRANK *goes up stage looking off stage; then leisurely down—in time for speech.*)

JOSH. Well, stop yer yawpin' and go get me a towel and I'll wash up out here. (*Exit* RICKETY *into house.*) And you help Aunt Tilda get supper ready. (*Throws hat and glasses on chair at* R. *and puts glasses in hat. Then, going to steps—rolling up shirt sleeves—calls off into house.*) And tell Miss O'Flaherty to get her milking done before night.

FRANK H. How is the fishing around here, Uncle Josh?

(*Enter* RICKETY *with towel, places it on bench by rain barrel and house and exits back into house.*)

JOSH. Gosh! I don't know! Ain't been fishin' since I was a boy.

FRANK H. How is that?

JOSH. Ain't had time. (*Goes to bench, takes tin wash bowl, dips water out of barrel at corner of house while he speaks—soaps his hands with a piece *of brown soap and washing his face —after speaking and then comes to* R. C. *with one eye closed to keep out soap, drying hands and face with towel.*)

FRANK H. No? (*Sitting on edge of bench at well.*)

JOSH. No, we have to scratch around up here like a hen with forty chickens to pay taxes and keep out of the poorhouse. We don't have much time for fishing, I can tell you. How's your father?

FRANK H. Quite well, thanks.

JOSH. Got rich, I hear. (*Crosses to wash bench, throwing down towel.*)

FRANK H. Yes, rated at over a million.

JOSH (*crossing, amazed, before speaking*). Christopher Columbus! A million dollars?

FRANK H. Quite a sum of money, isn't it?

JOSH. Gosh! I guess it is. Only think on't, he and I sit on the same bench together in the district school.

FRANK H. Yes; I've often heard him speak of it.

JOSH. You can see the old schoolhouse down there just over the tops of them trees. (*Points off stage.*) Stands right across from that old barn with a load of hay on it.

FRANK H. (*looking off stage*). Yes, I see it.

JOSH. 'Twas a new building then, but age is beginning to tell on it. We are growing old together. Many's the time that your old dad and I got our jackets tanned there, I can tell you.

FRANK H. I suppose so.

JOSH. New York must be a pretty smart sort of a village, I guess, ain't it?

FRANK H. Well, I should say it is. Were you never there?

JOSH. No, sir. Never sot foot in it. (*Goes to chair—takes hat and glasses and puts them on.*) But I'm going there one of these days to look for my boy.

FRANK H. (*rising*). Why, have you a son in New York?

JOSH (*reflectively*). I don't know; —I did have four or five months ago. Ain't heard nothin' from him since.

FRANK H. He went there thinking to make his fortune, I suppose?

JOSH. Well, not exactly. Might as well tell you first as last, 'cause you're sure to hear on't and I want you to hear on it right! Pull up a chair and sit down.

(*Gets chair and sits.*)

FRANK H. Yes, thank you, I will.

(*Takes chair near well and sits— about three feet from* JOSH.)

JOSH. About a year ago now he was cashier in the Cheshire Bank in Keene a few miles from here. Well, it seems one day, a party of sharps from Boston went to Keene and went into the bank and when some of them were talking to Reub one of the mean sneaks got into the vault and stole a lot of money.

FRANK H. He did?

JOSH. Gosh! Yes. It all came out on the trial. Well, they pitched on to my boy and had him arrested right before a lot of visitors from Boston, on suspicion of robbing the bank; but they let him go again pretty quick, I can tell you. When I think on't I get so mad, I perty near froth. Charged with stealing something he didn't know no more about than the man in the moon.

FRANK H. What a shame!

JOSH. I guess it was. And he felt it dreadfully, too. I don't believe the boy had a good night's rest since. He always imagined people p'inted at him and was downhearted and low-spirited so one day he packed his trunk and started for New York.

FRANK H. So you think of going there to look for him, do you?

JOSH. I certainly shall.

FRANK H. Why not go back with us?

JOSH. Gosh! I will if my new boots are done in time.

FRANK H. And I will assist you to look for your boy in every way I can.

JOSH. Thank'ee, thank'ee. Now I am going to ask you something and I know you will laugh at me.

FRANK H. Why should I?

JOSH. Because it is so foolish. (*Looking mysteriously to house.*) Say, do you believe in dreams? (FRANK *laughs.*) That's right, laugh—I don't blame you a mite.

FRANK H. Why do you ask?

JOSH. Because I've had 'em about my boy lately,—so nat'ral that it almost seems as though they must be true.

FRANK H. That is the result of constantly thinking of him,—nothing more, believe me.

JOSH. I hope not—I hope not.

(*Enter* RICKETY *from house and comes down beside* JOSH.)

RICKETY. Say, Uncle, Aunt Tildy says to ask you if you won't come in and cut some dried beef for supper.

JOSH. Why, sartin. (*Rises.*) Won't you come in the house, young man?

FRANK H. (*rises. Takes chair and replaces it by well*). No thanks—I'll stop out here and look around if you have no objections.

JOSH. Oh, no; make yourself at home. I don't care what you do as long as you don't set on my beehives—(*Goes to steps.*) be careful about that! (*Exits into house.*)

RICKETY (*looking about mysteriously*). Say, who be you anyway? I didn't know you was comin'.

FRANK H. No? Then there must be something wrong about it, isn't there?

RICKETY. Oh, I don't know.

FRANK H. Well, I'm Frank Hopkins and I am from New York. Now who are you?

RICKETY. Oh, well, I ain't very bright, folks say. My name is Mary Ann Maynard, but they call me Rickety Ann.

FRANK H. What for?

RICKETY. I don't know—guess 'cause I had the rickets when I was little.

FRANK H. Indeed!

RICKETY (*looking about before speaking*). Say, do you know what?

FRANK H. No, what is it?

RICKETY. Well, I can climb a tree jest as good as a boy,—want to see me? (*Turns up stage as if to look for a tree.* FRANK *stops her.*)

FRANK H. No, no!—I'll take your word for it.

RICKETY (*admiringly—surveying* FRANK). Say, do you know you're awful nice looking?

FRANK H. Thanks.

RICKETY. Yes, you be.

FRANK H. Say, Rickety Ann, have you always lived here?

RICKETY. No, I was borrowed out o' the poorhouse jest to help Aunt Tildy while the visitors are here. But I guess I'll never go back there any more.

FRANK H. No?

RICKETY. Aunt Tildy says if I am a good girl I may stay here jest as long as I want to, and I'm going to try and be good. Wouldn't you?

FRANK H. I certainly should.

RICKETY. Say, you never lived in the poorhouse, did you?

FRANK H. No indeed.

RICKETY. Oh, you wouldn't like it a bit, I bet!

FRANK H. No.

RICKETY. 'Cos you don't get half enough to eat only on prize days!

FRANK H. What do you get on prize days?

RICKETY. Well, on prize days the one that eats the most puddin' and milk gets a piece of pumpkin pie; and that last time I eat the most puddin' and milk.

FRANK H. And you got the pie of course.

RICKETY. No;—eat so much puddin' and milk couldn't eat no pie. (*Cow bells heard off stage.*) Oh, here comes the cows—I must go and drive them in the barnyard.

(*Exit calling "Co boss, co boss, co boss,"—calling cows.*)

FRANK H. Good-by.

(*Enter* MAGGIE *from house, singing an Irish ditty, looking around now and then at* FRANK *in a flirting way and exit.* FRANK *in meantime is following her up, returning the flirtation.*)

ANNIE H. (*appearing at door of house*). There, there! That will do, young man! Come and lift the tray out of my trunk. (*Exits in house.*)

FRANK H. (*speaking as he crosses*). Very well, Annie, but the next time I come to the country, I come alone. (*Exits into the house.*)

(*Enter* MATILDA *from house, who takes chair and picks the stems from strawberries, which she has, from one pan to the other.*)

MATILDA. Well, I guess I'll pick the berries out here—little mite cooler than it is inside.

(*Enter* RICKETY *from entrance.*)

RICKETY (*crosses stage, singing*). "Cy Prime had a wife but I guess he killed her, now I guess he's comin' over to court Aunt Tilda."

MATILDA (*rising indignantly*). What's that? What's that?

(RICKETY *exits hastily into house, laughing, and* MATILDA *sits, busy with strawberries.*)

CY P. (*enters with small tin pail with berries, singing "Roll on, silvery moon, guide the traveller on his way."—Sees* MATILDA*—speaks aside*). There she is—the smartest woman that ever fried a nut cake or turned a flapjack. I heve been trying for nigh on to thirty years to ask Tildy to have me for better or worse, but could never muster up courage enough to pop the question; but I'll do it now or bust my galluses. I got a bran new speech all rit out that I'm goin' to speak to her—hev been studying it for the last six months. (*Aloud.*) Well, Tildy, how de-do—how de-do? (*Comes down beside* MATILDA.)

MATILDA (*looking up, sees* CY P.). How de-do, Cyrus?

CY P. Here, I brought you a lettle mess o' rasberries. Found some pretty nice ones and I thought I might as well bring them to you. (*Hands small can of berries to* MATILDA.)

MATILDA. Thank you, Cyrus. (*Takes berries and turns them into can she has.*) Come in awful handy. Had some, but we got company, and I was a little might afraid they wouldn't go around.

CY P. Yes. Met Dr. Baxter—he told me you'd got company.

MATILDA. Been perty warm today, ain't it?

CY P. Warm? Should think it was! Been hotter than mustard. Oh, it got so hot today over to the store that the mercury jumped right up and knocked the top right off the thermometer!

MATILDA (*smiling*). Oh, I guess not!

CY P. Oh, I guess yes!

MATILDA (*looking archly at* CY P.). Oh, I guess not!

CY P. (*hitching trousers and scraping ground with toe of boot*). Well, that's what I was told; but folks lie so nowadays you can't believe more'n half you hear.

MATILDA. I should think so!

CY P. (*aside*). If she keeps on talking about the weather, I sha'n't get any chance to speak my new speech!

MATILDA. Cyrus, git a chair and sit down.

CY P. Yes, don't care if I do. As I said before, it has been perty hot and I've had a long walk and I'm nigh on tuckered out. (*Going to porch, near steps, sees cucumbers.*) Well, by jinks! That's a nice mess of cucumbers you got there, to be sure. (*Takes up biggest one.*) That's a whopper, ain't it? Got some nice tomatoes, too. (*Picks one up—then replaces it. He crosses down to* MATILDA *and speaks bashfully and hesitatingly.*) Say, Tildy, I can remember when folks around here used to call them things love apples.

MATILDA. Yes, so can I.

CY P. (*crosses to well—takes chair and sits by* MATILDA *after several movements as to proximity. He finally sits about two feet away.*) And they'd no more think of eatin' one o' them in them days than they 'ud think o' eatin' a toadstool now. (*Aside.*) I wonder how in Sam Hill my new speech begins? (*Thinks.*) Oh, yes—I know! (*Business.*) Well, Tilda——

(*She looks up at him as soon as he speaks, which knocks the lines out of his head.*)

MATILDA. Well, Cyrus?

CY P. (*weakening, aside*). 'Tain't no use—I can't do it. She's knocked the first lines of my new speech clean out o' my head. (*Recovering.*) Well, Tildy, as I was going to say—— (*Enter* EB GANZEY. *He crosses slowly, behind well, up, whistling "Devil's Dream," or other tune, in country style.* CY P. *is obviously nervous at the interruption and follows* GANZEY'S *movements till he exits back of house, then he speaks.*) Tildy, what's that Ganzey doin' around here?

MATILDA. Well, he's been helpin' the hired men down in the meadow and chorin' around here.

CY P. Well, I don't s'pose you have to pay him nothin', do you?

MATILDA. Oh, yes! Guess Joshua gives him a little suthin'. Why?

CY P. Well, I should think it would be a pretty tough match to get work enough out o' him to pay for what he eats.

MATILDA. Oh, well, he's growin', you know.

CY P. Growin'! Well, I should think he was! He's longer than a shootin' match! Well, Tildy, I thought I'd come over here today to see if you—that is, I thought I'd come over to ask you if you thought that——Tildy, what kind o'—what kind er ——

(*Re-enter* GANZEY *from above house, whistling softly and with an ear to the dialogue. He has an empty pail —goes to well—draws bucket of water —fills pail, and waits for cue.*)

MATILDA. What kind o' what?

CY P. Paint would you put on a house if you wanted to make it look yaller.

MATILDA. Yaller paint of course!

CY P. Yes, that would be a good idea. Wonder I didn't think of it before.

GANZEY (*from well, taking bucket in hand*). And if you want the house to look green put on green paint. (*Whistles and exits above house.*)

CY P. (*commencing to get angry and watching* GANZEY *off*). Tildy, does that boy whistle all the time?

MATILDA. Pretty much; he's got to be a chronic whistler.

CY P. A comic whistler?

MATILDA. Chronic whistler!

CY P. Oh, yes! A chronic whistler. Well, if he comes fooling around where I be again I'll give him somethin' that'll cure him of his chronicness. (CY P. *continues speaking as he takes soiled paper of speech from packet and gazes at it sideways, unobserved by* MATILDA.) Yes, Tildy, I thought I'd get some yaller paint and put it on my house and make it look yaller; and then I'd get some dark green paint and put on the door and make that look green; and then I'd get a new brass knocker and put that on the front door and make that look brassy; then get a half a dozen new cane seat chairs and put them in the parlor. (*Enter* RICKETY *from house; whispers to* MATILDA *and both exit in house hurriedly.*) I been laying awake pretty nigh all night thinkin' I'd come over here today and ask you to have me for better or worse, there! (*Business of astonishment, etc. Gets up from chair and looks all around for missing* MATILDA.) Well, I guess I'm about as far off as ever and, if anything, a little mite further off, but never mind, I've made up my mind to it and that's all there is about it. (*Sits again.*)

(*Enter* MATILDA *from house and sits in chair.*)

MATILDA. Well, Cyrus, what do you think?

CY P. I don't know, Tilda, what is it?

MATILDA. My cake is all crisp.

CY P. (*aside*). Well, I'm afraid mine is all dough.

MATILDA. That gal has gone and let that cake get all burned up and makes me so plaguey mad!

CY P. Oh, well, I wouldn't get mad if I was you. She couldn't help it,—she was born that way, wasn't she?

MATILDA. But we ain't got no cake in the house. Now what'll folks think on't to see no cake on the table for supper?

CY P. Well, that's a pretty serious question, Tilda, I must confess; but if I was in your place I'd put on plenty of applesass and nut cakes then I don't think they'd miss the cake much. And I was goin' to tell you furthermore, Tilda, I got a new kitchen stove put up in my kitchen, too!

MATILDA. Sho', have yer?

CY P. Yes, the old one is pretty nigh all burned out and I got my old horse and wagon all painted up fresh and my sister Betsy was asking me this very morning what I was gettin' things so all fired slicked up for, so I told her right out plump and plain that I was comin' over here and I was going to say to you——

(*Enter* RICKETY *from house, down steps.*)

RICKETY. Supper is ready. (*Goes up stage and exits above house.*)

CY P. (*aside*). Supper is ready. (*Disgusted.*) So am I pretty nigh ready for the crazy house.

MATILDA (*rising and placing chair at corner of house, down stage*). All right! Cyrus, come now and we'll set right down to supper. (*Exits in house.*)

CY P. Yes, Tilda, but before we go to supper I'd like to git a question o' mine answered. (*Arises from chair disgusted. Places chair by well.*) Now I'd like to know how a man supposed to have his head full of green paint and yaller paint and brass knockers and cane seat chairs—— (GANZEY *whistling outside.* CY P. *goes to where the cucumbers are—picks them up and lays for him.* GANZEY *enters and crosses to go to well, when* CY P. *pelts him with the cucumbers.* GANZEY *runs off, dropping pail at exit.* CY P. *kicks pail and cries.*) Oh!!

(MATILDA *enters from house to foot of step.*)

MATILDA. Well, Cyrus, what's the matter?

CY P. What's the matter? Why, it's all over with me.

MATILDA. Nonsense!

CY P. Yes; I have just kicked the bucket.

MATILDA. Come in to supper.

(*Exit both in house. Re-enter* GANZEY*—looks around cautiously while whistling—picks up pail and goes to well to draw water.*)

MAGGIE (*enters*). Hey, sonny! Mind yourself or you'll fall in the well and spile the water!

GANZEY. That's all right! You're going to catch it!

MAGGIE. And for what?

GANZEY. The cake is all burnt up!

MAGGIE. And what if it is? What have I got to do with it? I can't watch the cake and milk the cows all at one time, can I? I wonder do they think I'm twins? (*Exits in house.*)

(*Enter* QUARTETTE *as farmers, behind house. They cross down to positions at well, leaving rakes and pitchforks up stage.*)

GANZEY (*to* QUARTETTE). Say, boys, you'll have to wait a little while for supper. Uncle Josh has got visitors and the first table is full.

FIRST MAN. That's all right, we're in no hurry. I guess we can wait if you can. (*All laugh.*)

GANZEY (*laughing mockingly*). I can wait as long as any on ye, come right down to it. (*Exits, behind house.*)

FIRST MAN (*drinking water which he dips from bucket*). That tastes good.

I tell you, boys, there's nothing like water out of the bucket in a tin dipper, beats all your tomfool drinks in the country. It's as good as the song —as the old bucket itself. Let's sing it while we're waiting for supper?

(*They sing "Old Oaken Bucket," "Hard Times Come Again No More." During singing of encore* GANZEY *and* RICKETY *enter from above house.* RICKETY *sits on doorstep of house while* GANZEY *stands by water barrel down* R., *looking into it. Extra ladies can enter from above house,* R., *during first song as if they had been berrying. They stand listening and exeunt after singing is over. When* QUARTETTE *finishes it exits back of house.*)

GANZEY. Oh, Rickety, come here!

(*Looking earnestly into barrel.*)

RICKETY (*going to barrel*). What do you want?

GANZEY. Look! There's wigglers in the water barrel.

(*Tramp heard singing "White Wings" off stage.* GANZEY *and* RICKETY *both go up to entrance and look off stage.* GANZEY *runs off up* R. RICKETY *runs toward house until stopped by tramp. Enter* HAPPY JACK.)

RICKETY (*in doorway, startled*). I'll tell Uncle!

JACK. One moment, my pretty gazelle.

RICKETY. What's that?

JACK. Come here.

RICKETY (*timidly*). What do you want?

JACK. I would banquet, fair maid. I'm a prestidigitator.

RICKETY (*awed—dropping down step*). A what-a-ta-tor?

JACK. That is, I make things disappear.

RICKETY (*starts to go in house*). Well, I thought so!

JACK. Stay! For instance, I take a couple of slices of bread thusly—(*Pretends to palm pieces of bread.*) place a piece of cold meat between them, presto change! Gone!

RICKETY. Sho'! That's nothing! Anybody can do that. (*Tries to imitate him.*)

JACK. Well, to be plainly spoken I would eat, ma amie.

RICKETY (*starts to go in house*). No, you won't eat me, nuther!

JACK. Stay! Don't light a fire for me! Just plain every-day bread and a little cold meat will do; don't care for turkey.

RICKETY. Well, you won't get nothin' here. (*Exits in house.*)

JACK. No? Then I'll score my first failure. (*Strikes chest.*) Happy, old boy, how is your high C?

(*Business running scale and breaking into "Nobody's Darling," or other song. At the last strain he crosses to well, as* JOSH *enters from house.* MATILDA *and* RICKETY *enter from house and group at doorstep.*)

JOSH (*amused*). I can't help that.

JACK (*very polite*). Probably you would like something different.

(*Starts "Sixteen Dollars On My Inside Pocket" or other popular air.*)

JOSH. Tut! Tut! I got visitors. I don't want none o' that!

JACK (*very polite*). All right!

JOSH. How'd you get here?

JACK (*laughs*). Came in on a hot wave.

JOSH. Who be you?

JACK (*bows low*). A man without a home; poor, but a gentleman still.

JOSH. You're a tramp I guess, ain't you?

JACK. Well, vulgarly speaking, yes, properly, no!

JOSH. What be you?

JACK. A natural result.

JOSH. Of what?

JACK. Drink!

(MATILDA *throws hands up in horror and quietly exits into house.*)

JOSH. By gum! You look like it!

JACK (*bows low*). Thanks!

JOSH. You seem pretty sober now.

JACK. It's a dead force though, I can assure you.

JOSH. Shouldn't wonder. You've got one thing in your favor, Mr.——

JACK. What is it, sir?

JOSH. You ain't afraid to tell the truth.

JACK (*bows low*). Thank you.

(JACK *crosses to well, "sprucing up."*)

JOSH (*turning to* RICKETY *who has come down to* JOSH). Politer than a pair o' sugar tongs. (*To* JACK.) Git a chair and set down. (*Aside.*) Somethin' good about this fellow if he ain't a hypocrite. If he is, I'll find him out pretty quick.

(JOSH *takes chair and sits.*)

JACK (*has gone above well—looks in—takes dipper—then turns to* JOSH). Old gentleman, can I have a drink?

JOSH. Certainly, help yourself—pitch right in.

JACK. Won't you join me?

(*Business, laughs—drinks mouthful—makes face.*)

JOSH. That's pretty good—out o' my own well, too. What's the matter? Don't like it, do you?

JACK. Well, it tastes a little weak.

JOSH. 'Tain't quite so strong as you're used to drinking.

JACK. You struck it right the first time, old gentleman.

(*Turns water from dipper into bucket by well and puts dipper in bucket. Takes chair by well and placing it by* JOSH, *sits.*)

JOSH. I thought so. Now, are you hungry?

JACK. Well, I think I could manage to eat a tart if it were not too large.

RICKETY (*back of* JOSH). Well, if that ain't cheek. Guess I'd better shut up the hens. (*Starts to cross up entrance.*)

JOSH (*stopping her—she comes back to* JOSH *with a suspicious eye on* JACK). Here, Rick, come here. You go and tell Aunt Tildy to git a couple slices o' bread and butter and bring them here.

(RICKETY *starts for house slowly.*)

JACK (*rising—to* RICKETY). Skip!

(*Exit* RICKETY *quickly.* JACK *coughs as* JOSH *is stooping to look at* JACK'S *boots.* JACK *coughs violently over him, at which* JOSH, *rising, jumps away and puts handkerchief over top of head as if to protect himself.*)

JOSH. You got a cold, ain't you?

JACK (*coughing*). Yes, a slight one. Guess I must have left the bars down last night.

JOSH. Where did you stop?

JACK. At Widow Green's. (*Crossing to front of well.*)

JOSH. At Widow Green's?

JACK. Yes.

JOSH (*innocently*). I don't know no Widow Green around here.

JACK (*advancing to* JOSH.) Why, my dear old unsophisticated——

JOSH. Here, here! That'll do!

JACK. We knights of the road call a hay field "Widow Green."

JOSH. Oh, you do, do you?

JACK. Yes, I guess I must have crawled in the north side of a stack last night. The fact is, I am getting heedless of late. (*Feeling inside coat pocket as if he had cigarettes.*) Haven't got a cigarette about you, have you?

JOSH. No, sir, I don't smoke.

(*Decisively, as he sits.*)

JACK. Quite right—it's a pernicious habit, anyways. The fact is I only smoke occasionally.

(JACK *sits in his chair.*)

JOSH. Well, why don't you carry a pipe?

JACK. No; it makes your clothes smell.

JOSH. I guess you're kind of a comic, ain't you?

JACK. Well, there's no use crying over spilt milk, so I use a little philosophy now and then.

JOSH. Philosophy is all well enough in sunshine; but I should think you would want something a little more substantial in rough weather.

JACK. You're right there, old gentleman.

JOSH. Do you know, I often wonder how you fellows get along?

JACK. Yes?

JOSH. And what you think of, if you ever do think. What your aim in life is.

JACK (*rising and walking to well and turning*). Well, I merely log along, grab on when I can. I'm acclimated and adjusted to all countries and climes, whether in the everglades of Florida or on the snowy ranges of the Sierras, it's all the same. (*Pause, as he crosses back to chair—puts* R. *foot on same—and chants the remainder of speech.*) I'm often drunk and seldom sober, win or lose I take my booze, for I'm Happy Jack the rover.

JOSH. Well, I declare! You are a good one to speak a piece! I guess you're a good deal like a singed cat:—you feel better than you look.

JACK (*laughing*). That's a good one, old gentleman. Well, there's no use denying what everybody can see, is there?

JOSH. No, that's so.

JACK (*looking in front of him as if he sees coin, then picks it up*). Is this yours?

JOSH. What is it?

JACK. A ten-cent piece.

JOSH. Guess not. Ain't in the habit of carrying money around loose in my pockets. Maybe you dropped it yourself?

JACK (*feeling in side pockets*). No, my money is all right. I might have lost my reputation or a trifle like that; but ten cents? Never!

JOSH. Never mind, keep it—it might come in handy.

JACK (*sitting down*). Why, what would that little thing buy?

JOSH. A bar of soap.

JACK. Say, old gentleman, what are you trying to give me anyway?

JOSH. A little advice.

JACK. A little advice, eh?

JOSH. Yes, sir.

JACK. Advice is good. Say, did you ever try to live on it?

JOSH. Don't know as I ever did.

JACK. Well, try it, and you will find it an excellent substitute for anti-fat.

JOSH. What's your name?

JACK. Jack.

JOSH. Jack what?

JACK. Happy Jack.

JOSH. By gosh! It fits you, don't it?

JACK (*laughs*). Like a glove.

JOSH. Where do you come from?

JACK. Nowhere.

JOSH. Where do you live?

JACK. Everywhere.

JOSH. Sho'! I want to know!

JACK. I am the champion deadhead of America, the star truck rider of the world.

(*Rises, takes off hat, bows and sits again.*)

JOSH. What do you mean by that?

JACK. That I ride from one end of the country to the other, without a dollar.

JOSH. What on?

JACK. The cars.

JOSH. Don't they put you off?

JACK. They don't see me.

JOSH. What's the reason they don't?

JACK. I ride underneath on the trucks.

JOSH. O-ho!

JACK. I don't travel on a train unless they run a sleeper. (JOSH *whistles low in surprise.*) They are better than common passenger cars—the trucks are wider and more comfortable and don't come quite so near your head.

JOSH. By gum! It must be pretty risky business, ain't it?

(*Music cue for sympathetic music pp. in orchestra.*)

JACK (*with pathos*). Yes. Not a day passes that some poor fellow is not either killed or maimed. Now last winter on our way south, my partner lost his life. I was riding on the rear truck and he was on the front. In rounding a curve the brace of the truck bent and caught him between the truck and the brace and mashed him to death. I had to ride nearly thirty-two miles listening to his pitiful cries for help but I couldn't reach him, so he said: "Jack, old pard, you'll have to get another pal. I'm called in," and all was over with poor Tom. A higher power had put on the brakes. The engine of life was stopped.

(*Buries face in old dirty handkerchief. Enter* MATILDA *from house with two slices of bread, gives them to* JOSH *and exit into house.*)

JOSH. Here, here!

(JOSH *rises, handing bread to* JACK, *and sits again.*)

JACK (*rises and takes bread and puts in pocket as he speaks*). Thank you; I will not eat this now.

JOSH. Are your parents living?

JACK (*wipes eyes with handkerchief*). One of them, sir.

JOSH. Which one?

JACK. My mother.

(*Crossing a few steps to hide emotion.*)

JOSH. Where?

JACK. In New York City.

JOSH. Poor?

JACK. No, sir, rich.

JOSH. Why, what made you leave home?

JACK. Simply because I couldn't have my own way.

JOSH. Well, you look as though you had had it lately. Now, why don't you go home?

JACK. Have you any sons?

JOSH. Yes, sir—one.

JACK. Where?

JOSH. In New York, I believe; he was there the last time I heard on him.

JACK (*crossing back to chair*). Well, why doesn't he come home?

JOSH. Now by gosh! You have got me!

JACK. I'll tell you why I don't go home. Because I'm ashamed to! I'm no good—a wreck at thirty—look fifty, don't I?

JOSH. Pretty near.

JACK. Yes.

JOSH. Do you ever think?

JACK. Think of what?

JOSH (*with pathos*). Your mother. How she watched you all through the cares and dangers of childhood; worked for you; prayed for you. I tell you, boy, you owe that mother more than you can ever repay. Her care may have saved your life a dozen times—you can't tell.

JACK (*sits, penitently, with lowered head*). Say, old gentleman, you've set me thinking.

JOSH. I'm glad of it if I have. Now look here, will you go home if I give you money enough to pay your fare?

JACK. Yes.

JOSH. And stop drinking?

JACK. Whew! Say, old gentleman, that's a corker, but I'll try it. (*Rising and putting chair back by well then coming resolutely back to* JOSH.)

JOSH. All right, sir—there's a ten-dollar bill. (*Gives ten-dollar bill to* JACK.) It won't break me and it may make you. You can take a train and go as far as New Haven, then take a boat and be home in the morning.

JACK. Ten dollars, eh? (*Music stops.*)

JOSH. Yes, sir.

JACK (*reflectively and with wonder*). Ten great big dollars! Say, old gentleman, if you had set the dog on me it would have been more in my way.

JOSH. Why, what good would that do?

JACK. Oh, no good! It would seem more natural, that's all.

JOSH. I suppose so, poor fellow.

JACK (*starts up stage musingly*). Go home, yes! Stop drinking? (*Returns to* JOSH, *who still sits.*) Say, old gentleman—(*offering money to* JOSH.)—you had better take this money back. I don't honestly believe I can do as I have agreed.

JOSH (*rising*). Well, you can try, can't you?

JACK. Yes, I can try.

JOSH (*putting hand on* JACK'S *shoulder*). That's right! Go home and try to be somebody, it ain't too late.

JACK (*with determination*). Well, I will! And if I don't win, I'll give old

John Barleycorn the toughest scuffle he ever had for the underhold. Good-by, old friend, good-by!

(*Shakes hand and exits, walking as if footsore.*)

JOSH. Good-by, sir! (*Sits in chair, reflecting.*) Maybe I have done a foolish thing. Well, never mind—if he don't profit by it, it won't be my fault. But I kind of think he will. A man who can express so much feeling at another's misfortune must have a kind heart.

(*Pause, as* JOSH *gazes meditatively in front and the mixed quartette off stage sing "Oh, Where Is My Boy Tonight?" pp., then gradually f. till finish of song and slow.*)

CURTAIN

ACT TWO

SCENE—*A parlor of the* HOPKINS' *mansion, New York City. An opening, or arch, at back through which is seen a corridor. In the center of the corridor stands a large statue of Venus of Melos on a pedestal. The statue is flanked by palms, or flowering plants. Up stage, in the wall to the right of the audience, a door leads off to the smoking and billiard room. In the opposite wall is another door. A sofa, or divan, with pillows occupies the center of the room and back of it stands a library table with books, papers, a shaded lamp and a tap bell. In front of sofa lies a white, or black, bear rug. Down stage stands a piano and stool. An easy, or armchair, stands beside piano and a trifle above. A footrest, without legs, upholstered in the same material is in front of the armchair. Above the piano a standing piano lamp with shade. There is a so-called "self-rocker" rocking chair with a small table on which is a vase of flowers. Near by is a reception-hall chair. At back of arch, a bookcase and a writing desk and chair. Pictures on walls. Curtains on arch. Flowers in vases. The whole set symbolizes refined taste and culture.*

(*At rise of curtain* MRS. HOPKINS *is seated at piano playing.* MR. HENRY HOPKINS *reclines on sofa, or divan, reading New York paper.* FRANCOIS, *dressed in livery, enters with a card on tray, and coming down presents same to* MRS. HOPKINS. *She stops playing—looks at card and replaces it on tray. As* FRANCOIS *exits,* MRS. HOPKINS *rises.*)

HENRY H. (*rising—folds paper and throws it on table back of sofa*). Who is it, Lizzie?

MRS. H. Judge Patterson and his daughter.

HENRY H. Oh, I am glad of that. I was thinking of the Judge just a moment ago. I want his opinion regarding some real estate I think of purchasing.

(HENRY H. *awaiting arrivals. Enter* NELLIE PATTERSON *and* JUDGE PATTERSON. MRS. HOPKINS, *on their entrance, goes up stage, kisses* NELLIE *and shakes hands with* JUDGE. MRS.

H. *and* NELLIE *stand up stage until* JUDGE P. *and* HENRY H. *sit.)*

JUDGE P. (*as he enters*). Good evening, Mrs. Hopkins.

MRS. H. Good evening, Judge.

HENRY H. Well, Judge, how are you?

JUDGE P. (*coming down to* HENRY H.) Splendid. We have just returned from a drive through the park and Nellie insisted upon calling to see if Frank and Annie had returned.

HENRY H. I am very glad you did, as I desire your opinion respecting that 85th Street property belonging to the Lennox estate.

(*Business:* JUDGE P. *sits on reception chair and* HENRY H., *drawing chair from writing desk, sits beside him.)*

MRS. H. (*coming down with* NELLIE P.—*sitting on divan.*) We received a dispatch from the children this morning. They will be home this evening. The coachman has driven to the station to meet them—expect them every moment.

NELLIE P. (*sits by* MRS. HOPKINS). Why, how long have they been absent? A week or more, is it not?

MRS. H. A fortnight yesterday and how we have missed them!

NELLIE P. I am sure you must have! How tanned Annie will be! I do so long to see her!

(*Doorbell rings off stage.)*

MRS. H. That must be the children. Henry, they are here! (MRS. HOPKINS *and* NELLIE *rise at sound of bell.* MRS. HOPKINS *turns and goes up stage to arch. Enter* FRANK H. *and* ANNIE H. ANNIE H. *kisses* MRS. HOPKINS *followed by* FRANK H. HENRY H. *and* JUDGE P. *rise at their entrance.* ANNIE H. *kisses* HENRY H. *and bows to* JUDGE P. *and* NELLIE P. *—then back to* MRS. HOPKINS *who leads her down to divan* C., *speaking as they go, and sit.* FRANK H. *crosses and sits by* NELLIE P.: NELLIE P. *on piano stool and* FRANK H. *in armchair.* MRS. HOPKINS *at* L. *of* ANNIE H.—*on sofa.*) Now then, Annie, come tell me. What kind of a time did you have?

ANNIE H. Just lovely!

MRS. H. And how is dear old Matilda?

ANNIE H. She's splendid.

HENRY H. And Uncle Joshua?

JOSH (*outside*). How do you git in here, anyway?

FRANK H. Here he is—he can answer for himself.

ANNIE H. We brought him with us. He is awfully odd but you can't help liking him, he's so good. (*Going up stage to door and looking off.*) No, no;—not upstairs; this way, Uncle Josh.

JOSH (*coming on, taking* ANNIE H.'S *hand in his.*) I hain't got the hang o' the schoolhouse yit, but I'll fetch it. Annie, you got visitors, hain't ye?

(*At entrance of* JOSH MRS. HOPKINS, NELLIE P. *and* FRANK H. *rise.)*

ANNIE H. This is my father, Uncle.

(*Introducing.* HENRY H. *goes up and shakes hands heartily.* ANNIE H. *stands up, talking to* JUDGE P.)

JOSH. You ain't Henry Hopkins—Hank Hopkins, Redheaded Hank!

HENRY H. (*laughs*). Yes, the very same.

JOSH (*shaking hands warmly*). How de-do? Glad to see ye.

HENRY H. (*comes down stage to sofa, introducing*). My wife.

JOSH (*comes to sofa, shaking hands with* MRS. HOPKINS). I want to know if you are Henry's wife?

MRS. H. (*in front of sofa.*) Yes, Mr. Whitcomb.

JOSH. Let me see,—you was a Richardson, warn't ye?

MRS. H. Yes, Mr. Whitcomb.

JOSH. Betsy Richardson!

MRS. H. (*haughtily*). Elizabeth Richardson!

JOSH. Yes, I remember we used to call you Bets for short. I can remember the first time I ever saw you just as well as if 'twas yisterday.

(FRANK H. *crosses* R. *and joins* JUDGE. ANNIE H. *leaves, crosses, and stands with* NELLIE P., *below piano.*)

MRS. H. Indeed!

JOSH. Yes. You druv down to the store with your father on a load of wood. (MRS. HOPKINS *is very much mortified but appears pleased when he speaks of her good looks.*) I never will forget how pretty you looked that day in your new calico frock and sunbonnet and new yarn stockings, hanging down over that load of maple.

(*Business:* MRS. HOPKINS *appears very much annoyed.* FRANK H. *leaves* JUDGE P. *and goes down stage hurriedly and takes* JOSH *by left arm and leads him up to where the* JUDGE *stands.* HENRY H. *laughs heartily, which angers* MRS. HOPKINS *who crosses in front of him and seats herself.* HENRY *follows her and stands behind her chair and tries to pacify her.*)

FRANK H. (*introducing*). Judge Patterson, Mr. Whitcomb.

JUDGE P. (*shakes hands*). How do you do?

JOSH (*comes down stage, with* JUDGE P. *Shakes hands*). How de-do? (*Thinking.*) Let me see, you ain't any relation of old John Patterson that used to keep the soap factory at Chesterfield, be you?

(FRANK H. *stands by library table.*)

JUDGE P. (*laughs*). No, sir——

JOSH. Well, but I didn't know but what you was.

JUDGE P. No, sir; no, sir!

(*Sits.*)

JOSH (*turns, looks up casually and suddenly sees the statue of Venus. He stares at statue*). Henry——

HENRY H. Well?

JOSH. Was she a New York lady before she died?

(*All laugh heartily.* JOSH *stands talking with* JUDGE P. L.)

MRS. H. (*annoyed*). Henry, for goodness' sake, take him away or I shall grow frantic.

HENRY. Where shall I take him? (*Laughing.*)

MRS. H. Anywhere—to the stables!

JOSH. What's that about stables? What kind of a barn hev you got anyway, Henry?

HENRY H. A perfect beauty! Would you like to have a look at it?

JOSH. Sartin. I wanted to help your man onharness and fodder but he said he guessed he could do it all right. (*Looking to* MRS. HOPKINS.) They won't be mad if Henry and I go out to the barn, will they?

MRS. H. (*sarcastically*). No; I don't think they will!

(*Sitting on sofa.*)

JOSH. Well, I hope not. Frank, look out for my trunk.

FRANK H. (*standing by table*). I'll attend to that, Uncle.

JOSH. Hev you milked yet?

HENRY H. (*laughs*). Oh, long ago! Come along with me, I'll show you a beautiful barn. (*They exit.*)

JUDGE P. (*rises—crosses to sofa and sits.* FRANK H. *comes to sofa and stands*). Oh, there, never mind, Mrs. Hopkins—don't feel annoyed. We understand your position perfectly; let us treat it in the proper spirit. I know it's terribly embarrassing but it's awfully funny. (*Laughing.*)

MRS. H. (*seated on sofa*). Well, I suppose I might as well laugh as cry. (*Laughs.*)

JUDGE P. Certainly. But it's too funny for anything, isn't it? (*Laughs.*)

ANNIE H. Frank and I are really to blame. Ma and Pa knew nothing of his coming. We brought him with us because he wanted to see New York, and to find his son who left his home about a year ago. He has not heard from him for a long time and the fear that something had happened to him constantly worried him. He didn't look half so funny in the country.

JUDGE P. I suppose not.

FRANK H. And, Mother, we wished to surprise you with old recollections.

MRS. H. (*rising*). You have been entirely successful. (*All laugh.*)

ANNIE H. Come, Nellie, I have so much to tell you about Swanzey and Chesterfield.

(*Exit* NELLIE P. *and* ANNIE H., *followed by* MRS. HOPKINS *through arch.*)

FRANK H. (*to* JUDGE P.). Now, Judge, won't you come with me into the smoking room and join me in a cigar?

JUDGE P. (*rising*). The very thing, my boy. "Was she a New York lady before she died?"

(JUDGE P. *and* FRANK H. *exeunt door laughing. Hearty laughter heard off stage as* HENRY H. *and* JOSH *enter.*)

JOSH. I knowed you'd laugh when I told you about it. (*Looking around.*) Hello! Where's all the visitors gone?

HENRY H. Oh, they are about the house somewhere. Come, Joshua, sit down.

(HENRY H. *sits on divan offering* JOSH *a seat.*)

JOSH. You don't set on that, do you?

HENRY. H. Why, certainly.

JOSH. Go 'long—it'll spile it, won't it?

HENRY H. (*rising*). No—no.

JOSH. No danger of going through, is there?

HENRY H. No—no. (JOSH *sits down and then jumps up suddenly.*) What's the matter?

JOSH. Gosh! I thought I sot on a cat.

HENRY H. (*laughs; and both sit*). Well, Joshua, I suppose the old farms at Swanzey are pretty well worn out by this time?

JOSH. Well, the yield ain't quite so good as they used to be, and it's ben a leetle worse this year than ever. Then we hev had a good deal to contend with—the season's been dry and we've had two circuses and a balloon ascension, and a wrestling match, and one thing and another; and old Abe Hill always contended such things hurt crops worse than grasshoppers.

HENRY H. Joshua, is the old meetin' house there yet?

JOSH. The main part on't is—they got it raised up; new stained windows in, new belfry on, and one thing and another, so it don't look much as it did when you and I had our marriages published on the front of it.

HENRY H. No, I suppose not. Is the old house still standing?

JOSH. Our old house?

HENRY H. Yes.

JOSH. Jest the same. You remember the old kitchen, don't you?

HENRY H. Indeed I do.

JOSH. And that old fireplace where you and I and brother Bill and Eb and Dad Cross used to sit around cold winter nights, when we was boys popping corn and telling Injun stories.

HENRY H. (*laughing*). And we used to get so frightened we were almost afraid to go to bed.

JOSH. Bill was a master hand to tell stories, warn't he?

HENRY H. Indeed he was. Tell me, Joshua, are the Shaw boys living?

JOSH. All dead—every one o' them.

HENRY H. You don't say so!

JOSH. Yes.

HENRY H. And the Pattersons?

JOSH. All living but Bill and I guess he'd 'a' ben if he'd 'a' stayed to home.

HENRY H. How is that?

JOSH. Well, Bill always had a kind o' roving turn o' mind and he got oneasy and went out west somewhere, out to Montany I guess it was; and he got tangled up with politics and whiskey and a piece of rope and kind o' discouraged him a leetle mite. Henry, I guess you must remember the Divine boys?

HENRY H. (*thinking*). Divine boys?

JOSH. You must remember the youngest—Deuteronomy?

HENRY. Yes. Of course I do.

JOSH. Well, he got a new glass eye.

HENRY H. (*laughs*). NO!

JOSH. Yep—don't wear it only Sundays though. (HENRY H. *laughs.*) You see, Deut. lost an eye during the war and he never felt able to get one till t'other day he went up to Keene and got one o' the jewelers to send down to Boston and get him one. When he got it home it didn't fit very well—was a leetle mite too big I guess. However he put it in his eye and started for meetin' the fust Sunday he got it and he come pretty near breaking the meetin' up before he got home.

HENRY H. How was that?

JOSH. Well, it appears Deut. got to sleep during sarvice and commenced to snore.

HENRY H. Yes.

JOSH. And old Mrs. Munsel sot in the pew right in front him and she turned around to nudge him and there was Deut. fast asleep, one eye shut and the new one wide open. (*Both laugh heartily.*) Scart the old woman so she squawked right out in meetin', like a guinea hen.

HENRY H. I don't suppose Deut. ever wore it again.

JOSH. Oh, yes, he did—he took it to the blacksmith's and got it filed down and it works fust rate now.

HENRY H. Oh, go along! (*Shoving* JOSH *with left hand.*) Joshua, whatever became of Nick Ludlow?

JOSH. Dead.

HENRY H. No! (*Surprised.*)

JOSH. Yes; died last April.

HENRY H. You don't say so! What complaint?

JOSH. No complaint—everybody satisfied. (HENRY H. *laughs heartily.*) Now, Henry, I'm going to ask you suthin' jest to see if you remember it.

HENRY H. (*turns half back to* JOSH). Well, go on.

JOSH. Now look out!

HENRY H. Well, I'm waiting for you.

JOSH. Do you remember the first circus you and I ever went to see?

(*Both laugh heartily—*JOSH *falls back on divan—then recovers himself;*

rubs top of head with both hands and then sinks back laughing as though he was exhausted from laughing.)

HENRY H. (*laughing*). And how we laughed at the old clown!

JOSH. And et ginger bread!

HENRY H. Yes.

JOSH. Henry, do you remember that?

HENRY H. Remember it? I shall never forget it as long as I can remember anything.

JOSH. Me nuther! I spent forty-one cents that day!

HENRY H. We went together, don't you remember?

JOSH. So we did!

HENRY H. I called for you at your house.

JOSH. There! That's right.

HENRY H. It was the first you ever wore a roundabout suit.

JOSH (*proudly*). So it was!

HENRY H. Oh, you were dressed to kill that day!

JOSH. Gosh! I guess I was! You had on a new store hat and I had to wear the old one Till braided. You beat me on the hat but I kind o' cut you out on the clothes. (*Chucks* HENRY H. *in ribs—both laugh.*)

HENRY H. Yes.

JOSH. Both on us barefoot.

HENRY H. Yes, both of us.

(JOSH *gives* HENRY H. *affectionate shove.)*

HENRY H. And away we both started for Keene and the circus. (*With pathos*) and don't you remember, Joshua, that when we got on top of that little hill, near Jackson's, we looked back and there was your dear old mother, standing in the doorway. (*Rising and folding his hands in pantomime.*) Her hands wound up in her apron, with her head thrown back, the way she had a way of doing, looking at us through her big, bowed spectacles, wondering, I suppose, which one of us would be president first. (*Sitting down.*)

JOSH (*with feeling, shaking hands with* HENRY H. *and looking over glasses*). Happy days, Henry!

HENRY H. Happy, indeed, Joshua.

JOSH (*with pathos*). No use talking, children little know the anxiety parents have for them. I've got a boy all alone in this great city and I'm dreadfully worried about him.

HENRY H. Don't you know where he is stopping?

JOSH. No, I don't.

HENRY H. And hasn't he written you?

JOSH. Not for four or five months.

HENRY H. Oh, well—we must hunt him up for you. What was he doing when you last heard from him?

JOSH. He warn't doin' nothin'. Said he expected to get something to do before long and writ a little mite as though he was discouraged. And when I answered I guessed he'd better come back again;—but you know how it is with boys when they go away from home to make their living, they hate to come back and have folks say they warn't smart enough to do it; and Reub is kind o' proud-spirited. I don't know as I blame him much,—like as not he's out o' money, —maybe he's sick and perhaps he's——

(*Puts handkerchief to eyes and completely breaks down.*)

HENRY H. (*patting* JOSH *on back soothingly*). Come, come—old friend, this won't do—cheer up! We'll find him for you yet.

JOSH (*brightening*). Think so?

HENRY H. I know it.

JOSH (*grasping* HENRY H.'S *hand warmly*). Henry, I'll sleep all the better tonight for them few words of encouragement.

HENRY H. I hope so.

JOSH (*wiping eyes*). I feel sure on't.

HENRY H. By the way, Joshua, I had almost forgotten to ask you if you had your supper yet.

JOSH. No; I don't want any nuther. I ate two plates of beans at Springfield as I come along, and besides my carpet-bag is about half full of nut cakes, and I have been nibbling on them the biggest part of the way. Henry, I ain't very particular about my eatin' but if you could manage it, so I can sleep somewhere near the earth, I would like it fust rate. The fact on it is, I am a leetle mite skittish about fires, and I'd like to be where I can step right out in case of a flare-up. I am a poor hand to shin down a lightning rod.

HENRY H. (*laughs lightly*). Oh, well, we can arrange that for you very readily; you can sleep in my private office right on the ground floor here. (*Pointing at door down* L.)

JOSH. No; can I though?

HENRY H. Yes.

JOSH. That'll suit me fust rate. (HENRY H. *reaches back and strikes gong on table.* JOSH *is startled.*) Gosh! It ain't one o'clock, is it?

HENRY H. (*laughs*). One o'clock! What an idea!

(FRANCOIS *enters and comes and stands on* HENRY H.'S R. JOSH *on seeing* FRANCOIS *rises and bows very low to him.* HENRY H. *astonished—sees him bow—rises and pushes* JOSH *back gently on divan.*)

FRANCOIS. Yis, sur!

HENRY H. Where is Mrs. Hopkins? (*Sitting.*)

FRANCOIS. In the library, sur.

HENRY H. Very well. Tell Christina to have the folding bed in my private office let down for Mr. Whitcomb, who will occupy that room tonight.

FRANCOIS. Yis, sur!

JOSH (*watching him off*). Who is that, Henry?

HENRY H. My servant, Francois.

JOSH. Gosh! I thought it was some foreign lord!

HENRY H. (*laughs*). Oh, no; oh, no!

(*Doorbell rings.*)

JOSH. Got his trousers gallused up pretty high, ain't he?

HENRY H. He has indeed.

JOSH. Outgrowed them a leetle mite, I guess.

HENRY H. It looks like it, very much.

(*Re-enter* FRANCOIS C., *same business as before—presenting card on tray.*)

JOSH. There's the plate! Meetin's commenced.

(*Dives in pocket for change.* HENRY H. *sees mistake, takes card, laughing.* JOSH *also sees mistake—covers face with handkerchief and leans back against divan.* HENRY H. *looks at card.*)

HENRY H. Commissioner Nichols, eh?

FRANCOIS. Yis, sur. He says he won't detain you but a moment if you will jist step to the door.

HENRY H. Very well. (*To* JOSH.) Excuse me, Joshua, for a minute. (*Rises.*) I have a little private business to transact and will join you presently. (*Exit.*)

JOSH. That's all right, Henry. Frenchy and I will visit here. (*To* FRANCOIS.) Come, sit down.

FRANCOIS. No, sur! It's against the rules.

JOSH. What's agin the rules?

FRANCOIS. To sit down.

JOSH (*jumping up*). I want to know! It ain't agin the rules for me to stand up and talk to you a little while, is it?

FRANCOIS. No, sur!

JOSH (*going to* FRANCOIS). We ain't got very well acquainted, hev we?

(*Striking* FRANCOIS *playfully with handkerchief.*)

FRANCOIS. Well, not very well, sur.

JOSH. What's your politics?

FRANCOIS. What do you think?

JOSH. Well, I'm a leetle mite divided in my opinions. (*Places handkerchief across* FRANCOIS'S *throat.*) From here down, (*Business*) you look like a Republican; but from here up you look like a Democrat.

FRANCOIS. Now I'll lay you can't tell what I am, and I'll give you two guesses.

JOSH. I bet I can.

FRANCOIS. Well, go on then.

JOSH. You're a Democrat.

FRANCOIS. No, sur!

JOSH. Republican?

FRANCOIS (*approaching* JOSH—*whispering*). Hi-ber-ni-an!

JOSH (*surprised*). Well, that's the first one o' them critters I've seen. What makes you wear your trousers so short?

FRANCOIS. Shure an' they make me!

JOSH. Who makes you?

FRANCOIS. The boss.

JOSH. Must be pretty rough on you in fly time.

FRANCOIS. Faith an' you're a funny man, Mr. Whitecomb.

JOSH. Whitecomb? My name is Whitcomb!

FRANCOIS. Fitcomb!

JOSH. Gosh! If I didn't know you was French, I'd think you was Irish.

FRANCOIS. Oui-oui; certe mong!

JOSH. Hello, hello! What kind of lingo is that?

FRANCOIS. Shure, that's Frinch. I do be hearin' so much o' that kind o' talk I don't often know whether I am a New York French Irishman or an Irish French Canadian New Yorker, or a Bulgarian.

JOSH. Well, you'll get so mixed up some o' these days, they will have to run you through a separating machine. (*Accidentally puts hand on gong on table—jumps back surprised; then walks slowly up stage until he sees statuette; then jumps away.*) Now I don't want to ask any foolish questions but I would like to know what they hev got that wax figger stuck up there for?

FRANCOIS. Werra, man, dear—that's not wax, that's alabaster marble.

JOSH. I want to know!

FRANCOIS. Why, certainly!

JOSH. What do you do with it when the minister comes?

FRANCOIS. We don't do nothin' at all with it.

JOSH. You don't?

FRANCOIS. No, sur!

JOSH. I'll bet ten dollars if I put that up in my cornfield I would be arrested before night. (*Exit servant.*) It's darn lucky I didn't bring Matilda with me, she'd put for home jest as soon as she see any sich sight as that. (*Enter* HENRY H.)

HENRY H. (*putting hand on* JOSH'S *right shoulder*). Joshua, wouldn't you like to join us in the smoking room and have a little chat before you retire?

JOSH (*winding old-fashioned watch*). No; I guess not, Henry. I'm kind o' tired and sleepy and I'll go to bed so as to be up bright and arly and look for Reub, you know.

HENRY H. Is there anything I can do for you before going?

JOSH. Let me see—yes, you can ask your hired man if he won't bring my trunk up into my room—wish you would,—if he ain't too busy.

(HENRY H. *goes to table, strikes bell and rejoins* JOSH. *Enter* FRANCOIS. *Comes down and stands, awaiting.*)

HENRY H. (*laughs*). Have Mr. Whitcomb's trunk brought up immediately.

FRANCOIS. Yis, sur. (*Exits.*)

HENRY H. Now, Joshua, excuse me a moment or two and I'll see you before you retire.

JOSH. That's all right, Henry, I want to look around here a little while before I go to bed, anyway. (*Exit* HENRY H. JOSH *observes square footrest in front of armchair, upholstered in same material as the furniture. He looks about and sees all chairs supplied with cushions except the reception chair above* L. *door.*) Somebody must have knocked the cushion out of one of the chairs.

(*He picks up footrest and, crossing, places it in reception chair and, as he gapes about, exits. Enter* FRANCOIS, *followed by a porter with old-fashioned trunk on shoulder.* FRANCOIS *stands while porter deposits trunk in* JOSH's *room, then both exeunt. Enter* JOSH *in shirt sleeves, looking about as if in search for something. A slight pause and* HENRY H., JUDGE P. *and* FRANK H. *enter*—HENRY H. *preceding.*)

HENRY H. Well, Judge, you're not going so soon?

JUDGE P. Am very sorry but we must be going.

HENRY H. (*crossing to* JOSH. *Astonished, going and putting hand on* JOSH's *shoulder*). Why, Joshua, what are you doing here?

(FRANK H. *stands back of table.*)

JOSH. I'm looking for a boot-jack. (*All laugh.*) There! I suppose I've made some mistake agin. (*Sits on "self-rocker." It tips forward with him and he falls on floor. Gets up, sits way back, and falls backward. Chair and all is caught behind by two foot high stool.* FRANK H. *runs to his assistance each time he falls and helps him up. All laugh.*) Henry, rears up like a two-year-old, don't it? I know what I'd do with it if 'twas mine.

HENRY H. What?

JOSH. Put martin gills on it.

HENRY H. Joshua, we don't use boot-jacks here.

(*All laugh.*)

JOSH (*still sitting in chair*). You don't?

HENRY H. No.

JOSH. How do you get your boots off?

HENRY H. We have them made so they will come off easy.

JOSH. Well, that is what our shoemaker never learnt yet. (*Crosses legs and holds up boot.*) Henry, straddle that boot—why, you've done it lots o' times. (HENRY H. *appears surprised at first, then, remembering old times, crosses to* JOSH, *turns his back*—JOSH *puts his foot between* HENRY H.'S *legs and braces himself on* HENRY

H.'s *back. Same business with other foot. When boots off,* HENRY H. *crosses to* JUDGE P. *and places hand on* JUDGE P.'s *shoulder who is watching actions.* FRANK H. *by divan. All laughing heartily.* JOSH *picks up boot, crosses, and steps on white bear rug which tickles his foot and jumps off hurriedly and stands looking at* JUDGE P.) What's the matter, Judge? That's the fust boot-jack you ever see like that, I guess, ain't it?

JUDGE P. (*laughing heartily*). No; but it's the first one I have seen in a great many years.

JOSH. I suppose so. Some good leather in them boots, Henry.

HENRY H. Yes.

JOSH. Now I'm all ready to tumble into bed.

HENRY H. (*crossing to* JOSH). That's right.

JOSH. You tell the women folks I got kind o' sleepy and went to bed, won't you?

HENRY H. Certainly.

JOSH. Might as well leave a sasser o' taller alongside o' the fireplace. I may want to grease my boots before you get up in the morning.

HENRY H. All right.

JOSH. Good night, Judge. (*Exit.*)

HENRY H. Good night. Hope you will sleep soundly. Now, Frank, tell your mother to come in. (FRANK H. *exits through arch.*) Dear old Joshua, he is the very embodiment of honesty and rural simplicity.

JUDGE P. (*crosses back of* HENRY H.). He is indeed, Henry.

(*Enter* ANNIE H. *followed by* NELLIE P., MRS. HOPKINS *and* FRANK H. FRANK H. *and* MRS. HOPKINS *remain at back.* NELLIE P. *sits on sofa.* ANNIE H. *crosses.*)

ANNIE H. Well, Father, how do you like Uncle Josh?

HENRY H. (*crossing to* ANNIE H.). First rate, daughter—first rate! I like a man, I don't care what shape he is.

ANNIE H. (*taking* HENRY H.'s *hand*). Thank you. (*Sits on piano stool.*)

NELLIE P. Father, don't you think it is time we said good night?

JUDGE P. Presently, dear.

HENRY H. (*looking at watch*). Why this haste? It is scarcely ten.

JUDGE P. (*going to* HENRY H.). Henry, call at the house some time next week and we will look at the Lennox property together.

HENRY H. Very well, what day do you propose?

JUDGE P. Say Tuesday.

HENRY H. There! That will suit me to a T. Now, Judge, before you go will you oblige me by singing my old favorite?

JUDGE P. Certainly, Henry.

HENRY H. Thank you.

JUDGE P. (*going and standing by piano*). Miss Annie, will you kindly play for me?

ANNIE H. Why, certainly. What shall I play?

JUDGE P. Your father's favorite.

(ANNIE H. *plays accompaniment of song while* JUDGE P. *sings.*)

"The hush of midnight weaves its spell—
In peace the throbbing city lies;
When lo!—afar, a distant bell
Gives echo through the wintry skies.
'Awake!' 'Awake!' the warning tolls,
There's danger lurking—dread and dire—
'Awake!' 'Awake!' the warning rolls:
'The town's a-fire!' 'The town's a-fire!'

Chorus

"Lo! the engines clang and the pulsing roar
Of a thousand throats rise higher and higher;
Till the welkin swells with clamorous bells
Of 'Fire!'—'Fire!'—'Fire!'"

(*During the course of the song, when* JUDGE P. *sings "Fire!"—"Fire!"—"Fire!"* JOSH *enters in his night dress, boots in right hand, dragging his trunk with his left, shouting "Fire!" at the top of his voice.* HENRY H. *runs in front of him to stop him.* FRANK H. *catches hold of the end of his trunk, holding* JOSH *back who is struggling to get out of door* C. *All laugh.*)

CURTAIN

(*P. S.—At the end of this act there is generally a call.* JOSH *slips off his long night gown, pulls on his boots, goes before curtain in his shirt sleeves, bows awkwardly—never stepping out of his character,—is always* JOSHUA.)

ACT THREE

SCENE—*Exterior of Grace Church, Broadway and Tenth Street, New York, at night. The drop representing the church is hung about six feet from the curtain line, admitting of entrances at both sides. A lamp post, without the framework, glass or lamp, stands near the curtain line. A U. S. letter box is attached to the lamp post.*

(NOTE.—*To obviate a reproduction of the exterior of Grace Church a drop, or scene, representing a garden can be used; and at the extreme right of the audience, facing the audience, a portal, or entrance, to the church, will suggest that the main building and steeple stand off stage.*)

(*The curtain rises while chimes of bells are ringing off stage. When chimes stop an organ is heard with mixed quartette singing the "Psalms," or other selection, off in church. Near the conclusion of the singing* JOSH *and* HENRY H. *enter.*)

JOSH (*enters, followed by* HENRY H. *Both stand listening to singing of choir*). That's good music, Henry.

HENRY H. First class, Joshua, first class.

JOSH. That's a good melodeon they've got in there. What meetin' house is this, Henry?

HENRY H. Grace Church.

JOSH (*looking up at spire*). By gum! It's a whopper, ain't it?

HENRY H. It is indeed grand, Joshua. In my mind this is one of the prettiest sights in New York City, especially by moonlight, as you see it now.

JOSH. Pretty and no mistake; beats the old Baptist meetin' house at Swanzey all holler, don't it?

HENRY H. Comes pretty close to it, and we used to think that beat the world.

JOSH. So we did, Henry, so we did. (*In taking handkerchief out of right pocket, pulls a letter with it.*) There's that letter I wrote to Till and I forgot to put it in the post-office. Have to do it the first thing in the morning, just as soon as I get up.

HENRY H. No, no! Save yourself all that trouble; put it in the letter box. (*Points.*) There.

JOSH. Is that a letter box?

HENRY H. Yes.

JOSH. Gosh! Thought it was a knapsack strapped on there (*Hesitating.*) No; I guess not! Somebody will hook it. (*About to put letter back in pocket.*)

HENRY H. No! No! It will be perfectly safe there.

JOSH (*goes to letter box and tries to lift the top*). How do you get the lid up?

HENRY H. Oh, no; not that way! Here, I'll show you how.

(HENRY H. *crosses to box—lifts lid and* JOSH *drops letter in.*)

JOSH. By gum, that's handy, ain't it?

HENRY H. It is indeed.

JOSH. How they do improve now-a-days. (*Crossing to* HENRY H.)

HENRY H. Wonderful, perfectly wonderful!

JOSH. I suppose that's in the post-office by this time. (HENRY H. *laughs.*) Well, Henry, another day is pretty near gone and we ain't found Reuben yet.

HENRY H. Well, well! Don't get discouraged, New York is a large place. We'll run across him yet.

JOSH. I don't know; I got my doubts about it now.

HENRY H. (*comforting*). Come! Come, old friend, you mustn't be disheartened, we shall certainly find him. Now, Joshua, don't you think you'd better go home with me and have a good night's rest and you can start out nice and fresh in the morning.

JOSH (*gratefully*). Henry, it's real good of you to help me look for Reuben and I know I ought to do just as you say; but I would like to hang around a little while longer. It's right in the shank of the evening and I might run across him.

HENRY H. Very true; but you know that I——

JOSH. I know that you got visitors up to the house and you want to go and visit with them, so you run right along home and I won't be long.

HENRY H. Very well. You haven't forgotten the way there, have you?

JOSH. Well, I guess I ain't; let me see. (*Thinks.*) I go right straight up the road until you come to the first open lot. (*Pointing.*)

HENRY H. Yes, Union Square.

JOSH. Go right straight through that and keep right on till I get up as far as the Waldorf Tavern.

HENRY H. That is right.

JOSH. Then keep straight ahead to where I see the stage go out this morning——

HENRY H. The tallyho from the Plaza.

JOSH. Then cross over and it is a little ways up on the right-hand side.

HENRY H. That's correct; you'll not get lost.

JOSH. Well, I guess not! I didn't live in Boston two weeks, last summer, for nothin'.

HENRY H. No?

JOSH. No! Streets so crooked there pretty near made me cross-eyed afore I got home.

HENRY H. (*laughing*). They must be crooked indeed.

JOSH. Crooked! I guess they was. I had to get Jack Martin's boy to put a halter on me and take me up to the Common every morning and let me go. Didn't make no difference which way I struck out, I always fetched up on Boston Common.

HENRY H. Yes; but how did you get home at night?

JOSH. Same boy there with the halter and a hand full o' oats.

HENRY H. (*laughingly*). Oh, Joshua, not quite so bad as that, I guess!

JOSH. Well, perhaps not, Henry; but it warn't far from it.

HENRY H. (*starting off*). Well, I must be going.

JOSH. All right. Tell the folks I won't be out late.

HENRY H. See that you're not. Good-by for the present. Good-by. (*Exits.*)

JOSH. Good-by, Henry. Guess folks must think I'm crazy—staring at everybody as though I never see nothin' afore. I got to do it to look for Reub, and they go by so fast sometimes it almost makes me dizzy. I am like a dog that has lost its owner: I trot after one a little ways and then back and after another, and that's the way I go it from morning till night.

(*Enter apple woman*—MRS. MAGUIRE—*crying "Apples!" "Apples!"*)

MRS. MAGUIRE. Do you wish to buy any apples, sir?

JOSH. No; I ain't hungry.

MRS. MAGUIRE. Well, buy some to take home with you.

JOSH. I hain't got no home here; I'm visitin'.

MRS. MAGUIRE. Buy some to take to your frinds, thin.

JOSH. My friends are better able to buy them than I be.

MRS. MAGUIRE. Faith an' you're smart, ain't ye?

JOSH. Well, I manage to get along without taking up a collection, I guess.

MRS. MAGUIRE. Well, thin, take my advice about one thing.

JOSH. What's that?

MRS. MAGUIRE. Don't go to Philadelphia.

JOSH. Why not?

MRS. MAGUIRE. For the Cintinnial is over. Apples! Apples! (*Exit.*)

JOSH. Well, I must look all fired green when folks think I'm on my way to the Centennial, a year after it is over. I did not go there at all; wish I had now; they say it was worth seeing. I bet a ninepence I don't miss the next one! (*Enter* DUDE, *crossing, bumps his left shoulder against* JOSH'S *right. Turns and taps* JOSH *with cane and exits. When* DUDE *taps* JOSH *with cane, he puts his hand on his watch and keeps it there till* DUDE *makes same motion with cane second time at which* JOSH *takes off hat and makes motion as if to shoo him off.*) Shoo! Shoo! Gosh! I like to run over a goslin'. (*Exit.*)

(*Enter* HAPPY JACK *in evening dress, top coat, gloves and cane.*)

JACK. Well, there's no use talking, fine feathers make fine birds. By Jove! I must look like a winner!

(*Hums "After the Opera is Over," or other song, and crosses to exit, when he is stopped by voices of* POLICEMAN *and* REUBEN *off stage.*)

POLICE. Come on, you've been sitting here long enough.

REUBEN. Hold on, officer! I haven't done anything!

(*Enter* REUBEN *and* POLICEMAN; POLICEMAN'S *hand on* REUBEN'S *coat collar—preceding him.*)

POLICE. Come on; you can't stop here.

REUBEN. Hold on, officer—let me explain.

POLICE. You can tell the judge all about that in the morning.

JACK (*turning to* POLICEMAN). Say, what are you going to do with him?

POLICE. (*roughly*). Is that any of your business?

JACK. Oh, no! Oh, no; it is not any of my business but he's a friend of mine.

POLICE. Oh, he's a friend of yours, is he?

JACK. Yes, he isn't a bad sort of a fellow, officer. (*Taking note from breast pocketbook and pressing it in* POLICEMAN'S *hand.*) He's all right.

POLICE (*keeping right hand that holds club down by side, when* JACK *passes money into it, takes sly glance at it and changes tone*). Oh, well, if he is a friend of yours, of course that makes all the difference in the world. (*Exit, swinging club.*)

REUBEN. That was very kind of you, sir.

JACK. Don't mention it.

REUBEN. Do you know me?

JACK. No, sir.

REUBEN. How do you know that I'm worthy of your friendship?

JACK. Well, I'll take chances that you are.

REUBEN. I'm afraid you're taking long chances.

JACK. Never mind, I am used to it. Racing is a weakness of mine and I play a short horse occasionally if I think it a good one. Now tell me what did the King of Clubs want to take you in for?

REUBEN (*pointing*). I fell asleep in that doorway.

JACK. A little tired out, I suppose?

REUBEN. Yes; partly that.

JACK. A little discouraged, eh?

REUBEN (*nervously*). No, sir; I was sleeping off a drunk.

JACK. I thought so. (*Feeling* REUBEN'S *arm.*) Why, look here, old fellow, you're all over a-shake!

REUBEN. Yes; I know it.

JACK. You need a good strong milk punch to brace you up.

REUBEN. I think that would do me good.

JACK. Have you got the price?

REUBEN. Not a cent. (*Feeling in pockets.*)

JACK. Oh! Well, here's a dollar note for you. (*Taking bill from vest pocket.*) Now go and take a good bracer; get a shave; have your head rubbed; get something to eat and after that sit down and think a while.

REUBEN (*gratefully shaking hands with* JACK). Thank you, sir, thank you! (*Exits hurriedly.*)

JACK (*looking after him*). There he goes, poor fellow; struck a bee line for the nearest dive. Now he may take my suggestion about bracing up and he may not. (*Cross to* R. *while speaking.*) Well, never mind, if a man can make a dollar note win once in a hundred times in such a case he ought to feel himself well paid. (*Exits.*)

(*Enter apple woman—*MRS. MAGUIRE *—followed by* POLICEMAN.)

MRS. MAGUIRE. Apples! Apples!

POLICE. Well. Mrs. Maguire?

MRS. MAGUIRE (*turning and making courtesy*). Good evening, sir.

POLICE. How is business tonight?

MRS. MAGUIRE. Och! Surely there's nothing at all doing; I am jist waitin' for the weddin' party to come out of the church; thin I expect to sell out and go home.

POLICE. Nice apples you have there. (*Handling apples.*)

MRS. MAGUIRE. Faith 'n' they are splendid.

POLICE. How do you sell them? (*Putting hands in pants pockets.*)

MRS. MAGUIRE (*hands apple*). Och! Nothin' at all to you, sir; take one.

POLICE. Thank you.

MRS. MAGUIRE. Don't mention it.

POLICE. You are very kind. (*Salutes* MRS. MAGUIRE *and exits.*)

MRS. MAGUIRE (*looking after him*). Faith 'n' I am. Nice man is Mr. Doyle if you trate him decent and lave him eat all yer apples. Apples! (*Exit.*)

JOSH (*enters, followed by* POLICEMAN). Well, I guess I'll have to do as Henry says, give it up for tonight and take a fresh start in the morning; can't find Reuben nowhere. (*To* POLICEMAN.) Good evening, neighbor.

POLICE. Good evening, sir.

JOSH. You are a constable here, I guess.

POLICE. No, sir, I'm a policeman!

JOSH. Same thing, we call 'em constables up our way.

POLICE. Indeed?

JOSH. Yes. How long have you held office here?

POLICE (*thinking*). Well, let me see, I've been on the force about six years.

JOSH. How long you lived in New York?

POLICE. All my life; was born here.

JOSH. How old be you?

POLICE. Thirty.

JOSH. And you ain't killed yet?

POLICE. Nary a kill. (*Laughing.*)

JOSH. Well, that beats all! Had an idea man couldn't live in New York all his life without getting killed.

POLICE. Ha! Ha! Ha!

JOSH. You must know most everybody 'round here, I guess?

POLICE. Yes, I know a good many.

JOSH. You know Henry Hopkins?

POLICE. Henry Hopkins? What does he do?

JOSH. Don't do nothin' and got rich at it.

POLICE. Henry Hopkins,—can't say that I do.

JOSH. Well, that beats all! Thought everybody knew Henry. He's lived here more'n thirty years.

POLICE. Well, you're not in the country now, old gentleman.

JOSH. No, I wish I was.

POLICE. Why so?

JOSH. My feet are pretty near worn out walking over these stone pavements.

POLICE. Tires you, eh?

JOSH. Yes. You have to sot up all night, I suppose?

POLICE. Yes, sir.

JOSH. Gosh! I never could do that!

POLICE. Oh, that's nothing, you would soon get used to it. (*Exit.*)

JOSH. Well, I guess not. I never sot up all night but once or twice in my life and that was just before I got married. Darned if I ain't gettin' hungry; had nothing to eat since noon. Henry and I went into a tavern where they had a printed schedule of what they had to eat. Couldn't read it any more'n you could hog latin, not a mite! I didn't see only two down-East names on it, Baked Beans à la Boston. I took a mouthful but I spit them right out again. The "à la" they put in thim just spiled them. Henry eat the beans and I had some ice-cream and clams.

(*Enter* TERROR *with hat pulled down over eyes; cigar lit and touching rim of hat. He crosses to back of* JOSH *and knocks into right shoulder with his left shoulder as he passes and then turns to* JOSH.)

TERROR (*roughly*). Get out of the way! Do you want the whole sidewalk?

JOSH. Well, why don't you bump agin somebody? Who be you anyway?

TERROR. I'm de Hoboken Terror!

JOSH. Well, yer hat'll catch fire there if you ain't careful!

TERROR. What doo you soi? (*Approaching* JOSH.)

JOSH. I say, if you cock your cigar up like that you'll get your hat on fire.

TERROR. Oh, what's de matter wid you? (*Grabs* JOSH'S *hat from head and throws it on stage in front of him. Then flicks ashes from cigar —restores it, and assumes tough attitude.*)

JOSH. Well, I lasted longer than I thought I would. I expected to get scalped the first day I got here. (*Picking up hat slowly and deliberately.*) What did you do that for?

TERROR. Just for fun!

JOSH. Well, I ain't got no objection to your havin' a little fun but I don't want yer to have it all to yourself.

(*Knocks* TERROR'S *hat off and squares off at him, country style—jumping about and moving backwards.*)

TERROR (*dumbfounded*). Look here! If you wasn't an old man I'd come over there and make it pleasant for you.

JOSH. Well, I'll be right here when you come! (*Enter* POLICEMAN—*stands near* TERROR *who turns and sees him then crosses to* POLICEMAN—*stops, throws right lapel of coat back bravado style, blows cloud of smoke out and exits.*) If that feller ain't careful he'll scare somebody.

POLICE. You ran against a wrestler that time, old gentleman. (*Exit.*)

(*Enter* MRS. MAGUIRE.)

JOSH. So did he, too. Don't you worry about that. (*Off* L. *the bass drum, tambourines and singing of a stirring hymn is heard.*) Sounds like Fourth of July.

(*Enter the Salvation Army, consisting of bass-drummer—in advance—followed by two women beating tambourines—a flag bearer—and four other women. They exeunt, singing and playing.* JOSH *looks on in wonder.*)

MRS. MAGUIRE. Apples! Apples! (*Trips across stage* C. *to the music. Re-enter the Salvation Army and crosses stage followed by a drunken man and exit.*) Apples! Apples!

(*These lines are spoken as the Army passes. Enter again the Army—still singing and playing—and followed by the drunken man and the* HOBOKEN TERROR *and all exeunt. The singing and music die out in the distance.*)

JOSH. What's the militia out tonight for?

(*Enter* POSTMAN, *takes out key, opens box, places mail in bag.*)

MRS. MAGUIRE. Wusha, man dear, they ain't soldiers.

JOSH. No?

MRS. MAGUIRE. No. That's the Salvation Army.

JOSH. Gates of Garra! I wan ter know?

MRS. MAGUIRE. Apples! (*Exit.*)

JOSH. That beats all I ever see. (*Discovering* POSTMAN *at mail box.*) Robbing the mail, by gosh! Here! Here! You can't do that! (*Seizing* POSTMAN *and turning around. Both struggle for bag.*) I've got him! I've got him!

(*Enter* POLICEMAN, *running in and separating them.*)

POLICE. Here! Here! What's the matter here?

JOSH. Catch him! Catch him! He took my letter out of that box!

POLICE. Why, this man's appointed by the Government to collect the mail.

JOSH. Gosh all fish hooks! (*Hides behind lamp post.*) Now I'd sell out pretty cheap.

POSTMAN. What's the matter with the old jay?

POLICE. Oh, that's all right. It's only a mistake. (POSTMAN *exits.*) Say, look here, old gentleman, you'll have to be a little more careful in the future.

JOSH. That's all right. I didn't know he was the postmaster. (*Exit* POLICEMAN, *laughing*. JOSH *comes to center.*) No business to go 'round without a guide-board on. That was a pretty narrow escape for me. Guess I had better go home before I get in the lock up.

(*Enter* JACK. *Stops, surprised at seeing* JOSH. *Looks* JOSH *all over.* JOSH *puts right hand on watch and left hand in pocket.*)

JACK (*astonished*). Why, no!

JOSH. What's the matter?

JACK. It is.

JOSH. How do you know it is?

JACK. My preserver!

JOSH. Sho'!

JACK. Why, you saved my life!

JOSH. Well, that's the first time I ever knew I looked like a life preserver.

JACK. I met you in Swanzey.

JOSH (*very slowly and knowingly*). Well, I guess not! I have had that two or three times before. (*Turns up stage and balances first on one toe and then on other in a country smart way as much as to say, "I know a thing or two!"*)

JACK (*laughing*). Yes, I did. About three weeks ago. Don't you remember?

JOSH. No—the next Centennial ain't begun yet.

JACK. Your name is Whitcomb.

JOSH. Now, look here, Appetite Joe, I have heard on you; I have been tackled by about a dozen of you fellers since I have been here, and I'm gittin' kind o' tired on't. Now if you don't want ter get your feathers ruffled up, you go look for squashes somewhere else! I just hitched on to a feller and I feel pretty darned "kinky." Ain't quite so green as you think I be. I take the papers. Play none o' yer "hunker slidin' on me," by gosh!

(*Same business up stage.*)

JACK. Let me put you right.

JOSH. Oh, I'm all right! Don't you worry!

JACK. Don't you remember about three weeks ago giving a poor miserable wretch money enough to go to his home?

JOSH (*puzzled*). Now how did you find that out?

JACK. I am the man.

JOSH. You be darned! You ain't?

JACK. I can convince you.

JOSH (*putting his hands in his pockets*). Well, that's what you'll have to do before I talk to you much longer.

JACK. I can tell you the last words you said to me.

JOSH. Well, let's hear them.

JACK. Go home and try and be somebody. It isn't too late.

JOSH (*taking hands from pockets and slapping them together*). By gum! That's what I said! (JACK *holds out his hand to shake.* JOSH *puts hands in pockets again quickly, weakening.*) Hold on! Hold on! Tell me what you said and then I'll give up.

JACK. I told you I would try and if I didn't win, I'd give old John Barleycorn the toughest scuffle he ever had for the underhold.

JOSH. Well, that's just what you said. (*Shakes hands very cautiously and returns his hand to his pocket, still on his guard.*) And there's my hand. I'm glad to see you.

JACK. And I am glad to see you, old gentleman and old friend. (*Taking ten-dollar bill from pocket and handing to* JOSH.) Allow me to return your ten dollars.

JOSH (*taking money*). Now, by gosh! I know it's you. How de-do! (*Shaking hands.*) I guess your mother was glad to see you, wasn't she?

JACK. Yes, overjoyed!

JOSH. I knowed she'd be!

JACK. Did you find your boy yet, Mr. Whitcomb?

(*Organ plays piano—some very pretty church service.*)

JOSH (*with feeling*). No, sir; I didn't, and I have been trampin' up and down these streets for more'n a week searching for him everywhere; and I have seen more wickedness and misery in that time than I ever thought could exist in a civilized community. I am dreadfully afraid he has been led off, and took to drink.

JACK. What makes you think so?

JOSH. Because I have seen so much of it since I have been here. Henry Hopkins says drink is the ruination of more than half the young men of New York.

JACK. Well, Henry Hopkins isn't far from being right.

(*Organ stops. Commotion outside.*)

JOSH. There's a row! Don't go too near or you'll get stabbed. A lot of rowdies outside——

JACK. Here comes my dollar investment and about as drunk as they make them.

(*Voices outside shouting "Good night, old feller," etc. Enter* REUBEN *staggering.* JOSH *recognizes him. He falls into* JOSH'S *arms and then falls on his knees.* JOSH *bends over him.*)

JOSH. My boy Reub! Reub! Reub! (*When* REUBEN *falls,* POLICEMAN *runs on, and* JACK *stops him.*) Why, it's my boy Reub!

(*Organ in church plays "Wedding March," piano, till curtain, and then forte till final curtain.*)

CURTAIN

(SECOND CURTAIN: POLICEMAN *with head bowed.* REUBEN *stands with his head on* JOSH'S *shoulder.* JACK *removes his hat and stands with bowed head.*)

CURTAIN

ACT FOUR

SCENE—*Kitchen in the Old Homestead. To the left of the audience a door up opens off to outside. By door—in corner—a wood box and a kitchen chair. An old-fashioned fireplace with andirons, fire logs lit, bellows, fire shovel and tongs. A mantel on which an old lantern is lit, two candlesticks, an almanac and* JOSH'S *hat and mittens. In front of fireplace a rag rug and a plain rocking-chair. Beside fireplace, a tall grandfather's clock with key inside. Near clock a curtained window, the panes of which suggest snow on the outside. A small table below window. Midway in wall a kitchen cupboard—shelves papered—and filled with crockery. Leaning against cupboard a broom whose handle has been partly cut through the middle. Down stage, a door leading off into the "front" room. Midway on wall to the left, hangs a series of pegs on which hang* GANZEY'S *hat and mittens,* CY P.'S *hat and comforter and* SETH'S *hat and scarf, and down stage, a door. An old-fashioned cradle stands in the corner and a kitchen chair to left of it. To the right two kitchen chairs stand near cupboard and below door is a black hair-seated "front-room" chair. A few common pictures adorn the walls.*

(CY PRIME *and* SETH PERKINS *are seated near cupboard with checkerboard on knees, playing.* JOSH *is standing* R. *of them watching the game.* MATILDA *is up at fireplace talking to two of the* STRATTON *girls.* EB GANZEY *and* RICKETY ANN *are conversing over* R. *with the* QUARTETTE *and others.* ELINOR STRATTON *is seated by cradle.* CY P. *moves a "man" and laughs.*)

JOSH (*beside players*). What's the matter, Cy, got him penned?

CY P. (*with back to cupboard*). Yes; he can't make a move without losing two men. I sot a trap for him and he stepped right into it. I knowed he would.

ELINOR S. (*sitting by cradle*). Uncle Josh, what is the cradle doing here?

JOSH. Got it down to rock Stocky's baby in, when he was on here visitin' from Wesconsin—ain't used it sence Reub was a baby. Come now, let's all go into the front room, we've got a table sot in there. We'll have some pumpkin pie, cookies and games, playin' on the melodeon and one thing and another.

MATILDA. Joshua, has the fire got to going in the stove?

JOSH. Roarin' away like a mill dam.

MATILDA. Come on, boys and girls—come! (*Exits.*)

JOSH. Come on, all on ye.

(*Exit all except* SETH, CY P., RICKETY *and* GANZEY. GANZEY *eating almonds.* CY P. *rises, goes up by fireplace, and* SETH *rises and places checkerboard on cupboard.*)

RICKETY (*comes down to left of* GANZEY). Say, Eb, what you eatin'?

GANZEY. Almonds. Oh, here's a double one!

RICKETY. Gimme one?

GANZEY. Will if you play philopene.

RICKETY. All right, I will. (GANZEY *gives almond.*) Five or take, yes or no.

GANZEY. Yes or no.

RICKETY. All right. Now remember if I ask you anything and you say yes or no, I ketch you.

GANZEY. All right. Say, Rickety, goin' to dance with me tonight?

RICKETY. Oh, you jist want me to say yes so you can ketch me.

(*Exit laughing.* GANZEY *whistles; goes up stage.* CY P. *picks up iron shovel to strike him*—GANZEY *exits hurriedly.*)

CY P. (*laughing*). You play checkers! Ho, ho, ho!

SETH. Ho, ho, ho! Why don't you laugh?

CY P. Well, I be a-laughing, ain't I?

SETH. That's all right, go it—keep it up! It'll be my turn one of these days.

CY P. What do you mean by that?

SETH. I mean that I consider it pretty darn small potatoes when a man pins another playin' checkers to holler right out before the hull room full then laugh at him!

CY P. Oh, you do, do you?

SETH. Yes, I do!

CY P. Well, that ain't no wuss than what you done.

SETH. What did I do?

CY P. Didn't you blat right out before everybody that you could beat anybody in the house playin' checkers?

SETH. No, I didn't, nuther!

CY P. Yes, you did, tuther!

SETH. Said I'd play anybody in the house.

CY P. I took you up, didn't I?

SETH. Yes.

CY P. An' I beat you, didn't I?

SETH. Yes; and you crowed about it.

CY P. Well, supposin' I did?

SETH. That's all right. (*Sneeringly.*) You put me in mind of an old rooster I've got. He's always fightin'; wins one battle in about fifty and then crows so durn loud you can hear him all over town.

CY P. Oh, he do, do he?

SETH. Yes; that's what he do do.

CY P. Ha! Ha! Well, I won't tell you what you put me in mind on. But you'd better take my advice and not go through that pasture where the Hennesy folks keep their goats. (*Sits.*)

SETH. Why?

CY P. Because they're liable to put a bell on you.

SETH (*to* CY P., *angrily*). Cy Prime, I've stood your slurs about my personal appearance about as long as I'm going to. You ain't got nothin' to brag on. There ain't no more meat on you than there is on a hoe handle, not a mite. You ain't heavy enough to sink a fish line. You're that kind o' calf that lives all winter and dies in the spring.

CY P. Why, you gol darn picter out of a comic almanac, what you talking about? (*Rises and goes toward* SETH.)

SETH. That's what I said—(*Firmly*) —and so you are, too!

CY P. (*throwing off coat, displaying sleeveless arms*). Well, don't say it again, for I don't like it. (*Threatens* SETH *as* JOSH *enters followed by* MATILDA *and* GANZEY.)

JOSH (*going up to fireplace*). Here! Here! What you got your coat off for, Cy?

CY P. Well, I was jest showing Seth where I got vaccinated, that's all. (*Showing vaccinated arm and then puts on coat.*)

MATILDA. What is it, what is it?

JOSH (*takes hat and mittens from mantelplace and puts them on*). Oh, these two boys quarreling again, that's all.

SETH. Well, he commenced it.

CY P. I didn't nuther.

SETH. Now, Cy, you know very well—

JOSH (*comes down between them*). Boys!—boys!—boys!—stop it now!

(SETH *goes up stage and stands by window.*)

MATILDA. Where you goin', Joshua?

JOSH. Goin' out to the barn to see if the cattle's all right. Ebenezer, get your mittens on. (GANZEY *goes up to pegs and puts on hat and mittens.*) Run down the road and tell Len Holbrook to come up here and bring his fiddle.

(MATILDA *sits in armchair at fireplace and knits.*)

GANZEY. S'pose he's in bed?

JOSH. Tell him to get up.

GANZEY. All right. (*Hands* JOSH *lighted lantern from shelf.*)

JOSH. Come, Cy, fill your wood box, it's gettin' late.

CY P. All right, Joshua, all right. (*Exit* JOSH *and* GANZEY.) I snum! I forgot all about my wood for night. By Jinks! But never mind, I kin git it jist as well now as any other time. (*Puts on hat and comforter from pegs.*) Don't make any difference. (*Sees* SETH *at window.*) Now there is some maneuverin' goin' here and I know it. That feller is tryin' to pull the wool over my eyes. He's no more lookin' out o' that winder than he's lookin' up the chimley. (*Exits.*)

SETH. Tildy, do you know——

(CY P. *re-enters cautiously, sees* SETH *talking to* MATILDA; *goes down stage and stands beside him.* SETH *turns, sees* CY P., *puts hand to mouth and goes up to window again.*)

CY P. I knowed it! I'll keep my eye on that Swanzey dude!

(*Exit. Melodeon heard off stage with* QUARTETTE *singing, "I'll meet her when the sun goes down," or other melody.*)

SETH. The young folks in the front room 'pear to be enjoyin' theirselves, don't they, Tildy?

MATILDA. Yes, they do. Why don't you go in, Seth?

SETH (*takes chair from beside fireplace and sits*). No, no! Most too old to play games and cut up didoes as I used to.

MATILDA (*knitting*). Yes, that's so—both on us gettin' pretty old now.

SETH. Yes, yes——

MATILDA. So I thought arter the young folks get started playin' games and one thing another, I'd jest come out here and knit a spell.

SETH. Glad you did; glad you did.

MATILDA. Seth, why don't you come round here and see us oftener? I believe 'twas more'n a month sence you was here last.

SETH. I would come round oftener but you see it makes old Cy Prime so hoppin' mad.

MATILDA. Well, you mustn't mind him.

SETH. Well, I don't much. He's allus throwing out slurs about my sneakin' round here to see you.

MATILDA. Go long!

SETH. Yes. Warn't more'n a week ago, he twitted me right out before the hull store about the time I took you up to Keene to see old blind Dexter's wax figgers.

MATILDA. Why, Seth! That was thirty year ago or more!

SETH. I know that; but the mean way he said it made me so plaguey mad, I throwed a ten penny nail at him and broke his new clay pipe all to smash. (*Laughs.*) Guess we'd 'a' had a pitch battle right then and there if the neighbors had not interfered. Phew! That fire o' yours is pretty hot, don't you think it is, Tildy?

MATILDA. Pretty warm, Seth. Cold night outside and it takes considerable fire to warm up the house.

(*Enter* CY P. *Sees* SETH *sitting by* MATILDA—*throws bundle of wood which he carries in wood box.* SETH *jumps up, startled.*)

CY P. Well, Seth Perkins, couldn't keep on your own side of the fence, could you? What you doin' round here, anyhow?

SETH. Well, I ain't doin' chores for my board.

CY P. Nor I, nuther, ain't doin' chores for my board. I'm stoppin' here this winter with Joshua, 'cause my sister Betsy's gone out west visitin', and you know it, too, gol darn ye.

(*Both square off to fight—country style.* JOSH *enters, hastily throwing hat and mittens on mantel and comes down between* CY P. *and* SETH.)

JOSH. Here—here! Stop this, or I'll put you both in the trundle bed. What's this all about, Til?

MATILDA (L. C.). I don't know.

JOSH. Well, you go into the front room and turn the damper in the stovepipe; I'm afraid it'll draw all the heat up the chimney—the sparks are flyin' out like fury.

MATILDA. Be they! (*Exits.*)

JOSH. Yes, I'll settle this business pretty quick. It's ben goin' on jist about as long as it orter. Seth, you go over there and set down;—you go over there and set down, Cy. (SETH *in meantime goes up to wood box and gets a chip of wood, places it on left shoulder.* CY P. *sees it and goes and knocks it off. Both pretend to fight again.* JOSH *interferes and stops it.* SETH *and* CY P. *sit.*) Stop slammin' the chairs around—I won't have it. (*Sees a black, hair-seated chair, goes over, takes it up.*) Who brought this front-room chair out in the kitchen, I'd like to know? (CY P. *and* SETH *look at each other.* JOSH *takes chair off stage, leaves it and returns.*) Now what's the matter with you two old fools? (*Takes chair and sits.*) You've been snappin' and snarling at each other for more'n thirty years; and ain't ye ashamed o' yourselves and you boys together, raised on jinin' farms. Cy, don't you remember when you and Seth was barefooted boys ridin' saw logs round the mill pond; how you fell in one day where it was over your head and you would hev drownded if it hadn't ben for him? He jumped in and saved you. You couldn't swim and he could. Hev you forgot that, Cy? I hev heard your father tell it lots o' times. And, Seth—— (*Looking at* SETH.)

SETH. Eh?

JOSH. Don't you remember when your brother Bill came home from New Orleans sick, a good many years ago, and everybody thought he had the yellow fever and was afraid to go near him, how Cy jumped up in the store and said, "Hang yellow fever—I ain't afraid of it! Sha'n't leave no neighbor o' mine alone, I'll tend to him." And he did tend to him for a good many long weeks. (SETH *fills up and wipes eyes with handkerchief.*) Hev you forgot that, Seth?

SETH (*rises and takes* JOSH'S *hand.* JOSH *also rises*). No, Josh; I ain't and I never will either.

JOSH. That's right, that's right!

CY P. (*crying*). Well, I ain't got nothin' agin Seth and I could prove it too, if old Bill Jones was alive. (*Rises and goes to* JOSH.)

SETH. If Cy was taken sick I'd watch over him jest the same as he did my brother Bill; I would if it killed me!

JOSH. I know that, I know that. Come now, shake hands and be friends.

(JOSH *puts* CY P.'S *hand in* SETH'S, *crossing to back of them.*)

CY P. And, Seth, if you should fall overboard and was goin' to git drownded I'd jump in and save your life, and I can't swim a lick!

JOSH. There now! Don't you feel better? (*Patting both on back.*)

SETH. I do; a durned sight.

JOSH. Of course you do.

CY P. And so do I. If I had a dipper o' cider, I'd stay up till ten o'clock.

JOSH. Here! Don't get reckless! There, boys, go and fill your wood box.

CY P. All right, Joshua.

(*Replaces his chair by fireplace and gets hat and comforter.*)

SETH (*gets hat and scarf from peg, puts them on; goes down to where* CY P. *stands*). Hold on, Cy, I'll help you bring in your wood.

CY P. Will you, Sethy?

JOSH (*laughs*). Seth-y!

SETH. What's the use o' us two fallin' out?

CY P. Oh, not a bit o' use at all.

SETH. We're a couple o' ninny hammers.

CY P. Yes, we ain't got as much gumption as a sick woodchuck!

SETH. Have an apple? (*Takes apple from coat tail pocket, hands to* CY P.)

CY P. Yes. Don't care if I do.

SETH. Come along now, and I'll help you bring in your wood.

CY P. Will you? (*Exits running, followed by* SETH.)

JOSH. How true it is, once a man, twice a child. When they commenced to fill up I came near sloppin' over myself.

MATILDA (*enters*). Have they made up, Joshua?

JOSH. Better friends than ever.

MATILDA. Well, I'm glad of that—so much better than always hectorin' one another.

(CY P. *and* SETH *outside, laughing.*)

JOSH (*goes to window and knocks on window pane*). Boys! Boys!

SETH and CY P. What is it?

JOSH. March up here! (SETH *and* CY P. *come to window.*) Now stop your wrestling and get your wood in. (*They pretend to wrestle outside—* SETH *calling to* CY P. *to stop.* JOSH *laughs.*) Darned if Cy hain't flopped him flatter than a flounder in the snow bank. Well, no use talking, boys will be boys. By gum! It's sharp out tonight.

(*Goes and stands with back to fireplace.*)

MATILDA (*sitting in rocker*). Pretty cold, I guess.

JOSH. Cold and crisp as a new dollar bill.

MATILDA. Do you think the pigs hev got straw enough in the pen?

JOSH. Yes; pitched in a fresh bundle jest afore I come in. Hed the wust time a little while ago with that old brindle heifer you ever seen in your life.

MATILDA. What's she ben doin' now?

JOSH. Got loose agin and got on to the barn floor and was havin' a cotillion with the fannin' mill.

MATILDA. Well, of all things! How does she manage to git loose so often?

JOSH. I don't know unless she onties herself.

MATILDA. No, Joshua, that's impossible.

JOSH. I don't know about that: Cy says he saw her pick the padlock on the corn crib door the other day with her horn.

MATILDA. Well, Cyrus says more'n his prayers.

JOSH. Shouldn't wonder a mite.

MATILDA. Did you shet the hen house door?

JOSH. Yes. Everything's all snugged up—not a critter on the place but what'll sleep as warm as a meadow mouse under a haystack.

MATILDA. Well, I'm glad o' that—hate to know there's anything sufferin' belonging to us.

JOSH. Did you wind the clock?

(*Melodeon plays "Grandfather's Clock" off stage.*)

MATILDA. Not yet. Elinor Stratton's playin' the melodeon——

JOSH. Plays fust rate, too, for a gal that's got as bad a cold as she has. (*Goes to clock and winds slowly—during which* MATILDA *fills up and puts handkerchief to eyes, rises.*) What's the matter, Til?

MATILDA. Nothin',—nothin' much.

JOSH. Yes, there is, too. What you snivelling about?

MATILDA. Well, I was worrying a little mite about Reuben. Do you think he'll come home tonight, Joshua?

JOSH (*sits*). Jest as sartin as the world. Didn't his letter say, "Father, I'll be home New Year's if I'm spared my health"? Ain't his friends and schoolmates here to meet him? He's comin' by way o' Boston; train may be late comin' into Keene. Then he's got to drive six miles, you must remember that.

MATILDA. Yes, I know all that, Joshua; but why didn't you bring him home with you when you was in New York?

JOSH. Well, I'll tell you, Til. He did start to come but when he got as far as the depot, I noticed something troubled him. He hung back a leetle mite, and I said to him—"Reuben, don't you want to go home with me?" And he says, "Yes, Father, I do; but I hate to go back and have Swanzey people say that Reuben Whitcomb went away to make his own living and his father had to go and bring him back again." (*With pathos.*) And, Til, when he hung down his head and his eyes filled up with tears, and his voice was kind o' choked, he says, "Father, let me stick it out a little while longer"—I says, "Go it!" "Thank you," he says, "I'll be home by New Year's"; and he'll be here tonight, you see if he ain't.

MATILDA. I hope so.

JOSH. I feel sure on't. (*Rises and wipes eyes.*) Guess I'd better go down in the cellar and set my mouse trap before I go to bed. (*Exits hurriedly. Enter* CY P., *throwing wood in box and warming himself at fireplace. In meantime* MATILDA *takes chair and sits knitting.*)

CY P. Well, I tell you what it is—pretty cold night out tonight, Tildy.

MATILDA. Yes, Cyrus.

CY P. I'll bet it's as cold tonight as it was the night Washington crossed the Delaware.

MATILDA. Now what do you know about Washington crossing the Delaware?

CY P. What do I know about it? Well, I know old Bill Jones put him up to it—that's what I know about it.

(*Enter* SETH. *Throws wood in box.*)

SETH. There, there! I s'pose you ben telling Til how you flopped me over in the snow, ain't ye?

CY P. No, I never said a word about it, did I, Tildy?

MATILDA. No, you didn't.

SETH. He done it though—fair and square. S'pose you'll crow about that for the next twenty years.

(JOSH *enters—crosses up to fireplace and sits in rocking chair.*)

CY P. No, I won't—I won't say a word about it; I guess your foot slipped, anyway.

SETH. No, it didn't,—I was throwed fair.

CY P. Well, you know how it is with me, when I get that grape-vine lock o' mine sot—suthin's got to come.

(CY P. *seizes* SETH *about the waist—legs entwined—illustrating grape-vine lock. An approaching sound of sleigh bells is heard off stage.*)

JOSH. Whose bells be them outside?

SETH. Sounded a leetle mite like Deacon Frosser's.

CY P. More like David Wilson's.

JOSH (*rising*). You're both wrong. They don't belong around here for I can tell every string of bells in town.

(*Outside, "Whoa!" Enter* GANZEY *hurriedly.*)

GANZEY. Reub is here!

(*Enter* REUBEN. JOSH *clasps him to his breast and turns him over to* MATILDA *who does the same.*)

JOSH (*excitedly*). There he is! I told you he would come. (*Exit* GANZEY.)

MATILDA. My boy—my boy!

JOSH. Take him right in the front room. (*Exit* MATILDA *and* REUBEN.) All your friends and schoolmates there. (*Excitedly.*) Put the shed under the hoss, throw a blanket over the barn. Fly around! (*Exit* L.)

SETH. Did you ever hear anything like that in all your born days?

CY P. (*laughing*). So I'm to put the shed under the hoss, be I?

SETH. An' I'm to throw a blanket over the barn.

CY P. Well, never mind. Josh's so tickled to think Reuben's got home that he don't know whether he's on his head or his heels, do he?

(CY P. *picks up broom—goes up—sweeps around fireplace.*)

SETH (*sits in chair*). No; his heart's sot on that boy.

(*Enter* GANZEY *and* JACK.)

GANZEY. Come right in, Mister—I'll tell Uncle Josh.

JACK. All right, thank you. (*In passing* CY P. GANZEY *whistles*—CY P. *tries to strike him with broom but he is too quick for him and exits hurriedly.*) Good evening, gentlemen.

(*Takes off hat and coat, hangs them on pegs and, crossing, stands in front of fire, warms hands.*)

CY P. How de-do? (*Comes down and sits left of* SETH—*first placing broom above door.*)

SETH (*seated by* CY P.). Good evenin', good evenin'.

CY P. Did you drive Reub down from Keene?

JACK. Yes, came from New York with him.

CY P. How you talk! (*Snickers.*)

SETH. Purty cold weather out tonight, eh, stranger?

JACK. Yes, sir; it's a little tough on mosquitoes. (*Laughs.*)

CY P. Skeeters! (*Laughs and nudges* SETH.)

JACK. But then we didn't mind it much—young blood, you know.

SETH. That's so. Cold weather don't bother us youngsters much, does it, Cy? (*Chuckling quietly and nudging* CY P.)

CY P. Not a hooter. (*Hits breast and coughs.*)

SETH (*aside*). Citified lookin' chap, ain't he, Cy? (*Nudges* CY P.)

CY P. (*aside*). Yes, one o' them cute New Yorkers, I guess. Say, Seth, tell him some sort o' whopper to pay him off for that skeeter joke o' his.

SETH (*aside*). Hadn't you better tackle him?

CY P. No; you can lie better than I can.

SETH. Stranger——

JACK. Beg pardon——

SETH. Be you one o' the Hopkins o' New York?

JACK. No, sir, my name is Hazard.

SETH. Oh!—Any relation to hap-hazard?

(*Both laugh.* CY P. *and* SETH *both poke each other playfully as if they had said something smart. They rise and move off, chuckling.*)

JOSH. Where is he? Where is he? (*Enter.*) Happy Jack, sure as a gun!

JACK (*both shake hands*). How do, how do, Mr. Whitcomb?

JOSH. How de-do? I'm glad to see you.

JACK. Thank you. On time, you see. I told you we would be here on New Year's eve.

JOSH. So you did. I'd take your word for a million.

JACK. Thank you.

JOSH (*calling*). Til, come here.

(*Enter* MATILDA.)

MATILDA. What is it, Joshua?

JOSH. Mr. Hazard.

MATILDA. Mr. Hazard?

JOSH. Why, you don't know him, do you? He is the young man who was so good to Reub and me in New York—the one I was tellin' you about —here last summer; turned over a new leaf in life—that's him!

MATILDA. Oh, there now—you ain't the young man who was here last summer, be you?

JACK. The very same.

MATILDA (*crossing to* JACK, *shakes hands heartily*). Well, how do you do? I'm glad to see you.

JACK. Thank you.

MATILDA (*looking* JACK *over*). Of all things—how you have changed.

JOSH. Fooled me, too, and I've travelled most all over the world.

JACK. Yes, Miss Whitcomb—it was under the old elm at the corner of the lane I first began my reformation. I couldn't help drawing a mind picture of it as I passed by coming to the door; and, old friend, I owe it all to you.

JOSH. Don't say another word about it, if you do I'll knock you down. Come into the front room and get acquainted.

(*Exit* JOSH *and* JACK. MATILDA *follows them to door when knock is heard.*)

MATILDA. Come in.

(*Enter* LEN HOLBROOK—*takes off scarf and hat, hangs them up.*)

LEN H. How de-do, Aunt Tilda!

MATILDA. How do you do, Mr. Holbrook? (*Exit.*)

LEN H. Hello, Cy!

CY P. Hello, Len!

LEN H. How are you, Seth?

SETH. How de-do; how de-do?

CY P. Pretty cold out tonight, ain't it, Len?

LEN H. Yes, it's pesky cold.

SETH. Brought your old fiddle with you, I see.

LEN H. Yes. Jest goin' to bed when the Ganzey boy came and said Joshua was goin' to hev a frolic and wanted me to fiddle—so here I be.

CY P. That's right; that's right.

LEN H. Hope they won't serve me the same as they did over at Richmond t'other night.

CY P. How's that?

LEN H. Greased my bow! Didn't git it out for more'n two days. (*Exit.*)

CY P. Greased his bow! That's Richmond all over! (*Knock at door.*) Come in!

(SETH *joins* CY P.)

SETH. Hullo, hullo! More company, more visitors!

(*Enter* PAT CLANCEY.)

CLANCEY. Hello, boys! (*Takes chair, sits by fire, throws hat and mittens on floor by his side, pipe in mouth, and warms hands.*)

CY P. Why, how are you, Mr. Clancey?

CLANCEY. How are you? (*To* SETH.)

SETH. What's the news?

CLANCEY. Oh, nothin' strange—me hens has stopped layin', that's all.

CY P. No wonder. Pretty cold weather out.

CLANCEY. Faith an' it is. It's terribly frosty—the fire in my pipe is frozen stiff. (*Rising.*)

CY P. Why don't you wear an overcoat?

CLANCEY. Overcoat, is it? Wusha, now! I have been in this country twenty-seven years, and I never wore an overcoat but the one you see on me now.

CY P. You're a tough little man, Mr. Clancey!

CLANCEY. I'll warrant you. Faith and there's not a man my heft around here that will weigh within tin pounds o' me.

CY P. Well, you hev done well in this country.

CLANCEY. Oh, jist about as well as them that ha' done no better.

CY P. It's a wonder to me that you don't go over to Ireland once more jest to see the old folks.

CLANCEY. Is it me go over to Ireland? Why, man, I've been out here so long and I have got so Yankified I'm afraid they wouldn't understand what I'd be sayin'.

CY P. (*chuckling*). Yankified? So is a tater!

CLANCEY. Say, Cy, O'Rourke, the horseshoer, was tellin' me Joshua's boy is home agin from New York.

CY P. Yes, that's right.

CLANCEY. Faith an' I'm glad to know that. Well, I just thought I'd come over and wish him welcome home agin. He thought a great deal about me.

(*Enter* MATILDA.)

MATILDA. How do you do, Mr. Clancey?

CLANCEY. Well, well, Miss Whitcomb, how are you?

MATILDA. I'm pretty well, thank you.

CLANCEY. Faith an' you're lookin' well.

MATILDA. You've jest come in time.

CLANCEY. Yes.

MATILDA. We have got the table sot in the front room an' all the neighbors are there to welcome Reuben home. Go right in with the rest of them, Mr. Clancey.

CLANCEY. Why, certainly, of course. Say, whisper, I'm bashful, you know, in company, but if there's any ateing goin' on, I'm at home with ye. (*Exits. Knock at door.*)

MATILDA. Come in! (*Enter* MRS. MURDOCK, *with baby wrapped in small blanket.*) Well, how are you, Mrs. Murdock? Glad to see you.

MRS. M. How do—how do, Aunt Matilda? Good evenin', Cyrus.

CY P. Good evenin', Anna Maria.

MRS. M. How do—how do, Mr. Perkins?

SETH. Good evenin', Mrs. Murdock, good evenin'.

MRS. M. Wanted to see Reuben so bad, couldn't wait till mornin'. Knew he'd got home, 'cause I see him drive by. Had to bring baby long 'cause everybody has gone to watch-meetin' but me, and couldn't leave him alone, you know.

MATILDA. Of course not, Anna Maria. How he does grow, don't he? Fast asleep, too. Well, take him right into my room, put him between the blankets and let him have his sleep out.

MRS. M. Now, Tildy, if there's anything you want me to do jest let me know, and I'll roll up my sleeves and pitch right in. (*Exits.*)

MATILDA. Thank you, Anna Maria, you're real good but I guess I can get along pretty well now. (*Exits.*)

SETH (*taking broom*). I bet you I—I bet you I kin——

CY P. Oh, no; no-no! You think you kin pull me up with that broomstick—why, you couldn't pull up a hill o' taters.

SETH. Set down, then, I'll show ye—if this stick holds out I'll yank ye more'n forty rods. (*Both sit on floor, feet together, and catching hold of broom handle which has been cut so as to break easily.*) Now, Cy, you pull fair.

(*Both pull hard and stick breaks; both fall over backwards. Enter* JOSH, REUBEN *and* JACK. JACK *watches up at fireplace.*)

JOSH. Hello, hello, hello. What's all this about? (SETH *jumps up and rushes off and* CY P. *tries to put broom portion of his broken half up his coat tails and ties scarf over it; puts on hat and rushes off.*) Up to some o' their capers, I'll warrant you.

REUBEN. Father, you haven't said anything about——

JOSH. Not a word to a soul—not even to your aunt.

REUBEN. Thank you. (*Shakes hands.*)

JOSH. Let bygones be bygones. That's the best way, ain't it, Jack?

JACK (*by fireplace*). Right you are, Mr. Whitcomb. (*Takes* JOSH'S *hands.*)

JOSH. You two boys ought to be brothers as long as you live.

JACK. It can be done.

JOSH. How?

JACK. Mother is still a widow. (*Laughing.*)

JOSH. I never thought of that.

REUBEN. It's worth thinking of, Father.

JOSH. Tut, tut, boys! Don't put sich nonsense in my head.

GANZEY (*enters*). Uncle, the gals and boys are goin' to slide down hill and they want to know if they can pile into your old sleigh?

JOSH. Yes; have the new one if they want.

GANZEY. Can they?

JOSH. Yes.

GANZEY (*going to door*). Say, come on, all on ye—Uncle says you can hev the sleigh, come on, come on. Say, Reub, won't you go with us?

(*Enter* SETH, ELINOR, RICKETY ANN, STRATTON *girls,* QUARTETTE *who cross up stage and exeunt—all dressed for out of doors.*)

REUBEN. No; I'll stay here with Father.

ELINOR (*pausing—by* REUBEN). Come, Reuben, I brought your coat and hat.

(REUBEN *takes hat and coat and follows with* ELINOR *off stage.*)

JOSH. Run along and have a good time. Jack and I'll keep house till you come back. There they go as happy as robins in spring. Well, Mr. Hazard, how do you like driving over our New Hampshire hills?

JACK (*taking chair near fireplace, sits*). I think it's delightful. It's great to get the blood circulating.

JOSH (*sits in rocker*). I guess it is!

JACK. Why, it beats the Turkish bath out of sight.

JOSH. So it does. I tell you, for health, give me a good old-fashioned New

England winter. I have seen the time, boy, when I was at your age, I used to jump into a sled behind a pair o' steers, in my shirt sleeves and my hat off, and go flying over the snow when it was cold enough to freeze the hinges of the barn door. Bin to dancing school lots o' times on a bob sled. We didn't use to hev dyspepsa them days. We didn't used to pull our chairs up to the table and say, "What hev you got for dinner?" but "How much hev you got?" Worked hard, lived plain, slept well, money was scarce and luxuries a good sight scarcer.

JACK. Well, you are none the worse for it.

JOSH. All the better! Hard as a hickory nut and spry as a kitten at sixty-four. (*Enter* MATILDA.)

MATILDA. Josh, I wish you'd come and help me put the table back. (*Exits.*)

JOSH (*rising*). Sartin. Come, Jack, I want to talk to you about your mother.

JACK. Oh-ho!

(*Exit with* JOSH L. *Enter* RICKETY *and* GANZEY *and stand by fireplace.*)

RICKETY. Well, if that ain't the meanest thing I ever knowed! Got the sleigh out from under the barn, helped them draw it up the hill, then they wouldn't let us go at all. Told us we could take hold o' hands and slide standin' up! It's mean, that's just what it is!

GANZEY. Mean! Well, I guess it is, come right down to it.

RICKETY. Now you jist wait till they ask me to do anything agin, that's all! —jist wait now! Wouldn't let us slide with them 'cause we weren't dressed good enough, I s'pose.

GANZEY. Ain't them mittens pretty? (*Shows mittens.*)

RICKETY. Oh, they're awfully nice.

GANZEY. Mother knit 'em.

RICKETY. Honest?

GANZEY. Goin' to hev sleeve buttons when I'm big enough.

RICKETY. No!

GANZEY. It's all that Ed Bogus's fault. He's awful stuck up ever sence he went to Saratogy last summer and stayed all night. He thinks he can order folks around jest as he's a mind to. Jest you wait till I get him alone! Jest you wait! You'll see!

RICKETY. Well, I jest would! Oh, say, let's put red pepper on the pop corn.

GANZEY. No, I'll tell you something better than that!

RICKETY. What?

GANZEY. Let's eat up all the pie.

RICKETY. Oh, all right. Say, Eb, do you like me?

GANZEY. Yes.

RICKETY. Philopene! (*Exits, laughing.*)

GANZEY (*whistles; hears organ off stage. Goes to door—listens*). Oh, the baby's awaked up—I better hide or they'll make me rock the cradle.

(*Hides in corner. Enter* MRS. MURDOCK *with baby which she places in cradle. As she does so she sings a lullaby. During the lullaby* SETH, CY P., ELINOR, RICKETY ANN, *and the* STRATTON *girls enter laughing.* MRS. MURDOCK *holds up a warning finger as she sings. The characters tiptoe softly and exeunt. The* QUARTETTE *enter and remain standing by fireplace and join in chorus of lullaby. At finish they quietly exeunt. A pause and* MATILDA *enters.*)

MATILDA. Well, Anna Maria, is the baby asleep?

MRS. M. Yes.

MATILDA. Why, what's the matter? You ben crying, ain't you?

MRS. M. Yes; the boys jest sung such a sweet song. It made me feel bad. I boo-hoo dreadful easy and always did, from a gal.

MATILDA. Never mind, Anna Maria, I wouldn't cry.

CY P. (*enters.*) Say, Tildy——

MATILDA. What?

CY P. You better come in here and pat Seth Perkins on the back.

MATILDA. Why?

CY P. Because he's jest swallowed a fork.

(CY P. *goes up and stands by fireplace. Enter* JOSH *and* REUBEN *followed by all the characters:* JACK, SETH, PAT CLANCEY, EB GANZEY, LEN HOLBROOK, *the* QUARTETTE, RICKETY ANN, ELINOR STRATTON, *two* STRATTON *girls and neighbors.* JACK *gazes at* ELINOR *who sits at cradle.* SETH *joins* CY P. *at fireplace.* PAT CLANCEY, EB GANZEY *and* LEN HOLBROOK, *with violin, remain near door.*)

JOSH. Here, Til, it's all settled. Reub and I hev had a good talk—we hev agreed on every pint,—he works the old farm on shares, takes possession tomorrow, New Year's Day—what do you think of that?

MATILDA. Oh, tell me all about it.

JACK. Mr. Whitcomb——

JOSH. What is it?

JACK. Who were those young ladies Reuben introduced me to? I have really forgotten their names.

JOSH. They are the Stratton gals.

JACK. And the one sitting at the cradle?

JOSH. That's Elinor.

JACK. She's a very pretty girl.

JOSH. And a proper good gal, too. Shin up to her and I'll lend you my front room to spark in, and you can burn all the wood you want to.

JACK. All right, thank you.

(JACK *is greeted by* ELINOR.)

JOSH. Now move your chairs and we'll have a dance. (*Everyone becomes alert and active, removing chairs and rugs aside.* LEN HOLBROOK, *and [if available] another fiddler, tunes up while* PAT CLANCEY *and* GANZEY *rush on the small, portable melodeon. The musicians sit while* GANZEY, *back of them, manipulates a jew's harp.* JOSH *stops them.)* Hold on! I want to say a word to our neighbors before they go. Now, you fathers that have got wild boys, I want you to be kind o' easy with them. If they are kind o' foolish now and then, forgive them. Like as not, it is as much your fault as 'tis theirs—they might have inherited it, you can't tell. And, mothers,—well, what's the use of saying anything to you, bless your smilin' faces. Your hearts are always biling over with love and kindness for the wayward child! Now don't let this be your last visit to the Old Homestead. Come up in June when all natur' is at her best—come on, all on you, and let the scarlet runners chase you back to childhood.

(*Music cue. The musicians strike a few chords while the characters, amid laughter and jollity, seek partners and positions for the Virginia Reel. The couples form in two lines down the middle of the room, gentlemen on one side facing their lady partners in the opposite line. The respective partners beginning down stage are as follows:* JOSH *and* MRS. MURDOCK; JACK *and* ELINOR; REUBEN *and* RICKETY; CY P. *and* MATILDA; SETH *and* STRATTON *girl; one of* QUARTETTE *and other* STRATTON *girl.* LEN HOLBROOK, *or one of the* QUARTETTE, *mounting a chair, can call the figures of the dance, which progresses with hilarity and enthusiasm till finish and*)

CURTAIN

Rip Van Winkle

AS PLAYED BY

JOSEPH JEFFERSON

ROYALTY NOTICE

Especial notice should be taken that the possession of this book without a valid contract for production first having been obtained from the publisher confers no right or license to professionals or amateurs to produce the play publicly or in private for gain or charity.

In its present form this play is dedicated to the reading public only and no performance, representation, production, recitation, public reading or radio broadcasting may be given except by special arrangement with Walter H. Baker, *178 Tremont Street, Boston, Mass.*

On application to Walter H. Baker Company, *178 Tremont Street, Boston, Mass., royalty will be quoted for amateur use of this play.*

Whenever the play is produced the following notice must appear on all programs, printing and advertising for the play: "Produced by special arrangement with Walter H. Baker Company."

Attention is called to the penalty provided by law for any infringement of the author's rights, as follows:

"Section 4966:—*Any person publicly performing or representing any dramatic or musical composition for which copyright has been obtained, without the consent of the proprietor of said dramatic or musical composition, or his heirs and assigns, shall be liable for damages thereof, such damages in all cases to be assessed at such sum, not less than one hundred dollars for the first and fifty dollars for every subsequent performance, as to the court shall appear to be just. If the unlawful performance and representation be wilful and for profit such person or persons shall be guilty of a misdemeanor; and upon conviction shall be imprisoned for a period not exceeding one year."*—U. S. Revised Statutes: Title 60, Chap. 3.

Rip Van Winkle has been played by many casts and has often been revised. The version included in the text is one that was revised by Joseph Jefferson himself and differs in some particulars from the production in which he first appeared at the Winter Garden in New York City on December 24, 1860, in which the principal characters were as follows:

Rip Van Winkle	Joseph Jefferson
Derrick Van Slaus	J. H. Stoddart
Herman Van Slaus	Lingham
Rory von Clump	Gourlay
Knickerbocker	Davidge
Nick Vedder	Clarke
Clausen	Craig
Stein	Styles
Spirit of Hendrick Hudson	Wilson
Dwarf	Miss Flynn
Second Spirit	Miss Tree
Third Spirit	Miss Evans
Seth Peabody	Owen Marlowe
Judge of the Court	Tree
Gustaff	George Stoddart
Child	Master Gourlay
Dame Van Winkle	Mrs. Duffield
Alice	Mrs. Chaufrau
Rowena	Sophie Gimber

Act One: The village of Falling Waters.
Act Two: Kitchen of Rip's house.
Act Three: A rocky clove in the Kaatskill Mountains.
Act Four: *Scene I*—Same as Act III.
Scene II—A room in Derrick's house.
Scene III—The village of Falling Waters.
Scene IV—Same as Scene II.

RIP VAN WINKLE

ACT ONE

SCENE—*The village of Falling Waters, set amid familiar and unmistakable Hudson River scenery, with the shining river itself and the noble heights of the Kaatskills visible in the distance. In the foreground, to the left of the stage, is a country inn bearing the sign of George III. In the wall of the inn, a window closed by a solid wooden shutter. To the right of the stage, an old cottage with a door opening into the interior; before the cottage stands a bench holding a wash-tub, with washboard, soap, and clothes in the tub. In the centre of the stage, a table and chairs, and on the table a stone pitcher and two tin cups.*

As the curtain rises, GRETCHEN *is discovered washing, and little* MEENIE *sitting near by on a low stool. The sound of a chorus and laughter comes from the inn.*

GRETCHEN. Shouting and drinking day and night. (*Laughter is heard from the inn.*) Hark how they crow over their cups while their wives are working at home, and their children are starving.

(*Enter* DERRICK *from the inn with a green bag, followed by* NICK VEDDER. DERRICK *places his green bag on the table.*)

DERRICK. Not a day, not an hour. If the last two quarters' rent be not paid by this time tomorrow, out you go!

NICK. Oh, come, Derrick, you won't do it. Let's have a glass, and talk the matter over; good liquor opens the heart. Here, Hendrick! Hendrick! (*Enter* HENDRICK.)

HENDRICK. Yes, Father.

DERRICK. So that is your brat?

NICK. Yes, that is my boy.

DERRICK. Then the best I can wish him is that he won't take after his father, and become a vagabond and a penniless outcast.

NICK. Those are hard words to hear in the presence of my child.

HENDRICK. Then why don't you knock him down, Father?

GRETCHEN. I'll tell you why——

DERRICK. Gretchen!

GRETCHEN (*wiping her arms and coming to front of tub*). It's because your father is in that man's power. And what's the use of getting a man down, if you don't trample on him?

NICK. Oh, that is the way of the world.

GRETCHEN (*to* HENDRICK). Go in, boy. I want to speak to your father, and my words may not be fit for you to hear. Yonder is my little girl; go and play with her. (HENDRICK *and* MEENIE *exeunt into the cottage.*) Now, Derrick, Vedder is right: you won't turn him out of his house yonder.

DERRICK. And why not? Don't he owe me a year's rent?

GRETCHEN. And what do you owe him? Shall I sum up your accounts for you? Ten years ago, this was a quiet village, and belonged mostly to my husband, Rip Van Winkle, a foolish, idle fellow. That house yonder has since been his ruin. Yes; bit by bit, he has parted with all he had, to fill the mouths of sots and boon companions, gathered around him in yonder house. And you, Derrick,—you supplied him with the money to waste in riot and drink. Acre by acre, you've sucked in his land to swell your store. Yonder miserable cabin is the only shelter we have left; but that is mine. Had it been his, he would have sold it to you, Derrick, long ago, and wasted its price in riot. (NICK, *who has been enjoying* DERRICK'S *discomfiture during this speech, is unable to control himself, and at the end of speech bursts into a loud laugh.*) Aye, and you too, Nick Vedder; you have ruined my husband between you.

NICK. Oh, come, Mrs. Van Winkle, you're too hard. I couldn't refuse Rip's money in the way of business; I had my rent to pay.

GRETCHEN. And shall I tell you why you can't pay it? It is because you have given Rip credit, and he has ended by drinking you out of house and home. Your window-shutter is not wide enough to hold the score against him; it is full of chalk. Deny it if you can.

NICK. I do deny it. There now!

GRETCHEN. Then why do you keep that shutter closed? I'll show you why. (*Goes to inn, opens shutter, holds it open, pointing at* RIP'S *score.*) That's why. Nick Vedder, you're a good man in the main, if there is such a thing. (DERRICK *laughs.*) Aye, and I doubt it. (*Turning on him.*) But you are the pest of this village; and the hand of every woman in it ought to help to pull down that drunkard's nest of yours, stone by stone.

NICK. Come, Dame Van Winkle, you're too hard entire; now a man must have his odd time, and he's none the worse for being a jolly dog.

GRETCHEN. No, none the worse. He sings a good song; he tells a good story,—oh, he's a glorious fellow! Did you ever see the wife of a jolly dog? Well, she lives in a kennel. Did you ever see the children of a jolly dog? They are the street curs, and their home is the gutter. (*Goes up to wash-tub, and takes revenge on the clothing she scrubs.*)

NICK (*getting up and approaching* GRETCHEN *timidly*). I tell you what it is, Dame Van Winkle, I don't know what your home may be, but judging from the rows I hear over there, and the damaged appearance of Rip's face after having escaped your clutches—(GRETCHEN *looks up angrily;* NICK *retreats a few paces hastily*)—I should say that a gutter was a luxurious abode compared with it, and a kennel a peaceful retreat.

(*Exit hurriedly, laughing, into the inn.*)

(GRETCHEN *looks up angrily, and throws the cloth she has been wringing after him, then resumes washing.* DERRICK *laughs at* NICK'S *exit, walks up to* GRETCHEN, *and puts one foot on bench.*)

DERRICK. Is it true, Gretchen? Are you truly miserable with Rip?

GRETCHEN. Ain't you pleased to hear it? Come then and warm your heart at my sorrow. Ten years ago I might have had you, Derrick. But I despised you for your miserly ways, and threw myself away on a vagabond.

DERRICK. You and I shared him between us. I took his estate, and you took his person. Now, I've improved my half. What have you done with yours?

GRETCHEN. I can't say that I've prospered with it. I've tried every means to reclaim him, but he is as obstinate and perverse as a Dutch pig. But the worst in him—and what I can't stand—is his good-humor. It drives me frantic when, night after night, he comes home drunk and helplessly good-humored! Oh, I can't stand that!

DERRICK. Where is he now?

GRETCHEN. We had a tiff yesterday, and he started. He has been out all night. Only wait until he comes back! The longer he stops out, the worse it will be for him.

DERRICK. Gretchen, you've made a great mistake, but there is time enough to repair it. You are comely still, thrifty, and that hard sort of grain that I most admire in woman. (*Looks cautiously around. Leans on tub.*) Why not start Rip for ever, and share my fortune?

GRETCHEN. Oh, no, Derrick; you've got my husband in your clutches, but you can't get them around me. If Rip would only mend his ways, he would see how much I love him; but no woman could love you, Derrick; for woman is not a domestic animal, glad to serve and fawn upon a man for the food and shelter she can get; and that is all she would ever get from you, Derrick. (*Piling the clothes on the washboard, and shouldering it.*)

DERRICK. The time may come when you'll change your tune.

GRETCHEN. Not while Rip lives, bad as he is. (*Exit into cottage.*)

DERRICK (*sneeringly*). Then I'll wait until you've killed him. Her spirit is not broken yet. But patience, Derrick, patience; in another month I'll have my claws on all that remains of Rip's property,—yonder cottage and grounds; then I'll try you again, my lady. (*Enter* COCKLES, *with papers in his hand, running towards the inn.*) How now, you imp? What brings you here so full of a hurry? Some mischief's in your head, or your heels would not be so busy.

COCKLES. I've brought a letter for you from my employer. There it is.

DERRICK (*examining letter*). Why, the seal is broken!

COCKLES. Yes; I read it as I came along.

DERRICK. Now I apprenticed this vagabond to my lawyer, and this is his gratitude.

COCKLES. Don't waste your breath, Nunky, for you'll want it; for when you read that, if it don't take you short in the wind I'll admire you.

DERRICK (*reads*). "You must obtain from Rip Van Winkle a proper conveyance of the lands he has sold to you. The papers he has signed are in fact nothing but mortgages on his estate. If you foreclose, you must sell the property, which has lately much advanced in value; and it would sell for enough to pay off your loan, and all your improvements would enure to the benefit of Rip Van Winkle."

COCKLES. There, now, see what you've been doing of!—wasting your money and my expectations on another chap's property. Do you want to leave me a beggar?

DERRICK (*reads*). "I enclose a deed for him to sign that will make him safe."

COCKLES. Of course he'll sign it; he won't wait to be asked—he'll be in such a hurry.

DERRICK. All my savings—all my money—sunk in improving this village!

COCKLES. Yes, instead of physicking Rip, as you thought, you've been coddling him all the while.

DERRICK. All these houses I've built are on another man's land. What shall I do?

COCKLES. Pull them down again; pull them down.

DERRICK. Ass!—dolt that I have been!

COCKLES. Calling yourself names won't mend it, Nunky.

DERRICK. The imp is right. Rip must be made to sign this paper. But how —how?

COCKLES. How? How? How's a big word sometimes, ain't it, Nunky?

DERRICK. Rip would not do it if he knew what he was about. But he can't read—nor write, for the matter of that. But he can make his cross, and I can cajole him.

COCKLES. Look sharp, Nunky. The man that's looking round for a fool, and picks up Rip Van Winkle, will let him drop again very quick.

DERRICK. He is poor: I'll show him a handful of money. He's a drunkard: I'll give him a stomachful of liquor. Go in, boy, and leave me to work this; and let this be a lesson to you hereafter: beware of the fatal effects of poverty and drink.

COCKLES. Yes,—and parting with my money on bad security. (*Exit. Laughter outside.*)

DERRICK. Here he comes now, surrounded by all the dogs and children in the district. They cling around him like flies around a lump of sugar.

(RIP *enters, running and skipping, carrying one small child pickaback, and surrounded by a swarm of others hanging on the skirts of his coat. He is laughing like a child himself, and his merry blue eyes twinkle with delight. He is dressed in an old deerskin coat, a pair of breeches which had once been red, now tattered, patched, and frayed, leather gaiters and shoes equally dilapidated, a shapeless felt hat with a bit of the brim hanging loose,—the whole stained and weatherworn to an almost uniform clay-color, except for the bright blue of his jean shirt and the scarlet of his long wisp of a necktie. One of the boys carries his gun.*)

RIP (*taking his gun from the boy*). There, run along mit you; run along.

DERRICK (*The children scamper off*). The vagabond looks like the father of the village.

RIP (*who has stood laughing, and watching the children, suddenly calls after them*). Hey! You let my dog Schneider alone there; you hear that Sock der Jacob der bist eine for donner spits poo—yah——

DERRICK. Why, what's the matter, Rip?

RIP (*coming down, and shaking hands with* DERRICK). Oh, how you was, Derrick? How you was?

DERRICK. You seem in trouble.

RIP. Oh, yah; you know them fellers. Vell, I tole you such a funny thing. (*Laughing.*) Just now, as me and Schneider was comin' along through the willage,—Schneider's my dawg; I don't know whether you know him? (RIP *always speaks of Schneider as if he were a person, and one in whom his hearer took as profound an interest as he does himself.*) Well, them fellers went an' tied a tin kettle mit Schneider's tail, and how he did run then, mit the kettle hanging about. Well, I didn't hi him comin'. He run betwixt me an' my legs, an' spilt me an' all them children in the mud;—yah, that's a fact. (RIP *leans his gun against the cottage.*)

DERRICK (*aside*). Now's my time. (*Aloud.*) Vedder! Vedder! (NICK *appears at the door of the inn.*) Bring us a bottle of liquor. Bring us your best, and be quick.

NICK. What's in the wind now? The devil's to pay when Derrick stands treat! (*Exit. Re-enters, with bottle and cups in left hand. Hands bottle to* DERRICK. RIP *lounges forward, and perches on the corner of the table.*)

DERRICK (*rising and approaching* RIP). Come, Rip, what do you say to a glass?

RIP (*takes a cup, and holds it to be filled*). Oh, yah; now what do I generally say to a glass? I say it's a fine thing—when there's plenty in it. (Ve gates! Ve gates!) (*Shakes hands with* NICK.) An' then I says more to what's in it than I do to the glass. Now you wouldn't believe it, —that's the first one I've had today.

DERRICK. How so?

RIP (*dryly*). Because I couldn't get it before, I suppose.

DERRICK. Then let me fill him up for you.

RIP. No, that is enough for the first one.

NICK. Come, Rip, a bumper for the first one.

RIP. That is enough for the first one.

DERRICK. Come, Rip, let me fill him up for you.

RIP (*with ludicrous decision and dignity*). I believe I know how much to drink. When I says a thing, I mean it.

DERRICK. Oh, well—— (*Turns aside, and starts to fill his own cup.*)

RIP. All right; come along. (*Holding out his glass, and laughing at his own inconsistency.*) Here's your good health and your families'; and may they live long and prosper! (*They all drink. At the end,* NICK *smacks his lips and exclaims "Ah!"* DERRICK *repeats same, and* RIP *repeats after* DERRICK. *To* NICK, *sadly.*) Ah, you may well go "Ah!" and smack your chops over that. You don't give me such schnapps when I come. Derrick, my score is too big now. (*Jerking his head toward the shutter, he notices for the first time that it is open.*) What you go and open that window for?—That's fine schnapps, Nick. Where you got that?

NICK. That's high Dutch, Rip—high Dutch, and ten years in bottle. Why, I had that in the very day of your wedding. We broached the keg under yonder shed. Don't you recollect?

RIP. Is that the same?

NICK. Yes.

RIP. I thought I knowed that licker. You had it ten years ago? (*Laughing suddenly.*) I would not have kept it so long. But stop, mein freund; that's more than ten years ago.

NICK. No, it ain't.

RIP. It's the same day I got married?

NICK. Yes.

RIP. Well, I know by that. You think I forgot the day I got married? Oh, no, my friend; I remember that day long as I live. (*Serious for a moment. Takes off his hat, and puts it on the table.*)

DERRICK. Ah! Rip, I remember Gretchen then, ten years ago.—Zounds, how I envied you!

RIP (*looking up, surprised*). Did you? (*Winks at* NICK. *Then, suddenly remembering.*) So did I. You didn't know what was comin', Derrick.

DERRICK. She was a beauty.

RIP. What, Gretchen?—Yes, she was. She was a pretty girl. My! My! Yah, we was a fine couple altogether. Well, come along. (*Holding out his cup to* DERRICK, *who fills it from the bottle.*)

NICK. Yes, come along. (*Takes water pitcher from table, and starts to fill up* RIP'*s cup.* RIP *stops him.*)

RIP (*who has been lounging against the table, sits on it, and puts his feet on the chair*). Stop! I come along mitout that, Nick Vedder. (*Sententiously.*) Good licker and water is like man and wife.

DERRICK and NICK. How's that, Rip?

RIP (*laughing*). They don't agree together. I always like my licker single. Well, here's your good health, and your families', and may they live long and prosper! (*They all drink.*)

NICK. That's right, Rip; drink away, and drown your sorrow.

RIP (*drolly*). Yes; but she won't drown. My wife is my sorrow, and you cannick drown her. She tried it once, but couldn't do it.

DERRICK and NICK. Why, how so?

RIP (*puts down his cup and clasps his knee, still perched on the corner of the table*). Didn't you know that Gretchen like to got drown?

DERRICK and NICK. No.

RIP (*puts hat on*). That's the funniest thing of the whole of it. It's the same day I got married; she was comin' across the river there in the ferry-boat to get married mit me——

DERRICK and NICK. Yes.

RIP. Well, the boat she was comin' in got upsetted.

DERRICK and NICK. Ah!

RIP. Well, but she wasn't in it.

DERRICK and NICK. Oh!

RIP (*explaining quite seriously*). No, that's what I say: if she had been in the boat what got upsetted, maybe she might have got drowned. (*More and more reflective.*) I don't know how it was she got left somehow or other. Women is always behind that way—always.

DERRICK. But surely, Rip, you would have risked your life to save such a glorious creature as she was.

RIP (*incredulously*). You mean I would yump in and pull Gretchen out?

DERRICK. Yes.

RIP. Oh, would I? (*Suddenly remembering.*) Oh, you mean then—yes, I believe I would then. (*With simple conviction.*) But it would be more my duty now than it was then.

DERRICK. How so?

RIP (*quite seriously*). Why, you see when a feller gets married a good many years mit his wife, he gets very much attached to her.

NICK (*pompously*). Ah, he does indeed.

RIP (*winks at* DERRICK, *and points at* NICK *with his thumb*). But if Mrs. Van Winkle was a-drowning in the water now, an' she says to me, "Rip, come an' save your wife!" I would say, "Mrs. Van Winkle, I will yust go home and think about it." Oh, no, Derrick, if ever Gretchen tumbles in the water, she's got to swim now, you mind that.

DERRICK. She was here just now, anxiously expecting you home.

RIP. I know she's keeping it hot for me.

NICK. What, your dinner, Rip?

RIP. No, the broomstick. (*Exit* NICK *into house, laughing.* RIP, *confidentially.*) Derrick, whenever I come back from the mountains, I always stick the gamebag in the window and creep in behind.

DERRICK (*seating himself on the table by the side of* RIP). Have you anything now?

RIP (*dropping into the chair* DERRICK *has just left. Leaning back, and putting hands behind his head*). What for game? No, not a tail, I believe, not a feather. (*With humorous indifference.*)

DERRICK (*touching* RIP *on the shoulder and shaking a bag of money*). Rip, suppose you were to hang this bagful of money inside, don't you think it would soothe her down, eh?

RIP (*sitting up*). For me, is that?

DERRICK. Yes.

RIP (*with a shrewd glance*). Ain't you yokin' mit me?

DERRICK. No, Rip, I've prospered with the lands you've sold me, and I'll let you have a loan on easy terms. I'll take no interest.

RIP (*getting up and walking forward, with decision*). No, I'm afraid I might pay you again some day, Derrick.

DERRICK. And so you shall, Rip, pay me when you please. (*Puts the bag in* RIP'*s hands, and forces his fingers over it, turns, and goes to table, speaking as he goes.*) Say, in twenty years,—twenty years from this day. Ah, where shall we be then?

RIP (*quizzically, and half to himself*). I don't know about myself; but I think I can guess where you'll be about that time. (*Takes chair and sits down.*)

DERRICK. Well, Rip, I'll just step into the inn and draw out a little acknowledgment.

RIP (*who has been sitting, leaning forward with his elbows on his knees, softly chinking the bag of money in his hand, looks up suddenly*). Knowledgment—for what is that?

DERRICK. Yes, for you to put your cross to.

RIP (*indifferently*). All right; bring it along.

DERRICK. No fear of Gretchen now, eh, Rip?

RIP (*plunged in thought*). Oh, no.

DERRICK. You feel quite comfortable now, don't you, Rip? (*Exit into inn.*)

RIP. Oh, yah! (*Suddenly becoming serious and much mystified at* DERRICK'*s conduct.*) Well, I don't know about that, Derrick! Derrick! (*Holding up the bag and chinking it.*) It don't chink like good money neither. It rattles like a snake in a hole. (*Grimly.*)

GRETCHEN (*inside the cottage*). Out with that lazy, idle cur! I won't have him here. Out, I say!

RIP. I'm glad I'm not in there now. I believe that's Schneider what she's lickin'; he won't have any backbone left in him. (*Sadly.*) I would rather she would lick me than the dog;

I'm more used to it than he is. (*Gets up, and looks in at the window.*) There she is at the wash-tub. (*Admiring her energy, almost envying it.*) What a hard-workin' woman that is! Well, somebody must do it, I suppose. (*With the air of a profound moral reflection.*) She's comin' here now. She's got some broomstick mit her, too. (RIP *snatches up his gun and slinks off around the corner of the house.*)

(*Enter* GRETCHEN *with broomstick, followed by* HENDRICK *and* MEENIE, *carrying clothes-basket.*)

GRETCHEN. Come along, children. Now, you take the washing down to Dame Van Sloe's, then call at the butcher's and tell him that my husband has not got back yet, so I will have to go down myself to the marsh, and drive up the bull we have sold to him. Tell him the beast shall be in his stable in half an hour; so let him have the money ready to pay me for it. (*During this* RIP *has crept in and sat on the bench by the side of the tub behind* GRETCHEN.) Ah, it is the last head of cattle we have left. Houses, lands, beasts, everything gone,—everything except a drunken beast who nobody would buy or accept as a gift. Rip! Rip! Wait until I get you home! (*Threatening an imaginary* RIP *with broomstick. With a comical grimace,* RIP *tiptoes back behind the house.*) Come, children, to work, to work! (*Exits.*)

(*Re-enter* RIP *cautiously.*)

RIP (*laughing to himself*). She gone to look after the bull. She better not try the broomstick on him; he won't stand it. (*Drops into the chair with his back to the audience.*)

HENDRICK. Oh, Meenie, there's your father.

RIP (*holds out his arms, and* MEENIE *runs into them. Taking her in his arms, and embracing her with great tenderness*). Ah, little gorl, was you glad to see your father come home?

MEENIE. Oh, yes!

RIP (*holding her close*). I don't believe it, was you? Come here. (*Getting up and leading her to the chair by the side of the table.*) Let me look at you; I don't see you for such a long time; come here. I don't deserve to have a thing like that belong to me. (*Takes his hat off as if in reverence.*) You're too good for a drunken, lazy feller like me, that's a fact. (*Bites his underlip, looks up, and brushes away a tear.*)

MEENIE (*kneeling by him.*) Oh, no, you are a good papa!

RIP. No, I wasn't: no good father would go and rob his child; that's what I've done. Why, don't you know, Meenie, all the houses and lands in the village was mine—they would all have been yours when you grew up? Where they gone now? I gone drunk 'em up, that's where they gone. Hendrick, you just take warnin' by that; that's what licker do; see that? (*Holds up the skirt of coat.*) Bring a man to hunger and rags. Is there any more in that cup over there? Give it to me. (*Drinks.* RIP *makes his confession with a childlike simplicity. The tears come, and he brushes them away once or twice. When he asks for the cup, at the end, it seems but the natural conclusion of his speech.)*

HENDRICK (*hands him cup*). Don't cry, Rip; Meenie does not want your money, for when I'm a big man I shall work for her, and she shall have all I get.

MEENIE. Yes, and I'll have Hendrick, too.

RIP (*greatly amused*). You'll have Hendrick, too. (*With mock gravity.*) Well, is this all settled?

HENDRICK. Yes, Meenie and me have made it all up.

RIP. I didn't know, I only thought you might speak to me about it; but if it's all settled, Meenie, then git married mit him. (*Laughing silently, and suddenly.*) You goin' to marry my daughter? Well, now that's very kind of you. Marry one another? (*The children nod.* RIP, *with immense seriousness.*) Well, here's your good health, and your family, may they live long and prosper. (*To* HENDRICK.) What you goin' to do when you get married, and grow up and so? (*Leans forward.*)

HENDRICK. I'm not going to stop here with Father; oh, no, that won't do. I'm going with Uncle Hans in his big ship to the North Pole, to catch whales.

RIP. Goin' to cotch whales mit the North Pole? That's a long while away from here.

HENDRICK. Yes, but Uncle will give me ten shillings a month, and I will tell him to pay it all to Meenie.

RIP. There! He's goin' to pay it all to you; that's a good boy, that's a good boy.

MEENIE. Yes, and I'll give it all to you to keep for us.

RIP (*with one of his little explosive silent laughs*). I wouldn't do that, my darlin'; maybe if you give it to me, you don't get it back again. Hendrick! (*Suddenly earnest.*) You shall marry Meenie when you grow up, but you mustn't drink.

HENDRICK (*slapping* RIP *on the knee*). I'll never touch a drop.

RIP (*quite seriously*). You won't, nor me neither; shake hands upon it. Now we swore off together. (*With a change of tone.*) I said so so many times, and never kept my word once, never. (*Drinks.*)

HENDRICK. I've said so once, and I'll keep mine.

DERRICK (*outside*). Well, bring it along with you.

RIP. Here comes Derrick: he don't like some children; run along mit you. (*Exit children with basket.*)

(*Enter* DERRICK *from inn with document.*)

DERRICK. There, Rip, is the little acknowledgment. (*Handing it to him.*)

RIP. Knowledgment. (*Putting on hat.*) For what is that?

DERRICK. That is to say I loaned you the money.

RIP (*lounging back in his chair*). I don't want that; I would lose it if I had it. (*Fills his cup from the bottle.*) I don't want it. (*Blandly.*)

DERRICK. Don't you? But I do.

RIP (*with simple surprise*). For what?

DERRICK. Why, for you to put your cross to. Why, bless me, I've forgotten my pen and ink. (*Enter* COCKLES.) But luckily here comes my nephew with it. (*Aside.*) And in time to witness the signature.

RIP. Say, Derrick, have you been writing all that paper full in the little time you been in the house there? (*Turns the paper about curiously. Pours out more schnapps.*)

DERRICK. Yes, every word of it.

RIP. Have you? Well, just read it out loud to me. (*With an air of great simplicity.*)

DERRICK (*aside*). Does he suspect? (*Aloud.*) Why, Rip, this is the first time you ever wanted anything more than the money.

RIP (*clasping his hands behind his head with an air of lordly indifference*). Yes, I know; but I got nothing to do now. I'm a little curious about that, somehow.

COCKLES (*aside to* DERRICK). The fish has taken the ground bait, but he's curious about the hook.

DERRICK (*aside*). I dare not read a word of it.

COCKLES (*aside*). Nunky's stuck.

DERRICK. Well, Rip, I suppose you don't want to hear the formalities.

RIP. The what?

DERRICK. The preliminaries.

RIP (*indolently*). I'll take it all,— Bill, Claws, and Feathers. (*Leans forward and rests his head on his hand, and looks at the ground.*)

DERRICK. "Know all men by these presents that I, Rip Van Winkle, in consideration of the sum of sixteen pounds received by me from Derrick Von Beekman——" (*Looks around at* COCKLES; *they wink knowingly at each other. Continues as if reading. Watching* RIP—) Do promise and undertake to pay the same in twenty years from date. (RIP *looks up; as he does so,* DERRICK *drops his eyes on document, then looks as if he had just finished reading.*) There, now are you satisfied?

RIP (*takes the document. In childlike surprise*). Well, well, and does it take all that pen and ink to say such a little thing like that?

DERRICK. Why, of course it does.

COCKLES (*aside to* DERRICK). Oh, the fool! he swallows it whole, hook and all.

RIP (*spreading the paper on the table*). Where goes my cross, Derrick?

DERRICK (*pointing*). There, you see I've left a nice little white corner for you.

RIP (*folds up paper in a leisurely manner, and puts it in game-bag*).

W-e-l-l, I'll yust think about it. (*Looks up at* DERRICK, *innocently.*)

DERRICK. Think about it? Why, what's the matter, Rip, isn't the money correct?

RIP. Oh, yes, I got the money all right. (*Chuckling.*) Oh! you mean about signing it. (*Rising. At a loss, for a moment.*) Stop, yesterday was Friday, wasn't it?

DERRICK. So it was.

RIP (*with an air of conviction*). Well, I never do nothing like that the day after Friday, Derrick. (RIP *walks away toward his cottage.*)

DERRICK (*aside*). The idiot! What can that signify? But I must not arouse his suspicions by pressing him. (*Aloud.*) You are right, Rip: sign it when you please; but I say, Rip, now that you're in funds, won't you help your old friend Nick Vedder, who owes me a year's rent?

RIP (*coming back to the table*). Oh, yah, I will wipe off my schore, and stand treat to the whole willage.

DERRICK. Run, boy, and tell all the neighbors that Rip stands treat.

RIP (*leans on back of chair*). An', Cockles, tell them we'll have a dance.

COCKLES. A dance! (*Runs off.*)

DERRICK. And I'll order the good cheer for you. (*Exit.*)

RIP. So do! so do! (*Cogitating dubiously.*) I don't understand it. (*Re-enter* HENDRICK *with the basket over his head, followed by* MEENIE.) Oh, you've come back?

HENDRICK. Yes, we've left the clothes.

RIP. Meenie, you take in the basket. (*Exit* MEENIE *with basket into cottage.* HENDRICK *is following.*) Hendrick, come here. (HENDRICK *kneels between* RIP's *knees.*) So you are going to marry my daughter? (HENDRICK *nods.*) So, so. That's very kind of yer. (*Abruptly.*) Why you don't been to school today, you go to school sometimes, don't you?

HENDRICK. Yes, when Father can spare me.

RIP. What do you learn mit that school,—pretty much something? (*Laughing at his mistake.*) I mean, everything?

HENDRICK. Yes; reading, writing, and arithmetic.

RIP. Reading, and what?

HENDRICK. And writing, and arithmetic.

RIP (*puzzled*). Writing, and what?

HENDRICK. Arithmetic.

RIP (*more puzzled*). Whatmeticks is that?

HENDRICK. Arithmetic.

RIP (*with profound astonishment and patting* HENDRICK's *head*). I don't see how the little mind can stand it all. Can you read?

HENDRICK. Oh, yes!

RIP (*with a serious affectation of incredulity*). I don't believe it; now, I'm just goin' to see if you can read. If you can't read, I won't let you marry my daughter. No, sir. (*Very drolly.*) I won't have nobody in my family what can't read. (*Taking out the paper that* DERRICK *has given him.*) Can you read ritmatics like that?

HENDRICK. Yes, that's writing.

RIP (*nonplused*). Oh! I thought it was reading.

HENDRICK. It's reading and writing, too.

RIP. What, both together? (*Suspiciously looking at the paper.*) Oh, yes; I didn't see that before; go along with it.

HENDRICK (*reads*). "Know all men by these presents——"

RIP (*pleased, leaning back in his chair*). Yah! That's right, what a wonderful thing der readin' is; why, you read it pretty nigh as good as Derrick, yes, you do; go along.

HENDRICK. "That I, Rip Van Winkle ——"

RIP (*taking off his hat, and holding it with his hands behind his head*). Yah, that's right; you read it yust as well as Derrick; go long.

HENDRICK. "In consideration of the sum of sixteen pounds received do hereby sell and convey to Derrick Von Beekman all my estate, houses, lands whatsoever——" (*Hat drops.*)

RIP (*almost fiercely*). What are you readin', some rithmatics what ain't down there. Where you got that? (*Looking sharply at* HENDRICK.)

HENDRICK (*pointing*). There. Houses! Lands, whatsoever.

RIP (*looking not at the paper but at* HENDRICK *very earnestly, as if turning over in his mind whether the boy has read it correctly. Then satisfied of the deception* DERRICK *has practised upon him, and struck by the humor of the way in which he has discovered it, he laughs exultantly and looks toward the inn-door through which* DERRICK *disappeared a short time before*). Yes, so it is; go long mit the rest. (*He leans forward, and puts his ear close to* HENDRICK, *so as not to miss a word.*)

HENDRICK. "Whereof he now holds possession by mortgaged deeds, from time to time executed by me."

RIP (*takes paper, and looks toward the inn fiercely exultant*). You read it better than Derrick, my boy, much better. (*After a moment's pause recollects himself. Kindly, to* HENDRICK.) That will do; run along mit you. (*Exit* HENDRICK. *Triumphantly.*) Aha, my friend, Derrick! I guess you got some snakes in the grass. Now keep sober, Rip; I don't touch another drop so long what I live; I swore off now, that's a fixed fact.

(*Enter* DERRICK, NICK, JACOB STEIN, *and* VILLAGERS.)

DERRICK. Come, Rip, we'll have a rouse.

RIP (*seriously; half fiercely still*). Here, Nick Vedder, here is the gelt; wipe off my score, and drink away I don't join you; I swore off.

NICK. Why, Rip, you're king of the feast.

RIP (*absently. Still intent on* DERRICK). Am I dat?

OMNES. Swore off? What for?

RIP. I don't touch another drop.

STEIN (*coming down toward* RIP *with cup*). Come, Rip, take a glass.

RIP (*turning on him, almost angry*). Jacob Stein, you hear what I said?

STEIN. Yes.

RIP (*firmly*). Well, when I said a thing, I mean it. (*Leans back in chair with his hands behind his head.*)

STEIN. Oh, very well. (*Turns away.*)

(NICK *comes down and holds cup under* RIP'S *nose.* RIP *looks to see if they are watching him. He can resist no longer, and takes the cup.*)

RIP (*laughing*). Well, I won't count this one. Here's your good health and your families', may they all live long and prosper.

DERRICK. Here come the fiddlers and the girls.

(*Enter girls.* RIP *walks over and closes the shutter which has held his score, then returns and seats himself on a low stool, and keeps time to the music as the villagers dance. Finally, the rhythm fires his blood. He jumps to his feet, snatches one of the girls away from her partner, and whirls into the dance. After a round or two, he lets go of her, and pirouettes two or three times by himself. Once more he catches her in his arms, and is in the act of embracing her, when he perceives* GRETCHEN *over her shoulder. He drops the girl, who falls on her knees at* GRETCHEN'S *feet. There is a general laugh at his discomfiture, in which he joins half-heartedly. As the curtain descends,* RIP *is seen pointing at the girl as if seeking, like a modern Adam, to put the blame on her.*)

ACT TWO

SCENE—*The dimly lighted kitchen of* RIP'S *cottage. The door and window are at the back. It is night, and through the window a furious storm can be seen raging, with thunder, lightning, and rain.*

A fire smoulders on the hearth, to the right, and a candle gutters on the table in the center; a couple of chairs, a low stool, and a little cupboard, meagrely provided with cups and platters, complete the furniture of the room. Between the door and the window a clothes-horse, with a few garments hanging on it, forms a screen. To the left is a small door leading to the other rooms of the cottage.

As the curtain rises, MEENIE *is seen sitting by the window, and* GRETCHEN *enters, takes off cloak, and throws a broomstick on the table.*

GRETCHEN. Meenie! Has your father come yet?

MEENIE. No, Mother.

GRETCHEN. So much the better for him. Never let him show his face in these doors again—never!

MEENIE. Oh, Mother, don't be so hard on him.

GRETCHEN. I'm not hard; how dare you say so? (MEENIE *approaches her.*) There, child, that father of yours is enough to spoil the temper of an angel. I went down to the marsh to drive up the bull. I don't know what Rip has been doing to the beast; he was howling and tearing about. I barely escaped with my life. (*A crash outside.*) What noise is that?

MEENIE. That's only Schneider, Father's dog.

GRETCHEN (*picking up broomstick*). Then, I'll Schneider him. I won't have him here. (*Exit through the door leading to the rest of the cottage.*) Out, you idle, vagabond cur; out, I say!

MEENIE (*following her to the door, and crying*). Oh, don't, don't hurt the poor thing!

(*Re-enter* GRETCHEN.)

GRETCHEN. He jumped out of the window before I could catch him. He's just like his master. Now, what are you crying for?

MEENIE. Because my poor father is out in all this rain. (*A peal of thunder is heard.*) Hark, how it thunders!

GRETCHEN. Serve him right—do him good. Is the supper ready?

MEENIE. Yes, Mother; it is there by the fireside. (*Pointing to a soup bowl by the fire.*) Shall I lay the table?

GRETCHEN. Yes. (*Again it thunders.*) It's a dreadful night; I wonder where Rip is?

MEENIE (*bringing the cups and platters from the sideboard, together with a loaf of bread*). Shall I lay the table for two, Mother, or for three?

GRETCHEN. For two, girl; he gets no supper here tonight. (*Another peal of thunder.*) Mercy, how the storm rages! The fool, to stop out in such a downpour. I hope he's found shelter. I must look out the old suit I washed and mended for him last week, and put them by the fire to air. The idiot, to stop out in such a downpour! I'll have him sick on my hands next; that's all I want to complete my misery. (*She fetches clothes from the horse, and hangs them on the back of the chair in front of the fire.*) He knows what I am suffering now, and that's what keeps him out. (*Lightning.*) Mercy, what a flash that was! The wretch will be starved with the cold! Meenie!

MEENIE. Yes, Mother.

GRETCHEN. You may lay the table for three. (*There is a knock at the outer door.*) There he is now! (*Enter* HENDRICK, *who shakes the rain from his hat.*) Where's Rip? Is he not at your father's?

HENDRICK. No; I thought he was here.

GRETCHEN. He's gone back to the mountain. He's done it on purpose to spite me.

HENDRICK (*going to the fire*). Shall I run after him, and bring him home? I know the road; we've often climbed it together.

GRETCHEN. No; I drove Rip from his house, and it's for me to bring him back again.

MEENIE (*still arranging the supper table*). But, Mother—— (*She pauses, with embarrassment.*) If he hears your voice behind him, he will only run away the faster.

GRETCHEN. Well, I can't help it; I can't rest under cover, while he is out in the storm. I shall feel better when I'm outside sharing the storm with him. Sit down, and take your suppers. I'll take my cloak along with me. (*Exit.*)

(MEENIE *has seated herself by the window.* HENDRICK *carries stool to the centre of the stage, in front of the table.*)

HENDRICK. Meenie! Meenie!

MEENIE. Eh? (HENDRICK *beckons to her. She runs to him. He stops her suddenly, then puts the stool down with great deliberation, and sits on it, while* MEENIE *kneels beside him.*)

HENDRICK (*in a very solemn tone*). I hope your father ain't gone to the mountains tonight, Meenie?

MEENIE (*in distress*). Oh, dear! he will die of the cold there.

HENDRICK (*suddenly*). Sh! (MEENIE *starts.*) It ain't for that. (*Mysteriously.*) I've just heard old Clausen, over at Father's, saying, that on this very night, every twenty years, the ghosts—

MEENIE (*catching his wrist*). The what?

HENDRICK (*in an awed tone*). The ghosts of Hendrick Hudson, and his pirate crew, visit the Kaatskills above here. (*The two children look around, frightened.*)

MEENIE. Oh, dear, did he say so?

HENDRICK. Sh! (*Again they look around, frightened.*) Yes; and the spirits have been seen there smoking, drinking, and playing at tenpins.

MEENIE. Oh, how dreadful!

HENDRICK. Sh! (*He goes cautiously to the chimney, and looks up, while* MEENIE *looks under the table; then, he returns to the stool, speaking as he comes.*) Yes; and every time that Hendrick Hudson lights his pipe there's a flash of lightning. (*Lightning, and* MEENIE *gives a gasp of fear.*) And when he rolls the balls along, there is a peal of thunder. (*Loud rumble of thunder.* MEENIE *screams, and throws herself into* HENDRICK'S *arms.*) Don't be frightened, Meenie; I'm here. (*In a frightened tone, but with a manly effort to be courageous.)*

(Re-enter GRETCHEN *with her cloak.)*

GRETCHEN. Here, stop that! *(The children separate quickly.* HENDRICK *looks up at the ceiling and whistles, with an attempt at unconsciousness, and* MEENIE *assumes an innocent and unconcerned expression.)* Now, don't you be filling that child's head with nonsense, but remain quietly here until I return. Hush, what noise is that? There is some one outside the window. *(She steps behind the clothes-horse.* RIP *appears at the window, which he opens, and leans against the frame.)*

RIP. Meenie!

MEENIE and HENDRICK *(trying to make him perceive* GRETCHEN*, by a gesture in her direction).* Sh!

*(*RIP *turns, and looks around outside to see what they mean, then, discovering nothing, drops his hat in at the window, and calls again, cautiously.)*

RIP. Meenie!

MEENIE and HENDRICK *(with the same warning gesture).* Sh!

*(*GRETCHEN *shakes her fist at the children, who assume an air of innocence.)*

RIP. What's the matter? Meenie, has the wildcat come home? *(*RIP *reaches in after his hat.* GRETCHEN *catches him by his hair, and holds his head down.)* Och, my darlin', don't do that, eh!

HENDRICK and MEENIE *(who run toward* GRETCHEN*).* Don't, Mother! Don't, Mother! Don't!

RIP *(imitating their tone).* Don't, Mother, don't! Don't you hear the children? Let go my head, won't you? *(Getting angry.)*

GRETCHEN *(still holding his head down).* No; not a hair.

RIP *(bantering).* Hold on to it then, what do I care?

HENDRICK and MEENIE *(catching* GRETCHEN'S *dress).* Don't, Mother! Don't, Mother! Don't!

*(*GRETCHEN *lets go of* RIP*, and turns upon them. They escape, and disappear through the door to the left.)*

RIP *(getting in through the window, and coming forward, apparently drunk, but jolly; and his resentment for the treatment he has just received is half humorous).* For what you do dat, hey? You must want a bald-headed husband, I reckon!

*(*GRETCHEN *picks up chair, and bangs it down;* RIP *imitates her with the stool. She sits down, angrily, and slaps the table.* RIP *throws down his felt hat with a great show of violence, and it makes no noise, then seats himself on the stool.)*

GRETCHEN. Now, then!

RIP. Now, den; I don't like it den, neider. *(When* RIP *is drunk, his dialect grows more pronounced.)*

GRETCHEN. Who did you call a wildcat?

RIP (*with a sudden little tipsy laugh, and confused*). A wildcat—dat's when I come in at the window?

GRETCHEN. Yes; that's when you came in the window.

RIP (*rising, and with a tone of finality*). Yes; that's the time I said it.

GRETCHEN. Yes; and that's the time I heard it.

RIP (*with drunken assurance*). That's all right; I was afraid you wouldn't hear it.

GRETCHEN. Now, who did you mean by that wildcat?

RIP (*confused*). Who did I mean? Now, let me see.

GRETCHEN. Yes; who did you mean?

RIP. How do I know who-oo I mean? (*With a sudden inspiration.*) Maybe, it's the dog Schneider, I call that.

GRETCHEN (*incredulously*). The dog Schneider; that's not likely.

RIP (*argumentatively*). Of course it is likely; he's my dog. I'll call him a wildcat much as I please. (*Conclusively. He sits down in the chair on which his clothes are warming, in front of the fire.*)

GRETCHEN. And then, there's your disgraceful conduct this morning. What have you got to say to that?

RIP. How do I know what I got to say to that, when I don't know what I do-a, do-a? (*Hiccoughs.*)

GRETCHEN. Don't know what you do-a-oo! Hugging and kissing the girls, before my face; you thought I wouldn't see you.

RIP (*boldly*). I knowed you would—I knowed you would; because, because ——(*Losing the thread of his discourse.*) Oh-h, don't you bodder me. (*He turns, and leans his head against the back of the chair.*)

GRETCHEN. You knew I was there?

RIP (*laughing*). I thought I saw you.

GRETCHEN. I saw you myself, dancing with the girl.

RIP. You saw the girl dancin' mit me. (GRETCHEN *remembers* RIP's *clothes, and goes over to see if he is wet, and pushes him toward the center of the stage.* RIP *mistakes her intention.*) You want to pull some more hair out of my head?

GRETCHEN. Why, the monster! He isn't wet a bit! He's as dry as if he'd been aired!

RIP. Of course I'm dry. (*Laughing.*) I'm always dry—always dry.

GRETCHEN (*examines game-bag, and pulls out a flask, which she holds under* RIP'S *nose*). Why, what's here? Why, it's a bottle—a bottle!

RIP (*leaning against the table*). Yes; it's a bottle. (*Laughs.*) You think I don't know a bottle when I see it?

GRETCHEN. That's pretty game for your game-bag, ain't it?

RIP (*assuming an innocent air*). Somebody must have put it there.

GRETCHEN (*putting the flask in her pocket*). Then, you don't get it again.

RIP (*with a show of anger*). Now mind if I don't get it again—well—all there is about it—— (*Breaking down.*) I don't want it. I have had enough. (*With a droll air of conviction.*)

GRETCHEN. I'm glad you know when you've had enough.

RIP (*still leaning against the table*). That's the way mit me. I'm glad I know when I got enough—— (*Laughs.*) An' I'm glad when I've got enough, too. Give me the bottle; I want to put it in the game-bag.

GRETCHEN. For what?

RIP (*lounging off the table, and coming forward and leaning his arms on* GRETCHEN'S *shoulders*). So that I can't drink it. Here's the whole business—— (*He slides his hand down to* GRETCHEN'S *pocket, and tries to find the bottle while he talks to her.*) Here's the whole business about it. What is the use of anybody—well—wash the use of anybody, anyhow—well—oh—— (*Missing the pocket.*) What you talkin' 'bout—— (*Suddenly his hand slips into her pocket, and he begins to pull the bottle out, with great satisfaction.*) Now, now I can tell you all 'bout it.

GRETCHEN (*discovering his tactics, and pushing him away*). Pshaw!

RIP. If you don't give me the bottle, I just break up everything in the house.

GRETCHEN. If you dare!

RIP. If I dare! Haven't I done it two or three times before? I just throw everything right out of the window. (RIP *throws the plates and cups on the floor, and overturns a chair, and seats himself on the table.* GRETCHEN *picks them up again.*)

GRETCHEN. Don't, Rip; don't do that! Now stop, Rip, stop! (GRETCHEN *bangs down a chair by the table, and seats herself.*) Now, then, perhaps you will be kind enough to tell where you've been for the last two days. Where have you been? Do you hear?

RIP. Where I've been? Well, it's not my bottle, anyhow. I borrowed that bottle from another feller. You want to know where I been?

GRETCHEN. Yes, and I will know.

RIP (*good-humoredly*). Let me see. Last night I stopped out all night.

GRETCHEN. But why?

RIP. Why? You mean the reason of it?

GRETCHEN. Yes, the reason.

RIP (*inconsequently*). The reason is why? Don't bother me.

GRETCHEN (*emphasizing each word with a bang on the table*). Why—did—you—stop—out—all—night?

RIP (*imitating her tone*). Because—I—want—to—get—up—early—in—the—morning. (*Hiccough.*) Come, don't get so mad mit a feller. Why, I've been fillin' my game-bag mit game. (RIP *gets down off the table, and* GRETCHEN *comes toward him and feels his game-bag.*)

GRETCHEN. Your game-bag is full of game, isn't it?

RIP (*taking her hand and holding it away from her pocket*). That? Why, that wouldn't hold it. (*Finding his way into* GRETCHEN'S *pocket.*) Now I can tell you all about it. You know last night I stopped out all night——

GRETCHEN. Yes; and let me catch you again. (*He is pulling the bottle out, when* GRETCHEN *catches him, and slaps his hand.*) You paltry thief!

RIP. Oh, you ain't got no confidence in me. Now what do you think was the first thing I saw in the morning? (*Dragging a chair to the front of the stage.*)

GRETCHEN. I don't know. What?

RIP (*seating himself*). A rabbit.

GRETCHEN (*pleased*). I like a rabbit. I like it in a stew.

RIP (*looking at her, amused*). I guess you like everything in a stew—everything what's a rabbit I mean. Well, there was a rabbit a-feedin' mit the grass,—you know they always come out early in der mornin' and feed mit the grass?

GRETCHEN. Never mind the grass. Go on.

RIP. Don't get so patient; you wait till you get the rabbit. (*Humorously.*) Well, I crawl up——

GRETCHEN. Yes, yes!

RIP (*becoming interested in his own powers of invention*). An' his little tail was a-stickin' up so—— (*With a gesture of his forefinger.*)

GRETCHEN (*impatiently*). Never mind his tail. Go on.

RIP (*remonstrating at her interruption*). The more fatter the rabbit, the more whiter is his tail——

GRETCHEN. Well, well, go on.

RIP (*taking aim*). Well, I haul up——

GRETCHEN. Yes, yes!

RIP. And his ears was a-stickin' up so —— (*Making the two ears with his two forefingers.*)

GRETCHEN. Never mind his ears. Go on.

RIP. I pull the trigger.

GRETCHEN (*eagerly*). Bang went the gun, and——

RIP (*seriously*). And the rabbit run away.

GRETCHEN (*angrily*). And so you shot nothing?

RIP. How will I shot him when he run away? (*He laughs at her disappointment.*) There, don't get so mad mit a feller. Now I'm going to tell you what I did shot; that's what I didn't shot. You know that old forty-acre field of ours?

GRETCHEN (*scornfully*). Ours! Ours, did you say?

RIP (*shamefacedly*). You know the one I mean well enough. It used to be ours.

GRETCHEN (*regretfully*). Yes; it used, indeed!

RIP. It ain't ours now, is it?

GRETCHEN (*sighing*). No, indeed, it is not.

RIP. No? Den I wouldn't bodder about it. Better let somebody bodder about that field what belongs to it. Well, in that field dere's a pond; and what do you think I see in that pond?

GRETCHEN. I don't know. Ducks?

RIP. Ducks! More 'an a thousand.

GRETCHEN (*walking to where broomstick is*). More than a thousand ducks?

RIP. I haul up again——

GRETCHEN (*picking up broomstick*). Yes, and so will I. And if you miss fire this time—— (*She holds it threateningly over* RIP*'s shoulder.*)

RIP (*looking at it askance out of the corner of his eye, then putting up his hand and pushing it aside*). You will scare the ducks mit that. Well, I take better aim this time as I did before. I pull the trigger, and—bang!

GRETCHEN. How many down?

RIP (*indifferently*). One.

GRETCHEN (*indignantly*). What! only one duck out of a thousand?

RIP. Who said one duck?

GRETCHEN. You did.

RIP (*getting up, and leaning on the back of the chair*). I didn't say anything of the kind.

GRTECHEN. You said "one."

RIP. Ah! *One*. But I shot more as one duck.

GRETCHEN. Did you?

RIP (*crosses over, and sits on the low stool, and laughs silently*). I shot our old bull. (GRETCHEN *flings down the broomstick, and throws herself into the chair at the right of the table, in dumb rage.*) I didn't kill him. I just sting him, you know. Well, then the bull come right after me; and I come right away from him. O Gretchen, how you would laugh if you could see that—— (*With a vain appeal to her sense of humor.*) The bull was a-comin', and I was a-goin'. Well, he chased me across the field. I tried to climb over the fence so fast what I could—(*doubles up with his silent laugh*) an' the bull come up an' save me the trouble of that. Well, then, I rolled over on the other side.

GRETCHEN (*with disgust*). And then you went fast asleep for the rest of the day.

RIP. That's a fact. That's a fact.

GRETCHEN (*bursting into tears, and burying her head in her arms on the table*). O Rip, you'll break my heart! You will.

RIP. Now she gone crying mit herself! Don't cry, Gretchen, don't cry. My d-a-r-l-i-n', don't cry.

GRETCHEN (*angrily*). I will cry!

RIP. Cry 'way as much you like. What do I care? All the better soon as a woman gets cryin'; den all the danger's over. (RIP *goes to*

GRETCHEN, *leans over, and puts his arm around her.)* Gretchen, don't cry; my angel, don't. (*He succeeds in getting his hand into her pocket, and steals the bottle.*) Don't cry, my daarlin'. (*Humorously.*) Gretchen, won't you give me a little drop out of that bottle what you took away from me? (*He sits on the table, just behind her, and takes a drink from the bottle.*)

GRETCHEN. Here's a man drunk, and asking for more.

RIP. I wasn't. I swore off. (*Coaxingly.*) You give me a little drop, an' I won't count it.

GRETCHEN (*sharply*). No!

RIP (*drinking again*). Well, den, here's your good health, an' your family, and may they live long and prosper! (*Puts bottle in his bag.*)

GRETCHEN. You unfeeling brute. Your wife's starving. And, Rip, your child's in rags.

RIP (*holding up his coat, and heaving a sigh of resignation*). Well, I'm the same way; you know dat.

GRETCHEN (*sitting up, and looking appealingly at* RIP). Oh, Rip, if you would only treat me kindly!

RIP (*putting his arms around her*). Well, den, I will. I'm going to treat you kind. I'll treat you kind.

GRETCHEN. Why, it would add ten years to my life.

RIP (*over her shoulder, and after a pause*). That's a great inducement; it is, my darlin'. I know I treat you too bad, an' you deserve to be a widow.

GRETCHEN (*getting up, and putting her arms on* RIP'S *shoulders*). Oh, Rip, if you would only reform!

RIP. Well, den, I will. I won't touch another drop so long what I live.

GRETCHEN. Can I trust you?

RIP. You mustn't suspect me.

GRETCHEN (*embracing him*). There, then, I will trust you. (*She takes the candle, and goes to fetch the children.*) Here, Hendrick, Meenie. Children, where are you? (*Exit through the door on the left.*)

RIP (*seats himself in the chair to the right of the table, and takes out flask*). Well, it's too bad; but it's all a woman's fault anyway. When a man gets drinkin' and that, they ought to let him alone. So soon as they scold him, he goes off like a skyrocket.

(*Re-enter* GRETCHEN *and the* CHILDREN.)

GRETCHEN (*seeing the flask in* RIP'S *hand*). I thought as much.

RIP (*unconscious of her presence*). How I did smooth her down! I must drink her good health. Gretchen, here's your good health. (*About to drink.*)

GRETCHEN (*snatching the bottle, and using it to gesticulate with*). Oh, you paltry thief!

RIP (*concerned for the schnapps*). What you doin'? You'll spill the licker out of the bottle. (*He puts in the cork.*)

GRETCHEN (*examining the flask*). Why, the monster, he's emptied the bottle!

RIP. That's a fac'. That's a fac'.

GRETCHEN (*throwing down the flask*). Then that is the last drop you drink under my roof!

RIP. What! What!

(MEENIE *approaches her father on tiptoe, and kneels beside him.*)

GRETCHEN. Out, you drunkard! Out, you sot! You disgrace to your wife and to your child! This house is mine.

RIP (*dazed, and a little sobered*). Yours! Yours!

GRETCHEN (*raising her voice above the storm, which seems to rage more fiercely outside*). Yes, mine, mine! Had it been yours to sell, it would have gone along with the rest of your land. Out, then, I say—(*pushing open the door*) for you have no longer any share in me or mine. (*A peal of thunder.*)

MEENIE (*running over, and kneeling by* GRETCHEN). Oh, Mother, hark at the storm!

GRETCHEN (*pushing her aside*). Begone, man, can't you speak? Are you struck dumb? You sleep no more under my roof.

RIP (*who has not moved, even his arm remaining outstretched, as it was when* MEENIE *slipped from his side, murmurs in a bewildered, incredulous way*). Why, Gretchen, are you goin' to turn me out like a dog?

(GRETCHEN *points to the door.* RIP *rises and leans against the table with a groan. His conscience speaks.*) Well, maybe you are right. (*His voice breaks, and with a despairing gesture.*) I have got no home. I will go. But mind, Gretchen, after what you say to me tonight, I can never darken your door again—never—— (*Going toward the door.*) I will go.

HENDRICK (*running to* RIP). Not into the storm, Rip. Hark, how it thunders!

RIP (*putting his arm round him*). Yah, my boy; but not as bad to me as the storm in my home. I will go. (*At the door by this time.*)

MEENIE (*catching* RIP's *coat*). No, Father, don't go!

RIP (*bending over her tenderly, and holding her close to him*). My child! Bless you, my child, bless you!

(MEENIE *faints.* RIP *gives a sobbing sigh.*)

GRETCHEN (*relenting*). No, Rip—I——

RIP (*waving her off*). No; you have drive me from your house. You have opened the door for me to go. You may never open it for me to come back. (*Leans against the doorpost, overcome by his emotion. His eye rests on* MEENIE, *who lies at his feet.*) You say I have no share in this house. (*Points to* MEENIE *in profound despair.*) Well, see, then, I wipe the disgrace from your door. (*He staggers out into the storm.*)

GRETCHEN. No, Rip! Husband, come back! (GRETCHEN *faints, and the curtain falls.*)

ACT THREE

SCENE—*A steep and rocky clove in the Kaatskill Mountains, down which rushes a torrent, swollen by the storm. Overhead, the hemlocks stretch their melancholy boughs. It is night,* RIP *enters, almost at a run, with his head down, and his coat-collar turned up, beating his way against the storm. With the hunter's instinct, he protects the priming of his gun with the skirt of his jacket. Having reached a comparatively level spot, he pauses for breath, and turns to see what has become of his dog.*

RIP (*whistling to the dog*). Schneider! Schneider! what's the matter with Schneider? Something must have scared that dog. There he goes head over heels down the hill. Well, here I am again—another night in the mountains! Heigho! these old trees begin to know me, I reckon. (*Taking off his hat.*) How are you, old fellows? Well, I like the trees, they keep me from the wind and the rain, and they never blow me up; and when I lay me down on the broad of my back, they seem to bow their heads to me, an' say: Go to sleep, Rip, go to sleep. (*Lightning.*) My, what a flash that was! Old Hendrick Hudson's lighting his pipe in the mountains tonight; now, we'll hear him roll the big balls along. (*Thunder.* RIP *looks back over the path he has come, and whistles again for his dog.*) Well, I—no—Schneider! No; whatever it is, it's on two legs. Why, what a funny thing is that a-comin' up the hill? I thought nobody but me ever come nigh this place.

(*Enter a strange dwarfish figure, clad all in gray like a Dutch seaman of the seventeenth century, in short-skirted doublet, hose, and high-crowned hat drawn over his eyes. From beneath the latter his long gray beard streams down till it almost touches the ground. He carries a keg on his shoulder. He advances slowly toward* RIP, *and, by his gesture, begs* RIP *to set the keg down for him.* RIP *does so, and the dwarf seats himself upon it.*)

RIP (*with good-humored sarcasm*). Sit down, and make yourself comfortable. (*A long pause and silence.*) What? What's the matter? Ain't ye goin' to speak to a feller? I don't want to speak to you, then. Who you think you was, that I want to speak to you, any more than you want to speak to me; you hear what I say? (RIP *pokes the dwarf in the ribs, who turns, and looks up.* RIP *retreats hastily.*) Donner an' Blitzen! What for a man is das? I have been walking over these mountains ever since I was a boy, an' I never saw a queer-looking codger like that before. He must be an old sea-snake, I reckon.

(*The dwarf approaches* RIP, *and motions* RIP *to help him up the mountain with the keg.*)

RIP. Well, why don't you say so, den? You mean you would like me to help you up with that keg? (*The dwarf nods in the affirmative.*) Well, sir, I don't do it. (*The dwarf holds up his hands in supplication.*) No; there's no good you speakin' like that. I never seed you before, did I? (*The dwarf shakes his head.* RIP, *with great decision, walking away, and leaning against a tree.*) I don't want to see you again, needer. What have you got in that keg, schnapps? (*The dwarf nods.*) I don't believe you. (*The dwarf nods more affirmatively.*) Is it good schnapps? (The *dwarf again insists.*) Well, I'll help you. Go 'long pick up my gun, there, and I follow you mit that keg on my shoulder. I'll follow you, old broadchops.

(*As* RIP *shoulders the keg, a furious blast whirls up the valley, and seems to carry him and his demon companion before it. The rain that follows blots out the landscape. For a few moments, all is darkness. Gradually, the topmost peak of the Kaatskill Mountains becomes visible, far above the storm. Stretching below, the country lies spread out like a map. A feeble and watery moonlight shows us a weird group, gathered upon the peak,—*HENDRICK HUDSON, *and his ghostly crew. In the foreground, one of them poises a ball, about to bowl it, while the others lean forward in attitudes of watchful expectancy. Silently he pitches it; and, after a momentary pause, a long and rumbling peal of thunder reverberates among the valleys below. At this moment, the demon, carrying* RIP'S *gun, appears over the crest of the peak in the background, and* RIP *toils after with the keg on his shoulder. Arrived at the summit, he drops the keg on his knee, and gasps for breath.*)

RIP (*glancing out over the landscape*). I say, old gentleman, I never was so high up in the mountains before. Look down into the valley there; it seems more as a mile. I—— (*Turning to speak to his companion, and perceiving another of the crew.*) You're another feller! (*The second demon nods assent.*) You're that other chap's brother?

(*The demon again assents.* RIP *carries the keg a little further, and comes face to face with a third.*)

RIP. You're another brother? (*The third demon nods assent.* RIP *takes another step, and perceives* HENDRICK HUDSON *in the centre, surrounded by many demons.*) You're his old gran'father? (HUDSON *nods.* RIP *puts down the keg in perplexity, not untinged with alarm.*) Donner and Blitzen! here's the whole family; I'm a dead man to a certainty.

(*The demons extend their arms to* HUDSON, *as if inquiring what they should do. He points to* RIP, *they do the same.*)

RIP. My, my, I suppose they're speakin' about me! (*Looking at his gun, which the first demon has deposited on the ground, and which lies within his reach.*) No good shootin' at 'em; family's too big for one gun.

(HENDRICK HUDSON *advances, and seats himself on the keg facing* RIP. *The demons slowly surround the two.*)

RIP (*looking about him with growing apprehension*). My, my, I don't like that kind of people at all! No, sir! I don't like any sech kind. I like that old gran'father worse than any of them. (*With a sheepish attempt to be genial, and appear at his ease.*) How you was, old gentleman? I didn't mean to intrude on you, did I? (HUDSON *shakes his head.*) What? (*No reply.*) I'll tell you how it was; I met one of your gran'children, I don't know which is the one—— (*Glancing around.*) They're all so much alike. Well—— (*Embarrassed, and looking at one demon.*) That's the same kind of a one. Anyway this one, he axed me to help him up the mountain mit dat keg. Well, he was an old feller, an' I thought I would help him. (*Pauses, troubled by their silence.*) Was I right to help him? (HUDSON *nods.*) I say, was I right to help him? (HUDSON *nods again.*) If he was here, he would yust tell you the same thing anyway, because —— (*Suddenly perceiving the demon he had met below.*) Why, dat's the one; ain't it? (*The demon nods.*) Yes; dat is the one, dat's the same kind of a one dat I met. Was I right to come? (HUDSON *nods approval.*) I didn't want to come here, anyhow; no, sir, I didn't want to come to any such kind of a place. (*After a pause, seeing that no one has anything to say.*) I guess I better go away from it. (RIP *picks up his gun, and is about to return by the way he came; but the demons raise their hands threateningly, and stop him. He puts his gun down again.*) I didn't want to come here, anyhow—— (*Grumbling to himself, then pulling himself together with an effort, and facing* HUDSON.) Well, old gentleman, if you mean to do me any harm, just speak it right out—— (*Then with a little laugh.*) Oh! I will die game—— (*Glancing round for a means of escape, and half to himself.*) If I can't run away.

(HUDSON *extends a cup to* RIP, *as if inviting him to drink.*)

RIP (*doubtfully*). You want me to drink mit you? (HUDSON *nods.* RIP *approaches him cautiously, unable to resist the temptation of a drink.*) Well, I swore off drinkin'; but as this is the first time I see you, I won't count this one—— (*He takes the cup.* HUDSON *holds up another cup.* RIP *is reassured, and his old geniality returns.*) You drink mit me? We drink mit one another? (HUDSON *nods affirmatively.* RIP *feels at home under these familiar circumstances, and becomes familiar and colloquial again.*) What's the matter mit you, old gentleman, anyhow? You go and make so (*imitating the demon*) mit your head every time; was you deaf? (HUDSON *shakes his head.*) Oh, nein. (*Laughing at his error.*) If you was deaf, you wouldn't hear what I was sayin'. Was you dumb? (HUDSON *nods yes.*) So? You was dumb? (HUDSON *nods again.*) Has all of your family the same complaint? (HUDSON *nods.*) All the boys dumb, hey? All the boys dumb. (*All the demons nod. Then, suddenly, as if struck with an idea.*) Have you got any girls? (HUDSON *shakes his head.*) Don't you? Such a big family, and all boys? (HUDSON *nods.*)

RIP (*with profound regret*). That's a pity; my, that's a pity. Oh, my, if you had some dumb girls, what wives they would make—— (*Brightening up.*) Well, old gentleman, here's your good health, and all your family —(*turning, and waving to them*) may they live long and prosper.

(RIP *drinks. As he does so, all the demons lean forward, watching the effect of the liquor.* RIP *puts his hand to his head. The empty cup falls to the ground.)*

RIP *(in an awed and ecstatic voice).* What for licker is that!

(As he turns, half reeling, he sees HUDSON *holding out to him another cup. He snatches it with almost frantic eagerness.)*

RIP. Give me another one!

(He empties it at a draught. A long pause follows, during which the effect of the liquor upon RIP *becomes apparent; the light in his eyes fades, his exhilaration dies out, and he loses his grasp on the reality of his surroundings. Finally, he clasps his head with both hands, and cries in a muffled, terrified voice.)*

RIP. Oh, my, my head was so light, and now, it's heavy as lead!

(He reels, and falls heavily to the ground. A long pause. The demons begin to disappear. RIP *becomes dimly conscious of this, and raises himself on his elbow.)*

RIP. Are you goin' to leave me, boys? Are you goin' to leave me all alone? Don't leave me; don't go away. *(With a last effort.)* I will drink your good health, and your family's —— *(He falls back heavily, asleep.)*

CURTAIN

ACT FOUR

SCENE I

As the curtain rises, the same high peaks of the Kaatskills, and the far-stretching valley below, are disclosed in the gray light of dawn.

RIP *is still lying on the ground, as in the last act; but he is no longer the* RIP *we knew. His hair and beard are long and white, bleached by the storms that have rolled over his head during the twenty years he has been asleep.*

As he stirs and slowly rises to a half-sitting posture, we see that his former picturesque rags have become so dilapidated that it is a matter of marvel how they hold together. They have lost all traces of color, and have assumed the neutral tints of the moss and lichens that cover the rocks.

His voice, when he first speaks, betrays even more distinctly than his appearance the lapse of time. Instead of the full round tones of manhood, he speaks in the high treble of feeble old age. His very hands have grown old and weatherbeaten.

RIP *(staring vacantly around).* I wonder where I was. On top of the Kaatskill Mountains as sure as a gun! Won't my wife give it to me for stopping out all night? I must get up and get home with myself. *(Trying to rise.*) Oh, I feel very bad! Vat is the matter with my elbow? (*In trying to rub it, the other one gives him such a twinge that he cries out.*) Oh! The other elbow is more badder than the other one. I must have cotched the rheumatix a-sleepin' mit the wet grass. (*He rises with great difficulty.*) Och! I never had such rheumatix like that. (*He feels himself all over, and then stands for a moment pondering, and bewildered by a strange memory.*) I wasn't sleeping all the time, needer. I know I met a queer kind of a man, and we got drinkin', and I guess I got pretty drunk. Well, I must pick up my gun, and get home mit myself. (*After several painful attempts, he succeeds in picking up his gun, which drops all to pieces as he lifts it.* RIP *looks at it in amazement.*) My gun must have cotched the rheumatix too. Now that's too bad. Them fellows have gone and stole my good gun, and leave me this rusty old barrel. (RIP *begins slowly to climb over the peak toward the path by which he had ascended, his memory seeming to act automatically. When he reaches the highest point, where he can look out over the valley, he stops in surprise.*) Why, is that the village of Falling Waters that I see? Why, the place is more than twice the size it was last night. I—— (*He sinks down.*) I don't know whether I am dreaming, or sleeping, or waking. (*Then pulling himself together with a great effort, and calling up the image of his wife to act as whip and spur to his waning powers, he says, with humorous conviction, as he gets up painfully again:* —) I go home to my wife. She'll let me know whether I'm asleep or awake or not. (*Almost unable to proceed.*) I don't know if I will ever get home, my k-nees are so stiff. My backbone, it's broke already.

(*As the curtain falls,* RIP *stands leaning on the barrel of his gun as on a staff, with one hand raised, looking out over the valley.*)

SCENE II

A comfortable-looking room in DERRICK'S *house. As the curtain rises,* MEENIE *and* GRETCHEN *enter.* MEENIE *is a tall young woman of twenty-six, and* GRETCHEN *is a matronly figure with white hair. They are well dressed, and have every appearance of physical and material prosperity.*

GRETCHEN. I am sent to you by your father, Meenie.

MEENIE. Oh, don't call him so; he is not my father! He is your husband, Mother; but I owe him no love. And his cruel treatment of you——

GRETCHEN. Hush, child! Oh, if he heard you, he would make me pay for every disrespectful word you utter.

MEENIE. Yes; he would beat you, starve and degrade you. You are not his wife, Mother, but his menial.

GRETCHEN. My spirit is broken, Meenie. I cannot resent it. Nay, I deserve it; for as Derrick now treats me, so I treated your poor father when he was alive.

MEENIE. You, Mother? You, so gentle? You, who are weakness and patience itself?

GRETCHEN. Yes; because for fifteen years I have been Derrick's wife. But it was my temper, my cruelty, that drove your father from our home twenty years ago. You were too young then to remember him.

MEENIE. No, Mother, I recollect my dear father taking me on his knee, and saying to Hendrick that I should be his wife; and I promised I would.

GRETCHEN. Poor Rip! Poor, good-natured, kind creature that he was! How gently he bore with me; and I drove him like a dog from his home. I hunted him into the mountains, where he perished of hunger or cold, or a prey to some wild beast.–

MEENIE. Don't cry, Mother!

(*Enter* DERRICK, *now grown old and bent over his cane, and infinitely more disagreeable than before. He, too, has thriven, and is dressed in a handsome full suit of black silk.*)

DERRICK. Sniveling again, eh? Teaching that girl of yours to be an obstinate hypocrite?

MEENIE. Oh, sir, she——

DERRICK. Hold your tongue, miss. Speak when you're spoken to. I'll have you both to understand that there's but one master here. Well, mistress, have you told her my wishes; and is she prepared to obey them?

GRETCHEN. Indeed, sir, I was trying to——

DERRICK. Beating about the bush, prevaricating, and sneaking, as you usually do.

MEENIE. If you have made her your slave, you must expect her to cringe.

DERRICK (*approaching her threateningly*). What's that?

GRETCHEN. Meenie! Meenie! For Heaven's sake, do not anger him!

DERRICK (*raising his cane*). She had better not.

MEENIE (*defiantly*). Take care how you raise your hand to me, for I'll keep a strict account of it. And when Hendrick comes back from sea, he'll make you smart for it, I promise you.

DERRICK. Is the girl mad?

MEENIE. He thrashed your nephew once for being insolent to me. Go and ask him how Hendrick pays my debts; and then when you speak to me you'll mind your stops.

DERRICK (*to* GRETCHEN). Oh, you shall pay for this!

GRETCHEN. No, Derrick, indeed, indeed I have not urged her to this! O Meenie, do not speak so to him; for my sake forbear!

MEENIE. For your sake, yes, dear Mother. I forgot that he could revenge himself on you.

DERRICK. As for your sailor lover, Hendrick Vedder, I've got news of him at last. His ship, the "Mayflower," was lost, almost three years ago, off Cape Horn.

MEENIE. No, no. Not lost?

DERRICK. If you doubt it, there's the "Shipping Gazette," in on my office table. You can satisfy yourself that your sailor bully has gone to the bottom.

GRETCHEN. Oh, sir, do not convey the news to her so cruelly.

DERRICK. That's it. Because I don't sneak and trick and lie about it, I'm cruel. The man's dead, has been dead and gone these two years or more. The time of mourning is over. Am I going to be nice about it this time of day?

MEENIE. Then all my hope is gone, gone forever!

DERRICK. So much the better for you. Hendrick's whole fortune was invested in that ship. So there's an end of him and your expectations. Now you are free, and a beggar. My nephew has a fancy for you. He will have a share of my business now, and my money when—when I die.

GRETCHEN. Do not ask her to decide now!

DERRICK. Why not? If she expects to make a better bargain by holding off, she's mistaken.

GRETCHEN. How can you expect her to think of a husband at this moment?

DERRICK. Don't I tell you the other one is dead these two years?

GRETCHEN (*leading* MEENIE *away*). Come, my child. Leave her to me, sir; I will try and persuade her.

DERRICK. Take care that you do; for if she don't consent to accept my offer, she shall pack bag and baggage out of this house. Aye, this very day! Not a penny, not a stitch of clothes but what she has on her back, shall she have! Oh, I've had to deal with obstinate women before now, and I've taken them down before I've done with them. You know who I mean? Do you know who I mean? Stop. *Answer me! Do you know who I mean?*

GRETCHEN (*submissively*). Yes, sir.

DERRICK. Then why didn't you say so before? Sulky, I suppose. There, you may be off. (*Exeunt.*)

SCENE III

The village of Falling Waters, which has grown to be a smart and flourishing town, but whose chief features remain unchanged.

To the left, as of yore, is the inn, bearing scarcely any mark of the lapse of time, save that the sign of George III has been replaced by a portrait of George Washington. To the right, where RIP'S *cottage used to stand, nothing remains, however, but the blackened and crumbling ruins of a chimney. A table and chairs stand in front of the Inn porch.*

Into this familiar scene RIP *makes his entrance, but not as before,—in glee, with the children clinging about him. Faint, weak, and weary he stumbles along, followed by a jeering, hooting mob of villagers; while the children hide from him in fear, behind their elders. His eyes look dazed and uncomprehending, and he catches at the back of a chair as if in need of physical as well as mental support.*

KATCHEN (*as* RIP *enters*). Why, what queer looking creature is this, that all the boys are playing——

SETH. Why, he looks as though he'd been dead for fifty years, and dug up again!

RIP. My friends, *Kanst du Deutsch sprechen?*

FIRST VILLAGER. I say, old fellow, you ain't seen anything of an old butter-tub with no kiver on, no place about here, have you?

RIP (*bewildered, but with simplicity*). What is that? I don't know who that is.

SECOND VILLAGER. I say, old man, who's your barber?

(*The crowd laughs, and goes off repeating, "Who's your barber?" Some of the children remain to stare at* RIP; *but when he holds out his hand to them, they, too, run off frightened.*)

RIP. Who's my barber; what dey mean by dat? (*Noticing his beard.*) Why, is that on me? I didn't see that before. My beard and hair is so long and white—Gretchen won't know me with that, when she gets me home. (*Looking toward the cottage.*) Why, the home's gone away! (RIP *becomes more and more puzzled, like a man in a dream who see unfamiliar things amid familiar surroundings, and cannot make out what has happened; and as in a dream a man preserves his individuality, so* RIP *stumbles along through his bewilderment, exhibiting flashes of his old humor, wit, and native shrewdness. But with all this he never laughs.*)

SETH. I say, old man, hadn't you better go home and get shaved?

RIP (*looking about for the voice*). What?

SETH. Here, this way. Hadn't you better go home and get shaved?

RIP. My wife will shave me when she gets me home. Is this the village of "Falling Waters," where we was?

SETH. Yes.

RIP (*still more puzzled, not knowing his face*). Do you live here?

SETH. Well, rather. I was born here.

RIP (*reflectively*). Then you live here?

SETH. Well, rather; of course I do.

RIP (*feeling that he has hold of something certain*). Do you know where I live?

SETH. No; but I should say you belong to Noah's Ark.

RIP (*putting his hand to his ear*). That I belong mit vas?

SETH. Noah's Ark.

RIP (*very much hurt*). Why will you say such thing like that? (*Then, with a flash of humor, and drawing his beard slowly through his fingers.*) Well, look like it, don't I? (*Beginning all over again to feel for his clue.*) My friend, did you never hear of a man in this place whose name was Rip Van Winkle?

SETH. Rip Van Winkle, the laziest, drunken vagabond in the country?

RIP (*somewhat taken aback by this description, but obliged to concur in it*). Yah, that is the one; there is no mistaking him, eh?

SETH. I know all about him.

RIP (*hopefully*). Do you?

SETH. Yes.

RIP (*quite eagerly*). Well, if you know all about him; well, what has become of him?

SETH. What has become of him? Why, bless your soul, he's been dead these twenty years!

RIP (*looking at* SETH). Then I am dead, I suppose. So Rip Van Winkle was dead, eh?

SETH. Yes; and buried.

RIP (*humorously*). I'm sorry for that; for he was a good fellow, so he was.

SETH (*aside*). There appears to be something queer about this old chap; I wonder who he is. (*Rises, and taking chair over to* RIP.) There, old gentleman, be seated.

RIP (*seating himself with great difficulty, aided by* SETH). Oh, thank you; every time I move a new way, I get another pain. My friend, where is the house what you live in?

SETH (*pointing at inn*). There.

RIP. Did you live there yesterday?

SETH. Well, rather.

RIP. No; it is Nick Vedder what live in that house. Where is Nick Vedder?

SETH. Does he? Then I wish he'd pay the rent for it. Why, Nick Vedder has been dead these fifteen years.

RIP. Did you know Jacob Stein, what was with him?

SETH. No; but I've heard of him. He was one of the same sort as Rip and Nick.

RIP. Yes, them fellows was all pretty much alike.

SETH. Well, he went off the hooks a short time after Rip.

RIP. Where has he gone?

SETH. Off the hooks.

RIP. What is that, when they go off the hooks?

SETH. Why, he died.

RIP (*with an air of hopelessness*). Is there anybody alive here at all?

(*Then, with a sudden revulsion of feeling, convinced of the impossibility of what he hears.*) That man is drunk what talks to me.

SETH. Ah, they were a jolly set, I reckon.

RIP. Oh, they was. I knowed them all.

SETH. Did you?

RIP. Yes, I know Jacob Stein, and Nick Vedder, and Rip Van Winkle, and the whole of them. (*A new idea strikes him, and he beckons to* SETH, *whom he asks, very earnestly.*) Oh, my friend, come and see here. Did you know Schneider?

SETH. Schneider! Schneider! No, I never heard of him.

RIP (*simply*). He was a dog. I thought you might know him. Well, if dat is so, what has become of my child Meenie, and my wife Gretchen? Are they gone, too? (*Turning to look at the ruins of the house.*) Yah, even the house is dead.

SETH. Poor old chap! He seems quite cast down at the loss of his friends. I'll step in and get a drop of something to cheer him up. (*Exit.*)

RIP (*puzzling it out with himself*). I can't make it out how it all was; because if this here is me, what is here now, and Rip Van Winkle is dead, then who am I? That is what I would like to know. Yesterday, everybody was here; and now they was all gone. (*Very forlorn.*)

(*Re-enter* SETH, *followed by the* VILLAGERS.)

SETH (*offering* RIP *the cup*). There, old gent, there's a drop of something to cheer you up.

RIP (*shaking hands with* SETH *and* KATCHEN). Oh, thank you. I—I—I swore off; but this is the first time what I see you. I won't count this one. (*His voice breaks.*) My friend, you have been very kind to me. Here is your good health, and your family's, and may they all live long and prosper!

SETH. I say, wife, ain't he a curiosity fit for a show?

RIP (*aside*). That gives me courage to ask these people anodder question. (*He begins with difficulty.*) My friend, I don't know whether you knowed it or not, but there was a child of Rip,—Meenie her name was.

SETH. Oh, yes; that's all right.

RIP (*with great emotion, leaning forward*). She is not gone? She is not dead? No, no!

SETH. No. She's alive.

RIP (*sinking back with relief*). Meenie is alive. It's all right now,—all right now.

SETH. She's the prettiest girl in the village.

RIP. I know dat.

SETH. But if she wastes her time waiting on Hendrick Vedder, she'll be a middle-aged woman before long.

RIP (*incredulously*). She's a little child, only six years old.

SETH. Six-and-twenty, you mean.

RIP (*thinking they are making fun of him*). She's a little child no bigger than that. Don't bodder me; I don't like that.

SETH. Why, she's as big as her mother.

RIP (*very much surprised that* SETH *knows* GRETCHEN). What, Gretchen?

SETH. Yes, Gretchen.

RIP. Isn't Gretchen dead?

SETH. No; she's alive.

RIP (*with mixed emotions*). Gretchen is alive, eh! Gretchen's alive!

SETH. Yes; and married again.

RIP (*fiercely*). How would she do such a thing like that?

SETH. Why, easy enough. After Rip died, she was a widow, wasn't she?

RIP. Oh, yes. I forgot about Rip's being dead. Well, and then?

SETH. Well, then Derrick made love to her.

RIP (*surprised, and almost amused*). What for Derrick? Not Derrick Von Beekman?

SETH. Yes, Derrick Von Beekman.

RIP (*still more interested*). Well, and then?

SETH. Well, then her affairs went bad; and at last she married him.

RIP (*turning it over in his mind*). Has Derrick married Gretchen?

SETH. Yes.

RIP (*with a flash of his old humor, but still with no laughter*). Well, I didn't think he would come to any good; I never did. So she cotched Derrick, eh! Poor Derrick!

SETH. Yes.

RIP. Well, here's their good health, and their family's, and may they all live long and prosper! (*Drinks.*)

SETH. Now, old gent, hadn't you better be going home, wherever that is?

RIP (*with conviction*). Where my home was? Here's where it is.

SETH. What, here in this village? Now do you think we're going to keep all the half-witted strays that choose to come along here? No; be off with you. Why, it's a shame that those you belong to should allow such an old tramp as you to float around here.

VILLAGERS (*roughly, and trying to push him along*). Yes; away with him!

RIP (*frightened, and pleading with them*). Are you going to drive me away into the hills again?

FIRST VILLAGER. Yes; away with him! He's an old tramp.

(*Enter* HENDRICK, *with stick and bundle, followed by some of the women of the village.*)

VILLAGERS. Away with him!

HENDRICK (*throwing down bundle*). Avast there, mates. Where are you towing that old hulk to? What, you won't? (*Pushing crowd aside, and going forward.*) Where are you towing that old hulk to?

SETH. Who are you?

HENDRICK. I'm a man, every inch of me; and if you doubt it, I'll undertake to remove the suspicions from any two of you in five minutes. Ain't you ashamed of yourselves? Don't you see the poor old creature has but half his wits?

SETH. Well, this is no asylum for worn out idiots.

VILLAGERS (*coming forward*). No, it ain't!

HENDRICK. Ain't it?

OMNES. No, it ain't.

HENDRICK. Then I'll make it a hospital for broken heads if you stand there much longer. Clear the decks, you lubberly swabs! (*Drives them aside. Turns to* RIP, *who stands bewildered.*) What is the cause of all this?

RIP (*helplessly*). I don't know; do you?

HENDRICK (*to* VILLAGERS). Do any of you know him?

FIRST VILLAGER. No; he appears to be a stranger.

HENDRICK (*to* RIP). You seem bewildered. Can I help you?

RIP (*feebly*). Just tell me where I live.

HENDRICK. And don't you know?

RIP. No, I don't.

HENDRICK. What's your name?

RIP (*almost childishly*). I don't know; but I believe I know vat it used to be. My name, it used to be Rip Van Winkle.

VILLAGERS (*in astonishment*). Rip Van Winkle?

HENDRICK. Rip Van Winkle? Impossible!

RIP (*pathetically feeble, and old*). Well, I wouldn't swear to it myself. I tell you how it was: Last night, I don't know about the time, I went away up into the mountains, and while I was there I meet a queer kind o' man, and we got drinkin'; and I guess I got pretty drunk. And then I went to sleep; and when I woke up this morning, I was dead. (*All laugh.*)

HENDRICK. Poor old fellow; he's crazy. Rip Van Winkle has been dead these twenty years. I knew him when I was a child.

RIP (*clutching at a faint hope*). You don't know me?

HENDRICK. No; nor anybody else here, it seems.

(*The* VILLAGERS, *finding that there is to be no amusement for them, straggle off to their occupations.*)

SETH (*as he goes into the inn*). Why, wife, he's as cracked as our old teapot.

RIP (*with simple pathos*). Are we so soon forgot when we are gone? No one remembers Rip Van Winkle.

HENDRICK. Come, cheer up, my old hearty, and you shall share my breakfast. (*Assists* RIP *to sit at the table.* RIP *has fallen into a dream again. To* KATCHEN.) Bring us enough for three, and of your best.

KATCHEN. That I will. (*Exit into inn.*)

HENDRICK. So here I am, home again. And yonder's the very spot where, five years ago, I parted from Meenie.

RIP (*roused by the name*). What, Meenie Van Winkle?

HENDRICK. And she promised to remain true to Hendrick Vedder.

RIP. Oh, yah; that was Nick Vedder's son.

HENDRICK (*turning to* RIP). That's me.

RIP (*resentfully*). That was you! You think I'm a fool? He's a little child, no bigger than that,—the one I mean.

HENDRICK. How mad he is! (*Enter* KATCHEN *from inn with tray, on which is laid a breakfast. She puts it on table, and exits into inn.*) There, that's right. Stow your old locker full while I take a cruise around yonder house, where, five years ago, I left the dearest bit of human nature that was ever put together. I'll be back directly. Who comes here? It's surely Derrick and his wife. Egad, I'm in luck; for now the old birds are out, Meenie will surely be alone. I'll take advantage of the coast being clear, and steer into harbor alongside. (*Exit.*)

(*Enter* DERRICK, *followed by* GRETCHEN.)

DERRICK. So you have come to that conclusion, have you?

GRETCHEN. I cannot accept this sacrifice.

RIP (*starting from his reverie, and turning to look at her*). Why, that is Gretchen's voice. (*As he recognizes her, and sees how aged she is.*) My, my! Is that my wife?

DERRICK. Oh, you can't accept! Won't you kindly allow me a word on the subject?

RIP (*aside, humorously*). No, indeed, she will not. Now, my friend, you are going to cotch it.

GRETCHEN. There is a limit even to my patience. Don't drive me to it.

RIP (*aside, drolly*). Take care, my friend, take care.

DERRICK. Look you, woman; Meenie has consented to marry my nephew. She has pledged her word to do so on condition that I settle an annuity on you.

GRETCHEN. I won't allow my child to break her heart.

DERRICK. You won't allow? Dare to raise your voice, dare but to speak except as I command you, you shall repent it to the last hour of your life.

RIP (*expectantly*). Now she'll knock him down, flat as a flounder.

DERRICK (*sneeringly*). You won't allow? This is something new. Who are you; do you think you are dealing with your first husband?

GRETCHEN. Alas, no; I wish I was.

RIP (*lost in wonderment*). My, my, if Rip was alive, he never would have believed it!

DERRICK. So you thought to get the upper hand of me, when you married me; didn't you?

GRETCHEN. I thought to get a home for my little girl—shelter, and food; want drove me to your door, and I married you for a meal's victuals for my sick child.

DERRICK. So you came to me as if I was a poorhouse, eh? Then you can't complain of the treatment you received. You sacrificed yourself for Meenie; and the least she can do now, is to do the same for you. In an hour, the deeds will be ready. Now, just you take care that no insolent interference of yours spoils my plans; do you hear?

GRETCHEN. Yes, sir.

DERRICK. Why can't you be kind and affectionate to her, as I am to you? There, go and blubber over her; that's your way. You are always pretending to be miserable.

GRETCHEN. Alas, no, sir! I am always pretending to be happy.

DERRICK. Don't cry. I won't have it; come now, none of that. If you come home today with red eyes, and streaky cheeks, I'll give you something to cry for; now you know what's for supper. (*Exit.*)

RIP (*still amazed*). Well, if I hadn't seen it, I never would have believed it!

GRETCHEN (*absorbed in her grief*). Oh, wretch that I am, I must consent, or that man will surely thrust her out of doors to starve, to beg, and to become—— (*Seeing* RIP.) Yes, to become a thing of rags and misery, like that poor soul.

RIP. She always drived the beggars away; I suppose I must go. (*Getting up, and starting to go.*)

GRETCHEN (*taking penny from her pocket*). Here, my poor man, take this. It is only a penny; but take it, and may God bless you, poor wanderer, so old, so helpless. Why do you come to this strange place, so far from home?

RIP (*keeping his face turned away from her*). She don't know me; she don't know me!

GRETCHEN. Are you alone in the world?

RIP (*trying to bring himself to look directly at* GRETCHEN). My wife asks me if I'm alone.

GRETCHEN. Come with me. How feeble he is; there, lean on me. Come to yonder house, and there you shall rest your limbs by the fire. (GRETCHEN *takes his arm, and puts it in her own. As they move toward her house,* RIP *stops, and, with an effort, turns and looks her full in the face, with a penetrating gaze, as if imploring recognition, but there is none; and, sadly shaking his head, he shrinks into himself, and allows her to lead him tottering off.*)

SCENE IV

The same room in DERRICK'S *home as in Scene II.*

(*Enter* DERRICK.)

DERRICK. I don't know what women were invented for, except to make a man's life miserable. I can get a useful, hard-working woman to keep my house clean, and order my dinner for me, for half that weak snivelling creature costs me.

(*Enter* COCKLES.)

COCKLES: Well, Uncle, what news; will she have me?

DERRICK. Leave it to me; she must, she shall.

COCKLES. If she holds out, what are we to do? It was all very well, you marrying Rip's widow; that choked off all inquiry into his affairs; but here's Meenie, Rip's heiress, who rightly owns all this property; if we don't secure her, we're not safe.

DERRICK. You've got rid of Hendrick Vedder; that's one obstacle removed.

COCKLES. I'm not so sure about that. His ship was wrecked on a lonely coast; but some of the crew may have, unfortunately, been saved.

DERRICK. If he turns up after you're married, what need you care?

COCKLES. I'd like nothing better; I'd like to see his face when he saw my arm around his sweetheart—my wife. But if he turns up before our marriage——

DERRICK. I must put the screw on somewhere.

COCKLES. I'll tell you, Meenie will do anything for her mother's sake. Now you are always threatening to turn her out, as she turned out Rip. That's the tender place. Meenie fears more for her mother than she cares for herself.

DERRICK. Well, what am I to do?

COCKLES. Make Gretchen independent of you; settle the little fortune on her, that you are always talking about doing, but never keeping your word. The girl will sell herself to secure her mother's happiness.

DERRICK. And it would be a cheap riddance for me. I was just talking about it to Gretchen this morning. You shall have the girl; but I hope you are not going to marry her out of any weak feeling of love. You're not going to let her make a fool of you by and by?

COCKLES. I never cared for her until she was impudent to me, and got that sailor lover of hers to thrash me, and then I began to feel a hunger for her I never felt before.

DERRICK. That's just the way I felt for Gretchen.

COCKLES. 'Tain't revenge that I feel; it's enterprise. I want to overcome a difficulty.

DERRICK (*chuckling*). And so you shall. Come, we'll put your scheme in train at once; and let this be a warning to you hereafter, never marry another man's widow.

COCKLES. No, Uncle; I'll take a leaf out of your book, and let it be a warning to her. (*Exeunt.*)

SCENE V

A plain sitting-room in DERRICK'S *house. A table stands in the centre with several chairs around it. There are cups, a jug, and a work-basket on the table. As the curtain rises,* MEENIE *is discovered seated by the table.*

MEENIE. Why should I repine? Did my mother hesitate to sacrifice her life to make a home for me? No; these tears are ungrateful, selfish.

(*The door at the back opens, and* GRETCHEN *enters, leading* RIP, *who seems very feeble and a little wild.*)

GRETCHEN. Come in and rest awhile.

RIP. This your house, your home?

GRETCHEN. Yes. Meenie, Meenie, bring him a chair.

RIP (*turning aside so as to shield his face from* MEENIE). Is that your daughter?

GRETCHEN. That is my daughter.

RIP (*looking timidly at* MEENIE, *as* GRETCHEN *helps him into a chair*). I thought you was a child.

GRETCHEN (*crossing to go into another room, and speaking to* MEENIE, *who starts to follow her*). Stay with him until I get some food to fill his wallet. Don't be frightened, child, he is only a simple, half-witted creature whose misery has touched my heart. (*Exit.* MEENIE *takes her work-basket, and starts to follow.*)

RIP (*holding out his hand to detain her, and speaking with hardly suppressed excitement*). One moment, my dear. Come here, and let me look at you. (*Pathetically.*) Are you afraid? I won't hurt you. I only want to look at you; that is all. Won't you come? (MEENIE *puts down her work-basket; and* RIP *is relieved of his great fear that she might leave him. His excitement increases as he goes on in his struggle to make her recognize him.*) Yes; I thought you would. Oh, yah, that is Meenie! But you are grown! (MEENIE *smiles.*) But see the smile and the eyes! That is just the same Meenie. You are a woman, Meenie. Do you remember something of your father? (*He looks at her eagerly and anxiously, as if on her answer hung his reason and his life.*)

MEENIE. I do. I do. Oh, I wish he was here now!

RIP (*half rising in his chair, in his excitement*). Yah? But he isn't? No? No?

MEENIE. No; he's dead. I remember him so well. No one ever loved him as I did.

RIP. No; nobody ever loved me like my child.

MEENIE. Never shall I forget his dear, good face. Tell me——

RIP (*eagerly and expectantly*). Yah?——

MEENIE. Did you know him?

RIP (*confused by her question, and afraid to answer*). Well—I thought I did. But I—— When I say that here, in the village, the people all laugh at me.

MEENIE. He is wandering. (*She starts to go.*)

RIP (*making a great effort of will, and resolved to put the question of his identity to the test*). Don't go away from me. I want you to look at me now, and tell me if you have ever seen me before.

MEENIE (*surprised*). No.

RIP (*holding out his arms to her*). Try, my darlin', won't you?

MEENIE (*frightened*). What do you mean? Why do you gaze so earnestly and fondly on me?

RIP (*rising from his chair, in trembling excitement, and approaching her*). I am afraid to tell you, my dear, because if you say it is not true, it may be it would break my heart. But, Meenie, either I dream, or I am mad; but I am your father.

MEENIE. My father!

RIP. Yes; but hear me, my dear, and then you will know. (*Trying to be logical and calm, but laboring under great excitement.*) This village here is the village of Falling Waters. Well, that was my home. I had here in this place my wife Gretchen, and my child Meenie—little Meenie—(*a long pause, during which he strives to re-assemble his ideas and memories more accurately*) and my dog Schneider. That's all the family what I've got. Try and remembei me, dear, won't you? (*Pleadingly.*) I don't know when it was—— This night there was a storm; and my wife drived me from my house; and I went away—I don't remember any more till I come back here now. And see, I get back now, and my wife is gone, and my home is gone. My home is gone, and my child—my child looks in my face, and don't know who I am!

MEENIE (*rushing into his arms*). I do! Father!

RIP (*sobbing*). Ah, my child! Somebody knows me now! Somebody knows me now!

MEENIE. But can it be possible?

RIP. Oh, yah; it is so, Meenie! (*With a pathetic return of his uncertainty.*) Don't say it is not, or you will kill me if you do.

MEENIE. No. One by one your features come back to my memory. Your voice recalls that of my dear father, too. I cannot doubt; yet it is so strange.

RIP. Yah, but it is me, Meenie; it is me.

MEENIE. I am bewildered. Surely Mother will know you.

RIP (*smiling*). No, I don't believe she'll know me.

MEENIE. She can best prove your identity. I will call her.

RIP. No. You call the dog Schneider. He'll know me better than my wife. (*They retire to a sofa in the background, where* RIP *sits with his arm around* MEENIE.)[1]

(*Enter* DERRICK, *with documents.*)

DERRICK. What old vagabond is this?

(MEENIE *starts to resent insult.*)

RIP. Don't you say a word.

DERRICK. Here, give him a cold potato, and let him go. (*To* GRETCHEN, *who has entered, followed by* COCKLES. GRETCHEN *seats herself in the chair at the right of the table.*) Come you here, mistress. Here are the papers for the young couple to sign.

COCKLES (*aside*). And the sooner the better. Hush, Uncle. Hendrick is here.

DERRICK. Young Vedder? Then we must look sharp. (*To* GRETCHEN.) Come, fetch that girl of yours to sign this deed.

GRETCHEN. Never shall she put her name to that paper with my consent. Never.

DERRICK. Dare you oppose me in my own house? Dare you preach disobedience under my roof?

GRETCHEN. I dare do anything when my child's life's at stake. No, a thousand times, no! You shall not make of her what you have of me. Starvation and death are better than such a life as I lead.

DERRICK (*raising cane*). Don't provoke me.

GRETCHEN (*kneeling*). Beat me, starve me. You can only kill me. After all, I deserve it. (*Rising.*) But Meenie has given her promise to Hendrick Vedder, and she shall not break her word.

COCKLES (*seated at right of table*). But Hendrick Vedder is dead.

(*The door is flung open, and* HENDRICK *enters.*)

HENDRICK. That's a lie! He's alive!

[1]In reply to a question, why Rip should sit with his arm around Meenie, during the next scene, when the other persons in the drama are present, and are still ignorant of his identity, Mr. Jefferson said: "The other persons are occupied with their own affairs, and are not supposed to see this. It is natural that Rip should embrace his daughter whom he has just found; but the others are not supposed to see it. It is like a side speech on the stage. I went to a Chinese theatre once, and after the Chinese lady got through with her song, they brought her a glass of gin; she turned her back to the audience, and drank it, as much as to say, 'That's not in the play.' We are dealing with the impossible all the time on the stage; and we have got to make it appear possible. Dramatically, things may often be right, when, realistically, they are wrong. What we do is often the result of averaging the thing, determining how far good taste will admit of an error, you see; like the discord in music,—not good in itself, but good in its place."

GRETCHEN and MEENIE (*rushing to him*). Alive!

HENDRICK (*to* MEENIE). I've heard all about it. They made you believe that I was dead. (*To* DERRICK.) Only wait till I get through here. (*Embracing* MEENIE.) What a pleasure I've got to come! (*To* DERRICK.) And what a thrashing I've brought back for you two swabs.

DERRICK (*angrily*). Am I to be bullied under my own roof by a beggarly sailor? Quit my house, all of you. (*Seizes* GRETCHEN, *and drags her away from the crowd.*) As for you, woman, this is your work, and I'll make you pay for it.

GRETCHEN. Hendrick, save me from him. He will kill me.

HENDRICK. Stand off!

DERRICK (*raising cane*). No; she is my wife, mine.

GRETCHEN. Heaven help me, I am!

(RIP *has risen from the sofa, and come forward, and leans against the centre of the table, with one hand in his game-bag. He is fully awake now, and has recovered all his old shrewdness.*)

RIP. Stop. I am not so sure about that. If that is so, then what has become of Rip Van Winkle?

COCKLES. He's dead.

RIP. That's another lie. He's no more dead than Hendrick Vedder. Derrick Von Beekman, you say this house and land was yours?

DERRICK. Yes.

RIP. Where and what is the paper what you wanted Rip Van Winkle to sign when he was drunk, but sober enough not to do it? (*Taking an old paper out of game-bag, and turning to* HENDRICK.) Have you forgot how to read?

HENDRICK. No.

RIP. Then you read that.

(HENDRICK *takes the document from* RIP, *and looks it over.*)

DERRICK. What does this mad old vagabond mean to say?

RIP. I mean, that is my wife, Gretchen Van Winkle.

GRETCHEN (*rushing to* RIP). Rip! Rip!

COCKLES. I say, Uncle, are you going to stand that? That old impostor is going it under your nose in fine style.

DERRICK. I'm dumb with rage. (*To the* VILLAGERS, *who have come crowding in.*) Out of my house, all of you! Begone, you old tramp!

HENDRICK. Stay where you are. (*To* DERRICK.) This house don't belong to you. Not an acre of land, not a brick in the town is yours. They have never ceased to belong to Rip Van Winkle; and this document proves it.

DERRICK. 'Tis false. That paper is a forgery.

HENDRICK. Oh, no, it is not; for I read it to Rip twenty years ago.

RIP. Clever boy! Clever boy! Dat's the reason I didn't sign it then, Derrick.

DERRICK (*approaching* HENDRICK). And do you think I'm fool enough to give up my property in this way?

HENDRICK. No. You're fool enough to hang on to it, until we make you refund to Rip every shilling over and above the paltry sum you loaned him upon it. Now, if you are wise, you'll take a hint. There's the door. Go! And never let us see your face again.

RIP. Yah; give him a cold potato, and let him go.

(*Exit* DERRICK *in a great rage. All the* VILLAGERS *laugh at him.* HENDRICK *follows him to the door.*)

COCKLES (*kneeling by* MEENIE). O Meenie! Meenie!

HENDRICK (*coming down, and taking him by ear*). I'll Meenie you! (*Takes him and pushes him out. All the* VILLAGERS *laugh.* MEENIE *gives* RIP *a chair.*)

GRETCHEN (*kneeling by the side of* RIP). O Rip! I drove you from your home; but do not desert me again. I'll never speak an unkind word to you, and you shall never see a frown on my face. And Rip——

RIP. Yah.

GRETCHEN. You may stay out all night, if you like.

RIP (*leaning back in his chair*). No, thank you. I had enough of that.

GRETCHEN. And, Rip, you can get tight as often as you please. (*Taking bottle, and filling the cup from it.*)

RIP. No; I don't touch another drop.

MEENIE (*kneeling by the other side of* RIP). Oh, yes, you will, Father. For see, here are all the neighbors come to welcome you home.

(GRETCHEN *offers* RIP *the cup.*)

RIP (*with all his old kindliness and hospitality*). Well, bring in all the children, and the neighbors, and the dogs, and—— (*Seeing the cup which* GRETCHEN *is offering to him.*) I swore off, you know. Well, I won't count this one; for this will go down with a prayer. I will take my cup and pipe, and tell my strange story to all my friends. Here is my child Meenie, and my wife Gretchen, and my boy Hendrick. I'll drink all your good health, and I'll drink your good health, and your families', and may they all live long and prosper!

CURTAIN

The Man From Home

A Play in Four Acts

BOOTH TARKINGTON

AND

HARRY LEON WILSON

(Completely rewritten and revised)

Copy of program of first performance in New York of *The Man from Home,* as produced at The Astor Theatre, August 17, 1908.

WILLIAM HODGE

IN THE NEW FOUR-ACT PLAY

THE MAN FROM HOME

By Booth Tarkington and Harry Leon Wilson

Liebler & Co., Managers

Production staged by Hugh Ford

CAST

Daniel Voorhees Pike	William Hodge
The Grand Duke Vasili Vasilivitch	Henry Jewett
The Earl of Hawcastle	John Glendenning
The Hon. Almeric St. Aubyn	Echlin P. Gayer
Ivanoff	Henry Harmon
Horace Granger-Simpson	Hassard Short
Ribiere	Henry S. Lang
Mariano	Anthony Asher
Michele	Antonio Salerno
Carabiniere	A. Montegriffo
Valet de Chambre	C. L. Felter
Ethel Granger-Simpson	Olive Wyndham
Countess de Champigny	Alice Johnson
Lady Creech	Ida Vernon

SYNOPSIS OF SCENES

Act I: Terrace of the Hotel Regina Margherita at Taormina. (Morning.)
Act II: Entrance garden of the same. (Afternoon.)
Act III: An apartment in the hotel. (Evening.)
Act IV: The Terrace. (Morning.)

Time: The present. Place: Southern Italy.

NOTE

The original tryout of *The Man From Home* was in Louisville, Kentucky, and the play was intended as a satire, but the reception accorded the character of Daniel Voorhees Pike was such as to persuade the authors to revise the part for straight playing. William Hodge, then a successful player in vaudeville, was selected for the part and appeared in the first regular performance in Chicago in April 1908 with the same cast as subsequently appeared in New York, save for the part of the Earl of Hawcastle, which was played by E. J. Ratcliffe.

In the text here presented, in accordance with later revisions, some of the characters have been changed as follows:

THE GRAND DUKE VASILI VASILIVITCH *to* MONSIEUR LE BLANC.
THE HON. ALMERIC ST. AUBYN *to* ST. ULLBEYNNES.
IVANOFF *to* GEORGEOPOLIS.
COUNTESS DE CHAMPIGNY *to* MADAME DE CHAMPIGNY.

THE MAN FROM HOME

ACT ONE

SCENE—*Terrace of the Hotel Regina Margherita, on the cliff at Sorrento, overlooking the Bay of Naples. At back is the bay and semi-circular coast line, dotted with villages and Vesuvius gray in the distance. Across the stage at back runs a marble balustrade about three feet high, guarding the edge of the cliff. To the right, meeting end of balustrade, the wall of the hotel runs obliquely. There is a large double door in hotel wall. This door is modern Italian style—glass nearly to the base, with lace shade. A single step is before this door. The doors are approached by four or five marble steps with railing and a small stoop. There are windows in hotel wall—awnings shield all of them. The hotel is of pink and white stucco. At left of audience is a grove. Two or three small wicker tea-tables, covered bath chairs, broadly striped with pink and white, and a square table laid with white cloth complete the set.*

Eleven o'clock in the morning. Stage bright. Before the Curtain rises mandolins and guitars are heard and the Fisherman's songs—time very rapid and gay—off stage.

(MARIANO, *maître d'hôtel, is laying the table with eggs, coffee and rolls for two.*)

MARIANO (*looking off stage; crossly to* MUSICIANS). *Silenzio!*

MICHELE (*appears at doors*). *Par ici, Monsieur Ribière, pour le Maître d'hôtel.*

RIBIERE (*enters, carrying handsome leather brief case*). Ah, Mariano! (MICHELE *exits.*)

MARIANO (*bowing*). *Monsieur Ribière! J'espère que vous êtes——* (*Turns and shouts to* MUSICIANS.) *Silenzio!* (*Turning again to* RIBIERE.) *J'espère que vous——*

RIBIERE. *Monsieur Le Blanc est en automobile—avec un ami qu'il ne connait pas. Mais, c'est égal. L'ami connait pas Monsieur Le Blanc.*

MARIANO (*amused*). Monsieur Le Blanc! *Toujours l'excentrique!* (*Over to table and opens napkins.*)

RIBIERE (*amused*). *Grand poseur! Vive la démocratie, eh?*

MARIANO. *Son ami, il est de ce pays?*

RIBIERE. *Non. Il est un Américain—un Américain du Nord. C'est un "Yankee," Mariano, avec Monsieur Le Blanc pour le moment.*

MARIANO (*amused*). *Ah, ces "Yankees"!*

RIBIERE. *Le déjeuner est pour les deux: Monsieur Le Blanc et Monsieur le Yankee!* (*Pauses on step.*)

N'oubliez pas! M. le Blanc—il est toujours M. le Blanc! (Exits.)

MARIANO. *Va bene, signore! (Bows to door.)*

LORD HAWCASTLE (*enters*). Good morning, Mariano! (*He comes down.*)

MARIANO. Milor' Hawcastle is serve. (*Placing* HAWCASTLE's *hat and cane on table up stage.*)

MICHELE (*entering, hands* HAWCASTLE *newspaper*). *Il Mattino,* the yesterday morning journal from Napoli, Milor'.

HAWCASTLE. No English papers?

MICHELE. Milor', the mail is late. (*Exits.*)

HAWCASTLE (*sitting*). And Madame de Champigny?

MARIANO (*serves coffee, etc.*). Madame de Champigny is——

MME. DE CHAMPIGNY (*entering*). *Me voici.*

HAWCASTLE (*rising*). Waiting for you. (*They sit at table. He smiles cheerfully to her and she laughs pleasantly.*) You haven't seen my august sister-in-law yet—this morning? (*He reads paper, puzzlingly.*)

MME. DE CHAMPIGNY. She has *déjeuner* in her apartment.

HAWCASTLE (*reading*). "Dagli mani degli carabinière——" (*Letting his voice dwindle.*) Not very interesting! (*He tosses the paper aside.*)

MARIANO (*bowing*). *Permesso, signore*—if I might——

HAWCASTLE. I don't want it.

MME. DE CHAMPIGNY (*smiling*). You're interested in the Neapolitan papers, Mariano?

MARIANO. Will Milor' and Madame excuse me? And may I take the journal? There is someone who——

HAWCASTLE. Very well.

MARIANO. Thank you, Milor'! (*Bows and exits.*)

MME. DE CHAMPIGNY (*laughs*). Listen!

HAWCASTLE. To what?

MME. DE CHAMPIGNY. I think the little sunrise riding party is over.

(*Music off stage. Enter* ETHEL *followed by the* MUSICIANS, *who are unseen. She halts and throws them money. They go away singing.*)

HAWCASTLE (*rising*). Miss Granger-Simpson! Good morning, my dear.

ETHEL (*in lively spirits*). H'lo! Aren't you lazy though? Almeric and I've been all the way up to the Mola—but that isn't all we were up to, if you care to know it.

MME. DE CHAMPIGNY (*rising, running to her and kissing her*). Oh, I hope you mean——My dear, you look *happy*.

HAWCASTLE. You mean you have made my *son* happy?

ETHEL (*running to door*). Well, Taormina's a lovely place—everybody ought to be happy here—even your son! (*Runs off.*)

MME. DE CHAMPIGNY (*getting parasol from table as* HAWCASTLE *resumes his seat*). Ah! That is good! (*Piano off stage.*) Listen! She has flown to her piano. That's splendid. (*Lighting cigarette.*)

HAWCASTLE. Yes—and she's a nice little girl; I don't know what *better* Almeric could ask.

MME. DE CHAMPIGNY (*casually, but keen-eyed*). You think she will make no difficulties at *all?*

HAWCASTLE (*thoughtfully*). Why should she? I've talked of it with her brother—even the *details.*

MME. DE CHAMPIGNY. My friend! But *she*——

HAWCASTLE (*seriously, and in an honest mood, rather briskly*). But hang it, she ought to. Look what she's *getting*. She's fairly rolling in dollars, isn't she? And we're what she *wants,* aren't we? It isn't *pretty;* I don't *claim* it is, but, confound it! Let's face it. We're out-at-elbows and we have to sell what we've *got.* (*With pain in his voice.*) I've been sitting on the edge of the most damnable insolvency every minute of the last three months.

MME. DE CHAMPIGNY (*gently*). Dear, I will help in all ways. (*He pats her hand and turns away, moved.*)

ALMERIC (*as he enters*). Hello, Governor! Howdy, Helene! (*Drops in chair by table.*)

HAWCASTLE. Almeric! (*Significantly, meaning he wants the news.*)

ALMERIC. Ah, yes, I understand. Miss Granger-Simpson has been good enough to settle it definitely. She's just been that kind-hearted, poor dear. (*He speaks whimsically, but not without feeling.*)

HAWCASTLE (*quietly*). Thank heaven!

ALMERIC (*lightly*). Do you? Can't say I'd go quite *all* that way with my thanks, you know. She's a good little thing. I'm fond of her, too—but I don't set up to be a marryin' man, myself. Especially when it comes to sellin' out to *dollars.*

HAWCASTLE. You talk as if we were the first to have to do it. It's always been done ever since *they* began *having* dollars—and it always *will* be done.

ALMERIC. Oh, yes; my position as a dollar bridegroom will be *fashionable* enough.

HAWCASTLE. Don't play the fool, Almeric.

ALMERIC (*laughing ruefully*). *Play?* I'm damn serious! Look here, why couldn't you have done it yourself? You're a widower.

MME. DE CHAMPIGNY (*with quiet emotion*). You are not considerate. I have never asked your father to make that sacrifice of his liberty—even for me! (HAWCASTLE *touches her shoulder gently.*)

ALMERIC. And I suppose it wouldn't be cricket for him even to look at anyone *else?* Dear me! Oh, very well! *I'm* sorry!

HAWCASTLE. How *soon* did she say she's——

ALMERIC. She didn't say; but I'm afraid I make the poor child quite happy. (*As if he thought this matter grimly pathetic.*)

HAWCASTLE. How strange! But, think God! I believe you're right.

ALMERIC (*enter* HORACE). Here's the brother.

MME. DE CHAMPIGNY (*going toward him*). My dear Horace Granger-Simpson!

HORACE. My sister's just told me some pretty interesting news.

HAWCASTLE (*shaking hands*). It's interesting for us, too, you know.

HORACE. It's the most delightful, really loveliest——

MME. DE CHAMPIGNY. It *is* lovely; yes!

ALMERIC (*rising; smiling*). Most of all for *me*, of course.

HORACE (*with simple earnestness*). I simply can't deny I hoped for it. Of course I think my sister's a great girl; I hope you won't think I'm claiming too much when I say I know she'll be quite up to it in every way. She will indeed.

ALMERIC (*kindly*). Poor old chap!

HORACE. She will, indeed, Lord Hawcastle.

HAWCASTLE. Certainly she will.

HORACE. When do *you* think it ought to be?

HAWCASTLE (*surprised, apparently*). The wedding?

HORACE. Yes. Would you consider having it here—where she loves it so—in Sicily?

HAWCASTLE. Of course, if she wishes it.

ALMERIC (*satire in this; a little plaintive; but humorous*). Just as *you* like, Governor, just as *you* like.

MME. DE CHAMPIGNY. Enchanting! That settles *where*. Shall we turn to *when?* (*Sitting.*)

HORACE (*merrily*). Well, what's the good of long engagements?

HAWCASTLE. You Americans!

ALMERIC. Quite so! (*Exits.*)

HORACE. Oh—that matter we were speaking of the other day—— (*Sits back of table.*)

HAWCASTLE (*easily*). Oh, that—yes.

HORACE (*smiling apologetically*). Well, since this *has* happened as we hoped, shall we go into—ah—that other matter? The settlement——

HAWCASTLE (*smiling indulgently, as if* HORACE *had made a pardonable breach of taste*). My dear boy, you and I have already been into that as far as *we* can. The rest we may safely leave to my solicitor and your sister's man-of-business, I think. I'll wire our solicitor to come, and your sister's man-of-business you said you were expecting, didn't you?

HORACE. Yes; he may be here at any time. I think I told you he's rather more her guardian—technically, that is, you see.

HAWCASTLE. Yes, I understand that—vaguely. In that case his consent is—ah, legally—necessary, I suppose?

HORACE (*hurriedly*). Yes; but he won't make any difficulty. Seems always anxious to please——

HAWCASTLE (*smilingly amused*). Seems to be?

HORACE. You see, we've been on this side so many years—and there's been no occasion for the chap to look us up. When he comes my sister will just tell him what to sign. (*Laughing*). He's always done whatever she's written him to.

HAWCASTLE. Then, when my solicitor comes, he and your man can have the evening over a lot of musty papers and the rest of us needn't bother our heads about it. Again, my boy—(*rising and taking his hand*)—God bless you! (*Exits.*)

HORACE (*smiling*). It's delightful, you know, really!

MME. DE CHAMPIGNY. Yes, there is but these little arrangements between your advocate and Lord Hawcastle's—but you Americans you laugh at such things. You are big, so big, like your country. (*Lightly.*)

HORACE (*smiling*). Oh, in some things one is still willing to be quite American.

MME. DE CHAMPIGNY (*smiling*). Yes, and you are still American in that you are ab-om-inab-ly rich. The settlement, such matter as that, over which a Frenchman, an Italian, an Englishman, might hesitate—you laugh. You toss it aside! You say, "Oh yes—take it!"

HORACE. No, we *aren't* mercenary. We're like you in that, aren't we? (*Enter* ETHEL. *She has books.*)

MME. DE CHAMPIGNY (*quickly*). Indeed yes! (*Seeing* ETHEL; *runs and kisses her.*) Largesse, sweet Countess of Hawcastle, Largesse! (*Turns.*) I leave you with your dear brother. *Au plaisir!* (*Exits.*)

HORACE (*going to* ETHEL *and taking her hand*). Well, old thing! (*Elated and affectionate.*)

ETHEL. Think I'm a *nice* old thing, Hoddy? (*She is elated, and affectionate with him.*)

HORACE (*kneeling in chair*). You know I think *his* family are as pleased as *we* are. They really *like us*, d'you see?

ETHEL. This is Burke's Peerage, and this—(*indicating book*)—is Froissart's Chronicles. I've been reading it all over again—Almeric's ancestors at Crécy and Agincourt. (*She sits by table.*) I suppose I'm a little fanatic about that, Hoddy. *This* age seems so *tawdry* to me—just jazz and cheap mediocrity. Nobody has any reverence for anything any more. Well, here's a great name. It's always stood for something—here it is in history, in this old book. It's Almeric's—and it will be mine. It's a name to hold *up!* That's what *I* feel.

HORACE. Oh, it's a name like an old Norman bugle call.

ETHEL (*with a sudden anxiety to reassure herself*). *You're* keen on Almeric, aren't you, Hoddy—you really admire him, don't you?

HORACE. Well, rath-urr! I'm quite romantic about him, in fact. I think he's like the one of his forebears that went to the Crusades.

ETHEL (*very earnest, not pointing the youthfulness—simply*). Yes; the Crusader! He *has* that kind of nobility. He can't *help* having it, because it's come *down* to him. Even if you don't see it, you know it's *got* to be in him. You understand what I mean, don't you, Hoddy?

HORACE (*thoughtfully*). Certainly. Oh, by the way, about the settlement. It'll take the best part of your share of the estate, Sis; a hundred and fifty thousand pounds. That's seven hundred and fifty thousand dollars, you know.

ETHEL (*not too lightly*). What of that?

HORACE. You're magnificent, Ethel!

ETHEL. Isn't helping to hold up an historical house and name worth while? *They have* to have it done. *I* think it a privilege to be permitted to *do* it. And, besides, even eugenically it's correct.

HORACE (*puzzled*). Eugenically?

ETHEL. Yes. You see even the best old Nordic family stocks that have held the world up run out if they're not strengthened by other strains. Don't you know *any*thing about that? Why don't you ever *read* something? Well, Almeric's stock's an old, old one and we're a new one. Of course *our* stock's Nordic, too, but——

HORACE. Our stock! My heavens! Doesn't it seem impossible that we were born in Indiana?

ETHEL. Ah, but we got away young. That saved us. If we hadn't, we prob'ly wouldn't ever have known anything *at all*. Think of what we know *now*, Hoddy!

HORACE. It's pretty glorious! When Hawcastle dies, I'll be saying, quite offhand, you know, "My sister, the Countess of Hawcastle," and so on.

ETHEL (*shaking her head*). No; it isn't that I care for. I don't think anybody cares much about titles any more; that side of it's—well, a little shoddy, I think. Even this old Mr. Pike prob'ly won't be terribly impressed by the *title* part of it, I imagine. By the way, you don't s'pose he'll be—queer—do you? One hundred percent American—or anything horrid like that?

HORACE. Well, the Governor himself was a bit of the raw soil, you know, and you remember he said in his will he considered this Pike his best friend. But he's probably harmless.

ETHEL. I wish I knew. I shouldn't like Almeric and his father to think —You know what horrid types of Americans you *do* see sometimes——I—I couldn't bear it, Hoddy.

HORACE. Then keep him out of the way. That's simple enough. None of them, except the solicitor, need see him.

ETHEL. I rather wish he hadn't insisted on coming; he could have just as well forwarded his consent by mail. (*She rises; inspired.*) Hoddy, do you know, I have a feeling that today for the first time I've found out what life really means. I've never had a really great *purpose* before, and now I've got one. Gimme a cigarette. (*This last in a quick change of tone without any humor or consciousness of contrast. He is offering her a light when the noise outside breaks upon them. Mob shouts off stage, "Yankee Doodle."* HORACE *and* ETHEL *go up stage.*) What is that? (LADY CREECH *enters.*)

ETHEL (*going to* LADY CREECH). Lady Creech—dear Lady Creech—what is the trouble?

LADY CREECH. Some horrible people! Coming to this hotel. They've made a riot in the village. (MARIANO *enters with* MICHELE *and clears table.* MICHELE *exits with tray.*)

HORACE (*coming down stage*). Oh, dear me!

LADY CREECH (*sinking into chair.*) One of your fellow-countrymen, my dear. Your Americans are really too——

ETHEL. Not *my* Americans, Lady Creech! (*Mob heard off stage.*)

ALMERIC (*entering*). Curious habits of our dear American cousins. I beg your pardon, Ethel, but I'm afraid some of your Yankee friends do still amaze us sometimes.

ETHEL (*a little sharply*). I'm not a "Yankee." What is it?

ALMERIC. Car breaks down on the way from Messina. One of the chaps in it discharges the chauffeur and the other—unmistakably American, I fear—hires two absurd great oxen to pull it. Then he takes a walking stick and proceeds to conduct them himself, waving his stick and addressing the oxen in remarkable language.

LADY CREECH. Don't mumble your words, Almeric. I never understand people when they mumble their words. (VALET DE CHAMBRE *enters. He carries a tray. Crosses to table, sets tray on it and exits.*)

ALMERIC. I couldn't resist a bit of *blague,* myself. I went up to the Yankee chap, d'you see—and I pointed to the two very *dense*-lookin' oxen and I said: "I hope you don't mind bein' congratulated on showin' a lot of *fellow-feelin'*." Not *too* bad, was it?

LADY CREECH. Dreadful people!

ALMERIC. All he could answer was, no, he'd only decided to pick the best company in sight. An effort, of course; but a bit feeble. I think I had him rather; what? (*Not elaborately or stressing. Mob heard off stage.* MARIANO *exits.* MME. DE CHAMPIGNY *enters and goes toward* ETHEL. HAWCASTLE *enters with newspapers.*)

HAWCASTLE (*as he enters*). Annoying uproar.

MME. DE CHAMPIGNY (*to* ETHEL). But we know that such Americans are not of your type, cherie.

ETHEL. Well, gosh, *no;* naturally not!

HAWCASTLE. The English papers!

ALMERIC (*taking paper*). Thanks. I'm off.

ETHEL (*detaining him*). For a walk, Almeric? Would you like me to go with you?

ALMERIC (*regretting his paper a little, but only a little*). Oh, yes, surely. I'll be too pleased.

ETHEL (*she catches his tone—but cheerful*). No. I've changed my mind. (*Turns up with* MME. DE CHAMPIGNY. *Exit* ALMERIC *rapidly.*)

LADY CREECH (*in chair by table, looking at paper which* HAWCASTLE *gives her*). *The Church Register!*

(*Mob heard off stage.* MICHELE *laying table.* ETHEL *and* MME. DE CHAMPIGNY *are slightly toward back of stage.* HORACE *sits by table.* HAWCASTLE *back of table.* MARIANO *has entered.*)

HORACE. Mariano, how long is this noise to continue?

MARIANO. How can *I* know? We can do nothing. The people outside will not go while they think there is one more chance to see the North American who drive the automobile with those beefs in the American language. (*Mob heard off stage.*)

MARIANO. He will be not content with the dejeuner till he have the ham and the eggs.

RIBIERE (*enters*). *Cameriere!* (MICHELE *and* MARIANO *stand at attention.* RIBIERE *exits.*)

HAWCASTLE. Upon my soul, who's all this?

MARIANO. It is Monsieur le Blanc; he is coming—the—the traveler who own the automobile.

HAWCASTLE. Traveler? Commercial traveler, Mariano?

MARIANO (*disturbed*). Well, I can't say.

HAWCASTLE. Is it necessary to put such people in this particular part of the garden?

MARIANO (*fogged*). Well, it is the bes'! Excuse, please. (*Hearing* M. LE BLANC *about to enter, hurries up to greet him.*)

LE BLANC (*off stage*). *Niente, niente, Ribière!* (*He enters with* RIBIERE, *who is trying to show him an item in a newspaper.*) *Les anarchistes, ils ne m'amusent pas! Combien des temps faut il que je vous dirais ça?*

LADY CREECH. What a dreadful person! (LE BLANC *and* MARIANO *and* MICHELE *bow.*)

LE BLANC (*sitting by table*). See to my American friend. (MICHELE *exits.* MARIANO *takes* LE BLANC'S *cap.* ETHEL *and* MME. DE CHAMPIGNY *stroll off.*)

HAWCASTLE. Quite right, but take care; he speaks English.

LADY CREECH. Many thoroughly objectionable persons do.

LE BLANC. My American friend wishes his own national dish.

MARIANO (*serving* LE BLANC *to caviar*). Yes, Monsieur le Blanc, he will have the eggs on but one of two sides. (*Noise of the crowd outside; then a moment of dead silence.* PIKE *enters.*)

PIKE. Is the Colonel out here? (*Sees* OTHERS *first. He is a little bewildered and speaks to them.*) Where's the—oh, excuse me; I see him. (*Crosses to table, taking chair.* MARIANO *takes his hat.* MARIANO *and* MICHELE *both serve meal.*)

LE BLANC. Some ham with egg *is* the American national dish, I am right?

PIKE (*ruefully and gently*). Yes, but not petrified in olive oil with garlic on it.

LE BLANC. Will you have some of the pollo bollito?

PIKE (*shaking his head as he eats*). No, thank you. Everything I hear mentioned over here sounds to me like the name of a cigar. I've been all mixed up and heterogeneous ever since I landed. I ought never to have left home, Colonel.

LE BLANC. What a patriot! (*Pause.*) I trust you will be successful when you kindly repair that wicked motor of mine.

PIKE. I think so. I put a Pierce-Arrow together once after it had been run over by four Fords at the State Fair Grounds.

LE BLANC. Ah—sometimes I fail to comprehend your references. What is a Four-Fords?

PIKE (*staring*). It's almost worth the trip—to meet a man that never even heard of *one?*

LE BLANC. *Ah, c'est une blague, je crois!*

PIKE. Nix fer stay.

LE BLANC. May I offer you a little of this native antipasta?

PIKE (*a little distrustfully as he amiably accepts*). Native? It was *born* here, you mean? (*He eats, and is distressed.*) No, I see what you meant now. You meant this was where it went after it died. (*Speaks gently.*)

LE BLANC. A little of this Sicilian wine will take away the taste. (PIKE *takes wine, then hastily eats cheese.*) But I thought you did not like the antipasta?

PIKE. It's to take away the taste of the wine.

LE BLANC. Permit me to salute you! (*Drinks.*)

HAWCASTLE (*soothingly to* HORACE, *who is fuming*). My dear boy! We poor Britishers have our types of bounders, too. (*Low voice.*)

HORACE (*ruefully*). Ours travel, unfortunately.

PIKE (*looking at his wine glass pensively*). I expect it's too good for me because I'm not *used* to it, Colonel.

LE BLANC (*pleased and amused*). Why do you insist to call me "Colonel"?

PIKE. I've got to call you *some*thing. I couldn't pronounce "Moun-*Moun*seer" right if you were going to make me eat some more of that cheese.

LE BLANC. Then I accept my commission as colonel with gratitude. I understand this is your first journey to Europe?

PIKE. Yes—and last if it keeps on the way it's started. I can go sit around the American Express Company offices at home just as well as I can over here.

LE BLANC. You were not in France in the war?

PIKE. No; I had my flu in training-camp. They kept my regiment in Texas on account of the extra room they've got down there for buryin' people. It was a great excursion, Colonel. Anyhow, it was the biggest I've taken since I moved up to our county seat—and began to practice law.

LE BLANC. Your "county seat"? It is a city?

PIKE. City? (*pitying him*). Is it? Is it a *city?* Listen, Colonel! Over here where if a person just wants a common ordinary drink of water, he has to buy a quart *bottle with it—warm* —I don't expect I'd be rightly understood if I began to talk about what a *real city is.* Colonel, my city pays a seven eighths per cent tax rate for the maintenance of schools alone; we built the first automobile in the Western hemisphere; we are located just eighty-five and a quarter miles from the exact center of population of the whole United States of America. During the last fiscal year we manufactured one million, nine hundred and fifty-six thousand, four hundred and fifty-eight——

LE BLANC. And your architecture; your public buildings——

PIKE. Well, sir, of course I know you've got some mighty fine historical architecture and public buildings over here, but when you come right down *to* it, Colonel, I wouldn't trade our new State Insane Asylum for the worst ruined ruin in Europe—not for hygiene and real comfort.

LE BLANC. And your people?

PIKE (*with apologetic humor*). Well, we kind o' like each other. (HORACE *slaps paper sharply.*)

LE BLANC. But you have no leisure class.

PIKE. No leisure class? We've got a pretty good-sized colored population.

LE BLANC. I mean no aristocracy.

PIKE. We haven't? You ought to see somebody from Boston traveling out West, if you don't think so! Of course we don't pay taxes to support any kings and earls and first grooms of the bed-chamber and so on. If anybody wants our money for nothing, he has to show *energy* enough to *steal* it! And, of course, some *do.*

HAWCASTLE (*low voice. To* HORACE). Your fellow-countryman seems to be rather down on us.

HORACE (*to* HAWCASTLE). It's pretty mortifying.

LE BLANC. I wonder you make this long journey, my friend, instead of to spend your holiday at home.

PIKE. Holiday! Why, I haven't even gone fishing since Fourth of July, year before last.

LE BLANC (*to* MARIANO). *Finito!* (*Sets napkin on the table, and lights cigarette.*)

PIKE (*folds his napkin*). No, sir, you wouldn't catch me putting in any time over here unless I had to.

LADY CREECH (*not in an offensive tone*). Hawcastle, can you tell me how much longer these persons intend to remain here listening to our conversation?

HAWCASTLE (*lightly*). It *is* somewhat annoying not to be allowed to read one's paper in peace.

HORACE. Quite beastly annoying!

LADY CREECH. I had a distant impression that the hotel had reserved this part of the garden for our party.

LE BLANC (*quietly to* PIKE). I fear we have disturbed these good people.

PIKE. Do you think they're—hinting—at us?

LE BLANC. I fear so.

PIKE. Why, we haven't said anything to 'em.

LE BLANC. No, my friend.

PIKE. Well, I guess there's no bones broken. (*Enter* ETHEL *and* MME. DE CHAMPIGNY.) I expect it's about time for me to go and find the people I've come to look after.

LE BLANC. You are here for a duty, then?

PIKE. I shouldn't be surprised if that was the name for it.

LE BLANC. I trust they will not wholly monopolize you.

PIKE (*apologetically; smiling*). I expect prob'ly I won't be able to *eat* with you this evening. You see, I've come a mighty long way to look after her, and she—probably—that is, *they*'ll prob'ly want me to have my meals with them.

LE BLANC. Perfectly. Your friends, they have a villa?

PIKE. No; they're right here in this hotel.

LE BLANC. Seek them. I finish my cigarette.

PIKE (*rising and addressing* HORACE). I beg your pardon; but would you tell me if—— (HORACE *rises and walks away.*)

PIKE (*to* MARIANO). Waiter, tell that gentleman I'm speaking to him.

MARIANO (*to* HORACE). Monsieur—that gentleman speak with you.

HORACE (*coming back*). What gentleman? (MARIANO *bows toward* PIKE.)

PIKE. I thought from your looks you might be an American.

HORACE (*coming down stage to* PIKE). Are you speaking to me?

PIKE. Why, I shouldn't be surprised. Aren't you an American?

HORACE. I happen to have been born in the States.

PIKE. Well, that was luck, wasn't it? (*Genially affirmative.*) I wanted to ask you——

HORACE (*turning as if to go*). Will you kindly excuse me?

PIKE. Hold on a second! I'm looking for some Americans here, and I expect you might know 'em—a boy and girl named Simpson.

HORACE. Is there any possibility that you mean Granger-Simpson?

PIKE. No, just plain Simpson. Granger's their middle name. That's for old Jed Granger, grandfather on their mother's side. It's the girl I'm really looking for, though.

HORACE. Will you be good enough to state any possible reason why Miss Granger-Simpson should see you?

PIKE. Reason? Why, yes. I'm her guardian. (ETHEL *behind him.* MME. DE CHAMPIGNY *exits.*)

HORACE. What?

PIKE. Daniel Voorhees Pike, Attorney-at-Law, Kokomo, Indiana.

(HAWCASTLE *rises.* LADY CREECH *sweeps up to* ETHEL, *kisses her consolingly and sweeps out up* L. HAWCASTLE *goes out quietly, apparently reading his paper, though he glances back at* PIKE.)

HORACE. I will ask her if she will consent to an interview.

PIKE *You* will? Why, who—— (*He means "Who are you?"*) Don't you understand? I'm her *guardian.*

HORACE (*turning up stage*). I understand. (*He is overcome, but controls his emotion. Exits.*)

LE BLANC. When you have finished your affairs, my friend, remember my poor car. I will have it rolled out into the enclosure here for you.

PIKE (*puzzled*). I'll remember, Colonel.

LE BLANC. Then *au plaisir,* my friend. (*Strolls off.*)

PIKE (*watching him go*). Yes, sir.

ETHEL. I am Miss Granger-Simpson.

PIKE (*recognizing her breathlessly and solemnly.*) Yes—I see. Why, I thought more of your father than I ever thought of anybody else in my life, but—but it's your *mother* I think you *look* like! You don't remember *her* at *all,* I expect.

ETHEL. Do you think we might avoid the *personal* note? I believe it would be pleasanter.

PIKE. I don't see how it's possible to avoid—altogether, that is.

ETHEL (*sitting by table*). Will you please sit down?

PIKE. All right. (*He sits at table.*)

ETHEL. As you know, I—I—oh, are you *really* my guardian?

PIKE (*a little apologetic*). I've got the papers in my suitcase.

ETHEL. We certainly didn't expect——

PIKE. I know. You thought I'd be considerably older. It may seem queer to you, but your father and I took a liking to each other from the time when I was only a little boy on a farm that he owned. When I began to practice law, he put all his legal business in my hands right away. That was trusting me with a good deal. Well—he kept on trusting me—that's all.

ETHEL. I *never* understood my father.

PIKE (*gently*). No. *He* knew that. He was just a plain sort of man—maybe that's why *I* understood him better than his own children did. *He* knew you didn't want to be at home with him. I liked being with him, myself. (*Chuckles.*) I guess he and I must have played more than a million games of checkers.

ETHEL (*with cold distaste*). Do you suppose *that's* why he made you my guardian?

PIKE (*with a plaintive smile and shaking his head over the mystery*). Well—might-a *been!* Of course I did win a few lawsuits for him, too, and—well, I expect you prob'ly don't take the home papers?

ETHEL. No. Why?

PIKE (*meaning that if she did she'd known more about him*). Well, if you did, you'd—— (*He stops, deciding that modesty forbids his explaining more.*) Well—nothing. Anyhow, your father did appoint me, and I've put in a good deal of time looking after your estate. And I've got my practice, besides, you see, and it's a pretty good—well, that doesn't matter, except it's why I never came over here to see you. But when I got your letter, seventeen days ago, I had a talk with myself.

ETHEL (*lightly; annoyed*). Oh, did you?

PIKE. Yes, I said to myself: "What are you doing in Kokomo? John Simpson trusted you with more than his property: he trusted you with his daughter. *Now* she's come to a jumping-off place in her life! She's thinking of getting married. Isn't it about time you packed your grip and hiked over there to stand *by* her?"

ETHEL. Oh, dear me! Perhaps I'd better make it clear that I'm no longer *thinking* of marrying——

PIKE (*with quiet, deep relief*). Is that so? I'm certainly glad to——

ETHEL. I mean it's been decided upon. The wedding will be here at Taormina, and very soon.

PIKE (*swallowing*). Oh—will it?

ETHEL. There's no reason for delay.

PIKE. Well, I don't know that I could rightly say anything against that. He must be a mighty nice fellow, and you must think a lot of him! That's the way it should be. And you're—happy—are you?

ETHEL. Distinctly!

PIKE (*in sudden alarm*). It isn't that fellow I was talking to yonder?

ETHEL (*turning*). That was my brother!

PIKE (*hastily*). It was? Oh, yes. I wouldn't remember *him*. He couldn't have been more than twelve years old last time you were home. Of course, I'd have known you——

ETHEL. How? You couldn't have seen me since I was a child.

PIKE. From your picture. Though *now* I see—it *isn't* so much like you.

ETHEL (*looking at him*). You have a photograph of me?

PIKE. The last time I saw your father alive he gave me one.

ETHEL. Gave it to you?

PIKE. Gave it to me—to—to look at. (*He equivocates, seeing that she would resent his "owning" it.*)

ETHEL. And you remembered——

PIKE (*ruefully emphatic*). Yes, I certainly did.

ETHEL. It doesn't strike me as plausible. (*Rising.*) Have you any business connected with the estate you care to bring to my attention?

PIKE (*bothered*). I was thinking, if you'd like to—to introduce me to your—to your——

ETHEL. To my brother?

PIKE. No, to your—to the young *man*.

ETHEL. You feel it's—necessary?

PIKE (*apologetically*). Well, I'll *have* to have a talk with him—sort of look him over, so to speak; but I won't stay around here any longer than I can help.

ETHEL (*sitting*). Frankly, I don't see that you need have come at all.

PIKE (*looking at her gravely*). You mean you're sorry I took all the time and trouble to?

ETHEL. I don't think it was *necessary*.

PIKE. That isn't what you mean.

ETHEL. Have it your own way! Suppose we say we'd have *all* been more comfortable if you'd stayed at home where—well, where——

PIKE. Where I *belong*, you mean—in Kokomo. You needn't be afraid of hurting my feelings by saying *that! I like* to belong there.

ETHEL. I don't doubt it.

PIKE. What you really mean is that—well, that over *here* you're afraid I'll—well, that I'll mortify you. How?

ETHEL. On that point, where'd you pick up that—that *person* who's with you?

PIKE. The Colonel? Why, he isn't a "person." You only think he is because he's with me. I just got to talking with him on the steamer dock at Palermo, and so he——

ETHEL (*despairing of him*). Oh, dear me! Don't you see *yourself* you oughtn't to travel? (*Turns away, then back.*) You could perfectly well have just written your consent.

PIKE. Not without seeing the young man you're to——

ETHEL. And you could have arranged the settlement in the same way.

PIKE. Settlement? You seem to have settled things pretty well without me.

ETHEL. Of course you don't understand. Do you mind making an effort to?

PIKE. An effort—to understand. Yes—I'll do it. What about?

ETHEL. This isn't a Kokomo—wedding, Mr. Pike. It's what's sometimes called an alliance.

PIKE (*really puzzled*). Uh—well, all right——

ETHEL. Of course it's not your fault you're not man of the world enough to understand such things without explanation—I'll try to remember that—but a girl who enters into such an alliance as this is expected to bring her *dot*.

PIKE. Her what?

ETHEL (*wearily furious*). A dowry!

PIKE. Money, you mean?

ETHEL. If you choose to put it that way.

PIKE (*puzzled*). You mean you want to put aside something of your own to buy a house and fix up a place to start——

ETHEL (*interrupting sharply*). I mean a settlement upon my fiancé directly.

PIKE. You mean you want to *give* it to him?

ETHEL. If that's the only way to make you understand, *yes!*

PIKE. How *much* do you want to give him?

ETHEL. A hundred and fifty thousand pounds.

PIKE. Pounds?

ETHEL. Pounds.

PIKE. Seven hundred and fifty thousand dollars!

ETHEL. Precisely that!

PIKE (*solemnly*). He must be the Prince of the World! I expect you're right about my not meeting *him*. I prob'ly wouldn't stack up very high alongside of a man that's big enough for you to care *that* much for him. Why, I'd have to squeeze every bit of property your father left you.

ETHEL (*turning to* PIKE). Is it your property?

PIKE. I've worked pretty hard to take care of it for you.

ETHEL (*rising. Coming to him*). Forgive me for saying that.

PIKE (*meaning he doesn't mind*). Oh, pshaw!

ETHEL. I *don't* want to be irritated into mere petty exhibitions of temper, at a time like this, just when I've——

PIKE. Just when you've what?

ETHEL. Just when I've taken a great step toward doing a great thing.

PIKE (*puzzled. Mildly inquiring*). "A great"—Oh, yes. Have you talked with the young man about this present you want to make him?

ETHEL. Not with him.

PIKE. I thought not. You'll see, he wouldn't take it if I'd let you give it to him. He'll want to make his own way, of course. Mighty few men like to have everybody talking about their living on their wife's money.

ETHEL. Oh, I *can't* make you understand! A *settlement* is not a *gift*.

PIKE. How'd you happen to decide that just a hundred and fifty thousand pounds was what you wanted to give him?

ETHEL. It was his *father* who fixed the amount.

PIKE. His *father*? What's *he* got to do with it?

ETHEL. He is the Earl of Hawcastle, the head of Almeric's *house*.

PIKE. And he asks you for your property—asks you for it in so many words?

ETHEL. As a settlement.

PIKE. And the young man knows it?

ETHEL. I tell you I have not discussed it with him.

PIKE. I thought not! Do you know what's the first thing he'll do when he hears his father's made such a proposition to you? He'll take the old man out in the back yard and tie him down and run their lawnmower over him till there won't be enough left to rake up.

(Bugle and drum off stage twice. MARIANO *and* MICHELE *enter hurriedly. Lean over balustrade at back, looking off stage.* PIKE *and* ETHEL, *surprised, turn to look.)*

MARIANO *(coming down)*. It is a bandit! A bandit of Palermo, Mademoiselle. The soldiers think he hide in a grotto under the cliff. *(Bugle and drum once.)*

ALMERIC *(comes on rapidly carrying shotgun)*. Not bad sport, by Jove! Not so bad! I hope the beggar has a gun himself. Think he has a chance, Michele?

MICHELE. No, Signore, there are too many of the carabinière. *(Bugle and drum—twice. Exit* MICHELE *and* MARIANO.*)*

ETHEL. Almeric!

ALMERIC. Hello!

ETHEL. I wish to present my guardian to you. *(To* PIKE.*) This* is my fiancé, Mr.——*(She is interrupted by* ALMERIC.*)*

ALMERIC *(interrupting as he comes down)*. Hello—it's the oxen driver, isn't it? Hope you don't mind my having ragged you a bit about that. You'll have to see the governor and our solicitor about the settlement. I'm rather supposed gracefully to keep out of *that,* aren't I? Don't mind my toddlin'. The carabinière seem to be running down a bandit or somebody and I want to be in at the death. Yoicks! Tantivy, oh—tantivy! *(Exits.)*

PIKE. Seven hundred and—— Say—how much do they charge over here for a real man?

CURTAIN

ACT TWO

SCENE—*In the distance are green slopes of vineyards, castle and olive orchards leading up the mountain side. At back an old stone wall 7 feet high. This wall is almost covered with vines showing autumn tints, crowning the crest of the wall and hanging from it in profusion. In the center of the wall is a broad, green gate of the Southern Italian type, closed. A white columned pergola occupies the stage to the left. The top of the pergola is an awning formed by a skeleton of green-painted strips thickly covered by entwining lemon branches bearing ripening lemons. Between the columns of the pergola are glimpses of a formal Italian garden—flowers, hedges—and a broad, flat vase of marble on a slender pedestal. At the right, a two-story wing of the hotel meets the wall at the back and runs squarely across to the tree wings on the other side. The wall of the hotel shows windows. The wall of the hotel facing the audience shows open double doors near its upper corner, with windows upstairs and below with lowered awnings at the right. Flower boxes on ledges of all windows, and along base of hotel walls. A narrow strip of well-tended flowers except where a single broad step leading to doorway interrupts it. A Venetian well with strong wrought iron overwork showing hanging chain. A marble bench among shrubberies; an open touring car—dusty—*R. *under awning formed by the overhang of the pergola; bag of tools open on stage nearby; floorboards of car removed; apron lifted.*

PIKE *discovered in shirt sleeves, his hands dirty, and wearing a workman's long blue blouse, buttoned, is bending over engine, working and singing, at intervals whistling, "June Brought the Roses."*

HORACE (*enters from gate at back. He is flushed and angry, but controls himself with an effort, trying to speak politely*). Mr. Pike!

PIKE (*hammering at motor and singing*). "June brought the ro-ses——"

HORACE. Mr. Pike! Mr. Pike.

PIKE (*looks up*). Hum?

HORACE. I've decided the only thing to do is to have a talk with you, myself.

PIKE (*sings softly*). "The be-yoo-tiful *ro*-ses of June."

HORACE. I've been pretty thoroughly upset by what I have just learned from my sister.

PIKE. Why, that's too bad.

HORACE. She tells me that she had done you the honor to present you to the family with which we are forming an alliance—to the Earl of Hawcastle—her fiancé's father——

PIKE. Yes, sir!

HORACE. To her fiancé's aunt, Lady Creech——

PIKE. Yes, sir! The whole possetucky of them. (*Sings softly.*) "She was my hanky—panky—danky from the town of Kalamazack!" Yes, sir—that French lady, too. "She ran away with a circus clown—she never did come back —— Oh, Solomon Levi!"

HORACE. And she introduced you to her fiancé, himself.

PIKE. Yes, sir. He had to go help the Italian Army hunt a bandit, but after he—came back we had quite a talk. (*As by a sudden thought.*) Do you know if he plays the saxophone?

HORACE. Certainly not! Why?

PIKE. I forgot to ask him, and I couldn't find anything *else* he ever did. Seems as if he ought to do *something*!

HORACE. Do you know what he did during the war?

PIKE. No.

HORACE. He won a D. S. O. *You* didn't win anything in the war, did you, Mr. Pike?

PIKE. Not a thing but bad language from eleven different sergeants.

HORACE. *Only* eleven?

PIKE (*thoughtfully*). By the way, I've got to get these people straightened out in my mind, since they mean so much to your sister. What's the status of this French lady that's with them? I've placed the *others*, but I don't just——

HORACE (*frostily; interrupting*). Do you mean Madame de Champigny?

PIKE. I expect so. She a widow?

HORACE (*stiffly*). I believe so.

PIKE (*thoughtfully cynical*). Is she engaged to be married or anything to—to the father?

HORACE (*stiffly*). She is merely his good friend.

PIKE (*thoughtfully*). I see. Related to the family on her husband's side, maybe. (*Not a question, but as a probable conclusion.*)

HORACE. It is impossible for you to understand the motives of my sister and myself.

PIKE. I guess so.

HORACE. The type you belong to is always shouting that "one hundred percent American" stuff at us, and at Europe.

PIKE. You mean when I was talking to the Colonel this morning? Why, *I* wasn't criticizing Europe; I was only criticizing myself for *being* here.

HORACE. *You* make Europe laugh at us—you're precisely the type my sister and I are trying to get *away* from. You don't understand anything that isn't based on *dollars!*

PIKE (*innocently*). You don't think the people over here care for—any—dollars?

HORACE. Confound it, man, these people are the fine flower of Europe. And you're presuming to interfere between my sister and them.

PIKE. Well, I don't know that the folks around Kokomo ever used to speak of your father as a "fine flower," but everybody thought a lot *of* him, and, according to what *I've* always heard, when he married your mother he was so glad to get her—that—well, I never heard yet that he asked for any *settlement.*

HORACE. You *are* impossible.

PIKE. The fact is, when she took him he was a poor man, but if he'd had seven hundred and fifty thousand dollars, I'll bet he'd have given it for *her.* (*Goes to car.*)

HORACE (*turns on his heel and immediately turns again toward* PIKE, *who is apparently preoccupied*). I warn you, we shall act without paying the slightest attention to you. (*Triumphantly.*) What have you to say to that? (PIKE *blows horn twice.* HORACE *throws up hands and crosses. As* HORACE *crosses and returns,* LADY CREECH *and* ALMERIC *enter from gate.*)

PIKE (*thoughtfully, as if to himself*). Yes, the *horn* seems to be all right.

HORACE. The fellow is hopeless.

LADY CREECH. Dreadful person! I shall go to my room for my forty winks. (*Exits into hotel.*)

ALMERIC. (*As she goes out.*) Day-day, Aunt! (*Stops amusedly to look at* PIKE.) I see you're proving your admiration for industry by setting us all an example, Mr. Pike.

PIKE. Yes; somebody's got to work or nothing'll *run,* Mr. Hawcastle.

ALMERIC (*amusedly horrified at his ignorance*). Good heavens! My name isn't Hawcastle!

PIKE (*surprised*). Why, that's your father's name, isn't it?

ALMERIC (*amused*). Permit me! (*Gives him a card and exits into hotel.*)

PIKE (*studying the card*). The Honorable Almeric Saint—(*he spells out*) —Saint U-L-L-B-E-Y-N-N-E-S Ullbaines. The Honorable Almeric Saint Ullbaines. (*Enter* LE BLANC *at the gate.*)

HORACE. That's not the way to pronounce it. It's the *family* name. Hawcastle is the *title.* Good Lord, don't you even know *that* much?

PIKE. I'm learning.

HORACE. In regard to the settlement, Mr. Pike, will you, or will you *not*——

PIKE. Did you, or did you *not,* take an oil-can away from here? (HORACE *exits.*)

LE BLANC (*coming down*). You make progress, my friend? (*Saunters to well.*)

PIKE. Colonel, your machine's like a good many people—it's got too much engine for its rear axle. (MARIANO *enters from hotel and makes noise with lock at gate.*)

LE BLANC. Are you shutting us in?

MARIANO (*coming down*). No, Monsieur le Blanc, I have shut someone out—the convict from Palermo who have not been capture. The carabinièri warn us to close all gates for an hour. They will have that wicked one soon. There are now two companies. (*Exits into hotel.*)

PIKE. Two companies of soldiers! When they get after a bandit over *here* they seem to *mean* it!

LE BLANC (*inquiring slyly*). And with you in America?

PIKE. We send a policeman first and then an undertaker for the policeman. We're too busy to bother, Colonel.

LE BLANC. My friend, you are teaching me to respect your country, not for what you brag, but by what you do.

PIKE. How's that?

LE BLANC. I see how a son of that great democracy can apply himself to a dirty machine while his eyes are full of visions of one of its beautiful daughters.

PIKE. Colonel, you've got too much engine for your back axle. Will you please go get some of the help to give you a little clean bunch of rags?

LE BLANC. What is it you ask me to do?

PIKE. I want some more rags.

LE BLANC. My friend, I obey. (*Exits.*)

(PIKE *whistles, at work on the car.* MARIANO *has fastened the gate with a drop bar. A knife blade comes through between the gates and quietly lifts the bar, drops it from the catch, so that the gate may be opened, and is withdrawn. Then the gate opens, and* GEORGEOPOLIS *comes in quickly and quietly, closes the gate, and immediately stoops to examine some flowers nearby, his back to* PIKE. *There is a short bugle call in the distance; a voice outside calls:* "Non e qui"; *and another voice:* "Avanti, Avanti!" PIKE *is pausing in the attitude of labor, puzzled.* GEORGEOPOLIS *is in dark shabby clothes, with a dark old cap. He takes out a large pocket knife and appears to be pruning the roses.* PIKE, *looking at him, whistles an air thoughtfully.* GEORGEOPOLIS, *after a glance at him, begins to hum a Neapolitan tune as he prunes.* LADY CREECH *has been seen at window to the right.*)

PIKE (*finally*). So this is pruning time over here, is it?

GEORGEOPOLIS. *Siete lei Americano?*

PIKE. What say?

GEORGEOPOLIS. You are American tourist, gentleman?

PIKE (*affirming*). You one the hotel gardeners?

GEORGEOPOLIS. Yes, sir. You can see I am. (*Works.*)

PIKE (*this is lightly and covertly suspicious*). Um hum.

GEORGEOPOLIS (*laughing; but a little uneasiness shows*). Gardener!

PIKE. So, of course, you know all the other help here. If one of 'em were to step out here now it wouldn't embarrass you or anything?

GEORGEOPOLIS. Oh, no. (*Goes to the gate and listens.*) I go, now—excuse.

(*Is about to go out when voices are heard outside. He stops.*)

PIKE (*mildly*). Well, you said you were going; whyn't you go?

GEORGEOPOLIS (*swallowing; smiles feebly*). I go thees way. (*Turns and goes to enter the hotel. Something within the place deters him; he feels himself caught and moves back from the door.*)

PIKE. Why *don't* you go that way?

GEORGEOPOLIS (*again giving him a sick smile*). Excuse. (*He turns, but evidently finds that way blocked; he wipes his forehead, tries again to smile and repeats his word.*) Excuse!

PIKE. Funny! *You* don't look like any such hijackin' wild-cat they'd have to call out two companies o' the National Guard to coax you back to jail.

GEORGEOPOLIS (*with desperate simplicity*). You help me?

PIKE. I've got trouble enough of my own over here already. (*Voices outside and within the hotel.* GEORGEOPOLIS *becomes frankly desperate.*)

GEORGEOPOLIS. Listen! American good people.

PIKE. How do *you* know?

GEORGEOPOLIS. When I was sixteen I went to America to work, so I could learn the language. I work two year Urbana.

PIKE (*incredulous, but excited*). Urbana, *Ohio*? Why, you're almost a Hoosier.

GEORGEOPOLIS. I am old courier, educated man. I am foreigner here, same as you. In Sicily, no justice. After eight year I get away. I won't go back.

PIKE. Where do you *want* to go?

GEORGEOPOLIS. America!

PIKE. You can't. We hardly got jail-room enough for *ourselves* lately. Had to shut the doors.

GEORGEOPOLIS. *South* America I go to. Else you *see* me *kill* myself. If they touch me I do that. (*Indicates he will cut his throat.*)

PIKE. Seems to me I heard some talk of a *bandit*.

GEORGEOPOLIS (*hurried, desperate, plaintive, hushed*). I am old courier, I tell you! I knew Americans once would give a man one chance. Twenty minute? It's all. They don't know me except from photograph. Photograph in prison clothes. Don't look like me. Twenty minute?

PIKE (*slowly taking off his working blouse*). I don't believe I ought to. I don't believe I can do anything for you. (*Tosses the blouse on the car. There are knocks on the gate.*)

GEORGEOPOLIS. I only ask you not do anything at all. (*Bells are rung in the hotel.*)

PIKE (*with a glance at the blouse*). Well, maybe I could go that far. I don't know. (*Examining the blouse.*) I certainly did get this old jumper mighty dirty. Look here! Do you know anything about an automobile?

GEORGEOPOLIS. Nothing!

PIKE. Then you're a chauffeur, all right! (GEORGEOPOLIS *seizes the blouse and puts it on.*)

MARIANO (*off stage calling*). *Subito! Subito! Vengo, signore, Vengo.* (PIKE *puts on hat and coat.* MARIANO *entering from hotel and running to gates, opens them.*) *Corpo de Saint Costanzo! Non posso essere dapertutto allo stesso tempo. Vengo, Vengo!* (*Meanwhile* PIKE *lights cigar and stands by car.*) *Ecco! Dio mio!* (THREE CARABINIERI *are disclosed and* MOB.)

FIRST CARABINIERE. *Buon Giorno!* (Two CARABINIERI *enter, the* THIRD *keeping* MOB *back.*)

MARIANO (*closing gate; calling to* CROWD *outside*). No, no!

FIRST CARABINIERE. *Cerchimo l'assassino di Palerme!*

MARIANO. *Dio mio! Non nell' Albergo Regina Margherita.*

SECOND CARABINIERE. *Avete vista un uomo saltare il muro?*

PIKE. I didn't get those last two words.

SECOND CARABINIERE (*Repeats*). *Avete vista un uomo saltare il muro?*

PIKE (*to* MARIANO). Tell 'em to go on up Main Street with their Knights o' Pythias parade. I don't speak it.

MARIANO (*coming down to* PIKE). It is the bandit of Palermo. They think he climb the wall, the assassin. The other carabinieri, they surround wall yonder—these two they search here. They ask you, please, have you seen him *climb the wall?*

PIKE. *No.*

FIRST CARABINIERE (*coming down stage*). *E quelcuno passato de qui?*

MARIANO. He say has anyone *go across here?*

PIKE. *No.*

FIRST CARABINIERE (*pointing to* GEORGEOPOLIS, *who slowly looks up from the engine, over which he is stooping, then seems again engaged far under the hood*). *Chi Costui?*

MARIANO. He want to know who that is.

PIKE (*concealing some indecision*). That?

MARIANO, FIRST CARABINIERE, SECOND CARABINIERE. *Si, si.*

PIKE (*not liking it*). You mean that man there? (GEORGEOPOLIS *looks up.*)

MARIANO, FIRST CARABINIERE, SECOND CARABINIERE) *Si, si!* (GEORGEOPOLIS *looks at* PIKE *tragically.*)

PIKE. He's a Swede. Didn't you hear the colonel say he'd telephoned for a new Swedish chauffeur from Naples?

MARIANO. *E lo chauffeur di un illustre personaggio padrone dell' automobile.* (*The* CARABINIERI *glance at* GEORGEOPOLIS, *then bow to* PIKE.)

FIRST CARABINIERE (*bowing to* PIKE). *Grazia, signore.* (*Exit swiftly*

FIRST CARABINIERE *through pergola,* SECOND *left.*)

MARIANO. Dio mio! But those are the brave, Signore. Either one shall meet in a moment this powerful assassin who may take his lifes. (*Voices from back.* MARIANO *runs back to gate, opens it and exits into hotel.*) *Vate, vate! Devo dire al mareaciallo di cacciarvi?* (*Meanwhile* LE BLANC *has entered from hotel with bundle of clean rags in hand.*)

LE BLANC. Is there a new eruption of Etna?

PIKE (*meeting him and taking rags*). No; they're trying to arrest a high-school professor.

LE BLANC. What?

PIKE. I told them he's your new Swede chauffeur.

LE BLANC. My friend, do you realize the penalty for protecting a criminal from arrest?

PIKE. I can't help it now, Colonel; I'm committed to it. He used to live in Urbana.

LE BLANC. My friend, my friend!

PIKE (*quietly; looking off stage*). Look out, the governor's staff is coming back.

MARIANO (*entering*). *Lazzaroni!* (FIRST *and* SECOND CARABINIERI *enter.*)

SECOND CABABINIERE (*as he enters*). *Niente!*

FIRST CARABINIERE. *Niente la!* (*The* TWO CARABINIERI *stand up conferring.*)

MARIANO. *Grazia Dio!* It must be a mistake to think he came here.

PIKE. You'll have to get a new front tire, Colonel. This one's pretty bad. (FIRST CARABINIERE *beckons to* MARIANO *and speaks to him.*)

LE BLANC. Do you know what you are asking me to do?

PIKE. To put on a new *tire.*

MARIANO (*coming down to* PIKE). Because the chauffeur have been engage only today and have just arrive, the carabinièri ask ten thousand pardons, but inquire how long he have been known to his employer.

PIKE (*to* LE BLANC). Did you tell me you'd had him for a chauffeur three years ago all summer? (*Scratches his head, as if to remember.*)

MARIANO (*to* LE BLANC). Oh, if that is so——

PIKE (*going to auto*). I can't be mistaken about your having said that, can I, Colonel?

LE BLANC (*to* MARIANO). You have heard my friend say it.

MARIANO. Monseigneur graciously consents that I reveal his incognito to the carabinièri?

LE BLANC. Is it necessary?

MARIANO. Otherwise I fear they will not withdraw.

LE BLANC. Very well, tell them, but I rely upon them to——

MARIANO. Monseigneur, they will be discreet. (*Goes up to* CARABINIERI *and speaks to them.*) Monseigneur, they withdraw. (CARABINIERI *salute* LE BLANC.)

FIRST CARABINIERE. *Mille graze signore.* (CARABINIERI *go rapidly out gate.* MARIANO *closes gate and exits into hotel.*)

PIKE (*going to the car*). I guess you've got your twenty minutes.

GEORGEOPOLIS (*to* PIKE). I will pray God for you all my life. (*To* LE BLANC.) And you——

LE BLANC. My American friend yonder has too impulsively placed himself—in danger of the penal code of Italy. Perhaps you will be so good as to let us know for what he has incriminated himself.

GEORGEOPOLIS. You are Italian gentleman—an officer? (PIKE *leans against the car.* LE BLANC *at well.*)

LE BLANC. I am waiting.

GEORGEOPOLIS. I am a Greek. My name is Georgeopolis.

PIKE (*not meaning to be funny*). George who?

GEORGEOPOLIS. Georgeopolis. It is one name; Georgeopolis. (PIKE *studies this.*) I was courier, a professor of the languages and archaeology. I conduct parties to Timgad; to Girgenti, Rome, Cairo—anywhere you wish to go. Courier! Yes, sir! Brigand, *no!*

PIKE. How'd you get in trouble?

GEORGEOPOLIS. A very old, old way. I had a pretty *wife!*

LE BLANC. Ah!

GEORGEOPOLIS (*bitterly*). I was courier for a man—very kind to me. Spend money like water. In Athens, come to live at my 'ouse. I am *flatter!* He like to joke with my pretty young wife—*he,* the *great* man! He send me to Cairo to buy him some scarab. When I come back—— (*Makes a sweeping gesture.*)

PIKE (*impulsively, sadly, earnestly*). *Gone*—by the light o' the moon! I *guessed* it.

GEORGEOPOLIS. Gentlemans, I jus' go crazy. I hear they are gone to Sicily and I find them in a villa at Palermo. Gentlemans, I was *very* crazy then! I shot him.

LE BLANC. Finish him?

GEORGEOPOLIS (*emphatically*). No! He walk the streets again with my wife on his arm w'en I begin my sentence. Twenty-four years in prison —that is my sentence.

LE BLANC (*frowning*). What? Such a sentence here in *Sicily* for an *injured husband?* I don't credit you, man.

GEORGEOPOLIS (*explaining*). My wife face me in the court—she swear he had *pay* me—for her—she swear I come ask for *more,* and shoot him because I don' get it. They believe *her.* I got no friend in Sicily. You know this Sicily? She want to kill me because I hurt that man. Twenty-four year!

LE BLANC. He was still in the hospital when your wife gave evidence against you?

GEORGEOPOLIS (*excited*). You know my case? You *do* know it.

LE BLANC. I'm afraid the point for my friend here is that by your own confession to us you're an escaped convict.

GEORGEOPOLIS (*with desperation, yet resigned and quiet in a choked way*). Well—I ask him for twenty minute.—He give it to me. Well—all right—I go now. (*Moves.*)

PIKE. Where are you going?

GEORGEOPOLIS (*touching his throat*). I still got a remedy if they get me.

LE BLANC (*coldly*). I do not think you can get away.

PIKE (*going to* LE BLANC). Why, Colonel, he's *got* to *now*, on *your* account! You've just made yourself one of his confederates!

LE BLANC. Upon my soul, so I have! My friend, from my first sight of you in the hotel at Palermo, I saw that you were a great man.

PIKE. What are you doing? Running for Congress?

LE BLANC. I do not think that the carabinièri went away without suspicion.

GEORGEOPOLIS. They will watch every way out from the hotel. If I could find some hole till after the *dark* comes——

PIKE. Why, the colonel here's got the whole lower floor of this wing—you're his chauffeur——

LE BLANC. I was about to suggest it. I have a room that can easily be spared.

(HORACE *and* MME. DE CHAMPIGNY *heard laughing off stage.*)

GEORGEOPOLIS. You are good friends to me, gentlemans, I never——

PIKE. Don't waste time talking about *that.*

LE BLANC. My valet-de-chambre will attend to this person's needs. (*Exit* LE BLANC, GEORGEOPOLIS *and* PIKE *into hotel.*)

(*Enter* HORACE *and* MME. DE CHAMPIGNY, *laughing and talk ad lib.* LADY CREECH *enters from hotel, much flustered.*)

LADY CREECH. Have you seen my brother? Where is Lord Hawcastle?

HORACE. On the other side of the hotel, Lady Creech. (*Exit* LADY CREECH.)

HORACE. *Revenons à nos moutons, Madame.* My sister and I *do* feel that, although we may accomplish your *manner,* we never become your finest substance.

MME. DE CHAMPIGNY. You dear children! Shall I tell you what you may lack? You should not lose your own *bigness.* You and your sister! How long will you let this wild *avocat* say "She shall—she shall *not*"? Aren't you his masters?

HORACE (*worried*). Of course we are, but the trouble is, it's so hard to make *him* see it!

MME. DE CHAMPIGNY (*coldly*). I fear so. (HORACE *and* MME. DE CHAMPIGNY *go to car.* HAWCASTLE *and* LADY CREECH *enter,* LADY CREECH *talking excitedly.*)

LADY CREECH. I tell you I couldn't *hear* what they said—they mumbled their words so—but upon my soul, Hawcastle, if I couldn't hear, didn't I *see* enough?

HAWCASTLE. Possibly. (*Is thoughtful and serious.*)

ALMERIC (*entering*). Family pow-wow?

HAWCASTLE. Is there anything unusual in the village?

ALMERIC. Ra-ther! Carabinièri all over the shop—still huntin' their bandit.

LADY CREECH. Don't mumble your words so.

ALMERIC. I think it's all nonsense. I don't believe there *is* one.

LADY CREECH (*she is emphatic*). What!

HAWCASTLE (*to her*). Hermione, please.

ALMERIC. The officials insist on believing this mythical person still in the neighborhood.

LADY CREECH. What did I tell you?

HAWCASTLE. Never mind.

ALMERIC (*amused*). Something up?

HAWCASTLE. Do you feel able, my child, to exert yourself to the extent of speaking four words to your fiancée? (*He is not bitter, but has an annoyed, half-blasé sophistication—a kind of weary humor.*)

ALMERIC. *Je m'amuse!* What else *is* there for a sacrificial lamb like me to do?

HAWCASTLE (*more irritably*). Run along, sacrificial lamb, and ask Miss Granger-Simpson to come here.

ALMERIC (*with submissive mockery*). I run, Governor, I run! (*Exits into hotel.*)

PIKE (*as he enters from hotel*). Looks to me as if we were going to blow up cold. (*They* ALL *turn away from him. All up stage except* HAWCASTLE. *Exit* HORACE *and* LADY CREECH *into hotel.* MME. DE CHAMPIGNY *exits.*)

HAWCASTLE. Good afternoon, Mr. Pike.

PIKE. Howdy!

HAWCASTLE. As a father, I suppose one shouldn't press upon the subject of a son's merits.

PIKE. I don't want to talk any more about him with you—I don't want to hurt your feelings.

HAWCASTLE. I am already accustomed to your delicacy of sentiment, Mr. Pike. But upon the topic of your ward's wishes——

PIKE. I can't talk about it with anybody but her.

(*Enter* MARIANO *from hotel with letter on tray. Goes to* PIKE.)

HAWCASTLE. But mightn't I say—— (PIKE *stands examining letter.* HAWCASTLE *continues.*) I fear I do not have your attention. (MARIANO *exits into hotel.*)

PIKE. Go ahead!

HAWCASTLE (*casually and amused*). You won't discuss *any*thing with me?

PIKE. I'll talk about anything *else* with you.

ETHEL (*entering from hotel*). You wished me to come here?

HAWCASTLE (*cheerfully*). My child, I wish you to have another chat with our strangely prejudiced friend on the subject so near to all our hearts. Will you try your gentle hand with him again while I remain—so to speak, on call? (*Smiling and pleasant. Exits.*)

PIKE (*coming toward her*). I'm glad you've come. I have something here I want to read to you.

ETHEL (*coldly, plaintive*). I didn't come to hear you read.

PIKE. When I got your letter at home I wrote to Jim Cooley, our vice-consul at London, and asked him to look up the records of these Hawcastle people and write to me here about how they stand in their own community.

ETHEL. What!

PIKE. What's thought of them by the best citizens and so on.

ETHEL. You've had the audacity—*you*—to pry into the affairs of the Earl of Hawcastle?

PIKE. Why—I wouldn't have stopped at anything. I'd have done it if it had been the Governor of Indiana himself.

ETHEL. You didn't consider it indelicate to write to strangers about my intimate affairs?

PIKE. Why, Jim Cooley's office used to be right next to mine in the Citizen's National Bank Building in Kokomo.

ETHEL. Oh, hadn't you shamed me enough without this?

PIKE. Now, just let's sit down here and try to work things out together.

ETHEL. "Work things out *together!*"

PIKE. I'm sorry—for *you,* I mean. But I don't see any other way to do it, except—together. Won't you? (*She sits on well. He sits by her.*) I haven't opened the letter yet. I want you to read it first; but I ought to tell you there are probably things in it that will kind of hurt your feelings, sort of, maybe.

ETHEL. How?

PIKE. Well, I haven't much of a doubt but Jim'll have some statements in it that'll show you I'm right. If he's got the facts, I *know* he will.

ETHEL. How do you "know" it?

PIKE. Because I've had experience enough of life——

ETHEL. In Kokomo?

PIKE. Why, there are just as many kinds of people in Kokomo as there are in Pekin. This Earl's altogether too much on the stripe of T. Cuthbert Bentley to suit me. T. Cuthbert was a Chicago gentleman with a fur collar and horn spectacles—he opened up a brokerage office in our town, and when he caught the Canadian express three months later all he left in Kokomo was the sign on the front door. *It* was *painted* on. Here's the letter.

ETHEL (*reading*). "Dear Dan: The Earldom of Hawcastle is one of the oldest in the Kingdom and the holders of the title have distinguished themselves in the forefront of English battles, from Agincourt and Crécy to the Armistice. The present incumbent lives somewhere in Italy and has spent so much of his life out of England that I haven't been able to find out much about him. Nothing in his English record is seriously against him, though he is rather shot to pieces financially. (PIKE *rises.*) His son, the Honorable Almeric, is said to be rather a blasé and world-weary young man, but there's no objection whatever to be alleged against his character. That's all I've been able to learn." (ETHEL *rises.*) A terrible indictment! So that was what you counted on to convince me of my mistake?

PIKE (*ruefully*). Yes; it *was!*

ETHEL (*coming toward him*). Do you assert there is one word in this seriously discreditable to the reputation of *anybody?*

PIKE. No.

ETHEL. And, remember, it's the testimony offered by your own friend—by your own detective!

PIKE. Yes, but he doesn't seem to be much of a detective.

ETHEL. I shall tell Lord Hawcastle that you will be ready to take up the matter of the settlement the moment his solicitor arrives. (*She starts to the hotel.*)

PIKE (*at the well*). No, I wouldn't do that.

ETHEL (*coming to* PIKE). After *this,* have you any further objection to my alliance with——

PIKE (*dryly and sadly, interrupting*). It isn't an *"alliance"* you're after.

ETHEL. Then what *am* I—"after"?

PIKE. You're after something there isn't anything *to,* and if I'd let you buy what you want with your money—and your whole life—you'd find it as empty as the morning after Judgment Day.

ETHEL (*sits on well. Icily, in a low voice*). Would I?

PIKE. Don't you have any doubt about my understanding what you think of me.

ETHEL (*in a low voice*). I haven't.

PIKE. You think this—"How could that small-town American lawyer understand what I want—or understand *me?"* Yet I've seen a girl go through just the same thing at home.

ETHEL (*incredulous, scornful*). What?

PIKE. I used to go to school with her in the country: name was Annie

Hoffmeyer and her father was a good carpenter. When they moved up to Kokomo, Annie couldn't get into the Kokomo Ladies' Thackeray Club, so she got her father to give her the money to marry Artie Seymour. Artie was a minister's son—and he *was!* That was two years ago. Annie's working at the station candy-stand now while Artie's busy—busy drinking up what's left of old Hoffmeyer's settlement.

ETHEL. You say you understand! And you couple a tippling yokel with a gentleman of distinction like Almeric.

PIKE. Distinction? I didn't know he was distinguished.

ETHEL. His ancestors have fought with glory on every field of battle from Crécy and Agincourt to the Crimea.

PIKE. I don't believe you'd see *much* of *them,* would you?

ETHEL. He bears their name.

PIKE. Yes, and it's the name you want. And I'd let you buy it if it would make you happy—if you didn't have to take the people with it.

ETHEL. The "people"?

PIKE. Don't you *know* they're *all* counting on what your father left me to turn over to *you*—not to them?

ETHEL (*tensely, almost furiously, yet trying to control her sharp impatience with him*). Do you want me to *hate* you for making me explain it's an *exchange? I'm* getting the *privilege* of making a great name *mine* to hold *up*. Don't you see any *value* in *that?*

PIKE. I don't put a *money* value on it; no. But I think so *much* of it that I know John Simpson's daughter doesn't need anybody else's to help her out. (*Music P.P.*) She's fine enough and I think she's sweet enough, and I know from the way she goes for *me* that she's brave enough to stand on her own feet. (*First sunset effect with lights slowly changed.*) What is that?

ETHEL. Serenaders going up to the Greek theater. (*Music F. "Addio Bella Signora."* PIKE *stands listening.*)

PIKE (*as the song is heard approaching*). What does it mean?

ETHEL (*gently but demurely*). *Addio bella signora.*

PIKE. I mean in English.

ETHEL. Oh, it means "Good-by, beautiful lady!" (*Has an almost concealed humor here. But she looks at him significantly—just a glance.*)

PIKE (*applying it to himself and her*). Oh—yes! (*Ruefully. Music grows louder.*) It's mighty pretty. It's like this whole place. I don't blame you for liking it—it's the prettiest place I ever saw; but it's kind of foreign—and lonesome, too. I'd rather live somewhere that seems more—like home. I expect you've about forgotten everything of that kind, haven't you?

ETHEL. Yes.

PIKE. Seems funny, now; but out on the ocean, coming here, I kept kind of looking forward to hearing you sing some evening—"Sweet Genevieve," maybe. You know it, don't you?

ETHEL. I used to—but the music's a bit common, isn't it?

PIKE. I expect so. I expect that's why I like it so much.

ETHEL (*smiling*). Wouldn't you call it rather Victorian?

PIKE. Yes, worse'n that: Garfield and Arthur. My mother used to sing it—it's my favorite on the radio. I couldn't—I couldn't get you to sing it for me before I go back home—could I?

ETHEL (*after a moment*). No. (*She moves away; then turns; crosses.*) I know absolutely what I want in life. I gave Almeric my promise. It was forever, and I shall keep it.

PIKE. But you can't; I'm not going to let you.

ETHEL. Then I shall marry without your consent.

PIKE. Do you think *they'd* let you?

ETHEL. I think *you'll* let me—especially after this terrible letter.

PIKE. By the way, did you finish it?

ETHEL. I think so. No—it says "over."

PIKE. Won't you read it, please?

ETHEL (*reading impatiently*). "I'm sorry old man Simpson's daughter's got so——" (*Stops abruptly but reads more to herself. Then speaks to him with some anger.*) The rest of this is personal to yourself. Please remember I have not read it. (*Turns again, going.*)

PIKE. Neither have I. (*Reaching his hand for the letter.*)

ETHEL. Oh! (*Drops letter on bench.* PIKE *picks up letter and sits at well. She stands looking at him as he begins it, then exits quickly. He thinks she is still there.*)

PIKE (*reading letter*). "I'm sorry old man Simpson's daughter got so Europeanized. I haven't forgotten how you always kept that picture of her on your desk. The old man thought so much of you I had an idea he hoped she'd come back home some day and marry—(*reads on incredulously and with some embarrassment*)—marry some unornamented Hoosier or other." (*Shakes his head ruefully.*) I don't wonder you said you hadn't—— (*Looks round and discovers she isn't there.*) Oh! (*Blankly.*)

(HAWCASTLE *and* HORACE *enter.*)

HORACE. She says he absolutely refuses.

HAWCASTLE. That's a great pity. (HORACE *exits into hotel.*) Mr. Pike, I'm going to make a last effort to be reasonable with you—if you will with us.

PIKE. Go ahead.

HAWCASTLE. You think you're *protecting* the young lady—but, my dear chap, the young lady knows exactly what *she's* doing, and with her eyes open. Come, now! Aren't you merely being stubborn?

PIKE. I don't want to seem rude, but I meant what I said.

HAWCASTLE. Then I'm sorry. You *force* me to take another course with you.

PIKE. What's that?

HAWCASTLE (*sitting on bench facing* PIKE). Late this afternoon I developed an anxiety concerning the penalty prescribed by Italian law for conniving at the escape or concealment of certain unfortunates—ah—*wanted*—by the *police*. Believe me, I didn't *wish* to be interested. In the course of a rather hard-pushed career one does some things one wishes one weren't quite pushed to do, it's true; but one doesn't become so calloused as to *like* doing them. I'm really not such a hard fellow, Mr. Pike, as perhaps you'll think me.

PIKE. I'll take your word for it.

HAWCASTLE. I'd *much* rather we'd not been *so* hard-pushed as, frankly, we are, and when Providence simply *hurls* a weapon into the hands of a man as hard-pushed as *I* am—well, one can't blame one's self too much for using it. I'd merely be a fool if I *didn't* use it, Mr. Pike.

PIKE. All right. Use ahead.

HAWCASTLE. Italian jails, I regret to say, are not what they *should* be, Mr. Pike. (*Speaks with a real regret that he is forced to speak as he does. Is sincere throughout and not unkindly.*)

PIKE. Well, being in jail any place isn't much like an Elks' carnival.

(*Enter* MARIANO *from hotel with torch to light lamp on wall near gates.*)

HAWCASTLE. Mariano!

MARIANO. Milor'?

HAWCASTLE. Mariano, do you happen to know what the prison term is, here in Sicily, for helping to evade the police?

MARIANO. Oh, if they catch you—sometime they don't—but if——

HAWCASTLE. I mean when they *do* catch you.

MARIANO. Oh, Fascisti—Judge give maybe two year—maybe three year—maybe five year—maybe fifteen year—maybe twenty——

PIKE. Maybe what? Never mind! Don't go on! Some of you people over here never seem to know when to quit talking.

MARIANO. Yes, sir. (*Exits into hotel.*)

HAWCASTLE (*quietly but significantly*). There, Mr. Pike! Imagine that some too kind-hearted American and a friend of his had deceived the officers of the law and were now sheltering a fugitive—say in that lower suite yonder—anybody in so dangerous a position certainly wouldn't want to make enemies, would he? Especially not of people whose simple *duty required them* to mention their suspicions, would he? He'd need to keep everybody about him *friendly*, wouldn't he?

PIKE. Talk plain; talk plain!

HAWCASTLE. Well, frankly then, your mere prejudices can't be allowed to stand in our way, my dear chap. Now, remembering how necessary it *may* be for you to have *only friends* about you, don't you agree it will be better for you to think our whole matter over, Mr. Pike?

PIKE. How long will you give me?

HAWCASTLE. My poor dear man, I'm not—what do you clever people call it—"holding you up!"—I'm only suggesting that you think it over—oh, *any* time—any time fairly soon.

PIKE (*a little sharply*). *How* soon?

HAWCASTLE. Oh, I'll hope to have a glimpse of you, say this evening after dinner. By that time—

PIKE. By that time I've got to give you my answer?

HAWCASTLE. Perhaps you'd prefer to give it sooner, Mr. Pike? Don't you think you might right now?

PIKE. No. Right *now,* I feel the way the little American animal did.

HAWCASTLE. The what?

PIKE. It's a little one hundred percent American animal we call the polecat. The porcupine had been stingin' him and stingin' him all day, and the polecat began to feel he just couldn't stand much more of it.—Finally the porcupine walked up close to him. "You goin' to do what I tell you to?" he said. "Because if you don't I'm goin' to shoot every last quill I got right into you!" "All right, you go ahead and shoot," the polecat told him. "But I want to say one thing before you begin," he said. "Right *now* you're makin' a horrible mistake standin' this close to me an' talkin' about it!" (*His tone is vigorous and indignant.* HAWCASTLE, *after a brief glance at him, exits rather decisively.*)

CURTAIN

ACT THREE

SCENE—*A handsome private salon in the hotel. Cabinets against the walls buhl tables, luxurious tapestried chairs, etc. Walls panelled, Louis XV style Large double door and single door to the left of the audience—both closed To the right, a handsome fireplace with fire burning. A window with lambrequins and curtains. At back are wide double doors. Electric lights in sconces on the walls—not lit. The only light comes from the fireplace and the open doors, so that the room is dim. Beyond doors, is a brilliantly lighted conservatory hall which extends back as far as possible, showing among the plants, palms, oleanders in bloom, etc., one or two small coffee-tables with chairs. Off stage an orchestra is playing and a voice singing, "Addio Bella Signora."*

It is evening of the same day.

Rise of Curtain discloses PIKE *sitting at fire with his back to the audience.*

HAWCASTLE *and* LADY CREECH, *followed by* ALMERIC *and* ETHEL, *pass open doors at back. Enter* VALET C., *followed by* MICHELE. VALET *turns on lights and rings bell for* RIBIERE, *who enters. They stand, bowing at doors, as* LE BLANC *enters.*

LE BLANC (*as* VALET *takes his coat, turning to* RIBIERE). *Vous avez expidiez un petit bleu?*

RIBIERE. *Oui,* Monsieur le Blanc.

LE BLANC (*seeing* PIKE). Ah, you are enjoying our good old volcano, are you?

PIKE. Enjoying the volcano? No! I *think* I'm *sitting* on one.

LE BLANC. Why do you sit upon it—and how?

PIKE. I'm glad you've come, Colonel. I've been waiting to tell you.

LE BLANC (*signing to* MICHELE). Then perhaps we close the doors. Or perhaps you better like to hear the singing? (MICHELE *waits. The song is quite loud.*) You like that song?

PIKE (*ruefully*). Oh, just so so.

LE BLANC (*with secret enjoyment*). It is called "Farewell, Beautiful Lady!"

PIKE (*turning chair. More ruefully*). Yes, somebody told me that this afternoon.

LE BLANC. (*Smiles to himself and signs for the doors to be closed.* VALET, RIBIERE, MICHELE *exit. Sitting down at the table.*) I have dined with an old tutor of mine who lives here. Once every year I come to Taormina for that. (VALET *then returns with tray on which are cordials and cigarettes. Places on table and exits.*) And you, I suppose you dined with the charming young lady, your ward, and her brother, as you expected?

PIKE. No—they have friends of their own here.

LE BLANC. So I have observed. These friends of theirs are quite notables—even in Sicily.

PIKE. Oh, I don't mind their not asking me. Fact is, these friends of hers are trying to get me to do something I can't do.

LE BLANC. You need not tell me that, my friend. I have both eyes and ears; I understand.

PIKE. I wish you understood the rest, because it isn't easy—or—pleasant. Colonel, I'm afraid I may have got you into a pretty bad hole. *That's* the volcano I've been sitting on.

LE BLANC. And *that,* I fear, I do *not* understand.

PIKE. I'm afraid I *have* got you in pretty bad—all three of us: you and George and me.

LE BLANC. George? Who is George?

PIKE (*with a gesture toward the door*). *You know!* In *there.*

LE BLANC. Georgeopolis?

PIKE (*running into the plaintive*). Yes. What we did this afternoon has put you and me in the hole *with* George.

LE BLANC. How?

PIKE. Why, *some*body must have been looking out of a window.

LE BLANC (*nodding gravely*). I see.

PIKE. This Hawcastle knows—and he knows it as well as I know you're sitting in that chair—that we've got that poor fellow in there. (*Gesture.*)

LE BLANC. Surely you can trust Lord Hawcastle not to mention it. He must know that the consequences for you, as well as for me, would be, to say the least, disastrous. Surely you made that clear to him.

PIKE. No; he made it clear to me. Listen, do you know the maximum of what they *can* give you over here for it? Never *mind!* If you don't know it I won't tell you. What's the use of turning your hair white with just a simple bit of information like *that?*

LE BLANC. What does he want you to do?

PIKE. The young lady's father trusted me to look after her, and if I won't agree to let her pay seven hundred and fifty thousand dollars for—— (*Fumbles in his pocket.*) Wait a minute. He gave me his card this afternoon. (*Producing it with a feeble chuckle.*) For the Honorable Almeric Saint Ullbaines——

LE BLANC (*aware of* PIKE'S *mistake in pronunciation*). Ah! You refer to the son of Lord Hawcastle?

PIKE. I expect so. Well, if I don't agree to do that it seems George goes back to jail in Palermo; and you and I go *with* him! (*Tosses card on table.*)

LE BLANC. He threatens that?

PIKE. He'll *do* that! He isn't going to wait too *long,* either. He won't take the chance of anything slipping. I'm looking for something painful any minute.

LE BLANC. What do you mean to do?

PIKE. I *can't* do what they *want* me to, even to let you and George out. It isn't my money. All I can do is to ask you to forgive me, and warn you to get away before they come down on me. They've got me. You see how it stands: *George* can't get away——

LE BLANC. No; I think he can't.

PIKE. Why, they've got this militia all around the place.

LE BLANC. Yes, I passed through the cordon of carabinièri as I came in.

PIKE. But right now *you* can come and go as you like.

LE BLANC. So can you.

PIKE (*shaking his head*). No, I doubt it. Anyhow, I can't—I've got business here—— (*Uncomfortable about explaining it is on* ETHEL'S *account he must stick it out.*) Oh, *you* know? But, as for you——

LE BLANC (*rising and going up stage*). As for me—— (*Rings bell near door.*) I shall go.

PIKE. That's part of the load off my mind. I haven't known how to tell that poor wreck in *there*. (*Crosses.* VALET *enters; bows. Scene played quickly.*)

LE BLANC (*to* VALET, *indicating door*). *Appelez le Monsieur, la.* (VALET *goes to door, opens it to* GEORGEOPOLIS, *who appears.* GEORGEOPOLIS *comes in slowly; stands a few steps from door.* VALET *draws curtains on window and exits.*) You may come in, Georgeopolis, Some difficulties have arisen. Your presence here has been discovered by persons who do not mean well to this gentleman. He can do nothing more for you.

PIKE. It's the truth—I can't.

GEORGEPOLIS (*accepting it—swallowing*). Well—I thank you for what you did *try* for me.

LE BLANC. My friend here thinks that *I* would be permitted to leave. I have decided to attempt it.

GEORGEOPOLIS (*deferentially suspicious*). I think you succeed. You are not Frenchman—Italian, I think?

LE BLANC (*coldly and quickly*). We have spoken of that. What is more important, I have remembered a little of your trial.

GEORGEOPOLIS. "Remember"? That so? It was very quiet. There was influence against me for that. How you remember?

LE BLANC. I heard of it and I have a good memory. I think I recall that your wife was not, like you, a Greek?

GEORGEOPOLIS. *She?* French girl! Damn French girl! I am crazy! Marry damn French girl!

LE BLANC. And the *man,* I think I recall, was a noble?

GEORGEOPOLIS. Not a Milo; no—no title.

LE BLANC. I thought you said—

GEORGEOPOLIS. He was in that *class* —noble, but no title. His name was Stubbins.

PIKE. What?

GEORGEOPOLIS. Stubbins! Stubbins! Damn, *damn* Stubbins!

PIKE (*to* LE BLANC). You can't blame him. Stubbins would certainly be a terrible name for anybody to have your wife run away with!

(*Enter* VALET *with black hat and coat for* LE BLANC.)

LE BLANC. Stubbins! Yes, Stubbins is most strange. My friend, I leave you with your riddle.

PIKE (*ruefully*). Riddle? I guess so!

LE BLANC (*as* VALET *puts coat on*). But think how *much* has Europe been told of the resourcefulness of your people! You are always equal to *anything,* we learn. I hope you will prove it true. But as for me, I am *not* resourceful. You think Naples a safe place for me: I depart. *Au plaisir, mes amis!* (*All this with a tense gravity. That he has been humorous appears later.*)

PIKE (*shaking hands*). Good-by, Colonel, and take care of yourself.

LE BLANC. To our next meeting! (*Exits.* VALET *withdraws.* GEORGEOPOLIS *goes quickly to table, examining the cordial, etc.*)

PIKE. "Riddle"? Humph! (*Shakes his head ruefully, then dismisses it from his mind.*) Look here, George——

GEORGEOPOLIS (*at the table*). He call himself "Le Blanc"! He is Italian! Italian *officer!* I see it in one hundred things! You know him?

PIKE. No, *I* don't know him. I just got talking with him—on the dock over in Palermo. But whatever he is, he did what he could to help you.

GEORGEOPOLIS. He say he remember my trial. It was not even in a Palermo newspaper. How he remember? If he has been to the officials here tonight they would tell him. That is the only way he could "remember"!

PIKE. He wouldn't do that.

GEORGEOPOLIS (*in gloomy despair*). I knew when I come in these room I never get away. I know it. I am gone. (*Sinks into chair at table, miserably.*)

PIKE. Oh, look here! They're going to walk on us, all right, but anyhow, let's don't lie down on the floor with "Step on me" on our chests like a couple of doormats!

GEORGEOPOLIS. Doormat? Eh? Mat for door? (*Laughing bitterly.*) Yes. Doormat! That's me! (*Strikes his chest.*) Doormat! Damn, damn doormat ever since I marry damn French girl! Damn Stubbins! (*Knocks on door.*) They come for me!

PIKE. Not yet. Now, you go in there and stay till I send for you. (*Points to room to left.*) We won't throw our hands into the discard. We're going to raise till they *call* us. That's all you *can* do when you haven't got anything in your hand. (*Exit* GEORGEOPOLIS, *closing door after him. Another knock.*) Come in.

(MARIANO *enters.* HAWCASTLE *and* LADY CREECH *are seen at back.*)

MARIANO. Miladi Creesh—she ask you would speak with her a few minutes.

PIKE. Where is she? Oh, come right in. (LADY CREECH *gets a slight sign from* HAWCASTLE *and enters.* MARIANO *closes door and exits.*)

LADY CREECH. I need scarcely inform you that this interview is not of *my* seeking. On the contrary, it is intensely disagreeable to me.

PIKE (*mildly*). Yes'm, I should think so.

LADY CREECH. My brother-in-law feels that someone intimate with Miss Granger-Simpson's wishes should put the case finally to you. This is on *your* account, young man. My brother-in-law is anxious to avoid putting you in an unpleasant position.

PIKE. Yes'm.

LADY CREECH. My brother-in-law has made us quite aware of the state of affairs, and I am *not* in sympathy with his attitude that nothing should be done to you if it can be avoided.

PIKE (*mildly inquisitive*). What do *you* think ought to be done to me?

LADY CREECH. You've incurred penalties. Since you ask me, I think you deserve them. You'll certainly *get* them if you don't accede to my poor brother-in-law's request. (*Sits by table.*)

PIKE. You say your brother-in-law told you? Has he told Miss Ethel?

LADY CREECH. It hasn't been thought proper. Young girls should be shielded from disagreeable things.

PIKE (*ruefully*). Yes'm. I'm old-fashioned enough to think so, too. That's the idea that got me into this trouble.

LADY CREECH. I say, this young lady who seems to be technically your ward but who is considered by all of us who understand her infinitely more, *my* ward——

PIKE. Go on, ma'am.

LADY CREECH. She came to me something more than a year ago.

PIKE. Did *she* come to *you*? Are you sure about that?

LADY CREECH. I suppose it is your intention to be offensive.

PIKE. No, ma'am; I didn't mean to be at all. But, you see, I've handled all her accounts, and her payments to you——

LADY CREECH (*interrupting*). We are convinced that you have a preposterous sentimental interest yourself in Miss Granger-Simpson.

PIKE. What's that I have?

LADY CREECH. Upon what other grounds are we to explain your conduct?

PIKE. You mean that I'd only stand between her and you for my own sake?

LADY CREECH. We can comprehend no other grounds.

PIKE. I don't believe you can. But you *can* comprehend that I wouldn't have any hope, can't you?

LADY CREECH. Ah, but you strange creatures—you Americans! You hope *anything*. Oddest of all is your sometimes hoping to *lift* yourselves, and odder still, one or two of you sometimes *do*. Miss Granger-Simpson is one of those who has done so. If you stand in the way of her lifting herself higher, you take the responsibility for her health. Disappointment does kill sometimes. (*She uses a voice of great feeling.*)

PIKE (*encouragingly*). Yes'm, sometimes. Go on.

LADY CREECH. She had profited by my instruction. We have seen all along what we could make out of her.

PIKE (*politely, but dryly*). Yes'm. I'm sure you have.

LADY CREECH (*angrily*). That we could make something *better* of her! We offer her this alliance with a family which for seven hundred years——

PIKE. Yes, ma'am. Crécy and Agincourt, I know. The Saint Ullbaines family in all the battles that——

LADY CREECH (*interrupting coldly*). What family is that?

PIKE. *Your* family. Anyhow your brother-in-law's family. The Saint Ullbaines family.

LADY CREECH (*sharply*). Oh, dear me! (*Is more and more irritated with him.*)

PIKE. Why, see here, Mrs. Creech——

LADY CREECH. "*Mrs.* Creech"?

PIKE (*explaining*). I know Hawcastle is a title, or something, and isn't really Mr. Hawcastle's family name——

LADY CREECH (*interrupting again*). "*Mister* Hawcastle"?

PIKE (*apologetic*). Well, I can call a person Cap or Colonel or Doc, or anything like that but I just plain don't know how to get the words you have over here for those things into my mouth. Just let me run on in my own way. I don't mean to hurt your feelings.

LADY CREECH (*icily*). I thank you.

PIKE. Your nephew gave me his card this afternoon. I *had* it here a minute ago. Certainly, here it is: (*Taking it from the table.*) The Honorable Almeric Saint—— (*He spells out.*) U-l-l-b-e-y-n-n-e-s. Isn't that right?

LADY CREECH (*sharply*). Certainly!

PIKE. Well, I suppose, of course, if Hawcastle is a title, a person *oughtn't* to put Mister before it because if he were a Mister he'd be a Mister Saint Ullbaines too, like his son, of course. He was just a Mister before he *had* the title, wasn't he, or something?

LADY CREECH (*irritably*). Dear me, *yes!*

PIKE. Well, then, just let me speak of him that way. I can manage it easier. What I'm getting *at*, Mr. Saint Ullbaines, the father, sends you to me to say practically that he wants my answer and he wants it pretty soon. You're *really* here to notify me he isn't going to wait much longer. Isn't that the case?

LADY CREECH. I certainly *hope* it is.

PIKE. Yes. I thought so. Now, before I *give* you my answer, I want to ask one question. When he comes *down* on me and does what he *says* he will, the young lady is at least going to notice that I'm not *around* here any more, isn't she?

LADY CREECH. Possibly.

PIKE. She's going to find out then what happened and *how* it happened, isn't she?

LADY CREECH. Possibly—if she inquires.

PIKE. Well, when she understands *who* gave the information that did it, what's she going to think about it?

LADY CREECH. She will see it perfectly as *we* do—as a duty performed.

PIKE. A *painful* duty, maybe?

LADY CREECH. Not necessarily, considering your behavior toward herself!

PIKE. That's all I wanted to ask.

LADY CREECH (*rising*). Perhaps, then, you'll be so good as to—

PIKE. As to give you my answer to your brother-in-law? Certainly. Tell him I've thought it over and I'll be ready to talk to him at any time after the next half hour. I'll talk to him in the presence of the young lady and her brother.

LADY CREECH (*turning to go*). Her brother—certainly! As for Miss Granger-Simpson—no!

PIKE. No?

LADY CREECH. I shall not permit her to come near here. As her chaperone I refuse. (*She sweeps up to the doors.*) I shall tell Lord Hawcastle——

PIKE. Any time after half an hour, and in this room.

LADY CREECH (*at door*). But Miss Granger-Simpson under no condition whatever! (*Exits.*)

PIKE. Thank you. (PIKE *closes door behind her, presses button; crosses to desk and writes hurriedly. Knock at doors.*) Come in.

MARIANO (*entering*). Signore.

PIKE. Mariano, I want you to take this note to Miss Simpson. (*Quickly encloses note in envelope and addresses it.*)

MARIANO. The Mees Granger-Simpson?

PIKE. Yes! Do you know where she is?

MARIANO. She walks on the terrace alone.

PIKE. Give it to her yourself—to no one else, and I want you to hurry. (*Gives him note.*)

MARIANO. *Si,* Signor. (*Exits.*)

PIKE (*as* MARIANO *exits*). George! (*Crosses to window and draws curtains.* GEORGEOPOLIS *opens door and enters.*) I wanted to tell you. I believe I've got them held off for about half an hour, but I think then it will happen. I didn't dare try for more time than that because I don't think they'll take many chances of your not *being* here when they say the word. Do you see *any* way of *not* being here?

GEORGEOPOLIS. No, I told you I am gone. It must be I offend some god of my Olympus.

PIKE. Who?

GEORGEOPOLIS. Why did I come to Taormina? Because the Mafia tell me my wife is at Taormina. The gods let me get that *near.* (*Bugle outside.*) Now the carabinièri come for me. (*Going to the window.*)

PIKE (*thrusting* GEORGEOPOLIS *behind him*). Don't show yourself!

GEORGEOPOLIS (*looking out of window over* PIKE's *shoulder*). Look! There by the gates—the carabinièri.

PIKE. Yes—they've been there ever since this afternoon. Look there! Who on earth—who's that they've got with them?

GEORGEOPOLIS. It is Monsieur le Blanc. Did I not tell you he was

Italian? He has betray me himself. (*Turning from window again.*)

PIKE. Don't you believe it. They've arrested the poor old Colonel. They got him as he went out.

GEORGEOPOLIS (*pointing*). No; they speak respectfully to him. They bow to him—they bow to him.

PIKE. Yes. They'll be bowing to us in a minute. (*Sharp knock on doors.*)

PIKE. You go in there, and remember this is my fight and you're not going to do anything crazy.

GEORGEOPOLIS. I try to do what you tell me.

PIKE. Then don't you *forget* what I've been telling you—that car's got too much engine for the back axle. You be careful not to strain it! (GEORGEOPOLIS *bows meekly and exits, closing door.*)

MARIANO (*door opens.* MARIANO *appears*). Miss Grahnger-Seempson.

PIKE (*turning*). All right, Mariano. (ETHEL *enters, goes to sofa and sits.* MARIANO *exits.*)

PIKE. I'm much obliged to you for taking my note the right way. I have some pretty good reasons for not leaving this room.

ETHEL. Your note seemed so urgent.

PIKE. It had to be. Some people who want to see me are coming here, and I want you to see *them.* They'd have stopped you from coming if they could.

ETHEL. There was no effort to prevent me.

PIKE. No; I didn't give 'em time.

ETHEL. May I ask to whom you refer?

PIKE. The whole kit and boodle of 'em.

ETHEL. You are inelegant, Mr. Pike.

PIKE. I haven't time to be elegant—even if I knew how.

ETHEL. Do you mean that my chaperone would disapprove?

PIKE. I shouldn't be surprised. I expect the whole fine flower of Europe would disapprove. "Disapprove!" Why, they'd sandbag you to keep you away.

ETHEL (*rising quickly*). Oh, then I *can't* stay. (*Moves toward doors.*)

PIKE (*stepping in front of her*). Yes, you can, and you will, and you've got to!

ETHEL. "Got to"! I shall not!

PIKE. I'm your guardian and you'll obey me this once if you never do again. You'll stay here while I talk to these people, and you'll stay in spite of anything they say or do to make you go. (ETHEL *crosses to table.*) I hate to talk roughly to you; I wouldn't hurt your feelings for the world, but it's come to where I've got to use the authority I have over you.

ETHEL (*turning*). Authority? Do you think——

PIKE. You'll stay here if I have to make Crécy and Agincourt look like a Peace Conference. (ETHEL *sinks into chair by table.*) You and your brother have soaked up a society column notion of life over here; you're like old Peter Delaney of Terre Haute. Poor old Pete got so he'd even drink *tea* out of a bottle if there was a whiskey label on it. They've muddled you with *labels;* and it's my business to have you know the kind of people you're dealing with.

ETHEL. You're bullying me. You're talking *brutally* to me.

PIKE. Do you think I'd do it for anything but you?

ETHEL. You are odious.

PIKE. Don't you suppose *I* know how you despise me?

ETHEL (*hurriedly, defiantly, facing him*). I don't despise you.

PIKE (*indignantly*). What! Why, every *word* you've said to me——

ETHEL (*interrupting sharply and rapidly*). I don't care! I don't! I don't despise you. I think if I'd never left home I—— (*Has gone this far on a quick impulse; then stops abruptly.*)

PIKE (*coldly*). Well?

ETHEL. If I'd stayed home and grown up there, I'd prob'ly have been a provincial flapper of the kind you prob'ly like—I'd prob'ly have been playing "Sweet Genevieve" for you tonight. But my life hasn't been *that,* thank Heaven! And you've humiliated me from the moment of your coming here. You've made me ashamed both of you and of myself. (*Murmur of voices outside and knock at the door.*)

PIKE (*incredulously*). Of yourself, too?

ETHEL (*resentfully*). Oh, dear, but you do think you're superior!

PIKE (*a little grimly, but sadly*). You couldn't imagine being ashamed of—of these *other* people—could you?

ETHEL (*with feeling*). Of them? Never!

PIKE (*abruptly*). Did you ever see newsboys and street dogs run down a rat in the gutter? It makes you sorry for the poor old rat, doesn't it?

ETHEL (*surprised and puzzled*). What?

PIKE. This afternoon I saw a *man* in a hole like that. He was only a runaway jailbird, but to save my life I couldn't help being sorry for him. Eight or nine years ago another man ran away with his wife and he followed them and did some harm to the man—but the wife swore my poor old jailbird into the penitentiary. It seemed a pretty raw deal to me.

ETHEL. But what has that—— (*Means "What's it got to do with me?"*)

PIKE. I tried to help him get away.

ETHEL (*coldly but not sourly*). Don't you think *that* was rather foolish? When you're in a foreign country——

PIKE. Why, he used to work in a fruit store in *Urbana*. Urbana, *Ohio!*

ETHEL (*giving him up as lamentable*). Oh, *dear!*

PIKE. Why, of *course* I did all I could for him. But some of the friends you could never be ashamed of saw us bring him into these rooms. They know I've got him here now—and this is what I sent for you to tell you: If I don't hand over *you* and most of the money John Simpson made for you, it means that my poor old jailbird goes back to jail and I go with him for—well, two years is the shortest time they *can* make it.

ETHEL (*angrily*). You expect me to *believe* they'd do such a——

PIKE (*sharply*). You *don't?*

ETHEL. Oh, I *knew* you'd have some awful idea that would make everybody *ashamed* for me—to think you're in *charge* of me. Haven't you *got* any sense? Don't you know these are gentlefolk? (*Knock on door.*)

PIKE. I think the gentlefolk are here. Come in, gentlefolk. (LADY CREECH, HAWCASTLE, ALMERIC *and* HORACE *enter, leaving doors open.*)

LADY CREECH (*as she enters, coming toward* ETHEL, *followed by* OTHERS). My dear child, what are you doing in this dreadful place with this dreadful person? (*Crosses in front of* ETHEL.)

HORACE. Ethel.

PIKE. She's here by my authority; she'll *stay* by my authority.

HAWCASTLE (*appearing at door,* MME. DE CHAMPIGNY, *following him, stands in doorway*). Is she here?

HORACE. Lord Hawcastle, will you please insist upon Ethel's leaving?

HAWCASTLE (*coming down*). Yes. I think Miss Granger-Simpson would *better* go.

PIKE (*starting toward door*). Not yet.

ALMERIC (*joins* MME. DE CHAMPIGNY *in doorway. He speaks as he appears*). What's she doin' here? (*Calling to* ETHEL) Ethel——

PIKE (*to Almeric and* MME. DE CHAMPIGNY). Come in or stay out. (*They step in and he closes the doors, speaking sharply to* ETHEL.) You stay right where you are!

ALMERIC. Oh, I say!

LADY CREECH. The lynching ruffian!

HORACE. Ethel, do you mean to let this fellow dictate to you?

ETHEL. But he says I must!

PIKE. Why do you all want her to go?

MME. DE CHAMPIGNY. This man is an *Apache*.

LADY CREECH. Barbarian!

PIKE. I'll leave it to you to tell her.

HAWCASTLE. Don't you think a gentleman might spare her a "scene"?

PIKE. *I* won't! Speak out! Why do you mind her being here?

LADY CREECH. Don't mumble your words!

PIKE. I've told her why you don't want her here and she doesn't believe me.

ETHEL. Do you think I believe an English gentleman would stoop——

PIKE. Stoop? Mr. Saint Ullbaines wouldn't stoop that far? Then, if he wouldn't, Mr. Saint Ullbaines doesn't *know* I've got anybody in that room there at all, or if he *does* know it, he doesn't intend to do anything about it even if I don't consent to what you all want. But if I *have* got the man in there and if I *don't* consent and Mr. Saint Ullbaines *does* send the Knights of Pythias in on us, then would you think he stooped? Because he certainly knows now that out of the choice he gave me, I'm still Hoosier enough to take jail.

HAWCASTLE (*irritated*). Do you realize you've just admitted shielding a convict here? Is it "stooping" if we decline to violate the law of the country we're in? After what you've admitted, if we shield you, we're *all* subject to the same penalty that *you* are. Do you expect me to let these ladies be arrested, too?

PIKE (*in desperate triumph to* ETHEL). Do you believe me *now?* And that's what you're here to *do,* isn't it, Mr. Saint Ullbaines—to see that nobody's arrested except my jailbird and me? That's what you're going to do just about right now, isn't it?

HAWCASTLE. What else *can* we do since you've confessed, *yourself*——

PIKE. "Confessed"! You're not keeping your eye on the ball, Mr. Saint Ullbaines. I'm *proving* this to her! I'm *claiming* I've got him in there, Mr. Saint Ullbaines!

LADY CREECH (*breaking out fiercely*). Stulbins, man! Stulbins! Stulbins!

PIKE. What? It *isn't* Saint Ull——

LADY CREECH (*fiercer*). Stulbins! Stulbins!

PIKE. Is your grand old name *Stubbins?* Is it pronounced *Stubbins?* My soul! God does move in a mysterious way his wonders to perform.

LADY CREECH (*sharply*). Blasphemy now, is it?

HAWCASTLE (*sharply*). Haven't you finished this nonsense?

PIKE (*sharply*). Just about. (*To* ETHEL.) I told you of a man who stole a poor devil's wife and let her swear her husband into prison. Could you believe that of this man here? (*Indicating* HAWCASTLE.)

HAWCASTLE. What?

ETHEL (*angrily*). Believe it of *him?*

PIKE. Yes, and that now he's going to send that *same* poor devil *back* to jail and me along with him for trying to help him. *Could* you believe it?

HAWCASTLE (*fiercely*). Have you absolutely lost your senses?

PIKE. Either I have or I've got something for you. (*He goes to the door.*) George! There's somebody here says his name is Stubbins!

HAWCASTLE (*as* GEORGEOPOLIS *enters*). Who's this? What? (*His voice is horror-stricken.*)

(GEORGEOPOLIS *crosses to* MME. DE CHAMPIGNY *with arms over head as if to strike her.*)

MME. DE CHAMPIGNY (*as* GEORGEOPOLIS *crosses, calls wildly to* HAWCASTLE). My *dearest!* (*Then as* GEORGEOPOLIS *reaches her, sinks upon the floor.*) Oh, Mother of God! Don't kill me—don't kill me!

HORACE (*starting toward her*). Madame de Champigny!

PIKE. You keep back. She's—his wife. (HORACE *goes to the fireplace.*)

HAWCASTLE (*huskily*). Almeric, call the carabinièri.

PIKE. Call them in. We're ready. (MME. DE CHAMPIGNY *rises and goes to window, followed by* HAWCASTLE.)

ALMERIC (*At doors*). Tell that officer to bring his men in here.

PIKE (*to* ETHEL). But I want you always to remember, I consider it cheap at the price. (ETHEL *turns up stage and seats herself in chair by* HORACE *at mantel.* PIKE *crosses to* GEORGEOPOLIS *and puts his hand on his shoulder.*)

(LE BLANC *enters, passing by* ALMERIC, *who is at door.* RIBIERE *enters immediately after from same direction.*)

LE BLANC (*coming down.*) There will be no arrests tonight, my friends.

HAWCASTLE (*to* ALMERIC). Do as I say.

LE BLANC. The officer is not there; the carabinièri have been withdrawn. (*To* PIKE.) For your sake, I have relinquished my incognito. The man Georgeopolis is in my custody.

HAWCASTLE (*struggling to regain his dignity*). By whose authority? Do you know that you are speaking to the Earl of Hawcastle?

RIBIERE (*advancing a step*). Gently, sir. You are addressing His Highness, the Duke of Piedmont, Prince of Savoy, Count of Basilicata, Lieutenant General of Italian Cavalry, Governor of Romagna and cousin to the Royal House of Italy.

PIKE. Oh! And *think* of what *I've* been calling him!

LE BLANC. My friend, my study of you has been refreshing, simply refreshing. (*Exits.*)

(RIBIERE *comes down to* GEORGEOPOLIS, *touches him on the shoulder and starts for door.* GEORGEOPOLIS *rises to follow him and encounters* MME. DE CHAMPIGNY, *who has started up stage.*)

GEORGEOPOLIS. I won't touch you—not even to strangle you! (*To* HAWCASTLE.) You—it's different. I'm going to pay you. (*Exits rapidly.* RIBIERE *follows.* MME. DE CHAMPIGNY *sinks into chair by fireplace.*)

HAWCASTLE (*near door*). Almeric —— (*Makes a slight motion of the head toward* ETHEL). My dear—— (*He speaks appealingly.*)

ETHEL. Nothing is changed between us, Almeric. (*Deeply moved, she comes to* PIKE; *speaks appealingly, almost tearfully.*) He hasn't done anything wrong and he has my promise. Am I less bound to him because you've shown me the name I wanted to lift up is a disgrace?

PIKE (*incredulously, slowly*). What?

ETHEL (*tremulously*). You want me to be honorable, don't you?

PIKE (*plaintively, dryly, despairing of her*). I guess you take after a great-uncle of yours your father never told you about, old Linseed Simpson, that got hanged. When they asked him if he had anything to say, just before it—happened—he said, "Yes. This may convince a whole lot of other people, but for my part," he said, "I consider it practically no argument at all." (*As she stares at him, open-mouth and wondering.*)

CURTAIN

ACT FOUR

The morning of the next day.

SCENE—*Same as Act I, except that large table has been removed, and only one tea-table remains. A bench is to the left. On the steps leading to doors are some bags, hat-boxes, and rugs.*

HAWCASTLE *discovered at table, with* PORTER *back of table, strapping bags.*

PORTER. *Questi sono tutti?*

HAWCASTLE. *Si, si. E tutti. Va bene.* (*Exit* PORTER.)

ALMERIC. (*Enters.*) Ah, Governor! You off?

HAWCASTLE. That depends!

ALMERIC. Depends? Poor dear Madame de Champigny took the morning train to Naples, and your heavy luggage went with hers. Shouldn't say that looks much like dependin'.

HAWCASTLE. It does, though.

ALMERIC (*faintly amused*). You don't think that beggar'd be havin' a shot at you?

HAWCASTLE (*grimly looking at him*). He did once. Ah—he didn't *miss* me, you know.

ALMERIC (*sitting on bench*). No, that's true. I take it this Royalty personage assumes the responsibility for him now, though.

(LADY CREECH *enters.*)

HAWCASTLE. The Duke of Piedmont has the reputation of being a quixotic fool. I don't know what moment he may let the man loose.

LADY CREECH. Then I have the advantage over you, Hawcastle. He's just done it.

HAWCASTLE. What?

LADY CREECH. Arranged a pardon for him by telegraph.

HAWCASTLE. You don't mean that!

LADY CREECH. Ethel has just told me.

HAWCASTLE. That's pleasant for *me!* (*Enter* MARIANO. *Scene very sharp and fast.*) Mariano, I'm off for Naples. Put my things in the car. (MARIANO *calls* PORTER *and they exit with bags. To* ALMERIC.) I've got to trust you to see it through. You never *did* see anything through *yet*, but——

ALMERIC (*interrupting with a languid laugh*). Since you've always treated me as an ineffective ass, dare say I *am*—but am I *quite wrong* in thinking that what blew up our little party last night was your own *too* effective record, dear chap?

HAWCASTLE. Let that alone. I've been hard-pushed most of my life and the misfortunes of a hard-pushed man appear as crimes to inexperienced people like our young American lady. What's important *now* is that she gave you her word last night that she'd stick it.

LADY CREECH. But she's behaving very peculiarly this morning.

HAWCASTLE. How?

LADY CREECH. Shedding tears over this Georgeopolis's story. What's more, she's—sent the awful Pike person to him with *money*.

HAWCASTLE. Money?

ALMERIC. If you don't mind my seeming to have an idea, I'd say she might be trying to hush him up.

HAWCASTLE. You *have* hit it—for once. That's what she's trying to do.

LADY CREECH. Then why do you go?

HAWCASTLE. Because I'm not sure she can, and I'm better out of the way just now on *all* accounts. Wire me at the Bertolini. (*Turning at stoop.*) This shows she means to stick it.

LADY CREECH (*with a smile of pride in her teaching*). Naturally!

HAWCASTLE. She still wants what she wanted, thank Heaven! (*Exits.*)

(PIKE *enters, looking after* HAWCASTLE.)

PIKE (*mildly*). Your father seems to be on his way. (*Exit* LADY CREECH.)

ALMERIC. Oh, yes, possibly. He's always been a great one to worry over things, you see.

PIKE (*sits on bench, regarding him, puzzled*). *You're* not that way, are you?

ALMERIC. What's the good? Things happen—or else they don't. Haven't you Yankees a bit of slang to cover that? *Why* I should worry?

PIKE. I'm not a Yankee. I'm a Hoosier.

ALMERIC (*sits by table*). Are you? I'm sure the difference would be interesting to an anthropologist. But you hardly expect *us* to be "up" on all your intricate American tribal distinctions, do you? I mean to say, my poor dear chap, I'm *not* worrying about that—or about anything.

PIKE. No? As we say in our intricate American tribal way, I expect *you wouldn't*.

ALMERIC. Is it clever? So often we can't tell, you see. I mean to convey, if I can penetrate your intelligence, you rather over-reached yourself last night, didn't you? In your merry cowboy way "you shot up the town"—isn't it? Well, you hit my immediate ancestor but didn't touch *me*. You failed, you see. Ethel sticks it, you see.

PIKE (*honestly puzzled, not superior*). "It"? "Sticks—*it*"? Yes, she seems to.

ALMERIC. The Governor's—tactful. He won't rejoin us till things are settled. Certainly not, until Ethel's drawn off your friend, the bad hat.

PIKE (*gently puzzled, as if to himself*). "Bad hat"?

ALMERIC. The Georgeopolis chap. Come, now, wouldn't you call him a bit of a bad hat, yourself?

PIKE. I couldn't state. You say you think she's drawn off—drawn off this—this bad hat?

ALMERIC. Yes; the convict chap. What I understand you call in the States affixing him.

PIKE (*puzzled*). "Affixing him"? (*Then understanding.*) Oh, yes, go on telling me. I *like* to listen to you.

ALMERIC. She's been sending him money, hasn't she? You took it him yourself, didn't you?

PIKE (*not obviously mocking*). Yes, I took it him.

ALMERIC. Well, did he promise he'd keep quiet?

PIKE. Oh, *that's* what she sent the poor cuss the money for, was it?

ALMERIC. Why, what other reason could there be?

PIKE. You wouldn't gather that maybe it was because she thought he'd been wronged, maybe?

ALMERIC. I'm rather experienced, my chap. I don't look for quixotism. I'd say she shows she already identifies herself with *us* and shuts him up.

PIKE. Would you mind my being present when you thank her for it?

ALMERIC. I'm afraid you'd *never* understand us. (*Not ill-natured. Laughing.*) We don't love wallowin' about in passionate gratitude, young fellow Pike, my lad.

PIKE (*breaking out sincerely*). Oh, if I could only get you over to Kokomo!

ALMERIC (*coming back to bench*). Curious! You'd like to see me among your own wigwams—but I shouldn't be at all keen about treating Piccadilly to a sight of *you*. Daresay, we can muddle along amiably enough with these few differences between us. Bye-bye.

PIKE. Going?

ALMERIC (*indicating the approach of* ETHEL). Tactful of me. (*Smiles triumphantly.*) She may wish to consult her man of business again on certain matters. (*His smile indicates that he means the settlement; he produces a sort of chuckle.*) I'll be back soon, poor old chap. (*Exits.*)

ETHEL (*entering*). Mr. Pike, I——

PIKE (*rising*). George wants to thank you. Can I bring him?

ETHEL. Yes.

PIKE (*moving off*). I'll go for him.

ETHEL. I heard that Lord Hawcastle has left the hotel.

PIKE. Yes; he was afraid of—that is, he was afraid of not being tactful—or *something,* I guess! (*Not over-pointing it as he exits.*)

(*Enter* MARIANO *and* SERVANTS, *followed by* LE BLANC *and* RIBIERE, ALL *bowing deeply.*)

ETHEL (*making deep courtesy*). Monseigneur!

LE BLANC (*To* OTHERS.) I beg you, I beg you! (*Mariano,* RIBIERE *and* SERVANTS *exit. To* ETHEL.) Not you! I have come to make my adieux to your guardian. Incognito or out of it, he is my very good friend—no matter if he is an egotist.

ETHEL. Egotist! I shouldn't call him exactly an egotist.

LE BLANC. Ah? So? What do you call him?

ETHEL. I—I call him—— (*Turns away.*)

LE BLANC. Bravo! I call him an egotist because he will not pretend to be something he is not. I respect your country in him, my dear young lady; he cares nothing whether I am a King or a commoner. He salaams no more to the one than to the other.

ETHEL. But don't you think we should show reverence? *Shouldn't* he salaam?

LE BLANC. Not if he is both brave-minded and humble-minded enough to see that he doesn't know *how.* In the coast towns of Algeria sometimes you see an Arab trying to wear our European clothes. He does not look well. In the desert you meet the barbarian Bedouin who is fiercely *himself.* He does not know our forms of courtesy but he may show you his own. I like him better.

ETHEL (*gently*). Thank you. I'll remember you said that. (*Enter* PIKE *with* GEORGEOPOLIS.)

LE BLANC. I have come to bid you good-by, my friend. Life is a series of farewells, they say; but if you come to Rome, when I am there, you will be made welcome. Your Ambassador will tell you where to find me.

PIKE. And if you ever get out as far as Indiana, don't miss Kokomo—the station taxi-driver will tell you where to find me. You'd like it, Colonel. (*He is distressed by the word having slipped out.*)

LE BLANC. I'm sure I should.

PIKE. I don't even know how to call you rightly by name. Don't you ever think I don't understand how many things I don't know.

LE BLANC (*as they shake hands*). No, my friend, but I have confided to you that you are a great man. But a great man is sure to be set upon a pedestal by some pretty lady. (ETHEL *turns away.*) It is a great responsibility to occupy a pedestal. On that account—I depart in some anxiety for you.

PIKE. What do you mean?

LE BLANC. Ah, if you do not understand that, my friend—— What is it you have taught me to say? Ah, yes! You have too much engine for your rear axle! (LE BLANC *nods gravely to* GEORGEOPOLIS, *kisses* ETHEL'S *hand gallantly and exits.*)

GEORGEOPOLIS. Kind young lady—oh, kind!—I take what he give me from you; I *must*—I've got nothing. I have been convict; no one take me as courier again. I go to London; maybe I can teach some languages.

ETHEL. Are you following Lord Hawcastle and your wife?

GEORGEOPOLIS. She is nothing. Exist no longer for me.

ETHEL. But Lord Hawcastle?

GEORGEOPOLIS. Ah, *yes! He* exist; I don't forget 'im! Where does a man suffer? (*Striking his head.*) I 'ave foun' out it is 'ere, 'ere! It is in the mind! That man, it is *'ere* I can *'it* 'im! (*Striking his head again.*) What does he own now that is worth something to 'im? Only 'is name; 'e is Milor. Well, I am goin' tell everybody in the worl' what 'e has done to me! 'E shall not go in 'is club! That name of 'is, I am going to make it a *shame!* I will! God is goin' to 'elp me do that to 'im!

ETHEL (*with bent head*). Yes. (*In a low voice.*)

GEORGEOPOLIS. I forget myself! I talk so ugly!

ETHEL (*huskily*). No—you couldn't feel any other way, of course.

GEORGE. Miss, I thank you. (*Crosses; kisses her hand humbly.*) Miss, good-by! (*He shakes hands with* PIKE, *tries to speak, fails, and exits up.*)

PIKE (*somewhat affected emotionally*). I don't want you to think I don't understand there are plenty of fine people over here.

ETHEL (*gently*). When you're home again, I hope you'll remember them.

PIKE. I will.

ETHEL. And I hope you'll forget everything I've ever said.

PIKE. Somehow it doesn't seem as if I very likely would.

ETHEL (*coming toward him*). Oh, yes, you will! All those unkind things I've said to you——

PIKE. Oh, I'll forget *those*—easy!

ETHEL. Forget it all. And when you're among the home people again, that you like so well—I think prob'ly there's one of them you'll be gladdest of all to get back to—I can see her so easily. Doesn't she wait for you at her "front gate" in the twilight? Isn't she like that?

PIKE. No. Not like that.

ETHEL. But there *is* someone there? You—— (*She pauses.*)

PIKE. Yes—there is "someone there." That is, in a *way,* she's there. Sometimes when I go home in the evening she kind of *seems* to be there. I live in an old house you were born in—as it just happens. It gets kind of lonesome sometimes and then I get to thinking she *is* there, sitting at a tiny old piano that used to be my mother's, and singing——

ETHEL. Singing "Sweet Genevieve"?

PIKE. Yes. *You*—sing—sometimes, don't you?

ETHEL. *Only* when I'm very *happy.*

PIKE. "Sweet Genevieve" has always been my favorite. I expect it *isn't* very good music—or anyway not much in fashion. But, after all, nobody does sing it for me—except on the radio—and when I imagine *she* does, I come *to* before long—and there isn't anybody there but me—and the cat. (*His tone is gently serious.*)

ETHEL. But you'll find the singer some day, and—well, I'll think of you listening to her voice in that nice warm American summer twilight you have over there. I *know* it's a sensible, kindly life—pretty different from my *own* destiny.

PIKE. What destiny is that?

ETHEL. Why, it's bound up with poor Almeric's, isn't it? He's got to make the world forget his father and think of *him.* He's got to have a career that will *do* that. He's got to hold up his own *work*——

PIKE (*interrupting mildly*). Work?

ETHEL. You see I haven't *absolutely* forgotten my father. I'm afraid you've stirred something up in me that I *had* forgotten, though: I mean I—I seem to be—well—— (*She seems to be confessing something, with difficulty.*)

PIKE. You seem to be what?

ETHEL (*in a low voice*). I seem to be something of an—of an American, after all.

PIKE. Do you? Well, don't be afraid: nobody heard you but me and I won't tell on you.

ETHEL (*sharply*). You're unbearable! I'm not ashamed of it, and it's all the more reason for me to behave decently now. Isn't it true?

PIKE. Yes, of course it is.

ETHEL (*walking toward hotel*). I haven't seen Almeric since last night. I must see him now.

PIKE. He'll be along, I think.

ETHEL. He's always been so light and gay: I've been coward enough to keep out of his way this morning. I hated to see him bending under such a blow as this. But I must: I've got to show him how to get his head up in spite of it. That's my duty, isn't it?

PIKE. I agree: it's your duty.

(HORACE *enters unobserved.*)

ETHEL (*coming back*). Do you say that—as my guardian?

PIKE. I agree to it, I said.

ETHEL. Then that must mean that you consent—

PIKE. It does.—I give my consent to your marriage.

ETHEL. You do?

PIKE. I place it *all* in your hands.

HORACE. I protest against this! She's talking like a Victorian flapper! And I, for one, won't allow it.

ETHEL. Too late—he's consented! (*Exits.*)

HORACE. But, Ethel, I say—— (*Turning to* PIKE.) I tell you I won't permit her to throw herself away.

PIKE. Look here. Who's the guardian of this girl?

HORACE. A magnificent guardian *you* are! You came here to protect her from something you thought rotten—now we all *know* it's rotten, you hand her over. By Jove! I shouldn't be surprised if you consent to the settlement, too.

PIKE. I shouldn't be surprised if I did.

HORACE. Have I gone crazy? Do you know what you're *doing?*

PIKE. Oh, I'm just crossing my Rubicon. If you're going to cross the Rubicon, cross it; don't wade out to the middle and stand there. You only get hell from both banks.

LADY CREECH (*enters*). Mr. Granger-Simpson, have you seen my nephew?

HORACE. No; I've rather avoided that, if you don't mind my saying so.

LADY CREECH. Mr. Granger-Simpson!

HORACE. I'm sorry, Lady Creech, but I've had a most awful shaking-up and I'm almost thinking of going back home with Mr. Pike. I rather think he's about right in his ideas. You know we abused him, not only for himself but for his vulgar friend; yet his vulgar friend turned out to be a royal personage—and look at what our friends turned out to be! (*Exits.*)

(ALMERIC *is heard whistling "Funiculi" off stage.*)

LADY CREECH. Isn't that Almeric? (*Walking upstage.*)

ALMERIC (*entering*). Mariano, Mariano—I say, Mariano—— (MARINO *enters.*) Mariano, my breakfast tea tasted of olive oil.

MARIANO. Oil? Oh, no, gentleman!

ALMERIC. I swear it did. Oil's not pleasant in tea, you know. Just see it doesn't happen again, will you?

MARIANO. Intensely, I will, gentleman. Intensely. (*Exits.*)

ALMERIC. Can anything in the world be more upsetting than *oil* in one's *tea?*

LADY CREECH. Almeric, really, there *are* more important things, you know.

ALMERIC. I'm rather to be congratulated, you see, on not having to worry about *them,* Auntie. What?

PIKE. I think you are. I have given my consent.

ALMERIC (*laughing*). So you've come round to it, old son! I thought so.

LADY CREECH. And the settlement——?

PIKE. The settlement, too. Everything.

(*Enter* ETHEL, *followed by* HORACE.)

LADY CREECH (*starting toward* ETHEL). Ethel, my dear. I'm too overjoyed in your good fortune to remember any little bickerings between us. The sky has cleared wonderfully. Everything is settled.

ETHEL. Yes; it's all over; my guardian has consented.

ALMERIC. I fancy it will be a bit off the Governor's mind. I'll see that a wire catches him at Naples; and he'll be glad to know what came of your arrangement with that bad hat Georgeopolis.

ETHEL (*crossing to* ALMERIC). Almeric, I think it's stunning to be jaunty in trouble, but—— (HORACE *crosses back of* LADY CREECH *to* ETHEL. LADY CREECH *sits beside table.*)

ALMERIC. I say, you know, I'm afraid you've really *got* me.

ETHEL. I mean I do like your pluck in seeming unconcerned under disgrace, but——

ALMERIC. Disgrace? Dear me, how you wonderful Americans do put things! Don't you see it really was rather *funnily* raw on the poor old Governor? Old boy has a "grand passion"—devotes his *life* to the wild little woman who ran off with him—and then—after all these years—down comes the *husband* on him! For the *second* time! Bang! Like that! Haven't you *any* humor, you wonderful Yankees?

ETHEL. Almeric!

ALMERIC. You *did* get that bad hat called off, didn't you?

ETHEL. "Called off"?

ALMERIC (*with a gesture to* PIKE). He *told* me you sent the man money. Wouldn't he agree not to stir things up? I'm afraid the Governor'll be a bit *worried* if——

ETHEL (*breaking out at him*). Almeric!

ALMERIC (*surprised*). Oh, yes?

ETHEL. Are you *really* this, or is it just manner?

ALMERIC (*puzzled*). I don't——

ETHEL. Don't you see it's time *you* were worried?

ALMERIC. What's the good if I *worried?*

ETHEL. Don't you even see you've got to *do* something? That you've got to begin a career; that you've got to *work?*

ALMERIC (*smiling indulgently, though troubled*). Dear me! I really don't follow you. In the first place, there's the settlement.

ETHEL. Settlement! You talk of settlement, now.

LADY CREECH (*rising*). Settlement, certainly there's the settlement.

ETHEL (*turning to* LADY CREECH). What for?

LADY CREECH. You expect some day to be Countess of Hawcastle, don't you?

ETHEL. Do you think *that* had great weight with me—ever?

ALMERIC. Why—hasn't he told you—the only obstacle on earth between us was this fellow's consent to the settlement, and he's just given it.

ETHEL. Do you mean to say he's consented to *that?*

ALMERIC. Why, to be sure! He's just consented—with his own lips, didn't you?

PIKE. I did.

LADY CREECH. Don't you see—he's *consented?* Don't you hear?

ETHEL. I do and I don't believe my own ears. Yesterday when I wanted something I thought was of value, he refused. Today, when I know that what I wanted is worth less than *nothing,* he tells me to give my *fortune* for it. What kind of man *is* this?

LADY CREECH. But since he *does* tell you——

ETHEL (*interrupting fiercely*). And what are *you* when, after last night, you ask me for a *settlement?*

LADY CREECH. Would you expect to enter this family and *bring* nothing? (HORACE *goes upstage.*)

ETHEL (*with a half laugh, half sob in her voice*). "Nothing"? That's your word for my offering my *life* to him? (*Meaning* ALMERIC.)

ALMERIC (*speaking hurriedly*). No, indeed, my dear. But you see that's rather balanced by *my* life. It's like this, my dear. *You want* what *we've got;* we deucedly *need* what *you've got.* Well, you're upset just now by this mess the Governor got into, and you don't feel so liberal as you did. I'm sure the Governor'd wish me to say we shan't haggle.

ETHEL. You mean you'd be willing to accept a few thousand pounds less?

ALMERIC. I tell you I *hate* such awful ways of *putting* it. (*Desperately.*) Yes!

ETHEL (*crying out*). Oh! That's the end of it for me!

ALMERIC (*sharply*). Didn't you say you'd stick it?

ETHEL. To stand by you! To help you make yourself into something like a man! Now you ask me to *pay* for the privilege of making the sacrifice—I'm released! I'm free! (*Pointing furiously at* PIKE.) I'm not that man's property to give away.

ALMERIC (*deliberately*). You break your——

ETHEL (*wildly*). Yes; I break it! Into ten thousand thousand pieces! Go find some *other* poor little goose. And as for you—(*She turns furiously upon* PIKE) —never presume to speak to me again.

ALMERIC. (*To* LADY CREECH). Most extraordinary creatures, aren't they?

LADY CREECH. Stop mumbling your words! (*As they exit,* HORACE *exits also.*)

ETHEL. What have you to say to me?

PIKE. Nothing.

ETHEL. What explanation have you to make?

PIKE. None.

ETHEL. That's because you don't care what I think of you. Oh, you've already shown that when you were willing to give me up to those people, and to let me pay them for taking me. You let me romanticize to you about honor and duty—and you knew all the time it was *only* the money they were after. Didn't you understand me enough to see that your leaving me free to *give* it to them would make me free to *deny everything* to them if they *demanded* it? (*He looks at her.*) Oh, you mean you've given me another superior little lesson upon the *unreality* of my attitude toward these people—and toward life!

PIKE. No, no! I—— No!

ETHEL. You'll always say that. It's like you. You let me make a fool of myself and then you show it to me! After that you deny it! You're always showing off your superiority. Would you do that to the girl you told me of, to the girl you fancy singing for you in your empty house at home? I think you'd better go back to her.

PIKE. She won't be there.

ETHEL (*tremulously*). She might be.

PIKE No. The house will still be empty.

ETHEL. Are you sure?

PIKE. It will be emptier than ever, now.

ETHEL (*crossing to door.*) You might be wrong—for *once!* (*Exits.*)

(*After a pause, music of "Sweet Genevieve,"* ETHEL *singing.* PIKE *rises, slowly crosses stage as if spellbound. Noiselessly pushes door open —falls back a step, looking in.*)

CURTAIN

Peg O' My Heart

BY J. HARTLEY MANNERS

"Oh, there's nothing half so sweet in life
As Love's young dream."

TO
"LAURIE"

"—— in that which no waters can quench,
No time forget, nor distance wear away."

The following is a copy of the program of the first performance of *Peg o' My Heart* at the Cort Theatre, New York City.

FRIDAY, DECEMBER 20, 1912.

LAURETTE TAYLOR

IN A COMEDY OF YOUTH IN THREE ACTS

ENTITLED

PEG O' MY HEART

BY J. HARTLEY MANNERS

(Produced under the personal direction of the author)

"Oh, there's nothing half so sweet in life
As Love's young dream."

THE CAST

(*In the order of their first appearance*)

MRS. CHICHESTER	Miss Emilie Melville
FOOTMAN	Mr. Peter Bassett
ETHEL, *Mrs. Chichester's daughter*	Miss Christine Norman
ALARIC, *Mrs. Chichester's son*	Mr. Hassard Short
CHRISTIAN BRENT	Mr. Reginald Mason
PEG	Miss Laurette Taylor
MONTGOMERY HAWKES, *solicitor*	Mr. Clarence Handyside
MAID	Miss Ruth Gartland
JERRY	Mr. H. Reeves-Smith

THE SCENES OF THE COMEDY

Act I: The Coming of Peg.
Act II: The Rebellion of Peg.
Act III: Peg o' My Heart.

The entire action of the comedy passes in the living-room of Regal Villa, Mrs. Chichester's house in Scarborough, England, in early summer.

One month elapses between Acts I and II and a single night passes between Acts II and III.

NOTE: *The curtain will descend in Act II to denote the passing of a few hours.*

PEG O' MY HEART

ACT ONE

"THE COMING OF PEG"

SCENE—*The action of the entire comedy passes in a living-room in an old Tudor house in Scarborough, England. It is a solid, massive room on the ground level opening into a garden. Through the windows can be seen pathways winding away between lines of old, tall trees to the sea, and through the window R. can be seen an old garden with flowers in full bloom. Jasmine and creepers climb up the porch.*

The room is furnished for the most part with solid old furniture; an oak table on which are books, papers, magazines, methodically arranged; an armchair; against the wall a writing-desk; a grand piano on which is a mass of music, a marble statuette of Cupid, several framed photos, vases of flowers, etc. On the walls are some excellent pictures framed in oak. Lounges, comfortable armchairs, etc., are distributed about the room. The whole effect is of ease, comfort, and good taste.

A flight of twelve deep stairs runs up and off at the back to the right of the audience. In the same wall is a door.

The curtain rises on an empty stage.

MRS. CHICHESTER, *a woman of fifty, hurries in through alcove back.*

JARVIS *enters with letters on salver.*

MRS. CHICHESTER *comes down to table and* JARVIS *meets her. She takes letters and reads, then* JARVIS *goes up back, pulls open the curtains, and then goes down to door.*

MRS. CHICHESTER. Wait, Jarvis. My son! Miss Ethel! At once, I must see them at once. (MRS. CHICHESTER *finishes reading the letter, bursts into tears, sinks down shivering and crying on the armchair.*)

(ETHEL *enters. She has a copy of* The Morning Post *folded back at the General News Items. She goes across to her mother.* FOOTMAN *exits.*)

ETHEL. Mother! Have you seen this?

MRS. CHICHESTER. Oh, my dear Ethel!

(*Enter* ALARIC. ETHEL *goes to her mother.*)

ALARIC (*moves briskly and energetically, throwing his hat into window-seat at back*). Hallo, Mater! Hallo, Ethel!

MRS. CHICHESTER (*between gasps*). Alaric! My poor boy!

ALARIC. What's the matter? What's up?

MRS. CHICHESTER (*seated*). We're—(*Sob.*) We're—(*Sob.*) ruined! (*Cries bitterly.*)

ALARIC (*by his mother*). Ruined? Go on! Are we, really?

MRS. CHICHESTER (*looking at letter and staunching her tears*). Our bank has failed. Every penny your poor father left me was in it. We're beggars.

ALARIC. Oh, tush! Tush and nonsense! It can't be true.

MRS. CHICHESTER (*hands him letter*). Read.

ALARIC (*to* ETHEL). Eh!

ETHEL (*crossing to* ALARIC, *hands him* The Morning Post *with thumb on paragraph, and then sits*). Yes, look.

ALARIC (*looks at paper and reads*). "Failure of Gifford's Bank." (*Looks at letter and reads.*) "Gifford's Bank suspended business yesterday." (*Looks at newspaper.*) "Gifford's Bank has closed its doors." Eh? (*Looks blankly at* MRS. CHICHESTER *and* ETHEL.)

MRS. CHICHESTER (*seated*). Yes. We're ruined.

ETHEL. Beggars!

ALARIC. Now that's what I call a downright, rotten, black-guardly shame. Closed its doors, indeed! Why should it close its doors? That's what I want to know. Why—should—it? What right have banks to fail? Why isn't there a law against it? (*Looking from letter and paper, at which he glances alternately.*) They should be made to open their doors—and keep 'em open. That's what we give 'em our money for—so that we can take it out when we want to.

MRS. CHICHESTER. Everything gone! Ruined! And at my age!

ALARIC (*goes to table and puts down letter and paper*). A nice kettle of fish! That's all I can say. A nice kettle of fish, all a-boiling. Eh, Ethel?

ETHEL (*quite unmoved*). Pity!

(MRS. CHICHESTER *moans.*)

ALARIC (*crosses to* MRS. CHICHESTER). Don't worry, Mater. (*Buttons his coat determinedly.*) I'll go down and tell 'em just what I think of 'em. They can't play the fool with me. Don't you care, Mater. You've got a son, thank God. And one no bank can take liberties with. What we put in there we've got to have out. That's all I can say. We've simply—got—to—have—it—out. I've said it.

MRS. CHICHESTER. It's bankrupt!

ETHEL. Failed!

MRS. CHICHESTER. We're beggars. I must live on charity the rest of my life. The guest of relations I've always hated the sight of, and who've always hated me. Oh! (*Weeps.*)

ALARIC (*crosses to his mother, comforts her, and speaks to* ETHEL). Don't you think we'll get anything?

ETHEL (*shakes her head*). Nothing.

ALARIC (*unbuttoning his coat, goes limp*). I always thought bank directors were a lot of blighters. Good Lord, what a mess!

(MRS. CHICHESTER *looks up at him.*)

ALARIC. What's to become of Ethel?

MRS. CHICHESTER (*looking up at* ALARIC). Whoever shelters me must take Ethel as well.

ALARIC. Shocking tough, old girl. (*Looking across at* ETHEL.)

ETHEL (*shakes her head determinedly*). No.

ALARIC. No? What?

ETHEL. Charity.

ALARIC (*shivers*). Cold-blooded word. What will you do?

ETHEL. Work.

ALARIC. What at?

ETHEL. Teach.

ALARIC. Teach! Who in the wide world can you teach?

ETHEL. Children.

ALARIC. Oh, come! That's rich! Eh, Mater? Ethel teachin' grubby little children their A. B. C's. Tush!

ETHEL. Must.

ALARIC. A Chichester teach!

ETHEL (*with imperative gesture*). Settled! (*Rises to piano.*)

ALARIC (*determinedly buttoning up his coat again*). Very well then, I'll work too. (*Faces front.*)

MRS. CHICHESTER. Oh, Alaric!

ALARIC. I'll put my hand to the plough. (*With increased energy.*) The more I think of it the keener I am to begin. From today I'll be a workin' man.

ETHEL (*by piano, laughs mirthlessly and superciliously*). Ha!

ALARIC (*turning quickly to her*). And may I ask why that "Ha"? (*To* MRS. CHICHESTER.) There is nothing I couldn't do if I was really put to it, not a single thing.

MRS. CHICHESTER (*proudly*). I know that, dear. But it's dreadful to think of you working.

ALARIC. Not at all. I'm just tingling all over at the thought of it. Only reason I haven't so far is because I never had to. But now that I have, I'll just buckle on my armor, so to speak, and astonish you all. (*Leans on table.*)

ETHEL (*by piano, laughs again*). Ha!

ALARIC. Please don't laugh in that cheerless way, Ethel. (*Shivers.*) It goes all down my spine. Jerry's always telling me I ought to do something; that the world is for the worker, and all that. Now I'm goin' to show him. (*Suddenly.*) I say, what's today? (*Looks at date of newspaper.*) The first? June the first. Jerry's comin' today. All his family. They've taken Noel's Folly on the hill. He's sure to look in here. (JARVIS *enters with card on salver.*) Couldn't be better. I'll put it to him as man to man. He's the cove to turn to in a case like this. I'll—What is it? (*To* JARVIS, *who holds out salver to him, picks up card and reads it.*) Chris Brent!

MRS. CHICHESTER (*rising, goes to* ETHEL). Oh, I can't see anyone.

ALARIC. Nor I. I'm all strung up. (*To* JARVIS.) Tell Mr. Brent we're out. (*Puts card back on salver.*)

ETHEL. I'll see Mr. Brent here.

(*Exit* JARVIS.)

MRS. CHICHESTER. Thank you, dear. My head's throbbing. I'll go to my room. (*Goes to stairs, round back of table.*)

ALARIC (*following* MRS. CHICHESTER *to stairs*). All right, Mater. And don't worry. Leave everything to me. I'll thrash the whole thing out—absolutely thrash it out.

MRS. CHICHESTER (*on stairs, to* ETHEL). Come to me when he goes, dear.

ETHEL. Yes, Mother.

(MRS. CHICHESTER *passes up the stairs out of sight.*)

ALARIC (*crossing to window up back, picks up hat*). Awful business, Ethel.

ETHEL (*has come to front of table*). Pretty bad.

ALARIC. Really goin' to teach? (*Beside table.*)

ETHEL. Yes.

ALARIC. Right. I'll find something, too. We'll pull through somehow——

ETHEL (*indicating door*). Mr. Brent's coming.

ALARIC. Jolly good of you to let him bore you. (*Going to alcove.*) Hate the sight of the beggar myself. Always looks like the first conspirator at the play. (*The door opens.* ALARIC *hurries out through the alcove, back.*)

(JARVIS *shows in* CHRISTIAN BRENT, *a dark, eager, pleasure-loving looking young man of twenty-five.* ETHEL, *for the first time, shows some animation as he enters and shakes her hand.* JARVIS *exits.*)

BRENT. Well, how are you? (*They shake hands.*)

ETHEL. Fair. (*Draws her hand away, which he has kept.*)

BRENT. Your mother?

ETHEL. Lying down.

BRENT. Alaric?

ETHEL. Out there.

BRENT (*glances quickly at the garden*). Then we've a moment or two alone?

ETHEL. I suppose so.

BRENT. Oh, Ethel. (*He goes to embrace her, she draws back and crosses to couch and sits. He follows her.*) Glad to see me?

ETHEL. Why not?

BRENT (*he sits beside her*). I am to see you—more than glad.

ETHEL. Why?

BRENT. I'm at the cross-roads.

ETHEL. Really?

BRENT. It came last night.

ETHEL. Oh!

BRENT. This is the end between me and my wife.

ETHEL. Is it?

BRENT. Yes. The end. It's been wretched. We've not one thought in common. There's not a word of mine —not an action—that she doesn't misunderstand.

ETHEL. How boring!

BRENT. She'd see harm even in this.

ETHEL. Why?

BRENT. She'd think I was here to—to——

ETHEL. What?

BRENT. Make love to you.

ETHEL. Well. Aren't you?

BRENT. Ethel!

ETHEL. Don't you—always?

BRENT. How can you say that?

ETHEL. Don't you?

BRENT (*on couch*). Has it *seemed* like that to *you?*

ETHEL. Yes—by insinuation. Never straightforwardly.

BRENT. Has it offended you?

ETHEL. Ah! Then you admit it?

BRENT (*moves a little nearer*). Oh, I wish I had the right to——(*Stops.*)

ETHEL. Yes?

BRENT. Make love to you straightforwardly.

ETHEL. Then you wouldn't do it.

BRENT. Ethel!

ETHEL. It's only because you *haven't* the right that you do it—by suggestion.

BRENT (*starts back in disgust*). Why do you think that?

ETHEL. You don't deny it.

BRENT. What a contemptible opinion you must have of me. (*Rises.*)

ETHEL. Then we're quits, aren't we?

BRENT. How? (*Turns to her.*)

ETHEL. You have a contemptible opinion of me.

BRENT. Why? (*Comes down a little.*)

ETHEL. You must have. Every married man has a contemptible opinion of the woman he covertly makes love to. If he hadn't he couldn't do it.

BRENT. I don't follow you.

ETHEL. Haven't you had time to think of an answer?

BRENT. I don't know what you're driving at.

ETHEL (*smiles*). No? I think you do. (BRENT *makes movement away. Pause.*) What happened last night?

BRENT. Why, she—(*Moves toward her, then stops.*) No. I'd sound like a cad, blaming a woman.

ETHEL. Never mind how it sounds, tell it.

BRENT (*comes to couch, knee on it, over her*). The more I look at you and listen to you the more I realize I should never have married.

ETHEL. Oh! Why did you?

BRENT (*sits beside her, back to the audience*). Why? Have you ever seen a young hare, fresh from its kind, run headlong into a snare? Have you ever seen a young man straight from college dash into a net? I did. I wasn't trap-wise. Good God, what nurslings we are when we first feel our feet! We're like children just loose from the leading-strings. Anything that glitters catches us. Every trap that is set for our unwary feet we drop into. *I* did. Dropped in. Caught hand and foot, mind and *soul.*

ETHEL. Soul?

BRENT. Yes.

ETHEL. Don't you mean body?

BRENT. Well, body, mind, *and* soul.

ETHEL. Ah! Body anyway.

BRENT. And for what? Love? Companionship! That's what we build on in marriage. And what did I realize? Hate and wrangling. Then came the baby.

ETHEL. Ah! (*She turns away.*)

BRENT. One would think that would change things. But, no. Neither of us wanted her—neither of us loved her. (*Look from* ETHEL.) And then—(*Pause.*) I shouldn't tell you this. It's horrible. I see it in your face. (*Pause.*) What are you thinking?

ETHEL. I'm sorry.

BRENT. For me?

ETHEL. For your wife.

BRENT. My wife?

ETHEL. Yes. Aren't you? (*He turns away. Pause.*) No? (*Pause.*) Just sorry for yourself?

BRENT. You think me purely selfish?

ETHEL. Naturally. *I* am. (*Pause.* BRENT *turns away with a sulky movement.*) Don't sulk. Let's be truthful—sometimes.

BRENT (*suddenly, facing her*). We quarreled last night—about you.

ETHEL. Really?

BRENT. Gossip has linked us together. She heard it. Put the worst construction on it.

ETHEL. Well? What did you do?

BRENT (*rises and walks round table*). I left the house and walked the streets—hours. I looked my whole life back as if it were some stranger's. I tell you, we ought to be taught. We ought to be taught what marriage means. Just as we are taught not to steal or lie or sin. In marriage, when we are *ill-mated,* we do *all three.* We steal affection from someone else, we lie in our lives, we sin in our relationship.

ETHEL (*rises and crosses to table*). Do you mean that you're a sinner, a thief, and a liar?

BRENT. Ethel!

ETHEL (*sits by table*). Oh, take some of the blame. Don't put it all on the woman. (*He turns away.*) What do you intend to do?

BRENT (*front of table*). Separate. The only thing. You don't doctor a poisoned limb when your life is at stake. You cut it off. When *two lives* generate poison, face it as a surgeon would. Amputate.

ETHEL. And after the operation? What then?

BRENT (*leaning over front of table*). That is why I'm here—facing you.

ETHEL. But if *we* generate poison—what will you do? Amputate me?

BRENT. You are different from all other women.

ETHEL. Didn't you tell your wife that when you asked her to marry you?

BRENT (*turns away*). Don't say those things. They hurt. (*Going around table*).

ETHEL. I'm afraid, Chris, I'm too frank. Aren't I?

BRENT (*leaning over, at back of table*). You stand alone. You seem to look into the hearts of people and know why and how they beat.

ETHEL (*meaningly*). Do I? It's an awkward faculty sometimes, isn't it?

BRENT. How marvelously different two women can *be*—you and my wife. (*Again back of table.*)

ETHEL. We're not really very different. Only some natures like change. Yours does. And the new has all the virtues. I mightn't last as long as your wife did.

BRENT (*standing close to her, over her*). Don't say that. We have a common bond—understanding.

ETHEL. Think so?

BRENT. I understand you.

ETHEL. I wonder.

BRENT. You do me.

ETHEL. That's just it.

BRENT. I tell you I'm at the crossroads. The finger-post points the way to me distinctly. (*Pause. Sits on chair back of table, close to her.*) Would *you* risk it?

ETHEL (*turning on him*). What?

BRENT. I'll hide nothing. I'll put it all before you. The snubs of your friends, life in some little Continental village, dreading the passers-through, and then—— No. It wouldn't be fair to you.

ETHEL (*slowly*). No. I don't think it would. However, I'll think it over and let you know.

BRENT (*to* ETHEL, *eagerly*). When she sets me free we could—we could——(*Stops.*)

ETHEL. It is a difficult little word at times, isn't it?

BRENT. *Would* you *marry* me?

ETHEL. I never cross my bridges till I reach them, and we're such a long way from that one, aren't we?

BRENT (*rises*). Ethel! (*She rises. He puts his hand on hers, and she moves away down in front of bench.*) Then I'm to wait? (*Comes down level with her.*)

ETHEL. Yes, do. When the time comes to accept the charity of relations or do something useful for tuppence a week, who knows? When a woman has to choose between charity and labor—who knows?

BRENT. Charity? Labor?

ETHEL (*moves to bench and sits*). A tiresome bank has failed with all our sixpences locked up in it. Isn't it stupid?

BRENT (*follows her to couch*). Is all your money gone?

ETHEL. Everything.

BRENT. Good God!

ETHEL. Mamma knows as little about business as she does about me. Until this morning she has always had a rooted belief in her bank and her daughter. If I bolt with you her last cherished illusion will be destroyed.

BRENT. Let me help you.

ETHEL. How? Lend us money?

BRENT. I'll do that if——(ETHEL *looks at him.*) I beg your pardon.

ETHEL (*looking down*). So you see we're both, in a way, at the crossroads.

BRENT (*seizing her hand*). Let me take you away out of it all.

ETHEL (*slowly*). No. Not just now. (BRENT *turns away to table.*) I'm not in a bolting mood today. (*She turns to him saying:*) Chris, some time, perhaps in the dead of night, something will snap in me—the slack, selfish, luxurious me that hates to be roused into action—and the longing for adventure will come. Then I'll send for you. (*Rises.*)

BRENT. And you'll go with me?

ETHEL (*stretching lazily*). I suppose so. (*He goes to embrace her, but she keeps him off. Looking at him through half-closed eyes.*) Then Heaven help you.

BRENT. I want you—I need you.

ETHEL. Until the time comes for amputation? (*He turns away.*) You see I don't want you to have illusions about me. I've none about you. Let us begin fair, anyway. It will be much easier when the end comes. (*Moves away.*)

BRENT (*going quickly to her*). But there'll be no end. I love you—love you with every breath in my body, every thought in my mind, every throb of (*Embraces her.*) my nerves. (*Down the path comes a strange little figure—a beautiful girl of eighteen, shabbily but cleanly dressed in a simple print dress, a wide-brimmed cheap straw hat from under which hangs a profusion of short, natural curls of gleaming reddish hair. She is carrying a bag and a paper parcel somewhat the worse for wear under one arm, and under the other arm is a shaggy, unkempt, and altogether disgraceful looking Irish terrier. She walks quietly into the room, sees* BRENT *and* ETHEL *in the embrace, turns away and sits in chair by table with her back to them.*)

ETHEL. Please don't. It's so hot this morning. (*Sees* PEG *over* BRENT'S *shoulder, straightens up with a quick movement, and swings* BRENT *round. They look in horrified amazement at the strange little figure.* ETHEL *goes to her.*) How long have you been here? (*Crosses to table*).

PEG (*by table, with a delightfully slight Irish brogue, looking up innocently in* ETHEL'S *eyes*). I just came in.

ETHEL. What do you want?

PEG. I don't want anything. I was told I must wait at this place.

ETHEL. Who told you?

PEG. A gentleman.

ETHEL. What gentleman?

PEG. Just a gentleman. He told me to wait—at the place that is written down on the card. (*Hands her a soiled visiting card.* BRENT *is staring at* PEG.)

ETHEL (*in front of table, taking card, reads*). "Mrs. Chichester, Regal Villa." What do you want with Mrs. Chichester?

PEG. I don't want anything. I was told I must wait here. (*Taking card back.*)

ETHEL. Who are you?

PEG. I wasn't to say anything. I was only to wait.

(ETHEL *turns to* BRENT. BRENT *is looking admiringly at the little stranger.*)

ETHEL (*pauses and looks at* BRENT *then turns again to* PEG). You say you've only been here a minute?

PEG. Just a minute.

ETHEL. Were we talking when you came in?

PEG. Ye were.

ETHEL. Did you hear what we said?

PEG. Yes, I did. (*Look between* ETHEL *and* BRENT.)

ETHEL. What did you *hear*?

PEG. I heard you say "Please don't. It's so hot this morning."

ETHEL (*pauses*). You refuse to say why you're here or who you are?

PEG. I don't refuse at all. The gentleman said to me, he said, "You go to the place that's written down on the card, and you sit down at the house, and you wait, and that's all you do—just wait."

ETHEL (*turning to* BRENT). Eh?

BRENT. Extraordinary.

ETHEL (*coming back to table*). The servants' quarters are at the back of the house.

PEG. Yes.

ETHEL (*front of table*). And I may save you the trouble of waiting by telling you that we don't need any assistants. We're quite provided for.

PEG. Yes.

ETHEL (*pause*). If you insist on waiting, kindly do so there. (*Turns again to* BRENT.)

PEG. Well, we're not particular where we wait as long as we wait. They're sending us to the kitchen, Michael. (*Rising up to opening.*) At the back of the house, Miss?

ETHEL. Follow that path round until you come to a door. Knock, and ask permission to wait there. (PEG *gathers her bundles and her dog under her arms and goes to arch, to top of step.*) For your future guidance, go to the back door of a house and knock. Don't walk, unannounced, into a private room.

PEG (*in arch*). Ye see, ma'am, I couldn't tell it was a private room. The blinds were all up and the door was open. I couldn't tell it was a private room.

ETHEL. That will do. That will do.

PEG. And I couldn't knock on your door because it's a windy. (PEG *exits arch.*)

ETHEL (*after watching her off, very angry*). Outrageous!

BRENT (*crossing up to window*). Poor little wretch. She's rather pretty.

ETHEL (*looking intelligently at him*). Is she?

BRENT. Didn't you think so?

ETHEL (*comes up to table*). I never notice the lower orders. You apparently do.

BRENT (*comes down level with her*). She's the strangest little apparition——

ETHEL. She's only a few yards away if you care to—— (*Turns to* BRENT.)

BRENT. Ethel! (*Comes down nearer to her.*)

ETHEL. Suppose my mother had come in! Or Alaric! Never do such a thing again.

BRENT. I was carried away. I——

ETHEL. Kindly exercise a little more restraint. You'd better go now. (*Crosses to stairs.*)

BRENT (*following her to stairs round back of table*). May I come tomorrow?

ETHEL. No. Not tomorrow.

BRENT. Then the following day?

ETHEL. Perhaps.

BRENT. Ethel, remember I build on you.

ETHEL (*looking at him*). I suppose we are worthy of each other.

(*Voices off stage.*)

ALARIC (*off*). Come this way, Mr. Hawkes. I think we shall find some of the family in here.

ETHEL. (*To* BRENT.) Go now. (*Goes upstairs.*)

(*As* BRENT *goes to door,* ALARIC *hurries in through window, sees* ETHEL, *puts hat on piano.*)

ALARIC. Wait a minute, Ethel. (*Seeing* BRENT.) Hello, Brent! How are you? Disturbin' you?

BRENT. No. I'm just going.

ALARIC. Oh, don't go. I want to ask you something. (*He goes up to arch and calls to someone in the garden.*) Come in, Mr. Hawkes. (*Enter* MONTGOMERY HAWKES, *a suave, polished, important-looking man of forty.* ALARIC *comes back, introducing.*) Mr. Hawkes—my sister—Mr. Brent. (HAWKES *bows to* ETHEL *and to* BRENT *and puts hat on table.* ALARIC *to* ETHEL:) You might see if the Mater's well enough to come down, like a dear, will ye? This gentleman's come all the way from London just to see her. D'ye mind? Bring her down here, will you? (ETHEL *goes upstairs and out of sight. To* HAWKES.) Sit down, Mr. Hawkes. (HAWKES *sits in armchair.* ALARIC *goes toward* BRENT.) Must ye go? (ALARIC, *shaking him warmly by the hand and taking him to door.*) Sorry I was out. Run in any time. Always delighted to see you. Oh, I know what it was I wanted to ask you—Angel wife all right?

BRENT. Thank you.

ALARIC. And the darling child?

BRENT. Please give my remembrances to your mother.

ALARIC. Certainly. Look in any time. Any time at all. (*Exit* BRENT, ALARIC *closes door.* MRS. CHICHESTER *and* ETHEL, *carrying dog, a little French poodle, come down the stairs.* HAWKES *rises.* MRS. CHICHESTER *moves away,* ETHEL *to bench, sits.* ALARIC *goes up and brings* MRS. CHICHESTER *down.*) Here we are, Mater. I found this gentleman in a rose-bed inquiring for our lodge. He's come all the way from dear old London just to see *you.* (*Brings* MRS. CHICHESTER *down, bringing them together and introducing them.*) Mr. Hawkes—my mother.

MRS. CHICHESTER (*anxiously*). You've come to see me?

HAWKES. On a very important and very private family matter.

MRS. CHICHESTER. Important? Private?

ALARIC. We're the family, Mr. Hawkes.

MRS. CHICHESTER (*her eyes filling*). Is it bad news?

HAWKES (*genially*). Oh, no.

ALARIC. Is it good news?

HAWKES (*by table*). In a measure.

ALARIC (*helps* MRS. CHICHESTER *to couch*). Ah, then let's get at it. We can do with a bit of good news, can't we, Mater? Wait. Is it by any chance about the bank? (*Crosses to table.*)

HAWKES (*to* MRS. CHICHESTER). It's about your late brother, Nathaniel.

MRS. CHICHESTER. Late? Is Nathaniel dead?

(ALARIC *near table.*)

HAWKES (*pauses by table. Nods commiseratingly.*) Ten days ago. I am one of the executors of the late gentleman's estate. (*Sits by table and gets out his papers.*)

MRS. CHICHESTER (*weeps.*) Oh!

ALARIC. Poor old Nat! Eh, Ethel?

ETHEL (*at end of couch*). Never saw him.

MRS. CHICHESTER. I ought to have been informed. The funeral——

HAWKES (*seated by table*). There was *no* funeral.

ALARIC. No funeral?

HAWKES. In obedience to his written wishes he was cremated, and no one was present except his chief executor and myself. He said *he* so little regretted not having seen any of his relations for the last twenty years that he was sure *they* would equally little regret his death. On no account was anyone to wear mourning for him, nor to express any open sorrow. They wouldn't feel it, so why lie about it?

MRS. CHICHESTER. What?

ALARIC. Eh?

HAWKES. I use his own words.

ALARIC (*by table*). What a rum old bird! Eh, Mater?

MRS. CHICHESTER (*at right end of couch*). He was always the most unfeeling, the most heartless——

HAWKES. Now, in his will——

MRS. CHICHESTER (*checking herself*). Eh?

ALARIC. A will! Did the dear old gentleman leave a will?

(ETHEL *watches them smilingly and listens intently.*)

HAWKES. I have come here to make you acquainted with some of its contents.

ALARIC (*rubbing his hands gleefully*). Dear old Nat. I remember him when I was a baby. A portly, sandy-haired old buck, with three jolly chins.

HAWKES (*gravely*). He was white toward the end, and very thin.

ALARIC. Was he? It just shows, doesn't it? How much did he leave? (*Goes back of table.*)

HAWKES. His estate is valued approximately at two hundred thousand pounds.

ALARIC (*whistles*). Phew! (*Sits back of table.*)

MRS. CHICHESTER (*cries silently*). Perhaps it was my fault I didn't see him oftener——

ALARIC. How did he split it up?

HAWKES. To his immediate relations he left—

ALARIC. Yes?

(MRS. CHICHESTER *looks up through her tears, and* ETHEL *shows a little interest.*)

HAWKES. I regret to say—nothing.

ALARIC. What?

MRS. CHICHESTER. Nothing?

(ETHEL *turns away.*)

ALARIC. Not a penny piece to anyone?

HAWKES. No.

MRS. CHICHESTER. His own flesh and blood!

ALARIC (*back of table*). What a shabby old beggar!

MRS. CHICHESTER. He was always the most selfish, the most heartless——

HAWKES (*turning back the pages of the will and reading*). Here it is from the will. "I am not going to leave one penny of what I have spent my life accumulating to people who are already well provided for."

MRS. CHICHESTER. But we're not well provided for.

ALARIC (*rises*). No. Our bank's bust.

MRS. CHICHESTER. We're ruined.

ALARIC. Broke.

MRS. CHICHESTER. We've nothing. (ALARIC *hands letter from table to* MRS. CHICHESTER, *who hands it to* HAWKES.)

ALARIC. Not threppence.

HAWKES. Dear! Dear! How extremely distressing!

ALARIC. Distressin'! Disgustin'!

HAWKES (*hands letter back to* ALARIC, *who gives it to his mother*). Then perhaps a clause in his will may have a certain interest.

ALARIC (*helps* MRS. CHICHESTER *to chair by table, then sits again. All express interest*). Clause! Did the dear old gentleman leave a clause?

HAWKES. When Mr. Kingsnorth realized that he hadn't very much longer to live he spoke constantly of his other sister, Angela.

MRS. CHICHESTER (*seated at table*). But she's dead.

HAWKES (*looking up*). That was why he spoke of her.

MRS. CHICHESTER. Never a word of me?

HAWKES. We'll come to that later. (*Refers to papers.*) It appears that this sister, Angela, married at the age of eighteen a certain improvident Irishman by the name of O'Connell, was cut off by her family——

MRS. CHICHESTER. The man was a beggar! It was a disgrace!

ALARIC (*checking her*). Mater!

HAWKES (*continuing to read*)—went to the United States of America with her husband, where a daughter was born. After going through many conditions of misery with her husband, who never seemed to prosper, she died while her child was still a baby. Mr. Kingsnorth elsewhere expresses his lasting regret that in one of his sister's acute stages of distress she wrote to him, asking him for the first time to assist her. He replied (*Looking up.*) "You've made your bed—lie in it."

MRS. CHICHESTER. She had disgraced the family. He was quite right.

ALARIC (*checks her*). Mater! Mater! He hasn't got the old gentleman's clause out yet. Go on, Mr. Hawkes.

HAWKES. With death approaching, Mr. Kingsnorth's conscience began to trouble him, and the remembrance of his treatment of his unfortunate sister distressed him. If the child were still alive he wanted to see her. So I made inquiries and found that the girl was living with her father in very poor circumstances in the city of New York.

ALARIC. New York, eh? Fancy that, Ethel! New York!

HAWKES. We sent sufficient funds for the journey and a request to the father to allow her to visit Mr. Kingsnorth in England. The father consented. However, before she sailed, Mr. Kingsnorth died.

ALARIC (*seated back of table*). Died! Too bad! That really was too bad, Ethel. Eh? Died! (*To* ETHEL *and* MRS. CHICHESTER.)

HAWKES. Realizing that he would never see her he made the most extraordinary provision for her in his will.

MRS. CHICHESTER. He provided for her, and not—for—me?

(ALARIC *checks her and kisses her hand.*)

HAWKES. Here is the provision. (*Reads.*) "I hereby direct that to any respectable, well-connected woman of breeding and family who will undertake the education and up-bringing of my niece, Margaret O'Connell, in accordance with the dignity and tradition of the Kingsnorths there be paid the sum of one thousand pounds a year——"

ALARIC. A thousand pounds a year! Fancy that, Ethel! A thousand pounds!

HAWKES (*reading*). "If at the expiration of one year my niece is found to be, in the judgment of my executors, unworthy of further interest she is to be returned to her father and the sum of two hundred and fifty pounds a year paid her to provide her with the necessities of life. But if, on the other hand, she proves herself worthy of the best traditions of the Kingsnorth family the course of training is to be continued until she reaches the age of twenty-one, when I hereby bequeath to her the sum of five thousand pounds a year——"

ALARIC. Five thousand pounds a year! I mean to say—five thousand pounds.

HAWKES. "—to be paid her annually out of my estate during her lifetime, and to be continued after her death to any male issue she may have——"

MRS. CHICHESTER (*looks up*). Eh?

HAWKES. —by marriage.

MRS. CHICHESTER. And me—his own sister——

ALARIC. And I—who knew him as a baby——

HAWKES. "On no account is her father to be permitted to visit her, and she must not on any account visit her father. After the age of twenty-one she can do as she pleases." (*Looking up.*)

ALARIC. That clause doesn't interest *us* at all, Mr. Hawkes.

HAWKES. Now my dear Mrs. Chichester, it was Mr. Kingsnorth's wish that the first person to be approached on the matter of undertaking the training of the young lady should be you.

MRS. CHICHESTER (*rising*). I?

ALARIC (*rising*). My mother?

(ETHEL *rises also, and listens and watches intently.*)

HAWKES (*referring to will*). He said he would be "sure at least of a strict upbringing in the best traditions of the Kingsnorths, and though narrow and conventional in ideas"——

MRS. CHICHESTER. Well! Really!

HAWKES. Again I use his own words. —"still, his sister Monica was eminently fitted to undertake such a charge." There you have the whole object of my visit. (*Rises.*) Now will you undertake the training of the young lady?

MRS. CHICHESTER (*crosses to couch*). I never heard of such a thing.

ETHEL. Ridiculous!

ALARIC. Tush! Tush and nonsense!

HAWKES. Then I take it you refuse?

MRS. CHICHESTER. Absolutely.

ETHEL. Entirely.

ALARIC. I should say so.

HAWKES. Then there's nothing more to be said. Mr. Kingsnorth was of the opinion that you were well provided for, and that the additional thousand a year might be welcome as, say, pin-money for your daughter. (*Gathering up papers at table.* ETHEL *and* MRS. CHICHESTER *look at each other. They draw a little away to front of bench.*)

ETHEL (*with a note of biting sarcasm*). Pin-money! Ha!

ALARIC (*coming down level with* MRS. CHICHESTER). Mater! Ethel! A cool thousand, eh?

MRS. CHICHESTER (*pause*). It would keep things together.

ALARIC. The wolf from the door.

ETHEL. No charity.

MRS. CHICHESTER (*to* ALARIC). What do you think?

ALARIC. Whatever you say, Mater.

MRS. CHICHESTER (*to* ETHEL). Ethel?

ETHEL. You decide, Mamma.

MRS. CHICHESTER (*to* ALARIC). We might try it for a while, at least.

ALARIC. Until we can look round.

MRS. CHICHESTER. Something may be saved from the wreck.

ALARIC. Until *I* get really started.

MRS. CHICHESTER. (*to* ETHEL.) Ethel?

ETHEL. Whatever you decide, Mamma.

MRS. CHICHESTER. I'll do it. (ALARIC *turns upstage a little.*) It will be hard, but I'll do it. (*All turn round to* HAWKES. ETHEL *sits on couch.*)

HAWKES (*smiling*). Well?

MRS. CHICHESTER. For the sake of my poor dead sister I'll do as Nathaniel wished.

HAWKES. Good! I'm delighted. (MRS. CHICHESTER *turns to* ALARIC.) One thing more. (MRS. CHICHESTER *turns to* HAWKES *again.*) The young lady is not to be told of the conditions of the will unless at the discretion of the executors, should some crisis arise. She will be, to all intents and purposes, your guest.

ALARIC. Our guest? Fancy that, Ethel!

HAWKES. In that way we'll arrive at a more exact idea of her character. Is that understood?

MRS. CHICHESTER. Very well.

HAWKES. Where is your bell?

ALARIC. There. (*Points to bell and moves to foot of stairs.*)

HAWKES. May I ring?

ALARIC. Certainly. Want a sandwich or something?

HAWKES. I would like to send for the young lady. (*Smiling, he rings.*) The heiress.

MRS. CHICHESTER (*crossing to armchair.*) Where is she?

HAWKES. She arrived from New York this morning and I brought her straight here. I had to call on a client, so I gave her your address and told her to come here and wait. (ETHEL *rises.*) She ought to be here by now. (*Comes down above table.* JARVIS *enters.*) Is there a young lady waiting for Mr. Hawkes?

JARVIS. Young lady, sir? No, sir.

MRS. CHICHESTER. That will do.

(JARVIS *moves toward door.*)

HAWKES. That's strange.

ALARIC. There you are, you see.

JARVIS. Oh, there is a young person sitting in the kitchen. Won't give no account of herself. Says she's to wait until a gentleman calls. Can't get nothing out of her.

HAWKES. That must *be* the young lady. May I bring her in?

MRS. CHICHESTER (*indignantly*). My niece in the kitchen! Surely you should know the difference between my niece and a servant!

JARVIS. I'm truly sorry, Madam, but there was nothing to tell——

MRS. CHICHESTER (*front of armchair*). That will do. Bring my niece here at once. (*Exit* JARVIS.) It's monstrous! (*Comes to front of table.*)

ALARIC. Stoopid! That's what I call it —Stoopid!

(ETHEL *smiles.*)

HAWKES (*coming round table*). Perhaps it was my fault. I told her not to talk—to come here and say she was to wait.

MRS. CHICHESTER. She should have been brought straight to me. The poor thing! My niece in the kitchen! (*Goes back to armchair.*) A Kingsnorth mistaken for a servant!

(*The door opens and the astonished* JARVIS *enters and beckons someone in. Then he looks helplessly at* MRS. CHICHESTER *to indicate that anyone might have made the same mistake. Enter the stranger, quite composedly, still holding her parcels and the dog.* MRS. CHICHESTER, ALARIC, *and* ETHEL *look at her*—MRS. CHICHESTER *and* ALARIC *in horrified amazement,* ETHEL *with knit brows.* JARVIS *looks at them all, as much as to say "What did I tell you? No one could guess."* JARVIS *exits.*)

PEG (*alluding to* ETHEL'S *dog*). Where's the rest of that? (*Or.*) It's a dog, isn't it?

MRS. CHICHESTER. (*Sinks in chair*). Oh! *Oh!* (*Pause.*)

ALARIC (*by high chair. Stares at the stranger in astonishment and turns to* MRS. CHICHESTER. *Aside.*) Oh, I say! Really, you know! It isn't true. It can't be.

HAWKES (*crossing to meet* PEG.) Come here. We're all your friends. (*The stranger comes over slowly, looking from one to the other. She bobs a little curtsey to* MRS. CHICHESTER.)

MRS. CHICHESTER (*pause. Controls herself with an effort. Half-hysterically*). What is your name?

PEG. Peg.

MRS. CHICHESTER. What?

PEG (*bobbing a little curtsey*). Peg. Peg O'Connell, my name is, ma'am.

MRS. CHICHESTER. Good heavens! (*To* ALARIC.) Ring, Alaric.

ALARIC (*whispering to his mother*). It can't be, really. (*Goes up to bell at back and rings.* PEG *follows him round, then laughs to* MR. HAWKES.)

HAWKES (*pause. To* PEG). This lady is Mrs. Chichester.

PEG. Chich—Chich—ster.

(ALARIC *upstage by window.*)

HAWKES (*distinctly*). Chi-chest-er. Your aunt.

PEG. Where's my uncle?

HAWKES. Alas, my dear child, your uncle is dead.

PEG. Dead? After sending for me?

HAWKES. He died just before you sailed.

PEG. God rest his soul. I'm too late then. Good day to yez. (*Bobs and starts for door.*)

HAWKES (*intercepting her*). Where are you going?

PEG. Back to my father.

HAWKES. Oh, dear, no.

PEG. I must go back to my father if my uncle's dead. I must go back to my father. If my uncle's dead I must go back to my father.

HAWKES. It was your uncle's last wish that you should stay here under your aunt's care. She has kindly consented to give you a home.

PEG (*to* MRS. CHICHESTER). Have ye?

MRS. CHICHESTER (*faintly and angrily*). I have.

(ALARIC *moves, sits by* ETHEL.)

PEG. Thank ye, ma'am, but I think I'd be just as happy with my father.

HAWKES. Nonsense. You'll be very happy here.

(JARVIS *enters.*)

PEG (*looking from one to the other*). They don't seem crazy about us, do they?

MRS. CHICHESTER. Jarvis, take away those parcels and that dog.

PEG (*clutching the dog*). Oh, no, ma'am. Not Michael. Ye can't take Michael away from me. He was given to me by my father.

MRS. CHICHESTER. Take it away. And never let it inside the house again.

PEG (*with anger and pathos*). Well, if ye don't want Michael inside the house ye don't want me inside your house.

HAWKES (*interposing*). Come, come——

PEG. No. I'm not going to let go my dog. I had a hard time getting him ashore. You don't understand about Michael. He's a house-dog, not a watch-dog. A pet dog, Michael is.

HAWKES. Come, now. Don't let us have an argument.

PEG. I'm not having an argument. I'm making a statement. I don't know these people ten minutes, and they want to take my dog away from me. (*Pointing to* ETHEL.) She has a dog right in the house. (HAWKES *looks at* ETHEL'S *dog.* PEG, *under her breath.*) And well ye may look. I thought it was her knitting until it moved.

HAWKES. You must try to do whatever your aunt asks you. Come, now —you can see him whenever you want to.

PEG. Is he going to be in the house?

HAWKES. Yes.

PEG. If I ring the bell he'll bring him in? (*Pointing to* JARVIS.)

HAWKES. To be sure he will.

PEG. Well, I don't suppose my father would like me to start a fight first thing. (*Gives dog to* HAWKES.) But I don't understand why I can't have my dog. (HAWKES *gives dog to* JARVIS, *then takes the bag from her and hands it to* JARVIS, *who receives them in disgusted amazement. The parcel breaks open, and a prayer-book, a small Bible, a rosary, and a little dull-framed photograph fall out.* PEG *kneels, piles up the articles and hands them to* HAWKES, *who puts them on top of bag* JARVIS *is holding.* PEG *retains photo and rosary, caresses* MICHAEL, *and says appealingly to* JARVIS. *Crossing to* JARVIS.) Ye'll be very nice to him, won't ye? And if ye'll give him some water and a bone I'd be much obliged. He loves mutton-bones. Ye'll find he's crazy about mutton-bones. (*The astonished* JARVIS *goes out holding the dog and the parcels as far from him as possible.*) That was a grand turn he made, wasn't it? (*To* ALARIC, *sitting on couch.*) I hope he gives him a mutton-bone. Michael's crazy about mutton, so he is.

MRS. CHICHESTER (*sternly*). Come here. (PEG *backs to her, facing* ALARIC.) Look at me.

(PEG *turns to her.*)

PEG. Yes, ma'am.

MRS. CHICHESTER. Don't call me ma'am.

PEG. No, ma'am. (*Checks herself.*) Ant, I mean. No, ant, I mean.

MRS. CHICHESTER. Aunt—not "ant."

ALARIC (*to* ETHEL). "Ant"—like some little crawling insect.

PEG (*hears it, looks at* ALARIC *and* ETHEL, *then all round the room as if she missed someone, then turns back to* MRS. CHICHESTER). Are you my uncle Nat's widow?

MRS. CHICHESTER (*indignantly*). I am not.

PEG. Then how are you my ant—aurnt?

MRS. CHICHESTER. I am your mother's sister.

PEG. Then yer name's Monica?

MRS. CHICHESTER. It is.

PEG. What do you think of that, now? (*Looks covertly at the photo.*) You don't look a bit like my poor mother did.

MRS. CHICHESTER. What's that?

PEG (*softly*). It's my poor mother's picture, that is.

MRS. CHICHESTER. Let me see it. (PEG *hands it to her.*) She had changed very much since I saw her.

PEG. Sorrow and poverty did that, Aunt Monica.

MRS. CHICHESTER. *Aunt* will be sufficient. Put it away. (PEG *covers it with her hands.*) Do sit down.

PEG. All right. Where'll I sit? (*She looks at* ALARIC, *who does not move.* HAWKES *hands her to chair by table.* PEG *sits.*) Thank ye. (MRS. CHICHESTER *sighs.*) Don't ye feel well? I don't. I don't like the steamer. The steamer always upsets me, the steamer does. (*She looks round and laughs at* ALARIC, *who is smoking a cigarette in a long holder.*) Does that make you think it's a pipe? Sure, I'd no idea in the world I had such fine relations. Though my father always told me I had some very nice folks on my mother's side.

(HAWKES *back of table.*)

ALARIC (*on couch*). Folks! Really, Ethel! (*Holds his knee in his hands, lifting his leg*).

MRS. CHICHESTER (*severely, to* PEG). Don't sprawl like that. Sit up. (PEG *does so.*) Put your feet together. (PEG *puts one leg over the other.*) No, no. Look at your cousin.

PEG (*uncrosses her legs*). Yes, look at him. He had his feet in the air, he had.

MRS. CHICHESTER. I mean your cousin, Ethel.

PEG (*sits up demurely, then looks at* ETHEL *and turns back to* MRS. CHICHESTER). Her? Oh! Ethel's my cousin?

MRS. CHICHESTER. She is.

ALARIC (*rises and goes up level with her*). Yes. And I am, too. Cousin Alaric.

PEG (*looks at him a second and laughs, then looks very curiously at* ETHEL, *looks all round again, turns to* MRS. CHICHESTER). Where's her husband gone to? (*Looking round again.*)

(ETHEL *rises.*)

MRS. CHICHESTER. Husband?

PEG. Yes. I saw her husband. I've been in this room before, you know. I came in that door. She was with her husband.

ALARIC. What in Heaven's name does she mean?

PEG. She sent me to the kitchen. She and him.

ALARIC. Him? Who in the world——?

ETHEL. Mr. Brent. (*Sits.*)

ALARIC. Brent. Oh! Ha! Ha! Ha! Ha!

PEG. Ha! Ha! Ha! (ALARIC *stops laughing suddenly, turns away, and stands by desk. Pause. To* MRS. CHICHESTER.) She thought I was a servant lookin' for a place, and I've got my very best hat on, too. Mr. Hawkes told me not to say a word. He said, "you go up to the lady's house and you wait, and when I get there I'll do all the talking. That's my business. That's what I get paid for."

HAWKES (*comes down level with* PEG). Ssh! Ssh! Ssh! My time's short. You must do everything your aunt tells you. Try to please her in all things. On the first day of every month I'll call and find out what progress you're making. (*Crosses front of* PEG—*to* MRS. CHICHESTER, *handing card.*) This is my business address. (*Crossing to table*). Now I must take my leave. (*Takes up his hat.*)

PEG (*springing up breathlessly and frightenedly*). I'm going with ye, too.

HAWKES. Come, come.

PEG (*earnestly—her eyes filling*). My father mightn't like me to stay here, now that my uncle's dead.

HAWKES. It was your uncle's last wish that you should come here. Why, your father will be delighted at your good fortune. Good-by, Miss O'Connell.

PEG (*shaking hands with* MR. HAWKES). Good-by, Mr. Hawkes. And thank ye for bein' so kind to me.

(ALARIC *opens door for* HAWKES.)

HAWKES (*bows to her*). Miss Chichester. By Jove, I'll just catch the express. (*Looking at his watch.*)

ALARIC. Have a cab?

HAWKES (*crossing to door*). No. No luggage. Like the walk. Good day. (*Exits.*)

ALARIC (*calling off*). Jarvis, the door. (*He closes the door and remains by desk.*)

(PEG *wistfully watches* HAWKES *go, then looks dejectedly at the floor, then sits in chair again.*)

MRS. CHICHESTER (*severely*). Your name is Margaret.

PEG (*quickly*). Peg. (*Catches herself.*) My name is Peg.

(ALARIC *sits at desk.*)

MRS. CHICHESTER. That is only a corruption. We will call you Margaret.

PEG (*pause*). All right. But don't blame me if I'm not there, will ye? (ALARIC *bangs desk.*) I'm very much afraid indeed that I'll forget to answer to the name of Margaret. My name is Peg anyway. My father always calls me Peg. It will put me in mind of my father.

MRS. CHICHESTER. Kindly leave your father out of our conversation.

PEG (*rises, to* MRS. CHICHESTER, *with a sudden flash of anger*). Then it's all I will leave him out of.

MRS. CHICHESTER. No temper, if you please. (PEG *sits down breathing hard. Pause.*) You must take my daughter as your model in all things. (PEG *looks at* ETHEL, *half inclined to cry, half to laugh*). Everything she does you must try to imitate. You cannot have a better example. Mould yourself on her.

PEG (*tries to sit as* ETHEL *is sitting, to pose as she does, to arrange her dress as she has hers arranged. Imitates her*). "Please don't. It's so hot this mornin'." (*Laughs.*)

MRS. CHICHESTER. What do you mean?

PEG. We have a little joke together, haven't we? (*to* ETHEL.)

MRS. CHICHESTER (*rising, to* PEG). You have a great deal to learn.

PEG. Yes, Aunt.

MRS. CHICHESTER. Until some decent clothes can be procured for you we'll find some from my daughter's wardrobe.

PEG. Sure, I've got a beautiful silk dress that I wear to Mass on Sunday. It's a very pretty silk dress. I couldn't wear it on the ship because it would get all wet. I can't wear my Sunday clothes, ma'am. I must wear my traveling suit when I'm traveling.

MRS. CHICHESTER (*rising—checking* PEG). That will do. Ring, Alaric. (ALARIC *crosses back of table to bell and rings. To* PEG.) You must try to realize that you have an opportunity very few girls in your position are ever given. I only hope you will try to repay our interest and your late uncle's wishes by obedience, good conduct, and hard study.

PEG (*meekly, her eyes twinkling with mischief*). My dress has lace on it, too, you know. (MRS. CHICHESTER *turns away.*) Well, I don't want you to think my father doesn't buy me any pretty clothes. I have some grand dresses.

(*Enter* JARVIS.)

MRS. CHICHESTER. Jarvis, tell Bennett to show my niece to the Mauve Room and to attend her.

JARVIS. Yes, ma'am. (*Goes to top of stairs.*)

MRS. CHICHESTER. Now go with him.

PEG. Of course, I know this suit is very old, and should be mended and pressed. I wish I'd worn my silk dress. (*Rises and crosses to* ETHEL.) I've got two silk dresses, Miss. I've got a blue one and a pink one. The blue one is my going-to-Mass dress. It's dark blue. And the pink one is my party dress. It has a black velvet sash on it—a wide black velvet sash. (ETHEL *looks away.*) It's very black, too, it is. (ETHEL *takes no notice.* PEG *sees dog.*) Hello! I've got two silk dresses. Did you know that? (*As dog takes no notice* PEG *goes to table.*) Devil a bit he cares about dresses. (*If dog is friendly, and goes to* PEG, *she takes him up saying.*) Look at that now. He's very friendly. Dogs like me, dogs do. (*Puts down dog.*) You'll have to get over that, young fellow. Nice and friendly. I wonder where he picked it up. (*If dog jumps up and down, make him do it two or three times, and say.*) I'm a dog-trainer, I am. He should be on wheels.

MRS. CHICHESTER. Now go with him.

PEG. Yes, ma'am. (*Turns to* JARVIS *and laughs, then looks at* ETHEL, *then at* MRS. CHICHESTER, *then at* ALARIC.) Of course I'll try to do everything you want me to do, but I'm very far away, and it's all so strange, and I do miss my father so much— (*Checks herself.*)

MRS. CHICHESTER (*coldly*). Go with him.

PEG. Yes, ma'am. (*Bobs, then shrinks into herself, creeps quietly upstairs, looks at* JARVIS, *who does not move.*) He's not going. (*Or,* He doesn't know where to go. *Business with* JARVIS. *They exit.*)

(ALARIC, ETHEL *and* MRS. CHICHESTER *look at each other.*)

ALARIC (*to* ETHEL). Eh?

ETHEL (*on bench*). Awful!

MRS. CHICHESTER. Terrible!

ALARIC (*leaning on chair*). It's our unlucky day.

MRS. CHICHESTER. One thing is absolutely necessary. She must be kept away from everyone for the present.

ALARIC. I should say so. Good Lord! Jerry! He mustn't see her. He'd laugh his head off at the idea of me having a relation like that. He'll probably run in for lunch.

(ETHEL *rises, picks up dog, and crosses up to foot of stairs.*)

MRS. CHICHESTER. She must remain in her room until he's gone. Meanwhile I'll go into town and order some things for her and see about tutors. She's got to be taught, and at once. (*Crosses to desk and picks up list.*)

ETHEL. But why put up with it at all, Mother?

MRS. CHICHESTER. (*Turns to* ETHEL.) One thousand pounds a year. That's the reason. And rather than you should have to make any sacrifice, dear, I'd put up with worse than that.

ETHEL. Yes, I believe you would. I wouldn't. (*Up the stairs.*)

ALARIC. Where are you off to, Ethel?

ETHEL (*at head of stairs*). To make up my mind, if I can, about something. The coming of Peg may do it for me. (*Exit upstairs.*)

ALARIC. I'll go with you, Mater, as far as the Station Road, and see if I can head Jerry off. (*Looks at watch.*) His train is due if it's punctual. (*Crosses to piano and gets hat.*)

(*Enter* JARVIS *with fresh flowers.*)

MRS. CHICHESTER (*to* JARVIS). Oh, Jarvis, my niece is not to leave her room without my permission.

JARVIS. Yes, ma'am.

MRS. CHICHESTER. Come, Alaric. (*Goes to door, in front of* JARVIS, *who holds it open.*)

ALARIC. Any callers, Jarvis, we'll be back to lunch. One sharp. (*Exit, following* MRS. CHICHESTER *out.* MAID *comes downstairs laughing. They exchange looks. The maid nods in the direction of upstairs and laughs.*)

JARVIS (*to maid*). Bennett. (JARVIS *crosses to back of table,* MAID *to side of table.*)

MAID. Well? Have you seen her?

JARVIS. I have.

MAID. Have you ever seen anything like her?

JARVIS. Never in my life. Bring me over the vase, will you?

(MAID *gets vase from desk.*)

MAID. What do you make of her?

(JARVIS *goes up to back for vase.*)

JARVIS (*comes back to table*). Every family I've served had its family skeleton. That's ours.

MAID (*putting flowers in vase*). A niece?

JARVIS. So they say.

MAID. She hasn't a rag to her back. I'd be ashamed to be dressed as she is. You should see the one she goes to Mass in.

JARVIS. I did. All wrapped up in "The Irish Times." And I get ragged for putting her in the kitchen. (*Goes to back with flowers.*) Looked too good for her. And, what do you think? That dog tried to bite me.

MAID. Where is the dog now?

JARVIS. Tied up in the stables, worrying the horses.

(*Door bangs. Slam off stage.*)

MAID. They're gone. (*Goes to stairs, halfway up.*)

JARVIS (*comes to chair front of table*). Oh, Bennett. The niece is not to leave her room without permission. You'd better tell her.

MAID (*going upstairs*). Oh, my! These poor relations. (*Lightning.*)

(JARVIS *puts chair back by table, picks up paper, and crosses to desk. Down the path comes a man. He is* JERRY, *a tall, athletic, breezy, tanned, broad-shouldered, energetic young man of twenty-six, magnetic in all he says and does. He swings in briskly through arch.*)

JERRY. Hullo, Jarvis. How are you?

JARVIS. Quite nicely, thank you, sir.

JERRY (*puts hat on table.*) Where's everyone?

JARVIS. Just drove away, sir. (*Comes to table.*)

JERRY (*sits armchair*). What time's lunch?

JARVIS. One, sir.

JERRY. All well?

JARVIS. Yes, sir.

JERRY. Anything new?

JARVIS. No, sir. (*Coughs. Pause. Looks up the stairs.*) Yes, sir. There's a new—(*slight pause.*)—mare in the stable, sir. Came yesterday.

JERRY. Miss Ethel's?

JARVIS. Yes, sir.

JERRY. I'll go and have a look at her. (*Starts, picking up hat.*)

JARVIS. There's a strange dog tied to the door, sir. Better walk round him, sir. Snappy.

JERRY. A new dog, too, eh? Mr. Alaric's?

JARVIS. No, sir.

JERRY. Whose is it?

JARVIS. It just came, sir.

(*Thunder.*)

JERRY. What breed?

JARVIS. It might be anything, sir.

(*Thunder.*)

JERRY. I'll look that over, too. (*Thunder rolls in the distance.*) Hullo, storm's blowing up. If Mr. Alaric turns up send him out to me, will you? (*Goes off.*)

(*The sound of voices upstairs is heard, and the maid appears, followed by* PEG. PEG *is in her going-to-Mass dress.* JARVIS *arranges books and magazines on table.*)

MAID. The missus said——

PEG (*downstairs*). I'll come cut of my room if I want to.

MAID. The missus said you were not to leave your room.

PEG. I want to tell you something, Miss.— It's a long time since I had a nurse. (*Comes downstairs. Looks at* JARVIS.) It's a funny job you've got, isn't it? (*Goes to table.*) Standing round, looking mad all the time. I'll come down in your parlor if I want to. What's a parlor for but to keep company in? Well, I'm company and this is the parlor, so we're all right.

JARVIS (*to* MAID). Well?

MAID (*to* PEG). You'll only get me into trouble.

PEG. I wouldn't do that for all the world. I'll get all the throuble, Miss. I'll get it now. (*Goes to door, opens it, and calls.*) Ant! Aurnt! I want to see your parlor, and your nurse won't let me.

MAID. They've all gone out.

PEG (*comes back, closing door*). Well, why didn't you tell me they'd all gone out. You let me shout my head off, and then tell me they've all gone out. You'd better go out too. (*They do not move.*) Go on with you. (JARVIS *and* MAID *move toward door, then stop and turn. To* JARVIS.) I don't know whether to laugh or cry at him. (*Maid laughs. She and* JARVIS *look at each other in amazement, and exeunt. Lightning. Examines all the things, which are new to her. Laughs. Sees Cupid on piano, runs to it, and claps her hands.*) Hullo, Cupid, ye darling. You're the one that causes all the mischief in the world, ye devil. (*Thunder. Sits end of piano-stool and crosses herself.*) Oh, Holy Mary! (*She cowers into herself and prays.* JERRY *appears with Michael in his arms. It has grown very dark. Lightning.* PEG *trembles in terror, her back to* JERRY.)

JERRY. Hello!

PEG (*turns quickly*). Michael! (*Thunder. Runs to* JERRY, *snatches dog from him, and runs over to left, chattering with fear and looking suspiciously at* JERRY. JERRY *looks at* PEG *in astonishment. Two flashes of lightning.*) Shut it out! Shut it out! Shut the storm out! (JERRY *draws the curtains and comes down to* PEG.) That's right, sir. (*Explaining to* JERRY.) Don't go near the dog. You mustn't come near the dog. (*Puts dog outside door.*) Dogs attract lightning.

JERRY (*looking at her in amazement*). Does he belong to you?

PEG (*nods*). What were you doin' with him?

JERRY. I found him barking at a very high-spirited mare.

PEG. Mare? Where?

(*Lightning.*)

JERRY (*by table*). Tied to the stable door.

PEG. The stable? Is that where they put Michael?

(*Thunder.*)

JERRY. Don't be frightened. It's only a summer storm.

PEG (*in awe*). Summer or winter, they shrivel me up.

JERRY. Come and look at it. They're beautiful in this part of the country. Come and watch it. (*Going to window at back and lifting curtain.*)

(*Lightning.*)

PEG (*sits by table*). Shut it out! Shut it out! I'll not look at it at all. They say if you look at the sky when the lightning comes ye can see the Kingdom of Heaven. And the sight of it blinds some and kills others accordin' to the state of grace ye're in.

(*Lightning.*)

JERRY (*coming down by table*). You're a Catholic?

PEG. Of course I'm a Catholic. What else is anybody? (*Thunder.*) It does seem to me that He is very angry with us for our sins.

JERRY. With me, perhaps, not with you.

PEG. What do you mane by that?

JERRY. You don't know what sin is.

PEG. And who may you be, to talk to me like that?

JERRY. My name is Jerry. What's yours?

PEG. *Peg.* (*Looks round at stairs.*) That's what it is, too, Peg. Jerry, did ye say?

(*Rain.*)

JERRY. Just plain Jerry. And you're Peg?

PEG (*nods*). Just plain Peg.

JERRY (*comes down to table and sits*). I don't agree with you. I think you're very charming.

PEG (*seated at table*). You mustn't say things like that—with the storm outside.

JERRY. I mean it.

PEG. Ye don't. The man that thinks them things never says them to your face. My father always said to me "Now, Peg, there's one sort of a fellow you've got to be very careful of, and that the one that says flattering things right in your face. He's no good," he says. "He's no good."

JERRY. Who are you?

PEG. Did ye ever see such a funny-looking sofa as that one? What do ye do with it? Do ye sit on it, or lie down on it?

JERRY. Whichever you like.

PEG. I think it should have a back and some handles if it wants to be a sofa.

JERRY. Who are you?

PEG (*rises*). And look here. I've found another funny one over here. (*Crosses and sits in chair.*) Do you know what this is? It's a high-chair. I never heard of anybody keeping a high-chair in the parlor, did you? And I never heard of anybody buying a sofa that looks like a bench. (*Crosses to him, sliding on carpet.*) And the carpet—it's a slippery carpet. I can make poses on it. (*Slides back to him, posing.* JERRY *laughs.* PEG *slides to bench and back again.*) We have a carpet home. But our carpet's not slippery. This must be a cheap one. Our carpet has roses on it, big red and yellow roses. Makes the room more cheerful—more like a parlor.

JERRY. Who in the world are you?

PEG. Do you know Alaric?

JERRY. Yes, of course.

PEG. I wish I could take him home and show him to my father.

JERRY. Who are you?

PEG. And the big fellow. Are you acquainted with the big fellow who works in this house?

JERRY. The big fellow? I don't think I know him.

PEG. He's all in front of himself.

JERRY. Oh, you mean Jarvis.

PEG. Jarvis. Do you know all he does to make his living—that great big strong fellow? He just carries round a little card on a big plate, to tell who's coming to the house. (*She turns and points to the bench again.*)

JERRY. Now, who in the world are you?

PEG. You asked me that before, didn't you?

JERRY. Yes.

PEG. Well, I'm my aunt's niece, I am. (*Sitting on sofa. Pause.*)

JERRY (*on sofa, smiling*). And who is your aunt?

PEG. Mrs. Chi—ch—es—es—cher.

JERRY. Who?

PEG. Mrs. Chi—ch—es—es.

JERRY. Mrs. Chichester.

PEG. That's it. You have to jump it in the middle.

JERRY. Really? How extraordinary!

PEG. Isn't it? You wouldn't expect a fine lady like her to have a niece like me, would ye?

JERRY. That isn't what I meant.

PEG. Yes, it is. And you mustn't tell untruths with the storm outside.

JERRY. I was thinking that I don't remember Alaric ever telling me he had such a charming cousin. (*By sofa.*)

PEG. Alaric didn't know I was alive till I dropped down from the clouds this morning.

JERRY. Where did you drop from?

PEG. New York.

JERRY. Really? How odd!

(*Stop rain.*)

PEG. Not at all. It's just the same as any other big city. There's nothing odd about New York. It's a big place, New York is.

JERRY (*hesitatingly, and with pronounced English accent*). Were you born there?

PEG. What was that you said?

JERRY. I said, "Were you born there?"

PEG. Yes, I was.

JERRY. By way of Old Ireland?

PEG. How did you guess that?

JERRY. Your slight, but delightful, accent.

PEG. I've got an accent?

JERRY. Yes.

PEG. Well, I was much too polite to say anything, but I was thinking you had an accent. (JERRY *laughs.*) What are you laughing at? Haven't you ever listened to yourself?

JERRY. No. I can't say I have.

PEG. Well, you said to me just now "Were you born there?" (*Imitating him.*)

JERRY. Well, how would you say it?

PEG. I'd say it naturally—"Were you born there?" I'd say. "Were you born there?" I wouldn't fall over my words. I'd say it straight out of my face. I wouldn't make a song-and-dance out of it.

JERRY (*sits beside her. She moves a little away*). I see. (*Laughing.*) Hello! (*Goes to window and pulls curtains open.*) The storm's over. All the anger has gone from the heavens. See! (*Draws open the curtains.*)

PEG (*under her breath*). Praise be to God for that!

JERRY. Are you going to stay here?

PEG. Mebbe I will. Mebbe I won't.

JERRY. Did your aunt send for you?

PEG. No: my uncle Nat.

JERRY. Nat?

PEG. Nathaniel Kingsnorth, God rest his soul.

JERRY. Nathaniel Kingsnorth?

PEG (*seated on couch, nods*). Sleepin' in his grave, poor man!

JERRY (*crosses to back to bench*). Then you're Margaret O'Connell?

PEG. I am. How did you know that?

JERRY. Why, I—(*Goes to sit—sees her look.*) May I sit here?

PEG. That's what you said it was for. Go on and sit.

(JERRY *sits.*)

JERRY. I was with your uncle when he died.

PEG. Were ye?

JERRY. He told me all about you.

PEG. Did he? I wish the poor man 'd have lived. (*Pause.*) I wish he'd sent for me sooner. He with all his money and my father with none, and me his sister's only child.

JERRY. What does your father do?

PEG (*on couch, eagerly*). Anything. My father can do anything at all. Except make money. And when he does make it he can't keep it. He doesn't like money. Neither do I. (*Pause.*) I've never had much to like. But I've seen others around us with plenty, and we've been the happiest—that we have. When times were the hardest I never heard a word of complaint from my father or saw a frown on his face. (*Pause.*) Sure, we're more like boy and girl than father and daughter. (*Pause.*) And I'm sick for the sight of him. (*Pause.*) And I'm sure he is for me—for his "Peg—o'—my—heart," as he always calls me. (*Covers her eyes.*) I wish I was back home.

JERRY (*gently*). Don't do that.

PEG (*wiping her eyes with a large handkerchief, which is fastened—folded—by a safety-pin to her dress*). I don't cry very often. (*Pause.*) My father never made me. I never saw him cry but twice in my life. Once when he'd made a little money and we had a Mass said for my mother's soul and had the most beautiful candles lit on Our Lady's altar. And when I left him to come here. (*Pause.*) He laughed and joked with me up to the last minute, and when the ship swung away from the dock he just broke down and sobbed like a little child. "My Peg," he kept sayin', "My little Peg." And I wanted to get off the ship and go to him. But we'd started, and I didn't know how to swim. (*Pause.*) I cried myself to sleep that night. I'm not going to be happy here. (*Pause.*) I only came here because my father thought it'd be for my good. (*Pause.*) And they won't make a lady out of me if I can help it. (*Pause.*) Ye can't make a silk purse out of a sow's ear. That's what my father said. And that's what I am—a sow's ear.

JERRY (*rises. Gently*). I don't agree with you.

PEG (*wiping her eyes*). I don't care whether ye do or not. I'm—a sow's ear, I am.

JERRY. When the strangeness wears off you'll be very happy here.

PEG. What makes ye think that?

JERRY. Because you'll know that you are pleasing your father.

PEG. But I'm all alone——

JERRY. You're among friends.

PEG (*shakes her head*). They're ashamed of me.

JERRY. Oh, no.

PEG. They are. They sent me to the kitchen when I first came here. And they put Michael to sleep in the stable. I want to tell you Michael's not used to sleeping in a stable. We never had any. That was a quick joke, wasn't it? Michael has always slept with my father ever since he was a little bit of a puppy. Michael, I mean. I thought you might think I meant my father.

JERRY. When they really get to know you they'll be just as proud of you as your father is—as I'd be.

PEG (*to corner of piano, looks at him, then picks up music*). You'd be? (*Pause.*) Why should you be proud—(*pause*)—of me?

JERRY. I'd be more than proud if you'd look on me as a friend.

PEG. But I don't know who ye are at all, do I?

JERRY (*sitting on table.*) Oh, I can give you some very good references. For instance, I was up at the same college as your cousin Alaric.

PEG (*sits on piano-stool*). Were ye? Well, I would mention that to very few people.

JERRY. Don't you want me to be your friend?

PEG. I don't know. I'm like the widow's pig that was put in a rale bed to sleep in. The pig neither wanted it nor it didn't want it. It had done without it all its life, and it wasn't cryin' its heart out for the loss of somethin' it had never had and didn't miss. (JERRY *laughs heartily.*) I want to tell you that's one thing that's in your favor.

JERRY. What is?

PEG. The laughter's not dead in ye as it is in everybody else in this house. (*Looking at him with more interest, puts down music. He laughs three times.* PEG *laughs with him, then goes to him.*) Say, who are ye at all?

JERRY. No one in particular.

PEG. Well, I can see that. I mean, what do ye do?

JERRY (*on table*). Everything a little and nothing really well. I was a soldier for a while, then I took a splash at doctoring; read law; civil-engineered in South America for a year—now I'm farming.

PEG (*by table*). Ye're a farmer?

JERRY. Yes.

PEG (*laughs*). Where's your whiskers?

JERRY. I'm a new farmer. (*Laughs.*) To sum up my career, I can do a whole lot of things fairly well, and none of them well enough to brag about.

PEG. Like my father, that is.

JERRY. You flatter me.

PEG. I know I flatter you. There's not a man in the whole world like my father.

JERRY. No. Of course not.

PEG. No. Not one man in the whole world, there isn't. (*Pause, she goes round to back of table.* JERRY *comes to side of table.*) But he says he's a rolling stone, and they don't amount to much in a hard-hearted world that's all for making dollars.

JERRY. Your father's right. Money is the standard today, and we're all valued by it.

PEG. Yes. And he's got none. (*Pause.*) But he has got me. (*Pause. Looks ruefully all round, then gets up resolutely.*) I'm goin' right back to him now. (*Crosses to foot of stairs.*)

JERRY. No, no. (*Round back of table to newel post.*)

PEG (*on third step*). I must. Sure, it's easier to suffer the want of food than the want of love. (*Pause. Imitates her father, banging newel post.* JERRY *starts back.*) "And that's what the Irish are doing all over the world.

They're driven from their own country. They're made wanderers on the face of the earth, and nothin' they ever earn'll make up to them for the separation from their homes and from their loved ones." (JERRY *laughs.*) Do you know what that is?

JERRY (*shakes his head*). I haven't the slightest idea.

PEG. That's one of my father's speeches.

JERRY. One of his speeches?

PEG. My father makes grand speeches.

JERRY. Does he?

PEG. He makes them in the cause of Ireland.

JERRY (*smiles. Comes to newel post*). In the cause of Ireland?

PEG. Yes. My mother died when I was a little baby, and my father brought me back to Ireland. I lived there all my life till two months ago, when he had to go back to New York, and they sent for me to come here. I went all through Ireland with my father on his lecture tours. We had a cart. We traveled from place to place in the cart. He made his speeches from the tail of it, and we lived in the middle. My father practised all of his speeches on me first.

JERRY. Oh, did he?

PEG. I know fifty of them by heart.

JERRY. Fifty?

PEG. Yes. I'm going to recite them all to Mrs. Chichester. She'll be very pleased. Nice old lady, she is.

JERRY. Very nice.

PEG. Full of fun. (*They both laugh.*) I tell you I'm not used to sour faces. My father's full of jokes. I'm lost without my father. I get very lonesome without him. I'm going back to him, too. (*She goes upstairs.*)

JERRY (*following her and leaning over balustrade*). Wait! Think! Just give us one month's trial. One month. It's very little out of your life, and I promise you your father will not suffer by it, except in losing you for that one little month. (*Pause.*) Will you? Please do. Just a month?

PEG (*coming down to bottom step*). Why do you want me to stay here?

JERRY. Because—because your uncle was my friend. It was his last wish to do something for you. (*Pause.*) Will you? Just a month?

PEG. Not any more than a month.

JERRY. Not unless you wish it.

PEG. All right. I don't suppose I'll mind a month. It's going to seem like a lifetime in this place.

JERRY. I'm glad.

PEG. Glad it's going to seem like a lifetime?

JERRY (*smiling*). No. That you're going to stay.

PEG. That's a comfort anyway. Someone in the house'll be pleased at my stayin'——(*Pause.*)

JERRY (*following her*). I am—immensely.

PEG. Yes. I heard you say it.

JERRY (*nearer to her*). And will you look on me as your friend?

PEG (*looks at him quickly, then moves away*). I don't know who you are, do I?

JERRY (*following*). Is it so difficult?

PEG. I don't know at all. I don't know whether it's difficult or not till I thry it. (*Goes away.*)

JERRY (*following* PEG). Try.

PEG. I don't understand you.

JERRY. Yet I'm very simple.

PEG. Devil doubt that. (*Crosses to corner, sits in high chair, sees he is quite near her.*) Where do you think you'll go now? (JERRY *holds out his hand.*) What's that for?

JERRY. To our friendship.

PEG. I never met anybody like you in all my life before. (*Looks at his hand.*)

JERRY. Shake hands on it.

PEG. I don't think it's necessary.

JERRY. Do.

PEG. I don't shake hands with every Tom, Dick and Harry I meet.

JERRY. Come.

PEG. Queer fish, you are. (*Gives her hand.*)

JERRY (*holds it*). Friends?

PEG. Not yet. Not so fast.

JERRY. I'll wager we will be.

PEG. Don't put much on it. Ye might lose.

JERRY. I'll stake my life on it.

PEG. Ye don't value it much, then.

JERRY. More than I did. (PEG *looks at him.*) May you be very happy here, Peg.

(*Door slams.*)

PEG (*crosses and runs upstairs.* JERRY *watches her in amazement*). Don't tell anybody you saw me down in this room. (*She turns to go, meets* ETHEL *at top of stairs, turns, comes downstairs, meets* MRS. CHICHESTER *and* ALARIC *entering. She turns completely round, and finally sits at bottom of stairs.*)

(MRS. CHICHESTER *goes to* JERRY, *who shakes hands with her.*)

MRS. CHICHESTER. So sorry we were out. You'll stay to lunch?

JERRY. It's what I came for. (MRS. CHICHESTER *crosses to right.* JERRY *shakes hand with* ETHEL, *who also goes down to her mother, telling her that* PEG *is on the stairs.*)

ALARIC (*slouches over to* JERRY). What ho! Jerry!

JERRY (*slips his arm through* ALARIC'S *and takes him to windows, seeing* PEG *on stairs in passing*). I say, Al, your cousin's adorable.

ALARIC. What?

JERRY. Simply adorable.

(*They talk by windows.*)

ALARIC. Oh, I say, adorable!

(ETHEL *points out* PEG *to* MRS. CHICHESTER, *then sits on piano-stool.*)

MRS. CHICHESTER. Margaret! Margaret! (MRS. CHICHESTER *looks round at newel post and* PEG *comes out and goes to* MRS. CHICHESTER.) Who gave you permission to come in here?

PEG. No one at all. I just walked in.

MRS. CHICHESTER. Go to your room and stay there until I give you leave to come out.

PEG (*passionately*). Sure, if this house is going to be a prison I'm going back to my father.

(*Lunch gong off stage.*)

ALARIC. There we are! Lunch, everyone!

JERRY. At last! I'm starving!

PEG. So am I. I haven't had a bite since six.

JERRY (*offering* PEG *his arm*). Allow me.

MRS. CHICHESTER. My niece is tired after her journey. She will lunch in her room.

PEG. I'm not a bit tired, and I'd rather have lunch down here with Mr. Jerry.

ALARIC. Oh, I say,—Mr. Jerry!

JERRY. And so you shall have lunch with Mr. Jerry. Come along—let us lead the way. (*Goes off with* PEG *on his arm,* PEG *looking back impishly at the others and then smiling up at* JERRY.)

PEG. I'm not so sure about that wager of yours. I think your life is safe. I want to tell ye ye saved my life. I'm so hungry my soul is hanging by a thread.

SLOW CURTAIN

MRS. CHICHESTER. She must be taught, and at once.

ACT TWO

"THE REBELLION OF PEG"

SCENE—*A month afterward. A July evening.*

At rise of curtain PEG *is discovered lying on couch intently reading a large, handsomely-bound volume.* JARVIS *noiselessly shows in* BRENT, *who is in automobile garb—light overcoat on, cap in hand—and exits.* BRENT *puts coat and cap on window-seat, moves down* L. C. *near couch, sees* PEG, *and looks down at her as he takes gloves off. He bangs glove on hand.* PEG *looks up, meeting* BRENT'S *admiring gaze.*

BRENT (*comes to couch*). It must be absorbing. (PEG *shuts book and moves into sitting position. She is then seen to be charmingly gowned, her hair dressed à la mode.*) What's the book? (PEG *puts her hands over the title and looks at him distrustfully.* BRENT *walks round couch, sits beside* PEG, *smiling appreciatingly at her.* PEG *jumps up and stands defiantly, her eyes flashing angrily.*) You mustn't be angry, child. (*Points to book.*) What is it? Something *forbidden?* (*Leering.*) Show me. (*Holds out his hand.* PEG *smacks it.* PEG *crosses to corner of piano, puts book under piano cover, and faces* BRENT.) Aha! A hiding place! Now you make me really curious. Let me look at it. (*Goes to her.* PEG *stands at bay, ready to defend the identity of the book.*) I love spirit. Why, what a wonderful change in a month! You'd most certainly not be sent to the kitchen *now.* (*Pause. He sits on arm of armchair.*) Do you know you've grown into a most attractive young woman? (PEG *ejaculates.*) Oh, you are really delightful when you're angry. And you are angry, aren't you? And with me. I'm sorry I offended you. Let us kiss and be friends. (*He takes her left hand, and as he bends near her she gives him a resounding box on the ears.* BRENT *gives a muffled ejaculation and tries to take her in his arms. Enter* ETHEL. PEG, *panting with anger, glares at him, then rushes straight out through arch.* BRENT *follows her, swings round, sees* ETHEL, *stops, then goes to her with outstretched hand, and comes down to front of table.*) Why, my dear Ethel!

ETHEL (*ignoring his hand*). Why did she run away?

BRENT (*smiling easily and confidently*). I'd surprised one of her secrets and she flew into a temper. Did you see her strike me?

ETHEL. Secrets?

BRENT. Yes. Here we are. (*Goes to piano, turns up piano cover, takes out book, opens it, reads.*) "The Love Stories of the World"—"To Peg from Jerry." Jerry! Oho! No wonder she didn't want me to see it. (*Puts it back and covers it up.*) Jerry, eh? (*Goes to* ETHEL.) So *that's* how the land lies! Romantic little child! (*To* ETHEL.) Now, Ethel, I——

ETHEL (*looking steadily at him*). Why don't you go after her? (*Nodding in the direction in which* PEG *ran.*)

BRENT. Ethel!

ETHEL. She's *new* and has all the *virtues.*

BRENT. I assure you——

ETHEL. You needn't. If there's one thing I'm convinced of it's your *assurance.*

BRENT. Really, Ethel——

ETHEL (*sitting in armchair*). Were you *"carried away"* again?

BRENT. Do you think——?

ETHEL. Yes. I do.

BRENT (*hunting for an explanation*). I—I don't know what to say.

ETHEL. Better say nothing.

BRENT. Surely you're not jealous—of a—child?

ETHEL (*slowly*). No. I don't think it's *jealousy*.

BRENT. Then what is it?

ETHEL (*looking scornfully at him*). Disgust. (*Shrugs her shoulders contemptuously.*) Now I understand why the *kitchen* is sometimes the rival of the *drawing-room*. The love of *change*.

BRENT (*crosses and turns back*). This is not worthy of you.

ETHEL. That is what rankles. It isn't. You're not.

BRENT (*coming back*). Ethel——

ETHEL (*seated*). If that ever happened again I should have to—*amputate you*. (*Pause. He turns up to window-seat for coat.*) Chris! (*He turns.*) Come here! (BRENT *comes back to her. She smiles.*) My nerves have been tried this past month.

BRENT. Poor Ethel! (*Pause.*)

ETHEL. Put a mongrel into a kennel of thoroughbreds and they'll either destroy the intruder or be in a condition of unsettled, irritating intolerance. (*Pause.*) That's exactly my condition. (*Pause.*) I'm unsettled, irritable, intolerant.

BRENT (*crosses to* ETHEL). Then I came in time.

ETHEL (*smiles as she looks straight through him*). So did I. Didn't I?

BRENT. Don't. Please don't. (*Turns away.*)

ETHEL. Very well. I won't. (*Pause. He turns to her again.*) I'm sorry, Chris. (*Pause. She looks up at him.*) A month ago it wouldn't have mattered. Just now—it did. I'd rather looked forward to seeing you. It's been horrible here.

BRENT. It's been a month of misery for me toc. But I'm going away—out of it—tomorrow.

ETHEL. Are you? Where?

BRENT. Norway—Moscow—Siberia.

ETHEL. Oh! The *cold* places! Going alone?

BRENT (*bending over* ETHEL). Yes. Unless *someone* goes with me.

ETHEL. Naturally.

BRENT. *Will* you go?

ETHEL (*rises*). I wish *I'd* been here when you called—instead of that *brat*.

BRENT (*turns away to table*). Good God——

ETHEL. One doesn't mind an *equal* so much—but that——

BRENT. This is unbearable.

ETHEL. Your wife all over again, eh?

BRENT (*coming down to* ETHEL C.). No. I place you far above her—above all petty suspicion and carping narrowness. I value you as a woman of understanding.

ETHEL (*meaningly*). I am. From what you've told me about your wife, *she* is, too.

BRENT (*turns away distractedly*). Don't treat me like this.

ETHEL. What shall I *do?* (*He looks at her.*) Apologize? That's odd. I've been waiting for yours. (*Crosses to piano.*)

BRENT. Oh! (*Moves restlessly away.*)

(ALARIC *hurries in.*)

ALARIC. Hello! H'are ye? (*Shakes hands with* BRENT.) Disturbing you?

BRENT. Not at all—no.

ALARIC. The angel wife all right?

BRENT. Very well, thank you.

ALARIC. And the darling child?

BRENT. Quite well, thank you.

ALARIC. Splendid! (*Crossing to* ETHEL *at back of table.*) Seen Margaret?

ETHEL (*nods in direction of garden*). Out there.

ALARIC. Mater wants her. Got to have a family meetin' about her. Mater'll be here in a minute. (*To* BRENT.) Just the family! (*Hurries out.*)

BRENT (*hurries to* ETHEL *at back of table*). I'm at the hotel. I'll be there until morning. Send me a message. Will you? I'll wait up all night for one. Will you?

ETHEL (*at piano*). Perhaps, Chris.

BRENT. Oh, I'm sorry if anything I've said or done has hurt you.

ETHEL. Don't say any more.

BRENT. Oh, if you only——(ETHEL *checks him as door opens and* MRS. CHICHESTER *enters.* MAID *comes downstairs at same moment, opening curtain.*)

MRS. CHICHESTER. How do you do? (*Bowing to* BRENT. *Turns to maid.* ETHEL *sits.*) When did you see my niece last?

(BRENT *to window-seat, gets cap and coat.*)

MAID. Not this hour, ma'am.

MRS. CHICHESTER. Tell Jarvis to search the gardens.

MAID. Yes, ma'am. (*Starts toward arch.*)

MRS. CHICHESTER (*comes to table*). Tell Jarvis—(MAID *stops.*)—to search the stables.

MAID. Yes, ma'am. (*Starts off again.*)

MRS. CHICHESTER. Tell Jarvis—(MAID *stops.*)—to look up and down the road.

MAID. Yes, ma'am. (*Exit arch.* BRENT *comes toward* MRS. CHICHESTER.)

MRS. CHICHESTER (*turning to* BRENT). Forgive me, Mr. Brent. I'm sorry.

BRENT. Not at all. I'm just leaving. (*Crosses, bows to her, shakes hands.*)

MRS. CHICHESTER. Oh, you needn't —

BRENT (*going toward door*). I'm going abroad tomorrow. I just called to say good-by.

MRS. CHICHESTER. I trust *you and Mrs. Brent* will have a very pleasant trip.

BRENT. Thank you. (*Passes out.*)

(ALARIC *re-enters.* ETHEL *sits armchair.*)

ALARIC. Not a sign of Margaret anywhere. (*Fanning himself with his handkerchief.*)

MRS. CHICHESTER. This *cannot* go on. (*Sits at table.*)

ALARIC (*sits at table*). I should think not, indeed.

MRS. CHICHESTER. Mr. Hawkes writes that he will call tomorrow for his first report. What am I to *tell* him?

ALARIC. What *will* you? (JARVIS *and* MAID *enter.*)

MRS. CHICHESTER. Am I to tell him that every tutor I've engaged for her has resigned? That no maid will stay with her? Am I to tell him that?

ALARIC. Serve her jolly-well right if you did. Eh, Ethel?

ETHEL. It would.

MAID. I've searched everywhere, ma'am. Not a sign of her.

JARVIS. Not in the stables nor up or down the road. And the dog's missing.

ETHEL. Pet?

JARVIS. No, not Pet, Miss. *She's* gnawing a bone on the lawn. The *other*—Michael.

MRS. CHICHESTER. That will do. (*Exeunt* JARVIS *and* MAID.) Where *is* she?

ALARIC. Heaven knows.

MRS. CHICHESTER. If only I could throw the whole business up!

ALARIC. Wish to goodness we *could.* But the monthly cheque will be useful tomorrow, Mater. Let's give the little beggar another month of it. Let her off lightly this time, and the moment the lawyer-bird's gone read her the Riot Act. Pull her up with a jerk. Ride her on the curb, and no rot.

(*Suddenly through the open windows comes the sound of two dogs barking furiously and snapping at each other.*)

ETHEL. Pet! (*Jumps up and hurries out through arch.* ALARIC *and* MRS. CHICHESTER *go to windows.*)

MRS. CHICHESTER. Margaret!

ALARIC (*up at window, lifting the curtain*). And the mongrel! She's urging him on. The terrier's got Pet now (*Calling.*) Fight him, old girl! Maul him! Whoa there! Pet's down. There's Ethel on the scene.

MRS. CHICHESTER. Go and separate them.

ALARIC. Not me. I'll talk to 'em. Stop it! Stop it now, when I tell you! Ethel can handle 'em. I hate the little brutes—all hair and teeth. Can't understand women coddling those little masses of snarling, smelly wool.

(*The sound stops.* ETHEL *enters, flushed and angry, soothing the ruffled Pet. She goes down to couch. A little later* PEG *enters with the victorious Michael in her arms. She has a roguish look of triumph in her eyes. She, too, is flushed and excited, and follows* ETHEL *to bench.*)

MRS. CHICHESTER (*angrily*). Take that animal out of the room.

PEG. Come on, Ethel. Let him finish it.

MRS. CHICHESTER. Take that dog out of the room! (PEG *turns and walks out into the garden.* MRS. CHICHESTER *comes to front of table and lets her get some distance away.*) Margaret! Margaret! (*Pause.*) Come here! Do you hear me?

PEG (*outside. Without moving*). Can Michael come in?

MRS. CHICHESTER. *You* come in, and leave that brute outside. (*Pause.*) At once! (*Comes down center.*)

PEG (*leaves* MICHAEL *outside arch, and comes down to* MRS. CHICHESTER). I think it's the silliest thing, this class-distinction between dogs.

MRS. CHICHESTER. Where have you been?

(ALARIC *comes down to armchair.*)

PEG. Down to the seashore.

MRS. CHICHESTER. And why?

PEG. I wanted to give Michael a swim. The tide was high, but he wouldn't go in.

MRS. CHICHESTER. You took Michael down to the seashore in that dress?

(PEG *looks down at it.*)

PEG. No. He wasn't in this dress.

MRS. CHICHESTER. Look at your hair, all over your eyes. What do you think *will* become of you?

PEG. I have hopes of Heaven, like all the Catholics.

MRS. CHICHESTER (*despairingly, to* ALARIC *and* ETHEL). I give it up. (*Crosses to couch and sits beside* ETHEL.)

ALARIC. I should say so.

MRS. CHICHESTER. Is it that you don't wish to improve? Is it that?

PEG. I'll tell you what *I* think it is. I think—(*gets chair from table, brings it down, and sits* C.)—there's a devil in me some place, and every now and again he pops out.

MRS. CHICHESTER. A devil?

PEG (*demurely*). Yes, Aunt.

MRS. CHICHESTER. How dare you use such a word to me?

PEG. I didn't. I used it to myself. I don't know whether there's a devil in you or not. I don't think there is.

MRS. CHICHESTER. Tomorrow Mr. Hawkes will call for his first report on you. (PEG *laughs suddenly, then checks herself.*) And *why* did you do that?

PEG. I just had a picture of what you're goin' to tell him.

MRS. CHICHESTER. Your manners are abominable.

PEG. Yes, Aunt.

MRS. CHICHESTER. What *am* I to tell Mr. Hawkes?

PEG. I'd tell him the truth and shame the—devil. I would.

MRS. CHICHESTER. Oh! Don't you wish to remain here?

PEG. Sometimes I do. Sometimes I don't.

MRS. CHICHESTER. Don't I do everything possible for you?

PEG. Yes. You do everything possible *to* me—

MRS. CHICHESTER. What?

PEG. *For* me. (*Singing.*) *For* me.

MRS. CHICHESTER. Why do you constantly disobey me?

PEG. I suppose it's the original sin in me.

MRS. CHICHESTER. What?

ALARIC (*sitting on armchair*). Oh, I say, you know! Original sin! Ha! Ha! Ha!

PEG. Ha! Ha! Ha! I never know whether he's laughing or coughing. (*Catches* MRS. CHICHESTER'S *eye, and stops.*) Whenever I did anythin' wilful or disturbin' at home my father always said to me "Now, Peg, that is the original sin in ye, and ye're not to be punished, because ye can't help it." And then he used to punish himself for what I did, and when I saw how it hurt him I wouldn't do it any more. Now, I think that was a grand way to raise a daughter, and I did have an idea that an aunt might be very successful if she tried to raise a niece that way. (MRS. CHICHESTER *looks at her.*) Ye see, if you were to punish *yourself* for what I do—(MRS. CHICHESTER *stares at her.*)—I might be sorry. But, then, of course I might not, and that would be very hard on you. Ye see, I can't tell about myself.

MRS. CHICHESTER. Your father must have been a very bad influence on you.

PEG (*hotly*). My father's the best man in all the world.

MRS. CHICHESTER. Margaret!

PEG (*sullenly, looking down*). There was never a man on earth as good as my father. If more girls had fathers born to them as good as my father there'd be less trouble in this world.

MRS. CHICHESTER. Haven't I told you never to contradict me?

PEG. Well, you contradict me all the time. It's not fair if it doesn't work both ways.

MRS. CHICHESTER. Margaret!

PEG. I want to tell you I'd have a much sweeter disposition if you wouldn't talk against my father.

MRS. CHICHESTER. Really, Margaret!

PEG. I don't mind scolding—that has no effect on me whatever.

MRS. CHICHESTER. Margaret!

PEG. I'm surprised at you, I am. You know I'm mad about my father, and you should respect my feelings about him. I respect your feelings about Alaric, don't I?

(ALARIC *rises.*)

MRS. CHICHESTER. Stop!

PEG. I'd like to know who would have fed and clothed me all these years——

MRS. CHICHESTER. Stop!

PEG. It makes me furious when you talk against my father.

MRS. CHICHESTER. Stop! (PEG *opens her mouth to begin again.*) Stop!

PEG. All right. I've stopped. (*Rises, puts chair back, and goes round to table.*) I'll wipe out the whole of the Chichester family the next time you talk against my father, and that's my last word.

MRS. CHICHESTER (*to* ETHEL). Oh, it's hopeless. If I consent to take charge of you for another period will you promise me you will do your best to show some advancement during the next month?

PEG (*level with her*). Yes, Aunt.

MRS. CHICHESTER. And if I get fresh tutors for you will you try to keep them?

PEG. Yes. I will.

MRS. CHICHESTER (*to* ALARIC, *who has gone round back during foregoing, and is now seated on bench by* ETHEL). What do you think?

ALARIC. We might risk it, eh, Ethel?

ETHEL. Don't ask me.

MRS. CHICHESTER. Very well. Begin now. Get your books.

(JARVIS *enters.*)

PEG. Yes, Aunt. (*Hurriedly gets three books from piano and comes back to table.*)

MRS. CHICHESTER (*to* JARVIS). Well?

JARVIS. A letter for Miss Chichester. (*Hands it to* ETHEL.) By hand, Miss. No answer. (ETHEL *takes it unconcernedly, opens it and reads.* JARVIS *moves toward door.* PEG *slams book.*)

MRS. CHICHESTER (*starts*). Oh!

PEG. I beg your pardon. It shlipped out of my fist.

MRS. CHICHESTER. Fist!

PEG (*calls*). Jarvis! Michael's outside. He's had a fight. I'll be very much obliged if you'll put him to bed for me, please.

JARVIS. Yes, Miss. (*Exit.*)

PEG. That's a nice boy, Jarvis.

ALARIC. Boy, Ethel!

MRS. CHICHESTER (*by table*). Who's that from, Ethel?

ETHEL (*rising*). Mr. Brent.

(PEG *listens.*)

ALARIC. What on earth does *he* want?

ETHEL. He wants me to do something for him.

ALARIC. *Do* something?

ETHEL. Yes. I'll answer it here. (*Crosses over to writing-desk, sits, and writes.*)

MRS. CHICHESTER (*to* PEG). Margaret! Now, study for a little while. And do try to keep your hair out of your eyes. (*Business with curls.*)

PEG. Yes, Aunt.

MRS. CHICHESTER. Come, Alaric. (ALARIC *rises and crosses to table.* MRS. CHICHESTER *goes out.*)

ALARIC (*to* PEG). Original sin, eh? That's a good one!

PEG. I knew you would be the one to think it was good.

ALARIC. Study all the pretty maps. (*Leans over her.*) What's the population of Turkey?

PEG. There's going to be one less in England one day. (*Picks up book, grimaces, and looks threateningly at him.*)

ALARIC (*starts back*). Little devil!

PEG. He's tuggin' at me now. The little devil hates knowledge. He always tries to stop me gettin' any of it.

ALARIC (*laughs*). Ha! Ha! (*Glances across at* ETHEL.) Study your cousin. Model yourself on Ethel. Imitate her, eh, what? (*Hurries to door.* PEG *runs after him with book. Exits as she almost throws book at him. As* PEG *turns back from door he pops his head back into room, and laughs.*) Little devil! (PEG *goes for him again, but he shuts door again in time, and escapes.*)

(PEG *goes to table and sits watching* ETHEL, *who finishes her note, takes cigarette, and lights match. Imitating* ETHEL, PEG *puts down her book, takes cigarette and lights match.* ETHEL *sees* PEG *imitating her, gives impatient ejaculation, throws unlighted cigarette on ash-tray, and blows out match.* PEG, *still imitating her, does same.*)

ETHEL (*rising*). Why do you watch me?

PEG (*rising*). Aren't you my model? (*Mischievously. To front of table.* ETHEL *turns away angrily and starts upstairs.* PEG *goes to her.*) Ethel! I was only fooling. I was trying to have some fun. I was only trying to make you laugh. I want to talk to you.

ETHEL (*going up two stairs*). You were told to *study*.

PEG (*comes to newel-post. Pause*). Ye know we are both girls in the same house, of the same family, pretty much of the same age, and you've never said a kind word to me since I've been here. Ye like your dog better than me, don't ye? (ETHEL *fondles Pet.*) I'm sorry Michael hurt him. It was *my* fault. I set him on to do it.

ETHEL (*coming down to foot of stairs, turns to her*). You?

PEG (*at post back of table, nods*). I thought it was a rabbit at a distance. If a dog has got to be a dog it should be made to look like a dog. Ye'd know that Michael was a dog. (ETHEL *turns upstairs again.*) Ethel! I don't want to talk about dogs. Won't ye make friends with me? I want to ask ye something.

ETHEL (*goes up to third stair*). We have nothing in common.

PEG. That doesn't prevent us being decent to each other.

ETHEL (*pause*). Decent?

PEG. I'll meet ye threequarters of the way if ye'll only show one generous feeling toward me. (*Pause.*) Ye would if ye knew what was in my mind.

ETHEL (*goes to foot of stairs*). You're a strange creature.

PEG. You've got us mixed up. I'm not the strange one. *I'm* just what I am. I don't want to be anythin' else. But you, all of ye, are trying to be somethin' different from what ye are.

ETHEL (*by table*). What do you mean?

PEG (*by armchair beside table*). I watch ye and listen to ye. Ye turn yer face to the world as much as to say "Aren't I the easy-goin', sweet-tempered, calm young lady?" And ye're not quite that, are ye?

ETHEL. *What* am I? (*Sits at table.*)

PEG. Of course, ye've got the breedin' and the beautiful manners, but up in yer head and down in yer heart you worry your soul all the time. And ye have a temper. And it's a beautiful temper. It's a shame for ye not to let it out in the daylight so that every-one can see it. But ye can't, can ye? Because it's not good form. And with all yer fine advantages ye're not very happy, are ye? (ETHEL *turns her head away and down.*) Are ye, *dear*?

ETHEL (*slowly*). No. I'm not.

PEG. Nayther am I in this house. (*Pause.*) Couldn't we thry to comfort each other? (*Crosses to* ETHEL *at table.*)

ETHEL. *Comfort?* You?

PEG. Sure, a kindly impulse gives ye a warm feelin' around the heart, so they say. And ye'd have it if ye'd only be a little kind to me.

ETHEL (*rises, moved in spite of herself*). I'm afraid I *have* been a little inconsiderate.

PEG. Ye have.

ETHEL. What would you like me to do?

PEG. I'd like ye to spake to me as if I were a human bein', and not a clod of earth.

ETHEL. Very well, Margaret, I will.

PEG. Thank ye very much. (ETHEL *moves to go.* PEG *moves up, too.*) Ethel! I'd like very much to ask ye something else.

ETHEL (*turning back*). What is it? (*Comes back to table.*)

PEG (*close to* ETHEL). Do ye know anything about love?

ETHEL (*astonished*). *Love?*

PEG. Have ye ever been in love?

ETHEL (*puts letter slowly behind her back*). No.

PEG. Have ye ever thought about it?

ETHEL. Yes.

PEG (*turns to* ETHEL. *Eagerly*). What do ye think about it?

ETHEL. Rot! (*Comes down to front of bench, looks at letter.*)

PEG (*following her down*). Rot, is it?

ETHEL (*sits on bench*). Sentimental nonsense that exists only in novels.

PEG (*excitedly*). Ye're wrong. It's the most wonderful thing in the world. To love a good man who loves you. A man who made ye hot-and-cold, burnin' like fire one minute, and freezin' like ice the next. Who made yer heart leap with happiness when he came near ye, and ache with sorrow when he went away from ye. Haven't ye ever felt that?

ETHEL. Never.

PEG. Oh! It's mighty disturbin', so it is. (*Sits beside* ETHEL.) One day ye walk on air, and the next yer feet are like lead. One day the world's all beautiful flowers and sweet music and sunshine, and the next day it's all coffins and corpses. (*Shaking her head.*) It's mighty disturbin', so it is.

ETHEL. How do you know all this?

PEG (*hurriedly*). I read about it in a great, big book.

ETHEL. When you're a little older you'll think differently. You'll realize it's all very primitive.

PEG. Primitive?

ETHEL. Of the earth, earthy.

PEG (*suddenly*). Don't you like men?

ETHEL. Not much.

PEG (*at end of couch*). Just dogs?

ETHEL (*opposite end of couch*). You can trust them. (*Caresses Pet.*)

PEG. I like dogs, too. But I like children very much better. (*Suddenly.*) Wouldn't ye like to have a child of yer own?

ETHEL (*horrified*). Really, Margaret!

PEG. Well, I would. And that's the woman in us. Ye only fondle that thing—(*pointing to Pet*)—because ye haven't got a chick to call yer own. All the selfish women have dogs. They're afraid to have children. I like dogs, too. They're all very well in their way, but sure they can't laugh to ye, and cry to ye, and comfort ye, like a baby can. (*Points to

Pet.) Ye know, that thing could never be President of the United States. But if ye had a child he might grow up to be President.

ETHEL. That's very Irish.

PEG. It's very human, too. I wish you were a little more Irish. I think we'd get along better, I do.

ETHEL (*rises*). It is not customary for girls to talk about such things.

PEG. I know it isn't, and I can't understand why we shouldn't discuss events of national importance. I know it's not customary. We think about them—why can't we talk about them? If there was more honesty in the world there would be less sin.

ETHEL. Please, Margaret. (*Turning.*)

PEG (*rises and crosses to* ETHEL). Now, let *us* be honest with each other.

ETHEL. What do you mean?

PEG. You like Mr. Brent, don't ye?

ETHEL (*instinctively puts letter behind her back*). Certainly, I do. He's a very old friend of the family.

PEG. He has a wife?

ETHEL. He has.

PEG. He has a baby?

ETHEL. Well——!

PEG. Of course, I've never seen them. He never brings them along with him when he calls on you, but ye'd know he had 'em if ye ever heard Alaric ask after 'em.

ETHEL. What of that?

PEG. Is it customary for English husbands with babies to kiss other women—— (ETHEL *turns on her.*) Well, let us say, to kiss other women's hands?

ETHEL (*pause. Checks her anger*). It is a very old and very respected custom.

PEG. Devil doubt it it's *old*. I'm not so sure about the respect. Why doesn't he kiss my aunt when he comes to this house?

ETHEL. Oh! You don't understand. (*Crosses to foot of stairs.*)

PEG. I know I don't, but I'm trying to.

ETHEL (*at foot of stairs*). I suppose it is too much to expect that a child of the common people should understand the customs of *decent* people.

PEG. Why should the *common people* have all the decency and why should the aristocracy have *none* of the decency. (ETHEL *goes to stairs and up two steps.* PEG, *at foot of stairs, looks at her.*) Don't get mad. I didn't mean it. I've heard my father say that in one of his speeches, and it came to my tongue first thing.

ETHEL (*up third stair, indignantly*). Oh! Be good enough never to speak to me again as long as you're in this house. (*Enter* JARVIS.) If I had my way you'd leave it this moment. As it is—as it is—(*Looks at letter.* PEG *to front of table.* JARVIS *shows in* JERRY, *who is in evening-dress, light summer overcoat, and Homburg hat.*

ETHEL *shakes hands with* JERRY.) How do you do? Excuse me just a moment. Wait, JARVIS. (*Goes to writing-desk, tears envelope open, adds a postscript, addresses another envelope, and seals it. The moment* JERRY *enters* PEG'S *face lights up. She gives him her hand.*)

JERRY. Well, and how is Miss Peg?

PEG. Oh! I'm fine, Mr. Jerry. How are you? Let me take yer hat and coat.

JERRY. No, thank you. I'm not going to stay.

PEG (*disappointedly*). Ye're not?

JERRY. Is your aunt in?

PEG. Yes. Are you calling on her?

JERRY. Yes.

ETHEL (*rises, hands letter to* JARVIS). Send that, please.

(*Exit* JARVIS.)

JERRY (*bringing* ETHEL *into the scene*). I've come to ask your mother if she would let you both come to a dance tonight across at the Assembly Rooms.

ETHEL. I'm sorry. I can't go. I have a headache. (*Turns and crosses to door.*)

JERRY. What a pity! Do you suppose your mother would allow Miss Margaret to go?

ETHEL (*stops and turns*). I'll ask her. (*Goes to door.*)

PEG (*impulsively runs to her. In undertone*). I didn't mean to hurt ye. (ETHEL *exits.* PEG *comes back ruefully and sits on couch, after which* JERRY *puts hat and coat on chair by table.*)

JERRY. What's the matter?

PEG (*sits back of couch*). I tell you, one of us girls has been brought up all wrong. I tried to make friends with her, but only made her hopping-mad, as I make everybody else in this house. The minute I open my mouth away they go.

JERRY. Aren't you friends?

PEG. No. We're not. None of them are with me.

JERRY. What a shame!

PEG. Wait until ye hear me aunt when ye ask her about the dance.

JERRY. Don't you think she will let you go?

PEG. No. I know she won't let me go. I know that. The question is—are we going? (*Determinedly, rises and goes to him.*) I want to go to that dance, Jerry.

JERRY. Why, Peg——

PEG. I do want to go to that dance. I'm crazy mad to go to that dance.

(JERRY *shakes his head.*)

JERRY. We'll ask your aunt.

PEG. I know we will. We'll ask her tomorrow.

JERRY. No. We'll ask her tonight.

PEG. Don't let's take any chances. I do want to go that dance, Jerry.

JERRY. No, Peg, no.

PEG. Well, if you think I'm going to let a dance get by me you're very much mistaken. When the lights are all out and they're all asleep I'll creep down the stairs and meet you at the foot of the path. And if it goes against your tender conscience to take me—I'll take you—and that's how we'll settle that.

JERRY (*laughing*). But there may not be any occasion to do any such wild, foolish thing. Your aunt may be delighted.

PEG. My aunt doesn't know how to spell that.

JERRY (*sits on table, looking at books*). Are these your books? How are your studies progressing?

PEG. The way they always have. They're standing still. I can't see the sense of learnin' the heights of a lot of mountains I'm never goin' to climb. And I want to tell you, I'm surprised at my aunt allowing me to read about the doings of those dead kings. I think Charles II was a devil.

JERRY. They made history.

PEG. Did they? Well, they ought to have been ashamed of themselves. I don't care how high Mont Blanc is, and I don't care when William the Conqueror landed in England.

JERRY. Oh, nonsense——

PEG. And I tell ye, I hate yer English history—it makes all my Irish blood boil, so it does. "What is England? Do you know what it is? It's a bit of a counthry that's tramplin' down a fine race like ours." That's what my father says, and that's how my father says it, with his fist, and nobody ever contradicts him either.

(JERRY *laughs.*)

JERRY. Is it fair to your aunt?

PEG (*sullenly*). I don't know.

JERRY. Is it fair to yourself?

PEG. That sounds like my aunt, that does.

JERRY. You'll be at such a disadvantage by-and-by with other girls with half your intelligence just because they know the things you refuse to learn. Then you'll be ashamed.

PEG. Are *you* ashamed of me?

JERRY. Not a bit.

PEG. You're not ashamed of me, are ye?

JERRY. Of course not.

PEG. Then everything's all right then. What's the matter? (*Goes to piano and sits on stool.*)

JERRY. I was just the same at your age. (*Crosses to armchair.*) I used to scamp at school and shirk at college until I found myself so far behind fellows I despised that I was ashamed. Then I went after them tooth and nail until I caught them up and passed them. (*Kneels on chair.*)

PEG (*eagerly*). Did ye now?

JERRY. I did.

PEG. I am going to do that, too.

JERRY. Will you?

PEG (*nods vigorously*). From now on I'm going to learn everything they teach me, if it kills me.

JERRY. I wish you would.

PEG. And after I know more than anybody else in all the world ever knew are you going to be very proud of me? (*Wistfully.*)

JERRY (*kneeling on armchair.*) Very. Even more than I am now.

PEG. Are ye proud of me now?

JERRY. Yes, Peg, proud to think you're my friend.

PEG. Faith, that's not news. I know very well that we're friends.

JERRY. I am *yours.*

PEG. Sure, I guess I'm yours all right. (*Looks at him, laughs shyly, presses her cheeks.*) Did ye ever hear what Tom Moore wrote about friendship?

JERRY. No.

PEG (*excitedly*). Would ye like to hear what Tom Moore wrote about friendship?

JERRY. Yes.

PEG. See if anybody's comin'. (JERRY *crosses to stairs and listens.* PEG *starts playing.*)

JERRY (*crosses to armchair*). Oho! So you play?

PEG (*nods, laughing*). A little bit. My father taught me. But my aunt can't bear it. Do you know what the teacher here told me? She said I should do this—(*plays scale*)—for two years. I should do that before I played a tune. I told her I played by ear. She said I had no ear.

JERRY (*looking at her ears*). I think they're very pretty.

PEG. Do ye?

JERRY. I do.

PEG. Well, you watch them, and then you won't mind my singin'. Come on over in Jarvis' high-chair. (JERRY *crosses to chair below piano.* PEG *smiles up at him.*) About a girl, this is, who built a shrine. And she thought the best thing in the world to put in it was an image of "*Friendship.*"

JERRY. Yes.

PEG. Yes. You see she was like you. She thought there was nothing in the world as nice as friendship.

JERRY. Yes.

PEG. Yes. And this is what happened to her. (*Laughs a little elfish laugh, and then croons softly.*)

"She flew to a sculptor, who set
 down before her
A 'Friendship,' the fairest his art
 could invent.
But so cold and so dull that this
 Youthful adorer
Saw plainly that was not the
 Friendship she meant.

(*Sings.*)

"'Oh, never,' she cried, 'could I think of enshrining
An image whose looks are so joyless and dim,
But yon little Cupid—(*Points to Cupid.*)
—midst roses reclining,
We'll make, if you please, sir, a Friendship of him.'"

A Friendship of Cupid. (JERRY *looks at the statuette.* PEG *nods, smiling, and excitedly sings.*)

"'Farewell,' said the sculptor, 'Sure, you're not the first maiden
Who came but for Friendship and took away—

(*Pause.*)

Love.'"

(*Her voice dies away to a whisper.*)

JERRY (*amazed*). Where in the world did you learn that?

PEG. My father taught me that. Tom Moore's my father's prayer-book.

JERRY (*rises*). "Who came but for Friendship and took away Love."

PEG (*on piano-stool*). Isn't that beautiful?

JERRY. Is there anything better than friendship between man and woman?

PEG. Of course there is. (*Nods, goes to him.*) My father felt it toward my mother or I wouldn't be here now.

JERRY. Could you ever feel it, Peg?

(PEG *nods.*)

PEG. I wish I'd studied—I'd be more worthy of——(*Suddenly breaking off.* JERRY *turns to her.* PEG *covering up what is in her mind and on her tongue.*) I'm just an Irish nothing.

JERRY. Don't say that.

PEG. Yet I'm sure there is something good in me, but the bad little something always beats the good little something out, so it does.

JERRY. What you call the bad in you is just the cry of youth that resents being curbed, and the good in you is the *woman* struggling for an outlet.

PEG. Will you help me to give it an outlet, Mr. Jerry?

JERRY. Yes. In every way in my power.

PEG (*roguishly*). Well, would ye mind very much if the bad little something had just one more *spurt* before I killed it altogether.

JERRY. What do you mean?

PEG. I want to go to the dance. It's the last bad thing I'll ask you to let me do. I'll behave like a Saint from Heaven after that. I'll die happy if I can waltz once around the floor with you. (*Pleading. Dances up to him, and waltzes round him. Enter* MRS. CHICHESTER, *who looks at* PEG *in horrified amazement.*)

MRS. CHICHESTER. Oh! What does this mean?

JERRY (*crossing to* MRS. CHICHESTER). I want you to do something that will make the child very happy. Will you allow her to go to a dance at the Assembly Rooms tonight?

MRS. CHICHESTER. Certainly not. I'm surprised at your asking such a thing.

PEG (*sits armchair*). I could have told you that backwards.

JERRY (*straightening up*). I asked Ethel as well, but she can't go, as she's got a headache. I thought you might be pleased at giving your niece a *little* pleasure.

MRS. CHICHESTER. Go to a dance? Unchaperoned?

JERRY. My mother and sisters will be there.

MRS. CHICHESTER. A child of her age!

PEG (*vehemently*). A child of my age! My father lets me go any place I want to ever since I was six. Ye can't raise the Irish on a lot of books. It's never been done. They'll die on yer hands, they will. I'm crazy mad to go to that dance.

MRS. CHICHESTER. No, Margaret.

PEG. I'll study my head off in the morning if ye'll let me dance my feet off a little bit tonight.

MRS. CHICHESTER. No.

PEG (*pleadingly*). I ask ye on my bended knees—please let me go to the dance.

MRS. CHICHESTER. No, Margaret. No.

PEG. All right. I give ye fair warning, I'm going to the dance.

MRS. CHICHESTER (*to* JERRY). It was very good of you to trouble to come over. Forgive me if I seem ungracious, but it's quite out of the question.

(PEG *winks at* JERRY *behind* MRS. CHICHESTER'S *back, and rises.*)

JERRY (*gets hat and coat from chair*). I'm sorry. (*Shakes hands with* MRS. CHICHESTER.)

MRS. CHICHESTER. Kindly remember me to your mother and sisters.

JERRY. With pleasure. Good night! (*Goes to door.*)

PEG. Good night, Mr. Jerry. (*Pantomimes* JERRY *that she will be down to meet him and go to the dance after they're all in bed.* MRS. CHICHESTER *looking round and seeing her making signs,* PEG *pretends to be catching a fly. Exit* JERRY.)

MRS. CHICHESTER. What do you mean by twirling around in that disgraceful way? Are you ever going to learn how to behave?

PEG. Yes, Aunt. I'm never going to annoy you after tonight. I'm going to work very hard, too,—after tonight. Don't ye see what a disadvantage I'd be at with other girls of half my age and half my intelligence. I'm going after them tooth and nail, and I'll catch them up and pass them, and then he'll be proud of me, he will.

MRS. CHICHESTER. What?

PEG. Ye'll be proud of me, I said, ye will.

MRS. CHICHESTER. What is all this?

PEG. It's what I'm going to do—*after tonight.*

MRS. CHICHESTER. Well, I'm very glad to hear it.

PEG. I knew ye would be. And I'll never be any trouble to ye—*after to-night.*

MRS. CHICHESTER. I hope you will be of the same opinion in the morning.

PEG. I hope so, too. D'ye mind very much if I sit up for an hour——

MRS. CHICHESTER. What?

PEG. Study, I mean.

(MRS. CHICHESTER *crosses to piano.*)

MRS. CHICHESTER. Study just one hour. That will be very nice.

(PEG *goes to back of table, sits, and opens atlas.*)

PEG. Are you going to bed now?

MRS. CHICHESTER. Yes.

PEG. Everybody in the house going to bed now?

MRS. CHICHESTER. Yes. Everybody. (*Shuts piano, goes up and closes windows, turns off hall lamp.*)

PEG. That's good. (*Sings song.*)

"Man, dear, I remember when coming home the rain began.
I wrapped my frieze coat round her, and devil a waistcoat had I on.
My shirt was rather fine-drawn, but, oh, the false and cruel one.
For all o' that she's gone and left me here for to die."

MRS. CHICHESTER. Where on earth did you hear a song like that?

PEG. That's a fine song, that is. That's my father's best song. An Irish song, that is.

MRS. CHICHESTER. I should think it was. (*Closes curtains.*)

PEG. It has twenty-two verses.

MRS. CHICHESTER. (*Comes down to* PEG.) Has it, indeed?

PEG. Yes. I know them all, too. (*Sings again.*)

"Man, dear, and did ye never hear of pretty Molly Brannigan?
Faith, and she has left me, and I'll never be a man again."

MRS. CHICHESTER. Now, now! Don't make any noise.

PEG. That's not a noise. That's my best singing. That's very discouraging to a young singer.

MRS. CHICHESTER. Good night, Margaret. And, oh, if only you would keep your hair out of your eyes.

PEG. Well, why don't you let me wear one of your fishnets? (MRS. CHICHESTER *goes upstairs saying "Fishnets!"* PEG *calling.*) Oh, Aunt!

MRS. CHICHESTER. Yes?

PEG. Do you remember I said I had to be getting back home? Well, I've changed my mind. I'd like to stay here another month, please.

MRS. CHICHESTER (*top of stairs*). Well, we'll talk it over with Mr. Hawkes in the morning.

(*Warning.*)

PEG. Yes, Aunt.

MRS. CHICHESTER. Good night, Margaret.

PEG. God bless you. (*Exit* MRS. CHICHESTER. *Business. Sings.*)

"The left side of my carcass is as
    weak as water-gruel, man.
There's not a pick upon my bones
    since Molly's proved so cruel,
    man.
And if I had a blunder-gun I'd go
    and fight a duel, man.
'Tis better I should shoot myself
    than live here to die."

(*Or*)

"The place where my heart was you
    could easy roll a turnip in.
'Tis as wide as old Dublin, and
    from Dublin to the Devil's Glyn.
If she wished to take another, sure,
    she might have left mine back
    again,
And not have gone and left me here
    alone for to die."

(ETHEL *enters, goes upstairs, and exits without a word as* PEG *sings.*)

"I'm cool and determined as any Al-
    exander man
Will ye come to my wake when I go
    the long meander, man?"

Hello, Ethel! (*Mimics* ETHEL.) "How do ye do, Margaret?" "I'm studying for an hour." (*Turning leaves of atlas.*) "I'm trying to find England." (*Pauses.*) "Good night, Ethel." "Good night, Margaret, dear." "Sleep tight, Ethel." "Oh, that's all right, Margaret." "Don't mention it, Ethel." (*Mimics* ALARIC.) "What's the population of Turkey? Ye little devil! Study all the pretty maps. Model yourself on Ethel. Sit down like Ethel." (*Noise with mouth. Goes and pulls curtains open. Clock strikes nine.*) I wonder if he's coming back. (*Comes down and sits chair by table. Mimics* MRS. CHICHESTER *and* JERRY.) "Go to a dance unchaperoned? Oh, no. Not unchaperoned." "My mother and sisters will be there. Eh, what? What, what?" "Go to a dance? A child of her age? Margaret, I'm surprised. No, sir. No dance. Not until she's—eighty."

Curtain falls for about ten seconds.

(*As soon as curtain is down start music under stage.*)

CURTAIN

(*Curtain rises. Dance music "Valse Mauve" heard faintly in the distance.* JERRY *enters, goes to stairs, listens, then turns back.*)

JERRY. It's all right. (PEG *enters, goes to stairs, listens, then comes to* JERRY, *who has gone to piano and put down his hat.*)

PEG. Oh, I'm so happy! So happy! The whole world's goin' round in one grand waltz, and it's all been through you, Mr. Jerry. (*Dances to the distant music.*)

JERRY. I'm glad it's been through me, Peg.

PEG. I don't see why it can't all be like this. Why can't we laugh and dance our way through it all?

JERRY. I wish I could make the world one great ballroom for you.

PEG. And no creepin' back like a thief in the night!

JERRY. No—your own mistress, free to do whatever you wish.

PEG (*suddenly, with a little elfish laugh*). Yet, you know, half the fun tonight has been that while I'm supposed to be sleepin' upstairs I've been at the dance stealin' time. Do ye know "the best of all ways to lengthen your days"?

JERRY. No.

PEG. "It's to steal a few hours from the night, my dear."

JERRY (*by piano*). Well, you've stolen them.

PEG. I'm a thief, I am.

JERRY. No. You're the sweetest, dearest—— (*Bends over her, checks himself, goes to piano for hat.*) I think you'd better go to bed now.

PEG. I know that. But what were ye goin' to say to me?

JERRY. Something it would be better to say in daylight.

PEG. But why in the daylight, with the beautiful bright moon so high in the heavens?

JERRY. Go now. Someone may hear us.

PEG. I'll not sleep a wink thinkin' of all the wonderful things that have happened this night. Must I go?

JERRY. You must.

PEG. With the music coming in across the lawn?

JERRY. Someone might come.

PEG. And the moon so high in the heavens?

JERRY. I don't want to cause you any trouble.

PEG. That's a grand moon, so it is.

JERRY. Go, Peg, go.

PEG. All right. I suppose you do know best, but that's a magnificent moon. Good night, Mr. Jerry.

JERRY. Good night, Peg. (*Kisses her hand. She gives a little sigh and looks at her hand. Footsteps are heard in the garden.*) Take care! Someone is coming. (*Goes out.* PEG *sits on stairs, hiding behind newel post.* BRENT *appears outside opening.*) Hello, Brent!

BRENT. Why, what in the world——?

JERRY. Ssh! The house is asleep.

BRENT. So I see.

JERRY. Just coming from the dance? I didn't see you there.

BRENT. No. I was restless, and just strolled here.

JERRY (*takes* BRENT'S *arm*). Shall we go along to the road together?

BRENT. Right——

JERRY. *Strolled* here? Why, you've got your car.

BRENT. Car? Yes. It's a bright night for a spin. (*They disappear.*)

(PEG *remains in the same position till they are out of hearing, then she creeps up the stairs. At the top she starts back, and* ETHEL *appears, fully dressed, carrying a small dressing-bag.* ETHEL *waits to come down till* PEG *is nearly at the top of the stairs.*)

PEG. Ethel!

ETHEL (*at head of stairs. In guarded tones*). Go down into the room. (PEG *goes downstairs.* ETHEL *following her to front of table.*)

PEG (*front of table*). Ye won't tell your mother, will ye? She'd send me away, and I don't want to go away now. I've been to the dance.

ETHEL. To the dance?

PEG. Yes. Mr. Jerry took me.

ETHEL. Jerry?

PEG. Yes. Ye won't tell your mother, will ye? (*Backing*).

ETHEL (*following*). I most certainly shall see that my mother knows it.

PEG. You will?

ETHEL. I will. You had no right to go.

PEG. Why are you so hard on me, Ethel?

ETHEL. Because I detest you.

PEG. I'm sorry. Ye've spoilt all my pleasure now, so you have. (*Starts to stairs and goes slowly up. Stops, thinks, looks at* ETHEL.) Wait a minute! What are you doin' yourself with your hat and coat on at this time of night? (*Coming back.*)

ETHEL (*turning to* PEG). Go to your room!

PEG. Were you goin' away?

ETHEL. Keep your voice down.

PEG. *He* was here a minute ago—Jerry took him away.

ETHEL. Who was here?

PEG. Mr. Brent was here. (ETHEL *starts.* PEG *grips her wrist.*) Were ye goin' away with him? Were ye?

ETHEL. Take your hands off me.

PEG. Were ye? Answer me.

ETHEL. Yes. And I *am*.

PEG (*turns* ETHEL *round*). No, ye're not.

ETHEL. Let me go.

PEG. Ye're not going out of this house tonight if I have to wake everyone in it.

ETHEL (*front of table*). Wake them! They can't stop me. Nothing can stop me now. I'm sick of this living on charity, sick of meeting you every day—an implied insult in your every tone and look, as much as to say, "I'm giving you your daily bread, I'm keeping the roof over you." I'm sick of it, and I end it tonight. Let me go, or I'll—I'll—— (*Starts.*)

PEG. What d'ye mean, I'm keepin' the roof over ye, I'm givin' ye yer daily bread? What are ye ravin' about?

ETHEL. I'm at the end tonight. I'm going—— (*Struggles with* PEG.)

PEG. And what d'ye suppose ye'd be agoin' to? A wakin' and sleepin' hell, sure!

ETHEL. *I'm* going.

PEG. Ye'd take him from his wife and her baby?

ETHEL. He hates them, and I hate *this*. And I'm going——

PEG. So ye'd break yer mother's heart and his wife's just to satisfy yer own selfish pleasures? Well, I'm glad I sinned tonight in doin' what I wanted to do, since it's given me the chance to save *you* from doin' the most shameful thing a woman ever did.

ETHEL (*turns*). Will you——?

PEG. Ye'll stay here if I have to wake up the whole world.

ETHEL (*frightenedly*). No, no, you mustn't do that!

PEG. Ye just told me yer own mother couldn't stop ye.

ETHEL. She mustn't know! She mustn't know! (*Sobs.*) Let me go. He's waiting. (*Moves forward.*)

PEG. You let him wait. He gave his name and his life to a woman, and it's your duty to protect her and the child she brought him.

ETHEL. I'd kill myself first.

PEG. Not first. That's what would happen to ye after ye'd gone with him. He'd lave ye in an hour to sorrow alone. Doesn't he want to leave the woman he swore to cherish at the altar of God? What do ye suppose he'd do to one he took no oath with at all? You have some sense about this. And I want to tell ye it's no compliment the man's payin' ye either. Faith, he'd have made love to me if I'd let him.

ETHEL (*turns to* PEG *slowly*). What? To you?

PEG. If ye hadn't come in when ye did today I'd have taught him a lesson he'd have carried to his grave, so I would.

ETHEL (*crossing to* PEG). He tried to make love to you?

PEG. A dozen times since I've been in yer house. And today he walked toward me with his arms outstretched, saying, "Come. Let's kiss and be friends," and in you came.

ETHEL (*coming forward*). Is that true?

PEG. On my poor mother's memory that's true, so it is.

ETHEL. Oh! The wretch! The wretch! (*Sinks in chair by table, drops bag.*)

PEG. That's what he is. And ye'd give yer life into his keepin' to blacken so that no decent man or woman would ever look at ye again.

ETHEL. No. That's over. It's over. I hate myself. Oh, how I hate myself! (*Crying and sobbing.*)

PEG (*In a moment all pity*). Ethel! Acushla! Don't cry. Don't do that. Don't. Don't ye know he's not worth it? Don't ye know ye've got to kape yer life and yer heart clean till the one man in all the world comes to ye, and then ye'll know what real happiness means. Don't cry, dear. (ETHEL *buries her face in her hands to deaden the sobs.* PEG *beside her, comforting her.* ETHEL *still crying.*) Well, then, cry. And may the salt of yer tears wash away the sins of this night and fall like holy water on yer soul! And with the sunlight the thought of all this will go from ye. Come to my room and I'll sit by yer side till morning. (PEG *helps her up.* ETHEL, *on the verge of fainting, picks up bag, her body trembling with suppressed sobs, totters.* PEG *walks her across to staircase.*) I don't know at all how you could think of going away with a married man, Ethel.

ETHEL (*cries*). Oh, Margaret!

PEG. Ssh, dear! You'll wake yer mother up. Not a sound! Not a sound now! We'll talk when we get upstairs. Aisy now! (*Both creep up the stairs. When they are almost at the top* PEG *slips and rolls all the way to the bottom, knocking over a brass jardiniere at the top of the stairs, which rolls all the way down.* PEG *rises, runs across to* R. *corner.* ETHEL *follows her.* PEG *listens.*)

PEG. Holy Mary!

ETHEL. What shall we do? What shall we do?

PEG. Well, that's all I'm going to do, I tell you. If that doesn't wake them up they're sleeping the sleep of the dead.

(*Voices off stage.*)

ALARIC (*off*). Hello, Mater! Did you hear it, too? Etc.——

MRS. CHICHESTER (*off*). Oh, Alaric! A most fearful crash! Etc.——

ETHEL. Oh, what shall we do, Margaret? What shall we do?

PEG. Give me your hat and coat, and sit in that chair. (*Takes off her cap and cloak and puts on* ETHEL'S *hat and coat.*) I'll do all the talking, though what the devil I'll say I don't know. Don't you say a word. Your mother mustn't know you were going out of the house with that man. It would break her heart. Where's your bag? (*Takes bag quickly from* ETHEL. *Door opens and* JARVIS *enters.* MRS. CHICHESTER *and* ALARIC *coming down the stairs with candles,* MRS. CHICHESTER *in wrapper,* ALARIC *in dressing-gown.*)

ALARIC. It's all right, Mater. Don't be frightened. I'm not a bit timid. Thank God you've got a man in the house.

JARVIS. Who's there? (ALARIC *moves carefully, collides with* JARVIS, *and takes him by the throat.*)

ALARIC. Ah! I've got you!

JARVIS. It's only me, sir.

ALARIC. Oh, get out of the way, Jarvis. (JARVIS *exits.* ALARIC *moves slowly, flashing his light all over the room.*) Now then, come out! Where are you? (*Sees the two girls.*) Ethel!

MRS. CHICHESTER. Margaret!

ALARIC. Well! I mean to say! What I want to know is—(*switches on lights.* ETHEL *is discovered very white and tear-stained in the chair,* PEG *standing beside her, wearing* ETHEL'S *coat and hat and carrying her hand-bag in her right hand*)—what are you two girls playing at?

MRS. CHICHESTER (*to* PEG). What does this mean?

PEG. Sure, I was going out, and when I came in Ethel said to me——

MRS. CHICHESTER. Where were you going?

PEG. I was going out, and—when I came in—Ethel said to me——

MRS. CHICHESTER. Where were you going?

PEG. I was going out, I said, and—Ethel came in——

MRS. CHICHESTER. Why, that's Ethel's cloak.

PEG. I got her hat on, too. And I've got her bag. (*Trying to distract* MRS. CHICHESTER'S *attention from* ETHEL, *who is half-fainting, puts bag on corner of table.*)

MRS. CHICHESTER. Her bag! Ethel's bag! (*Opens bag, takes out wash-leather bag.*) Her jewel-bag!

PEG. Jewel-bag!

MRS. CHICHESTER. Where did you get this?

PEG. I took them.

MRS. CHICHESTER. You took them?

PEG. Yes. I took them.

MRS. CHICHESTER. You were *stealing them?*

PEG. No. I wasn't stealing them. I took 'em.

MRS. CHICHESTER. *Why* did you take them?

PEG. I wanted to wear them.

MRS. CHICHESTER. *Wear* them?

PEG. I always had an idea I should like to wear Ethel's jewels and her hat and coat.

MRS. CHICHESTER. At this time of night?

PEG (*jumping at the explanation*). I went to the dance, I did.

MRS. CHICHESTER. *What* dance?

PEG. I went to the dance with Mr. Jerry, and I thought it would be a good chance to wear Ethel's jewels and her hat and coat. So I put on her hat and coat, and I wore her jewels, and I went to the dance, and when I came back I made a noise, and Ethel heard me. She put on some clothes and came downstairs and said, "Where have you been?" I said, "I've been to the dance with Mr. Jerry." She said, "You'd better go to bed," and I said, "All right," and I started up the stairs, and some noisy thing came all the way down and forninst me.

ALARIC (*crosses back of table to arch*). There's someone prowling in the garden.

MRS. CHICHESTER. Oh, Alaric! (*Puts back jewel-bag and closes hand-bag.*)

ALARIC. He's on the path.

ETHEL (*rises, but sits again as* PEG *soothes her*). Mr. Brent!

ALARIC. He's coming here. Don't be frightened, Mater. I'll deal with him. (ETHEL *straightens up, her eyes distended.* PEG *grips her hand to quiet her.*) Now, then! What do you want here? Good Lord! Jerry!

(*Music Valse Mauve begins again very faint in the distance. Enter* JERRY.)

JERRY. I saw your lights go up and I ran back. I guessed something like this had happened. Don't be hard on your niece. The whole thing was entirely my fault. I asked her to go.

MRS. CHICHESTER. You took my niece to a dance in spite of my absolute refusal to allow her to go?

PEG. He had nothing to do with it all. I took him to the dance, I did. I took him.

MRS. CHICHESTER. Surely Sir Gerald Adair knows better than to take a girl of eighteen to a public ball without the sanction of her relatives?

PEG. Sir Gerald? (*To* JERRY.) So you have a title, have yez?

JERRY. Yes, Peg.

MRS. CHICHESTER. Now I hope you realize what you've done.

PEG. I am just beginning to realize what I've done, so I am.

MRS. CHICHESTER. You've disgraced us all.

PEG (*fiercely*). Have I?

MRS. CHICHESTER. I'm ashamed of you.

PEG. Are you? Well, I'm going back to my father, who's never ashamed of me. Everything I do is right because I do it. I've disgraced you, have I? There's not one of you in this house will tell the truth to me—(*to* JERRY) —and I'm going back to my father.

MRS. CHICHESTER. Well, go back to your father.

PEG (*starts forward angrily to* MRS. CHICHESTER). I've never been mad about your house.

ETHEL (*hysterically. Rising from chair*). No, no! Wait! Don't go. Mother, we are not treating her fairly. You found her here tonight because—because——(*Faints in chair. General movement.* PEG *bends over her.*)

PEG. She's fainted. Get some water and some smelling-salts. (JERRY *exits for water.*)

ALARIC (*runs upstairs*). Smelling-salts.

MRS. CHICHESTER (*comes running over to chair*). Ethel?

PEG (*hysterically*). That's all right. What help can you be to her now that she's fainted, I'd like to know. You don't know how to raise her. You don't know one thought in your daughter's mind. You don't know who she sees or who she goes with.

Why don't you try to find out something about your own child once in a while? A lot you know about motherhood! My father knows more about motherhood than any man in the world.

FIRST CURTAIN

(JERRY *comes in with water, hands it to* MRS. CHICHESTER, ALARIC *comes downstairs with smelling-salts.*)

SECOND CURTAIN

ACT THREE

SCENE—*Same as Act One. N. B. Same flowers as in Act Two, a few fallen leaves on table and floor (on writing desk wild flowers).*

TIME: *Next morning.*

DISCOVERED: ALARIC *sitting on window-seat up at back reading a newspaper.*

(*Enter* MRS. CHICHESTER, *pale and weary, from upstairs.*)

ALARIC (*jumps up, puts down paper, meets* MRS. CHICHESTER *at foot of stairs*). Mornin', Mater. (*Kisses her on forehead.*) How are you feelin'?

MRS. CHICHESTER (*crossing him to table*). I didn't close my eyes all night.

ALARIC. Isn't that rotten? I was a bit plungy myself. You know—first one side and then the other. (*Yawns.*)

MRS. CHICHESTER (*sits*). What is to be done?

ALARIC (*stretching his arms*). Get in forty winks during the day, I suppose.

MRS. CHICHESTER. I mean about Margaret.

ALARIC. Oh! The little devil. (*Crosses and sits on couch.*) Nothin' that I can see. She's got it into her stubborn little head that she means to leave us, and that's the end of it.

MRS. CHICHESTER. And the end of our income.

ALARIC. Well, you were a bit rough on her, Mater. Now I come to think, we've all been a bit rough on her, except me. I did make her laugh once or twice. Poor little soul! After all, suppose she did want to dance. What's the use of fussing? Let her, I say. Let her dance. Let her dance.

MRS. CHICHESTER. A child of her age?

ALARIC. Child! Why, in America they're grown women with families at her age.

MRS. CHICHESTER. Thank Heaven they're not in England.

ALARIC. No. But they will be, Mater. They're kickin' over the traces every day. One time they kept to the pavement. Now they're out in the middle of the road, and in thousands. What ho!

MRS. CHICHESTER. Yes. That's true.

ALARIC. Bless me, yes. I know it's true. I've met 'em. And some of 'em were *rippers*. Why, there's one little woman I know—well, when I say little—she's—she's—you might say magnificent——

MRS. CHICHESTER. Oh, Alaric——

ALARIC. Well, perhaps you're right.

MRS. CHICHESTER. And just when I had begun to have some hope of her.

ALARIC. Who?

MRS. CHICHESTER. Why, Margaret.

ALARIC. Oh! The imp. (*Rises and goes to back of table.*) Well, I never did. Not a hope. I've always felt she ought to have the inscription on dear old Shakespeare's grave waving in front of her all the time. How does it go? You know, Mater. "Good friend, for goodness sake forbear."

MRS. CHICHESTER. But under *our* influence—in time——

ALARIC. *No,* no, Mater. Peg will always be a Peter Pan. (*Crosses around table.*) She'll never grow up. She'd play elfish tricks if she had a nursery full of infants.

MRS. CHICHESTER. Some good man, some day, might change that.

ALARIC. Ah! But where is he? No. Back she goes today, and off I go tomorrow to work.

MRS. CHICHESTER. Oh, Alaric.

ALARIC. Must hold the roof up, Mater, and pacify the tradesmen. (*Sits on table.*)

MRS. CHICHESTER (*with a sudden thought*). Alaric!

ALARIC. Yes?

MRS. CHICHESTER. Do you *like* her?

ALARIC. Oh, here and there. She amuses me like anything at times. She drew a map of Europe the other day that was the most fearful and wonderful thing I ever saw. Looked like some marvellous sin. Mostly Ireland.

MRS. CHICHESTER (*rising*). Oh, my boy!

ALARIC. What is it? (*Rises.*) You're not going to cry?

MRS. CHICHESTER (*weeps*). Oh, if you only could!

ALARIC. *Could? What?*

MRS. CHICHESTER. Take that little wayward child into your life and mould her.

ALARIC. Me?

MRS. CHICHESTER. Yes.

ALARIC. No, Mater. I can do most things, but as a "Moulder" oh, no. Let Ethel do it. (*Moves away.*)

MRS. CHICHESTER (*following him*). I mean to take her really into your life—to have and to hold!

ALARIC. I don't want to hold her.

MRS. CHICHESTER. It would be the *saving* of her.

ALARIC. That's all very well, but what about me?

MRS. CHICHESTER. It would be the saving of us.

ALARIC. How would my holding and moulding her save us?

MRS. CHICHESTER. She'd stay with us if you were engaged.

ALARIC. Engaged! Don't, Mother, please. (*Sits armchair, shivers.*) Good Lord! Engaged to that tomboy!

MRS. CHICHESTER. She has the blood of the Kingsnorths.

ALARIC. Pretty well covered up in O'Connell—Irish.

MRS. CHICHESTER. She has the breeding of my sister, Angela.

ALARIC (*in armchair*). Well, you wouldn't think it to watch her.

MRS. CHICHESTER. And she'll have five thousand a year when she's twenty-one.

ALARIC (*whistles—business. Rises and looks at* MRS. CHICHESTER). Five thousand of the very best, eh?

MRS. CHICHESTER (*embraces him*). Oh, my boy!

ALARIC. Wait a minute. One can't burn all one's boats.

MRS. CHICHESTER. Think what it means. Your family preserved, and a brand snatched from the burning.

ALARIC. Ah! That's just it! I cannot see myself as a brand-snatcher. Besides, there's that little girl wild about me, and I don't dislike her at all, and I've half-promised——

MRS. CHICHESTER (*crossing to him*). It would unite our blood.

ALARIC. Oh, hang our blood.

MRS. CHICHESTER. It would settle you for life.

ALARIC. Yes. It certainly would.

MRS. CHICHESTER. Think what it would mean.

ALARIC. I am. I'm thinking really awfully hard. (*She moves to him.*) Just a minute! Give me a chance, Mater. (*Reasoning.*) Of course she's not half bad lookin', here and there. (*Mildly enthusiastic, sits on bench.*)

MRS. CHICHESTER. At times she's beautiful.

ALARIC (*depressed*). She has a shockin' temper.

MRS. CHICHESTER. That would soften under the restraining hand of affection.

(ALARIC, *shaking his head, turns to* MRS. CHICHESTER.)

ALARIC. She'd have to dress her hair and drop that dog. I will *not* have that dog all over the place. In that I would be obeyed.

MRS. CHICHESTER. The woman who loves always obeys.

ALARIC. Ah! There we have it. *Does* she love me?

MRS. CHICHESTER. How could she be near you for the last month and not love you? (*Crossing to him, embracing him.*)

ALARIC. Of course there *is* that. (*Thinks.*) Well, as you say, if she loves me—and for your sake, Mother, —and for darling Ethel's sake—and for me—*well*, anyway, it's a go! I'll do it. (*Straightens up.* MRS. CHICHESTER *turns to him.*) It'll take a bit of doin' but I'll do it.

(*Enter* PEG *from stairs. She, too, is pale and worried, her eyes sleepless. When she sees* MRS. CHICHESTER *she stops at bottom of stairs.*)

MRS. CHICHESTER. Good morning, Margaret!

PEG. Good mornin', Ant.

MRS. CHICHESTER. Now, Alaric. (*Puts his tie straight, then exits.*)

(PEG *looks quickly at* ALARIC, *who is nervously arguing with himself, his back to her. She hurries to* R. *corner, turns piano-cover up, and takes out book.* ALARIC *turns and sees her. She puts book under her arm.*)

ALARIC. Hello! What have we got there all tucked away?

PEG (*holding it up*). The only thing I'm takin' away that I didn't bring with me.

ALARIC. Oh! A book?

PEG. Shure, you're a very good guesser when you see a thing. That's what it is, a book.

ALARIC. You're takin' it away?

PEG. That's what I said, I'm takin' it away. (*Crossing behind table to stairs.*)

ALARIC (*following* PEG). You're not really goin' to leave us, Cousin?

PEG. I am, Cousin. And ye can forget the relationship the minit the cab drives away from yer door, Cousin. (*Goes to stairs, stops on third step.*)

ALARIC (*runs upstairs above her*). Wait a minute. There's something I want to tell you. Do you know, I've grown really——(*he swallows.*)—awfully fond of you.

PEG. It nearly choked ye, didn't it?

ALARIC. Awfully fond of you. Sit down. (PEG *goes to sit on stairs.*) Not there. Over there. Someone may hear us.

PEG (*sitting on chair below stairs, looking at him with a mischievous twinkle in her eyes*). When did ye find out ye were fond of me, Alaric?

ALARIC. Just now. Over there. No, over there. When the thought flashed through me that perhaps you really meant to leave us. The idea bruises me—

PEG. Does it?

ALARIC. —positively bruises!

PEG. You'll get over that.

ALARIC. I don't think I will. (*With a supreme effort.*) You know, meeting a girl like you day after day for a month has an awful effect on a fellow.

PEG. Awful effect?

ALARIC. Awful! Not to see you running up and downstairs, lying about the place, studying all those jolly maps and things, it hurts, really hurts. (*Comes down to her.*) Do you know, I'm goin' to do something I've never done before in all my life.

PEG. Somethin' useful?

ALARIC. No, no. I'm goin' to ask a very charming young lady to marry me, eh?

PEG. What do you think of that, now?

ALARIC. And—who—do—you—think—it—is?

PEG. I don't know.

ALARIC. Guess.

PEG. I couldn't guess who'd marry you, Alaric.

ALARIC. Who would it be?

PEG. That's the question, who would it be?

ALARIC. Who is it?

PEG. Who is it?

ALARIC. Who is it?

PEG. Who is it?

ALARIC. Who is it?

PEG. I'm asking you. You're not asking me. Who is it?

ALARIC (*with all the fervor he can muster*). *You.*

PEG. Me? (*She falls back against the balustrade, then laughs long and unrestrainedly.*)

ALARIC (*cheerfully*). Aha! Laughing! That's a splendid sign. Splendid! I always heard that girls cry when they're proposed to.

PEG. *I'm* half laughin' and half cryin'.

ALARIC. 'course ye know I've nothin' to offer you——

PEG. I know that.

ALARIC. —except a life-long devotion, a decent old name, and my career——

PEG. What?

ALARIC. —my career, when once I get it goin'. I only need a little incentive to make no end of a splash in the world. And *you'd* be my little incentive.

PEG. That's fine.

ALARIC (*runs upstairs again a few steps and then back*). Then it's all right?

PEG. That's the most wonderful thing I've ever heard in my life.

ALARIC (*runs upstairs again*). Good! Fine! Splendid!

PEG. Can't you make up your mind whether you want to be upstairs or downstairs.

ALARIC. Of course there are one or two little things to be settled first. (*Sits, top of stairs, facing front.*)

PEG. Only one or two?

ALARIC. Just little things. (*Emboldened by her manner.*) A little obedience.

PEG. You must obey me?

ALARIC. No, no. You must obey me.

PEG. That's funnier.

ALARIC. That's most essential. A little care about ordinary things, such as dress, speech, hair, etc., and—*no Michael.*

PEG. Oh! Couldn't I have Michael?

ALARIC (*firmly*). In that I'm absolutely determined. (*Rises.*) No Michael.

PEG. You're very firm about it.

ALARIC. Very firm.

PEG. It wouldn't be, love me love my dog?

ALARIC (*prepared to compromise*). No. It would not. I've never seen a dog I loved less than Michael.

PEG (*pause. Rises and goes up level with him*). What could you offer me in place of Michael?

ALARIC. What could I offer you in place of—? Oh! There we have it, dear Cousin, *Myself.*

PEG. I'll keep my dog.

ALARIC. *Oh,* come, I say! *You don't mean that?*

PEG. I get more affection out of his bark of greetin' than I've ever got from any human bein' in this house. If it makes no difference to you I'd rather have Michael.

ALARIC. You don't mean to say you refuse me?

PEG. I refuse you.

ALARIC. You actually decline my hand and heart?

PEG. I decline your hand, and I wouldn't deprive you of what you've got left of a heart.

ALARIC (*unable to believe his ears*). Really?

PEG (*on the brink of laughing*). Really!

ALARIC. Positively?

PEG. Positively!

ALARIC (*overjoyed. All the tension relieved*). I say! You're a brick! (*Shakes her hand violently.*)

PEG. Am I?

ALARIC. It's really awfully good of you. Some girls in your position would have jumped at me. But you're a genuine, hall-marked, A-number-one little brick. I'm extremely obliged to you. (*Shakes her warmly by the hand over balustrade.*) You're a plucky little girl, that's what you are. A plucky little girl. (*Goes toward alcove.*)

PEG. Am I?

ALARIC (*comes back to her. She hands him book*). I'll never forget it. Never. If there's anything I can do—at any time—call on me. I'll be there—on the spot. (*puts down book on newel post, crosses behind table.*) Bless you, Cousin! You've taken an awful load off my mind. I was really worried. Had to ask you—promised to.

PEG. Well, I said, "No." I refused to have you.

ALARIC. Yes. I know. I know. Ta, ta! See you before you go. Whew! What an escape! (*Hurries out through alcove into garden.* PEG *watches him go through window, and laughs.*)

PEG. But I said I wouldn't have you. (*Door opens and* HAWKES *and* MRS. CHICHESTER *enter.* HAWKES *looks around for* PEG. PEG *shakes hands with* HAWKES.) Hello, Mr. Hawkes! How do ye do?

HAWKES. Well, and how is our little protegée? I declare you're quite a young lady.

PEG. Am I? Ask my aunt.

MRS. CHICHESTER. Mr. Hawkes wishes to talk to you, dear.

PEG. And I'd like to talk to him.

MRS. CHICHESTER. Margaret! Why do you always have your hair over your eyes? Excuse me, Mr. Hawkes. (*To door.*) Oh, it's hopeless. (*Exits.*)

PEG (*comes and sits on bench*). I tell you, if I ever cut my hair off her occupation will be gone. I have to pin it up, and band it up. My father used to cut it every six months, and that's all the trouble we had with it.

HAWKES. What's all this nonsense about your going away?

PEG. I'm going back to my father.

HAWKES. Why are you going back to him?

PEG. I'm going back.

HAWKES. Aren't you happy here?

PEG. Devil a bit.

HAWKES. What's the trouble?

PEG. All the men have gone crazy in this house.

HAWKES. Has anyone been making love to you?

PEG. Yes. Two of them.

HAWKES. What?

PEG. One man tried to kiss me and I slapped his face——

HAWKES. Good.

PEG. The other man asked me to marry him and I sassed him.

HAWKES. Who was it?

PEG. Alaric.

HAWKES. What did you say to him?

PEG. I told him I'd rather have Michael.

HAWKES. Michael?

PEG. Yes. My dog.

HAWKES (*laughing*). Oh, the dog. So you refused him?

PEG. Of course. What would I be doing marrying Alaric?

HAWKES. Oh, I don't know. Is he too young?

PEG. Too young, too silly, and too selfish. And everything I don't like in a man Alaric is.

HAWKES. And what do you like in a man?

PEG. Precious little.

HAWKES. Listen, my dear Miss O'Connell. I'm speaking now as your late uncle's friend, and your well-wisher. You've a wonderful chance here. Remain with Mrs. Chichester. Continue your course of training. Then marry. Marry in England. And uphold the dignity and traditions of the Kingsnorths.

PEG. There's not a man in the world I'd marry now.

HAWKES. Really, Miss O'Connell, your future would then be absolutely assured. (*Taking her hand.*) Come, now. Marry here.

PEG. Are you proposing to me?

HAWKES (*laughingly*). Well, I didn't mean to, but now you suggest it——

PEG. I suggest it?

HAWKES. You're alone in the world. I'm alone in the world.

PEG (*rises and goes to staircase*). And as far as I'm concerned you'll stay alone in the world. I'm going to get out of this crazy house. You're all mad.

HAWKES. You're determined to go back to America?

PEG. Yes, I am. And I was going to ask you to buy me a passage on the steamer.

HAWKES (*comes to foot of stairs*). I'll see that a passage is reserved for you, and will escort you down to the steamer myself.

PEG. Thank you very much, Mr. Hawkes.

(MRS. CHICHESTER *enters with* JERRY.)

MRS. CHICHESTER. Margaret.

JERRY (*going to foot of stairs*). Peg.

PEG (*looking at* JERRY). I'm going back to my father in half-an-hour.

JERRY. In half-an-hour?

PEG. Yes. In thirty minutes. (*Exits.*)

JERRY (*turning to* HAWKES). What does she mean, Hawkes, by going in thirty minutes?

HAWKES. She's returning to America. She appears absolutely discontented here. I've reasoned with her, but she seems determined to go.

(*Enter* ALARIC.)

ALARIC. Hello, Jerry! (ALARIC *shakes hands with* HAWKES. *They talk.*)

JERRY. Hello, Al! (*Turns to* MRS. CHICHESTER.) I was entirely to blame for last night's unfortunate business. It was my fault.

MRS. CHICHESTER. I've tried to tell her I'd overlook it, but she insists on returning to America at once. (*Enter* JARVIS, *coming downstairs with dog and bundle.* MRS. CHICHESTER *turns to* JARVIS.) Where are you going with these?

JARVIS. To put them in a cab, ma'am. Miss O'Connell's orders.

MRS. CHICHESTER. Put those articles in a bag. Use one of my daughter's.

JARVIS. Miss O'Connell objects, ma'am. Says she'll take nothing away she didn't bring with her.

MRS. CHICHESTER. (*Crosses to armchair.*) That will do.

(ALARIC *drops down* R. *to armchair.* JARVIS *exits.* ALARIC *and* JERRY *look at each other.*)

ALARIC. Never mind, Mater. It can't be helped. We've done our best. I know I have—even offered to marry her if she'd stay.

HAWKES. So I believe.

JERRY. You offered to marry her?

ALARIC. Yes.

JERRY. What did she say?

HAWKES. Yes, what did she say?

ALARIC (*confusedly*). Oh! Er—er—what did she say? Oh, yes. The little beggar laughed in my face. Said she'd rather have Michael.

(*All laugh except* MRS. CHICHESTER.)

HAWKES. Now, Sir Gerald. My duties in regard to Miss O'Connell end today. Good-by. (*Starting to door.*)

JERRY. I think not, Hawkes.

HAWKES (*turning to* JERRY). I beg your pardon.

JERRY. I must be satisfied that the conditions of the late Mr. Kingsnorth's will are complied with, in the spirit as well as to the letter. Remember, I am the chief executor.

ALARIC (*by high chair*). What! An executor! Oh, fancy that, Mater. Executor!

HAWKES. Exactly, and——

JERRY. He expressly stipulated that a year was to elapse before any definite conclusion was arrived at. So far only a month has gone by.

HAWKES. But she seems determined to return to her father.

ALARIC. I never saw anyone so determined.

JERRY. Have you told her the conditions of the will?

HAWKES. Why, no. Mr. Kingsnorth distinctly stated that she was not to know them.

JERRY (*behind chair at table*). Except under exceptional circumstances. Well, I consider the circumstances most exceptional, and I intend to make known the conditions to Miss O'Connell and then let her decide as to whether she wishes to abide by them or not.

HAWKES. As a lawyer I must strongly object to such a course.

ALARIC. I should say so, indeed. What on earth do you want to do a silly thing like that for, Jerry?

MRS. CHICHESTER. Absolutely unnecessary!

HAWKES. Entirely uncalled for!

ALARIC. Stupid. Deuced stupid!

JERRY. I don't think so, Alaric. In my opinion Margaret ought to be told.

ALARIC. Ought to be told! Tush and nonsense!

JERRY. I intend telling her why she was brought here, and what Mr. Kingsnorth wished should be done for her.

ALARIC. I never heard of such a thing.

MRS. CHICHESTER. It's absurd.

JERRY. Is it? Do you think you have treated her quite fairly?

MRS. CHICHESTER. Fairly?

JERRY. Yes. Fairly. Pardon me speaking in this way, but I am responsible to a certain extent for her being here. It was at my suggestion that your late brother decided to give you the first opportunity of taking care of her. You have benefited by the arrangement, haven't you? Come! Think! What have you done for her in return?

MRS. CHICHESTER. What more could I have done?

ALARIC. Or I?

JERRY. Well, for one thing, you might at least have tried to make this a home for her. If you had, she would not be going away now.

MRS. CHICHESTER. How could I make it a home for such a girl as she is?

ALARIC. I should think not. Home, indeed!

JERRY. I suppose it was out of the question.

MRS. CHICHESTER. Absolutely.

ALARIC. I should say so.

JERRY. Very well. (*To* HAWKES.) Then it is our duty to find some other lady who will carry out Mr. Kingsnorth's wishes. Under those circumstances she may be persuaded to remain in England.

MRS. CHICHESTER. What?

ALARIC. There goes our thousand-a-year, Mater.

(*Enter* PEG *and* ETHEL *coming downstairs.*)

ETHEL. Peg, don't go.

PEG. The cab's at the door. There's nothing to keep me here now. (*Crossing to* MRS. CHICHESTER.) Good-by, Mrs. Chichester. I'm sorry I've been so much trouble.

MRS. CHICHESTER. Good-by, Margaret. (*Pointing to her dress.*) But why this dress? Why not one of the dresses I gave you?

PEG. This is the way I left my father—this is the way I'm going back to him. Good-by, Alaric.

ALARIC. Good-by, you little devil.

(*They shake hands.*)

PEG. Good-by, sir.

JERRY. One moment, please. Have you ever wondered at the real reason why you were brought to this house, and the extraordinary interest taken in you by relatives who, until a month ago, had never bothered about even your existence?

PEG. Yes. I have wondered.

JERRY (*impatiently*). First of all I must introduce myself to you in a new capacity—as the executor of your late uncle's will. One of his keenest wishes was to atone in some way for his unkindness to your mother.

PEG. Nothing could do that. "Ye've made yer bed, lie in it," was what he wrote to my mother when she was starvin', and why? Because she loved my father. Well, I love my father, and if he thought his money could separate us he's very much mistaken. No man can separate us—no dead man.

JERRY. In justice to yourself you must know that he set aside the sum of one thousand pounds a year to be paid to the lady who would undertake your training.

(HAWKES *sits by desk.*)

PEG. A thousand pounds a year? (*To* MRS. CHICHESTER.) You got paid for abusing me?

JERRY (*by table*). No. For taking care of you. I tell you this because I don't want you to feel that you have been living on charity. You haven't.

PEG. I've been made to feel it. (*To* MRS. CHICHESTER.) Who are ye, I'd like to know, to bring me up any better than my father? I want you to know that my father is just as much a gentleman as you are. He never hurt a girl's feelings just because she didn't have any money. I'd like to know if it's a crime not to have any money. (*Crosses over to* ETHEL.)

ETHEL. Don't cry, dear. You have literally fed and housed us for the last month. The day you came here we were beggars.

PEG (*looks up at her in astonishment*). Ye were beggars?

ETHEL. Yes. We have nothing but the provision made for your training.

PEG. And will ye have nothing if I go away?

ETHEL. Nothing.

PEG. Is that what ye meant last night by the roof over ye? (ETHEL *checks her.*) And I was drivin' ye to it. (ETHEL *drops her eyes.*) Well, I wouldn't see ye a beggar for the world, Ethel. I've been raised one, and I know what it's like. Bring in my bundles and my dog. I've changed my mind. I'm going to stay here.

(PEG *sits by table.* ETHEL *crosses behind table.*)

JERRY (*coming down*). That is just what I would have expected you to do, but there's no need for such a sacrifice. I came here this morning with some very good news for you, Mrs. Chichester. I happen to hold some shares in Gifford's Bank, and I am happy to say it will shortly reopen its doors.

ALARIC (*down to* MRS. CHICHESTER). Reopen its doors! So it jolly-well ought to. What right had it to close 'em? That's what I want to know.

MRS. CHICHESTER. Oh, Ethel—Alaric.

ALARIC. Now, Mater, listen to me. Every ha'penny goes out of Gifford's Bank and into something that's got a bottom to it. In future I'll manage the business of this family.

PEG (*rises*). That settles that. You don't need me any more. Good-day to yez. (*Starts to go.* HAWKES *rises to open door for her.*)

JERRY (*stopping her*). Just a moment. There is just one more condition of Mr. Kingsnorth's will, that you must know. Should you go through your course of training satisfactorily to the age of twenty-one you will inherit the sum of five thousand a year.

PEG. I get five thousand pounds a year when I'm twenty-one? No wonder all the men were mad to marry me this morning. (*Looking at* ALARIC.) I might forgive you, Alaric. (*Looking at* HAWKES.) But I'd like to know what you meant, Mr. Hawkes.

HAWKES (*by door, turning*). Oh, nonsense! Come, now, Miss O'Connell——

JERRY. Did you propose to Miss O'Connell, too? (*Turning to* HAWKES.)

HAWKES (*hesitatingly*). Well—er—in a measure.

PEG. Yes. It was very measured.

HAWKES. It seemed to be an admirable solution of the difficulty.

PEG. He's a solution, he is.

HAWKES. Well, there's no harm done.

PEG. No. It didn't go through, did it?

HAWKES No. Always your friend and well-wisher.

PEG. But never my husband.

HAWKES. Unfortunately, no. Good-day, everybody. I will wait to escort you to the boat, Miss O'Connell. (*Exits.*)

JERRY. Now, may I have a few minutes alone with my ward?

MRS. CHICHESTER. Certainly.

PEG. Your what?

JERRY. Ward.

PEG. Who's that? Me?

JERRY. I am your legal guardian—appointed by Mr. Kingsnorth.

PEG. Shareholder in a bank, executor of an estate, and now you're my guardian. What do you do with your spare time?

JERRY (*to the others*). Just a second, please.

(MRS. CHICHESTER *crosses to go upstairs.* PEG *stops her.*)

PEG. Aunt Monica, would you mind very much saying "Good-by" to me?

MRS. CHICHESTER. Certainly not. Good-by, Margaret. It is unlikely we'll meet again. I hope you have a safe journey. (*Exits upstairs.*)

(*Lights slowly down.*)

ALARIC (*lounging over to* PEG). Jolly decent of ye to offer to stay here—awfully decent. You are certainly a wonder. Miss you terribly.

PEG. Did you know about that five thousand, Alaric?

ALARIC. 'course I did. That was why I proposed. To save the roof.

PEG. Ye'd have sacrificed yerself by marryin' me?

ALARIC. Like a shot.

PEG. There's a great hero lost in you, Alaric.

ALARIC (*crosses to door*). Oh, I mustn't boast. It's all in the family.

PEG. Well I'm glad you didn't have to do it.

ALARIC. So am I.

PEG. Don't get sassy. (*Exit* ALARIC. PEG *looks at* ETHEL. *To* JERRY.) Look out of the window a minute, please. (*Pointing to windows.*) I want to speak to Ethel. (JERRY *goes to windows.* PEG *crosses to* ETHEL.) Is that all over?

ETHEL. Yes.

PEG. You're never going to see him again?

ETHEL. Never. I'll write him that. What must you think of me?

PEG. I thought of ye all last night. Ye seem like someone lookin' for happiness in the dark with yer eyes shut. Open them wide, dear. Look at the sunlight and ye'll know happiness.

ETHEL. I feel today that I'll never know happiness.

PEG. I've felt like that ever since I've been in this house. I tell you, three meals a day, a soft bed to slape in, and everythin' ye want, makes ye mighty discontented, so it does.

ETHEL. Last night you saved me from myself, and then you shielded me from my family.

PEG. I'd do that for any poor girl—much less my own cousin.

ETHEL (*crosses to door. Turns to* PEG). Don't think too hardly of me.

PEG. I don't, dear. Sure, it wasn't your fault. It was your mother's.

ETHEL. My mother's?

PEG. Yes. She doesn't understand children. You can't raise them in a hothouse. You've got to thrust them out into the cold wind and let them get used to it while they're young. I had the advantage of you all the time. It isn't every girl has the bringing up I had from my father. Good-by, Ethel.

ETHEL. Good-by, dear. (*Cries.*)

PEG. Don't do that, dear. Don't cry. (*Suddenly takes* ETHEL *in her arms and kisses her.*)

ETHEL (*goes to door, turns*). Good-by, Peg.

PEG. Good-by, Ethel. God bless you! (ETHEL *exits.*) All right. The door is shut.

JERRY (*coming down and round table*). Are you still determined to go?

PEG. I am.

JERRY. And you'll leave here without a regret?

PEG (*looks down*). I didn't say that, did I?

JERRY. We've been good friends, haven't we?

PEG. I thought we were, but friendship must be honest. Why didn't ye tell me ye had a title? How could I know you were a gentleman? Sure, Jerry might mean anybody.

JERRY. Are we never to play like children again?

PEG. No. We're not equals.

JERRY. Would nothing make you stay?

PEG. Nothing. I'm aching for my home.

JERRY. Peg! (*Comes forward to her.*)

PEG. Sir Gerald!

JERRY (*tenderly*). Peg, my dear——

PEG. Are you goin' to propose, too? (JERRY *straightens up, hurt.*) What the devil made me say that? (*Pause.*)

(*Enter* JARVIS.)

JARVIS. Mr. Hawkes says if you're goin' to catch the train, Miss——

PEG. All right. I'll catch the train. (JARVIS *exits.*) It's my Irish tongue, I suppose. (*Creeps quietly to door, rattles knob to attract* JERRY'S *attention, then goes out of door.*)

(*Lightning and thunder.* JERRY *stands still, passes the back of his hand across his eyes. Goes to window* R. *and looks toward the lane. It is now very much darker. Suddenly the pent-up storm breaks with redoubled fury. The rain comes in torrents. Lightning and thunder follow in quick succession. Door opens and* PEG *staggers in half-fainting, shuts the door quickly and leans against the door, deathly white, and trembling with fear.* JERRY *turns, gives a cry, and hurries to her.*)

JERRY. Peg!

PEG. Shut it out! Shut the storm out! (JERRY *draws the blinds. Faintly.*) I'm sorry for what I said just now. You're not going to be cross with me about that, are you?

JERRY. I couldn't be cross with you, Peg. I love you. Be my wife.

PEG. Don't be mad if I ask ye, but have ye proposed to me now?

JERRY. I have. Be my wife.

PEG. Ye have a title, Jerry.

JERRY. Share it with me.

PEG. Ye'll be ashamed of me.

JERRY. I love you.

PEG. Do ye love me?

JERRY. I do.

PEG. I love you, too, I do.

JERRY (*starting toward her*). Peg, my dear—(*Stops and hesitates.*)

PEG. Go on. Go on. What's the matter?

(*Lightning.*)

JERRY. Why, Peg, what will your father say?

PEG. My father always said: "Sure, there's nothing half so sweet in life as love's young dream." (*Loud crash of thunder. She hides her head on* JERRY'S *shoulder. Thunder and lightning till final curtain.*)

THE CURTAIN FALLS

Lightnin'

A PLAY IN PROLOGUE

AND THREE ACTS

BY

WINCHELL SMITH

AND

FRANK BACON

LIGHTNIN' was first presented at the Gaiety Theatre, August 26, 1918, with the following cast:

Lightnin' Bill Jones	Frank Bacon
John Marvin	Ralph Morgan
Raymond Thomas	Paul Stanton
Lemuel Townsend	Thomas Maclarnie
Rodney Harper	Lionel Adams
Everett Hammond	E. J. Blunkall
Nevin Blodgett (Sheriff)	Sam Coit
Oscar Nelson	George Thompson
Fred Peters	Sidney Coburn
Walter Lennon	William F. Granger
Zeb Crothers	George Spelvin
Liveryman	Fred Conklin
Hotel Clerk	James C. Lane
Mildred Buckley	Beatrice Nichols
Mrs. Jones	Jessie Pringle
Mrs. Margaret Davis	Jane Oaker
Mrs. Harper	Bessie Bacon
Freeda	Beth Martin
Emily Jarvis	Sue Ann Wilson
Mrs. Moore	Phyllis Rankin
Mrs. Jordan	Minnie Palmer
Mrs. Brainerd	May Duryea
Mrs. Starr	Frances Kennon
Mrs. Corshall	Ruth Towle
Mrs. Brewer	Florence Goddard

SYNOPSIS OF SCENES

Prologue—John Marvin's Cabin in Nevada.

Act One: The next day. Scene I—Office of the Calivada Hotel on the state line between Nevada and California. Scene II—That night.

Act Two: Six months later. Superior Court at Reno.

Act Three: The Hotel—the same evening.

LIGHTNIN'

PROLOGUE

JOHN MARVIN's cabin in Nevada, near Lake Tahoe. Rough log cabin of one room. Small window to the right of the audience, door to the left. On the wall near window is a shelf built out and held up by two rough sticks; wooden water pail, tin wash basin. Over shelf is a box nailed to wall, with comb, brush, soap, tooth-brush, shaving cup, razor strop, etc. Above box is a small cheap mirror. An old kerosene oil-stove in front of a rough fireplace, with tea kettle on stove. Above fireplace, on wall, are frying pans and a few other cooking utensils. On a little shelf a few cheap plates, cups, knives, spoons.

To the right, an old bunk with blanket and old quilt; sheets and pillows; left of bunk a small trunk, locked. Old piece of carpet just below bunk. Hanging on wall a pair of old rubber boots; on floor, laces, shoes and old slippers. Hanging above trunk, which is beside door, a suit of clothes (which JOHN wears in Act One) carefully stretched on hanger; also hat.

To the left a rough table with ten or a dozen law books on it, chair beside it, also writing materials, a tin alarm clock. Kerosene lamp hangs above table (all cheap). A cabinet picture in a plain black leather frame, not new. Beside this, a small china mug with a few wild flowers drooping. Between this table and door, a rifle, a shot gun and two axes in rack.

At the right, a rough table. On the table some unwashed dishes, tin coffee cup, sugar bowl, and opened can of condensed milk. Two chairs supposed to have been made by JOHN, solid but very rough. One is back of table and facing it, one is to the right.

(At rise stage is empty. There is a rapid knock on the door.)

OSCAR (*enter behind window looking back*). Mr. Marvin! Mr. Marvin! (*Opens door hurriedly, peers in, sees cabin empty, comes in quickly, closing door, goes to window, looks out. As door shuts, there is a pause.* SHERIFF *crosses window, knocks on door.*) Come in! (*Enter* SHERIFF—OSCAR *drops down stage front of table.*) What you want?

SHERIFF. You're John Marvin, ain't you?

OSCAR. No, sir.

SHERIFF. Well, then, you're working for him. (*Pause.*) Ain't you?

OSCAR. Who I work for ban my business.

SHERIFF. None of that. You're with the gang that's been chopping down that timber. (OSCAR *turns.*) You know Marvin is stealing it, don't you?

OSCAR (*turns to* SHERIFF). Stealing!

SHERIFF. Yes, from the Pacific Railroad Company. Now, I'm Sheriff of this county and I've got a warrant for Marvin's arrest.

OSCAR. Huh! (*Goes to window.*)

SHERIFF. You know where he is, don't you?

OSCAR. I know he gone away.

SHERIFF. Where?

OSCAR. I not know.

SHERIFF (*moves to* OSCAR). When did he go?

OSCAR (*goes to shelf*). He go yesterdy.

SHERIFF. When is he coming back?

OSCAR (*at window, looking at stove*). I not think he's coming back at all.

SHERIFF. It's goin' to be mighty bad if you're lyin' to me.

OSCAR (*goes to him, menacingly*). If you call me liar—(*crosses up to door, opens it, comes toward* SHERIFF.)—I throw you out that door.

SHERIFF (*crosses to* OSCAR). If you threaten me, the next thing you know you'll find yourself in jail. Don't forget that. (*Exits.*)

OSCAR (*goes to window and looks off stage. Door opens quietly.* JOHN *enters.* OSCAR *turns quickly and sees him.* JOHN *holds finger to his lips.* OSCAR *turns again and looks out of window.* JOHN *goes close to him*).

JOHN (*to table. Puts flowers in glass, takes old ones and puts them in box under table and ax against front of table*). Do you see him?

OSCAR. He get on his horse and start down the trail. There he goes, look!

JOHN. Good. You got rid of him very well, Oscar. Much obliged to you. (*Collects dirty dishes from table, crosses and puts them in pan.*)

OSCAR. He tell me——

JOHN. I know what he told you. I was out there listening to him.

OSCAR. Then do that land belong to railroad?

JOHN (*lights stove, gets water from bucket, puts it in coffee pot, puts pot on stove*). It does now, Oscar. But I sold the timber a long time before the railroad got the property and I'm trying to save it for the man who bought it.

OSCAR. And can they arrest you for that?

JOHN. Not unless they can find me.

OSCAR. And me and my boys. Can they arrest us too?

JOHN. No. They won't touch the boys. You fellows are working for me.

OSCAR (*goes over to table*). Oh! You know that from your law books?

JOHN (*puts coffee in pot*). Yes, Oscar. Anyhow, you'll be gone in the morning. That job's done, thank heaven. Did you have the boys sign the payroll? (*Going to* OSCAR.)

OSCAR (*handing over paper*). Yes, sir.

JOHN (*taking paper*). Thank you, Oscar—oh, and Oscar, if that Sheriff or anybody else asks the boys when the timber was cut, tell 'em not to remember, will ye?

OSCAR. Oh, ye don't want anybody find out when we do it?

JOHN. That's the idea, Oscar——

OSCAR. Nobody find out from us ye bet ye life. (*Exits* R. C.)

HARPER'S VOICE (*outside*). Say, who's the boss of this gang here?

OSCAR'S VOICE (*savagely*). Boss gone away!

(JOHN, *on hearing the voice, goes to door, swings it open and calls off stage.*)

JOHN. Hello, Mr. Harper, come in. (*After a pause* HARPER *enters and stands in doorway.*)

HARPER. I didn't expect to find you here.

(HARPER *is a keen, honest, gruff American of forty. Clothes plain and ill fitting; flannel shirt and collar; slouch hat. Although dressed roughly, his clothes must not look cheap. His appearance, despite a good deal of dust, is cleanly.*)

JOHN (*friendly*). I'm mighty glad to see you. Sit down, won't you? (*Offers chair by table.*)

HARPER (*grimly, eyeing* JOHN). Wait a minute—till I get our relations straightened out a bit. (*Closes door.*) I had a notion that when I met up with you, I'd put a bullet into you.

JOHN (*pleasantly*). Well, can't you shoot sitting down?

HARPER. You don't think I mean it, eh?

JOHN (*smiling and speaking lazily*). I don't think you figured on what I'd be doing.

HARPER. We'll see what you'd be doing when I find out how the land lays. Just before my trip East I bought a grove of timber from you and paid you cash for it. And when I get back yesterday I learn you've *sold* the property, timber and all, to the railroad.

JOHN. I didn't know your timber was still on the property. When you bought it you were going to cut it down right away.

HARPER (*turns away from* JOHN *thinking, then turns back to him quickly*). But you told me you were never going to part with a foot of the property because your mother was so crazy over it.

JOHN. That's right. It was her dream that we'd have a home here sometime. Do you remember why I sold you that timber?

HARPER (*front of table*). I remember what you said. Your mother was sick—and you needed the money.

JOHN (*by table*). Yes. I brought her to San Francisco where she had the best care and the best doctors in the town.

HARPER. Is she there now?

JOHN (*shaking his head; then speaking simply*). No, she's dead.

HARPER. Oh. (*Crosses to table, picks up picture of* JOHN'S *mother.*) I'm sorry to hear that. (HARPER *looks at the picture and sits as* JOHN *speaks.*)

JOHN (*goes to* HARPER, *talking rapidly*). When we got to San Francisco, a lawyer named Raymond Thomas came to see my mother at the hospital and said he wanted to buy a piece of this property and build a home here after he'd retired from practice. He found out that I was studying law and he offered to take me into his office, and help me in every way he could. I was mighty glad of the chance and spent all my time at his office when I wasn't with mother. One day she told me she thought we ought to sell Mr. Thomas the land he wanted because he had taken such an interest in me. Mother got worse right after that, and I didn't think any more about it. When she—after the funeral was over—I found she had sold Thomas the property he wanted and had taken in payment some stock in a Land Company that I don't believe is worth the paper it's written on.

HARPER (*rises*). As soon as this lawyer got the property he sold it to the railroad for a big price?

JOHN. Yes.

HARPER. Well, when you found that out, why the devil didn't you kill him?

JOHN (*smiles*). It was just about that time I found you hadn't cut down your timber, and you were way off in the East.

HARPER. Well, you couldn't do anything about that, could you?

JOHN. Only one thing I could think of.

HARPER. What was that?

JOHN. Cut it down and get it over on my property.

HARPER. What! (*Goes to door, opens it, looks off stage.*) You've got all my timber over on your property!

JOHN. Yes, we finished the job today.

HARPER. Oh, I had it all wrong. I thought that gang out there were working for the railroad.

JOHN. No, they've been working for me; the next thing is to get the timber away.

HARPER. Oh, I'll take care of that. (*Closes door.*)

JOHN. It may not be as easy as you think. We've just had a visit from a Sheriff.

HARPER (*coming down to* JOHN). What did he want?

JOHN. He wanted me. The railroad company sent him after me. Of course, if they can prove when the timber was taken down, they can recover. In that case if you will give me time I'm going to return every cent you paid for it.

HARPER. You'll do nothing of the sort. I'll take all the chances from now on. I guess I was a little sharp when I first came in.

JOHN. Oh, that's all right.

HARPER. But everything's gone wrong with me today. (*Front of table.*)

First, there was a strike at the sawmill, then I heard about this thing, and just as I was starting out here to look into it, I had a row with my wife. (*Sits at table.*)

JOHN. Oh, I'm sorry. (*Crosses and sits on front of table.*)

HARPER. I didn't mind the strike and this timber mix-up so much, but the other thing—well, that ain't in my line. And there's no reason for it. (*Rises, crosses to* JOHN.) That's what makes me sore. I bought her a present when I was East and had it shipped home by express. It arrived at the office this morning and I was showing it to Miss Robbins—she's my stenographer—when my wife walks in, saw it, and thought I bought it for Miss Robbins.

JOHN. But surely you could explain that?

HARPER. Do you think so?

JOHN. Yes.

HARPER. That's because you've never been married. The more I tried to explain the worse it looked, and I—oh, hell, what's the use talking about it? Let's get back to business. I figured it would cost eight hundred dollars to do that job out there. (*Reaching in pocket.*) And that's just what I'm going to hand you for it.

JOHN (*to front of table*). I couldn't take it, Mr. Harper.

HARPER. Why not?

JOHN. Because you haven't got that timber yet.

HARPER. Well, the railroad will have some job on their hands to get it away from me, and unless they do, I owe you eight hundred dollars, you understand——

(JOHN *facing front as though he hears something at door. As* JOHN *tiptoes to door,* HARPER *goes guardedly, puts hand to back pocket reaching for gun.* JOHN *jerks open the door and* BILL JONES *wanders past him.* BILL *is a little old man, rather shabbily dressed. He has a slight and a very quiet jag. He carries a few honeysuckle shoots wrapped in a newspaper.*

JOHN (*comes down by* BILL). Why, hello, Lightnin'. You were so still out there I thought it was somebody spying on us.

BILL. I was a spy once—with Buffalo Bill. (BILL *stares at* HARPER *as he speaks.*)

JOHN. This is Lightnin' Bill Jones, Mr. Harper.

HARPER. How d'you do? (*Takes chair from beside table, and places it in front of it—takes out notebook and pencil and starts to write—puts hat on table.*)

BILL. How are you?

JOHN. What were you so quiet about, Bill?

BILL. I knocked on the door. (*He goes up and deposits hat and packages on bunk.*)

JOHN. Well, it wasn't a very loud one.

BILL. I didn't want to disturb you. I always make 'em knock easy like that at the hotel. (*Comes down to table.*)

JOHN. Mr. Jones is a hotel proprietor.

HARPER (*looks up at* BILL). That so?

BILL. Got the best hotel on the Lake.

JOHN. Sit down, Bill.

BILL. No. Can't stop. Got to be home at supper time to see everything's going right.

JOHN. What time do you have supper at your hotel?

BILL. Supper's at—what time is it now?

JOHN (*looks at clock on shelf*). Nearly seven o'clock.

BILL (*after a moment's thought*). They can get along without me. I got everything s-sys-sysmitized.

JOHN (*looking at him sharply*). I'm afraid you've been drinking, Bill. (JOHN *lights lamp that is hanging above table.*)

BILL. No. Just saying good-by to the boys out there. They're breaking camp.

JOHN. And they wanted to have you take a few farewell drinks.

BILL. I didn't like to hurt their feelings. (*To* HARPER.) Railroad man?

JOHN (*smiling*). Oh, no. Mr. Harper's the man I sold that timber to.

HARPER (*looking up to* JOHN). Does he know about it?

JOHN (*crosses front of table to stove*). Bill knows the property belongs to the railroad and he's been a little worried.

BILL (*looking at* HARPER). That's the best timber in Washoe County.

HARPER. Yes, I know it is.

BILL. Except a piece I got. (JOHN *prepares supper,* BILL *sits on table.*)

HARPER (*looking at him amused*). Is your place in Nevada?

BILL. Some of it is, more of it's in California. The state line runs right through my hotel.

JOHN (*fixes coffee*). You've heard of Lightnin's hotel, haven't you, Mr. Harper?

HARPER (*turning to* JOHN). I'm afraid not.

BILL. I guess you're the only one.

JOHN. (*putting beans on fire*). He just got back from the East, Bill. He would have heard of it, if he'd been at home.

HARPER. Why, what about it?

JOHN (*washes hands*). Well, you see, Bill's house was on the state line and his wife got the idea of turning it into a summer hotel.

BILL. I give her the idea.

JOHN. So they enlarged the house, called it the *Calivada Hotel* and got ready for a rush of guests—and nobody came. But just when it looked like a failure and they were about ready to close up, the miracle happened. (*Drying hands.*)

BILL. It wasn't no miracle. I knew it would happen all the time.

HARPER (*to* BILL). What was it?

JOHN. Women began to arrive and they all wanted rooms on the Nevada side and they wanted them for six months.

HARPER (*laughs*). The Reno divorce brigade!

JOHN. Yes. Of course, everybody knows what a woman goes to Reno for, but at Bill's hotel she can get a room on the Nevada side and make her friends think she's at a California resort. (*Takes two plates, knives, forks and spoons and puts them on table.*) So, instead of failing, the Calivada's a big success. Of course this is Bill's story.

BILL. No, it ain't. I can tell it better than that. (JOHN *goes back to stove.*)

BILL. John's never seen the hotel.

JOHN. I haven't had time. And we haven't known each other long.

BILL. I never saw John till I happened by here about a month ago.

HARPER. Oh. Been in this part of the country long?

BILL (*on corner of table*). Came out during the gold excitement.

HARPER. The gold excitement was back in '49.

BILL. Well, they was still excited when I got here.

HARPER (*laughs*). And you didn't happen to be one of the lucky ones?

BILL. Lucky? I located more claims than any man ever that came out here. I'm a civil engineer.

HARPER. Oh, you ought to be a mighty rich man.

BILL. Always cheated out of my share.

HARPER. How was that?

BILL. Crooked partners.

HARPER. Well, couldn't you do anything to them?

BILL. I shot some, put all the others in the penitentiary—except one.

HARPER. What happened to him?

BILL. He died before I got him.

HARPER (*laughs and turns front*). Died of fright, perhaps.

BILL. I guess so. (*Goes over to table.*)

HARPER (*picks up hat—puts chair by table. Rises, laughs*). Well, I'll get out before you tell me any more. I've got all I can remember at one time, and I shouldn't like to forget any of it. (*Goes up to door.*)

JOHN (*coming to table with coffee cups*). I'm trying to fix some supper for you.

HARPER (*with a slight glance at the food*). No, thanks. I'll be in Truckee in two hours.

BILL (*looking out window*). That's your automobile out there, ain't it?

HARPER (*coming down*). Yes.

BILL. And it'll get you to Truckee in two hours?

(JOHN *brings food to table.* HARPER, *coming back, meets him in front of table.*)

HARPER (*to* BILL). That's what it will. (*To* JOHN. *Coming down to front of table.*) Well, Marvin! I'm going to send the trucks down here tomorrow and start hauling.

JOHN (*coming in front of table*). Had I better be around?

HARPER. No, I don't think so. You take a vacation. Then if there's a kick, no one here will know anything about it. I'll keep you posted or I'd just as soon give you that eight hundred right now. (*Pulls out money;* BILL *looks at it.*)

JOHN. No, thank you, sir. And I shan't forget the way you've treated me.

HARPER (*patting* JOHN *on his shoulder*). How would you expect me to treat you after that job out there? (*Shakes hands.*) Good-by, Marvin; good-by, Mr. Jones. (*Starts up to door.*)

BILL. Oh! If you want to get rid of some of that money, perhaps you'd cash a check for me.

HARPER. (*Shrewdly. Comes down to* BILL.) Let's see it.

BILL (*taking check from pocket; hands it to* HARPER). Oh, it's good, I guess.

HARPER (*looking at it*). Oh; pension! So you were in the war, too?

BILL. First man to enlist!

HARPER (*handing it back*). Endorse it.

BILL. What's that?

HARPER. Write your name on the back of it.

BILL. I always do that. (*Showing* HARPER *check.*) See all those names on there, Secretary of the Treasury and all of them? (HARPER *nods.*) It ain't no good unless I sign it. (*Goes to table, sits, endorses check.* HARPER *counts out money, hands it to* BILL, *laughing as he does so.*)

HARPER (*hands him money—takes check*). Here you are, Mr. Jones. Good night, Marvin.

JOHN. Good night, Harper. (HARPER *exits.* JOHN *brings beans, bread and coffee to table.*) He's a fine man, Bill.

BILL (*rising*). He's a fast driver.

JOHN (*offering* BILL *chair back of table*). Sit down and have some supper.

BILL. No. Just had a snack outside with the boys.

JOHN (*sits and begins to eat beans and bread*). Oh.

BILL (*coming to table*). But I don't want to be unfriendly. I'd just as soon take a drink with you.

JOHN (*eating*). I haven't got anything, Bill.

BILL. Yes, you have. (*Produces bottle.*)

JOHN. You mean you have.

BILL. No, Oscar made you a present of it, and he asked me to bring it in to you. (*Hands bottle to* JOHN.)

JOHN. Oh. (*Takes it.*)

BILL (*holds coffee cup expectantly;* JOHN *puts bottle down on table.*)

JOHN. I don't think you ought to drink any more tonight, Bill. Try some coffee.

BILL. No, go on and eat. Don't mind me. (*Puts cup down.* JOHN *pours coffee.*) Hear the railroad had a sheriff after you.

JOHN. How did you know?

BILL. Oscar told me. You remember what I promised you?

JOHN. What was that, Bill?

BILL. If they go to Court, I'll come and be a witness. (*Raising voice; positive for first time.*) I can swear those trees was cut before you sold the property.

(JOHN *stops eating and looks at him. Beside table.*)

JOHN (*smiling and going on with supper*). I couldn't let you swear to that, Bill.

BILL. You can't help yourself. I got a right to swear to what I like.

JOHN. But I haven't got to prove when those trees were cut; they have.

BILL. I know it.

JOHN. Oh, do you?

BILL. Yes, used to be a lawyer.

JOHN. Well, why don't you practice?

BILL. I don't need any practice. And I promise you if they go to Court I'll be there, and I never broke a promise yet. (*Crosses, taking out cigarette papers, makes cigarette.*)

JOHN. Lightnin', does anybody home know where you are?

BILL. Not unless they're mind-readers.

JOHN. How far is it to your hotel?

BILL. Seven miles.

JOHN. Is it all right for you to be here, Bill?

BILL (*turning to* JOHN—*starting out*). Do you want me to go?

JOHN. Of course not. You know better than that. But I mean, won't they worry about you?

BILL. Who, the boarders?

JOHN. No. Your wife.

BILL. Oh, Mother—she's got plenty to do.

JOHN. Sometimes I wonder if she approves of your going off as you do.

And your drinking. She certainly doesn't like to have you drink, does she, Bill?

BILL. I don't drink.

JOHN. Well, if you did drink, she wouldn't like it, would she?

BILL. You know how some women are. They're curious about some things.

JOHN. Then all these tall yarns you tell—Now what does your wife think about them?

BILL. I don't tell her none. (JOHN *gives it up, smiles and goes on eating.* BILL *smiles at him affectionately. He goes to table, picks up picture and turns with it in his hand.* JOHN *looks up and their eyes meet.*) I was over there this afternoon.

JOHN. Were you, Bill?

BILL (JOHN *stops eating.* BILL *returns the picture to table*). You got things growing there, ain't you? Looks fine! When did you get time to do it?

JOHN (*goes and puts out stove*). Sunday.

BILL (*gets package from bunk*). I brought these honeysuckle shoots to plant there, but I guess you got plenty without 'em now.

JOHN (*crosses to* BILL.) No, I want them. (*Takes package and crosses to table.*) Thank you for remembering, Bill; thank you very much. I know just the place for them. I'll set them out in the morning. (*Puts package front of table, sits, picks up picture.*)

BILL. They're off the finest vine in California. I suppose it's a little lonesome for you now without her, ain't it?

JOHN. Well, it's all different, Bill. But I have too much to do to be lonesome. (*Turns, starts to work on law books.*) If you have trouble, Bill, keep busy, that's the best thing.

BILL. I could stay here tonight, if you thought I'd be any company for you.

JOHN (*laying his hand on* BILL'*s arm*). You'd be great company for anybody, Bill, but I don't believe you'd better. They'll worry about you at home. (*Goes back to work on law books.*)

BILL. And you've got studying to do, ain't you?

JOHN. Yes.

BILL (*turning at bunk as he picks up hat*). Well, good night.

JOHN. Good night, Bill.

BILL (*sees bottle—looks at him, then goes and takes bottle from table and puts it in pocket—goes up to door, opens it.*)

JOHN (*rises*). Bill! (BILL *turns and faces him.*) You won't drink any more tonight, will you? (BILL *looks at him a moment sheepishly, then slowly closes door, takes bottle out of pocket and offers it to* JOHN.) No, you can keep it, Bill. (BILL *puts bottle quickly into pocket.*) Only I want you to go home sober.

BILL. I don't drink nothin'.

JOHN. And you won't take a drink out of that bottle tonight?

BILL (*after a pause*). No. (*Starts out.*)

JOHN (*going up to* BILL). Are you going straight home?

BILL (*avoiding his eye*). Uh-huh.

JOHN. You're not going to stop anywhere on the way?

BILL. No.

JOHN. You just told me you never broke a promise, Bill.

BILL (*emphatically*). That's right.

JOHN. Will you promise me to take home all that pension money, every cent of it?

BILL (*thinks it over first*). Yes.

JOHN. Good night, Lightnin'.

(BILL *goes to door at once.* JOHN *goes to table and settles down to study.* BILL *tries to tear himself away but wanders back toward* JOHN *again.*)

BILL (*pause. After looking at* JOHN). I'd just as soon leave the bottle here now, if you want me to. (*Pause,* JOHN *is buried in his work.*) I won't touch it tonight . . . now that I promised you. . . . (*Pause—waits for* JOHN *to answer—he doesn't.*) That'll be all right, won't it? (BILL *gives it up. Once more, however, he comes down and watches him, then muses.*) Studying. (*Starts up to door.*) That's how I got my start. (*He is going out as curtain falls slowly.*)

CURTAIN

ACT ONE

SCENE—*A small hotel on the border between California and Nevada. There is a door to the left of the audience that leads to dining-room, a door on the same wall to parlor and a door in back to the road. In alcove to the right, there is a door to the kitchen and a door in alcove not used.*

There are two staircases; one to the left and one to the right, that lead to the rooms. At the top of each an arch with curtains. In the circle of the stairways there are two counters with a register on each. A large fish hangs over the center of arch at back. There are two rugs running up and down stage with about six inches between marking the state line. The ground cloth is brown, striped to represent boards. On the railing of stairways, both sides, there is a letter box with keys or tags. Down in front of stairway to the left is an old-fashioned hall rack and umbrella stand. At right in front of stairway an old whatnot filled with old pieces of bric-a-brac, an upholstered chair just right of this. There is a small old-fashioned round table with chairs beside it—camera on table—off in doorway right a small stand with toothpicks in a glass vase, on it. It is placed to hold door open. A small rug in front—and off stage—of doors outside, a fence running across the stage in the center of which there is a sign reading "California—Nevada." A drop with mountains and a lake and waterfall on it, a ground row in front of this with part of lake on it; this is removed for last act and shows the power plant on the drop—this power plant not to be seen in first act.

There are brackets on either side of door center and above doors right and left. A chandelier hangs in center.

As curtain rises MRS. JORDAN *is seated in chair right of table center.* MRS. STARR *enters from down right. Waitress comes down Nevada stairs with tray of dishes, crosses and exits.* MRS. COGSHALL *enters. All women are dressed for a walk.*

MRS. JORDAN (*to* MRS. STARR). Have you had enough?

MRS. STARR. Goodness, yes. (MRS. MOORE *comes down Nevada stairs.*)

MRS. MOORE (*to* MRS. STARR). Hello!

MRS. STARR (*to* MRS. COGSHALL). Sorry if I kept you waiting.

MRS. COGSHALL. That's all right, dear.

(MRS. STARR *meets* MRS. COGSHALL. *They exit.*)

MRS. MOORE (*to* MRS. JORDAN). Are you ready?

MRS. JORDAN. Yes. But don't you think we ought to ask Mrs. Preston to come with us?

MRS. MOORE (*comes to table*). Oh, Lord! (*Sits.*)

MRS. JORDAN. I know what you mean but I feel so awfully sorry for her.

MRS. MOORE. Well, I have no sympathy for a woman who can't hold her husband.

MRS. JORDAN. But I have and I've heard Mr. Preston is only waiting to get this divorce . . . until he can . . .

(*Enter* MRS. PRESTON *from dining-room, takes parasol from hall rack.*)

MRS. MOORE (*seeing* MRS. PRESTON). Sh!

MRS. JORDAN (*rises*). Oh—Mrs. Preston! (MRS. PRESTON *comes down.*) We're going over to the waterfall to take some snapshots and we thought you might like to come along too.

MRS. MOORE (*rises; comes down*). Yes, do come, Mrs. Preston.

MRS. PRESTON. Why, thank you. I'd love to. (*Crosses to look in mail box.*) But—do you know if the mail has come yet?

MRS. MOORE. I know it hasn't and it's disgraceful.

MRS. JORDAN. I suppose Mr. Jones has gone for it again.

MRS. MOORE. No wonder they call him Lightnin'. Monday he didn't get back until supper time and when he did come back he could hardly walk. I'm going to speak to Mrs. Jones about it.

MRS. PRESTON (*up and over to* MRS. MOORE). Oh, please don't. There probably wasn't anything for me anyway.

MRS. JORDAN. And you can't find Mrs. Jones now. She's always in the kitchen at meal time.

MRS. MOORE. Then I'll speak to her daughter. If I can pry her away from that young man for a moment. (*To* MRS. PRESTON:) He's still in the dining-room, isn't he? (MRS. JORDAN *crosses to table.*)

MRS. PRESTON. But he's not Millie's young man. She was employed in his office in San Francisco.

MRS. MOORE. Well, there's no reason because she worked for him that he can't be in love with her.

MRS. JORDAN. Such a man would hardly be in love with a head waitress. (*Picking up camera.*)

MRS. MOORE (*starts off*). Whether he's in love with her or not, I'm going to ask her about the mail. (*Calls off.*) Millie! May I speak to you for a moment? (*Slight pause.* MILLIE *enters from dining-room.*)

MILLIE. Yes, Mrs. Moore?

MRS. MOORE. Do you know why the mail hasn't arrived?

MILLIE. Perhaps the train is late today.

MRS. JORDAN. It couldn't be this late. It's nearly two o'clock and the train's due at ten.

MRS. MOORE. Who went for the mail? Your father?

MILLIE. Yes, I believe he did. (*Goes up back of desk.*)

MRS. JORDAN. Why in the world do they let him go for it? (*Gets bags.*)

MRS. PRESTON. You see, dear, the mail is the most exciting event of the day. (*At counter.*)

MILLIE. I'm very sorry.

MRS. MOORE. Well, I suggest another mail carrier.

(*Gets bag from table. Women gather up their things and start up stage.* THOMAS *enters from dining-room, takes hat from rack, crosses up stage.*)

MILLIE. Did you have all you wanted?

THOMAS. No, but I had all I could hold. (*He joins women, who turn back when he enters.*) The food here is ripping, isn't it?

(*Together:*)
MRS. JORDAN. Yes, indeed! Perfectly delicious.
MRS. MOORE. Yes. Mrs. Jones sets a wonderful table. Everyone says that.
MRS. PRESTON. Oh, splendid!

THOMAS. Going for a stroll?

ALL. Yes, we were.
MRS. MOORE. Won't you come with us?

(*Together:*)
MRS. JORDAN. Oh, do.
MRS. PRESTON. Yes, come along.

THOMAS. I'm sorry, but I can't possibly. I've got my packing to do. I'm leaving on the afternoon boat.

MRS. MOORE. Oh, I didn't know that!

MRS. JORDAN. I'm awfully sorry you're going so soon.

MRS. PRESTON. Why, you only came three days ago. (*Women exit, saying:*)

MRS. JORDAN. Good-by.

MRS. MOORE. So pleased to have met you.

MRS. PRESTON. I hope you'll be back before long.

THOMAS (*to* MILLIE). It's a shame to miss a stroll with them. (*Coming back to* MILLIE, *front of counter.*) What's the matter, Millie?

MILLIE (*comes below counter front of it*). Daddy!

THOMAS. Anything happened to him?

MILLIE. He went for the mail at nine o'clock this morning and hasn't got back yet.

THOMAS. Oh, well, don't let that worry you. After I get my things packed, I'll go out and see if I can hunt him up.

MILLIE (*coming over to him*). As if you hadn't done enough for us already.

THOMAS. But now I think of it I've got to see Lightnin' before I go.

MILLIE. Must you? Why, the place belongs to mother.

THOMAS. But Bill happens to be her husband—so we need his name too.

MILLIE. Oh, dear, what if we can't find him before you go?

THOMAS (*crosses to back of counter, gets keys*). Well, in that case, I can leave the papers here and you can get his signature and send them on to me. So that's all right.

MILLIE. You do know how much I appreciate all you've done for us, don't you?

THOMAS. Why, it's nothing at all, Millie.

MILLIE. Nothing at all? When I didn't know which way to turn and mother was about frantic, and then you come here and in no time arrange everything so that mother and daddy are going to be better off than they ever dreamed of?

THOMAS. But it was the simplest thing in the world! I just happened to think what to do. That was all. (MRS. JONES *enters from kitchen—starts for stairs.* THOMAS *sees her.*) Oh, hello, Mrs. Jones.

MRS. JONES. Oh, excuse me. (*Starts back for kitchen.*)

MILLIE (*going to her and catching her*). Oh! Mother—No—you're not going back into that hot kitchen. (*Brings her down to chair by table*). You've been working out there three mortal hours.

MRS. JONES (*looking at* THOMAS). But I don't look presentable.

THOMAS. Come now, you mustn't mind me, Mrs. Jones.

MILLIE (*back of table*). Do sit down, Mother. You look ready to drop. (MRS. JONES *sits beside table.*)

MRS. JONES (*to* THOMAS—*rolling down sleeves*). She's always telling me that. Some time I think I'll fall down just to satisfy her.

THOMAS. Millie's right. You do work a great deal too hard.

MRS. JONES. The work has to be done. (*Fixing hair.*)

THOMAS. Well, it won't be long before you can say good-by to hard work for the rest of your life.

MRS. JONES. I can scarcely realize that yet. (*Rises.*) But I do realize that I owe it all to you. I only wish I could tell you how grateful I am.

THOMAS (*starts upstairs*). Well, I'm going to get out for fear you'll try. Hang on to her, Millie, and make her take a rest. (THOMAS *exits up California stairs.*)

MRS. JONES (*crosses toward California desk*). There! Now I've driven him away. (*Turns to* MILLIE.)

MILLIE. Why, no, you haven't. He was going up to pack.

MRS. JONES. Is he really leaving this afternoon?

MILLIE. Yes.

MRS. JONES. I don't see why he wants to hurry away. (*In front of chair*).

MILLIE. Why, he's arranged everything about selling the place. There's nothing more to stay for. (*Takes chair, places it front of California desk.*)

MRS. JONES. You're here, ain't you?

MILLIE. Oh, Mother. (*Coming down toward* MRS. JONES.) Please get that foolish idea out of your head.

MRS. JONES. Foolish idea? (*Sits.*) Why, Millie, every letter you wrote home all the time you was working in his office showed that he cared for you.

MILLIE. Why! I never wrote you anything of the sort—never.

MRS. JONES. I could read between the lines and if he isn't in love with you, why is he planning for us to come and live in San Francisco?

MILLIE. I'm planning that. (*Crosses to* MRS. JONES *and places arm around her and leans cheek on* MRS. JONES'S *head.*) For years you've worked like a slave and now you deserve to see something of life and have some good times.

MRS. JONES. The very idea of the city frightens me.

MILLIE (*surprised—moves back*). Why, you've talked of going to the city ever since I can remember.

MRS. JONES (*looking at* MILLIE). I know I have, but now that I can go I'm afraid I'm going to look out of place—that I won't know how to dress right and——

MILLIE. I'm going to see that you have just as nice things as any of the women who are stopping here. (*They look at each other and smile.*)

MRS. JONES (*to front*). Then there's Bill. (*Rises.*) I'm so afraid of the way he'll behave. (*Turns to* MILLIE.) When his pension comes you must take him to town and buy him some new clothes.

MILLIE (*with sudden thought*). Is it time for his pension to be here? (*Crosses to* MRS. JONES.)

MRS. JONES. Why? (*Turns and looks at letter box* L. *then turns back to* MILLIE.) Ain't he back with the mail yet?

MILLIE. Not yet.

MRS. JONES. Oh!

MILLIE. Oh, Mother, then you think his pension has come?

MRS. JONES (*turns to* MILLIE). I think it's come—and gone. (*Crosses to back of Nevada desk, looks under desk, turns and looks at mail box, then back at the desk. After* MRS. JONES *is back of desk* L. MILLIE *crosses to desk* R. *watching* MRS. JONES.) I found him hanging around this desk this morning and it took him forever to get started. I wonder —— (*Opens register and finds flask, holds it up.*) There! He was waiting for a chance to get at this.

MILLIE (*crosses to* MRS. JONES). Anyway—(*goes and puts her arm around her*)—don't let's blame him for anything until we're sure. Now please go up and have a good rest. (*Crosses to dining-room door.*)

MRS. JONES (*crosses to kitchen door*). I've got to go to the kitchen first.

MILLIE. What for? (*Turns.*)

MRS. JONES (*hesitating*). Why—if he should come home sober——

MILLIE. Oh—you want to keep something hot for him!

MRS. JONES. He don't deserve a mouthful.

MILLIE (*imitating* MRS. JONES). No, of course not. (MRS. JONES *exits into kitchen.*) I'll set a place for him. (*Exits.* BILL *enters slowly from porch, papers and letters under his arm. He looks about then beckons to* ZEB *off. Whistling "Darling, I Am Growing Old."*)

BILL (*starts, stops, looks up.* ZEB CROTHERS *appears cautiously in doorway. He is a very old man, shabbily dressed. Turning and seeing* ZEB). Come on, Zeb. What are you 'fraid of?

ZEB. Where's your old woman?

BILL. That's all right. She ain't here.

ZEB. I don't believe ye got a drop. (*Takes one step in door.* BILL *goes to desk and raises lid of register.*)

BILL. I'll show ye. (MRS. JONES *enters briskly from kitchen.* ZEB *seeing her, hurries out.* BILL *closes desk quickly, goes to letter rack and begins sorting mail.*)

MRS. JONES (*rushes to door to* ZEB *who has run out door*). Clear out now. (*Comes back and turns, sees* BILL, *walks deliberately down to chair.*) Bill Jones—where have you been? (*Hard, angry tone.* BILL *looks around as though surprised to see her there. Holds position a moment, then speaks pleasantly as if she hadn't spoken to him. Still whistling.*)

BILL. Hello, Mother. (*Goes on sorting mail. She watches him angrily and advances a step.*)

MRS. JONES (*pause*). Do you know what time it is? (BILL *pays no attention. Pause.*) It's after two o'clock. (*She stands glaring at him. He goes on whistling.*)

BILL (*looking at letter in his hand*). Mrs. Taft's in number four, ain't she? (*Corrects his mistake—changes letter to No. Four.*) There! That's right. This one is for Mr. Thomas. (*Turns as if to go up stage. She makes slight move in that direction, he alters his course and makes a wide detour down stage, looking at letter in his hand. Pauses—and reads envelope.*) "Raymond Thomas, Es—Q."

MRS. JONES. Bill, have you been drinking?

BILL (*turns suddenly and breathes in her face*).

MRS. JONES. Thank the Lord.

BILL. What's he got to do with it? (*Turns and puts* THOMAS's *letter in California rack.*)

MRS. JONES (*in much mollified tone*). You know it's way past dinner time. If you won't work, the least you can do is to be on time for your meals.

BILL. I been working. (*Crosses, speaking as he goes.*)

MRS. JONES. Working? At what?

BILL. I got the mail. (*Passing* MRS. JONES.)

MRS. JONES. The mail came at ten o'clock.

BILL. Well, I got it.

MRS. JONES. Was there a letter for you? (*Looking into* BILL's *face.*)

BILL (*slightly shaking head*). No.

MRS. JONES. Bill Jones, didn't your pension come today? (*Still looking at* BILL.)

BILL (*Puts hand in trousers pocket —feeling money*). Not—today——

MRS. JONES (*pleasantly*). Well, when it does come, Millie's going to buy you some clothes with it.

BILL. I got clothes enough.

MRS. JONES. You've got nothing fit to wear in the city. When you began calling on me you had good clothes.

BILL. Well, this is the same suit. (*Crosses toward California desk, meets* MILLIE. MILLIE *enters from dining-room, leaving door open.*)

MILLIE (*comes to* BILL). Oh, Daddy —you're back!

BILL. What of it?

MILLIE (*goes to him*). Are you all right?

BILL (*breathes into her face*). Now are you satisfied?

MILLIE (*kisses him*). Do go in to your dinner, won't you? (*Crosses to dining-room door.*)

MRS. JONES. Millie has saved you something hot. (*Crosses close to* BILL.)

MILLIE. Please come now. The girls want to get their work done up.

BILL. I'd have been in there long ago if mother hadn't stopped me. (MILLIE *goes back of California desk. Glances at Nevada desk.*) You and Millie go in. I'll be there in a moment.

MRS. JONES. Oh, no. You march yourself in *now*. (*Points to dining room.*)

BILL. No.

MRS. JONES. What?

BILL. Yes. (*Exits. Enter* LEMUEL TOWNSEND, *from dining room.* BILL *crosses* LEM *and exits.* LEM *gets his hat and portfolio from hat rack.* MRS. JONES *goes up California stairs.*)

MRS. JONES. Call me when the boat comes, Millie. (*Exits.*)

MILLIE. Yes, ma'am. (*Back of California desk, looking in letter box.*)

LEM (*with a low bow*). Who do I pay? (*Coming in front of desk. Puts hat and portfolio on desk.*)

MILLIE. Are you only staying for dinner?

LEM. That's all this trip.

MILLIE. Four bits.

LEM. Cheap enough for that dinner. (*Gives* MILLIE *money. She puts it in drawer under desk.*) I never heard of this hotel until a week ago. (LEM *looking about.*)

MILLIE. It's only been running about three months.

LEM. Well, it certainly is a great idea. Who thought of it?

MILLIE. It just happened.

LEM. How was that?

MILLIE (*back of desk*). Mother's plan was just to take summer boarders and we didn't get any; but all of a sudden the women began coming and asking for rooms in Nevada. So we had to put in the Nevada desk and register.

LEM (*looks from one desk to the other*). Oh—and now you're all filled up.

MILLIE. Nevada's about full, but California's about empty.

LEM. Well, if I'm elected—(*opening portfolio, taking out cards*)—your guests will be coming up before me later on. I'm running for Judge, at the next election. (*Takes card bearing his picture and "Vote for Lemuel Townsend for Superior Judge of the Second Judicial District." Hands her one.*)

MILLIE (*looking at card*). Indeed?

LEM. Yes, I'm on a sort of personally conducted campaign tour. Do you mind if I tack up a card or two?

MILLIE. Not at all.

LEM (*taking cards, etc., to other desk*). Thank you. (*Crosses around to hat rack, puts card on post of staircase.*)

(MILLIE *back of desk. Enter* LIVERYMAN *carrying several bags.* LEM *goes behind desk and puts up cards.*)

LIVERYMAN. I drove some folks up from the landing. (*Putting two grips by Nevada desk.*)

MILLIE. Oh! the boat's in.

(*Enter* C. MRS. HARPER *and Maid* FREEDA, EVERETT HAMMOND *and* SHERIFF NEVIN BLODGETT. MRS. HARPER *is twenty-four and looks younger; she is pretty, trim little figure and girlish manner. She is a little overdressed, wears a heavy veil and is much agitated and embarrassed.* FREEDA, *the maid, is dressed in dark blue street dress; she is tall and thin but good looking. She stands helplessly about with her arms full of bundles.* HAMMOND *is a large, important man about forty. His clothes are well fitting, well pressed and a bit flashy. He continually tries to be genial.* SHERIFF BLODGETT *is a tall, long-legged, raw-boned, hatchet-faced man. He wears slouch hat and high boots.* MRS. HARPER *gives* LIVERYMAN *money,* R. *of him.*)

LIVERYMAN (*receiving money from* MRS. HARPER). Thank you, marm.

HAMMOND. I want to pay for two. (*Comes to* LIVERYMAN.)

LIVERYMAN (*going past him and out*). I'll be back in a minute. I got to help the lame lady.

SHERIFF. How are you, Mr. Townsend? (*Crossing down to* LEM.)

LEM. Hello, Sheriff. (*They shake hands.*)

MILLIE (*going to* SHERIFF). Do you want to register?

HAMMOND. No, thanks. We just wanted to find out if—— (*Notices* MRS. HARPER—SHERIFF *turns and looks at* MRS. HARPER. LEM *sticks card on end of desk and then watches* MRS. HARPER.) Suppose you attend to the others first. (MILLIE *turns to* MRS. HARPER, *who advances much embarrassed.*)

MILLIE. Would you like to register?

MRS. HARPER (MRS. HARPER *looks around at everybody*). How do you do—I understand—(*sees* HAMMOND *looking on.*)—I've been told that—(*sees* SHERIFF *watching from the other side.*) Could I speak to you privately?

MILLIE (*going to parlor door which she opens*). Certainly. Will you come in here? (LEM *goes back of desk,* SHERIFF *turns to* LEM *and makes remark about* MRS. HARPER.)

MRS. HARPER (MRS. HARPER *and* FREEDA *exit into parlor*). Thank you. (*Crossing to door.*) Come, Freeda. (FREEDA *picks up bag and follows* MRS. HARPER *off stage.*)

HAMMOND. Can we hire an automobile here?

MILLIE. No, sir. But you can get a team from the liveryman.

HAMMOND. Thanks. (MILLIE *exits, closing door.* LIVERYMAN *enters with* MRS. MARGARET DAVIS. *She is on one crutch and he has her arm.*) Can I get a rig from you?

LIVERYMAN (*holding open door*). Not until I get back to the stable.

HAMMOND. That's soon enough. Come on, Blodgett. (HAMMOND *and* SHERIFF *exit.* HAMMOND *points to waterfall as they exit.* MARGARET DAVIS *is a woman of thirty, of medium height, pretty, well-formed, well and quietly dressed. Though she is quite independent, she is simple and straightforward, never fresh and seldom slangy. She is on one crutch.* LEM *turns to watch.)*

MARGARET. Now I'm all right, thank you.

LIVERYMAN. Is this your bag? (*He turns and picks up bag and puts it on desk.)*

MARGARET. Yes. (*Sees* LEM.) Oh; wait a minute and I'll get some change from the clerk. (*Going to desk—opening purse.*) Will you change five dollars for me? (*In front of desk.)*

LEM (*laughs—embarrassed*). I'm afraid I can't.

MARGARET. Well then, pay the bus man, please. (*Turns away.)*

LEM (*realizing whom she has taken him for*). Why—er—er——

MARGARET (*looks at him*). What's the matter with you?

LEM. I shall be delighted. (*He crosses to* LIVERYMAN.) How much is it?

LIVERYMAN. Four bits; two bits apiece.

MARGARET. Apiece?

LIVERYMAN. Two for you and two for your trunk.

MARGARET (*laughing*). Oh, I didn't know but you were charging for the crutch. (LEM *laughs.* MARGARET *stops laughing and glares at* LEM—*he stops laughing.)*

LEM (*gives him money*). Here you are.

LIVERYMAN. Thank you, marm. (*Exits.)*

MARGARET. Charge that, please.

LEM (*hesitating*). Well—er——

MARGARET. I'm Mrs. Davis—Mrs. Margaret Davis.

LEM (*crosses to her, as if being introduced*). I'm very glad to meet you. My name is Lemuel Townsend. And I——

MARGARET. Will you show me my room?

LEM. I'm afraid I don't know where it is——(*Amused.)*

MARGARET. Why, you were expecting me, weren't you?

LEM. No, no, I wasn't.

MARGARET. I wrote you I was coming.

LEM. No, you didn't write to me. You see I'm only a guest here. (LEM *joins in the laugh and laughs louder than she, as if it were a great joke.)*

MARGARET. And I said——(MARGARET *looks front. Laughs suddenly.*) And I took you for the clerk. (*Still laughing.)*

LEM. Yes. (*Laughs.*)

MARGARET (*laughs*). And I made you pay the bus man.

LEM. That was a pleasure. (*Laughs.*)

MARGARET (*laughs through speech*). Oh! I couldn't allow that. Just as soon as somebody comes, I'll return it. I hope you'll forgive me. (*Seriously.*)

LEM (*gets chair.*) I'm so glad it happened. Oh! won't you sit down? (*Offers chair.*)

MARGARET. I'll try but (*Sits. Takes crutch in left hand.* LEM *moves to her in back and helps her*) it's not so easy for me to sit down as it used to be. (*When seated.*) There—now I'm all right till I have to get up again.

LEM. Will you allow me to introduce myself properly? (*Sees card on desk and gets it.*) Permit me—my card. (MARGARET *takes card.*) I'm candidate for judge at the next election.

MARGARET (*looking at card*). Oh, really. (*Turns to him suddenly, handing back card. Pause.*) Where will you be judge?

LEM. If I'm elected—in Reno.

MARGARET (*quickly*). Will you try divorce cases?

LEM. Oh, yes.

MARGARET (*offers hand*). Eh! I'm awfully glad to meet you.

LEM. The pleasure is mutual, believe me. (*Puts card back on desk—gets chair and brings it down to* MARGARET.) Do you intend remaining here long? (*Sits.*)

MARGARET. I'm in for six months.

LEM (*seriously*). Oh! I'm very sorry for you, Mrs. Davis—if——

MARGARET. Oh, my case doesn't call for sympathy.

LEM. No?

MARGARET. No! Congratulations.

LEM (*changing manner—laughing*). Oh—it's that way?

MARGARET. Yes, and I'd probably never been able to get a divorce if it hadn't been for this. (*Indicates leg.*)

LEM (*shocked and very indignant*). You don't mean that your husband was brute enough to . . . ?

MARGARET. Oh, heavens no! This was an accident.

LEM. Oh—Is it—Is it serious?

MARGARET (*emphatically*). I should say it is.

LEM. Something that will be permanent?

MARGARET (*laughing*). Oh, no. Not so bad as that.

LEM. Oh!

MARGARET. It's a sprain. See? (*Crosses knees, puts hand on ankle.*)

LEM (*a trifle embarrassed*). I'm very sorry.

MARGARET. It's probably all for the best. You see, I'm a dancer.

LEM. A dancer?

MARGARET. Yes. I play vaudeville theaters. I've wanted a divorce for years but I'm always booked solid and never could stay in one place long enough to get one. When this happened it gave me just the chance I've been looking for. Now I can get a good long rest and my freedom into the bargain.

LEM. That certainly *is* a great scheme.

MARGARET. It's nice of you to listen to it all—I don't often tell the story of my life.

LEM (*romantically*). I'm glad you told it to me—because from the moment I saw you walk in that door—I—— (MARGARET *looks at* LEM.) But then I was afraid—that you—well, it was a great relief to find you had two good—— (*Indicates leg.*)

MARGARET. Anyone that has seen me dance can inform you about that. (*Look at each other and laugh.*) Are you stopping here for pleasure or are you doing time too?

LEM. I'm a bachelor.

MARGARET (*looks at him; he smiles; she looks away*). How nice! (BILL *enters from dining room.*) Oh, here's someone now. (LEM *rises, moves chair.* LEM *helps her to rise.* BILL *watches as she limps toward him.*) Are you connected with the hotel? (LEM *puts his chair near desk and crosses at back, watching following scene.*)

BILL. Rheumatism?

MARGARET. No.

BILL. This is the best climate in the world for rheumatism.

MARGARET (*in front of desk*). I'm Mrs. Davis. You're reserving a room for me. (*Takes pen.*)

BILL. How long do you expect to stay? (*Goes back of desk.*)

MARGARET. The usual. (*In front of desk starting to register.*)

BILL. Eh?

MARGARET. Six months.

BILL (*takes away pen and crossing to the other desk front of it*). This is the six months side over here. (MARGARET *turns.* MRS. JONES *enters from upstairs. She has changed dress and combed hair. Crosses to* MRS. DAVIS.)

MRS. JONES. Oh, is this Mrs. Davis?

MARGARET. Yes.

MRS. JONES. I'm reserving number eight for you. Do you want to go up now?

MARGARET. Good heavens—is it up?

MRS. JONES. Only one flight. (*Turns and sees bag on upper end of desk.*) Is this your bag?

MARGARET. Yes. (MRS. JONES *crosses and gets bag, goes upstairs and waits at top.*)

LEM (*who has been watching eagerly, to* MARGARET). Won't you let me help you?

MARGARET. Why, thank you very much, Judge. (LEM *takes crutch, puts left arm about her, starts for stairs.*)

(*Enter* MILLIE, MRS. HARPER *and* FREEDA. MRS. HARPER *starts for California desk.*)

LEM. I'm not a judge yet.

MARGARET. Oh, but you will be. I'm sure of that. (*She puts her arm on his shoulder and he assists her.* MRS. JONES *stands aside to let them pass.*)

BILL (*to* MRS. HARPER *and* FREEDA). Is either of you getting a divorce?

MILLIE. Daddy! (*Goes behind desk.*)

BILL. Well, if they are, they are going to the wrong desk. (MRS. HARPER *goes to Nevada desk and registers.*)

MARGARET. Will you have my trunk sent up please? (*Exits*).

MRS. JONES. Bill.

BILL. Yes?

MRS. JONES. Bring Mrs. Davis's trunk up to eight right away.

BILL. It'll be right up there. (MRS. JONES *exits up Nevada stairs.*)

MRS. HARPER. All right, Freeda.

MILLIE (*taking keys from rack, comes around and up to steps*). It's a very small room but the only one we have left. (MILLIE *comes from behind desk, starts up stairs as does* FREEDA *who has picked up luggage*).

BILL (*reading name in register*). Mrs. Harper, Truckee. (MRS. HARPER *turns and looks at him. Looking up.*) Does your husband drive a green automobile?

MRS. HARPER (*surprised*). Yes.

BILL. I met him last night. (MRS. HARPER *looks at* BILL *in surprise.*) He's a fast driver, ain't he? Gets to Truckee in two hours.

MILLIE (*from stairs*). Will you come up now?

MRS. HARPER (*following her*). Thank you.

BILL (*talking to* MRS. HARPER *as she goes*). Yes, sir, he's got a pile of money. Carries it all with him.

MILLIE (*from landing*). Daddy! (MRS. HARPER *and* FREEDA *exit up Nevada stairs.*)

BILL. Well, seems like she was making a mistake, leaving a man like that. (HAMMOND *and* SHERIFF *enter.*)

MILLIE. Daddy! (*Exits.*)

HAMMOND. How are you?

BILL (*looking them over*). All right. Want to register? (*Starts for California desk.*)

HAMMOND. No, thanks. We're just waiting for a rig from the livery stable. Is it too late to get something to eat? (*Looks toward dining room.*)

BILL. Dinner's over. Supper at six.

SHERIFF. Got a bar?

BILL. Having one put in next week. Do you want a drink?

SHERIFF. Where'll I get it?

BILL (*suddenly thinking*). I think I can find you something. (*Crosses above* SHERIFF *to desk.*)

SHERIFF. Good. (*Gets chair, brings it around and sits.*)

(BILL *goes to Nevada desk and looks for flask.* HAMMOND *gets chair, brings it down and sits*).

HAMMOND. By the way, is there a man stopping here named Raymond Thomas?

BILL. Huh! (*Taking letters out of register.*)

HAMMOND. I heard there was a Mr. Thomas stopping here.

BILL (*looking in his pockets*). Yeh. He's here.

HAMMOND. Is he in now?

(BILL *looks behind desk. Raises lid of register.*)

HAMMOND. I say, do you know if he's here now?

(MILLIE *enters from Nevada stairs.*)

BILL. I know it was here last night.

MILLIE (*sees* BILL *hunting*). Daddy? (BILL *slams down register.* SHERIFF *and* HAMMOND *rise, remove hats.* SHERIFF *puts his chair front of counter.*)

BILL. He wants to see Mr. Thomas. (*Comes out.*)

MILLIE (*crossing to* HAMMOND—*looks at* HAMMOND *interested*). He's in his room.

HAMMOND (*rises*). Would you send up my card, please? (*Takes out card case.*)

BILL (*crosses to* MILLIE). They wanted dinner. But I told them it was too late.

MILLIE (BILL *feels for bottle*). I can get you some sandwiches if you'd like them.

HAMMOND. Well, we are a little hungry, but I don't like to trouble you. (*Hands* MILLIE *card.*)

MILLIE. It isn't a bit of trouble. Daddy, take this card to Mr. Thomas. (*Gives* BILL *card.*) Won't you come in here . . . (*She crosses to dining-room door*—HAMMOND *and* SHERIFF *follow.*)

HAMMOND (*going*). That's right nice of you. Come along, Blodgett. (*He goes—hangs hat on rack.* FREEDA *starts downstairs.*)

MILLIE. I'll try to find you something. (*Exits.*)

BILL. I've been trying to find them something. (*Tearing up card.* SHERIFF *exits, hanging hat on rack.* FREEDA *comes down Nevada stairs—looks about.*)

FREEDA (*to* BILL). Which way is the kitchen?

BILL. Through there. (*Points; thinks, turns and goes back to Nevada desk and again searches in register.*

FREEDA *exits to kitchen.* JOHN, *neatly dressed, enters, watches* BILL.)

JOHN (*loudly, coming down before speaking*). Front! (BILL *swings around guiltily—closing register quickly.*) Hello, Lightnin'.

BILL (*stands looking at* JOHN *in surprise*). I never saw you dressed up before. Had your dinner?

JOHN. Yes, Lightnin'. (*Laughing.*)

BILL. I can get you some sandwiches.

JOHN. No, thanks. I want to look around. (*Turns.*) Is this the room that's in both states?

BILL (*pointing*). Yes, the state line runs right across there. (*Points to line.*)

JOHN. You're in California and I'm in Nevada? I had no idea you had such a place.

BILL (*crossing back absent-mindedly to Nevada desk*). How about a little something to drink?

JOHN. No, nothing, thanks.

BILL. Sure?

JOHN. No, nothing, Bill.

BILL. Well, I can't find it anyhow. (JOHN *crosses to* BILL. *With a sudden thought, crosses to register and points at name.* JOHN *looks at register.*)

JOHN. Mrs. Harper?

BILL. Just got here. Come for a divorce.

JOHN. How do you know?

BILL. That's what they all come for.

JOHN. Why, Mr. Harper told me all about that trouble. It's the silliest thing in the world. I wonder if I could talk to her.

BILL. I tried that. Don't do no good. (FREEDA *enters from kitchen with glass of milk and saucer of crackers on tray—starts for stairs.*) There's her hired girl.

JOHN (*going toward her, crosses in front of* BILL). Oh, Miss—are you here with Mrs. Harper?

FREEDA (*stopping—surprised*). I am.

JOHN. My name is John Marvin. I'm a friend of Mr. Harper. Will you please ask Mrs. Harper if I may see her for a few minutes?

FREEDA (*doubtfully*). Yes, sir, I'll ask her. (*Goes to foot of stairs—waits for* LEM *to pass.*)

JOHN. Thank you. (LEM *enters down Nevada stairs.* FREEDA *exits.*)

LEM (*sees* BILL). Mrs. Davis is waiting for her trunk.

BILL. It'll be right up there.

LEM (*crosses to desk, picking up hat and portfolio as he goes.* JOHN *goes to upper end California desk and puts hat there*). Well, hurry it up, will you? She wants to change her dress and I'm going to take her for a buggy ride. (*Hurries off stage.*)

BILL (*starts to sit in chair*). They're always wanting something. (MRS.

JONES *enters from Nevada stairs. Comes downstairs hurriedly.*)

MRS. JONES. Bill Jones, where's that lady's trunk?

BILL (*rises*). Oh, Mother, this is Mr. Marvin. (JOHN *rises—backing up.*)

JOHN. How'd you do, Mrs. Jones. (*Crosses to* MRS. JONES.)

MRS. JONES (*shortly*). How de do. (*To* BILL *as she goes toward kitchen.*) Don't you know how long that lady's been waiting for her trunk?

BILL. It'll be right up there. (*Crosses and points to chair.*) Sit down, John. (MRS. JONES *turns at the kitchen door.*)

MRS. JONES. Well, you get it up there. (*He turns.*) Start!

BILL (*going toward porch*). Wait here, John. I won't be a minute. (*Exits.*)

MRS. JONES. Excuse me. (*She exits into kitchen.* JOHN *looks after her in amused surprise, then turns, goes to Nevada desk.* MILLIE *enters from dining room—starts.*)

JOHN. Why, Miss Buckley!

MILLIE (*seeing him*). Mr. Marvin! (*Goes to him.*) This is a surprise. (*They shake hands.*)

JOHN. Good heavens! You're not married!

MILLIE (*puzzled*). Married?

JOHN. I—I thought people came here to get divorced.

MILLIE (*laughs*). Oh—they do. But I work here.

JOHN. You what?

MILLIE. The hotel belongs to my mother and father.

JOHN. Mr. and Mrs. Jones?

MILLIE. Yes.

JOHN. Are your mother and father?

MILLIE. Well, they're not really, but I've always called them that, I've lived with them ever since I can remember.

JOHN. And I've been seeing Lightnin' for the last month and never knew anything about it.

MILLIE. Have you got a camp over on High Ridge?

JOHN. Yes.

MILLIE. Why, Daddy's always talking about you and I hadn't an idea who you were. You haven't given up law, have you?

JOHN. Only for the time being.

MILLIE. I was sure you'd never give that up.

JOHN. Why?

MILLIE. The way you studied at Mr. Thomas' office. I never saw anyone study so hard.

JOHN. Not when you were in the room, I wasn't—because I was looking at you most of the time.

MILLIE. Oh, no. If you'd been looking at me, I'd have seen you.

JOHN. Would you? (*Crosses close to* MILLIE—*both laugh.* MILLIE *turns and sits chair.*)

MILLIE. Uh, huh! (*Sits.*)

JOHN. You haven't left Mr. Thomas' office?

MILLIE. Why yes, I left the week after you did.

JOHN. Why? Was there any trouble?

MILLIE. Of course not. How could there be any trouble with Mr. Thomas?

JOHN (*bringing chair to* MILLIE *and sitting*). Oh! You like Mr. Thomas—like him very much, don't you?

MILLIE. I more than like him. I adore him. Why, he's done everything for me. You've no idea how fine he is.

JOHN. Well, I know a little about him.

MILLIE. Oh, yes, he sold some property for your mother, didn't he?

JOHN. Yes. He sold it to the railroad.

MILLIE. He'll be awfully glad to see you again.

JOHN (*pause*). You don't mean Mr. Thomas is here?

MILLIE. Yes, he's upstairs packing now. He's leaving by the afternoon boat. He came way up from San Francisco to help me.

JOHN. In what way?

MILLIE. Well, mother had just opened the hotel. He said I ought to go home and see how she was getting on—and I found her in the biggest lot of trouble.

JOHN. What trouble?

MILLIE. Why, it seems a big hotel company found out how well she was doing and they planned to put up a huge hotel just back of us, and mother was nearly crazy, for she saw that would take away all her business.

JOHN. And you wrote to Mr. Thomas all about it?

MILLIE (*surprised*). Yes.

JOHN. And he wrote you he'd do everything in his power to help you?

MILLIE. He telegraphed. Wasn't that just like him?

JOHN. Exactly. Wouldn't it be wonderful if Mr. Thomas could get the hotel company to buy your property and build the big hotel here?

MILLIE. You're awfully clever to think of that. That's just what he has done. (JOHN *looks front.*) And they're going to pay enough to make mother and daddy comfortable for the rest of their lives.

JOHN. Are they going to pay cash?

MILLIE. Oh, it's much better than cash. It's shares of their stock that pay you ten per cent a year. It seems almost too good to be true.

JOHN (*rises*). It does, doesn't it?

MILLIE (*rises*). Well, the hotel company telegraphed they'd take it and Mr. Thomas is going to fix up all the papers as soon as he gets back to the city.

JOHN. Miss Buckley, I'm afraid that you—— (*Sees* MRS. JONES, *who enters from kitchen and starts for stairs.*)

MILLIE. Why—what is it?

JOHN. I must see Bill for a moment right away if you'll excuse me. (*Crosses up to door.*)

MILLIE. Oh, Mother, this is Mr. Marvin.

MRS. JONES. I've met the gentleman.

JOHN. Yes, Mr. Jones introduced us. (*At door.*)

MILLIE. Do you know where Daddy is?

JOHN. He went out here somewhere after a trunk.

MRS. JONES. My land—ain't he got back with that trunk yet? (*Turns and speaks to* JOHN.)

JOHN (*to* MRS. JONES). I'll go out and find him. (MILLIE *crosses to right of* JOHN.) I hope I may see you again, Miss Buckley.

MILLIE. I shan't run away.

JOHN. I—I'll be right back. (*Goes out, turning to left.*)

MILLIE (*comes down to right of* MRS. JONES). Oh, is that for Mrs. Davis? (*Indicating tray* MRS. JONES *brought in.*)

MRS. JONES. Just to last her till supper time.

MILLIE. I'll take it up to her. (*Crosses to Nevada stairs.*)

MRS. JONES. What's that man doing around here? (*Crosses to door, looking after him.*)

MILLIE (*turns to* MRS. JONES). He's an awfully nice man, Mother. Why, he's been living near here for over a month and I didn't know anything about it.

MRS. JONES (*crosses to* MILLIE). Why should you? He's one of Bill's cronies, ain't he?

MILLIE. Yes, but I met him in Mr. Thomas' office.

MRS. JONES (*comprehending*). Oh—the poor young man that studied so hard and that you were so sorry for—I thought there was more to that story than you ever let on.

MILLIE (*starts up Nevada stairs*). Why, I hardly know Mr. Marvin. (*Goes upstairs, exits.*)

MRS. JONES (*crosses to stairs, calling after her*). It looked to me as though you knew each other pretty well.

(*Enter* BILL *with trunk on his back.* MRS. JONES *turns and sees* BILL.)

MRS. JONES (*to* BILL). Do you realize how long that lady's been waiting for her trunk?

BILL. I realize it's heavy. (*Going up steps.*)

MRS. JONES (*scolding, but really afraid of trunk's weight*). Oh, well—don't try to take it up if it's too much for you.

BILL (*turns and comes down to her*). Oh, it's easy when you know how. Just a knack.

MRS. JONES. Did you see that Mr. Marvin out there?

BILL. No.

MRS. JONES. Well, I don't want him hanging around here, Bill.

BILL. John's all right. (*Starts upstairs.*)

MRS. JONES. I won't have him here, I've got my reasons. (*Exits into kitchen.* MRS. HARPER *enters from top of stairs as* BILL *gets to top step with trunk.*)

MRS. HARPER (*almost running into* BILL). Oh!

BILL. Excuse me. (*Comes down steps.* MRS. HARPER *comes down.*)

MRS. HARPER. Does a Mr. Marvin want to see me?

BILL. Yes—just wait there in the parlor and I'll send him to you in a minute. (MRS. HARPER *goes into the parlor.* BILL *starts up the stairs again.* JOHN *enters.*)

JOHN. Oh, Bill—I want to see you right away—— (*Comes down, throws chair up center.*)

BILL. Mrs. Harper's in the parlor. (*Coming downstairs to* JOHN.)

JOHN. I'll see her in a minute. Bill, they're trying to rob you.

BILL. Wait a minute. (*Puts trunk on desk, turns to* JOHN.) What did you say?

JOHN. They're trying to rob you, Bill.

BILL (*taking money out of packet*). No, they ain't.

JOHN. Listen, Bill, this man Thomas is trying to cheat you out of your place.

BILL. Mr. Thomas?

JOHN. Yes, Mr. Thomas.

BILL. What makes you think that?

JOHN. I'm sure of it. The stock he's going to give you isn't worth a dollar.

BILL. What can I do about it? The place belongs to mother.

JOHN (*looks front*). Oh! well, tell Thomas your wife won't consider selling until you consult your lawyer. Then I'll talk to him. (BILL *gets trunk on his back again at desk.*)

BILL. What'll I tell him? (*With trunk on back at desk.*)

JOHN. That you won't sell until you consult your lawyer.

BILL. I'd have told him that anyway. (*Crosses up stage and goes upstairs.*)

JOHN. Good. Now I've got to see Mrs. Harper.

BILL (*at top of stairs leaning over railing*). Oh, John! What makes you think that about Thomas?

JOHN. Because he's the man who cheated me out of my property and sold it to the railroad. (*Exits into parlor and* THOMAS *enters.* BILL *stands on landing looking at* THOMAS. THOMAS *enters from California stairs as* JOHN *exits.*)

THOMAS. Oh, Bill, I want to see you for a minute.

BILL. Can't you see me from there?

THOMAS (*looks up at him*). Why, what's the matter? (*Puts hat and coat on desk.*)

BILL. Can't tell you 'till I consult my lawyer. (*Exit* BILL, *enter* MRS. JONES *from kitchen.*)

MRS. JONES. So you are all ready to go?

THOMAS. Yes, all ready.

MRS. JONES. I'd like to have a little talk with you if you don't mind.

THOMAS. Why, certainly not, Mrs. Jones. (*Comes down to* MRS. JONES.)

MRS. JONES. There's something that's worrying me and I just wanted to speak to you about it.

THOMAS. Why then do so by all means.

MRS. JONES. Well, I've had an idea that you are—(*Laughs.*) well, that you're fond of Millie.

THOMAS. Oh! (*Laughing.*) Fond of her? I should say I am.

MRS. JONES. And I know that Millie is very fond of you. And I've been wondering if there was any reason why you hadn't told each other about it.

THOMAS. Oh, well, I guess Millie doesn't see me in that light.

MRS. JONES. Do you think she sees Mr. Marvin in that light?

THOMAS (*hesitatingly*). Marvin?

MRS. JONES. Ain't that the name of the man you had in your office?

THOMAS (*after a moment's pause*). Why, yes—yes—I did have a John Marvin in my office for a short time. Has—has Millie talked to you about him?

MRS. JONES (*looking front*). It is not what Millie said—(*looks at* THOMAS) —it's the way he looked at her. A blind man could see he was in love with her.

THOMAS. He—he was here?

MRS. JONES. He's here now.

THOMAS. Where?

MRS. JONES (*pointing out*). Outside there somewhere.

THOMAS (*going to door—moving chair as he goes*). I'd no idea that fellow had been coming here.

MRS. JONES (*hastily*). Oh, I don't think he has ever been here before.

THOMAS (*coming down*). Mrs. Jones, I think it's only fair to tell you—this Marvin is not a proper person for her to see. I thought he was a splendid fellow when I took him into my office. And I could hardly believe it when I found out the sort of a man he really is.

MRS. JONES. What sort is he?

THOMAS. Why—he's in with a gang that goes about the country stealing timber.

MRS. JONES. Mercy on us. (MILLIE *comes down Nevada stairs.*)

MILLIE. Oh, Mr. Thomas.

THOMAS (*cautioning* MRS. JONES). Sh!

MILLIE. Did you see the man that was waiting for you? (*Crosses to* THOMAS.)

THOMAS. No!

MILLIE (*crossing to door*). Oh! dear —I sent Daddy up to you with his card. (*As she exits into dining-room.*) Mr. Thomas is here now.

HAMMOND. Thank you! (*A moment's pause—then enter* HAMMOND.)

HAMMOND. Is this Mr. Thomas? (*Crosses to* THOMAS.)

THOMAS. Yes, sir.

HAMMOND. My name is Hammond, Everett Hammond.

THOMAS. How do you do, Mr. Hammond?

MRS. JONES. Excuse me!

THOMAS (*to* MRS. JONES). Oh, I shall see you before I go, Mrs. Jones?

MRS. JONES. Oh, yes. (*Exits in the kitchen.*)

THOMAS (*after looking around*). What's up?

HAMMOND. I'm on my way over to that Marvin fellow's place. The railroad sent a Sheriff after him yesterday but he couldn't get him so they told me I'd better come along with the Sheriff and see what I could do. I thought I'd stop here and see you first because I don't know whether it's a good idea to jail Marvin or not.

THOMAS. Why not?

HAMMOND. He'll squeal, won't he?

THOMAS. He can't prove anything. And if he talks, he'll do more harm out of jail than he will in. Where's the Sheriff?

HAMMOND. In the dining-room.

THOMAS. Well, you don't need to go over to Marvin's camp.

HAMMOND. Why?

THOMAS. Because he's here.

HAMMOND. Here, he? Does he know anything about our buying the hotel?

THOMAS. I don't know.

HAMMOND. You've got it, haven't you?

THOMAS. Well, they've agreed to sell.

HAMMOND. Then you'd better have it transferred to me right away.

THOMAS. That's what I was going to do. Now call in the Sheriff. (HAM-

MOND *crosses toward door.* MILLIE *enters, crosses to* THOMAS.) Oh, Millie—will you tell your mother that Mr. Hammond, of the Golden Gate Land Company, is here? She's in the kitchen.

MILLIE. I'll get her. (*Exits into kitchen.* THOMAS *takes chair up.*)

HAMMOND. Ready, Blodgett? (*Crosses to rack, gets hat.*)

SHERIFF. Yes, just waiting for you. (SHERIFF *enters, closes door and gets hat.*)

HAMMOND. Sheriff, this is Mr. Thomas.

THOMAS. How do you do?

SHERIFF. How are you? (*Crosses to* THOMAS.)

HAMMOND. He tells me your man is here.

SHERIFF (*to* THOMAS). Where? (*Looks at* HAMMOND, *then to* THOMAS.)

THOMAS. He's apt to come in that door any minute.

HAMMOND. You wait for him out there, and don't let him in this room.

SHERIFF. Huh!

HAMMOND. You see, if you nabbed him in the house it might cause a lot of talk.

SHERIFF. Oh! (*Starts up, turns to* THOMAS.) How'll I know him?

THOMAS. I'll point him out to you. (MRS. JONES *enters with* MILLIE. MRS. JONES *comes down.* SHERIFF *exits.*) This is Mr. Hammond, Mrs. Jones—and Miss Buckley.

HAMMOND. How do you do? (MILLIE *comes over to* MRS. JONES.)

MRS. JONES. Pleased to meet you.
MILLIE. How do you do?
(*Spoken together.*)

THOMAS. Mr. Hammond represents the Golden Gate Land Company and he tells me they are ready to take over this place at once. (THOMAS *left of* MRS. JONES, *enter* BILL *on stairs.*)

MRS. JONES. You mean you want to have us leave right away?

HAMMOND. Oh, that isn't necessary. But we prefer to have the transfer made so that we can take over the management immediately.

THOMAS. You've no objection to that, have you, Mrs. Jones? (BILL *starts downstairs.* SHERIFF *crosses window with back to audience, stands there.*)

MRS. JONES. Certainly not! (*Looking at* THOMAS. *Crosses to* HAMMOND.) I want to leave the whole matter in Mr. Thomas' hands—and I'll do anything he advises me to.

THOMAS. Then we'll give you a deed this afternoon, Mr. Hammond. (BILL *comes down to* THOMAS.)

BILL. Hold on, Thomas. We ain't goin' to sell the hotel until I consult my lawyer.

MRS. JONES (*crossing to* THOMAS). Bill—do be quiet. What in the world's the matter with you?

BILL (*enter* JOHN). Mother—they're trying to rob you.

MRS. JONES. Bill! (*Crosses to* BILL.)
MILLIE. Daddy!
(*Spoken together.*)

MRS. JONES. You apologize for saying such a thing to Mr. Thomas. (BILL *turns up to desk.*)

JOHN (*comes to* MRS. JONES). There's no need for an apology, Mrs. Jones. Bill's right. (THOMAS *goes up to door. Beckons to* SHERIFF *and points to* JOHN.)

MRS. JONES. So it's you who's been putting Bill up to this! Now I know all about you and I don't want any of your advice. (*She goes up to kitchen door,* JOHN *follows her. The* SHERIFF *enters.*)

JOHN. Mrs. Jones, you—— (SHERIFF *enters, meets* JOHN.)

SHERIFF. Is your name John Marvin? (JOHN *turns and eyes* SHERIFF *for a moment.*)

JOHN. Don't interrupt me now. (*Comes down* C. *California side.* SHERIFF *follows down Nevada side.*)

SHERIFF. You better not get fresh with me.

HAMMOND. That's the man you're after, Sheriff.

SHERIFF. I got a warrant for your arrest.

MILLIE. Oh! (*Starts up.*)

JOHN (*to* SHERIFF). I can't be bothered with you just now. Now I——

SHERIFF. None of your lip! Now, come along. (*Grabs* JOHN. *They are right on the state line.*)

JOHN (*throwing him back*). Take your hands off me. (*Throws* SHERIFF *to Nevada side; he stays on California side.*)

SHERIFF. Now you're worse off than you was before, resisting an officer of the law. (*Taking handcuffs from coat pocket starts for* JOHN.)

JOHN. Law! Don't you know any more about law than to try to serve me with a Nevada warrant when I'm in California?

BILL. By Jiminy—he's right. (*Ring curtain.*)

JOHN (*as curtain descends*). Now understand, Bill—they can't get a good title to this place without your signature—so don't you sign any paper till you see what they're after. (*Starts for* BILL, *crosses line,* SHERIFF *starts for* JOHN. BILL *motions for* JOHN *to get back as Curtain comes down. All exit quickly, except* BILL *and* SHERIFF. BILL *goes back of desk,* SHERIFF *goes up, takes* BILL'*s hat up, puts it on hook with coat, brings small table down—goes back up stage.*)

CURTAIN

ACT ONE

SCENE II

SCENE—*Same as Scene I. Moonlight outside—lamps on stage lighted. Curtain down one minute.* MRS. STARR *enters from parlor, takes chair from front of stairs, places it, back to audience, sits. She has eight quarters.* MRS. MOORE *enters from Nevada stairs, gets chair from foot of Nevada stairs, places it back of table facing front, sits.* MRS. MOORE *brings the bridge scores and pencil and cards.* MRS. JORDAN *enters from parlor, brings chair front parlor and bridge score. Places chair at table, sits.* MRS. PRESTON *enters from dining-room followed by* MRS. COGSHALL. MRS. PRESTON *gets chair at California desk, places it* R. *of table, sits.* MRS. COGSHALL *crosses back of table by* MRS. MOORE, *watching game.* LIVERYMAN *enters, puts coat and hat on chair by door, sits on them.* SHERIFF *stands talking to him.*

BILL *is behind Nevada desk getting out keys. The ladies are adding up the bridge score as curtain rises.*

MRS. MOORE. I make it thirty-one cents. (*Adding up on card.*)

MRS. JORDAN. That's correct.

(MRS. STARR *puts chair at Nevada desk.* MRS. JORDAN *takes chair up left of door center, goes to foot of Nevada stairs.* MRS. COGSHALL *crosses and goes up to top of Nevada stairs. As* MRS. JORDAN *goes up with chair,* MRS. PRESTON *crosses and follows* MRS. COGSHALL *upstairs;* MRS. JORDAN *follows* MRS. PRESTON *up;* MRS. STARR *follows* MRS. MOORE; *and* MRS. JORDAN *follows* MRS. STARR.)

MRS. STARR. I'm through for tonight.

SHERIFF (*to* LIVERYMAN). Then I can't get back tonight?

LIVERYMAN. Not unless I drive you over.

SHERIFF. What'll that cost?

LIVERYMAN. Eight dollars.

SHERIFF. I'll wait and take the train back in the morning.

MRS. COGSHALL (*from stairs*). Good night, Mr. Jones. (*Exits.*)

ALL THE LADIES. Good night, Mr. Jones.

BILL. Good night—good night. (*All ladies exit.* BILL *comes from behind Nevada desk, takes chair, puts it at Nevada desk and table up left of door center.*) Jim, keep your eye on that fellow, will you?

LIVERYMAN. Sure. (*Exits.*)

BILL (*crosses to kitchen door, raps on it.* JOHN *enters from kitchen*).

Sheriff's just gone out but he's going to stay here over night.

JOHN (*crosses in front of* BILL, *looks through window*). Has Thomas said anything more to you? (*Coming down to* BILL.)

BILL. No—but he and the other fellow have been talking to mother.

JOHN. Where are they now?

BILL. In the dining-room—going over the books.

JOHN. Is your wife with them?

BILL. No. She's up in her room with that lame lady.

JOHN. You won't sign that deed, will you, Bill?

BILL. Not unless you tell me to.

JOHN. That's right. They don't care about this hotel. They want the property for some other reason and I've got to find out what that reason is.

BILL. I can find that out for you.

JOHN. How?

BILL. I used to be a detective.

JOHN. Did you tell Miss Buckley I hadn't gone?

BILL. She ain't been down since supper.

JOHN. I must see her before I go, Lightnin', I must.

LIVERYMAN (*enters through door*). Look out, he's comin' back. (*Goes down to Nevada desk.*)

BILL (*to* JOHN). Go in there. I'll let you know the minute she comes down. (JOHN *exits quickly into kitchen.* SHERIFF *enters, looks at* BILL, *closes door, sits at table.* LIVERYMAN *crosses up to* SHERIFF, *takes* BILL'S *coat and hat from hook back of curtain, puts them on table.* LIVERYMAN *and* SHERIFF *cut cards that have been left on table by the ladies.* THOMAS *enters from dining-room with small account books, goes behind California desk, leaves books, gets papers.* BILL *comes to counter.*) I thought you was going away this afternoon?

THOMAS. You prevented that. And you nearly spoiled your wife's chances of selling this place. (*Making notation on papers.*)

BILL. Well, I'm not going to do anything 'till I consult my lawyer.

THOMAS. Oh, he calls himself a lawyer, does he, eh?

BILL. He is a lawyer. The smartest lawyer on the Coast.

THOMAS (*smiling*). Are you trying to hurt my feelings, Bill?

BILL. No, I mean the smartest honest lawyer. (LEM *comes to door, enters, comes down to* BILL.)

THOMAS (*scowls at* BILL, *then recovers himself*). Well, you go up and tell your wife Mr. Hammond and I want to see her. (*Exits door, taking papers with him.*)

BILL. Tell her yourself. (BILL *sits in chair.*)

LEM (*to* BILL). Do you know who Mrs. Davis is?

BILL. Yep, she's the lame lady.

LEM. Well, will you go up and tell her that Mr. Townsend's been waiting for her for over an hour?

BILL. That won't do no good.

LEM. What?

BILL. She's got another one now.

LEM. Another one!

BILL. Mr. Thomas. He's cut you out. He grabbed her the minute you brought her back from the buggy ride.

(LIVERYMAN *who has been watching this, laughs.* LEM *turns, sees* LIVERYMAN, *comes down left.*)

LEM. Are you the liveryman?

LIVERYMAN. Yes, sir.

LEM. I want my horse hitched up.

LIVERYMAN. You said you were going to stay over night.

LEM. I changed my mind. (LIVERYMAN *takes hat and coat from chair by door—coming down to* BILL.) Who the devil is Mr. Thomas?

BILL. If you want to get even with him, I'll send him out to you. (BILL *goes behind counter.* SHERIFF *comes down left.*

SHERIFF. Say, you going to drive to Reno tonight, Mr. Townsend?

LEM. Yes. You want to come along?

SHERIFF. Thanks. I'd like to. (HARPER *enters quickly. He carries bag.* LEM *exits after he's on.*)

HARPER (*to* LIVERYMAN). Do you know where I can find Mr. Marvin?

SHERIFF (*hears* HARPER *say* "MARVIN," *turns to him, comes down left of* HARPER). What's that? Who do you want to find?

HARPER (*turns to* SHERIFF). John Marvin. I got a telegram from him and I want to see him. (*Comes from behind to front of counter.*)

BILL. He's gone.

SHERIFF (*to* BILL). Yes, he has!

BILL. How are you, Mr. Harper?

HARPER (*comes down left of* BILL). Oh, why hello, Mr. Jones.

SHERIFF (*to* LIVERYMAN). Come along, I'll help you hitch up. (SHERIFF *starts out, followed by* LIVERYMAN. *They exit*).

BILL (*shaking his hand*). How do you do, Mr. Harper? (*Looking around cautiously. To* HARPER.) John's here. But they don't know it.

HARPER. Where's Mrs. Harper?

BILL (*pointing*). In Nevada.

HARPER. What?

BILL. I told her I thought you'd be here.

HARPER (*anxiously*). What did she say?

BILL (*after glancing at him*). Guess I better not tell you. It ain't encouraging. (HARPER *moves chair up, sits limply.*)

HARPER. Of all the damn fool things.

BILL. I wouldn't call her that.

HARPER (*rises*). Who is calling her that? I mean what happened—it was all a mistake.

BILL. Why don't you tell her?

HARPER (*up center and back to* BILL). She wouldn't believe it.

BILL (*crosses behind desk*). Same trouble I have. Folks don't believe nothin' I tell them either. Why don't you write it to her?

HARPER (*comes to front of desk*). Good idea. Can I get a room?

BILL (*behind California desk*). All you want on this side. Just register.

HARPER (*puts bag down front of desk. Registering*). Where's the bar?

BILL. Down to the saloon.

HARPER. Never mind, I've got a flask in my bag.

BILL (*picking up bag with alacrity, starts for California stairs*). I'll show you right up. (*Bill knocks on kitchen door. To* HARPER.) John wants to see you.

HARPER. What's that?

(MILLIE *enters down Nevada stairs.*)

BILL. Millie, come right down. (*Seeing her.*) Up in number four—at the end of the hall. (*Pushes* HARPER *up California stairs.* BILL *stops, looks at* JOHN *and* MILLIE *from balcony.* HARPER *exits,* BILL *follows him.* MILLIE *leaves stairs and starts down toward dining-room door.* JOHN *enters from kitchen, steps in her way.*)

JOHN. Miss Buckley. (MILLIE *looks at him. A moment's pause.*) I suppose you are surprised to find me still here.

MILLIE. I don't think anything you could do would surprise me, after what happened today.

JOHN. That's what I've waited to explain. I couldn't go without telling you why I tried to stop that sale.

MILLIE. I don't care to hear it. Mr. Thomas is the best friend I have in the world. And I won't listen to a word against him.

JOHN. But Mrs. Jones is being cheated—robbed——

MILLIE. I don't believe it. I'll never believe it. And I can't see how this concerns you anyway.

JOHN. It concerns me because—well, because I care for you.

MILLIE. Why didn't you tell me what you suspected when you first saw me today?

JOHN. Well, you see, you told me how much you thought of him. I hadn't realized before that you——

MILLIE. Do you mean, I told you I loved Mr. Thomas?

JOHN. That's what I understood.

MILLIE. Oh, you're always wrong.

JOHN. You—you mean you don't love him?

MILLIE (*turning back to* JOHN). I told you he was my best friend; I never said I loved him.

JOHN. Well, say it now—I mean, say you don't, and then give me time. I'll find out what their game is.

MILLIE (*coming to* JOHN). Oh, I don't want you to find out because I know you're mistaken, and you can't prevent mother's selling because she has sold already, only they won't pay her for it until they have daddy's name.

JOHN. They shan't have that.

MILLIE (*turns away from him*). So that's it?

JOHN. But don't you see——

MILLIE (*turning back to* JOHN). Yes, I see now. You're doing all this just to hurt Mr. Thomas.

JOHN. He told you that?

MILLIE. Yes, he did.

JOHN (*coming close to* MILLIE). Just the same I'll never let Bill sign that deed if I can prevent it, and some day you'll thank me for it.

MILLIE. Thank you! I'll always hate and despise you! Always, always, always. I hope I shall never see you again, and if I do—I'll never notice (SHERIFF *starts on*) you or speak to you the longest day I live. (SHERIFF *comes in.*) Look out, *John!* (JOHN *jumps over to California side as* SHERIFF *comes down and tries to catch him.*)

JOHN. Thank you, Miss Buckley. You saved me. (MILLIE *rushes up the Nevada stairs.*) And, Miss Buckley, I shall be grateful to you always, always, always. (MILLIE *exits.* JOHN *goes up to door—to* SHERIFF.) I'm on my own side, Sheriff. (*Exits.* SHERIFF *runs for door, tries to catch* JOHN *as he jumps and disappears.* BILL, *a bit worse for liquor, enters from California stairs, coming down.* SHERIFF *comes back and closes door.*)

SHERIFF (*to* BILL). That fellow hadn't gone after all.

BILL. Mind your business.

SHERIFF (*coming down to* BILL). Say, you're collecting something, ain't you?

BILL. I didn't get nothing from you.

SHERIFF. Don't get sore. I wish'd I was in your place. (SHERIFF *sits.* THOMAS *enters from dining room.*)

BILL (*starts for Nevada stairs*). In my place? You're like that other fellow. (*Indicates* THOMAS.)

THOMAS (*goes back of California desk consulting paper*). Did you tell your wife we were waiting for her?

BILL. No, I didn't. I've been up visiting my friend Mr. Harper. (*To* SHERIFF.) Big millionaire. Havin' trouble with his wife. I got him to write this note and I'm going to deliver it. He gave me this bottle for the idea. (*Holding up bottle.* BILL *goes up Nevada stairs, exits.* MARGARET *and* MRS. JONES *enter from California stairs.* MRS. JONES *in evening gown;* MARGARET *is carrying crutch in her left hand.* MRS. JONES *has her arm around* MARGARET'S *waist helping her.*)

MARGARET. Oh, Mr. Thomas—look who's here.

THOMAS (*sees* MRS. JONES, *comes from behind desk to front of it*). Well, upon my word—what does this mean?

MRS. JONES. It means she's been fixing me up in one of her theater dresses.

MARGARET. Now, Mrs. Jones—you know you wanted to put it on.

MRS. JONES. Well, I didn't want to come down here in it. She's been so worried, about how she was going to look when she gets to San Francisco that I dressed her up in this.

THOMAS. Why, you look stunning.

MRS. JONES. Well, I feel foolish.

THOMAS. Well, you've no reason to. (*Goes and opens door.*)

MARGARET. Of course you haven't. (MRS. JONES *looks at* MARGARET.)

THOMAS. Do you know, Mr. Hammond and I've been waiting for you for an hour?

MRS. JONES (*crossing to* THOMAS). I'm sorry. (*To* MARGARET.) It's the business about the hotel. Will you excuse me? (*Exits.*)

MARGARET. Of course. (*Goes to* THOMAS. LEM *enters, comes down stage watching* THOMAS *and* MARGARET.)

THOMAS (*goes to* MARGARET). It's mighty nice of you to go to all this trouble, Mrs. Davis. I appreciate it a lot.

MARGARET. Don't speak of it. I've enjoyed it immensely.

SHERIFF (*rises and comes down to* JUDGE). Is the team ready, Mr. Townsend? (THOMAS *exits.*)

JUDGE (*starts up center.*)

MARGARET (*goes above chair to* LEM). Why, Judge, you're not going? (SHERIFF *exits.*)

LEM (*stops*). Yes. (*Starts out.*)

MARGARET. Why, you said you'd wait until tomorrow.

LEM. I've changed my mind.

MARGARET. But I haven't seen you all evening.

LEM (*coming to her*). Oh, have you noticed that?

MARGARET. But I'd no idea you were leaving tonight—and there are so many things I wanted to talk to you about—oh, don't go just yet—(BILL *enters Nevada stairs, comes down*)—please, Judge! (*Hands him crutch.*) We'll go out on the porch. (*Takes his arm and leads him up.*) It wouldn't be at all nice to go without even saying good-by. (*They exit. As they exit,* BILL *closes door, comes to bottom of Nevada stairs, calls up Nevada stairs.*)

BILL. Mrs. Harper—Mrs. Harper—— (MRS. HARPER *appears top of Nevada stairs; wears kimono.*)

BILL. He's in number four. Hurry now before anybody sees you. (MRS. HARPER *comes down, crosses to foot of California stairs.*)

MRS. HARPER (*going to* BILL). Do they all know he's my husband?

BILL. No, I won't say nothin' about it. He's in number four. Hurry before somebody sees you. (BILL *leans on counter.* MRS. HARPER *goes up California stairs and exits.* HAMMOND *enters from dining-room with books and papers, goes behind California desk.* SHERIFF *enters.*)

SHERIFF. This is a hard place to get away from. Now that the rig's ready that woman's got Townsend out there buzzin' him like a Dutch uncle. (*Turns up, looks off through window.*)

BILL (*to* HAMMOND). Oh, you running the place now? (SHERIFF *brings chair.*)

HAMMOND. Well, I've just settled everything with your wife. All that's needed now is for you to sign that deed.

BILL. I'll take a drink with you.

HAMMOND (*laughing*). Sorry, I haven't got anything.

BILL (*takes out bottle*). I have.

SHERIFF. You look as if you've had enough.

BILL. Oh, I don't want it for myself, it's just sociability. I don't drink.

SHERIFF. Don't tell me that. You're a booze fighter. (*Sits.*)

BILL. No, I ain't—I'm a Indian fighter.

SHERIFF. Is that so?

BILL. Yes, that's so. Did you ever know Buffalo Bill?

SHERIFF. Yes, I knew him well. (BILL *turns, takes a good look at him.*)

BILL. I learned him all he knew about killing Indians. (*Sits.*) Did he ever tell you about the duel I fought with Settin' Bull?

SHERIFF. Settin' Bull?

BILL. He was standin' when I sho˛ him. I never took advantage of nobody, not even a Indian.

SHERIFF. Say, you got a bee in your bonnet, ain't you?

BILL. What do you know about bees?

SHERIFF. Not much, do you?

BILL. Yes, I do—I know all about 'em. I used to be in the bee business. Why, I drove a swarm of bees across the plains in the dead of winter. And never lost a bee. Got stung twice.

SHERIFF (*rises*). I got enough. (SHERIFF *replaces his chair by desk and exits.*) I'm going out and set in the buggy.

HAMMOND. Now look here, Mr. Jones——

BILL. Won't do no good. I promised John not to sign nothing, and I ain't going to sign nothing—understand that.

HAMMOND. Well, if you don't you'll find yourself without a home. (*Enter* MRS. JONES *and* THOMAS, *he stops at lower end of desk, and* MRS. JONES *crosses to Nevada desk.*) You understand that—if you're not too drunk.

BILL. Do you think I'm drunk? (*Turns, sees* MRS. JONES *crossing to left; thinks she is one of the guests. Rises. Crosses to* MRS. JONES.) Do you want your key? (MRS. JONES *turns with key in one hand and pen in the other.* BILL *recognizes her.*) Mother, it ain't you?

MRS. JONES (*angrily*). Yes, it's me.

BILL (*to* HAMMOND). You're right. I'm drunk.

THOMAS (*suddenly assuming pleasant manner*). Don't you approve, Lightnin'? Why, she's dressed in the height of fashion.

BILL. Looks higher'n that to me. (MRS. JONES *starts for door.*) Mosquitoes will give you hell in that this summer.

MRS. JONES. Oh! (*Exits quickly into dining room, slamming door.*)

THOMAS (*going up California stairs, speaking to* BILL). You'll get yourself disliked around here, if you don't look out.

BILL. So'll you.

THOMAS. Know where your room is, Mr. Hammond?

HAMMOND. Yes. Good night.

THOMAS. Good night. (*Exits.*)

HAMMOND (*to* BILL). See here, Jones, I've taken over the management of this place and I don't propose to stand any more nonsense from you, and unless you do as your wife tells you to, I'll kick you out of here.

BILL. No, you won't.

HAMMOND. What's the reason I won't?

BILL. 'Cause you talk too much about it.

HAMMOND (*going up California stairs*). You'll see whether I will or not. (*He exits.* MRS. JONES *enters from dining room, comes slowly toward* BILL *with deed and pen still in her hand.*)

BILL. Mother, ain't you cold?

MRS. JONES (*almost in tears*). No, I'm hot all over at your insulting me before those gentlemen. (*Cries.*) Makin' fun of me because I try to look presentable for once in my life.

BILL (*goes to her, puts hand on her arm*). It's gettin' late, Mother, you're tired, you've been working hard, you're all tuckered out. Now you go upstairs and put on some clothes and go to bed.

MRS. JONES (*crossing*). Oh! You ought to be ashamed of yourself with that gentleman here to buy the place and you around the office drinking liquor.

BILL. No, I ain't. (MRS. JONES *pulls flask from his pocket.*)

BILL. That belongs to Mr. Harper. You can go up and ask him if you don't believe it. (*Puts it on Califor-*

nia desk; opens deed, holds it out in front of him.)

MRS. JONES. Now I want you to put your name to this paper.

BILL. I can't, Mother.

MRS. JONES. What's the reason you can't?

BILL. Because I promised.

MRS. JONES. Now, see here, Bill, I've been working my fingers to the bone for years and now that I've sold the place, I'm entitled to a rest and you shan't stop my having it. Mr. Thomas is taking Millie and me to San Francisco tomorrow and if you'll sign that, he'll bring you with us. If you don't, you'll have to look out for yourself a while.

BILL (*pauses, points upstairs*). That fellow said he'd throw me out, do you want me to get out, Mother? Is that what you mean?

MRS. JONES. I mean just that, Bill.

BILL. All right, I'll go.

MRS. JONES. Go where?

BILL. I'll be all right.

MRS. JONES (*Goes up to right of* BILL). Well, I mean every word I've said, Bill. (*She goes to foot of California stairs.*) It's one thing or the other. (*Going up the stairs.*) Either you make up your mind to sign this or I'm through with you. (*Exits.*)

(BILL *gets his hat and coat from table, comes to desk, picks up flask, looks upstairs, changes his mind, sets it back on desk, goes to door, opens it, turns and looks at flask, goes back and gets it, puts it in his pocket, exits, closing door behind him.*)

CURTAIN

ACT TWO

SCENE—*A court room in Reno, Nevada, the* JUDGE'S *bench is to the left of the audience, with door at back of it. This platform and door is about three feet high. There is a door to the left below this. There are four steps coming down at lower end of* JUDGE'S *platform. At the lower down-stage side of* JUDGE'S *platform there is a small desk and six-inch platform for the Clerk of the Court—up stage is the witness box on a two-foot platform. A railing with a gate runs from the witness box to the wall. In railing there is a break up enough for the* SHERIFF'S *chair. Up and down stage in two rows there are ten chairs for witnesses. There are two windows to the right, one up and one down stage. There is a large old-fashioned stove with a long stovepipe going to the ceiling just back of rail. At back there are two rows of benches, one in front of the other, fourteen feet long; these are up back of railing. Down stage and to the right there is a large table with legal papers on it, and two law books and a Reno newspaper. There are two chairs—one in front and one in back of table—there are three chairs in front of* JUDGE's *bench—between* JUDGE *and witness stand there is a small desk on platform for* COURT STENOGRAPHER. *There is a large office clock on back wall, one over door left, one over door right center. There are two brackets at back, one right, one left, a bracket between windows. A chandelier hangs in the center of ceiling.*

SCENE—*At rise of curtain,* SHERIFF *slouched down in chair, his feet on lawyer's table, is reading Reno* News. MISS EMILY JARVIS *enters. She is an old maid of forty to forty-five, medium size, quiet and business-like; not exaggerated character part. Though she takes an interest in all that goes on in Court, her mind is constantly on her own work. A nice, good-natured, matter of fact woman, with a sense of humor. She enters from right in a business-like way; carries a roll of papers and a bunch of flowers.*

EMILY. Good morning, Nevin. (*Crosses to her desk.*)

SHERIFF (*looking up from paper*). Hello, Emily. (*Goes back to paper.*)

EMILY (*puts paper and flowers on her chair*). My, but it's stuffy in here. (SHERIFF *snaps paper closed, looks up.*) Why don't you let in a little fresh air? It's lovely and warm outside. (*She crosses, taking off wraps and exits left, leaving door open.* SHERIFF *pays no attention till she has gone. Then he looks about, sniffs as though to test the air's freshness, and throws open the two windows, grumbling.*)

SHERIFF. No chance to read the papers—why don't they get a man stenographer? (*Meanwhile* WALTER LENNON *enters from right—the* JUDGE's *room, and puts papers on* JUDGE's *desk. He is short, chunky and genial.*)

WALTER (*going behind clerk's desk*). What you doing, Sheriff—playing freeze-out? (SHERIFF *scowls at him.*)

SHERIFF. Miss Jarvis says it's stuffy in here.

WALTER. A court room is supposed to be stuffy.

SHERIFF. Well, if it gets too cold I'll shut them before court opens. (*Sits in chair front of table.* EMILY *re-enters without wraps, bringing two glasses of water.*)

EMILY (*noticing windows*). Ah, that's better, Nevin. (*Closes door, goes to her desk.*)

WALTER (*coming down steps, to clerk's desk*). Morning, Emily.

EMILY. Good morning, Walter. (*Sits, puts glasses on rail of witness stand.*)

WALTER (*crosses up to* EMILY). Have you noticed the first case on the list this morning? (*Glances at* SHERIFF. *Places list on clerk's desk glancing at it.*)

EMILY. No. (*Takes paper cuffs from side of desk, puts them on.*)

WALTER (*winking at her and nodding at* SHERIFF). Pacific Railroad Company versus John Marvin. (SHERIFF *pretends to be much absorbed in paper.*)

EMILY. What of it?

WALTER. Why, you've heard of Marvin, haven't you? (*Crosses, glancing at* SHERIFF.)

EMILY (*comes down to* WALTER). Not that I remember.

WALTER. Well, about six months ago, they got a warrant out for his arrest and sent a Sheriff after him. (*Crosses to table.*) They told the Sheriff to be careful because his man was a pretty slippery customer—but he was a smart Sheriff and said that was just the kind he liked to tackle—then he got handcuffs and a gun and everything and went out and nabbed the fellow in great style. The only mistake was that it was a Nevada Sheriff and he tried to grab his man in California. Did you ever hear of that case, Nevin? (*Laughing.*)

SHERIFF. Oh, shut up! (WALTER *laughs.*)

EMILY. Oh, Nevin—were you the Sheriff? (*Laughs.*)

SHERIFF (*swings around*). Yes, I was the Sheriff. (EMILY *crosses up stage to her desk, covers drinking glass with card, puts it on* JUDGE'S *desk, puts flowers in the other glass and puts that up.*) It happened six months ago and it looks as if I'd never hear the last of it. How was I going to know he was on the other side of the state line? (WALTER *laughs,* SHERIFF *up, crosses to* WALTER.) Go on; laugh! But it may not be so funny before I get through.

WALTER. Why? What you going to do?

SHERIFF. His case is comin' up today and they've got his property attached. If he don't show up, they'll get a judgment. And if he does show up—(*Turns.*) Well, I've still got that warrant. (*Indicates inside of pocket, starts to read paper.*)

WALTER. But you can't arrest a man in the courtroom.

SHERIFF. I know I can't. Now don't try to tell me the law. (*Looks into paper.*) I can arrest him outside the courtroom.

WALTER. Yes, but you've got to be in here. (*Goes to clerk's desk.*)

SHERIFF. Oh, have I? You wait and see. (*Turns.* TEDDY, *a newspaper reporter, enters, comes through gate to right of* SHERIFF.)

TEDDY. Hello, Sheriff.

SHERIFF. Hello, Teddy.

TEDDY. Well, did you see it?

SHERIFF. Yes, I've just been reading it. (*Looks at paper.*)

TEDDY. What do you think of it?

SHERIFF. Fine. I don't care anything about having my name in the paper but it tickles my wife to death.

TEDDY. Oh, that's all right. But say —— (*Turns to* SHERIFF.) If you come across a good story, you know me. (TEDDY *crosses up to* EMILY. *She puts a flower in his buttonhole.*)

SHERIFF. Bet your life I won't forget. (THOMAS *enters from outside. Comes with an air of importance.*

Puts his books, etc., on table.) How do, Mr. Thomas.

THOMAS. Good morning, Sheriff. *Crosses to clerk.*) Good morning, Miss Jarvis.

EMILY. Good morning, Mr. Thomas.

THOMAS. How do you do? How are you, Lennon?

(MRS. COGSHALL *and* MRS. STARR *enter and go to front visitors' bench.* SHERIFF *meets them at gate and points to visitors' bench. They cross and sit there.* SHERIFF *sits with back to audience at his desk and reads paper.*)

WALTER. Good morning. (*Smiles.*)

THOMAS. Have you got the list?

WALTER. Yes. Your case is first. (*Picks up list.*)

THOMAS. Which one? I've got two today.

WALTER. Railroad versus Marvin is first.

THOMAS. Good. When is my divorce case?

(*Two men enter, one stops by door, the other comes down stage, looks around and they both go and sit in back row.* TEDDY *goes and sits in back row and talks to ladies in front of him.*)

WALTER. Which is it? There are four here.

THOMAS. Jones is mine.

WALTER. Jones versus Jones. That's third.

THOMAS. Thanks. (*Crosses to* SHERIFF.) Sheriff!

SHERIFF. Yes. (SHERIFF *comes to meet him.*)

THOMAS. That Marvin case is on first this morning.

SHERIFF. I know it is.

THOMAS. I'm going to use you as a witness.

SHERIFF (*confidential tone*). You goin' to bring up that story of my serving the warrant?

THOMAS (*laughing*). No, I don't think we'll have to go into that.

SHERIFF. Don't if you can help it.

THOMAS. But I want to ask you about the time you went to Marvin's camp.

SHERIFF (*relieved*). Oh, that's all right.

THOMAS. I want to show when he was taking down the timber. I'm going to ask you what time you were there—the date, I mean.

SHERIFF. I didn't get out where the timber was.

THOMAS. But you know he had a gang of wood-choppers there?

SHERIFF. Yes.

THOMAS. And they drove you off by force?

SHERIFF. Yes.

THOMAS. And you remember the date?

SHERIFF. Yes.

THOMAS (*goes to above table and gets paper out of portfolio and sits*). Good. That's all I need.

SHERIFF (*goes up to gate, turns to* THOMAS). You don't think Marvin will be here, do you?

THOMAS (*back of table*). I don't care whether he is or not. The case is a cinch.

SHERIFF. I got a notion he won't be here. Not in here. (THOMAS *crosses to* EMILY.) Say, Walter, look out for things till court opens, will you? And if I'm wanted, let me know.

WALTER. Where you going?

SHERIFF. I'll be jest outside the door. (*Going to gate.*)

WALTER. Oh—going to lay for Marvin out there, are you?

SHERIFF. Never mind what I'm going to do.

(WALTER *crosses back to his desk and sits writing.* HAMMOND, MRS. JONES *and* MILLIE *enter from outside,* SHERIFF *holds the gate for them.*)

HAMMOND. This is the way. (*Starts down,* MRS. JONES *following,* THOMAS *turns, and sees them.*)

THOMAS. Oh, good morning. I'm glad to see you. Come right in. (MILLIE *goes to him.*) How fine you look, Millie.

MILLIE. I don't feel that way.

THOMAS. Oh, the trial won't amount to anything. How are you, Mrs. Jones? (*She has turned and followed* MILLIE. HAMMOND *comes around in front of the table.*)

MRS. JONES. Well, I'm here.

HAMMOND. Mrs. Jones is a mighty brave woman, Thomas.

THOMAS. You can't tell me anything about Mrs. Jones. (*To her.*) It's like going to the dentist's; the worst part is making up your mind to it.

HAMMOND. I tell her she'll be in a much better position to find her husband and tell him after the divorce is over and she gets the money from the place.

THOMAS. Of course. No doubt of that. Oh, this is the only thing to do, Mrs. Jones.

MRS. JONES (*unsteadily*). I know it's for the best.

MILLIE. You haven't heard anything of Daddy?

THOMAS. No, we haven't been able to locate him.

MRS. JONES. I wonder where he can be?

THOMAS. Your case is fourth. It will be some time before they get to it. (*Two men enter, come to gate, then sit in front row extreme left of bench.*)

MILLIE. Oh, dear!

THOMAS. But you needn't wait here. (*Turns to* LENNON.) Lennon, my client and her friends can wait in there, can't they?

WALTER (*opening door*). Certainly, Mr. Thomas.

THOMAS. Just step right in here, Mrs. Jones, Millie.

MRS. JONES. Thank you, Mr. Thomas. (*They exit.*)

THOMAS (MILLIE *and* MRS. JONES *go*). You better go too, Hammond. (*In a lower tone, as* HAMMOND *turns, disgusted.*) Keep them cheered up.

HAMMOND. That's about all I've been doing for the last six months. (*He follows the women off stage.*)

THOMAS. Thank you, Lennon.

(SHERIFF *opens door.* MRS. DAVIS *enters, crosses to sit in visitors' bench.*)

WALTER. Not at all. (*Closes door.*)

SHERIFF (*opens gate*). This way! (MARGARET *comes through gate, crosses to* CLERK'S *desk, speaks to him.*)

MARGARET. Could I see Judge Townsend?

WALTER. Not 'till after court.

MARGARET. Oh!

WALTER. Are you party to a case?

MARGARET. Yes.

WALTER. Then just take a seat over there, please. (*Points to chairs.*)

MARGARET (*sees* THOMAS). Oh! Mr. Thomas! (THOMAS *crosses below table to* MARGARET.)

THOMAS. Yes?

MARGARET. Don't you remember me?

THOMAS. Why, yes, Mrs. Davis, isn't it?

(SHERIFF *enters, glances at them, looks off door.*)

MARGARET. Yes. (*They shake hands.*)

THOMAS. You were on crutches the last time I saw you. Have you quite recovered?

MARGARET. Oh! long ago.

THOMAS. Does your case come up today?

MARGARET. Yes, and I'm worried sick about it. Do you think I could see Lemuel, I mean the Judge—for a moment?

THOMAS. I'm afraid not just now. Is there anything I can do? (TEDDY *comes around and sits in front row.*)

MARGARET. I don't know. My lawyer's sick.

THOMAS (*laughing*). Well, you ought to see a doctor about that.

MARGARET. I have. That is, the doctor telephoned me and said he couldn't allow him to come to Court. And if I could only tell the Judge——

THOMAS. Why, that's nothing to worry about. You can explain to the

Judge when your case is called, and he'll postpone it.

MARGARET (SHERIFF *glances at them*). But I don't want to have it postponed. A Court room scares me to death and now I'm here, I want to get it over.

THOMAS. Well, I'd be very glad to represent you if you care to have me. (SHERIFF *shows amusement and listens.*)

MARGARET. Oh, could you?

THOMAS. Certainly. Delighted. There's nothing to your case anyhow. The Judge is a friend of yours, isn't he? (SHERIFF *looks out door.*)

MARGARET. Oh, yes, he's a—well, that is, I know him.

THOMAS. Then don't give it another thought. Just leave everything to me. (*Crosses to table, gets paper.*)

MARGARET. That does take a load off my mind. (*Goes* C. *to him.*) If anything went wrong after waiting all these months, I'd die, that's all.

THOMAS (*goes to door*—SHERIFF *comes through gate to right of chair at back of table, stands*). No chance of that. Mrs. Jones and Millie are here.

MARGARET. Are they? Where?

THOMAS. In the next room. Come in and say hello to them, won't you? (*Opens door.*)

MARGARET. But I want to be here when I'm called.

THOMAS. Oh, they won't get to you for quite a while. Another case of mine goes on first. (*Opens door.*) Right in here.

MARGARET. I'm certainly glad I ran into you. (*She goes—followed by* THOMAS. *Off stage*—"Why how do you do." THOMAS *closes door.*)

SHERIFF. Say, Teddy, I got your story.

TEDDY. What's up? (*Comes through gate to* SHERIFF.)

SHERIFF. Did you notice that woman?

TEDDY. The one that got Thomas to take her case?

SHERIFF. Watch the Judge when he hears that Thomas is to be her lawyer.

TEDDY. Why?

SHERIFF. Judge Townsend's crazy about her and thinks Thomas is trying to steal her away from him.

TEDDY. Good! Thanks.

SHERIFF. Don't say I said anything about it.

TEDDY. Sure I won't. (*Crosses up to rail between witness chair and* SHERIFF'S *chair. One man and one woman enter, sit in back room.* JOHN *jumps through window.*)

EMILY. Oh! (*Screams, rises.*)

WALTER (*going toward him to gate, holds it so* JOHN *can't get through*). Here—what are you doing?

JOHN (*trying to get through gate*). I've got business here.

WALTER. Then wouldn't it be just as handy for you to come in through the door?

JOHN. I'm afraid not. I saw someone there I didn't want to meet.

WALTER (*suddenly thinking*). Oh—is your name Marvin?

JOHN. Yes. John Marvin.

WALTER. The Sheriff's out there with a warrant, waiting for you.

JOHN. So I noticed.

WALTER. Come in. (*Opens gate.*)

JOHN. Thanks.

WALTER. Hide over there. (*Points to chairs. Stands laughing.* JOHN *goes toward chairs.* HARPER, MRS. HARPER *and* FREEDA *enter. The women sit in row of visitors' benches.* HARPER *goes to* JOHN—TEDDY *goes through gate and sits in back row of visitors' bench.*)

HARPER. Hello, Marvin. (SHERIFF *opens gate and shows in* MRS. PRESTON *and* MRS. JORDAN.)

JOHN. Hello, Mr. Harper. This wasn't necessary.

SHERIFF. Walter!

WALTER. What?

SHERIFF. Look out for these ladies, will you?

WALTER. Why don't you do it?

SHERIFF. I'm busy. (WALTER *looks at* JOHN *and points to door.* JOHN *and* WALTER *laugh. He exits, closes door.*)

WALTER. Are you ladies parties to a case?

MRS. JORDAN. Yes, this lady's divorce case comes up this morning, and I'm a witness.

WALTER. This way. (*He lets them through gate.* MRS. JORDAN *starts for second row, but seeing her companion going to first row, she follows.*)

(MARGARET, HAMMOND *and* THOMAS *enter.* MARGARET *crosses and shakes hands with* MRS. JORDAN *and sits in chair down stage in first row.* HAMMOND *crosses and sits in chair up stage in back row.* THOMAS *crosses to his chair back of table,* MRS. COGSHALL *and* MRS. STARR *come through gate and sit in back row of witness chairs.* PERKINS *enters, carries a portfolio and sits in chair up stage front row.*)

MRS. JORDAN. Oh, there's Mr. Perkins now!

(HARPER *exits. A man and woman enter, sit in back row of visitors' seats.*)

WALTER. Come along, Sheriff. (SHERIFF *takes his place by gate, raps with gavel. The Judge,* LEM, *enters from Judge's room and ascends to his place. All rise but one woman in witness chairs and one man on visitors' bench.*)

SHERIFF (*to lady seated*). Stand up—please. (*To man seated.*) Stand up! (*They do so.*)

LEM. Open court, Sheriff. (TEDDY *rises, comes to front row of visitors' bench, sits.*)

SHERIFF (*raps with gavel*). Oyez, Oyez, Oyez. The honorable District Court of Washoe County, second judicial district, is now open and in session. All persons having cause for action therein will give their attendance according to law. (*The people sit.* SHERIFF *hurries to door and looks out.*)

LEM (*looking over papers*). First case. (SHERIFF *closes door and comes down to gate.*)

WALTER (*rises*). Pacific Railroad versus John Marvin. (*Sits.*)

THOMAS (*advancing*). Plaintiff's ready. (*Crosses to* JUDGE, SHERIFF *starts to speak to* JUDGE.)

JOHN (*going in front of table*). Defendant ready.

SHERIFF. Huh! (SHERIFF *wheels about,* WALTER *snickers with hand over mouth.* EMILY *smiles.* THOMAS *gives him one glance, then ignores him.* SHERIFF *comes through gate and sits, two women enter and sit in back row of visitors' bench.*)

LEM. How long do you think this case will take? (*Takes out watch.*)

THOMAS. Probably all morning, your honor.

LEM (*to* JOHN). You represent the defendant?

JOHN. I am the defendant, your honor, and I represent him too.

LEM. Oh, you are counsel for yourself?

JOHN. Yes, sir.

THOMAS. If it please your honor, this is an action for the wrongful taking down of timber. The defendant was a former owner of the property. (MARGARET *clears her throat and bows to* JUDGE. *He sees her, bows too, and smiles at her.* THOMAS *turns and looks at* MARGARET *who has risen. She sits.*)

LEM (*who hasn't been listening*). Eh? What's that?

THOMAS. I have been saying, your honor, that—

LEM. Oh, yes. Just a moment. (*To* WALTER.) Let me see the list. (WALTER *hands* JUDGE *the list.*) It may be best to dispose of these short cases first. (*Looks about court room —hands back list.*) Mrs. Davis. (*She rises.* C.) Are you ready?

MARGARET (*stops abruptly*). Why, yes; I think so.

LEM (*to* THOMAS *and* JOHN). I'll take this case at two o'clock, Mr. Thomas. (JOHN *returns to seat;* MR. PERKINS *tells the ladies they must wait, then he goes. Two men enter and join other men on back seat of visitors' benches.* HAMMOND *rises and says something to* THOMAS, *who nods; then* HAMMOND *goes out.*)

WALTER (*rises*). Davis versus Davis. (*Sits.* MARGARET *sits front of table.*)

THOMAS (*crosses to* JUDGE). If it please your honor, this case——

LEM. This case is Davis versus Davis, Mr. Thomas.

THOMAS. I am quite aware of that, your honor, I am counsel for Mrs. Davis.

LEM (*surprised.* REPORTER *and* SHERIFF *look at each other*). You are?

THOMAS. Yes. In place of Mr. Brainerd.

LEM (*displeased; glancing from* THOMAS *to* MARGARET). Oh.

THOMAS. As I believe your honor is familiar with the complaint and has gone over the depositions submitted by the plaintiff, and as the defendant has entered no denial or appeared in court or been represented by counsel, I move that the plaintiff be granted an absolute separation, from the defendant forthwith.

LEM (*after glancing from* THOMAS *to* MARGARET). Motion denied.

MARGARET (*rises*). Oh. (SHERIFF *raps desk,* MARGARET *turns and looks at him.*)

THOMAS. But, your honor—I understood that your honor considered the evidence——

LEM. I deny the motion.

MARGARET. Does that mean I can't get my divorce?

THOMAS. No, no, Mrs. Davis.

LEM. It means that the motion of your counsel is unusual and that I have good and sufficient reasons for denying it.

THOMAS. I should be glad to try the case if your honor considers that necessary.

LEM (*pause*). All right. Go ahead.

THOMAS. Certainly, your honor. Mrs. Davis, will you take the stand? (MARGARET *wanders down toward* CLERK'S *desk—*THOMAS *crosses to back of table.*) No; there. (*He indicates witness chair. She, in a half frightened, puzzled way, goes there and sits.*)

WALTER. Stand up, please.

MARGARET. Who, me?

WALTER. Yes. Hold up your right hand. (*She does so. He stands with his hand raised waiting for her.*) You solemnly swear the evidence you give to be the truth, the whole truth and nothing but the truth, so help you God?

MARGARET (*nodding her head*). I do. (*Sits, lowers her hand.*)

WALTER. What is your full name?

MARGARET (*very distinctly—rises—raising her hand before speaking*). Margaret Davis.

THOMAS (*turning and seeing her still standing with hand up*). Just sit down, please, Mrs. Davis. (*Comes center—she sits.*) Mrs. Davis, where do you live?

MARGARET. New York. (LEM *glances at her; she notices it and adds quickly.*) Oh, no, I don't! I live here —in Nevada; and I've lived here long enough to get a divorce. The Judge —— (*Looks up at* JUDGE, *then front*) his honor can tell you that. (*She looks at* THOMAS, *anxiously as if afraid she had said something to hurt her cause.*)

THOMAS (*pleasant tone*). Just answer the questions please, Mrs. Davis.

MARGARET. Well, that's not so easy when you're sworn to tell the truth. (*Several smile,* MARGARET *glances at* LEM, *but he takes no notice.* STENOGRAPHER *writes in shorthand all evidence.*)

THOMAS. You are the wife of Gerald Davis?

MARGARET. I was. I mean, yes, sir.

THOMAS. When were you married to him?

MARGARET. Seven years ago—October fifth.

THOMAS. Where?

MARGARET (*shortly*). Peoria.

EMILY. I didn't get that.

MARGARET (*turning to* STENOGRAPHER—*distinctly*). Peoria. It's a place.

THOMAS. You were living in Peoria?

MARGARET (*quickly*). I should say not.

THOMAS. Oh, your husband living there?

MARGARET. No! We were playing there. We were partners, doing a dancing act.

THOMAS. When did your husband first show signs of not loving you?

MARGARET (*not trying to be funny but remembers she is under oath*). About a year before we were married.

THOMAS (*walks right. Then back to her*). Then why did you marry him?

MARGARET. That's hard to explain. But you see we were in Peoria—and we were partners, and—and—it rained all week. Well, somehow it seemed a good idea at the time.

THOMAS. But, after you were married he was cruel to you.

MARGARET (*hesitating*). Er—yes, sir.

THOMAS. What did he do that was cruel?

MARGARET. A lot of things.

THOMAS. Will you name one?

MARGARET. He put his name on the bill in larger type than mine——

THOMAS. And he fought with you, didn't he?

MARGARET. Er—yes, sir.

THOMAS. Did he strike you?

MARGARET. Well, he was a poor judge of distance.

THOMAS. But his treatment was sufficient to cause you mental anguish?

MARGARET. Yes, sir.

THOMAS. And then he deserted you?

MARGARET. Well—we parted.

THOMAS. And after he deserted you?

LEM. The witness has not testified that her husband deserted her.

MARGARET. Why, it's just the same thing, we were playing in Chicago and I went West and he stayed there.

THOMAS. Oh!

LEM. That sounds as if you deserted him.

MARGARET. Well, I didn't do anything of the sort.

LEM. Um—so—far, Mrs. Davis, your testimony has not brought out anything to substantiate your complaint.

MARGARET (*indicating* THOMAS). That's because he told me to do nothing but answer his questions, and then he asked me all the wrong things. (*She bursts into tears.*)

THOMAS. Your honor—I——

MARGARET. Oh, I didn't mean to blame you. (*To* LEM.) He doesn't know anything about my case.

LEM (*glances from one to the other, sternly*). Then why is he appearing for you?

MARGARET. Because my lawyer's sick.

LEM. What's that?

MARGARET. And I wanted to tell you about it but Mr. Thomas said I couldn't see you.

LEM. Oh, he did? (*Glares at* THOMAS.)

MARGARET. Yes, and he said he'd do everything for me, and you'd give me a divorce without any trouble at all.

LEM. When did he tell you all this? (*Glaring at* THOMAS.)

MARGARET. Just now—when I came into court. This is the only time I've seen him since you were at the hotel.

LEM (*much relieved*). Then why didn't you say so?

MARGARET (*more tears*). How could I, if he didn't ask me? (*She wipes her eyes with handkerchief.*)

LEM. There—there—don't let it upset you. (*Rises and offers her glass of water.*)

MARGARET (*looking up at him*). Water?

LEM. Yes.

MARGARET. No, thanks.

THOMAS. Your honor, I was simply acting from a friendly standpoint. In the case, I thought——

LEM. No matter what your motives were, Mr. Thomas, you presumed when you told the plaintiff what the court's rulings would be—Now—(*Sweetly.*) Mrs. Davis, why did you leave your husband in Chicago? (THOMAS *crosses, sits back of table.*)

MARGARET. Because he didn't show up for a performance and I had to go on alone—and afterward the manager told him the act was better without him than with him. And then he stayed away from the theatre all the rest of the week and on our next jump he refused to go with me.

LEM. And so you were obliged to go without him?

MARGARET. Yes. I was under contract.

LEM. Did you try to have him go with you?

MARGARET. Of course I did—I mean, yes, your honor. But he said he'd show me how long I'd last on my own.

LEM. And you showed him.

MARGARET (*in a deep voice imitating* JUDGE). Yes, your honor.

LEM. And since that time he has never contributed to your support?

MARGARET. No, sir. I've contributed to his. (*Bursts into tears.*)

LEM. Have you ever heard from him since?

MARGARET. Only when he wrote for money.

LEM. Have you ever seen him since?

MARGARET. No, sir. (*In tears, broken up.*)

LEM. But you've tried to see him, haven't you? (*Pause, then nods suggesting that she say yes, then she nods with him.*)

MARGARET. Yes, your honor, I got Mr. Blackmore's sworn statement to prove that.

LEM (*looking over papers*). Yes; it's here; also deposition dated Chicago stating that Davis left you without warning and refused to dance with you again.

MARGARET. Yes, your honor.

LEM (*after a moment's examination of papers*). Your decree is granted. (*Very pleasantly.*)

MARGARET (*going to front of* JUDGE'S *desk*). Oh! Your honor. (*Bursts into tears and crosses to door.*)

LEM. There, there, Mrs. Davis, please. (*He rises.*)

MARGARET. I'm so emotional, you know. (*Exits.*)

LEM (*watches her exit*). Mr. Sheriff, announce a temporary recess. (*He rises and exits.*)

SHERIFF (*hitting table with gavel*). Short recess. (SHERIFF *humors laugh.*)

(SHERIFF *after his line "short recess" goes over and leans on lower left arm of witness box talking to* EMILY *three-quarters back to audience so he can see doors.*)

(THOMAS *goes out.*)

(MRS. MOORE *and* MRS. JORDAN *and two men in the back row leave the room. An old man on the end seat of back row has to stand up to let others out.*)

(BILL *enters from outside. He is in G.A.R. uniform, comes to railing, looking about timidly, starts to come through.*)

(*The extra people cover* BILL'S *entrance all they can.*)

(*Two men off.*)

SHERIFF. Here—what do you want? (*Stops him at gate.*)

BILL (*after a look at* SHERIFF). Been arrestin' anybody in California lately?

JOHN (*turning and rushing to him at sound of his voice*). Why, hello, Lightnin'! How in the world did you get here?

BILL. The train was late. Your case ain't over, is it?

JOHN. No, it's called for two o'clock.

BILL (*to* SHERIFF). I'm a witness for him.

SHERIFF. Oh, you are?

BILL. I got to testify how you served a warrant on him. (*Comes through gate.* WALTER *laughs and turns away;* SHERIFF *glares. Threatens him with fist.* EMILY *laughs.*)

JOHN. Come over here, Lightnin'. How in the world did you happen to show up?

BILL. I promised you, didn't I? (*During scene* SHERIFF *stands with back to audience reading paper.*)

JOHN. But that was a long time ago. I supposed you'd forgotten all about it.

BILL. I haven't forgotten nothing since I was four years old.

JOHN. How did you know the trial was today?

BILL. You told me last time you was at the Home.

JOHN. But you didn't say anything about coming. If you had, I'd have told you it wasn't necessary. (*In front of table.*)

BILL. That's why I didn't say nothing.

JOHN. How did you get the money?

BILL. Pension.

JOHN. You told me you sent the pension to your wife.

BILL. I did some of it. I sent Mother six dollars, but I didn't get no answer.

JOHN. Did you tell her you were in the Soldiers' Home?

BILL. No.

JOHN. Then she probably didn't know where you were.

BILL. Where else could I be? And six dollars is six dollars.

SHERIFF. The Judge.

(MRS. MOORE *and* MRS. JORDAN *re-enter.* LEM *comes from Judge's room.* SHERIFF *raps. All rise.* LEM *motions to* SHERIFF *as he is sitting, at which time all except* BILL *sit, and whispers to him to get* MRS. DAVIS. SHERIFF *nods and goes to door, down* R. *Calls* MRS. DAVIS. MARGARET *enters,* SHERIFF *gives her a seat front of Judge's desk.* THOMAS *enters, crosses toward his desk, pauses as he sees* BILL, *then crosses to end of table.* HAMMOND *follows and whispers to* THOMAS *about* BILL.)

BILL. There's Thomas. (HAMMOND *comes in behind him, both pause a moment in surprise at seeing* BILL. BILL *wanders forward keeping his eyes on* THOMAS, *and doesn't see* MRS. JONES *who now enters, till they are almost face to face.* MILLIE *enters.*) Why, mother? What are you doing here?

MILLIE. Oh, Daddy! (SHERIFF *raps,* MARGARET *helps* MRS. JONES *to seat by her.* THOMAS *sits.*)

LEM. Come along, Mr. Clerk. I want to get through promptly at noon today. (*Glances at* MARGARET.) I've got an important engagement. (*He smiles at* MARGARET *and she turns and smiles at him.*) Call the next case.

WALTER. Jones versus Jones. (*Rises and then sits.*)

JOHN (*going to* BILL). By Jove! I believe that's you, Bill.

BILL. Me?

JOHN. Did you know your wife was —— (SHERIFF *raps,* BILL *turns and looks at him.*)

LEM. Read the complaint.

WALTER (*rises, reads*). "To the people of the State of Nevada, Mary Jones, Plaintiff *vs.* William Jones, Defendant. A civil action wherein the said plaintiff deposes and says she was lawfully married to the said defendant on the 14th day of June, eighteen hundred and ninety six, in the State of Nevada. The said plaintiff prays this court for a permanent annulment of her marriage vows, the defendant, William Jones, having disregarded and broken all obligations of the marriage contract, thereby causing the plaintiff great suffering and mental agony and the said Mary Jones claims a final separation and divorce from the said William Jones on the grounds of failure to provide, habitual intoxication and intolerable cruelty. (BILL *goes to* JOHN.) Subscribed and sworn to me on the fifth day of April, nineteen hundred and seventeen. Alexander Bradshaw, Notary; Raymond Thomas, Attorney for the plaintiff." (WALTER *sits.*)

BILL. Is that all about me? (*To* JOHN. SHERIFF *raps,* BILL *looks at him.*)

LEM (*looking at* BILL). What did you say?

JOHN (*crosses to* JUDGE). Your honor, this is Mr. Jones, the defendant. He happens to be in court as a witness in another case and has had no previous knowledge whatever of this action.

THOMAS. The defendant's whereabouts were unknown, your honor, and the court allowed us to serve notice by publication.

JOHN. Publication in what? (*Turns to* THOMAS.)

LEM (*looks at* JOHN). Proper service was given if the defendant couldn't be located. (*To* BILL.) Is that what you asked about?

BILL (*turns to* JUDGE. *Pauses*). Who, me?

LEM. Yes—you made some remark after the complaint was read.

BILL. I wasn't sure I'd got it straight.

LEM. You mean the grounds on which this action is based?

BILL (*pause*). I guess so.

LEM (*to* WALTER). Repeat that part of the complaint.

WALTER (*rising—finding place*). The grounds are—failure to provide, habitual intoxication and intolerable cruelty. (WALTER *sits.*)

BILL. Is that all?

LEM. Don't you think it's enough?

BILL. Sounded as if there was more the first time he read it.

JOHN. The defendant enters a general denial, your honor.

LEM. Are you counsel for the defense?

BILL (*before* JOHN *can speak*). Yes, sir, he's my lawyer.

LEM. Call your witnesses, Mr. Thomas. (JOHN *sits.*)

THOMAS. Mrs. Jones. (HAMMOND *anticipating this, comes to* THOMAS, *and whispers, then goes back to seat.*) I don't think it will be necessary for you to testify after all, Mrs. Jones. (MRS. JONES *returns to her seat.*) Miss Buckley, will you take the stand, please?

(MILLIE *rises, surprised, looks about and goes toward stand.* BILL *smiles at her. She stands in front of witness chair. Then goes up on stand.* JOHN *sits beside table.* BILL *is seated in front of it.*)

WALTER. Raise your right hand. (*He and* MILLIE *raise hands.*) You solemnly swear the evidence you give to be the truth, the whole truth and nothing but the truth—so help you God!

MILLIE (*faintly*). I do. (*She sits.*)

WALTER. What is your full name?

MILLIE. Mildred Buckley.

THOMAS (*crosses to the stand*). Miss Buckley, you make your home with Mrs. Jones, the plaintiff, do you not?

MILLIE (*faintly answers all questions*). Yes, sir.

THOMAS. How long have you lived with her?

MILLIE. Since I was three years old.

THOMAS. You were an orphan and Mrs. Jones took you into her home and brought you up as though you were her own daughter, isn't that so?

MILLIE (*turns front*). Yes, sir.

THOMAS. And ever since you can remember, Mrs. Jones has toiled and slaved early and late to provide for the family?

MILLIE (*looking at* MRS. JONES). Yes, sir.

THOMAS. About three years ago you left home, did you not? That is, Mrs. Jones' home?

MILLIE. Yes, sir. (*Front.*)

THOMAS. Why did you leave?

MILLIE. To try and earn my living. (*To Thomas.*)

THOMAS. And you obtained employment as a stenographer?

MILLIE. Yes, sir. (*To* THOMAS.)

THOMAS. What did you do with your wages?

MILLIE. Why I—I— (*Turns front.*)

THOMAS (*leaning on witness stand speaks low*). I'm sorry to be obliged to ask these questions, Miss Buckley, because I know how you dread to testify in this case, but it's unavoidable—you sent the greatest part of your wages home, did you not?

MILLIE (*looks front, drops head*). Yes, sir!

THOMAS. And you felt obliged to leave home and earn money in order to contribute to the support of the Jones family?

MILLIE (*to* THOMAS). Why—yes—but I——

THOMAS. Did you ever see Mrs. Jones' husband drunk—(*looks at* BILL)—under the influence of liquor? (*Pause.*) Answer the question, please. (*Looks at* MILLIE.) Did you ever see Mr. Jones intoxicated?

MILLIE (*drops head*). Yes, sir.

THOMAS. You've seen him in that condition hundreds of times, haven't you?

MILLIE. Why I—I never counted. (*Drops head.*)

THOMAS. But he was in the habit of coming home drunk, wasn't he? (*Looks at* MILLIE.)

MILLIE. Sometimes. (*Front.*)

THOMAS. And because of the poverty brought about by Jones' bad habits, you were obliged to leave home? (*At* BILL.)

MILLIE. Why, no, I—— (*To* THOMAS.)

THOMAS. Well, you knew something had to be done—and you felt it was your duty to help them?

MILLIE. Yes, sir. (*Drops head.*)

THOMAS. Thank you—Miss Buckley, that's all. (*Sits at table.* MILLIE *half rises, to leave stand.*)

JOHN. (*Coming to her* L.) Miss Buckley. (MILLIE *stands still, surprised.*) When you took a position as stenographer, by whom were you employed?

(*After a pause—*MILLIE *walks toward her seat.*)

LEM. One moment, Miss. (*She stops angry and frightened.*) The counsel for the defence has asked you a question.

MILLIE. I—I refuse to answer it.

LEM (*after a surprised pause*). What is your reason for refusing?

MILLIE (*turns to him*). Must I tell the reason?

LEM. Yes, you must.

MILLIE. Because I swore I would never speak to the man who asked it.

LEM (*looks from* JOHN *to* MILLIE). Oh—well, this is embarrassing. (*Pause.*) Will you answer if I ask the question?

MILLIE. Certainly, sir. (*Smiles.* LEM *motions her back to stand. She goes back to witness box.*)

LEM. Who employed you as stenographer?

MILLIE. Mr. Thomas. (*All through following scene she looks at* JUDGE, *her back to* JOHN.)

JOHN. This Mr. Thomas? The gentleman whose questions you did answer?

LEM. The plaintiff's counsel?

MILLIE. Yes, sir.

JOHN. And did Mr. Thomas give you this position because you told him you wanted to be of financial assistance to the Jones family?

THOMAS (*rises*). Your honor, I object to that question. It is quite irrelevant.

JOHN (*to* JUDGE—*facing him*). I am quite willing to withdraw it, if Mr. Thomas—(*turns to* THOMAS)—finds it objectionable. (MILLIE *looks front.*)

THOMAS. Don't flatter yourself that I mind it, or anything else you can ask —only it has no bearing on this case. (*Facing each other.*)

LEM. Objection sustained.

JOHN. Well, Miss Buckley, Mr. Thomas has taken an interest in your affairs and given you advice?

MILLIE (*quickly*). He—(*To* JOHN, *then turns to* JUDGE. *She stops, angry that she forgot herself, turns away.*)

LEM. The question was—has Mr. Thomas taken an interest in your affairs and given you advice?

MILLIE (*to* LEM). Mr. Thomas has been more than kind to me always. He is kind to everybody. And he has given me advice that has been of the greatest help.

JOHN. And you have always followed his advice?

LEM. Have you?

MILLIE. Always—implicitly, in spite of what others have said against it.

JOHN. Now, Miss Buckley, you never knew Mr. Jones to be cruel—or even unkind to his wife, did you?

THOMAS. I object. (*Rises.*)

LEM. Cruelty is one of the counts in your complaint. Objection overruled. (*To* EMILY.) What was the question?

EMILY (*reading notes*) "Now, Miss Buckley, you never knew Mr. Jones to be cruel or even unkind to his wife, did you?"

MILLIE. No, sir, never.

JOHN. You never saw him unkind to anyone or anything, did you?

LEM. Did you?

MILLIE. No, sir, I never did. (*To* LEM.)

JOHN. The complaint which was read claims a divorce on the ground of drunkenness, failure to provide and cruelty. You know that none of these is the real object for getting the divorce. Don't you, Miss Buckley?

THOMAS. I object. (*Rises.*)

LEM (*pause*). Objection sustained. (*To* JOHN.) If the plaintiff can prove any one of the three counts enumerated in the complaint, it will be sufficient cause to grant a divorce no matter what other reasons or objects there are.

JOHN. Miss Buckley, you know that Mr. Jones loved his wife—loved her devotedly, don't you?

LEM. How can she know that?

JOHN. If it please your honor, that is something that a woman does know. She may believe a man to be a contemptible liar—she may say she'll hate and despise him—always—always—always, but somehow, down in her heart, if he really loves her, she knows it. If she is his ideal—his hope, his all, if he would willingly, gladly lay down his life for her, she can't help knowing it; and no matter what she says about him, or thinks about him, the knowledge that he cares more for her than for all else in the entire universe, must count for something and I contend—your honor—— (MILLIE *turns and weeps.*)

LEM. Hold on there—wait a minute—are you trying a divorce case or making love?

JOHN. I beg pardon, your honor. That's all, Miss Buckley. (*Returns to chair at table.*)

LEM. And I should say it's quite enough. Now suppose we get back to business.

THOMAS (*rises*). That will do, Miss Buckley. (MILLIE *goes to seat.*)

(MRS. MOORE *enters, looks around, then comes through gate and comes to* MRS. PRESTON, *takes her chair and* MRS. PRESTON *takes* HAMMOND'S *chair.*)

THOMAS. Mr. Hammond. (HAMMOND *rises promptly, goes to witness stand and raises right hand.*)

WALTER (*rises*). You solemnly swear the evidence you give shall be the truth, the whole truth, and nothing but the truth, so help you God?

HAMMOND (*matter of course*). I do. (*Sits.*)

WALTER. What is your full name? (*Sits.*)

HAMMOND. Everett Hammond. (*Crosses right leg.*)

THOMAS. Mr. Hammond, what is your place of residence? (*Crosses to stand.*)

HAMMOND. San Francisco. (*Pleasantly until* JOHN *questions him.*)

THOMAS. You are in the real-estate business, are you not?

HAMMOND. I am, yes, sir.

THOMAS. You know the plaintiff, Mrs. Jones—and her husband the defendant?

HAMMOND. I do. (*Looks at* MRS. JONES *and then at* BILL.)

THOMAS. How long have you known them?

HAMMOND. I met them first about—(*Pause*)—seven months ago.

THOMAS. Kindly tell the court how you happened to meet them.

HAMMOND (*to* JUDGE). I was—asked to consider the purchase of a piece of property belonging to Mrs. Jones.

THOMAS. And you went to see it?

HAMMOND. I had some other business nearby and stopped off at the Jones' place.

THOMAS. What was the other business?

HAMMOND. The Pacific Railroad was being robbed of timber in that locality and sent me with a sheriff to arrest the thief. (SHERIFF *looks at* HAMMOND.)

THOMAS. Who was the sheriff? (SHERIFF *looks at* THOMAS.)

HAMMOND. Mr. Blodgett; the sheriff of this court. (*Nods toward* SHERIFF.)

THOMAS. And who was the thief?

HAMMOND. His name is John Marvin. (*Doesn't look at* JOHN.)

THOMAS. The same, er—gentleman who has been playing Romeo?

HAMMOND. Yes, sir—the same gentleman. (*Front.*)

THOMAS. Since that time you have had business dealings with Mrs. Jones?

HAMMOND. I have. (*Looks at her.*)

THOMAS. And you have always found her to be upright and honest?

HAMMOND. Absolutely.

THOMAS. And was Mr. Jones a source of trouble and great embarrassment to Mrs. Jones?

HAMMOND. Yes, sir—he was. (*Looks at* BILL.)

THOMAS. In what way?

HAMMOND. By his shiftlessness, drunkenness, cruelty and untruthfulness.

THOMAS. So he was untruthful into the bargain?

HAMMOND. He has a local reputation for being the biggest liar in the county. (BILL *rises, starts to take off his coat.* JOHN *persuades him not to.* SHERIFF *rises with the gavel, and sits after* BILL *sits.*)

THOMAS. Did you ever see Mr. Jones drunk?

HAMMOND. Yes, sir. I never saw him any other way.

THOMAS. And you saw him abuse his wife?

HAMMOND. Yes, sir.

THOMAS. You heard him tell lies?

HAMMOND. I did indeed—he was also breaking the law by harboring a fugitive from justice in his house.

THOMAS. Thank you, Mr. Hammond. That's all.

JOHN (*coming to* HAMMOND *who is beside stand.*) You say, Mr. Hammond, that you had business dealings with Mrs. Jones?

HAMMOND. Yes. (*Crosses leg. Turns away from* JOHN, *speaks roughly all through following scene.*)

JOHN. Do you mind telling what that business was?

HAMMOND. Not at all. (*To* JUDGE.) I purchased for the Golden Gate Land Company, three hundred and twenty-nine acres of land, including buildings.

JOHN. By buildings you mean the hotel?

HAMMOND. I mean the property and everything on it. (*Sneering.*)

JOHN. And you bought the property from Mrs. Jones?

HAMMOND. I did.

JOHN. Why didn't you consult Mr. Jones?

HAMMOND. Because Mrs. Jones was the sole owner.

JOHN. You had seen the records?

HAMMOND. Yes—I'd seen the records.

JOHN. Now, you testified that you first met Mr. and Mrs. Jones about seven months ago.

HAMMOND. I did.

JOHN. Do you remember the date?

HAMMOND. I don't recall the exact date. (*Pauses, looks at him.*) Perhaps you can—it was the day I brought a sheriff there with a warrant for your arrest.

JOHN. Possibly the sheriff will remember the date. (SHERIFF *looks at* HAMMOND, *then starts toward* JOHN *in chair.*)

HAMMOND. Possibly.

JOHN. And you had not met Mr. and Mrs. Jones before?

HAMMOND. No, I had not.

JOHN. And you also met Mr. Thomas on that same day?

HAMMOND. Yes, he represented Mrs. Jones.

JOHN. And Miss Buckley was there, too?

HAMMOND. Yes, they were all there.

JOHN (*facing front*). And you had never met Miss Buckley or Mr. Thomas before?

HAMMOND (*pause*). No, I don't think so.

JOHN. Well. (*Pause.*) At least you are sure you had not met them before to your knowledge?

HAMMOND. Yes, I'm sure of that.

JOHN. All right. (*Comes down, goes up.*) Mr. Hammond, you have told the Court that Mr. Jones was a lawbreaker.

HAMMOND. Yes. You were a fugitive from justice and Jones was harboring you in his house.

JOHN. Didn't you just testify that Mrs. Jones was the sole owner of that house? (*Pause.*) Didn't you?

HAMMOND (*pause*). Yes, and my testimony was correct.

JOHN. Then how could Mr. Jones harbor a fugitive in his house if he didn't have a house?

HAMMOND. Well, I don't suppose he could.

JOHN. Then will you withdraw the statement that he broke the law?

HAMMOND. It's a technical point.

JOHN. Will you withdraw it?

HAMMOND. Yes, I withdraw it. (BILL *is pleased—proud of* JOHN.)

JOHN. Now, up to the time you met Mr. Jones, you didn't know anything about him, did you?

HAMMOND. Of course not. But it didn't take me long to find out about him.

JOHN (*strangely*). I agree with you there, Mr. Hammond. Eight hours after you first saw Mr. Jones he was driven out of the house and you have never set eyes on him since—yet you have testified that he is a drunkard, a loafer, a liar, and a lawbreaker.

HAMMOND (*pause*). It didn't take me one hour to see what Jones was.

JOHN. You also said he was cruel to his wife.

HAMMOND. He was.

JOHN. In what way?

HAMMOND (*pause*). His manner was insulting.

JOHN. What did he do that was insulting?

HAMMOND (*pause*). He criticized the dress she was wearing—(*pause*)—before the other guests.

JOHN. And do you think the claim of intolerable cruelty is substantiated by a husband criticizing his wife's dress?

THOMAS. I object to that question. (*Rises.*)

JOHN. I should think you would. (*Goes down stage and turns.*)

LEM. Objection sustained.

JOHN (*comes up stage and to stand*). You testified that Mr. Jones was a drunkard—that you'd never seen him sober.

HAMMOND. I never have.

JOHN (*taking* BILL *by the arm.* BILL *stands back to audience near* JOHN). Is he drunk now?

HAMMOND. I don't know.

JOHN (*goes back to stand.* BILL *sits*). Then how did you know the other time you saw him?

HAMMOND. It was plain enough then.

JOHN. Now you couldn't get a good title to the Jones' property unless Mr. Jones signed the deed, could you?

THOMAS (*rises*). I object to that question. That matter is quite irrelevant.

JOHN. If it please your honor, this complaint charges intoxication. My question has a direct bearing on that point.

LEM. Objection overruled. (THOMAS *sits.*)

HAMMOND (*to* LEM). I don't mind answering in the least.

LEM (*to* EMILY). Read the question.

EMILY. "Now you couldn't get a good title to the property unless Mr. Jones signed the deed, could you?"

HAMMOND (*to* LEM). The property belonged entirely to Mrs. Jones but the husband's signature was wanted on the deed.

JOHN. And he refused to sign it?

HAMMOND. Yes—after you told him not to.

JOHN. Was he drunk then?

HAMMOND (*pause*). I think he was.

JOHN (*with force*). I'm not asking you what you think. You have said under oath that you never saw him sober—was he drunk when he refused to sign that deed?

HAMMOND (*quickly*). Yes, he was.

JOHN. And you tried to induce him to sign such an important document as that when he was drunk?

HAMMOND (*pause*). I never tried to get him to sign.

JOHN. Then Mr. Thomas did.

HAMMOND. Well, I didn't. And he didn't sign it.

JOHN. No, he wasn't drunk enough for that. He wasn't drunk at all. He was as sober as he is at this moment—and you know it.

HAMMOND. You mean to call me a liar? (*Leans forward.*)

JOHN. No: I mean to prove it. (*Goes down stage—comes up again.*) Now, you called Mr. Jones a liar.

HAMMOND. Yes, and everybody who knows him will say the same thing

JOHN. Did you testify he was a liar because you heard others say so?

HAMMOND. No; because he lied to me.

JOHN. What did he tell you that was untrue?

HAMMOND. Everything he told me was untrue.

JOHN (*strangely*). Repeat one lie that he told you, can you?

HAMMOND. He told me so many I can't recall them.

JOHN. They couldn't have amounted to much if you can't remember one.

HAMMOND (*pause*). He said he drove a swarm of bees across the plains in dead of winter. (BILL, *facing front, tries to keep a straight face, but finally bursts out laughing.*)

JOHN. Well, how do you know that's a lie?

HAMMOND. Of course, it's a lie.

JOHN. Can you prove it?

HAMMOND. Oh, I know the thing's impossible.

JOHN. How? Have you ever tried it?

HAMMOND. That's all nonsense.

JOHN. That's precisely what it is, Mr. Hammond—nonsense and that's just what Mr. Jones meant it to be. (*Pause.*) What else did he say?

HAMMOND. What's the difference? You say it's all nonsense.

JOHN. Not all, Mr. Hammond. He said at least one thing that wasn't nonsense. He said to his wife: "Mother, these two men are trying to rob you." Do you remember that? You were all there—do you remember his saying you and Mr. Thomas were trying to rob Mrs. Jones? (*Points to each.*)

HAMMOND (*at top of his voice—rises —*SHERIFF *rises*). I don't propose to sit here and be insulted by a criminal like you——

THOMAS. This is insufferable, your honor, that a gentleman coming here to give disinterested testimony, as a favor——

LEM. I think the defense has brought out quite clearly that this witness' testimony is not disinterested. This divorce has got to be obtained to give him a good deed to the Jones' property, hasn't it?

THOMAS. Mr. Hammond didn't testify on that account.

LEM. Perhaps not—but I wouldn't call him exactly disinterested.

THOMAS. Nevertheless, your honor, I protest against this man's insulting manner. How it is possible for such a person—a person who even now should be serving a jail sentence—to be admitted to the Bar, I can't conceive. (*Turns away—sits, slams books.*)

LEM (*to* JOHN). You are an attorney in good standing, are you not? (THOMAS *turns back quickly.*)

JOHN (*goes down stage. Pauses*). No, your honor.

LEM. What? Do you mean to tell me you've never been admitted to the Bar?

JOHN (*crosses to* LEM). No, I haven't, your honor, but this defendant has just taken a long journey to help me He came today from the Soldiers' Home, of his own accord and at his own expense, to testify in my case—and when, without warning, this action against him for divorce was called, I knew it was conspiracy—that these two conspirators—— (*Crosses to stand.* HAMMOND *rises.*)

THOMAS (*jumping up*). Your honor! (SHERIFF *raps.*)

LEM. Sit down, Mr. Thomas. (THOMAS *sits.*) I'll attend to this. You are making a very serious charge,

Mr. Marvin—and if you believe you can substantiate it, you will have due recourse to the Courts. In the meantime, you must be aware that you had no right whatsoever to undertake the trial of this case under the guise of being an attorney. You are guilty of a reprehensible act. (*To* EMILY.) The stenographer will strike from the records all the evidence in this case that has been brought out by your cross-examination. (HAMMOND *sits.*) Mr. Thomas, have you finished with your witness?

THOMAS (*rises*). If the cross-examination is to be thrown out, I will not take up the Court's time by re-direct testimony.

JOHN (*as* HAMMOND *starts from seat*). One moment! If it please your honor, before the witness is excused——

LEM. You have no standing in this Court. If you wish to remain, you will take a seat on the visitors' bench. (JOHN *turns slowly—thinking hard.*)

SHERIFF. This way.

JOHN (*as* JOHN *reaches gate* SHERIFF *opens it. Rushing quickly to front of table—puts arm around* BILL). But your honor, the defendant has a legal right to plead his own case.

LEM. Yes; he has.

JOHN (*helping* BILL *to his feet*). Then, if it please your honor, he will take up the examination.

LEM (*to* BILL). You have the right to do that if you care to.

JOHN (*crosses toward* JUDGE). He does, your honor.

SHERIFF (*to* JOHN). You come out here.

JOHN. I'm a witness for the defense, your honor.

LEM (*pointing to witness chair*). Then sit there. (SHERIFF *sits after applause.* JOHN *goes to front row, down stage.* BILL *looks confused.*)

LEM (*to* BILL). Examine your witness.

BILL. What's the matter with him? (*During the laugh,* JOHN *sneaks to chair at table.*) The things John asked him was all right. (*To* HAMMOND.) Answer them.

LEM. You mean the testimony he has already given? (JOHN *sneaks in chair front of table.*)

BILL. I got a right to ask 'em over again, ain't I?

LEM (JOHN *moves to end of table*). Yes. (JOHN *steals up and takes* BILL'S *seat.*)

HAMMOND. Do I have to go all over that, your honor?

LEM. Would your replies be the same?

HAMMOND (*after a moment's hesitation*). Certainly.

LEM (*to* EMILY). Re-instate the cross-examination—(BILL *smiles at* JOHN) —questions put by the defendant.

HAMMOND (*about to get up*). Is that all? (BILL *looks at* JOHN *who shakes his head violently.*)

BILL (*repeating gesture*). No! No! Hold on—I got some more for you. (JOHN *whispers to him.*) Yeh. I was going to. (*Going to* HAMMOND *with legal pose—important.*) Ah—Mr. Hammond—you—wait a minute.— (*Goes back to* JOHN—*where* JOHN *can whisper questions to him.*) When you went after Mr. Marvin with a sheriff what was the charge against him?

HAMMOND. Trespassing on the property of the Pacific Railroad Company.

BILL. Uh huh! (*Crosses back to* JOHN.) If he was on their property—(*To* JOHN.) What's that—(*Has to bend down to* JOHN *to get rest of sentence*) what did you have to do with it?

HAMMOND. I went at the request of the President of the Road.

BILL. You sold the railroad the land he was trespassin' on, didn't you?

THOMAS (*jumping up*). I object to that question.

LEM. Mr. Thomas, you and your witness have been accused of conspiracy. If I were you, I'd allow the witness to answer that question. (BILL *back to* JOHN.)

THOMAS. Your honor, I don't propose to defend the witness and myself from such a ridiculous charge at this time. We are not on trial. This is a divorce action.

LEM. Objection overruled. If there is any conspiracy about this action, the court wants to know it. Answer the question.

HAMMOND (*angry*). I purchased the property for the railroad acting as their agent.

BILL (JOHN). Who did you buy it from?

HAMMOND. Mr. Thomas.

BILL (JOHN). When did you buy it?

HAMMOND. About ten months ago.

BILL (*by himself*). That's three months before you bought mother's place?

HAMMOND. Yes.

BILL (*going up to him. By himself*). Then why did you swear you'd never met him till you saw him at the hotel?

HAMMOND. Because I never did.

BILL. You bought all that land of him and never saw him about it? (*To* LEM—*crossing to him.*) And he called me a liar. (*As* HAMMOND *moves.*) Don't go away; we got some more for you. (*To* JOHN.) Ain't we? I got one for him. You know the Railroad company leased the waterfall on mother's place and put up a power plant there?

HAMMOND. I believe they have.

BILL. And you know that the Railroad pays you more for that lease in a month than you agreed to give mother in a year.

HAMMOND. I don't know anything about that, the railroad lease is with the Golden Gate Land Company.

BILL. Who controls the Golden Gate Land Company?

HAMMOND. I don't know.

BILL. Don't you know it's controlled by you and Mr. Thomas?

THOMAS. Your honor, I object.

BILL. And that all your stock's in the name of rummies? (JOHN *stops him.* JOHN *to* BILL:) Dummies, Dummies!

BILL. Dummies! Dummies!

THOMAS (*rises*). I protest against this. (HAMMOND *rises.*)

LEM. Sit down, Mr. Thomas. You're beginning to make me believe in this fraud story.

BILL. Then let him go on talking.

HAMMOND. Judge Townsend, I absolutely refuse to submit to this any longer—to stand here and be made to look like a criminal.

BILL. Well—you look natural.

HAMMOND. Do you expect me to stand for this?

BILL. You can sit down if you want to. I'm all through with you. (*Goes to* JOHN.)

THOMAS. All this absurd testimony has no possible connection with the case in point, but I propose to prove beyond the shadow of a doubt, that the insinuations against the integrity of the witness and myself are not only groundless, but positively malicious—and I shall do this at the first opportunity. (*Sits.*)

JOHN (*to* LEM, *crosses to front of* JUDGE'S *bench*). Your honor, Mr. Thomas will have that opportunity at two o'clock this afternoon when the Pacific Railroad's action against me comes before this court. At that time I will submit positive documentary proof that these men control the Golden Gate Company and that Company has been buying up all the property wanted by the Pacific Railroad. I will submit to the Court twenty cases where the Golden Gate Company has swindled innocent victims out of property and paid them for it with worthless stock. I will prove to the Court——

LEM. Just a moment, Mr. Marvin, it will be most interesting for you to prove your statements at two o'clock. I must remind you again, however, that you are not a party to this divorce action and have no standing in this Court.

JOHN. Yes, your honor.

LEM. If the defendant wishes you for a witness, you may be sworn.

BILL. I don't want no witnesses for the divorce. (BILL *crosses to center—* JOHN *goes up to rail near* SHERIFF.) I didn't know anything about it till I got here. But I been thinking it over ever since and I've made up my mind mother's right. If mother can prove them things he read, she can get a divorce, can't she?

LEM. Yes.

BILL. Well, I can prove them for her.

LEM. You can prove them?

BILL. Oh, yes, I used to be a judge. Now first it said I got drunk; well,

I can prove that. And it—then it said I was cruel to mother; well, I can—no, I can't prove that one, because it ain't true, Judge—and I don't believe mother ever said it. But then it said I failed to provide. That's the one that's on my mind. I have failed, Judge. I never thought anything about it before, but I don't see no chance to provide now that I do think of it. Mother and Millie can get along better without me, so you can see mother ought to have a divorce, Judge—and I'm all right. I can go back to the Home, and stay there until—until—that's all, Judge. (*Turns. He goes toward seat*).

MRS. JONES (*going before* JUDGE'S *desk*). No, Judge! Please don't give me a divorce if you can help it. Please, Judge—I don't want it. I didn't know what I was doing. They said it was the only way I could take care of Bill and myself in our old age—but they was just telling me lies. (*Goes to* BILL. *Turns.*) Bill, I've done you a wrong, and I can't blame you if you never look at me again—but I didn't mean to, Bill—I—didn't mean to and if you'll forgive me and take me back—I'll try all my life to make up for it—will you? Will you, Bill? (*She holds out her arms to him.* BILL *turns to* MRS. JONES.)

BILL. Did you ever get six dollars I sent you?

(MRS. JONES *crosses toward* JOHN—MILLIE *crosses to* BILL.)

LEM. This complaint is dismissed. Call the next case.

WALTER. Preston versus Preston. (MRS. PRESTON *crosses to stand.* JOHN *comes to* BILL, PERKINS *crosses to* JUDGE *and hands up paper.*)

SECOND CURTAIN

CLERK (*to* PERKINS). Raise your right hand. (*She does so.*) You solemnly swear the evidence you give shall be the truth, and nothing but the truth so help you God.

CURTAIN

ACT THREE

SCENE—*Same as Act One, except that there is a small table with chairs, right and left of it. Small cigar case with cigars, on California desk.*

Electric fixtures have taken the place of those used previously. In the distance waterfall is seen, with power-plant building near it. This spot is lighted with a number of electric lights, making small blaze of light.

DISCOVERED: *At rise,* FRED PETERS, *the Golden Gate Hotel Company manager, is behind Nevada desk, shooting dice with the* LIVERYMAN *opposite. As the curtain rises the* LIVERYMAN *throws.*

LIVERYMAN. Four threes.

PETERS (*gathers up dice—shakes them—throws. Leaves three dice—picks up two*). All I need is another six. (*Throws again.*) It ain't there.

(*Picks up the two dice—returns them to shaker—throws again.*)

LIVERYMAN (*sweeping off coins from desk*). I thought four threes'd be enough.

PETERS. I can't throw a shadow tonight. (ZEB *enters.* PETERS *sees* ZEB.) Now what do you want?

ZEB. I jest dropped in.

PETERS. How'd you like to drop out? (*To* ZEB *front of table.*) You know I don't allow no loafin' in this office.

ZEB. Who's a-loafin'? I want a segar.

PETERS. Then show me your nickel.

ZEB. Oh, I got it. (*Finds coin and gives it to* PETERS.)

PETERS (*taking nickel*). Go over and get one—you know the box! (*Crosses to Nevada desk. Puts money in drawer under desk.*) And don't take but one—I got my eye on you.

ZEB. One's all I want.

PETERS (*behind desk counting change*). And don't take a good one.

ZEB (*looking at him*). Eh! What?

PETERS (*fixing keys in letter rack*). I mean a ten cent one.

ZEB. Oh, I like the fives better'n the tens.

PETERS. You never had a ten.

ZEB. Well, that's why I like the fives better. (LIVERYMAN *and* CLERK *look at* ZEB. *He has taken cigar and comes back.*) Say, nobody ain't seen Lightnin', has they? (*Lights cigar.*)

LIVERYMAN (*crosses down to* ZEB *front of table*). So that's what you're doin' over here, is it?

ZEB. I heared his old woman and Millie come back this afternoon.

PETERS (*turns to* ZEB *and* LIVERYMAN). And they got put in their place, too.

LIVERYMAN (*to* PETERS). What do you mean?

PETERS. I mean I'm manager here now and the old woman can't put anything over on me just because she used to own the hotel.

ZEB. Did they say where Lightnin' was?

PETERS (*at desk*). No.

LIVERYMAN. Say, Zeb, Bill wouldn't be with her—don't you know there's talk of their bein' divorced?

ZEB. I don't pay no attention to talk—but if Lightnin' should come back, I'd like to see him.

PETERS (*comes from behind* ZEB *sniffing at cigar, puts him out*). Hey, go on now and smoke that damned thing outside. (PETERS *goes behind desk.* LIVERYMAN *goes to desk.*)

ZEB (*going up*). That's right, take all a man's money, and then throw him out. (*Enter* LEM *and* MARGARET. LEM *carries bags and flowers.* MARGARET *wears auto veil, opens door for him.* ZEB *exits* C. *after* LEM *enters.*)

LEM (*sees* LIVERYMAN—*recognizes him*). Oh, Liveryman!

LIVERYMAN. Yes, sir.

LEM. Will you look after my team?

LIVERYMAN. Yes, sir.

LEM (MARGARET *crosses to desk*). And there's a basket under the seat I wish you'd bring in.

LIVERYMAN. Right away. (*Exit*—LEM *goes to California desk, puts hat on cigar case, comes down center.*)

PETERS. Hello, Mrs. Davis.

MARGARET (*to* PETERS). Good evening. Will you give me my key, Mr. Peters?

PETERS. Sure. (*Giving her the key.*) I didn't expect you back tonight.

MARGARET. Well, I wasn't expecting it myself.

PETERS (*coming from desk*). Did your case come out all right? (LEM *and* MARGARET *look at each other and smile.*)

MARGARET (*giggling*). Wonderfully! (*Indicating* LEM.) This is Judge Townsend, Mr. Peters. (PETERS *crosses to* JUDGE.) Mr. Peters is the manager of the hotel.

PETERS (*posing with his own importance*). The pleasure's all mine, Judge.

LEM (*looking at* PETERS). That's right. See here, have you got a suite? (MARGARET *turns quickly.*)

PETERS. Got a what?

LEM. Have you got a——

MARGARET (*breaking in on* JUDGE). Oh, Mr. Peters, we'd like to see Miss Buckley and Mrs. Jones.

PETERS. All right, I'll go up and tell them you're here. (*Starts up Nevada stairs.*)

MARGARET (*down at desk*). Thank you.

LEM. But young man, I want to get a——

MARGARET. Wait till he comes down, Judge.

PETERS. Yes, I can't do but one thing at a time. (*He exits.*)

LEM (MARGARET *comes down to* JUDGE). What's the matter, dear? Didn't you want the clerk to know we're married?

MARGARET. Well, he's got to know it, I suppose; but I hated to have you tell him so right before me.

LEM. You're not ashamed of it, are you?

MARGARET. No, I'm proud of it. But it is embarrassing to leave here this morning to get rid of number one and come back this evening with number two. (JUDGE *turns away a little from her—she notices this.*) You're not angry, are you, dear? (*Taking his arm.*)

LEM. Well, it's a little jarring to be referred to as number two.

MARGARET. Oh, I didn't mean that, Lemuel. But I couldn't bear to have everyone staring and smirking at us.

LEM. But this isn't a secret marriage, Maggie.

MARGARET. Oh, I don't mind them knowing about it tomorrow, after we're gone—but let's be sure they don't find it out tonight.

LEM. All right, my dear. Just as you say. (*He starts to embrace her, as* PETERS *comes down Nevada stairs.*)

PETERS. Mrs. Jones will be down in a few minutes. (*Sees* MARGARET *and* JUDGE *embracing.*) Oh!

MARGARET. Oh! (*Bursts out laughing.*) Judge Townsend is my husband, Mr. Peters.

PETERS. What?

MARGARET. We were married this afternoon.

PETERS. You don't say so! (*Crosses to* LEM.) Quick work, eh, Judge?

LEM (*glares at* PETERS *and turns away*).

MARGARET. But we don't want you to say a word about it to anybody——

PETERS. Oh, I can keep a secret. My congratulations, and I hope this one turns out better than the other one did.

MARGARET. Oh! (*Starts up Nevada stairs.* LIVERYMAN *brings in basket.*)

LEM. If you don't mind, we won't discuss that, Mr. Peters. (PETERS *goes to basket.*)

MARGARET. I'll go upstairs and take off my wraps. (*Going upstairs.*) Tell Mrs. Jones I'll be down in five minutes. (*At top of stairs, she blows kiss to* LEM. *Exits.* JUDGE *blows kiss back to* MARGARET.)

PETERS (*breaking in on this*). Do you want anything done with that basket, Judge?

LEM. Yes. I want to arrange a little special supper.

PETERS. What? Tonight?

LEM. You don't suppose I want it tomorrow morning, do you?

PETERS. But everybody's gone to bed.

LEM (*taking a bill out of his pocket*). Well, do you think that would get the cook up?

PETERS. That would get the whole hotel up.

LEM (*takes another bill and offers it to* PETERS). And would that make you willing to help a little and not be so damned fresh?

PETERS (*after hesitation—taking money*). Why I—well—thank you, Judge. (*Crosses back to California desk.*)

LEM (*crossing to desk*). Now I've got everything there. (*Indicating basket.*) Tell the cook to fix up the crabmeat salad.

PETERS. She ain't no good on crabmeat.

LEM. She can put it on a platter, can't she?

PETERS (*laughing*). Yes, she can do that.

LEM (*registering*). And make some coffee?

PETERS. She makes rotten coffee.

LEM. Well, then, put the champagne on ice.

PETERS. We ain't got a bit of ice left.

LEM. Oh, Lord! (*Turns away, then back to* PETERS.)

LEM. What's the best room you got?

PETERS (*looking at register, then at key rack*). I can give you number two.

LEM. Number two—my God! I don't want number two. (*Looking upstairs after* MARGARET.)

PETERS. Well, here's five.

LEM. What sort of a room is that?

PETERS. Nothing to be proud of.

LEM. Well, let's see it.

PETERS (*comes from back of desk to table, takes grips, starts upstairs with them*). I'll show you right up. This way, Judge.

LEM. And Peters, can you get me a vase for these flowers? (*Unwraps parcel and takes out bunch of flowers.*)

PETERS. No, sir, but I can get you a water pitcher. (*Exits upstairs.*)

LEM. Waited thirty years for a honeymoon, then come to a damned joint like this! (*Follows* PETERS *off upstairs.* MRS. JONES *enters from Nevada side as* MR. *and* MRS. HARPER *enter from* C., HARPER *first, then* MRS. HARPER, *and closes door.* MRS. HARPER *comes down to table.* MR. HARPER *is beside table.*)

HARPER. Ah, the place is deserted. Oh—Mrs. Jones, don't you remember us?

MRS. JONES. Why, it's Mr. and Mrs. Harper. (*Comes down by desk.*)

HARPER. We just brought Mr. Marvin and your husband over from Reno.

MRS. JONES. Oh, where are they?

HARPER. John went over to see the Probate Judge and Bill's out there telling a friend about being a lawyer. (*Laughs.*)

MARGARET (*enters from Nevada stairs*). Hello.

MR. HARPER. Why, good evening, Mrs. Davis.
MRS. HARPER. How do you do?
(*Spoken together.*)

MARGARET. Good evening. (*Between* MRS. JONES *and* HARPER.)

MRS. JONES. How did you get back tonight?

MARGARET. Why, my—Judge Townsend drove me over.

MRS. HARPER. Wasn't that romantic?

MARGARET. What do you know about it? (*Crosses to* MRS. HARPER.)

MRS. HARPER. Only that the Judge seemed to be so taken with you in Court. (LEM *enters down California stairs.* PETERS *follows him down, takes basket and exits into kitchen during following.*)

MARGARET. Oh, Judge Townsend—this is Mr. and Mrs. Harper.

LEM (*bowing to each in turn*). How do you do, Mrs. Harper.

MRS. HARPER. How do you do?

HARPER. How are you, Judge?

LEM (*to* MRS. JONES). I am very glad to see you under more pleasant circumstances, Mrs. Jones.

MRS. JONES. Thank you, sir. Can you tell me what happened in Mr. Marvin's case this afternoon?

MARGARET. Oh, don't you know about that? (*Crosses to* JUDGE.)

LEM. They had to do everything Marvin demanded—they were lucky to keep out of jail. They gave up this place without a murmur.

MRS. JONES. What?

HARPER. Why, didn't you know the place was yours again?

MRS. JONES. Ours again?

HARPER. Why, yes.

MARGARET. Yes (*Crosses to her.*) and you get all the money the Company pays for the waterfall. It's an awful lot. How much is it, dear? (*To* LEM. MRS. JONES *looks at* MARGARET. *She stops suddenly—puts hand over her mouth.*)

LEM. Why, Mrs. Davis——

MARGARET (*begins laughing*). I called you dear. (*To* MRS. JONES.) I called him dear. (*To others.*) Well, you see—he's my husband!

MRS. HARPER. Why?

MRS. JONES. Your husband?

HARPER. You don't say.

LEM. But she doesn't want anybody to know about it.

MARGARET. We were married this afternoon.

MRS. HARPER (*kisses* MARGARET). What a surprise!

MRS. JONES (*crosses and kisses her*). Well, of all things. (*Then* HARPER *kisses her—and turns her into* PETERS' *arms, who enters from dining-room during the above—he also kisses her, goes down extreme right.* HARPER *crosses behind* MRS. HARPER. MARGARET'S *head on* MRS. HARPER'S *shoulder.*)

LEM. Will you return her when you are through with her?

PETERS. Excuse me, can I speak to you, Judge?

LEM. What is it? (*Crosses to* PETERS.)

PETERS. I've found a piece of ice, and I've got the champagne on the table.

LEM (*turns to the others.* MARGARET *comes down between* LEM *and* PETERS). Mrs. Davis and I—

MAFGARET. Lemuel!

LEM. I mean my wife and I are going to have a little special supper. Won't you all do us the honor of——

MARGARET. Oh, yes, do—that would be lovely! (*Crosses between* MRS. JONES *and* HARPER.)

HARPER. Why that's fine!

MRS. JONES. Splendid!

MRS. HARPER. We'd be delighted!

PETERS (*starts up California stairs*). Now, I'll get the cook up.

MRS. JONES. Oh, Judge! Let me do the cooking, won't you? (*Crosses to* LEM. PETERS *stops.*)

MARGARET. Oh, no——

MRS. JONES (*turning to* MARGARET). I'm just dying to get back in that kitchen again.

LEM. Well, if you want to do it, it would be a crime to stop you. I know what your cooking is like.

MRS. JONES. Thank you, Judge. (*Goes up and exits into kitchen.*)

MRS. HARPER. And can't we set the table?

PETERS (*coming down center*). You can do anything you like, ladies.

HARPER. Come along, Judge, we'll all set the table. (*Crosses right, opens door.*)

MARGARET. Come along, it'll be great fun. (*The four exit into dining room, chatting.*)

PETERS (*as they go through dining-room door*). Am I invited, Judge?

LEM (*turns at door*). Certainly—you're invited to wait on the table. (LEM *exits.*)

PETERS. All right, I'll do that. (*Exits into kitchen.* BILL *enters, comes down, looking about, followed by* ZEB, *who coughs as he starts on.*)

ZEB. Go on, Bill, then what happened?

BILL. And after that the Judge never decided nothin' till he looked at me. (*Leaning against Nevada counter.*) Why, they was getting all the best of it till I went after them. Come on, Zeb—what are you afraid of?

ZEB (*coming down*). I hate to tell you, Bill, but I reckon you got to know: your wife's here.

BILL. I know it.

ZEB. Oh, you do?

BILL. Yes.

ZEB. Seems curious her comin' here now you're divorced.

BILL. We ain't divorced.

ZEB. You ain't divorced?

BILL. No.

ZEB. I thought you said you won the case. Didn't you say you won it? (BILL *looks at* ZEB*—pauses.*)

BILL. Question overruled. (*Turns.* PETERS *enters kitchen door, crosses to California desk, discovers* ZEB.)

PETERS (*to* ZEB). You're back again, are you?

BILL (*turns.*) I object to that question.

ZEB. That fellow's the manager.

BILL. No, he ain't.

PETERS. What's the reason I ain't? (*Crosses to* BILL.)

BILL. Because you're fired.

PETERS. That's what Mrs. Jones just said, but I take my orders from Mr. Hammond.

BILL. Oh, you do. Well here they are. (*Hands* PETERS *letter.*)

PETERS (*opening letter*). Well, if I am fired I can go back to my old job.

BILL. What's that?

PETERS. I'm a bartender.

BILL (*comes down looking at* PETERS). A good one?

PETERS. Yes, a good one.

BILL. Well, I'll fix it so you can stay here.

PETERS. I guess I better talk to Mrs. Jones about that. (*Exits into kitchen.* MILLIE *enters from Nevada stairs.*)

ZEB (*sees* MILLIE). Look out. (*Starts for door.*)

BILL. Hold on, Zeb. What are you afraid of? It's only Millie.

ZEB. Well, I'll see you tomorrow when the women folks is working. It's safer then. (*Exits*).

MILLIE. Did you just get here, Daddy?

BILL. Yes. (*Crosses and leans on chair.*)

MILLIE. Have you seen Mother? (*Crosses to* BILL.)

BILL. That's all right. I ain't had a drink in a month.

MILLIE. Did you come alone? (*Looking front.*)

BILL. Huh! Oh, why didn't you speak to John before you left the court?

MILLIE (*trying to hold back the tears*). I—I couldn't.

BILL (*sorry for her*). Well, it's all right—I fixed it for you.

MILLIE (*turns*). What?

BILL. I got him to promise he'd come over here and see you. (*Leaning on chair.*)

MILLIE. You asked him to come over and see me? (*Crosses to him.*)

BILL. No. I told him you was just crazy to see him.

MILLIE. Oh, Daddy!

BILL. You'd a lost him if it hadn't been for me. Why, every girl in Reno is after John, but I got him so he's willing to marry you.

MILLIE (*turns to* BILL, *horror-stricken*). You asked him to marry me?

BILL. Yes, and it was a tough job, after the way you treated him.

MILLIE. What did you say?

BILL. I told him you'd made a fool of yourself—but all women do that now and then—and if you'd own up that you was ashamed, like mother did, he'd better give you another chance.

MILLIE. Oh!

BILL. Now if you'll beg his pardon when he comes——

MILLIE. I won't see him when he comes. (*Starts toward stairs.*)

BILL (*putting hand in his pocket—crosses above table*). If you don't see him, what's he going to do with this? (*Pulls out ring in a box and shows it to her.*)

MILLIE. What is it? (*Crosses to him.*)

BILL. It's a ring he got for you. He sent me out to buy it while he was in court.

MILLIE. Oh! (*Turns and runs into kitchen.* BILL *looks after* MILLIE *a moment, turns back and puts ring in pocket.*)

BILL (*looks at register desk, raises lid looking for bottle, closes it slowly, hand on counter, looks at hand, wipes hand on coat*). St—st—never like that when I was here. (*Sees electric button behind counter.*) What's that? (*Pushes button No. 1.*) Well—— (*Pushes button No. 2.*) That's funny. (*Pushes button No. 3.*) Now I broke it. (MRS. JONES *enters, crosses to desk. As* BILL *pushes No. 1 button, bracket above door goes out; when he presses No. 2 brackets right and left go out. When he presses No. 3 everything goes out. When* MRS. JONES *is on,* BILL *presses button—everything comes on.*) Now, I fixed it. (*Comes from behind counter, turns back to* MRS. JONES.)

MRS. JONES (*slowly comes down to him*). Are you all right, Bill? (*He breathes into her face.*) I didn't mean that. Ain't you all tired out?

BILL. No.

MRS. JONES (*placing chair for him*). Sit down and rest yourself. (*She seats him—places pillow behind him, he turns and watches her, then settles back.*)

BILL (*after he is fixed in chair*). What's the matter, Mother—you sick?

MRS. JONES. No, Bill. (BILL *looks curiously about room, notices electric fixtures, while* MRS. JONES *takes chair from in front of table and placing it beside* BILL's, *sits down and takes his hand. He pulls it away.* MRS. JONES *holds on to it.*) You have forgiven me, ain't you, Bill?

BILL. Yes.

MRS. JONES. Bill——

BILL. Huh——

MRS. JONES. Just think—just think of the place being ours again.

BILL. It's yours again.

MRS. JONES. No, ours after this, Bill.

BILL. All right.

MRS. JONES (*lets go of his hand*). How did Mr. Marvin manage to get it away from them?

BILL. I saw to it. Did anybody tell you how much money you get out of the water-fall?

MRS. JONES (*looking front and back at* BILL). Yes, but please say *we* get it.

BILL. You mean I get half of it?

MRS. JONES. Yes.

BILL (*looks at her*). Oh, and you're going to keep it for me. (MRS. JONES *smiles at* BILL.) How'd you know about my getting the place back?

MRS. JONES. Judge Townsend told me.

BILL. Is he here!

MRS. JONES. Yes, and he and Mrs. Davis are married.

BILL. What?

MRS. JONES. Judge Townsend and Mrs. Davis got married this afternoon.

BILL. I fixed it.

MRS. JONES. We won't have any more divorce people here, Bill.

BILL. Then you'll have to close up.

MRS. JONES (*takes* BILL'S *hand*). I want to close up, Bill. I want to have a home again.

BILL. All right. (*Smiles; she smiles back—rises—takes her chair—puts it beside table*).

MRS. JONES. We're all going to have some supper.

BILL. Where'd you get it?

MRS. JONES. I've been cookin' it. (*Crosses to* BILL.)

BILL. Mother, I found out one thing when I was at the Home.

MRS. JONES (*puts her arm about* BILL'S *neck*). What was that, Bill?

BILL (*looks up at her*). I found out that you was a good cook. (MRS. JONES *smiles happily—suddenly puts her arms around* BILL'S *neck and kisses him.* BILL *looks front in great surprise—then looks slowly at* MRS. JONES *and smiles at her—she turns slowly but does not see* BILL *smiling.*)

MRS. JONES. You didn't mind my doing that, did you, Bill?

BILL (*after a pause*). No.

MRS. JONES. Bill—— (*He looks at her.*) Would you kiss me?

BILL. Yeh! (*After thinking it over, rises, goes slowly to* MRS. JONES. *His face close to hers—suddenly laughs.* MRS. JONES *goes toward the kitchen door.*) Now, Mother, I was going to.

MRS. JONES (*at door*). I guess you better have your supper first. (*She exits as* JOHN *enters* C. *Closes door. He carries a bag—puts it on table*).

BILL. Did you see Judge Tuttle?

JOHN (*coming down to* BILL). Yes, it's all right. They'd never had their deed recorded—they were waiting for the divorce. Did you see your wife?

BILL. She's all right—she's cooking supper.

JOHN (*hesitating*). And is—is——

BILL. Millie—Oh! she's waiting for you.

JOHN. Is she?

BILL. Yes, only she's afraid you ain't going to forgive her.

JOHN. I think I can convince her about that.

BILL. When you do just give her this and it'll be all settled. (*He gives* JOHN *ring.*)

JOHN. Now I know why you went into that jewelry store.

BILL. Now you know why I borrowed that two dollars. (*Going toward dining-room door.*) After you give it to her, come in to the party.

JOHN. What party?

BILL. Celebration—in here. (*Opens door short distance. Laughter heard inside.* BILL *peeks in—then calls in low tone.*) Millie! (*A cork is heard to pop off stage.*)

HARPER (*off stage*). Ah! Champagne! (BILL *exits quickly into dining room as* MILLIE *enters.* BILL *closes door after him.* MILLIE *sees* JOHN*—he stands looking at her.*)

MILLIE (*crosses to him, then*). Daddy has told me what I ought to say to you.

JOHN (*smiling*). What is it?

MILLIE. That I've made a fool of myself—and I'm ashamed of myself and I beg you to forgive me.

JOHN (*laughing*). I can tell you something much better than that to say. Say, "John"—you might even make it "John, dear," "John, dearest, I know that you love me—always, always, always, because——"

MILLIE. Because that is something a woman must know.

JOHN. Yes, that's it.

MILLIE. So I ought to say, please marry me.

JOHN. And I'll say, I will, Millie—if you'll have me. Millie, I want to show you something. (*Shows her ring.*)

MILLIE. I've seen it.

JOHN. Oh, have you?

MILLIE. It was very thoughtful of you to get it, before you even spoke to me.

JOHN. I didn't get it—I never saw it 'til just now—Bill bought it for me to give you.

MILLIE. How can you help marrying me with everyone trying to force you to?

JOHN. I don't want to help it. There's only one thing I want to know—do you care for me?

MILLIE (*turning away from* JOHN). I can't tell you that now. (*Dining-room door opens and* MR. HARPER, *then* MRS. HARPER, LEM *and* MRS. JONES *enter—all have glasses filled with champagne.* MARGARET *and* LEM *have two glasses each.* LEM *gives* JOHN *and* MILLIE *theirs, then takes one from* MARGARET.)

HARPER. Yes, here they are. We've caught you.

MARGARET. Mr. Jones has just told us the great news.

MILLIE. What?

MARGARET. Of your engagement.

LEM. And we all want to drink your health.

HARPER. May your life together be as happy as—(*indicating* MRS. HARPER *and himself*)—ours has been.

LEM. And as ours is going to be.

BILL (*enters, raising glass*). Come on, John.

MARGARET. Oh, they can't drink yet.

BILL. Then I'll do it for you. Here's to both of them. (*To* MR. *and* MRS. HARPER, LEM *and* MARGARET.) Now turn your backs. (*All laugh and do so.*)

JOHN. Don't let's disappoint them.

MILLIE. John. (*They kiss.* BILL *turns and sees them kiss.*)

BILL. Mother, look. (*She turns and sees them.*) I fixed that.

CURTAIN

The Bat

A PLAY OF MYSTERY IN THREE ACTS

BY

MARY ROBERTS RINEHART

AND

AVERY HOPWOOD

The following is a copy of program of the first performance of *The Bat* as produced at the Morosco Theatre, New York, August 23, 1920, with the following principals:

LIZZIE	May Vokes
MISS CORNELIA VAN GORDER	Effie Ellsler
BILLY	Harry Morvil
BROOKS	Stuart Sage
MISS DALE OGDEN	Anne Morrison
DOCTOR WELLS	Edward Ellis
ANDERSON	Harrison Hunter
RICHARD FLEMING	Richard Barrows
REGINALD BERESFORD	Kenneth Hunter
AN UNKNOWN MAN	Robert Vaughan

SYNOPSIS

Act One: Living room in Miss Van Gorder's Long Island house.
Act Two: The same.
Act Three: The garret of the same house.

THE BAT

SCENE—*A combined living room and library of a country house. Open book shelves (four) in the set. Single door to the left of the audience leads to front door; dining room. Double doors leading to alcove, small staircase and terrace door, and exit below the stairs and off to the library up in the back to the left. All along the back of set, are french windows. Six small frames in these windows. Double doors in the* C. *of window to open on stage. On the right, a single door leads to billiard room and a fireplace.*

The six small windows in french window effect are fitted with long narrow shades. Light in color. Shades remain down throughout Acts I and II.

Beyond the double doors a small and supplementary staircase, showing stair rail, two steps, newel post (supposed to be newly varnished). Platform and steps carry off to the left. Terrace door in the alcove at right angle to the french windows. Thus one enters the house from the terrace past the french windows and the terrace door opens directly on foot of small staircase.

DISCOVERED: CORNELIA VAN GORDER *and* LIZZIE. CORNELIA *is knitting by the light of the lamp on center table. She is seated in armchair by the table.* LIZZIE *is at the city telephone. When Curtain is well up,* LIZZIE *sets down the phone, with angry snap; hangs up the receiver.*

LIZZIE. He says the reason they turned the lights off last night was because there was a storm threatening. He says it burns out their fuses. (*Low rumble of thunder in the distance.*) There! They'll be going off again tonight! (*Scared.*)

CORNELIA. Humph! I hope it will be a dry summer. Ask Billy to bring some candles and have them ready.

LIZZIE (*frightened, moves down to back of table*). You're not going to ask me to go out into that hall alone?

CORNELIA (*putting down knitting*). What's the matter with you, anyhow, Lizzie Allen?

LIZZIE (*pleadingly, and shivering with terror*). Oh, Miss Neillie, I don't like it! I want to go back to the city.

CORNELIA (*firmly*). I have rented this house for four months, and I am going to stay.

LIZZIE (*clutching at* CORNELIA'S *arm*). There's somebody on the terrace!

CORNELIA (*also nervous and looking over her shoulder*). Don't do that!

LIZZIE (*relieved*). I guess it was the wind.

CORNELIA. *You* were born on a brick pavement. You get nervous out here at night when the crickets begin to sing, or scrape their legs together, or whatever it is they do.

LIZZIE. Oh, it's more than that, Miss Neillie, I——

CORNELIA (*turning to her fiercely*). What did you really see last night?

LIZZIE. I was standing right at the top of that there staircase with your switch in my hand—then I looked down and I saw a gleaming eye. It looked at me and *winked*. I tell you, this house is haunted!

CORNELIA (*skeptically*). A flirtatious ghost? Humph! Why didn't you yell?

LIZZIE. I was too scared to yell. And I'm not the only one. Why do you think the servants left all of a sudden? Did you really believe that the housemaid had a pain in her side? Or that the cook's sister had twins? (*Moves slowly up and back of table.*) I bet a cent the cook never had any sister—and her sister never had any twins. No, Miss Neillie, they couldn't put it over on me like that. They were scared away. (*Impressively.*) They saw—*it.*

CORNELIA. Fiddlesticks! What time is it?

LIZZIE (*looks at mantel clock*). Half past ten.

CORNELIA (*yawns*). Miss Dale won't be home for half an hour. Now you forget that superstitious nonsense! There's nothing in that sort of thing. (*Rolls up her knitting and puts in bag.*) Where's that Ouija Board? (*Rises and turns armchair.*)

LIZZIE (*shuddering; indicating; points*). It's up there—with a prayer book on it—to keep it quiet.

CORNELIA. Bring it here.

LIZZIE (*hesitates; shuddering; protesting in every movement, brings the Ouija Board, places it in* CORNELIA'*s lap*). You can do it yourself.

CORNELIA. It takes two people, and you know it, Lizzie Allen.

LIZZIE (*gets small chair*). I've been working for you for twenty years. I've been your goat for twenty years, and I've got a right to speak my mind.

CORNELIA. You haven't got a mind. Sit down. (LIZZIE *sits.*) Now make your mind a blank.

LIZZIE (*frightfully; she and* CORNELIA *put their fingers on Ouija Board*). You just said I haven't got any mind.

CORNELIA. Well, make what you haven't got a blank.

LIZZIE (*mumbles*). I've stood by you through thick and thin—I stood by you when you were a Vegetarian—I stood by you when you were a Theosophist—and I seen you through Socialism, Fletcherism and Rheumatism—but when it comes to carrying on with ghosts——

CORNELIA. Be still! Nothing will come if you keep chattering.

LIZZIE. That's *why* I'm chattering! My teeth are, too. I can hardly keep my upper set in. (*She starts.*) I've got a queer feeling in my fingers all the way up my arms. (*Wiggles arms.*)

CORNELIA. Hush! (*Pause.*) Now, Ouija, is Lizzie Allen right about this house—or is it all stuff and nonsense?

LIZZIE. My Gawd! It's *moving.*

CORNELIA. You shoved it!

LIZZIE. I did not—cross my heart, Miss Neillie, I——

CORNELIA. Keep quiet! (*A moment's pause. Ouija wildly writes, then stops;* CORNELIA *calls off the letters.*) B—M—C—X—P—R—S—K—I.

LIZZIE (*breathlessly*). Russian! (*Ouija Board continues to move. Pause.*)

CORNELIA. B—A—T—Bat! (*Pause. Ouija stops.* CORNELIA *takes her hands off board.*) That's queer.

LIZZIE (*turns round, to front*). Bats are unlucky—everybody knows it. There's been a bat flying around inside this house all evening. (*Rises. Steps back.*) Oh, Miss Neillie, please let me sleep in your room tonight. It's only when my jaw drops that I snore. I can tie it up with a handkerchief.

CORNELIA (*who is evidently revolving a thought in her mind*). I wish you'd tie it up with a handkerchief now. (*Still thinking. Rises. Puts board on table.*) B—A—T—Bat! Give me the evening paper and my glasses. (*Straightens the armchair to face front, then crosses front of table and sits by table.*)

LIZZIE (*turns, looks around, then sees newspaper on settee. Brings it to* CORNELIA. *Then over to fireplace, feels mantel over fireplace*). I don't see your glasses here. You'll hurt your eyes reading without 'em. (*Returns to table.*)

CORNELIA (*seated, holding newspaper at arm's length. Testily*). My eyes are all right—but my arms aren't long enough. (*She reads.*) "Police again baffled by the Bat! (LIZZIE *stands, scared.*) This unique criminal, known to the underworld as 'The Bat,' has long baffled the Police. The record of his crimes shows him to be endowed with almost diabolical ingenuity. So far there is no clue to his identity—but Anderson, City Detective, today said—'We must cease combing the criminal world for The Bat and look higher. He may be a merchant—a lawyer—a doctor, honored in his community by day—and at night a blood-thirsty assassin.'"

LIZZIE. I'm going to take the butcher knife to bed with me!

CORNELIA (*puts hand on Ouija Board*). That thing certainly spelled *Bat!* (*Sits facing front; glances at paper.*) I wish I were a *man!* I'd like to see any doctor, lawyer or merchant of my acquaintance lead a double life without my suspecting it! (*Lays down paper on table.*)

LIZZIE (*over to chair she brought down earlier*). A man takes to a double life like a woman does to a kimono—it rests him! (LIZZIE *takes up chair; puts it back below billiard-room door.*)

CORNELIA (*knits*). If I had the clues the Police have about that man, I could get him. If I were a detective——

LIZZIE (*overcome*). Now it's Detective-ism!

(*Enter* BILLY. *He is an impassive Jap. Carries tray with small glass pitcher of water, and two glasses.*

Places tray on table. He starts to exit. CORNELIA *calls him. He stops.)*

CORNELIA. Billy. What's all this about the cook's sister not having twins—did she? (LIZZIE, *scared watching Jap, moves to top of table; pours out two glasses of water; places one for* CORNELIA.)

BILLY (*has come down, facing* CORNELIA). Maybe she have twins—— It happen sometime.

CORNELIA. Do you think there was any other reason for her leaving?

BILLY. Maybe!

CORNELIA (*knits*). What *was* the reason?

BILLY. All say same thing—house haunted!

CORNELIA (*slight laugh*). You know better than that, don't you?

BILLY (*shrugs shoulders*). Funny house—find window open—nobody there—door slam—nobody there! (*Door slam.* LIZZIE *gives a little jump and squeal. All three look off stage.*)

CORNELIA (*irritably*). Stop that! It was the wind.

BILLY (*impassively*). I think not wind.

CORNELIA (*look of slight uneasiness. Knitting rapidly*). How long have you lived in this house?

BILLY. Since Mr. Fleming built.

CORNELIA. And this is the first time you have been disturbed?

BILLY. Last two days only. (LIZZIE *scared.*)

CORNELIA. What about the face you saw last night at the window?

BILLY. Just face—that's all!

CORNELIA. A man's face!

BILLY. Don't know—maybe! It there! It gone!

CORNELIA. Did you go out after it?

BILLY (*shakes head*). No, thanks!

LIZZIE. Oh, Miss Neillie—last night when the lights went out I had a token. My oil lamp was full of oil, but do what I would to keep it going, the minute I shut my eyes, out that lamp would go. There ain't a surer token of death! The Bible says, "Let your light shine"—— When a hand you can't see puts your lights out—good night! (*There is a moment's silence. Even* CORNELIA *is uncomfortable.*)

CORNELIA. Well, now that you have cheered us up. (*Distant roll of thunder.* CORNELIA *rises. Pause.*) Bring some candles, Billy, the lights may be going out any moment. (BILLY *starts off.*) And Billy—— (BILLY *stops.*) There's a gentleman arriving on the last train. After he comes you may go to bed. I shall wait up for Miss Dale. (BILLY *starts off.*) Oh, and Billy. (BILLY *stops.*) See that all the outer doors on this floor are locked and bring the keys here. (*Exit* BILLY.)

LIZZIE. I know what all this means! I tell you, there's going to be a death sure!

CORNELIA. There certainly will be if you don't keep quiet. Lock the billiard room windows and go to bed. (*Sits by table. Knits.*)

LIZZIE (*angry*). I am not going to bed. I am going to pack up and to-morrow I'm going to leave. (*Pause; look.*) I asked you on my bended knees not to take this place, two miles from a railroad. For mercy's sake, Miss Neillie, let's go back to the city.

CORNELIA. I am not going. You can make up your mind to that. I'm going to find out what's wrong about this place, if it takes all summer. I came out to the country for a rest, and I'm going to stay and *get* it.

LIZZIE (*grimly*). You'll get your Heavenly rest.

CORNELIA (*puts knitting away*). Besides—I might as well tell you, Lizzie, I'm having a detective sent down tonight from Police Headquarters, in the city.

LIZZIE (*startled.*) A detective? Miss Neillie, you're keeping something from me! You know something I don't know.

CORNELIA. I hope so. I don't know that I need him—but it will be interesting to watch a good detective's methods. (*She picks up newspaper off table. Reads.*) "His last crime was a particularly atrocious one. The body of the murdered man——"

LIZZIE (*with a wail—quickly to billiard-room door*). Why don't you read the funny page once in a while? (*Exits quickly, closing door behind her.*)

(*Lightning flashes across french windows.* CORNELIA *reads on to herself, then thinks she hears something; goes into alcove; bolts terrace door; then comes into room and pushes light button. Lights all out. Thunder, distant flashes lightning. While lights are out,* CORNELIA *crosses over to french windows, slowly pulls one shade aside and looks out. Then she goes back to switch button; pushes it. Lights full up.*)

BILLY (*enters with three candles and box of parlor matches. He crosses to small table, puts them on table*). New gardener come! (*Puts water glasses on tray, at large table.*)

CORNELIA. Nice hour for him to get here! What's his name? (*Takes out knitting.*)

BILLY. Say name Brook.

CORNELIA. Ask him to come in—and Billy—where are the keys?

BILLY (*takes two keys out of pocket; places on table center. Then crosses to left with tray, pitcher and glasses. As* BILLY *crosses* CORNELIA, *he turns around and faces her and points up at terrace door*). Door up there—spring lock. (*Exits.*)

CORNELIA. I know, spring lock.

LIZZIE (*enters from billiard room as if she had been shot out of a gun; leaves door partly open as she enters. Loud whisper. To* CORNELIA). I heard somebody yell out in the grounds. Away down by the gate!

CORNELIA. What did they yell?

LIZZIE. Just yelled a yell!

CORNELIA (*crosses front of table and sits chair. Knits*). You take a liver pill and go to bed. (BILLY *opens hall door. Unseen.* BROOKS *enters.* BROOKS *is a handsome young fellow, shabbily dressed, but very neat, and carries a cap in his hand.* BILLY *closes the door behind him.* BROOKS *is smooth shaven.*) You are Brooks, the new gardener?

BROOKS. Yes, madam. The butler said you wanted to speak to me.

CORNELIA (*pause. Looks at him*). Come in. (BROOKS *comes forward two steps. Faces* CORNELIA.) You're the man my niece engaged in the city, this afternoon?

BROOKS. Yes, madam.

CORNELIA (*knitting*). I could not verify your references, as the Brays are in Canada.

BROOKS. I am sure, if Mrs. Bray *were* here——

CORNELIA (*turns in chair; looks at* BROOKS). Were here? (*She eyes him with quick suspicion*). Are you a professional gardener?

BROOKS (*doubtful*). Yes.

CORNELIA. Know anything about hardy perennials?

BROOKS. Yes, they—they're the ones that keep their leaves during the winter—aren't they?

CORNELIA. Come over here. (BROOKS *steps over to* R.C. CORNELIA *scrutinizes him carefully*). Have you had any experience with rubeola?

BROOKS. Oh, yes—yes—indeed! (LIZZIE *stands; watches* BROOKS.)

CORNELIA. And—alopecia?

BROOKS. The dry weather is very hard on alopecia.

CORNELIA. What do you think is the best treatment for urticaria?

BROOKS. Urticaria frequently needs —er—thinning.

CORNELIA (*rises. Faces him across table*). Needs scratching, you mean. Young man, urticaria is hives, rubeola is measles and alopecia is baldness. (*Slight pause. She crosses front of table to* BROOKS. *Suspiciously.*) Why did you tell me that you were a professional gardener? Why have you come here at this hour of the night, pretending to be something you are not?

BROOKS (*suddenly smiles at her, boyishly*). I know I shouldn't have done it. You'd have found me out anyhow. I don't know *anything* about gardening. The truth is, I was desperate! I *had* to have *work*.

CORNELIA. That's *all*, is it?

BROOKS. That's enough, when you're down and out! (*Turns to front.*)

CORNELIA (*somewhat melted*). How do I know you won't steal the spoons?

BROOKS (*turns to* CORNELIA. *Lighten up*). Are they *nice* spoons?

CORNELIA. Beautiful spoons.

BROOKS (*again engagingly boyish*). Spoons are always a great temptation to me, Miss Van Gorder, but if you'll take me, I'll promise to leave them alone.

CORNELIA (*with grim humor*). That's *extremely kind* of you. (*She goes to bell and pushes button.*)

LIZZIE (*quickly over and up to* CORNELIA). I don't trust him! He's too smooth! (CORNELIA *to window,* LIZZIE *following her, their backs to* BROOKS.)

CORNELIA. I haven't asked for your opinion, Lizzie.

LIZZIE. You're just as bad as all the rest of 'em. A good-looking man comes in the door and your brains fly out the window. (*During this,* BROOKS *has a chance to make a stealthy survey of the room. He does this in such a way that from that time on it is perfectly plain to the audience that his interest in the house is not that of a gardener only.* BROOKS *quickly runs up to alcove, looks off and quickly back, so that when* CORNELIA *turns to him, he is where she saw him last.*)

CORNELIA. Have you had anything to eat lately?

BROOKS. Not since this morning.

(BILLY *enters from the left.*)

CORNELIA. Billy, give this man something to eat, and then show him where he is to sleep. (*To* BROOKS, *holding out candle and matches. He takes a step up to her.*) Take a candle and a box of matches to your room with you. The local light company crawls under its bed every time there is a thunderstorm. Good night, Brooks.

BROOKS. Good night, ma'am. (*Over to door.*) You're being mighty good to me. (CORNELIA *smiles at him as* BROOKS *exits.* BILLY *exits, closing door.*)

LIZZIE. Haven't you any sense, taking strange men into the house? How do you know that isn't the Bat? (*Distant thunder, lights blink.*) There go the lights.

CORNELIA (*crosses front of table to right*). We'll put the detective in the blue room when he comes. You'd better go up and see if it's all ready. (LIZZIE *lifts newspaper off Ouija, gets board off table, puts prayer book on Ouija and on small table, starts for alcove doors.*) Lizzie! (LIZZIE *stops; looks at* CORNELIA.) You know that stair rail's just been varnished—use the other stairs. (LIZZIE *starts for hall door*)—and Lizzie——

LIZZIE. Yes'm.

CORNELIA. No one is to know that he is a detective—not even Billy.

LIZZIE. What'll I *say* he is?

CORNELIA (*sits at table*). It's nobody's business.

(*Doorbell off stage.*)

LIZZIE. A detective! Tiptoeing around with his eyes to all the keyholes. A body won't be safe in the bathtub—— (*Exits. Pause.*)

(*Enter* BILLY *from left.*)

BILLY (*as he comes and goes to table for key*). Front door key, please.

CORNELIA. Find out who it is before you unlock the door. (BILLY *gets key off table and exits, leaving door open.* CORNELIA *rises; looks toward door.*)

DALE (*off stage*). Won't you come in for a few minutes?

DOCTOR (*off stage*). Oh, thank you. (CORNELIA *sits with knitting.*)

(*Enter* DALE OGDEN. *She is a beautiful young girl of twenty-five. She wears a pale-colored charming evening frock and evening wrap. She enters quietly and without animation.*)

CORNELIA. Aren't you back early, Dale?

DALE (*throws off her wrap*). I was tired——

CORNELIA. Not worried about anything?

DALE (*comes down to chair by table. Sits. Unconvincingly*). No, but I've come out here to be company for you, and I don't want to run away all the time.

DOCTOR (*off stage*). How have you been, Billy?

BILLY (*off stage*). Very well, thanks.

CORNELIA. Who's out there, Dale?

DALE. Dr. Wells—he brought me over from the club. I asked him to come in for a few minutes—Billy's just taking his coat.

CORNELIA. Your trunks have come.

DALE (*listlessly*). That's good. (*Rises and turns; goes up back of table.*)

CORNELIA. I hope this country air will pick you up. I promised your mother before she sailed that I'd take good care of you. (DALE *leans over; kisses* CORNELIA. *Then* DALE *goes and sits on settee, which is up and down stage to the right. Faces fireplace.*)

(DR. WELLS *enters. He is in dinner clothes; good looking man in his early forties—with a shrewd, rather aquiline face.* BILLY *enters, goes to table, puts key on table, then exits; closes door.*)

DOCTOR (*crosses to table; shakes hands with* CORNELIA). Well, how are we this evening, Miss Van Gorder?

CORNELIA. Very well, thank you, Doctor. Well, many people at the Country Club?

DOCTOR. Not very many. This failure of the Union Bank has knocked a good many of the club members sky high.

CORNELIA. Just how did it happen?

DOCTOR. Oh, the usual thing. The cashier, a young chap named Bailey, looted the bank to the tune of over a million. (CORNELIA *surprised.*)

DALE (*visibly agitated*). How do you *know* the cashier did it?

DOCTOR. Well, he's run away, for one thing. The Bank Examiner found the deficit this morning. Bailey, the cashier, went out for lunch and didn't come back. The method was simple—blank paper substituted for securities.

DALE. Couldn't somebody else have done it? (CORNELIA *looks at* DALE, *then at* DOCTOR.)

DOCTOR. Of course the President of the bank had access to the vaults. But as you know, Mr. Courtleigh Fleming, the late President, was buried last Monday.

CORNELIA. Dale dear, did you know this young Bailey?

DALE (*controlling herself with an effort*). Yes—slightly.

CORNELIA. What with bank robberies and Bolshevism and the Income Tax, the only way to keep your money these days is to spend it.

DOCTOR (*sits at table*). Or *not* to *have* any! Like myself!

CORNELIA. You know, Dale, this is Courtleigh Fleming's house. I rented it from his nephew only last week.

DOCTOR. As a matter of fact, Dick Fleming had no right to rent you this property before the estate was settled. He must have done it the moment he received my telegram announcing his uncle's death.

CORNELIA. Were you with him when he died?

DOCTOR. Yes—— In Colorado—— It was very sudden.

CORNELIA (*knitting and in an innocent tone*). I suppose there is no suspicion that Courtleigh Fleming robbed his own bank?

DOCTOR. Well, if he did—I can testify he didn't have the loot with him. No, he had his faults—but not that.

CORNELIA. Doctor, I think I ought to tell you something. Last night and the night before, attempts were made to enter this house. Once an intruder actually got in, and was frightened away by Lizzie, at the top of that staircase. (*Indicating rear.*) And twice I have received anonymous communications threatening my life if I did not leave this house.

DALE (*startled*). I didn't know that, Auntie. How dreadful!

CORNELIA. Don't tell Lizzie. She'd yell like a siren. It's the only thing she can do like a siren, but she does it superbly. (*At this moment, pane of one of the French windows is smashed in, and a stone with a note tied to it with a piece of string is thrown into the room.* ALL *rise quickly and look up at windows.*)

DALE. What's that?

CORNELIA. Somebody smashed a window pane.

DALE. And threw in a stone.

DOCTOR. Wait a minute. I'll—— (*He hurries up to alcove and terrace door.*)

CORNELIA (*follows up a few steps*). It's bolted at the top. (DOCTOR *unbolts door leading to terrace, and goes out. Meanwhile,* DALE *has picked up stone; unties string off stone, hands note to* CORNELIA *after she has closed terrace door.* DALE *drops stone on settee.* CORNELIA *to top of table, unfolds the note and reads it.*) "Take warning. Leave this house at once!

It is threatened with disaster, which will involve you if you remain."

DALE. Who do you think wrote it?

CORNELIA. A fool, that's who! If anything was calculated to make me remain here, this sort of thing would do it. (*Slaps paper.*)

DALE. But—something may happen.

CORNELIA. I hope so! That's the reason I——

(*Doorbell rings off stage.*)

DALE (*startled*). Oh, don't let anyone in. (*Down a step below* CORNELIA.)

BILLY (*enters. Crosses to table, gets key before he speaks*). Key front door, please; bell ring.

CORNELIA (*crosses front of table*). See that the chain is on the door. And get the visitor's name before you admit him. (*Crosses to* BILLY.) If he gives the name Anderson, let him in and take him to the library. (BILLY *exits; closes door.*)

DALE. Anderson—— Who is——

CORNELIA (*pause; thinks*). Dale dear—perhaps you had better go back to the city.

DALE (*surprised*). Tonight?

CORNELIA (*impassively*). There is something *behind* all this disturbance—something I don't understand. But I mean to. (*Looks to see if* DOCTOR'S *returning, then moves close to* DALE. *Lowers voice.*) The man in the library is a detective from Police Headquarters.

DALE (*unaccountably aghast*). Not—the Police.

CORNELIA. Sh—— Be careful. It's not necessary to tell the *doctor*. I think *he's* a sort of perambulating bedside gossip. (*Slight pause.*) If it's *known* that the police are here, we'll *never* catch the criminals.

(DOCTOR *enters terrace door, trifle out of breath. Takes out handkerchief; shakes off rain.*)

DOCTOR. He got away in the shrubbery.

CORNELIA (*steps from front of table to* DOCTOR; *hands him note*). Read this. (DALE *sits settee, stares front, clearly terrified.*)

DOCTOR (*reads, pauses, then looks at* CORNELIA). Were the others like this?

CORNELIA. Practically.

DOCTOR. Miss Van Gorder, may I speak frankly?

CORNELIA. Generally speaking, I detest frankness.

DOCTOR. I think you *ought* to leave this house.

CORNELIA (*takes it lightly*). Because of that letter?

DOCTOR (*seriously*). There is some deviltry afoot. You are not safe here.

CORNELIA. I have been safe in all kinds of houses for sixty years. It's time I had a bit of a change. Besides, this house is as nearly impregnable as I can make it. (*She faces the French *windows.*) The window locks are sound—the doors are locked and the keys are here. (*Steps to back of table; points to keys on table.*) On that door to the terrace—(*looks*)—I had Billy today place an extra bolt. By the way, did you bolt that door again? (*She is about to go up to terrace door.* DOCTOR *takes a step up to stop her.*)

DOCTOR. Yes, I did. (CORNELIA *stops.*) Miss Van Gorder, I confess I'm very anxious for you. This letter is ominous. Have you any enemies?

CORNELIA. Don't insult me! Of course I have. Enemies are an indication of character.

DOCTOR. Why not accept my hospitality in the village tonight. It's a little house, but I'll make you comfortable. Or, if you won't come, let *me* stay *here.*

CORNELIA. Thank you, no, Doctor, I'm not easily frightened. (DOCTOR *looks at letter.*) And tomorrow I intend to equip this entire house with burglar alarms on doors and windows. (*She goes up into alcove and to terrace door; pushes bolt.*) I knew it. (*Triumphantly.*) Doctor, you *didn't* fasten that bolt!

DOCTOR (*facing up stage*). Oh, I'm sorry—

CORNELIA. You pushed it only part of the way. (*Sees door is bolted.*) The only thing that worries me now is that broken window. Anyone can reach a hand through it and open the latch. (*She goes to settee.* DALE *rises to see what* CORNELIA *intends to do.*) Please, Doctor!

DOCTOR. What do you mean to do?

CORNELIA. I'm going to barricade that window. (DOCTOR *and* DALE *push up settee until it is against French windows.*)

DOCTOR. It would take a furniture mover to get in there now.

CORNELIA. Well, Doctor, now I'll say good night—and thank you very much. (*Faces* DOCTOR.) Don't keep this young lady up too late—she looks tired.

DOCTOR. I'll only smoke a cigarette. You won't change your mind?

CORNELIA (*smiles*). I've got a great deal of mind. It takes a long time to change it. (*She exits; closes door.*)

DOCTOR (*rather nettled*). It may be mind—but—forgive me if I say I think it is foolhardy stubbornness.

DALE. Then you think there is really danger?

DOCTOR. Well, those letters—(*he has placed it on table*)—mean *something* —— Here you are—isolated—the village two miles away—and enough shrubbery around the place to hide a dozen assassins.

DALE. But what enemies can she have?

DOCTOR (*takes cigarette from case*). Any man will tell you what I do. This is no place for two women, practically alone. (DALE *walks away to fireplace; back to* DOCTOR. *Unseen by her, he steps down right of table, takes match box off match holder and slips it into his side pocket. Then with assumed carelessness*) I don't seem to see any matches. (*Looks up at stand.*)

DALE (*turns; faces him*). Oh, aren't there any? I'll get you some. (DALE *quickly crosses front of table and exits* R.; *closes door.* DOCTOR *watches her off, then swiftly he runs up into alcove and unfastens bolt on terrace door. He quickly comes back to same position, picks up a book and opens it. Enter* DALE *with matches. She crosses to him; gives him matches.*)

DOCTOR. I'm so sorry to trouble you —but tobacco is the one drug every doctor forbids his patients and prescribes for himself. (DALE *smiles at his little joke.* DOCTOR *lights cigarette.*) By the way, has Miss Van Gorder a revolver?

DALE (*turns; faces him*). Yes, she fired it off this evening to see if it would work.

DOCTOR. If she tries to shoot at anything, for goodness' sake stand behind her. Oh, I must be going. (*Starts to go; looks at wrist watch.*)

DALE. If anything happens, I shall *telephone* you at once.

DOCTOR (*stops on word "telephone," hesitates; then*). I'll be home shortly after midnight. I'm stopping at the Johnsons'. One of the children is ill. (*Faces* DALE.) Take a parting word of advice. The thing to do with a midnight prowler is—let him alone. Lock your bedroom doors, and don't let anything bring you out until morning. (*Goes to door.*)

DALE. Thank you. Billy will let you out. He has the key.

DOCTOR (*at door*). By jove, *you're* careful, aren't you? (*Looks around.*) The place is like a fortress! Well, good night, Miss Dale.

DALE. Good night. (*Exit* DOCTOR. *Pause. Door slam off stage.* DALE *is left alone. Stands motionless, takes out handkerchief, dabs eyes. She is distressed for some unknown reason. Crosses to fireplace.* BILLY *enters, puts door key on table.* DALE *picks up book.*) Billy, has the new gardener come?

BILLY. He here—name Brook. (*Exit* BILLY, *leaving door open. Stands in sight while they enter.* CORNELIA *sweeps in, followed by* ANDERSON. *He is a man of probably fifty, an aggressive person with a loud voice. Not at all the typical stage detective.*)

CORNELIA. Dale, dear, this is Mr. Anderson.

DETECTIVE. How do you do? (DALE *bows; does not speak.*)

CORNELIA. This is the room I spoke of. All the disturbances have taken place around that door. (*Indicating terrace door.*)

DETECTIVE (*up to alcove*). This is not the main staircase?

CORNELIA. No, the main staircase is out there. (*Indicating.*)

DETECTIVE (*looking over at french windows*). I think there must be a conspiracy between architects and the House Breakers Union these days. Look at all that glass. All a burglar needs is a piece of putty and a diamond cutter to break in.

CORNELIA. But the curious thing is that whoever got into the house evidently had a key to that door. (*Indicating terrace door.*)

DETECTIVE. Hello—what's that? (*Sees broken glass on floor in front of settee. He crosses up and over to window.* CORNELIA *comes down to table, watching* DETECTIVE. DETECTIVE *picks up piece of glass off floor front of settee. Places glass on settee.*)

DALE. It was broken from the outside, a few minutes ago. (DETECTIVE *pulls aside one of the blinds; looks out.*)

DETECTIVE. The outside?

DALE. And then that letter was thrown in. (*Points to table.* DETECTIVE *comes down to top of table* C. CORNELIA *hands him the note that was thrown in.* DETECTIVE *pauses; looks at letter.*)

DETECTIVE (*calm; self-assured*). Um! Coy, isn't it? Somebody wants you *out* of here, all right!

CORNELIA (*facing him across table*). There are some things I haven't told you *yet*. This house belonged to the late Courtleigh Fleming.

DETECTIVE (*with interest*). The Union Bank?

CORNELIA. Yes. I rented it for the summer and moved in last Monday. I have not had a really quiet night since I came. The very first night I saw a man with an electric flashlight making his way through that shrubbery. (*Points.* DETECTIVE *is looking up at window.*)

DALE. You poor dear! And you were here alone!

CORNELIA. Well, I had Lizzie—(*she opens drawer in side of table. Takes out a small revolver*)—and I had a revolver. I know so little about these things that if I didn't hit a burglar I'd certainly hit *somebody* or something. (*Looks into the barrel; then waves it about carelessly.*)

DETECTIVE (*turns; faces* CORNELIA. *Sees revolver. Starts*). Would you mind putting that away? I like to get in the papers as much as anybody, but I don't want to have them say "omit flowers." (CORNELIA *replaces revolver in drawer; closes it.* DETECTIVE *goes up, facing alcove doors.*) Now, you say, you don't think anybody has got upstairs yet?

CORNELIA. I think not. I'm a very light sleeper, especially since the papers have been so full of the exploits of this criminal they call "The Bat." I was just reading your statement about him in the evening paper. (*Sits beside table.*)

DETECTIVE (*comes down, professional manner*). Yes. He's contrived to surround himself with such an air of mystery that it verges on the supernatural.

CORNELIA. I confess I have thought of him in *this* connection. (DETECTIVE *laughs.*) Nevertheless, somebody has been trying to get into this house—night after night.

DETECTIVE (*looks around. Seriously*). Any liquor stored here?

CORNELIA. Yes.

DETECTIVE (*interested*). What?

CORNELIA (*with pride; knits*). Eleven bottles of home-made elderberry wine.

DETECTIVE. You're safe. (*Moves to table; looks newspaper. Shakes head.*) You can always tell when The Bat has anything to do with a crime. When he's through he signs his name to it. (*Sits; plays with box of matches.*)

CORNELIA. His name? I thought nobody knew his name.

DETECTIVE. That was a figure of speech. The newspapers named him "The Bat" because he moved with incredible rapidity—always at night—and he seemed to be able to see in the dark.

CORNELIA. I wish I could. These country lights are always going out.

DETECTIVE. Within the last six months he's taken up the name himself—pure bravado—— Sometimes he draws the outline of a bat, at the scene of the crime. Once, in some way, he got hold of a real bat and nailed it to the wall. (*Shudder from* DALE *and* CORNELIA.) He seems to have imagination. (*Slaps knee, rises, takes step determinedly.*) I've got imagination, too. (*Stands second, then with effort brings himself back to present situation.*) How many people in this house, Miss Van Gorder? (DALE *starts to cross to table. She does this slowly.*)

CORNELIA. My niece and myself; Lizzie Allen, who has been my personal maid for twenty years—the Japanese butler and the gardener. The cook, parlor maid and house maid left yesterday—frightened away. (*Smiles.* DALE *picks up her wrap from chair and exits.* DETECTIVE *just glances at her as she goes.*)

DETECTIVE. Well, you can have a good night's sleep tonight. I'll stay right here in the dark and watch.

CORNELIA. Would you like some coffee to keep you awake?

DETECTIVE. Thank you. Do the servants know who I am?

CORNELIA. Only Lizzie—my maid.

DETECTIVE. I wouldn't tell anyone that I am remaining up all night.

CORNELIA. You don't suspect my household?

DETECTIVE. I'm not taking any chances.

LIZZIE (*enters; stands at door*). The gentleman's room is ready.

CORNELIA (*knitting at table*). The maid will show you your room now, and you can make yourself *comfortable* for the night.

DETECTIVE (*facing up stage*). My toilet is made for an occasion like this when I've got my gun loaded. (LIZZIE *gives a start. His hand on hip pocket.* DETECTIVE *stares at* LIZZIE, *and goes over to her.*) This is the maid you referred to? (LIZZIE *stiffens.*) What's your name?

LIZZIE. Elizabeth Allen.

DETECTIVE. How old are you? (LIZZIE *looks across at* CORNELIA.)

LIZZIE. Have I got to answer that? (CORNELIA *nods her head. Cute-like.*) Thirty-two.

CORNELIA. She's forty. (LIZZIE *gives a start.*)

DETECTIVE. Now, Lizzie, do you ever walk in your sleep?

LIZZIE. I do not.

DETECTIVE. Don't care for the country, I suppose?

LIZZIE. I do not.

DETECTIVE (*facetiously*). Or detectives?

LIZZIE. *I do not.*

DETECTIVE. All right, Lizzie. Be calm! I can stand it! (*He goes to table, picks up note that was thrown through window, crosses back beside* LIZZIE, *holds out note so* LIZZIE *can read it. Quick.*) Ever see this before?

LIZZIE (*reads it; is horrified. Makes gesture with arm, nearly hitting* DETECTIVE *in face*). Mercy on us!

DETECTIVE (*watching her*). Didn't write it yourself, did you?

LIZZIE (*angrily*). I did *not!*

DETECTIVE. You're sure you don't walk in your sleep?

LIZZIE (*strong*). When I get into bed in this house I wouldn't put my feet out for a million dollars.

DETECTIVE. Well, that's more money than I'm worth.

LIZZIE. Well, *I'll say it is.* (*She flounces out; slams door behind her.* CORNELIA *laughs.*)

DETECTIVE (*turns and goes to table; puts note back on table*). Now, what about the *butler?*

CORNELIA. Nothing about him—except that he was Courtleigh Fleming's servant.

DETECTIVE. Do you consider that significant?

(DALE *enters from below stair alcove. Stands watching and listening to* DETECTIVE.)

CORNELIA. Is it not possible that there is a connection between this colossal theft at the Union Bank and *these* disturbances?

DETECTIVE (*looks at* DALE. *Pause*). Just what do you mean? (DALE *slowly moves to table.*)

CORNELIA. Suppose Courtleigh Fleming took that money from his own bank and concealed it in this house?

DETECTIVE. That's the theory you gave Headquarters, isn't it? But I'll tell you how Headquarters figures it out. In the first place, the cashier is missing. In the second place, if Courtleigh Fleming did it, and got as far as Colorado, he'd have had it with him. In the third place, suppose he had hidden the money in or around this house. Why did he rent it to you?

CORNELIA. But he didn't. I leased this house from his nephew—his heir.

DETECTIVE. Well, I wouldn't struggle like that for a theory. The cashier's *missing*—that's the answer.

CORNELIA (*resents with pride*). I've read a great deal on the detection of crime, and——

DETECTIVE (*interrupting her*). Huh! I suppose so—there are a lot of amateur detectives crawling around over the country today, measuring foot prints with a tape measure. Much as your life's worth to leave a thumb print on a soda water glass. The only real detectives outside the profession are married women.

CORNELIA. Then *you* don't think there's a chance that the money from the Union Bank is in this house? (*Puts knitting away.*)

DETECTIVE. Very unlikely!

CORNELIA (*rises*). If you come with me, I'll show you to your room. (*She crosses front of table.* DETECTIVE *follows her toward door.*)

DETECTIVE. Well, I suppose I might as well see where I park my toothbrush.

(CORNELIA *exits, followed by* DETECTIVE. DALE *is now seen to be in a state of violent excitement. She goes to hall door; then to alcove door; quick to center of stage. Alcove door opens cautiously.* BROOKS *enters.*)

DALE. Sh! Sh! Be careful! That man's a detective! (BROOKS *looks quickly off stage, then closes door, and goes to table.* DALE *follows him over.*)

BROOKS. Then they've traced me here?

DALE. I don't think so.

BROOKS. I couldn't get back to my rooms. If they've searched them—(*pause*)—as they're sure to—they'll find your letters to me. (*Pause.*) Your aunt doesn't suspect anything?

DALE. No, I told her I'd engaged a gardener—and that's all there was about it.

BROOKS. Dale! (*Turns and faces* DALE.) You *know* I didn't take that money.

DALE. Of course! I believe in you absolutely.

BROOKS (*he catches her in his arms, kisses her, then breaks*). But—the Police here—what does that mean?

DALE. Aunt Cornelia says people have been trying to break into this house for a week—at night.

BROOKS (*sharply*). What sort of people? (*Steps back.*)

DALE. She doesn't know.

BROOKS. That proves exactly what I have contended right along. (*Turns; looks at* DALE.) Courtleigh Fleming took that money and put it here. And somebody knows that he did.

DALE. The detective thinks you're guilty because you ran away.

BROOKS. Ran away? (*Turns front; smiles.*) The only chance I had was a few hours to myself, to try to prove what actually happened.

DALE. Why don't you tell the detective what you think? That Courtleigh Fleming took the money, and that it's still here?

BROOKS. He'd take me into custody at once—and I'd have no chance to search.

DALE. Why are you so *sure* it is here?

BROOKS (*crosses to* DALE). You must remember, Fleming was no ordinary defaulter—and *he* had no intention of being exiled to a foreign country. He wanted to come back here and take his place in the community while I was in the Pen.

DALE. But even then——

BROOKS (*interrupting*). Listen, dear. The architect who built this house was an old friend of mine. We were together in France and you know the way fellows get to talking when they're far away. Just an hour or two before a shell got him, he told me he had built a *hidden room* in this house.

DALE (*pauses; then speaks*). Where?

BROOKS. I don't know. We never got to finish that conversation. But I remember what he said—— He said "You watch old Fleming. If I get mine over here, it won't break his heart." He didn't want any living being to know about that room.

DALE (*excitedly; whisper*). Then you think the money is in this hidden room?

BROOKS. I do. I don't think Fleming took it West with him. He knew the minute this thing blew up he'd be under suspicion. (*Looks off stage.*) Only if he left the money here, why did he rent this house?

DALE. He didn't. His *nephew* rented it to us. (*Pause. She takes a step, looks and then crosses to* BROOKS.) Jack, could it be the nephew who's trying to break in?

BROOKS. He wouldn't *have* to break in. He could make an excuse and come at any time. (*Looks around.*) If I could only get hold of a blueprint of this place.

DALE. (BROOKS *crosses to fireplace.*) Oh, Jack, I'm so confused and worried!

BROOKS (*he stops her; hands on shoulders in effort to cheer her. Pause*). Now, listen—this isn't as hard as it sounds. I've got a clear night to work in—and as true as I'm standing here, that money's in the house. Now listen, honey, it's like this. (*Pantomime action of house on floor.*) Here's the house that Courtleigh Fleming built—here, somewhere, is the Hidden Room in the house that Courtleigh Fleming built—and here, somewhere—pray Heaven—is the money, in the Hidden Room, in the house that Courtleigh Fleming built! When you're low in your mind, just say that over!

DALE (*smiles faintly*). I've forgotten it already!

BROOKS (*still trying to cheer her*). Why, look here! (*Hands on her shoulders, turns her around*). It's a sort of game, dearest—"Money, money, who's got the money." You know. (*Looks around room*). For that matter, the Hidden Room may be behind these very walls. (BROOKS *sees golf sticks in bag leaning against small table; quickly up and gets one club. Comes down to fireplace.* DALE *watches him.* BROOKS *taps wall above fireplace. Roll of thunder. Lights blink. Lightning.*)

DALE. The lights are going out again.

BROOKS. Let them go. The less light the better for me. The only thing to do is to go over this house room by room. (*Indicates billiard-room door*). What's in there?

DALE. The billiard room. (BROOKS *starts toward billiard-room door.*) Jack! Perhaps Courtleigh Fleming's nephew would know where the blueprints are!

BROOKS. It's a chance, but not a very good one. (*Exit* BROOKS *and* DALE *into billiard room, leaving door open.*)

(BROOKS *raps with golf club off stage. Pause, then raps again. Enter* LIZZIE *with white table napkin. As soon as she gets inside, thunder. Lightning.* LIZZIE *looks nervously about. She shows she is scared; to table with napkin; spreads it on upper end of table.* BROOKS *repeats raps.* LIZZIE *starts off stage, looking back.*)

LIZZIE. Spirits! (*Over to door*). Go back to Hell, where you *started* from. (*Exits. Lights out. Lightning and thunder stop. Enter* BROOKS *and* DALE.)

BROOKS. Well, here we are, back where we started from.

DALE. There's a candle on the table, if I can find the table. Here it is. (*Finds candle on table.*)

BROOKS. I have matches. (*He lights candle. Places candle on table.*) It's pretty nearly hopeless. If all the walls are panelled like that. (*Rappings heard overhead—four dull raps.*)

DALE (*suddenly interrupting*). What's that?

BROOKS (*in tense voice and looking up at ceiling*). Someone else is looking for the Hidden Room. (*Four dull raps heard again.*)

DALE (*looking up at ceiling.*) Upstairs!

BROOKS. Who's in this house besides ourselves?

DALE. Only the detective—Aunt Cornelia—Lizzie and Billy.

BROOKS. Billy's the Jap?

DALE. Yes.

BROOKS. Belong to your aunt?

DALE. No, he was Courtleigh Fleming's butler. (*Four raps upstairs.*)

BROOKS (*looks up at ceiling*). He was, eh? (*Quickly puts down candle; crosses to alcove doors and into alcove.*) It may be the Jap. (*Four more raps upstairs.*) If it is, I'll get him. (BROOKS *exits quickly but quietly. Closes door behind him.* DALE, *left alone, stands thinking. Her distress and anxiety are evident. At last she forms a resolution. Goes up to city phone.*)

DALE (*at phone*). One-two-four. (*She looks around before calling number, her voice is cautious*). Is that the Country Club? Is Mr. Richard Fleming there? Yes—I'll hold the wire. (*Moment's pause. She looks around nervously.*) Hello—— Is this Mr. Fleming?—This is Miss Ogden. —Do you remember my aunt has rented your house, Cedarcrest? I know it's rather odd my calling you so late, but—I wonder if you could come over here for a few minutes. Yes—tonight. I wouldn't trouble you but—it's awfully important. Hold the wire a moment. (*She puts the receiver down; glances up the stairs; goes, listens at door, then back again to phone.*) Hello. I shall wait outside the house on the drive. It—it's a confidential matter.—Thank you so much. (*She hangs up phone. A moment's pause, then* DETECTIVE *enters with unlighted candle in his hand.*)

DETECTIVE. Spooky sort of place in the dark, isn't it?

DALE. Yes—rather!

DETECTIVE. Left me upstairs without a match. I found my way down by walking part of the way and falling the rest. I don't suppose I'll ever find the room I left my toothbrush in! (*Lights his candle from the lighted candle on table.*)

DALE. You're not going to stay up all night, are you?

DETECTIVE (*takes cigar out*). Oh, I may doze a bit. What's your opinion of these intrusions your aunt complains of?

DALE. I don't know. I only came today.

DETECTIVE. Is she a pretty nervous temperament usually? Imagines she sees things and all that?

DALE. I don't think so.

DETECTIVE. Know the Flemings?

DALE. I've met Mr. Richard Fleming once or twice.

DETECTIVE (*turns to table*). Know the cashier of the Union Bank?

DALE (*after a barely perceptible pause*). No. (*Moves to fireplace.*)

DETECTIVE. Fellow of good family, I understand—very popular. That's what's behind most of these bank embezzlements. Men getting into society and spending more than they make. (*Phone rings.* DETECTIVE *starts for house phone.*)

DALE. No, the other one; that's the house phone.

DETECTIVE (*looking at house phone*). No connection with the outside, eh?

DALE. No, just from room to room, in the house.

DETECTIVE (*goes to city phone*). Hello! Hello! (*Pause. Hangs up phone.*) This line sounds dead.

DALE. It was all right a few minutes ago.

DETECTIVE. You were using it a few minutes ago?

DALE (*hesitates, then*). Yes. (*Phone rings again.*)

DETECTIVE (*picks up phone*). Yes, yes—*this* is Anderson—go ahead—— (*Rather impatiently.*) You're sure of that—are you?—I see—— All right! 'Bye! (*Hangs up phone; turns and looks at* DALE *intently.*) Did I understand you to say that you are not acquainted with the cashier of the Union Bank? (*Pause.* DALE *stares ahead; does not reply.*) That was Headquarters, Miss Ogden. They have found some letters in Bailey's room which seem to indicate that you were not telling the entire truth just now.

DALE. What letters?

DETECTIVE. From you to Jack Bailey—showing that you had recently become engaged to him.

DALE. Very well. That's true.

DETECTIVE. Why didn't you say so before?

DALE (*frankly*). It's been a secret. I haven't even told my aunt yet. (*Rises*). How can the Police be so stupid as to accuse Jack Bailey—a young man about to be married? Do you think he would wreck his future like that?

DETECTIVE. Well, some folks wouldn't call it wrecking a future to lay away a million dollars. (*Speaks slowly and ominously.*) Do you know *where* he is now?

DALE. No.

DETECTIVE. Miss Ogden, in the last minute or so the Union Bank case and certain things in this house begin to tie up pretty close together. (*Steps a little nearer to her.*) Bailey disappeared at three o'clock this afternoon. Have you heard from him since then?

DALE. No.

DETECTIVE. You used the telephone a few minutes ago. Did you *call* him?

DALE. No.

DETECTIVE. I'll ask you to bring Miss Van Gorder here.

DALE. Why do you want her?

DETECTIVE. Because this case is taking on a new phase.

DALE. You don't think I know anything about that money?

DETECTIVE. No, but you know—somebody who does.

(DALE *hesitates, about to reply, finding none. Taking a lighted candle with her, exits.* DETECTIVE, *left alone, reflects for a moment, then he picks up lighted candle from table; proceeds to make a systematic examination of walls.* MAN *appears outside windows. His shadow shows on shades. He then disappears to terrace door. At same time* LIZZIE *appears at hall door with tray of dishes and food, Parker House roll, chop, plate, cup and saucer. She walks slowly, with her head turned to look behind her. The faint light of a candle from the hall gives her enough light to advance. As she gets to table, she hears key turn in terrace door. Registers fright. She has tray poised over the table.* MAN *who passed the windows now enters terrace door. He closes the door, reaches out his left arm, as if feeling his way to stairs. On his wrist he has a wrist watch with luminous face. It glows in darkness.* LIZZIE *stands galvanized with fright.* MAN *about to go up staircase.* LIZZIE *drops the tray on top of the table with a crash. She makes three attempts to scream before her voice responds. Then she shrieks. The* MAN *quickly runs up the stairs and off stage.* CORNELIA *runs on from the left. She is carrying a lighted candle.* CORNELIA *also carries a coffee pot, half filled with burnt sugar and water (coffee) and spills it at every step. At same time* DETECTIVE *enters with candle lighted.*)

CORNELIA. For the love of Heaven, what's wrong? (CORNELIA, *holding the coffee pot inclined, the coffee pours out of the spout on* LIZZIE'S *foot.*)

LIZZIE (*screams*). Oh, my foot! My foot!

CORNELIA. My patience! Did you yell like that because you stubbed your toe?

LIZZIE (*wildly*). You scalded it! It went up the staircase.

CORNELIA. Your toe went up the staircase?

LIZZIE (*stands on one foot*). No, no! An eye—as big as a saucer! It ran right up that staircase—(CORNELIA *puts pot and candle on table.*)

DETECTIVE (*sternly*). Now, see here. Stop this chicken-on-one-leg business, and tell me what you saw.

LIZZIE (*still holding up one leg*). A ghost! It came right through that door and went up the stairs! (DALE *and* BROOKS, *with lighted candle, come on, followed by* BILLY.)

DALE. Who screamed?

LIZZIE. I did. I saw a ghost. (*Then to* CORNELIA.) I begged you not to come here. I begged you on my bended knees. There's a graveyard not a quarter of a mile away.

CORNELIA. Yes, and one more scare like that, Lizzie Allen, and you'll have me lying in it.

LIZZIE (*holding foot*). Oh, my foot! If anything tries to get me now, I won't even be able to run away. (BROOKS *up with candle.* CORNELIA *goes up to terrace door in alcove.*)

DETECTIVE (*sore*). Now, Lizzie—what did you really see?

LIZZIE. I told you what I saw.

DETECTIVE (*rather threateningly*). You're not trying to frighten Miss Van Gorder into leaving this house and going back to the city?

LIZZIE (*grimly*). Well, if I am, I'm giving myself a good scare too, ain't I?

CORNELIA (*coming down from terrace door; annoyed*). Somebody who had a key could have got in here, Mr. Anderson. That door's been unbolted from the inside.

LIZZIE (*hysterically*). I *told* you so! I *knew* something was going to happen tonight. I heard rappings all over the house today, and the Ouija Board spelled "Bat"!

DETECTIVE. I think I see the answer to your puzzle, Miss Van Gorder! An hysterical and not very reliable woman—(LIZZIE *glares at him*)—anxious to go back to the city, and terrified over and over by the shutting off of the electric light.

CORNELIA. I wonder!

DETECTIVE. A good night's sleep and——

LIZZIE (*interrupting, aghast*). My *God!* We're not going to bed, are we?

DETECTIVE (*kindly to* LIZZIE). You'll feel better in the morning. Lock your door and say your prayers and leave the rest to me.

CORNELIA. That's very good advice. You take her, Dale. (CORNELIA *puts arm around* LIZZIE. DALE *comes down* R. *of* CORNELIA. LIZZIE *is passed along by* CORNELIA *to* DALE, *who puts arm around her shoulder, leads her toward door.*)

LIZZIE (*does not want to go, but does*). I'm not going to bed. Do you think I'm going to wake up in the morning with my throat cut? (DALE *and* LIZZIE *exit.*)

DETECTIVE (*speaking to* CORNELIA). There are certain things I want to discuss with you, Miss Van Gorder, but they can wait till tomorrow morning.

CORNELIA (*looks off stage*). Do you think all this pure imagination?

DETECTIVE (*close to table*). Don't you?

CORNELIA. I'm not sure.

DETECTIVE (*laughs a little*). I'll tell you what I'll do. (*Puts candle down.*) You go upstairs and go to bed comfortably. I'll make a careful search of the house before I settle down.

CORNELIA (*turns; looks at* DETECTIVE; *picks up coffee pot off table*). I'm afraid Lizzie has *absorbed* most of your coffee. Billy shall make you some more. (*She turns to* BILLY. *He steps forward and takes pot. Registers it is hot. He bows and exits with coffee pot*). Well, I hope we're at the end of our troubles. (*She crosses to table.* DETECTIVE *hands her candle.*)

DETECTIVE. Sure you are. Now you go upstairs. (CORNELIA *starts off with candle.*) Get your beauty sleep. I'm sure you need it. (*Earnestly, without intention, then realizing what he said.*)

CORNELIA (*has reached door, turns, smiles caustically at him*). I begin to understand why The Bat has so long eluded you! (*Exits majestically.*)

DETECTIVE (*takes out handkerchief; mops his face*). Whew! (*Then looks at* BROOKS. BROOKS *about to exit, when* DETECTIVE *speaks*). So you're the gardener, are you?

BROOKS (*lightly*). Yes.

DETECTIVE. Well, I don't need any gardening done just now—you can —— (*Looks attentively at* BROOKS.) I've seen you somewhere—and I'll place you before long. (*There is a little threat in his voice.*) Not in the portrait gallery at Headquarters, are you?

BROOKS (*resentfully*). Not yet.

DETECTIVE. Well, we slip up now and then. All right, Brooks. If you're needed during the night you'll be *called.*

BROOKS. Very well, sir. (BROOKS *exits. Closes door.*)

(DETECTIVE *watches him off with expression of suspicion. With noiseless step,* DETECTIVE *goes to hall door; listens. Opens door suddenly. Then closes door. Takes out revolver. To table; picks up candle;* DETECTIVE *proceeds to make a careful search of the entry, floor, walls, stair and stair rail. He looks up staircase. Then bolts terrace door; comes back into room.* DETECTIVE *draws revolver from hip pocket; examines it; then exits with candle. Wind, thunder, lightning. Pause.* DALE *comes down the stairs holding a lighted candle high. She carries a rubber slicker and a pair of rubbers. She is cautious. She unbolts the terrace door; comes into the room from alcove. She places the candle on table and sits by table; places coat on back of chair. She is about to put on her rubbers when she hears a knock on terrace door. She starts at the sound, terrified, as she opens drawer right side of the table, takes out revolver. Steps up back of table with revolver pointed up at alcove. Noise as of opening terrace door with key.*)

DICK (DICK FLEMING *enters terrace door; closes it. He steps into room from alcove; stands there a moment. He is a man of perhaps thirty, rather dissipated as to face, foppish in dress, with collar of his dinner coat turned up against the rain*). Did I frighten you?

DALE. Oh, Mr. Fleming—yes! (*She puts revolver on table. She goes toward him.*)

DICK. I rapped—but as nobody heard me, I used my key.

DALE. You're wet through.

DICK. Oh, no! (*Takes off cap and raincoat; places them on back of chair.*) Reggie Beresford brought me over in his car. He's waiting down the drive.

DALE (*Closes double door*). Mr. Fleming, I'm in dreadful trouble!

DICK (*over a few steps to her*). I say! That's too bad.

DALE. You know the Union Bank closed today.

DICK. Yes, I know it! I didn't have anything in it—or in *any* bank, for that matter—but I hate to see the old thing go to smash.

DALE. Well, even if *you* haven't lost anything by this failure, a lot of your friends have, surely?

DICK. I'll say so! Beresford is sitting down the road in his Rolls-Royce now—writhing with pain!

DALE (*pause*). Lots of awfully poor people are going to suffer, too.

DICK (*rather heartlessly*). Oh, well, the poor are always in trouble. They specialize in suffering. (*Takes out cigarette case and cigarette; moves closer to table.*) But look here—you didn't send for me to discuss the poor depositor, did you? Mind if I smoke?

DALE. No! (DICK *takes up candle from table; lights cigarette; slight pause.*) Mr. Fleming, I'm going to say something rather brutal. Please don't mind. I'm merely desperate. You see, I happen to be engaged to the cashier—Jack Bailey.

DICK (*whistles and sits on edge of table*). I *see!* And he's beat it!

DALE. He has not! I'm going to tell you something—he's here now, in this house. My aunt thinks he's a new gardener. He is here, Mr. Fleming, because he knows he didn't take the money, and the only person who could have done it—was—your uncle. (DICK *drops cigarette on tray. Pause. Turns; faces her.*)

DICK. That's a pretty strong indictment to bring against a dead man.

DALE. It is true.

DICK. All right. (*Smiles.*) Suppose it's true? Where do I come in? (*Steps toward her.*) You don't think I know where the money is?

DALE. No, but I think you might help to find it. (*She turns to make sure no one is listening, then faces* FLEMING.) If anybody comes in—you've just come to get something of yours. (*Comes close to him.*) Do you know anything about a Hidden Room in this house?

DICK. A Hidden Room—that's good. (*Laughs.*) Never heard of it. Now, let me get this straight. The idea is—a Hidden Room—and the money is in it—is that it?

DALE (*nods "yes"*). The architect who built this house told Jack Bailey he had built a Hidden Room in it. (DICK'S *expression has changed. A slowly growing look of avarice and calculation has taken the place of his smile. He no longer looks at* DALE. *His eyes are shifty and uncertain. They open and close as though already he has them on the treasure.*) Do you know where there are any blueprints of the house?

DICK (*starts; restrains himself*). Blueprints? (*It is evident to the audience that he does know.*) Why, there may be some—— (*He formulates; one can see almost the plot growing in his mind.*) Have you looked in that old secretary in the morning room? My uncle used to keep all sorts of papers there.

DALE. Why, don't you remember, you locked it when we took the house?

DICK (*gets out his keyring and selects the key*). So I did. Suppose you go and look. Don't you think I'd better stay here? (DALE *takes key.*)

DALE (*cheerful; grateful*). Yes—— Oh, I can hardly thank you enough! (*She quickly crosses and exits; closes door.*)

(DICK *quickly looks around room, then goes around room from bookcase to bookcase. Turns; looks around room again. Pause. Decides to try the bookcase above fireplace. All these moves are quick. He takes out the books in top shelf and puts them quickly on mantel at fireplace; reaches behind books on shelf and pulls out a roll of three blueprints. He leans over to see what they are at fireplace. Then over to table. Holds blueprints close to candle on table. Looking carefully at each blueprint, finds the third one is the one he wants. He tears off a corner of it.*)

DALE (*enters; closes door behind her. Quickly over to him, rejoiced*). Oh, you found it! (*Gives him the key.*) Please let me have it. I *know* that's it.

DICK (*his manner changed*). Just a moment. (*He steps away from her.*

Picking up candle and looking at the piece of blueprint in his hand; then turns; looks at DALE.) Do you suppose, if that money is actually here, that I can simply turn this over to you—and let you give it to Bailey? Every man has his price. How do I know that Bailey's isn't a million dollars? (*He inspects piece of blueprint closely.*)

DALE. What do you mean to do, then?

DICK (*turning over blueprint in his hand. Pause*). I don't know. (*Puts candle down on table. Looks at* DALE.) What is it you want me to do?

DALE. Aren't you going to give it to me?

DICK. I'll have to think about that. So the missing cashier is in the house posing as a gardener?

DALE. If you won't give it to me—there's a detective in the house. (*She makes a turn as if to call him. Then to* DICK.) Give it to him—let him search.

DICK (*quickly, facing her, startled*). A detective? What's a detective doing here?

DALE. People have been trying to break in.

DICK. What people?

DALE. I don't know.

DICK (*to himself, looking out front*). Then it is here. (*At this one of the alcove doors opens noiselessly just an inch or so. Evidently someone is listening.*) I'm not going to give it to the detective. (DICK *picks up the roll of blueprints; quickly goes to fireplace; throws in the roll of blueprints.* DICK *takes the small piece of blueprint from pocket; watches papers burn.* DALE *has followed him over to fireplace.*)

DALE (*as she follows* DICK). What do you mean? What are you going to do?

DICK (*turns and faces* DALE, *near fireplace*). Let us suppose a few things, Miss Ogden. Suppose my price is a million dollars—suppose I need money very badly—and my uncle has left me a house containing that amount in cash—suppose I choose to consider that that money is mine—then it wouldn't be hard to suppose, would it, that I'd make a pretty sincere attempt to get it?

DALE (*close up to him*). If you go out of this room with that paper, I'll scream for help.

DICK. To carry on our little game of supposing—suppose there is a detective in this house—and that if I were cornered I should tell him where to lay his hands on Jack Bailey, do you suppose you would scream? (DALE *stands helpless. He quickly crosses and stops by table, looks up at alcove doors a moment, then he hurries up and opens them; makes for stairs in alcove.*)

DALE (*follows him over to table. When he starts to move off, she picks up revolver off table and hurries up after him. Speaks as she goes. Suddenly desperate*). No! No! Give it to me! Give it to me! (DALE *up to* DICK *at foot of stairs in alcove. He turns and waits for her. He snatches the revolver from her. A very short scuffle in the darkness of the entry in effort to secure the revolver. He unguards the piece of blueprint, which she tears from him, leaving only a corner of it in his grasp.)*

(A light flashes on from the top of stairs and covers DICK *at foot of stairs. Supposed to be a pocket flash, held by an invisible hand. Light shows him poised ready to come down after the girl, his face shown distorted with fury. Shot off stage.* DICK *falls forward, dead. The revolver* DALE *carried falls between them.* DICK *lies with head just inside the double doors into the room proper, face downward.)*

DALE *(backs away into room; hides the blueprint in dress. With a little whimpering cry of horror).* Oh, no, no! *(The storm dies out. Pause. Voices off stage heard ad lib.)*

VOICES. The noise came from this room—I think it is in here.

(General entrance. (1) DETECTIVE. *Sees body.* (2) BROOKS. (3) BILLY, *the Jap.* (4) CORNELIA. LIZZIE *enters last and stands in doorway. They all perceive* DALE *and the body. A tense silence.)*

DALE *(stepping back until she is almost to door).* Oh! I didn't do it! I didn't do it!

DETECTIVE *(goes to body; examines it; takes plenty of time).* He's dead. *(Pause. Picks up revolver, looks at it, then turns, and looks at* DALE *curiously.)* Who is he?

DALE *(hysterically).* Richard Fleming— Somebody shot him!

DETECTIVE *(takes a step toward her).* What do you mean by somebody? *(*CORNELIA *sinks into chair.)*

DALE. Oh, I don't know. *(Hysterically.)* Somebody on the staircase.

DETECTIVE. Did you see anybody?

DALE. No—there was a light from somewhere—like a pocket flash.

LIZZIE *(in doorway, hysterically points up at stairs).* I *told* you I saw a man go up that staircase. *(Pause.* DETECTIVE *has turned from facing* DALE. *He looks at* LIZZIE *and* CORNELIA.*)*

CORNELIA. That's the only explanation, Mr. Anderson.

DETECTIVE. I've been all over the house. There's nobody there. *(House phone rings.)*

CORNELIA *(rises. Slight pause).* The house phone—— *(Looks at the other characters.)* But we're all here. *(They* ALL *stand, pause, aghast. Then* CORNELIA *goes up to phone.)* Hello! Hello! *(*ALL *stand, listening rigidly. She gasps. An expression of horror comes over her face.)*

THE CURTAIN SLOWLY FALLS

ACT TWO

SCENE—*Same as Act. I.*

DISCOVERED: ALL CHARACTERS *as at end of Act I. The action being continuous. They are staring aghast at* CORNELIA, *who still stands clutching the phone.*

CORNELIA (*gasps*). Somebody groaning! It's horrible! (DETECTIVE *crosses to* CORNELIA. *She gives him the phone. She steps down to table.*)

DETECTIVE (*listens in phone*). I don't hear anything. (*Slight pause.*)

CORNELIA. I heard it! I couldn't *imagine* such a dreadful sound! I tell you somebody in this house is in terrible distress.

DETECTIVE. Where does this phone connect?

CORNELIA. Practically every room in the house.

DETECTIVE (*puts receiver to ear again*). Just what did you hear?

CORNELIA. Dreadful groans, and what seemed to be an inarticulate effort to speak.

LIZZIE (*trembling violently*). I'd go somewhere, if I had somewhere to go! (*Rises.*)

CORNELIA (*faces up to* DETECTIVE). Won't you send these men to investigate? Or go yourself?

DETECTIVE. My place is here—you two men. (*To* BROOKS *and* BILLY.) Take another look through the house. (BILLY *opens door.*) Don't leave the building—I'll want you pretty soon.

BROOKS. If you'll give me that revolver—— (*Indicating* CORNELIA'S *revolver, which* DETECTIVE *still holds in his hand.*)

DETECTIVE. This revolver will stay where it is. (*Exit* BILLY, *followed by* BROOKS. *Close door. As* BROOKS *goes reluctantly, puzzled and anxious glance at* DALE, DETECTIVE *looks at body, then turns quickly on* DALE.) Now I want the real story. You lied before.

CORNELIA (*indignantly*). That is no tone to use! You'll only terrify her.

DETECTIVE (*turns; looks at* CORNELIA). Where were you when this happened? (DALE *moves down a little.*)

CORNELIA. Upstairs in my room.

DETECTIVE (*to* LIZZIE). And you?

LIZZIE. In *my* room, brushing Miss Cornelia's hair.

DETECTIVE (*goes to table; breaks revolver and looks at it*). One shot has been fired from this revolver.

CORNELIA (*looking over shoulder*). I fired it myself, this afternoon.

DETECTIVE. You're a quick thinker. (*Places revolver on table.*)

CORNELIA. I demand that you get the Coroner here.

LIZZIE. Dr. Wells is the Coroner.

DETECTIVE (*to* DALE). I'm going to ask you some questions.

CORNELIA. Do you mind covering that body first? (DETECTIVE *eyes her in a rather ugly fashion, then gets* FLEMING'S *raincoat on chair. Goes up to body. Throws coat over it.*) Shall I telephone for the Coroner?

DETECTIVE (*goes to phone*). I'll do it. What's his number?

DALE. He's not at his office—he's at the Johnsons'.

CORNELIA (*up to phone*). I'll get the Johnsons, Mr. Anderson. (DETECTIVE *relinquishes phone to* CORNELIA; *gives her a look.*)

DETECTIVE (*to* DALE). Now what was Fleming doing here? (DALE *down to fireplace.*)

DALE. I don't know.

DETECTIVE. Well, I'll ask that question another way. How did he get into the house?

CORNELIA (*at phone*). One—four——

DALE. He had a key. He used to live here.

DETECTIVE. A key to what door?

DALE. To that door over there. (*Indicating terrace door.*)

CORNELIA (*at phone*). Hello—is that Mr. Johnson's residence? Is Dr. Wells there? No? (DETECTIVE *turns during this; watches* CORNELIA. CORNELIA *pauses; listens in on phone.*) All right, thank you. Good night! (*Hangs up phone, puzzled. She comes down table center. Same time* DETECTIVE *registers, sees ashes of blueprints in fireplace.*)

DETECTIVE (*to* DALE). When did you take that revolver out of the table drawer?

DALE. When I heard him outside, on the terrace, I was frightened.

LIZZIE (*tiptoes over to* CORNELIA). You wanted a detective! I hope you're happy now you've got one! (CORNELIA *gives* LIZZIE *a look.*)

DETECTIVE (*to* DALE). When he came in, what did he say to you? (CORNELIA *sits by table.*)

DALE. Just—something about the weather.

DETECTIVE. You didn't have any quarrel with him?

DALE (*after hesitation*). No.

DETECTIVE. He just came in that door —said something about the weather —and was shot from that staircase? Is that it?

DALE (*after moment's hesitation*). Yes.

CORNELIA. Are all these questions necessary? You can't for a moment believe that Miss Ogden shot that man? (DALE *sits at fireplace.*)

DETECTIVE (*looks at* DALE). I think she knows more than she's telling. She's concealing something. The nephew of the President of the Union Bank shot in his own house on the day the Bank has failed—that's queer enough. (*He turns; looks at* CORNELIA.) But when the only person present at his murder is the girl who is engaged to the guilty cashier—— (*Looks at* DALE.) I want to know more about it! (*Picks up cigarette* DICK *put on ash tray Act I.*)

CORNELIA (*rises*). Is that true, Dale?

DALE. Yes.

CORNELIA. What has *that* got to do with it? (*To* DETECTIVE.)

DETECTIVE (*turning to* CORNELIA). I'm not accusing this girl, but behind every crime there is a motive. When we've found the motive for *this* crime we'll have found the criminal.

(DALE'*s hand instinctively goes to her bosom where she has concealed the blueprint. Her expression shows that she realizes that her having the blueprint is damaging evidence against her.*)

DETECTIVE (*who has been facing* CORNELIA, *now turns on* DALE). What papers did he burn in that grate? (*Slight pause.*)

DALE. Papers!

DETECTIVE. Papers! The ashes are still there.

CORNELIA. Miss Ogden has said he didn't come into this room.

DETECTIVE. I hold in my hand proof that he was in this room for some time. (*Holding up half-burnt cigarette.* CORNELIA *sits.*) His cigarette with his monogram on it. (*He goes to fireplace and picks up small piece of blueprint from the fender; looks at* DALE.) A fragment of what is technically known as a blueprint. What were you and Richard Fleming doing with a blueprint? (DALE *hesitates.*) Now think it over! The truth will come out sooner or later! Better be frank *now!*

BROOKS (*runs on, followed by* BILLY. BROOKS, *a trifle breathlessly*). Nothing in the house, sir.

BILLY. Me go all over house. Nobody. (BOTH *start off as if to continue search.*)

DETECTIVE. You men stay here! I want to ask you some questions. (*Then to* DALE.) Now, what about this blueprint?

DALE (*still seated*). I'll tell you just what happened. I sent for Richard Fleming, and when he came I asked him if he knew where there were any blueprints of the house.

DETECTIVE. *Why* did you want blueprints?

DALE. Because I believed old Mr. Fleming took the money himself, from the Union Bank, and *hid* it here.

DETECTIVE. Where did you get that idea?

DALE. I won't tell you.

DETECTIVE. What had the blueprints to do with it?

DALE. I'd heard there was a Hidden Room built in the house.

DETECTIVE (*leans forward*). Did you locate that room?

DALE (*hesitates*). No.

DETECTIVE. Then why did you burn the blueprints?

DALE. *He* burned them. I don't *know* why.

DETECTIVE. Then you didn't locate this Hidden Room?

DALE. No.

DETECTIVE. Did he?

CORNELIA. What's that? (DALE *rises.*)

DETECTIVE. What's what?

CORNELIA. I heard something.

(THEY ALL *turn and look up stage at windows.* BROOKS *is near windows,* BILLY *beside him.* CORNELIA *at table. Suddenly from outside a circle of brilliant white light is thrown on the window shades up stage. In the* C. *of the light area is seen a vivid black shadow resembling a gigantic Black Bat. For an instant it glows there, travelling across and disappears.*)

LIZZIE (*wails*). Oh, my God—it's The Bat! That's his sign. (BROOKS *starts for terrace door.*)

CORNELIA. Wait, Brooks! (*Then to* DETECTIVE.) Mr. Anderson, you are familiar with the sign of The Bat. Did that look like it?

DETECTIVE (*puzzled and evidently disturbed*). Well—it looked like the shadow of a bat—I'll say that. (*Doorbell rings.* ALL *look at hall door.*)

BROOKS. I'll answer that!

CORNELIA (*gives him key off table*). Don't admit anyone till you know who it is.

(BROOKS *exits.* ALL *stand and wait.* CORNELIA, *hand over her revolver on table where* DETECTIVE *had laid it.* BROOKS' *and* WELLS' *voices heard off stage, raised in angry dispute. Some evidence of a slight scuffle. Ad lib. "What do I know about a flashlight?" "I haven't got a pocket flash." "Take your hands off me." Then* WELLS *enters, cap on, followed by* BROOKS. *He comes down and faces* CORNELIA. *He is ruffled and enraged.* BROOKS *close behind him, vigilant and watchful.* CORNELIA, *relieved, quickly drops revolver.*)

DOCTOR. My dear Miss Van Gorder! Won't you instruct your servants that, even if I do make a late call, I am not to be received with violence. (*Takes off cap; bag on chair by table.*)

BROOKS (*strong*). I asked you if you had a pocket flash about you. If you call a question like that violence——

CORNELIA. It's all right, Brooks. (BROOKS *places key on table.*) You see, Dr. Wells, just a moment before you rang the doorbell a circle of white light was thrown on those window shades.

DOCTOR. Why—that was probably the searchlight from my car—I noticed as I drove up that it fell directly on that window.

LIZZIE (*with deep suspicion*). "He may be a merchant, a lawyer, a doctor——"

CORNELIA (*suspiciously watching the* DOCTOR. *Lift scene*). In the center of this ring of light there was an almost perfect silhouette of a bat.

DOCTOR. A bat? Ah—I see—the symbol of the criminal of that name. (*Laughs.*) I think I can explain what you saw—quite often my lamps collect insects at night. A large moth spread on the glass would give precisely the effect you speak of. Just to satisfy you—I'll go out and take a look. (*He turns and is about to go when he sees body on floor. At same time* CORNELIA *turns and faces* DOCTOR.) Why—— (*Startled, stares at covered body. Then he glances from covered body on floor to the faces of the* OTHERS.)

CORNELIA (*at table, facing* DOCTOR). We have had a very sad occurrence here, Doctor.

DOCTOR (*turns; looks at* CORNELIA). Who?

CORNELIA. Richard Fleming.

DOCTOR (*pause. Horrified*). Richard Fleming! (*Bends over body; turns raincoat back.*)

CORNELIA. Shot and killed, from that staircase.

DETECTIVE. Shot and killed, anyhow.

DOCTOR (*on knees, beside body. He has been blithe and gay up to that moment; seems almost instantly to become aged. His face is stricken. He repeats*). From that stairway. (*Rises. Straightens up and glances up the stairs, then.*) What was Richard Fleming doing in this house at this hour?

DETECTIVE. That's what I'm trying to find out. (DOCTOR *looks over at* DETECTIVE. DOCTOR *is puzzled.*)

CORNELIA. Doctor—this is Mr. Anderson. (DOCTOR *crosses to* DETECTIVE. *They shake hands.*)

DETECTIVE (*To* DOCTOR). Headquarters!

LIZZIE (*loud whisper to* CORNELIA). Don't you let him fool you with any of that moth business. He's The Bat! (*She sits by table.*)

CORNELIA (*to* DOCTOR). I didn't tell you, Doctor, I sent for a detective this afternoon. (*Then suspiciously.*) You happened in very opportunely.

DOCTOR (*pulling himself together*). After I left the Johnsons I felt very uneasy. I determined to make one more effort to get you away from this house. As this shows, my fears were *justified.* (CORNELIA *sits.* DOCTOR *takes off muffler; puts it in pocket of overcoat. Takes off overcoat; throws it upstage on settee, front of french windows. He takes out handkerchief, mops face and neck as though under great mental excitement. Looks over at body, then looks at* CORNELIA.) Died instantly, I suppose. (*Looks at* DETECTIVE.) Didn't have time to say anything?

DETECTIVE (*looking at* DALE). Ask the young lady. She was here when it happened. (DOCTOR *looks at* DALE.)

DALE (*pitifully*). He just fell over.

DOCTOR (*there is no question but that the* DOCTOR *is relieved. He draws a long breath. Looking at body. Speaks as he crosses above table*). Poor Dick has proved my case for me better than I expected. (*Stops. Turns; looks at* DETECTIVE, *who stands up.*) Mr. Anderson, I ask you to use your influence to see that these two ladies find some safer spot than this for the night.

LIZZIE (*half rises*). *Two?* If you *know* any safe spot, lead *me* to it! (DOCTOR *up to body.*)

CORNELIA. I have a strange feeling that I'm being watched by unfriendly eyes.

(BILLY *up to window, scared, pulls shade aside, looks out; sees something outside when he looks out window. Moves down while the others are not looking at him. Pretending to straighten the tray which* LIZZIE *brought on in Act I, he gets possession of front door key from table, and exits.* LIZZIE *speaks on word cue; does not wait for* BILLY'S *business.*)

LIZZIE (*clutching at* CORNELIA, *across table*). I wish the lights would go out again. (CORNELIA *slaps* LIZZIE.) No, I don't neither! (LIZZIE *crosses to door; stands there.*)

DETECTIVE (*steps to table. To* DOCTOR). You say, Doctor, you came back to take these women away from the house. Why?

DOCTOR. Miss Van Gorder has explained.

CORNELIA (*at table. To* DOCTOR). Mr. Anderson has already formed a theory of the crime.

DETECTIVE. I haven't said that. (*House phone rings.* ALL *are startled. Turn; look at phone.* CORNELIA *and* DALE *rise.*)

DALE. The house telephone—again! (CORNELIA *makes movement as if to answer it.*)

DETECTIVE (*going to phone. Takes up phone.*) I'll answer that! Hello! Hello! (*The* DOCTOR'S *face is a study in fear. He clutches the back of chair by table to steady himself.*) There's nobody there! (*Hangs up phone.*) Where's that Jap? (*Looking at door.* DALE, *relieved, sits down.* LIZZIE *sits.*)

CORNELIA. He just went out.

DETECTIVE (*to* DOCTOR). That Jap rang that phone. Miss Van Gorder believes that this murder is the culmination of the series of mysterious happenings which caused her to send for me. I do not.

CORNELIA. Then what is the significance of the anonymous letters? Of the man Lizzie saw going up the stairs, of the attempt to break into the house? Of the ringing of that telephone bell?

DETECTIVE (*deliberately*). Terrorization.

DOCTOR (*moistening his dry lips*). By whom?

DETECTIVE (*with cold deliberation*). I imagine by Miss Van Gorder's own servants. By that woman. (*Points at*

LIZZIE. LIZZIE *rises.*) Who probably writes the letters—by the gardener, who may have been the man Lizzie saw slipping up the stairs—by the Jap, who goes out and rings the telephone.

CORNELIA. With what object?

DETECTIVE. That's what I'm going to find out.

CORNELIA. Absurd—the butler was in this room when the telephone rang the first time.

(*Ad lib. noise between* BERESFORD *and* BILLY *off stage. Violent scuffle.* ALL *turn to hall door. Door opens and* REGINALD BERESFORD *is catapulted into the room by* BILLY. BERESFORD *falls to floor.* BILLY *stands in doorway, arms folded; he is impassive.* BERESFORD *speaks as he picks himself up; brushes clothes off. He is in dinner clothes; carries straw hat.*)

BERESFORD (*turning on* BILLY). Damn you! What do you mean by this?

BILLY (*impassively, in doorway*). Jujitsu. Pretty good stuff. Found on terrace with searchlight.

DETECTIVE. With searchlight!

BERESFORD. Well, why shouldn't I be on the terrace with a searchlight? (CORNELIA *crosses to side of table.*)

DETECTIVE. Who *are* you?

BERESFORD. Who are you? (DETECTIVE *flashes his police badge, which is on inside of lapel of coat, right side.* BERESFORD *looks at it.*) H'm! (*Takes out gold cigarette case.*) Very pretty—nice, neat design—very chaste! (*He takes a swift glance around room; sees* DALE; *suddenly senses the situation without suspecting a tragedy.*)

DETECTIVE. If you've finished admiring my badge, I'd like to know what you were doing on that terrace?

BERESFORD (*hesitates, glances at* DALE, *then*). I've had some trouble with my car down the road. (*Looks again at* DALE.) I came to ask if I might telephone.

CORNELIA. Did it require a searchlight to find the house?

BERESFORD. Look here—why are you asking me all these questions?

CORNELIA (*stepping toward* BERESFORD). Do you mind letting me see that flashlight? (BERESFORD *hands it to her. She examines it.* DETECTIVE *takes it from her; examines lens, then down* R. *of* BERESFORD. CORNELIA *gives way for* DETECTIVE. *She is now at table.*)

DETECTIVE (*to* BERESFORD). Now—what's your name? (*Hands flash back to* BERESFORD.)

BERESFORD (*sulkily*). Beresford—Reginald Beresford—if you doubt it—I've probably got a card somewhere. (*Goes through his pockets.*)

DETECTIVE. What's your business?

BERESFORD. What's my business *here?*

DETECTIVE (*sharply*). How do you earn your living?

BERESFORD (*flippantly*). I don't. I'm a *lawyer*.

LIZZIE (*sepulchrally, quoting from newspaper*). "He may be a lawyer."

DETECTIVE (*to* BERESFORD). And you came here to telephone about your car?

DALE. Oh, don't you see—he's trying to protect me—— It's no use, Mr. Beresford. (CORNELIA *turns, and steps beyond chair by table.* DALE *comes over to left of table.* CORNELIA *places* DALE *in chair by table, placing her hand on* DALE'S *shoulder.*)

BERESFORD. I see. Well, the plain truth is—I didn't know the situation—and I thought I'd play safe, for Miss Ogden's sake.

DALE (*to* DETECTIVE). He doesn't know anything about—(*pause*)—this. He brought Mr. Fleming here in his car—that's all.

DETECTIVE (*to* BERESFORD). Is that true?

BERESFORD. Yes—I got tired waiting and so I—

DETECTIVE (*breaks in curtly*). All right—— (*Turns.*) Now, Doctor. (*Nods toward body.* BERESFORD *turns, follows* DETECTIVE'S *glance, stands rigid.*)

BERESFORD (*tensely*). What's that? (DOCTOR *uncovers body and kneels beside it.* BERESFORD, *thickly.*) That's not—Fleming—is it? (*Looks at* DETECTIVE. DETECTIVE *nods head.*)

DOCTOR. If you've looked over the ground— (*To* DETECTIVE.) I'll move the body to where I can have a better light.

BERESFORD (*takes another step up and says, with force*). Do you mean to say that Dick Fleming—— (DOCTOR *takes paper from* DICK'S *hand; throws cigarette to floor as he starts up.*)

DETECTIVE (*interrupting, eyes on* DOCTOR, *silences* BERESFORD *with an uplifted hand. Then, menacingly, to* DOCTOR). What have you got there, Doctor?

DOCTOR (*on knees beside body*). What do you mean?

DETECTIVE. You took something just then, out of Fleming's hand.

DOCTOR. I took nothing out of his hand.

DETECTIVE. I warn you not to obstruct the course of Justice. Give it here.

DOCTOR (*gets up, and hands* DETECTIVE *small piece of blueprint he took out of* FLEMING'S *hand*). Why, it's a scrap of paper—— Nothing at all. (DOCTOR *crosses around body.*)

DETECTIVE (*with blueprint, down to table, eyes the* DOCTOR). Scraps of paper are sometimes very important. (*Looks at* DALE.)

BERESFORD (*angry. Crosses few steps over and up to* DETECTIVE). Look here—I've got a right to know about this thing. I brought Fleming over here—and I want to know what happened to him.

LIZZIE (*overcome*). You don't have to be a mind-reader to know that!

BERESFORD (*to* DETECTIVE). Who killed him? That's what *I* want to know.

DETECTIVE. Well, you're not alone in that.

DOCTOR (*nervously*). As the Coroner —if Mr. Anderson is satisfied—I suggest that the body be taken where I can make a thorough examination. (DETECTIVE *up to body; turns body half over, then lets it fall back on face. Same as before.* DETECTIVE *steps back; glances from blueprint in his hand to* DOCTOR. DETECTIVE *takes off the overcoat from body.*)

DETECTIVE. All right.

CORNELIA. Into the library, please. (CORNELIA *goes over to fireplace while body is being moved.* DALE *watches* DETECTIVE. DOCTOR, *in alcove, takes hold of body by legs.* BERESFORD, *right side, hands* BILLY *his hat, takes body under arm.* BROOKS, *left side, under arm.* DOCTOR *going off first.* DETECTIVE *follows body off. As body disappears,* LIZZIE *up to double doors. Then* BILLY *picks up the rug where* DETECTIVE *dropped it.* BILLY *exits with rug.* DALE *gets piece of blueprint from front of dress and gets roll from floor, front of table. She puts blueprint in the roll, replaces roll on floor.* BILLY *returns from door. Enters; goes to table; picks up tray. Sees roll on floor; places it on tray.* DETECTIVE *comes back on as* BILLY *enters.*)

CORNELIA. Take that tray out to the dining room.

DETECTIVE (*steps down in front of* BILLY). Wait, I'll look at that tray. (*Makes a thorough search of the tray; even examines the napkin, lifts the dishes, etc.* DALE *sits, tensely apprehensive.* DETECTIVE *fails to find anything.*) All right, take it away. (BILLY *exits with tray.*)

CORNELIA. Lizzie, go out in the kitchen and make some fresh coffee. I'm sure we'll all need it.

LIZZIE. Go out in that kitchen—alone.

CORNELIA (*sits*). Billy's there.

LIZZIE. That Jap and his jujitsu! One twist, and I'd be folded up like a pretzel! (*Exits.*)

DETECTIVE (*to back of table. Looks at piece of blueprint in his hand, and then at* DALE). Now, Miss Ogden—I have here a scrap of blueprint which was in Dick Fleming's hand when he was killed. I'll trouble you for the rest of it.

DALE (*is seated by table*). The rest of it?

DETECTIVE. Don't tell me that he started to go out of this house holding a blank scrap of blue paper in his hand. He didn't start to go out at all!

DALE (*rises*). Why do you say that?

DETECTIVE. His cap's there on that table.

CORNELIA (*is seated at table. Disturbed*). If you're keeping anything back, Dale, tell him.

DETECTIVE. She's keeping something back, all right. She's told part of the truth but not all. You and Fleming located that room by means of a blueprint of the house. He started—not to go out, but probably to go up that staircase. And he had in his hand the rest of this. (*He holds out the scrap of blueprint.*)

DALE (*slight pause, then, rather pitifully*). He was going to take the money and go away with it.

CORNELIA (*alarmed*). Dale!

DALE. He changed the minute he heard about it. He was all kindness before that, but afterwards—— (*She closes her eyes.*)

DETECTIVE (*turns triumphantly to* CORNELIA). She started in to find the money—and save Bailey, but to do it she had to take Fleming into her confidence, and he turned yellow. Rather than let him get away with it—she—— (*He makes expressive gesture, hand on hip pocket.* DALE *registers. He indicates revolver. Then to* DALE.) Is that true?

DALE. I didn't kill him.

DETECTIVE. Why didn't you call for help? You—you knew I was here?

DALE (*hesitates*). I couldn't. (*Steps toward him.*)

CORNELIA (*agitated*). Dale! Be careful what you say!

DETECTIVE (*advances step to* DALE). Now I mean to find out two things—*why* you didn't call for help, and *what* you have done with the blueprint.

DALE. Suppose I could find that piece of blueprint for you? Would that establish Jack Bailey's innocence?

DETECTIVE. If the money's there—yes.

CORNELIA (*rises, crosses to* DALE; *turns on* DETECTIVE). But her own guilt! No, Mr. Anderson—granting that she knows where that paper is—and she has not said that she does, I shall want more time, and much legal advice, before I allow her to turn it over to you.

(*Enter from below the stairs,* DOCTOR, BERESFORD *and* BROOKS *silently.*)

DETECTIVE (*turns and looks up at them*). Well, Doctor?

DOCTOR. Well, poor fellow—straight through the heart!

CORNELIA. Were there any powder marks?

DOCTOR. No—and the clothing was not burned. He was apparently shot from some little distance—and I should say, from above.

DETECTIVE. Beresford, did Fleming tell you why he came here tonight?

BERESFORD. No. He seemed to be in a great hurry; said Miss Ogden had telephoned for him, and asked me to drive him over.

DETECTIVE. Why did you come up to the house?

BERESFORD. Well—— (*Looks over at* DALE.) I thought it was putting rather a premium on friendship to keep me sitting out in the rain all night, so I came up the drive, and by the way—— (*Suddenly remembering*) I picked this up, about a hundred feet from the house. (*Pulls out a man's battered open-face silver watch from pocket; holds it out on his hand.*) A man's watch. It was partly crushed into the ground, and you see it's stopped running.

DETECTIVE (*taking it, and examining it*). Yes! (*Thoughtfully.*) At ten-thirty——

BERESFORD. I was using my pocket flash to find my way, and what first attracted my attention was the ground torn up. Anyone here recognize the watch? (DETECTIVE *shows watch, holding it up so* ALL *can see it. No one replies.*) You didn't hear any evidence of a struggle, did you?

CORNELIA. Just about ten-thirty Lizzie heard somebody cry out, in the grounds. (DETECTIVE *looks* BERESFORD *over.*)

BERESFORD. I don't suppose it has any bearing on this case, but it's interesting. (DETECTIVE, *having finished his examination of the watch, slips it into his pocket.*)

CORNELIA (*suspiciously*). Do you always carry a flashlight, Mr. Beresford?

BERESFORD. Always at night in the car.

DETECTIVE. This is all you found?

BERESFORD. Yes.

CORNELIA (*sits by table*). Someday I hope to meet the real estate agent who promised me that I would sleep here as I never slept before. He's right. I've slept with my clothes on every night since I came.

BILLY (*enters hurriedly. He carries a butcher knife in one hand, his face is excited; comes over to* CORNELIA). Key, kitchen door, please.

CORNELIA. Key? What for?

BILLY. Somebody outside try to get in. I see knob turn so—— (*Illustrating turning hand.*) And so—three times. (*They are all startled.*)

DETECTIVE (*quickly puts hand to revolver in pocket*). You're sure of that, are you? (*Roughly to* BILLY.)

BILLY. Sure I sure!

DETECTIVE (*looks at* CORNELIA). Where's that hysterical woman, Lizzie? She may get a bullet in her if she's not careful. (DALE *sits fireplace.*)

BILLY. She see too. She shut in closet. Say prayers maybe.

DETECTIVE. Doctor, have you a revolver?

DOCTOR. No.

DETECTIVE. How about you, Beresford?

BERESFORD (*hesitates*). Yes. Always carry one at night in the country. (CORNELIA *registers this.*)

DETECTIVE. Beresford, will you go with this Jap to the kitchen? (*Exit* BILLY, *leaving door open.*) If anyone's working at the knob, shoot through the door. I'm going round to take a look outside. (*Starts up for doors.*)

BERESFORD (*going to hall door, turns, looks up at* DETECTIVE. DETECTIVE *stops, looks at* BERESFORD *as he speaks*). I advise you not to turn the doorknob yourself, then.

DETECTIVE. Much obliged. (*Exit* DETECTIVE *terrace door. Closes door. At same time* BERESFORD *exits to hall.*)

BROOKS (*to* BERESFORD). I'll go with you if you don't mind. (*Exit* BROOKS, *closing door.* DOCTOR *crosses up to below staircase.*)

CORNELIA (*at table, to* DOCTOR). Doctor.

DOCTOR. Yes?

CORNELIA. Have *you* any theory about this occurrence tonight? (*Watching him closely.*)

DOCTOR. None whatever—it's beyond me.

CORNELIA. And yet you warned me to leave the house. (*Stop knitting.*) You didn't have any reason to believe that the situation was even as serious as it has proved to be?

DOCTOR. I did the perfectly obvious thing when I warned you. Those letters made a distinct threat.

CORNELIA (*pause*). You said he'd probably been shot from above.

DOCTOR. Yes, apparently.

CORNELIA (*suddenly*). Have you a pocket flash, Doctor?

DOCTOR (*hesitates*). Why—yes—a flashlight is more important to a country doctor than castor oil.

CORNELIA (*turns to* DALE). Dale, you said you saw a white light shining down from above?

DALE. Yes.

CORNELIA (*crosses to* DOCTOR). May I borrow your flashlight? (DOCTOR *gives her his pocket flash.*) Now that I've got that fool detective out of the way, I want to do something. Doctor, I shall ask you to stand at the foot of the small staircase, facing up.

DOCTOR. Now?

CORNELIA. Now, please. (DOCTOR *walks up and takes position foot of stairs.* CORNELIA *turns, looks at* DALE.) And, Dale—when I give the word, put out the lights here, and then tell me when I have reached the point on the staircase from which the flashlight seemed to come. All ready. (DALE *moves up toward door, ready to turn out stand lamp.* CORNELIA *at door.*) I shall go up this way and down the other. (*Exit* CORNELIA, *closing door.* DOCTOR, *looking up staircase. His face changes, showing surprise and apprehension. He glances back into room to see if* DALE *can see him. She cannot. To somebody, evidently at top of stairs, he makes an insistent gesture, "Go back, go back."* DALE *turns out stand lamp.* DALE *then walks by the French windows to electric button. Stands with finger on button.* THE UNKNOWN *reaches hand in through the broken pane in French window, turns knob on window, unlocking the window door. Then the window door is pushed inward, evidently to admit a crouching figure. When* UNKNOWN *is in and behind couch, which he pushes down to make room for his body, he closes the door in window.*

Only his hand seen during this business. When UNKNOWN *is on stage, back of settee and window closes.)* All right! Put out the lights! (DALE *pushes button on wall. Lights out.* DALE *steps just inside alcove, looks up and off stairs. She leans heavily against the double door.* CORNELIA *off.)* Was it here? (*Spot focuses on* DOCTOR'S *face.* DOCTOR *stands at foot of stairs, looking up.)*

DALE. Come down a little.

DOCTOR (*to* CORNELIA *with an attempt at jocularity*). I hope you have no weapon.

CORNELIA (*off*). How's this?

DALE. That's about right.

CORNELIA (*off*). Lights please. (DALE *pushes the wall button. Lights up.* CORNELIA *has evidently left the staircase.* DALE *back into room. She goes down to table.* DOCTOR *backs into room.)*

DALE (*by table; sits*). Doctor, I'm so frightened!

DOCTOR (*down to her*). Why, my dear child, because you happened to be in the room when a crime is committed?

DALE. But he has a perfect case against me.

DOCTOR. That's absurd!

DALE. No.

DOCTOR. *You don't mean?*

DALE (*horrified*). I *didn't kill* him, but you know the piece of blueprint you found in his hand?

DOCTOR. (*Tensely.*) Yes?

DALE. There was another piece—a large piece—I tore it from him just before——

DOCTOR (*trying to control his excitement*). Why did you do such a thing?

DALE. Oh, I'll explain that later. It's not safe where it is—Billy may throw it out, or burn it without knowing——

DOCTOR. Let me understand this. The butler has that paper now?

DALE. He doesn't know he has it. It was in one of the rolls that went out on the tray.

DOCTOR (*slight pause*). Now don't you worry about it. I'll get it. (*He starts, stops, turns to* DALE.) But you oughtn't to have it in your possession. (*Comes a step toward her.*) Why not let it be burned?

DALE (*startled*). Oh, no! It's important—it's vital!

DOCTOR. The tray is in the dining room?

DALE. Yes.

(DOCTOR *exits to hall, closing door.* UNKNOWN *back of settee raises himself, just for a second. Audience just sees top of his head. Moves settee slightly.* DALE *crosses slowly to fireplace. Enter* BROOKS *from hall; closes door behind him. He carries two logs of wood for fire.* DALE *turns; sees him.)*

DALE (*as soon as* BROOKS *is on*). Oh! Things have gone awfully wrong, haven't they?

BROOKS. Be careful! (*Turns, looks around room.*) I don't trust even the furniture in this house tonight. (*Moves to* DALE, *kisses her, then crosses back of her to fireplace. Raises his voice very formally.*) Miss Van Gorder wishes the fire kept up! (*Drops the wood, turns back to* DALE, *speaks in undertone.*) Play up!

DALE (*distinctly*). Put some logs on the fire, please. (*Then, in undertone, facing away from him.*) Jack, I'm nearly distracted! (BROOKS *drops the wood at fireplace, and quickly comes up behind her; puts his arms around her.*)

BROOKS. Dale, pull yourself together. We've got a fight ahead of us. (*As he releases her and starts back to fireplace.*) These old-fashioned fireplaces eat up a lot of wood. (*Drops on knees; places wood inside fender.*)

DALE (*turns and goes toward him; leans on arms of armchair, which is between them*). You know why I sent for Richard Fleming, don't you?

BROOKS (*on knees, turns and faces her*). Yes—but who in God's name killed him?

DALE. You don't think it was Billy?

BROOKS (*half rises*). More likely the man Lizzie saw going upstairs. I've been all over the upper floors.

DALE. And nothing?

BROOKS. Nothing. (*Leaning over armchair toward* DALE.) Dale, do you think that——

DALE (*is conscious that someone is coming. To* BROOKS). Be careful! (BROOKS *turns to fireplace; works with logs.* CORNELIA *enters from hall; closes door behind her. She carries her black bag. She sees* BROOKS *at fireplace as soon as she enters. Coming to table.*)

CORNELIA. Well, Mr. Alopecia—Urticaria, Rubeola—otherwise Bailey. (BROOKS *rises with a start; faces her. Stares at her. Look between* DALE *and* BROOKS.) I wish you young people would remember that even if hair and teeth have fallen out at sixty the mind still functions. (*She reaches into her black knitting-bag and brings out a cabinet photograph of* BROOKS.) His photograph—sitting on your dresser! (DALE *crosses to table, across from* CORNELIA. *To* DALE, *as* CORNELIA *holds out the photo toward her.*) And that detective with as many eyes as a potato. Burn it and be quick about it!

DALE (*takes photo, but continues to stand facing* CORNELIA. *Then glances at* BROOKS, *and back at* CORNELIA). Then—you knew?

CORNELIA (*sitting by table*). My dear child, I have employed many gardeners in my time, and never before had one who manicured his finger nails, who wore silk socks, who talked like Harvard condescending to Yale—(BROOKS *registers this by looking down*)—and who regards baldness as a plant instead of a calamity. (DALE *crosses to fireplace; throws photo in fire.*)

BROOKS (*facing* CORNELIA). Do you know why I'm here?

CORNELIA. I do—and a pretty mess you've put me in by coming here. If that detective was as smart as he thinks he is, he'd have had you an hour ago. (*She rises, crosses toward* DALE; *then* DALE *becomes very grave.*) Now, I want to ask *you* something. Was there a blueprint and did you get it from Richard Fleming?

DALE. Yes.

BROOKS (*facing* CORNELIA *and* DALE). Dale! Don't you see where this places you? If you had it, why didn't you give it to Anderson when he asked for it?

CORNELIA. Because she had sense enough to see that Mr. Anderson considered that piece of paper the final link in the evidence against *her!*

BROOKS. But she could have no *motive.*

CORNELIA. Couldn't she? The detective thinks she could—to save you!

BROOKS (*takes step back; slight pause*). Good God!

CORNELIA (*close to* DALE). Where is the paper now?

DALE. The Doctor is getting it for me.

CORNELIA. *What!*

DALE. It was on the tray Billy took out.

CORNELIA (*puts hands up, depressed*). Well, I'm afraid everything's over. (*She crosses to front of table.*)

DALE (*plaintively*). I didn't know what else to do.

CORNELIA (*looks at hall door*). One of two things will happen now. Either the Doctor's an honest man, in which case, as Coroner, he will hand that paper to the detective, or he is *not* an honest man, and he will keep it for himself. *I* don't think he's an honest man.

DALE (*goes, meets* CORNELIA *back of table*). Then you think the Doctor may give the paper to Mr. Anderson?

CORNELIA. He may, or he may not. (*Enter* BILLY. CORNELIA *takes a step toward* BILLY.) I want to know the moment *anybody goes upstairs.* I want to know—immediately. (BILLY *is about to go.*) Oh, Billy—— (*She looks up stairs, then.*) Where is the Doctor?

BILLY. In dining room, having cup coffee.

CORNELIA. And Mr. Beresford?

BILLY. Sit on kitchen floor, inside door, with gun. (CORNELIA *motions* BILLY *to go. Exit* BILLY.)

CORNELIA (*to* DALE). Dale, watch that door. (*Indicating hall door.* DALE *crosses to door.*) And warn me if anyone is coming. (CORNELIA *gets* DOCTOR'S *bag, carries it to table, places on table, turns to* BROOKS.) Get some soot.

BROOKS. Soot?

CORNELIA. Yes, soot, from the back of that fireplace. (BROOKS *takes envelope from pocket, goes to fireplace, reaches far in, scrapes back of fireplace; envelope blackened. At same time* CORNELIA *steps up to stand, gets piece of writing paper, places it with lead pencil on table.*)

BROOKS (*to table*). Is this all right?

CORNELIA. Yes. Now rub it onto the handle of that bag. (*Indicating* DOCTOR'S *bag.* BROOKS *blackens the handle.*)

DALE. Somebody's coming! (BROOKS *quickly to fireplace; pretends to work at fireplace.*)

CORNELIA (*pretending to carry on conversation and carries bag back to chair. She does not touch the handle of bag*). We all need sleep and I think—— (*Motions to others.*)

BILLY (*enters just inside of hall door*). Doctor just go upstairs. (*Exits, leaving door open.*)

CORNELIA (*steps to door; looks off; calls*). Oh, Doctor! Doctor!

DOCTOR (*off stage. Apparently from stairway*). Yes? (*A moment's pause.* DOCTOR *enters; he takes a furtive glance around the room. Faces* CORNELIA; *just about to speak.*) Your maid insists that a man went up that staircase before the crime. I was going to take a look around.

CORNELIA (*pleasantly*). The gardener has just made a thorough search.

DALE (*coming down to* DOCTOR). Doctor, did you? (DETECTIVE *knocks on terrace door. On the knock* DOCTOR *half turns, looks up.*)

DETECTIVE (*outside on terrace; muffled voice*). It's Anderson.

BROOKS (*crosses up to terrace door*). The detective. (*Unbolts door for* DETECTIVE.)

DALE (*following* DOCTOR). Did you get it?

DOCTOR (*turns; looks at* DALE). My dear child, are you sure you put it there?

DALE (*dismayed*). Why, yes, I—— (*She looks at him; suddenly distrusts him.* DALE *turns; exchanges looks with* CORNELIA. BROOKS *stands near window.* DETECTIVE *comes in terrace door, slams it behind him.*)

DETECTIVE (*stays up in doorway; irritably*). I couldn't find anybody. I think that Jap's crazy.

DOCTOR (*getting coat from settee*). Well, I think I've fulfilled all the legal requirements. I must be going.

DETECTIVE (*turns and faces* DOCTOR). Doctor, did you ever hear Courtleigh Fleming mention a Hidden Room in this house?

DOCTOR (*does not look directly at* DETECTIVE). No—and I knew him rather well.

DETECTIVE. You don't think, then, that such a room and the money in it could be the motive of this crime?

DOCTOR. I don't believe Courtleigh Fleming robbed his own bank. If that's what you mean. (DOCTOR *crosses to get his bag.* DOCTOR, *to* CORNELIA.) Well, I can't wish you a comfortable night, but I can hope it will be a quiet one. (DOCTOR *gets bag in right hand, cap in left.*)

CORNELIA (*crosses to* DOCTOR). We're naturally upset. Perhaps you will write a prescription. Some sleeping medicine.

DOCTOR. Why, certainly. (*He comes toward table.* CORNELIA *hands him paper and pencil. He is about to write on paper, using the bag as a pad.*)

CORNELIA. I hoped you would. Here is paper and pencil.

DOCTOR (*taking the paper in right hand*). I don't generally advise these drugs, but—— (*Then stopping short.*) What time is it?

CORNELIA (*looks at clock on mantel*). Half-past eleven.

DOCTOR. Then I'd better bring you the powders. The pharmacy closes at eleven. (*She takes the paper from* DOCTOR; *puts it down on table without looking at it. From the blackened handle of the bag his thumb has made a clear impression on the paper. He is quite unconscious of this.* CORNELIA *picks up the paper, with apparent carelessness, glances at it, and lays it with the print down. She picks up a key off table.* DOCTOR *goes toward door.*)

CORNELIA. Dale will let you out, Doctor. (DALE *gets key from* CORNELIA.)

DOCTOR (*stops, turns, smiles at* CORNELIA). That's right. Keep things locked up. Discretion is the better part of valor. (DALE *waits just in hall doorway for* DOCTOR.)

CORNELIA. I've been discreet for sixty years, and sometimes I think it was a mistake. (DALE *exits* R. DOCTOR *follows her off.*)

DETECTIVE (*looks with angry eye on* BROOKS). I guess we can do without you!

BROOKS. All right, sir. (*Exits. Closes door.*)

DETECTIVE (*comes over to table. To* CORNELIA). Now, I want a few words with you! (*His tone is surly.*)

CORNELIA (*beside table*). Which means that you mean to do all the talking. Very well! But first I want to show you something. Will you come here, please? (*She starts up to alcove.*)

DETECTIVE. I've examined that staircase.

CORNELIA. Not with me! I have something to show you. (DETECTIVE *follows her up. They exit up the staircase. The room is now empty.*)

(LIZZIE *enters, carrying hot-water bottle and a large butcher knife.* UNKNOWN *opens the door in French windows. He is getting out of the room by the window, unseen.* LIZZIE, *after closing door, sees the French window move. It closes. She gives a wild screech; drops the water bag on chair by stand.* CORNELIA *and* DETECTIVE *run down the stairs. When* LIZZIE *sees them she points at window.* DALE *enters from hall.*)

LIZZIE (*wildly*). That window! It closed—without human hands! (CORNELIA *goes up to window; looks out.* DETECTIVE *stands in alcove door; looks at* LIZZIE.)

DETECTIVE (*speaks to* CORNELIA, *but looking at* LIZZIE). I wish you'd put this screech owl to bed!

LIZZIE (*agitatedly*). You'd screech owl yourself if you saw what I saw! (LIZZIE *collapses into chair; sits on water bottle. She gives a scream, jumps up and points to water bottle on chair.*) I'm scalded again! I can't walk and now I can't sit. (DETECTIVE *takes her by the shoulder and pushes her. They exit. Close door.*)

DALE (*starting over cautiously to* CORNELIA). It isn't there. The Doctor says he didn't see it and I've looked. It's gone.

CORNELIA. Then the Doctor—— (*She stops; hears doorknob move to left.* DALE *sits chair. Enter* DETECTIVE; *closes door.*)

DETECTIVE (*to* CORNELIA). Now, your point about that thumb-print on the stair-rail is very interesting. But just what does it prove?

CORNELIA. It points down——

DETECTIVE. It does—and what then?

CORNELIA. It shows that somebody stood there, for some time, listening to my niece and Richard Fleming, in this room below.

DETECTIVE. All right, I'll grant that to save argument, but the moment that shot was fired the lights came on. If somebody on that staircase shot him, and then came down and took the blueprint, Miss Ogden would have seen him. (*He turns to* DALE.) Did you?

DALE. No, nobody came down.

CORNELIA. Now, Mr. Anderson——

DETECTIVE. Now, I'm not hounding this girl. I haven't said yet that she committed the murder, but she took that blueprint, and I want it.

CORNELIA. You want it to connect her with the murder.

DETECTIVE (*savagely*). It's rather reasonable to suppose that I might want to return the funds to the Union Bank, isn't it? Provided they're here.

CORNELIA. I see. Well, I'll tell you this much, Mr. Anderson, and I'll ask you to believe me as a gentlewoman, granting that at one time my niece knew something of that blueprint, at this moment we do not know where it is or who has it.

DETECTIVE. Damnation—— (*Mutters.*) That's the truth, is it?

CORNELIA. That's the truth. (*She sits by table* C.; *takes out knitting; knits. Pause. To* DETECTIVE.) Did you ever try knitting when you wanted to think?

DETECTIVE. No. (*He crosses over to table, takes out cigar, lights it. Matches on table.*)

CORNELIA. You should some time! I find it very helpful!

DETECTIVE. I don't need knitting to think straight!

CORNELIA. I wonder! You seem to have so much evidence left over. (DETECTIVE *turns; looks at her.*) Did you ever hear of the man who took a clock apart, and when he put it together again he had enough left over to make another clock? (DETECTIVE *comes down, looking at* DALE.)

DETECTIVE (*ignoring* CORNELIA. *To* DALE). What do you mean by saying that paper isn't where you put it?

CORNELIA (*quickly*). She hasn't said that. (DETECTIVE *walks up, impatient movement.*) Do you believe in circumstantial evidence?

DETECTIVE. It's my business.

CORNELIA. While you have been investigating, I too have not been idle. (DETECTIVE *gives a mean laugh.*) To me it is perfectly obvious that one *intelligence*—(DETECTIVE *stops; looks at* CORNELIA)—has been at work, behind many of the things that have occurred in this house.

DETECTIVE. Who?

CORNELIA. I'll ask you that! Some one person who, knowing Courtleigh Fleming well, probably knows of the existence of a Hidden Room in this house—and who, finding us in occupation of the house, has tried to get rid of me in two ways: First by frightening me with anonymous threats, and second, by urging me to leave. Someone who very possibly entered this house tonight, shortly before the murder, and slipped up that staircase.

DETECTIVE (*startled*). The Doctor? (*Step down.*)

CORNELIA (*still knitting*). When Dr. Wells said he was leaving here earlier in the evening for the Johnsons', he did not go there. He was not expected to go there. I found that out when I telephoned.

DETECTIVE (*moves head, eyes narrowing*). The Doctor!

CORNELIA. As you know, I had a supplementary bolt placed on that door. (*Refers to terrace door.*) Earlier this evening Dr. Wells said that he had bolted it when he had left it open, purposely as I now realize, in order that later he might return. You may recall that Dr. Wells took a scrap of paper from Richard Fleming's hand and tried to conceal it. Why did he do *that?* (*Slight pause; changes tone.*) May I ask you to look at this? (*She picks up from the table the paper containing* DOCTOR WELLS' *thumb-print.*)

DETECTIVE (*over to table; takes the paper*). A thumb-print—— (*Looks at it.*) Whose is it?

CORNELIA. Dr. Wells'. (*She picks up reading-glass and offers it to* DETECTIVE. *He takes it; looks through it at paper.*) They say thumb-prints never lie.

DETECTIVE (*slight pause, looking at paper. Sarcastically*). You don't really think you *need* a detective, do you?

CORNELIA (*quietly ironical*). I am a humble follower in your footsteps.

DETECTIVE (*ironically bows to her; then she bows*). Well, I'll bite! Anything to help a sister in the profession!

CORNELIA (*calmly*). You'll find that the same hand that made that left the imprint on the staircase. (DETECTIVE *looks at* CORNELIA, *then up; goes up to foot of staircase. He turns and surveys the two women, then he goes slowly up the staircase and off.* DALE *half rises, as if to speak to* CORNELIA. CORNELIA *makes a warning gesture.* DALE *sinks back into chair.*)

BERESFORD (*enters. Closes door. Comes over and faces* CORNELIA). Miss Van Gorder, may I ask you to make an excuse and call your gardener here? (DALE *starts violently.* CORNELIA *betrays no emotion, save that she knits a trifle more rapidly.*)

CORNELIA. The gardener? Certainly—if you'll touch that bell. (BERESFORD *pushes button on wall; stands there.* DALE *is in an agony of suspense.*)

DETECTIVE (*comes quietly down the stairs into the room*). It's no good, Miss Van Gorder. The prints are not the same.

CORNELIA. Not the same!

DETECTIVE (*smoking cigar; lays down the reading-glass and paper on table*). If you think I'm mistaken, I'll leave it to any unprejudiced person or your own eyesight. Thumbprints never lie. Did you ever try a good cigar when you wanted to think?

CORNELIA. I still believe it was the Doctor.

DETECTIVE. And yet the Doctor was in this room tonight, according to your own statement, when the anonymous letter came through the window. (BILLY *enters.*)

BERESFORD (*steps down a little; to* BILLY). Tell the gardener Miss Van Gorder wants him—and don't say we're all here. (BILLY *exits.*)

DETECTIVE (*to* BERESFORD, *rather grimly*). I seem to have plenty of *help* in this case!

DALE (*rises; to* BERESFORD). Why have you sent for the gardener?

BERESFORD (*grimly*). I'll tell you that in a moment. (*Enter* BROOKS; *takes a swift survey of the room; closes door. Slight pause.*)

BROOKS (*to* CORNELIA). You sent for me?

BERESFORD (*with eye on* BROOKS, *speaks to* CORNELIA *brusquely*). How long has this man been in your employ?

CORNELIA (*still seated*). Why does that interest you?

BROOKS. I came this evening.

BERESFORD. Exactly. (*To* DETECTIVE.) I've been trying to recall this man's face ever since I came tonight—I know now who it is.

DETECTIVE. Who is he?

BROOKS (*straightening*). It's all right, Beresford. I know you think you're doing your duty, but I wish to God you could have *restrained* your sense of duty for about three hours more.

BERESFORD. To let you get away?

BROOKS. No—to let me finish what I came here to do.

BERESFORD. Don't you think you've done enough? (*Turns to* DETECTIVE.) This man has imposed on the credulity of these women. I am quite sure, without their knowledge. His name is Bailey, of the Union Bank.

DETECTIVE (*puts cigar on ashtray. To* BROOKS). That's the truth, is it?

BROOKS. It's true, all right.

BERESFORD. I accuse him not only of the thing he is wanted for but of the murder of Richard Fleming.

BROOKS (*fiercely to* BERESFORD). You lie!

DETECTIVE (*turns; goes down a step toward* DALE). You knew this? (*Turns to* CORNELIA.) Did you?

CORNELIA. Yes.

DETECTIVE. Then it's a conspiracy, is it? All this case against the Doctor! (*Wheels on* BROOKS.) What did you mean by that—"three hours more"?

BROOKS. I could have cleared myself in three hours. (*Doorbell rings off stage.*)

CORNELIA. Probably the Doctor. He was to come back with some sleeping-powders. (*Enter* BILLY. *He goes to table, upper end; gets key.*)

DETECTIVE (*to* BILLY). If that's the Doctor, admit him. If it's anybody else, call me. (BILLY *exits; leaves door open. To* BROOKS.) Have you got a gun on you?

BROOKS. No.

DETECTIVE. I'll just make sure of that. (*Crosses to* BROOKS. DETECTIVE *frisks* BROOKS; *then takes pair handcuffs out of pocket and puts them on table.*)

DALE (*at sight of handcuffs*). Oh, no! I can't bear it! I'll tell you everything. (ALL *the characters turn and face* DALE. DOCTOR *enters from hall, leaving the door open behind him. In the intensity of the scene the* DOCTOR'*s entrance is ignored.* DALE *continues.*) He got to the foot of the staircase—Richard Fleming, I mean. (*To* DETECTIVE.) And he had the blueprint you've been talking about. I had told him Jack Bailey was here as the gardener, and he said if I screamed he would tell that. I was desperate—I threatened him with the revolver, but he took it from me. Then I tore the blueprint from him—he was shot—from the stairs.

BERESFORD. By Bailey!

BROOKS (*strong*). I didn't even know he was in the house.

DETECTIVE. What did you do with the blueprint? (DOCTOR *is listening intently.*)

DALE. I put it first in the neck of my dress—then, when I found you were watching me, I hid it, somewhere else. (*She glances over at the* DOCTOR. *He is apprehensive and anxious. It is evident that he would make his escape, but* BILLY *at that moment enters with key.*)

BILLY. Key—front door. (*He crosses in front of* DOCTOR *and behind the* OTHER CHARACTERS *to table, upper end; places key there, and exits.*)

DALE (*does not wait for this business*). I put it—somewhere else. (*Again she glances at* DOCTOR.)

DETECTIVE. Did you give it to Bailey?

DALE. No—I hid it, and then I told where it was—to the Doctor. (ALL *turn in surprise to* DOCTOR, *who is at hall door.* CORNELIA *rises.*)

DOCTOR (*smiles grimly, then slowly comes down into scene*). That's rather inaccurate. You told me where you had placed it, but when I went to look for it it was gone.

CORNELIA (*strongly*). Are you quite sure of that?

DOCTOR (*gaining courage*). Absolutely. (*Then to* DETECTIVE.) She said she had hidden it inside one of the rolls that were on the tray. (*He crosses to table, front of the* OTHERS, *takes out a box of powders from overcoat pocket and places them on table.*) On that table. She was in such distress that I finally agreed to look for it—it wasn't there.

DETECTIVE (*has come down behind the* DOCTOR. *To* DOCTOR). Did you realize the significance of this paper?

DOCTOR (*turns to* DETECTIVE). Nothing beyond the fact that Miss Ogden was afraid it linked her with the crime.

DETECTIVE (*considers a moment, then to* CORNELIA). I'd like to have a few minutes with the Doctor alone.

(CORNELIA *and* DALE *cross front of table toward hall door.* CORNELIA *with arm around* DALE. BROOKS *stands by hall door. As* DALE *passes him she puts out her hand to him.* BROOKS *grasps* DALE'S *hand. Exit* CORNELIA *and* DALE.)

DETECTIVE (*as* CORNELIA *and* DALE *are crossing to right*). Beresford, take Bailey to the library and see that he stays there.

(DOCTOR *has crossed to left; takes off his overcoat and places it on settee.* BROOKS *and* BERESFORD *exit.* BERESFORD *closes the door behind them.* DETECTIVE *up to alcove doors; closes them; then he comes down a few steps, facing the* DOCTOR.)

DETECTIVE. Now, Doctor, I'll have that blueprint.

DOCTOR (*eyeing him warily*). I've just made the statement that I didn't find that blueprint.

DETECTIVE (*dryly*). I heard you! Now, this situation is between you and me, Dr. Wells—it has nothing to do with that poor fool of a cashier. He didn't take that money and you know it. It's in this house, and you know that too.

DOCTOR. In this house?

DETECTIVE. In this house! Tonight when you claimed to be making a professional call, you were in this house—and I think you were on that staircase when Richard Fleming was killed!

DOCTOR. No, Anderson, I'll swear I was not.

DETECTIVE. I'll tell you something. Miss Van Gorder very cleverly got a thumb-print of yours tonight. Does that mean anything to you?

DOCTOR. Nothing. I have not been upstairs in this house in three months. (*Up to this point he is obviously telling the truth.* DETECTIVE *is puzzled.*)

DETECTIVE. Before Courtleigh Fleming died, did he tell you anything about a Hidden Room—in this house?

DOCTOR (*his air of honesty lessens; he becomes furtive*). No.

DETECTIVE. You haven't been trying to frighten those women out of here with anonymous letters so you could get in?

DOCTOR. No—certainly not. (*Slight pause.* DETECTIVE *walks toward* DOCTOR.)

DETECTIVE. Let me see your key-ring?

(DOCTOR *unwillingly produces key-ring.* DOCTOR *hands out keys to* DETECTIVE, *who takes them.* DETECTIVE, *with revolver in hand, goes up into alcove, unlocks terrace door, goes out, leaving terrace door open.* DOCTOR *glances upstage to see if* DETECTIVE *is out of sight. He gets piece of blueprint out of his pocket and tiptoes to the fireplace with it. He throws paper toward grate, but it falls on floor outside of grate. A flash of lightning reveals through the broken pane in window* DETECTIVE, *who is on terrace, and has drawn the shade aside. Slight rumble of thunder, lightning, while* DETECTIVE *on terrace looking through window.*)

DETECTIVE (*sees* DOCTOR *throw the paper to floor; with noiseless swiftness the* DETECTIVE *is back in the room, and has the* DOCTOR *covered with revolver*). Pick that up. (DOCTOR *does pick it up.*) And put it on the table. (DOCTOR *slowly to table with paper.*) Now—stand away from the table—— (DOCTOR *backs away. A low rumble of thunder. Lightning.* DETECTIVE *lowers revolver, puts keys on table and stands back of table, looking at the blueprint. Lays the revolver on table. Looks up at* DOCTOR *with a half-sardonic smile, then examining blueprint.*) Behind a fireplace, eh? What fireplace? In what room?

DOCTOR (*sullenly*). I won't tell you!

DETECTIVE (*by table*). All right. I'll find it, you know. (*Consulting blueprint again, leaning over table.*)

(DOCTOR *maintains a furious silence. Slight pause. Then with a leap the* DOCTOR *is on top of the* DETECTIVE. *There follows a silent, furious struggle.* DOCTOR *pins* DETECTIVE'S *arms behind him.* DETECTIVE *bends down; gets his right arm free; gets revolver off table, but he drops it to floor. Then* DOCTOR *gets* DETECTIVE'S *both arms pinned behind him, and reaches back to stand up* C. *and gets hold of the telephone.* DOCTOR *hits the* DETECTIVE *over the head with base of phone, rendering* DETECTIVE *insensible. Thunder, lightning, wind.* DETECTIVE *falls.* DOCTOR *straightens up; listens tensely. There is no sound from the rest of the house. Only the thunder and lightning.* DOCTOR *picks up the revolver, puts in pocket, gets the blueprint, puts in pocket. Now gets down on his knees beside* DETECTIVE. *Rapidly gags him with handkerchief.* DOCTOR *then takes his own muffler and wraps it around head of* DETECTIVE. *After the gag is on,* DOCTOR *listens and looks around, then he gets the handcuffs off the table, left there in scene with* BROOKS. DOCTOR *now locks the handcuffs on* DETECTIVE'S *wrists; not behind his back, but in front of him. Then he puts arms under* DETECTIVE'S *arms and drags* DETECTIVE *off into billiard room. Comes into the room again. Closes and locks door. And then cautiously starts to go up into alcove. He makes a dash for the staircase. There is a knock on terrace door behind him. He backs down quickly, looks at door where the knocks come from. Backs into room. Then he is about to start up into alcove again when* BERESFORD *enters from below staircase. Goes to terrace door.* BERESFORD *looks at* DOCTOR. DOCTOR *points at door, and backs into room.*)

BERESFORD (*four knocks. Speaking through the door*). Who's that? (*No answer.* BERESFORD *draws revolver from pocket.* THE UNKNOWN, *outside terrace door, repeats knocks on terrace door. All the other characters now enter from hall.* CORNELIA, LIZZIE, DALE, BROOKS *and* BILLY. BILLY *closes door behind him.*)

CORNELIA (*as she enters and goes up toward alcove doors; sees* BERESFORD). What was that noise?

DOCTOR. Someone at that door.

BERESFORD (*still in alcove at door*). Sh! Sh! Shall I open it? (*Thunder, wind, lightning throughout this scene.* CORNELIA, *up to double doors; stands.*)

LIZZIE (*with a low wail*). If it ain't human, it's dead! If it *is* human, we're dead! (*Four knocks repeated by* UNKNOWN.)

CORNELIA. Be careful, Mr. Beresford.

LIZZIE (*moans*). It's The Bat!

(BERESFORD *very cautiously opens the terrace door. As he does so—clap of thunder, wind, lightning, lights blink. At the same moment* UNKNOWN, *who has been leaning against the terrace door, falls into* BERESFORD'S *arms.* BERESFORD *drops his revolver and catches the man so he does not fall to floor in alcove.* UNKNOWN *straightens up himself, achieves a certain measure of action and balances himself; staggers into room.* UNKNOWN *is rather good looking. It is seen that there is dried blood on his forehead. His feet and hands have been tied, and pieces of rope still dangle from his wrists and ankles.* UNKNOWN *staggers to table.* DOCTOR *beside him.* BERESFORD *on his other side. When clear of the table,* UNKNOWN *gives a couple of steps forward and falls prone on his face.*)

BERESFORD (*beneath his breath*). Good God!

CORNELIA (*comes down toward* DOCTOR. *General movement when* UNKNOWN *fell*). Doctor!

(*Thunder and lightning and wind die out.* DOCTOR *stoops down over prostrate man, turns him over, puts hand over heart.*)

DOCTOR. He's fainted! Struck on the head, too.

CORNELIA. Who is it?

DOCTOR. I never saw him before. Does anyone recognize him? (ALL *look at* UNKNOWN. *Slight pause. No one recognizes him.*)

CORNELIA. Is he badly hurt?

DOCTOR. It's hard to say. I think not. (UNKNOWN *moves, and makes effort to sit up.* BERESFORD *and* DOCTOR *assist him. He gets to his feet. He sways.*) A chair—— (BROOKS *quickly steps forward from table and places the chair for* UNKNOWN *who collapses into it.*) You're all right now, my friend. (*In professional, cheerful voice*). Dizzy a bit, aren't you?

UNKNOWN (*makes no answer, stretches his arms, rubs his wrists*). Water!

CORNELIA (*to* BILLY). Bring some water. (BILLY *crosses right*).

DOCTOR. Whisky would be better.

CORNELIA. Billy! (BILLY *stops and turns.*) There's whisky in my room.

BILLY (*brightening*). Yes—hid in closet—I know. (CORNELIA *stares at him. He exits through alcove and goes up and off by stairs.*)

DOCTOR (*to* UNKNOWN). Now, my man, you're in the hands of friends. Brace up.

BERESFORD. Where's Anderson? (UNKNOWN *starts, then controls himself. From this point on it is evident to the audience that the* UNKNOWN *is not as dazed as he seems to be.*) This is a police matter. (*Makes a movement as if to go.*)

DOCTOR (*raises hand to stop* BERESFORD). He was here a moment ago. He'll be back presently. (*Gives* UNKNOWN *a little shake*). Rouse yourself, man! What has happened to you?

UNKNOWN (*slowly and apparently with difficulty*). I'm dazed—I don't remember!

CORNELIA. What a night! (*Front of table; turns to* DALE.) Richard Fleming murdered in this house—and now —this! (UNKNOWN *is sitting so that his face is visible to the audience but not to those on the stage. He gives a swift, stealthy glance at* CORNELIA, *then his eyes fall again.*)

DALE. Why doesn't somebody ask him his name? (BROOKS *over to* UNKNOWN.)

BERESFORD. Where the devil is that detective? (*He rushes off through hall door. Leaves door open.*)

BROOKS (*to* UNKNOWN). What's your name? (UNKNOWN *makes no reply.*)

CORNELIA. Look at his papers. (BROOKS *and* DOCTOR *look in his pockets. Trousers only. He has no coat or vest on. Slight pause.*)

BROOKS. Not a paper on him.

(*Glass crash off stage, apparently at head of stairs.* BERESFORD *rushes on and* ALL *turn up; look at the alcove doors, except the* UNKNOWN, *who half rises in his chair. Tense and alert.* BILLY, *terrified, backs down the small staircase and into the room. He stands with his back to the audience, a rigid little figure, with horror in every outline.*)

CORNELIA (*sharply*). Billy!

DALE. Billy! What is it?

BILLY (*moistens his dry lips with his tongue*). It—nothing. (UNKNOWN *sinks back into his chair, and resumes his pose of immobility.*)

BERESFORD (*crosses and catches* BILLY *by the shoulders; swings* BILLY *round to face him*). Now, see here! You've seen something! What was it?

BILLY (*trembling*). Ghost! Ghost!

CORNELIA. He's concealing something. Look at him!

BILLY. No! No! No! (BERESFORD *releases* BILLY *and steps back.*)

CORNELIA (*To* BROOKS). Brooks, close that door. (*Points up at terrace door in alcove.* BROOKS *quickly up into alcove. Terrace door is slammed shut in his face. At same time lights out. All dark.*)

BROOKS (*in alcove*). This door's locked—the key's gone. (*To* BERESFORD.) Where's your revolver, Beresford? (*Goes over to table.*)

BERESFORD. I dropped it, in the alcove.

CORNELIA. I have one. Quick, there's a candle on the table. Light it, somebody!

BERESFORD (*over to table, quickly*). Righto! (*He tricks light in his wrist watch on.* LIZZIE *sees wrist watch light; points at it.*)

LIZZIE. The eye! The eye! (*Meanwhile* BERESFORD *has struck match and lighted candle.*)

(LIZZIE *and* BILLY *back away toward hall door to get out.* BROOKS *has come down to door.*)

BROOKS. This door's locked.

CORNELIA (*taking the candle and revolver off table*). I know there's somebody upstairs. We'll go this way. (*She starts up to alcove doors.* OTHERS *all turn and take a step toward doors.* BROOKS *up to doors. Doors are closed and locked.*)

BROOKS. Locked!

CORNELIA (*holds up the lighted candle*). *A Bat!*

(*Black paper Bat is tacked to the door* R.C. *The* UNKNOWN *rises and stands looking up at alcove doors.* ALL THE CHARACTERS *are facing up toward doors.*)

CURTAIN

ACT THREE

SCENE—*The trunk room on the third floor.*

The walls of room, except fireplace up Center, window to the right of the audience and a door to the left, are lined with high closets, with practical doors in each. At the rear, a wooden fireplace (mantel).

Instead of the grate, there is an iron fireplate fastened in, making the mantel, when it moves, as solid as a door. Mantelpiece swings open on concealed hinges, revealing behind it a room, perhaps 6 feet by 6, in which is a tall iron safe. Next to the mantel is a row of drawers. The mantel is opened by pushing aside a panel in the drawers, revealing a knob which, when turned, swings the mantel out like a door.

To the left is a large wicker hamper. Beside this two small old battered trunks. Set up and down stage, one on top of the other. Next to hamper, a kitchen chair without back.

To the right a kitchen chair with back. Two old boxes behind door. Some paper bundles up on high shelf above closets at the left. Old sewing-machine against wall. A box pin-hinged to set below the casement window, for characters to step on, getting in and out of window. Two old dress-suit cases, to dress scene. Important: Woman's satchel, on floor, front of hamper; matches on top of trunk.

AT RISE: *Stage dark.*

DISCOVERED: MASKED MAN (DETECTIVE) *at safe, up stage, Center, back of the open mantelpiece. He is working at the knob of safe. After a moment* MASKED MAN *swings open the safe. He takes out the money-bag, shuts safe, blows out the candle on floor beside safe, shuts off his pocket flash, and closes the mantel.*

Remote hammering heard off stage. MASKED MAN *to door, about to open door. Crash of splintering wood heard off stage. Ad lib.*

BERESFORD (*off stage*). You go this way. I'll go that.

BROOKS (*off stage*). Have your revolver ready.

(*During this ad lib.* MASKED MAN *darts back, drops the money-bag into hamper, and closes lid of hamper. He runs to window. Gets out of window; goes up ladder below window, up onto the roof. Footsteps heard coming up stairs. Door flung open,* BROOKS *rushes on, stands a second, then runs to window.*)

CORNELIA (*suddenly enters with revolver and dead candle*). Hands up —or I'll shoot!

BROOKS (*is seen silhouetted against window. He turns, faces* CORNELIA, *throws up his hands*). Don't shoot! It's Bailey!

CORNELIA (*to front of trunk*). What brought you up here? (*She lights candle.*)

BROOKS. The others will search downstairs. But, Miss Van Gorder, you mustn't run over the house by yourself. Don't you realize that the man who locked us in was probably The Bat?

CORNELIA (*crosses room*). That's why I'm running! Anyway, where would a body *be* safe? When eight of us could be locked up together in one room and have to break out, it's a pretty kettle of fish!

BROOKS. That window's open.

CORNELIA. It's a good forty feet to the ground.

BROOKS (*looks around room*). Well, he isn't here. I'll take a look over the rest of this floor. (*He gets to door.*)

CORNELIA (*suddenly looks at floor, and sees candle grease, near window*). Candle grease! (BROOKS *stops, turns and looks at* CORNELIA. CORNELIA *touches the grease on floor with finger.*) Fresh candle grease! Now, who do you suppose did that? Do you remember how Mr. Gillette, in Sherlock Holmes—when he—— (*Voice trails off; she stoops down, follows the candle grease marks to fireplace.*) It leads straight to the fireplace. (*She stands erect and surveys the mantel.*) It's been going through my mind for half an hour that no chimney flue runs up this side of the house.

BROOKS. Then why the fireplace?

CORNELIA. That's what I'm going to find out.

DALE (*off stage*). Jack! Jack! (*Cautiously.*)

(CORNELIA *raps on mantel.*)

BROOKS (*beckons* DALE, *who enters*). Come in—— Lock the door behind you. (DALE *closes and locks door.*) Where are the others?

DALE. They're searching the house. There's no sign of anybody.

BROOKS. Where's Anderson?

DALE. I haven't seen him.

CORNELIA (*up at mantel; raps on wall above mantel with her revolver*). Hollow as Lizzie's head. (*She carefully examines the painted small drawers left of mantel.*) Some of these ought to slide or push or something. (*She works small drawer. It slides slowly open* (*panel*), *revealing a white doorknob behind the panel.*) Merciful powers! It's moving! (DALE *backs away.*)

BROOKS (*up to* CORNELIA). Give me the revolver, and stand back. (BROOKS *and* CORNELIA *back away. Pause.* BROOKS *up to the open panel; turns the knob. It opens slowly, swinging back against wall.* BROOKS *faces mantel as it moves.*)

DALE. Look! (*The black aperture of room beyond revealed.* BROOKS *takes candle from* CORNELIA *and revolver; goes up.*)

DALE. Jack! Be careful!

BROOKS (*goes in. A pause*). Nobody home! (*Then triumphantly.*) Money! money! We've got the money! (*Stoops, turns lever and opens safe. Stands a moment. Comes out of safe with candle.*)

CORNELIA. Well!

BROOKS. The safe's empty—— (*For a moment no one speaks, their disappointment is so great.*) The money's gone. Well, that settles me! (*With forced laugh.*)

CORNELIA (*over to him. She takes candle from him*). Nonsense! The location of this room—the presence of that safe—is enough to establish the facts.

DALE. Jack, get Mr. Anderson and show him. (*Violent hammering on door and a loud scream from* LIZZIE *off stage.*)

LIZZIE (*hysterically*). Let me in! For the love of Heaven, let me in! (BROOKS *runs over, unlocks and opens the door.* LIZZIE *staggers in, her candle hanging down in her hand. Almost immediately she gives a cry, and candle goes out. Candle light burns her. Her movement puts it out.*)

CORNELIA. Good Heavens, what's the matter?

LIZZIE (*in front of hamper; hysterically*). I saw him! I saw The Bat! He dropped through that skylight out there—(*points*)—and run along the hall. He was eight feet tall and he had a face like a demon.

BROOKS. Did you see his face?

LIZZIE. No, he didn't have any face. He was all black where his face ought to be.

DALE. A mask!

LIZZIE (*crosses over toward* DALE; *volubly*). Yes'm, that's what it was, a mask! (BROOKS, *followed by* CORNELIA, *has started for the door. He carries* CORNELIA'S *revolver.* CORNELIA *carries the lighted candle.* LIZZIE *turns; sees* CORNELIA *going toward door; steps quickly after* CORNELIA.) Where are you going, Miss Neillie? (BROOKS *stands at open door, waiting for* CORNELIA.)

CORNELIA (*turns to* LIZZIE). Keep quiet and don't stick to me like a porous-plaster.

LIZZIE. It's not you I'm sticking to, it's the candle!

CORNELIA (*to* LIZZIE, *as* CORNELIA *starts for door*). Go back and stay with Miss Dale. (CORNELIA *and* BROOKS *exit with lighted candle. Room in darkness.*)

DALE. Lizzie, give me your candle and the matches. (LIZZIE *crosses over to* DALE; *gives her the candle and matches.*)

LIZZIE (*terrified*). I won't stay here and be murdered in the dark. (*Starts for door.*) If I've got to die, I want to see myself do it! (*She bolts out; closes door after her.*)

(DALE *tries to light candle, striking matches on box. They do not light. Slight pause.* DALE *looks around the room, then door very slowly opens about an inch. At first a thread of light from flashlight gradually widening, then it is extinguished.* DALE *sees this. She is frightened. She darts up to Hidden Room, goes in and closes the two iron doors noiselessly. All dark.* MASKED MAN, *overcoat on, large flash, opens door very slowly; backs in; flash off. Sweeps room with flashlight. It is the man who was discovered at safe, opening of the Act. He locks the door. Goes to hamper; puts flash for a moment on satchel, front of hamper; picks satchel up; empties its contents into the hamper (old clothes and two paper-backed novels); thrusts the bag of money into satchel; uses flash; works with feverish haste; closes the grip; turns to go to door; hears footsteps off stage. He uses flash sparingly. With satchel in hand, he starts for the window. As he nears the window, extension ladder comes up and leans against the window. He drops the satchel up stage above window. He is plainly trapped. He darts for the mantel room; closes the mantel behind him. There is absolute silence. Pause.*

Then the ladder moves as someone climbs it. Stealthily a MAN'S SILHOUETTE (DOCTOR) *is seen outside. The* FIGURE *on the ladder, as he is about to step through the window into the room, is heard to hiss cautiously.)*

DOCTOR. Sssssst! (*Receiving no reply, with infinite caution he crawls in through window. Then he starts for mantel; uses flash—off—on.*) Ssst! (*Doorknob heard turning.* DOCTOR *starts.*)

BROOKS (*off*). Dale!

CORNELIA (*off stage*). Dale! Dale! The door's locked——

BROOKS (*off stage*). Dale! (BROOKS *rattles the knob; pounds on door; tries to break in.*)

DOCTOR (*after a moment*). Wait a moment! (*He goes to door; unlocks it.* BROOKS *hurls himself into room. He is followed by* CORNELIA *with candle.* LIZZIE *stands in doorway.*)

BROOKS (*turns on* DOCTOR). Why did you lock that door? (BROOKS *takes a look around the room, and realizes the amazing fact that* DALE *is not there.*)

DOCTOR. But I didn't.

BROOKS (*turns on* DOCTOR). You—you—— Where is Miss Ogden? What have you done with her?

DOCTOR. Done with her! I don't know what you're talking about. I haven't seen her.

BROOKS (*threateningly*). You didn't lock that door?

DOCTOR. Absolutely not. I was coming through the window when I heard your voice at the door.

LIZZIE (*in doorway, in shaking tones*). In at the window, just like a bat! (CORNELIA *places candle and revolver on hamper.*)

DOCTOR. I saw lights up here from outside, and I thought——

CORNELIA (*interrupting*). That mantel's closed.

DOCTOR (*starts as he discovers their knowledge of the Hidden Room*). Damn!

BROOKS (*to* DOCTOR). Did you close it?

DOCTOR. No!!

BROOKS (*as he starts up to mantel*). I'll see whether you closed it or not. (*Leans against mantel; speaks loud.*) Dale! Dale!

(DOCTOR *turns front of hamper, back to audience. Picks up the candle from hamper where* CORNELIA *placed it.* BROOKS *starts to open mantel. As it begins to swing out,* DOCTOR *deliberately extinguishes candle. Dark stage.* DOCTOR *drops the candle to floor, front of hamper.* MASKED MAN *rushes out of Hidden Room, back of hamper, to door. Bumps* LIZZIE *in doorway. She falls to stage, as* MASKED MAN *exits.*)

CORNELIA (*as the lights go out*). Doctor, why did you put out that candle?

DOCTOR. I didn't—I——

CORNELIA. You did—I saw you do it. (*Door slams.*)

BROOKS. What was that?

LIZZIE (*on floor at doorway*). Oh! Oh! Somebody knocked me down and tramped on me.

CORNELIA (*beside hamper*). Matches —quick! Where's the candle?

DOCTOR (*front of hamper*). Awfully sorry. I assure you it dropped out of the holder. (*Stoops down; gets candle.*) Here it is! (BROOKS *to* DOCTOR; *strikes match; lights candle as* DOCTOR *holds it.*)

(CORNELIA *takes the candle after* BROOKS *lights it.* BROOKS *up to Hidden Room.* DALE *is seen on floor in Hidden Room, in front of the safe.* BROOKS *carries* DALE *down to chair.* DALE'S *eyes closed.*)

BROOKS (*as he comes out of Hidden Room with* DALE). Doctor! (DOCTOR *crosses to chair; feels* DALE'S *pulse.* CORNELIA *holds up candle.*)

CORNELIA. Lizzie, get some whisky.

LIZZIE (*as she gets up off floor*). Oh, Miss Neillie, I can't stand any more of this. My spine's driven clean up through my brains.

CORNELIA (*going with candle*). You haven't got any spine and you haven't got any brains! Get that whisky. (LIZZIE *turns to go out door; sees* DETECTIVE *in doorway.* DETECTIVE *a grim and menacing figure. He carries a lighted candle.*)

LIZZIE (*facing* DETECTIVE *in doorway*). That's right! Come in when everything's over. (DETECTIVE *steps in, and* LIZZIE *exits.*)

DOCTOR (*with back turned toward* DETECTIVE, *looking at* DALE). She'll be all right in a moment.

DETECTIVE (*to* DOCTOR). You took my revolver from me downstairs. (*Places lighted candle on trunk, beside hamper.* DOCTOR *turns and faces him.*) I'll trouble you for it. (*The* OTHERS *are startled.* DOCTOR *sullenly gives up revolver to* DETECTIVE, *who examines and puts it in his hip pocket.*) I've something to settle with you, pretty soon, and I'll settle good and proper. (*Crosses over to* DALE.) Now what's this? (*Indicating* DALE. *Meanwhile* DOCTOR *walks slowly and quietly toward door.*)

CORNELIA. She's coming to. We found her shut in there, Mr. Anderson. (*Indicating Hidden Room.* DETECTIVE *goes over and looks at open Hidden Room. As* DOCTOR *is about to exit,* DETECTIVE *turns; sees* DOCTOR.)

DETECTIVE. Wells! (CORNELIA *and* BROOKS *work over* DALE. BROOKS *rubs her hands.* CORNELIA *beside* DALE. DOCTOR *stops and turns; faces* DETECTIVE.) Where were you when she was locked in this room? (*Points up at Hidden Room.*)

DOCTOR (*front of hamper*). I didn't shut her in—if that's what you mean! There was someone shut in there—(*points up at Hidden Room*)—with her. Ask these people here. (*Indicating* CORNELIA *and* BROOKS.)

CORNELIA (*angry*). The fact remains, Doctor, that we left her here alone. When we came back you were here. That door was locked. (*Indicates *door to Hidden Room.)* And she was in that room. (DETECTIVE *goes in Hidden Room. Pause.* CORNELIA *up with candle.)* Unconscious! As we opened that door—(*indicates mantel*)—the Doctor deliberately extinguished the candle.

DETECTIVE (*wheeling on* DOCTOR. CORNELIA *comes down.)* Do you know who was in that room?

DOCTOR (*sullenly*). No—I didn't put out the candle. It fell. And I didn't lock that door. (*Indicates door.)* I found it locked. (DALE *opens her eyes and sits up. She looks around; suddenly realizes where she is and what is happening. She looks over her shoulder; sees open Hidden Room.* DALE *shudders; half rises.)*

DALE. Please close that awful door. I don't want to see it again. (DETECTIVE *goes up; closes the iron doors to Hidden Room.)*

BROOKS (*gets down on his knees beside* DALE). What happened to you? Can you remember?

DALE. I was here alone in the dark —then that door opened—(*indicates door*)—and I saw a man come in. I hid in there. (*Indicates Hidden Room.)* It was the only thing I could think of.

DETECTIVE (*facing* DALE). And then——

DALE. He came in too, and closed the door, and I think he heard me gasp, for he turned a flashlight on me and said, "If you make a sound I'll kill you!" That's all I remember.

DETECTIVE (*looks at* DOCTOR, *then looks at* DALE; *suspiciously*). Do you *know* who that man was?

DALE. No. (DETECTIVE *looks at* DOCTOR.)

CORNELIA. But I do—it was The Bat!

DETECTIVE (*turns on her rather sardonically*). Ha! Still harping back to The Bat!

CORNELIA. I have every reason to believe The Bat is in this house.

DETECTIVE (*jeeringly*). And that he took the Union Bank money out of that safe, I suppose? No, Miss Van Gorder! (*Turns; faces* DOCTOR.) Ask the Doctor who took the Union Bank money out of that safe. Ask the Doctor who attacked *me* downstairs in the drawing room; knocked *me* senseless, and locked *me* in the billiard room! (*To* DOCTOR. *Pause.)* The next time you put handcuffs on a man, be sure to take the key out of his vest pocket! (*An astounded pause, then* CORNELIA *speaks.)*

CORNELIA. Perhaps I am an obstinate old woman, but the Doctor and all the rest of us were locked in the drawing room not ten minutes ago.

DETECTIVE (*sneeringly*). By The Bat, I suppose!

CORNELIA (*obstinately*). By The Bat! (DETECTIVE *looks at* DOCTOR.) He went to the trouble to leave his visiting card fastened to the door!

DETECTIVE. The Bat, eh? (*Confronts the* DOCTOR). You knew about this room, Wells?

DOCTOR (*looking up at* DETECTIVE). Yes.

DETECTIVE. And you knew the money was in the room?

DOCTOR. Well, I was wrong, wasn't I?

DETECTIVE. You were up in this room, earlier tonight.

DOCTOR. No. I couldn't *get* up.

DETECTIVE. You know where that money is, Wells, and I'm going to find out!

DOCTOR (*goaded beyond endurance*). Good God! Do you suppose if I knew where it is I'd be here? I've had plenty of chances to get away. No, you can't pin anything on me, Anderson. It isn't criminal to have known that room is here.

DETECTIVE. Don't be so damned virtuous. Maybe you haven't been upstairs, but unless I miss my guess, you know who was. (DOCTOR'S *face changes. Crosses to* DOCTOR.) What about Richard Fleming?

DOCTOR (*impressively*). I never killed him! I don't even own a revolver!

DETECTIVE (*crosses down stage and front of* DOCTOR. *As he goes*). You come with me, Wells. This time I'll do the locking up. (DETECTIVE *stands by door; looks at* CORNELIA. *He takes lighted candle off trunk.*) Better get the young lady down to bed. I think that I can promise you a quiet night, from now on.

CORNELIA (*sardonically*). I'm glad you think so, Mr. Anderson! (DOCTOR *crosses past* DETECTIVE; *exits.* DETECTIVE *follows* DOCTOR.)

(CORNELIA *swiftly crosses over to door; closes it. Then she turns and faces* DALE *and* BROOKS.)

DALE (*with force*). I can't believe the Doctor killed Richard Fleming. (CORNELIA *crosses back to center with lighted candle.*)

CORNELIA (*swiftly moves to center*). Of course he didn't. He's just guilty enough to look more guilty than he is. (*She stands for a moment, then says to* DALE.) But the man who was shut in the, mantel room with you was the man who *killed* Richard Fleming, and took the money. But what brought him back? (*Pause. She looks at door, then down at floor.*) It's clear as a pikestaff. In some way he heard me coming—got out on the roof—(*points*)—through the skylight —(*points*)—and back here again. (*To verify her theory about the roof, she goes up to window; looks out.* BROOKS *follows and stands watching her. She then faces into room again; stands looking around.*) But what brought him back? (*Pause, while* CORNELIA, *candle in hand, moves quickly, now stooping to examine floor. Now straightens, looks about her. She also makes a careful search of the Hidden Room. As she comes out of Hidden Room she partly closes the two iron doors.*)

BROOKS (*watching her.*) Is this something else you saw Mr. Gillette do?

CORNELIA (*over to hamper*). I'm using my wits! I never saw *any* man do that. (*At last, with an air of great satisfaction, she sets candle on hamper. Evidently she has made *some important discovery.*) I know very little about bank currency. Could such a sum be carried away in a man's pocket?

BROOKS. Even in bills of large denomination it would make a pretty sizable bundle.

(*Enter* LIZZIE *with tumbler of wine in one hand and a lighted candle in the other.* CORNELIA *pursues her search of the room up.*)

LIZZIE (*front of hamper*). That Jap broke the whisky, but here's some of that elderberry wine. It's kind of comforting. Say, that assault and battery case is wandering all over the second floor. Think he's out of his head. I ran into him in the dark. I thought all my goose-flesh was standing on end before, but I raised a whole new crop. (*She goes back to door; kicks it shut with her foot.* CORNELIA *crosses with candle to front of hamper.* LIZZIE *toward* DALE, *who is still seated.*) I think there's a whole gang of crooks in this house. That Beresford—the Jap—and that assault and battery case—— Everybody pretending to be somebody he isn't! (*Starts.*) Oh! (*She offers the wine to* DALE, *who shakes her head in refusal.*)

BROOKS (*beside* DALE, *with his arm about her*). Take it, Sweetheart.

LIZZIE (*stares, astounded; looks over at* CORNELIA). The gardener's calling her "Sweetheart."

CORNELIA. Oh, be still! He's *not* a gardener.

LIZZIE. My God! Another one! (*Then she raises wine to her lips; drinks it.* CORNELIA, *with the lighted candle, looking around room near hamper. As she gets near door, she hears something. She makes gesture to others. The* OTHERS *stand and watch. The door is suddenly thrown open and* BERESFORD *stands in the doorway, crouching, ready to spring. Sees them. His attitude relaxes. He looks rather sheepish.*)

BERESFORD (*smiles—in doorway*). Oh—it's you?

CORNELIA (*suspiciously*). Who did you *think* it was?

BERESFORD (*relieved*). I've been making a rather hectic search for the man who locked us in. But I didn't find a sign. (*He shuts the door. His eyes travel to* BROOKS. *He crosses over to him. In ugly tone.*) Oh, still at large, Bailey?

BROOKS (*up close to him.*) I am, but the Doctor is not. Now, see here, Beresford, the situation has changed in the last few minutes—— (CORNELIA *puts candle on hamper.*) Dr. Wells is under arrest! I didn't mind your recognition of me—that was your duty—but I do object to the implication in your tone that I am a criminal. You've done your damnedest—now cut it. (*Doorknob turns.* CORNELIA *lifts up candle.*)

CORNELIA (*faces door*). That doorknob's moving. (ALL *turn and look at door.*)

BERESFORD (*in whisper to* CORNELIA). I'll open it. (*He crosses front of* CORNELIA *to door. Jerks open door.* BILLY, *who has hold of the off-stage side of doorknob, is jerked into room. Pause.*)

BILLY (*evidently very nervous, turns, steps back to door; looks off, then turns, faces others in room*). I come in, please? I not like to stay in dark.

CORNELIA. Come in. What is it, Billy? (*Steps forward a step or two.*)

BILLY (*nervously*). Man with sore head.

CORNELIA. What about him?

BILLY. Act very strange.

BERESFORD (*near door*). The man who fell into the room, downstairs?

BILLY. Yes—on second floor, walking around.

BERESFORD (*to* CORNELIA). I was watching that fellow downstairs that fell in the room. I didn't think he was as dazed as he pretended to be.

CORNELIA (*to* BILLY, *brightly*). Bring him up, Billy. (BILLY *starts to go, then turns back; faces* CORNELIA.)

BILLY (*nervously—over to* CORNELIA). You give candle, please? Don't like dark.

CORNELIA (*hands lighted candle to trembling* BILLY). Billy, what did you see when you came running down the stairs, before we were locked in?

BILLY (*candle shakes in his hand, nervously*). Nothing! (BROOKS *now stands between* CORNELIA *and* LIZZIE.)

LIZZIE (*feeling the wine somewhat*). It must have been some nothing to make him drop a bottle of whisky.

BILLY. Ghost walk in house! (*Backs away toward door.*)

LIZZIE (*leaning close to* BROOKS, *shivering*). Ghosts! It makes my very switch stand on end! (*She puts the bottom of the glass on the flame of candle. Candle out. Almost at same time* BILLY *disappears through door with lighted candle. Stage dark.*)

BERESFORD. Can't we have a light?

BROOKS. Wait, I'll——

(*Strange flapping sound is heard, first in one part of the room and then the other. Hits near ceiling.*)

CORNELIA (*sharply, after a moment*) What's that?

LIZZIE (*plaintively*). If you hear anything, it's my teeth chattering.

CORNELIA. Take them out and put them in your pocket. (*Flapping sound again.*)

BERESFORD (*after a moment*). That's odd! There *is* something moving around the room. (*Flapping sound again.*)

BROOKS. It's up near the ceiling.

LIZZIE (*slow wail*). Oh—h—h—— (*Flapping sound again.*)

BERESFORD. Good God! It hit me in the face. (*He slaps hands together.*)

LIZZIE. I'm going! I don't know where, but I'm going. (*She quickly crosses to hamper. Flapping sound again. She screams.*) It's in my hair! It's in my hair!

BROOKS (*voice in the dark, crosses right, then back to left*). I've got it! It's a Bat! (*Scream from* LIZZIE. *He goes up quickly to window, throws something out. There is a pause.*)

CORNELIA (*facing up stage*). Lizzie—(*Pause.*) Lizzie, where are you?

LIZZIE (*on her knees back of hamper—voice out of the gloom*). Trying to crawl under the floor. I'd go down a rathole if there was one. (*Door slowly opens and* BILLY, *leading the* UNKNOWN MAN, *enters.* LIZZIE *gets rid of her glass and dead candle as she kneels behind hamper. She places them on floor behind hamper.*)

BERESFORD. Come in. (*Steps to end of hamper; gets the chair without back; places it.*) Sit down. (BERESFORD *steps back and stands above* UNKNOWN.)

CORNELIA (*to* UNKNOWN, *who sits down*). Are you better now?

UNKNOWN (*slowly*). Somewhat.

CORNELIA. Lizzie, give him some wine.

LIZZIE (*back of hamper, head just in sight*). Somebody drank it.

CORNELIA (*speaks to* BILLY). Billy, you can go.

BILLY (*turns to* CORNELIA. *His tone is fairly pitiful*). I stay, please.

BROOKS (*by* CORNELIA. *Watches* BILLY *suspiciously, then to* CORNELIA). Anderson intimated that the Doctor had an accomplice in the house. (*Crosses to* BILLY, *front of the other characters.* BROOKS *close up to* BILLY.) Why isn't this the man? (*Takes the candle from* BILLY.)

BILLY (*cringing*). Please, no.

BROOKS (*puts candle on hamper, catches* BILLY *by the shoulders and half turns him to look up at the Hidden Room*). Did you know that room was there?

BILLY. No.

CORNELIA. He couldn't have locked us in. He was *with* us.

BROOKS. He may *know* who did it. (*To* BILLY.) Do you? (BILLY *shivers.*) Who did you see at the head of the small staircase? (BROOKS *swings* BILLY *in half circle around.*) Now we're through with nonsense. I want the truth.

BILLY. See face. That's all.

BROOKS (*strong*). *Whose* face?

BILLY (*evidently lying*). Don't know. (*Looks down.*)

CORNELIA. Never mind Billy—(*Looks at* UNKNOWN MAN.) Solve the mystery of *this* man and we may get at the facts. (BERESFORD *holds lighted candle above* UNKNOWN. BROOKS *has turned when* CORNELIA *speaks. Takes eyes off* BILLY, *who has started on tiptoes for door. Just as he gets to door,* BROOKS *turns and sees* BILLY *trying to get away.*)

BROOKS (*takes a step or two toward* BILLY). You stay here. (BILLY *stops; stands by door.*)

BERESFORD. This chap—(*indicating* UNKNOWN)—claims to have lost his memory. I suppose a blow on the head might do that. I don't know.

LIZZIE (*back of hamper*). I wish somebody would knock *me* on the head. *I'd* like to forget a few things.

CORNELIA (*to* UNKNOWN). Don't you remember even your name?

UNKNOWN (*shakes head*). Not—yet.

CORNELIA. Or where you came from? (UNKNOWN *shakes his head.*) Do you remember how you got into this house?

UNKNOWN (*with difficulty*). Yes, I remember that, all right. (*He puts hand to his head.*) My head aches—to beat the band.

CORNELIA. How did you happen to come to this house?

UNKNOWN (*slowly*). Saw the lights.

BROOKS (*quickly*). Where were you when you saw the lights?

UNKNOWN. I broke out of the garage.

BERESFORD. How did you get there?

UNKNOWN. I don't know.

BROOKS (*with keen suspicion*). Had you been robbed?

UNKNOWN. Everything gone—out of my pockets.

BROOKS (*stepping closer to* UNKNOWN). Including your watch?

UNKNOWN. If I had a watch, it's gone. All my papers—are—gone.

CORNELIA (*suspiciously*). How do *you* know you *had* papers?

UNKNOWN (*looks front; haltingly*). Most men—carry papers, don't they? I'm dazed, but my mind's all right. If you ask me—I think I'm d-d-damned funny. (BROOKS *and* BERESFORD *exchange glances.*)

CORNELIA. Did you ring the house phone? (BROOKS *and* BERESFORD *change places.*)

UNKNOWN. Yes. (*A start from* CORNELIA *and* BROOKS.) I leaned against the button in the garage—then, I think maybe I fainted. That's not clear. (DALE *rises.*)

DALE (*leaning over, and looking at* UNKNOWN; *brightly*). You don't remember how you were hurt?

UNKNOWN. No. The first thing I remember I was in the garage, tied. I was gagged, too—that's what's the matter with my tongue now. Then I got myself free—and got out of a window.

BERESFORD. Just a moment, Miss Van Gorder—Anderson ought to be here for this. (*On word "Anderson,"* DALE *sits again.*)

(BERESFORD *starts for door.* DETECTIVE *enters. Closes the door after him. On word "Anderson,"* UNKNOWN'S *face shows intense alertness. The* UNKNOWN *gets to his feet.* DETECTIVE *has closed the door before he catches sight of the* UNKNOWN. *He stands rigid, his hand still on the knob of the door. It is to be remembered the* DETECTIVE *has not yet seen or heard of the* UNKNOWN.)

CORNELIA (*raises voice, watching* ANDERSON). A new element in our mystery, Mr. Anderson. (*Slight pause.* DETECTIVE *and* UNKNOWN *look at each other for a moment. The* UNKNOWN'S *face is blank and expressionless.*) Quite dazed, poor fellow! (UNKNOWN *sways.*)

DETECTIVE (*slowly*). How did *he* get into the house?

CORNELIA. He came through the terrace door some time ago, just before we were locked in.

DETECTIVE (*dryly*). Doesn't remember anything, eh? (*Crosses to* UNKNOWN. BERESFORD *crosses over same time with candle.* DETECTIVE *speaks roughly and puts hand under* UNKNOWN'S *chin; jerks* UNKNOWN'S *head up.*) Look up here! (UNKNOWN *looks up at* DETECTIVE *with a blank face.*) Look up, you—— (*Same business.*) This losing your memory stuff doesn't go down with me!

UNKNOWN (*weakly*). It doesn't go down very well with me, either!

DETECTIVE. Did you ever see me before? (BERESFORD *holds the candle a little nearer* DETECTIVE'S *face.*)

UNKNOWN (*looks at* DETECTIVE; *slight pause, haltingly*). You're the Doctor I saw downstairs, aren't you?

DETECTIVE (*takes the watch of Act II from his pocket; holds it out toward* UNKNOWN). Does this watch belong to you? (*Looks suspiciously at* UNKNOWN.)

UNKNOWN (*looks at watch*). Maybe —— (*Falls back against* BROOKS.) I don't know.

CORNELIA. He has evidently been attacked. He claims to have recovered consciousness in the garage, where he was tied, hand and foot.

DETECTIVE. He does, eh? If you'll give me five minutes alone with him, I'll get the *truth* out of him!

CORNELIA (*half turning back to* DETECTIVE). Do you believe that money is irrevocably gone?

DETECTIVE. There's no such word as "irrevocable" in my vocabulary, but I believe it's out of the house, if that's what you mean.

CORNELIA. Suppose I tell you that there are certain facts that you have overlooked?

DETECTIVE (*sardonically, to* CORNELIA, *but looks at* UNKNOWN). Still on the trail!

CORNELIA. I was right about the Doctor, wasn't I? (*Goes to door.*)

DETECTIVE. Just fifty per cent right, and the Doctor didn't turn the trick alone. Now, if you'll all go out and close that door—— (CORNELIA *looks off stage. Takes candle from* BROOKS.)

CORNELIA (*starts out*). Quick! A man just went through that skylight and out onto the roof.

DETECTIVE. Out onto the roof!

BROOKS. Come on, Beresford!

(CORNELIA *exits.* BROOKS (2), DETECTIVE (3), BERESFORD (4), BILLY (5), *and closes door behind him. Ad lib. from the* MEN *as they run off, "A man on the roof," etc. Talking and excitement and noise of running. As the* DETECTIVE *goes off he draws his revolver.)*

BERESFORD. Righto—— (DALE, LIZZIE *and* UNKNOWN *remain in room. In the dark, except for the light from doorway.)*

LIZZIE *(goes over to* DALE*)*. I'd *run* if my legs would!

DALE. Hush!

LIZZIE *(wails)*. How do we know *this fellow right here* isn't *The Bat*? *(Indicating the* UNKNOWN, *who has half risen, back into chair.* CORNELIA *re-enters with lighted candle.* CORNELIA *comes in very cautiously, looks over her shoulder, and quietly closes the door.)*

DALE. What did you see?

CORNELIA *(calmly)*. I didn't see anything! I had to get rid of that dratted detective before I assassinated him.

DALE. Nobody went through the skylight?

CORNELIA. They have now—the whole outfit.

DALE. Then why did you——

CORNELIA *(interrupting)*. Because that money's in this room. If the man who took it out of the safe had got away with it, why did he come back and hide there? *(Indicates Hidden Room. They look up at Hidden Room.)* He got it out of the safe, and that's as far as he *did* get it! There's a *hat* behind that safe—a man's soft felt hat.

LIZZIE. Oh, I wish he'd take his hat and go home. (UNKNOWN *listens intently.)*

CORNELIA *(disregarding* LIZZIE; *goes over in front of the closets, back of the hamper. On floor she picks up a half-burned candle)*. A half-burned candle. Another thing the detective overlooked. *(She steps back; looks from candle to closet. Suddenly at the window* BROOKS *quickly lowers himself in from the roof ladder on downstage side of window.)*

LIZZIE *(horrified)*. Oh, my God, another one! (CORNELIA *gets her revolver from top of hamper; points at the figure of* BROOKS.)

DALE *(recognizes* BROOKS; *puts her hand up so* CORNELIA *won't shoot)*. It's Jack! (DALE *moves over to* BROOKS *as he comes in window.* CORNELIA, *on seeing that it is* BROOKS, *lays her revolver on top of hamper.* UNKNOWN *sees her do this.)*

BROOKS *(up at window)*. The man Lizzie saw drop from the skylight probably reached the roof from this window—easiest thing in the world.

CORNELIA *(looks at the closets)*. Never mind the window! When that detective comes back I may have a *surprise party* for him! (DALE *crosses toward* CORNELIA.)

LIZZIE. No more surprises for me. I've been surprised pretty near to death all night.

DALE *(up to* BROOKS*)*. Aunt Cornelia thinks the money's still here. (LIZZIE *sits in chair.)*

CORNELIA (*over to closets; opens three, one after another.*) I *know* it's here. (BROOKS *crosses to* CORNELIA.)

(LIZZIE *sits still, her eyes riveted on the* UNKNOWN, *who is looking at revolver on hamper.* DALE *looks at* LIZZIE, *then steps down to* LIZZIE.)

DALE (*nervously*). Lizzie—— What are you looking at?

(UNKNOWN *is again sunk in apathy.* CORNELIA *resumes trying of the closet doors. She is now at one of the closets.*)

CORNELIA. This one is locked, and the key gone.

LIZZIE (*seated; crying*). If there's anything locked up in that closet, you'd better let it stay. There's enough running around loose in this house as it is. (*There is no question about the interest in the* UNKNOWN'S *face.* BROOKS *up and stands back of* CORNELIA. CORNELIA *hands* BROOKS *the candle.*)

CORNELIA. Lizzie, did you ever take that key?

LIZZIE (*seated*). No'm.

CORNELIA. It may be locked from the inside. (DALE *up beside* BROOKS; *watches* CORNELIA *at closet.*) I'll soon find out. (CORNELIA *takes from her hair a wire hairpin and runs it through the keyhole.*) There's no key inside. (BROOKS *shakes the door of closet but it does not yield.*) I want to see the inside of that closet.

LIZZIE. If you could see *my* insides, you wouldn't recognize them.

CORNELIA. Bring me the other closet keys. (DALE, *with the candle, goes from closet to closet; then down to closet below the window. Gets key.* LIZZIE *follows* DALE *and the candle.*)

(DALE *up to* CORNELIA *and gives her key.* LIZZIE *follows her. Meanwhile* BROOKS *goes to closets against back wall, gets keys. During above business,* UNKNOWN, *with infinite caution, moves his chair over toward revolver* CORNELIA *has left on top of hamper. He reaches out, gets revolver, moves back chair, and sits same as before, revolver partly covered.*)

CORNELIA. There! That unlocked it!

BROOKS. I'd keep *back* a little. You don't know *what* may be inside. (CORNELIA *and* DALE *draw back.*)

LIZZIE (*shivering, speaks as she crosses front of* UNKNOWN, *over to front of hamper*). Mercy sakes, who *wants* to know! (LIZZIE *sits on the hamper.* BROOKS *takes the candle, and slowly and cautiously opens the door of the closet. He stands for a moment and stares, appalled at something on the floor of the closet.*)

(BROOKS *looks into closet. Pause.*)

DALE (*aghast*). What is it? What did you see? (*Staring at* BROOKS.)

BROOKS (*does not answer; then pulling himself together*). Miss Cornelia, I think we have found the ghost the Jap butler saw. How are your nerves?

CORNELIA (*holds out her hand*). Give me the candle. (*He does.* BROOKS *crosses over to* DALE. *They stand and watch* CORNELIA.)

(CORNELIA *opens closet door.* CORNELIA *closes door of closet and comes down again.* UNKNOWN *half turns and watches the others out of the corner of his eye. A tense pause.*)

CORNELIA. It is Courtleigh Fleming.

BROOKS. It *was* Courtleigh Fleming.

DALE (*with hand on back of chair*). Then he did not die in the West.

BROOKS. He died in this house—within the last hour. The body is still warm, and Dr. Wells killed him.

CORNELIA. I wonder! (*Then to* BROOKS *as she crosses to* DALE.) Please look and see if Courtleigh Fleming wore a wrist watch with a luminous dial. (BROOKS *up to closet; opens down-stage door; gets on his knees; puts arm in closet. Time for brief examination. Rises; closes closet door.*)

BROOKS. Yes.

CORNELIA (*to* DALE). The *eye* Lizzie saw was the wrist-watch. (*The* UNKNOWN *sinks down in chair, but listens intensely.*)

BROOKS. Isn't it clear, Miss Van Gorder? The Doctor and old Mr. Fleming formed a conspiracy—Fleming to rob the bank and hide the money here. Wells to issue a false death certificate in the West, and bury a substitute body, secured God knows how. It was easy—it kept clear the name of the President of the Union Bank—and it put the blame on me. (*Turns quickly and looks up at* CORNELIA) Only they slipped up in one place. Dick Fleming leased the house to you, and they couldn't get it back.

CORNELIA (*quickly*). Then you think that tonight Courtleigh Fleming broke in, with the Doctor's assistance, and that he killed Dick, his own nephew, from the staircase?

BROOKS. Don't you?

CORNELIA. No.

BROOKS (*facing* CORNELIA). It's as clear as crystal. Wells tried to get out of the house tonight with that blueprint. *Why?* He knew the minute we got it we'd come up here, and Fleming was here.

CORNELIA. Perfectly true, and then?

BROOKS. Old Fleming killed Dick, and Wells killed Fleming. (*Crossing over to* DALE.) *You can't get away from it!*

CORNELIA. No—no the Doctor is not a murderer. He's as puzzled as we are about some things. He and Courtleigh Fleming were working together, but remember this—Dr. Wells was locked in the drawing room with us. He's been trying all evening to get up the stairs and failed.

BROOKS. He was here ten minutes ago, locked in this room.

CORNELIA. I grant you that—but at the same time an unknown masked man was locked in that mantel room with Dale. The Doctor put out the candle when you opened that Hidden Room. *Why?* Because *he thought Courtleigh Fleming was hiding there.* But at this moment he believes that Fleming has made his escape. No—we haven't solved the mystery yet——There's another element—an *unknown* element—and that element is—the *Bat!*

DALE (*half hysterically*). Oh, call the detective. Let's get through with this thing. I can't *bear* any more.

CORNELIA. Wait. Not yet. Nobody can help Courtleigh Fleming, and I'm not through.

LIZZIE (*seated on hamper*). Well, I'm through, all right!

CORNELIA (*looks and sees hamper*). Open the lid of that hamper. (*Indicates hamper which* LIZZIE *is sitting on.*) And see what's inside. (BROOKS *crosses over to hamper; opens lid; looks inside.*)

BROOKS. Nothing here but some clothes and books.

CORNELIA (*beside* BROOKS). Books? I left no books in that hamper.

BROOKS (*reading title of cheap paper novel*). *Little Rosebud's Lovers, or a Cruel Revenge,* by Laura Jean——

LIZZIE (*beside hamper*). That's mine! Oh, Miss Neillie, I tell you this house is haunted. I left that book in my satchel, along with *Wedded But No Wife* and—— (BROOKS *closes lid.*)

CORNELIA. Where's your satchel?

LIZZIE (*looks around front of hamper and leans over hamper; looks behind it and around on the floor of hamper*). Where's my satchel? My satchel —— My satchel's gone. (*Over hamper at end.* CORNELIA *holds candle high.*)

CORNELIA (*at last sees satchel, by window on floor, where* MASKED MAN *left it when he darted into the Hidden Room earlier in act. Indicating it*). Isn't that your satchel, Lizzie?

(LIZZIE *quickly over to* CORNELIA, *then crosses to above window; looks scared; then looks at* CORNELIA.)

LIZZIE. Yes, ma'm.

CORNELIA (*points to chair*). Put it there. (LIZZIE *stalls, scared.* CORNELIA *continues to point at chair.*)

LIZZIE. I'm scared to touch it. It may have a bomb in it! (*She reluctantly gets the satchel; carries it very slowly between thumb and forefinger as she might carry a loaded gun.*)

CORNELIA. Do as I tell you—put it on that chair. (LIZZIE *deposits the satchel on chair and backs away up near window.* CORNELIA *starting up stage, looking at* BROOKS *and* DALE. DALE, *behind hamper.* BROOKS *beside her. To* BROOKS.) You open it. If the money's there, you're the one who ought to find it.

(BROOKS *looks at* DALE, *then with a smile crosses front of* CORNELIA. DALE *follows him.* CORNELIA, *with candle, follows them.* BROOKS *fumbles at catch of satchel on chair,* DALE *beside him. While they are occupied with this business,* UNKNOWN *rises and quickly gets to door; faces the others, his back to door. With hand behind him, he locks the door, takes the key out, and puts it in his pocket. Meanwhile* BROOKS *has succeeded in opening the satchel.* BROOKS *and* DALE *show they are delighted as they see the canvas bag with the packages of money in it.*)

BROOKS. The money is here.

DALE. Oh, thank God!

(*Red glow starts faintly outside window, increases and goes up and down.*

Flame effect. Crackling of burning wood heard off stage. ALL *stand; watch window as red glare fills room.*)

LIZZIE. Fire!

BERESFORD (*off stage*). The garage is burning!

(*Sound of men's voices and running of feet on tin, supposed to be the roof.* CORNELIA, BROOKS, DALE *and* LIZZIE *all turn towards door. Suddenly their attention is rivetted on the* UNKNOWN, *who is standing in front of door. His back to door, facing the other characters, he has the revolver in his hand.*)

UNKNOWN (*savage tone*). This door is locked and the key is in my pocket —— (LIZZIE *opens her mouth to scream. He looks at her and in an ominous tone.*) Not a sound out of *you.* (*To* BROOKS.) Close that bag—(*referring to satchel*)—and put it back where you found it.

BROOKS (*starts toward him a step*). *You!*

DALE. Jack!

CORNELIA (*to* BROOKS). Do what he tells you! (BROOKS *closes bag, and puts it up by window.*)

LIZZIE (*horrified whisper*). It's the Bat!

UNKNOWN (*at door*). Blow out that candle! (CORNELIA, *after a moment's hesitation, blows out candle. Only light in room now is the flicker from fire outside window.*)

LIZZIE (*hysterically*). I'm going to scream! I can't keep it back.

UNKNOWN (*over at door; savagely*). Put that woman in that mantel room —(*points*)—and shut her up. (BROOKS *pushes* LIZZIE *up to mantel.*)

LIZZIE (*as she goes*). Don't shove! I'm damn glad to go. (*She goes in Hidden Room.* BROOKS *closes the iron doors behind her.*)

UNKNOWN (*unlocks the door; opens it a little; listens; closes it without locking it*). Not a sound, if you value your lives. (*Pause.*) In a moment or two a man will come into this room, either through the door or by that window. (*Steps toward window.*) The man who started the fire to draw you out of this house.

BROOKS (*steps toward* UNKNOWN). For God's sake don't keep these women here!

UNKNOWN. Keep them here where we can watch them! Don't you understand? There's a *killer* loose!

(*The red glow dies out.*)

CORNELIA (*to* UNKNOWN). I have understood very clearly for the last hour. The man who struck you down and tied you in the garage, the man who killed Dick Fleming and stabbed that poor wretch in the closet, the man who locked us in downstairs, and removed the money from the safe—the man who started that fire outside is——

UNKNOWN (*as if hearing someone outside window, puts up his hand*). Sh! (*He runs quickly over to door, locks it, and hurries back.*) Stand back out of the light. The ladder!

(DALE *and* CORNELIA *stand back.* BROOKS *up stage by window.* UN-

KNOWN *flattens his body against wall beside* BROOKS. *The ladder is seen to shake, outside the window. A breathless pause, then outside on the ladder* THE BAT *is faintly outlined coming up ladder, in cap and black silk handkerchief disguise. He steps in window, and backs up to get the grip. As he does this,* UNKNOWN *and* BROOKS *grab him, just as* BAT *focuses flashlight on the satchel. There is a struggle in the dark.* BROOKS *and* UNKNOWN *overpower* THE BAT.)

UNKNOWN (TO BROOKS). Get his gun. (*Pause.*) Got it?

BROOKS. Yes.

UNKNOWN. Hold out your hands, Bat, while I put on the bracelets! (*Puts handcuffs on* BAT'S *wrists.*) Sometimes even the *cleverest* Bat comes through a window at night and is caught! Double murder—burglary, and arson—— That's a good night's work even for you, Bat! (UNKNOWN *turns flashlight on* THE BAT'S *face.*) Take off that handkerchief. (BROOKS *does this business, revealing* ANDERSON, *the detective.* UNKNOWN *above* ANDERSON, BROOKS *below him.* DETECTIVE *is covered with two revolvers. The storm being over, the lights flash on.*)

DALE (*with* CORNELIA). It's Mr. Anderson!

UNKNOWN (*without taking his eyes off* THE BAT). I'm Anderson. This man has been impersonating me. You're a good actor, Bat, for a fellow that's such a *bad* actor! How did you get your dope on this case? Did you tap the wires to Headquarters?

THE BAT (*with sardonic smile*). I'll tell you that when I—— (*With swift movement, though handcuffed, he jerks the revolver by the barrel from the real* ANDERSON, *wheels on* BROOKS *with lightning rapidity, brings down the butt of revolver on* BROOKS' *wrist.* BROOKS' *revolver drops to floor.* THE BAT *swings around, keeping the characters covered with gun. Speaks as he moves or backs away.*) Hands up, everybody! (CORNELIA *has not raised her hands.*) Hands up—you! (*Savagely to* CORNELIA.)

CORNELIA. Why, I took the bullets out of that revolver two hours ago. (THE BAT *throws the revolver toward her. It drops in front of her on floor. As soon as* THE BAT *drops revolver, the* UNKNOWN *picks up the other gun, and runs back of* CORNELIA *and blocks* THE BAT'S *getaway.* UNKNOWN *covers* BAT *with gun.*)

UNKNOWN (*to* BAT). Don't move! (CORNELIA *picks up her gun from the floor.*) You see, you never know what a woman will do! (*Tauntingly to* BAT, *who turns and growls at* UNKNOWN.)

CORNELIA (*breaks the revolver and the loaded shells fall to floor.* THE BAT *wheels and looks at her, and bullets on floor.*) As it happened, I didn't. The first lie of an otherwise stainless life!

CURTAIN FALLS

On SECOND CURTAIN, LIZZIE *sticks her head out of Hidden Room, scared, and disappears into Hidden Room again.*

Abie's Irish Rose

A COMEDY IN THREE ACTS

BY ANNE NICHOLS

"ABIE'S IRISH ROSE" was first produced by Miss Nichols at the Fulton Theatre in New York City, May 23, 1922. The play was directed by Laurence Marston and the cast was as follows:

Mrs. Isaac Cohen	Mathilde Cottrelly
Isaac Cohen	Bernard Gorcey
Dr. Jacob Samuels	Howard Lang
Solomon Levy	Alfred Wiseman
Abraham Levy	Robert B. Williams
Rose Mary Murphy	Marie Carroll
Patrick Murphy	John Cope
Father Whalen	Harry Bradley
Flower Girl	Dorothy Grau

SYNOPSIS OF SCENES

Act One: Solomon Levy's Apartment, New York.

Act Two: Same as Act One. (One week later.)

Act Three: Abie and Rose Mary's Apartment, New York. (Christmas Eve, one year later.)

ABIE'S IRISH ROSE

ACT ONE

SCENE—*The home of a New York business man, a prosperous one. The living room is comfortably furnished, without particular effort made to follow any special period, both as to architecture and decoration. The ensemble is rich in appearance and denotes very good taste.*

There are glass doors in the right and left walls, and two arches right and left center in the back wall. There are glass double doors in these arches, opening off; the draperies on these doors cut off the view beyond when the doors are closed. In the right center hall is a stairway leading to the upper part of the house; and the main entrance is off right. Beyond the left center arch is the conservatory. There is a window up right.

At right center is a davenport with a library table behind it; a stand above the right door and a table above the window; a hat tree in the hall together with a large lamp; a table and a chair up center; a table and two chairs in the room up left center; a table up left; a chair below left door; a table and two chairs left center; a heavy chandelier hangs from the ceiling center. The chandelier is very ornate of the New York gas and electricity combined period.

In Act Two the room is decorated with orange trees in upper right and left corners. These are about eight feet high, with real oranges. There are smaller trees, poppies and other California flowers placed on the tables to give the room an atmosphere of California. Ribbons are attached to the chandelier and carried to the four corners of the room. The ribbons are orange in color with a small vine entwined around them, preferably bridal wreath or smilax.

The left center table has been removed and the chairs pushed aside. The left center doors are closed.

As the curtain goes up COHEN *is on the davenport. He has the funny part of the evening paper which he is reading with evident enjoyment.* MRS. COHEN *and* RABBI *are seated at table left center.* MRS. COHEN *in chair right and* RABBI *in chair left.*

At rise COHEN *laughs.* MRS. COHEN *gives him a look and continues speech.*

MRS. COHEN. Yes sir, I says to Isaac, says I, "Isaac call the doctor, I know ven I god a differend pain. Ven my indegestive tablets don't voik, I know how I veel!" (COHEN *laughing uproariously at the funny paper. The* RABBI *looks at him.* MRS. COHEN *is furious at this interruption. Continues with her monologue.*) So Isaac he calls the doctor. (COHEN *laughs again, which interrupts* MRS. COHEN. *She looks at him, then at the* RABBI.) Such a foolishness! (*She gives* COHEN *another look which he doesn't see, so interested in his paper is he, then she turns back again to the* RABBI.) Vhere was I?

RABBI (*impatiently*). Isaac had just called the doctor.

MRS. COHEN. Oh, yess! Und de doctor came und:—(COHEN *laughs again.* MRS. COHEN *stops, looks at* COHEN *furiously.* COHEN *takes paper down from his face.*) Will you stop dot laughing at nodings! (*Crosses to* COHEN.)

COHEN (*laughs to himself, vaguely hearing her, then it penetrates that he has been spoken to. There is a deep silence. He looks up.* MRS. COHEN *is looking daggers at him. The* RABBI *is trying not to laugh.*) Huh? Vot? You speak to me, Mama?

MRS. COHEN. Such a foolishness! Laughing at nodings!

COHEN (*hurt*). Mama. I was laughing at Maggy and Jiggs. Such a vife!

MRS. COHEN (*sore now and ready for an argument*). Oh, so you voss laughing at the vife?

COHEN. No. No, I'm keeping up with Maggy and Jiggs. (*He picks up the paper again. His face beams as he starts to read. Reading— "What a man—What a man, just like me."* MRS. COHEN *sits at the table.*) Mama, listen. "You big walrus why don'd you go into some pizzness, instead of loafing all day; ged oud of my sight." Dod's Maggy vot she says. Und Jiggs he says, vid de cigar in his mout and his hands on his hips, "Vell," says Jiggs, "Maggy" dods the wife from Jiggs. "Vell," says Jiggs, "Maggy, you soitantly kin tink of disagreeable tings." (COHEN *laughs. The* RABBI *is also interested.*)

MRS. COHEN (*rises, with her face all set for a fight. Her mouth gathered together into a little knot*). Is dod funny?

COHEN. Vait a minute! (*Laughs.*) Und Jiggs goes oud for a pizzness!

RABBI. Is that the one, Isaac, where he goes into business with Mr. Duem?

COHEN (*laughing uproariously*). Yess, und meets all the pretty girls. (*Crossing to* MRS. COHEN; *shows her paper and nudges her.*) Und Maggy catches him making lofe to the stenographer. (*Laughing, crosses back to davenport; sits.*) Ain't that funny, Mama?

MRS. COHEN (*now thoroughly disgusted with both of them*). I'm dying with laughing! (RABBI *laughing at the thought of it.* MRS. COHEN *sits.* COHEN *looks at her; stops laughing, then picks up his paper, turns it over and looks at another page.* MRS. COHEN *looks at him satisfied she will not be interrupted again. The* RABBI *yawns behind his hand.*) Vot vass I talking aboud?

RABBI. Your operation!

MRS. COHEN. Oh, yes. Where vas I—in the hospital?

RABBI. Oh, no. Isaac had just called the doctor.

MRS. COHEN. Und the doctor he came. Und I said—"good evening, Doctor." Und the doctor he say "good evening"—and——

RABBI. And did he diagnose the case as appendicitis?

MRS. COHEN. Like that. Didn't he, Isaac? (*There is a pause, then* COHEN *looks up.*)

COHEN. Oh yes, sure, Mama. (*He turns back—then.*)

RABBI. And did he operate immediately?

MRS. COHEN. No, he didn't want to.

RABBI. Didn't want to?

MRS. COHEN. He didn't want to. Did he, Isaac? (*Pause.*) *Did he Isaac?!!!!?*

COHEN. No.—No. (*Pause.*) Didn't want to what, Mama?

MRS. COHEN. Didn't want to operate.

COHEN. Oh, the doctor. No. (*He turns back again to paper.*)

RABBI. I sympathize with you, Mrs. Cohen.

MRS. COHEN. I tell you, Dr. Samuels, it is the woman what silently suffers.

COHEN. Yes, Mama—you were silent with the ether, but you haven't been silent ever since.

MRS. COHEN. Oh, I don't talk so much.

COHEN. Yes, you do, Mama. Always you talk about ether.

MRS. COHEN. I didn't say a word about the ether.

COHEN. But, Mama——

MRS. COHEN. Ssh—Isaac!!!

COHEN. All right, noo——

RABBI. I wonder what is keeping our good host.

MRS. COHEN. He went to find Sarah —someone called him on the phone, and Sarah couldn't hear the message. He's waiting for it to ring any minute. Poor Solomon.

COHEN. See. Why do you say "poor Solomon," Mama? He ain't poor.

MRS. COHEN. Papa—always you—argue——

COHEN. But, Mama. Poor is arem and arem is poor. If he ain't arem how can he be poor——

MRS. COHEN. But why should you always argue—*Shweig Shtill!*

RABBI. You know—we three might help Solomon——

MRS. COHEN. How?

RABBI. Have you ever tried concentration?

COHEN. Concentration?

RABBI. I mean, keep quiet—not talk.

COHEN. Mama did vonce, but it didn't agree vid her.

RABBI. I mean to concentrate, to think!

MRS. COHEN. All I can think of vos dod operation.

RABBI. If we three concentrate, think, all together, that we want that telephone to ring again and relieve Solomon's mind about Abie it might result successfully.

COHEN. If it does, I'll concentrate on a million dollars.

MRS. COHEN. Let's try. It don't cost nothink!

RABBI. Very well! Now for one minute think hard that you want *that telephone to ring.*

(ALL *sit thinking. Fifteen seconds pass; the clock strikes one,* ALL *sit up nervously.* COHEN *assumes a pose of "The Thinker."* MRS. COHEN *looks at the time.*)

MRS. COHEN. How early it iss of late!

RABBI. Ssh! Concentrate, *my friends! Concentrate!*

(COHEN *repeats "Thinker" pose.* ALL *sit again quietly. The doorbell rings violently.* SOLOMON *enters from door left.*)

SOLOMON. Vos dod the phone? (*Sees the* RABBI.)

MRS. COHEN. No. Mr. Levy, dot vas the doorbell.

SOLOMON (*to* MRS. COHEN). Thank you. Hello, Dr. Samuels; glad to see you! Eggscuse me blease! Sarah can't hear a void over the phone and she can'd hear the doorpell any more —keeps me busy running my servant's errands. (*Doorbell rings again.*) Hello, Isaac. (*Said as he goes to door. He exits quickly out right center.*)

MRS. COHEN. Why he don't discharge Sarah is more than I could learn.

COHEN. Poor Solomon! He's worried about Abie. (*This is to the* RABBI.) He vosn't to the store all day!

MRS. COHEN. Sowin' his vild oats!

RABBI. Nonsense. I know his son Abie as well as I know his father, and if Abie has been away from the store all day, he has had a very good reason, you'll see.

MRS. COHEN. Dod's *vod you say!* (*She squints her eye knowingly. The telephone rings,* SOLOMON *rushes in like mad. Answers telephone on table right center.*) Yess, dod vos the phone dod time, Solomon. (*She says this in a most sympathetic manner as much as to say "poor thing, I pity you."*)

SOLOMON (*grabs the telephone, picking it up*). Thank God! (*He has the receiver off the hook by this time.*) Hello! Who iss it? Yes vot? Me! Yes, it's me! Who am me? Say who am you? What number? I don't know the number! I didn't get the phone to call myself! Oh, Abie wishes to speak vid his fadder? Pud him on! (*To* RABBI.) Abie. (SOLOMON *laughs at* OTHERS. MRS. COHEN *makes a knowing face at* COHEN, *they are* ALL *interested.* SOLOMON *seems very angry at the telephone.*) Hello! Iss dod you? Oh it iss? Vell you—you—loafer! V-here have you been all tay and vot iss it? I've a good notion to—Vot? Huh? A vod vid you? You vont to bring a lady home to dinner? (*He turns to* COHEN *and winks, belying his bad humor. In a whisper, as though* ABIE *could hear.*) He vonts to bring a lady home to dinner! (*Then back in the telephone again.*)

COHEN (*to* SOLOMON, *who with his eyes warns* COHEN *of* MRS. COHEN'S *presence*). Oy, I can't wait! (*Throws one leg excitedly over the other. Turns around, sees* MRS. COHEN—*and is squelched.*)

SOLOMON. Vot, I didn't heard you—say it twice! Oh, she's a very sweet girl? Oh I vill, vill I? (*He turns to them again.*) He says I'll like her! She's a sveet girl. (*Then immediately back into telephone.*) Jewish? (*He smiles and turns to them again.*) He says, vait till I see her! (*Then back in the telephone again.*) You little goniff—I smell a mices! Sure! I'll tell Sarah. Good-by, Abie, good-by. (*He hangs up receiver. They* ALL *sit waiting for him to tell them everything.*) Ha, ha, peoples, my Abie's got a girl. Maybe the good Rabbi will soon officiate at a wedding. Eh? (*Crosses to center. He is delighted.*)

COHEN. Is she Hebrew?

SOLOMON. Of course. Hebrew. Jewish Hebrew. (*He is delighted. He nudges* COHEN.) Abie! says, vait till I see her! (*Turns to* RABBI.) Dr. Samuels—"Lieber Freund"—maybe we'll all be goin' to a vedding soon! Yes! (*Crosses to back of table left center.*)

COHEN. Solomon, why are you trying to get Abie married? He's happy.

MRS. COHEN. You mean to say he wouldn't be happy if he was married?

COHEN. Mama, can't I talk at all?

RABBI. Oh, Isaac didn't mean to infer he isn't happy. He is happy, aren't you, Isaac?

COHEN. Perfectly.

SOLOMON. No, it isn't the idea that I want my Abie married exactly, but I want his grandchildren. (*Crosses center.*)

COHEN. You don't want him to get married. But you want him to have children. Mama listen to that.

MRS. COHEN. Isaac, you don't know what Solomon means.

COHEN. Sure, I do, he——

MRS. COHEN. You don't understand a word he says——

COHEN. Concentrate, Mama, concentrate.

SOLOMON. Yes, Isaac, I want grandchildren—dozens of them. (*Crosses to* COHEN.)

COHEN. Right away you talk wholesale.

SOLOMON. You see before my Abie was born, Rebecca and I we always used to plan for him. I wanted him to be a politician. Rebecca says, "no, Solomon. I want my boy—our son—to stay close by his father."

COHEN. And he certainly has.

SOLOMON. Yes.

RABBI. Yes, I don't know what your business would have done without him.

SOLOMON. Neither do I. But don't you tell him I said so.

MRS. COHEN. Why don't you take him into the firm?

RABBI. Right. Solomon Levy and Son—that wouldn't sound bad at all.

SOLOMON. *That's* just exactly what I am going to do. When he's married—not before.

RABBI. Why must you wait until he's married?

SOLOMON. Did you ever see any of Abie's girls?

RABBI. No.

SOLOMON. Not one Jewish and my Abie is not going to marry anyone but a Jewish girl if I can help it.

COHEN. Maybe you won't be able to help it.

SOLOMON. Who said it, not be able to help it? Let him try and you'll see how I could help it.

MRS. COHEN. Are you sure that this new girl is the right one?

SOLOMON. Didn't he say wait till I see her? Oh, what a relief when I'll see that son of mine safely married. I must tell Sarah dinner for three—— (*Crosses to door left.*)

MRS. COHEN (*rises and starts to go*). Ve must be going.

SOLOMON. Den please come back later and take a look at her.

MRS. COHEN. If ve can, ve vill.

COHEN. Vhy can't we, Mama? (*Rises, crosses to center.*)

MRS. COHEN (*to* COHEN). Because I'm awfully tired and you ought to go to bed early.

COHEN (*crestfallen; to door right center*). See—she's tired, and I got to go to bed early. (*Going out through hall followed by* MRS. COHEN.)

RABBI (*starting for the door. Right center*). I'll drop in later, Solomon.

SOLOMON. Good-by, peoples, good-by, and don't forget. When my Abie says a thing you can build a bank on it. (*Going to arch right center. To photograph on table up center.*) Abele, Boyele meiner.

(SOLOMON *takes out cigarette paper, puts in two pinches of tobacco, singing "Masseltof" as he reaches left center door, moistens cigarette, causes discord in song, and exits left center.* ABIE *enters the room from right center cautiously looking about, then he beckons to* ROSE MARY *who enters after him. They are both nervous and frightened.* ABIE *looks upstairs, listens a moment, then comes down to door left, opens it, listens, then closes it carefully, not making any noise. He goes to door right and repeats business, then back to arch right center.*)

ABIE. Well, the coast is clear. (*Crosses to* ROSE MARY, *center.*)

ROSE MARY (*coming down to* ABIE). Oh, Abie, I'm so frightened!

ABIE. With a perfectly good husband to protect you?

ROSE MARY. Oh, I forgot!

ABIE (*takes her in his arms*). You haven't been married long enough yet to be used to it. Let's see—— (*Looks at his watch.*) Just one hour and thirty-three minutes. Do you realize, young lady, you are no longer Rose Mary Murphy? You are Mrs. Abraham Levy.

ROSE MARY. Mrs. Abraham Levy! Glory be to God!

ABIE. Isn't it wonderful?

ROSE MARY. Abie, we will both be disowned.

ABIE. Well, that's better than being separated for the rest of our lives, isn't it?

ROSE MARY (*hesitating over it*). Yes.

ABIE. Why do you say it that way?

ROSE MARY. I am not so sure that they won't try to separate us.

ABIE. Oh, yes, try. But we're not going to let them. Are we?

ROSE MARY. No.

ABIE (*takes her in his arms*). We were married good and tight by a nice Methodist minister.

ROSE MARY. "Till death do us part."

ABIE (*breaks embrace and takes her hands*). Oh, that reminds me, why did you refuse to say "I do" to the obey me?

ROSE MARY (*with a slight brogue, smiling*). Shure—I'm that Irish!

ABIE. I didn't balk when he said "repeat after me, With all my worldly goods I thee endow." You know it's fifty-fifty.

ROSE MARY. To be sure it is. Faith you haven't any worldly goods and your father is liable to disown you when he finds out you haven't married a nice little Jewish girl.

ABIE. So is your father, when he find out you haven't married a nice little Irish boy.

ROSE MARY (*with true Irish foresight*). That would be fifty-fifty. (*Backs to front of davenport.*)

ABIE. You know, Rose Mary, I was just thinking. (*Crosses down left of davenport.*)

ROSE MARY. You are liable to have to do a whole lot of thinking, so you had better get into practice. (*Sits on davenport. He sits with her.*)

ABIE. No, in all seriousness, Rose Mary, you know I'm sure Father will be crazy about you.

ROSE MARY (*lapsing into brogue*). He might be crazy about me all right, but when he hears about "me religion" he'll be crazier.

ABIE. Silly, isn't it, to be so narrow-minded. Well, he can't any more than tell us to go, can he?

ROSE MARY. But Abie—you work for your father!

ABIE. Yep! (*Sighing.*) And if you don't make a hit with him, I'm liable to lose my job. I should worry. I'll find another.

ROSE MARY. And if you lost your job I'll have to do my own housework, and learn to cook.

ABIE. You can fry eggs, can't you?

ROSE MARY. I can, but I can't turn them over.

ABIE (*with his arm around her*). I'll turn them over for you. (*She cuddles close to him, forgetting for an instant what is coming.*)

ROSE MARY. Oh, Abie! Will you always be willing to do so much for me?

ABIE. Always! (ABIE *and* ROSE MARY *sigh.*)

ROSE MARY. Abie!

ABIE (*holding her close*). Yes, dear?

ROSE MARY. Wouldn't it be wonderful if our fathers would take our marriage nicely!

ABIE (*hugging her closer*). Wonderful!

ROSE MARY. Then we wouldn't have to worry about a thing. You could go on with your job—and—

ABIE. Now, you stop worrying about that, dear. I'm sure Father will fall in love with you as I did, on first sight.

ROSE MARY. Abie, you're a dear! You know sometimes (*Lapsing into brogue.*) I think you've a bit of the Irish tucked away in you somewhere. Faith, I believe you're half Irish.

ABIE (*right back at her with a brogue*). To be sure Mavourneen, my better half is Irish.

ROSE MARY (*laughing*). And my better half is Jewish. (*Puts right hand on his cheek.*)

ABIE. What could be sweeter? (*Kiss. In embrace.* SOLOMON *sings off left.*) That's Father!

ROSE MARY (*frightened. Both rise*). Oh, Abie!

ABIE. Don't weaken, dear! And no matter what he says, remember he's a peach when you get under his skin.

ROSE MARY. I hope it isn't a long way under.

(ABIE *crosses to center.* ROSE MARY *behind him walking lockstep. Hides behind* ABIE *on* SOLOMON'S *entrance.* SOLOMON *enters; front of table left center to center. He is a good-natured man with a round Jewish face. Hard work has made him older than his years, but hard luck has only softened his nature. He is a prosperous business man now, but still wears the comfortable old clothes of his other years. He is not stingy, but having known the want of things in days gone by he wastes nothing extravagantly. He sees* ABIE*—does not notice* ROSE MARY *who is standing back of* ABIE*—*SOLOMON *singing "Oi—Oi—")*

ABIE (*trying to be casual*). Hello, Dad.

SOLOMON. Vell? (*Hands behind him. Stopping short.*) You loafer! Vhere hafe you peen all afternoon?

ABIE. Away. (*Crosses to* SOLOMON. ROSE MARY *follows close behind, unseen by* SOLOMON.)

SOLOMON. Is dod an excuse—away?

ABIE. Certainly not, but——

SOLOMON (*not letting him get in a word edgeways*). Und de pizzness! Pi! Such a day! Vid everybody esking for you.

ABIE. Missed me, eh, Dad?

SOLOMON (*angrily*). Loafer! (*Turns to left. On word "Loafer"* ROSE MARY *quickly goes to arch right center and watches the two from behind the dra-*

peries. ABIE *tries to find* ROSE MARY *with hands behind him.*) Nobody vants me to vait on dem. It's "vhere is Abraham, Mr. Levy? Vhere your son iss, Mr. Levy? No tank you, Mr. Levy. I'll vait for your son, Mr. Levy, he knows eggsactly vot I vant, Mr. Levy." All tay long! Abie I'm not going to stand for this nonsense——

ABIE (*with a winning smile*). Now, Dad——

SOLOMON (*holds* ABIE *off, and looks at him fondly, then he hugs him to him*). Abie—Boyele meiner——

(ROSE MARY *enters laughing; comes down center.* SOLOMON *sees* ROSE MARY, *who has been standing watching this scene intently. He looks at her first as if he cannot believe his eyes—drops* ABIE *and steps back. Her smile fades.*)

ABIE. Dad—this—is—the lady I just phoned you about. (*Looking at* ROSE MARY—*then back again at his father. Taking* ROSE MARY *by the hand and leading her to his father.*) Dad, I want you to meet a very dear friend of mine!

SOLOMON (*looks at* ROSE MARY *skeptically*). Who's de name blease?

ABIE (*ignoring the question*). I met her just before the Armistice was signed!

SOLOMON (*not at all friendly*). Iss dod so?

ROSE MARY. Yes, in France!!

(ABIE *and* ROSE MARY *do not know what to say.*)

SOLOMON. A trained nurse, dod's a pizzness!

ROSE MARY. Well, I wasn't exactly a trained nurse.

SOLOMON (*looking at her skeptically*). No? Well, I had a trained nurse vonce and she wasn't eggsactly von either.

ABIE (*trying to break the tenseness of the situation*). She was an entertainer, Dad. You know, keeping the boys' minds off the war. Making it easier for them, you know!

SOLOMON. Yes, I know. (*Looking at* ROSE MARY'S *prettiness and believing it.*)

ROSE MARY. I used to sing for the boys in back of the lines.

SOLOMON. Oy—an actress!

ROSE MARY. Mercy, no!

ABIE (*impatiently*). Dad!

SOLOMON. Vell, you introduced me *vonce* to an actress. And believe me *dod* girl could act. Her name was O'Brien! Oi! Vod a name! (ABIE *backs up a step.* ABIE *and* ROSE MARY *exchange glances.* ROSE MARY *crosses to front of davenport.*) I tought you vos an actress, too, by the dress.

ROSE MARY (*trying to laugh*). You think this dress is loud?

SOLOMON. It's not so quiet—und there ain'd much of id. (*He motions with his hands that the dress is short.*) Maybe it shrunk!

ABIE (*coming down center*). Of course, it didn't shrink. All the girls are wearing their dresses short this year, Dad.

SOLOMON. Iss dod so? Well, boy, your mudder always wore long dresses. (*Looking skeptically at* ROSE MARY'S *legs.*)

ABIE. I'll bet if Mother were alive today she would be wearing short dresses too. (*Crosses up.*)

ROSE MARY (*steps toward him*). It's much more sanitary, Mr. Levy. Long skirts trailing along the ground get full of microbes.

SOLOMON. The microbes would have some high jump to make dod hem.

(*She turns away.*)

ABIE (*who is dreadfully ill at ease*). Never mind, Rose. (*Crosses to left of davenport.*)

SOLOMON (*suspiciously*). Rose? Rose vot?

ROSE MARY. Rose Mary.

SOLOMON (*closing up like a clam toward her*). Dot's vot I thought.

ABIE. You thought what! (*Crosses center to* SOLOMON.)

SOLOMON. Ven my son goes vid a girl, dot girl must speak the English language like a Jewess.

ABIE (*goes up a step*). Father!

SOLOMON (*sternly*). Still!!! (*Crossing to* ROSE MARY. ABIE *drops his head and goes up.*) I have nodings against you. I like Rose. I like the name of Rose. *Mary* might have been a grand old name, but I don't like it.

ROSE MARY. My name was good enough for my mother, sure it's good enough for me.

ABIE (*comes down left of* SOLOMON). Of course it is!

SOLOMON. Vell, tell me, vhere did you learn does Irish expressions? Sure!

ROSE MARY (*very proudly*). From my father.

SOLOMON (*now highly suspicious*). Hah! Iss dod so?

ABIE (*interrupting hastily*). Why yes, Dad. He was once an actor.

SOLOMON. *So*? Vell vot is *his* name? Is it Mary too?

ROSE MARY. My father's name Mary?

SOLOMON. You just said your name vos Rose *Mary*.

ABIE (*interrupting hastily again*). His name is Solomon!

SOLOMON. Oh! Your name is Rose Mary Solomon?

ROSE MARY (*very indignant*). Certainly not!

SOLOMON (*quickly*). Oh, your father's *first* name is Solomon?

ABIE (*quickly*). Yes! (ROSE MARY *looks at him—he is too fast for her—she gasps, so quickly has* ABIE *retorted.*)

SOLOMON. Oh! Well, Solomon vhot? (*Turns to* ROSE MARY.)

ROSE MARY. Murphy—— (SOLOMON *looks at her quickly;* ABIE *interrupts and finishes before* ROSE MARY *knows exactly what he is doing.*)

ABIE (*quickly*). Miss Murpheski.

SOLOMON. Murpheski! say dod's a fine nize name! Now there you are. (ROSE MARY *is so taken back by this interruption of* ABIE'S *she is speechless.*) At first I tought you vouldn't have a name like dod. You don'd look id!

ABIE. No, she doesn't, does she?

SOLOMON (*looking at* ROSE MARY). Faces are very deceiving! (*Smiling benignly for the first time on* ROSE MARY.) Take off your coad, Miss Murpheski! (*He turns to* ABIE *very reprovingly.*) Abie, I'm surprised at your inhospitality! Honest! (*He turns back to* ROSE MARY, *takes her wrap, looks at the material very closely, putting his glass on to do so.*) You buy fine materials, Miss Murpheski.

ROSE MARY. Thank you.

SOLOMON. Noo, Abe, *voss shtaistie vie a laimener goilem.* Hang it up. (*Gives coat to* ABIE. ABIE *takes coat to hall, hangs it up and returns to rear of davenport.*) Sit down, Miss Murpheski. Ay, ay, ay! (*Sitting on davenport.*) Dod's some ring you are varing, yes? (*Breathes on ring.* ABIE *standing behind davenport makes motions over* SOLOMON'S *shoulder to* ROSE MARY.)

ROSE MARY. Yes, my father gave me that.

SOLOMON. Oh, your papa! (*After* ROSE MARY *has seated herself at right of table he settles himself back contentedly for a chat.*) So you and Abie have known each odder a long time, eh?

ROSE MARY. Oh, yes. We met in France! Your son's a wonderful hero, Mr. Levy, do you realize that?

SOLOMON. Ain'd he my son? How could he be anything else? (ABIE *comes down.* SOLOMON *smiles on him proudly.*)

ABIE. With such a father, eh! Dad? (ABIE *is kidding, but* SOLOMON *hasn't that kind of a sense of humor.* ABIE *comes down to left center.*)

SOLOMON. Dod's vhat I *say!*—You know every time dot—— (*He turns to* ROSE MARY, *rising, offering his hand.*) Oi! I'm pleased to meet you, Miss Murpheski!

(*This comes as a surprise to* ROSE MARY. SOLOMON *goes to* ABIE.)

ROSE MARY. Thank you.

SOLOMON. Abie, ve must esk Miss Murpheski to stay to supper, yes?

ABIE. I phoned you that she would stay to dinner.

SOLOMON (*crosses to left center*). Oh, yes, dod's so.

ROSE MARY. I don't want to be any trouble.

SOLOMON. *Nod* at all! Miss Murpheski. Eggscuse me, I'll speak to Sarah. Murpheski! Abele boyele meiner! Murpheski!

(*He exits left, leaving* ROSE MARY *and* ABIE *together.* ROSE MARY *turns to* ABIE *furiously.*)

ROSE MARY (*rises*). Murpheski!

ABIE. Rose Mary, I just had to do it. I saw that he wasn't even going to give himself a chance to like you.

ROSE MARY. I don't want him to like me! Murpheski! (*Hides her face.*) Oh, Shades of St. Patrick!

ABIE (*trying to calm her*). Rose Mary, dear——

ROSE MARY. He even objects to my first name. First thing I know you'll be calling me Rebecca!

ABIE. Sssh! He'll hear you. (*Looking off left.*)

ROSE MARY. I want him to hear me. I was never so insulted in my life. Sure, Murphy's a grand name—I don't know why you had to tack "ski" on to it. (*Crying.*)

ABIE. I know, dear, but if I had told him your name was Murphy we wouldn't have had a chance. It's our happiness *I'm* fighting for!

ROSE MARY. But he'll have to know someday that I'm Irish!

ABIE. I have a grand idea.

ROSE MARY. If it's anything like the last few you've sprung on me, please don't tell me. (*Crosses and sits on davenport.*)

ABIE (*slight pause—then crosses to her. Sits beside her*). Listen! You love me, don't you? (*Pause.*)

ROSE MARY. Ah, Abie darling, that's the trouble, I do love you.

ABIE (*sits—embraces her—slight pause*). And you want our married life to be a happy one, don't you?

ROSE MARY. It's going to be, I can see that much from here.

ABIE. Then listen, dear, let him think your name is Murpheski. Make him like Miss Murpheski, then maybe Miss Murpheski can persuade him to open his heart a little bit to Miss Murphy. See what I mean?

ROSE MARY. You mean, I'm to let him think I'm Jewish until he likes me?

ABIE. Yes.

ROSE MARY. If he learns to like me, you think he might sanction our marriage?

ABIE. I'm sure of it. You know when you married me this morning you took me for better or for worse.

ROSE MARY. This is the worst I ever heard of.

ABIE. I'd do as much for you. You know your father isn't going to be easy either.

ROSE MARY. Don't remind me of my father at this minute. Your father is enough trouble for one day.

ABIE. That's what I say, dear, let's win my father over to our side, then when your father comes on from California, we'll have my father to help win your father.

ROSE MARY. You don't know my *father—— (They kiss.)*

SOLOMON *(enter* SOLOMON *to front of table left center)*. Vell, dod's dod! *(Smiling again upon them, they stop kissing—look a bit uneasy and separate as they turn to him.)* Go right ahead, don't let me inderrupt!

ABIE *(rising)*. Oh, Dad, come over here—I want you to know Miss Murpheski better. *(Brings him to davenport.)*

SOLOMON *(sits on davenport)*. Vell, dod's fair enough! I am glad of vone thing totay! *(*BOTH *look at* SOLOMON *expectantly.)* Dod you ain't an actress!

ROSE MARY. Then I'm glad I'm not too!

SOLOMON. What do you do for a living?

ROSE MARY *(the question has been fired so quickly at her she is stunned)*. Nothing.

SOLOMON. *Dod's* a great way to live. I don't believe in it.

ROSE MARY. My father never would let me work. I must study.

SOLOMON *(smiling again)*. Your father he has money!

(All this time ABIE *is fidgeting about, embarrassed.)*

ABIE. He's in business on the Coast.

SOLOMON. Vat business, Abie? Clioding?

ROSE MARY. No, contracting!

SOLOMON *(immediately freezing again)*. Murpheski—contracting?

ABIE. Contracting for clothes.

SOLOMON. What!

ROSE MARY *(getting* ABIE'S *meaning quickly)*. Yes, contracting for clothes.

SOLOMON. Contracting for—— Oh yes, yes I know. I know. I must—look him up. *(Pleased at this—takes out notebook, writes.)* Look him up. You know a lod aboud her father's business, Abie. *(Jokingly.)*

ABIE. Why, I know what Miss Murpheski has told me.

SOLOMON. Vell the cloiding is a good pizzness. *(*ABIE *and* ROSE MARY *exchange glances,* BOTH *are nervous and trying to make a hit.)* Abie!

ABIE. Yes, Dad?

SOLOMON. Vhy didn't you speak before of Miss Murpheski to me?

ABIE. Oh, I don't know.

SOLOMON *(nudges* ROSE MARY*)*. I hate to tell you, Miss Murpheski, never before has Abie had such a nice little Jewish girl.

ROSE MARY *(trying to laugh)*. Is that so?

SOLOMON. You tell 'em! But, Rose Mary—that's a fine name for a Jewish girl. Rose Mary!

ABIE. Why don't you tell Dad how you got the Mary part of it.

SOLOMON (*turning to* ROSE MARY). Vod does he mean got the Mary's?

ROSE MARY (*not knowing what* ABIE *is thinking of saying*). Why you see, Mr. Levy—— You tell him, Abie.

ABIE (*short embarrassed pause*). Well, you see, Dad, her name is really Rosie!

SOLOMON (*smiling broadly*). Rosie! Vell, I thought so!

ABIE. Rosie Murpheski!

SOLOMON. Yeh, but the Mary's?

ROSE MARY (*coming to* ABIE'S *rescue, who is hardly able to come up for air*). Well, I thought Mary was such a pretty name, so I took it.

SOLOMON. Give it back! Rosie is a peautiful name. You don't need the rest of it. (ABIE *sits on right arm of davenport.*)

ROSE MARY. All right, if you say so.

SOLOMON (*this flatters him*). You hear dod, Abie? If I say so! Oh, Abele—— (*Laughs.*) I never knew you had such a good taste. (*Looking at* ROSE MARY *and pinching her cheek.*) And Abie—has known you ever since the var?

ROSE MARY. Yes—but you see I live in California. I went home as soon as I came back from France.

SOLOMON. Are you visiting somebody here now?

ROSE MARY. No, I'm staying at the Pennsylvania.

SOLOMON. In the depot?

ABIE. Dad! The Pennsylvania Hotel!!!!

SOLOMON. Oi, such an expense! Abie right away quick you should get Rosie's trunk away from dod place.

ROSE MARY. But Mr. Levy!

SOLOMON. Tut—tut—tut! *This* is your New York home. I like you, Rosie. I vouldn't have you staying in such a hotel.

ABIE. But Dad, maybe Miss Murpheski prefers to stay in a hotel.

SOLOMON. Nonsense! Rosie stays here, where she can get some nice Kosher food. (*Turns to* ROSIE.) You like dod?

ROSE MARY (*isn't able to say anything to it*). I love it.

SOLOMON (*to* ABIE). See, she loves it. I vouldn't think of letting her go avay from here. (*He turns to* ROSE MARY, *smiles—she smiles back—*ABIE *is frantic—but can say nothing.*) Abie, run over to the Cohens', and ask Mrs. Cohen if Mr. Cohen can come over. I want him to meet Rosie.

ABIE. Why not ask Mrs. Cohen too. She's a peach, Miss Murpheski—you'd like her.

SOLOMON (*skeptically*). Yes. Esk *her* too. She hasn't any appendix, but she's a nice woman.

ROSE MARY. Oh, I see—she's just been operated on?

SOLOMON. Yes. About three or four years ago. She'll tell you about it.

ABIE. You might as well hear it tonight and get it over with. She tells everybody.

ROSE MARY. I love to hear of operations.

SOLOMON. Then run along, Abie. And, Abie——

ABIE (*up to arch right center*). Yes, Dad.

SOLOMON. Don't hurry back. Joke. Yes. (*Crosses up to arch right center. He laughs at his own jokes all the time.*)

ABIE (*laughs*). Dad, shall I ask the Cohens to stay for dinner?

SOLOMON. For vhat? We're not celebrating anything. A business for giving dinners for nothing. (ABIE *exits, going right through hall, smiling.* SOLOMON *turns to* ROSE MARY. *Pause.*) I don't know how Abie ever kept you a secred so long.

ROSE MARY. Well, we were afraid you wouldn't like me.

SOLOMON. Ain't dod foolishness? (*Comes down to her.*)

ROSE MARY. Abie wanted to tell you about me.

SOLOMON. Abie is it? (*Nudging her jokingly.*)

ROSE MARY. Hearing you call him Abie—it came natural to me.

SOLOMON. That's right. Keep it up! I like to hear you call him Abie! He's a vonderful boy, my Abie!

ROSE MARY. Indeed he is!

SOLOMON. You like him?

ROSE MARY. Very much; he's a splendid man.

SOLOMON. You don't know the half of it. All by myself I raised him.

ROSE MARY (*softly*). Yes, I know. Abie told me his mother died when he was born. (SOLOMON *nods his head, "yes."*) My mother died when I was born, too.

SOLOMON (*turning to her*). Your father raised you, too? (ROSE MARY *nods her head.* SOLOMON *throws up his hands.*) I can sympathize with him.

(*At this* ROSE MARY *is taken aback.*)

ROSE MARY. My father is a wonderful man!

SOLOMON. Of course he is, isn't his name Murpheski! (*Turns away.*) What did Abie say his first name was?

ROSE MARY (*thinking quickly*). Why—Solomon!

SOLOMON. Solomon Murpheski! (ROSE MARY *quickly crosses herself.*) I'd like to shake the hand of Solomon Murpheski.

ROSE MARY (*with double meaning*). I wish you could. (*Laughing.*)

(MRS. COHEN *enters right center. She is a tall good-looking woman, very well dressed.*)

MRS. COHEN. Hello, Mr. Levy. Abie gave me the key and told me to walk right in.

SOLOMON (*rises, goes to her*). Mrs. Cohen—I vant you to know Rosie. Miss Rosie Murpheski.

MRS. COHEN (*crosses to her.* ROSE MARY *rises*). Miss Murpheski! I am glad to know anybody what iss a friend of Abie's.

SOLOMON. Sid down Mrs. Cohen. Make yourself homely. (MRS. COHEN *sits on davenport.*) Oh, won't you lay off your furs for a minute?

MRS. COHEN. No thanks, I have to be goink in a few minutes.

SOLOMON (*center*). You von't feel the good of it. What's the use of havin' furs if you can't feel them when you go oud. (*Gets chair at back.*)

MRS. COHEN. I always wear somethink around me in the house, ever since my operation—— (SOLOMON *drops chair.*) don't I, Solomon?

SOLOMON (*puts chair center, facing davenport. Paying no attention*). Yes. Yes—just think, Mrs. Cohen, Abie has known Rosie ever since the var.

MRS. COHEN. Ve can blame a lod of things on the var, can't ve?

ROSE MARY. I hope you won't blame the war for me.

MRS. COHEN. Vat a nize pleasant blame. Did you go over?

SOLOMON. Dod's vhere she met Abie.

MRS. COHEN. Oh, you poor dear, what a lot of suffering you must have seen.

ROSE MARY. I did.

SOLOMON. Abie got shot in the Argonne. He laid in the hospital for weeks.

MRS. COHEN. I can sympathize with anybody in a hospital.

SOLOMON (*trying to stop her*). Yes ve know, your appendix was amputated.

MRS. COHEN. You know, Miss Murpheski, it started with a little pain, right here. (*Indicating her abdomen.*) Or was it here——

SOLOMON. Make up your mind.

MRS. COHEN. Now come to think of it——

SOLOMON. Don'd think of it, Mrs. Cohen. Forged it!

MRS. COHEN. I vish I could.

SOLOMON. So do I. (*She looks at him. He smiles, changing the meaning.*) It would be so much better for you, Mrs. Cohen.

MRS. COHEN. That is just what Isaac says. (*She sighs.*) But I can't.

SOLOMON (*to* ROSE MARY). Isaac is Mrs. Cohen's husband. He'll be here in a few minutes. You'll like him, von't she, Mrs. Cohen?

MRS. COHEN. Oh, yes, he's *just a husband*——

(ROSE MARY *is amused at their conversation. The doorbell rings.*)

SOLOMON. Now I vonder who dod can be?

MRS. COHEN. Abie, maybe, he gave me his key. I forgod to leave the door open maybe for him.

SOLOMON (*rises and puts chair back*). I'll have to answer it. Sarah is so deaf she can't even hear the *doorbell anymore.* (*Doorbell rings again.*) Stop ringling. Can't you see I'm coming! (*He exits out into the hall right center.*)

MRS. COHEN. Miss Murpheski have you ever had an operation?

ROSE MARY. No, not yet.

MRS. COHEN. Then you've never taken ether.

ROSE MARY. No.

MRS. COHEN. Dey had to give me twelve smells! I was in the hospital for three weeks. Oh vat a time I had. Miss Murpheski you should know vat I suffered after my appendix was oud.

ROSE MARY. I thought you suffered while it was in.

MRS. COHEN. And oud too.

(SOLOMON *enters followed by* ABIE.)

SOLOMON. Mrs. Cohen, Abie says Isaac will be right over.

ABIE. Will you give me the key to the front door, Mrs. Cohen, before we both forget it.

MRS. COHEN. Now where did I pud that key? (*Finds key on neck of dress.*) Oh, here it is.

SOLOMON (ABIE *and* SOLOMON *exchange glances*). Mrs. Cohen, vhy don'd you take off your fur?

MRS. COHEN. I'm a sight.

ABIE. We don't mind. Do we, Miss Murpheski?

ROSE MARY. I'm a sight myself. I haven't combed my hair since morning.

SOLOMON. Mrs. Cohen, vill you please take Rosie upstairs to the spare room.

ABIE (*up to arch right center*). I'll show her where it is.

SOLOMON (*center*). You'll do nothing of the kind. Mrs. Cohen, you know the house as vell as ve do.

MRS. COHEN (*rising and going up right center*). Of course I do. Come on Miss Murpheski. You probably feel as dirty as I do.

(ROSE MARY *crosses to her.*)

ROSE MARY (*to* SOLOMON). I would like to wash my hands and powder my nose a bit.

SOLOMON. Run along, Rosie. (MRS. COHEN *leads the way.* ROSE MARY *follows her up the stairs.* ROSE MARY *takes* ABIE'*s hand in passing. Throws a kiss at him.* ABIE *looks after them.* SOLOMON *crosses to chair left of table left center. Sits chuckling all the while—then says*) *Abie—kim a hare —tzurn-taten.* (*His father's voice calls his attention.* ABIE *comes down and sits right of table.*) Well, my son, you're getting some senses at last.

ABIE. You like her, Dad?

SOLOMON. She's a nice girl, Jewish and everything.

ABIE (*not so sure*). Yeh!

SOLOMON. How much money has she got?

ABIE. Oh, I don't know exactly. Her father is comfortably fixed, that is all I know.

SOLOMON. And your father is comfortably fixed, too! (*Smiling knowingly.*)

ABIE. What do you mean?

SOLOMON. You like her, don'd you?

ABIE. Do I! (*This speaks volumes.*)

SOLOMON. Who could help it?

ABIE. Do you really like her, Dad?

SOLOMON. She's a nice girl. Didn't I told you to vait ven you brought all those girls around, those Christian girls? Didn't I say "Abie, vait—someday you'll meet a nize little Jewish girl." Didn't I say that?

ABIE. You did, Dad!

SOLOMON. Uh—Bahama, aren't you glad you vaited?

ABIE. I'm glad I waited for Rose Mary!

SOLOMON (*grabs his hand angrily, almost yelling at him*). Please don'd call her Rose Mary. (*Smiles.*) She's Rosie!

ABIE. All right—Rosie! But I don't care what she is; it's the girl I like, not her religion.

SOLOMON. Sure—fine! You don'd care, but I care! We'll have no "Schickies" in this family. (*He hits table.*)

ABIE. You mean to say if Rosie were a Christian you wouldn't like her?

SOLOMON. Bud she isn't!

ABIE. Oh, piffle!

SOLOMON (*getting angry*). Don'd you peefle me!

ABIE. I didn't mean it for you——

SOLOMON (*hitting table. Paying no attention to* ABIE's *semi-apology*). I von'd be peefled!

ABIE (*meekly*). All right.

SOLOMON. No sir!

(ABIE *says nothing, sits with his hands deep in his pockets, hunched down in chair.*)

SOLOMON. *Positivill! Ein umglik mit dem ziem meinen zoog ich azoi zoogt er azoi shut up.* (ABIE *still says nothing.* SOLOMON *talks long strings of Jewish, then awakes to the fact that he is arguing against the wind; he looks at* ABIE. ABIE *pays no attention—seems lost in his own thoughts.*) Vhy don'd you say something?

ABIE. There is nothing to say.

SOLOMON. Don'd argue with me. You get a nice little Jewish girl and you don'd hang on to her.

ABIE (*with double meaning*). I'm hanging on to her all right!

SOLOMON. Yeh, all right vhy don'd you marry her qvick?

ABIE. Dad, have I your consent?

SOLOMON. Do you vant *me* to ask her for you?

ABIE. No. I can do that.

SOLOMON. Vell do it, and—if she says yes, I'll start you in some kind of a business. What would you like?

ABIE. I hate business.

SOLOMON. You'll need a business ven you start raising a fambly! Esk Rosie! She's got a common senses!

ABIE (*apprehensively*). Say, Dad—don't mention anything about a family to Rose Mary.

SOLOMON (*grabs head angrily*). *Oi —Ich platz*. Didn't I just tell you not to call her dod Rose Mary. (*Smiles.*) She's Rosie!

ABIE. All right, Rosie! But say please don't mention anything about a family to her, will you?

SOLOMON. Vat's the matter? She pelieves in a fambly, don't she?

ABIE (*nervously*). Why, I don't know. I've never asked her that.

SOLOMON. Vell, say, if she don'd, after you marry her make her change her mind.

ABIE. Well, it is just as well not to say anything to her about it anyhow.

SOLOMON. Sure! Ve know, don'd ve! (*Nudging* ABIE *in the side.*)

ABIE (*uncomfortably*). Yes!

(MR. COHEN *enters right center. He is an undersized little man, very much stoop shouldered, slightly bald, and absolutely dominated by* MRS. COHEN. *He is the direct antithesis of his wife. She is beautiful big and loud. He is undersized, quiet and—retiring.*)

COHEN. Hello, Solomon! (*Down to* SOLOMON. *Shakes hands.*)

SOLOMON (*rising and going to* COHEN *—very excited*). Isaac, my friend, congratulate me.

COHEN. What's the matter? Has somethink happened?

SOLOMON (*smiling blandly*). You should esk me! You should esk me!

COHEN (*smiling too*). I am esking you. Abie has somebody died and left him some money?

SOLOMON. Money—money—there are greater things in life than money.

COHEN. Vell, don't keep me in suspenses!

SOLOMON. Go on, boy—you tell him.

ABIE (*nervously*). Why there is nothing to tell him yet—

SOLOMON (*angrily*). Vot? Nothink to tell! Ain'd you going to esk Rosie to marry you?

ABIE (*nervously*). Yes—— (*Hesitating on the "yes" a bit.*)

SOLOMON (*mimicking him*). Yes —— Dod's no vay to feel.

COHEN. Rosie? Who iss it Rosie?

SOLOMON (*very expressively*). Oi! You should see Abie's Rosie! Such a hair! Such a teeth! Such a figure!

COHEN (*reprovingly*). Solomon!

SOLOMON (*turning again very angrily*). And dot schlimiel he's known her since de var! They should have been married with the childrens py this time.

ABIE (*looking toward the stairs*). Ssh!

SOLOMON (*indignantly*). I von't be shushed.

COHEN. Vhere is Rosie?

ABIE. She's upstairs with Mrs. Cohen.

SOLOMON (*almost weeping; slapping* COHEN, *nearly knocking him over*). Isaac, I love dod girl! She's vine vife for Abie! Und dod loafer he won't esk her yet.

COHEN (*he walks sideways until he hits the davenport*). Solomon, control yourself! Abie hasn't esked her yet, maybe she won't hab 'em. (*Sits on arm of davenport.*)

SOLOMON (*immediately forgetting his sadness*). Vot! Nod marry my Abie! Look what's talking. Who could refuse my Abie. Ain'd he my son?

ABIE (*rises*). Listen, Dad!

SOLOMON (*turning to* ABIE). Vell, I'm listening!

ABIE. Do you like Rosie?

SOLOMON. Isaac, listen to him after all I have——

ABIE (*interrupting him*). Now wait a minute!

SOLOMON. Oi! Such a talk!

ABIE. Do you want Rosie for a daughter-in-law?

SOLOMON. Do I vant a million dollars?

ABIE. All right, I'll ask her. But you are quite sure *you* like her?

SOLOMON (*smiling at* COHEN *blandly*). Ain'd dod a son to hev?

COHEN. Vell, Solomon, you hev been hard to blease! I'll say dod for you! Abie has prought at least a dozen girls I've seen my own eyes with.

SOLOMON. But dey vere not Jewish!

(*As though this statement was the Alpha and Omega. At this* ABIE *gets a bit nervous again.*)

ABIE (*a bit angrily*). Well, I want you both to know that I'm not marrying Rosie because she's Jewish— (*Walks away to left.*) I wouldn't care if she were Turkish!

COHEN (*at the word "Turkish"*). Vell dod wouldn't be so bad!

SOLOMON (*looks sternly at* COHEN. *Pause. Turns to* ABIE. *Sternly*). But I vould care!

ABIE. Then you don't like Rosie for herself. (*Up to him.*)

SOLOMON. Well, boy, I think I like her preddy vell, for vone day.

ABIE (*the idea striking him*). Then the longer you know her the better you'll like her.

(MRS. COHEN *enters coming down the stairs followed by* ROSE MARY. MRS. COHEN *is talking.*)

MRS. COHEN. And the doctor said he never saw a case like mine. My appendix was so small you could hardly see it! (ROSE MARY *smiles.* COHEN *rises and crosses to right. Comes down left of davenport and sits.*) Papa here. (*Motioning casually toward* COHEN.) Thought he was going to lose his mama. Didn't you, Papa?

COHEN (*he is right of davenport*). Yes, Mama. Yeh, yeh——

SOLOMON. Rosie! (ROSIE *does not recognize her name, continues to be deeply interested in* ABIE *up right center.*) Rosie! (*Still does not turn. He calls louder.*) Rosie! (*He is so loud this time they* BOTH *turn at the noise. When they turn he smiles.*) Rosie, don't you know your name?

ROSE MARY. Oh, I beg your pardon. (*She leaves* ABIE *and comes down right center.* SOLOMON *crosses to her.*)

SOLOMON. I vant you to meed a very dear friend of mine, Mr. Cohen, Mrs. Cohen's husband.

(COHEN *crosses to left of davenport.*)

ROSE MARY (*holds out her hand which he takes*). How do you do, Mr. Cohen?

COHEN. So this is Rosie! (*Takes her hand.*)

SOLOMON (*smiling delightedly*). Is she the same I told you?

COHEN. Also, and more. It's a pleasure—— (MRS. COHEN *pulls his coat-tail. He is looking at* ROSE MARY *full length. He looks at* MRS. COHEN *for a second. She pulls him onto the davenport*)—I'm sure, to meet you. (*Ad lib, to* MRS. COHEN.)

SOLOMON. You know, Rosie, ve vere talking aboud you while you vas gone.

(ABIE *eases to above table left center.*)

ROSE MARY (*turning to* SOLOMON). How lovely! What were you saying?

SOLOMON. Ve vere saying vot a lucky man he would be, who god you.

ROSE MARY. Oh, thank you.

SOLOMON. If I was young enough—I would try myself.

ROSE MARY. Oh, Mr. Levy, your blarney is wonderful!

(ABIE *crosses to left of table left center.*)

SOLOMON (*immediately changing. Grabs his head*). Please don'd say dod void to me. I never allow it to be used in my house.

ROSE MARY. Why! (*This is more an exclamation than a question. She is so surprised by the change.*)

SOLOMON. I had once dealings with a fellow named Murphy and what he didn't do to me. Every time I hear dot void blarney it reminds me of dot Irisher.

ROSE MARY (*nervously*). Then you don't like the Irish?

SOLOMON. Could you like the Irish? I'm asking you?

ABIE. Dad!

SOLOMON (*turning to him*). Vot's the matter?

ABIE. You don't have to get so excited about it.

SOLOMON (*gritting his teeth*). I am not excited. (*Turning to* ROSE MARY.) Could you marry an Irishman?

ROSE MARY (*looking at* ABIE *with double meaning*). No, I couldn't! (*Laughing.*)

SOLOMON. There! Vot did I told you? You know, Rosie—— (*Thinking he has won the argument.*) Ven you marry, you get a nize little Jewish boy what keep his Yom Kippur. (*He passes* ROSE MARY *over to* ABIE.)

ROSE MARY. I intend to.

SOLOMON. You hear dod, Abie? (COHEN *and* MRS. COHEN *listening to all this and smiling benignly upon* ABIE *and* ROSE MARY *too.* COHEN *nudges* MRS. COHEN, *who nods as much as to say "It meets with my approval."*) She is going to marry a little Jewish boy, ain'd dod nize? (*He turns to* COHEN *for his approval.* COHEN *nods his head.* ROSE MARY *and* ABIE *go up to arch left center. They are a bit embarrassed but cannot help themselves.*)

MRS. COHEN (*rises*). Come on, Papa! Ve hev to hev supper. (*Crosses to center.*)

SOLOMON. You are goink to hev supper here! I should let you go home! Never!

COHEN. Bud, Solomon——

MRS. COHEN. Shud up, Isaac, didn't you hear vot Solomon said, he invited us.

COHEN (*melting immediately, he knows he had better*). Oh, is dod so, tanks! (*Shaking* SOLOMON'S *hand; goes up right center.*)

SOLOMON. Mrs. Cohen, you run and tell Sarah you are staying and if she don'd like it, you fix it yourself.

MRS. COHEN. Sarah won'd mind, she likes me. Ever since my operation, she likes to hear about it.

SOLOMON. Tell her again! (MRS. COHEN *exits door left.*) It looks like a party! Yes? (*Beaming on them.*)

MRS. COHEN (*sticks her head through the door left and yells for* COHEN). Isaac! Come here vonce, I vant you! (*She immediately exits, knowing her word is law.*)

SOLOMON. Maybe she's got another appendicitus!

COHEN. I ain'd so lucky.

MRS. COHEN (*off left*). Isaac, come here, I want you.

COHEN. Oh, Mama! Always you want something. I vantcha—*I vantcha*—— (*He rushes to left door and exits. The doorbell rings.*)

SOLOMON. Now, who can dod be? (*Crosses up right.*)

ABIE. Let Sarah answer the bell, Dad, you spoil her.

SOLOMON. She can't hear the pell!

ABIE. Then get somebody who can.

SOLOMON. And discharge Sarah?

ABIE. Certainly.

SOLOMON (*turns at the arch to speak*). I know, Abie, bud if I discharge Sarah she can't get another job. (*He exits right center.*)

ROSE MARY. Oh, Abie, he's really a dear!

ABIE. Of course he is, and so are you.

(*Looks around to see that no one is looking and takes* ROSE MARY *in his arms. He kisses her. As he does so,* SOLOMON *enters right center again, followed by the* RABBI. SOLOMON *motions the* RABBI *to be quiet;* SOLOMON *beams. The* RABBI *looks at the lovers in their embrace. He cannot understand the situation; he looks at* SOLOMON *gesticulating like a mad man, he is so happy.* SOLOMON *comes further down into the room;* ABIE *and* ROSE MARY *still hold the kiss.* SOLOMON *cannot contain himself any longer, so he yells, almost scaring the lovers to death.*)

SOLOMON (*looks at watch; counts five*). Time!

(ROSE MARY *and* ABIE *jump as though shot.* RABBI *goes down right of davenport.*)

ROSE MARY. Oh!

ABIE (*undertone*). Dad!

SOLOMON (*beaming*). Don't plush, Rosie! I kissed Abie's mama just the same vay vonce!

ROSE MARY. Oh, Mr. Levy! (*Goes to* SOLOMON'S *arms—embarrassed to tears.*)

SOLOMON. Call me Papa! (*He takes her in his arms. Her head is on his shoulder.*)

COHEN (*enters. To* RABBI). Hello, Doctor.

SOLOMON. Isaac, my friend, Abie did it. (*Shakes* COHEN'S *hand, turning to* RABBI *as he does so.*) Didn't he did it Dr. Samuels? Didn't he did it?

RABBI. I don't know what you are talking about, Solomon.

SOLOMON. Didn't you see what I saw before we came into the room just now, vid Abie and Rosie?

RABBI. Oh, you mean the kiss?

SOLOMON (*turning to* COHEN *delightedly*). You hear vod he say! He saw the same thing. Oh such a happiness! (*Crossing to the* RABBI.)

COHEN (*opens door left and yells at the top of his voice*). Mama! Quick! Abie did it! Abie did it!

ABIE. (*Embarrassed for* ROSE MARY; *also a little for himself.*) Dad, please!

(ABIE *and* ROSE MARY *come down center. He takes her in his arms.*)

MRS. COHEN (*entering out of breath. She has on an apron as though cooking*). Isaac, what iss it?

COHEN. Abie did it.

MRS. COHEN (*sees the* RABBI. *Crosses to center.* COHEN *crosses to left*). Dr. Samuels, what is it?

SOLOMON. Mrs. Cohen—(*beaming*) —Abie asked her!

MRS. COHEN (*loudly*). Oh! You sveet child! Ven you going to be married by the good Rabbi here?

ROSE MARY (*to* ABIE'S *arms*). Rabbi!

SOLOMON. Next week!

ROSE MARY. Abie!

SOLOMON (*interrupting*). Oh, you can be ready by next week, Rosie! I'll get the trousseaus—the svellest in the city! I'll go to Greenbergs. He gives me a discount.

ABIE. But, Father—Rose Mary and I want to tell you——

SOLOMON (*incensed at the interruption*). Young man, whose vedding iss dis?

ABIE (*now thoroughly going*). It's mine!

SOLOMON. Den keep *quiet, I'll run it!*

(SOLOMON *and* MRS. COHEN *go to the* RABBI *in consultation.* ROSE MARY *in consternation is gathered into* ABIE'S *arms trying to pacify her.* COHEN *is in the seventh heaven of delight as*

THE CURTAIN FALLS

ACT TWO

SCENE—*Same as Act One. With the exception that the entire room is decorated with oranges. There are orange trees of all different sizes. Oranges in bunches hanging on the walls which are festooned with orange ribbons. The place looks like a veritable orange bower.*

TIME: *One week later.*

AT RISE: ROSE MARY *in her wedding dress steals into the living room from upstairs making sure no one is there; she is very mysterious about her movements. Then she goes to the telephone, picks it up and calls:*

ROSE MARY. Pennsylvania-6-5600. (*Then she looks around cautiously again.*) Yes, hurry please! (*There is a pause as she waits for the number.*) Hello, hello! (*She seems very agitated.*) Pennsylvania-6-5600. Information? Can you tell me if the 6.30 from Chicago is on time? (*She pauses.*) One hour late, but you think it will make up some of the time? Thank you. Good-by. (*Hangs up, crosses to arch right center.*)

ABIE (*enters from right, stops, listening to* ROSE MARY, *placing his hat on table right center*). Rose Mary! (*She turns and sees* ABIE; *almost shrieks.*) Why, what is it, dear?

ROSE MARY. You shouldn't see me in my wedding dress until we're married! It's bad luck! (*She almost weeps —together with her agitation over the telephone.*)

ABIE (*putting his arms around her soothingly*). Nonsense, it's good luck to see you at any time.

ROSE MARY. I know, but we should be very careful. It might be true.

ABIE (*laughing*). Well, I didn't see you in your wedding dress before we were married. You forget we've been married a week today. This is our anniversary. We're celebrating our wedding by being wedded again.

ROSE MARY. I forgot! Oh, Abie, it's been an awful week!

ABIE. I know it, dear! (*Holding her in his arms.*) But it will soon be over.

ROSE MARY. Abie, Father's train is an hour late.

ABIE. Good!

ROSE MARY. But they said they would probably make up some of the time.

ABIE. We mustn't delay the wedding a minute.

ROSE MARY. If my father arrives before the Rabbi marries us, both your father and my father will prevent it.

(*Down center looking left.*)

ABIE (*to her; shakes her*). Mrs. Abraham Levy, you speak as if you weren't married to me at all.

ROSE MARY. I know, Abie. But your father wouldn't believe we've ever been married with only a minister officiating. (*Turns to him.*) Neither would my father. My father won't even pay any attention to the Rabbi. (*Crosses to davenport.*)

ABIE. But my father will. According to him, we'll be married good and tight this time. And it is all his fault, he has arranged every bit of it.

ROSE MARY. Then, please God, he doesn't find out I'm not a little Jewish girl until the good Rabbi ties the knot. (*Sits on davenport.*)

ABIE. Amen! (*Sits beside her.*)

ROSE MARY. The knot that we had tied a week ago, a little tighter. Abie, I'm getting awfully nervous!

ABIE. Now don't worry, dear. Everything is going to be all right.

ROSE MARY. What time is it?

ABIE (*looking at his watch*). Six-fifteen.

ROSE MARY. I hope Father's train doesn't make up any time!

ABIE. In fifteen minutes you will be married to me for the second time.

ROSE MARY (*fervently*). I hope so!

SOLOMON (SOLOMON *comes down the stairs. He is all dressed for the wedding. He has on a suit a trifle large. He walks down center, pirouettes.*) Abie—Rosie—give a look—a regular dandy!

(*They both rise.*)

ABIE. Father, I told you to have that suit made smaller.

SOLOMON (*facing him*). Vot? I paid fifty-nine dollars and ninety-eight cents for this suit. Und den you vont dot I should have some of it out? No, sir. I vant all I paid for. (*Faces left.*)

ABIE. But, it doesn't fit!

SOLOMON. I don't vant it to fit.

ROSE MARY. Abie, it's lovely. (*Crosses to* SOLOMON.)

SOLOMON. You hear. That boy has no idea of the money. I could hire a suit but he says no, und I buy this to please him und den he ain't pleased yet.

ABIE. Yes I am, Dad. (*Crosses to right of davenport.*)

SOLOMON. Fifty-nine dollars and ninety-eight cents to wear a suit for von night. I could hire a suit for three dollars und save fifty-six dollars and ninety-eight cents.

ROSE MARY. Never mind; you look wonderful.

SOLOMON (*holding out his arm*). And how sveet you look! Oi! Such a bride! Abie, look at her. Look at her! Und den tank me!

ABIE. The Rabbi hasn't married us yet. (*Crosses to front of davenport.*)

SOLOMON. He'll soon be here! Oi! I hope nothink happens to his texes keb!

(ROSE MARY *goes up right center to arch.*)

ABIE. Father, please don't borrow trouble! I'm nervous enough.

SOLOMON. You're nervous! Vot do you tink I am? But I shall nod rest until I see you two lovers unided for life.

ABIE. Neither shall I.

SOLOMON. Unided you stand, divided you don'd.

ROSE MARY (*crossing down to* ABIE). Abie and I are never going to be divided, are we, Abie?

ABIE (*she is in his arms*). I'll say we're not.

SOLOMON. Dod's de vay my childrens should speak up. Dod's de vay, Rosie! (*Crosses to left center.*) Vell, vod you tink of the decorations, you haven't said it yet. I did it all for you, Rosie.

ROSE MARY. They're beautiful.

SOLOMON (*to center*). Does dod bring California back to you?

ROSE MARY. It certainly does. I love oranges.

SOLOMON. Now I'm glad now I couldn't get the blossoms. You know this is more of an economical idea.

Ven the wedding is over, we can *eat* the fruit.

ABIE (*reprovingly*). Dad!!

SOLOMON (*not getting the tone*). Vod do I care for expenses, ven it's all for my little Rosie. I told Cohen this vedding vos goink to be the svellest blow-up in the Bronx. (*He stops for a second.*) I vonder if dos musicians have come yet? I ordered dem for a quarter past six. (*Crossing to left.* ROSE MARY *up to arch right center.*)

ABIE (*looking at his watch*). It's only that now!

SOLOMON. Den they should be here.

ABIE (*nervous and a bit impatient with his father's chatter*). Oh, Dad, give them a chance! (*Crosses to him left center.*)

SOLOMON. I'm givink them money; why should I give dem chances, a business with chances, dey should be here playing already!

(ABIE *crosses down right.* SOLOMON *moves chair at back to down center.*)

ABIE. Not until after the ceremony, Dad. I'm too nervous for music just now! (*To right center.*)

SOLOMON (*teasing him*). Abie! For why are you nervous?

ROSE MARY (*down to* ABIE). Abie, isn't it time to begin?

SOLOMON. But, Rosie, your father isn't here yet.

ABIE (*nervously*). His train is late.

SOLOMON (*sits in chair left center*). Den ve'll vait for him.

ROSE MARY. No—no! (SOLOMON *looks at her in surprise.*) It's bad luck to wait, isn't it, Abie?

ABIE. Positively.

SOLOMON (*perplexed*). Yeh, but who vill give the bride avay?

ROSE MARY. I'll give myself away!

SOLOMON. Oi! I never did hear of such a talk!

ABIE. I know how to get around it!

SOLOMON. Giving the bride away?

ABIE. Yes.

SOLOMON. Ven the Rabbi esks, who gives the bride avay, you speaks oud of your turn and says, "Nobody, I take her myself!"

ABIE. Just tell the Rabbi to omit that part of the ceremony.

SOLOMON. Vat, leave oud sometink, ven it costs me so much money for the decoratings?

ROSE MARY (*pleadingly; hugs* SOLOMON). Please don't make us wait!

SOLOMON (*changing immediately*). Abie! You see she can't vait!

ABIE (*crosses to door right*). I'm more impatient than Rosie!

SOLOMON. Never did I see such love. (*Doorbell rings.* ROSE MARY *and* ABIE *start nervously,* SOLOMON *smiles broadly. He rises.*) Rosalie, maybe dod is your papa, our very good friend Solomon Murpheski! I vond to shake his hands! (*Goes to arch right center and exits, going to door. Slight pause.* ROSE MARY *almost in tears.* ABIE *reassuringly embraces her.*)

ROSE MARY (*almost in tears*). Abie!

ABIE. Don't weaken! If it's your father—— (*She starts.*) We'll have to face it. That's all!

(*Voices are heard out in hall. They face up stage.*)

SOLOMON, MR. AND MRS. COHEN. Maziltof! (*Leads the way in from hall, followed by* COHEN *and* MRS. COHEN *who go to left and right end of table up center respectively.* ABIE *is standing with his arm protectingly about* ROSE MARY *waiting for the blow to fall.*) Isaac, look! (*Coming down center.*)

COHEN. A regular tscotska.

SOLOMON (*very proudly*). *Ain'd* she a bride?

MRS. COHEN (*going down to* ROSE MARY). My dear, your gown is beautiful!

COHEN. But, Mama, look vots in the gown.

MRS. COHEN. Isaac!!!!

(MRS. COHEN *gives him a hard look, and he goes up left and brings a chair down to left center.*)

SOLOMON. Yess! (*Beaming—as doorbell rings again.*) Rosie, maybe dod is de papa!

(*He is delighted to think so.* ABIE *and* ROSE MARY *look almost frightened to death again.*)

COHEN. Ain'd her papa here yet? (*Sits left center.* MRS. COHEN *sits right of him.*)

ABIE. No!

SOLOMON. Answer the door, Abie, and leave it open so the peoples can valk right in.

(ABIE *looks at* ROSE MARY. *She crosses herself surreptitiously.* ABIE *goes up to right center and exits.*)

MRS. COHEN. Ain'd you afraid to leave the door open?

SOLOMON (*center*). Vid a vedding goink on? Nefer! Always leave the door open for veddings and funerals! It's stylish.

COHEN. Rosie, have you heard from the papa?

ROSE MARY. Yes, his train is an hour late.

MRS. COHEN. Musd ve vait an hour?

SOLOMON. Rosie von'd vait! (*Thinking this is a huge joke.* ROSE MARY *doesn't pay much attention to their chatter. She is back of the davenport looking apprehensively at the hall arch, thinking it might be her father.*)

MRS. COHEN. Vell, I don't blame her. It's bad luck! Ve delayed our vedding fifteen minutes, und I always said, dod's de reason I god my appendicitis!

(ISAAC *puts hat under chair,* RABBI *enters right center followed by* ABIE. RABBI *goes to shake hands with* SOLOMON. ABIE *goes back of davenport to* ROSE MARY.)

SOLOMON (*disappointed*). Oh! I thought dod vos Rosie's papa! Hello, Dr. Samuels! Vell, I guess you is as much importance.

RABBI (*center*). Yes—I'm the one who does it.

SOLOMON. Vell, Dr. Samuels, do it vell!

RABBI. I will, Solomon, have no fear. (*Smiling.*) Well, how are the Cohens tonight?

COHEN (*rises*). Perfect. Couldn't be perfecter.

MRS. COHEN (*falls in chair*). Isaac, speak for yourself! I have my own feeling, vod you don'd know aboud.

(COHEN *is squelched and sits meekly.*)

ABIE. Dr. Samuels, hadn't we better start things?

RABBI. I'm ready! Rosie, where are your bridesmaids?

SOLOMON. They're upstairs vaiting. Go on up, Rosie, you've god to come down vid dem!

RABBI. Is her father here?

SOLOMON. No, his train is late.

RABBI. Then what is the hurry?

SOLOMON. Rose vonts to be married!

RABBI. Yes, of course. But who will give the bride away?

SOLOMON. That's just it!

MRS. COHEN. Isaac, you give the bride avay.

COHEN. Sure I don'd care.

SOLOMON. Sure, you don'd care. It don'd cost you noddings.

RABBI. Does that meet with your approval, Rosie?

ROSE MARY (*who is by now very nervous*). Oh, yes, yes!

SOLOMON. Vell run along den, Rosie!

ROSE MARY (*picking up her skirts preparing to go*). Good-by, Abie. I'll meet you at the altar, if I'm lucky!

(*She rushes out and upstairs. They* ALL *look after her.* SOLOMON *goes up to left of arch right center.* ABIE *in arch.* RABBI *looks after her; then crosses back of davenport to front of it.*)

SOLOMON. She's so afraid sometink is going to happen. I don't know vod!

MRS. COHEN. She is nervous! All brides are! I remember I was dreadfully nervous. Vosn't I, Papa?

COHEN. Oh yes, Mama! Bud you soon god over your nervousness, Mama!

MRS. COHEN. A vedding is almost as bad as an operation.

COHEN. Concentrate, Mama, concentrate!

(RABBI *is looking around room in perplexity.* SOLOMON *sees him, he swells all up again. Comes down center.*)

SOLOMON. Vell! Vod you tink? Some decorations, yes?

RABBI. Splendid, Solomon, but why all the oranges?

SOLOMON. All for Rosie! She comes from California! Ve couldn't ged the flowers, so I ged's the fruit! Real California *Navy* oranges. *Ain'd* dod an idea?

COHEN. Peautiful! Significance!

MRS. COHEN. Are they sveet?

SOLOMON. Yes, bud don't eat them! If you ged hungry please vait!

COHEN. Solomon, I don'd know how you thought of it. You're a genius!

SOLOMON. Vell, my Abie vill only be married vonce.

(ABIE *standing in arch right center glances at* SOLOMON *and exits.*)

COHEN. Dr. Samuels, vod shall I do ven you ask for the bride?

RABBI. Well——

MRS. COHEN. Isaac, don'd led them know how already dumb you are yet!

COHEN. What you mean how dumb I am yet?

(*Ad lib argument.*)

SOLOMON. Order—order—order—Mrs. Cohen, Isaac vonts to know!

MRS. COHEN. He's been married! He vent to his own vedding!

COHEN. I didn' vent. Dey took me. Dr. Samuels what shall I do when you esk for the bride?

RABBI. Don't get nervous, Isaac, it is very easy. You'll know exactly what to do when the time comes.

MRS. COHEN. Pud me somevhere so I can nudge him.

COHEN. Mama, I don'd vont to be nudged!

(MRS. COHEN *gives him a look.*)

SOLOMON (*center. Looks disgustedly at* COHENS). Mrs. Cohen, I don'd tink anybody should be nudged at this vedding.

RABBI (*looking at his watch*). It is time to begin, Solomon.

SOLOMON. I'll tell them to start the moosic! They should be earning their money already before! (*Crossing to door left.*)

MRS. COHEN. Iss everybody here?

SOLOMON. You should see. I god it all fixed like a theater, everybody is seated holding the front seats to see the show good.

RABBI. Isaac you go upstairs and wait for the bride! You bring her down on your arm.

(COHEN *gets hat and immediately starts for the stairs.*)

COHEN. The bride! Sure! Fine!

MRS. COHEN (*follows him to arch*). Und Isaac, vait outside the door! (COHEN *exits upstairs, very quickly.*) If I don't tell him, he goes right in by the bride. (*Exits left.*)

(ABIE *enters.* SOLOMON *moves chair up left and when* MRS. COHEN *exits, he puts other chair up.*)

RABBI (*going over to* ABIE *and slapping him affectionately on the shoulder*). Good luck, son!

(*Music—"Oh, Promise Me"—starts softly as* RABBI *goes to door left.* SOLOMON *goes to left center, and stands with back to the audience.*)

ABIE (*smiles at the* RABBI) Thanks!

(RABBI *goes to* SOLOMON, *pats him affectionately, and exits left.* SOLOMON *has been looking at* ABIE *affectionately, he goes up to him, puts his arm around him.* ABIE *gets hat from table right center and crosses to* SOLOMON.)

SOLOMON. My little Abie! Sure it seems like only yesterday, I vos vaiting for your mama, just like you are vaiting for Rosie now. My son, I hope you can keep Rosie by your side until your hair is white like mine!!! My Rebecca didn't stay so long wid me. Only a little vhile—bud no one couldn't take her place. I tink you lofe Rosie the same way.

ABIE (*center*). I do, Dad. I love Rosie better than my life.

SOLOMON. Dod's the vay, Abie! Und I lofe Rosie too!

ABIE. I'm so glad of that, Dad! Will you always love her?

SOLOMON. Sure, why nod? Ain'd she Jewish and everything?

(*At this* ABIE *is squelched again. The music stops.* RABBI *enters.*)

RABBI (*to left center*). Solomon, everything is all ready and waiting. The best man is here!

SOLOMON. Iss it time for the moosic?

RABBI. Yes!

SOLOMON (*getting excited*). Vait till I gife the high sign! (*He goes to door left and waves his hand frantically to the orchestra which is off stage.*) Go on—start to commence! Go on! Ve're vaiting. (*Music begins, the wedding march, off left.*) There! Now vod do ve do?

(*The music softens.*)

RABBI. Abie. (*Indicates* ABIE'S *hat, he puts it on.*) Now come. (*Exit* RABBI *left.*)

ABIE. Dad, I'm nervous as a cat!

SOLOMON. It vill soon be over. (*He slaps his back affectionately.*) Don't be nervous! (ABIE *exits left.* SOLOMON *is more nervous than* ABIE. *He goes to table up center, gets his hat, puts it on, starts out left, then rushes to the foot of stairs and putting his hand to his mouth, calls.*) Isaac! Don'd forget to bring up the rear! Abie's goink in now! Come on! (*He runs about like a madman. All of this time the "Wedding March" is being softly played off left. The* SIX BRIDESMAIDS *are seen coming down the stairs. Then a* LITTLE FLOWER GIRL *strewing flowers in front of the bride,* ROSE MARY, *who comes down the steps on* COHEN'S *arm. Her eyes downcast.* THE BRIDESMAIDS *exit left.* COHEN *and* ROSE MARY *with* LITTLE FLOWER GIRL *in front of them, follow the* BRIDESMAIDS *off left.* SOLOMON *looks about, to see that they are all in.*) I guess dod's all! (*Puts on his hat and slowly crosses to door left. As* SOLOMON *gets to door, music strikes up loudly. Very pleased, he exits same door, closing it behind him. The music is still heard playing through the closed door. The room is empty. Only the music which finally stops. There is another long pause. The doorbell rings one short ring. Then there is another pause. Then the bell rings again, a longer ring. Another pause. Then a long definite ring. Then voice is heard with a distinct brogue in the hall.*)

PATRICK. Come on in, Father. This must be the house. (*He enters, hangs hat on tree, goes down left.* PATRICK MURPHY, ROSIE'S *father, enters the room, followed by* FATHER WHALEN. PATRICK *is a big, burly Irishman, red-faced, brawny. The kind who fights at the drop of a hat, but if appealed to in the right way, would give his last dollar.* FATHER WHALEN, *the priest, is a good-looking man of the scholarly type. Gentle, and kind. Irish, but of the esthetic type.*)

FATHER WHALEN. Patrick, we shouldn't enter a man's house without an invitation.

PATRICK. This is the house all right. Didn't the children outside the door say the wedding was to be here. (*As he starts away from* FATHER WHALEN, *he spies the decoration of oranges; he looks about the place, blinking his eyes to make sure he is not "seeing things."*) Father Whalen, do you see what I see?

FATHER WHALEN (*looks about the room. He is surprised, too*). Yes!

PATRICK (*center*). What do you see?

FATHER WHALEN (*smiles*). I see oranges.

PATRICK. Dozens of them?

FATHER WHALEN (*surprised at this unusual feature*). Why, yes!

PATRICK (*in sudden fear*). Glory be to God, Father, she's marrying a Protestant!

FATHER WHALEN. Don't jump at conclusions!

PATRICK. I'm going to get to the bottom of this! (*He yells. Through door left.*) Oh, Rose Mary! Rose Mary!!

FATHER WHALEN. Take it easy, son, take it easy!

PATRICK. Take it easy, with all them oranges staring me in the face! Rose Mary! Rose Mary!! (*Going to door right, opening it and calling.*)

FATHER WHALEN. Patrick! You know love has never been a respecter of religion!

PATRICK. Who said anything about love? I'm talking about them oranges! (*To* FATHER WHALEN.) I hate orange! 'Tis the color of the damned A.P.A.'s—Rose Mary! Rose Mary!

(*He goes up right.* FATHER WHALEN *comes down to front of davenport.* PATRICK *goes to center. The left door flies open and* SOLOMON *enters, closing the door behind him. Pantomimes* PATRICK *to hush.* PATRICK *walks down to him.*)

SOLOMON (*on entrance*). Shh! Sh! Shush, shush, please be qviet! You're interrupting the whole works!

PATRICK (*to* FATHER WHALEN, *seeing* SOLOMON *and getting his dialect*). He's no A.P.A.

SOLOMON (*suddenly beaming*). Is your name Murpheski?

PATRICK (*not getting him yet*). What?

SOLOMON. Are you Solomon Murpheski?

PATRICK (*looking at* FATHER WHALEN *then back to* SOLOMON). Say, are you trying to kid me?

SOLOMON. No. I'm expecting Solomon Murpheski.

PATRICK. My name is Patrick Joseph Murphy.

SOLOMON. Gewald!

PATRICK. Not Gewald—Murphy! And I'm looking for my daughter. Is she here?

SOLOMON (*making a face at the name* MURPHY). Nobody by dod name is here. Voddo you vant?

PATRICK. I'm looking for the home of Michael Magee!

SOLOMON (*laughs*). Michael Magee! Listen to him! Efeter I've been telling you——

PATRICK. What is your name?

SOLOMON (*proudly*). Solomon Levy! Does dod sound like Michaels Magee?

PATRICK. Well, I'll tell the world it doesn't!

SOLOMON. Den please go vay!

FATHER WHALEN. Come, Patrick, I told you we were in the wrong house. (*Goes up to arch right center.*)

SOLOMON (*starts for the door left*). Absitivle! Close the door und lock id ven you go oud.

PATRICK (*following*). Wait a minute!

SOLOMON (*impatiently*). Oi, please be qvick! It vill soon be over. Isaac is giving the bride avay. Und I vont to see it. It's the first thing in his life he ever gave avay, I'm telling you.

(*Laughs heartily.* PATRICK *walks slowly down to him.*)

PATRICK (*laughs*). I'm very sorry. But I'm looking for my daughter. She is to be married tonight to a young fellow by the name of Michael Magee. I thought this was the address she gave me.

SOLOMON. No, sir! A girl by the name of Rosie Murpheski is marrying my son, Abraham Levy.

PATRICK. Ah, I see! Oh, but would you mind telling me, what you are doing with all the A.P.A. decorations?

SOLOMON. Oh, you liked id?

PATRICK. I'm not saying anything about that. But it seems very funny to have oranges for decorations.

SOLOMON. Vell, I'll tell you why! The girl's from California!

PATRICK (*cutting him short*). So's my daughter!

SOLOMON. Bud my son is marrying a Jewish girl!

PATRICK. My daughter is marrying an Irish boy!

SOLOMON (*almost shouting*). My son isn't Irish!

PATRICK. Well my God! My daughter isn't Jewish!

FATHER WHALEN. Come, Patrick!

PATRICK (*turning to* FATHER WHALEN). But, Father, where can Rose Mary be? (*Crossing up stage.*)

SOLOMON. Wait a minute! (*In terror.*) Did you say Rose Marys?

PATRICK (*Coming close to him*). Shure I said it! That's my daughter's name!

SOLOMON (*suddenly grabbing his head*). Oi vey is mire. Do you suppose it could be true?

PATRICK (*looking at him in amazement*). What's the matter, are you having a fit?

SOLOMON (*pays no attention to* PATRICK, *but starts for door left, yelling at the top of his lungs.*) Vait a minute! Stob id! Vait a minute! Stob it!

VOICE (*off left*). *Mas ameah, hoosen veim ha calo!*

(*As* SOLOMON *gets to the door, the music starts up, which denotes the end of a Jewish ceremony.* GUESTS *cry "Masseltof," music plays.*)

SOLOMON (*holding his head*). It's too late! It's too late! (*He staggers into chair down left.*)

PATRICK. What's that? Sounds like a riot!

(COHEN *enters left. Does a wild sort of a dance.*)

COHEN. Solomon, did you see me give the bride avay?

SOLOMON. Vhere is Abie?

COHEN. He'll be here in a minute. Everybody is kissing the bride. Und, believe me, Solomon, she is some bride! I hated to give her avay! (*Crosses to left center.*)

PATRICK (*to* FATHER WHALEN). There is something wrong here?

COHEN (*seeing him; crossing to him*). Oh, is it a detective, vatching the vedding presents?

PATRICK (*turns to him*). I'm no detective! I'm a contractor!

SOLOMON. Oi! Oi! The contractor! (*Holds his head.*)

COHEN (*advances*). Oh, you're the papa?

PATRICK. What do you mean, the papa?

COHEN. Don't you know bot iss it, a papa?

PATRICK (*raising his fist*). Don't you "papa" me!

FATHER WHALEN (*softly*). Control yourself, Patrick! (*Crosses down right of davenport.*)

SOLOMON. Oi! Patrick!

COHEN. Abie heard the doorbell ring und he thought it vos the papa. He sent me on ahead to see for sure.

PATRICK. Abie! And who in the hell is Abie?

COHEN. He's your new son-in-law!

PATRICK (*crosses to left of davenport. To* FATHER WHALEN). Did you hear that, Father? Abie! My new son-in-law! Well, that name better have an O or a Mac stuck in front of it!

COHEN. A Mac or an O in the front of a beautiful name like Levy?

PATRICK (*crosses down to* FATHER WHALEN). My God! Did you hear that other name, Father? Abie Levy, my new son-in-law!

FATHER WHALEN. Sit down, Patrick, sit down!

(PATRICK *and* FATHER WHALEN *ad lib., both shaking heads and arguing, sit on davenport.*)

COHEN. And a fine boy he is too! He met Rose Marys when the Var vas here.

SOLOMON. Oi! Oi!

COHEN. Solomon, for why do you do dod? Oi! Oi!

(MRS. COHEN *enters left. She is all aglow.*)

MRS. COHEN (*to* SOLOMON). Vod a vedding! Solomon, you have did yourself proud for vonce.

SOLOMON. Oi! Oi!

MRS. COHEN. Vod's the matter? Iss the expense worrying you already yet?

COHEN (*now thoroughly alarmed at* SOLOMON'S *distress*). Mama, he's been doink dod since I came in, after the wedding.

MRS. COHEN. Solomon, heve you god a pain?

SOLOMON. I've god a sometink. I didn't vont, but now I've god it!

MRS. COHEN. That's the way I felt too about my appendix.

SOLOMON. It ain't my appendixes! I vish it vas!

MRS. COHEN. Solomon! If you vished it vas, you vish it vasn't! I know, I had the operation. Didn't I, Papa? (*She goes up.*)

COHEN (*center*). Yes, Mama!

(*All this time* PATRICK *is looking on as though he would like to wring them* ALL *by the necks.*)

FATHER WHALEN. Well, Patrick, if our Rose Mary has married this boy, we'll have to make the best of it!

COHEN. Sure! They are crazy aboud each other. Never did I see such love. (*Crosses to* PATRICK.)

SOLOMON. They are both crazy!

COHEN. Solomon, Rosie is a wonderful girl. I vould take her in a minute. (*Crosses back to center.*)

MRS. COHEN. Isaac! (*She swings about her fan, just grazing* COHEN's *face.*)

COHEN (*covering himself*). Vouldn't ve, Mama? (*Crosses to* MRS. COHEN. *Enter* RABBI *left.*)

MRS. COHEN. I vould take her in a minute, vouldn't ve, Papa? (BOTH *go up left.*)

SOLOMON. I'd sell her for a nickel!

PATRICK (*rising, crosses to center*). You don't have to! I'm going to take her away for nothing.

SOLOMON. Oi! If you vould do me such a favor!

COHEN. But, Solomon, you had the Rabbi marry them yourself, for vhy have you changed?

SOLOMON. Esk him! (*Pointing to* PATRICK.)

COHEN (*crosses to* PATRICK). Do you know?

PATRICK. I have a sneaking suspicion I do! (*Doubles up his fist.*)

COHEN (*crosses to* MRS. COHEN). Mama, I don'd like dose sneaking suspiciousness!

(RABBI *goes to* PATRICK.)

RABBI. Are you Rosie's father?

PATRICK. *Rosie's* father? (*Turning to* FATHER WHALEN.)

SOLOMON. Oi! Oi!

RABBI (*center*). Why, Solomon, what is the matter, has something happened?

SOLOMON (*pointing to* PATRICK). Look at him! And ask me! I shall die from shame! His name's Murphy!

PATRICK (*in a rage*). You'll die for shame at looking at me! Shure, you won't be able to see me, you won't be able to see anybody—you won't have room enough to open your eyes, you poor little abbreviated excuse for an apostrophe! (*Starts for* SOLOMON. FATHER WHALEN *stops him.*)

SOLOMON (*rising, to* PATRICK). I didn't hear a word you said, but I'll get even for it!

RABBI. Solomon, don't do anything rash.

SOLOMON. Dod little Irisher! Marrying my son Abie against his vill. No vonder, she vouldn't vait. She vas afraid he'd back oud. The—the—the little—Irish A.P.A.

(*He exits left quickly.* PATRICK *starts right after him;* FATHER WHALEN *holding his arm.*)

PATRICK. Let me loose, Father—let me loose.

FATHER WHALEN. Patrick, where are you going?

PATRICK (*breaking away at the door left*). I'm going after that little runt and make him eat those words along with every damned orange in this place!

(*Exits left;* FATHER WHALEN *crosses to front of davenport.*)

COHEN. Come on, Mama! Ve god to help Solomon. (*Starting after* PATRICK.)

MRS. COHEN. Isaac! Don'd bud in. If you come between them you'll get hit both vays! (*She exits left.*)

COHEN (*following her*). When I get through with that Irishman, I'll make him eat all the oranges in California.

(FATHER WHALEN *and* RABBI *look at each other for a second, then they smile.* RABBI *crosses to left of davenport.*)

MRS. COHEN (*off left*). Isaac! Isaac!

FATHER WHALEN. It looks like war between the Murphys and the Levys.

RABBI. Yes, I pity the young folks!

FATHER WHALEN. So do I. They are going to have their hands full. Poor Rose Mary!

RABBI. I feel sorry for Abie, too. He's a fine lad.

FATHER WHALEN. And Rose Mary's a wonderful girl. But what are we going to do about it?

RABBI. Seems to me, it's a little too late to do anything.

FATHER WHALEN. Yes, there is no use locking the barn door after the mare has gone. You married them, didn't you?

RABBI. Yes, and Solomon asked me to tie the knot good and tight.

(*He smiles at this.* FATHER WHALEN *laughs too.*)

FATHER WHALEN (*looking at* RABBI, *closely*). You know, your face is very familiar.

RABBI. I have been thinking the same of yours. You live here in New York?

FATHER WHALEN. No! California. I came on with Patrick for Rose Mary's wedding. (RABBI *indicates davenport.* FATHER WHALEN *sits and then the* RABBI *sits.*) Have you ever been in California?

RABBI. No—never west of Pittsburgh!

FATHER WHALEN. And I have never been East, except during the war. I went over there!

RABBI. I went over there too!

FATHER WHALEN. Maybe that's where we met.

RABBI. Most likely. That is where Abie and Rosie met—Abie did his bit. He was quite a hero.

FATHER WHALEN. Wounded?

RABBI. Very badly!

FATHER WHALEN. Shure, I have comforted a great many boys of your faith in their last hours when there wasn't a good rabbi around.

RABBI. And I did the same thing for a good many boys of your faith—when we couldn't find a good priest.

FATHER WHALEN. We didn't have much time to think of any one religion on the battle fields.

RABBI. I'll say not!

FATHER WHALEN. Shure they all had the same God above them. And what with all the shells bursting, and the shrapnel flying, with no one knowing just what moment death would come, Catholics, Hebrews and Protestants alike forgot their prejudice and came to realize that all faiths and creeds have about the same destination after all.

RABBI (*shaking his head*). True. Very true.

FATHER WHALEN. Shure, we're all trying to get to the same place when we pass on. We're just going by different routes. We can't all go on the same train.

RABBI. And just because you are not riding on my train, why should I say your train won't get there?

FATHER WHALEN. Exactly!

RABBI. You know (*Rises.*) I wish I could remember where I met you.

FATHER WHALEN (*rises*). I feel the same way. However, as long as we both feel that we have met before, we're old friends. My name's Whalen. John Whalen. (*Holding out his hand cordially.*)

RABBI. And mine is Samuels! Jacob Samuels! (*Taking* FATHER WHALEN'S *hand, clasping it warmly.*)

FATHER WHALEN. John Whalen and Jacob Samuels! (*Laughs.*) Shure, 'tis almost as bad as Murphy and Levy!

RABBI (*laughing too*). Yes, except that we're not married! (*They* BOTH *laugh heartily at this.*)

(PATRICK *and* SOLOMON *heard quarreling off left.* BRIDESMAIDS *scream and rush on to* RABBI; *where he tries to pacify them.* ROSE MARY *dashes out of door left. She stops on seeing* FATHER WHALEN. *Goes to him, throws herself into his arms.*)

ROSE MARY. Oh, Father Whalen!

FATHER WHALEN. There—there—child!

ROSE MARY. Can't you do something with Father? He's gone mad!

FATHER WHALEN. Such a pretty bride too! (*He looks around at the* GIRLS.) Faith, dear, you look frightened to death!

ROSE MARY. I have reason to be, Father! You ought to hear Abie's father and my father fight! Oh, such language!!

RABBI. Girls, wait in here, out of the way. It is just as well to keep out of sight of both fathers. Don't you think so, Father Whalen? (*The* GIRLS *exeunt with bit of chatter left center.*)

FATHER WHALEN. I do that! Shure, there's no use waving a red flag at a bull, unless you want more trouble.

(RABBI *closes doors after them, and remains up left center.*)

ROSE MARY. We couldn't have any more trouble!

RABBI. Oh, yes you can, my child—much more than this!

(ABIE *enters on the run; he stops on seeing* ROSE MARY; *takes a deep breath of relief.*)

ABIE. Oh!—I thought you had gone! (*Goes to her.*)

ROSE MARY. Isn't it awful? (*Crosses to* ABIE.)

ABIE. It's worse than I expected!

FATHER WHALEN (*right center*). Is this Abie?

ROSE MARY. Oh, pardon me, Father—I thought you'd met him! Abie, this is Father Whalen.—Father brought him all the way from California to marry us!

FATHER WHALEN (*holds out his hand as* ABIE *hesitates, before he sees* FATHER WHALEN *is so cordial*). I'm glad to know you, Son!

ABIE. Father Whalen, I'm glad to know *you!*

RABBI. Where are the fond fathers? (*Loud ad lib off left.*)

SOLOMON (*off left*). I tell you, don't push!

PATRICK (*also off left. A growl*).

FATHER WHALEN. Ah! (*Crosses to front of davenport.*)

ABIE. There they are.

ROSE MARY. Oh, dear!

ABIE. It's all your father's fault, if he hadn't come, everything would have been all right!

ROSE MARY. It is not my father's fault! It's your father's! I never saw such a man!

(FATHER WHALEN *turns away right, smiling.*)

ABIE. My father is wonderful, he is just a little stirred up right now, that is all!

ROSE MARY. *All!* (*Turning away; crosses to front of davenport.*) If he is only stirred up now, what is he like when he's really mad?

FATHER WHALEN. Here—here! Don't you two start to fight too! (*Pats* ROSE MARY *on the shoulder.*)

RABBI. That is just what the two fathers would like!

ABIE (*crosses to her*). There—there—Rose Mary dear! Don't cry!

ROSE MARY (*crying*). But your father said he'd sell me for a nickel!

(FATHER WHALEN *goes to right of davenport, crosses center to* RABBI.)

ABIE (*taking her in his arms*). But you don't belong to my father, you belong to me! And I wouldn't sell you for the whole world with a fence around it!

(FATHER WHALEN *and the* RABBI *exchange glances and smile.*)

ROSE MARY. And my father said he was going to take me away from you and have the marriage annulled. He says that no rabbi cuts any ice with him!

ABIE. Well, the rabbi didn't marry him, he married us!

SOLOMON (*runs in to center; stops*). Abie, take your arm avay from her!

PATRICK (*entering after* SOLOMON; *stops too, left center*). The marriage isn't legal!

SOLOMON. No, ve just found out that you ain'd married at all!

RABBI (*down left*). I beg your pardon. I have married a great many people—I know my business!

SOLOMON. No reflection, Dr. Samuels! It ain'd your fault this vone didn't took!

ABIE. What do you mean we are not married?

PATRICK. Her name isn't Murpheski! It's Murphy. Murpheski!! (*Making a face.*) And another thing—that license you got isn't legal with that name on it!

SOLOMON (*smiling delightedly*). You see! Dr. Samuels, you merried Rose Murpheski—dhere ain'd no Rose Murpheski, so dhere ain'd no merriage! Oi! Vod a relief!

PATRICK. Rose Mary—take off that dress and veil! I am going to take you home!

SOLOMON. I'll send you a letter of tenks for it!

PATRICK (*looking down belligerently on him*). I don't want anything from you but silence, and plenty of that!

SOLOMON. All right! All right!

PATRICK (*turns back to* ROSE MARY). Rose Mary! (*She hasn't moved from* ABIE'S *side.*)

ABIE (*holding her in his arms*). She isn't going with you or anyone else.

SOLOMON. Abie, don'd be foolish. You ain'd merried!

ABIE. Yes we are!!

SOLOMON. Bud id didn't took! Esk anybody! They'll tell you the same thing! You merried Rosie Murpheski. She ain'd!

RABBI. I'm afraid there might be some truth in what your father says, Abie!

ROSE MARY. We are married whether you like it or not! Aren't we, Abie?

ABIE. Yes, dear, and if this marriage didn't take——

SOLOMON. I von'd let you merry her again!

ABIE. You can't prevent it!

PATRICK. But I can!!

ABIE. Well, I married Rose Mary Murphy just one week ago today in Jersey City!

(ABIE *takes* ROSE MARY *in his arms.* SOLOMON *grabs his head.*)

SOLOMON. Oi!! I nefer did like dod town! (*Up center.*)

PATRICK (*to left center*). Rose Mary, is this true?

ROSE MARY. Yes.

SOLOMON. Oi, such a headache!

PATRICK. Were you married by a priest?

(ROSE MARY *frightened—looks at* ABIE.)

ABIE. No. By a Methodist minister!

SOLOMON. It's gettink worse!

PATRICK. Then you are not married!

ABIE. Well, try and take her away from me!

PATRICK. If you thought you were married so good and tight last week, why did you do it over again?

SOLOMON. To make it vorser!

(SOLOMON *and* PATRICK *look at one another as if to start another fight.*)

ABIE. To satisfy my father.

SOLOMON (*getting furious*). To satisfy me! Say, do you tink I am satisfied? Look at me!

PATRICK (*shouting, starting toward* SOLOMON). *You* have nothing on me!

(SOLOMON, *frightened, goes to the* RABBI, *his hand on his heart.*)

FATHER WHALEN (*crosses to* PATRICK). Patrick, as I told you before, you'd better make the best of it! The children have done all they could to satisfy both fathers.

PATRICK. Did they try to satisfy me? No! They get a Methodist minister first and a rabbi next—would I let a minister or a rabbi marry me?

FATHER WHALEN. Well, marriages by ministers and Rabbis are as legally binding as by priests or others!

PATRICK. They are not married!

ROSE MARY (*crying*). Abie!

SOLOMON. I'm going to phone my lawyer! (*He starts for the door left yelling.*) Cohen! Oh, Isaac!!

(PATRICK *follows him.* SOLOMON *exits.*)

PATRICK (*to* ROSE MARY). Get into your street clothes, young lady. Father Whalen you see that she doesn't run away with him! I'm going after this poor fish and see what his lawyer has to say. They're not going to put anything over on me. (*Exits left.*)

(*This leaves* RABBI, FATHER WHALEN, ROSE MARY *and* ABIE.)

ROSE MARY (*crying*). Abie!

ABIE. What is it, dear? (*Trying to soothe her.*)

ROSE MARY. He doesn't believe we are married. He says it didn't take!

ABIE. But we are!

ROSE MARY. Oh, I told you we should have been married by a priest in Jersey City!

ABIE. Your father wouldn't be satisfied no matter who married us!

RABBI (*down left*). Father Whalen, I wouldn't suggest it, but as long as the young folks have made a business of getting married, I don't think it would do any harm to marry them again in her faith, do you?

FATHER WHALEN. I don't think so!

ROSE MARY. Father Whalen, would you? (*Crosses to him.*)

FATHER WHALEN. Where is the telephone?

ABIE. On the table! (*Indicates telephone.*)

FATHER WHALEN. I must get permission from my superior. (FATHER WHALEN *goes to telephone. Looks in address book for number. Then takes telephone.*)

ABIE (*crosses to him*). But Dr. Samuels, why all this red tape?

RABBI (ROSE MARY *goes to left of* FATHER WHALEN. *Up left*). Every great institution must have organization, my boy, and we must respect their rules and regulations.

FATHER WHALEN. Give me Vanderbilt zero, two, three, four. That's right. Vanderbilt zero, two, three, four.

ROSE MARY (*nervously*). Suppose your superior says no?

ABIE (*to* ROSE MARY). Suppose he isn't in?

FATHER WHALEN. Sssh—Hello—— Vanderbilt zero, two, three, four? Is his Grace, the Archbishop in? Father Whalen from California, speaking. I'm sorry to trouble, but it's a very serious matter. Yes, yes, I must speak to him personally.

ROSE MARY. Tell him to hurry. Father will be here any minute!

RABBI. Father Whalen, there is a phone extension in the other room. You had better talk from it.

ABIE. But they are liable to want to use this one, and then they'll hear!

RABBI. I'll guard this phone, until the matter is settled one way or the other. (*To* ABIE.) Show Father where it is!

ABIE. This way, Father Whalen. (*Up to arch left center and exits.*)

RABBI. Hurry, you haven't much time.

FATHER WHALEN (*starts for arch left center*). Come, Rose Mary! (*Turns in doorway.*) And if his Grace says yes, I'll tie the charmed knot so tight, it'll make you dizzy! (*Exits left center.*)

ROSE MARY. Dr. Samuels! Say a prayer for us.

RABBI. What will I say?

ROSE MARY. Say please God, make the Archbishop say yes. (*She exits.*)

RABBI. All right! (RABBI *closes door with a satisfied smile on his face.*)

MRS. COHEN (*enters left; sees* RABBI). Nefer did I see such a night! (*Sits on davenport.*) Nefer was I so tired! Oh dear! If my appendix wasn't out, I know I'd have it again!

RABBI (*down to* MRS. COHEN). You mustn't worry about it. Everything is going to be all right!

(PATRICK *enters left. He looks around.*)

PATRICK. Where is my daughter?

RABBI. I think you told her to change her dress.

PATRICK (*center*). Oh, she has gone to do it?

RABBI. You told her to, didn't you?

PATRICK. Where's the telephone in this house? I want to make reservations for California. I'm going to get out of this town on the first train and take me daughter with me!

RABBI (*goes to telephone*). I'll get your number for you, Mr. Murphy. What road do you want to go by? The Penn?

PATRICK. The fastest road out of New York, and the soonest. (RABBI *takes receiver off and listens.*) What's the matter, won't Central answer?

RABBI. The line's busy!

PATRICK. You never can get a number when you want it! (*Starts for telephone.*) Here, give me that phone. I'll show you how to get it!

RABBI. No, no, Mr. Murphy—I insist on getting your number for you!

PATRICK (*ad lib*). I know but—

RABBI. There is someone speaking now, and we must not disturb them!

PATRICK. But if you'll allow—

RABBI. It would not be the right thing to do!

PATRICK. Yes, but if you'll—

RABBI. You wouldn't want to be disturbed, would you?

PATRICK. (*turns away center, disgusted*). Ah!

RABBI. Central—give me Penn—six, five, six hundred.

PATRICK. Whoever it is, by this time they should be through talking!

RABBI. All right, thank you! (*Hangs up.*)

PATRICK. What's the matter now?

RABBI. The line's busy!

PATRICK (*in rage*). Oh, I'll never get out of this damn town!

(RABBI *crosses to arch left center.* SOLOMON *enters left, followed by* COHEN.)

SOLOMON. Oo—ah—

COHEN. Oo-ah—oo!

SOLOMON (*to* RABBI). My lawyer says dod no matter vod I say, dhey are married so tight, it would make your head curl! (*Sits in big chair left.*)

MRS. COHEN. Vod you tink! Didn't you tell Dr. Samuels to tie a good knot?

SOLOMON (*almost a scream*). I should be so foolish! Oi! Oi!

PATRICK (*bounds across room to* SOLOMON *and just misses tramping on* COHEN, *who is in the way*). If you don't stop saying Oi, Oi, you'll drive me to drink!

(PATRICK *turns, looks at* COHEN, *who frightened, crosses and sits left of* MRS. COHEN. *As* PATRICK *continues to look at him,* MRS. COHEN *passes* COHEN *to right of her and then looks defiantly at* PATRICK.)

SOLOMON. Did you hear that I'll drive him to drink! I'd like to drive you to something for wishing an Irish wife on my Abie!

PATRICK. Wishing it on him! The devil take him and all his.

RABBI. Ssh! Ssh! You know what it says in the Scriptures about family quarrels?

PATRICK. Family quarrels! Do I look like a member of this family? (*He looks around at them.*) No, and my daughter isn't going to be. Thank heaven, she wasn't married by a priest!

RABBI. And would that make any difference to you, Mr. Murphy?

SOLOMON. Dod's vhere he is lucky! He can do something widout fear or trembling. Bud wid me! (*Pointing to* RABBI.) You tie the knot and I'm tied to it!

PATRICK. I'm going to untie that knot, don't you worry!

SOLOMON. Worry if you untie it? If you please, I'll be very much obliged.

PATRICK (*goes to telephone*). I don't want you to be anything but out of my life. Penn six, five, six hundred and don't you tell me the line's busy!

ABIE (*off left center*). With this ring I do thee wed.

(RABBI *opens the door, disclosing wedding party—*FATHER WHALEN'S *voice is heard coming out clear and strong.*)

FATHER WHALEN. I now pronounce you man and wife. "Those whom God hath joined together, let no man put asunder."

(*As this is heard,* SOLOMON *comes to; he listens as though he cannot believe his ears.* PATRICK *is spellbound for the second, too.*)

PATRICK. My God! They've done it again!

(SOLOMON *turns, looks up at left center door, where is the picture of* ABIE *and* ROSE MARY *with* FATHER WHALEN *between them, the* BRIDESMAIDS *grouped around them, collapses in chair as*

THE CURTAIN FALLS

ACT THREE

SCENE—*In* ABIE'S *and* ROSE MARY'S *little modest apartment.*

It is small and not elegantly furnished, but everything shows that a woman's hand has tastefully arranged everything.

There is a door direct center at back, which leads into a foyer. Another door center at back of foyer leads to the hall outside. A door down right leads into the dining room. A window up right. Another door up left leads into the bedroom. There is a table left center with a chair on either side of it. A console with mirror above it, is down left. A Christmas tree stands in the upper right corner. Other furniture to dress the room.

There is a small table with a chair between right door and window; a service table left of the center arch; a chair above the console down left.

TIME: *It is Christmas Eve. One year later than Act Two.*

DISCOVERED: ABIE *and* ROSE MARY *are discovered. She sitting on chair just left of Christmas tree.* ABIE *kneeling left of her. She is holding a baby. The moonlight is streaming through the window right, on them. All lights are out.* ROSE MARY *is singing an Irish lullaby "Too-ro-la too."*

Together, they rise, and walk slowly to door, left, she singing softly. She goes out. ABIE *looks after her for a second, then turns on lights.*

ROSE MARY (*re-enters*). Oh, I hope that baby sleeps now.

ABIE. So do I. Hurry up, dear. (*Gets up on chair at tree.*)

ROSE MARY. Well, what do you want next? (*Holding two ornaments up to him.*)

ABIE. Where's the star that goes on the top?

ROSE MARY (*getting it from table left center*). Here it is. (*She takes it over to him, he puts it on the highest part of the tree. They kiss.* ABIE *gets off chair.*)

ABIE. The star of Bethlehem! Only we haven't any Wise Men to see it!

ROSE MARY. This is the baby's Christmas tree, star and all. (ABIE *gets off chair.*)

ABIE. Of course it is! So we should worry about the Wise Men, eh what? (*They embrace.*)

ROSE MARY (*goes over to the table, picks up another ornament which she takes back to* ABIE). Say, Abie, did your father ever have a Christmas tree for you? (*Crosses to the table.*)

ABIE. My father, a Christmas tree? (*He laughs.*)

ROSE MARY. Christmas wouldn't be Christmas to me without a tree.

ABIE. Well, my father doesn't believe there is such a day in the year.

ROSE MARY (*handing him another ornament*). Didn't you ever get things?

ABIE (*putting it on the tree*). You mean presents? (*Kiss.*)

ROSE MARY. Yes.

ABIE. Not directly from Father. But I found out later that he used to give Sarah money to get things for me, so I would have toys and things. Like the other boys.

ROSE MARY. You know, Abie, I can't understand. Our fathers seemed to love us so much, yet they won't forgive us for marrying.

ABIE (*gets down from the chair and puts his arm around her*). Now, don't start to worry again about that. You are not strong enough yet. Aren't we happy?

ROSE MARY. Oh, Abie! (*Looking up into his face lovingly.*) But you worry too!

ABIE. Oh, I know it. But every time I do, I say to myself, "Well, old boy, you've got the dearest—(*kiss*)—sweetest—(*kiss*)—wife in the world, so why worry?"

ROSE MARY. That's right, we have each other.

ABIE. Don't forget our family, too!

ROSE MARY (*running to the door left*). Oh, Abie, I put the baby's bottle of milk on the electric stove to heat, and forgot all about it. I bet I've broken another bottle. I'm always breaking them. (*She tiptoes off.*)

(ABIE *sings "Too ra loo ra." As she shuts the door. The door bell rings. He goes to the door center. As he opens the outside door in the foyer,* MR. *and* MRS. COHEN *are there. They enter.* MRS. COHEN *first,* COHEN *behind so close he cannot be seen until she steps aside.* COHEN *pulls cane out of coat and frightens* MRS. COHEN.)

ABIE. Well, look who's here! Come in, Mrs. Cohen! How are you, Mr. Cohen?

MRS. COHEN. Hello, Abie! (*Bustling in with her regular spirit.*) Ve vere just goink home from the theater und I said to Isaac come on, let's go see Abie and Rosie a minute. Didn't I, Papa?

COHEN. You did, Mama.

ABIE. I'm glad you did. Won't you take off your things?

COHEN. Yes, Abie!

MRS. COHEN. Sure, why not? Isaac! Be a gentleman once in a while! (*She stoops and* COHEN *takes off her coat, and places it off center.*) Where's our little Rose Mary? (*Sits right of table.*)

ABIE. She went to fix the baby's milk.

MRS. COHEN. Oh, how I love babies!

ABIE. Yes, I've been a proud father just a month today.

COHEN (*back from foyer, hanging up things*). Don' the time fly? And you can do so much in a little while!

MRS. COHEN. Have you heard from your father yet?

ABIE (*crosses to* MRS. COHEN). No. Not a word.

COHEN (*brings chair down to left of table; sits.* ABIE *is between them*). Ve haven't mentioned it to him at all. Hev ve, Mama?

MRS. COHEN. Not a word! But he keeps talking about children all the time.

ABIE (*eagerly*). Does he really?

MRS. COHEN. Says he's goink to leave all his moneys to poor children.

COHEN. Yeh and I esked him, if the money vos goink to be left just for Jewish children, und he said——

MRS. COHEN. Yes, Abie, he said it!

ABIE. Said what?

MRS. COHEN. Go on, Isaac, tell him what he said.

COHEN. How can I tell him when always you butts in? All the time!

MRS. COHEN. I butts in?

COHEN. Yes, always you butts in, Mama! (BOTH *ad lib.*)

ABIE. Well, come, come, what did he say? (*Standing between them.*)

COHEN and MRS. COHEN (*together*). Well, he said——

COHEN (*excited*). Mama, we can't say it together individually!

MRS. COHEN. All right, go on tell him, I don't care.

COHEN. You said tell him in the first place.

MRS. COHEN (*angry*). Well, tell, I'm shut! Shtum shoin! (*Puts hand over mouth.*)

COHEN. Well, he said, he said—now you made me forget it, see that?

MRS. COHEN (*laughing*). I made him forget it! (BOTH *ad lib.*)

COHEN. Abie, vhere vas I?

ABIE. Why you were saying that my father was going to leave his money to Jewish children.

MRS. COHEN. Dots it, Abie!

COHEN. Fangst shoin vider un! Don't you know the old saying silence is fourteen carats—he said "Certainly nod! His money vas goink to be all kins of childrens."

MRS. COHEN. Yes sir, Abie! He said, "can children help it vhen dhere parents are voolish?"

COHEN. Und I said, "vell vhy nod leave id to Abie's children, they're poor?"

MRS. COHEN. He said, "I'm goink to leave my money to many childrens."

COHEN. Und I said, "vell give Rose and Abie a chance, dey might hev a lot, dey certain heven't wasted any time yet."

ABIE. Poor Dad! You know I think he is just dying to see what a son of his son's looks like. (*Crosses up to above tree.*)

COHEN. *Shure!* Vhy nod? I'd like to see it too!

MRS. COHEN. Isaac, you ain'd got a son. How can you see vhat his son looks like?

COHEN. I said if I had vone, I'd like to see it!

MRS. COHEN. But you haven't!

(ROSE MARY *enters the room.*)

COHEN (*crossing to* MRS. COHEN). Mama always you argue with me here.

MRS. COHEN. But how can you see your son——

COHEN (*crosses to her*). Yeh, but vhy argue in other people's houses? Soon we'll be home. Home! (*Goes up to door center. Back to right.*)

ROSE MARY (*crosses down left of table*). Hello, there!

MRS. COHEN (*goes to her and kisses her*). Didn't expect us so late, did you?

ROSE MARY. Awfully glad you stopped in. We're waiting up for Christmas. Hello, there. (*Crosses to* COHEN.)

COHEN (*comes down right*). I'm sorry, ve can't stay a minute.

MRS. COHEN. Isaac! (*She gives him look.*)

COHEN (*quickly*). Yes, ve can!

ROSE MARY. I have something awfully good to eat.

ABIE. And it's Kosher. (*Coming down left.*)

MRS. COHEN. Papa, we're goink to stay! (*Takes off hat, puts it on service table up left center.*)

COHEN. Mama say we stay! We stay!

ROSE MARY. How do you like the tree? (*They* ALL *turn, look at it.*)

COHEN (*not very enthusiastic*). Fine!

ROSE MARY. Abie trimmed it all by himself. (*She is bustling about like a good little housewife.*)

COHEN. You don't say so?

ROSE MARY. Excuse me, I must see about my ham, it's in the oven. (*She exits right.* ABIE *reacts to* MRS. COHEN.)

COHEN (*crosses to* ABIE, *delighted*). Abie, did she say ham?

MRS. COHEN (*crosses to* COHEN). Isaac, do you ead ham?

COHEN. Vell, Mama, I tasted it vonce. You would like id!

MRS. COHEN. Abie, ham ain'd Kosher food!

ABIE. I know it isn't! The ham is for Rose Mary and her friends. The Kosher food is for me and my friends.

COHEN. I hope Rosie ain'd god too many friends.

MRS. COHEN. Isaac!! Over there! Zits!

(COHEN *jumps and goes to left of table.*)

ABIE. Don't you worry though, it is a large ham. I bought it myself! (*The doorbell rings.*) Excuse me.

MRS. COHEN. Sure. Vy not?

(ABIE *answers bell, going to center door. It is* FATHER WHALEN. MRS. COHEN *sits right of table and* COHEN *left.*)

FATHER WHALEN. Good evening, Abie!

ABIE (*delighted*). Father Whalen! Come right in! Give me your hat and coat. I was never so glad to see anyone in my life! How have you been?

FATHER WHALEN. Splendid—(*Taking off his coat at the center door.*) And how is the good wife?

ABIE. Wonderful!!

FATHER WHALEN. And the family?

ABIE. Great! You know the Cohens, Father?

(FATHER WHALEN *comes down center.*)

FATHER WHALEN. Why, of course. (*Taking off gloves.*)

COHEN. Shure! I know de Father! Merry Christmas!

(*Both* MR. *and* MRS. COHEN *rise.*)

FATHER WHALEN. How are you both?

MRS. COHEN. Ve haven't seen you since the vedding! Oi! Vod a battle!

FATHER WHALEN. Everything seems peaceful enough now.

(ABIE *crosses toward door right.*)

MRS. COHEN. Yes, seems dod vay.

(FATHER WHALEN *nods for them to sit, which they do.*)

ABIE (*calls*). Rose Mary! Look!

ROSE MARY (*entering*). Oh, Father Whalen, I can't believe my eyes! Is it really you?

FATHER WHALEN. Your eyes are not deceiving you, Rose Mary!

MRS. COHEN (*smiling benignly*). She's glad to see somebody from home!

ROSE MARY. How's Father! Have you seen him lately? Is he well? He won't even write to us.

FATHER WHALEN. To be sure he's well. Fit as a fiddle!

ROSE MARY. Did he send his love?

FATHER WHALEN. No dear, not by me. (*She looks disappointed.*) But I think he would have liked to. (ROSE MARY *turns away, hides her face.*) There—there—Rose Mary! (*He motions to* ABIE *to go to her.*)

ABIE (*seeing that* ROSE MARY *is sad, taking her in his arms.*) Don't you care, dear! We should worry about your old father!

ROSE MARY. But I do care! He's my father!

MRS. COHEN. Vell, dod ain'd your fault!

(COHEN *shows his disgust at this remark. Bangs hand on table.* MRS. COHEN *turns to him.* COHEN *points to* FATHER WHALEN *and bangs hand on table again.* MRS. COHEN *turns back to* COHEN *and bangs table.* COHEN *is squelched.*)

ROSE MARY. (*Crosses to* MRS. COHEN *smiling, puts arm on her shoulder.*) Father Whalen come with me, I want to show you something. (*She is very sweet about this, takes* FATHER WHALEN'S *hand and leads him to door left.*) You've never seen anything so cunning in your life!

COHEN. Oi! Such a sveetness! If I vos the papa of a sveetness like dod, I vouldn't speak to anybody!

FATHER WHALEN. Lead me to it! I'm crazy about babies! (ROSE MARY *leads the way into the room left,* FATHER WHALEN *following.* ABIE *fixes tree.*)

ROSE MARY. Right in there, and don't make any noise. You know young babies sleep all the time!

FATHER WHALEN (*tiptoeing into room*). I won't.

ROSE MARY (*before she exits*). Mrs. Cohen will you look at my ham and see that it doesn't burn? (ROSE MARY *exits after* FATHER WHALEN, *closing the door.* MRS. COHEN *looks in blank amazement at* ABIE *and* COHEN.)

MRS. COHEN. Look at a ham! I never looked at a ham in my life!

COHEN (*amused*). Go on, Mama, look at it! It von't bite you.

ABIE. If I knew anything about it, I'd attend to it myself!

COHEN. So vould I! (*Rising.*)

MRS. COHEN. Never mind! Zits! I'll do id—(*crosses to door right*)—I'll do id, bud it's against my vill! (*With great effort she says the last and exits.* ABIE *smiles to himself.*)

COHEN (*crosses to* ABIE, *right*). I hope she don'd do anythink to spoil dod ham! I don'd trust Mama vid pork!

ABIE (*laughing*). She can't do anything to hurt it!

COHEN. Vell, I'd feel safer vatching her! I'm nod goink to take any chances. She's liable to make a fish out of it. (*Exits right.* ABIE *laughs.*)

ROSE MARY (*enters, followed by* FATHER WHALEN, *who closes the door*). Abie, did she go?

ABIE. Right in where the ham is. (*Exits right.*)

FATHER WHALEN. Where is everybody?

ROSE MARY. They're all in with the ham. Will you excuse me a second till I see if everything is all right? You know I'm chief cook and bottle washer now.

FATHER WHALEN. To be sure I will. Go right ahead! I understand! (ROSE MARY *starts to go.*) And Rose Mary—— (*Goes to her.*) I have a little Christmas present for you.

ROSE MARY. Oh, what is it?

FATHER WHALEN. I'll tell you later. Go in the kitchen until I call you.

(*As soon as* ROSE MARY *exits right,* FATHER WHALEN *goes to center door. Opens same, beckons, walks down center. A second later* PATRICK *enters. He has Christmas toys wrapped in paper. Everything for a girl.*)

PATRICK (*puts package back of table*). I wondered where you had gotten to!

FATHER WHALEN. They have company.

PATRICK. They have?

FATHER WHALEN (*pause*). The Cohens! (PATRICK, *who is taking off coat, makes motion as if to put it on again.*) You remember them?

PATRICK. I'd like to forget them! (*Puts coat on again, sees tree, hangs coat on tree in hall.*)

FATHER WHALEN. So you've been shopping, eh?

PATRICK. Yes, I saw a little store down the street and thought I'd get a few things for my granddaughter. (*Crosses to back of table.*)

FATHER WHALEN. Suppose it isn't that kind of a baby?

PATRICK. What—they have a boy?

FATHER WHALEN. I said, suppose!

PATRICK. A boy would have to have the name of Levy tacked on to him forever. That would be terrible!

FATHER WHALEN (*crosses to* PATRICK). Well, Levy isn't a bad name.

PATRICK. Huh!

(ABIE *enters, stands very quietly. They do not see him.*)

FATHER WHALEN. If it's good enough for Rose Mary; it ought to be good enough for her baby.

PATRICK. That's the trouble! It isn't good enough for Rose Mary! Why, she is a direct descendant of the Kings of Ireland!

FATHER WHALEN. Well, Abie might be a direct descendant of the Kings of Jerusalem!

ABIE. No! Just plain Jew. But I love Rose Mary, Mr. Murphy, more than you do!

PATRICK. Oh, you do, do you?

ABIE. Yes, for I wouldn't do anything in the world to cause her the tiniest bit of unhappiness. Can you say as much?

PATRICK. Listen to him! (*Turns away left, to sideboard, looks at decanter.*)

FATHER WHALEN. The lad is right, Patrick. (*Crosses to* ABIE.) Abie, will you do something for me?

ABIE. Anything, Father!

FATHER WHALEN. Keep everybody in the kitchen as long as you can, will you?

ABIE. Don't you want Rose Mary?

FATHER WHALEN. Not yet, laddie! I'll call you! (*The doorbell rings.*) I'll answer the door! You keep them in there!

ABIE. All right! I suppose you know what you are doing, Father!

FATHER WHALEN. I do, lad, trust me!

(*As* ABIE *exits,* FATHER WHALEN *turns to see* PATRICK *looking into a whisky decanter on sideboard. He smiles and goes to center door, opening same. It is the* RABBI.)

RABBI. Well, well, if it isn't my old friend, John Whalen!

FATHER WHALEN. Jacob Samuels, how are you?

(*The* RABBI *enters, takes off hat and coat.* PATRICK *is sore at the interruption.*)

PATRICK. Huh! The Jew parson!

FATHER WHALEN (*down center*). Come in!

RABBI. Where are the young folks? (*Comes down center.*)

FATHER WHALEN (*in soft tone; pointing to kitchen*). In there.

(RABBI *starts to go.* FATHER WHALEN *touches him on shoulder, and points to* PATRICK.)

RABBI (*looks at* PATRICK). Is that Mr. Murphy?

PATRICK (*looking at him as though he would like to fight*). It is that!

RABBI. You came all the way from California to spend your Christmas with Rosie?

PATRICK. I did not. I didn't come to see Rose Mary! 'Tis the child I came to see and if it looks Irish, it gets all my money. (*Crosses to center.* RABBI *and* FATHER WHALEN *smile at each other. Turning to* FATHER WHALEN.) Father Whalen, I'll be right back. I couldn't carry everything up the stairs at once. (*He turns and exits center.*)

FATHER WHALEN. His bark is far worse than his bite. He's dying to see his daughter.

(BOTH *sit at table—*RABBI *left—* FATHER WHALEN *right.*)

RABBI. Of course he is. So is Solomon just as anxious to see his son.

FATHER WHALEN. The young folks have stuck it out. They deserve to be forgiven.

RABBI. 'Tis the young folks who should do the forgiving. Their only crime is loving not wisely but well.

FATHER WHALEN. Abie's a fine boy!

RABBI (*not to be outdone*). And Rosie's a fine girl!

FATHER WHALEN. Indeed she is!

RABBI. Father, did you show Patrick the—— (*Pointing to bedroom.*)

FATHER WHALEN. No, not yet. I knew he was anxious so I thought a little punishment would be good for him. The stubborn old Mick! (*They laugh.*) Patrick is sure it's a girl.

RABBI. And Solomon is just as sure it's a boy. I must take a peek myself! (*Goes to left door, and looks out. Motions for* FATHER WHALEN *to come.*) Father did you ever see anything so sweet in your life?

FATHER WHALEN. Never! (*Looking over* RABBI'S *shoulder.*) And I've seen a great many babies too!

(*They exit left, tiptoeing off; closing the door. The door center opens cautiously, and* SOLOMON *sticks his head in the door. He has overcoat, hat and earmuffs on; looks in; removes coat and hat, looks in door again, then removes earmuffs, hangs them up; then enters with pillow sham containing Teddy Bear, horse, engine, drum and sticks; goes to back of table. Crosses to right, listens, then sits on chair up right of tree; takes out toys, places them on the floor: takes out horse, whose tail is off. He looks it over, finally finding where tail belongs and puts it on. As he puts engine on floor* PATRICK *enters with phonograph.* PATRICK *puts phonograph left of tree, then goes to package back of table, and begins to open it,* SOLOMON *puts drum down and* PATRICK *hears it. He looks toward door right, then they* BOTH *spy each other.* SOLOMON *and* PATRICK *turn, face each other,* BOTH *come center, then sniff—turn away two steps and look at each other; then* SOLOMON *gets Teddy Bear and places it under the tree—*PATRICK *pushes Teddy Bear* *over to make room for his doll—triumphant attitude.* PATRICK *gets dolls placed under tree—same business as* SOLOMON, SOLOMON *gets horse and places Teddy Bear on it—same business.* PATRICK *unwraps go-cart, places doll in it, same business.* SOLOMON *gets engine, runs it on table several times.* PATRICK *gets phonograph, starts it—it has a record, an Irish jig—places it under tree—dances a few steps.* SOLOMON *gets toy drum, beats it, trying to drown out jig.* PATRICK *gets toy horn, faces* SOLOMON, *blowing it.* RABBI *enters from left followed by* FATHER WHALEN.)

RABBI. Here, here!

FATHER WHALEN. Glory be to God!

RABBI. What is this? Your second childhood? (PATRICK *and* SOLOMON *both look foolish.* PATRICK *turns off phonograph.*)

PATRICK. I wanted to see that everything worked right for my granddaughter. (*Crosses to front of table.*)

SOLOMON (*rising, laughing sarcastically*). Listen to him, he thinks it's a girl!

PATRICK (*glowering at him*). Do you know what it is?

SOLOMON. No! But I know it isn't a girl!

FATHER WHALEN. Come on, Patrick, be reasonable!

SOLOMON. Oi! Oi! Such a name! Patrick! Patrick Murphy!

PATRICK. Patrick's a grand old name! It speaks for itself!

SOLOMON. Vell, ven you call Solomon, you don'd have to use your imagination.

(*All this time* FATHER WHALEN *and* RABBI *are standing back; trying to get a chance to stop them.*)

RABBI. Solomon! Solomon! (*Down to* SOLOMON.)

FATHER WHALEN (*down to* PATRICK). Patrick!

SOLOMON. Oi! Dod I should live to see my son married to a Murphy!

PATRICK. Well, you may not know it, but your time has almost come!

RABBI. Come, come, this will never do! If you are going to fight like this, it would have been better to have stayed away!

PATRICK. What? Me stay away from my granddaughter on Christmas?

SOLOMON. She would be better, if she didn't have a grandpapa?

PATRICK. And are you speaking for yourself?

SOLOMON. I heven't a granddaughter!

FATHER WHALEN. Well, if you had one, I don't think she'd own you!

PATRICK. And that's no lie! (*Turning away.*)

FATHER WHALEN. Or you either, Patrick!

PATRICK (*surprised*). What's the idea?

FATHER WHALEN. She'd be ashamed of the fighting. You know, Patrick, the Irish are a great people!

PATRICK. Don't I know it! (*Throwing out his chest.*)

SOLOMON. Huh! Say some more funny things!

FATHER WHALEN. And the Jews are a wonderful people!

PATRICK. That's the best joke tonight!

FATHER WHALEN. Now if the Jews and the Irish would only stop fighting, and get together, they'd own a corner of the world!

RABBI. You're right, Father, and I think they ought to start getting together right here!

PATRICK (*starting for* SOLOMON). That suits me, by golly, that suits me!

SOLOMON. Pas kudnack!

FATHER WHALEN (*stops him; crosses to* SOLOMON). I'm an Irishman, and I never saw a finer lad in my life than Abraham Levy!

RABBI (*crosses to* PATRICK). I'm a Jew, and I never saw a finer girl in the world than Rosie!!

PATRICK. Her name isn't Rosie! It's Rose Mary!

RABBI. Very well, Rose Mary, if that pleases you better!

SOLOMON. The Rose Mary's don'd please me better! It's Rosie!

PATRICK. Whose daughter is she?

SOLOMON. She ain'd your daughter any more. You disowned her, you said so. Ain'd you?

RABBI. Here, here, neither of you should say anything! Both of you ought to be ashamed. Instead of making the best of a bad situation, you make it worse!

FATHER WHALEN. 'Tis the truth he's speaking, Patrick! (*Walks up.*)

RABBI. Now Abie and Rosie—
PATRICK. Rose Mary!
SOLOMON. Rosie!
(*Spoken together.*)

RABBI. Very well, Abie and his wife have been very happy here. For one year—neither one of you have given a cent toward helping them. And some of the times have been pretty hard. Abie only makes a small salary and Rosie has had to do all the work, even do her own washing.

SOLOMON. Vell, dod's a good pizzness for the Irish!

(*Pause.* RABBI *and* FATHER WHALEN *go up center.* PATRICK *starts for* SOLOMON, *but* FATHER WHALEN *motions him back.*)

PATRICK. Well, that's better than peddling shoestrings!

SOLOMON. They named vonce a song "The Irish Washerwoman."

PATRICK. I could say something insulting, but I won't, you funny wizened-up old Shylock! (*Turns away.*)

SOLOMON. Did you give them any money yourself this year? No! You stingy old A.P.A. (*Walks toward center.*)

PATRICK (*starting after* SOLOMON). Don't call me an A.P.A. I belong to the Ancient Order of Hibernians—and believe me, that ain't no A.P.A. hangout!

(FATHER WHALEN *stops him.* RABBI *goes to* SOLOMON.)

RABBI. Solomon, why do you call him an A.P.A.?

SOLOMON. I don't know. It makes him mad. (*To* FATHER WHALEN.) I never knew there vos any difference between them.

PATRICK. My God! Will you listen to the dumb thing. Any difference between them? And I live to hear such a thing!

SOLOMON. Vell, nod being Irish myself, I should know the difference. Bud—I'm glad I insulted you. I'll say it again. (RABBI *and* FATHER WHALEN *go up a few steps.*)

PATRICK (*going toward him threateningly*). If you say it once more, it will be the last thing you say in this world! Now speak up, or forever hold your peace!! (*By this time he is standing over* SOLOMON.)

SOLOMON (*smiling up at him*). Vell, if I say id, I vill forever hold my peace!

PATRICK. You bet you will! (*He walks away.*)

SOLOMON. I don'd have to say id!

PATRICK (*satisfied that he has won the battle*). You're wise!

SOLOMON. I'll tink it! (*Laughs.*)

PATRICK (*spinning around immediately to him*). Oh, you'll tink it, will you? (*Raising his fist.*)

SOLOMON (*blandly*). Vell, I'm not tinking it now!

PATRICK (*walking away again*). It's a good thing!

SOLOMON. Bud I have an active mind! (PATRICK *immediately turns to him again.*) I can tink of the weather—(*snapping his fingers*)—like dod!

PATRICK. In a few minutes, you're going to go where the weather is so hot a thermometer can't register it!

SOLOMON. Dod is good! I'll keep it dod vay for your arrival!

FATHER WHALEN (*center*). Now, aren't you two ashamed of yourselves?

RABBI. Grown men! Fathers!

FATHER WHALEN. Grandfathers!

PATRICK. If you will only let me see my granddaughter, I'll go!

SOLOMON. I vont to see Abie's first born!

RABBI. I'll bring the baby to you. (*Exits left.*)

PATRICK (*right of table*). My granddaughter!

SOLOMON. If it's a girl, you can hev it, I don'd vant it!

FATHER WHALEN (*up right*). Oh, yes you will, Mr. Levy!

PATRICK. If it's a girl she gets all my money!

SOLOMON. If she's a boy, she gets all mine!

RABBI (*enters*). Father Whalen! Will you take little Patrick Joseph.

PATRICK. Patrick Joseph! A boy named for me?

FATHER WHALEN. Yes. (FATHER WHALEN *exits left.* PATRICK *follows smiling, a few steps then faces front.*)

PATRICK (*gloating over the name*). Patrick Joseph Murphy—Levy. *Oh!!!* I won't say the rest! (*Crosses front of table.*) It ought to be the happiest day of your life to think you're lucky enough! (*Places chair right of table, and sit facing off left.*)

SOLOMON. Tut, tut—I thought you wouldn't hev a boy!

PATRICK. This is different. 'Tis named for me! (*Slams chair down in rage.*)

SOLOMON. Dod's enough! Patrick Joseph! Ph! To tink I should live to have that name in my family! (PATRICK *sits—his back to* SOLOMON.) To think my Abie's first born should be called Patrick Joseph!

PATRICK. I'm going to call my grandson Pat, for short!

SOLOMON (*looks daggers at* PATRICK. *Picks up chair, places it back to back to* PATRICK'S *with a bang, and sits facing off right.*) I won't call him Patrick. I'll call him Mr. Levy!

PATRICK. That's the trouble with your race; they won't give in; acknowledge when they're beaten!

SOLOMON. Give in, is it? That's the trouble with the Irish! Dod's the reason it took you so long to get free!

PATRICK. Well, at least we've always had a country—that's more than you can say!

SOLOMON. Ve god a country, too! Jerusalem is free! Ve god it back!

PATRICK. Now that you got it, what are you going to do with it?

SOLOMON. Ve really don'd need it! Ve own all the other peoples!

PATRICK. Well, you don't own Ireland, thank God!!

SOLOMON. No, maybe dod's vot's the matter wid it! (PATRICK *rises and starts after him.* SOLOMON *holds chair up to defend himself.*)

PATRICK. I won't stand it, I won't—I'll break every bone—— (*Ad lib.*)

FATHER WHALEN (*enters with baby, he sees the two fighting*). Patrick! (PATRICK *turns and sees* FATHER WHALEN *with the baby which he brings to* PATRICK. PATRICK *takes the baby.*) Look out for its head.

PATRICK (*takes baby and crosses to chair left of table with the greatest of care. While* SOLOMON *sorrowfully looks on*). Hello, Pat! (*Sits.*)

SOLOMON. Oi, Pat! (*Cries, sits right.*)

RABBI (*enters with other baby. He goes to* SOLOMON *while* FATHER WHALEN *closes door, and comes to right of table.* RABBI *stands beside* SOLOMON). Solomon!

SOLOMON (*his head bowed, gradually raises his head, sighing*). Ah, what's the use? (*He sees baby, looks at* PATRICK, *sees other baby, then rises delighted.*) Twinses?

RABBI. Yes.

PATRICK. Glory be to God!

SOLOMON (*stands up*). My Abie is a smart boy; you see—he wouldn't forget his old papa. Dr. Samuels, is this one named after my papa?

RABBI. No, Solomon, it couldn't be. It's a girl!

SOLOMON (*his expression changes*). Take it back—I don't vant it!

RABBI. Oh, yes you do—it's a wonderful baby. Come, Solomon, look at her!

SOLOMON. I wouldn't do it.

RABBI. Poor little Rebecca——

SOLOMON. (*His heart softens.*) Rebecca—that's a fine name. Give me a look. (*He takes baby quickly from* RABBI.)

RABBI. Look out, Solomon, look out for its head.

SOLOMON. Dot's all right, I was a baby vonce. (*He goes to chair right of table, sits.*)

PATRICK. Father Whalen. (*Motions for him, whispers.* FATHER WHALEN *goes to him.*) Are you sure this is the boy?

FATHER WHALEN. Certainly, it has the pink ribbon.

PATRICK. I haven't much confidence in ribbon.

SOLOMON (*motions for* RABBI). Dr. Samuels, sometimes they get twinses mixed.

RABBI. They haven't been mixed, Solomon. You have little Rebecca!

SOLOMON (*playing with baby*). Yeh! Coochy coo! (*Takes rattle from pocket, and shakes it.*)

PATRICK (*takes chicken balloon from his pocket and blowing it up, stands it on table. Holds baby to see*). Look, Pat!

(RABBI *and* FATHER WHALEN *laugh and exeunt right.*)

SOLOMON. Rebecca, look! (*After wind is out of chicken.*) Look for nothing.

PATRICK (*who is beginning to get lost in the interest of the baby*). Shure, I have to give Abie credit—the boy here is the dead image of him!

SOLOMON (*delighted*). No, is it?

PATRICK. Look! (BOTH *rise.* SOLOMON *goes a bit closer and looks at the baby.*)

SOLOMON. He is, isn't he?

PATRICK. Didn't I tell you?

SOLOMON. Und the girl is just like Rosie! She's beautiful! Give a look!

(*Each is looking at the baby in the other man's arms.*)

PATRICK. She looks just like my little Rose Mary! It takes me back to the time I first held her in my arms—her mother didn't live!

SOLOMON (*softly*). Abie's didn't too!

PATRICK. I wonder if you'd mind if I held little Rebecca in me arms for a while!

SOLOMON. Certainly nod! Give me little Patrick! (*They look for some place to put the babies to exchange. Finally* PATRICK *puts his on table, and takes baby from* SOLOMON.) Look out for the cup.

PATRICK. What???

SOLOMON. Excuse me, please, look out for its head!

PATRICK. Ah, talk United States! Ah shure, I feel more natural with a girl! Guess I'm more used to it!

SOLOMON (*puzzled at how to pick up the baby, picks it up*). Me too! I feel more natural vid a boy! Patricka! (*They both sing lullabies,* SOLOMON *singing "Oyitzki Iz Gegangen, etc."* PATRICK *singing "Too-ra-loo-ra-loo-ra."*)

PATRICK. She ought to be called Rose Mary.

SOLOMON. Yes, maybe some day she could marry a good Irishman like yourself, and keep it all alike, yes?

PATRICK. You know, Sol.

SOLOMON. Yes, Pat?

PATRICK. That boy should be named for you. Solomon Levy.

SOLOMON. Solomon. It does sound better!

PATRICK. Let's change the names!

SOLOMON. Maybe Abie and Rosie vont let us!

(ROSE MARY *enters right followed by* ABIE. *They go over to their parents and look down over their shoulders; the men do not see them.*)

PATRICK. To be sure, they'll let us!

SOLOMON. Maybe we could apologize and esk them to fergive us.

PATRICK. Well, if I can feel ashamed of myself, and I am—God knows you ought to be!

SOLOMON (*resents the insult, then smiles*). I feel like ten cents worth of liverwurst!

(ROSE MARY *and* ABIE *run to their fathers,* ROSE MARY *kisses* PATRICK *and* ABIE *puts his arm around* SOLOMON.)

ROSE MARY. Daddy!

ABIE. Oh, Dad!

SOLOMON. It's all right!

(MRS. COHEN *enters right followed by* COHEN *carrying four plates.* RABBI *and* FATHER WHALEN *also enter right.*)

MRS. COHEN. Merry Christmas! (*She is carrying the ham.*)

SOLOMON. Mrs. Cohen, vod is dod you're carrying?

MRS. COHEN. It's a baked ham! (*She crosses and puts it on table, followed by* COHEN *with plates.*)

(SOLOMON'S *smile disappears. The Christmas bells start to ring out.*)

SOLOMON. Vod iss it? A fire?

PATRICK. A fire! 'Tis Christmas! Merry Christmas, Sol!

SOLOMON. Goot Yonteff, Patrick!

CURTAIN

Tobacco Road

A THREE-ACT PLAY BY

JACK KIRKLAND

FROM THE NOVEL BY

ERSKINE CALDWELL

PRINTED IN U. S. A.

Reprinted by permission of the Publishers, Duell, Sloan & Pearce, Inc.

ORIGINAL CAST OF CHARACTERS

AS THEY APPEARED IN THE FIRST PERFORMANCE, DECEMBER 4, 1933, AT THE FORTY-EIGHTH STREET THEATRE, NEW YORK CITY

	Played by
DUDE LESTER	Sam Byrd
ADA LESTER	Margaret Wycherly
JEETER LESTER	Henry Hull
ELLIE MAY	Ruth Hunter
GRANDMA LESTER	Patricia Quinn
LOV BENSEY	Dean Jagger
HENRY PEABODY	Ashley Cooper
SISTER BESSIE RICE	Maude Odell
PEARL	Reneice Rehan
CAPTAIN TIM	Lamar King
GEORGE PAYNE	Edwin Walter

Produced and directed by Anthony Brown.
Settings by Robert Redington Sharpe.

Act One: Late afternoon.

Act Two: Next Morning.

Act Three: Dawn, the following day.

The entire action of the play takes place at the farm of Jeeter Lester, situated on a tobacco road in the back country of Georgia.

TOBACCO ROAD

ACT ONE

TIME—*The present.*

PLACE—*The back country, Georgia—thirty miles or so from Augusta. It is a famished, desolate land, once given over to the profitable raising of tobacco, then turned into small cotton plantations, which have been so intensively and stupidly cultivated as to exhaust the soil. Poverty, want, squalor, degeneracy, pitiful helplessness and grotesque, tragic lusts have stamped a lost, outpaced people with the mark of inevitable end. Unequipped to face a changing economic program, bound up in traditions, ties, and prejudices, they unknowingly face extinction. It is a passing scene, contemporary and fast fading, hurling the lie at nature's mercy and challenging a god who reputedly looks after his own. Grim humor pervades all, stalking side by side with tragedy on the last short mile which leads to complete, eventual elimination. The pride and hope of a once aggressive group, pioneers in a great new world, thus meet ironic conclusion. The world moves on, unmindful of their ghosts.*

SCENE—*The squalid shack of* JEETER LESTER, *where live his wife, his mother, and two children, last of a multiple brood and last of many generations of deep Georgia crackers. Left stage, angled to curtain line, is the front of the cracked and bleeding house. A small porch, one step up from the yard, projects beyond the building front. Rear, running parallel with the curtain line and disappearing—left, behind the house, and, right, behind a clump of bushes—is the immediate section of the Tobacco Road. Center stage, from road rear to foots, is a sandy yard. Right center stage is a leafless chinaberry tree, under which is a broken, weatherworn bench. Downstage from this, to within two feet of the curtain line, is a well structure, behind which, masking right stage to curtain, is a broken corn crib. A sprawling, broken log fence separates the yard from the road, beyond which fields of sedge brush stretch away in the distance.*

AT RISE—JEETER, *dressed in dirty, torn overalls and dark shirt, an old, battered hat on his head, and heavy, worn boots on his feet, is sitting on the edge of the porch, trying vainly to patch a rotted inner tube. He is really concentrating on his work, but that does not hinder an almost constant run of chatter, most of it a complaining monotone. Standing in the yard and hurling a ball, which he retrieves on the rebound, against the side of the house, upstage beyond the porch, is* DUDE, *last son of* JEETER *to remain at home.* DUDE *is just sixteen, dirty, skinny, and not too bright. He is dressed like his father in dirty overalls and a shirt. Underfeeding has had its effect on both* JEETER *and* DUDE. *They are scrawny and emaciated.* DUDE *continues thumping the ball against the house and catching it on the rebound in spite of the fact that the old boards aren't capable of much resistance. The ball hits the house several times before* JEETER *complains.*

JEETER. Stop chunkin' that ball against that there old house, Dude. You've clear about got all the weatherboards knocked off already. (DUDE, *ignoring him, throws the ball three more times.*) Don't you never do what I tell you? Quit chunkin' that ball at them there weatherboards. The durned old house is going to pitch over and fall on the ground one of these days if you don't stop doing that.

DUDE (*casually*). Aw, go to hell, you dried-up old clod. Nobody asked you nothin'.

(*Throws ball again.*)

JEETER (*an edge of supplication in his voice*). Now, Dude, is that a way to treat your old Pa? You ought to sort of help me out instead of always doing something contrary. You ought to be helping me fix up this old inner tube instead of chunking that ball at that old house all the time.

DUDE. That there old inner tube ain't going to stay fixed noway. You might just as well quit tryin'.

JEETER. Maybe you're right. Maybe I ought to try filling the tires with cotton hulls and drivin' on them that way. A man told me that was the way to do it.

DUDE (*between throwing the ball*). That old automobile ain't no good. It ain't got no horn on it no more and there ain't no sense drivin' an automobile unless you got a horn.

JEETER. It had one of the prettiest horns in the country when it was new.

DUDE. Well, it ain't got no horn now, and it don't hardly run neither.

JEETER. It used to be one of the prettiest runnin' and prettiest soundin' automobiles you ever saw. I used to put you children in it and let you blow the horn all you liked.

DUDE. That was so long ago it ain't doing me no good now.

JEETER. That old automobile is just about the last of my goods. It looks like a man can't have any goods no more.

DUDE (*suddenly—fierce*). Some day I'm going to have me a new automobile. I'm going to have me a new automobile and a new horn on it and I'm going to ride through the country just a raisin' of hell. (GRANDMA LESTER, *an old, bent hag in ragged, black clothes comes around the far corner of the house just as* DUDE *throws his ball with particular viciousness, almost striking her. In fright, she drops to her knees and begins crawling downstage toward the porch.* DUDE *catches the ball on the rebound and prepares to hurl it again.*) Look out of the way, old woman, or I'll knock your head off. (DUDE *hurls the ball against the house just above the old woman as she crawls, whimpering, along the ground in the direction of the porch steps. He takes savage delight in her fears. She moves painfully and slowly and he has time for two throws before she reaches the comparative safety of the steps, under which she crawls.*)

JEETER. Now, Dude, is that a way to act toward your old grandma? You got her scared half to death.

DUDE. Aw, shut up. You wish she was dead just as much as anybody, even if she is your own ma.

JEETER. Now, Dude . . . I never wished no harm to nobody.

DUDE. You're a dirty old liar. You don't even give her nothing to eat.

JEETER. I don't give her nothing because there ain't nothing.

DUDE. Even when there is you don't give it to her. You needn't go telling me you don't want her dead.

JEETER. Now, Dude, is that a way to talk? It don't seem to me like that's a way a son should talk to his father.

DUDE. Then keep your mouth out of it when nobody's asked you nothing. (DUDE *throws the ball against the house, beginning his game again.* JEETER *resumes work on the inner tube, sitting on the patch.* GRANDMA *comes slowly from under the edge of the porch, rises and starts cautiously to move around* DUDE *in the direction of the Tobacco Road. She is carrying an old gunny sack.*)

DUDE (*seeing the old woman and stopping*). Where you going now? There ain't no use you picking up firewood today. There ain't going to be anything to eat. (*The* OLD WOMAN *shuffles on toward right rear hole in the log fence.* DUDE *looks after her, the spirit of hurt in his heart and mind.*) You better run, old woman, I'm going to chunk this ball at you. (*He holds ball to throw. She sees his gesture, moves more quickly, stumbles, falls, gets up.*) Look out now, I'm going to hit you in the head—I'm going to hit you in the head. (GRANDMA *stumbles again in her hurry, but this time doesn't rise, continuing her exit on hands and knees.* DUDE *is on the point of throwing the ball at her, when his eye catches the torn cover and checks him. He looks at the ball more closely.*) Goddam, just look at that ball. Just look at what that old house done to that ball.

JEETER (*wiggling on tube to make the patch stick*). Let me see it here. (DUDE *hands him the ball. He looks at it and shakes his head.*) Yes, sir, it's plumb wore out.

DUDE (*taking back the ball, holding it up, and looking at it*). It ain't even round no more. That old house just about ruined it for good. (*Sits on ground, inspecting ball.*)

JEETER. Looks like about everything around here is wore out. Seems like the Lord just ain't with us no more at all.

DUDE. I'm going down to Fuller tomorrow and steal me a new ball. That's what I'm going to do.

JEETER. Stealing is powerful sinful, Dude. I wouldn't want you doing that. I guess stealing is about the most sinful thing a man can do.

DUDE. Go on, you old liar. You're always stealing something if you can find it.

JEETER. Now, Dude! Maybe I have been a powerful sinner in my time, but ain't nobody never been sorrier than me when he's done something against the Lord.

DUDE. You're always praying and shouting after you been stealing something, but that ain't never stopped you from doing it. I'd like to hear you tell me of one time when it stopped you. Just tell me. (*Pauses while* JEETER *fiddles with inner tube.*) You just won't tell me—that's what.

JEETER (*avoiding the issue, pulls at the patch, which comes off in his hand*). Just look at that old inner tube. . . . (*Inspects it for an instant, tosses it aside.*) Well, I guess there ain't no use trying to fix that no more. Looks to me like I got to figure some other way of getting a load of wood down to Augusta. (*Yawns, stretches.*) I got to do some thinking about that. (*Lies back on porch, tilting his hat over his eyes.* DUDE *continues to pound ball on rock.*) I know what I'm going to do. I'm going down to Fuller one of these days and borrow me a mule. I expect I could take a load of wood to Augusta almost every day that way.

DUDE (*laughs*). Ho! Ho! Ain't nobody going to loan you a mule. You can't even get seed-cotton and guano to plant a crop with.

JEETER. Never you mind now. That way I could do about everything I wanted. When I wasn't hauling wood I could cultivate the fields. That's what a man ought to be doing anyway. When February comes like this and the ground gets right for plowing a man ought to be planting in the ground and growing things. That's what the Lord intended a man should do. But he can't do much without a mule to plow with. (*Nods his head, sits up.*) Yes, sir, that's what I'm going to do. I'm going down to Fuller or maybe even McCoy one of these days and borrow me a mule. (*Lies down on his back again, tilting hat over his eyes.*) I got to do some thinking about that. (DUDE *makes no comment, concentrating on pounding the ball back into shape. Hits it twice on the ground.*)

DUDE. Goddam that old house. This ball never will get round no more.

(*Enter* ADA *through doorway on to the porch and taking in* JEETER'S *recumbent form with a quick, irritated glance.* ADA *is a thin, gaunt, pellagra-ridden woman. Her shapeless dress is dirty and ragged. She was never a beauty, and pellagra and forty years of living with* JEETER *have not helped to improve her appearance. Her hair is a stringy, colorless gray-brown. She shambles rather than walks, and leans against anything strong enough to bear her weight. An inevitable snuff stick protrudes from her lips. She speaks when* DUDE *stops pounding the ball to inspect it again.*)

ADA. What are you doing laying down there on the porch, Jeeter Lester? Ain't you going to haul no wood to Augusta?

JEETER (*pushing back hat and sitting up. Even in that short time he has fallen asleep. He regards his wife vaguely*). What's that?

ADA. When you going to haul some wood to Augusta?

JEETER (*sinking back*). I'm aiming to take a load over there tomorrow or the next day.

DUDE. The hell he is, Ma. He's just trying to lie out of it.

JEETER. Now, Dude.

ADA. You're just lazy, that's what's wrong with you. If you wasn't lazy you could haul a load every day, and I'd have me some snuff when I wanted it most.

JEETER. I ain't no durn wood-chopper. I'm a farmer. The wood-choppers hauling wood to Augusta ain't got no farming to take up their time like I has. Why, I expect I'm going to grow near about fifty bales of cotton this year.

ADA. That's the way you talk every year about this time, but you don't never get started.

JEETER. This year I'm going to get at it. Dude and me'll burn the broom sedge off the fields one of these days and it won't take long then to put in a crop.

ADA. I been listening to you talk like that so long I don't believe nothing you say now. It's a big old whopping lie.

JEETER. Now leave me be, Ada. I'm going to start in the morning. Soon as I get all the fields burned off I'll go borrow me some mules. I wouldn't be surprised if me and Dude growed more than fifty bales of cotton this year, if I can get me some seed-cotton and guano.

DUDE. Who's going to give you seed-cotton and guano this year any more than they did last year or the year before, or the year before that?

JEETER. God is aiming to provide for me. I'm getting ready right now to receive His bounty.

ADA. You just lay there and see! Even the children has got more sense than you has. Didn't they go off and work in the mills as soon as they was big enough? If I wasn't so old I'd go up there right now and make me some money, myself, just like you ought to be doing.

JEETER (*intensely—sitting bolt upright*). It's wicked, you saying that, Ada. City ways ain't God-given. It wasn't intended for a man with the smell of the land in him to live in a mill in Augusta.

ADA. It's a whole lot better to live in the mills than it is to stay out here on the Tobacco Road and starve to death.

DUDE. Cuss the hell out of him, Ma.

JEETER (*sadly. Again lying down*). The Lord sends me every misery He can think of just to try my soul. He must be aiming to do something powerful big for me because He sure tests me hard. I reckon He figures if I can put up with my own people I can stand to fight back at the devil.

ADA. Humph! If He don't hurry up and do something about it, it will be too late. My poor stomach gives me a powerful pain all day long when I ain't got the snuff to calm it.

JEETER (*without moving*). Yes, I reckon you women folks is about near as hungry as I is. I sure feel right sorry for you women folks. (*Pulls hat over his eyes and dozes off again.*)

(*Enter* ELLIE MAY *right on Tobacco Road.* ELLIE MAY *is eighteen, and not unattractive as to figure. Her eyes are good; her hair is brown. The outstanding feature, however, is a slit lip, red and fiery, the opening running from about the center of the lip to the left side of her nose. When she speaks, which is seldom, she has the garbled pronunciation and nasal emphasis of those afflicted with a harelip. She is barefoot and hatless, and her light cotton dress is old, rumpled, and streaked with dirt. She comes forward shyly, like a frightened doe, her eyes watching the three other people. She only comes in as far as the chinaberry tree, half edging behind it.*)

ADA. You talk like an old fool. . . . Where you been there, Ellie May?

ELLIE MAY. No place, Ma.

ADA (*eagerly*). You didn't maybe go to see Pearl, did you?

ELLIE MAY. No, Ma.

ADA (*more to herself than to anyone*). I declare I don't know what's got into that girl. I ain't seen hide nor hair of her since she and Lov got married.

DUDE (*with deliberate cruelty.*) Why should Pearl want to see you?

ADA. She loves her old ma, that's why.

DUDE. Well, she ain't been back, has she?

ADA. Pearl is different. There ain't one of the whole seventeen she's like.

DUDE (*pointedly—leering*). She sure ain't like the rest of us, all right. . . . What was you doing, Ma, horsing around some man besides that old fool over there?

ADA. You ain't no right talking like that to your old ma, Dude Lester. The Lord will strike you dead one of these days.

DUDE. I ain't afraid of the Lord. He ain't never done nothing for me one way or the other. . . .

ADA. If you was a good son, you wouldn't be saying things like that. You'd be helping to get rations and snuff for your old ma. I declare to goodness I don't know when I've had enough to eat. It's getting so if I had a stylish dress to be buried in I'd like to lie down right now and die.

DUDE (*with vicious humor*). You ain't never going to get a new dress to die in. You're going to die and be buried in just what you got on. They're going to bury you in that same old dress.

ADA. Now, Dude, don't start fooling with your old ma like that.

(JEETER *is aroused and straightens up sleepily.* ELLIE MAY *moves a step nearer the porch, but is still close to the chinaberry tree.* DUDE *gets to his feet, leering with joy at the effect of his cruel tormenting.* ADA *steps down from the porch, but one hand still holds the upright.*)

DUDE. I ain't fooling. I guess I know . . . Yeh, and they're going to bury Pa just like he is, too. They're going to lay you in the corn crib and then they're going to bury you both just like you is.

JEETER (*plaintively*). What are you saying, Dude? You're always saying that when you know how I feel about it. They ain't going to lay me in no corn crib. Lov swore to me he'd dig a hole and put me right in it.

DUDE. What do I care what Lov promised? I know what they're going to do.

ADA. Make him say they ain't, Jeeter.

JEETER. Dude, you can't let them do that. My pa was laid in the corn crib before they buried him and the rats ate off half his face. You can't let them do that to me.

DUDE. What you so worried about? You'll be dead, anyhow.

JEETER. My old pa was dead and I know he minded.

DUDE. There ain't no rats in that old corn crib no more. There ain't been no corn in there for five years. They've all gone away.

JEETER. They'll come back, when they know I'm layin' there. They got it in good and heavy for me because there ain't been no corn in that old crib all this time. They'll just be waitin' to come back when I'm dead and eat off me when I can't do nothing to keep 'em away.

DUDE. What do I care about that?

ADA. You're the only boy left to see your old ma is buried in a stylish dress. You got to swear to me, Dude.

DUDE (*getting up*). I ain't going to swear to nothing.

JEETER (*coming forward a few steps*). Now, Dude, boy——

DUDE. Aw, go to hell. What do I care about you? (*Turns—starts to chant*): You're going to die and get laid in the corn crib—you're going to die and get laid in the corn crib.

JEETER (*threateningly*). You shut up, Dude Lester. You shut up your mouth.

DUDE (*continuing chant, walking toward gate*). You're going to die and get laid in the corn crib—you're going to die, etc.

(JEETER *rushes at* DUDE.)

JEETER (*striking weakly at* DUDE'S *back*). Shut up. You hear me—shut up!

DUDE (*turning—blocking blows easily*). What you trying to do, you old fool? Get away from me. (*Pushes* JEETER, *who stumbles back, falling.*) You keep away from me when I tell you. (*Turns—breaks again into chant.*) You're going to die and get laid in the corn crib . . . etc. (*Exits.*)

ADA (*plaintively*). Dude, you come back here. You can't go off like that without making a promise to your old ma.

(ADA *is answered only by* DUDE'S *grim chant, diminishing in the distance.* JEETER *gets up, goes back to the porch and sits, abstractedly picking up the inner tube and working on it.* ADA *at bench.*)

JEETER (*after a pause*). I reckon Dude is about the worst child of the whole lot. Seems like a boy would have the proper respect for his old pa.

ADA. I know Lizzie Belle'd help me get a stylish dress if I could find out where she is at. She used to love her old ma a heap. Clara might help some, too. She used to tell me how pretty I looked when I combed my hair mornings and put on a clean apron. I don't know if the others would want to help none or not. It's been such a long time since I saw the rest of them I've just about forgot what they was like. Seems like I can't recall their names even.

JEETER. Lizzie Belle might be making a lot of money over in the mills. Maybe if I was to find her and ask her about it, she might come sometime and bring us a little money. I know Bailey would. Bailey was just about the best of all the boys.

ADA. Reckon any of the children is dead?

JEETER. Some, I reckon. . . . But Tom ain't dead. I know that for sure. I ain't got around to doing it yet, but one of these days I'm going over to Burke County and see him. Everybody in Fuller tells me he's hauling cross ties out of the camp by the wagon load day and night. From what people say about him he's a powerful rich man now. He sure ought to give me some money.

ADA. When you see Tom tell him that his old ma would like to see him. You tell him that I said he was near about the best of the whole seventeen. Clara and Lizzie Belle was about the best, I reckon, but Tom and Bailey led the boys when it came to being good children. You tell Tom I said he was the best and maybe he'll send me some money for a stylish dress.

JEETER. Pearl is the prettiest. Ain't none of the other gals got pretty yellow hair like she has. Nor them pale blue eyes, neither.

ADA. Pearl is my real favorite. But I wish she'd come to see me sometime. What do you think makes her stay away since she got married, Jeeter?

JEETER. There never was no telling what Pearl was going to do. You was much like her yourself in that respect when you was twelve or thirteen.

ADA. Do you think she's happily married to Lov?

JEETER. Happy? I don't know anything about that. When a gal is mated to a man that's all there is to it.

ADA. Maybe she should've gone off to Augusta like the others done, even if she was scared. That's where a pretty girl ought to be. She ought to be where there's pretty clothes and shoes to wear and windows to look at.

JEETER. I don't agree to that. People that's born on the land should stay on the land. The Lord intended such. I made her go to live with Lov because that was the best thing for her to do.

ADA. Humph! Well, it might be she's satisfied. Maybe she don't care about seeing her old ma right now. When girls is satisfied they sometimes don't like to talk about their husbands any more than they do when they ain't satisfied.

JEETER. Pearl don't talk none anyway. Reckon she talks to Lov, Ada?

ADA. When girls sleep in the bed with their husbands they usually talk to them, I've discovered.

JEETER. By God and by Jesus you was certainly in no hurry to talk to me even then.

ADA. I'll go down to see her one of these days if she don't come to see me. You go see Lov, too. It's time you done that.

JEETER. Don't bother me about that now. I got to figure out some way to plant me a crop this year. (*Leans against upright.*) I got to do some thinking about that right away. (JEETER *pulls hat over his eyes and promptly goes to sleep.* ADA *shakes her head.* ELLIE MAY *starts out gate, but* ADA *sees her.*)

ADA. Ellie May! Hey you, Ellie May! You come inside and fix up the beds. They ain't been made all day and somebody's got to do something around here.

(ELLIE MAY *turns and reluctantly starts toward house, when* DUDE *enters excitedly from right and comes to right of porch.*)

DUDE. Hey, Lov's coming! Lov's coming down the road.

(ELLIE MAY *crosses to right end of fence; looks down road.*)

JEETER (*drowsily*). What?

ADA (*kicks* JEETER). Wake up, you old fool—Lov's coming. Maybe he wants to talk about Pearl.

JEETER. What do I care about that now? By God, woman, can't you see I'm thinking?

DUDE. He's toting a croker sack that's got something in it.

JEETER (*suddenly wide awake*). A croker sack! (*Rises.*) What does it look like is in that croker sack, Dude?

DUDE. He's just coming over the ridge now and I couldn't make out. But nobody carries a sack that ain't got nothing good in it.

(JEETER *runs to the fence and looks over it down the road.* ELLIE MAY *also goes to the fence, but as far right stage from the others as possible. Enter* GRANDMA LESTER *with a sackful of twigs which she drags along the ground. She does not even glance at the others, who are gazing in the opposite direction down the road, but crosses to the porch, releases the sack, and sits, pressing her hands to her side in pain and swaying back and forth.*)

JEETER (*peering over fence*). By God and by Jesus, that's Lov all right. Do you think them's turnips he's toting, Dude? Do you think them's turnips in that croker sack?

DUDE. It's something all right.

JEETER (*delighted*). By God and by Jesus, I just been waiting to have me some turnips.

ADA. If them's turnips do you reckon he'll let me have some?

JEETER. I'll mention it when I talk to him, but I don't know how he'll take it. He must have paid a good stiff price if they's winter turnips.

DUDE. Lov ain't giving away nothing he paid a good stiff price for.

JEETER. I ain't concerning myself about that. Lov and me think a heap of each other.

DUDE. If he don't give you none, is you going to try and steal some?

JEETER (*admonishingly*). Now, Dude! Stealing is about the most sinful thing a man can do. The Lord don't have no truck with stealing. (ELLIE MAY *giggles foolishly.* JEETER *turns to her.*) Get away from that fence, Ellie May. Lov ain't likely to come in here at all if he sees that face of yours. (ELLIE MAY *giggles foolishly again and moves behind chinaberry tree, from where she peeks.* GRANDMA LESTER *shuffles downstage and flattens herself against the corner of the porch nearest the curtain line.* JEETER *and* DUDE *stretch far over the fence to watch* LOV'*s approach.*)

ADA. Is he near about here, Jeeter?

JEETER. Near about. He's just about here now.

ADA. Is them turnips?

JEETER. By God, if they ain't, I sure is doing a hell of a lot of stretching for nothing.

(JEETER *gives his full attention to the approaching man for a second, then turns and motions to the others.*)

JEETER. Get away from that fence—all of you. Come on, sit down. Act unconcerned.

(JEETER *goes to side of house;* ADA *to the well;* DUDE *sits on fence. Enter* LOV BENSEY. LOV *is a man about thirty, dressed in coal-grimed overalls and wearing a dirty, floppy hat. When he removes the hat to wipe the sweat from his face a shock of unruly hair is seen rising above a sunburned face. He is not unattractive in his dull, slow way, and his body shows the result of hard work and a reasonable amount of food. He is not a big man, but he is stronger and better nourished than either* DUDE *or* JEETER. *He carries a partly filled gunny sack over his shoulder. Caution and suspicion mark his every move in dealing with the Lesters, and this is in evidence now as he comes into the scene.*)

JEETER (*hiding his eagerness by trying to be casual*). Hi there, LOV.

LOV. Hi. (*He moves on beyond them toward center stage.*)

JEETER. Ain't seen you in a long time.

LOV. No. (*He stops near the gate, and shifts bag.*)

JEETER. You must be plumb wore out toting that croker sack. Come in off the Tobacco Road and rest yourself.

LOV. I ain't tired.

JEETER. You must of come a far piece off if you come from down Fuller way.

LOV. Umm.

JEETER. Come inside and get yourself a drink.

LOV. I ain't thirsty.

JEETER (*with calculated amiability*). We was just talking about you, Lov. We ain't seen you since a way long the first of the winter. How is you and Pearl getting on down there at the coal chute?

ADA (*a trace of anxiety*). Pearl—is she all right?

LOV. Humph! (*He glances suspiciously at all of them.*) I want to talk to you, Jeeter.

JEETER. Sure. Come inside the yard and sit down. No use toting that croker sack while you're talking. (LOV *repeats his glance of suspicion, but comes hesitatingly inside and drops the sack against fence near gate. He stands in front of it, guarding it.* JEETER *tries to make his voice casual, but every eye on the stage is on that sack, giving the lie to their pretended indifference.*) What you got in that croker sack, Lov? (*Innocently, as* LOV *doesn't answer*): I heard it said that some people has got turnips this year. (LOV's *eyes narrow with suspicion and he backs even more protectively against the sack.*)

LOV (*shrewdly*). It's Pearl I want to talk to you about.

ADA. She ain't sick, is she?

LOV (*suddenly angry*). By God, she's something! (*He lets himself to ground, sitting beside turnips and gripping neck of sack.*)

JEETER (*archly*). Why don't you go over on the porch? That ain't no place to sit.

LOV. I'll sit right where I is.

JEETER (*agreeably*). What you got to say to me, Lov? You must have a heap to say, toting that sack all this way to do it.

LOV. I sure has. You got to go talk to Pearl. That's what I got to say.

JEETER. What's that gal up to? I never could understand her. What's she done now?

LOV. It's just like she done ever since she went down to live with me at the chute, only I'm getting pretty durn tired of it by this time. All the niggers make fun of me because of the way she treats me.

JEETER. Pearl is just like her ma. Her ma used to do the queerest things in her time.

ADA (*sharply*). Is you treating her right?

LOV. That ain't got a goddam thing to do with it. She's married to me, ain't she?

JEETER. You got leave of the county. I remember that all right.

LOV. Then why the hell don't she act like she ought to? Every time I want to have her around, she runs off in the broom sedge. She won't talk to me, neither, and she won't cook nothing I want to eat.

JEETER. Great day in the morning, now what do you think makes her do that?

LOV. I don't know and I don't care. But I call it a hell of a business.

JEETER. About the cooking you is just about right. But when it comes to not talking I don't see no harm in that. Ada, there, didn't used to talk neither, but, by God and by Jesus, now you can't make her shut up.

LOV (*stubbornly*). I want Pearl to talk to me. I want her to ask me if my back is sore when I come home from the chute, or if it's going to rain, or when I is going to get a hair cut. There's a hell of a lot of things she could ask me about, but she don't talk at all.

JEETER. Maybe you don't try the right way to make her.

LOV. I tried kicking her and I tried pouring water on her and chunking rocks and sticks at her, but it don't do no good. She cries a lot when she's hurt, but, by God, I don't call that talking.

ADA. Don't you dare hurt her, Lov Bensey.

LOV. You keep out of this. I guess I know my rights. (*He pauses, looking belligerently from* ADA *to* JEETER.) And they is something else she don't do neither.

JEETER. For one little gal they sure is a heap of things she don't do. What else don't she do, Lov?

LOV. She don't sleep in the bed with me, that's what. (*Viciously to* ADA.) And what you got to say about that?

JEETER (*much more interested*). Now that's something. By God and by Jesus, that's something.

LOV (*turning back to* JEETER). She ain't never slept in the bed. It's a durn pallet on the floor she sleeps on every night. Now what I say is, what the hell is the sense in me marrying a wife if I don't get none of the benefits?

ADA. If you don't like what she's doing, you send her right home and get yourself another girl. Her old ma will look after her.

LOV. No. I ain't going to do that neither. I want Pearl. She's about the prettiest piece in the whole country and I want her.

JEETER. You give her time and she'll get in the bed.

LOV. By God. I already give her enough time. Right now I feel like I got to have me a woman. (*He looks at* ELLIE MAY. ELLIE MAY *catches his glance and giggles. She begins the wriggling movement, which at the right time brings her near* LOV.)

JEETER. I know how you feel, Lov. When the time to plow and put seed in the ground comes along a man feels just like that. Even at this day and age I could do a little of that myself.

LOV. Well, then, you go down and talk to her. You tell her to stop sleeping on that durn pallet and get in the bed—and tell her to talk to me, too, by God.

JEETER. I might do that if I felt you was ready and willing to do something for me in return.

LOV (*suspiciously*). What do you mean by that, Jeeter?

JEETER (*unable longer to restrain himself*). By God and by Jesus, Lov, what you got in that croker sack? I been looking at it ever since you been here and I sure got to know.

LOV. I don't see what that's got to do with it?

JEETER. What is they, I tell you!

LOV (*after a short pause for emphasis and a hard, proud glance around*). Turnips, by God. (*His announcement causes a noticeable reaction on everyone. Their bodies stiffen and lean forward—a look of greed appears in their faces. But wisely they refrain from taking any actual steps forward. Instinctively they wait for* JEETER *to see it through. Only* ELLIE MAY *forgets her hunger in the sharpening force of passion brought on by proximity to* LOV, *and continues her sex-conscious wriggling.*)

JEETER (*keyed up, but holding himself in*). Turnips! Where'd you get turnips, Lov?

LOV. Wouldn't you like to know?

JEETER. Turnips is about the thing I want most of all right now. I could just about eat me a whole croker sackful between now and sundown.

LOV. Well, don't look to me to give you none because I ain't.

JEETER. That's a mean thing to say, Lov. It's a whopping mean thing to say to Pearl's old Pa.

LOV. To hell with that. I had to pay fifty cents for this many in a sack and I had to walk clear to the other side of Fuller to fetch them.

JEETER. I was thinking maybe you and me could fix up some sort of trade. I could go down to your house and tell Pearl she's got to sleep in the bed, and you could give me some of them——

LOV. No, by God. You're Pearl's daddy, and you ought to make her behave for nothing.

JEETER. By God and by Jesus, Lov, you oughtn't to talk to me like that. I just got to have me some turnips. I ain't had a good turnip since a year ago this spring. All the turnips I raised this year has got them damn-blasted green-gutted worms in them.

LOV. I don't see what that's got to do with Pearl one way or another. I gave you seven dollars when she came to live with me and that's enough.

JEETER. Maybe it was then, but it ain't now. We is about starved around here. What God made turnip-worms for I can't make out. It appears to me like He just naturally has got it in good and heavy for a poor man. I worked all the fall last year digging up a patch of ground to grow turnips in, and when they're getting about big enough to pull up and eat, along come them damn-blasted green-gutted worms and bore clear to the middle of them.

(LOV *is entirely indifferent to* JEETER'S *plea. Cruelly he takes a turnip from the sack and takes a big bite. Chewing the bite to the agony of the starving Lesters, he points the stub of the turnip at the wriggling* ELLIE MAY, *sitting on the ground near the bench and looking at him with avid eyes. She giggles.*)

LOV. Now if Pearl was anything like Ellie May there, she wouldn't act like she does. You go down and tell her to act like Ellie May.

JEETER. Is you in mind then to make a trade with them turnips?

LOV (*eating*). I ain't trading turnips with nobody.

JEETER. That's a hell of a thing to say, Lov. I'm wanting turnips God himself knows how bad.

LOV. Go over to Fuller and buy yourself some, then. I went over there to get mine.

JEETER. Now, Lov, you know I ain't got a penny to my name. You got a good job down there at the chute and it pays you a heap of money.

LOV. I don't make but a dollar a day. House rent takes up near about all that and eating the rest of it.

JEETER. Makes no difference. You don't want to sit there and let me starve, do you?

LOV. I can't help it if you do. The Lord looks at us with equal favor, they say. He gives me mine and if you don't get yours you better go talk to Him about it.

DUDE. You give him hell, Lov. If he wasn't so durn lazy he'd do something instead of cussing about it all the time. He's the laziest son-of-a-bitch I ever seen.

JEETER. My children all blame me because God sees fit to make me poverty-ridden, Lov. They and their Ma is all the time cussing me because we ain't got nothing to eat. It ain't my fault that Captain John shut down on giving us rations and snuff, and then went away and died.

LOV (*indifferently*). It ain't my fault neither.

JEETER. I worked all my life for Captain John, Lov. I worked harder than any four of his niggers in the field; then the first thing I knowed he came down here one morning and says he can't be letting me get no more rations and snuff at the store. After that he sells all the mules and goes up to Augusta to live. He said there wasn't no use trying to run a farm no more—fifty plows or one plow. He told me I could stay on the land as long as I liked, but that ain't doing me no good. Ain't no work I can find to do for hire and I can't raise a crop of my own because I ain't got no mule and I ain't got no credit. (LOV's *attention turns from* JEETER *to* ELLIE MAY, *whose wriggling movement is bringing her inch by inch closer to him.*) That's what I'm wanting to do powerful strong right now—raise me a crop. When the winter goes and when it gets time to burn off the broom sedge in the fields, I sort of want to cry. I reckon it is the smell of that sedge smoke this time of year near about drives me crazy. Then pretty soon all the other farmers start plowing. That's what's the worst. When the smell of that new earth turning over behind the plows strikes me, I get all weak and shaky. It's in my nature—burning broom sedge and plowing in the ground this time of year. I did it for near about fifty years, and my Pa and his Pa before him was the same kind of men. Us Lesters sure like to stir up the earth and make plants grow in it. The land has got a powerful hold on me, Lov.

(LOV *is giving his full attention to* ELLIE MAY *now, a half-eaten turnip arrested on its way to his mouth.* ELLIE MAY *leans back until she rests on the ground and continues her wriggling and squealing.* LOV *begins to edge toward her.* DUDE *watches them closely.*)

DUDE. Hey, Pa.

JEETER. Shut up, Dude. It didn't always used to be like it is now, neither, Lov. I can remember a short time back when all the merchants in Fuller was tickled to give me credit. Then all of a sudden Captain John went away and pretty soon the sheriff comes and takes away near about every durn piece of goods I possessed. He took every durn thing I had, excepting that old automobile and the cow. He said the cow wasn't no good because she wouldn't take no freshening, and the automobile wasn't no good neither. I reckon he was right, too, because the automobile won't run no more and the cow died.

DUDE (*throwing a broken piece of weather-boarding at* JEETER). Hey, you.

JEETER (*angrily*). What you want, Dude? What's the matter with you —chunking weather-boarding at me like that?

DUDE. Ellie May's horsing. That's horsing from way back yonder, hey, Pa?

JEETER (*giving the action conscious attention for the first time*). By God and by Jesus, Lov, has you been paying attention to what I was saying? You ain't answered me about them turnips yet.

DUDE. Lov ain't thinking about no turnips. He's wanting to hang up with Ellie May. Look at her straining for him. She's liable to bust a gut if she don't look out.

(*It's* JEETER'S *turn now to be indifferent to conversation. He watches while* LOV *creeps several yards from the turnip sack up to* ELLIE MAY *and awkwardly begins to fondle her. Their backs meet and rub together in a primitive love gesture.*

Slowly and silently, JEETER *puts aside the inner tube which he has been holding and vaguely trying to fix, and gets to his feet. Inch by inch he begins edging toward the sack.* LOV *has worked his way around in back of* ELLIE MAY *and his hands are around her, stroking her arms and legs.*

JEETER *moves closer and closer to the sack, unseen by* LOV. *Only* ADA *and* GRANDMA LESTER *notice him.* DUDE *is too occupied watching* LOV *and* ELLIE MAY.) By God, Lov ain't never got that close before. He said he wouldn't never get close enough to Ellie May to touch her with a stick. But he ain't paying no mind to that now. I bet he don't even know she's got a slit-lip on her. If he does know it, he don't give a good goddam.

(*And now* JEETER *makes his play. In one swift lunge he crosses the intervening distance and grabs up the sack.* LOV *sees him, turns swiftly, and reaches for him, but misses. He starts to rise as* JEETER *backs a step away, but* ELLIE MAY *grabs his leg, tripping him up. Before he can shake her off,* ADA *hurries from the well, picking up a stick on the way.* GRANDMA LESTER *totters from her place, also brandishing a stick. The two* OLD WOMEN *move down on* LOV *to help* ELLIE MAY.)

LOV. Drop them turnips, Jeeter! Drop them turnips. (ELLIE MAY, *quicker than* LOV, *practically leaps on top of him, holding him down. They roll and struggle. To* ELLIE MAY). Get off me, you. Get off me. (LOV *struggles to rise.* ADA *and* GRANDMA *slap and jab at him with their sticks.*)

JEETER (*at the gate*). You tell Pearl I said be good to you, Lov. I'll be down to see about that first thing in the morning. (*He exits, running.*)

LOV. Goddam you! (LOV, *by dint of great effort, throws off the women, literally hurling* ELLIE MAY *to the ground and dashes to the gate. He stops there, looking down the road, trying to spy* JEETER.)

DUDE. Ain't no use trying to catch Pa. He's run off in the brush and there ain't nobody can catch Pa when he runs off in the brush.

(LOV *realizes the truth of* DUDE'S *statement, and, winded and panting, leans against the fence, making no effort to run.* ELLIE MAY *lies on the ground, also breathing hard, but her eyes still are on* LOV.)

ADA. Go on back to Ellie May, Lov. Don't be scared of her. You might even get to like her and let Pearl come back here to me.

(LOV *doesn't answer, pulling a huge colored handkerchief from his pocket and wiping his streaming face.* DUDE *moves to the fence, center.*)

DUDE. How many scoops-full does that No. 17 freight engine empty at the chute every morning, Lov? Looks to me like them freight engines takes on twice as much coal as the passenger ones does. (LOV *pays no attention.* ADA *goes back to the porch.* GRANDMA LESTER *picks up her sack of twigs, and, groaning, goes into the house.*) Why don't the firemen blow the whistles more than they do, Lov? If I was a fireman I'd pull the whistle cord near about all the time. (DUDE *makes noise like locomotive whistle.* LOV *turns from the fence, goes back into the yard, recovers his hat, glances at* ELLIE MAY, *who lies sprawled on the ground. Then he turns and starts off.* DUDE *follows* LOV *to the gate.* LOV *finishes adjusting his overalls and crosses to the gate,* DUDE *following.*) When is you going to buy yourself an automobile, Lov? You make a heap of money at the chute. You ought to get one that has got a great big horn on it. (*Repeats locomotive sound. Ecstatically.*) Whistles and horns sure make a pretty sound.

(*Ignoring* DUDE, LOV *exits through the gate and down the road.*) I reckon Lov don't feel much like talking today.

ADA. Dude, you run right out in the brush and find your pa before he eats up all them turnips. (DUDE *starts.*) See you bring some of them back to your old ma, too. (*Exit* DUDE. ADA *watches him through the gate, then calls*). Ellie May . . . Ellie May!

ELLIE MAY (*looking up—blinking*). Yes, Ma.

ADA. You get inside the house and fix up them beds like I told you a long time ago. (ELLIE MAY *stretches and yawns, showing no disposition to move.*) I declare to goodness there ain't nobody around here got gumption enough to do anything. Now you get inside the house and do like I tell you. Do you hear me? Come on.

ELLIE MAY (*slowly getting to her feet*). All right—I'm a coming.

(*Enter* HENRY PEABODY, *a man who, except for his voice and slight differences in his dress, might well be* JEETER. HENRY *is very excited. He doesn't come into the yard, but hangs over the fence.* ELLIE MAY *promptly sits again.*)

HENRY. Hey you, Ada. Is Jeeter home?

ADA (*shaking her head negatively*). He went out into the brush a little while back. I'm expecting him pretty soon, but I ain't certain.

HENRY. You tell him I was here.

ADA. What's got you so excited, Henry Peabody? I ain't seen you hurry like that since you was a boy.

HENRY. I ain't got time to tell you about it now, but you tell Jeeter I been here and I'll stop again on my way home.

(*Enter* SISTER BESSIE RICE, *a rather portly woman of about forty. She is dressed in a faded apron and wears a sunbonnet over her large, round face.* BESSIE *is one of the brood of itinerant women preachers peculiar to certain sections of the deep South. She owes allegiance to no church, and her creed and method of divine teaching are entirely her own. She is loud and sure of voice, and is generally accepted at her own value by the God-fearing innocents among whom she moves. She enters by way of the gate, coming inside the yard, and takes off her sunbonnet, fanning herself, as she gives her greeting.*)

BESSIE. Good evening, Brother Henry —good evening, Sister Ada. The Lord's blessing be with you.

HENRY. Good evening, Sister Bessie. . . . Well, I got to be rushing off. (*Starts off.*)

BESSIE. What's hurrying you, Brother Henry? You been sinning against the Lord?

HENRY. No, praise God, but I got to hurry. (*Exits.*)

BESSIE (*calling after him*). I'm coming down to your house for preaching and praying one of these days, Brother Henry. (*There is no answer and she turns to* ADA.) Now what do you suppose that Henry Peabody's been up to? I bet he's been a powerful wicked man here of late to hurry off like that. Looks like the devil's got into him sure.

ADA. Come inside, Bessie. I reckon Jeeter will be right glad to see you.

BESSIE. I'll be right pleased to, Sister. I reckon I walked near about three miles getting here. (*Walks to the porch, stands for a second.*)

ADA. Set down.

BESSIE. Has you got a chair, Sister? My poor back's so weary it feels like it's mighty near breaking in half.

ADA. H'mm. (*She exits into house.* BESSIE, *looking around and fanning herself, sees* ELLIE MAY. ELLIE MAY *giggles.*)

BESSIE. How is you, child? God be with you. (*She goes onto the porch singing the hymn "Shall We Gather at the River." Midway in the song* ADA *returns from the house dragging an old rocking chair which she thumps down.* BESSIE *abruptly stops singing. To* ADA:) Bless you, Sister. (*She sits, rocking back and forth, fanning herself.* ADA *stands on the ground, leaning against the porch upright, chewing on her snuff stick.*) Where is Jeeter at this time of day, Sister Ada? Has that man been up to something sinful again?

ADA. He's out in the broom sedge, eating up turnips he stole from Lov a while back.

BESSIE. Lord, O Lord, he's been stealing again. Jeeter's a powerful sinful man. Ain't no sin like stealing. . . . Was they good eating winter turnips, Sister?

ADA. I reckon.

BESSIE. Lord forgive us our sins, and particularly forgive Jeeter. . . . Is he coming back with any of them turnips, Ada?

ADA. I told Dude to fetch him before he eats them all up. Maybe he will and maybe he won't.

BESSIE. Dude will do right by the Lord. Dude's a mighty fine boy, Sister.

ADA. Humph.

BESSIE. We got to be careful against delivering him to the Hardshell Baptists, though. They're sinful people. They don't know the working of the Lord like I does.

ADA. What do you call your religion, Sister Bessie? You ain't never said what name you called it.

BESSIE. It ain't got a name. I generally just call it "Holy." It's just me and God. God talks to me in prayer and I answer him back. I get most things done that way.

ADA. I want you to say a prayer for Pearl before you go away, Bessie. I reckon Lov's mad about Jeeter stealing his turnips and he might beat Pearl more than he ought to.

BESSIE. I'll be right happy to say a prayer for Pearl. But she ought to pray for herself, too. That sometimes helps a lot with the Lord.

ADA. Pearl don't talk to nobody except me—not even the Lord. I reckon what praying's done for her has got to be done by somebody else.

BESSIE. I'll mention that to the Lord and see if he'll let loose her tongue. There's sin someplace in her or she'd talk like everybody else. The Lord didn't intend for a woman not to talk.

ADA. Ellie May don't talk much, either. But that's because of her lip. It sounds funny when she talks.

BESSIE. There's been a powerful lot of sinning among you Lesters, or Ellie May wouldn't have that lip. One way or another I reckon you Lesters is about the most sinful people in the country. (*They are interrupted by the off-stage sound of* JEETER *and* DUDE *quarreling.*)

DUDE (*off stage*). You ain't the only one that likes turnips. I ain't had no more to eat this week than you has.

JEETER (*off stage*). You had five already.

DUDE. Give me some more. Do you hear me?

JEETER. You don't need no more.

DUDE. I'll wham you. (*At this point* JEETER *comes running to the gate. He has his pockets filled with turnips.* DUDE *is right on his heels and catches him in the gate, throws one arm around him from behind and holds him as he extracts turnips from his pockets with his right hand.*)

JEETER (*trying to free himself*). Stop that, Dude, you stop that!

DUDE (*laughing at him*). Ho! Ho! You can't hurt nobody. You're as weak as an old cat. (*Pushes* JEETER, *who falls on the ground near the corner of the house.* DUDE *crosses to right of gate eating a turnip.*)

JEETER (*lying on ground*). Now that's all you're going to git. (*Picks himself up.*)

BESSIE (*oracularly*). You been sinning again, Jeeter Lester.

JEETER (*seeing* BESSIE *for the first time*). Sister Bessie! The good Lord be praised. (*He rushes to the porch.*) I knowed God would send His angel to take away my sins. You come just at the right time.

BESSIE. The Lord always knows the right time. I was at home sweeping out the kitchen when He come to me and said, "Sister Bessie, Jeeter Lester is doing something evil. You go to his house and pray for him right now before it's too late." I looked right back at the Lord and said, "Lord, Jeeter Lester is a powerful sinful man, but I'll pray for him until the devil goes clear back to hell." That's what I told Him and here I is.

JEETER (*dancing ecstatically in front of* BESSIE'S *chair on the porch*). I knowed the good Lord wouldn't let me slip and fall in the devil's hands. I knowed it! I knowed it!

BESSIE. Ain't you going to give me a turnip, Jeeter? I ain't had so much to eat lately. Times is hard for the good and bad alike.

JEETER. Sure, Bessie. (JEETER *selects several of the largest, gives them to* BESSIE. *Turns to* ADA.) Here you is, Ada. (*Gives her some. As others get theirs,* GRANDMA *enters, comes to* JEETER, *and starts pulling at his coat. To* BESSIE.) I wish I had something to give you to take home, Sister. When I had plenty, I used to give Brother Rice a whole armful of chickens and potatoes at a time. Now I ain't got nothing but a handful of turnips, but I ain't ashamed of them. The Lord growed them and His doings is good enough for me.

BESSIE (*with full mouth*). Praise be the Lord.

JEETER *and* ADA. Amen, Sister! Amen.

BESSIE (*finishing her turnip with a sigh*). I feel the call of the Lord. Let's have a little prayer. (BESSIE *gets up and crosses to the center of the yard,* JEETER *following, as does*

ADA *and* GRANDMA LESTER, *who groans as she moves.* ELLIE MAY *and* DUDE *sit on the porch, eating the turnips and watching.*) Some people make an objection to kneeling down and having prayer out of doors. They say, "Sister Bessie, can't we go in the house and pray just as good?" And do you know what I do? I say, "Brothers and Sisters, I ain't ashamed to pray out here in the open. I want folks passing along the road to know that I'm on God's side. It's the old devil that's always whispering about going in the house out of sight." That's what I tell them. That's the way I stick up for the Lord.

JEETER. Praise the Lord.

BESSIE. Let's get ready to pray. (*They all kneel.*) Sister Ada, is you still suffering from pleurisy?

ADA. All the time. (JEETER *and* ADA *bow their heads and close their eyes, but* GRANDMA LESTER *stares straight ahead, her eyes open, her head raised a bit.* BESSIE *nods to* ADA, *then prays.*)

BESSIE. Dear God, here I is again to offer a little prayer for sinful people. Jeeter Lester and his family want me to pray for them again. The last time helped a whole lot, but Jeeter let the devil get hold of him today and he went and done a powerful sinful thing. He stole all of Lov's turnips. They're just about all et up now, so it's too late to take them back. That's why we want to pray for Jeeter. You ought to make him stop stealing like he does. I never seen a more stealing man in all my days. Jeeter wants to quit, but it seems like the devil gets hold of him almost as soon as we get through praying for him. You ain't going to let the old devil tell You what to do, is You? The Lord ought to tell the devil what he should do. . . . And Sister Ada has got the pleurisy again. You ought to do something for her this time sure enough. The last time didn't help none too much. If You'll make her well of it she'll quit the devil for all time. Won't you, Sister Ada?

ADA. Yes, Lord.

BESSIE. And old Mother Lester has got a misery in her sides. She's in pain all the time with it. She's kneeling down right now, but she can't do it many more times. . . . You ought to bless Ellie May, too. Ellie May has got that slit in her lip that makes her an awful sight to look at. (ELLIE MAY *buries her face in her hands.* DUDE *looks at her and grins.*)

JEETER. Don't forget to pray for Pearl, Sister Bessie. Pearl needs praying for something awful.

BESSIE. I was just going to do that. Sister Ada told me to pray Lov wouldn't beat her too hard because of them turnips you stole.

JEETER. It ain't that. It's what Pearl's done herself.

BESSIE. What has Pearl done sinful, Brother Jeeter?

JEETER. That was what Lov spoke to me about today. He says Pearl won't talk to him and she won't let him touch her. When night comes she gets down and sleeps on a durn pallet on the floor, and Lov has got to sleep in the bed by himself. That's a pretty bad thing for a wife to do, and God ought to make her quit it.

BESSIE. Brother Jeeter, little girls like Pearl don't know how to live married lives like we grown-up women do. So maybe if I was to talk to her myself instead of getting God to do it, she would change her ways. I expect I know more about what to tell her than He does, because I been a married woman up to the past summer when my former husband died. I expect I know all about it. God wouldn't know what to tell her.

JEETER. Well, you can talk to her, but maybe if you asked God about it He might help some, too. Maybe He's run across gals like that before, though I don't believe there's another durn gal in the whole country who's as contrary-minded about sleeping in the bed as Pearl is.

(DUDE *stands up and takes his ball from his pocket.*)

BESSIE. Maybe it wouldn't hurt none if I was to mention it.

JEETER. That's right. You speak to the Lord about it, too. Both of you together ought to get something done. (DUDE *hurls the ball against the house and catches it.* JEETER *speaks angrily.*) Quit chunking that there ball against that old house, Dude. Don't you see Sister Bessie's praying. I declare I wish you had more sense.

DUDE. Aw, go to hell.

BESSIE. Now, Dude. . . . (*Waits until he stops.*) Now, Lord, I've got something special to pray about. I don't ask favors unless they is things I want pretty bad, so this time I'm asking for a favor for Pearl. I want You to make her stop sleeping on a pallet on the floor while Brother Lov has to sleep by himself in the bed. I was a good wife to my former husband. I never slept on no pallet on the floor. Sister Ada here don't do nothing like that. And when I marry another man, I ain't going to do that neither. I'm going to get in bed just as big as my new husband does. So You tell Pearl to quit doing that.

JEETER. What was that you was saying, Sister Bessie? Didn't I hear you say you was going to marry yourself a new husband?

BESSIE. Well, I ain't made up my mind yet. I been looking around some, though.

JEETER. Now if it wasn't for Ada there . . .

BESSIE (*giggling*). You hush up, Brother Jeeter. How'd you know I'd take you anyway? You're pretty old, ain't you?

JEETER. Maybe I is and maybe I ain't, but if I is I ain't too old for that.

ADA (*stiffly*). I reckon you'd better finish up the prayer. You ain't done like I asked you about Pearl yet.

BESSIE. So I ain't. . . . Please, Lord, Sister Ada wants me to ask You not to let Lov beat up Pearl too much. And I guess that's about all. . . . Save us from the devil and——

JEETER. Hey, wait a minute. You clear forgot to say a little prayer for Dude. You left Dude out all around.

DUDE. No, sir, not me, you don't. I don't want no praying. (BESSIE *jumps up and runs to* DUDE. *Clutching him by the arm she starts dragging him back to the praying circle.)*

BESSIE. Come on, Dude. Come and kneel with me.

DUDE (*angrily*). I don't want to do that. I don't want no praying for me. (BESSIE *puts one arm around his waist, holding him very close, and with her free hand strokes his shoulder.)*

BESSIE (*tenderly*). I got to pray for you, Dude. The Lord didn't leave you out no more than He did Ellie May. (*She kneels, but keeps his legs encircled in her arms.)* Come on now. All of us has got to have prayer some time or another. (DUDE *finds the pressure of her arms on his legs quite stimulating and exciting, and he begins giggling and squirming.)*

JEETER. Quit that jumping up and down, Dude. What ails you?

(DUDE *puts his arms around her neck and begins rubbing her as she is rubbing him.)*

BESSIE. You kneel down beside me and let me pray for you. You'll do that, won't you, Dude?

DUDE (*snickering*). Hell, I don't give a damn if I do. (*He kneels, continuing to keep his arms about her, and she keeps her arms around him.)*

BESSIE. I knowed you would want me to pray for you, Dude. It will help you get shed of your sins like Jeeter did. (*Closes her eyes, lifts her head.)* Dear God, I'm asking You to save Brother Dude from the devil and make a place for him in heaven. That's all. Amen.

JEETER. Praise the Lord, but that was a durn short prayer for a sinner like Dude. (*He gets to his feet.* BESSIE *and* DUDE *continue to hold each other.)*

BESSIE (*smiling fondly at* DUDE). Dude don't need no more praying for. He's just a boy, and he's not sinful like us grown-ups is.

JEETER. Well, maybe you're right. But I sort of recollect the Bible says a son shouldn't cuss his Ma and Pa like he does other people.

BESSIE (*stroking* DUDE'S *hair*). Dude won't do that again. He's a fine boy, Dude is. He would make a handsome preacher, too. He's mighty like my former husband in his younger days. (*She and* DUDE *stop kneeling, but sit on the ground and continue to hold each other.)*

JEETER. Dude's about sixteen years old now. That makes him two years younger than Ellie May. He'll be getting a wife pretty soon, I reckon. All my other male children married early in life, just like the gals done. If it wasn't for Ellie May's lip she'd been married as quick as any. Men here around Fuller all want to marry gals about eleven or twelve years old, like Pearl was. Ada, there, was just turning twelve when I married her.

BESSIE. The Lord intended all of us should be mated. He made us that way. My former husband was just like the Lord in that respect. They both believed in the same thing when it came to mating.

JEETER. I reckon the Lord did intend for us all to get mated, but He didn't take into account a woman with a slit in her mouth like Ellie May's got.

BESSIE. The Lord's ways is wise, Jeeter.

JEETER. Well, maybe, but I don't believe He done the right thing by her when He opened up her lip. That's the only contrary thing I ever said about the Lord, but it's the truth. What use is a slit like that for? You can't spit through it, and you can't whistle through it, now can you? It was just meanness on His part when He done that—just durn meanness.

BESSIE. You shouldn't talk about the Lord like that. He knows what He done it for. He had the best reason in the world for doing it.

JEETER. What reason?

BESSIE. Maybe I ought not to say it, Jeeter.

JEETER. You sure ought to tell me if you tell anybody. I'm her Pa.

BESSIE. He done that to save her pure body from you, Brother Jeeter.

JEETER. From me?

BESSIE (*nodding*). He knowed she would be safe in this house when He made her like that. He knowed that you was once a powerful sinner, and that you might be again.

JEETER. That's the truth. I used to be a powerful sinful man in my time. I reckon at one time I was the most powerful sinful man in the whole country. Now you take them Peabody children over across the field. I reckon near about all of them is half mine, one way or another.

BESSIE. You wait till I finish accusing you, Jeeter, before you start lying out of it.

JEETER. Praise God, I ain't lying out of it. I just now told you how powerful sinful I once was.

BESSIE. Don't think the Lord didn't know about it.

JEETER (*chuckles; crossing to well*). Henry Peabody didn't know nothing about it, though.

ADA. Humph.

JEETER (*turns left; really noticing* BESSIE'S *and* DUDE'S *goings on*). Say, Sister Bessie, what in hell is you and Dude doing? You and him has been squatting there, hugging and rubbing of the other, for near about half an hour. (BESSIE *manages as much of a blush as she is capable of.*)

BESSIE (*removing* DUDE'S *arm from around her waist, trying to rise*). The Lord was speaking to me. (DUDE *replaces his arm about her waist.*) He was telling me I ought to marry a new husband.

JEETER. He didn't tell you to marry Dude, did he?

BESSIE. Dude would make a fine preacher. He would be just about as good as my former husband was, maybe better. He is just suitable for preaching and living with me. Ain't you, Dude?

DUDE (*quickly*). You want me to go home with you now? (*Takes a step toward her.*)

BESSIE. Not now, Dude. I'll have to ask the Lord if you'll do. (*Crosses left of* DUDE.) He's sometimes particular about his male preachers, especially if they is going to marry women preachers. I got to pray over it first—(*with a knowing glance at* DUDE)—and Dude, you pray over it, too.

DUDE (*giggles in embarrassment*). Aw, like hell I will. (*Crosses to left of gate.*)

JEETER (*crossing to* DUDE). What's the matter with you, Dude? Didn't you hear Sister Bessie tell you to pray over that? You is the luckiest man alive. What's the matter with you, anyway? Great day in the morning, if you ain't the goddamdest boy I ever heard tell of. (JEETER *starts down left;* DUDE *crosses to right of gate.*)

(*Enter* HENRY PEABODY. *He comes running to the gate.*)

PEABODY (*coming to gate*). Hey, you, Jeeter—Jeeter.

JEETER (*crosses to* PEABODY). What's the matter, Henry?

PEABODY. Didn't Ada tell you nothing?

JEETER. She didn't tell me nothing.

PEABODY. Didn't she tell you I was here before?

JEETER (*impatiently*). No. What is it you've got to say?

PEABODY. It's big news, Jeeter.

JEETER. Well, start telling it. It ain't going to do me no good keeping it to yourself.

PEABODY (*impressively*). Captain John's coming back.

JEETER (*shocked*). Captain John! Captain John's dead.

PEABODY. Well, not Captain John, but his boy is.

JEETER. He is! (*Turning on* ADA.) Do you hear that, Ada? Captain John's coming back!

ADA. He didn't say Captain John. He said Captain John's boy.

JEETER. That don't make no difference. Captain Tim is Captain John's boy, ain't he? (*To* PEABODY:) He figures on giving credit to the farmers again, don't he?

PEABODY. I reckon so. That's what everybody thinks. He's down in Fuller now, but he'll be around about here tomorrow.

JEETER. God be praised. I knowed the Lord was aiming to provide. (*To* ADA:) Well, what has you got to say now, woman? Didn't I tell you I was going to plant me a crop this year? (*To* DUDE, *as* ADA *shrugs and doesn't answer:*) Hey, you, Dude. Get out in the fields and start burning off that broom sedge. You go to the far side and I'll go to the near. We're going to burn off all the fields this year. We're going to grow us the biggest crop you ever seen.

PEABODY. Well, I got to be going, Jeeter. I reckon I'll burn off my own fields now myself.

(JEETER *nods and he exits.*)

JEETER. Good-by, Henry. . . . Now you go in that house, Ada, and fix us something to eat. We're going to be hungry when we come back.

ADA. There ain't nothing to fix.

JEETER. You're the contrariest woman I ever seen. By God and by Jesus, if you ain't. You do like I tell you and quit saying all them damn fool things. . . . Come on, Dude, Captain John's boy has got to see we is all ready when he comes around tomorrow. Hurry up now . . . come on.

(JEETER *climbs over fence, left, in his hurry, exiting down the Tobacco Road.* DUDE *gives a hungry glance at* BESSIE, *then hurries to the gate and exits.* BESSIE *runs to fence and calls after* DUDE.)

BESSIE. Hey, you, Dude. Don't you forget. You pray like I told you and I'll be back here in the morning and let you know. (*Turns to* ADA *with a benevolent smile.*) Something tells me the Lord is going to like Dude a whole lot.

CURTAIN

ACT TWO

SCENE—*Same as Act One.*

TIME—*The following day.*

AT RISE—*It is still early morning and the amber glow of dawning day haunts the scene. Slowly, as time passes, the light comes on fuller and brighter until full day has arrived. As the curtain rises, no one is seen, the rotting house enjoying the dawn in solitude. In a moment, however,* BESSIE *enters swiftly through the gate, crosses to the porch, and hammers loudly on the door with her fists.*

BESSIE. Dude. . . . Hey, you, Dude. . . . Dude! (*She waits impatiently a few seconds, glancing first to the upstage corner of the house, then to the window downstage of the porch. Then she flings open the door and yells inside.*) Where is you, Dude?

(JEETER, *yawning and scratching, sticks his head out of the window and rubs his mouth with the back of his hand before speaking. He is still sleepy but is wearing, already, his tattered hat, although the rest of his body is, apparently, as naked as a blue jay.*)

JEETER. What you want with Dude this time of day, Bessie?

BESSIE. Never you mind. I want Dude. . . . Hey, you, Dude. (*She exits through the door, calling.*) Dude. . . . You, Dude. (JEETER *draws back from the window, looking inside, as* BESSIE'*s voice continues, off.*) Where is you, Dude? . . .

(*For an instant the stage is empty. Then* DUDE *enters left down Tobacco Road and crosses yard to the well, where he draws up water and drinks. He pays no attention to* BESSIE'*s oc-*

casionally repeated cry for him. Enter JEETER *through the house door. He is getting into his overalls, and is carrying his shirt, also socks and shoes in his hands. He sees* DUDE.)

JEETER. Hey, you, Dude, where you been? Bessie's been looking all over for you. (DUDE *doesn't answer, continuing to drink water.* JEETER *drops shoes and socks and slips into overalls.*) She just about tore up every bed in the house. Why don't you tell her where you is?

DUDE. Aw, to hell with her. (*Drinks.*)

JEETER (*dressing*). By God and by Jesus, I never seen a woman so anxious to see anybody. I reckon she wants to get married to you after all. (*Glances up as* DUDE *doesn't answer.*) Is you thinking about getting yourself married to her if that's what she wants?

DUDE. Aw, what do I want to do that for?

JEETER. You sure looked like you was set on doing that yesterday—all that hugging and rubbing of the other. What do you think about that now, Dude?

DUDE. Aw, hell, it don't always look the same to a man in the morning.

BESSIE (*off*). Dude! . . . Hey, you, Dude.

JEETER. Listen to her yelling. She must of gone clear through to the backyard by this time. Why don't you answer her, Dude? Where was you when she went looking in the bed for you? Where was you anyway?

DUDE. Out in the fields.

JEETER (*excitedly*). What about them fields? Is they finished burning?

DUDE (*nodding*). Most. Them to the north is still burning some.

JEETER. I is sure glad to hear that. We want to be ready to start the plowing and planting when Captain John's boy comes around today.

BESSIE (*off*). Dude. . . . Where is you, Dude? (BESSIE *enters around upstage corner of house, sees* DUDE.) There you is! (*Crosses swiftly to him. He glances at her, but keeps his back to her as she comes up.*) Didn't you hear me call you? (*Affectionately—putting her arms around his waist from the rear.*) Don't you know I been looking for you, Dude boy? (*Her arms tighten in a sudden and sharp squeeze that causes the water to slosh from the bucket he is holding.*)

DUDE. Hey, now look what you made me go and do.

BESSIE. Now that ain't nothing, Dude. Ain't you glad to see me? (*She presses him closer.*) Don't that make you feel good?

DUDE (*grinning*). H'mm. (*He puts down the bucket, turns and embraces her. Their posture is awkward and amusing. On the steps,* JEETER *continues to pick his feet and slowly put on shoes and socks, the while he watches the amorous couple.*)

JEETER. You must be figuring on getting married after all, Bessie. (BESSIE *starts to smooth down* DUDE'S *wet hair.* ADA *appears in doorway,* ELLIE MAY *at window.)*

BESSIE (*confidentially—nodding affirmatively*). The Lord told me to do it. I asked Him about it last night and He said, "Sister Bessie, Dude Lester is the man I want you to wed. Get up early in the morning and go to the Lester place and marry Dude the first thing." That's what He said, so I got out of bed and ran up here as fast as I could, because the Lord don't like to be kept waiting. (BESSIE *affectionately regards* DUDE, *who grins self-consciously.*)

JEETER. You hear what the Lord told Sister Bessie. What do you think of doing that now, Dude?

DUDE. Shucks! I don't know.

JEETER. What's ailing you? Ain't you man enough?

DUDE. Maybe I is, and maybe I ain't.

BESSIE. There ain't nothing to be scared of, Dude. You'll like being married to me because I know how to treat men fine. (DUDE *hesitates.* ADA *moves forward from doorway and rests against the porch upright.* GRANDMA LESTER *appears around the upstage corner of the house but keeps crouched and hidden so as not to attract attention.*)

JEETER. Well, is you going to do it, Dude?

DUDE (*self-consciously*). Aw, hell, what do I want to go marry her for? (DUDE *pulls ball out of his pocket and throws it against house.* BESSIE *glances swiftly at* DUDE'S *averted face, then plays her trump card. She turns to* JEETER.)

BESSIE (*wisely to* JEETER). Do you know what I is going to do, Jeeter?

JEETER. What?

BESSIE. I is going to buy me a new automobile. (*The effect of this on all of them is electric.* JEETER *comes quickly to his feet, and* DUDE *stops throwing ball with sudden awed interest.*)

JEETER. A new automobile? A sure enough brand-new automobile?

BESSIE (*nodding*). A brand-new one. (BESSIE *shakes her head emphatically.* DUDE *looks at her wide-eyed and unbelieving.*)

JEETER. Is you got money?

BESSIE (*proudly*). Eight hundred dollars.

JEETER. Eight hundred dollars! Where did you get all that money, Bessie?

BESSIE (*nodding*). My former husband had that in insurance and when he died I got it and put it in the bank.

JEETER. That sure is a heap of money. I didn't think there was that much real money in the whole country.

ADA. You ain't going to spend all that on a new automobile, is you?

BESSIE (*nodding*). Dude and me wants the best there is. Don't we, Dude? (DUDE *can only look at her wide-eyed.*)

ADA. It don't seem right to me. It seems to me like if you wanted to do right you'd give some of that money to Dude's old Ma and Pa. We could sure use it for snuff and food.

BESSIE. No, Sister Ada, the Lord didn't intend for it to be used like that. He intended I should use it to carry on the preaching and the praying. That's what I'm buying the new automobile for, so Dude and me can drive around when we take a notion to go somewheres in the Lord's work.

JEETER. Sister Bessie's right, Ada. There ain't nothing like working for the Lord. It don't make no difference to us about that money noway. Captain John's boy, Captain Tim, is back now and I'll get all the credit I need.

ADA. Humph. You is sure mighty high-handed with something you ain't got yet.

JEETER. Never you mind about her, Bessie. When you going to buy that new automobile?

BESSIE. I'm going over to Fuller and get it right now. (*Glances at* DUDE *eagerly.*) That is, if Dude and me gets married.

JEETER. What do you say to that now, Dude? Will you be wanting to marry Sister Bessie and ride around the country preaching and praying in a new automobile?

DUDE. Will it have a horn on it?

BESSIE. I reckon it will. Don't all new automobiles have horns?

DUDE. Can I drive it?

BESSIE. That's what I'm buying it for.

DUDE. Can I drive it all the time?

BESSIE. Sure, Dude. I don't know how to drive an automobile.

DUDE. Then why the hell not?

BESSIE (*joyfully hugging him and trying to kiss him*). Oh, Dude! (DUDE *escapes from her embrace and begins to put on his shoes.*)

ADA. When is you and Dude going to do all this riding around and preaching and praying? Is you going to get married before or after?

BESSIE. Before. We'll walk over to Fuller right now and buy the new automobile and then get married.

JEETER. Is you going to get leave of the county, or is you just going to live along without it?

BESSIE. I'm going to get the license for marrying.

JEETER. That costs about two dollars. Is you got two dollars? Dude ain't—Dude ain't got nothing.

BESSIE. I ain't asking Dude for one penny of money. I'll attend to that part myself. I've got eight hundred dollars in the bank and a few more besides. Dude and me won't have nothing to worry about. Will we, Dude?

DUDE (*impatiently*). Naw. Come on. We ain't got no time to lose. (DUDE *starts to walk away, while* BESSIE *is delayed arranging her hair, walking more slowly to the gate.*)

ADA. You'll have to make Dude wash his feet every once in a while, Bessie, because if you don't he'll dirty up the quilts. Sometimes he don't wash himself all winter long, and the quilts get that dirty you don't know how to go about the cleaning of them.

BESSIE (*pleasantly to* DUDE, *who is waiting at gate*). Is you like that, Dude?

DUDE (*impatiently*). If we is going to buy that new automobile, let's buy it.

ADA. Dude is just careless like his Pa. I had the hardest time learning him to wear his socks in the bed, because it was the only way I could keep the quilts clean. Dude is just going on the way his Pa done, so maybe you'd better make him wear his socks, too.

BESSIE. That's all right. Me and Dude'll know how to get along fine. (*Exit* DUDE. *Exit* BESSIE.)

ADA (*calling after* BESSIE *and* DUDE). If you get down around where Pearl lives, I wish you'd tell her that her Ma sure would like to see her again. (JEETER, ADA, *and* ELLIE MAY *move to fence to look after* DUDE *and* BESSIE. *Even* GRANDMA LESTER *looks from behind the trunk of the chinaberry tree.*)

JEETER (*shakes his head emphatically*). That Dude is the luckiest man alive. (*Directly to others:*) Now, ain't he? . . . He's going to get a brand-new car to ride around in and he's going to get married all at the same time. There's not many men get all that in the same day, I tell you. There ain't nobody else that I know of between here and the river who has got a brand-new automobile. And there ain't many men who has a wife as fine-looking as Sister Bessie is, neither. Bessie makes a fine woman for a man—any man, I don't care where you find him. She might be just a little bit more than Dude can take care of, though. Now if it was me, there wouldn't be no question of it. I'd please Sister Bessie coming and going right from the start, and keep it up clear to the end.

ADA (*in disgust*). Huh!

JEETER (*speaks now to* ELLIE MAY). Now you, Ellie May, it's time you was finding yourself a man. All my other children has got married. It's your time next. It was your time a long while ago, but I make allowances for you on account of your face. I know it's harder for you to mate up than it is for anybody else, but you ought to get out and find yourself a man to marry right away. It ain't going to get you nowhere fooling around with Lov like you was doing, because he's married already. He might have married you if it wasn't for the way you looked, but don't show your face too much and it won't stop the boys from getting after you. (*He pauses, and to his amazement* ELLIE MAY *bursts into heartbroken sobs, hiding her face in her hands.*) What's the matter? What's the matter with you, Ellie May? (*Still sobbing,* ELLIE MAY *runs to the gate and exits down the road.* JEETER *turns helplessly to* ADA.) Now I never seen the likes of that before. I wonder what I said to make her carry on like that? (JEETER *sits on porch.*) I declare to goodness I don't know what gets into women folks sometimes. There ain't never no way to figure them out. (*Starts to lie down, but* ADA *is in the way.*) By God and by Jesus, woman, can't you move over when a man wants to lay down?

ADA. Ain't you going to take no wood to Augusta today?

JEETER. Are you going to start that talk again? Ain't I told you Captain Tim is coming and I'm going to plant me a crop. I've got to save my strength for that.

ADA. Humph! There ain't a bite in the house, and nobody never saved their strength by not eating.

JEETER. Never mind that now. Captain Tim will fix that. Anyhow, I couldn't make that old automobile go even if I wanted to.

ADA. Do you reckon Dude and Bessie will let you take a load in their new car?

JEETER. I ain't aiming to carry no more wood to Augusta. But I sure is going to take a ride in that new car. I reckon I'll be riding clear over into Burke County one of these days to see Tom.

ADA. If you see him you might mention that his old ma sure would like a stylish dress to die in. I know he won't stand back with his money for a little thing like that.

JEETER. I'll mention it, but I don't know how he'll take it. I expect he's got a raft of children to provide for.

ADA. Reckon he has got some children?

JEETER. Maybe some.

ADA. I sure would like to see them. I know I must have a whole heap of grandchildren somewhere. I'm bound to have, with all them boys and girls off from home.

JEETER. Clara has got a raft of children, I bet. She was always talking about having them. And they say over in Fuller that Lizzie Belle has got a lot of them, too. I don't know how other folks know more about such things than I do. Looks like I ought to be the one who knows most about my own children. (*Enter* LOV, *who stands just inside gate, panting heavily and looking at* ADA *and* JEETER. JEETER *glances up and sees* LOV, *whose heaving chest and haunted eyes make him believe* LOV *has come for revenge for stealing the turnips.*) Lov, by God! (*He springs to his feet and darts for the downstage corner of the well.*)

LOV (*through quick breathing*). Never mind running, Jeeter, I ain't going to hurt you.

JEETER (*at corner of house, still ready to run*). Ain't you peeved about me stealing them turnips yesterday?

LOV (*wearily*). I don't care about that no more.

JEETER. What's the matter with you, Lov? You look like you run all the way here. What's wrong with you, anyway? (LOV *doesn't answer and sits.*) Is you sick? (LOV *nods negatively.*)

ADA (*higher note—stepping forward*). It's Pearl! That's what it is—it's Pearl! (LOV *looks at her and nods. She comes forward hysterically.*)

JEETER. What's the matter with her, Lov?

LOV. She run off.

ADA. No! She didn't! She wouldn't have done that without seeing her ma first.

LOV (*coming forward—shaking head*). She just run off.

JEETER. How do you know, Lov? Maybe she's just hiding in the woods someplace.

LOV (*shakes his head*). Jones Peabody saw her walking along the road to Augusta this morning.

ADA. Augusta!

LOV. He said he stopped and asked her where she was going, but she wouldn't talk to him. She just kept on going.

ADA (*fiercely to* LOV). You done something to her. Don't tell me you didn't.

LOV. No, I didn't, Ada. I woke up early this morning and looked at her down on that pallet on the floor and I just couldn't stand it no longer. I got down and hugged her in my arms. I wasn't going to hurt her. I just wanted to hold her for a minute. But she got loose from me and I ain't seen her since.

(ADA *rocks, heartbroken, on the porch.*)

JEETER. Well, I figured that she was going to run off to Augusta one of these days, only she was always afraid before.

LOV. Jones Peabody said she acted like she was about scared to death this morning. (*Desperately:*) I got to get her back, Jeeter. I just got to get her back.

JEETER. Ain't much use you figuring on that. All them girls went off all of a sudden. Lizzie Belle up and went to Augusta just like that. (*He snaps his fingers.*)

LOV. Ain't there something I can do, Jeeter?

JEETER. About the best thing you can do, Lov, is let her be.

LOV. If I was to go up to Augusta and find her, do you reckon she'd let me bring her back home to stay? . . . Reckon she would, Jeeter?

JEETER. I wouldn't recommend that. You'll lose your time down there at the chute while you was looking for her, and if you was to bring her back she'd run off again twice as quick.

LOV. She might get hurt up there.

JEETER. Lizzie Belle and Clara took care of themselves all right, didn't they?

LOV. Pearl ain't like them.

JEETER. In many ways she ain't, but in many she is, too. She wasn't never satisfied living down here on the Tobacco Road. She's just like Lizzie Belle and Clara and the other gals in that respect. I can't call all their names right now, but it was every durn one of them, anyhow. They all wanted stylish clothes.

LOV. Pearl never said nothing to me about wanting stylish clothes. She never said anything to me at all.

JEETER. It's just like I said. They're like their Ma. Ada there ain't satisfied neither, but she can't do nothing about it. I broke her of wanting to run off, but them gals was more than I could take care of. There was too durn many of them for one man to break. They just up and went.

LOV (*thinking aloud*). I sort of hate to lose her, for some reason or another. All them long yellow curls hanging down her back always made me hate the time when she would grow up and be old.

JEETER. That sure ain't no lie. Pearl had the prettiest yellow hair of any gal I ever saw. I wish Ada had been that pretty. Even when Ada was a young gal she was that durn ugly it was a sin. I reckon I ain't never seen an uglier woman in the whole country.

LOV. I been the lonesomest man in the whole country for the longest time, Jeeter. Ain't there something you can do to get her back again?

JEETER. I might try something, but it wouldn't do no good. One way or another I've said about everything I can to that girl, but she won't even answer me. She won't talk to nobody but her Ma. It wouldn't do no good for me to do anything, even if you could find her.

LOV. Ada, will you? . . . (*Sees hopelessness of help from* ADA. *Abjectly:*) Well, I've got to get back to the chute. That morning freight will be coming along pretty soon now and it always empties all the scoops. They raise hell if they ain't filled up again. (*Turns; crosses to gate; leans against post.*)

JEETER. I sure am glad you wasn't riled about the turnips, Lov. I meant to go down first thing this morning and talk to you about that, but Dude and Bessie went off to get married and I forgot all about it. Did you hear about that, Lov? Dude and Bessie went off to Fuller to get married and buy them a new automobile all at the same time. Now ain't that something! (LOV *nods.*)

LOV. If you happen to see or hear anything about Pearl, you let me know. (LOV *exits down road left.*)

JEETER (*turning back to* ADA, *who still sits on the porch, staring blankly into space*). Lov sure is a funny one. He just can't think about anything but Pearl. It looks to me like he wouldn't want a gal that won't stay in the bed with him. I don't understand him at all. I don't understand Pearl, for that matter, neither. I'd of bet almost anything she would have come up here and told us good-by before running off. But it's like I always said. Coming or going, you can't never tell about women. (*Looks at* ADA, *hoping she'll talk to him. Crosses closer to her, but her eyes stare straight ahead. Finally he hits her gently with the back of his hand.*) That's all right, Ada. (*He crosses to fence, left, climbs it, glances back at her.*) If Captain John's boy comes along, you tell him I'll be back soon. I'm going out to look at them fields.

(JEETER *exits.* ADA *sits staring ahead, her eyes holding a depth of suffering. Suddenly there is an offstage cry from* JEETER *and she turns to look toward the gate.*)

JEETER (*off—calling*). Ada—Ada! (*Lower, but still off.*) Come on, child—come on. (*He appears at the edge of the gate, pulling someone after him.* ADA, *eyes wide with wonder, stands up.*) Come on—there ain't nothing to be afraid of. Your old Pa ain't going to hurt you. (*He pulls* PEARL *through the gate.*) Look, Ada—look what I found hiding in the broom sedge.

ADA (*lifts her hands, palms turned up, toward her daughter*). Pearl!

PEARL. Ma!! (*Pulling away from* JEETER, PEARL *rushes across stage and flings herself, sobbing, into her mother's arms.* JEETER, *eager and alive with excitement and admiration, comes up to the two women.* PEARL *is a beautiful child. She looks at least sixteen, in spite of the fact that she is much less than that, and is almost as tall as* ADA. *She is barefoot, and wears only a shabby, dark gray calico dress. Her hair hangs down over her shoulders like a cloud of spun gold.* ADA *soothes her.*)

ADA. There, now—there, now, don't cry. You got your old ma again.

JEETER (*prancing around* PEARL). Now ain't that somethin'! I was just turning to go across the fields when I saw that yellow head of hers moving in the broom sedge and there she was. If she hadn't stumbled I never would of caught her. Ain't she pretty! She's about the prettiest piece in the whole country. . . .

ADA. Go away, Jeeter.

JEETER (*who hasn't the slightest intention of going away*). Ain't she growed some in the past year, though? She's most a grown woman by now. (*Moves* PEARL'S *dress the better to see her figure.*) By God and by Jesus if she ain't.

ADA (*sharply—slapping* JEETER'S *hand away*). Stop that, Jeeter.

JEETER. What for? She is, ain't she? Look how white and gold she looks with that yellow hair hanging down her back. . . . What are you standing there crying for, Pearl? Why didn't you go on to Augusta like you started to anyway? Was you scared? Was that it, Pearl?

ADA. She wanted to see her old ma first. (*To* PEARL:) That was it, wasn't it, child? (PEARL *nods, her head still on her mother's shoulder, and* ADA *speaks to* JEETER.) There, you see that, Jeeter. Now you go on away like I tell you. She ain't going to talk none while you're here.

JEETER. I got to speak to her about Lov first. Now that she ain't run away she'll have to begin treating him right.

ADA. Hush up, Jeeter. Maybe she ain't going to go back and live with Lov at all. Just because she didn't go all the way to Augusta, don't mean she's going to stay with Lov again.

JEETER. What's that? Now you wait a minute. That ain't right. When a gal is mated up with a man she's got to live with him.

ADA. Mind your own business, Jeeter.

JEETER. I is minding my own business. I'm minding my business and Lov's business, too. A gal's got no right to act like Pearl's been acting. No, sir. I say Pearl has got to go back and live in the house with Lov and let him have his rights with her.

ADA (*angrily*). Now you listen to me, Jeeter Lester. You keep out of this. If I says so Pearl can do just like she wants. You ain't got the right to tell her what she's got to do.

JEETER. What! Who you talking to, anyway? I'm her pa, ain't I?

ADA. No, you ain't.

JEETER. What?

ADA. That's what.

JEETER. By God and by Jesus! Do you know what you're saying, woman?

ADA. I sure do. You ain't her pa. You never was and never will be.

JEETER (*lightly amazed*). Well, by damn—now what do you think of that?

ADA. Whatever made you think you was, anyway? Do you think a lazy old fool like you could be the daddy of a gal like Pearl?

JEETER (*without rancor*). Well, I thought about that now and then. She didn't look to me like none of the Lesters I ever heard of.

ADA. There ain't no Lester in her. Her real pa wouldn't have no truck with any of you.

JEETER. It wasn't that Henry Peabody down the road, was it?

ADA (*with disgust*). No.

JEETER. I didn't think it was. He couldn't have a pretty piece like Pearl for a child any more than I could. Who was it, Ada?

ADA. Nobody you ever knew. He came from South Carolina and was on his way to Texas.

JEETER. H'mm. I don't remember nobody like that. I must of been in Fuller, or even maybe in Augusta at the time.

ADA. You was down seeing Captain John about a mule to plow with.

JEETER. By God and by Jesus, I remember now. I remember that old mule just like I remember that old cow I used to have. Remember that old mule, Ada?

ADA. I reckon.

JEETER. It was the last one I ever got off Captain John. Pretty soon after that he moved up to Augusta and I ain't heard a word from him since, until just now when his boy is coming back. (*To* PEARL:) Did you hear about that, Pearl? Captain John's boy is coming back this morning and I'm going to plant me a crop this year sure.

ADA. Pearl ain't interested in that now.

JEETER (*indignantly*). Well, she ought to be. Everybody ought to be when they's been born and raised on the land like I was. Captain John was and Captain John's boy that comes after him is interested just as much, you'll find out. You can't keep nobody like Captain John or me away from the land forever.

ADA. Shut up, Jeeter. Can't you see Pearl is all wore out? If Jones Peabody saw her on the road to Augusta she must of walked about ten miles this morning to get here. (*To* PEARL:) Is you hungry, Pearl? (PEARL *shakes her head affirmatively.*)

JEETER (*watching the girl with disapproval*). Now what's the sense to all that shaking of your head? (*Mimics her.*) What's the meaning of all that? It's plain to see you ain't no child of mine all right. Coming and going us Lesters has always talked about as much as anybody in the whole country. Can't you speak up?

ADA. Quit your nagging, Jeeter. You know what she means all right. She's hungry. You get busy and find her something to eat.

JEETER. Ain't you got no sense at all, Ada? How can I get her something to eat when there ain't even nothing for myself.

ADA. You got something yesterday from Lov when *you* was hungry.

JEETER. Is you aiming to make me steal again, woman? (ADA *shrugs.*) Well, if you is I ain't. The Lord's a wise old somebody. He's watching around the corner every minute for just such as that. You can't fool Him about stealing. . . . Besides there ain't nothing between here and Fuller to steal noway.

ADA. I heard tell Morgan Prior bought hisself a sack of corn meal down to McCoy the other day.

JEETER. Corn meal! I ain't et corn meal since—— (*Checks himself.*) No, sir! Maybe he did and maybe he didn't, but I ain't going near Morgan Prior's house no matter what the circumstance. I promised the Lord——

ADA (*shrewdly*). They say he's got some bacon and fat back, too.

JEETER. Woman, you is a sinner in the eyes of God! . . . (*Whistles.*) Morgan Prior must be a powerful rich man to have all that to eat. Maybe if I went down there and asked him he might let me borrow some for a little while.

ADA. Humph! I don't build no hopes on that. Morgan Prior ain't going to let you borrow nothing.

JEETER. I don't see why he oughtn't. The Lord says the rich should share their bounty with the poor. You come along with me, Ada, and we'll see if Morgan Prior is ready to do like the Lord says.

ADA. Me? What do you want me for?

JEETER. Don't you know nothing, woman? If I want to borrow me something from Morgan Prior somebody's got to talk to him at the front door, while I go around to the back, don't they? (*A full, belligerent pause.*) Now, hurry up. Morgan Prior might be out early plowing the fields and it would be an almighty temptation and a sin if we borrowed something when he wasn't at home.

ADA. You go get my old hairbrush first. Pearl ain't brushed her hair this morning.

JEETER (*eagerly*). Is she going to do that?

ADA (*with an abrupt nod*). While I'm gone off. (JEETER *exits quickly into house.*)

PEARL (*gripping* ADA). Oh, Ma, don't go off from me.

ADA (*comforting her*). There now. You don't need to worry no more. Your old ma's looking out for you from now on. You don't have to go back and live with Lov no matter what Jeeter says.

PEARL. I don't never want to go back!

ADA. You don't have to. But one of these days you got to go down to Augusta to live. I've made up my mind to that.

PEARL. I'm scared, Ma.

(JEETER *enters with hairbrush.*)

JEETER (*eagerly*). Here you is, Ada. Great day, we ought to see something now! Lov says there ain't a prettier piece in the whole country than Pearl when she's brushing her hair and I'm inclined to agree with him.

ADA (*snatching brush*). Go along, Jeeter. Don't think you're going to stay around here all day watching Pearl.

JEETER. Lord, Ada, don't get so peeved. I ain't doing nothing.

ADA. No, and you never would if I didn't make you. Hurry up now. You go along. I'll catch up with you down the road.

JEETER. Well—— (*Reluctantly crossing to gate.*) Pearl, if Captain John's boy comes here, you tell him I won't be gone long. You tell him I got a little business down the way and to wait right here for me. (*Exits.*)

ADA. Now you listen to me, honey. There ain't no sense you being scared about going off to Augusta. All my other gals went there or someplace else to live and they don't regret it.

PEARL (*fervently*). I want to stay here with you.

ADA. Never mind that. I ain't going to be here long. One of these days I'm going to die.

PEARL. No—no, you ain't!

ADA. That's all right, honey. It don't matter—only sometimes I do wish I had me a stylish dress to be buried in.

PEARL. I'll get you a stylish dress, Ma. Honest I will.

ADA. Don't you care about me. You got to look out for yourself. You got to have a hat to put on and shoes and dresses to wear like the gals in Augusta.

PEARL. I don't want none.

ADA. Sure you do. You don't want to stay here like your old ma, raising a raft of children and no snuff to calm you when there ain't nothing to eat. None of my other children was as pretty as you, or as smart, neither, when you want to talk, and if they can do it you can do it.

(JEETER *appears on Tobacco Road.*)

JEETER. Hey, you, Ada. Is you coming or ain't you?

ADA. I heard you, I'm coming. (*Gets up. Speaks to* PEARL.) Now, honey, you just think about that while I'm gone. And don't fret none. I won't be off long. (*Enter* GRANDMA LESTER *from around house, as* ADA *crosses to gate.*) Hey, you, old woman. You go out in the broom sedge and pick up some sticks for the fire. We might be wanting to cook around here pretty soon now. (*To* PEARL:) Fix up your hair now, honey.

(ADA *exits and* GRANDMA LESTER *hurries to the porch and pulls her old croker sack from beneath it.* PEARL *watches her. Straightening up, the old woman looks long at* PEARL. *Hobbling forward she tries to touch the girl's hair, but* PEARL *backs away from her.* GRANDMA LESTER *stops, her eyes reflecting her deep hurt and disappointment. For a moment more she gazes at the girl, then turns and shuffles off.* PEARL *stands looking after her, and when the* OLD WOMAN *has quite gone, she goes to the well and dips her brush in the bucket. She has taken a stroke or two with the brush when she suddenly stops and listens. The audience hears nothing, but she does. Moving quickly in back of the well, she drops to her knees, listening and waiting. Presently* HENRY PEABODY *enters down the road, running. He glances inside the yard, sees nothing, and then comes through the gate to the porch. Pushing open the door he calls inside.*)

PEABODY. Jeeter—hey, you, Jeeter—Ada. . . . Aw, to hell with them. (*No answer and he comes down from the porch and goes to upstage corner of the house; he glances around. Seeing nothing, then, he moves quickly to the gate and exits. Slowly and cautiously* PEARL *now comes around from behind the well, runs to the road to see if* PEABODY *has gone, then comes back to the porch and sits, her back to the gate, brushing her hair. She is so preoccupied she does not hear* LOV *enter quietly on the Tobacco Road. He sees her. He pauses. He moves silently through the gate across the yard on the balls of his feet and stands in back of her, watching. Suddenly he reaches down and takes her hand firmly as it makes a stroke with the brush. She leaps to her feet, panic-stricken, to run off, but his hold is too strong and he pulls her back.*)

LOV (*pleading*). Don't run off, Pearl. I ain't going to hurt you. (*She won't answer or look at him.*) If you only wouldn't run away, I'd leave hold of you now and just watch you brush your hair again. I'd rather see you do that than anything I can think of. There ain't nobody got pretty hair like you. I used to sit on the porch and watch through the window when you was combing and brushing it and I just couldn't keep my eyes off it. Will you promise you won't run off again if I leave you go? (*Pause as he waits for her to answer.*) Won't you talk to me? Won't you say nothing to me at all? You don't know how I been missing you since you run off. I didn't mean nothing by what I done this morning. It's just that you won't stay in the bed with me or talk to me. Sometimes I just shake all over, for wanting to squeeze you so hard. I keep on thinking how pretty your eyes is early in the morning. They's pretty any time of the day, but early in the morning they's the prettiest things a man could ever want to look at. Won't you come back again sometime? You won't even have to stay in the bed with me. Will you come back if I do that, Pearl? (*He waits, but still there is no answer.*) Remember that last pretty I got for you? I can remember like it was yesterday. They was green beads on a long string and when you put them around your neck I swear to God if it didn't make you about the prettiest girl I ever heard tell about. (*Pitiful enthusiasm.*) I tell you what . . . one of these days we'll ride up to Augusta and buy you a hat—and a stylish dress, too. Would you like to do that? Maybe Dude and Bessie will take us in the new automobile they're buying today. Did you know about that, Pearl? Dude and Bessie is getting married and is buying a new automobile. (*Not a flicker of interest shows in* PEARL'S *impassive expression.* LOV *has a dream.*) A new automobile! That's what we'll get one of these days, and we'll ride all over the whole country faster than that old No. 7 passenger ever thought of going—— (*In the excitement stimulated by imagination,* LOV *has released his hold on* PEARL'S *wrist and she has sprung clear of him. His pleading, broken cry falls on unhearing ears. Swiftly—much more swiftly than his clumsiness will permit him to follow—she steps away from the porch, whirls, and dashes to the gate.*) Pearl! (*Just as* PEARL *reaches the gate,* ADA *appears and the girl throws herself into her mother's arms.*)

PEARL. Ma! Ma! (ADA *says nothing, but over* PEARL'S *shoulder her eyes fasten malevolently on the innocent* LOV. *Appearances are against him, he knows it, and he is so emotionally upset his sense of guilt gains upper hand. For a full pause they regard each other.*)

LOV (*pitifully apologetic*). I didn't do nothing, Ada. We was just talking. I didn't hurt her none. (ADA *pushes* PEARL *behind her, picks up stick, and advances grimly and silently on him. He takes an involuntary step back.*) I just wanted her to come back and live in the house with me. (ADA *comes up to him, her fury blazing in her eyes. The stick falls across* LOV'S *hunched shoulders. He stands his ground, but lowers his head and raises his arms to protect himself.* PEARL *is thrilled.*) Don't do that, Ada—don't do that. (*Her answer is to strike him again. Enter* JEETER, *carrying a couple of small packages. His eyes light up as he sees the action.*)

JEETER. Great day in the morning, will you look at that! What you beating Lov for, Ada? What's he done to make you beat him like that?

LOV. I ain't done nothing, Jeeter—— (*He is stopped by a whack.*)

JEETER. By God and by Jesus, maybe you ain't, but you sure is getting a beating for it just the same. I don't remember when I ever seen such a good, round beating as you is getting right this minute.

(LOV *gives ground slowly, so that* ADA *misses now and again.*)

LOV. I tell you I ain't done nothing!

JEETER. That don't stand to reason to me. In my experience I found that people usually get what's coming to them in this world or the next and it looks to me like right now you is getting yours in this.

LOV. I swear to God I ain't, Jeeter.

JEETER. Do you hear that, Ada? Lov says he ain't done nothing. What have you got to say about that?

ADA. Shut up.

JEETER. By God, woman, don't talk like that. Put down that stick, do you hear me? You has already done one whopping big sin today. You ought to be mighty sorry to do another. (LOV *manages to grab* ADA's *stick and stop the attack.* JEETER *nods approval.*) I'm glad to see you do that, Lov. That was no way for Ada to treat you. But what did you do to her anyway to make her keep hitting you with that old stick all the time?

LOV. I only wanted Pearl to come back and live with me.

ADA (*holding* PEARL). Pearl ain't never going back and live with you. There ain't no use you trying to make her, either. She's going to Augusta just like she set out to do this morning and nothing you do can stop her.

LOV. I'm her husband, ain't I? I can stop her and by God I will!

ADA (*belligerently*). You just try it.

JEETER. There ain't no sense you trying to carry your point, Lov. Ada's made up her mind Pearl's going to Augusta and there ain't nothing I know can change it.

LOV. You can't be letting Pearl do that. It ain't right.

JEETER. Right or wrong ain't got nothing to do with it where Ada is concerned. Just a little while ago she made me borrow something when Morgan Prior wasn't at the house. That's about the biggest sin a woman can make a man do, but she don't care none. There ain't no use talking to her about right or wrong.

LOV. Augusta ain't no place for a girl as pretty as she is.

JEETER. I sure would like to stand in her way, but I ain't got no more right than that—— (*Snaps his fingers characteristically.*) Ada's the one you got to talk to, about that.

LOV. Ada's her ma, but you're her pa, ain't you?

JEETER. By God and by Jesus, no! Ada there was horsing around big as you please with some man while I was down borrowing me a mule one time. That don't make me her pa no more than you is.

LOV. You took care of her until she was married to me. That's the same thing.

JEETER. No, it ain't. The Lord don't take no recognition of that. The Lord is a wise old somebody. He said His flesh is His flesh. That don't make no provision for Ada horsing around while I'm down borrowing me a mule.

(*Enter* ELLIE MAY, *who hides bashfully behind tree when she sees* LOV.)

ADA. You might just as well go away, Lov. I ain't lettin' Pearl go back with you no matter how much you talk, less'n she wants to. . . . And I don't reckon she wants to.

LOV. Pearl—won't you come back? (*Pearl shrinks farther back.* LOV *glances pleadingly at* ADA.) Ada—— (LOV *glances helplessly from* ADA *to* PEARL, *then lowers his head and reaches down to pick up his hat, which has fallen off. He dusts it off on his knee and is starting away when* JEETER *stops him.*)

JEETER. Hold on there, Lov. No sense you going off without a gal just because Pearl don't want to go with you. Why don't you take Ellie May there? (ELLIE MAY, *behind her chinaberry tree, giggles and puts her arm over her mouth to hide the torn lip.* LOV *glances from* JEETER *to* ELLIE MAY, *then back to* JEETER *again. Without a word he pulls his hat tighter and again starts off.* JEETER *takes a step forward as he sees* LOV'S *indifference.* LOV *takes another step and* JEETER *follows.*) Ellie May's got to get a man somewhere. When me and Ada's dead and gone there won't be nobody to watch after her. The niggers would haul off and come here by the dozen. The niggers would get her in no time if she was here by herself. (ELLIE MAY *sets up her giggling and wriggling again and* LOV *once more regards her objectively and solemnly.*)

LOV (*looking away from* ELLIE MAY. *He speaks stubbornly*). I want Pearl.

JEETER (*exasperated*). By God and by Jesus, you know you ain't going to get Pearl, so what's the sense going on talking about that? Now Ellie May there's got a lot of——

LOV. Ellie May's got that ugly-looking face.

(ELLIE MAY, *standing in* LOV'S *path, giggles and squirms.* LOV *looks at her hard as* JEETER *continues.*)

JEETER. You and her was hugging and rubbing of each other to beat all hell just yesterday. Wouldn't you like to do that some more?

LOV (*still looking hard at* ELLIE MAY). No, by God! I want Pearl or nothing. (*He moves past her and exits.* JEETER *shakes his head as he watches* LOV *disappear down the road.*)

JEETER (*chiefly to* ADA). Now that's something I can't understand at all. It looks to me when a man loses one gal he'd be thankful to get another—hey, stop that! What you doing there, Ellie May? (*His sentence has been broken by* ELLIE MAY'S *attack on* PEARL. *She pushes* PEARL *to the ground, picks up the stick* ADA *dropped after beating* LOV, *and belabors her pretty sister furiously.* JEETER *steps forward to stop her, but he is slower than the infuriated* ADA, *who grabs the stick away from* ELLIE MAY *and starts beating her in turn.* ELLIE MAY *fights back for a moment.* GRANDMA LESTER *enters furtively and goes behind the chinaberry tree where she observes scene.*)

ADA (*swinging stick sharply*). I'll show you—I'll show you. (ELLIE MAY *gives up the unequal fight and flees through the gate and left down road.* PEARL *gets up and seeks protection behind her mother.*) Don't you worry none, Pearl. She won't do that no more. (*She starts dusting off* PEARL'S *dress.*)

JEETER (*shaking his head*). Great day in the morning! I never seen such beating one of the other as I seen here today. What do you suppose Ellie May done that for, Ada? (ADA *shoots him a baleful glance, but the disdainful reply she is forming is checked by the sudden muffled blast of a motor car horn. All of them look up. The horn, louder, sounds again.* JEETER'S *face lights up.*) That's Dude! That's Dude and Bessie in that new automobile. (JEETER *goes through gate, works to center stage, and looks down the road.* ADA *crosses to fence and looks. Even* PEARL *is moved by sudden interest and goes to the fence.*

Only GRANDMA LESTER *comes further in, taking her place downstage of the well, where she huddles, listening and waiting.*) Here they come! Just look at them! It's a brand-new automobile, all right—just look at that shiny black paint! Great day in the morning! Just look at them coming yonder! (*The horn sounds again—closer.* JEETER *speaks with pride.*) Listen to Dude blow that horn. Don't he blow it pretty, though?

(ELLIE MAY *enters left and flashes down the Tobacco Road on a dead run, exiting right to meet the car.*)

ADA. Ain't that the prettiest sight to see, Pearl? Look at that dust flying up behind. It makes it look like a big black chariot, running away from a cyclone. (*The horn sounds again, to the same rhythm of an engineer blowing a locomotive whistle.*)

JEETER. That's Dude driving it and blowing the horn, too. (*Mounting excitement.*) Hi, there, Dude! Hi, Bessie. (*Swinging down from the fence, he runs through gate and exits down road toward car. The horn continues to sound.* ADA, PEARL, *and* GRANDMA LESTER *wait, watching. We hear* JEETER *returning before we see him.*) By God, Bessie, I been seeing you come a far piece off in that new automobile. (BESSIE *and* JEETER *enter.*) In all my days I never seen a finer looking machine. Is it real brand new?

BESSIE (*vigorously and proudly*). I paid the whole eight hundred dollars for it.

(*The horn sounds.*)

JEETER (*listens to* DUDE, *then speaks*). By God and by Jesus, it sure does make me feel happy again to know there's such a handsome automobile around. Don't you reckon you could take me for a little trip, Bessie? I sure would like to go off in it for a piece.

BESSIE (*looking pretentiously at marriage license she carries.*) I reckon when Dude and me gets back you can go riding.

JEETER. Where is you and Dude going to, Bessie?

BESSIE (*proudly*). We're going to ride around like married folks.

ADA. Did you and Dude get married in Fuller?

BESSIE. Not all the way. I got leave of the county, however. It cost two dollars to do that little bit. (*Waves license at them.*) There's the paper to show it.

ADA. Ain't you going to get a preacher?

BESSIE. I is not! Ain't I a preacher of the gospel? I'm going to do it myself. Ain't no Hardshell Baptist going to fool with us.

JEETER. I knowed you would do it the right way. You sure is a fine woman preacher, Sister Bessie. (DUDE *blows horn again.* JEETER *smiles complacently.*) That there old Dude sure does like fooling around with that there old horn.

BESSIE (*a bit peeved*). He's been doing that about every minute all the way up from Fuller. Looks to me like he'd want to stop now that we is about to do the rest of the marrying.

ADA. Did you and Dude have any trouble getting leave from the county?

BESSIE. None to speak of. At first the man said Dude was too young and that I'd have to get the consent of his ma and pa. I told him the Lord said for me to marry Dude, but he told me that didn't make no difference. So I started praying right then and there, and pretty soon the man said if I would just stop he'd do anything I wanted.

JEETER. You sure is a powerful pray-er, all right, Sister Bessie. You is about the best pray-er and Dude is about the best automobile driver in the country. Coming and going that makes you just about equal. (*Enter* DUDE *lugging, with quite some noise, a torn-off, dented fender.* JEETER *whirls to look at him.*) Great day, Dude, what you got there? Ain't that a fender off your new car?

DUDE (*dropping fender without concern*). Uh-huh.

JEETER. Now how did that happen? Did you run into something?

DUDE. We was coming back from Fuller and I was looking out at a big turpentine still, and then the first thing I knowed we was smashed smack bang into the back of a two-horse wagon.

JEETER. Didn't hurt the running of the automobile, though, did it?

DUDE. Naw. It runs like it was brand new yet. The horn wasn't hurt none at all. It blows just as pretty as it did at the start.

JEETER (*nodding in agreement*). Don't pay no attention to it, Bessie. Just leave it be and you'll never know that machine was any different than when you got it.

BESSIE. That's right. I ain't letting it worry me none, because it wasn't Dude's fault. He was looking at the big turpentine still alongside the road, when the wagon got in our way. The nigger driving it ought to have had enough sense to move over.

JEETER. Was you blowing the horn then, Dude?

DUDE. Not right then I wasn't. I was busy looking at that big still. I never saw one that big nowhere. It was most as big as a corn-liquor still, only it wasn't so shiny-looking.

BESSIE (*bending down and wiping dust from fender with her skirt*). It's a shame to get the new car smashed up so soon, however. It was brand new not more than an hour ago.

DUDE. It was that damn nigger. If he hadn't been asleep on the wagon it wouldn't have happened at all. He was plumb asleep till it woke him up and threw him out in the ditch.

JEETER. He didn't get hurt much, did he?

DUDE. I don't know about that. The wagon turned over on him and mashed him some. His eyes was wide open all the time, but I couldn't make him say nothing. He looked like he was dead.

JEETER. Niggers will get killed. Looks like there just ain't no way to stop it.

(DUDE *takes out ball and hurls it against house.*)

ADA. When is you and Dude going to go on with the marrying?

BESSIE (*turning from fender and resuming her aggressive manner*). Right this minute. (*Smooths her skirt. Unrolls license again.*) Come on, Dude.

DUDE (*turning impatiently with ball in hand*). What do you want to do now?

BESSIE. Marry us.

DUDE. Didn't you get that all done at the courthouse in Fuller?

BESSIE (*still extending his end of license*). That wasn't all. We got to get married in the sight of the Lord.

DUDE. Humph! (*Throws ball again.*)

JEETER. By God and by Jesus, Dude, stop chunking that ball against that old house and do what Bessie tells you

DUDE. I want to take a ride.

BESSIE. We got plenty of time to ride around after we is married.

DUDE. Will we go then?

BESSIE. Yes, Dude.

DUDE. Is you sure?

BESSIE. Sure, Dude.

DUDE. What the hell, then. Then what do I do?

BESSIE (*extending license*). You hold your end of the license while I pray. (DUDE *gingerly takes one end of license, and* BESSIE *the other.* BESSIE *lowers her head and closes her eyes for several seconds of silent prayer, while* DUDE *looks down on her with a slight, rather perplexed frown. Presently* BESSIE *lifts her head, but her eyes are still closed as she intones*): I marry us man and wife. So be it. That's all, God. Amen. (*She opens her eyes and smiles gently up at* DUDE.)

DUDE (*pulling away*). Come on.

BESSIE. I got to pray now. You kneel down on the ground while I make a little prayer. (BESSIE *and others all kneel and* DUDE *reluctantly follows, still watching her with his expression of bored annoyance. Praying*): Dear God, Dude and me is married now. We is wife and husband. Dude, he is an innocent young boy, unused to the sinful ways of the country, and I am a woman preacher of the gospel. You ought to make Dude a preacher, too, and let us use our new automobile in taking trips to pray for sinners. You ought to learn him how to be a fine preacher so we can make all the goats into sheep. That's all this time. We're in a hurry now. Save us from the devil and make a place for us in heaven. Amen. (*She opens her eyes and smiles brightly at* DUDE.)

JEETER (*jumping up*). Bless the Lord, that was one of the prettiest marriages I ever seen. Dude sure got hisself good and wed, didn't he, Ada?

ADA. Humph!

JEETER (*goes to* BESSIE *and kisses her*). Praise God, Sister Bessie, that Dude is a lucky man. I'd sure like to be in his place right now.

BESSIE (*laughing coyly*). Be still, you old sinner.

JEETER (*to* DUDE). Yes, sir, Dude, boy. You sure is lucky to get a fine woman like Bessie.

DUDE (*shaking him off*). Aw, shut up, you old fool.

(BESSIE *raps on the porch and* JEETER *turns to look at her.*)

JEETER. What you knocking on the porch for, Bessie? (*She raps again and* JEETER'S *face clears.*) Great day! Now, why didn't I think of that? . . . You, Dude—can't you see how bad Sister Bessie wants to go into the house?

DUDE. What for?

JEETER. Never mind what for. (*He starts pushing* DUDE.)

BESSIE (*taking* DUDE'S *arm*). Just for now. Come on, Dude.

DUDE. You said we was going for a ride.

BESSIE. We can go after a little while.

JEETER (*pushing him harder*). What's the matter with you, Dude? Go on in with Sister Bessie.

(*Slowly and grudgingly* DUDE *allows himself to be shoved and pulled on to the porch. At the door he pauses.*)

DUDE. This is a hell of a time to be going indoors. (BESSIE *and* DUDE *exit into the house, the door closing.* JEETER *stands almost center stage, his eyes shining with excitement.* ELLIE MAY *crosses quickly to the window and draws herself up on her toes, her fingers on the sill, as she tries to look into the house.* JEETER *crosses to window and pulls* ELLIE MAY *away.*)

JEETER. You got no business trying to see inside. Sister Bessie and Dude is married. (*Shoving* ELLIE MAY *aside, he promptly pulls himself up on the sill to see.* ELLIE MAY *suddenly turns and crosses swiftly toward porch, where* ADA *leans against an upright.* PEARL *stands on the ground at the edge of the porch near her mother.*)

ELLIE MAY (*passing* PEARL). Come on around to the back.

(PEARL *hesitates for an instant, then joins her, and the two girls exit around upstage corner of house.* JEETER *hasn't much success seeing into the window, and he suddenly stops trying and scampers around the upstage corner of the house. He returns almost immediately with a chopping block on which he climbs to see into the room. A smile of approval beams on his weathered face.*)

JEETER. Sister Bessie sure is a fine-looking woman, ain't she, Dude?

BESSIE (*appearing at window*). Get away from there, Jeeter Lester.

JEETER. What's the matter, Bessie? I ain't done nothing.

BESSIE. Never you mind. You get away from there.

JEETER. Now don't get peeved, Bessie. This time of year puts a queer feeling into a man. I feel that way every late February and early March. No matter how many children a man's got, he always wants to get more.

BESSIE. That don't matter. I don't want to have nothing to do with you. You is an old sinner.

JEETER (*complacently*). Yes, I reckon I is. I reckon I is one of the biggest sinners in the whole country. (*Suddenly changes and roars*). But, by God and by Jesus, woman—what's a man going to do!

(DUDE *comes up to window and starts pushing at* JEETER *as enter* CAPTAIN TIM *and* GEORGE PAYNE)

DUDE. Get away from there, you old fool, or I'll wham you one.

TIM (*amused*). Well, Jeeter, what's all the excitement?

JEETER (*turning on block*). Captain John's boy!—Captain Tim!

(JEETER *steps from the box and runs swiftly to meet* TIM *at the gate, almost frantic with excitement.* ADA *stands on the porch, eying the strangers impassively and sucking on her snuff brush. The old* GRANDMOTHER *peers out from behind the protecting well.* TIM *extends his hand as* JEETER *comes running up.*)

TIM. How are you, Jeeter, how are you?

JEETER (*eagerly*). Captain Tim, I sure is glad to see you!

TIM. Jeeter, this is Mr. Payne, from Augusta.

PAYNE. How do you do, Mr. Lester?

JEETER. Morning, sir.

TIM (*seeing* ADA *on porch*). That's Ada, isn't it? Good morning, Ada.

ADA (*coldly*). Morning.

TIM (*indicating* DUDE). I don't recognize the boy, Jeeter. Which one is he?

JEETER. That's Dude.

TIM. Oh, yes. I remember Dude now. (*To* DUDE). Hello there, Dude. Do you remember me?

DUDE (*impudently*). Naw! (*Giggles self-consciously.*)

JEETER. That there next to Dude is Sister Bessie. They just married themselves before you came.

PAYNE. Married *themselves?*

JEETER. Sister Bessie is a woman preacher and she done it.

PAYNE (*dubiously*). I see.

TIM (*to* DUDE). Well, congratulations, Dude. Congratulations, Sister Bessie. (*To* JEETER). Is Dude the only one of your children left, Jeeter?

JEETER. Ellie May and Pearl is around someplace.

TIM (*looking about*). Well, the place hasn't changed much. What keeps it from falling down, Jeeter?

JEETER. Praise God, Captain Tim, I don't know. I expect it will one of these days. . . . Now you come on the porch and sit down. . . . Dude, you bring some chairs out here.

PAYNE. Don't bother. I'm afraid we won't be able to stay very long.

JEETER. Ain't no bother at all. Could you do with a drink of water, Captain Tim?

TIM. Thanks, Jeeter.

(PAYNE *crosses up left, glancing about the property and inspecting the house.*)

JEETER (*crossing to well for water*). Dude, you go do what I told you. (*While* JEETER *is getting the water,* PAYNE *glances around curiously. His eyes meet* TIM'S *and he shakes his head to suggest his reaction to the surroundings.* DUDE *pulls a chair on to the porch.*) Here you is. (*Crossing to* TIM *with dipper of water.*)

TIM. Much obliged. (*Drinks.*)

JEETER. I sure is glad to see you back, Captain. I knowed you couldn't stay away from the land any more than your Daddy could. Maybe city ways is all right for a short time, but when they start cleaning off the fields and burning the broom sedge, a man ain't happy unless he can be seeing it and be doing it, too.

TIM. You must be getting pretty old, Jeeter. I'd think you'd be tired of it by this time.

JEETER. No, sir. I is ready to do just as big a day's work as the next one. Ada there is always saying I is lazy, but there ain't no truth in that when it comes to planting a crop.

TIM (*going to well and putting cup down*). How have crops been lately?

JEETER. Praise God there ain't been none in seven years. We just ain't been able to get credit down here on the Tobacco Road. Ain't nobody got no money. By God and by Jesus, I is glad you came back to provide that again.

TIM (*turning—surprised*). What?

JEETER. Yes, sir, Captain Tim. I was just telling Ada a short time back that the Lord was aiming to take care of me out of His bounty. I wasn't thinking about you at the time, but soon as I heard you was here again Dude and me set to burning off the fields. Them north fields is burning some right this minute.

TIM (*after a glance at* PAYNE). Well, I don't know how that idea got around. I'm sure sorry, but I'm—well; Jeeter, I'm afraid I can't help you.

I'm in pretty much the same fix you are.

JEETER (*unbelieving*). What's that, Captain Tim?

TIM (*turning to* PAYNE). You'd better tell him, Payne.

PAYNE. Well, you see, Mr. Lester, I'm from the bank in Augusta. We're down here to collect money, not lend it.

JEETER. You mean I can't have no credit to grow me a crop this year?

PAYNE. I'm afraid not.

JEETER. But I just got to have credit. Me and my folks is starving out here on the Tobacco Road.

PAYNE. Well, then you ought to be glad we came. We're ready to help you to get away from here to where you have a chance of making a living.

JEETER. I don't want to get away from here. If you mean go off and work in the mills, I say, by God and by Jesus, no!—I ain't going to do it.

PAYNE. But if you're really starving——

JEETER. That ain't got nothing to do with it. Captain John said I could live here as long as I wanted. He said he couldn't give me credit at the stores in Fuller no more, but he told me I could stay here and live until I died. You know that, Captain Tim.

TIM. Yes, Jeeter, I remember, and that was all right as long as the land was ours. But it's not any more. I had to borrow money on every farm we owned around here and now I can't pay it back. Like your granddaddy used to own the land and Captain John took it over, the bank's doing it with me.

JEETER (*heatedly*). I don't understand that. This was my daddy's place and his daddy's before him, and I don't know how many Lesters before that. There wasn't nothing here in the whole country before they came. They made that road out there hauling tobacco kegs fifteen miles down the ridge to the river. Now I don't own it and you don't own it and it belongs to a durn bank that ain't never had nothing to do with it even.

TIM. That's the way things just seem to happen, Jeeter.

JEETER. Praise God, it ain't the way things just happen. It's the rich folks in Augusta that's doing it. They don't work none, but they get all the money us farmers make. One time I borrowed me three hundred dollars from a loan company there to grow a crop and when I gave them interest and payments and every other durn thing they could think of I didn't make but seven dollars the whole year working every day. By God, that ain't right, I tell you. God won't stand for such cheating much longer. He ain't so liking of the rich people as they think He is. God, He likes the poor.

PAYNE. Now, Mr. Lester. We don't want to be hard on you old farmers, but we're going to try putting this whole section under scientific cultivation and there wouldn't be any use for you.

JEETER. Why not? If you is going to grow things on the land, why can't I stay right here and do it, too? I'd work for you just like I did for Captain John and no nigger ever worked harder than that.

PAYNE. I'm afraid that's impossible.

DUDE. What did I tell you, you old fool? Nobody ain't going to give you nothing.

JEETER. You shut up, Dude Lester. You shut up and get away from here. Captain Tim ain't going to let them send me away. Is you, Captain Tim?

PAYNE. Be reasonable, Mr. Lester. You've proved you can't get along here. Why don't you move your family up to Augusta or across the river in South Carolina where the mills are?

JEETER. No! By God and by Jesus, no! That's one thing I ain't never going to do. Them durn cotton mills is for the women folks to work in. I say it's a hell of a job for a man to spend his time winding strings on spools.

PAYNE. It shouldn't be any harder than trying to grow a crop here. Even if you do get one, you can't make enough out of it to live on.

JEETER. I don't care. God made the land, but you don't see Him building no durn cotton mills.

PAYNE. That hasn't anything to do with it. You old farmers are all the same. You don't realize that times have changed.

JEETER. That's no concern of mine. I is ready to look after my own like the Bible says, but that don't include no goddam mill! (*Turning to* TIM.) Please, Captain Tim, don't let them make me do that. I'm like to die pretty soon now, anyway, but up there I'd go before my time. You ain't going to let them do that to me, is you?

TIM. Lord, Jeeter, what can I do? That's up to Mr. Payne now. (*Turning to* PAYNE.) How about it, Payne? Couldn't you do something for this man?

PAYNE. I'm sorry, Mr. Harmon, but if we made an exception for one we'd have to for all of them. Of course, if he could pay rent——

JEETER. Rent! No use asking that. I couldn't pay no rent. Praise God, I hasn't even got money to buy food with.

TIM. What about your children? Couldn't one of them help you?

JEETER. I don't know where none of them is except Tom—— (*A sudden idea.*) By God and by Jesus—Tom!

TIM. I remember Tom. What's Tom doing?

JEETER. They say down in Fuller he's a powerful rich man now. They tell me he hauls all the ties for the railroad. (*Turns to* PAYNE.) How much money would you be wanting for rent, mister?

PAYNE. Well—this place ought to be worth a hundred dollars a year.

JEETER. That's a heap of money, but Tom ought to be ready to help out his old pa at a time like this. When would you be wanting that hundred dollars?

PAYNE. We ought to be starting back early tomorrow.

JEETER. I got time for that. Tom's only over in Burke County. (*Turns and calls:*) Hey, you, Dude. You and Bessie get in that new automobile and ride over and see Tom. You tell him his old Pa has got to have a hundred dollars. Don't lose no time about doing it neither.

DUDE (*jumping off porch—eager for a ride*). Come on, Bessie. We is going for a ride. (BESSIE *hesitates, glancing back into the house.*)

JEETER. You hurry up there, Bessie. Ain't no time to be thinking about going in the house now. (*With a last disappointed glance,* BESSIE *comes down off the porch.* DUDE *moves ahead of her to the gate.*)

TIM. Don't you think you ought to go and speak to Tom yourself, Jeeter?

JEETER. He might not like that so much. He might have changed some since he was a boy. He'll talk to Dude and Bessie, though. (BESSIE *and* DUDE *disappear down the road, and* JEETER *runs to the gate to call after them*): Hey, you, Dude. You tell Tom his old pa needs that money powerful bad. You tell him we ain't got anything to eat here, either, and his Ma needs snuff to calm her stomach with. (*Turns back to* TIM.) Tom was just about the best of all the boys. I reckon Bailey was the best, but Tom was good, too. He always said he was going to make a heap of money. (*The horn sounds off in* DUDE'S *inimitable manner.* JEETER *speaks proudly.*) That's Dude doing that. Don't he blow the horn pretty, though? Just listen to it. (*The horn sounds again, somewhat fainter, and* JEETER *again smiles with pride at* TIM.) That's Dude. (*He is listening again as the curtain falls.*)

ACT THREE

SCENE—*The same.*

TIME—*Dawn the following morning.*

AT RISE—JEETER, *shoeless, is discovered asleep on the porch, his back against one of the uprights, head slumped forward on his chest. Again the early sun spreads its soft golden glow, soon to become a fierce white glare as the morning advances.* JEETER *awakens abruptly, as one does who all night has tried to fight off sleep, and crosses swiftly to the gate, where he gazes off right stage down the empty, silent road. Disappointed, he comes back into the yard to the well, where he performs his casual morning ablutions, using, as always, his shirt for a towel. Fingers through his hair serve as a comb for his scraggly hair; his hat goes back on his head. He is ready for the day. Again he crosses to the road, where his anxious gaze once more sweeps the horizon right for a glimpse of* DUDE *and* BESSIE. ADA *appears on the porch, pressing her sides to ease the early morning pains of a body that sleep can no longer refresh.*

ADA. Is they coming yet?

JEETER. No. (*Comes inside to porch where he sits and starts putting on shoes.*) By God and by Jesus, I don't understand that. They been gone long enough to go to Burke County and back three times over.

ADA. It's that Bessie. She ain't going to hurry none just because you want her to.

JEETER. They must of seen Tom all right if they been gone this long. Maybe he made them stay all night. Do you think he done that, Ada?

ADA. Maybe he did and maybe he didn't. But if he asked them, you can bet that Bessie stayed all right. She ain't going to come home as long as there is any other place to go.

JEETER. What is you so peeved at Bessie for? She's a fine woman preacher.

ADA. She's a old hussy, that's what she is.

JEETER. Now what makes you say that? Sister Bessie is——

ADA. Don't tell me what she is. I know. Walking around here so uppity because she bought herself that new automobile. Why didn't she buy us some rations and snuff instead of spending all that money. That's what a good woman preacher would have done.

JEETER. She wants that new automobile to carry on the preaching and the praying. Women preachers ain't like the rest of us. They is got the Lord's work to do.

ADA. Humph. Looks to me like the Lord's work would be done better if she bought Dude's Ma a stylish dress. The Lord would understand that.

JEETER (*suddenly and impatiently*). Say, when is we going to eat this morning, anyway? Ain't there none of that meal left we borrowed from Morgan Prior yesterday?

ADA (*crossly*). There's some meal all right, but there ain't no kindling wood. Ellie May's ready to cook it as soon as she gets some.

JEETER. You tell Ma Lester to go get it then.

ADA. Ma Lester ain't here.

JEETER. Where is she?

ADA. I don't know. She didn't sleep in the bed last night.

JEETER. H'mm. Maybe she went out in the broom sedge yesterday and couldn't get back. Maybe she even died out there.

ADA. Maybe. She ain't never stayed away before.

JEETER. I'll go out and look around one of these days. . . . Well, you tell Ellie May to go out and get some wood. I sure got to have my chicory before long. . . .

ADA (*calling inside house*). Ellie May—Ellie May!

ELLIE MAY (*off—in house*). What you want, Ma?

ADA. You go out in the fields and get some sticks for the fire.

ELLIE MAY (*off*). Oh, make that old woman go.

ADA. She ain't here.

ELLIE MAY (*complaining*). Well, where is she?

ADA. She's likely dead. You go on do like I tell you.

(ELLIE MAY *enters yawning and scratching her head.*)

ELLIE MAY. Why don't you make Pearl go? She don't never do nothing.

ADA. Never you mind now. I got other things for Pearl to do.

ELLIE MAY. Aw, gee!

JEETER. You hurry up. I is near about dying for my chicory.

ELLIE MAY (*complaining*). Can't I even get me a drink of water?

JEETER. All right, you get you some water, then get along. But keep away from them north fields. They might be burning some yet. That's probably what happened to your old Grandma. The fire come up on her and she couldn't get away from it. (*He is filled with sudden energy, gets up, crosses to the road, and looks down it, shakes his head.* ELLIE MAY *drinks leisurely from the water dipper.*) By God and by Jesus, they ought to be back with that money before this. First thing you know Captain Tim and that man will be along here looking for it.

ADA (*calling into house—ignoring* JEETER). Pearl—Pearl, git up, honey. Come out here and freshen up. We'll be having something to eat pretty soon now. Bring that old brush with you, too. I want to pretty up your hair. (ELLIE MAY *hears* ADA *and takes the dipper slowly down from her mouth. She looks at* ADA, *her face livid with unspoken rage. Suddenly she flings the dipper at* ADA, *the water spilling.* JEETER, *coming through the gate, regards* ELLIE MAY *with anger.*)

JEETER. Great day in the morning, what's the meaning of all that! (ELLIE MAY, *disregarding* JEETER, *looks at her mother with blazing eyes, her breath coming hard.* ADA *returns the look with level coldness.* ELLIE MAY'S *throat contracts with half-stifled sobs and she turns and rushes to the gate. She starts down the Tobacco Road left when something she sees offstage stops her. For an instant she is rigid, then, with the first pronounced sob, she turns, and exits right, running down the road.* JEETER *follows* ELLIE MAY *with a puzzled glance, then turns to* ADA.)

JEETER. Now if that ain't the durndest gal. What do you suppose made her turn around like that for? (*He answers his own curiosity by crossing to the road and looking off left. He turns back with some surprise.*) It's Lov coming down the road.

ADA. Don't you let him come in here.

JEETER. What the hell, woman. He ain't going to do no harm. He looks too durned tired.

ADA. He ain't going to have Pearl.

JEETER. Who said he was. I just said he was coming down the road.

ADA (*calling inside*). Pearl, Lov's coming. Stay where you is and get ready to run case he starts trying to get at you. (ADA *shuts the door and stands with her back to it.*)

JEETER. Great day, he's toting something again. Now whatever could be in that anyway? I bet you one thing, by God—it ain't turnips! (*Twitching with eagerness, he comes inside the yard and takes his familiar place, hanging over the fence, his back to the audience, straining to see down the road.*) Whatever he's got, I sure could use some, even if I can't see it. I certainly is happy Lov and me is friends about this time.

ADA. Humph! The only way you'll ever get anything from him is stealing it.

JEETER. No, sir! The Lord forgave me for that before and I ain't going to risk his wrath again.

ADA. Humph.

JEETER (*again stretching over fence to peer down the road*). Now, Ada, don't be too hard on Lov and I might be able to prevail on him to give us a little something.

ADA. Then he better keep away from Pearl. (JEETER *waves her quiet and turns back to the fence, but he restrains his eagerness, as he did in the first act, so that* LOV *will not be frightened off.* LOV *enters disconsolately, carrying a small flour sack, the bottom of which bulges somewhat from an object the size of a brick.*)

JEETER (*casually*). Hi, there, Lov. (LOV *stops.*)

LOV (*after a pause*). I want to talk to you, Jeeter.

JEETER. Sure, Lov. Come inside and rest yourself. (LOV *slowly comes through the gate.*) What you got in that sack, Lov? What you got there anyway?

LOV (*after a significant pause and a glance from* JEETER *to* ADA *and back to* JEETER. *Knowing the bombshell effect of his words*). Salt pork.

JEETER (*electrified*). Salt pork! Lord a'mighty! I ain't had salt pork since the Lord himself knows how long. Is you going to give me some of that, Lov? I sure could do with a small piece about this time.

LOV. Take it. (*He holds sack to the astounded* JEETER.)

JEETER (*unbelieving*). Take it? You mean take it all?

LOV. I bought it for that.

JEETER (*taking sack*). Great day in the morning, I never heard of such bounty! (*Turns.*) Did you hear that, Ada? Lov has give me all this salt pork.

ADA (*coldly*). What does he want for it?

JEETER. He don't want nothing for it. Lov just give it to me, that's all.

ADA. Ask him.

JEETER (*doubtfully*). Well now . . . What have you got to say about that, Lov? *Is* you after something from me in return for this salt pork?

LOV. I want to talk to you about Pearl.

ADA. That's just what I thought. Well, you ain't going to have her back. No use you trying to talk Jeeter into it, neither. He ain't got nothing to say about it. You give him back that salt pork, Jeeter.

JEETER. Now, Ada, there ain't no sense in being hasty about this matter. What you say is right, but there can't be no harm in talking about it.

ADA. You just want to hold on to that salt pork.

JEETER. Now, Ada——

LOV (*with sudden desperation*). I got to have Pearl back, Jeeter, no matter what you said yesterday. I just got to have her back.

JEETER. Now, Lov, we talked all about that before. I told you——

LOV. I don't care what you told me. Maybe you ain't Pearl's real Pa, but you got the right of her.

JEETER. I wish I could agree with you on that matter, Lov, but it ain't right in the eyes of God.

LOV. I'll pay you, Jeeter. I'll give you a dollar every week out of the money I make at the chute.

JEETER (*whistles*). That's a heap of money, Lov, and coming and going I might have considered it a short time back. But I ain't going to need money bad enough now to make me fly against the wrath of the Lord. Dude and Bessie is over with Tom right this minute and he'll be sending me all the money I want for my needs.

LOV. I'll give you two dollars.

JEETER. Two dollars a week! Now, Lov Bensey, you quit tempting me.

LOV (*with sudden fury*). By God, I want my wife. (ADA *plants her back more firmly against the door and the movement tells* LOV *where* PEARL *is. He takes a few steps to the edge of the porch.* ADA'S *arms raise to cover the door.*)

ADA. You come any closer, and I'll call to her to run off. (LOV, *checked by the threat, stops, his sudden anger cooling.*)

LOV (*defeated*). No, don't do that. (JEETER *takes this opportunity to hide the sack behind the well.* LOV *slowly turns to* JEETER.) Jeeter, I don't see how I can make it more than two dollars every week. But that's a heap of money.

JEETER. Praise God, I know it, Lov.

ADA. Get out of here, Lov Bensey—get out. (LOV *slowly turns and crosses to the gate;* JEETER *keeps himself in front of the well to lessen any chance of* LOV *seeing and remembering the salt pork.* LOV *exits left.* JEETER *waits until* LOV *has gone, then runs to the fence and looks after him.*)

JEETER. He's gone all right. He's gone and forgot that salt pork, too. (*Running back to the well, he picks up the sack and takes out the pork.*) Now ain't that something! That must be near about two pounds. Lov sure is a generous provider. (*Crosses to* ADA.) There you is, Ada. You fix up some of this with the corn meal when Ellie May comes back with the kindling. (ADA *takes the sack. She has moved away from the door on* LOV'S *exit and is in her usual position, leaning against an upright.*) Now what do you think's happened to Ellie May, anyway? What's happened to Dude and Bessie for that matter? By God and by Jesus, they ought to be back with that money before this.

ADA. What is you going to do with that money, Jeeter?

JEETER (*pausing with foot half raised to put on other shoe. He is outraged*). What is I going to do? Is you crazy, woman! I got to give it to that man with Captain Tim.

ADA. Humph! That don't make no sense to me.

JEETER. Great day in the morning, you *is* crazy! That money's going to keep me my land, ain't it? That money's going to let me stay here and raise a crop. By God and by Jesus, what do you mean there ain't no sense in that?

ADA. You give the money to that man and what has you got left? Nothing! You ain't got no seed cotton to plant in the fields, you ain't got nothing to eat and you ain't no better off than you was before.

JEETER. I ain't aiming to be better off. I'm aiming to keep my land.

ADA. You're an old fool, Jeeter Lester. With that money we could get us a place to live up in Augusta. Maybe we could even buy us an automobile like Bessie's. (*Wisely:*) You wouldn't have to worry none about being laid in the corn crib when you die neither. Ain't no telling what's going to happen if you stay here.

JEETER. Shut up! You just say that to scare me into doing what you want. Well, I ain't going to be laid in no corn crib, and I ain't going to work in no cotton mill neither.

ADA. Maybe you wouldn't have to work none up there. (*Glances toward door.*) Maybe Ellie May and Pearl could do that. Pearl would like that a lot. She wouldn't be scared of going if her old Ma went.

JEETER. You ain't thinking about my wants when you talk like that. It's Pearl you is thinking about. Well, you can take her if that's what you want, and leave me here alone. I was born here on the land, and by God and by Jesus that's where I'll die.

ADA (*fiercely*). I hope you do. I hope you die and they lay you in the corn crib and the rats eat off your face just like they done your Pa.

JEETER (*rising—threatening and furious, raising his shoe to strike her*). Goddam you, woman! (*The horn, sounded in* DUDE'S *inimitable style, checks* JEETER'S *descending blow. Radiance replaces black fury in his face as he hears it again.*) Here they is. That's them, all right. That's Dude blowing that old horn. (PEARL *and* ELLIE MAY *enter on to porch. Hobbling because of the one shoe,* JEETER *crosses to the gate, where he stops and starts to pull on his shoe, while the horn continues its bleat.*

JEETER'S *shoe goes on with difficulty. Once or twice he starts off with it half on, but is so impeded that he stops and works on it again. The horn stops.* JEETER, *giving up the job of putting on the shoe while standing, plumps to the ground, puts it on, and gets through the gate, starting down the road right, when* BESSIE *enters.*) Here you is, Bessie. I been waiting all night and day for you and Dude to come back. Where you been anyway?

BESSIE (*proudly*). In Augusta.

JEETER. Augusta! Didn't you go see Tom?

BESSIE. We saw Tom first. Then we rode up to Augusta and had us a honeymoon.

JEETER. Honeymoon? What the hell is that?

BESSIE. A honeymoon is when two people is married and they get in the bed together.

JEETER. Where did you do that?

BESSIE (*proudly*). At a hotel.

JEETER. Great day in the morning! Didn't that take a heap of money?

BESSIE. It took two bits.

JEETER. Hear that, Ada? Dude and Bessie stayed at a hotel in Augusta.

ADA (*dourly*). Did they bring us anything back?

BESSIE. I didn't have no money left to do that. That two bits was the last piece of money I had.

ADA. Humph! Looks to me like you might have brought some snuff back to Dude's old Ma instead of wasting money like that. (*Enter* DUDE *carrying broken headlight.*)

JEETER. Now, Ada, you let Bessie alone. (*Sees* DUDE.) Here you is, Dude. Bessie just told us about staying all night in Augusta—— (*Sees headlight.*) Great day, just look at that old headlight. What done that?

DUDE. A goddam old pine tree. That's what.

JEETER (*inspecting light*). H'mm. Was you looking where you was going?

DUDE. I just looked back once and there it was—smack in front of me.

JEETER. Well, it don't look like it's going to be much good no more.

DUDE. If I had me an ax, I'd have chopped that tree down right then and there.

JEETER. I wouldn't concern myself much about it. One headlight is plenty to drive with.

DUDE. Oh, to hell with it. (*He drops light on ground, crosses to gate.*) It's just the way that pine tree got in front of me, that's all.

JEETER. Looks like they will do that sometimes. Hey, Dude. Where is the money Tom sent me?

DUDE. Tom didn't send you no money. Why the hell did you think he would anyway? (*Exits.*)

JEETER. Hey, Dude—— (*Turning back to* BESSIE.) Dude's lying, ain't he, Bessie?

BESSIE (*nodding*). Tom ain't at all like he used to be, Jeeter.

JEETER (*desperately*). Now, Bessie—don't fool with me. Give me the money.

BESSIE. There ain't no money, Jeeter. Tom just didn't send any—that's all.

JEETER. You is crazy, woman. He did send it. Tom wouldn't do that to me.

BESSIE. Yes, he did, Jeeter. He's a wicked man, Tom is.

JEETER. No, sir, I don't believe it. You is got the money and I want it. Give it to me, hear me—give it to me.

BESSIE. I ain't got it, Jeeter.

JEETER. You is a liar. That's what you is—an old liar. Tom did send it. (*Enter* DUDE *rolling an auto wheel.* JEETER *rushes over to him inside the gate and grabs him.*) Dude, give me that money—hear me, give me that money.

DUDE (*shaking him off*). Didn't I tell you once! There ain't no money. Now get away from me and shut up. (*Bends over wheel, his back half to* BESSIE.)

JEETER. No. Tom wouldn't do that. He was my special boy. You just didn't go see him.

DUDE. We saw him all right. We saw him and he said to tell you to go to hell. (BESSIE *grabs him by the neck and shakes him so that the wheel falls to the ground.* DUDE *is furious.*) Damn you, turn loose of me. (*Shakes free.*) What the hell you doing?

BESSIE. You shouldn't have told Jeeter that. That's a wicked thing to say.

DUDE. I didn't say it—Tom said it. And you keep off me. I didn't do nothing to you.

BESSIE. Praise the Lord, you won't be fit to preach a sermon next Sunday if you cuss like that. Good folks don't want to have God send them sermons by cussing preachers.

DUDE. All right, I won't cuss no more. But don't you go jumping on my neck no more neither. (*He picks up wheel and rolls it against fence near the other broken pieces of the automobile, and sits.* JEETER *sits on fence, staring blankly ahead.* PEARL *and* ELLIE MAY *exit into the house.*)

ADA. What does Tom look like now? Has he changed much?

BESSIE. He looks a lot like Jeeter. There ain't much resemblance in him and you.

ADA. Humph! There was a time when I'd have declared it was the other way around.

BESSIE. Maybe one time, but now he looks more like Jeeter than Jeeter does hisself.

ADA. What did he say when you told him you and Dude was married?

BESSIE. He didn't say nothing much. Looked to me like he didn't care one way or the other.

DUDE (*over his shoulder from where he sits, back to audience, appraising the damaged parts*). Tom said she used to be a two-bit slut when he knowed her. (*With a bound* BESSIE *is on his neck again, choking him. He jerks away from her quickly and pushes his hand at her face, getting up, threatening.*) Goddam you! You keep off me.

BESSIE (*tenderly as she backs off*). Now, Dude, you promised me you wasn't going to cuss no more.

DUDE. Then, by God, quit choking me. I'm getting damned sick and tired of you doing that.

BESSIE. You shouldn't talk like that about the woman you is mated to.

DUDE. Well, that's what Tom said. He told it right to you and you didn't do nothing. Why didn't you do something to him if he was telling a lie?

BESSIE. Tom is a wicked man. The Lord punishes wicked men like that.

DUDE. Well, then, you let the Lord punish me and keep your hands off my neck. (DUDE *pulls wheel down and begins trying to straighten spokes by pulling on them with his hands and pounding them with a hand-sized rock.*)

ADA. Did Tom say he had any children?

BESSIE. He didn't mention it if he had. He didn't seem to want to talk very much, not even when I told him you and Jeeter didn't have meal nor meat in the house.

DUDE (*looking up from his work*). He just said he didn't give a damn and went on driving his team of ox.

ADA (*briskly—pleased*). Well, I reckon we better be getting ready to go off, Jeeter.

JEETER. What?—— (*Snapped back from his stunned silence.*) No, I ain't going, I tell you.

ADA (*exasperated*). Tom didn't send you no money. How you going to stay here?

JEETER. By God, I'm going to stay, that's all.

(ADA, *realizing the uselessness of arguing with him, turns and exits into the house.* BESSIE *turns to* DUDE *and watches him work.*)

BESSIE. Do you reckon you'll ever get that wheel straight again, Dude?

DUDE (*crossly*). I'm trying, ain't I?

JEETER (*abstractedly, pointing to wheel*). What done that?

DUDE. Remember that old pine tree that busted the headlight?

JEETER. Um.

DUDE. Well, I was backing away from that and some durn fool left a pile of cross ties right where I'd run smack into them.

JEETER (*easily*). Well, now what do you think?

DUDE. It busted the back of the car in, too.

BESSIE. It looks like everything's trying to ruin my new automobile. Ain't nothing like it was when I paid eight hundred dollars for it in Fuller just yesterday.

JEETER. It ain't hurt the running of it none, though, has it? It runs good yet.

BESSIE. I reckon so, but it makes a powerful lot of noise when it's running up hill—and down hill, too.

DUDE. That's because we was running it without oil. The man at the gasoline station said something was burned out inside.

JEETER. That's a pity.

DUDE. It runs pretty good, though, even if it does make all that racket.

JEETER. Some automobiles is like that. (*Jumps down from fence, suddenly his old self again.*) By God and by Jesus, now why didn't I think of that before. Quit pounding on that old wheel, Dude. You come with me.

DUDE (*still sitting*). What you want to do now? I done enough running around for one morning.

JEETER. You get up from there and do like I say. You and me is going to start hauling wood to Augusta right this minute.

DUDE. You're just an old fool. That old machine of yours can't carry no wood to Augusta.

JEETER. No, but that there new one can. You come on.

DUDE. What do I want to haul wood to Augusta for?

JEETER. So I can get me some money for the bank—that's what for.

DUDE. You ain't going to get no hundred dollars for no load of wood, or nothing else like it.

JEETER. I can get a couple of dollars maybe, and every day doing that I can get me more than a hundred.

BESSIE. You stop right where you is. Jeeter. You ain't going to use my new automobile for no such purpose.

JEETER. Now, Bessie, ain't I always shared what I had with you and your former husband? You ain't going to see me lose my land, is you?

BESSIE. That ain't no concern of mine. Hauling wood in my new machine would punch holes in the seat and the top just like it done to your old one.

JEETER. I won't let it hurt it none.

BESSIE. It's already broke up enough. I ain't going to let you do it.

JEETER. Now, Bessie——

BESSIE. You can't have it and that's all.

JEETER (*with heat*). That's a hell of a way to act toward me. You ain't got the mercy of the Lord in you. I say you is a hell of a woman preacher.

BESSIE (*angrily*). You shut up cussing at me, Jeeter Lester.

JEETER. I won't. You is an old bitch, that's what you is. You is an old bitch.

BESSIE (*with equal fury*). You is an old bitch, too. You is an old son-of-a-bitch. All you Lesters is sons-of-bitches.

(DUDE *looks up, amused.*)

JEETER (*coming up to her threateningly*). Get off my land. If I can't borrow me that automobile, you get off my land.

BESSIE. It ain't your land. It's the bank's land and *you* got to get off it.

JEETER. It's the old Lester place, and I ain't going to get off it while I'm alive. But durned if I can't run you off—— (*Enter* PEARL *from house with small, blackened pot.*) Now git! —You hear me, gi——
(JEETER *sees* PEARL, *who has hesitated on the porch at sight of the quarrel, and suddenly stops his tirade, the hand raised to strike* BESSIE *halted in midair.* PEARL *comes down from the porch and crosses to the well,* JEETER'S *eyes following her and his hand slowly lowering to his side. The fury in his eyes dies to a strange, puzzled, contemplative expression.* DUDE, *who has been amused by the quarrel, a smile wreathing his face, follows his father's glance curiously, but without enlightenment.* BESSIE *glances from* JEETER *to* PEARL *and back to* JEETER *again, a frown wrinkling her forehead.*)

BESSIE. What's the matter with you, you old fool? Has you lost your mind?

JEETER (*suddenly turning away from regarding* PEARL *at the well, smiling at* BESSIE, *and moving away a few steps*). Ain't no sense you and me fighting, Bessie. You and me always thought a heap of each other. You can stay here just as long as you has a mind to.

BESSIE. H'mm. (*Suspicious and uncompromising.*) You ain't going to have the use of my new automobile to haul wood to Augusta.

JEETER. I gave up thinking about that a long time back. Don't concern yourself about that no more. However, I might be wanting you and Dude to take a little trip for me pretty soon now. Will you do that?

BESSIE (*suspiciously*). Maybe. What you want us to do?

JEETER. Never you mind. It won't be far.

BESSIE. Well, if it ain't far.

JEETER. It won't hardly take no time. (*Crosses to* DUDE.) How is you getting on there, Dude?

DUDE (*back trying to straighten spokes*). Maybe it will be all right. It don't much matter if all the spokes ain't straight.

JEETER. Umm. (*Out of the corner of his eye* JEETER *watches* PEARL, *who, having filled the kettle, crosses back from well to house and exits.* JEETER *leaves his place at the fence and nonchalantly ambles to the porch and leans, taking out his knife and whittling on a piece of broken weather-boarding. Although he tries to appear at ease, his tenseness is apparent, and occasional swift glances at the door reveal his real interest.*)

DUDE (*hitting at spokes with a stone harder than before*). This is a hell of a job.

JEETER. Don't worry too much about that. The wheels of my old machine wasn't straight much after the first few days and it didn't hurt the running of it hardly any.

BESSIE. I don't like my new car busted up like that though. (*Indicating headlight.*) Look there, Dude. There ain't hardly a piece of glass left in that headlight.

DUDE. Don't I know it. Goddam it, can't you let me be? Can't you see I'm trying to fix this old wheel?

BESSIE. Now, Dude, is that a way to talk? Good folks don't want to go and hear a Sunday sermon by a cussing preacher. I thought you wasn't going to swear no more.

DUDE. Then don't be always poking around. Go sit down someplace.

(*Enter* PEARL *with pan.* JEETER *watches her sharply as she crosses to well.*)

JEETER (*pretending interest*). When's Dude going to start being a preacher, Bessie? (*Follows* PEARL *slowly to well.*)

BESSIE. He's going to preach a little short sermon next Sunday. I is already telling him what to say when he preaches.

JEETER. Dude might make a fine man preacher at that under your direction, although I never thought he had right good sense. I used to think he was going to stay on the land like I always done, but I reckon he'll be better off riding around the country preaching and praying with you. (*Edges forward a bit as* PEARL *fills her bucket and starts back to door. With a spring,* JEETER *is at* PEARL'S *side and grabs her firmly by the wrist. The bucket falls—the girl's cry rings out, as she makes a desperate effort to pull away and run.*)

PEARL. Ma!

(BESSIE *and* DUDE *whirl around to look.*)

JEETER. Hey, Dude—you and Bessie ride down to the chute and get Lov. Tell him I got Pearl for him. (*The door flies open and an infuriated* ADA *takes in the scene. She rushes down on* JEETER *and begins hitting at him furiously.*)

ADA. You let her be—you let her be!

JEETER (*pushing off* ADA *with his free hand*). Hurry up there, Dude. You tell Lov if he's still ready to pay that two dollars a week I'll make Pearl go back and live with him.

BESSIE. Jeeter, that ain't the right thing to do.

JEETER (*fighting off* ADA). Maybe it wasn't right before, but it sure is now. You get the hell out of here!

DUDE (*grabbing* BESSIE). Come on. (DUDE *half pulls* BESSIE *through gate.*)

ADA (*clawing at* JEETER *and yelling at* DUDE). Don't you go, Dude—don't you go.

JEETER. Go on, Dude. You do like I tell you.

(DUDE *and* BESSIE *exit right.* ADA *strikes at* JEETER, *but when she sees* DUDE *and* BESSIE *exit, she suddenly stops her attack and runs after them.*)

ADA. Don't go, Dude. Wait! Wait!

(ADA *exits.* PEARL *continues to scratch and fight against* JEETER, *her gasping sobs the only sound she utters.* JEETER *holds her, but looks off in direction the others have gone. For an instant there is silence, broken only by* PEARL'S *sobs. Then the sound of an engine starting up and the blare of a horn come from the road below, and hard on this rings out the high shriek of a woman in agony. Again the scream cuts the silence, and even* PEARL'S *sobs are hushed, as she and* JEETER *listen. Suddenly she again struggles to free herself in a frenzy of effort to be with her mother, but* JEETER'S *hold does not relax. Nothing is spoken, no voice is heard, for a full pause. Then, on hands and knees, crawling along the Tobacco Road and whimpering like a hurt puppy, comes* ADA. PEARL'S *struggles cease and she stands horrified, still in* JEETER'S *grasp, as* ADA *continues forward. At the gate her strength deserts her, and she sinks to her side, now dragging herself along by her arms alone, until she is in the yard.*)

PEARL. Ma! . . . Let me go, goddam you—let me go. (*But* JEETER *holds fast,* DUDE *and* BESSIE *come running up to fence outside, followed by* ELLIE MAY. DUDE *leans over the fence, looking at his mother. There is no grief in his voice, only calm explanation.* JEETER *holds* PEARL, *who stands transfixed.*)

DUDE. We was backing on to the road and she got in the way. I guess the wheels ran over her. (ADA *makes a last movement forward and a stifled groan comes from her crushed, racked body as she props herself on her arm. A sob escapes* PEARL *and she tries to pull away from* JEETER.)

ADA. Let her go, Jeeter. Let her come to me.

JEETER. Praise God, I'd like to do that for you, Ada, but she'll run away.

ADA. Just let her come close to me, that's all. (JEETER *yields several steps, so that* PEARL, *kneeling, can reach out her hand to touch* ADA. ELLIE MAY *enters and stands outside the fence.*)

PEARL (*kneeling—touching her mother—sobbing*). Ma! Ma! Don't die. You can't, Ma—you can't!

ADA. That's all right, Pearl. I was going pretty soon now anyway. (*Glances around as best she can.*) I wish I had that stylish dress to be buried in, though. Reckon you can get me one, Jeeter?

JEETER. I sure would like to promise you that, Ada, but it ain't likely.

PEARL. I'll get you one, Ma. I'll get you one.

ADA (*matter-of-factly, without either self-pity or bitterness*). Never mind, honey. I never really thought I'd get it. It would have sort of pleased me, though. (*Pauses, looks at* PEARL, *then* JEETER.) Let her go, Jeeter? I never asked for nothing before, but now I'm going to die.

JEETER. I sure would like to, Ada, but I'm going to die pretty soon myself now. I feel it inside me. But I got to die on the land. Don't you understand? If I don't hold on to her for Lov I won't be able to do that.

ADA. Please, Jeeter, don't make her go back.

JEETER. Praise God, Ada, I got to.

ADA. All my life I been working for you. I picked cotton in the fields and turned over the furrows. I took care of your house and raised your children, and now when I'm going to die you won't even do what I want you to.

JEETER. My concern is with the living. The dead has to look out for themselves.

ADA. You're a sinful man, Jeeter Lester. You're a sinful man, and you're going to hell. (*Holds out arm to* PEARL.) Come here, child. Just put your arm around me so I can sit up.

(JEETER *allows* PEARL *to come close enough to* ADA, *so that her free arm goes around her mother, and* JEETER'S *hand works close to* ADA'S *mouth. Suddenly* ADA *leans forward the few necessary inches and her teeth sink into* JEETER'S *hand. With a smothered exclamation* JEETER *jerks back his hand, releasing* PEARL. *With flashing quickness the girl is on her feet. A dash carries her through the gate before* JEETER *recovers from the shock of his pain. Pausing,* PEARL *looks back at her mother, propped on her arm in the yard.*)

PEARL. Good-by, Ma.

(JEETER *springs forward toward her, but with a last wave of her hand,* PEARL *flashes down the road and is gone.* JEETER *reaches the fence, makes to run after her, then stops, realizing the hopelessness of overtaking the girl.* ADA, *holding herself up with her last strength, sees his defeat. A low laugh escapes her and she rolls forward on her face and is dead.* JEETER *slowly turns and comes back inside. He stops to look down at* ADA *for a moment and then crosses to the porch where he sits. His hand doesn't hurt much now, but he continues to hold it.* LOV *enters.*)

DUDE. Hi there, Lov. Jeeter was looking for you, but I guess it's too late now. Pearl's done gone.

LOV (*after a pause, indicating* ADA). What's the matter with her?

DUDE. Me and Bessie run over her in the new automobile a while back.

LOV. Is she hurt bad?

DUDE. Looks like she's dead.

(LOV *comes inside, kneels down, looks at* ADA. *Then goes up to* JEETER.)

LOV. Ada's dead, Jeeter. (JEETER *nods, half dazed. Crossing to* ADA, *he stands over her for a long pause. At last he speaks.*)

JEETER. Lov, you and Dude go out in the fields and find the best place to bury her. Make a deep hole—Ada would like that. . . . Bessie, you do some praying, too. It would please Ada a whole lot.

BESSIE. Praise the Lord, I'll be glad to, Brother Jeeter.

(LOV, DUDE, *and* BESSIE *exit.* ELLIE MAY *moves forward tentatively and* JEETER *notices her.*)

JEETER. Ellie May, you better go down to Lov's house and fix it up for him. He'll be coming home to supper tonight and you cook him what he wants. Be nice to him and maybe he'll let you stay. He'll be wanting a woman pretty bad now.

(ELLIE MAY, *frantic with delight, drops her sticks and crosses on a run down the road. Just before she exits, she stops and looks back.*)

ELLIE MAY. Good-by, Pa.

(JEETER *nods.* ELLIE MAY *exits, running.* JEETER *looks down at* ADA.)

JEETER. You shouldn't have done that, Ada. One way and another it didn't do anybody much good except maybe Pearl.

(*For a brief second* JEETER *looks down at* ADA, *then he crosses to the porch and sits. He bends down slowly, takes a pinch of the earth between his fingers and rubs it into dust. He sits back, leaning against the upright, and tilts his hat forward over his eyes. It is the same posture he has assumed so many times before when he has suddenly and unexpectedly fallen asleep. For a moment he continues abstractedly to rub the dirt between his fingers. Then all movement ceases. Seconds of somber silence pass. A rotten shingle falls from the sagging porch, and the curtain falls slowly.*)

CURTAIN

CLARENCE DAY'S

Life With Father

MADE INTO A PLAY

BY

HOWARD LINDSAY

AND

RUSSEL CROUSE

To

OSCAR SERLIN

who started as our producer

and remains our friend

LIFE WITH FATHER

was produced by Oscar Serlin *at the*

Empire Theatre

New York City, on the night of Nov. 8, 1939

with the following Cast:

Annie	Katherine Bard
Vinnie	Dorothy Stickney
Clarence	John Drew Devereaux
John	Richard Simon
Whitney	Raymond Roe
Harlan	Larry Robinson
Father	Howard Lindsay
Margaret	Dorothy Bernard
Cora	Ruth Hammond
Mary	Teresa Wright
The Reverend Dr. Lloyd	Richard Sterling
Delia	Portia Morrow
Nora	Nellie Burt
Dr. Humphreys	A. H. Van Buren
Dr. Somers	John C. King
Maggie	Timothy Kearse

staged by *Bretaigne Windust*
settings & costumes by *Stewart Chaney*

SYNOPSIS OF SCENES

The time: late in the 1880's.
The entire action takes place in the morning room of the Day home on Madison Avenue.

ACT ONE

Scene I: Breakfast time. An early summer morning.
Scene II: Tea time. The same day.

ACT TWO

Scene I: Sunday, after church. A week later.
Scene II: Breakfast time. Two days later.
(During Scene II the curtain is lowered to denote a lapse of three hours.)

ACT THREE

Scene I: Mid-afternoon. A month later.
Scene II: Breakfast time. The next morning.

ACT ONE

SCENE I

The morning room of the Day home at 420 Madison Avenue. In the custom of the Victorian period, this was the room where the family gathered for breakfast, and because it was often the most comfortable room in the house, it served also as a living room for the family and their intimates.

There is a large arch in the center of the upstage wall of the room, through which we can see the hall and the stairs leading to the second floor, and below them the rail of the stairwell leading to the basement. The room can be closed off from the hall by sliding doors in the archway. The front door of the house, which is stage right, can't be seen, but frequently is heard to slam.

In the morning room the sunshine streams through the large window at the right which looks out on Madison Avenue. The room itself is furnished with the somewhat less than comfortable furniture of the period, which is the late 1880's. The general color scheme in drapes and upholstery is green. Below the window is a large comfortable chair where FATHER *generally sits to read his paper. Right of center is the table which serves as a living-room table, with its proper table cover and fruit bowl; but now, expanded by extra leaves, it is doing service as a breakfast table. Against the back wall, either side of the arch, are two console tables which are used by the maid as serving tables. Left of center is a sofa, with a table just above its right end holding a lamp, framed photographs, and other ornaments. In the left wall is a fireplace, its mantel draped with a lambrequin. On the mantel are a clock and other ornaments, and above the mantel is a large mirror in a Victorian frame. The room is cluttered with the minutiæ of the period, including the inevitable rubber plant, and looking down from the walls are the Day ancestors in painted portraits. The room has the warm quality that comes only from having been lived in by a family which enjoys each other's company—a family of considerable means.*

As the curtain rises, ANNIE, *the new maid, a young Irish girl, is finishing setting the table for breakfast. After an uncertain look at the result she crosses over to her tray on the console table.* VINNIE *comes down the stairs and into the room.* VINNIE *is a charming, lovable, and spirited woman of forty. She has a lively mind which darts quickly away from any practical matter. She has red hair.*

ANNIE. Good morning, ma'am.

VINNIE. Good morning, Annie. How are you getting along?

ANNIE. All right, ma'am, I hope.

VINNIE. Now, don't be worried just because this is your first day. Everything's going to be all right—but I do hope nothing goes wrong. (*Goes to the table.*) Now, let's see, is the table all set? (ANNIE *follows her.*) The cream and the sugar go down at this end.

ANNIE (*placing them where* VINNIE *has indicated*). I thought in the center, ma'am; everyone could reach them easier.

VINNIE. Mr. Day sits here.

ANNIE (*gets a tray of napkins, neatly rolled and in their rings, from the console table*). I didn't know where to place the napkins, ma'am.

VINNIE. You can tell which go where by the rings. (*Takes them from the tray and puts them down as she goes around the table.* ANNIE *follows her.*) This one belongs to Whitney—it has his initial on it, "W"; that one with the little dog on it is Harlan's, of course. He's the baby. This "J" is for John and the "C" is for Clarence. This narrow plain one is mine. And this is Mr. Day's. It's just like mine—except that it got bent one morning. And that reminds me—always be sure Mr. Day's coffee is piping hot.

ANNIE. Ah, your man has coffee instead of tea of a morning?

VINNIE. We all have coffee except the two youngest boys. They have their milk. And, Annie, always speak of my husband as Mr. Day.

ANNIE. I will that.

VINNIE (*correcting her*). "Yes, ma'am," Annie.

ANNIE. Yes, ma'am.

VINNIE. And if Mr. Day speaks to you, just say: "Yes, sir." Don't be nervous—you'll get used to him.

(CLARENCE, *the eldest son, about seventeen, comes down the stairs and into the room. He is a manly, serious, good-looking boy. Because he is starting in at Yale next year, he thinks he is grown-up. He is red-headed.*)

CLARENCE. Good morning, Mother. (*He kisses her.*)

VINNIE. Good morning, Clarence.

CLARENCE. Did you sleep well, Mother?

VINNIE. Yes, thank you, dear. (CLARENCE *goes to* FATHER'S *chair and picks up the morning paper.*) (*To* ANNIE): We always start with fruit, except the two young boys, who have porridge. (ANNIE *brings the fruit and porridge to the table.* CLARENCE, *looking at the paper, makes a whistling sound.*)

CLARENCE. Jiminy! Another wreck on the New Haven. That always disturbs the market. Father won't like that.

VINNIE. I do wish that New Haven would stop having wrecks. If they knew how it upset your father—— (*Sees that* CLARENCE'S *coat has been torn and mended.*) My soul and body, Clarence, what's happened to your coat?

CLARENCE. I tore it. Margaret mended it for me.

VINNIE. It looks terrible. Why don't you wear your blue suit?

CLARENCE. That looks worse than this one. You know, I burnt that hole in it.

VINNIE. Oh, yes—well, you can't go around looking like that. I'll have to speak to your father. Oh, dear!

(JOHN, *who is about fifteen, comes down the stairs and into the room.* JOHN *is gangly and a little overgrown. He is red-headed.*)

JOHN. Good morning, Mother. (*He kisses her.*)

VINNIE. Good morning, John.

JOHN (*to* CLARENCE). Who won?

CLARENCE. I haven't looked yet.

JOHN. Let me see. (*He tries to take the paper away from* CLARENCE.)

CLARENCE. Be careful!

VINNIE. Boys, don't wrinkle that paper before your father's looked at it.

CLARENCE (*to* JOHN). Yes!

(VINNIE *turns to* ANNIE.)

VINNIE. You'd better get things started. We want everything ready when Mr. Day comes down. (ANNIE *exits.*) Clarence, right after breakfast I want you and John to move the small bureau from my room into yours.

CLARENCE. What for? Is somebody coming to visit us?

JOHN. Who's coming?

VINNIE. I haven't said anyone was coming. And don't you say anything about it. I want it to be a surprise.

CLARENCE. Oh! Father doesn't know yet?

VINNIE. No. And I'd better speak to him about a new suit for you before he finds out he's being surprised by visitors.

(ANNIE *enters with a tray on which are two glasses of milk, which she puts at* HARLAN'S *and* WHITNEY'S *places at the table.*)

(WHITNEY *comes down the stairs and rushes into the room. He is about thirteen. Suiting his age, he is a lively active boy. He is red-headed.*)

WHITNEY. Morning. (*He kisses his mother quickly, then runs to* CLARENCE *and* JOHN.) Who won?

JOHN. The Giants, 7 to 3. Buck Ewing hit a home run.

WHITNEY. Let me see!

(HARLAN *comes sliding down the banister. He enters the room, runs to his mother, and kisses her.* HARLAN *is a roly-poly, lovable, good-natured youngster of six. He is red-headed.*)

VINNIE. How's your finger, darling?

HARLAN. It itches.

VINNIE (*kissing the finger*). That's a sign it's getting better. Now don't scratch it. Sit down, boys. Get in your chair, darling. (*The boys move to the table and take their places.* CLARENCE *puts the newspaper beside his father's plate.* JOHN *stands waiting to place* VINNIE'S *chair when she sits.*) Now, Annie, watch Mr. Day, and as soon as he finishes his fruit—— (*Leaves the admonition hanging in mid-air as the sound of* FATHER'S *voice booms from upstairs.*)

FATHER'S VOICE. Vinnie! Vinnie!

(*All eyes turn toward the staircase.* VINNIE *rushes to the foot of the stairs, speaking as she goes.*)

VINNIE. What's the matter, Clare?

FATHER'S VOICE. Where's my necktie?

VINNIE. Which necktie?

FATHER'S VOICE. The one I gave you yesterday.

VINNIE. It isn't pressed yet. I forgot to give it to Margaret.

FATHER'S VOICE. I told you distinctly I wanted to wear that necktie today.

VINNIE. You've got plenty of neckties. Put on another one right away and come down to breakfast.

FATHER'S VOICE. Oh, damn! Damnation!

(VINNIE *goes to her place at the table.* JOHN *places her chair for her, then sits.* WHITNEY *has started eating.*)

CLARENCE. Whitney!

VINNIE. Wait for your father, Whitney.

WHITNEY. Oh, and I'm in a hurry! John, can I borrow your glove today? I'm going to pitch.

JOHN. If I don't play myself.

WHITNEY. Look, if you need it, we're playing in that big field at the corner of Fifty-seventh and Madison.

VINNIE. 'Way up there!

WHITNEY. They're building a house on that vacant lot on Fiftieth Street.

VINNIE. My! My! My! Here we move to Forty-eighth Street just to get out of the city!

WHITNEY. Can't I start breakfast, Mother? I promised to be there by eight o'clock.

VINNIE. After breakfast, Whitney, you have to study your catechism.

WHITNEY. Mother, can't I do that this afternoon?

VINNIE. Whitney, you have to learn five questions every morning before you leave the house.

WHITNEY. Aw, Mother—

VINNIE. You weren't very sure of yourself when I heard you last night.

WHITNEY. I know them now.

VINNIE. Let's see. (WHITNEY *rises and faces his mother.*) "What is your name?"

WHITNEY. Whitney Benjamin.

VINNIE. "Who gave you this name?"

WHITNEY. "My sponsors in baptism, wherein I was made a member of Christ, the child of God and an inheritor of the Kingdom of Heaven." Mother, if I hadn't been baptized wouldn't I have a name?

VINNIE. Not in the sight of the Church. "What did your sponsors then for you?"

WHITNEY "They did promise and vow three things in my name——"

(FATHER *makes his appearance on the stairway and comes down into the room.* FATHER *is in his forties, distinguished in appearance, with great charm and vitality, extremely well dressed in a conservative way. He is red-headed.*)

FATHER (*heartily*). Good morning, boys. (*They rise and answer him.*) Good morning, Vinnie. (*He goes to her and kisses her.*) Have a good night?

VINNIE. Yes, thank you, Clare.

FATHER. Good! Sit down, boys.

(*The doorbell rings and a postman's whistle is heard.*)

VINNIE. That's the doorbell, Annie. (ANNIE *exits.*) Clare, that new suit looks very nice.

FATHER. Too damn tight! (*He sits in his place at the head of the table.*) What's the matter with those fellows over in London! I wrote them a year ago they were making my clothes too tight!

VINNIE. You've put on a little weight, Clare.

FATHER. I weigh just the same as I always have. (*Attacks his orange. The boys dive into their breakfasts.* ANNIE *enters with the mail, starts to take it to* VINNIE. FATHER *sees her.*) What's that? The mail? That goes to me.

(ANNIE *gives the mail to* FATHER *and exits with her tray.*)

VINNIE. Well, Clarence has just managed to tear the only decent suit of clothes he has.

FATHER (*looking through the mail*). Here's one for you, Vinnie. John, hand that to your mother. (*He passes the letter on.*)

VINNIE. Clare dear, I'm sorry, but I'm afraid Clarence is going to have to have a new suit of clothes.

FATHER. Vinnie, Clarence has to learn not to be so hard on his clothes.

CLARENCE. Father, I thought——

FATHER. Clarence, when you start in Yale in the fall, I'm going to set aside a thousand dollars just to outfit you, but you'll get no new clothes this summer.

CLARENCE. Can't I have one of your old suits cut down for me?

FATHER. Every suit I own still has plenty of wear in it. I wear my clothes until they're worn out.

VINNIE. Well, if you want your clothes worn out, Clarence can wear them out much faster than you can.

CLARENCE. Yes, and, Father, you don't get a chance to wear them out. Every time you get a new batch of clothes, Mother sends the old ones to the missionary barrel. I guess I'm just as good as any old missionary.

(ANNIE *returns with a platter of bacon and eggs and a pot of coffee.*)

VINNIE. Clarence, before you compare yourself to a missionary, remember the sacrifices they make.

FATHER (*chuckling*). I don't know, Vinnie, I think my clothes would look better on Clarence than on some Hottentot. (*To* CLARENCE:) Have that black suit of mine cut down to fit you before your mother gets her hands on it.

(ANNIE *clears the fruit.*)

CLARENCE. Thank you, Father. (*To* JOHN:) One of Father's suits! Thank you, sir!

FATHER. Whitney, don't eat so fast.

WHITNEY. Well, Father, I'm going to pitch today and I promised to get there early, but before I go I have to study my catechism.

FATHER. What do you bother with that for?

VINNIE (*with spirit*). Because if he doesn't know his catechism he can't be confirmed!

WHITNEY (*pleading*). But I'm going to pitch today.

FATHER. Vinnie, Whitney's going to pitch today and he can be confirmed any old time.

VINNIE. Clare, sometimes it seems to me that you don't care whether your children get to Heaven or not.

FATHER. Oh, Whitney'll get to Heaven all right. (*To* WHITNEY:) I'll be there before you are, Whitney; I'll see that you get in.

VINNIE. What makes you so sure they'll let you in?

FATHER. Well, if they don't I'll certainly raise a devil of a row.

(ANNIE *is at* FATHER'S *side with the platter of bacon and eggs, ready to serve him, and draws back at this astounding declaration, raising the platter.*)

VINNIE (*with shocked awe*). Clare, I do hope you'll behave when you get to Heaven.

(FATHER *has turned to serve himself from the platter, but* ANNIE, *not yet recovered from the picture of* FATHER *raising a row at the gates of Heaven, is holding it too high for him.*)

FATHER (*storming*). Vinnie, how many times have I asked you not to engage a maid who doesn't even know how to serve properly?

VINNIE. Clare, can't you see she's new and doing her best?

FATHER. How can I serve myself when she's holding that platter over my head?

VINNIE. Annie, why don't you hold it lower?

(ANNIE *lowers the platter.* FATHER *serves himself, but goes on talking.*)

FATHER. Where'd she come from anyway? What became of the one we had yesterday? I don't see why you can't keep a maid.

VINNIE. Oh, you don't!

FATHER. All I want is service. (ANNIE *serves the others nervously. So far as* FATHER *is concerned, however, the storm has passed, and he turns genially to* WHITNEY.) Whitney, when we get to Heaven we'll organize a baseball team of our own. (*The boys laugh.*)

VINNIE. It would be just like you to try to run things up there.

FATHER. Well, from all I've heard about Heaven, it seems to be a pretty unbusinesslike place. They could probably use a good man like me. (*Stamps on the floor three times. It is his traditional signal to summon* MARGARET, *the cook, from the kitchen below.*)

VINNIE. What do you want Margaret for? What's wrong?

(ANNIE *has reached the sideboard and is sniffling audibly.*)

FATHER (*distracted*). What's that damn noise?

VINNIE. Shhh—it's Annie.

FATHER. Annie? Who's Annie?

VINNIE. The maid. (ANNIE, *seeing that she has attracted attention, hurries out into the hall where she can't be seen or heard.*) Clare, aren't you ashamed of yourself?

FATHER (*surprised*). What have I done now?

VINNIE. You made her cry—speaking to her the way you did.

FATHER. I never said a word to her—I was addressing myself to you.

VINNIE. I do wish you'd be more careful. It's hard enough to keep a maid—and the uniforms just fit this one.

(MARGARET, *the cook, a small Irishwoman of about fifty, hurries into the room.*)

MARGARET. What's wanting?

FATHER. Margaret, this bacon is *good.* (MARGARET *beams and gestures deprecatingly.*) It's *good.* It's done just right!

MARGARET. Yes, sir! (*She smiles and exits.* ANNIE *returns, recovered, and starts serving the coffee.* VINNIE *has opened her letter and glanced through it.*)

VINNIE. Clare, this letter gives me a good idea. I've decided that next winter I won't give a series of dinners.

FATHER. I should hope not.

VINNIE. I'll give a big musicale instead.

FATHER. You'll give a what?

VINNIE. A musicale.

FATHER (*peremptorily*). Vinnie, I won't have my peaceful home turned into a Roman arena with a lot of hairy fiddlers prancing about.

VINNIE. I didn't say a word about hairy fiddlers. Mrs. Spiller has written me about this lovely young girl who will come for very little.

FATHER. What instrument does this inexpensive paragon play?

VINNIE. She doesn't play, Clare, she whistles.

FATHER. Whistles? Good God!

VINNIE. She whistles sixteen different pieces. All for twenty-five dollars.

FATHER (*stormily*). I won't pay twenty-five dollars to any human peanut stand. (*He tastes his coffee, grimaces, and again stamps three times on the floor.*)

VINNIE. Clare, I can arrange this so it won't cost you a penny. If I invite fifty people and charge them fifty cents apiece, there's the twenty-five dollars right there!

FATHER. You can't invite people to your own house and charge them admission.

VINNIE. I can if the money's for the missionary fund.

FATHER. Then where will you get the twenty-five dollars to pay that poor girl for her whistling?

VINNIE. Now, Clare, let's not cross that bridge until we come to it.

FATHER. And if we do cross it, it will cost me twenty-five dollars. Vinnie, I'm putting my foot down about this musicale, just as I've had to put my foot down about your keeping this house full of visiting relatives. Why can't we live here by ourselves in peace and comfort?

(MARGARET *comes dashing into the room.*)

MARGARET. What's wanting?

FATHER (*sternly*). Margaret, what is this? (*He holds up his coffee cup and points at it.*)

MARGARET. It's coffee, sir.

FATHER. It is not coffee! You couldn't possibly take water and coffee beans and arrive at that! It's slops, that's what it is—slops! Take it away! Take it away, I tell you!

(MARGARET *takes* FATHER'S *cup and dashes out.* ANNIE *starts to take* VINNIE'S *cup.*)

VINNIE. Leave my coffee there, Annie! It's perfectly all right!

(ANNIE *leaves the room.*)

FATHER (*angrily*). It is not! I swear I can't imagine how she concocts such an atrocity. I come down to this table every morning hungry——

VINNIE. Well, if you're hungry, Clare, why aren't you eating your breakfast?

FATHER. What?

VINNIE. If you're hungry, why aren't you eating your breakfast?

FATHER (*thrown out of bounds*). I am. (*He takes a mouthful of bacon and munches it happily, his eyes falling on* HARLAN.) Harlan, how's that finger? Come over here and let me see it. (HARLAN *goes to his father's side. He shows his finger.*) Well, that's healing nicely. Now don't pick that scab or it will leave a scar, and we don't want scars on our fingers, do we? (*He chuckles.*) I guess you'll remember after this that cats don't like to be hugged. It's all right to stroke them, but don't squeeze them. Now go back and finish your oatmeal.

HARLAN. I don't like oatmeal.

FATHER. (*kindly*). It's good for you. Go back and eat it.

HARLAN. But I don't like it.

FATHER (*quietly, but firmly*). I'll tell you what you like and what you don't like. You're not old enough to know about such things. You've no business not to like oatmeal. It's good.

HARLAN. I hate it.

FATHER (*firmly, but not quietly*). That's enough! We won't discuss it! Eat that oatmeal at once!

(*In contrast to* HARLAN, WHITNEY *has been eating his oatmeal at a terrific rate of speed. He pauses and puts down his spoon.*)

WHITNEY. I've finished *my* oatmeal. May I be excused?

FATHER. Yes, Whitney, you may go. (WHITNEY *slides off his chair and hurries to the stairs.*) Pitch a good game.

VINNIE. Whitney!

WHITNEY. I'm going upstairs to study my catechism.

VINNIE. Oh, that's all right. Run along.

WHITNEY (*on the way up*). Harlan, you'd better hurry up and finish your oatmeal if you want to go with me.

(*Throughout breakfast* FATHER *has been opening and glancing through his mail. He has just reached one letter, however, that bewilders him.*)

FATHER. I don't understand why I'm always getting damn fool letters like this!

VINNIE. What is it, Clare?

FATHER. "Dear Friend Day: We are assigning you the exclusive rights for Staten Island for selling the Gem Home Popper for popcorn——"

CLARENCE. I think that's for me, Father.

FATHER. Then why isn't it addressed to Clarence Day, Jr.? (*He looks at the envelope.*) Oh, it is. Well, I'm sorry. I didn't mean to open your mail.

(MARGARET *returns and slips a cup of coffee to the table beside* FATHER.)

VINNIE. I wouldn't get mixed up in that, Clarence. People like popcorn, but they won't go all the way to Staten Island to buy it.

(FATHER *has picked up the paper and is reading it. He drinks his coffee absentmindedly.*)

FATHER. Chauncey Depew's having another birthday.

VINNIE. How nice.

FATHER. He's always having birthdays. Two or three a year. Damn! Another wreck on the New Haven!

VINNIE. Yes. Oh, that reminds me. Mrs. Bailey dropped in yesterday.

FATHER. Was she in the wreck?

VINNIE. No. But she was born in New Haven. Clarence, you're having tea with Edith Bailey Thursday afternoon.

CLARENCE. Oh, Mother, do I have to?

JOHN (*singing*). "I like coffee, I like tea. I like the girls and the girls like me."

CLARENCE. Well, the girls don't like me and I don't like them.

VINNIE. Edith Bailey's a very nice girl, isn't she, Clare?

FATHER. Edith Bailey? Don't like her. Don't blame Clarence.

(FATHER *goes to his chair by the window and sits down with his newspaper and a cigar. The others rise.* HARLAN *runs upstairs.* ANNIE *starts clearing the table and exits with the tray of dishes a little later.* VINNIE *speaks in a guarded tone to the two boys.*)

VINNIE. Clarence, you and John go upstairs and do—what I asked you to.

JOHN. You said the small bureau, Mother?

VINNIE. Shh! Run along.

(*The boys go upstairs, somewhat unwillingly.* MARGARET *enters.*)

MARGARET. If you please, ma'am, there's a package been delivered with a dollar due on it. Some kitchen knives.

VINNIE. Oh, yes, those knives from Lewis & Conger's. (*She gets her purse from the drawer in the console table and gives* MARGARET *a dollar.*) Here, give this dollar to the man, Margaret.

FATHER. Make a memorandum of that, Vinnie. One dollar and whatever it was for.

VINNIE (*looking into purse*). Clare, dear, I'm afraid I'm going to need some more money.

FATHER. What for?

VINNIE. You were complaining of the coffee this morning. Well, that nice French drip coffee pot is broken—and you know how it got broken.

FATHER (*taking out his wallet*). Never mind that, Vinnie. As I remember, that coffee pot cost five dollars and something. Here's six dollars. (*He gives her six dollars.*) And when you get it, enter the exact amount in the ledger downstairs.

VINNIE. Thank you, Clare.

FATHER. We can't go on month after month having the household accounts in such a mess.

VINNIE (*she sits on the arm of* FATHER'S *chair*). No, and I've thought of a system that will make my bookkeeping perfect.

FATHER. I'm certainly relieved to hear that. What is it?

VINNIE. Well, Clare dear, you never make half the fuss over how much I've spent as you do over my not being able to remember what I've spent it for.

FATHER. Exactly. This house must be run on a business basis. That's why I insist on your keeping books.

VINNIE. That's the whole point, Clare. All we have to do is open charge accounts everywhere and the stores will do my bookkeeping for me.

FATHER. Wait a minute, Vinnie——

VINNIE. Then when the bills come in you'd know exactly where your money had gone.

FATHER. I certainly would. Vinnie, I get enough bills as it is.

VINNIE. Yes, and those bills always help. They show you just where I spent the money. Now if we had charge accounts everywhere——

FATHER. Now, Vinnie, I don't know about that.

VINNIE. Clare dear, don't you hate those arguments we have every month? I certainly do. Not to have those I should think would be worth something to you.

FATHER. Well, I'll open an account at Lewis & Conger's—and one at McCreery's to start with—we'll see how it works out. (*He shakes his head doubtfully. Her victory gained,* VINNIE *moves away.*)

VINNIE. Thank you, Clare. Oh—the rector's coming to tea today.

FATHER. The rector? I'm glad you warned me. I'll go to the club. Don't expect me home until dinner time.

VINNIE. I do wish you'd take a little more interest in the church. (*Goes behind* FATHER'S *chair and looks down at him with concern.*)

FATHER. Vinnie, getting me into Heaven's your job. If there's anything wrong with my ticket when I get there, you can fix it up. Everybody loves you so much—I'm sure God must, too.

VINNIE. I'll do my best, Clare. It wouldn't be Heaven without you.

FATHER. If you're there, Vinnie, I'll manage to get in some way, even if I have to climb the fence.

JOHN (*from upstairs*). Mother, we've moved it. Is there anything else?

FATHER. What's being moved?

VINNIE. Never mind, Clare. I'll come right up, John. (*She goes to the arch, stops. Looks back at* FATHER.) Oh, Clare, it's eight thirty. You don't want to be late at the office.

FATHER. Plenty of time. (VINNIE *looks nervously toward the door, then goes upstairs.* FATHER *returns to his newspaper.* VINNIE *has barely disappeared when something in the paper arouses* FATHER'S *indignation.*) Oh, God!

(VINNIE *comes running downstairs.*)

VINNIE. What's the matter, Clare? What's wrong?

FATHER. Why did God make so many damn fools and Democrats?

VINNIE (*relieved*). Oh, politics. (*She goes upstairs again.*)

FATHER (*shouting after her*). Yes, but it's taking the bread out of our mouths. It's robbery, that's what it is, highway robbery! Honest Hugh Grant! Honest! Bah! A fine mayor you've turned out to be. (FATHER *launches into a vigorous denunciation of Mayor Hugh Grant, addressing that gentleman as though he were present in the room, called up on the Day carpet to listen to* FATHER'S *opinion of Tammany's latest attack on his pocketbook.*) If you can't run this city without raising taxes every five minutes, you'd better get out and let someone who can. Let me tell you, sir, that the real-estate owners of New York City are not going to tolerate these conditions any longer. Tell me this—are these increased taxes going into public improvements or are they going into graft—answer me that, honestly, if you can, Mr. Honest Hugh Grant. You can't! I thought so. Bah! (ANNIE *enters with her tray. Hearing* FATHER *talking, she curtsies and backs into the hall, as if uncertain whether to intrude on* FATHER *and the Mayor.* VINNIE *comes downstairs.*) If you don't stop your plundering of the pocketbooks of the good citizens of New York, we're going to throw you and your boodle Board of Aldermen out of office.

VINNIE. Annie, why aren't you clearing the table?

ANNIE. Mr. Day's got a visitor.

FATHER. I'm warning you for the last time.

VINNIE. Oh, nonsense, he's just reading his paper, Annie. Clear the table. (VINNIE *goes off through the arch.* ANNIE *comes in timidly and starts to clear the table.*)

FATHER (*still lecturing Mayor Grant*). We pay you a good round sum to watch after our interests, and all we get is inefficiency! (ANNIE *looks around trying to see the Mayor and, finding the room empty, assumes* FATHER'S *remarks are directed at her.*) I know you're a nincompoop and I strongly suspect you of being a scalawag. (ANNIE *stands petrified.* WHITNEY *comes downstairs.*) It's graft—that's what it is—Tammany graft—and if you're not getting it, somebody else is.

WHITNEY (*to* FATHER). Where's John? Do you know where John is?

FATHER. Dick Croker's running this town and you're just his cat's-paw.

(VINNIE *comes in from downstairs, and* HARLAN *comes down from upstairs.* FATHER *goes on talking. The others carry on their conversation simultaneously, ignoring* FATHER *and his imaginary visitor.*)

HARLAN. Mother, where's John?

VINNIE. He's upstairs, dear.

FATHER. And as for you, Richard Croker—don't think, just because you're hiding behind these minions you've put in public office, that you're going to escape your legal responsibilities.

WHITNEY (*calling upstairs*). John, I'm going to take your glove!

JOHN (*from upstairs*). Don't you lose it! And don't let anybody else have it either!

VINNIE. Annie, you should have cleared the table long ago.

(ANNIE *loads her tray feverishly, eager to escape.*)

FATHER (*rising and slamming down the paper in his chair*). Legal responsibilities—by gad, sir, I mean *criminal* responsibilities.

(The boys start toward the front door.)

VINNIE *(starting upstairs)*. Now you watch Harlan, Whitney. Don't let him be anywhere the ball can hit him. Do what Whitney says, Harlan. And don't be late for lunch.

(FATHER has reached the arch on his way out of the room, where he pauses for a final shot at Mayor Grant.)

FATHER. Don't forget what happened to William Marcy Tweed—and if you put our taxes up once more, we'll put you in jail!

(He goes out of the archway to the left. A few seconds later he is seen passing the arch toward the outer door wearing his square derby and carrying his stick and gloves. The door is heard to slam loudly.)

(ANNIE seizes her tray of dishes and runs out of the arch to the left toward the basement stairs. A second later there is a scream from ANNIE and a tremendous crash.)

(JOHN and CLARENCE come rushing down and look over the rail of the stairs below. VINNIE follows them almost immediately.)

VINNIE. What is it? What happened?

CLARENCE. The maid fell downstairs.

VINNIE. I don't wonder, with your father getting her so upset. Why couldn't she have finished with the table before she fell downstairs?

JOHN. I don't think she hurt herself.

VINNIE. And today of all days! Boys, will you finish the table? And, Clarence, don't leave the house until I talk to you. *(She goes downstairs.)*

(During the following scene CLARENCE and JOHN remove VINNIE'S best breakfast tablecloth and cram it carelessly into the drawer of the console table, then take out the extra leaves from the table, push it together, and replace the living-room table cover and the bowl of fruit.)

JOHN. What do you suppose Mother wants to talk to you about?

CLARENCE. Oh, probably about Edith Bailey.

JOHN. What do you talk about when you have tea alone with a girl?

CLARENCE. We don't talk about anything. I say: "Isn't it a nice day?" and she says: "Yes," and I say: "I think it's a little warmer than yesterday," and she says: "Yes, I like warm weather, don't you?" and I say: "Yes," and then we wait for the tea to come in. And then she says: "How many lumps?" and I say: "Two, thank you," and she says: "You must have a sweet tooth," and I can't say: "Yes" and I can't say: "No," so we just sit there and look at each other for half an hour. Then I say: "Well, it's time I was going," and she says: "Must you?" and I say: "I've enjoyed seeing you very much," and she says: "You must come again," and I say "I will," and get out.

JOHN *(shaking his head)*. Some fellows like girls.

CLARENCE. I don't.

JOHN. And did you ever notice fellows, when they get sweet on a girl—the silly things a girl can make them do? And they don't even seem to know they're acting silly.

CLARENCE. Well, not for Yours Truly!

(VINNIE *returns from downstairs.*)

VINNIE. I declare I don't see how anyone could be so clumsy.

CLARENCE. Did she hurt herself?

VINNIE. No, she's not hurt—she's just hysterical! She doesn't make sense. Your father may have raised his voice; and if she doesn't know how to hold a platter properly, she deserved it—but I know he didn't threaten to put her in jail. Oh, well! Clarence, I want you to move your things into the front room. You'll have to sleep with the other boys for a night or two.

CLARENCE. You haven't told us who's coming.

VINNIE (*happily*). Cousin Cora. Isn't that nice?

CLARENCE. It's not nice for me. I can't get any sleep in there with those children.

JOHN. Wait'll Father finds out she's here! There'll be a rumpus.

VINNIE. John, don't criticize your father. He's very hospitable after he gets used to the idea.

(*The doorbell rings.* JOHN *and* VINNIE *go to the window.*)

JOHN. Yes, it's Cousin Cora. Look, there's somebody with her.

VINNIE (*looking out*). She wrote me she was bringing a friend of hers. They're both going to stay here. (*A limping* ANNIE *passes through the hall.*) Finish with the room, boys.

CLARENCE. Do I have to sleep with the other boys and have tea with Edith Bailey all in the same week?

VINNIE. Yes, and you'd better take your father's suit to the tailor's right away, so it will be ready by Thursday.

(VINNIE *goes down the hall to greet* CORA *and* MARY. CLARENCE *hurries off, carrying the table leaves.*)

VINNIE'S VOICE (*in the hall*). Cora dear——

CORA'S VOICE. Cousin Vinnie, I'm so glad to see you! This is Mary Skinner.

VINNIE'S VOICE. Ed Skinner's daughter! I'm so glad to see you. Leave your bags in the hall and come right upstairs.

(VINNIE *enters, going toward the stairs.* CORA *follows her, but, seeing* JOHN, *enters the room and goes to him.* MARY *follows* CORA *in timidly.* CORA *is an attractive country cousin of about thirty.* MARY *is a refreshingly pretty small-town girl of sixteen.*)

CORA (*seeing John*). Well, Clarence, it's so good to see you!

VINNIE (*coming into the room*). Oh, no, that's John.

CORA. John! Why, how you've grown! You'll be a man before your mother! (*She laughs herself at this time-worn quip.*) John, this is Mary Skinner. (*They exchange greetings.*) Vinnie, I have so much to tell you. We wrote you Aunt Carrie broke her hip. That was the night Robert Ingersoll lectured. Of course she couldn't get there; and it was a good thing for Mr. Ingersoll she didn't. (CLARENCE *enters.*) And Grandpa Ebbetts hasn't been at all well.

CLARENCE. How do you do, Cousin Cora? I'm glad to see you.

CORA. This can't be Clarence!

VINNIE. Yes, it is.

CORA. My goodness, every time I see you boys you've grown another foot. Let's see—you're going to St. Paul's now, aren't you?

CLARENCE (*with pained dignity*). St. Paul's! I was through with St. Paul's long ago. I'm starting in Yale this fall.

MARY. Yale!

CORA. Oh, Mary, this is Clarence—Mary Skinner. (MARY *smiles, and* CLARENCE, *the woman-hater, nods politely and walks away.*) This is Mary's first trip to New York. She was so excited when she saw a horse car.

VINNIE. We'll have to show Mary around. I'll tell you—I'll have Mr. Day take us all to Delmonico's for dinner tonight.

MARY. Delmonico's!

CORA. Oh, that's marvelous! Think of that, Mary—Delmonico's! And Cousin Clare's such a wonderful host.

VINNIE. I know you girls want to freshen up. So come upstairs. Clarence, I'll let the girls use your room now, and when they've finished you can move, and bring up their bags. They're out in the hall. (*Starts upstairs with* CORA.) I've given you girls Clarence's room, but he didn't know about it until this morning and he hasn't moved out yet.

(VINNIE *and* CORA *disappear upstairs.*)

(MARY *follows more slowly and on the second step stops and looks back.* CLARENCE *has gone into the hall with his back toward* MARY *and stares morosely in the direction of their luggage.*)

CLARENCE. John, get their old bags.

(JOHN *disappears toward the front door. The voices of* VINNIE *and* CORA *have trailed off into the upper reaches of the house.* CLARENCE *turns to scowl in their direction and finds himself looking full into the face of* MARY.)

MARY. Cora didn't tell me about you. I never met a Yale man before.

(*She gives him a devastating smile and with an audible whinny of girlish excitement she runs upstairs.* CLARENCE *stares after her a few seconds, then turns toward the audience with a look of "What happened to me just then?" Suddenly, however, his face breaks into a smile which indicates that, whatever has happened, he likes it.*)

CURTAIN

SCENE II

The same day. Tea time.

VINNIE *and the* RECTOR *are having tea.* THE REVEREND DR. LLOYD *is a plump, bustling man, very good-hearted and pleasant.* VINNIE *and* DR. LLOYD *have one strong point in common: their devotion to the Church and its rituals.* VINNIE'S *devotion comes from her natural piety;* DR. LLOYD'S *is a little more professional.*

At rise, DR. LLOYD *is seated with a cup of tea.* VINNIE *is also seated and* WHITNEY *is standing next to her, stiffly erect in the manner of a boy reciting.* HARLAN *is seated next to his mother, watching* WHITNEY'S *performance.*

WHITNEY (*reciting*). "—to worship Him, to give Him thanks; to put my whole trust in Him, to call upon Him——" (*He hesitates.*)

VINNIE (*prompting*). "—to honor——"

WHITNEY "—to honor His Holy Name and His word and to serve Him truly all the days of my life."

DR. LLOYD. "What is thy duty toward thy neighbor?"

WHITNEY. Whew! (*He pulls himself together and makes a brave start.*) "My duty toward my neighbor is to love him as myself, and to do to all men as I would they should do unto me; to love, honor, and succor my father and my mother; to honor and obey——"

VINNIE. "—civil authorities."

WHITNEY. "—civil authorities. To—to —to——"

VINNIE (*to* DR. LLOYD). He really knows it.

WHITNEY. I know most of the others.

DR. LLOYD. Well, he's done very well for so young a boy. I'm sure if he applies himself between now and Sunday I could hear him again—with the others.

VINNIE. There, Whitney, you'll have to study very hard if you want Dr. Lloyd to send your name in to Bishop Potter next Sunday. I must confess to you, Dr. Lloyd, it's really my fault. Instead of hearing Whitney say his catechism this morning I let him play baseball.

WHITNEY. We won, too; 35 to 27.

DR. LLOYD. That's splendid, my child. I'm glad your side won. But winning over your catechism is a richer and fuller victory.

WHITNEY. Can I go now?

VINNIE. Yes, darling. Thank Dr. Lloyd for hearing you and run along.

WHITNEY. Thank you, Dr. Lloyd.

DR. LLOYD. Not at all, my little man.

(WHITNEY *starts out, turns back, takes a piece of cake and runs out.*)

VINNIE. Little Harlan is very apt at learning things by heart.

HARLAN (*scrambling to his feet*). I can spell Constantinople. Want to hear me? (DR. LLOYD *smiles his assent.*) *C-o-ennaconny—annaconny—*sissaconny—tan-tan-tee—and a nople and a pople and a Constantinople!

DR. LLOYD. Very well done, my child.

VINNIE (*handing him a cake from the tea-tray*). That's nice, darling. This is what you get for saying it so well.

(HARLAN *quickly looks at the cake and back to* DR. LLOYD.)

HARLAN. Want me to say it again for you?

VINNIE. No, darling. One cake is enough. You run along and play with Whitney.

HARLAN. I can spell "huckleberry pie."

VINNIE. Run along, dear.

(HARLAN *goes out, skipping in rhythm to his recitation.*)

H-a-huckle — b-a-buckle — h-a-huckle-high. H-a-huckle — b-a-buckle — huckleberry pie!

DR. LLOYD (*amused*). You and Mr. Day must be very proud of your children. (VINNIE *beams.*) I was hoping I'd find Mr. Day at home this afternoon.

VINNIE (*evasively*). Well, he's usually home from the office by this time.

DR. LLOYD. Perhaps he's gone for a gallop in the park—it's such a fine day. He's very fond of horseback riding, I believe.

VINNIE. Oh, yes.

DR. LLOYD. Tell me—has he ever been thrown from a horse?

VINNIE. Oh, no! No horse would throw Mr. Day.

DR. LLOYD. I've wondered. I thought he might have had an accident. I notice he never kneels in church.

VINNIE. Oh, that's no accident! But I don't want you to think he doesn't pray. He does. Why, sometimes you can hear him pray all over the house. But he never kneels.

DR. LLOYD. Never kneels! Dear me! I was hoping to have the opportunity to tell you and Mr. Day about our plans for the new edifice.

VINNIE. I'm so glad we're going to have a new church.

DR. LLOYD. I'm happy to announce that we're now ready to proceed. The only thing left to do is raise the money.

VINNIE. No one should hesitate about contributing to that.

(*The front door slams.*)

DR. LLOYD. Perhaps that's Mr. Day now.

VINNIE. Oh, no, I hardly think so. (FATHER *appears in the archway.*) Why, it is!

FATHER. Oh, damn! I forgot.

VINNIE. Clare, you're just in time. Dr. Lloyd's here for tea.

FATHER. I'll be right in. (*He disappears the other side of the archway.*)

VINNIE. I'll send for some fresh tea. (*She goes to the bell-pull and rings for the maid.*)

DR. LLOYD. Now we can tell Mr. Day about our plans for the new edifice.

VINNIE (*knowing her man*). After he's had his tea.

(FATHER *comes back into the room.* DR. LLOYD *rises.*)

FATHER. How are you, Dr. Lloyd?

(CLARENCE *comes down the stairs and eagerly looks around for* MARY.)

CLARENCE. Oh, it was Father.

DR. LLOYD. Very well, thank you. (*They shake hands.*)

CLARENCE (*to* VINNIE). They're not back yet?

VINNIE. No! Clarence, no!

(CLARENCE *turns, disappointed, and goes back upstairs.*)

DR. LLOYD. It's a great pleasure to have a visit with you, Mr. Day. Except for a fleeting glimpse on the Sabbath, I don't see much of you.

(FATHER *grunts and sits down.* DELIA, *a new maid, enters.*)

DELIA. Yes, ma'am.

VINNIE. Some fresh tea and a cup for Mr. Day. (DELIA *exits and* VINNIE *hurries down to the tea table to start the conversation.*) Well, Clare, did you have a busy day at the office?

FATHER. Damn busy.

VINNIE. Clare!

FATHER. Very busy day. Tired out.

VINNIE. I've ordered some fresh tea. (*To* DR. LLOYD). Poor Clare, he must work very hard. He always comes home tired. Although how a man can get tired just sitting at his desk all day, I don't know. I suppose Wall Street is just as much a mystery to you as it is to me, Dr. Lloyd.

DR. LLOYD. No, no, it's all very clear to me. My mind often goes to the businessman. The picture I'm most fond of is when I envision him at the close of the day's work. There he sits —this hard-headed man of affairs— surrounded by the ledgers that he has been studying closely and harshly for hours. I see him pausing in his toil—and by chance he raises his eyes and looks out of the window at the light in God's sky and it comes over him that money and ledgers are dross. (FATHER *stares at* DR. LLOYD *with some amazement.*) He realizes that all those figures of profit and loss are without importance or consequence —vanity and dust. And I see this troubled man bow his head and with streaming eyes resolve to devote his life to far higher things.

FATHER. Well, I'll be damned!

(*At this moment* DELIA *returns with the fresh tea for* FATHER.)

VINNIE. Here's your tea, Clare.

(FATHER *notices the new maid.*)

FATHER. Who's this?

VINNIE (*quietly*). The new maid.

FATHER. Where's the one we had this morning?

VINNIE. Never mind, Clare.

FATHER. The one we had this morning was prettier. (DELIA, *with a slight resentment, exits.* FATHER *attacks the tea and cakes with relish.*) Vinnie, these cakes are *good.*

DR. LLOYD. Delicious!

VINNIE. Dr. Lloyd wants to tell us about the plans for the new edifice.

FATHER. The new what?

VINNIE. The new church—Clare, you knew we were planning to build a new church.

DR. LLOYD. Of course, we're going to have to raise a large sum of money.

FATHER (*alive to the danger*). Well, personally I'm against the church hop-skipping-and-jumping all over the town. And it so happens that during the last year I've suffered heavy losses in the market—damned heavy losses——

VINNIE. Clare!

FATHER. —so any contribution I make will have to be a small one.

VINNIE. But, Clare, for so worthy a cause!

FATHER. —and if your Finance Committee thinks it's too small they can blame the rascals that are running the New Haven Railroad!

DR. LLOYD. The amount everyone is to subscribe has already been decided.

FATHER (*bristling*). Who decided it?

DR. LLOYD. After considerable thought we've found a formula which we believe is fair and equitable. It apportions the burden lightly on those least able to carry it and justly on those whose shoulders we know are stronger. We've voted that our supporting members should each contribute a sum equal to the cost of their pews.

(FATHER'S *jaw drops.*)

FATHER. I paid five thousand dollars for my pew!

VINNIE. Yes, Clare. That makes our contribution five thousand dollars.

FATHER. That's robbery! Do you know what that pew is worth today? Three thousand dollars. That's what the last one sold for. I've taken a dead loss of two thousand dollars on that pew already. Frank Baggs sold me that pew when the market was at its peak. He knew when to get out. (*He turns to* VINNIE.) And I'm warning you now that if the market ever goes up I'm going to unload that pew.

VINNIE. Clarence Day! How can you speak of the Lord's temple as though it were something to be bought and sold on Wall Street!

FATHER. Vinnie, this is a matter of dollars and cents, and that's something you don't know anything about!

VINNIE. Your talking of religion in the terms of dollars and cents seems to me pretty close to blasphemy.

DR. LLOYD (*soothingly*). Now, Mrs. Day, your husband is a businessman and he has a practical approach toward this problem. We've had to be practical about it too—we have all the facts and figures.

FATHER. Oh, really! What's the new piece of property going to cost you?

DR. LLOYD. I think the figure I've heard mentioned is eighty-five thousand dollars—or was it a hundred and eighty-five thousand dollars?

FATHER. What's the property worth where we are now?

DR. LLOYD. Well, there's quite a difference of opinion about that.

FATHER. How much do you have to raise to build the new church?

DR. LLOYD. Now, I've seen those figures—let me see—I know it depends somewhat upon the amount of the mortgage.

FATHER. Mortgage, eh? What are the terms of the amortization?

DR. LLOYD. Amortization? That's not a word I'm familiar with.

FATHER. It all seems pretty vague and unsound to me. I certainly wouldn't let any customer of mine invest on what I've heard.

(*The doorbell rings.*)

DR. LLOYD. We've given it a great deal of thought. I don't see how you can call it vague.

(DELIA *passes along the hall toward the front door.*)

FATHER. Dr. Lloyd, you preach that some day we'll all have to answer to God.

DR. LLOYD. We shall indeed!

FATHER. Well, I hope God doesn't ask you any questions with figures in them.

(CORA'S *voice is heard in the hall, thanking* DELIA. VINNIE *goes to the arch just in time to meet* CORA *and* MARY *as they enter, heavily laden with packages, which they put down.* FATHER *and* DR. LLOYD *rise.*)

CORA. Oh, Vinnie, what a day! We've been to every shop in town and—— (*She sees* FATHER.) Cousin Clare!

FATHER (*cordially*). Cora, what are you doing in New York?

CORA. We're just passing through on our way to Springfield.

FATHER. We?

(CLARENCE *comes downstairs into the room with eyes only for* MARY.)

VINNIE. Oh, Dr. Lloyd, this is my favorite cousin, Miss Cartwright, and her friend, Mary Skinner. (*They exchange mutual how-do-you-do's.*)

DR. LLOYD. This seems to be a family reunion. I'll just run along.

FATHER (*promptly*). Good-by, Dr. Lloyd.

DR. LLOYD. Good-by, Miss Cartwright. Good-by, Miss—er——

VINNIE. Clarence, you haven't said how-do-you-do to Dr. Lloyd.

CLARENCE. Good-by, Dr. Lloyd.

VINNIE (*to* DR. LLOYD). I'll go to the door with you. (DR. LLOYD *and* VINNIE *go out, talking.*)

FATHER. Cora, you're as welcome as the flowers in May! Have some tea with us. (*To* DELIA:) Bring some fresh tea—and some more of those cakes.

CORA. Oh, we've had tea! We were so tired shopping we had tea downtown.

(*With a gesture* FATHER *countermands his order to* DELIA, *who removes the tea table and exits.*)

MARY. At the Fifth Avenue Hotel.

FATHER. At the Fifth Avenue Hotel, eh? Who'd you say this pretty little girl was?

CORA. She's Ed Skinner's daughter. Well, Mary, at last you've met Mr. Day. I've told Mary so much about you, Cousin Clare, that she's just been dying to meet you.

FATHER. Well, sit down! Sit down! Even if you have had tea you can stop and visit for a while. As a matter of fact, why don't you both stay to dinner?

(VINNIE *enters just in time to hear this and cuts in quickly.*)

VINNIE. That's all arranged, Clare. Cora and Mary are going to have dinner with us.

FATHER. That's fine! That's fine!

CORA. Cousin Clare, I don't know how to thank you and Vinnie for your hospitality.

MARY. Yes, Mr. Day.

FATHER. Well, you'll just have to take pot luck.

CORA. No, I mean——

(VINNIE *speaks quickly to postpone the revelation that* FATHER *has house guests.*)

VINNIE. Clare, did you know the girls are going to visit Aunt Judith in Springfield for a whole month?

FATHER. That's fine. How long are you going to be in New York, Cora?

CORA. All week.

FATHER. Splendid. We'll hope to see something of you, eh, Vinnie?

(CORA *looks bewildered and is about to speak.*)

VINNIE. Did you find anything you wanted in the shops?

CORA. Just everything.

VINNIE. I want to see what you got.

CORA. I just can't wait to show you. (*She goes coyly to* FATHER.) But I'm afraid some of the packages can't be opened in front of Cousin Clare.

FATHER. Shall I leave the room? (*Laughs at his own joke.*)

CORA. Clarence, do you mind taking the packages up to our room—or should I say your room? (*To* FATHER:) Wasn't it nice of Clarence to give up his room to us for a whole week?

FATHER (*with a sudden drop in temperature*). Vinnie!

VINNIE. Come on, Cora, I just can't wait to see what's in those packages.

(CORA, MARY, *and* VINNIE *start out.* CLARENCE *is gathering up the packages.*)

FATHER (*ominously*). Vinnie, I wish to speak to you before you go upstairs.

VINNIE. I'll be down in just a minute, Clare.

FATHER. I wish to speak to you now!

(*The girls have disappeared upstairs.*)

VINNIE. I'll be up in just a minute, Cora.

(*We hear a faint* "All right" *from upstairs.*)

FATHER (*his voice is low but stern*). Are those two women encamped in this house?

VINNIE. Now, Clare!

FATHER (*much louder*). Answer me, Vinnie!

VINNIE. Just a minute—control yourself, Clare.

(VINNIE, *sensing the coming storm, hurries to the sliding doors.* CLARENCE *has reached the hall with his packages and he, too, has recognized the danger signal and as* VINNIE *closes one door he closes the other, leaving himself out in the hall and* FATHER *and* VINNIE *facing each other in the room.*)

VINNIE (*persuasively*). Now, Clare, you know you've always liked Cora.

FATHER (*exploding*). What has that got to do with her planking herself down in my house and bringing hordes of strangers with her?

VINNIE (*reproachfully*). How can you call that sweet little girl a horde of strangers?

FATHER. Why don't they go to a hotel? New York is full of hotels built for the express purpose of housing such nuisances.

VINNIE. Clare! Two girls alone in a hotel! Who knows what might happen to them?

FATHER. All right. Then put 'em on the next train. If they want to roam—the damned gypsies—lend 'em a hand! Keep 'em roaming!

VINNIE. What have we got a home for if we can't show a little hospitality?

FATHER. I didn't buy this home to show hospitality—I bought it for my own comfort!

VINNIE. Well, how much are they going to interfere with your comfort living in that little room of Clarence's?

FATHER. The trouble is, damn it, they don't live there. They live in the bathroom! Every time I want to take my bath it's full of giggling females —washing their hair. From the time they take, you'd think it was the Seven Sutherland Sisters. I tell you, I won't have it! Send 'em to a hotel. I'll pay the bill gladly, but get them out of here!

(CLARENCE *puts his head through the sliding door.*)

CLARENCE. Father, I'm afraid they can hear you upstairs.

FATHER. Then keep those doors closed!

VINNIE (*with decision*). Clarence, you open those doors—open them all the way! (CLARENCE *does so.*)

VINNIE (*to* FATHER, *lowering her voice, but maintaining her spirit*). Now, Clare, you behave yourself! (FATHER *glares at her angrily.*) They're here and they're going to stay here.

FATHER. That's enough, Vinnie! I want no more of this argument. (*He goes to his chair by the window, muttering.*) Damnation!

CLARENCE (*to* VINNIE). Mother, Cousin Cora's waiting for you.

FATHER. What I don't understand is why this swarm of locusts always descends on us without any warning. (*He sits down.* VINNIE *looks at him; then, convinced of her victory, she goes upstairs.*) Damn! Damnation! Damn! (*He follows her upstairs with his eyes; he remembers he is very fond of her.*) Vinnie! Dear Vinnie! (*He remembers he is very angry at her.*) Damn!

CLARENCE. Father, can't I go along with the rest of you to Delmonico's tonight?

FATHER. What's that? Delmonico's?

CLARENCE. You're taking Mother, Cora, and Mary to Delmonico's for dinner.

FATHER (*exploding*). Oh, God! (*At this sound from* FATHER, VINNIE *comes flying downstairs again.*) I won't have it. I won't have it. (FATHER *stamps angrily across the room.*)

VINNIE (*on the way down*). Clarence, the doors!

FATHER. I won't stand it, by God! I won't stand it! (VINNIE *and* CLARENCE *hurriedly close the sliding doors again.*)

VINNIE. Clare! What's the matter now?

FATHER (*with the calm of anger that has turned to ice*). Do I understand that I can't have dinner in my own home?

VINNIE. It'll do us both good to get out of this house. You need a little change. It'll make you feel better.

FATHER. I have a home to have dinner in. Any time I can't have dinner at home this house is for sale!

VINNIE. Well, you can't have dinner here tonight because it isn't ordered.

FATHER. Let me tell you I'm ready to sell this place this very minute if I can't live here in peace. And we can all go and sit under a palm tree and live on breadfruit and pickles.

VINNIE. But, Clare, Cora and Mary want to see something of New York.

FATHER. Oh, that's it! Well, that's no affair of mine! I am not a guide to Chinatown and the Bowery. (*Drawing himself up, he stalks out, throwing open the sliding doors. As he reaches the foot of the stairs,* MARY *comes tripping down.*)

MARY. I love your house, Mr. Day. I could just live here forever. (FATHER *utters a bark of disgust and continues on upstairs.* MARY *comes into the room a little wide-eyed.*) Cora's waiting for you, Mrs. Day.

VINNIE. Oh, yes, I'll run right up. (*She goes upstairs.*)

CLARENCE. I'm glad you like our house.

MARY. Oh, yes, I like it very much. I like green.

CLARENCE. I like green myself. (*She looks up at his red hair.*)

MARY. Red's my favorite color.

(*Embarrassed,* CLARENCE *suddenly hears himself talking about something he has never thought about.*)

CLARENCE. It's an interesting thing about colors. Red's a nice color in a house, too; but outside, too much red would be bad. I mean, for instance, if all the trees and the grass were red. Outside, green is the best color.

MARY (*impressed*). That's right! I've never thought of it that way—but when you do think of it, it's quite a thought! I'll bet you'll make your mark at Yale.

CLARENCE (*pleased, but modest*). Oh! (*The outer door is heard to slam.*)

MARY. My mother wants me to go to college. Do you believe in girls going to college?

CLARENCE. I guess it's all right if they want to waste that much time—before they get married, I mean. (JOHN *comes in, bringing* The Youth's Companion.)

JOHN. Oh, hello! Look! A new *Youth's Companion!* (*They say* "Hello" *to him.*)

CLARENCE (*from a mature height*). John enjoys *The Youth's Companion.* (JOHN *sits right down and starts to read.* CLARENCE *is worried by this.*) John! (JOHN *looks at him nonplussed.* CLARENCE *glances toward* MARY. JOHN *remembers his manners and stands.* CLARENCE *speaks formally to* MARY.) Won't you sit down?

MARY. Oh, thank you! (*She sits.* JOHN *sits down again quickly and dives back into* The Youth's Companion. CLARENCE *sits beside* MARY.)

CLARENCE. As I was saying—I think it's all right for a girl to go to college if she goes to a girls' college.

MARY. Well, Mother wants me to go to Ohio Wesleyan—because it's Methodist. (*Then almost as a confession.*) You see, we're Methodists.

CLARENCE. Oh, that's too bad! I don't mean it's too bad that you're a Methodist. Anybody's got a right to be anything they want. But what I mean is—we're Episcopalians.

MARY. Yes, I know. I've known ever since I saw your minister—and his collar. (*She looks pretty sad for a minute and then her face brightens.*) Oh, I just remembered—my father was an Episcopalian. He was baptized an Episcopalian. He was an Episcopalian right up to the time he married my mother. *She* was the Methodist. (MARY's *tone would have surprised her mother—and even* MARY, *if she had been listening.*)

CLARENCE. I'll bet your father's a nice man.

MARY. Yes, he is. He owns the livery stable.

CLARENCE. He does? Well, then you must like horses.

MARY. Oh, I love horses! (*They are happily united again in their common love of horses.*)

CLARENCE. They're my favorite animal. Father and I both think there's nothing like a horse! (FATHER *comes down the stairs and into the room. The children all stand.*)

MARY. Oh, Mr. Day, I'm having such a lovely time here!

FATHER. Clarence is keeping you entertained, eh?

MARY. Oh, yes, sir. We've been talking about everything—colors and horses and religion.

FATHER. Oh! (*To* JOHN.) Has the evening paper come yet?

JOHN. No, sir.

FATHER. What are you reading?

JOHN. *The Youth's Companion,* sir. (WHITNEY *and* HARLAN *enter from the hall,* WHITNEY *carrying a small box.*)

WHITNEY. Look what we've got!

FATHER. What is it?

WHITNEY. Tiddle-dy-winks. We put our money together and bought it.

FATHER. That's a nice game. Do you know how to play it?

WHITNEY. I've played it lots of times.

HARLAN. Show me how to play it.

FATHER. Here, I'll show you. (*Opens the box and arranges the glass and disks.*)

MARY (*hopefully to* CLARENCE). Are you going out to dinner with us tonight?

CLARENCE (*looking at* FATHER). I don't know yet—but it's beginning to look as though I might.

FATHER. It's easy, Harlan. You press down like this and snap the little fellow into the glass. Now watch me. (*He snaps it and it goes off the table.*) The table isn't quite large enough. You boys better play it on the floor.

WHITNEY. Come on, Harlan, I'll take the reds, and you take the yellows.

FATHER. John, have you practiced your piano today?

JOHN. I was going to practice this evening.

FATHER. Better do it now. Music is a delight in the home. (JOHN *exits, passing* CORA *and* VINNIE *as they enter, coming downstairs.*)

VINNIE. Clare, what do you think Cora just told me? She and Clyde are going to be married this fall!

FATHER. Oh, you finally landed him, eh? (*Everybody laughs.*) Well, he's a very lucky man. Cora, being married is the only way to live.

CORA. If we can be half as happy as you and Cousin Vinnie——

VINNIE (*who has gone to the children*). Boys, shouldn't you be playing that on the table?

WHITNEY. The table isn't big enough. Father told us to play on the floor.

VINNIE. My soul and body! Look at your hands! Delia will have your supper ready in a few minutes. Go wash your hands right away and come back and show Mother they're clean. (*The boys pick up the tiddle-dy-winks and depart reluctantly. From the next room we hear* JOHN *playing "The Happy Farmer."*)

FATHER (*sitting down on the sofa with* MARY). Vinnie, this young lady looks about the same age you were when I came out to Pleasantville to rescue you.

VINNIE. Rescue me! You came out there to talk me into marrying you.

FATHER. It worked out just the same. I saved you from spending the rest of your life in that one-horse town.

VINNIE. Cora, the other day I came across a tin-type of Clare taken in Pleasantville. I want to show it to you. You'll see who needed rescuing. (*She goes to the table and starts to rummage around in its drawer.*)

FATHER. There isn't time for that, Vinnie. If we're going to Delmonico's for dinner hadn't we all better be getting ready? It's after six now.

CORA. Gracious! I'll have to start. If I'm going to dine in public with a prominent citizen like you, Cousin Clare—I'll have to look my best. (*She goes to the arch.*)

MARY. I've changed already.

CORA. Yes, I know, but I'm afraid I'll have to ask you to come along and hook me up, Mary.

MARY. Of course.

CORA. It won't take a minute and then you can come right back.

(FATHER *rises.* MARY *crosses in front of* FATHER *and starts toward the hall, then turns and looks back at him.*)

MARY. Mr. Day, were you always an Episcopalian?

FATHER. What?

MARY. Were you always an Episcopalian?

FATHER. I've always gone to the Episcopal church, yes.

MARY. But you weren't baptized a Methodist or anything, were you? You were baptized an Episcopalian?

FATHER. Come to think of it, I don't believe I was ever baptized at all.

MARY. Oh!

VINNIE. Clare, that's not very funny, joking about a subject like that.

FATHER. I'm not joking—I remember now—I never was baptized.

VINNIE. Clare, that's ridiculous, everyone's baptized.

FATHER (*sitting down complacently*). Well, I'm not.

VINNIE. Why, no one would keep a little baby from being baptized.

FATHER. You know Father and Mother—free-thinkers, both of them—believed their children should decide those things for themselves.

VINNIE. But, Clare——

FATHER. I remember when I was ten or twelve years old, Mother said I ought to give some thought to it. I suppose I thought about it, but I never got around to having it done to me. (*The shock to* VINNIE *is as great as if* FATHER *had calmly announced himself guilty of murder. She walks to* FATHER *staring at him in horror.* CORA *and* MARY, *sensing the coming battle, withdraw to the neutral shelter of the hall.*)

VINNIE. Clare, do you know what you're saying?

FATHER. I'm saying I've never been baptized.

VINNIE (*in a sudden panic*). Then something has to be done about it right away.

FATHER (*not the least concerned*). Now, Vinnie, don't get excited over nothing.

VINNIE. Nothing! (*Then, as only a woman can ask such a question:*) Clare, why haven't you ever told me?

FATHER. What difference does it make?

VINNIE (*the panic returning*). I've never heard of anyone who wasn't baptized. Even the savages in darkest Africa——

FATHER. It's all right for savages and children. But if an oversight was made in my case it's too late to correct it now.

VINNIE. But if you're not baptized you're not a Christian!

FATHER (*rising in wrath*). Why, confound it, of course I'm a Christian! A damn good Christian, too! (FATHER'S *voice tells* CLARENCE *a major engagement has begun. He hurriedly springs to the sliding doors and closes them, removing himself,* MARY, *and* CORA *from the scene of action.*) A lot better Christian than those psalm-singing donkeys in church!

VINNIE. You can't be if you won't be baptized.

FATHER. I won't be baptized and I will be a Christian! I beg to inform you I'll be a Christian in my own way.

VINNIE. Clare, don't you want to meet us all in Heaven?

FATHER. Of course! And I'm going to!

VINNIE. But you can't go to Heaven if you're not baptized!

FATHER. That's a lot of folderol!

VINNIE. Clarence Day, don't you blaspheme like that! You're coming to church with me before you go to the office in the morning and be baptized then and there!

FATHER. Vinnie, don't be ridiculous! If you think I'm going to stand there and have some minister splash water on me at my age, you're mistaken!

VINNIE. But, Clare——

FATHER. That's enough of this, Vinnie. I'm hungry. (*Draws himself up and starts for the door. He does not realize that he and* VINNIE *are now engaged in a battle to the death.*) I'm dressing for dinner. (*Throws open the doors, revealing* WHITNEY *and* HARLAN, *who obviously have been eavesdropping and have heard the awful revelation of* FATHER'S *paganism.* FATHER *stalks past them upstairs. The two boys come down into the room staring at their mother, who has been standing, too shocked at* FATHER'S *callous impiety to speak or move.*)

WHITNEY. Mother, if Father hasn't been baptized he hasn't any name. In the sight of the Church he hasn't any name.

VINNIE. That's right! (*To herself.*) Maybe we're not even married!

(*This awful thought takes possession of* VINNIE. *Her eyes turn slowly toward the children and she suddenly realizes their doubtful status. Her hand goes to her mouth to cover a quick gasp of horror as the curtain falls.*)

CURTAIN

ACT TWO

SCENE I

The same.

The following Sunday. After Church.

The stage is empty as the curtain rises. VINNIE *comes into the archway from the street door, dressed in her Sunday best, carrying her prayer book, hymnal, and a cold indignation. As soon as she is in the room,* FATHER *passes across the hall in his Sunday cutaway and silk hat, carrying gloves and cane.* VINNIE *looks over her shoulder at him as he disappears.* CORA, WHITNEY, *and* HARLAN *come into the room,* CORA *glancing after* FATHER *and then toward* VINNIE. *All three walk as though the sound of a football might cause an explosion, and speak in subdued tones.*

HARLAN. Cousin Cora, will you play a game of tiddle-dy-winks with me before you go?

CORA. I'm going to be busy packing until it's time to leave.

WHITNEY. We can't play games on Sunday. (*We hear the door close and* JOHN *enters and looks into the room apprehensively.*)

CORA. John, where are Clarence and Mary?

JOHN. They dropped behind—'way behind! (*He goes upstairs.* WHITNEY *takes* HARLAN'S *hat from him and starts toward the arch.*)

VINNIE. Whitney, don't hang up your hat. I want you to go over to Sherry's for the ice-cream for dinner. Tell Mr. Sherry strawberry—if he has it. And take Harlan with you.

WHITNEY. All right, Mother. (*He and* HARLAN, *trained in the good manners of the period, bow and exit.*)

CORA. Oh, Vinnie, I hate to leave. We've had such a lovely week.

VINNIE (*voice quivers in a tone of scandalized apology*). Cora, what must you think of Clare, making such a scene on his way out of church today?

CORA. Cousin Clare probably thinks that you put the rector up to preaching that sermon.

VINNIE (*tone changes from apology to self-defense with overtones of guilt*). Well, I had to go to see Dr. Lloyd to find out whether we were really married. The sermon on baptism was his own idea. If Clare just hadn't *shouted* so—now the whole congregation knows he's never been baptized! But he's going to be, Cora —you mark my words—he's going to be! I just couldn't go to Heaven without Clare. Why, I get lonesome for him when I go to Ohio. (FATHER *enters holding his watch. He's also holding his temper. He speaks quietly.*)

FATHER. Vinnie, I went to the dining room and the table isn't set for dinner yet.

VINNIE. We're having dinner late today.

FATHER. Why can't I have my meals on time?

VINNIE. The girls' train leaves at one-thirty. Their cab's coming at one o'clock.

FATHER. Cab? The horse cars go right past our door.

VINNIE. They have those heavy bags.

FATHER. Clarence and John could have gone along to carry their bags. Cabs are just a waste of money. Why didn't we have an early dinner?

VINNIE. There wasn't time for an early dinner and church, too.

FATHER. As far as I'm concerned this would have been a good day to miss church.

VINNIE (*spiritedly*). I wish we had!

FATHER (*flaring*). I'll bet you put him up to preaching that sermon.

VINNIE. I've never been so mortified in all my life! You stamping up the aisle roaring your head off at the top of your voice!

FATHER. That Lloyd needn't preach at me as though I were some damn criminal! I wanted him to know it, and as far as I'm concerned the whole congregation can know it, too!

VINNIE. They certainly know it now!

FATHER. That suits me!

VINNIE (*pleading*). Clare, you don't seem to understand what the church is for.

FATHER (*laying down a new Commandment*). Vinnie, if there's one place the church should leave alone, it's a man's soul!

VINNIE. Clare, dear, don't you believe what it says in the Bible?

FATHER. A man has to use his common sense about the Bible, Vinnie, if he has any. For instance, you'd be in a pretty fix if I gave all my money to the poor.

VINNIE. Well, that's just silly!

FATHER. Speaking of money—where are this month's bills?

VINNIE. Clare, it isn't fair to go over the household accounts while you're hungry.

FATHER. Where are those bills, Vinnie?

VINNIE. They're downstairs on your desk. (FATHER *exits almost eagerly. Figures are something he understands better than he does women.*) Of all times! (*To* CORA.) It's awfully hard on a woman to love a man like Clare so much.

CORA. Yes, men can be aggravating. Clyde gets me so provoked! We kept company for six years, but the minute he proposed—the moment I said "Yes"—he began to take me for granted.

VINNIE. You have to expect that, Cora. I don't believe Clare has come right out and told me he loves me since we've been married. Of course I know he does, because I keep reminding him of it. You have to keep reminding them, Cora. (*The door slams.*)

CORA. That must be Mary and Clarence. (*There's a moment's pause. The two women look toward the hall—then at each other with a knowing sort of smile.* CORA *rises, goes up to the arch, peeks out—then faces front and innocently asks:*) Is that you, Mary?

MARY (*dashing in*). Yes! (CLARENCE *crosses the arch to hang up his hat.*)

CORA. We have to change our clothes and finish our packing. (*Goes upstairs.*)

(CLARENCE *returns as* MARY *starts up the stairs.*)

MARY (*to* CLARENCE). It won't take me long.

CLARENCE. Can I help you pack?

VINNIE (*shocked*). Clarence! (MARY *runs upstairs.* CLARENCE *drifts into the living room, somewhat abashed.*

VINNIE *collects her hat and gloves, starts out, stops to look at* CLARENCE, *then comes down to him.*) Clarence, why didn't you kneel in church today?

CLARENCE. What, Mother?

VINNIE. Why didn't you kneel in church today?

CLARENCE (*troubled*). I just couldn't.

VINNIE. Has it anything to do with Mary? I know she's a Methodist.

CLARENCE. Oh, no, Mother! Methodists kneel. Mary told me. They don't get up and down so much, but they stay down longer.

VINNIE. If it's because your father doesn't kneel—you must remember he wasn't brought up to kneel in church. But you were—you always have—and, Clarence, you want to, don't you?

CLARENCE. Oh, yes! I wanted to today! I started to—you saw me start—but I just couldn't.

VINNIE. Is that suit of your father's too tight for you?

CLARENCE. No, it's not too *tight*. It fits fine. But it *is* the suit. Very peculiar things have happened to me since I started to wear it. I haven't been myself since I put it on.

VINNIE. In what way, Clarence? How do you mean?

(CLARENCE *pauses, then blurts out his problem.*)

CLARENCE. Mother, I can't seem to make these clothes do anything Father wouldn't do!

VINNIE. That's nonsense, Clarence—and not to kneel in church is a sacrilege.

CLARENCE. But making Father's trousers kneel seemed more of a sacrilege.

VINNIE. Clarence!

CLARENCE. No! Remember the first time I wore this? It was at Dora Wakefield's party for Mary. Do you know what happened? We were playing musical chairs and Dora Wakefield sat down suddenly right in my lap. I jumped up so fast she almost got hurt.

VINNIE. But it was all perfectly innocent.

CLARENCE. It wasn't that Dora was sitting on my lap—she was sitting on Father's trousers. Mother, I've got to have a suit of my own. (CLARENCE'S *metaphysical problem is one that* VINNIE *can't cope with at this particular minute.*)

VINNIE. My soul and body! Clarence, you have a talk with your father about it. I'm sure if you approach him the right way—you know—tactfully—he'll see——

(MARY *comes downstairs and hesitates at the arch.*)

MARY. Oh, excuse me.

VINNIE. Gracious! Have you finished your packing?

MARY. Practically. I never put my comb and brush in until I'm ready to close my bag.

VINNIE. I must see Margaret about your box lunch for the train. I'll leave you two together. Remember, it's Sunday. (*She goes downstairs.*)

CLARENCE. I was hoping we could have a few minutes together before you left.

MARY (*not to admit her eagerness*). Cora had so much to do I wanted to get out of her way.

CLARENCE. Well, didn't you want to see me?

MARY (*self-consciously*). I did want to tell you how much I've enjoyed our friendship.

CLARENCE. You're going to write me when you get to Springfield, aren't you?

MARY. Of course, if you write me first.

CLARENCE. But you'll have something to write about—your trip—and Aunt Judith—and how things are in Springfield. You write me as soon as you get there.

MARY. Maybe I'll be too busy. Maybe I won't have time. (*She sits on the sofa.*)

CLARENCE (*with the authority of* FATHER'S *trousers*). You find the time! Let's not have any nonsense about that! You'll write me first—and you'll do it right away, the first day! (*Sits beside her.*)

MARY. How do you know I'll take orders from you?

CLARENCE. I'll show you. (*He takes a quick glance toward the hall.*) Give me your hand!

MARY. Why should I?

CLARENCE. Give me your hand, confound it!

(MARY *gives it to him.*)

MARY. What do you want with my hand?

CLARENCE. I just wanted it. (*Holding her hand, he melts a little and smiles at her. She melts, too. Their hands, clasped together, are resting on* CLARENCE'S *knee and they relax happily.*) What are you thinking about?

MARY. I was just thinking.

CLARENCE. About what?

MARY. Well, when we were talking about writing each other I was hoping you'd write me first because that would mean you liked me.

CLARENCE (*with the logic of the male*). What's writing first got to do with my liking you?

MARY. Oh, you *do* like me?

CLARENCE. Of course I do. I like you better than any girl I ever met.

MARY (*with the logic of the female*). But you don't like me well enough to write first?

CLARENCE. I don't see how one thing's got anything to do with the other.

MARY. But a girl can't write first—because she's a *girl*.

CLARENCE. That doesn't make sense. If a girl has something to write about and a fellow hasn't, there's no reason why she shouldn't write first.

MARY (*starting a flanking movement.*) You know, the first few days I was here you'd do anything for me and then you changed. You used to be a lot of fun—and then all of a sudden you turned into an old sober-sides.

CLARENCE. When did I?

MARY. The first time I noticed it was when we walked home from Dora Wakefield's party. My, you were on your dignity! You've been that way ever since. You even dress like an old sober-sides. (CLARENCE'S *face changes as* FATHER'S *pants rise to haunt him. Then he notices that their clasped hands are resting on these very pants, and he lifts them off. Agony obviously is setting in.* MARY *sees the expression on his face.*) What's the matter?

CLARENCE. I just happened to remember something.

MARY. What? (CLARENCE *doesn't answer, but his face does.*) Oh, I know. This is the last time we'll be together. (*She puts her hand on his shoulder. He draws away.*)

CLARENCE. Mary, please!

MARY. But, Clarence! We'll see each other in a month. And we'll be writing each other, too. I hope we will. (*She gets up.*) Oh, Clarence, please write me first, because it will show me how much you like me. Please! I'll show you how much I like you! (*She throws herself on his lap and buries her head on his shoulder.* CLARENCE *stiffens in agony.*)

CLARENCE (*hoarsely*). Get up! Get up! (*She pulls back her head and looks at him, then springs from his lap and runs away, covering her face and sobbing.* CLARENCE *goes to her.*) Don't do that, Mary! Please don't do that!

MARY. Now you'll think I'm just a bold and forward girl.

CLARENCE. Oh, no!

MARY. Yes, you will—you'll think I'm bold!

CLARENCE. Oh, no—it's not that.

MARY (*hopefully*). Was it because it's Sunday?

CLARENCE (*in despair*). No, it would be the same any day—(*He is about to explain, but* MARY *flares.*)

MARY. Oh, it's just because you didn't want me sitting on your lap.

CLARENCE. It was nice of you to do it.

MARY. It was nice of me! So you told me to get up! You just couldn't bear to have me sit there. Well, you needn't write me first. You needn't write me any letters at all, because I'll tear them up without opening them! (FATHER *enters the archway, a sheath of bills in his hand and his account book under his arm.*) I guess I know now you don't like me! I never want to see you again. I— I—— (*She breaks and starts to run toward the stairs. At the sight of* FATHER *she stops, but only for a gasp, then continues on upstairs, unable to control her sobs.* CLARENCE, *who has been standing in unhappy indecision, turns to follow her, but stops short at the sight of* FATHER, *who is standing in the arch looking at him with some amazement.* FATHER *looks from* CLARENCE *toward the vanished* MARY, *then back to* CLARENCE.)

FATHER. Clarence, that young girl is crying—she's in tears. What's the meaning of this?

CLARENCE. I'm sorry, Father, it's all my fault.

FATHER. Nonsense! What's that girl trying to do to you?

CLARENCE. What? No, she wasn't—it was—I—how long have you been here?

FATHER. Well, whatever the quarrel was about, Clarence, I'm glad you held your own. Where's your mother?

CLARENCE (*desperately*). I have to have a new suit of clothes—you've got to give me the money for it.

(FATHER'S *account book reaches the table with a sharp bang as he stares at* CLARENCE *in astonishment.*)

FATHER. Young man, do you realize you're addressing your father?

(CLARENCE *wilts miserably and sinks into a chair.*)

CLARENCE. I'm sorry, Father—I apologize—but you don't know how important this is to me. (CLARENCE'S *tone of misery gives* FATHER *pause.*)

FATHER. A suit of clothes is so——? Now, why should a——? (*Something dawns on* FATHER *and he looks up in the direction in which* MARY *has disappeared, then looks back at* CLARENCE.) Has your need for a suit of clothes anything to do with that young lady?

CLARENCE. Yes, Father.

FATHER. Why, Clarence! (*Suddenly realizes that women have come into* CLARENCE'S *emotional life and there comes a yearning to protect this inexperienced and defenseless member of his own sex.*) This comes as quite a shock to me.

CLARENCE. What does, Father?

FATHER. Your being so grown up! Still, I might have known that if you're going to college this fall—yes, you're at an age when you'll be meeting girls. Clarence, there are things about women that I think you ought to know! (*He goes up and closes the doors, then comes down and sits beside* CLARENCE, *hesitating for a moment before he speaks.*) Yes, I think it's better for you to hear this from me than to have to learn it for yourself. Clarence, women aren't the angels that you think they are! Well, now—first, let me explain this to you. You see, Clarence, we men have to run this world and it's not an easy job. It takes work, and it takes thinking. A man has to be sure of his facts and figures. He has to reason things out. Now, you take a woman—a woman thinks—no I'm wrong right there—a woman doesn't think at all! She gets stirred up! And she gets stirred up over the damnedest things! Now, I love my wife just as much as any man, but that doesn't mean I should stand for a lot of folderol! By God! I won't stand for it! (*Looks around toward the spot where he had his last clash with* VINNIE.)

CLARENCE. Stand for what, Father?

FATHER (*to himself*). That's the one thing I will not submit myself to. (*Has ceased explaining women to* CLARENCE *and is now explaining himself.*) Clarence, if a man thinks a certain thing is the wrong thing to do he shouldn't do it. If he thinks a thing is right he should do it. Now that has nothing to do with whether he loves his wife or not.

CLARENCE. Who says it has, Father?

FATHER. They do!

CLARENCE. Who, sir?

FATHER. Women! They get stirred up and then they try to get you stirred up, too. If you can keep reason and logic in the argument, a man can hold his own, of course. But if they can *switch* you—pretty soon the argument's about whether you love them or not. I swear I don't know how they do it! Don't you let 'em, Clarence! Don't you let 'em!

CLARENCE. I see what you mean so far, Father. If you don't watch yourself, love can make you do a lot of things you don't want to do.

FATHER. Exactly!

CLARENCE. But if you do watch out and know just how to handle women——

FATHER. Then you'll be all right. All a man has to do is be firm. You know how sometimes I have to be firm with your mother. Just now about this month's household accounts——

CLARENCE. Yes, but what can you do when they cry?

FATHER (*he gives this a moment's thought*). Well, that's quite a question. You just have to make them understand that what you're doing is for their good.

CLARENCE. I see.

FATHER (*rising*). Now, Clarence, you know all about women. (*Goes to the table and sits down in front of his account book, opening it.* CLARENCE *rises and looks at him.*)

CLARENCE. But, Father——

FATHER. Yes, Clarence.

CLARENCE. I thought you were going to tell me about——

FATHER. About what?

CLARENCE. About women.

(FATHER *realizes with some shock that* CLARENCE *expected him to be more specific.*)

FATHER. Clarence, there are some things gentlemen don't discuss! I've told you all you need to know. The thing for you to remember is—be firm! (CLARENCE *turns away. There is a knock at the sliding doors.*) Yes, come in.

(MARY *opens the doors.*)

MARY. Excuse me!

(MARY *enters.* FATHER *turns his attention to the household accounts.* MARY *goes to the couch and picks up her handkerchief and continues around the couch.* CLARENCE *crosses to meet her above the couch, determined to be firm.* MARY *passes him without a glance.* CLARENCE *wilts, then again assuming firmness, turns up into the arch in an attempt to quail* MARY *with a look.* MARY *marches upstairs ignoring him.* CLARENCE *turns back into the room defeated. He looks down at his clothes unhappily, then decides to be firm with his father. He straightens up and steps toward him. At this moment* FATHER, *staring at a bill, emits his cry of rage.*)

FATHER. Oh, God!

(CLARENCE *retreats.* FATHER *rises and holds the bill in question between thumb and forefinger as though it were too repulsive to touch.* VINNIE *comes rushing down the stairs.*)

VINNIE. What's the matter, Clare? What's wrong?

FATHER. I will *not* send this person a check!

(VINNIE *looks at it.*)

VINNIE. Why, Clare, that's the only hat I've bought since March and it was reduced from forty dollars.

FATHER. I don't question your buying the hat or what you paid for it, but the person from whom you bought it—this Mademoiselle Mimi—isn't fit to be in the hat business or any other.

VINNIE. I never went there before, but it's a very nice place and I don't see why you object to it.

FATHER (*exasperated*). I object to it because this confounded person doesn't put her name on her bills! Mimi what? Mimi O'Brien? Mimi Jones? Mimi Weinstein?

VINNIE. How do I know? It's just Mimi.

FATHER. It isn't just Mimi. She must have some other name, damn it! Now, I wouldn't make out a check payable to Charley or to Jimmy, and I won't make out a check payable to Mimi. Find out what her last name is, and I'll pay her the money.

VINNIE. All right. All right. (*She starts out.*)

FATHER. Just a minute, Vinnie, that isn't all.

VINNIE. But Cora will be leaving any minute, Clare, and it isn't polite for me——

FATHER. Never mind Cora. Sit down. (CLARENCE *goes into the hall, looks upstairs, wanders up and down the hall restlessly.* VINNIE *reluctantly sits down opposite* FATHER *at the table.*) Vinnie, you know I like to live well, and I want my family to live well. But this house must be run on a business basis. I must know how much money I'm spending and what for. For instance, if you recall, two weeks ago I gave you six dollars to buy a new coffee pot——

VINNIE. Yes, because you broke the old one. You threw it right on the floor.

FATHER. I'm not talking about that. I'm simply endeavoring——

VINNIE. But it was so silly to break that nice coffee pot, Clare, and there was nothing the matter with the coffee that morning. It was made just the same as always.

FATHER. It was not! It was made in a damned barbaric manner!

VINNIE. I couldn't get another imported one. That little shop has stopped selling them. They said the tariff wouldn't let them. And that's your fault, Clare, because you're always voting to raise the tariff.

FATHER. The tariff protects America against cheap foreign labor. (*He sounds as though he is quoting.*) Now I find that——

VINNIE. The tariff does nothing but put up the prices and that's hard on everybody, especially the farmer. (*She sounds as though she is quoting back.*)

FATHER (*annoyed*). I wish to God you wouldn't talk about matters you don't know a damn thing about!

VINNIE. I do too know about them. Miss Gulick says every intelligent woman should have some opinion——

FATHER. Who, may I ask, is Miss Gulick?

VINNIE. Why, she's that current-events woman I told you about and the tickets are a dollar every Tuesday.

FATHER. Do you mean to tell me that a pack of idle-minded females pay a dollar apiece to hear another female gabble about the events of the day? Listen to me if you want to know anything about the events of the day!

VINNIE. But you get so excited, Clare, and besides, Miss Gulick says that our President, whom you're always belittling, prays to God for guidance and—

FATHER (*having had enough of Miss Gulick*). Vinnie, what happened to that six dollars?

VINNIE. What six dollars?

FATHER. I gave you six dollars to buy a new coffee pot and now I find that you apparently got one at Lewis & Conger's and charged it. Here's their bill: "One coffee pot—five dollars."

VINNIE. So you owe me a dollar and you can hand it right over. (*She holds out her hand for it.*)

FATHER. I'll do nothing of the kind! What did you do with that six dollars?

VINNIE. Why, Clare, I can't tell you now, dear. Why didn't you ask me at the time?

FATHER. Oh, my God!

VINNIE. Wait a moment! I spent four dollars and a half for that new umbrella I told you I wanted and you said I didn't need, but I did, very much.

(FATHER *takes his pencil and writes in the account book.*)

FATHER. Now we're getting somewhere. One umbrella—four dollars and a half.

VINNIE. And that must have been the week I paid Mrs. Tobin for two extra days' washing.

FATHER (*entering the item*). Mrs. Tobin.

VINNIE. So that was two dollars more.

FATHER. Two dollars.

VINNIE. That makes six dollars and fifty cents. And that's another fifty cents you owe me.

FATHER. I don't owe you anything. (*Stung by* VINNIE'*s tactics into a determination to pin her butterfly mind down.*) What you owe me is an explanation of where my money's gone! We're going over this account book item by item. (*Starts to sort the bills for the purposes of cross-examination, but the butterfly takes wing again.*)

VINNIE. I do the very best I can to keep down expenses. And you know yourself that Cousin Phoebe spends twice as much as we do.

FATHER. Damn Cousin Phoebe!—I don't wish to be told how she throws her money around.

VINNIE. Oh, Clare, how can you? And I thought you were so fond of Cousin Phoebe.

FATHER. All right, I am fond of Cousin Phoebe, but I can get along without hearing so much about her.

VINNIE. You talk about your own relatives enough.

FATHER (*hurt*). That's not fair, Vinnie. When I talk about my relatives I criticize them.

VINNIE. If I can't even speak of Cousin Phoebe——

FATHER. You can speak of her all you want to—but I won't have Cousin Phoebe or anyone else dictating to me how to run my house. Now this month's total——

VINNIE (*righteously*). I didn't say a word about her dictating, Clare—she isn't that kind!

FATHER (*dazed*). I don't know what you said, now. You never stick to the point. I endeavor to show you how to run this house on a business basis and you wind up by jibbering and jabbering about everything under the sun. If you'll just explain to me——

(*Finally cornered,* VINNIE *realizes the time has come for tears. Quietly she turns them on.*)

VINNIE. I don't know what you expect of me. I tire myself out chasing up and down those stairs all day long—trying to look after your comfort—to bring up our children—I do the mending and the marketing and as if that isn't enough, you want me to be an expert bookkeeper, too.

FATHER (*touched where* VINNIE *has hoped to touch him*). Vinnie, I want to be reasonable; but can't you understand?—I'm doing all this for your own good. (VINNIE *rises with a moan.* FATHER *sighs with resignation.*) I suppose I'll have to go ahead just paying the bills and hoping I've got money enough in the bank to meet them. But it's all very discouraging.

VINNIE. I'll try to do better, Clare.

(FATHER *looks up into her tearful face and melts.*)

FATHER. That's all I'm asking. (*She goes to him and puts her arm around his shoulder.*) I'll go down and make out the checks and sign them. (VINNIE *doesn't seem entirely consoled, so he attempts a lighter note to cheer her up.*) Oh, Vinnie, maybe I haven't any right to sign those checks, since in the sight of the Lord I haven't any name at all. Do you suppose the bank will feel that way about it too—or do you think they'll take a chance? (*He should not have said this.*)

VINNIE. That's right! Clare, to make those checks good you'll have to be baptized right away.

FATHER (*retreating angrily*). Vinnie, the bank doesn't care whether I've been baptized or not!

VINNIE. Well, I care! And no matter what Dr. Lloyd says, I'm not sure we're really married.

FATHER. Damn it, Vinnie, we have four children! If we're not married now we never will be!

VINNIE. Oh, Clare, don't you see how serious this is? You've got to do something about it.

FATHER. Well, just now I've got to do something about these damn bills you've run up. (*Sternly.*) I'm going downstairs.

VINNIE. Not before you give me that dollar and a half!

FATHER. What dollar and a half?

VINNIE. The dollar and a half you owe me!

FATHER (*thoroughly enraged*). I don't owe you any dollar and a half! I gave you money to buy a coffee pot for me and somehow it turned into an umbrella for you.

VINNIE. Clarence Day, what kind of a man are you? Quibbling about a dollar and a half when your immortal soul is in danger! And what's more——

FATHER. All right. All right. All right. (*He takes the dollar and a half from his change purse and gives it to her.*)

VINNIE (*smiling*). Thank you, Clare. (VINNIE *turns and leaves the room. Her progress upstairs is a one-woman march of triumph.*)

(FATHER *puts his purse back, gathers up his papers and his dignity, and starts out.* CLARENCE *waylays him in the arch.*)

CLARENCE. Father—you never did tell me—can I have a new suit of clothes?

FATHER. No, Clarence! I'm sorry, but I have to be firm with you, too!

(*He stalks off.* JOHN *comes down the stairs carrying a traveling bag, which he takes out toward the front door. He returns empty-handed and starts up the stairs again.*)

CLARENCE. John, come here a minute.

JOHN (*coming into the room*). What do you want?

CLARENCE. John, have you got any money you could lend me?

JOHN. With this week's allowance, I'll have about three dollars.

CLARENCE. That's no good. I've got to have enough to buy a new suit of clothes.

JOHN. Why don't you earn some money? That's what I'm going to do. I'm going to buy a bicycle—one of those new low kind, with both wheels the same size—you know, a safety.

CLARENCE. How are you going to earn that much money?

JOHN. I've got a job practically. Look, I found this ad in the paper. (*He hands* CLARENCE *a clipping from his pocket.*)

CLARENCE (*reading*). "Wanted, an energetic young man to handle household necessity that sells on sight. Liberal commissions. Apply 312 West Fourteenth Street, Tuesday from eight to twelve." Listen, John, let me have that job.

JOHN. Why should I give you my job? They're hard to get.

CLARENCE. But I've got to have a new suit of clothes.

JOHN. Maybe I could get a job for both of us. (*The doorbell rings.*) I'll tell you what I'll do, I'll ask the man.

FATHER (*hurrying to the foot of the stairs*). Vinnie! Cora! The cab's here. Hurry up! (*Goes through the arch toward the front door.*)

CLARENCE. John, we've both got to get down there early Tuesday—the first thing.

JOHN. Oh, no you don't—I'm going alone. But I'll put in a good word with the boss about you.

FATHER (*off*). They'll be right out. Vinnie! Cora! (*He comes back to the foot of the stairs and calls up.*) Are you coming? The cab's waiting!

VINNIE (*from upstairs*). We heard you, Clare. We'll be down in a minute.

(FATHER *comes into the room.*)

FATHER. John, go upstairs and hurry them down.

(JOHN *goes upstairs.* FATHER *crosses to the window and looks out, then consults his watch.*)

FATHER. What's the matter with those women? Don't they know cabs cost money? Clarence, go see what's causing this infernal delay!

(CLARENCE *goes out to the hall.*)

CLARENCE. Here they come, Father.

(MARY *comes sedately downstairs. She passes* CLARENCE *without a glance and goes to* FATHER.)

MARY. Good-by, Mr. Day. I can't tell you how much I appreciate your hospitality.

FATHER. Not at all! Not at all!

(VINNIE *and* CORA *appear at top of stairs and come down.* JOHN *follows with the bags and takes them out.*)

CORA. Good-by, Clarence. (*She starts into the room.*)

FATHER. Cora, we can say good-by to you on the sidewalk.

VINNIE. There's no hurry. Their train doesn't go until one-thirty.

FATHER. Cabs cost money. If they have any waiting to do they ought to do it at the Grand Central Depot. They've got a waiting room there just *for* that.

VINNIE (*to* MARY). If there's one thing Mr. Day can't stand it's to keep a cab waiting.

CORA. It's been so nice seeing you again, Clarence. (*She kisses him.*)

(MARGARET *enters with a box of lunch.*)

MARGARET. Here's the lunch.

FATHER. All right. All right. Give it to me. Let's get started.

(MARGARET *gives it to him and exits.*)

CORA. Where's John?

FATHER. He's outside. Come on. (*Leads the way.* CORA *and* VINNIE *follow.* MARY *starts.*)

CLARENCE. Mary, aren't you going even to shake hands with me?

MARY. I don't think I'd better. You may remember that when I get too close to you you feel contaminated. (*Starts out.* CLARENCE *follows her.*)

CLARENCE. Mary! (*She stops in the arch. He goes to her.*) You're going to write me, aren't you?

MARY. Are you going to write first?

CLARENCE (*resolutely.*) No, Mary. There are times when a man has to be firm.

(JOHN *enters.*)

JOHN. Mary, Mother says you'd better hurry out before Father starts yelling. It's Sunday.

MARY. Good-by, John. I'm very happy to have made *your* acquaintance.

(*She walks out. We hear the door close.* JOHN *goes out.* CLARENCE *takes a step toward the door, stops, suffers a moment, then turns to the writing desk, takes paper and pen and ink to the table, and sits down to write a letter.*)

CLARENCE (*writing.*) Dear Mary—

CURTAIN

SCENE II

The same.

Two days later. The breakfast table.

HARLAN *and* WHITNEY *are at the table, ready to start breakfast.* CLARENCE *is near the window reading the paper. The places of* JOHN *and* VINNIE *and* FATHER *are empty.* NORA, *a new maid, is serving the fruit and cereal.* NORA *is heavily built and along toward middle age. The doorbell rings and we hear the postman's whistle.* CLARENCE *drops the paper and looks out the window toward the door.* NORA *starts toward the arch.*

CLARENCE. Never mind, Nora. It's the postman. I'll go. (*He runs out through the arch.*)

WHITNEY (*to* NORA). You forgot the sugar. It goes here between me and Father.

(CLARENCE *comes back with three or four letters which he sorts eagerly. Then his face falls in utter dejection.* FATHER *comes down the stairs.*)

FATHER. Good morning, boys! John late? (*He shouts.*) John! John! Hurry down to your breakfast.

CLARENCE. John had his breakfast early, Father, and went out to see about something.

FATHER. See about what?

CLARENCE. John and I thought we'd work this summer and earn some money.

FATHER. Good! Sit down, boys. (*Goes to his chair.*)

CLARENCE. We saw an ad in the paper and John went down to see about it.

FATHER. Why didn't you go, too?

CLARENCE. I was expecting an answer to a letter I wrote, but it didn't come. Here's the mail. (*He seems depressed.*)

FATHER (*sitting*). What kind of work is this you're planning to do?

CLARENCE. Sort of salesman, the ad said.

FATHER. Um-hum. Well, work never hurt anybody. It's good for them. But if you're going to work, work hard. King Solomon had the right idea about work. "Whatever thy hand findeth to do," Solomon said, "do thy damnedest!" Where's your mother?

NORA. If you please, sir, Mrs. Day doesn't want any breakfast. She isn't feeling well, so she went back upstairs to lie down again.

FATHER (*uneasily*). Now, why does your mother do that to me? She knows it just upsets my day when she doesn't come down to breakfast. Clarence, go tell your mother I'll be up to see her before I start for the office.

CLARENCE. Yes, sir. (*He goes upstairs.*)

HARLAN. What's the matter with Mother?

FATHER. There's nothing the matter with your mother. Perfectly healthy woman. She gets an ache or a twinge and instead of being firm about it, she just gives in to it. (*The postman whistles. Then the doorbell rings.* NORA *answers it.*) Boys, after breakfast you find out what your mother wants you to do today. Whitney, you take care of Harlan.

(NORA *comes back with a special-delivery letter.*)

NORA. It's a special delivery. (*She hands it to* FATHER, *who tears it open at once.* CLARENCE *comes rushing down the stairs.*)

CLARENCE. Was that the postman again?

WHITNEY. It was a special delivery.

CLARENCE. Yes? Where is it?

WHITNEY. It was for Father.

CLARENCE (*again disappointed*). Oh—— (*He sits at the table.*)

(FATHER *has opened the letter and is reading it. Bewildered, he turns it over and looks at the signature.*)

FATHER. I don't understand this at all. Here's a letter from some woman I never even heard of.

(FATHER *tackles the letter again.* CLARENCE *sees the envelope, picks it up, looks at the postmark, worried.*)

CLARENCE. Father!

FATHER. Oh, God!

CLARENCE. What is it, Father?

FATHER. This is the damnedest nonsense I ever read! As far as I can make out this woman claims that she sat on my lap and I didn't like it. (CLARENCE *begins to turn red.* FATHER *goes on reading a little further and then holds the letter over in front of* CLARENCE.) Can you make out what that word is? (CLARENCE *begins feverishly to read as much as possible, but* FATHER *cuts in.*) No, that word right there. (*He points.*)

CLARENCE. It looks like—"curiosity."

(FATHER *withdraws the letter,* CLARENCE'S *eyes following it hungrily.*)

FATHER (*reads*). "I only opened your letter as a matter of curiosity." (*Breaks off reading aloud as he turns the page.*)

CLARENCE. Yes? Go on.

FATHER. Why, this gets worse and worse! It just turns into a lot of sentimental lovey-dovey mush. (*Crushes the letter, stalks across the room, and throws it into the fireplace.* CLARENCE *watching him with dismay.*) Is this someone's idea of a practical joke? Why must I be the butt——

(VINNIE *comes hurrying down the stairs. Her hair is down in two braids over her shoulders. She is wearing a lacy combing jacket over her corset cover, and a striped petticoat.*)

VINNIE. What's the matter, Clare? What's wrong?

FATHER (*going to her*). Nothing wrong—just a damn fool letter. How are you, Vinnie?

VINNIE (*weakly*). I don't feel well. I thought you needed me, but if you don't I'll go back to bed.

FATHER. No, now that you're here, sit down with us. (*He moves out her chair.*) Get some food in your stomach. Do you good.

VINNIE (*protesting*). I don't feel like eating anything, Clare.

(NORA *enters with a tray of bacon and eggs, stops at the serving table.*)

FATHER (*heartily*). That's all the more reason why you should eat. Build up your strength! (*He forces* VINNIE *into her chair and turns to speak to* NORA, *who has her back to him.*) Here—— (*Then to* CLARENCE.) What's this one's name?

CLARENCE. Nora.

FATHER. Nora! Give Mrs. Day some of the bacon and eggs.

VINNIE. No, Clare! (NORA, *however, has gone to* VINNIE'S *side with the platter.*) No, take it away, Nora. I don't even want to smell it.

(*The maid retreats, and serves* FATHER; *then* CLARENCE; *then serves coffee and exits.*)

FATHER. Vinnie, it's just weak to give in to an ailment. Any disease can be cured by firmness. What you need is strength of character.

VINNIE. I don't know why you object to my complaining a little. I notice when you have a headache you yell and groan and swear enough.

FATHER. Of course I yell! That's to prove to the headache that I'm stronger than it is. I can usually swear it right out of my system.

VINNIE. This isn't a headache. I think I've caught some kind of a germ. There's a lot of sickness around. Several of my friends have had to send for the doctor. I may have the same thing.

FATHER. I'll bet this is all your imagination, Vinnie. You hear of a lot of other people having some disease and then you get scared and think you have it yourself. So you go to bed and send for the doctor. The doctor—all poppycock!

VINNIE. I didn't say anything about my sending for the doctor.

FATHER. I should hope not. Doctors think they know a damn lot, but they don't.

VINNIE. But Clare, dear, when people are seriously ill you have to do something.

FATHER. Certainly you have to do something! Cheer 'em up—that's the way to cure 'em!

VINNIE (*with slight irony*). How would you go about cheering them up?

FATHER. I? I'd tell 'em—bah! (VINNIE, *out of exasperation and weakness, begins to cry.* FATHER *looks at her amazed.*) What have I done now?

VINNIE. Oh, Clare—hush up! (*She moves from the table to the sofa, where she tries to control her crying.* HARLAN *slides out of his chair and runs over to her.*) Harlan dear, keep away from Mother. You might catch what she's got. Whitney, if you've finished your breakfast——

WHITNEY (*rising*). Yes, Mother.

VINNIE. I promised Mrs. Whitehead to send over Margaret's recipe for floating-island pudding. Margaret has it all written out. And take Harlan with you.

WHITNEY. All right, Mother. I hope you feel better.

(WHITNEY *and* HARLAN *exit.* FATHER *goes over and sits beside* VINNIE *on the sofa.*)

FATHER. Vinnie. (*Contritely.*) I didn't mean to upset you. I was just trying to help. (*He pats her hand.*) When you take to your bed I have a damned lonely time around here. So when I see you getting it into your head that you're sick, I want to do something about it. (*He continues to pat her hand vigorously with what he thinks is reassurance.*) Just because some of your friends have given in to this is no reason why you should imagine you're sick, Vinnie.

VINNIE (*snatching her hand away*). Oh, stop, Clare!—get out of this house and go to your office!

(FATHER *is a little bewildered and somewhat indignant at this rebuff to his tenderness. He gets up and goes out into the hall, comes back with his hat and stick, and marches out of the house, slamming the door.* VINNIE *rises and starts toward the stairs.*)

CLARENCE. I'm sorry you're not feeling well, Mother.

VINNIE. Oh, I'll be all right, Clarence. Remember last fall I had a touch of this and I was all right the next morning.

CLARENCE. Are you sure you don't want the doctor?

VINNIE. Oh, no. I really don't need him—and besides doctors worry your father. I don't want him to be upset.

CLARENCE. Is there anything I can do for you?

VINNIE. Ask Margaret to send me up a cup of tea. I'll try to drink it. I'm going back to bed.

CLARENCE. Do you mind if John and I go out today or will you need us?

VINNIE. You run right along. I just want to be left alone. (*She exits up the stairs.* CLARENCE *starts for the fireplace eager to retrieve Mary's letter.* NORA *enters. He stops.*)

CLARENCE. Oh!—Nora—will you take a cup of tea up to Mrs. Day in her room?

NORA. Yes, sir. (*Exits.*)

(CLARENCE *hurries around the table, gets the crumpled letter, and starts to read it feverishly. He reads quickly to the end, then draws a deep, happy breath. The door slams. He puts the letter in his pocket.* JOHN *enters, carrying two heavy packages.*)

CLARENCE. Did you get the job?

JOHN. Yes, for both of us. Look, I've got it with me.

CLARENCE. What is it?

JOHN. Medicine.

CLARENCE (*dismayed*). Medicine! You took a job for us to go out and sell medicine!

JOHN. But it's wonderful medicine. (*Gets a bottle out of the package and reads from the label.*) "Bartlett's Beneficent Balm—A Boon to Mankind." Look what it cures! (*He hands the bottle to* CLARENCE.)

CLARENCE (*reading*). "A sovereign cure for colds, coughs, catarrh, asthma, quinsy, and sore throat; poor digestion, summer complaint, colic, dyspepsia, heartburn, and shortness of breath; lumbago, rheumatism, heart disease, giddiness, and women's complaints; nervous prostration, St. Vitus' dance, jaundice, and la grippe; proud flesh, pink eye, seasickness, and pimples." (*As* CLARENCE *has read off the list he has become more and more impressed.*)

JOHN. See?

CLARENCE. Say, that sounds all right!

JOHN. It's made "from a secret formula known only to Dr. Bartlett."

CLARENCE. He must be quite a doctor!

JOHN (*enthusiastically*). It sells for a dollar a bottle and we get twenty-five cents commission on every bottle.

CLARENCE. Well, where does he want us to sell it?

JOHN. He's given us the territory of all Manhattan Island.

CLARENCE. That's bully! Anybody that's sick at all ought to need a bottle of this. Let's start by calling on friends of Father and Mother.

JOHN. That's a good idea. But wait a minute. Suppose they ask us if we use it at our house?

CLARENCE (*a little worried*). Oh, yes. It would be better if we could say we did.

JOHN. But we can't because we haven't had it here long enough. (NORA *enters with a tray with a cup of tea. She goes to the table and puts the sugar bowl and cream pitcher on it.*)

CLARENCE. Is that the tea for Mrs. Day?

NORA. Yes. (*The suspicion of a good idea dawns on* CLARENCE.)

CLARENCE. I'll take it up to her. You needn't bother.

NORA. Thank you. Take it up right away while it's hot. (*She exits.* CLARENCE *watches her out.*)

CLARENCE (*eyeing* JOHN). Mother wasn't feeling well this morning.

JOHN. What was the matter with her?

CLARENCE. I don't know—she was just complaining.

JOHN (*getting the idea immediately and consulting the bottle*). Well, it says here it's good for women's complaints. (*They look at each other.* CLARENCE *opens the bottle and smells its contents.* JOHN *leans over and takes a sniff, too. Then he nods to* CLARENCE, *who quickly reaches for a spoon and measures out a teaspoonful, which he puts into the tea.* JOHN, *wanting to be sure* MOTHER *has enough to cure her, pours still more into the tea from the bottle as the curtain falls.*)

(THE CURTAIN *remains down for a few seconds to denote a lapse of three hours.*)

(*When the curtain rises again, the breakfast things have been cleared and the room is in order.* HARLAN *is kneeling on* FATHER'S *chair looking out the window as if watching for someone.* MARGARET *comes down from upstairs.*)

MARGARET. Has your father come yet?

HARLAN. Not yet. (NORA *enters from downstairs with a steaming tea-kettle and a towel and meets* MARGARET *in the hall.*)

MARGARET. Hurry that upstairs. The doctor's waiting for it. I've got to go out.

NORA. Where are you going?

MARGARET. I have to go and get the minister. (NORA *goes upstairs.*)

HARLAN. There's a cab coming up the street.

MARGARET. Well, I hope it's him, poor man—but a cab doesn't sound like your father. (*She hurries downstairs.*)

(HARLAN *sees something through the window, then rushes to the stairwell and shouts down to* MARGARET.)

HARLAN. Yes, it's Father. Whitney got him all right. (*Runs back to the window. The front door slams and* FATHER *crosses the arch and hurries upstairs.* WHITNEY *comes into the room.*) What took you so long?

WHITNEY. Long? I wasn't long. I went right down on the elevated and got Father right away and we came all the way back in a *cab.*

HARLAN. I thought you were never coming.

WHITNEY. Well, the horse didn't go very fast at first. The cabby whipped him and swore at him and still he wouldn't gallop. Then Father spoke to the horse personally—How is Mother?

HARLAN. I don't know. The doctor's up there now.

WHITNEY. Well, she'd better be good and sick or Father may be mad at me for getting him up here—'specially in a cab. (FATHER *comes down the stairs muttering to himself.*)

FATHER (*indignantly*). Well, huh!—It seems to me I ought to be shown a little consideration. I guess I've got some feelings, too!

WHITNEY (*hopefully*). Mother's awfully sick, isn't she?

FATHER. How do I know? I wasn't allowed to stay in the same room with her.

WHITNEY. Did the doctor put you out?

FATHER. No, it was your mother, damn it! (*He goes out and hangs up his hat and stick, then returns.* FATHER *may be annoyed, but he is also worried.*) You boys keep quiet around here today.

WHITNEY. She must be pretty sick.

FATHER. She must be, Whitney! I don't know! Nobody ever tells me anything in this house. Not a damn thing! (DR. HUMPHREYS *comes down the stairs. He's the family-doctor type of the period, with just enough whiskers to make him impressive. He carries his satchel.*)

DR. HUMPHREYS. Mrs. Day is quieter now.

FATHER. How sick is she? What's the matter with her?

DR. HUMPHREYS. She's a pretty sick woman, Mr. Day. I had given her a sedative just before you came—and after you left the room I had to give her another. Have you a telephone?

FATHER. A telephone! No—I don't believe in them. Why?

DR. HUMPHREYS. Well, it would only have saved me a few steps. I'll be back in ten minutes. (*He turns to go.*)

FATHER. Wait a minute—I think I'm entitled to know what's the matter with my wife. (DR. HUMPHREYS *turns back.*)

DR. HUMPHREYS. What did Mrs. Day have for breakfast this morning?

FATHER. She didn't eat anything—not a thing.

DR. HUMPHREYS. Are you sure?

FATHER. I tried to get her to eat something, but she wouldn't.

DR. HUMPHREYS (*almost to himself*). I can't understand it.

FATHER. Understand what?

DR. HUMPHREYS. These violent attacks of nausea. It's almost as though she were poisoned.

FATHER. Poisoned!

DR. HUMPHREYS. I'll try not to be gone more than ten or fifteen minutes. (*He exits.*)

FATHER (*trying to reassure himself*). Damn doctors! They never know what's the matter with anybody. Well, he'd better get your mother well, and damn soon or he'll hear from me.

WHITNEY. Mother's going to get well, isn't she? (FATHER *looks at* WHITNEY *sharply as though he is a little angry at anyone even raising the question.*)

FATHER. Of course she's going to get well!

HARLAN (*running to* FATHER). I hope she gets well soon. When Mamma stays in bed it's lonesome.

FATHER. Yes, it is, Harlan. It's lonesome. (*He looks around the room and finds it pretty empty.*) What were you boys supposed to do today?

WHITNEY. I was to learn the rest of my catechism.

FATHER. Well, if that's what your mother wanted you to do, you'd better do it.

WHITNEY. I know it—I think.

FATHER. You'd better be sure.

WHITNEY. I can't be sure unless somebody hears me. Will you hear me?

FATHER (*with sudden willingness to be useful*). All right. I'll hear you, Whitney. (WHITNEY *goes to the mantel and gets* VINNIE'S *prayer book.* FATHER *sits on the sofa.* HARLAN *climbs up beside him.*)

HARLAN. If Mamma's still sick will you read to me tonight?

FATHER. Of course I'll read to you. (WHITNEY *opens the prayer book and hands it to* FATHER.)

WHITNEY. Here it is, Father. Just the end of it. Mother knows I know the rest. Look, start here. (*He points.*)

FATHER. All right. (*Reading.*) "How many parts are there in a Sacrament?"

WHITNEY (*reciting*). "Two; the outward visible sign, and the inward spiritual grace." (FATHER *nods in approval.*)

FATHER. "What is the outward visible sign or form in Baptism?"

WHITNEY. "Water; wherein the person is baptized, in the name of the Father, and of the Son, and of the Holy Ghost." You haven't been baptized, Father, have you?

FATHER (*ignoring it*). "What is the inward and spiritual grace?"

WHITNEY. If you don't have to be baptized, why do I have to be confirmed?

FATHER (*ignoring this even more*). "What is the inward and spiritual grace?"

WHITNEY. "A death unto sin, and a new birth unto righteousness; for being by nature born in sin, and the children of wrath, we are hereby made the children of grace." Is that why you get mad so much, Father—because you're a child of wrath?

FATHER. Whitney, mind your manners! You're not supposed to ask questions of your elders! "What is required of persons to be baptized?"

WHITNEY. "Repentance, whereby—whereby——" (*He pauses.*)

FATHER (*quickly shutting the book and handing it to* WHITNEY). You don't know it well enough, Whitney. You'd better study it some more.

WHITNEY. Now?

FATHER (*softening*). No, you don't have to do it now. Let's see, now, what can we do?

WHITNEY. Well, I was working with my tool chest out in the back yard. (*Edges toward the arch.*)

FATHER. Better not do any hammering with your mother sick upstairs. You'd better stay here.

WHITNEY. I wasn't hammering—I was doing wood-carving.

FATHER. Well, Harlan—how about you? Shall we play some tiddle-dy-winks?

HARLAN (*edging toward* WHITNEY). I was helping Whitney.

FATHER. Oh—all right. (*The boys go out.* FATHER *goes to the stairwell.*) Boys, don't do any shouting. We all have to be very quiet around here. (*He stands in the hall and looks up toward* VINNIE, *worried. Then he tip-toes across the room and stares gloomily out of the window. Then he tiptoes back into the hall and goes to the rail of the basement stairs, and calls quietly.*) Margaret! (*There is no answer, and he raises his voice a little.*) Margaret! (*There is still no answer and he lets loose.*) Margaret! Why don't you answer when you hear me calling? (*At this moment* MARGARET, *hat on, appears in the arch from the right, having come through the front door.*)

MARGARET. Sh—sh—— (FATHER *turns quickly and sees* MARGARET.)

FATHER. Oh, there you are!

MARGARET (*reprovingly*). We must all be quiet, Mr. Day—Mrs. Day is very sick.

FATHER (*testily*). I know she's sick. That's what I wanted you for. You go up and wait outside her door in case she needs anything. (MARGARET *starts upstairs.*) And what were you doing out of the house, anyway?

MARGARET. I was sent for the minister!

FATHER (*startled*). The minister!

MARGARET. Yes, he'll be right in. He's paying off the cab. (MARGARET *continues upstairs. The door slams.* THE REVEREND DR. LLOYD *appears in the archway and meets* FATHER *in the hall.*)

DR. LLOYD. I was deeply shocked to hear of Mrs. Day's illness. I hope I can be of some service. Will you take me up to her?

FATHER (*with a trace of hostility*). She's resting now. She can't be disturbed.

DR. LLOYD. But I've been summoned.

FATHER. The doctor will be back in a few minutes and we'll see what he has to say about it. You'd better come in and wait.

DR. LLOYD. Thank you. (*Comes into the room.* FATHER *follows him reluctantly.*) Mrs. Day has been a tower of strength in the parish. Everyone liked her so much. Yes, she was a fine woman.

FATHER. I wish to God you wouldn't talk about Mrs. Day as if she were dead. (NORA *comes down the stairs and looks into the room.*)

NORA. Is the doctor back yet?

FATHER. No. Does she need him?

NORA. She's kinda restless. She's talking in her sleep and twisting and turning. (*She goes downstairs.* FATHER *looks up toward* VINNIE'S *room, worried, then looks angrily toward the front door.*)

FATHER. That doctor said he'd be right back. (*He goes to the window.*)

MARGARET (*coming downstairs*). Here comes the doctor. I was watching for him out the window. (*She goes to the front door. A moment later* DR. HUMPHREYS *enters.*)

FATHER. Well, Doctor—seems to me that was a pretty long ten minutes.

DR. HUMPHREYS (*indignantly*). See here, Mr. Day, if I'm to be responsible for Mrs. Day's health, I must be allowed to handle this case in my own way.

FATHER. Well, you can't handle it if you're out of the house.

DR. HUMPHREYS (*flaring*). I left this house because—— (DR. SOMERS, *an imposing medical figure, enters and stops at* DR. HUMPHREYS' *side.*) This is Dr. Somers.

DR. SOMERS. How do you do?

DR. HUMPHREYS. I felt that Mrs. Day's condition warranted my getting Dr. Somers here as soon as possible for consultation. I hope that meets with your approval.

FATHER (*a little awed*). Why, yes, of course. Anything that can be done.

DR. HUMPHREYS. Upstairs, Doctor! (*The two doctors go upstairs.* FATHER *turns back into the room, obviously shaken.*)

DR. LLOYD. Mrs. Day is in good hands now, Mr. Day. There's nothing you and I can do at the moment to help. (*After a moment's consideration* FATHER *decides there is something that can be done to help. He goes to* DR. LLOYD. FATHER *indicates the seat in front of the table to* DR. LLOYD *and they both sit.*)

FATHER. Dr. Lloyd, there's something that's troubling Mrs. Day's mind. I think you know what I refer to.

DR. LLOYD. Yes—you mean the fact that you've never been baptized.

FATHER. I gathered you knew about it from your sermon last Sunday. (*Looks at him a second with indignant memory.*) But let's not get angry. I think something had better be done about it.

DR. LLOYD. Yes, Mr. Day.

FATHER. When the doctors get through up there I want you to talk to Mrs. Day. I want you to tell her something.

DR. LLOYD (*eagerly*). Yes, I'll be glad to.

FATHER. You're just the man to do it! She shouldn't be upset about this—I want you to tell her that my being baptized would just be a lot of damn nonsense. (*This isn't what* DR. LLOYD *has expected and it is hardly his idea of how to help* MRS. DAY.)

DR. LLOYD. But, Mr. Day!

FATHER. No, she'd take your word on a thing like that—and we've got to do everything we can to help her now.

DR. LLOYD (*rising*). But baptism is one of the sacraments of the Church——

FATHER. (*rising*). You're her minister and you're supposed to bring her comfort and peace of mind.

DR. LLOYD. But the solution is so simple. It would take only your consent to be baptized.

FATHER. That's out of the question! And I'm surprised that a grown man like you should suggest such a thing.

DR. LLOYD. If you're really concerned about Mrs. Day's peace of mind, don't you think——

FATHER. Now see here—if you're just going to keep her stirred up about this, I'm not going to let you see her at all. (*He turns away.* DR. LLOYD *follows him.*)

DR. LLOYD. Now, Mr. Day, as you said, we must do everything we can —— (*The doctors come downstairs.* FATHER *sees them.*)

FATHER. Well, Doctor, how is she? What have you decided?

DR. HUMPHREYS. We've just left Mrs. Day. Is there a room we could use for our consultation?

FATHER. Of course (MARGARET *starts downstairs.*) Margaret, you go back upstairs! I don't want Mrs. Day left alone!

MARGARET. I have to do something for the doctor. I'll go back up as soon as I get it started.

FATHER. Well, hurry. And, Margaret, show these gentlemen downstairs to the billiard room.

MARGARET. Yes, sir. This way, Doctor—downstairs. (*Exits, followed by* DR. SOMERS. FATHER *delays* DR. HUMPHREYS.)

FATHER. Dr. Humphreys, you know now, don't you—this isn't serious, is it?

DR. HUMPHREYS. After we've had our consultation we'll talk to you, Mr. Day.

FATHER. But surely you must——

DR. HUMPHREYS. Just rest assured that Dr. Somers will do everything that is humanly possible.

FATHER. Why, you don't mean——

DR. HUMPHREYS. We'll try not to be long. (*Exits.* FATHER *turns and looks at* DR. LLOYD. *He is obviously frightened.*)

FATHER. This Dr. Somers—I've heard his name often—he's very well thought of, isn't he?

DR. LLOYD. Oh, yes indeed.

FATHER. If Vinnie's really—if anyone could help her, he could—don't you think?

DR. LLOYD. A very fine physician. But there's a greater Help, ever present in the hour of need. Let us turn to Him in prayer. Let us kneel and pray. (FATHER *looks at him, straightens, then walks to the other side of the room.*) Let us kneel and pray. (FATHER *finally bows his head.* DR. LLOYD *looks at him and, not kneeling himself, raises his head and speaks simply in prayer.*) Oh, Lord, look down from Heaven—behold, visit, and relieve this Thy servant who is grieved with sickness, and extend to her Thy accustomed goodness. We know she has sinned against Thee in thought, word, and deed. Have mercy on her, O Lord, have mercy on this miserable sinner. Forgive her——

FATHER. She's not a miserable sinner and you know it! (*Then* FATHER *speaks directly to the Deity.*) O God! You know Vinnie's not a miserable sinner. She's a damn fine woman! She shouldn't be made to suffer. It's got to stop, I tell You, it's got to stop! (VINNIE *appears on the stairway in her nightgown.*)

VINNIE. What's the matter, Clare? What's wrong?

FATHER (*not hearing her*). Have mercy, I say, have mercy, damn it!

VINNIE. What's the matter, Clare? What's wrong? (FATHER *turns, sees* VINNIE, *and rushes to her.*)

FATHER. Vinnie, what are you doing down here? You shouldn't be out of bed. You get right back upstairs. (*He now has his arms around her.*)

VINNIE. Oh, Clare, I heard you call. Do you need me?

FATHER (*deeply moved*). Vinnie—I know now how much I need you. Get well, Vinnie. I'll be baptized. I promise. I'll be baptized.

VINNIE. You will? Oh, Clare!

FATHER. I'll do anything. We'll go to Europe, just we two—you won't have to worry about the children or the household accounts—— (VINNIE *faints against* FATHER'S *shoulder.*) Vinnie! (*He stoops to lift her.*)

DR. LLOYD. I'll get the doctor. But don't worry, Mr. Day—she'll be all right now. (FATHER *lifts* VINNIE *up in his arms.*) Bless you for what you've done, Mr. Day.

FATHER. What did I do?

DR. LLOYD. You promised to be baptized!

FATHER (*aghast*). I did? (*With horror* FATHER *realizes he has been betrayed—and by himself.*) OH, GOD!

CURTAIN

ACT THREE

SCENE I

The same.

A month later. Mid-afternoon.

VINNIE *is seated on the sofa embroidering petit point.* MARGARET *enters, as usual uncomfortable at being upstairs.*

MARGARET. You wanted to speak to me, ma'am?

VINNIE. Yes, Margaret, about tomorrow morning's breakfast—we must plan it very carefully.

MARGARET (*puzzled*). Mr. Day hasn't complained to me about his breakfasts lately. As a matter of fact, I've been blessing my luck!

VINNIE. Oh, no, it's not that. But tomorrow morning I'd like something for his breakfast that would surprise him.

MARGARET (*doubtfully*). Surprising Mr. Day is always a bit of a risk, ma'am. My motto with him has always been "Let well enough alone."

VINNIE. But if we think of something he especially likes, Margaret—what would you say to kippers?

MARGARET. Well, I've served him kippers, but I don't recall his ever saying he liked them.

VINNIE. He's never said he didn't like them, has he?

MARGARET. They've never got a stamp on the floor out of him one way or the other.

VINNIE. If Mr. Day doesn't say he doesn't like a thing you can assume that he does. Let's take a chance on kippers, Margaret.

MARGARET. Very well, ma'am. (*She starts out.*)

VINNIE (*innocently*). And, Margaret, you'd better have enough breakfast for two extra places.

MARGARET (*knowingly*). Oh—so that's it! We're going to have company again.

VINNIE. Yes, my cousin, Miss Cartwright, and her friend are coming back from Springfield. I'm afraid they'll get here just about breakfast time.

MARGARET. Well, in that case I'd better make some of my Sunday morning hot biscuits, too.

VINNIE. Yes. We *know* Mr. Day likes those.

MARGARET. I've been getting him to church with them for the last fifteen years. (*The door slams.* MARGARET *goes to the arch and looks.*) Oh, it's Mr. Clarence, ma'am. (*Goes off downstairs and* CLARENCE *enters with a large package.*)

CLARENCE. Here it is, Mother. (*He puts it on the table.*)

VINNIE. Oh, it was still in the store! They hadn't sold it! I'm so thrilled. Didn't you admire it, Clarence? (*She hurries over to the table.*)

CLARENCE. Well, it's unusual.

VINNIE (*unwrapping the package*). You know, I saw this down there the day before I got sick. I was walking through the bric-a-brac section and it caught my eye. I was so tempted to buy it! And all the time I lay ill I just couldn't get it out of my head. I can't understand how it could stay in the store all this time without somebody snatching it up. (*She takes it out of the box. It is a large china pug dog.*) Isn't that the darlingest thing you ever saw! It does need a ribbon, though. I've got the very thing somewhere. Oh, yes, I know. (*Goes to the side table and gets a red ribbon out of the drawer.*)

CLARENCE. Isn't John home yet?

VINNIE. I haven't seen him. Why?

CLARENCE. Well, you know we've been working, and John went down to collect our money.

VINNIE. That's fine. (*She ties the ribbon around the dog's neck.*) Oh, Clarence, I have a secret for just the two of us; who do you think is coming to visit us tomorrow?—Cousin Cora and Mary.

CLARENCE. Yes, I know.

VINNIE. How did you know?

CLARENCE. I happened to get a letter.

(JOHN *enters, carrying two packages of medicine.*)

VINNIE. John, did you ever see anything so sweet?

JOHN. What is it?

VINNIE. It's a pug dog. Your father would never let me have a real one, but he can't object to one made of china. This ribbon needs pressing. I'll take it down and have Margaret do it right away. (*Exits with the beribboned pug dog.*)

CLARENCE. What did you bring home more medicine for? (*Then, with sudden fright.*) Dr. Bartlett paid us off, didn't he?

JOHN. Oh, yes!

CLARENCE (*heaving a great sigh of relief*). You had me scared for a minute. When I went down to McCreery's to get that pug dog for Mother, I ordered the daisiest suit you ever saw. Dr. Bartlett owed us sixteen dollars apiece, and the suit was only fifteen. Wasn't that lucky? Come on, give me my money.

JOHN. Clarence, Dr. Bartlett paid us off in medicine.

CLARENCE. You let him pay us off with that old Beneficent Balm!

JOHN. Well, he thanked us, too, for our services to mankind.

CLARENCE (*in agony*). But my suit!

JOHN. You'll just have to wait for your suit.

CLARENCE. I can't wait! I've got to have it tomorrow—and besides they're making the alterations. I've got to pay for it this afternoon! Fifteen dollars!

JOHN (*helpfully*). Why don't you offer them fifteen bottles of medicine?

(CLARENCE *gives it a little desperate thought.*)

CLARENCE. They wouldn't take it. McCreery's don't sell medicine.

(JOHN *is by the window and looks out.*)

JOHN. That's too bad. Here comes Father.

CLARENCE. I'll have to brace him for that fifteen dollars. I hate to do it, but I've got to—that's all—I've got to.

JOHN. I'm not going to be here when you do. I'd better hide this somewhere, anyway. (*Takes the packages and hurries upstairs. The door slams.* FATHER *enters and looks into the room.*)

CLARENCE. Good afternoon, sir.

FATHER. How's your mother, Clarence? Where is she?

CLARENCE. She's all right. She's downstairs with Margaret. Oh, Father——

(FATHER *goes off down the hall and we hear him calling downstairs.*)

FATHER. Vinnie! Vinnie! I'm home. (*Comes back into the room, carrying his newspaper.*)

CLARENCE. Father, Mother will be well enough to go to church with us next Sunday.

FATHER. That's fine, Clarence. That's fine.

CLARENCE. Father, have you noticed that I haven't been kneeling down in church lately?

FATHER. Clarence, don't let your mother catch you at it.

CLARENCE. Then I've got to have a new suit of clothes right away!

FATHER (*after a puzzled look.*) Clarence, you're not even making sense!

CLARENCE. But a fellow doesn't feel right in cut-down clothes—especially your clothes. That's why I can't kneel down in church—I can't do anything in them you wouldn't do.

FATHER. Well, that's a damn good thing! If my old clothes make you behave yourself I don't think you ought to wear anything else.

CLARENCE (*desperately*). *Oh, no!* You're you and I'm me! I want to be myself! Besides, you're older and there are things I've got to do that I wouldn't do at your age.

FATHER. Clarence, you should never do anything I wouldn't do.

CLARENCE. Oh, yes,—look, for instance: Suppose I should want to kneel down in front of a girl?

FATHER. Why in Heaven's name should you want to do a thing like that?

CLARENCE. Well, I've got to get married *sometime*. I've got to propose to a girl *sometime*.

FATHER (*exasperated*). Before you're married, you'll be earning your own clothes, I hope. Don't get the idea into your head I'm going to support you and a wife, too. Besides, at your age, Clarence——

CLARENCE (*hastily*). Oh, I'm not going to be married right away, but for fifteen dollars I can get a good suit of clothes.

FATHER (*bewildered and irritated*). Clarence! (*He stares at him. At this second,* VINNIE *comes through the arch.*) Why, you're beginning to talk as crazy as your mother. (*He sees her.*) Oh, hello, Vinnie. How're you feeling today?

VINNIE. I'm fine, Clare. (*They kiss.*) You don't have to hurry home from the office every day like this.

(CLARENCE *throws himself in the chair by the window, sick with disappointment.*)

FATHER. Business the way it is, no use going to the office at all.

VINNIE. But you haven't been to your club for weeks.

FATHER. Can't stand the damn place. You do look better, Vinnie. What did you do today? (*Drops on the sofa.* VINNIE *stands behind the sofa. Her chatter does not succeed in diverting* FATHER *from his newspaper.*)

VINNIE. I took a long walk and dropped in to call on old Mrs. Whitehead.

FATHER. Well, that's fine.

VINNIE. And, Clare, it was the most fortunate thing that ever happened. I've got wonderful news for you! Who do you think was there? Mr. Morley!

FATHER (*not placing him*). Morley?

VINNIE. You remember—that nice young minister who substituted for Dr. Lloyd one Sunday?

FATHER. Oh, yes! Bright young fellow, preached a good sensible sermon.

VINNIE. It was the only time I ever saw you put five dollars in the plate!

FATHER. Ought to be more ministers like him. I could get along with that young man without any trouble at all.

VINNIE. Well, Clare, his parish is in Audubon—you know, 'way up above Harlem.

FATHER. Is that so?

VINNIE. Isn't that wonderful? Nobody knows you up there. You'll be perfectly safe!

FATHER. Safe? Vinnie, what the devil are you talking about?

VINNIE. I've been all over everything with Mr. Morley and he's agreed to baptize you.

FATHER. Oh, he has—the young whippersnapper! Damn nice of him!

VINNIE. We can go up there any morning, Clare—we don't even have to make an appointment.

FATHER. Vinnie, you're just making a lot of plans for nothing. Who said I was going to be baptized at all?

VINNIE (*aghast*). Why, Clare! *You* did!

FATHER. Now, Vinnie!——

VINNIE. You gave me your promise—your Sacred Promise. You stood right on that spot and said: "I'll be baptized. I promise—I'll be baptized."

FATHER. What if I did?

VINNIE (*amazed, she comes down and faces him*). Aren't you a man of your word?

FATHER (*rising*). Vinnie, that was under entirely different circumstances. We all thought you were dying, so naturally I said that to make you feel better. As a matter of fact, the doctor told me that's what cured you. So it seems to me pretty ungrateful of you to press this matter any further.

VINNIE. Clarence Day, you gave me your Sacred Promise!

FATHER (*getting annoyed*). Vinnie, you were sick when I said that. Now you're well again.

(MARGARET *enters with the pug dog, which now has the freshly pressed ribbon tied around its neck. She puts it on the table.*)

MARGARET. Is that all right, Mrs. Day?

VINNIE (*dismissingly*). That's fine, Margaret, thank you. (MARGARET *exits.*) My being well has nothing to do with it. You gave me your word! You gave the Lord your word. If you had seen how eager Mr. Morley was to bring you into the fold. (FATHER, *trying to escape, has been moving toward the arch when suddenly the pug dog catches his eye and he stares at it fascinated.*) And you're going to march yourself up to his church some morning before you go to the office and be christened. If you think for one minute that I'm going to——

FATHER. What in the name of Heaven is that?

VINNIE. If you think I'm going to let you add the sin of breaking your Solemn and Sacred Promise——

FATHER. I demand to know what that repulsive object is!

VINNIE (*exasperated in her turn*). It's perfectly plain what it is—it's a pug dog!

FATHER. What's it doing in this house?

VINNIE (*defiantly*). I wanted it and I bought it.

FATHER. You spent good money for that?

VINNIE. Clare, we're not talking about that! We're talking about you. Don't try to change the subject!

FATHER. How much did you pay for that atrocity?

VINNIE. I don't know. I sent Clarence down for it. Listen to me, Clare——

FATHER. Clarence, what did you pay for that?

CLARENCE. I didn't pay anything. I charged it.

FATHER (*looking at* VINNIE). Charged it! I might have known. (*To* CLARENCE:) How much was it?

CLARENCE. Fifteen dollars.

FATHER. Fifteen dollars for that eyesore?

VINNIE (*to the rescue of the pug dog*). Don't you call that lovely work of art an eyesore! That will look beautiful sitting on a red cushion by the fireplace in the parlor.

FATHER. If that sits in the parlor, I won't! Furthermore, I don't even want it in the same house with me. Get it out of here! (*He starts for the stairs.*)

VINNIE. You're just using that for an excuse. You're not going to get out of this room until you set a date for your baptism.

(FATHER *turns at the foot of the stairs.*)

FATHER. I'll tell you one thing! I'll never be baptized while that hideous monstrosity is in this house. (*He stalks upstairs.*)

VINNIE (*calling after him*). All right! (*She goes to the pug dog.*) All right! It goes back this afternoon and he's christened first thing in the morning.

CLARENCE. But, Mother——

VINNIE. Clarence, you heard him say that he'd be baptized as soon as I got this pug dog out of the house. You hurry right back to McCreery's with it—and be sure they credit us with fifteen dollars.

(*The fifteen dollars rings a bell in* CLARENCE'S *mind.*)

CLARENCE. Oh, say, Mother, while I was at McCreery's, I happened to see a suit I would like very much and the suit was only fifteen dollars.

VINNIE (*regretfully*). Well, Clarence, I think your suit will have to wait until after I get your father christened.

CLARENCE (*hopefully*). No. I meant that since the suit cost just the same as the pug dog, if I exchanged the pug dog for the suit——

VINNIE. Why, yes! Then your suit wouldn't cost Father anything! Why, how bright of you, Clarence, to think of that!

CLARENCE (*quickly*). I'd better start right away before McCreery's closes. (*They have collected the box, wrapper, and tissue paper.*)

VINNIE. Yes. Let's see. If we're going to take your father all the way up to Audubon—Clarence, you stop at Ryerson & Brown's on your way back and tell them to have a cab here at eight o'clock tomorrow morning.

CLARENCE. Mother, a cab! Do you think you ought to do that?

VINNIE. Well, we can't walk to Audubon.

CLARENCE (*warningly*). But you know what a cab does to Father!

VINNIE. This is an important occasion.

CLARENCE (*with a shrug*). All right! A brougham or a Victoria?

VINNIE. Get one of their best cabs—the kind they use at funerals.

CLARENCE. Those cost two dollars an hour! And if Father gets mad——

VINNIE. Well, if your father starts to argue in the morning, you remember——

CLARENCE (*remembering his suit*). Oh, he agreed to it! We both heard him!

(VINNIE *has removed the ribbon and is about to put the pug dog back in the box.*)

VINNIE (*regretfully*). I did have my heart set on this. (*An idea comes to her.*) Still—if they didn't sell him in all that time, he might be safe there for a few more weeks. (*She gives the dog a reassuring pat and puts him in the box. She begins to sing "Sweet Marie" happily.* FATHER *comes down the stairs.* CLARENCE *takes his hat and the box and goes happily and quickly out.* FATHER *watches him.*) I hope you notice that Clarence is returning the pug dog.

FATHER. That's a sign you're getting your faculties back. (VINNIE *is singing quietly to herself in a satisfied way.*) Good to hear you singing again, Vinnie. (*Suddenly remembering something.*) Oh!—on my way uptown I stopped in at Tiffany's and bought you a little something. Thought you might like it. (*He takes out of his pocket a small ring box and holds it out to her. She takes it.*)

VINNIE. Oh, Clare. (*She opens it eagerly.*) What a beautiful ring! (*She takes the ring out, puts it on her finger, and admires it.*)

FATHER. Glad if it pleases you. (*He settles down to his newspaper on the sofa.*)

VINNIE. I don't know how to thank you. (*She kisses him.*)

FATHER. It's thanks enough for me to have you up and around again. When you're sick, Vinnie, this house is like a tomb. There's no excitement.

VINNIE (*sitting beside him*). Clare, this is the loveliest ring you ever bought me. Now that I have this, you needn't buy me any more rings.

FATHER. Well, if you don't want any more.

VINNIE. What I'd really like now is a nice diamond necklace.

FATHER (*alarmed*). Vinnie, do you know how much a diamond necklace costs?

VINNIE. I know, Clare, but don't you see?—your giving me this ring shows that I mean a little something to you. Now, a diamond necklace——

FATHER. Good God, if you don't know by this time how I feel about you! We've been married for twenty years and I've loved you every minute of it.

VINNIE. What did you say? (*Her eyes well with tears at* FATHER'S *definite statement of his love.*)

FATHER. I said we'd been married twenty years and I've loved you every minute of it. But if I have to buy out jewelry stores to prove it—if I haven't shown it to you in my words and actions, I might as well—— (*He turns and sees* VINNIE *dabbing her eyes and speaks with resignation.*) What have I done now?

VINNIE. It's all right, Clare—I'm just so happy.

FATHER. Happy!

VINNIE. You said you loved me! And this beautiful ring—that's something else I didn't expect. Oh, Clare, I love surprises. (*She nestles against him.*)

FATHER. That's another thing I can't understand about you, Vinnie. Now, *I* like to know what to expect. Then I'm prepared to meet it.

VINNIE (*putting her head on his shoulder*). Yes, I know. But, Clare, life would be pretty dull if we always knew what was coming.

FATHER. Well, it's certainly not dull around here. In this house you never know what's going to hit you tomorrow.

VINNIE (*to herself*). Tomorrow! (*She starts to sing,* FATHER *listening to her happily.*)

"Every daisy in the dell,
Knows my secret, knows it well,
And yet I dare not tell,
Sweet Marie!"

CURTAIN

SCENE II

The same.

The next morning. Breakfast. All the family except JOHN *and* VINNIE *are at the table and in good spirits.*

JOHN (*entering*). Mother says she'll be right down. (*He sits at the table.*)

(MAGGIE, *the new maid, enters with a plate of hot biscuits and serves* FATHER. *As* FATHER *takes a biscuit, he glances up at her and shows some little surprise.*)

FATHER. Who are you? What's your name?

MAGGIE. Margaret, sir.

FATHER. Can't be Margaret. We've got one Margaret in the house.

MAGGIE. At home they call me Maggie, sir.

FATHER (*genially*). All right, Maggie. (MAGGIE *continues serving the biscuits.*) Boys, if her name's Margaret, that's a good sign. Maybe she'll stay awhile. You know, boys, your mother used to be just the same about cooks as she is about maids. Never could keep them for some reason. Well, one day about fifteen years ago—yes, it was right after you were born, John—my, you were a homely baby. (*They all laugh at* JOHN'S *expense.*) I came home that night all tired out and what did I find?—no dinner, because the cook had left. Well, I decided I'd had just about enough of that, so I just marched over to the employment agency on Sixth Avenue and said to the woman in charge: "Where do you keep the cooks?" She tried to hold me up with a lot of red-tape folderol, but I just walked into the room where the girls were waiting, looked 'em over, saw Margaret, pointed at her, and said: "I'll take that one." I walked her home, she cooked dinner that night, and she's been cooking for us ever since. Damn good cook, too. (*He stamps on the floor three times.*)

VINNIE *comes down the stairs dressed in white. Somehow she almost has the appearance of a bride going to her wedding.*)

VINNIE. Good morning, Clare. Good morning, boys.

(*The boys and* FATHER *rise.* VINNIE *takes her bonnet and gloves and lays them on the chair below the fireplace.* FATHER *goes to* VINNIE'S *chair and holds it out for her, glancing at her holiday appearance.* VINNIE *sits.*)

FATHER. Sit down, boys. (*As* FATHER *returns to his own chair, he notices that all of the boys are dressed in their Sunday best.*) Everyone's dressed up this morning. What's on the program for this fine day?

(VINNIE, *who always postpones crises in the hope some miracle will aid her, postpones this one.*)

VINNIE. Well, this afternoon May Lewis's mother is giving a party for everyone in May's dancing class. Harlan's going to that.

HARLAN. I don't want to go, Mamma.

VINNIE. Why, Harlan, don't you want to go to a party and get ice cream and cake?

HARLAN. May Lewis always tries to kiss me.

(*This is greeted with family laughter.*)

FATHER (*genially*). When you get a little older, you won't object to girls' wanting to kiss you, will he, Clarence?

(MARGARET *comes hurrying in.*)

MARGARET. What's wanting?

FATHER. Margaret, these kippers are good. (MARGARET *makes her usual deprecatory gesture toward him.*) Haven't had kippers for a long time. I'm glad you remembered I like them.

MARGARET. Yes, sir.

(MARGARET *and* VINNIE *exchange knowing looks.* MARGARET *goes out happy.*)

FATHER. What's got into Margaret this morning? Hot biscuits, too!

VINNIE. She knows you're fond of them. (*The doorbell rings.* MAGGIE *goes to answer it.* VINNIE *stirs nervously in her chair.*) Who can that be? It can't be the mail man because he's been here.

FATHER (*with sly humor*). Clarence has been getting a good many special deliveries lately. Is that business deal going through, Clarence?

(*The family has a laugh at* CLARENCE. MAGGIE *comes back into the arch with a suit box.*)

MAGGIE. This is for you, Mr. Day. Where shall I put it?

CLARENCE (*hastily*). Oh, that's for me, I think. Take it upstairs, Maggie.

FATHER. Wait a minute, Maggie, bring it here. Let's see it.

(CLARENCE *takes the box from* MAGGIE, *who exits. He holds it toward his father.*)

CLARENCE. See, it's for me, Father—Clarence Day, Jr.

FATHER. Let me look. Why, that's from McCreery's and it's marked "Charge." What is it?

VINNIE. It's all right, Clare. It's nothing for you to worry about.

FATHER. Well, at least I think I should know what's being charged to me. What is it?

VINNIE. Now, Clare, stop your fussing. It's a new suit of clothes for Clarence and it's not costing you a penny.

FATHER. It's marked "Charge fifteen dollars"—it's costing me fifteen dollars. And I told Clarence——

VINNIE. Clare, can't you take my word it isn't costing you a penny?

FATHER. I'd like to have you explain why it isn't.

VINNIE (*triumphantly*). Because Clarence took the pug dog back and got the suit instead.

FATHER. Of course, and they'll charge me fifteen dollars for the suit.

VINNIE. Nonsense, Clare. We gave them the pug dog for the suit. Don't you see?

FATHER. Then they'll charge me fifteen dollars for the pug dog.

VINNIE. But, Clare, they can't! We haven't got the pug dog. We sent that back.

FATHER (*bewildered, but not convinced*). Now wait a minute, Vinnie. There's something wrong with your reasoning.

VINNIE. I'm surprised, Clare, and you're supposed to be so good at figures. Why, it's perfectly clear to me.

FATHER. Vinnie! They're going to charge me for one thing or the other.

VINNIE. Don't you let them!

(FATHER *gets up and throws his napkin on the table.*)

FATHER. Well, McCreery's aren't giving away suits and they aren't giving away pug dogs. (*He walks over to the window in his irritation.*) Can't you get it through your—— (*Looking out the window.*) Oh, God!

VINNIE. What is it, Clare? What's wrong?

FATHER. Don't anybody answer the door.

VINNIE. Who is it? Who's coming?

FATHER. Those damn women are back!

WHITNEY. What women?

FATHER. Cora and that little idiot. (CLARENCE *dashes madly up the stairs clutching the box containing his new suit.*) They're moving in on us again, bag and baggage! (*The doorbell rings.*) Don't let them in!

VINNIE. Clarence Day, as if we could turn our own relatives away!

FATHER. Tell them to get back in that cab and drive right on to Ohio. If they're extravagant enough to take cabs when horse cars run right by our door——

(MAGGIE *crosses the hall to answer the doorbell.*)

VINNIE. Now, Clare—you be quiet and behave yourself. They're here and there's nothing you can do about it. (*She starts toward the hall.*)

FATHER (*shouting after her*). Well, why do they always pounce on us without warning?—the damn gypsies!

VINNIE (*from the arch*). Shhh!—Clare! (*Then in her best welcoming tone.*) Cora! Mary! It's so nice to have you back again.

CORA. How are you, Vinnie? We've been so worried about you.

VINNIE. Oh, I'm fine now!

(CORA *and* MARY *and* VINNIE *enter and* CORA *sweeps right down into the room.*)

CORA. Hello, Harlan! Whitney! Well, Cousin Clare. Here we are again! (*Kisses* FATHER *on the cheek. He draws back sternly.* MARY *looks quickly around the room for* CLARENCE, *then greets and is greeted by the other boys.*) And John! Where's Clarence?

MARY. Yes, where is Clarence?

VINNIE. John, go find Clarence and tell him that Cora and Mary are here.

JOHN. Yes, Mother. (*Goes upstairs.*)

VINNIE. You got here just in time to have breakfast with us.

CORA. We had breakfast at the depot.

VINNIE. Well, as a matter of fact, we'd just finished.

FATHER (*with cold dignity*). I haven't finished my breakfast!

VINNIE. Well, then sit down, Clare. (*To* CORA *and* MARY): Margaret gave us kippers this morning and Clare's so fond of kippers. Why don't we all sit down? (*Indicates the empty places and the girls sit.* FATHER *resumes his chair and breakfast in stony silence.* MAGGIE *has come into the room to await orders.*) Maggie, clear those things away. (*She indicates the dishes in front of the girls, and* MAGGIE *removes them.* FATHER *takes a letter from his stack of morning mail and opens it.*) Clare, don't let your kippers get cold. (*To* CORA): Now—tell us all about Springfield.

CORA. We had a wonderful month—but tell us about you, Cousin Vinnie. You must have had a terrible time.

VINNIE. Yes, I was pretty sick, but I'm all right again now.

CORA. What was it?

VINNIE. Well, the doctors don't know exactly, but they did say this—that they'd never seen anything like it before, whatever it was.

CORA. You certainly look well enough now. Doesn't she, Clare?

(*Whatever is in the letter* FATHER *has been reading comes to him as a shock.*)

FATHER. Oh, God!

VINNIE. What's the matter, Clare? What's wrong?

FATHER. John! John!

(JOHN *is seen halfway up the stairs with the girls' bags. He comes running down the stairs, going to* FATHER.)

JOHN. Yes, Father?

FATHER. Have you been going around this town selling medicine?

JOHN (*a little frightened.*) Yes, Father.

FATHER. Dog medicine?

JOHN (*indignantly*). No, Father, not dog medicine!

FATHER. It must have been dog medicine!

JOHN. It wasn't dog medicine, Father——

FATHER. This letter from Mrs. Sprague says you sold her a bottle of this medicine and that her little boy gave some of it to their dog and it killed him! Now she wants ten dollars from me for a new dog.

JOHN. Well, he shouldn't have given it to a dog. It's for humans! Why, it's Bartlett's Beneficent Balm—"Made from a secret formula"!

FATHER. Have you been going around among our friends and neighbors selling some damned Dr. Munyon patent nostrum?

JOHN. But it's good medicine, Father. I can prove it by Mother.

FATHER. Vinnie, what do you know about this?

VINNIE. Nothing, Clare, but I'm sure that John——

JOHN. No, I mean that day Mother——

FATHER. That's enough! You're going to every house where you sold a bottle of that concoction and buy it all back.

JOHN (*dismayed*). But it's a dollar a bottle!

FATHER. I don't care how much it is. How many bottles did you sell?

JOHN. A hundred and twenty-eight.

FATHER (*roaring*). A hundred and twenty-eight!

VINNIE. Clare, I always told you John would make a good businessman.

FATHER (*calmly*). Young man, I'll give you the money to buy it back—a hundred and twenty-eight dollars. And ten more for Mrs. Sprague. That's a hundred and thirty-eight dollars. But it's coming out of your allowance! That means you'll not get another penny until that hundred and thirty-eight dollars is all paid up.

(JOHN *starts toward the hall, counting on his fingers, then turns and addresses his father in dismay.*)

JOHN. I'll be twenty-one years old!

(FATHER *glares at him.* JOHN *turns and goes on up the stairs, with the bags.*)

VINNIE (*persuasively*). Clare, you know you've always encouraged the boys to earn their own money.

FATHER. Vinnie, I'll handle this. (*There is a pause. He buries himself in his newspaper.*)

CORA (*breaking through the constraint*). Of course, Aunt Judith sent her love to all of you——

VINNIE. I haven't seen Judith for years. You'd think living so close to Springfield—maybe I could run up there before the summer's over.

CORA. Oh, she'll be leaving for Pleasantville any day now. Grandpa Ebbetts has been failing very fast and that's why I have to hurry back.

VINNIE. Hurry back? Well, you and Mary can stay with us a few days at least.

CORA. No, I hate to break the news to you, Vinnie, but we can't even stay overnight. We're leaving on the five o'clock train this afternoon.

VINNIE (*disappointed*). Oh, what a pity!

(FATHER *lowers the paper.*)

FATHER (*heartily*). Well, Cora, it certainly is good to see you again. (*To* MARY): Young lady, I think you've been enjoying yourself—you look prettier than ever.

(MARY *laughs and blushes.*)

WHITNEY. I'll bet Clarence will think so.

(*The doorbell rings.* MAGGIE *crosses to answer it.*)

FATHER. That can't be another special delivery for Clarence. (*To* MARY, *slyly*): While you were in Springfield our postman was kept pretty busy. Sure you girls don't want any breakfast?

MARY. No, thank you. (*Rises and goes to the arch and stands looking upstairs, watching for* CLARENCE.)

CORA. Oh, no, thank you, Cousin Clare, we've had our breakfast.

FATHER. At least you ought to have a cup of coffee with us. Vinnie, you might have thought to order some coffee for the girls.

CORA. No, no, thank you, Cousin Clare.

(MAGGIE *appears again in the arch.*)

MAGGIE. It's the cab, ma'am. (*Exits.*)

FATHER. The cab! What cab?

VINNIE. The cab that's to take us to Audubon.

FATHER. Who's going to Audubon?

VINNIE. We all are. Cora, the most wonderful thing has happened!

CORA. What, Cousin Vinnie?

VINNIE (*happily*). Clare's going to be baptized this morning.

FATHER (*not believing his ears*). Vinnie—what are you saying?

VINNIE (*with determination*). I'm saying you're going to be baptized this morning!

FATHER. I am not going to be baptized this morning or any other morning!

VINNIE. You promised yesterday that as soon as I sent that pug dog back you'd be baptized.

FATHER. I promised no such thing!

VINNIE. You certainly did!

FATHER. I never said anything remotely like that!

VINNIE. Clarence was right here and heard it. You ask him!

FATHER. Clarence be damned! I know what I said! I don't remember exactly, but it wasn't that!

VINNIE. Well, I remember. That's why I ordered the cab!

FATHER (*suddenly remembering*). The cab! Oh, my God, that cab! (*He rises and glares out the window at the cab, then turns back and speaks peremptorily.*) Vinnie! You send that right back!

VINNIE. I'll do nothing of the kind. I'm going to see that you get to Heaven.

FATHER. I can't go to Heaven in a cab!

VINNIE. Well, you can start in a cab! I'm not sure whether they'll ever let you into Heaven or not, but I know they won't unless you're baptized.

FATHER. They can't keep me out of Heaven on a technicality.

VINNIE. Clare, stop quibbling! You might as well face it—you've got to make your peace with God.

FATHER. I never had any trouble with God until you stirred Him up!

(MARY *is tired of waiting for* CLARENCE *and chooses this moment to interrupt.*)

MARY. Mrs. Day? (VINNIE *answers her quickly, as if expecting* MARY *to supply her with an added argument.*)

VINNIE. Yes, Mary?

MARY. Where do you suppose Clarence is?

FATHER. You keep out of this, young lady! If it hadn't been for you, no one would have known whether I was baptized or not. (MARY *breaks into tears.*) Damn! Damnation!

VINNIE. Harlan! Whitney! Get your Sunday hats. (*Calls upstairs.*) John! Clarence! (HARLAN *and* WHITNEY *start out, but stop as* FATHER *speaks.*)

FATHER (*blazing with new fire*). Vinnie, are you mad? Was it your plan that my own children should witness this indignity?

VINNIE. Why, Clare, they'll be proud of you!

FATHER. I suppose Harlan is to be my godfather! (*With determination.*) Vinnie, it's no use. I can't go through with this thing and I won't. That's final.

VINNIE. Why, Clare dear, if you feel that way about it——

FATHER. I do!

VINNIE. —the children don't have to go. (JOHN *enters.*)

JOHN. Yes, Mother?

(FATHER *sees* JOHN *and an avenue of escape opens up.*)

FATHER. Oh, John! Vinnie, I can't do anything like that this morning. I've got to take John down to the office and give him the money to buy back that medicine. (*To* JOHN.) When I think of you going around this town selling dog medicine!——

JOHN (*insistently*). It wasn't dog medicine, Father.

FATHER. John, we're starting downtown this minute!

VINNIE. You're doing no such thing! You gave me your Sacred Promise that day I almost died——

JOHN. Yes, and she would have died if we hadn't given her some of that medicine. That proves it's good medicine!

FATHER (*aghast*). You gave your mother some of that dog medicine!

VINNIE. Oh, no, John, you didn't! (*Sinks weakly into the chair below the fireplace.*)

JOHN. Yes, we did, Mother. We put some in your tea that morning.

FATHER. You did what? Without her knowing it? Do you realize you might have killed your mother? You did kill Mrs. Sprague's dog. (*After a solemn pause*): John, you've done a very serious thing. I'll have to give considerable thought as to how you're going to be punished for this.

VINNIE. But, Clare——

FATHER. No, Vinnie. When I think of that day—with the house full of doctors—why, Cora, we even sent for the minister. Why, we might have lost you! (*He goes to* VINNIE, *really moved, and puts his hand on her shoulder.*) It's all right now, Vinnie, thank God. You're well again. But what I went through that afternoon —the way I felt—I'll never forget it.

VINNIE. Don't talk that way, Clare. You've forgotten it already.

FATHER. What do you mean?

VINNIE. That was the day you gave me your Sacred Promise.

FATHER. But I wouldn't have promised if I hadn't thought you were dying—and you wouldn't have almost died if John hadn't given you that medicine. Don't you see? The whole thing's illegal!

VINNIE. Suppose I had died! It wouldn't make any difference to you. You don't care whether we meet in Heaven or not—you don't care whether you ever see me and the children again. (*She almost succeeds in crying.* HARLAN *and* WHITNEY *go to her in sympathy, putting their arms around her.*)

FATHER (*distressed*). Now, Vinnie, you're not being fair to me.

VINNIE. It's all right, Clare. If you don't love us enough there's nothing we can do about it. (*Hurt,* FATHER *walks away to the other side of the room.*)

FATHER. That's got nothing to do with it! I love my family as much as any man. There's nothing within reason I wouldn't do for you, and you know it! All these years I've struggled and worked just to prove —— (*He has reached the window and looks out.*) There's that damn cab! Vinnie, you're not well enough to go all the way up to Audubon.

VINNIE (*perkily*). I'm well enough if we ride.

FATHER. But that trip would take all morning. And those cabs cost a dollar an hour.

VINNIE (*with smug complacence*). That's one of their best cabs. That costs two dollars an hour. (FATHER *stares at her a second, horrified—then explodes.*)

FATHER. Then why aren't you ready? Get your hat on! Damn! Damnation! Amen! (*Exits for his hat and stick.* VINNIE *is stunned for a moment by this sudden surrender, then hastily puts on her bonnet.*)

WHITNEY. Let's watch them start! Come on, Cousin Cora, let's watch them start!

CORA. I wouldn't miss it! (WHITNEY, HARLAN, *and* CORA *hurry out.* VINNIE *starts, but* JOHN *stops her in the arch.*)

JOHN (*contritely*). Mother, I didn't mean to almost kill you.

VINNIE. Now, don't you worry about what your father said. (*Tenderly.*) It's all right, dear. (*She kisses him.*) It worked out fine! (*She exits.* JOHN *looks upstairs, then at* MARY, *who has gone to the window.*)

JOHN. Mary! Here comes Clarence! (JOHN *exits.* MARY *sits in* FATHER'S *chair.* CLARENCE *comes down the stairs in his new suit. He goes into the room and right to* MARY. *Without saying a word he kneels in front of her. They both are starry-eyed.*)

(FATHER, *with hat and stick, comes into the arch on his way out. He sees* CLARENCE *kneeling at* MARY'S *feet.*)

FATHER. *Oh, God!* (CLARENCE *springs up in embarrassment.* VINNIE *re-enters hurriedly.*)

VINNIE. What's the matter? What's wrong?

CLARENCE. Nothing's wrong, Mother. (*Then, for want of something to say:*) Going to the office, Father?

FATHER. No! I'm going to be baptized, damn it! (*He slams his hat on angrily and stalks out.* VINNIE *gives a triumphant nod and follows him. The curtain starts down, and as it falls,* CLARENCE *again kneels at* MARY'S *feet.*)

CURTAIN

Arsenic and Old Lace

A COMEDY BY

JOSEPH KESSELRING

First Printing

Arsenic and Old Lace was produced by Howard Lindsay and Russel Crouse at the Fulton Theatre, New York City, on the night of January 10, 1941, with the following cast:

Abby Brewster	Josephine Hull
Reverend Doctor Harper	Wyrley Birch
Teddy Brewster	John Alexander
Officer Klein	Bruce Gordon
Officer Brophy	John Quigg
Martha Brewster	Jean Adair
Elaine Harper	Helen Brooks
Mortimer Brewster	Allyn Joslyn
Mr. Gibbs	Henry Herbert
Jonathan Brewster	Boris Karloff
Dr. Einstein	Edgar Stehli
Officer O'Hara	Anthony Ross
Lieutenant Rooney	Victor Sutherland
Mr. Witherspoon	William Parke

Staged by Bretaigne Windust
Setting and Costumes by Raymond Sovey

SCENES

ACT ONE

Late afternoon, in September

ACT TWO

Later that night

ACT THREE

SCENE I: Still later that night

SCENE II: Early next morning

The entire action takes place in the Brewster home in Brooklyn.
Time, the present.

ACT ONE

The living room of the old Brewster home in Brooklyn. It is just as Victorian as the two sisters, Abby and Martha Brewster, who occupy the house with their nephew, Teddy.

Down stage, right, is the front door of the house, a large door with frosted glass panels in the upper half, beyond which, when it is open, can be seen the front porch and the lawn and shrubbery of the front garden of the Brewster house. On either side of the door are narrow windows of small panes of glass, curtained. Over the door is a small arch of colored glass. The remainder of the right wall is taken up by the first flight of stairs leading to the upper floors. In the up-stage corner is a landing where the stairs turn to continue along the back wall of the room. In the right wall of the landing is an old-fashioned window, also looking out on to the porch. At the top of the stairs, along the back wall, is another landing, from which a door leads into the second-floor bedrooms, and an arch at the left end of this landing suggests the stairs leading to the third floor.

On stage level under this landing is a door which leads to the cellar. To the left of this door is a recess which contains a sideboard, on the top of which at either end are two small cabinets, where the sisters keep, among other things, bottles of elderberry wine. On the sideboard, among the usual impedimenta, are colored wine glasses. To the left of the recess is the door leading to the kitchen.

In the left wall of the room, there is a large window looking out over the cemetery of the neighboring Episcopal Church. This window has the usual lace curtains and thick drapes, which open and close by the use of a heavy curtain cord. Below the window is a large window seat, the lid of which has a thin pad of the same material as the drapes. When this lid is raised, the hinges creak audibly.

At the left of the foot of the stairs is a small desk, on which stands a dial telephone, and by this desk is a stool. Along the back wall, to the right of the cellar door, is an old-fashioned sofa. Left center in the room is a round table. There is a small chair right of this table and behind it, to the left of the table, a larger, comfortable armchair. On the walls are the usual pictures, including several portraits of the rather eccentric Brewster ancestors.

The time is the present. Late afternoon in September. As the curtain rises, ABBY BREWSTER, *a plump little darling in her late sixties, is presiding at tea. She is sitting behind the table in front of a high silver tea service. At her left, in the comfortable armchair, is the* REVEREND DR. HARPER, *the elderly rector of the near-by church. Standing, stage center, thoughtfully sipping a cup of tea, is her nephew,* TEDDY, *in a frock coat, and wearing pince-nez attached to a black ribbon.* TEDDY *is in his forties and has a large mustache.*

ABBY. My sister Martha and I have been talking all week about your sermon last Sunday. It's really wonderful, Dr. Harper—in only two short years you've taken on the spirit of Brooklyn.

DR. HARPER. That's very gratifying, Miss Brewster.

ABBY. You see, living here next to the church all our lives, we've seen so many ministers come and go. The spirit of Brooklyn, we always say, is friendliness—and your sermons are not so much sermons as friendly talks.

TEDDY. Personally, I've always enjoyed my talks with Cardinal Gibbons—or have I met him yet?

ABBY. No, dear, not yet. (*Changing the subject.*) Are the biscuits good?

TEDDY. Bully! (TEDDY *retires to the sofa, with his teacup and his thoughts.*)

ABBY. Won't you have another biscuit, Dr. Harper?

DR. HARPER. Oh, no, I'm afraid I'll have no appetite for dinner now. I always eat too many of your biscuits just to taste that lovely jam.

ABBY. But you haven't tried the quince. We always put a little apple in with it to take the tartness out.

DR. HARPER. No, thank you.

ABBY. We'll send you over a jar.

DR. HARPER. No, no! You keep it here so I can be sure of having your biscuits with it.

ABBY. I do hope they don't make us use that imitation flour again. I mean with this war trouble threatening us. It may not be charitable of me, but I've almost come to the conclusion that this Mr. Hitler isn't a Christian.

DR. HARPER (*with a sigh*). If only Europe were on another planet!

TEDDY (*sharply*). Europe, sir?

DR. HARPER. Yes, Teddy.

TEDDY. Point your gun the other way!

DR. HARPER. Gun?

ABBY (*trying to calm him*). Teddy!

TEDDY. To the West! There's your danger! There's your enemy! Japan!

DR. HARPER. Why, yes—yes, of course.

ABBY. Teddy!

TEDDY. No, Aunt Abby! Not so much talk about Europe and more about the Canal!

ABBY. Let's not talk about war. Have another cup of tea, dear?

TEDDY. No, thank you, Aunt Abby.

ABBY. Dr. Harper?

DR. HARPER. No, thank you. I must admit, Miss Abby, that war and violence seem far removed from these surroundings.

ABBY. It is peaceful here, isn't it?

DR. HARPER. Yes—peaceful. The virtues of another day—they're all here in this house. The gentle virtues that went out with candlelight and good manners and low taxes.

ABBY (*glancing about her contentedly*). It's one of the oldest houses in Brooklyn. It's just as it was when Grandfather Brewster built and furnished it—except for the electricity. We use it as little as possible—it was Mortimer who persuaded us to put it in.

DR. HARPER (*dryly*). Yes, I can understand that. Your nephew Mortimer seems to live only by electric light.

ABBY. The poor boy has to work so late. I understand he's taking Elaine to the theater again tonight. Teddy, your brother Mortimer will be here a little later.

TEDDY (*baring his teeth in a broad grin*). Dee-lighted!

ABBY. We're so happy it's Elaine Mortimer takes to the theater with him.

DR. HARPER. Well, it's a new experience for me to wait up until three o'clock in the morning for my daughter to be brought home.

ABBY. Oh, Dr. Harper, I hope you don't disapprove of Mortimer.

DR. HARPER. Well . . .

ABBY. We'd feel so guilty if you did—sister Martha and I. I mean since it was here in our home that your daughter met Mortimer.

DR. HARPER. Of course, Miss Abby. And so I'll say immediately that I believe Mortimer himself to be quite a worthy gentleman. But I must also admit that I have watched the growing intimacy between him and my daughter with some trepidation. For one reason, Miss Abby.

ABBY. You mean his stomach, Dr. Harper?

DR. HARPER. Stomach?

ABBY. His dyspepsia—he's bothered with it so, poor boy.

DR. HARPER. No, Miss Abby, I'll be frank with you. I'm speaking of your nephew's unfortunate connection with the theater.

ABBY. The theater! Oh, no, Dr. Harper! Mortimer writes for a New York newspaper.

DR. HARPER. I know, Miss Abby, I know. But a dramatic critic is constantly exposed to the theater, and I don't doubt but that some of them do develop an interest in it.

ABBY. Well, not Mortimer! You need have no fear at all. Why, Mortimer hates the theater.

DR. HARPER. Really?

ABBY. Oh, yes! He writes awful things about the theater. But you can't blame him, poor boy. He was so happy writing about real estate, which he really knew something about, and then they just made him take this terrible night position.

DR. HARPER. My! My!

ABBY. But as he says, the theater can't last much longer and, in the meantime, it's a living. (*Complacently.*) I think if we give the theater another year or two . . . (*There is knock at the door.* TEDDY *starts toward it. They all rise.*) Now who do you suppose that is? (*To

TEDDY.) Never mind, Teddy, I'll go. (*She goes to door and opens it.*) Come right in, Mr. Brophy. (*Two uniformed policemen enter. They are* BROPHY *and* KLEIN.)

BROPHY. Hello, Miss Brewster.

ABBY. How are you, Mr. Klein?

KLEIN. Very well, Miss Brewster.

TEDDY (*to the policemen*). Gentlemen, what news have you brought me?

BROPHY (*as he and* KLEIN *salute him*). Colonel, we have nothing to report.

TEDDY (*returning the salute*). Splendid! Thank you, gentlemen! At ease!

ABBY (*to the policemen*). You know Dr. Harper.

KLEIN. Sure! Hello, Dr. Harper.

BROPHY (*to* ABBY). We've come for the toys for the Christmas Fund.

ABBY. Oh, yes!

DR. HARPER. That's a splendid work you men do—fixing up discarded toys to give poor children a happier Christmas.

KLEIN. It gives us something to do when we have to sit around the station. You get tired playing cards and then you start cleaning your gun and the first thing you know you've shot yourself in the foot.

ABBY. Teddy, go upstairs and get that box in your aunt Martha's room. (TEDDY *starts for the stairs.*) How is Mrs. Brophy today? Mrs. Brophy has been quite ill, Dr. Harper.

BROPHY (*to* DR. HARPER). Pneumonia.

DR. HARPER. I'm sorry to hear that. (TEDDY *has reached the landing, where he stops and draws an imaginary sword.*)

TEDDY (*shouting*). Charge! (*He charges up the stairs and exits through the door to the bedrooms. The others pay no attention to this.*)

BROPHY. Oh, she's better now. A little weak still . . .

ABBY. I'm going to get you some beef broth to take to her.

BROPHY. Don't bother, Miss Abby! You've done so much for her already.

ABBY. We made it this morning. Sister Martha is taking some to poor Mr. Benitzky right now. I won't be a minute. Sit down and be comfortable, all of you. (*She goes into the kitchen.* DR. HARPER *sits again.*)

BROPHY. She shouldn't go to all that trouble.

KLEIN. Listen, try to stop her or her sister from doing something nice—and for nothing! They don't even care how you vote. (*He sits on the window seat.*)

DR. HARPER. When I received my call to Brooklyn and moved next door, my wife wasn't well. When she died—and for months before—well, if I know what pure kindness and absolute generosity are, it's because I've known the Brewster sisters. (*At this moment* TEDDY *steps out on the balcony with a large brass bugle and blows a bugle call.*)

BROPHY (*to* TEDDY). Colonel, you promised not to do that!

TEDDY. But I have to call a Cabinet meeting to get the release of those supplies. (*He wheels and exits.*)

BROPHY. He used to do that in the middle of the night. The neighbors raised Cain with us. They're a little afraid of him, anyway.

DR. HARPER. Oh, he's quite harmless.

KLEIN. Suppose he does think he's Teddy Roosevelt. There's a lot worse people he could think he was.

BROPHY. Damn shame—a nice family like this hatching a cuckoo.

KLEIN. Well, his father—the old girls' brother—was some sort of a genius, wasn't he? And their father—Teddy's grandfather—seems to me I've heard he was a little crazy, too.

BROPHY. Yeah—he was crazy like a fox. He made a million dollars.

DR. HARPER. Really? Here in Brooklyn?

BROPHY. Yeah—patent medicine. He was kind of a quack of some sort. Old Sergeant Edwards remembers him. He used the house here as sort of a clinic—tried 'em out on people.

KLEIN. Yeah, I hear he used to make mistakes occasionally, too.

BROPHY. The department never bothered him much because he was pretty useful on autopsies sometimes, especially poison cases.

KLEIN. Well, whatever he did, he left his daughters fixed for life. Thank God for that.

BROPHY. Not that they ever spend any of it on themselves.

DR. HARPER. Yes, I'm well acquainted with their charities.

KLEIN. You don't know a tenth of it. When I was with the Missing Persons Bureau I was trying to trace an old man that we never did find . . . (*Rising.*) Do you know there's a renting agency that's got this house down on its list for furnished rooms? They don't rent rooms, but you can bet that anybody who comes here looking for a room goes away with a good meal and probably a few dollars in their kick.

BROPHY. It's just their way of digging up people to do some good to. (*The door-knob rattles, the door opens and* MARTHA BREWSTER *enters.* MARTHA *is also a plump, sweet, elderly woman with Victorian charm. She is dressed in the old-fashioned manner of* ABBY, *but with a high lace collar that covers her neck.*)

MARTHA (*closing the door*). Well, isn't this nice?

BROPHY. Good afternoon, Miss Brewster.

MARTHA. How do you do, Mr. Brophy?

DR. HARPER. Good afternoon, Miss Brewster.

MARTHA. How do you do, Dr. Harper, Mr. Klein?

KLEIN. How do you do, Miss Brewster? We dropped in to get the Christmas toys.

MARTHA. Oh, yes! Teddy's Army and Navy. They wear out. They're all packed.

BROPHY. The Colonel's upstairs after them—it seems the Cabinet has to OK it.

MARTHA. Yes, of course. I hope Mrs. Brophy's better?

BROPHY. She's doing fine, ma'am! Your sister's getting some soup for me to take to her.

MARTHA. Oh, yes, we made it this morning. I just took some to a poor man who broke ever so many bones. (ABBY *enters, carrying a small pail, covered.*)

ABBY. Oh, you're back, Martha. How was Mr. Benitzky?

MARTHA. It's pretty serious, I'm afraid. The doctor was there. He's going to amputate in the morning.

ABBY (*hopefully*). Can we be present?

MARTHA. No. I asked him, but he says it's against the rules of the hospital.

DR. HARPER. You couldn't be of any service—and you must spare yourselves something. (TEDDY *enters with a box of toys and comes downstairs and puts the box down on the stool by the desk.*)

ABBY. Here's the broth, Mr. Brophy. (*She hands the pail to* BROPHY.)

BROPHY. Thank you, Miss Brewster.

ABBY. Be sure it's good and hot.

KLEIN (*looking into the box of toys*). This is fine—it'll make a lot of kids happy. (*Holding up a toy soldier.*) That O'Mally boy is nuts about soldiers.

TEDDY. That's General Miles. I've retired him. (KLEIN *holds up a toy ship.*) What's this! The *Oregon!* (*He takes the ship from* KLEIN.)

MARTHA. Put it back, dear.

TEDDY. But the *Oregon* goes to Australia.

ABBY. Now, Teddy . . .

TEDDY. No, I've given my word to Fighting Bob Evans.

MARTHA. But, Teddy . . .

KLEIN. What's the difference what kid gets it—Bobby Evans, Izzy Cohen? We'll run along, ma'am, and thank you very much. (*He picks up the box and he and* BROPHY *salute* TEDDY *and exit.*)

ABBY (*closing door*). Not at all. Good-by.

MARTHA. Good-by.

DR. HARPER. I must be getting home.

ABBY. Before you go, Doctor——

(TEDDY *has reached the landing.*)

TEDDY. Charge! (*He dashes up the stairs. At the door, he stops.*) Charge the blockhouse! (*He dashes through the door.*)

DR. HARPER. The blockhouse?

MARTHA. The stairs are always San Juan Hill.

DR. HARPER. Have you ever tried to persuade him that he wasn't Teddy Roosevelt?

ABBY. Oh, no!

MARTHA. He's so happy being Teddy Roosevelt.

ABBY. Once, a long time ago, we thought if he would be George Washington it would be a change and we suggested it to him.

MARTHA. But he stayed under his bed for days and wouldn't be anybody.

ABBY. And we'd so much rather he'd be Mr. Roosevelt than nobody.

DR. HARPER. Well, if he's happy—and what's more important, you're happy. You will see that he signs these. (*He takes some legal documents from his pocket and hands them to* ABBY.)

MARTHA. What are they?

ABBY. Dr. Harper has made all the arrangements for Teddy to go to Happy Dale Sanitarium after we pass on.

MARTHA. But why should Teddy sign any papers now?

DR. HARPER. It's better to have it all settled. If the Lord should take you away suddenly, perhaps we couldn't persuade Teddy to commit himself and that would mean an unpleasant legal procedure. Mr. Witherspoon understands they're to be filed away until the time comes to use them.

MARTHA. Mr. Witherspoon? Who's he?

DR. HARPER. He's the Superintendent of Happy Dale.

ABBY (*to* MARTHA). Dr. Harper has arranged for him to drop in tomorrow or the next day to meet Teddy.

DR. HARPER. I'd better be running along or Elaine will be over here looking for me. (*He exits.*)

ABBY. Give Elaine our love . . . (*Calling after him:*) And please don't think harshly of Mortimer because he's a dramatic critic. Somebody has to do those things.

MARTHA (*noticing the tea things*). Did you just have tea?

ABBY (*as one who has a secret*). Yes—and dinner's going to be late, too. (TEDDY *enters on the balcony.*)

MARTHA. So? Why? (TEDDY *starts downstairs.*)

ABBY. Teddy! (*He stops halfway downstairs.*) Good news for you! You're going to Panama and dig another lock for the Canal.

TEDDY. Dee-lighted! Bully! Bully, bully! I shall prepare at once for the journey. (*He turns to go upstairs, stops as if puzzled, then hurries to the landing and cries:*) Charge! (*Exits.*)

MARTHA (*elated*). Abby! While I was out?

ABBY. Yes, dear! I just couldn't wait for you. I didn't know when you'd be back and Dr. Harper was coming.

MARTHA. But all by yourself?

ABBY. Oh, I got along fine!

MARTHA. I'll run right downstairs and see! (*She starts happily for the cellar door.*)

ABBY. Oh, no, there wasn't time. I was all alone. (MARTHA *looks around the room and toward the kitchen.*)

MARTHA. Well?

ABBY. Martha . . . (*Coyly.*) You just look in the window seat. (MARTHA *almost skips to the window seat, but just as she gets there, a knock is heard on the door. She stops. They both look toward the door.* ABBY *hurries to the door and opens it.* ELAINE HARPER *enters.* ELAINE *is an attractive girl in her twenties. She looks surprisingly smart for a minister's daughter.*) Oh, it's Elaine! Come in, dear.

ELAINE. Good afternoon, Miss Abby. Good afternoon, Miss Martha. I thought Father was here.

MARTHA. He just this minute left. Didn't you meet him?

ELAINE (*pointing to the window*). No, I took the short cut through the cemetery. Mortimer hasn't come yet?

ABBY. No, dear.

ELAINE. Oh? He asked me to meet him here. Do you mind if I wait?

MARTHA (*cordially*). Not at all.

ABBY. Why don't you sit down?

MARTHA. But we really must speak to Mortimer about doing this to you.

ELAINE. Doing what?

MARTHA. He was brought up to know better. When a gentleman is taking a young lady out he should call for her at her house.

ELAINE. Oh, there's something about calling for a girl at a parsonage that discourages any man who doesn't embroider.

ABBY. He's done this too often—we're going to speak to him!

ELAINE. Don't bother! After young men whose idea of night life was to take me to prayer meeting, it's wonderful to go to the theater almost every night of my life.

MARTHA. It's comforting for us too, because if Mortimer has to see some of those plays he has to see, at least he's sitting next to a minister's daughter.

ABBY. My goodness, Elaine, what must you think of us—not having tea cleared away by this time. (*She picks up the tea tray and starts toward the kitchen.*)

MARTHA (*to* ABBY). Now don't bother with anything in the kitchen until Mortimer comes. Then I'll help you. (ABBY *exits into the kitchen. To* ELAINE:) He should be here any minute now.

ELAINE. Yes. Father must have been surprised not to find me at home—I'd better run over and say good night to him.

MARTHA. It's a shame you missed him.

ELAINE. If Mortimer comes you tell him I'll be right back. (*She has opened the door, but sees* MORTIMER *just outside.*) Hello, Mort!

(MORTIMER BREWSTER *walks in. He is a dramatic critic.*)

MORTIMER. Hello, Elaine. (*As he passes her going toward* MARTHA, *thus placing himself between* ELAINE *and* MARTHA, *he reaches back and pats* ELAINE *on the fanny.*) Hello, Aunt Martha. (*He kisses her.*)

MARTHA (*calling off*). Abby, Mortimer's here!

MORTIMER (*to* ELAINE). Were you going somewhere?

ELAINE. I was just going over to tell Father not to wait up for me.

MORTIMER. I didn't know that was still being done, even in Brooklyn.

(ELAINE *closes the door, staying inside, as* ABBY *comes in from the kitchen.*)

ABBY. Hello, Mortimer.

MORTIMER. Hello, Aunt Abby. (*He kisses her.*)

ABBY. How are you, dear?

MORTIMER. All right. And you look well. You haven't changed much since yesterday.

ABBY. It was yesterday, wasn't it? We're seeing a great deal of you lately. (*She laughs and looks at* ELAINE.) Sit down! Sit down! (*It looks as though she's going to settle down, too.*)

MARTHA (*knowingly*). Abby—haven't we something to do in the kitchen? You know—the tea things.

ABBY (*getting it*). Oh, yes! Yes! (*Backing toward kitchen, joining* MARTHA.) Well—you two just make yourselves at home. Just . . .

MARTHA. Just make yourselves at home!

(ABBY *and* MARTHA *exit happily into the kitchen.* ELAINE *moves over to* MORTIMER *ready to be kissed.*)

ELAINE. Well, can't you take a hint?

MORTIMER. No. That was pretty obvious. A lack of inventiveness, I should say.

ELAINE. Yes—that's exactly what you'd say! (*She walks away, ruffled.*)

MORTIMER (*not noticing the ruffle*). Where do you want to go for dinner?

ELAINE. I don't care. I'm not very hungry.

MORTIMER. Well, I just had breakfast. Suppose we wait until after the show?

ELAINE. But that'll make it pretty late, won't it?

MORTIMER. Not with the little stinker we're seeing tonight. From what I've heard about it, we'll be at Bleeck's by ten o'clock.

ELAINE. You ought to be fair to these plays.

MORTIMER. Are these plays fair to me?

ELAINE. I've never seen you walk out on a musical.

MORTIMER. That musical isn't opening tonight.

ELAINE (*disappointed*). No?

MORTIMER. Darling, you'll have to learn the rules. With a musical there are always four changes of title and three postponements. They liked it in New Haven but it needs a lot of work.

ELAINE. Oh, I was hoping it was a musical.

MORTIMER. You have such a light mind.

ELAINE. Not a bit! Musicals somehow have a humanizing effect on you. (*He gives her a look.*) After a serious play we join the proletariat in the subway and I listen to that lecture on the drama. After a musical you bring me home in a taxi and you make a few passes.

MORTIMER. Now wait a minute, darling, that's a very inaccurate piece of reporting.

ELAINE. Oh, I will admit that after the Behrman play you told me I had authentic beauty—and that's a hell of a thing to say to any girl. It wasn't until after our first musical you told me I had nice legs. And I have, too. (MORTIMER *stares at her legs for a moment, then walks over and kisses her.*)

MORTIMER. For a minister's daughter you know a lot about life. Where did you learn it?

ELAINE (*casually*). In the choir loft.

MORTIMER. I'll explain that to you sometime, darling—the close connection between eroticism and religion.

ELAINE. Religion never gets as high as the choir loft. Which reminds me, I'd better tell Father please not to wait up for me tonight.

MORTIMER (*almost to himself*). I've never been able to rationalize it.

ELAINE. What?

MORTIMER. My falling in love with a girl who lives in Brooklyn.

ELAINE. Falling in love? You're not stooping to the articulate, are you?

MORTIMER (*ignoring this*). The only way I can regain my self-respect is to keep you in New York.

ELAINE. Did you say keep?

MORTIMER. No, I've come to the conclusion you're holding out for the legalities.

ELAINE. I can afford to be a good girl for quite a few years yet.

MORTIMER. And I can't wait that long. Where could we get married in a hurry—say tonight!

ELAINE. I'm afraid Father will insist on officiating.

MORTIMER. Oh, God! I'll bet your father could make even the marriage service sound pedestrian.

ELAINE. Are you, by any chance, writing a review of it?

MORTIMER. Forgive me, darling. It's an occupational disease. (*She smiles at him lovingly and walks toward him. He meets her halfway and they forget themselves for a moment in a sentimental embrace and kiss. When they come out of it, he turns away from her quickly.*) I may give that show tonight a good notice!

ELAINE. Now, darling, don't pretend you love me that much. (MORTIMER *looks at her with polite lechery.*)

MORTIMER. Be sure to tell your father not to wait up tonight.

ELAINE (*aware that she can't trust either of them*). I think tonight I'd better tell him to wait up.

MORTIMER (*reassuringly*). Darling, I'll telephone Winchell to publish the banns.

ELAINE. Nevertheless . . .

MORTIMER. All right, everything formal and legal. But not later than next month.

ELAINE. Darling. (*She kisses him.*) I'll talk it over with Father and set the date.

MORTIMER. Oh, no! We'll have to consult the Zolotow list. There'll be a lot of other first nights in October.

(TEDDY *enters from above and comes down the stairs carrying his bugle and dressed in tropical clothes and a solar topee. He sees* MORTIMER.)

TEDDY. Hello, Mortimer! (*He goes to* MORTIMER *and they shake hands.*)

MORTIMER (*gravely*). How are you, Mr. President?

TEDDY. Bully, thank you. Just bully. What news have you brought me?

MORTIMER. Just this, Mr. President —the country is squarely behind you.

TEDDY (*beaming*). Yes, I know. Isn't it wonderful? (*He shakes* MORTIMER'*s hand again.*) Well, good-by. (*He shakes hands with* ELAINE.) Good-by.

ELAINE. Where are you off to, Teddy?

TEDDY. Panama. (*He exits through the cellar door.* ELAINE *looks at* MORTIMER *inquiringly.*)

MORTIMER. Panama's the cellar. He digs locks for the Canal down there.

ELAINE. You're so sweet with him— and he's very fond of you.

MORTIMER. Well, Teddy was always my favorite brother.

ELAINE. Favorite? Were there more of you?

MORTIMER. There's another brother —Jonathan.

ELAINE. I never heard of him. Your aunts never mention him.

MORTIMER. No, we don't like to talk about Jonathan. He left Brooklyn very early—by request. Jonathan was the kind of boy who liked to cut worms in two—with his teeth.

ELAINE (*shuddering*). What became of him?

MORTIMER. I don't know. He wanted to be a surgeon like Grandfather, but he wouldn't go to medical school—and his practice got him into trouble.

(ABBY *enters from the kitchen.*)

ABBY. Aren't you going to be late for the theater?

MORTIMER. We're skipping dinner. (*Consulting his wrist watch, then to* ELAINE:) We won't have to start for half an hour.

ABBY. Then I'll leave you two alone again.

ELAINE. Don't bother, darling. I'm going to run over to speak to Father. (*To* MORTIMER:) Before I go out with you, he likes to pray over me a little. I'll be right back—I'll cut through the cemetery.

MORTIMER. Well, if the prayer isn't too long, I'd have time to lead you beside distilled waters. (*She laughs, and exits.*)

ABBY (*happily*). That's the first time I ever heard you quote the Bible! We knew Elaine would be a good influence on you.

MORTIMER. Oh, by the way—I'm going to marry her.

ABBY. Oh, Mortimer! (*She runs to him and embraces him. Then she dashes to the kitchen door, as* MORTIMER *crosses toward the window.*) Martha, Martha! Come right in here! I've got wonderful news for you! (MARTHA *hurries in from the kitchen.*) Mortimer and Elaine are going to be married!

MARTHA. Married! Oh, Mortimer. (*She runs over to* MORTIMER, *who is looking out the window, embraces and kisses him.*)

ABBY. We hoped it would happen just like this!

MARTHA. Elaine must be the happiest girl in the world!

MORTIMER (*looking out the window*). Happy! Just look at her leaping over those gravestones! (*He and* ABBY *wave to* ELAINE, *outside. He starts to turn away from the window but his attention is drawn to something.*) Say! What's that?

MARTHA (*looking out*). What's what, dear?

MORTIMER. See that statue there? That's a horundinida carnina.

MARTHA. Oh, no—that's Emma B. Stout ascending to heaven.

MORTIMER. No—standing on Mrs. Stout's left ear. That bird—that's a red-crested swallow. I've only seen one of those before in my life.

ABBY. I don't know how you can think of birds now—with Elaine and the engagement and everything.

MORTIMER. It's a vanishing species. Thoreau was very fond of them. By the way, I left a large envelope around here last week. It's one of the chapters of my book on Thoreau. Have you seen it?

MARTHA. Well, if you left it here, it must be here somewhere.

(MORTIMER *starts searching the room, looking in drawers, cupboards, desks, etc.*)

ABBY. When are you going to be married? What are your plans? There must be something more you can tell us about Elaine.

MORTIMER. Elaine? Oh, yes, Elaine thought it was brilliant.

MARTHA. What, Mortimer?

MORTIMER. My chapter on Thoreau!

ABBY. Well, when Elaine comes back I think we ought to have a little celebration. We must drink to your happiness. Martha, isn't there some of that Lady Baltimore cake left?

MARTHA. Oh, yes!

ABBY. And we'll open a bottle of wine.

MARTHA. And to think that it happened in this room! (*She exits into the kitchen.*)

MORTIMER. Now, where could I have put that . . .

ABBY. Well, with your fiancée sitting beside you tonight, I do hope the play will be something you can enjoy for once. It may be something romantic. What's the name of it?

(MORTIMER *is still searching for the envelope with the chapter in it.*)

MORTIMER. *Murder Will Out!*

ABBY. Oh, dear! (*She disappears into the kitchen.* MORTIMER *doesn't notice her absence and goes on talking. He is beside the window seat.*)

MORTIMER. When the curtain goes up the first thing you see will be a dead body . . . (*He lifts the window seat and sees one. Not believing it, he drops the window seat again and turns away. He looks back quickly toward the window seat, opens it again, stares in. He goes slightly mad for a moment. He drops the window seat again and sits on it, as if to hold it down.* ABBY *comes into the room, carrying the silencer and tablecloth, which she puts on a chair and turns to the table, clearing it of its impedimenta. When* MORTIMER *speaks to her it is in a somewhat strained voice.*) Aunt Abby!

ABBY. Yes, dear.

MORTIMER. You were going to make plans for Teddy to go to that sanitarium—Happy Dale.

ABBY. Yes, dear, it's all arranged. Dr. Harper was here today and brought the things for Teddy to sign. Here they are. (*She takes the papers from the sideboard and hands them to him.*)

MORTIMER. He's got to sign them right away.

ABBY. That's what Dr. Harper thinks . . . (MARTHA *enters from the kitchen, carrying a tray with the table silver. Throughout the scene the two sisters go ahead setting the table—three places.*) Then there won't be any legal difficulties after we pass on.

MORTIMER (*glancing through the papers*). He's got to sign them this minute! He's down in the cellar—get him up here right away.

MARTHA. There's no such hurry as that.

ABBY. When he starts working on the Canal you can't get his mind on anything else.

MORTIMER. Teddy's got to go to Happy Dale now—tonight!

MARTHA. Oh, no, Mortimer! That's not until after we're gone!

MORTIMER. Right away, I tell you! —right away!

ABBY. Mortimer, how can you say such a thing? Why, as long as we live we won't be separated from Teddy.

MORTIMER (*trying to be calm*). Listen, darlings, I'm frightfully sorry, but I've got some shocking news for you. (*The sisters stop work and look at him with some interest.*) Now, we've all got to try to keep our heads. You know, we've sort of humored Teddy because we thought he was harmless.

MARTHA. Why, he *is* harmless!

MORTIMER. He *was* harmless. That's why he has to go to Happy Dale—why he has to be confined.

ABBY. Mortimer, why have you suddenly turned against Teddy?—your own brother!

MORTIMER. You've got to know sometime. It might as well be now. Teddy's killed a man.

MARTHA. Nonsense, dear.

(MORTIMER *rises and points to the window seat.*)

MORTIMER. There's a body in the window seat!

ABBY (*not at all surprised*). Yes, dear, we know.

MORTIMER. You *know?*

MARTHA. Of course, dear, but it has nothing to do with Teddy. (*Relieved, they resume setting the table.*)

ABBY. Now, Mortimer, just forget about it—forget you ever saw the gentleman.

MORTIMER. Forget!

ABBY. We never dreamed you'd peek.

MORTIMER. But who is he?

ABBY. His name's Hoskins—Adam Hoskins. That's about all I know about him—except that he's a Methodist.

MORTIMER. That's all you know about him? Well, what's he doing here? What happened to him?

MARTHA. He died.

MORTIMER. Aunt Martha, men don't just get into window seats and die.

ABBY. No, he died first.

MORTIMER. But how?

ABBY. Mortimer, don't be so inquisitive! The gentleman died because he drank some wine with poison in it.

MORTIMER. How did the poison get in the wine?

MARTHA. We put it in wine because it's less noticeable. When it's in tea it has a distinct odor.

MORTIMER. *You* put it in the wine?

ABBY. Yes. And I put Mr. Hoskins in the window seat because Dr. Harper was coming.

MORTIMER. So you knew what you'd done! You didn't want Dr. Harper to see the body!

ABBY. Not at tea! That wouldn't have been very nice! Now you know the whole thing and you can forget all about it. I think Martha and I have the right to our own little secrets.

MARTHA. And don't you tell Elaine! (MORTIMER *stands looking at his aunts, stunned.* MARTHA *turns to* ABBY.) Oh, Abby, while I was out I dropped in on Mrs. Schultz. She's much better, but she would like to have us take Junior to the movies again.

ABBY. We must do that tomorrow or the next day. (*They start toward the kitchen.*)

MARTHA. This time we'll go where *we* want to go. Junior's not going to drag me into another one of those scary pictures.

ABBY. They shouldn't be allowed to make pictures just to frighten people. (*They exit into the kitchen.* MORTIMER, *dazed, looks around the room, goes to the telephone and dials a number.*)

MORTIMER (*into telephone*). City desk. . . . Hello, Al. Do you know who this is? (*Pause.*) That's right. Say, Al, when I left the office, I told you where I was going, remember? (*Pause.*) Well, where did I say? (*Pause.*) Uh-huh. Well, it would take me about half an hour to get to Brooklyn. What time have you got? (*He looks at his watch.*) That's right. I must be here. (*He hangs up, sits for a minute looking round the room, then suddenly leaps out of the chair toward the kitchen.*) Aunt Martha! Aunt Abby! Come in here! (*The two sisters bustle in.* MORTIMER *turns to them in great excitement.*) What are we going to do? What are we going to do?

MARTHA. What are we going to do about what, dear?

MORTIMER. There's a body in there.

ABBY. Yes, Mr. Hoskins'.

MORTIMER. Good God, I can't turn you over to the police. But what am I going to do?

MARTHA. Well, for one thing, stop being so excited.

ABBY. And for pity's sake stop worrying. We told you to forget the whole thing.

MORTIMER. Forget it? My dear Aunt Abby, can't I make you realize that something has to be done!

ABBY (*a little sharply*). Mortimer, you behave yourself! You're too old to be flying off the handle like this!

MORTIMER. But Mr. Hotchkiss . . .

ABBY. Hoskins, dear.

MORTIMER. Well, whatever his name is, you can't leave him there.

MARTHA. We don't intend to, dear.

ABBY. Teddy's down in the cellar now digging a lock.

MORTIMER. You mean you're going to bury Mr. Hotchkiss in the cellar?

MARTHA. Why, of course, dear. That's what we did with the others.

MORTIMER. Aunt Martha, you can't bury Mr. . . . Others?

ABBY. The other gentlemen.

MORTIMER. When you say others—do you mean—others? More than one others?

MARTHA. Oh, yes, dear. Let me see, this is eleven, isn't it, Abby?

ABBY. No, dear, this makes twelve.

(MORTIMER *backs up and sinks stunned on the stool beside the desk.*)

MARTHA. Oh, I think you're wrong, Abby. This is only eleven.

ABBY. No. When Mr. Hoskins first came in, it occurred to me that he would make a round dozen.

MARTHA. Well, you really shouldn't count the first one.

ABBY. Oh, *I* was counting the first one. So that makes it twelve.

(*The telephone rings.* MORTIMER, *in a daze, turns toward it and without picking up the receiver speaks.*)

MORTIMER. Hello! (*It rings the second time and he realizes it's the telephone and picks up the receiver.*) Hello. Oh, hello, Al. My, it's good to hear your voice!

ABBY (*to* MARTHA). But he is in the cellar, dear.

MORTIMER (*to aunts*). Ssh! (*Into telephone:*) Oh, no, Al, I'm as sober as a lark. No, I just called you because I was feeling a little Pirandello. Pirandel . . . You wouldn't know, Al. Look, I'm glad you called. Get hold of George right away. He's got to review the play tonight. I can't make it. No, you're wrong, Al. I'll tell you about it tomorrow . . . No— Well, George has got to cover the play tonight! This is my department and I'm running it! You get hold of George! (*He hangs up and sits for a moment, trying to collect himself.*) Now, let's see, where were we? (*He suddenly leaps from his chair.*) *Twelve!*

MARTHA. Yes, Abby thinks we ought to count the first one and that makes twelve.

MORTIMER. Now, let me get this. . . . (*Grabs* MARTHA *and sits her in a chair.*) Who was the first one?

ABBY. Mr. Midgely. He was a Baptist.

MARTHA. Of course, I still think we can't take full credit for him because he just died.

ABBY. Martha means without any help from us. You see, Mr. Midgely came here looking for a room.

MARTHA. It was right after you moved to New York.

ABBY. And it didn't seem right that your nice room should go to waste when there were so many people who needed it.

MARTHA. He was such a lonely old man.

ABBY. All his kith and kin were dead and it left him so forlorn and unhappy.

MARTHA. We felt so sorry for him.

ABBY. And then when his heart attack came, and he sat dead in that chair, so peaceful—remember, Martha?—well, we decided then and there that if we could help other lonely old men to find that peace, we would.

(MORTIMER *is immersed in their story for a moment.*)

MORTIMER. He dropped dead, right in that chair. How awful for you!

MARTHA. Not at all! It was rather like old times. Your grandfather always used to have a cadaver or two around the house. You see, Teddy had been digging in Panama and he thought Mr. Midgely was a yellow fever victim.

ABBY. That meant he had to be buried immediately.

MARTHA. So we all took him down to Panama and put him in the lock. (*Rising.*) You see, that's why we told you not to bother about it. We know exactly what's to be done.

MORTIMER. And that's how all this started? That man walking in here and dropping dead?

ABBY. Well, we realized we couldn't depend on that happening again.

MARTHA. Remember those jars of poison that have been up on the shelves in Grandfather's laboratory all these years?

ABBY. You know the knack your Aunt Martha has for mixing things. You've eaten enough of her piccalilli!

MARTHA. Well, Mortimer, for a gallon of elderberry wine I take a teaspoonful of arsenic, and add a half-teaspoonful of strychnine, and then just a pinch of cyanide.

MORTIMER (*appraisingly*). Should have quite a kick.

ABBY. As a matter of fact, one of our gentlemen found time to say, "How delicious!"

MARTHA. Well, I'll have to get things started in the kitchen. (*She starts out.*)

ABBY (*to* MORTIMER). I wish you could stay to dinner, dear.

MARTHA. I'm trying out a new recipe.

MORTIMER. I couldn't eat a thing.

(MARTHA *exits into the kitchen.*)

ABBY (*calling after* MARTHA). I'll come and help you. (*She turns to* MORTIMER, *relieved.*) Well, I feel better now that you understand. You have to wait for Elaine, don't you? (*She smiles.*) How happy you must be! I'll leave you alone with your thoughts. (ABBY *exits, smiling.*)

(MORTIMER *stands dazed and then summons his courage and goes to the window seat, opens it and peeks in, then closes it and backs away. He backs around the table and is still looking at the window seat when there is a knock on the door, immediately followed by* ELAINE'S *entrance. This, however, does not arouse him from his thought. She smiles at him softly.*)

ELAINE. I'm sorry I took so long, dear. (*She starts slowly toward him. As she approaches he looks in her direction and as her presence dawns on him he speaks.*)

MORTIMER. Oh, it's you!

ELAINE. Don't be cross, darling! Father saw I was excited—so I told him about us and that made it hard for me to get away. (*She goes to him and puts her arm around him.*) But, listen, darling—he's not going to wait up for me tonight.

MORTIMER. Elaine—you run on back home and I'll call you up tomorrow.

ELAINE. Tomorrow!

MORTIMER (*irritated*). You know I always call you up every day or two.

ELAINE. But we're going to the theater tonight.

MORTIMER. No—no, we're not.

ELAINE. Well, why not?

MORTIMER. Elaine, something's come up.

ELAINE. What, darling? Mortimer—you've lost your job!

MORTIMER. No—no! I haven't lost my job! I'm just not covering the play tonight. Now, you run along home, Elaine.

ELAINE. But I've got to know what's happened. Certainly, you can tell me.

MORTIMER. No, I can't, dear.

ELAINE. But if we're going to be married . . .

MORTIMER. Married?

ELAINE. Have you forgotten that not fifteen minutes ago you proposed to me?

MORTIMER. I did? Oh—yes! Well, as far as I know, that's still on. But you go home now. I've got to do something.

ELAINE. Listen, you can't propose to me one minute and throw me out of the house the next.

MORTIMER. I'm not throwing you out of the house, darling. Will you get out of here?

ELAINE. No, I won't get out of here. Not until I've had some kind of explanation! (*She stalks across the room and almost sits on the window seat. He intercepts her.*)

MORTIMER. Elaine! (*The telephone rings. He goes to it and answers.*) Hello! Oh, hello, Al. Hold on just a minute, will you, Al? I'll be right with you. All right, it's important! But it can wait a minute, can't it? Hold on! (*He puts the receiver down on the table and goes back to* ELAINE.) Elaine, you're a sweet girl and I love you. But I have something on my mind now and I want you to go home and wait until I call you.

ELAINE. Don't try to be masterful!

MORTIMER (*annoyed to the point of being literate*). When we're married and I have problems to face I hope you're less tedious and uninspired!

ELAINE. And when we're married, *if* we're married, I hope I find you adequate. (*She exits.*)

MORTIMER. Elaine! (*She doesn't answer him so he runs out on the porch and we hear:*) Elaine! (*He runs back in, slamming the door after him, and runs across to call to her out of the window. When he kneels on the window seat, he remembers Mr. Hoskins and starts for the kitchen, then he remembers "Al" is waiting on the telephone. He hurries across the room and picks up the receiver.*) Al. . . . Al. . . . (*He hangs up and starts to dial again, when the doorbell rings. He lifts the receiver and speaks into it.*) Hello . . . Hello . . .

(ABBY *enters from the kitchen, followed by* MARTHA.)

ABBY. It's the doorbell ringing. (*She goes to door and opens it, as* MORTIMER *hangs up and starts to dial.*) How do you do? Come in.

(MR. GIBBS *enters. A very disgruntled old man.*)

GIBBS. I understand you have a room to rent.

ABBY. Yes. Won't you step in?

GIBBS. Are you the lady of the house?

ABBY. Yes, I'm Miss Brewster. This is my sister, another Miss Brewster.

GIBBS. My name is Gibbs.

ABBY. Oh, won't you sit down? I'm sorry we're just setting the table for dinner.

MORTIMER (*into the telephone*). Hello . . . Let me talk to Al again. City desk! Al! City desk! What . . . I'm sorry . . . wrong number. (*He hangs up and dials again.*)

GIBBS. May I see the room?

MARTHA. Why don't you sit down and let's get acquainted?

GIBBS. That won't do much good if I don't like the room.

ABBY. Is Brooklyn your home?

GIBBS. Haven't got a home. Live in a hotel. Don't like it.

MORTIMER (*into the telephone*). Hello. City desk.

MARTHA. Are your family Brooklyn people?

GIBBS. Haven't got any family.

ABBY. All alone in the world. Why, Martha . . . (MARTHA *crosses to the sideboard for the wine.)* Well, you've come to just the right place. Do sit down. *(She eases* GIBBS *into a chair by the table.)*

MORTIMER *(into the telephone).* Hello. Al, Mort. We got cut off. . . . Al, I can't cover the play tonight. That's all there is to it. I can't.

MARTHA. What church do you go to? There's an Episcopal church practically next door.

GIBBS. I'm Presbyterian. Used to be.

MORTIMER *(into the telephone).* What's George doing in Bermuda? Certainly, I told him he could go to Bermuda. . . . It's my department, isn't it? Well, Al, you've got to get somebody. Who else is there around the office?

GIBBS. *(rising).* Is there always this much noise?

MARTHA. Oh, he doesn't live with us.

MORTIMER *(into the telephone).* There must be somebody around the place. How about the office boy? You know, the bright one. The one we don't like. Well, look around the office . . . I'll hold on.

GIBBS. I'd really like to see the room.

ABBY. It's upstairs. Won't you try a glass of our wine before we start up?

GIBBS. Never touch it.

MARTHA. We make this ourselves. It's elderberry wine.

GIBBS *(to* MARTHA*).* Elderberry. *(Looking at the wine.)* Haven't tasted elderberry wine since I was a boy. Thank you. *(He sits.* ABBY *pours a glass of wine for* MR. GIBBS.*)*

MORTIMER *(into the telephone).* Well, there must be some printers around. Look, Al, the fellow who sets my copy. He ought to know about what I'd write. His name is Joe. He's the third machine from the left. . . . But, Al, he might turn out to be another Burns Mantle!

GIBBS. Do you have your own elderberry bushes?

MARTHA. No, but the cemetery's full of them.

MORTIMER *(into the telephone).* No, I'm not drinking, but I'm going to start now. *(He hangs up and starts for the sideboard. When he sees the wine bottle on the table, he rushes and gets a glass from the sideboard and starts pouring himself a glass of wine.)*

MARTHA *(seeing* MORTIMER *pouring the poisoned wine).* Mortimer, eh . . . eh . . . eh!

MORTIMER *(engrossed in pouring the wine).* Huh?

MARTHA *(to* MORTIMER*).* Eh . . . eh . . . eh! . . .

ABBY *(seeing what* MORTIMER *is doing).* Mortimer! Not that! *(She drags his arm down as he is about to drink.* MORTIMER *puts his glass down, then realizes that it must be the poisoned wine. Suddenly, he sees* MR. GIBBS *is about to drink.* MORTIMER *utters a blood-curdling cry and points his finger at* MR. GIBBS, *who puts his glass down on the table and stares at* MORTIMER, *terrified.*)

MORTIMER. Get out of here! Do you want to be killed? Do you want to be poisoned? Do you want to be murdered? (*In the middle of the above speech,* MR. GIBBS *starts to run and dashes out of the house, with* MORTIMER *chasing him.* MORTIMER *slams the door behind* MR. GIBBS *and leans against it weakly.*)

ABBY (*to* MORTIMER). Now, you've spoiled everything.

MORTIMER. You can't do things like that! I don't know how I can explain this to you. But it's not only against the law, it's wrong! It's not a nice thing to do! People wouldn't understand. *He* wouldn't understand.

MARTHA. Abby, we shouldn't have told Mortimer.

MORTIMER. What I mean is . . . Well—this has developed into a very bad habit.

ABBY. Now, Mortimer, we don't try to stop you from doing the things you like to do. I don't see why you should interfere with us.

(*The telephone rings.* MORTIMER *answers it.*)

MORTIMER (*into the telephone*). Hello? Yes, Al. . . . All right, Al, I'll see the first act and I'll pan the hell out of it. But, Al, you've got to do this for me. Get hold of O'Brien. Our lawyer . . . the head of our legal department! Have him meet me at the theater. Now, don't let me down. O.K. I'm starting now. (*He hangs up, then speaks to his aunts.*) I've got to go to the theater. I can't get out of it. But before I go will you promise me something?

MARTHA. We'd have to know what it was first.

MORTIMER. I love you very much and I know you love me. You know I'd do anything in the world for you and I want you to do this little thing for me.

ABBY. What do you want us to do?

MORTIMER. Don't do anything. I mean—don't do anything! Don't let anyone in the house—and leave Mr. Hoskins right where he is.

MARTHA. Why?

MORTIMER. I want time to think—and I've quite a little to think about. You know I wouldn't want anything to happen to you.

ABBY. Well, what on earth could happen to us?

MORTIMER. Anyway—you'll do that for me, won't you?

MARTHA. Well, we were planning to hold services before dinner.

MORTIMER. Services?

MARTHA (*a little indignant*). You don't think we'd bury Mr. Hoskins without a full Methodist service? He was a Methodist.

MORTIMER. Can't that wait until I get back?

ABBY. Oh, then you could join us!

MORTIMER. Yes! Yes!

ABBY. You'll enjoy the services, Mortimer—especially the hymns. (*To* MARTHA): Remember how beautifully Mortimer sang in the choir before his voice changed?

MORTIMER. And you're not going to let anybody in the house until I get back? It's a promise.

MARTHA. Well . . .

ABBY. Oh, Martha—we can do that now that Mortimer's co-operating with us. All right, Mortimer.

MORTIMER. Have you got any paper? (ABBY *goes to the desk and gets a sheet of stationery.*) I'll be back as soon as I can. (MORTIMER *takes out the commitment papers, looks at them.*) There's a man I've got to see.

ABBY. Here's some stationery. Will this do?

MORTIMER (*taking it*). That's fine. I can save some time if I write my review on the way to the theater. (*He hurries out.* MARTHA *closes the door behind him.* ABBY *returns to setting the table.*)

MARTHA. Mortimer didn't seem quite himself today.

ABBY (*lighting the candelabra*). Well, that's only natural—I think I know why.

MARTHA (*going up to landing to close the drapes on the window of the landing*). Why?

ABBY. He's just become engaged to be married. I suppose that always makes a man nervous.

MARTHA. I'm so happy for Elaine. And their honeymoon ought to give Mortimer a real vacation. I don't think he got much rest this summer. (*She comes down into the room again, turns off the electric lights, straightens the telephone on the desk, lights the standing lamp beside the desk.*)

ABBY. Well, at least he didn't go kiting off to China or Spain.

MARTHA. I could never understand why he wanted to go to those places.

ABBY. Well, I think to Mortimer the theater has always seemed pretty small potatoes. He needs something really big to criticize—something like the human race.

MARTHA. Abby, if Mortimer's coming back for the services for Mr. Hoskins, we'll need another hymnal. There's one in my room. (*She starts upstairs.*)

ABBY. It's really my turn to read the services, but since you weren't here when Mr. Hoskins came I want you to do it. (MARTHA *stops on the stairs.*)

MARTHA (*pleased*). That's very nice of you, dear. Are you sure you want me to?

ABBY. It's only fair.

MARTHA. I think I'll wear my black bombazine—and Mother's old brooch. (*She starts up again and* ABBY *starts toward the kitchen. The doorbell rings.*)

ABBY. I'll go, dear.

MARTHA (*hushed*). We promised Mortimer we wouldn't let anyone in.

ABBY. Who do you suppose it is?

MARTHA. Wait a minute—I'll look. (*She is at the landing and turns to the landing window and peeks out the curtains.*) It's two men—and I've never seen them before.

ABBY. Are you sure?

MARTHA (*peeking out again*). There's a car at the curb—they must have come in that.

ABBY. Let me look! (*She hurries up the stairs. There is a knock at the door.* ABBY *peeks out the window.*)

MARTHA. Do you recognize them?

ABBY. They're strangers to me.

MARTHA. We'll just have to pretend we're not home. (*There is another knock, then the door is slowly opened and a tall man walks into the center of the room. He walks in with assurance and ease as though the room were familiar to him. He stands and looks about him—in every direction but that of the stairs. There is something sinister about the man—something that brings a slight chill in his presence. It is in his walk, his bearing and his strange resemblance to Boris Karloff. From the stair landing,* ABBY *and* MARTHA *watch him, almost afraid to speak. Having completed his survey of the room, the man turns and addresses someone outside the front door.*)

JONATHAN. Come in, Doctor. (DR. EINSTEIN *enters. He is somewhat ratty in his appearance. His face wears the benevolent smirk of a man who lives in a haze of alcohol. There is something about him that suggests the unfrocked priest. He stands just inside the door, timid but expectant.*) This is the home of my youth. (DR. EINSTEIN *looks about him timidly.*) As a boy, I couldn't wait to escape from this house. And now I'm glad to escape back into it.

EINSTEIN. Yah, Chonny, it's a good hideout.

JONATHAN. The family must still live here. There's something so unmistakably Brewster about the Brewsters. I hope there's a fatted calf awaiting the return of the prodigal.

EINSTEIN. Yah, I'm hungry. (*He sees the fatted calf in the form of the two glasses of wine.*) Look, Chonny! Drinks!

JONATHAN. As if we were expected! A good omen. (EINSTEIN *almost scampers to the table, passing* JONATHAN, *also on his way to the table. As they are about to reach for the glasses,* ABBY *speaks.*)

ABBY. Who are you? What are you doing here? (EINSTEIN *and* JONATHAN *turn and see the two sisters.*)

JONATHAN. Aunt Abby! Aunt Martha! It's Jonathan.

MARTHA. You get out of here.

JONATHAN. I'm Jonathan! Your nephew, Jonathan!

ABBY. Oh, no, you're not! You're nothing like Jonathan, so don't pretend you are! You just get out of here! (*A little belligerent, she comes two or three steps down the stairs.*)

JONATHAN. Yes, Aunt Abby. I *am* Jonathan. And this is Dr. Einstein.

ABBY. And he's not Dr. Einstein either.

JONATHAN. Not Dr. Albert Einstein —Dr. Herman Einstein.

ABBY. Who are you? You're not our nephew, Jonathan!

JONATHAN. I see you're still wearing the lovely garnet ring that Grandma Brewster bought in England. (ABBY *gasps, looks at the ring and then looks toward* MARTHA.) And you, Aunt Martha, still the high collar—to hide the scar where Grandfather's acid burned you. (MARTHA'S *hand goes to her throat. The two sisters stare at each other, then back at* JONATHAN.)

MARTHA. His voice is like Jonathan's.

ABBY. Have you been in an accident?

JONATHAN. No . . . (*His hand goes up to his neck.*) My face . . . (*He clouds.*) Dr. Einstein is responsible for that. (*The two sisters look at* EINSTEIN.) He's a plastic surgeon. (*Flatly.*) He changes people's faces.

MARTHA. But I've seen that face before. (*To* ABBY): Remember when we took the little Schultz boy to the movies—and I was so frightened. It was that face! (JONATHAN *grows tense and looks toward* EINSTEIN.)

EINSTEIN. Easy, Chonny—easy! (*He goes quickly between* JONATHAN *and his aunts.*) Don't worry! The last five years I give Chonny three faces. I give him another one right away. The last face—I saw that picture, too—chust before I operate. And I was intoggsicated.

JONATHAN (*with a growing and dangerous intensity*). You see, Doctor—what you've done to me. Even my own family . . .

EINSTEIN (*to calm him*). Chonny—you're home!—in this lofely house! (*To the aunts*): How many times he tells me about Brooklyn—about this house—about his aunts that he lofes so much! (*To* JONATHAN): They know you, Chonny. (*To the aunts:*) You know it's Chonny. Speak to him! Tell him so! (ABBY *starts slowly downstairs.*)

ABBY. Well—Jonathan—it's been a long time—what have you been doing all these years? (MARTHA *starts to follow her cautiously.*)

MARTHA. Yes, Jonathan, where have you been?

JONATHAN (*recovering his composure*). England, South Africa, Australia—the last five years, Chicago. Dr. Einstein and I have been in business together there.

ABBY. Oh! We were in Chicago for the World's Fair.

MARTHA (*for want of something to say*). We found Chicago awfully warm.

EINSTEIN. Yah—it got hot for us, too.

JONATHAN (*turning on the charm*). It's wonderful to be in Brooklyn again. And you—Abby—Martha—

you don't look a day older. Just as I remembered you—sweet, charming, hospitable. (*They exchange a quick look.*) And dear Teddy? (*He indicates with his hand a lad of eight or ten.*) Did he go into politics? (*Turns to* EINSTEIN.) My little brother, Doctor, was determined to become President.

ABBY. Oh, Teddy's fine! Just fine. Mortimer's well, too.

JONATHAN (*grimly*). I know about Mortimer. I've seen his picture at the head of his column. He's evidently fulfilled all the promise of his early nasty nature.

ABBY (*defensively*). We're very fond of Mortimer. (*There is a pause.*)

MARTHA (*uneasily*). Well, Jonathan, it's very nice to have seen you again.

JONATHAN (*expanding*). Bless you, Aunt Martha! It's good to be home again. (*He sits down. The two women look at each other with dismay.*)

ABBY. Martha, we mustn't let what's on the stove boil over. (*She tugs at* MARTHA.)

MARTHA. Yes. If you'll excuse us for just a minute, Jonathan—unless you're in a hurry to go somewhere. (JONATHAN *looks at her balefully.* ABBY *exits to the kitchen taking the glasses of wine with her.* MARTHA *takes the bottle of wine from the table, puts it in the compartment of the sideboard, then hurries out after* ABBY.)

EINSTEIN. Well, Chonny, where do we go from here? We got to think fast. The *police!* They got pictures of that face. I got to operate on you right away. We got to find some place—and we got to find some place for Mr. Spenalzo, too.

JONATHAN. Don't waste any worry on that rat.

EINSTEIN. But, Chonny, we got a hot stiff on our hands.

JONATHAN. Forget Mr. Spenalzo!

EINSTEIN. But we can't leave a dead body in the rumble seat! You shouldn't have killed him, Chonny. He's a nice fellow—he giffs us a lift—and what happens . . . ? (*He gestures strangulation.*)

JONATHAN. He said I looked like Boris Karloff. That's your work, Doctor. You did that to me.

EINSTEIN. Now, Chonny—we find a place somewhere—I fix you up quick.

JONATHAN. Tonight!

EINSTEIN. Chonny, I got to eat first. I'm hungry. I'm weak. (ABBY *enters and comes spunkily up to* JONATHAN. MARTHA *hovers in the doorway.*)

ABBY. Jonathan, we're glad that you remembered us and took the trouble to come and say "Hello." But you were never happy in this house and we were never happy while you were here. So we've just come in to say good-by.

JONATHAN (*smoothly*). Aunt Abby, I can't say your feeling toward me comes as a surprise. I've spent a great many hours regretting the heartaches I must have given you as a boy.

ABBY. You were quite a trial to us, Jonathan.

JONATHAN. But my great disappointment is for Dr. Einstein. (*The aunts look at* EINSTEIN.) I promised him that no matter how rushed we were in passing through Brooklyn, I would take the time to bring him here for one of Aunt Martha's home-cooked dinners. (MARTHA *rises to this a bit.*)

MARTHA. Oh?

ABBY. I'm sorry. I'm afraid there wouldn't be enough.

MARTHA. Abby, it's a good-sized pot-roast.

JONATHAN. Pot-roast!

MARTHA. I think the least we can do is . . .

JONATHAN. Thank you, Aunt Martha! We'll stay to dinner!

ABBY. Well, we'll hurry it along.

MARTHA. Yes! (*She exits into the kitchen.*)

ABBY. If you want to freshen up, Jonathan—why don't you use the washroom in Grandfather's laboratory?

JONATHAN. Is that still there?

ABBY. Oh, yes! Just as he left it. Well, I'll help Martha get things started—since we're all in a hurry. (*She exits into kitchen.*)

EINSTEIN. Vell, ve get a meal, anyway.

JONATHAN. Grandfather's laboratory! (*He looks upstairs.*) And just as it was! Doctor, a perfect operating room!

EINSTEIN. Too bad we can't use it.

JONATHAN. After you finished with me . . . Doctor, we could make a fortune here! The laboratory—that large ward in the attic—ten beds, Doctor—and Brooklyn is crying for your talents.

EINSTEIN. Why work yourself up, Chonny? Anyway, for Brooklyn we're a year too late.

JONATHAN. You don't know this town, Doctor. Practically everybody in Brooklyn needs a new face.

EINSTEIN. But so many of the old faces are locked up.

JONATHAN. A very small percentage—and the boys in Brooklyn are famous for paying generously to stay out of jail.

EINSTEIN. Take it easy, Chonny. Your aunts—they don't want us here.

JONATHAN. We're here for dinner, aren't we?

EINSTEIN. Yah—but after dinner?

JONATHAN. Leave that to me, Doctor, I'll handle it. This house will be our headquarters for years.

EINSTEIN. Oh, that would be beautiful, Chonny! This nice quiet house! Those aunts of yours—what sweet ladies! I lofe them already. (*Starts to the door.*) I get the bags, yah?

JONATHAN. Doctor! We must wait until we're invited.

EINSTEIN. But you chust said . . .

JONATHAN. We'll be invited.

EINSTEIN. And if they say no?

JONATHAN (*grimly*). Doctor—two helpless old women . . . ? (*He sits on the sofa.*)

EINSTEIN (*taking out flask, and relaxing on the window seat*). It's like comes true a beautiful dream. Only I hope you're not dreaming. (*Takes a swig from the flask*) It's so peaceful.

JONATHAN (*stretching out on the sofa*). Yes, Doctor, that's what makes this house so perfect for us. It's so peaceful. (TEDDY *enters from the cellar, blows a blast on his bugle, then marches to the stairs and on up to the landing as the two men look at his tropical garb with some astonishment.*)

TEDDY (*on the landing*). Charge! (*He rushes up the stairs and off through the balcony door.* JONATHAN *has risen, watching him.* EINSTEIN *stares and takes another hasty swig from his flask.*)

CURTAIN

ACT TWO

JONATHAN, *smoking an after-dinner cigar, is occupying the most comfortable chair, completely at his ease.* ABBY *and* MARTHA, *sitting together on the window seat, are giving him a nervous attention in the attitude of people who wish their guests would go home.* EINSTEIN *is relaxed and happy. The dinner dishes have been cleared and the room has been restored to order.*

JONATHAN. Yes, those five years in Chicago were the busiest and happiest of my life.

EINSTEIN. And from Chicago, we go to South Bend, Indiana. (*He shakes his head as though he wishes they hadn't.* JONATHAN *gives him a look.*)

JONATHAN. They wouldn't be interested in our experience in Indiana.

ABBY. Well, Jonathan, you've led a very interesting life, I'm sure. But we shouldn't have allowed you to talk so late. (*She starts to rise.*)

JONATHAN. My meeting Dr. Einstein in London, I might say, changed my whole life. Remember, I had been in South Africa in the diamond business—then Amsterdam, the diamond market. I wanted to go back to South Africa—and Dr. Einstein made it possible for me.

EINSTEIN. A good job, Chonny. (*To the aunts*): We take off the bandages. He look so different the nurse had to introduce me.

JONATHAN. I loved that face. I still carry the picture with me. (*He pro-*

duces a picture from his pocket, looks at it a moment and then hands it to MARTHA, *who takes it.* ABBY *looks over her shoulder.)*

ABBY. That looks more the way you used to look, but still I wouldn't know you. (MARTHA *returns the picture to* JONATHAN.)

JONATHAN. I think we'll go back to that face, Doctor.

EINSTEIN. Yah! It's safe now.

ABBY (*rising*). I know that you both want to get to—where you're going.

MARTHA. Yes. (*She rises, too, hintingly.*)

JONATHAN. My dear aunts—I am so full of that delicious dinner that I just can't move a muscle. (*He takes a puff of his cigar.*)

EINSTEIN. Yes, it's nice here. (*He relaxes a little more.*)

MARTHA. After all, it's very late and . . .

(TEDDY *appears at the head of the stairs, wearing his solar topee, carrying an open book and another solar topee.*)

TEDDY. I found it! I found it!

JONATHAN. What did you find, Teddy?

TEDDY (*descending*). The story of my life—my biography. (*Goes to* EINSTEIN.) Here's the picture I was telling you about, General. Here we are, both of us. (*He shows the open book to* EINSTEIN.) "President Roosevelt and General Goethals at Culebra Cut." That's me, General, and that's you. (EINSTEIN *looks at the picture.*)

EINSTEIN. My, how I've changed! (TEDDY *looks at* EINSTEIN, *a little puzzled, but makes the adjustment.*)

TEDDY. Well, you see that picture hasn't been taken yet. We haven't even started work on Culebra Cut. We're still digging locks. And now, General, we will go to Panama and inspect the new lock. (*He puts the book down and hands* EINSTEIN *the solar topee.*)

ABBY. No, Teddy—not to Panama!

EINSTEIN. We go some other time. Panama's a long way off.

TEDDY. Nonsense, it's just down in the cellar.

JONATHAN. The cellar?

MARTHA. We let him dig the Panama Canal in the cellar.

TEDDY. General Goethals, as President of the United States, Commander-in-Chief of the Army and Navy, and the man who gave you this job, I demand that you accompany me on the inspection of the new lock.

JONATHAN. Teddy! I think it's time for you to go to bed. (TEDDY *turns and looks at* JONATHAN.)

TEDDY. I beg your pardon. Who are you?

JONATHAN. I'm Woodrow Wilson. Go to bed.

TEDDY. No—you're not Wilson. But your face is familiar. (JONATHAN *stiffens.*) Let me see. You're not anyone I know now. Perhaps later—on my hunting trip to Africa—yes, you look like someone I might meet in the jungle. (JONATHAN *begins to burn.*)

ABBY. It's your brother, Jonathan, dear . . .

MARTHA. He's had his face changed.

TEDDY. So that's it—a nature faker!

ABBY. Perhaps you had better go to bed—he and his friend have to get back to their hotel. (JONATHAN *looks at* ABBY *and then, rising, turns to* EINSTEIN.)

JONATHAN. General Goethals—inspect the Canal.

EINSTEIN. All right, Mr. President. We go to Panama.

TEDDY (*on his way to the cellar door*). Bully! Bully! (EINSTEIN *follows him.* TEDDY *opens the cellar door.*) Follow me, General. It's down south, you know. (EINSTEIN *puts on the solar topee.*)

EINSTEIN. Well—bon voyage. (TEDDY *exits,* EINSTEIN *follows him off. When the cellar door closes* JONATHAN *turns to* ABBY.)

JONATHAN. Aunt Abby, I must correct your misapprehension. You spoke of our hotel. We have no hotel. We came directly here . . .

MARTHA. Well, there's a very nice little hotel just three blocks down the street . . .

JONATHAN. Aunt Martha, this is my home!

ABBY. But, Jonathan, you can't stay here. (JONATHAN *gives her a look.*) We need our rooms.

JONATHAN. You need them?

ABBY. Yes, for our lodgers.

JONATHAN (*alarmed for a moment*). Are there lodgers in this house?

MARTHA. Well, not just now, but we plan to have some.

JONATHAN. Then my old room is still free.

ABBY. But, Jonathan, there's no place for Dr. Einstein.

JONATHAN. He'll share the room with me.

ABBY. No, Jonathan, I'm afraid you can't stay here.

JONATHAN (*coldly*). Dr. Einstein and I need a place to sleep. This afternoon, you remembered that as a boy I could be disagreeable. It wouldn't be pleasant for any of us if . . .

MARTHA (*to* ABBY, *frightened*). Perhaps we'd better let them stay here tonight.

ABBY. Well, just overnight, Jonathan.

JONATHAN. That's settled. Now, if you'll get my room ready . . .

MARTHA (*starting upstairs*). It only needs airing out . . .

ABBY. We keep it ready to show to our lodgers. I think you and Dr. Einstein will find it comfortable.

JONATHAN. You have a most distinguished guest in Dr. Einstein. I'm afraid you don't appreciate his skill. But you shall. In a few weeks you'll see me looking like a very different Jonathan.

MARTHA (*stopping on the balcony*). But he can't operate here!

JONATHAN. When Dr. Einstein and I get organized . . . When we resume practice . . . I forgot to tell you—we're turning Grandfather's laboratory into an operating room. We expect to be very busy.

ABBY (*on the balcony*). Jonathan, we're not going to let you turn this house into a hospital.

JONATHAN. A hospital! Heavens, no! It will be a beauty parlor! (EINSTEIN *enters excitedly from the cellar.*)

EINSTEIN. Hey, Chonny! Down in the cellar . . . (*He sees the aunts and stops.*)

JONATHAN. Dr. Einstein. My dear aunts have invited us to live with them.

EINSTEIN. Oh, you fixed it?

ABBY. Well, you're sleeping here tonight.

JONATHAN. Please get our room ready immediately.

MARTHA. Well . . .

ABBY. For tonight. (*They exit to the third floor.*)

EINSTEIN. Chonny, when I was in the cellar, what do you think I find?

JONATHAN. What?

EINSTEIN. The Panama Canal.

JONATHAN. The Panama Canal!

EINSTEIN. Chonny, it just fits Mr. Spenalzo! A hole Teddy dug, four feet wide and six feet long.

JONATHAN (*pointing*). Down there?

EINSTEIN. You'd think they knew we was bringing Mr. Spenalzo along. Chonny, that's hospitality.

JONATHAN. Rather a good joke on my aunts, Doctor, their living in a house with a body buried in the cellar.

EINSTEIN. How do we get him in, Chonny?

JONATHAN. Yes, we can't just walk him through the door. (*Looks from door to window.*) We'll drive the car up between the house and the cemetery and, after they've gone to bed, we'll bring Mr. Spenalzo in through the window.

EINSTEIN. Bed! Just think! We got a bed tonight. (*He takes out his bottle and starts to take a swig.*)

JONATHAN. Easy, Doctor. Remember you're operating tomorrow. And this time you'd better be sober.

EINSTEIN. I fix you up beautiful.

JONATHAN. And if you don't . . . (ABBY *and* MARTHA *enter on the balcony.*)

ABBY. Your room's all ready, Jonathan.

JONATHAN (*crossing to the outside door*). Then you can go to bed. We're moving the car up behind the house.

MARTHA. It will be all right where it is—until morning. (EINSTEIN *has opened the door.*)

JONATHAN. I don't want to leave it in the street—that might be against the law. (*He and* EINSTEIN *exit.*)

MARTHA. Abby, what are we going to do?

ABBY (*coming downstairs*). Well, we're not going to let them stay more than one night in this house, for one thing. What would the neighbors think? People coming into this place with one face and going out with another.

MARTHA. What are we going to do about Mr. Hoskins?

ABBY. Oh, yes, Mr. Hoskins. It can't be very comfortable for him in there. He's been so patient, the poor dear. I think Teddy ought to get Mr. Hoskins downstairs right away.

MARTHA. Abby, I will not invite Jonathan to the services.

ABBY. Oh, no, dear—we'll wait until they've gone to bed and then come down and hold the services. (TEDDY *enters from the cellar.*)

TEDDY. General Goethals was very pleased. He said the Canal was just the right size.

ABBY. Teddy, there's been another yellow fever victim.

TEDDY. Dear me—that will be a shock to the General.

MARTHA. Then we mustn't tell him about it.

TEDDY. But it's his department.

ABBY. No, we mustn't tell him about it. It would just spoil his visit, Teddy.

TEDDY. I'm sorry, Aunt Abby. It's out of my hands—he'll have to be told. Army regulations, you know.

ABBY. No, Teddy, we'll have to keep it a secret.

MARTHA. Yes!

TEDDY. A state secret?

ABBY. Yes, a state secret.

MARTHA. Promise?

TEDDY. You have the word of the President of the United States. Cross my heart and hope to die. (*Following the childish formula, he crosses his heart and spits.*) Now let's see—how are we going to keep it a secret?

ABBY. Well, Teddy, you go back down in the cellar and when I turn out the lights—when it's dark—you come up and take the poor man down to the Canal. Go along, Teddy.

MARTHA. We'll come down later and hold services.

TEDDY. You may announce the President will say a few words. (*He starts to the cellar door, then stops.*) Where is the poor devil?

MARTHA. In the window seat.

TEDDY. It seems to be spreading. We've never had yellow fever *there* before. (*He exits into the cellar.*)

ABBY. When Jonathan and Dr. Einstein come back, let's see whether we can't get them to go to bed right away.

MARTHA. Yes, then they'd be asleep by the time we got dressed for the funeral. Abby, I haven't even seen Mr. Hoskins yet.

ABBY. Oh, my goodness, that's right—you were out. Well, you just come right over and see him now. (*They go to the window seat.*) He's really very nice-looking—considering he's a Methodist.

(MARTHA *is about to lift the window seat when* JONATHAN *thrusts his head through the window curtains. They jump back in fright.*)

JONATHAN. We're bringing our luggage through here. (*He climbs into the room.*)

ABBY. Your room's waiting for you. You can go right up. (*Two bags and a large instrument case are passed through the window.* JONATHAN *puts them down.*)

JONATHAN. I'm afraid we don't keep Brooklyn hours. You two run along to bed.

ABBY. You must be very tired—both of you—and we don't go to bed this early.

JONATHAN. Well, you should. It's time I came home to take care of you.

MARTHA. Oh, we weren't planning to go until . . .

JONATHAN (*sternly*). Did you hear me say go to bed, Aunt Martha? (MARTHA *retreats upstairs.* EINSTEIN *comes through the window.*) Take the bags upstairs. The instruments can go to the laboratory in the morning. (*Putting the instrument case beside the window seat.*) Doctor, we can take this up to the laboratory in the morning. (*He closes the window.*) Now we're all going to bed. (EINSTEIN *starts upstairs, reaching the upper landing, where he stops.*)

ABBY. I'll wait till you're up and turn out the lights. (*Retreats toward the light switch.*)

JONATHAN. Another flight, Doctor. Run along, Aunt Martha. (MARTHA *goes to the upstairs door and opens it.* EINSTEIN *goes through the arch with the bags and* JONATHAN *stops on the landing, looks down at* ABBY.) All right, Aunt Abby.

ABBY (*looking toward cellar door.*) I'll be right up.

JONATHAN. Now, Aunt Abby! Turn out the lights.

(ABBY *snaps out the lights.* JONATHAN *waits until* ABBY *has come upstairs and she and* MARTHA *have gone through their door and closed it, then turns and goes up through the arch. The stage is entirely dark.* TEDDY *opens the cellar door, looks out and sees everything is safe, then switches the cellar light on and moves toward the window seat. In the darkness we hear the familiar creak of the window seat as it is opened. A few seconds later we see the faint shadow of* TEDDY *carrying a burden, passing through the cellar door, then this door is closed behind him shutting off the light. After a second or two* JONATHAN *and* EINSTEIN *come out on the upper landing.* JONATHAN *lights a match and in its light he comes down the stairs.)*

EINSTEIN *(on the balcony, listening at the aunts' door).* It's all right, Chonny. *(He comes downstairs.)*

JONATHAN. I'll open the window. You go around and hand him through.

EINSTEIN. Chonny, he's too heavy for me. You go outside and push. I stay here and pull. Then together we get him down to Panama.

JONATHAN. All right. But be quick. I'll take a look around outside the house. When I tap on the glass you open the window. *(*JONATHAN *goes out front door, closing it behind him.* EINSTEIN *moves toward the window, holding lighted match. He bumps into the table, burns his finger, and we hear him suck the burnt place. He continues to window in darkness. Then we hear a crash.)*

EINSTEIN. Ach! Himmel! *(He lights a match and in its wavering light we see that he has fallen into the window seat.)* Vere did I go? Oh, here I am. Who left dis open, the dumbkopf? *(We hear tapping on the glass, as he closes the window seat and then we hear him open the window.)* Chonny? O.K. Allez oop! Wait a minute, Chonny. You lost a leg somewhere. Ach. Now I got him. *(There is a crash of a body and then the sound of a "Sh-h!" from outside.)* That was me, Chonny. I schlipped.

JONATHAN'S VOICE *(off).* Quiet!

EINSTEIN. Well, his shoe came off. *(Pause.)* All right, Chonny. I got him. Whew! *(In the silence there is a knock at the door.)* Chonny! Somebody at the door! Go quick. No, I manage here. Go quick! *(There is a second knock at the door. There is a moment's silence and we hear the creak of the window seat, the noise of* EINSTEIN *struggling with Mr. Spenalzo's body, then another creak of the window seat. There is a third knock at the door, then it is opened and by the dim glow of a remote street light we see* ELAINE *peering into the room.)*

ELAINE *(calling softly).* Miss Abby! Miss Martha! *(In the dim path of light she comes in and moves toward the center of the room, calling toward the staircase.)* Miss Abby! Miss Martha! *(*JONATHAN *enters hurriedly and we hear the closing of the door.* ELAINE *whirls and gasps.)* Who is it? Is that you, Teddy? *(*JONATHAN *advances on her.)* Who are you?

JONATHAN. Who are you?

ELAINE. I'm Elaine Harper—I live next door.

JONATHAN. What are you doing here?

*(*EINSTEIN *circles around* ELAINE *toward front door.)*

ELAINE. I came over to see Miss Abby and Miss Martha.

JONATHAN. Turn on the lights, Doctor. *(*EINSTEIN *switches on the lights.)* I'm afraid you've chosen an untimely moment for a social call. *(He moves past her toward the window expecting to see Mr. Spenalzo* *there. He doesn't, and this bewilders him.*)

ELAINE (*trying to summon courage*). I think you'd better explain what you're doing here.

JONATHAN. We happen to live here. (JONATHAN *looks out the window in his search for the missing Mr. Spenalzo.*)

ELAINE. You don't live here. I'm in this house every day and I've never seen you before. Where are Miss Abby and Miss Martha? What have you done to them?

JONATHAN. Perhaps we had better introduce ourselves. May I present Dr. Einstein . . .

ELAINE. Dr. Einstein!

(JONATHAN *moves toward the table and looks under the tablecloth for Mr. Spenalzo.*)

JONATHAN. A surgeon of great distinction—and—(*not finding Mr. Spenalzo*)—something of a magician.

ELAINE. And I suppose you're going to tell me you're Boris . . .

(JONATHAN *stiffens and speaks sharply.*)

JONATHAN. I'm Jonathan Brewster!

ELAINE (*almost with fright*). Oh—you're Jonathan.

JONATHAN. I see you've heard of me.

ELAINE. Yes—just this afternoon—for the first time . . .

JONATHAN. And what did they say about me?

ELAINE. Only that there was another brother named Jonathan—that's all that was said. Well, that explains everything. Now that I know who you are I'll run along back home—(*she runs to the door and finds it locked*)—if you'll kindly unlock the door. (JONATHAN *goes to the door and unlocks it.* ELAINE *starts toward the door, but* JONATHAN *turns and stops her with a gesture.*)

JONATHAN. "That explains everything?" Just what did you mean by that? Why did you come here at this time of night?

ELAINE. I thought I saw someone prowling around the house. I suppose it was you.

(JONATHAN *reaches back and locks the door again, leaving the key in the lock.* EINSTEIN *and* JONATHAN *both move slowly toward* ELAINE.)

JONATHAN. You thought you saw someone prowling about the house?

ELAINE. Yes—weren't you outside? Is that your car?

JONATHAN. Oh, you saw someone at the car!

ELAINE. Yes.

JONATHAN. What else did you see?

ELAINE. Just that—that's all. That's why I came over here. I wanted to tell Miss Abby to call the police. But if it was you, and that's your car, I don't need to bother Miss Abby. I'll be running along. (*She takes a step toward the door.* JONATHAN *blocks her way.)*

JONATHAN. What was the man doing at the car?

ELAINE. I don't know. You see I was on my way over here.

JONATHAN. I think you're lying.

EINSTEIN. Chonny, I think she tells the truth. We let her go now, huh?

JONATHAN. I think she's lying. Breaking into a house at this time of night. I think she's dangerous. She shouldn't be allowed around loose. (*He seizes* ELAINE'S *arm. She pulls back.*)

ELAINE (*in a hoarse frightened tone*). Take your hands off me . . .

JONATHAN. And now, young lady . . .

(*The cellar door suddenly opens and* TEDDY *comes through and closes it with a bang. They all jump.* TEDDY *looks them over.*)

TEDDY (*blandly*). It's going to be a private funeral. (*He starts for the steps.*)

ELAINE (*struggling*). Teddy! Teddy! Tell these men who I am!

TEDDY. That's my daughter, Alice. (*She struggles to get away from* JONATHAN.)

ELAINE. No! No! Teddy! Teddy! (*Still struggling.*)

TEDDY. Now, Alice, don't be a tomboy. Don't play rough with the gentlemen. (*He has reached the landing on the stairs, draws his imaginary sword.*) Charge! (*He charges up the stairs and off.*)

ELAINE. Teddy! Teddy! (JONATHAN *pulls her arm behind her back and claps a hand over her mouth.*)

JONATHAN. Doctor, your handkerchief! (JONATHAN *takes* EINSTEIN'S *handkerchief in his free hand and starts to stuff it in her mouth. As he releases his hand for this,* ELAINE *lets out a scream.* JONATHAN *claps his hand over her mouth again.*) Doctor, the cellar! (EINSTEIN *opens the cellar door, then dashes for the light switch and turns off the lights.* JONATHAN *forces* ELAINE *into the cellar and waits until* EINSTEIN *joins him and takes hold of her. In the dark, we hear:*)

ABBY. What's the matter?

MARTHA. What's happening down there?

(JONATHAN *closes the cellar door on* EINSTEIN *and* ELAINE *as* ABBY *turns on the lights from the balcony switch and we see* ABBY *and* MARTHA *on the balcony. They are dressed for Mr. Hoskins' funeral. Mr. Hoskins is being paid the respect of deep and elaborate mourning.*)

ABBY. What's the matter? What are you doing?

(JONATHAN *is holding the cellar door.*)

JONATHAN. We caught a burglar—a sneak thief. Go back to your room.

ABBY. I'll call the police! (*She starts downstairs.*)

JONATHAN. We've called the police. We'll handle this. You go back to your room. (*They hesitate.*) Did you hear me? (ABBY *turns as if to start upstairs when the knob of the outside door is rattled followed by a knock. They all turn and look toward the door.* ABBY *starts down again.*) Don't answer that! (ELAINE *rushes out of the cellar.* EINSTEIN *follows, grabbing for her.*)

ELAINE. Miss Abby! Miss Martha!

MARTHA. Why, it's Elaine!

(*There is a peremptory knock at the door.* ABBY *hurries over, unlocks it and opens it.* MORTIMER *enters carrying a suitcase. At the sight of him* ELAINE *rushes into his arms. He drops the suitcase and puts his arms around her. Einstein and* JONATHAN *have withdrawn toward the kitchen door, ready to make a run for it.*)

ELAINE. Oh, Mortimer, where have you been?

MORTIMER. To the Nora Bayes Theatre—and I should have known better. (*He sees* JONATHAN.) My God, I'm still there!

ABBY. This is your brother Jonathan —and this is Dr. Einstein.

(MORTIMER *surveys the roomful.*)

MORTIMER. I know this isn't a nightmare, but what is it?

JONATHAN. I've come back home, Mortimer.

MORTIMER (*looking at him and then at* ABBY). Who did you say that was?

ABBY. It's your brother Jonathan. He's had his face changed. Dr. Einstein performed the operation on him.

MORTIMER. Jonathan, you always were a horror, but do you have to look like one?

(JONATHAN *takes a step toward him.* EINSTEIN *pulls his sleeve.*)

EINSTEIN. Easy, Chonny! Easy!

JONATHAN. Mortimer, have you forgotten the things I used to do to you? Remember the time you were tied to the bedpost—the needles—under your fingernails. I suggest you don't ask for trouble now.

MORTIMER. Yes, I remember. I remember you as the most detestable, vicious, venomous form of animal life I ever knew.

(JONATHAN *gets tense and takes a step toward* MORTIMER. ABBY *steps between them.*)

ABBY. Now, don't you boys start quarreling again the minute you've seen each other.

MORTIMER. There won't be any fight, Aunt Abby. Jonathan, you're not wanted here, so get out!

JONATHAN. Dr. Einstein and I have been invited to stay.

MORTIMER. Oh, no—not in this house!

ABBY. Just for tonight.

MORTIMER. I don't want him anywhere near me.

ABBY. But we did invite them for tonight, Mortimer, and it wouldn't be very nice to go back on our word.

MORTIMER (*reluctantly giving in*). All right, tonight—but the first thing in the morning—out. Where are they sleeping?

ABBY. We put them in Jonathan's old room.

MORTIMER (*picking up his suitcase and starting for the stairs*). That's my old room. I'm moving into that room. I'm here to stay.

MARTHA. Oh, Mortimer, I'm so glad!

EINSTEIN (*to* JONATHAN). Chonny, we sleep down here.

MORTIMER. You bet your life you'll sleep down here.

EINSTEIN. You sleep on the sofa—I sleep on the window seat.

MORTIMER (*stopping suddenly, as he remembers Mr. Hoskins*). The window seat! Oh, well, let's not argue about it. That window seat's good enough for me tonight. (*Descending as he talks.*) I'll sleep on the window seat.

EINSTEIN. Chonny—all this argument—it makes me think of Mr. Spenalzo.

JONATHAN. Spenalzo! Well, Mortimer, there's no real need to inconvenience you. We'll sleep down here.

MORTIMER. Jonathan, this sudden consideration for me is very unconvincing.

EINSTEIN. Come, Chonny, we get our things out of the room, yes?

MORTIMER. Don't bother, Doctor.

JONATHAN. You know, Doctor, I've completely lost track of Mr. Spenalzo.

MORTIMER. Who's this Mr. Spenalzo?

EINSTEIN (*on the stairs*). Just a friend of ours Chonny's been looking for.

MORTIMER. Don't you bring anybody else in here.

EINSTEIN (*reassuringly*). It's all right, Chonny. While we pack I tell you about him.

(JONATHAN *starts upstairs.*)

ABBY. Mortimer, you don't have to stay down here. I could sleep with Martha and you could have my room.

JONATHAN (*on the balcony*). No trouble at all, Aunt Abby. We'll be packed in a few minutes, and then you can have the room, Mortimer.

MORTIMER. You're just wasting time. I told you I'm sleeping down here. (JONATHAN *exits through the arch.* MORTIMER *starts for stairs and almost bumps into* ELAINE.) Oh, hello, Elaine!

ELAINE. Mortimer!

MORTIMER (*taking her in his arms*). What's the matter with you, dear?

ELAINE. I've almost been killed!

MORTIMER. You've almost been . . . Abby! Martha! (*He looks quickly at the aunts.*)

MARTHA. It was Jonathan.

ABBY. He mistook her for a sneak thief.

ELAINE. No, it was more than that. He's some kind of a maniac. (*She draws close to* MORTIMER *again.*) Mortimer, I'm afraid of him.

MORTIMER. Why, darling, you're trembling. (*Sitting* ELAINE *on sofa. To the aunts:*) Have you got any smelling salts?

MARTHA. No, but do you think some hot tea or coffee . . . ?

MORTIMER. Coffee. Make some for me too—and some sandwiches. I haven't had any dinner.

MARTHA. We'll get something for both of you.

(ABBY *takes off her hat and gloves and puts them on sideboard.*)

ABBY. Martha, we can leave our hats downstairs here.

MORTIMER. You weren't going out anywhere, were you? Do you know what time it is? It's after twelve. Twelve! (*He glances hurriedly at the cellar door, remembering.*) Elaine, you go along home.

ELAINE. What?

ABBY. Why, Mortimer, you wanted some sandwiches for you and Elaine. It won't take us a minute.

MARTHA. Remember, we wanted to celebrate your engagement . . . That's what we'll do. We'll have a nice supper for you—and we'll open a bottle of wine.

MORTIMER (*reluctantly*). All right. (*The aunts exit to the kitchen. He calls after them.*) No wine!

ELAINE (*rising*). Mortimer, what's going on in this house?

MORTIMER. What do you mean—what's going on in this house?

ELAINE. You were supposed to take me to dinner and the theater tonight . . . You called it off. You asked me to marry you . . . I said I would . . . five minutes later you threw me out of the house. Tonight, just after your brother tries to strangle me, you want to chase me home. Now, listen, Mr. Brewster . . before I go home, I want to know where I stand. Do you love me?

MORTIMER (*going to her*). I love you very much, Elaine. In fact, I love you so much I can't marry you.

ELAINE (*drawing away*). Have you suddenly gone crazy?

MORTIMER. I don't think so—but it's just a matter of time. (*He seats her on sofa.*) You see, insanity runs in my family. (*He looks toward the kitchen.*) It practically gallops! That's why I can't marry you, dear.

ELAINE (*unconvinced*). Now wait a minute. You've got to do better than that.

MORTIMER. No, dear—there's a strange taint in the Brewster blood.

If you really knew my family—well—it's what you would expect if Strindberg had written *Hellzapoppin!*

ELAINE. Now, just because Teddy . . .

MORTIMER. No, it goes way back. The first Brewster—the one who came over on the *Mayflower*. You know, in those days the Indians used to scalp the settlers—he used to scalp the Indians.

ELAINE. Mortimer, that's ancient history.

MORTIMER. No, the whole family! Take my grandfather—he tried his patent medicines out on dead people to be sure he wouldn't kill them!

ELAINE. He wasn't so crazy. He made a million dollars.

MORTIMER. And then there's Jonathan. You just said he was a maniac. He tried to kill you.

ELAINE. But he's your brother, not you. I'm in love with you.

MORTIMER. And Teddy! You *know* Teddy. He thinks he's Roosevelt.

ELAINE. Even Roosevelt thinks he's Roosevelt.

MORTIMER. No, dear, no Brewster should marry. I realize now that if I'd met my father in time I would have stopped him.

ELAINE. Now, darling, all of this doesn't prove you're crazy. Just look at your aunts—they're Brewsters, aren't they?—and the sanest, sweetest people I've ever known.

MORTIMER (*glancing at the window seat and moving toward it*). Well, even they have their peculiarities. (ELAINE *walks away from him.*)

ELAINE. Yes, but what lovely peculiarities!—kindness, generosity, human sympathy!

(MORTIMER *lifts the window seat to take a peek at Mr. Hoskins and sees Mr. Spenalzo.*)

MORTIMER (*to himself*). There's another one!

ELAINE (*turning to* MORTIMER). There are plenty of others! You can't tell me anything about your aunts.

MORTIMER. I'm not going to! (*Crossing to* ELAINE.) Elaine, you've got to go home. Something very important has just come up.

ELAINE. Come up from where? We're here alone together.

MORTIMER. Elaine, I know I'm acting irrationally, but just put it down to the fact that I'm a mad Brewster.

ELAINE. If you think you're going to get out of this by pretending you're insane, you're crazy. Maybe you're not going to marry me, but I'm going to marry you. I love you, you dope!

MORTIMER (*pushing her toward the door*). Well, if you love me, will you get the hell out of here?

ELAINE. Well, at least take me home. I'm afraid!

MORTIMER. Afraid! A little walk through the cemetery.

ELAINE (*changing tactics*). Mortimer, will you kiss me good night? (MORTIMER *goes over to her.*)

MORTIMER. Of course. (*What* MORTIMER *plans to be a desultory peck,* ELAINE *turns into a production number.* MORTIMER *comes out of it with no loss of poise.*) Good night, dear. I'll call you up in a day or two. (*She walks to the door in a cold fury, opens it and starts out, then wheels on* MORTIMER.)

ELAINE. You—you critic! (*She exits, slamming the door.* MORTIMER *turns and rushes determinedly to the kitchen door.*)

MORTIMER. Aunt Abby, Aunt Martha! Come in here!

ABBY'S VOICE. We'll be in in just a minute, dear.

MORTIMER. Come in here now! (ABBY *enters from the kitchen.*)

ABBY. What do you want, Mortimer? Where's Elaine?

MORTIMER. I thought you promised me not to let anyone in this house while I was gone.

ABBY. Well, Jonathan just walked in.

MORTIMER. I don't mean Jonathan.

ABBY. And Dr. Einstein was with him.

MORTIMER. I don't mean Dr. Einstein. Who is that in the window seat?

ABBY. We told you—it's Mr. Hoskins.

MORTIMER. It is *not* Mr. Hoskins. (*He opens the window seat.* ABBY *goes over and looks down at Mr. Spenalzo.*)

ABBY (*puzzled at the sight of a stranger*). Who can that be?

MORTIMER. Are you trying to tell me you've never seen this man before?

ABBY. I certainly am! Why, this is a fine how-do-you-do! It's getting so anyone thinks he can walk into our house.

MORTIMER. Now, Aunt Abby, don't try to get out of this. That's another one of your gentlemen.

ABBY. Mortimer, that man's an impostor! Well, if he came here to be buried in our cellar, he's mistaken.

MORTIMER. Aunt Abby, you admitted to me that you put Mr. Hoskins in the window seat.

ABBY. Yes, I did.

MORTIMER. Well, this man couldn't have just got the idea from Mr. Hoskins. By the way, where is Mr. Hoskins?

ABBY. He must have gone to Panama.

MORTIMER. You buried him!

ABBY. Not yet, he's just down there waiting for the services, poor dear! We haven't had a minute what with Jonathan in the house.

MORTIMER. Jonathan . . . (*At the mention of* JONATHAN'S *name, he closes the window seat.*)

ABBY. We've always wanted to hold a double funeral, but we're not going to read services over a perfect stranger.

MORTIMER. A stranger! Aunt Abby, how can I believe you? There are twelve men in the cellar and you admit you poisoned them.

ABBY (*drawing herself up*). I did. But you don't think I'd stoop to telling a fib? (*She bustles indignantly into the kitchen, calling*): Martha!

(MORTIMER *starts to pace.* JONATHAN, *having learned where Mr. Spenalzo is, enters from above and comes down the stairs hurriedly, making for the window seat. He sees* MORTIMER *and stops.*)

JONATHAN. Mortimer, I'd like to have a word with you.

MORTIMER. A word's about all you'll have time for, Jonathan, because I've decided you and your doctor friend are going to have to get out of this house as quickly as possible.

JONATHAN. I'm glad you recognize the fact that you and I can't live under the same roof. But you have arrived at the wrong solution. Take your suitcase and get out! (*He starts toward the window seat.*)

MORTIMER. Jonathan, you're beginning to bore me. (*He circles around the table, heading* JONATHAN *off.*) You've played your one-night stand in Brooklyn. Move on.

JONATHAN. My dear Mortimer, just because you've graduated from the back fence to the typewriter, don't think you're grown up. (*He slips past* MORTIMER, *and sits on window seat.*) I'm staying—you're leaving—and I mean now.

MORTIMER. If you think I can be frightened, Jonathan, if you think there's anything I fear . . .

JONATHAN (*rising and facing* MORTIMER). I've led a strange life, Mortimer. But it's taught me one thing—to be afraid of nothing.

(*For a second they glare at each other with equal courage.* ABBY *marches in from kitchen, followed by* MARTHA.)

ABBY. Martha, you just look and see what's in that window seat.

(*Both men throw themselves on the window seat and speak and gesture simultaneously.*)

MORTIMER AND JONATHAN. Now, Aunt Abby . . . (*Light dawns on* MORTIMER'S *face. He rises with smiling assurance.*)

MORTIMER. Jonathan, let Aunt Martha see what's in the window seat. (JONATHAN *freezes dangerously.*) Aunt Abby, I owe you an apology. I have very good news for you. Jonathan is leaving. He's taking Dr. Einstein and their cold companion with him. (*He walks to* JONATHAN.) You're my brother, Jonathan. You're a Brewster. I'm giving you a chance to get away and take the evidence with you. You can't ask for more than that. (JONATHAN *doesn't more.*) All right. In that case, I'll have to call the police. (MORTIMER *starts for the telephone.*)

JONATHAN. Don't reach for that telephone. (*He crosses quickly toward*

MORTIMER.) Are you still giving me orders after seeing what's happened to Mr. Spenalzo?

MARTHA. Spenalzo?

ABBY. I knew he was a foreigner.

JONATHAN (*to* MORTIMER). Remember, what happened to Mr. Spenalzo can happen to you, too.

(*There is knock at the door; it opens and* OFFICER O'HARA *sticks his head in.*)

O'HARA. Oh, hello . . .

ABBY. Hello, Officer O'Hara. Is there anything we can do for you?

O'HARA. Saw your lights on—thought there might be sickness in the house. Oh, you got company. Sorry I disturbed you. (MORTIMER *hurries to* O'HARA *and pulls him through the door into the room.*)

MORTIMER. No! Come in!

ABBY. Yes, come in!

MARTHA. Come right in, Officer O'Hara. This is our nephew, Mortimer.

O'HARA. Pleased to meet you.

ABBY. And this is another nephew, Jonathan.

O'HARA. Pleased to make your acquaintance. Well, it must be nice having your nephews visiting you. Are they going to stay with you for a bit?

MORTIMER. I'm staying. My brother Jonathan is just leaving.

(JONATHAN *starts for stairs.* O'HARA *stops him.*)

O'HARA. I've met you here before, haven't I?

ABBY. I'm afraid not. Jonathan hasn't been home for years.

O'HARA (*to* JONATHAN). Your face looks familiar to me. Perhaps I've seen a picture of you somewhere.

JONATHAN. I don't think so.

(*He hurries up the stairs.*)

MORTIMER. I'd hurry if I were you, Jonathan. You're all packed anyway, aren't you?

(JONATHAN *exits upstairs.*)

O'HARA. Well, you'll be wanting to say your good-bys. I'll be running along. (*He starts for the door.*)

MORTIMER (*stopping him*). What's the rush? I'd like to have you stick around till my brother goes.

O'HARA. I just dropped in to make sure everything was all right.

MORTIMER. We're going to have some coffee in a minute. Won't you join us?

ABBY. Oh, I forgot the coffee. (*She hurries out.*)

MARTHA. I'd better make some more sandwiches. I ought to know your appetite by this time, Mr. O'Hara. (*She exits into the kitchen.*)

O'HARA (*calling after her*). Don't bother. I'm due to ring in in a few minutes.

MORTIMER. You can have a cup of coffee with us. My brother will be going soon.

O'HARA. Haven't I seen a photograph of your brother around here some place?

MORTIMER. I don't think so.

O'HARA. He certainly reminds me of somebody.

MORTIMER. He looks like somebody you've probably seen in the movies.

O'HARA. I never go to the movies. I hate 'em. My mother says the movies is a bastard art.

MORTIMER. Yes. It's full of them. Your mother said that?

O'HARA. Yeah. My mother was an actress—a stage actress. Perhaps you've heard of her—Peaches Latour.

MORTIMER. Sounds like a name I've seen on a program. What did she play?

O'HARA. Her big hit was *Mutt and Jeff*. Played it for three years. I was born on tour—the third season.

MORTIMER. You were?

O'HARA. Yeah. Sioux City, Iowa. I was born in the dressing-room at the end of the second act and mother made the finale.

MORTIMER. What a trouper! There must be a good story in your mother. You know, I write about the theater.

O'HARA. You do? Say, you're not Mortimer Brewster, the dramatic critic? (MORTIMER *nods.*) Say, I'm glad to meet you. We're in the same line of business.

MORTIMER. We are?

O'HARA. Yes, I'm a playwright. This being on the police force is just temporary.

MORTIMER. How long have you been on the force?

O'HARA. Twelve years. I'm collecting material for a play.

MORTIMER. I'll bet it's a honey.

O'HARA. Well, it ought to be. With all the drama I see being a cop. Mr. Brewster, you got no idea what goes on in Brooklyn.

MORTIMER. I think I have.

O'HARA. What time you got?

MORTIMER. Ten after one.

O'HARA. Gee, I got to ring in. (*He starts to go.*)

MORTIMER (*stopping him*). Wait a minute. On that play of yours—you know, I might be able to help you.

O'HARA. You would? Say, it was fate my walking in here tonight. Look, I'll tell you the plot.

(JONATHAN *and* EINSTEIN *enter on the balcony carrying suitcases.*)

MORTIMER. Oh, Jonathan, you're on your way, eh? Good! You haven't got much time, you know.

ABBY (*entering from kitchen*). Everything's about ready. (*She sees

JONATHAN *and* EINSTEIN.) Oh, you leaving now, Jonathan? Well, good-by. Good-by, Dr. Einstein. (*She notices the instrument case by the window.*) Oh, doesn't this case belong to you?

MORTIMER. Yes, Jonathan. You can't go without all of your things. (*To* O'HARA): Well, O'Hara, it was nice meeting you. I'll see you again—we'll talk about your play.

O'HARA. Oh, I'm not leaving now, Mr. Brewster.

MORTIMER. Why not?

O'HARA. Well, you just offered to help me with my play, didn't you? You and me are going to write my play together.

MORTIMER. No, O'Hara, I can't do that. You see, I'm not a creative writer.

O'HARA. I'll do the creating. You just put the words to it.

MORTIMER. But, O'Hara . . .

O'HARA. No, sir, Mr. Brewster, I ain't going to leave this house till I tell you the plot. (O'HARA *sits on the window seat.*)

JONATHAN. In that case, Mortimer, we'll be running along. (*He starts toward the outside door.*)

MORTIMER. No, Jonathan! Don't try that! You can't go yet. You're taking everything with you. . . . (*To* O'HARA:) Look, O'Hara, you run along now. My brother's just going and . . .

O'HARA. I can wait. I've been waiting twelve years.

(MARTHA *enters with sandwiches and coffee on a tray.*

MARTHA. I'm sorry I was so long.

MORTIMER. Don't bring that in here! O'Hara, would you join us for a bite in the kitchen?

MARTHA. The kitchen?

ABBY. Jonathan's leaving.

MARTHA. Oh, that's nice! Come along, Mr. O'Hara. (*She takes the tray back into the kitchen.*)

ABBY. Mr. O'Hara, you don't mind eating in the kitchen?

O'HARA. Where else would you eat? (*He exits to the kitchen.*)

ABBY. Good-by, Jonathan, it's nice to have seen you again. (*She hurries into kitchen.*)

MORTIMER (*closing the kitchen door after* ABBY). Jonathan, I'm glad you came back to Brooklyn because it gives me a chance to throw you out. (*He opens window seat.*) And the first one out is your boy friend, Mr. Spenalzo.

O'HARA (*appearing in doorway*). Look, Mr. Brewster! (MORTIMER *hurriedly closes the window seat.*) We can talk in here.

MORTIMER. No. I'll be right out, O'Hara. (*He pushes* O'HARA *back into the kitchen.*)

JONATHAN (*scornfully*). I might have known you'd grow up to write a play with a policeman.

MORTIMER. Get going, now—all three of you! (*He exits, closing the door.*)

JONATHAN (*putting the bags down*). Doctor, this affair between my brother and me has got to be settled.

EINSTEIN. Now, Chonny, we got trouble enough. Your brother gives us a chance to get away—what more could you ask?

JONATHAN. You don't understand, Doctor. (*Opening window seat.*) This goes back many years.

EINSTEIN. Now, Chonny, let's get going.

JONATHAN. We're not going—we're going to sleep right here tonight.

EINSTEIN. With a cop in the kitchen and Mr. Spenalzo in the window seat?

JONATHAN. That's all he's got on us, Doctor. (*He closes the window seat.*) We'll take Mr. Spenalzo down and dump him in the bay. That done, we're coming back here. And then if he tries to interfere . . .

EINSTEIN. Now, Chonny!

JONATHAN. Doctor, you know when I make up my mind . . .

EINSTEIN. Yeah—when you make up your mind, you lose your head! Brooklyn ain't a good place for you, Chonny.

JONATHAN (*peremptorily*). Doctor!

EINSTEIN. OK. We got to stick together. Some day we get stuck together. (*He points to the bags.*) If we're coming back do we got to take them with us?

JONATHAN. No. Leave them here. (*He looks toward upstairs, then toward the cellar door.*) Hide them in the cellar. (EINSTEIN *moves toward the cellar with the instrument case.*) Move fast! Spenalzo can go out the same way he came in.

(EINSTEIN *exits into the cellar.* JONATHAN *goes to the foot of the staircase, takes the other bags to the cellar door, goes to the window and opens it.* EINSTEIN *comes up from the cellar, excited.*)

EINSTEIN. Hey, Chonny! Come quick!

JONATHAN. What's the matter?

EINSTEIN. You know that hole in the cellar?

JONATHAN. Yes.

EINSTEIN. Well—we got an ace in the hole. (*They both disappear down the cellar steps.* MORTIMER *enters from kitchen, finishing a sandwich and looks around the room. He sees their two bags and notices the open window. He goes to the window seat, looks in and sees Mr. Spenalzo is still there, closes the window seat and, kneeling on it, leans out the window and calls softly.*)

MORTIMER. Jonathan! Jonathan! (JONATHAN *and* EINSTEIN *come in through the cellar door unnoticed by* MORTIMER *and walk into the room.*) Jonathan!

JONATHAN. Yes, Mortimer!

MORTIMER (*turning around and seeing* JONATHAN, *he speaks angrily*). Where have you two been? I thought I told you . . .

JONATHAN. We're not going.

MORTIMER. Oh, you're not? You think I'm not serious about this, eh? Do you want the police to know what's in that window seat?

JONATHAN (*firmly*). We're staying here.

MORTIMER. All right! You asked for it! This gets me rid of you and O'Hara both at the same time. (*He goes to the kitchen door.*) Officer O'Hara!

JONATHAN. If you tell O'Hara what's in the window seat, I'll tell him what's in the cellar.

MORTIMER (*closing the door swiftly*). The cellar?

JONATHAN. There's an elderly gentleman down there who seems to be very dead.

MORTIMER. What were you doing in the cellar?

EINSTEIN. What's *he* doing in the cellar?

(OFFICER O'HARA'S *voice is heard off stage.*)

O'HARA (*off stage*). No, thank you, ma'am. I've had plenty! They were fine!

JONATHAN. Now, what are you going to say to Officer O'Hara? (O'HARA *walks in.*)

O'HARA. Say, your aunts want to hear it, too. Shall I get them in here?

MORTIMER (*pulling him toward the outside door*). No, O'Hara! You can't do that now! You've got to ring in!

O'HARA. The hell with ringing in! I'll get your aunts in and tell you the plot.

MORTIMER. No, O'Hara, not in front of all these people. We'll get together alone someplace, later.

O'HARA. Say, how about the back room at Kelly's?

MORTIMER (*hurrying him toward door*). Fine! You go ring in and I'll meet you at Kelly's.

JONATHAN. Why don't you two go down in the cellar?

O'HARA. That's all right with me. (*He starts for the cellar door.*) Is this the cellar?

MORTIMER (*grabbing him*). No! We'll go to Kelly's. But you're going to ring in on the way, aren't you?

O'HARA. All right, that will only take a couple of minutes. (MORTIMER *pushes him through the outside door, then turns to get his hat.*)

MORTIMER (*to* JONATHAN). I'll ditch this guy and be back in five minutes. I expect to find you gone. Wait for me. (*He exits, closing the door.*)

JONATHAN. We'll wait for him, Doctor. I've waited a great many years for a chance like this.

EINSTEIN. We got him where we want him. Did he look guilty!

JONATHAN. Take the bags back to our room, Doctor. (*He goes to the window and closes it.*)

(ABBY, *who is wiping her hands on her apron, enters, followed by* MARTHA, *who has a saucer and dish towel in her hand.*)

ABBY. Have they gone? (*She sees* JONATHAN *and* EINSTEIN.) Oh—we thought we heard somebody leave.

JONATHAN. Just Mortimer—he'll be back in a few minutes. Is there any food left in the kitchen? I think Dr. Einstein and I would enjoy a bite.

MARTHA. You won't have time . . .

ABBY. Yes, if you're still here when Mortimer gets back, he won't like it.

EINSTEIN. He'll like it! He's gotta like it!

JONATHAN. Get something for us to eat, while we bury Mr. Spenalzo in the cellar.

MARTHA. Oh, no!

ABBY (*spiritedly*). He can't stay in our cellar, Jonathan. You've got to take him with you.

JONATHAN. There's a friend of Mortimer's downstairs waiting for him.

ABBY. A friend of Mortimer's?

JONATHAN. He and Mr. Spenalzo will get along fine together. They're both dead.

MARTHA. They must mean Mr. Hoskins.

EINSTEIN. Mr. Hoskins?

JONATHAN. So you know about what's downstairs?

ABBY. Of course we do, and he's no friend of Mortimer's. He's one of our gentlemen.

EINSTEIN. Your chentlemen?

MARTHA (*firmly*). And we won't have any strangers buried in our cellar.

JONATHAN. But Mr. Hoskins . . .

MARTHA. Mr. Hoskins isn't a stranger.

ABBY. Besides, there's no room for Mr. Spenalzo. The cellar's crowded already.

JONATHAN. Crowded? With what?

ABBY. There are twelve graves down there now.

JONATHAN. Twelve graves!

ABBY. That leaves very little room and we're going to need it.

JONATHAN. You mean you and Aunt Martha have murdered . . .

ABBY. Murdered! Certainly not! It's one of our charities.

MARTHA. What we've been doing is a mercy.

ABBY (*with a gesture of dismissal*). So you take your Mr. Spenalzo out of here.

JONATHAN (*amazed and impressed*). You've done that—right in this house—and buried them down there?

EINSTEIN. Chonny, we been chased all over the world . . . They stay right here in Brooklyn and do just as good as you do.

JONATHAN. What?

EINSTEIN. You got twelve, Chonny. They got twelve.

JONATHAN (*his pride wounded*). I've got thirteen.

EINSTEIN. No, twelve, Chonny.

JONATHAN. Thirteen! There's Mr. Spenalzo! Then the first one in London. Two in Johannesburg—one in Sydney—one in Melbourne—two in San Francisco—one in Phoenix, Arizona . . .

EINSTEIN. Phoenix?

JONATHAN. The filling station—the three in Chicago, and the one in South Bend. That makes thirteen.

EINSTEIN. But, Chonny, you can't count the one in South Bend. He died of pneumonia.

JONATHAN (*his record at stake*). He wouldn't have got pneumonia if I hadn't shot him.

EINSTEIN. No, Chonny, he died of pneumonia. He don't count.

JONATHAN. He counts with me! I say thirteen!

EINSTEIN. No, Chonny. You got twelve. They got twelve. The old ladies is just as good as you are.

JONATHAN (*wheeling on them*). Oh, they are, are they? That's easily taken care of! All I need is one more! —that's all—just one more!

(MORTIMER *enters hastily, closing the door behind him and turns to them with a nervous smile.*)

MORTIMER. Well—here I am!

(JONATHAN *looks at* MORTIMER *with the widening eyes of someone who has just solved a problem.*)

CURTAIN

ACT THREE

SCENE I

The curtain rises on an empty stage. We hear voices, voices in disagreement, from the cellar, through the open cellar door.

MARTHA (*off stage*). You stop doing that!

ABBY (*off stage*). This is our house and this is our cellar and you can't do that!

EINSTEIN (*off stage*). Ladies! Please go back upstairs where you belong.

JONATHAN (*off stage*). Abby! Martha! Go upstairs!

MARTHA (*off stage*). There's no use of your doing what you're doing because it will just have to be undone!

ABBY (*off stage*). I tell you we won't have it! (MARTHA *enters from the cellar.*)

MARTHA. You'll find out! You'll find out whose house this is! (*She goes to the street door, opens it and looks out.* ABBY *enters from the cellar. Both women are wearing their hats.*)

ABBY. I'm warning you! You'd better stop! (*To* MARTHA): Hasn't Mortimer come back yet?

MARTHA (*she closes the door*). No.

ABBY. It's a terrible thing—burying a good Methodist with a foreigner!

MARTHA. I won't have our cellar desecrated!

ABBY. And we promised Mr. Hoskins a full Christian funeral. . . . Where do you suppose Mortimer went?

MARTHA. I don't know. But he must be doing something. He said to Jonathan, "You just wait, I'll settle this!"

ABBY. Well, he can't settle it while he's out of the house. (*Turning to the cellar door.*) That's all we want settled—what's going on down there. (MORTIMER *enters from the street carrying* TEDDY'S *commitment papers in his hand.*)

MORTIMER (*grimly*). All right. Now, where's Teddy?

ABBY. Mortimer, where have you been?

MORTIMER. I've been over to Dr. Gilchrist's. I've got his signature on Teddy's commitment papers.

MARTHA. Mortimer, what's the matter with you?

ABBY. Running around getting papers signed at a time like this.

MARTHA. Do you know what Jonathan is doing?

ABBY. He's putting Mr. Hoskins and Mr. Spenalzo in together.

MORTIMER. Oh, he is, is he? Well, let him. Is Teddy in his room?

MARTHA. Teddy won't be any help.

MORTIMER. When he signs these commitment papers, I can tackle Jonathan.

ABBY. What have they got to do with it?

MORTIMER. You had to tell Jonathan about those twelve graves! If I can make Teddy responsible for those, I can protect you, don't you see?

ABBY. No, I don't see. And we pay taxes to have the police protect us.

MORTIMER (*starting upstairs*). I'll be back down in a minute.

ABBY. Come, Martha. (*To* MORTIMER): We're going for the police. (*The sisters get their gloves.*)

MORTIMER. All right. (*He suddenly realizes what has been said.*) The police! You can't go for the police. (*He rushes downstairs to the street door.*)

MARTHA. Why can't we?

MORTIMER. Because, if you told them about Mr. Spenalzo, they'd find Mr. Hoskins too; and that might make them curious, and they'd find out about the other gentlemen.

ABBY. Mortimer, we know the police better than you do. I don't think they'd pry into our private affairs if we asked them not to.

MORTIMER. But if they found your twelve gentlemen they'd have to report to headquarters.

MARTHA (*pulling on her gloves*). I'm not so sure they'd bother. They'd have to make out a very long report. And if there's one thing a policeman hates to do, it's to write.

MORTIMER. You can't depend on that! It might leak out! And you couldn't expect a judge and jury to understand.

MARTHA. Judge Cullman would.

ABBY (*drawing on her gloves*). We know him very well.

MARTHA. He always comes to church to pray just before election.

ABBY. And he's coming here to tea some day. He promised.

MARTHA. We'll have to speak to him again about that, Abby. (*To* MORTIMER): His wife died a few years ago and it's left him very lonely.

ABBY. Come along, Martha. (*She starts toward the door.* MORTIMER, *however, gets there first.*)

MORTIMER. You can't do this. I won't let you. You can't leave this house and you can't have Judge Cullman to tea!

ABBY. Well, if you're not going to do something about Mr. Spenalzo, we are.

MORTIMER. But I am going to do something. We may have to call the police in later, but if we do, I want to be ready for them.

MARTHA. You've got to get Jonathan out of this house!

ABBY. And Mr. Spenalzo, too!

MORTIMER. Will you please let me do it my own way? I've got to see Teddy. (*He starts upstairs.*)

ABBY. If they're not out of here by morning, Mortimer, we're going to call the police. (MORTIMER *turns at the top of the stairs.*)

MORTIMER. They'll be out. I promise you that! Go to bed, will you? And for God's sake get out of those clothes. You look like Judith Anderson. (*He exits upstairs.*)

MARTHA. Well, that's a relief, Abby.

ABBY. If Mortimer is doing something at last then Jonathan's just going to a lot of unnecessary trouble. We'd better tell him. (JONATHAN *comes up the cellar steps and into the room.*) Jonathan, you might as well stop what you're doing.

JONATHAN. It's all done. Did I hear Mortimer?

ABBY. Well, it will just have to be undone. You're all going to be out of this house by morning.

JONATHAN. Oh, we are? In that case, you and Aunt Martha can go to bed and have a peaceful night's sleep.

MARTHA (*always a little frightened by* JONATHAN). Yes. Come, Abby. (*They start up the stairs.*)

JONATHAN. Good night, aunties.

(*The sisters turn at the top of the stairs.*)

ABBY. Not good night, Jonathan. Good-by! By the time we get up you'll be out of this house. Mortimer's promised.

MARTHA. And he has a way of doing it, too!

JONATHAN. Then Mortimer is back?

ABBY. Yes, he's up here talking to Teddy.

MARTHA. Good-by, Jonathan.

ABBY. Good-by, Jonathan.

JONATHAN (*quietly*). Perhaps you'd better say good-by to Mortimer.

ABBY. Oh, you'll see Mortimer.

JONATHAN (*tense*). Yes, I'll see Mortimer. (ABBY *and* MARTHA *exit.* JONATHAN *stands without moving. There is murder on his mind. After an appreciable pause* EINSTEIN *comes up from the cellar dusting himself off. He is wearing Mr. Spenalzo's shoes.*)

EINSTEIN. Whew! That's all fixed up. Smooth like a lake. Nobody'd ever know they're there. (JONATHAN *still stands without moving.*) That bed feels good already. Forty-eight hours we didn't sleep. Whew! Come on, Chonny, let's go up, yes? (JONATHAN'S *eyes move to* EINSTEIN.)

JONATHAN. You're forgetting, Doctor.

EINSTEIN. Vas?

JONATHAN. My brother Mortimer.

EINSTEIN. Chonny, tonight? I'm sleepy. We do that tomorrow—the next day.

JONATHAN. No, tonight. Now!

EINSTEIN. Chonny, please! I'm tired . . . Tomorrow I got to operate . . .

JONATHAN. You're going to operate tomorrow, Doctor. But tonight we take care of Mortimer.

EINSTEIN. Chonny, not tonight—we go to bed, eh?

JONATHAN. Doctor, look at me! (EINSTEIN *looks and straightens up.*) You can see that it's going to be done, can't you?

EINSTEIN. Ach, Chonny! I can see! I know that look!

JONATHAN. It's a little late for us to dissolve our partnership.

EINSTEIN. OK, Chonny. We do it. But the quick way? The quick twist, like in London. (*He gives that London neck another twist with his hands.*)

JONATHAN. No, Doctor, I think this calls for something special. (JONA-

THAN *begins to anticipate a rare pleasure.*) I think, perhaps, the Melbourne method.

EINSTEIN. Chonny—No!—Not that! Two hours! And when it was all over —what? The fellow in London was just as dead as the fellow in Melbourne.

JONATHAN. We had to work too fast in London. There was no aesthetic satisfaction in it. Now, Melbourne—ah, there was something to remember.

EINSTEIN. Remember! (*He shivers.*) I wish I didn't. No, Chonny—not Melbourne—not me . . .

JONATHAN. Yes, Doctor. Where are the instruments?

EINSTEIN. I won't do it, Chonny! I won't do it!

JONATHAN. Get your instruments!

EINSTEIN. No, Chonny!

JONATHAN. Where are they? Oh, yes. You hid them in the cellar. Where?

EINSTEIN. I won't tell you!

JONATHAN. I'll find them, Doctor. (*He exits to the cellar.* EINSTEIN *paces desperately for a moment.* TEDDY *steps out on the balcony with his bugle and lifts it as if to blow.* MORTIMER *dashes out after him and grabs his arm.*)

MORTIMER. Don't do that, Mr. President!

TEDDY. I cannot sign any proclamation without consulting my cabinet.

MORTIMER. But this must be secret.

TEDDY. A secret proclamation? How unusual!

MORTIMER. Japan mustn't know until it's signed.

TEDDY. Japan? Those yellow devils! I'll sign it right away. You have my word for it. I can let the cabinet know later.

MORTIMER. Yes, let's go and sign it.

TEDDY. You wait here. If it's a secret proclamation it has to be signed in secret.

MORTIMER. At once, Mr. President.

TEDDY. I'll put on my signing clothes. (*He exits.* MORTIMER *comes downstairs.* EINSTEIN *takes* MORTIMER'S *hat from the hall-tree and meets him at the foot of the stairs.*)

EINSTEIN. You go now, eh? (*He hands* MORTIMER *his hat.*)

MORTIMER. No, Doctor, I'm waiting for something—something important. (MORTIMER *tosses his hat on the couch.*)

EINSTEIN (*urging* MORTIMER *to the door*). Please, you go now!

MORTIMER. Dr. Einstein, I have nothing against you personally. You seem to be a nice fellow. If you'll take my advice, you'll get out of this house and get just as far away as possible . . . There's going to be trouble.

EINSTEIN. Trouble, yah! You get out!

MORTIMER. All right, don't say I didn't warn you.

EINSTEIN. I'm warning you—get away quick!

MORTIMER. Things are going to start popping around here any minute.

EINSTEIN (*glancing nervously toward the cellar*). Chonny is in a bad mood. When he is like dis—he iss a madman! Things happen—terrible things!

MORTIMER. Jonathan doesn't worry me now.

EINSTEIN. Ach! Himmel! Don't those plays you see teach you anything?

MORTIMER. About what?

EINSTEIN. At least people in plays act like they got sense.

MORTIMER. Oh, you think so, do you? You think people in plays act intelligently. I wish you had to sit through some of the ones I have to sit through. This little opus tonight—for instance. In this play, there's a man . . . (JONATHAN *enters from the cellar, carrying the instrument case. He pauses in the doorway, unseen by* MORTIMER.) . . . he's supposed to be bright. He knows he's in a house with murderers—he ought to know he's in danger. He's even been warned to get out of the house. Does he go? No, he stays there. I ask you—is that what an intelligent person would do?

EINSTEIN. You're asking me!

MORTIMER. He didn't even have sense enough to be scared—to be on guard. For instance, the murderer invites him to sit down.

EINSTEIN. You mean "Won't you sit down"?

MORTIMER. Believe it or not, that one was in there, too.

EINSTEIN. And what did he do?

MORTIMER. He sat down! Mind you—this fellow is supposed to be bright. (MORTIMER *sits down.*) There he is—all ready to be trussed up. And what do they use to tie him with?

EINSTEIN. What?

MORTIMER. The curtain cord.

(JONATHAN *finds an idea being thrust on him, draws his knife, and goes to the window.*)

EINSTEIN. Well, why not? A good idea. Very convenient. (JONATHAN *cuts the curtain cord.*)

MORTIMER. A little too convenient. When are playwrights going to use some imagination? (JONATHAN *has coiled the curtain cord and is moving behind* MORTIMER.) The curtain cord!

EINSTEIN. He didn't see him get it?

MORTIMER. See him? He sat there with his back to him. That's the kind of stuff we have to suffer through night after night. And they say the critics are killing the theater. It's the playwrights that are killing the theater. So there he sat—the big dope—this guy that's supposed to be bright—waiting to be tied up and gagged. (JONATHAN *drops the looped curtain cord over* MORTIMER'S *shoulders, pulls it taut and ties it behind the back of the chair. Simultaneously* EINSTEIN *leaps to* MORTIMER, *pulls* MORTIMER'S *handkerchief out of his pocket and gags him with it.* JONATHAN *steps to* MORTIMER'S *side.*)

EINSTEIN (*tying* MORTIMER'S *legs*). You're right about that fellow—he wasn't very bright.

JONATHAN. Now if you don't mind, Mortimer—we'll finish the story. (MORTIMER *is making muted, unintelligible sounds.* JONATHAN *goes to the sideboard and brings the candelabra down to the table and lights the candles.*) Mortimer, I've been away for twenty years, but never, my dear brother, were you out of my mind. . . . In Melbourne one night —I dreamt of you. . . . When I landed in San Francisco—I felt a strange satisfaction—Once again I was in the same country with you. (JONATHAN *turns out the lights, throwing the room into an eerie candlelight. He picks up the instrument case and sets it down on the table between the candelabra.*) Now, Doctor—we go to work.

EINSTEIN. Please, Chonny—for me—the quick way—eh?

JONATHAN. Doctor, this must be an artistic achievement! After all, we're performing before a very distinguished critic.

EINSTEIN. Chonny . . .

JONATHAN (*flaring*). Doctor . . .

EINSTEIN. All right. Let's get it over! (JONATHAN *takes several instruments out of the case, handling them as potential accessories to torture. The last is a long probe, which he measures to* MORTIMER'S *face. Finally he begins to put on rubber gloves.* EINSTEIN *takes a bottle from his pocket, finds it empty.*) Chonny, I gotta have a drink, I can't do this without a drink.

JONATHAN. Pull yourself together, Doctor!

EINSTEIN. I gotta have a drink! Chonny, when we walked in this afternoon—there was wine there . . . (*He points to the table.*) Remember? Where did she put it? (*He remembers.*) Ah . . . (*He goes to sideboard and opens it, finding the wine.*) Look, Chonny! (*He takes the wine bottle to the table with two wine glasses.*) We got a drink. (*He pours the wine into the two glasses, the second glass emptying the bottle.* MORTIMER, *who has been squirming, stops, eyeing the bottle, then* JONATHAN *and* EINSTEIN.) That's all there is. I split it with you. We both need a drink! (EINSTEIN *hands one glass to* JONATHAN, *then raises the glass of poisoned wine and is about to drink.*)

JONATHAN. One moment, Doctor! Please! Where are your manners? (*To* MORTIMER:) Yes, Mortimer. I realize now that it was you who brought me back to Brooklyn. We drink to you! (*He raises his glass, sniffs the wine, hesitates, then proposes a grim toast.*) Doctor—to my dear dead brother! (*They are raising their glasses to their lips, when* TEDDY, *fully dressed and formally, steps out of the upper door onto the balcony and blows a terrific blast on his bugle.* EINSTEIN *and* JONATHAN *drop their glasses, spilling the wine.* TEDDY *turns around and goes out again.*)

EINSTEIN. Ach, Gott!

JONATHAN. Damn that idiot! He goes next! That's all. He goes next! (*He rushes to the staircase.*)

EINSTEIN. No, Chonny, not Teddy! That's where I shtop—not Teddy!

(*He intercepts* JONATHAN *at the stairs.*)

JONATHAN. We'll get to him later.

EINSTEIN. We don't get to him at all!

JONATHAN. Now we *have* to work fast!

EINSTEIN. Yah—the quick way—eh, Chonny?

JONATHAN. Yes—the quick way. (*He darts behind* MORTIMER, *pulling a large silk handkerchief from his pocket and drops it around* MORTIMER'S *neck. There is a knock on the door.* JONATHAN *and* EINSTEIN *are startled. The door opens and* OFFICER O'HARA *enters.*)

O'HARA. Hey, the Colonel's gotta quit blowing that horn!

(JONATHAN *and* EINSTEIN *quickly stand between* MORTIMER *and* O'HARA.)

JONATHAN. It's all right, officer. We're taking the bugle away from him.

O'HARA. There's going to be hell to pay in the morning. We promised the neighbors he wouldn't do that any more.

JONATHAN. It won't happen again, officer. Good night.

O'HARA. I better speak to him myself. Where are the lights? (O'HARA *turns on the lights.* EINSTEIN *and* JONATHAN *break for the kitchen door but stop when the lights go on.* O'HARA *closes the door and starts up the stairs.* MORTIMER *mumbles through the gag.* O'HARA *turns and sees him.*) Hey, you stood me up. I waited an hour at Kelly's for you (*He comes downstairs.* MORTIMER *is trying to talk.* O'HARA *turns to* EINSTEIN.) What happened to him?

EINSTEIN. He was explaining the play he saw tonight. That's what happened to a fellow in the play.

O'HARA. Did they have that in the play you saw tonight? (MORTIMER *nods his head.*) Gee, they practically stole that from the second act of *my* play. In the second act just before . . . I'd better begin at the beginning. It opens in my mother's dressing room, where I was born—only I ain't born yet. (MORTIMER *mumbles and moves his head.*) Huh? Oh, yes. (*He goes to* MORTIMER *and starts to remove the gag, then hesitates.*) No! You've got to hear the plot. (O'HARA *goes enthusiastically into his plot as the curtain is coming down.*) Well, she's sitting there making up, see—when out of a clear sky the door opens—and a man with a black mustache walks in . . .

CURTAIN

SCENE II

When the curtain rises again, daylight is streaming through the windows. MORTIMER *is still tied in his chair and seems to be in a semi-conscious state.* JONATHAN *is asleep on the couch near the stairs.* EINSTEIN, *pleasantly intoxicated, is seated, listening. There is a bottle of whisky on the table and two glasses.* O'HARA, *with his coat off and his collar loosened, has progressed to the most exciting scene of his play.*

O'HARA. . . . there she is lying unconscious across the table—in her longeray—the Chink is standing over her with a hatchet . . . (*He takes the pose.*) . . . I'm tied up in a chair just like you are . . . The place is an inferno of flames—it's on fire—great effect we got there—when all of a sudden—through the window—in comes Mayor La Guardia! (MORTIMER *is startled into consciousness, then collapses again.* O'HARA *is pacing with self-satisfaction.* EINSTEIN *pours himself a drink.*) Hey, remember who paid for that—go easy on it.

EINSTEIN. Well, I'm listening, ain't I?

O'HARA. How do you like it, so far?

EINSTEIN. It put Chonny to sleep. (EINSTEIN *goes over and shakes* JONATHAN.) Hey, Chonny!—Chonny!—want a drink?

O'HARA (*pouring drink*). Let him alone—if he ain't got no more interest than that—he don't get a drink. (O'HARA *tosses a drink down and is ready to resume his story.*) All right . . . it's three days later . . . I been transferred and I'm under charges—that's because somebody stole my badge—all right, I'm walking my beat on Staten Island—forty-sixth precinct—when a guy I'm following, it turns out is really following *me* . . . (*There is a knock at the door.*) Don't let anybody in. (EINSTEIN *hurries to the landing window and looks out.*) So I figure I'll outsmart him. There's a vacant house on the corner. I goes in.

EINSTEIN (*looking out*). It's cops!

O'HARA. I stands there in the dark and I sees the door handle turn.

EINSTEIN (*shaking* JONATHAN'S *shoulder*). Chonny! It's cops! It's cops! (EINSTEIN *hurries up the stairs.*)

O'HARA. I pulls my gun, I braces myself against the wall and I says "Come in!" (OFFICERS BROPHY *and* KLEIN *walk in, see* O'HARA *with his gun pointed toward them, and start to raise their hands.* EINSTEIN *exits upstairs.*) Hello, boys!

BROPHY (*recognizing* O'HARA). What the hell's going on here?

O'HARA. Hey, Pat, what do you know? This is Mortimer Brewster! He's going to write my play with me! I'm just telling him the story.

KLEIN. Did you have to tie him up to make him listen? (*He goes over and unties* MORTIMER.)

BROPHY. Joe, you'd better report in at the station. The whole force is out looking for you.

O'HARA. Did they send you boys here for me?

KLEIN. We didn't know you was here.

BROPHY. We came to warn the old ladies that there's hell to pay. The Colonel blew that bugle again in the middle of the night.

KLEIN. From the way the neighbors have been calling in about it you'd think the Germans had dropped a bomb in Flatbush Avenue.

BROPHY. The lieutenant's on the warpath. He says the Colonel's got to be put away some place.

(KLEIN *helps* MORTIMER *to his feet.*)

MORTIMER (*weakly*). Yes! (*He staggers toward the stairs.* O'HARA *follows him.*)

O'HARA. Listen, Mr. Brewster. I got to go, so I'll just run through the third act quick.

MORTIMER. Get away from me! (BROPHY *goes to the telephone and dials.*)

KLEIN. Say, do you know what time it is? It's after eight o'clock in the morning.

O'HARA. It is? Gee, Mr. Brewster, them first two acts run a little long. But I don't see anything we can leave out.

MORTIMER. You can leave it all out.

(BROPHY *sees* JONATHAN *on the couch.*)

BROPHY. Who the hell is this guy?

MORTIMER. It's my brother.

BROPHY. Oh, the one that ran away? So he came back.

MORTIMER. Yes, he came back. (*He has reached the balcony.*)

BROPHY (*into the telephone*). This is Brophy. Get me Mac. (*To* O'HARA): I'd better let them know I found you, Joe. (KLEIN *has wandered over to the other side of* JONATHAN *and looks down at him.* BROPHY *is looking at* O'HARA.) Mac? Tell the lieutenant he can call off the big man hunt. We got him. In the Brewster house. (JONATHAN *hears this and suddenly becomes very awake, looking up to see a policeman on each side of him.*) Do you want us to bring him in? Oh, all right—we'll hold him right here. (*He hangs up.*) The lieutenant's on his way over. (JONATHAN *is now on his feet between the two policemen, under the impression that he is cornered.*)

JONATHAN. So, I've been turned in, eh? (BROPHY *and* KLEIN *look at him with interest.*) All right, you've got me! I suppose you and my stool-pigeon brother will split the reward.

KLEIN. Reward? (*Instinctively* KLEIN *and* BROPHY *both grab* JONATHAN *by an arm.*)

JONATHAN. Now I'll do some turning in! You think my aunts are charming, sweet old ladies, don't you? Well, there are thirteen bodies buried in their cellar!

MORTIMER (*exits upstairs, calling*). Teddy! Teddy!

KLEIN. What the hell are you talking about?

BROPHY. You'd better be careful what you say about your aunts—they happen to be friends of ours.

JONATHAN. I'll show you! I'll prove it to you! Come down in the cellar with me! (*He starts to drag them toward the cellar door.*)

KLEIN. Wait a minute!

JONATHAN. Thirteen bodies—I'll show you where they're buried!

KLEIN (*refusing to be kidded*). Oh, yeah?

JONATHAN. Oh, you don't want to see what's down in the cellar! (BROPHY *releases* JONATHAN'S *arm.*)

BROPHY. Go on down in the cellar with him, Abe.

KLEIN (*stepping away from* JONATHAN). I'm not so sure I want to be down in the cellar with him. Look at that puss. He looks like Boris Karloff. (JONATHAN, *at the mention of Boris Karloff, leaps at* KLEIN'S *throat.*)

BROPHY. What d'you think you're doing?

KLEIN. Get him off me. Pat! Grab him! (BROPHY *swings on* JONATHAN *with his nightstick.* JONATHAN *falls, unconscious.*) Well, what do you know about that?

(*There is a knock on the door.*)

O'HARA. Come in!

(LIEUTENANT ROONEY *bursts in. He is a very tough, driving, dominating police officer.*)

ROONEY. What the hell are you men doing here? I told you *I* was going to handle this.

KLEIN. Well, sir, we was just . . . (KLEIN'S *eyes go to the prostrate* JONATHAN *and* ROONEY *sees him.*)

ROONEY. What happened? Did he put up a fight?

BROPHY. This ain't the guy that blows the bugle. This is his brother. He tried to kill Klein.

KLEIN (*feeling his throat*). All I said was he looked like Boris Karloff.

(ROONEY *gives them a look.*)

ROONEY. Turn him over!

BROPHY. We kinda think he's wanted somewhere.

(KLEIN *and* BROPHY *turn* JONATHAN *over and* ROONEY *takes a look at him.*)

ROONEY. Oh, you kinda *think* he's wanted somewhere? If you guys don't look at the circulars we hang up in the station, at least you could read *True Detective*. Certainly he's wanted! In Indiana! Escaped from the Prison for the Criminal Insane—

he's a lifer. For God's sake, that's how he was described—he looked like Karloff!

KLEIN. Was there a reward mentioned?

ROONEY. Yeah—and I'm claiming it.

BROPHY. He was trying to get us down in the cellar.

KLEIN. He said there was thirteen bodies buried down there.

ROONEY. Thirteen bodies buried in the cellar? And that didn't tip you off he came out of a nuthouse?

O'HARA. I thought all along he talked kinda crazy.

(ROONEY *sees* O'HARA *for the first time.*)

ROONEY. Oh—it's Shakespeare! Where have you been all night—and you needn't bother to tell me.

O'HARA. I've been right here, sir, writing a play with Mortimer Brewster.

ROONEY. Yeah? Well, you're going to have plenty of time to write that play. You're suspended!

O'HARA (*getting his hat and coat*). Can I come over some time and use the station typewriter?

ROONEY. No! Get out! (O'HARA *gets out.* TEDDY *enters on the balcony and comes downstairs.*) Take that guy somewhere else and bring him to. See what you can find out about his accomplice—the guy that helped him escape. He's wanted, too. (KLEIN *and* BROPHY *are bending over* JONATHAN.) No wonder Brooklyn's in the shape it's in. With the police force full of flatheads like you. Falling for that kind of a story—thirteen bodies buried in the cellar. (TEDDY *has reached* ROONEY'S *side.*)

TEDDY. But there are thirteen bodies in the cellar.

ROONEY (*turning on him*). Who are you?

TEDDY. I'm President Roosevelt.

(ROONEY *goes slightly crazy.*)

ROONEY. What the hell is this?

BROPHY. He's the fellow that blows the bugle.

KLEIN. Good morning, Colonel.

(BROPHY *and* KLEIN *salute* TEDDY. TEDDY *returns the salute.* ROONEY *almost salutes but stops halfway.*)

ROONEY. Well, Colonel, you've blown your last bugle!

(TEDDY'S *attention has been attracted to the body on the floor.*)

TEDDY. Dear me, another yellow fever victim!

ROONEY. What!

TEDDY. All the bodies in the cellar are yellow fever victims.

(ROONEY *takes a walk on this.*)

BROPHY. No, Colonel, this is a spy we caught in the White House.

ROONEY (*pointing to* JONATHAN). Will you get that guy out of here? (BROPHY *and* KLEIN *pick up* JONATHAN.) Bring him to and question him.

(MORTIMER *enters on the balcony carrying* TEDDY'S *commitment papers, and starts downstairs.*)

TEDDY. If there's any questioning of spies—that's my department!

(BROPHY *and* KLEIN *drag* JONATHAN *into the kitchen.* TEDDY *starts to follow.*)

ROONEY. Hey, you—keep out of that.

TEDDY. You're forgetting. As President, I'm also head of the Secret Service. (*He exits into the kitchen.* MORTIMER *has come down.*)

MORTIMER. Captain—I'm Mortimer Brewster.

ROONEY (*dizzy by this time*). Are you sure?

MORTIMER. I'd like to talk to you about my brother Teddy—the one who blew the bugle.

ROONEY. Mr. Brewster, we ain't going to talk about that—he's got to be put away.

MORTIMER. I quite agree with you, Captain. In fact, it's all arranged for. I had these commitment papers signed by Dr. Gilchrist last night. Teddy has just signed them himself—you see. And I've signed them as next of kin.

(ROONEY *looks at the papers.* EINSTEIN *enters hurriedly through the arch, sees the policeman and sneaks back out of sight.*)

ROONEY. Where's he going?

MORTIMER. Happy Dale . . .

ROONEY. All right. I don't care where he goes as long as he goes.

MORTIMER. Oh, he's going all right. But I want you to understand that everything that's happened around here Teddy's responsible for. Now, those thirteen bodies in the cellar . . .

ROONEY. Yeah—those thirteen bodies in the cellar! It ain't enough that the neighbors are afraid of him and his disturbing the peace with that bugle—but can you imagine what would happen if that cockeyed story about thirteen bodies in the cellar got around? And now he's starting a yellow fever scare. Cute, ain't it?

MORTIMER (*greatly relieved and with an embarrassed laugh*). Thirteen bodies! Do you think anybody would believe that story?

ROONEY. You can't tell. Some people are just dumb enough. You don't know what to believe sometimes. A year ago, a crazy guy started a murder rumor over in Greenpernt and I had to dig up a half-acre lot, just to prove . . .

(*There is a knock at the door.*)

MORTIMER. Excuse me! (*He goes to the door and admits* ELAINE *and* MR. WITHERSPOON, *an elderly, tight-lipped disciplinarian. He is carrying a briefcase.*)

ELAINE (*briskly*). Good morning, Mortimer!

MORTIMER. Good morning, dear.

ELAINE. This is Mr. Witherspoon. He's come to meet Teddy.

MORTIMER. To meet Teddy?

ELAINE. Mr. Witherspoon's the superintendent of Happy Dale.

MORTIMER (*eagerly*). Oh, come right in! This is Captain . . .

ROONEY. Lieutenant Rooney. I'm glad you're here, Super, because you're taking him back with you today.

WITHERSPOON. Today! I had no idea . . .

ELAINE. Not today!

MORTIMER. Elaine, I've got a lot of business to attend to, so you run along home and I'll call you up.

ELAINE. Nuts! (*She walks over and plants herself on the window seat.*)

WITHERSPOON. I didn't realize it was this immediate.

ROONEY. The papers are all signed. He goes today.

(TEDDY *enters from the kitchen.*)

TEDDY (*looking back*). It's insubordination. You'll find out I'm no mollycoddle. (*He advances into the room angrily.*) When the President of the United States is treated that way, what's this country coming to?

ROONEY. There's your man, Super.

MORTIMER. Just a minute! (*He goes to* TEDDY *and speaks with great dignity.*) Mr. President! I have very good news for you. Your term of office is over.

TEDDY. Is this March fourth?

MORTIMER. Practically.

TEDDY. Let's see! (*He thinks it over.*) Oh—now I go on my hunting trip to Africa! Well, I must get started immediately. (*He starts across, sees* WITHERSPOON, *steps back to* MORTIMER, *and speaks sotto voce.*) Is he trying to move into the White House before I've moved out?

MORTIMER. Who, Teddy?

TEDDY (*indicating* WITHERSPOON). Taft!

MORTIMER. This isn't Mr. Taft, Teddy. This is Mr. Witherspoon. He's going to be your guide in Africa.

TEDDY. Bully! Bully! (*He shakes* MR. WITHERSPOON'S *hand.*) Wait right here—I'll bring down my equipment. (MARTHA *and* ABBY *enter on the balcony and come downstairs.*) When the safari comes tell them to wait. (*To his aunts as he passes them on the stairs:*) Good-by, Aunt Abby. Good-by, Aunt Martha. I'm on my way to Africa. Isn't it wonderful? (*He has reached the landing.*) Charge! (*He charges up and out.*)

MARTHA. Good morning, Mortimer.

MORTIMER. Good morning, darlings.

MARTHA. Good morning, Elaine. Well, we have visitors.

MORTIMER. This is Lieutenant Rooney.

ABBY (*going to him*). Well, Lieutenant, you don't look like the fussbudget the policemen say you are.

MORTIMER. Why, the Lieutenant is here—you know Teddy blew that bugle again last night.

MARTHA. Yes, we're going to speak to Teddy about that.

ROONEY. It's a little more serious than that, Miss Brewster.

MORTIMER. And you haven't met Mr. Witherspoon—he's the superintendent of Happy Dale.

ABBY. How do you do?

MARTHA. Oh—you've come to meet Teddy.

ROONEY. He's come to take him.

MORTIMER. Aunties, the police want Teddy to go there today.

ABBY. Oh—no!

MARTHA. Not as long as we're alive!

ROONEY. I'm sorry, Miss Brewster, but it has to be done. The papers are all signed and he's going along with the superintendent.

ABBY. We won't permit it! We'll promise to take the bugle away from him.

MARTHA. We won't be separated from Teddy!

ROONEY. I know how you feel, ladies, but the law's the law. He's committed himself and he's going.

ABBY. Well, if he goes, we're going too.

MARTHA. Yes, you'll have to take us with him.

MORTIMER. Well, why not?

WITHERSPOON (*to* MORTIMER). It's sweet of them to want to, but it's impossible. You see, we can't take sane people at Happy Dale.

MARTHA. Mr. Witherspoon, if you'll let us live there with Teddy, we'll see that Happy Dale is in our will and for a very generous amount.

WITHERSPOON. The Lord knows we could use the money, but I'm afraid . . .

ROONEY. Now, let's be sensible about this, ladies. For instance, here I am wasting my morning when I've got serious work to do. You know there are still murders to be solved in Brooklyn.

MORTIMER. Yes! (*He remembers a few.*) Oh, are there?

ROONEY. It ain't only his bugle-blowing and the neighbors all afraid of him, but things would just get worse. Sooner or later we'd be put to the trouble of digging up your cellar.

ABBY. Our cellar?

ROONEY. Yeah—your nephew is telling around that there are thirteen bodies buried in your cellar.

ABBY. But there are thirteen bodies in our cellar.

MARTHA. If that's why you think Teddy has to go away—you come down to the cellar with us and we'll prove it to you.

ABBY. There's one, Mr. Spenalzo—who doesn't belong there and is going to have to leave—and the other twelve are our gentlemen.

(MORTIMER *crosses and stands in front of the cellar door to head them off.*)

MORTIMER. I don't think the lieutenant wants to go down in the cellar. He was just telling me that last year he had to dig up a half-acre lot—weren't you, Lieutenant?

ABBY. Oh, he doesn't have to dig here. The graves are all marked. We put flowers on them every Sunday.

ROONEY. Flowers! (*He thinks that one over and looks at* WITHERSPOON.) Superintendent—don't you think you can find room for these ladies?

WITHERSPOON. Well, I . . .

ABBY. You come along with us—and see the graves.

ROONEY. I'll take your word for it, lady—I'm a busy man. How about it, Super?

WITHERSPOON. They'd have to be committed.

MORTIMER. Teddy committed himself. Can't they do that? Can't they sign the papers?

WITHERSPOON. Certainly.

MARTHA. Oh, if we can go with Teddy we'll sign the papers. Where are they?

ABBY. Yes, where are they?

(*The sisters cross to the table and sit, ready to sign.* WITHERSPOON *produces the papers from his briefcase.* KLEIN *enters from kitchen.*)

KLEIN (*to* ROONEY). He's coming around, Lieutenant.

ABBY. Good morning, Mr. Klein.

MARTHA. Good morning, Mr. Klein. Are you here, too?

KLEIN. Yeah, me and Brophy have got your other nephew out in the kitchen.

ROONEY. Sign 'em up, Superintendent. I want to get this all cleaned up. Thirteen bodies! (*He and* KLEIN *exit into the kitchen.* WITHERSPOON *and* MORTIMER *produce fountain pens.*)

WITHERSPOON (*to* MARTHA). If you'll sign right here.

(MARTHA *takes his pen.*)

MORTIMER (*handing* ABBY *his pen*). And you here, Aunt Abby.

ABBY. I'm really looking forward to going. The neighborhood here has changed so.

MARTHA. Just think, a front lawn again!

(*They both sign.* EINSTEIN *enters on the balcony and comes downstairs stealthily.*)

WITHERSPOON. Oh—we're overlooking something.

MARTHA. What?

WITHERSPOON. Well, we're going to need the signature of a physician.

(MORTIMER *straightens up, sees* EINSTEIN *slipping out the door.*)

MORTIMER. Oh, Dr. Einstein! Will you come over here and sign some papers?

EINSTEIN. Please . . .

MORTIMER. Come right along, Doctor. At one time last night, I thought the doctor was going to operate on me. (EINSTEIN *crosses nervously to the table.*) Just sign right here.

(ROONEY *enters and goes to the telephone, unseen by* EINSTEIN, and *starts dialing.* KLEIN *has come in through the kitchen door.*)

ABBY. Were you leaving, Doctor?

EINSTEIN. Yes, I think so.

MARTHA. Aren't you going to wait for Jonathan?

EINSTEIN. I don't think we're going to the same place. (EINSTEIN *signs the papers hurriedly.* MORTIMER *suddenly rediscovers* ELAINE *patiently sitting on the window seat.*)

MORTIMER. Oh, hello, darling! Glad to see you. Stick around.

ELAINE. Don't worry. I'm going to.

ROONEY (*into the telephone*). Hello, Mac. Rooney. We've picked up that guy that's wanted in Indiana. There's a description of his accomplice on the circular—it's right on the desk there. Read it to me. (EINSTEIN *starts for the kitchen but sees* KLEIN. *He retreats toward the front door but is stopped by* ROONEY'S *voice.* ROONEY'S *eyes are somewhat blankly on* EINSTEIN *through the following description.*) Yeah—about fifty-four—five-foot-six—a hundred and forty pounds—blue eyes—talks with a German accent—poses as a doctor—— Thanks, Mac. (*He hangs up.*)

WITHERSPOON (*to* ROONEY). It's all right, Lieutenant. The doctor here has just completed the signatures.

ROONEY (*going to* EINSTEIN *and shaking his hand*). Thanks, Doc. You're really doing Brooklyn a service. (ROONEY *and* KLEIN *exit into kitchen.*)

EINSTEIN (*bolts for the front door*). If you'll excuse me, I'd better hurry. (*He exits, waving a good-by. The aunts wave gaily back.*)

WITHERSPOON (*to* MORTIMER). Mr. Brewster, you sign now as next of kin.

ABBY. (*a little upset by this*). Martha . . .

(*The sisters go into a huddle.*)

MORTIMER. Oh, yes, of course. Right here? (*He signs the papers.*)

WITHERSPOON. Yes. . . . That's fine.

MORTIMER. That makes everything complete? Everything legal?

WITHERSPOON. Oh, yes.

MORTIMER. Well, Aunties, now you're safe!

WITHERSPOON (*to the aunts*). When do you think you'll be ready to start?

ABBY (*nervously*). Well, Mr. Witherspoon, why don't you go up and tell Teddy what he can take along?

WITHERSPOON. Upstairs? (*He starts across the room.*)

MORTIMER. I'll show you. (*He starts, but* ABBY *stops him.*)

ABBY. No, Mortimer, you stay here. We want to talk to you. (*To* WITHERSPOON:) Just up the stairs and turn left. (WITHERSPOON *starts up, the sisters keeping an eye on him while talking to* MORTIMER.)

MARTHA. Mortimer, now that we're moving—this house is really yours.

ABBY. Yes, Mortimer, we want you to live here.

MORTIMER. No, Aunt Abby, I couldn't do that. This house is too full of memories.

MARTHA. But you'll need a home when you and Elaine are married.

MORTIMER. Darlings, that's very indefinite.

ELAINE (*still in there fighting*). It's nothing of the kind. We're going to be married right away.

(*The sisters watch* WITHERSPOON *as he exits through the balcony door, then turn to* MORTIMER.)

ABBY. Mortimer, we're really very worried about something.

MORTIMER. Now, Aunt Abby, you're going to love it at Happy Dale.

MARTHA. Oh, yes, we're very happy about the whole thing! That's just it! We don't want anything to go wrong.

ABBY. Will they investigate those signatures?

MORTIMER. Now, don't worry—they're not going to look up Dr. Einstein.

MARTHA. It's not his signature, dear, it's yours.

ABBY. You see, you signed as next of kin.

MORTIMER. Of course. Why not?

MARTHA. It's something we've never wanted to tell you, Mortimer. But now you're a man—and it's something Elaine should know, too. You see, you're not really a Brewster.

(MORTIMER *stares.*)

ABBY. Your mother came to us as a cook—and you were born about three months afterward. But she was such a sweet woman—and such a good cook—and we didn't want to lose her—so brother married her.

MORTIMER. I'm — not — really — a — Brewster?

MARTHA. Now don't feel badly about it, Mortimer.

ABBY. And you won't let it make any difference, Elaine?

MORTIMER. Elaine! Did you hear—do you understand? I'm a bastard!

(ELAINE *leaps into his illegitimate arms.*)

MARTHA (*relieved*). Well, I'll have to see about breakfast. (*She starts for the kitchen.*)

ELAINE. Mortimer's coming to my house. Father's gone to Philadelphia and Mortimer and I are going to have breakfast together.

MORTIMER. Yes, I need some coffee. I've had quite a night.

ABBY. Well, Mortimer, in that case, I should think you'd want to get to bed.

MORTIMER (*with a glance at* ELAINE). I do. (*He leads her out.* ABBY *closes the door.* WITHERSPOON *enters from balcony door, carrying an armful of canteens.* TEDDY *enters with an enormous, two-bladed canoe paddle.*)

TEDDY. Just a minute, Mr. Witherspoon. Take this with you. (*He hands the paddle to* WITHERSPOON *and goes back through the balcony door.* WITHERSPOON, *encumbered, comes downstairs.* ROONEY *enters from the kitchen, followed by* JONATHAN, *handcuffed to* KLEIN *and* BROPHY.)

ROONEY. We won't need the wagon. My car's out front.

MARTHA (*pleasantly*). Oh, you leaving now, Jonathan?

ROONEY. Yes. He's going to Indiana. Some people out there want to take care of him the rest of his life. (*To* JONATHAN:) Come on. (*The handcuffed three start.*)

ABBY. Well, Jonathan, it's nice to know you have some place to go.

(JONATHAN *stops.*)

JONATHAN. Good-by, Aunt Abby. Good-by, Aunt Martha.

MARTHA. We're leaving, too.

ABBY. We're going to Happy Dale.

JONATHAN. Then this house is seeing the last of the Brewsters.

MARTHA. Unless Mortimer would like to live here.

JONATHAN. I have a suggestion. Why don't you turn this property over to the church?

(*The aunts look at each other.*)

ABBY. Well, we never thought of that.

JONATHAN (*dryly*). After all, it should be a part of the cemetery. (*He starts, then turns back.*) Well, I won't be able to better my record now, but neither will you. At least, I have that satisfaction. The score stands even—twelve to twelve. (JONATHAN *and the policemen exit. The aunts bristle slightly, looking out after* JONATHAN.)

MARTHA. Jonathan always was a mean boy. He never could stand to see anyone get ahead of him. (*She closes the door.*)

ABBY. I wish we could show him he isn't so smart. (*She turns and her eyes fall on* WITHERSPOON, *standing looking out the window. She studies him.* MARTHA *turns from the door and sees* ABBY'S *contemplation.*) Mr. Witherspoon, does your family live with you at Happy Dale?

WITHERSPOON. I have no family.

ABBY. Oh . . .

MARTHA. Well, I suppose you consider everyone at Happy Dale your family.

WITHERSPOON. I'm afraid you don't understand. As head of the institution, I have to keep quite aloof.

ABBY. That must make it very lonely for you.

WITHERSPOON. It does. But my duty is my duty.

ABBY (*benignly*). Well, Martha . . . (MARTHA *immediately starts for the sideboard.*) If Mr. Witherspoon won't have breakfast with us, I think at least we should offer him a glass of elderberry wine.

WITHERSPOON. Elderberry wine?

(MARTHA *takes out a wine bottle but it is the one* EINSTEIN *has emptied. She reaches in for another.*)

MARTHA. We make it ourselves. (*She uncorks the fresh bottle.*)

WITHERSPOON. Why, yes! Of course, at Happy Dale our relationship will be more formal, but here . . . (*He sits, as* MARTHA *brings the wine with a single wine glass to the table.*) You don't see much elderberry wine nowadays. I thought I'd had my last glass of it.

ABBY. Oh, no . . .

MARTHA (*handing it to him*). Here it is!

(WITHERSPOON *bows to the ladies and lifts the glass to his lips, but the curtain falls before he does.*)

CURTAIN

Oklahoma!

A MUSICAL PLAY BY

RICHARD RODGERS

AND

OSCAR HAMMERSTEIN, 2ND

BASED ON *Lynn Riggs'*

GREEN GROW THE LILACS

BOOK AND LYRICS BY

OSCAR HAMMERSTEIN, 2ND

OKLAHOMA! was first produced by The Theatre Guild on April 1, 1943, at the St. James Theatre, New York City, with the following cast:

(IN ORDER OF APPEARANCE)

AUNT ELLER	Betty Garde
CURLY	Alfred Drake
LAUREY	Joan Roberts
IKE SKIDMORE	Barry Kelley
FRED	Edwin Clay
SLIM	Herbert Rissman
WILL PARKER	Lee Dixon
JUD FRY	Howard da Silva
ADO ANNIE CARNES	Celeste Holm
ALI HAKIM	Joseph Buloff
GERTIE CUMMINGS	Jane Lawrence
ELLEN	Katharine Sergava
KATE	Ellen Love
SYLVIE	Joan McCracken
ARMINA	Kate Friedlich
AGGIE	Bambi Linn
ANDREW CARNES	Ralph Riggs
CORD ELAM	Owen Martin
JESS	George Church
CHALMERS	David Tihmar
MIKE	Paul Shiers
JOE	George Irving
SAM	Hayes Gordon

DIRECTED BY Rouben Mamoulian
DANCES BY Agnes de Mille
SETTINGS BY Lemuel Ayers
COSTUMES BY Miles White
ORCHESTRA DIRECTED BY Joseph Schwartzdorf
ORCHESTRATIONS BY Russell Bennett
PRODUCTION UNDER THE SUPERVISION OF
Theresa Helburn and Lawrence Langner

SCENES

ACT ONE

Scene I: The Front of Laurey's Farmhouse
Scene II: The Smokehouse
Scene III: A Grove on Laurey's Farm

ACT TWO

Scene I: The Skidmore Ranch
Scene II: Skidmore's Kitchen Porch
Scene III: The Back of Laurey's House
TIME: *Just after the turn of the century*
PLACE: *Indian Territory (Now Oklahoma)*

MUSICAL NUMBERS

ACT ONE

SCENE I

Oh, What a Beautiful Mornin'	Curly
The Surrey with the Fringe on Top	Curly, Laurey, Aunt Eller
Kansas City	Will, Aunt Eller and the Boys
I Cain't Say No	Ado Annie
Many a New Day	Laurey and the Girls
It's a Scandal! It's a Outrage!	Ali Hakim and the Boys and Girls
People Will Say We're in Love	Curly and Laurey

SCENE II

Pore Jud	Curly and Jud
Lonely Room	Jud

SCENE III

Out of My Dreams	Laurey and the Girls

ACT TWO

SCENE I

The Farmer and the Cowman	Sung by Carnes, Aunt Eller, Curly, Will, Ado Annie, Fred and Ensemble
All er Nuthin'	Ado Annie and Will and Two Dancing Girls

SCENE II

Reprise: People Will Say We're in Love	Curly and Laurey

SCENE III

Oklahoma	Curly, Laurey, Aunt Eller, Ike, Fred and Ensemble
Oh, What a Beautiful Mornin'	Laurey, Curly and Ensemble
Finale	Entire Company

ACT ONE

SCENE I

SCENE: *The front of* LAUREY'S *farmhouse.*

"It is a radiant summer morning several years ago, the kind of morning which, enveloping the shapes of earth men, cattle in a meadow, blades of the young corn, streams—makes them seem to exist now for the first time, their images giving off a golden emanation that is partly true and partly a trick of the imagination, focusing to keep alive a loveliness that may pass away."

AUNT ELLER MURPHY, *a buxom hearty woman about fifty, is seated behind a wooden, brass-banded churn, looking out over the meadow (which is the audience), a contented look on her face. Like the voice of the morning, a song comes from somewhere, growing louder as the young singer comes nearer.*

CURLY (*off stage*).

There's a bright, golden haze on the meadow,
There's a bright, golden haze on the meadow.
The corn is as high as a elephant's eye
An' it looks like it's climbin' clear up to the sky.

(CURLY *saunters on and stands tentatively outside the gate to the front yard.*)

Oh, what a beautiful mornin',
Oh, what a beautiful day.
I got a beautiful feelin'
Ev'rythin's goin' my way.

(CURLY *opens the gate and walks over to the porch, obviously singing for the benefit of someone inside the house.* AUNT ELLER *looks straight ahead, elaborately ignoring* CURLY.)

All the cattle are standin' like statues,
All the cattle are standin' like statues.
They don't turn their heads as they see me ride by,
But a little brown mav'rick is winkin' her eye.
Oh, what a beautiful mornin',
Oh, what a beautiful day.
I got a beautiful feelin'
Ev'rythin's goin' my way.

(CURLY *comes up behind* AUNT ELLER *and shouts in her ear.*)

Hi, Aunt Eller!

AUNT ELLER.

Skeer me to death! Whut're you doin' around here?

CURLY.

Come a-singin' to you. (*Strolling a few steps away.*)

All the sounds of the earth are like music—
All the sounds of the earth are like music.
The breeze is so busy it don't miss a tree
And a ol' weepin' willer is laughin' at me!

Oh, what a beautiful mornin',
Oh, what a beautiful day.
I got a beautiful feelin'
Ev'rythin's goin' my way. . . .
Oh, what a beautiful day!

(AUNT ELLER *resumes churning.* CURLY *looks wistfully up at the windows of the house, then turns back to* AUNT ELLER.)

AUNT ELLER.

If I wasn't a ole womern, and if you wasn't so young and smart-alecky—why, I'd marry you and git you to set around at night and sing to me.

CURLY.

No, you wouldn't neither. Cuz I wouldn't marry you ner none of yer kinfolks, I could he'p it.

AUNT ELLER (*wisely*).

Oh, none of my kinfolks, huh?

CURLY (*raising his voice so that* LAUREY *will hear if she is inside the house*).

And you c'n tell 'em that, *all* of 'm includin' that niece of your'n, Miss Laurey Williams! (AUNT ELLER *continues to churn.* CURLY *comes down to her and speaks deliberately.*) Aunt Eller, if you was to tell me whur Laurey was at—whur would you tell me she was at?

AUNT ELLER.

I wouldn't tell you a-tall. Fer as fer as I c'n make out, Laurey ain't payin' you no heed.

CURLY.

So, she don't take to me much, huh? Whur'd you git sich a uppity niece 'at wouldn't pay no heed to me? Who's the best bronc buster in this yere territory?

AUNT ELLER.

You, I bet.

CURLY.

And the best bull-dogger in seventeen counties? Me, that's who! And looky here, I'm handsome, ain't I?

AUNT ELLER.

Purty as a pitcher.

CURLY.

Curly-headed, ain't I? And bow-legged from the saddle fer God knows how long, ain't I?

AUNT ELLER.

Couldn't stop a pig in the road.

CURLY.

Well, whut else does she want then, the damn she-mule?

AUNT ELLER.

I don't know. But I'm shore sartin it ain't you. Who you takin' to the Box Social tonight?

CURLY.

Ain't thought much about it.

AUNT ELLER.

Bet you come over to ast Laurey.

CURLY.

Whut 'f I did?

AUNT ELLER.

You astin' me too? I'll wear my fascinator.

CURLY.

Yeow, you too.

LAUREY (*singing off stage*).

Oh, what a beautiful mornin'
(*She enters.*)
Oh, what a beautiful day

(*Spoken as she gives* CURLY *a brief glance.*)

Oh, I thought you was somebody.

(*She resumes singing, crosses to clothesline and hangs up an apron.*)

I got a beautiful feelin'
Ev'rythin's goin' my way.

(*Spoken as she comes down to* AUNT ELLER.)

Is this all that's come a-callin' and it a'ready ten o'clock of a Sattiddy mornin'?

CURLY.

You knowed it was me 'fore you opened the door.

LAUREY.

No sich of a thing.

CURLY.

You did, too! You heared my voice and knowed it was me.

LAUREY.

I heared a voice a-talkin' rumbly along with Aunt Eller. And heared someone a-singin' like a bullfrog in a pond.

CURLY.

You knowed it was me, so you set in there a-thinkin' up sump'n mean to say. I'm a good mind not to ast you to the Box Social.

(AUNT ELLER *rises, crosses to clothesline, takes down quilt, folds it, puts it on porch.*)

LAUREY.

If you did ast me, I wouldn't go with you. Besides, how'd you take me? You ain't bought a new buggy with red wheels onto it, have you?

CURLY.

No, I ain't.

LAUREY.

And a spankin' team with their bridles all jinglin'?

CURLY.

No.

LAUREY.

'Spect me to ride on behind ole Dun, I guess. You better ast that ole Cummin's girl you've tuck sich a shine to, over acrost the river.

CURLY.

If I was to ast you, they'd be a way to take you, Miss Laurey Smarty.

LAUREY.

Oh, they would?

(CURLY *now proceeds to stagger* LAUREY *with an idea. But she doesn't let on at first how she is "tuck up" with it.* AUNT ELLER *is the one who falls like a ton of bricks immediately and helps* CURLY *try to sell it to* LAUREY.)

CURLY.

When I take you out tonight with
me,
Honey, here's the way it's goin' to be;
You will set behind a team of snow-
white horses
In the slickest gig you ever see!

AUNT ELLER.

Lands!

CURLY.

Chicks and ducks and geese better
scurry
When I take you out in the surrey,
When I take you out in the surrey
with the fringe on top!
Watch thet fringe and see how it
flutters
When I drive them high-steppin'
strutters!
Nosey-pokes'll peek through their
shutters and their eyes will pop!
The wheels are yeller, the uphol-
stery's brown,
The dashboard's genuine leather,
With isinglass curtains y'c'n roll right
down
In case there's a change in the
weather—
Two bright side-lights, winkin' and
blinkin',
Ain't no finer rig, I'm a-thinkin'!
You c'n keep yer rig if you're thinkin'
'at I'd keer to swap
Fer that shiny little surrey with the
fringe on the top!

(LAUREY *still pretends unconcern, but she is obviously slipping.*)

AUNT ELLER.

Would y'say the fringe was made of silk?

CURLY.

Wouldn't have no other kind but silk.

LAUREY (*she's only human*).

Has it really got a team of snow-white horses?

CURLY.

One's like snow—the other's more like milk.

AUNT ELLER.

So y'can tell 'em apart!

CURLY.

All the world'll fly in a flurry
When I take you out in the surrey,
When I take you out in the surrey
with the fringe on top!
When we hit that road, hell fer
leather,
Cats and dogs'll dance in the heather,
Birds and frogs'll sing all together
and the toads will hop!
The wind'll whistle as we rattle
along,
The cows'll moo in the clover,
The river will ripple out a whispered
song,
And whisper it over and over:
(*In a loud whisper.*)
Don't you wisht y'd go on ferever?
Don't you wisht y'd go on ferever?

(AUNT ELLER'S *and* LAUREY'S *lips move involuntarily, shaping the same words.*)

Don't you wisht y'd go on ferever
and ud never stop
In that shiny little surrey with the
fringe on the top?
(*Music continues under dialogue.*)

AUNT ELLER.

Y'd shore feel like a queen settin' up in *that* carriage!

CURLY (*over-confident*).

On'y she talked so mean to me a while back, Aunt Eller, I'm a good mind not to take her.

LAUREY.

Ain't said I was goin'!

CURLY (*the fool*).

Ain't ast you!

LAUREY.

Whur'd you git sich a rig at? (*With explosive laughter, seeing a chance for revenge.*) Anh! I bet he's went and h'ard a rig over to Claremore! Thinkin' I'd go with him!

CURLY.

'S all you know about it.

LAUREY.

Spent all his money h'arin' a rig and now ain't got nobody to ride in it!

CURLY.

Have, too! . . . Did not h'ar it. Made the whole thing up outa my head.

LAUREY.

What! Made it up?

CURLY.

Dashboard and all.

LAUREY (*flying at him*).

Oh! Git offa the place, you! Aunt Eller, make him git hisse'f outa here. (*She picks up a fly swatter and chases him.*) Tellin' me lies!

CURLY (*dodging her*).

Makin' up a few—look out now! (*He jumps the fence to save himself.* LAUREY *turns her back to him, and sits down. He comes up behind her. The music, which had become more turbulent to match the scene, now softens.*) Makin' up a few purties ain't agin' no law 'at I know of. Don't you wisht they *was* sich a rig, though? (*Winking at* AUNT ELLER.) Nen y'could go to the play party and do a hoe-down till mornin' if you was a mind to. . . . Nen when you was all wore out, I'd lift you onto the surrey, and jump up alongside of you —And we'd jist point the horses home. . . . I can jist pitcher the whole thing. (AUNT ELLER *beams on them as* CURLY *sings very softly:*)

I can see the stars gittin' blurry
When we ride back home in the
surrey,
Ridin' slowly home in the surrey
with the fringe on top.
I can feel the day gittin' older,
Feel a sleepy head near my shoulder,
Noddin', droopin' close to my shoul-
der till it falls, kerplop!
The sun is swimmin' on the rim of a
hill,

The moon is takin' a header,
And jist as I'm thinkin' all the earth is still,
A lark'll wake up in the medder. . . .
Hush! You bird, my baby's a-sleepin'—
Maybe got a dream worth a-keepin'
(*Soothing and slower.*)
Whoa! You team, and jist keep a-creepin' at a slow clip-clop.
Don't you hurry with the surrey with the fringe on the top.

(*There is silence and contentment, but only for a brief moment.* LAUREY *starts slowly to emerge from the enchantment of his description.*)

LAUREY.

On'y . . . on'y there ain't no sich rig. You said you made the whole thing up.

CURLY.

Well . . .

LAUREY.

Why'd you come around here with yer stories and lies, gittin' me all worked up that-a-way? Talkin' 'bout the sun swimmin' on the hill, and all —like it was so. Who'd want to ride 'longside of you anyway?

(IKE *and* FRED *enter and stand outside the gate, looking on.*)

AUNT ELLER.

Whyn't you jist grab her and kiss her when she acts that-a-way, Curly? She's jist achin' fer you to, I bet.

LAUREY.

Oh, I won't even speak to him, let alone 'low him to kiss me, the braggin', bow-legged, wisht-he-had-a-sweetheart bum!

(*She flounces into the house, slamming the door.*)

AUNT ELLER.

She likes you—quite a lot.

CURLY.

Whew! If she liked me any more she'd sic the dogs onto me.

IKE.

Y'git the wagon hitched up?

AUNT ELLER.

Whut wagon?

CURLY.

They's a crowd of folks comin' down from Bushyhead for the Box Social.

FRED.

Curly said mebbe you'd loan us yer big wagon to bring 'em up from the station.

AUNT ELLER.

Course I would, if he'd ast me.

CURLY (*embarrassed*).

Got to talkin' 'bout a lot of other things. I'll go hitch up the horses now 'f you say it's all right.

(*As he exits, a group of boys run on, leaping the fence, shouting boisterously and pushing* WILL PARKER *in front of them.* WILL *is apparently a favorite with* AUNT ELLER.)

SLIM.

See whut we brung you, Aunt Eller!

AUNT ELLER.

Hi, Will!

WILL.

Hi, Aunt Eller!

AUNT ELLER.

Whut happened up at the fair? You do any good in the steer ropin'?

WILL.

I did purty good. I won it.

(The following three speeches overlap.)

IKE.

Good boy!

FRED.

Always knowed y'would.

AUNT ELLER.

Ain't nobody c'n sling a rope like our territory boys.

WILL.

Cain't stay but a minnit, Aunt Eller. Got to git over to Ado Annie. Don't you remember, her paw said 'f I ever was worth fifty dollars I could have her?

AUNT ELLER.

Fifty dollars! That whut they give you fer prize money?

WILL.

That's whut!

AUNT ELLER.

Lands, if Ado Annie's paw keeps his promise we'll be dancin' at yer weddin'.

WILL.

If he don't keep his promise I'll take her right from under his nose, and I won't give him the present I brung fer him.

(He takes "The Little Wonder" from his pocket. This is a small cylindrical toy with a peep-hole at one end.) Look, fellers, whut I got for Ado Annie's paw! *(The boys crowd around.)* 'Scuse us, Aunt Eller. *(Illustrating to the boys, lowering his voice.)* You hold it up to yer eyes, like this. Then when you git a good look, you turn it around at th' top and the pitcher changes.

IKE *(looking into it)*.

Well, I'll be side-gaited!

(The boys line up, and take turns, making appropriate ejaculations.)

WILL.

They call it "The Little Wonder"!

AUNT ELLER.

Silly goats! *(But her curiosity gets the better of her. She yanks a little man out of the line, takes his place, gets hold of "The Little Wonder" and takes a look.)* The hussy! . . . Ought to be ashamed of herself.

(*Glaring at* WILL.) You, too! . . . How do you turn the thing to see the other pitcher? (*Looking again, and turning.*) Wait, I'm gettin' it. . . . (*When she gets it, she takes it away from her eye quickly and, handing it to* WILL, *walks away in shocked silence. Then she suddenly "busts out laughin'."*) I'm a good mind to tell Ado Annie on yer.

WILL.

Please don't, Aunt Eller. She wouldn't understand.

AUNT ELLER.

No tellin' what you been up to. Bet you carried on plenty in Kansas City.

WILL.

I wouldn't call it carryin' on. But I shore did see some things I never see before. (*Sings.*)

I got to Kansas City on a Frid'y.
By Sattidy I l'arned a thing or two.
For up to then I didn't have an idy
Of whut the modren world was comin' to!
I counted twenty gas buggies goin' by theirsel's
Almost ev'ry time I tuck a walk.
Nen I put my ear to a Bell Telephone
And a strange womern started in to talk!

AUNT ELLER.

Whut next!

BOYS.

Yeah, whut!

WILL.

Whut next?

Ev'rythin's up to date in Kansas City.
They've gone about as fur as they c'n go!
They went and built a skyscraper seven stories high—
About as high as a buildin' orta grow.
Ev'rythin's like a dream in Kansas City.
It's better than a magic-lantern show!
Y'c'n turn the radiator on whenever you want some heat.
With ev'ry kind o' comfort ev'ry house is all complete.
You c'n walk to privies in the rain an' never wet yer feet!
They've gone about as fur as they c'n go!

ALL.

Yes, sir!
They've gone about as fur as they c'n go!

WILL.

Ev'rythin's up to date in Kansas City.
They've gone about as fur as they c'n go!
They got a big theayter they call a burleeque.
Fer fifty cents you c'n see a dandy show.
One of the gals was fat and pink and pretty,
As round above as she was round below.
I could swear that she was padded from her shoulder to her heel,
But later in the second act when she begun to peel
She proved that ev'rythin' she had was absolutely real!
She went about as fur as she could go!

ALL.

Yes, sir!
She went about as fur as she could go!

(WILL *starts two-stepping.*)

IKE.

Whut you doin'?

WILL.

This is the two-step. That's all they're dancin' nowadays. The waltz is through. Ketch on to it? A one and a two—a one and a two. Course they don't do it alone. C'mon, Aunt Eller.

(WILL *dances* AUNT ELLER *around. At the end of the refrain she is all tuckered out.*)

AUNT ELLER.

And that's about as fur as I c'n go!

ALL.

Yes, sir!
And that's about as fur as she c'n go!

(WILL *starts to dance alone.*)

FRED.

Whut you doin' now, Will?

WILL.

That's rag-time. Seen a couple of colored fellers doin' it.

(*And* WILL *does his stuff, accompanied by four of the dancing boys. At end of number* CURLY *enters.*)

CURLY.

Team's all hitched.

WILL.

'Lo, Curly. Cain't stop to talk. Goin' over to Ado Annie's. I got fifty dollars.

IKE.

Time we got goin', boys. Thanks fer the loan of the wagon, Aunt Eller. (*They all start to leave.*) Come on, Curly.

CURLY.

I'll ketch up with you. (*He makes sure* IKE *is well on his way, then turns to* AUNT ELLER.) Aunt Eller, I got to know sumpin'. Listen, who's the low, filthy sneak 'at Laurey's got her cap set for?

AUNT ELLER.

You.

CURLY.

Never mind 'at. They must be plenty of men a-tryin' to spark her. And she shorely leans to one of 'em. Now don't she?

AUNT ELLER.

Well, they is that fine farmer, Jace Hutchins, jist this side of Lone Ellum—Nen thet ole widder man at Claremore, makes out he's a doctor or a vet'nary——

(JUD, *a burly, scowling man enters, carrying firewood.*)

CURLY.

That's whut I thought. Hello, Jud.

JUD.

Hello, yourself.

(JUD *exits into house.*)

AUNT ELLER (*significantly, looking in* JUD'S *direction*).

Nen of course there's someone nearer home that's got her on his mind most of the time, till he don't know a plow from a thrashin' machine.

CURLY (*jerking his head up toward the house*).

Him?

AUNT ELLER.

Yeah, Jud Fry.

CURLY.

That bullet-colored, growly man?

AUNT ELLER.

Now don't you go and say nuthin' agin' him! He's the best hired hand I ever had. Jist about runs the farm by hisself. Well, two women couldn't do it, you orta know that.

CURLY.

Laurey'd take up 'th a man like that!

AUNT ELLER.

I ain't said she's tuck up with him.

CURLY.

Well, he's around all the time, ain't he? Lives here.

AUNT ELLER.

Out in the smokehouse.

(JUD *and* LAUREY *enter from the house.* JUD *crosses and speaks to* AUNT ELLER.)

JUD.

Changed my mind about cleanin' the henhouse today. Leavin' it till tomorrow. Got to quit early cuz I'm drivin' Laurey over to the party tonight.

(*A bombshell!*)

CURLY.

You're drivin' Laurey?

JUD.

Ast her.

(*Pointing to* LAUREY, *who doesn't deny it.* JUD *exits.* CURLY *is completely deflated.*)

CURLY.

Well, wouldn't that just make you bawl! Well, don't fergit, Aunt Eller. You and me's got a date together. And if you make up a nice box of lunch, mebbe I'll bid fer it.

AUNT ELLER.

How we goin', Curly? In that rig you made up? I'll ride a-straddle of them lights a-winkin' like lightnin' bugs!

CURLY.

That there ain't no made-up rig, you hear me? I h'ard it over to Claremore.

(*This stuns* LAUREY.)

AUNT ELLER.

Lands, you did?

CURLY.

Shore did. (*Refrain of the "Surrey Song" starts in orchestra.*) Purty one, too. When I come callin' fer you right after supper, see that you got yer beauty spots fastened onto you proper, so you won't lose 'em off, you hear? 'At's a right smart turnout. (*His voice, a little husky, picks up the refrain.*)

The wheels are yeller, the upholstery's brown,
The dashboard's genuine leather,
With isinglass curtains y'c'n roll right down,
In case there's a change in the weather—

(*He breaks off in the song.*)

See you before tonight anyways, on the way back from the station—

(*Turning, singing to himself as he saunters off.*)

Ain't no finer rig, I'm a-thinkin' . . . 'at I'd keer to swap
Fer that shiny little surrey with the fringe on the top—

(*He is off.*)

AUNT ELLER (*calling off stage to him*).

Hey, Curly, tell all the girls in Bushyhead to stop by here and freshen up. It's a long way to Skidmore's. (*Maybe* LAUREY *would like to "bust out" into tears, but she bites her lip, and doesn't.* AUNT ELLER *studies her for a moment after* CURLY *has gone, then starts up toward the house.*) That means we'll have a lot of company. Better pack yer lunch hamper.

LAUREY (*a strange, sudden panic in her voice*).

Aunt Eller, don't go to Skidmore's with Curly tonight. If you do, I'll have to ride with Jud all alone.

AUNT ELLER.

That's the way you wanted it, ain't it?

LAUREY.

No. I did it because Curly was so fresh. But I'm afraid to tell Jud I won't go, Aunt Eller. He'd do sumpin turrible. He makes me shivver ever' time he gits clost to me. . . . Ever go down to that ole smokehouse where he's at?

AUNT ELLER.

Plen'y times. Why?

LAUREY.

Did you see them pitchers he's got tacked onto the walls?

AUNT ELLER.

Oh, yeah, I seed them. But don't you pay them no mind.

LAUREY.

Sumpin wrong inside him, Aunt Eller. I hook my door at night and fasten my winders agin' it. Agin' *it*—and the sound of feet a-walkin' up and down out there under that tree outside my room.

AUNT ELLER.

Laurey!

LAUREY.

Mornin's he comes to his breakfast and looks at me out from under his eyebrows like sumpin back in the bresh som'eres. I know whut I'm talkin' about.

(*Voices off stage. It's* ADO ANNIE *and the* PEDDLER.)

AUNT ELLER.

You crazy young 'un! Stop actin' like a chicken with its head cut off! Now who'd you reckon that is drove up? Why, it's that ole peddler! The one that sold me that egg-beater!

LAUREY (*looking off*).

He's got Ado Annie with him! Will Parker's Ado Annie!

AUNT ELLER.

Ole peddler! You know whut he tol' me? Tol' me that egg-beater ud beat up eggs, and wring out dishrags, and turn the ice-cream freezer, and I don't know whut all!

LAUREY (*calling off stage*).

Yoohoo! Ado Annie!

AUNT ELLER (*shouting off stage*).

Hold yer horses, Peddler-man! I want to talk to you!

(*She starts off, as* ADO ANNIE *enters with lunch hamper.*)

ADO ANNIE.

Hi, Aunt Eller!

AUNT ELLER.

Hi, yourself.

(AUNT ELLER *exits.*)

ADO ANNIE.

Hello, Laurey.

LAUREY.

Hello. Will Parker's back from Kansas City. He's lookin' fer yer.

(ADO ANNIE'S *brows knit to meet a sudden problem.*)

ADO ANNIE.

Will Parker! I didn't count on him bein' back so soon!

LAUREY.

I can see that! Been ridin' a piece?

ADO ANNIE.

The peddler-man's gonna drive me to the Box Social. I got up sort of a tasty lunch.

LAUREY.

Ado Annie! Have you tuck up with that peddler-man?

ADO ANNIE.

N-not yit.

LAUREY.

But yer promised to Will Parker, ain't yer?

ADO ANNIE.

Not what you might say *promised.* I jist told him mebbe.

LAUREY.

Don't y' like him no more?

ADO ANNIE.

'Course I do. They won't never be nobody like Will.

LAUREY.

Then whut about this peddler-man?

ADO ANNIE (*looking off wistfully*).

They won't never be nobody like *him*, neither.

LAUREY.

Well, which one d'you like the best?

ADO ANNIE.

Whutever one I'm with!

LAUREY.

Well, you air a silly!

ADO ANNIE.

Now, Laurey, you know they didn't nobody pay me no mind up to this year, count of I was scrawny and flat as a beanpole. Nen I kind of rounded up a little and now the boys act diff'rent to me.

LAUREY.

Well, whut's wrong with that?

ADO ANNIE.

Nuthin' wrong. I like it. I like it so much when a feller talks purty to me I git all shaky from horn to hoof! Don't you?

LAUREY.

Cain't think whut yer talkin' about.

ADO ANNIE.

Don't you feel kind of sorry fer a feller when he looks like he wants to kiss you?

LAUREY.

Well, you jist cain't go around kissin' every man that asts you! Didn't anybody ever tell you that?

ADO ANNIE.

Yeow, they *told* me. . . . (*Sings.*)

It ain't so much a question of not
  knowin' what to do,
I knowed whut's right and wrong
  since I been ten.
I heared a lot of stories—and I
  reckon they are true—
About how girls're put upon by men.
I know I mustn't fall into the pit,
But when I'm with a feller—I fergit!

I'm jist a girl who cain't say no,
I'm in a turrible fix.
I always say, come on, le's go—
Jist when I orta say nix!
When a person tries to kiss a girl
I know she orta give his face a smack.
But as soon as someone kisses me
I somehow sorta wanta kiss him back!
I'm jist a fool when lights are low.
I cain't be prissy and quaint—
I ain't the type thet c'n faint—
How c'n I be whut I ain't?
I cain't say no!

Whut you goin' to do when a feller
  gits flirty
And starts to talk purty?
Whut you goin' to do?
S'posin' 'at he says 'at yer lips're like
  cherries,
Er roses, er berries?
Whut you goin' to do?
S'posin' 'at he says 'at you're sweet-
  er'n cream
And he's gotta have cream er die?

Whut you goin' to do when he talks
thet way?
Spit in his eye?

I'm jist a girl who cain't say no,
Cain't seem to say it at all.
I hate to disserpoint a beau
When he is payin' a call.
Fer a while I ack refined and cool,
A-settin' on the velveteen settee—
Nen I think of thet ol' golden rule,
And do fer him whut he would do
fer me!
I cain't resist a Romeo
In a sombrero and chaps.
Soon as I sit on their laps
Somethin' inside of me snaps
I cain't say no!

(*She sits on her hamper, and looks discouraged.*)

I'm jist a girl who cain't say no.
Kissin's my favorite food.
With er without the mistletoe
I'm in a holiday mood!
Other girls are coy and hard to catch
But other girls ain't havin' any fun!
Ev'ry time I lose a wrestlin' match
I have a funny feelin' that I won!
Though I c'n feel the undertow,
I never make a complaint
Till it's too late fer restraint,
Then when I want to I cain't.
I cain't say no!

(*Resuming dialogue, after applause.*)

It's like I tole you, I git sorry fer them!

LAUREY.

I wouldn't feel sorry fer any man, no matter whut!

ADO ANNIE.

I'm shore sorry fer pore Ali Hakim now. Look how Aunt Eller's cussin' him out!

LAUREY.

Ali Hakim! That his name?

ADO ANNIE.

Yeah, it's Persian.

LAUREY.

You shore fer sartin you love him better'n you love Will?

ADO ANNIE.

I *was* shore. And now that ole Will has to come home and first thing you know he'll start talkin' purty to me and changin' my mind back!

LAUREY.

But Will wants to marry you.

ADO ANNIE.

So does Ali Hakim.

LAUREY.

Did he ast yer?

ADO ANNIE.

Not direckly. But how I know is he said this mornin' that he wanted fer me to drive like that with him to the end of the world. Well, 'f we drove only as fur as Catoosie that'd take to sundown, wouldn't it? Nen we'd have to go som'eres and be all night together, and bein' together all night means he wants a weddin', don't it?

LAUREY.

Not to a peddler it don't!

(*Enter* PEDDLER *and* AUNT ELLER.)

PEDDLER.

All right! All right! If the egg-beater don't work I give you something just as good!

AUNT ELLER.

Jist as good! It's got to be a thousand million times better!

(*The* PEDDLER *puts down his bulging suitcase, his little beady eyes sparkling professionally. He rushes over and, to* LAUREY'S *alarm, kisses her hand.*)

PEDDLER.

My, oh, my! Miss Laurey! Jippity crickets, how high you have growed up! Last time I come through here, you was tiny like a shrimp, with freckles. Now look at you—a great big beautiful lady!

LAUREY.

Quit it a-bitin' me! If you ain't had no breakfast go and eat yerself a green apple.

PEDDLER.

Now, Aunt Eller, just lissen——

AUNT ELLER (*shouting*).

I ain't yer Aunt Eller! Don't you call me Aunt Eller, you little wart. I'm mad at you.

PEDDLER.

Don't you go and be mad at me. Ain't I said I'd give you a present? (*Getting his bag.*) Something to wear.

AUNT ELLER.

Foot! Got things fer to wear. Wouldn't have it. Whut is it?

PEDDLER (*holding up garter*).

Real silk. Made in Persia!

AUNT ELLER.

Whut'd I want with a ole Persian garter?

ADO ANNIE.

They look awful purty, Aunt Eller, with bows onto 'em and all.

AUNT ELLER.

I'll try 'em on.

PEDDLER.

Hold out your foot.

(AUNT ELLER *obeys mechanically. But when he gets the garter over her ankle, she kicks him down.*)

AUNT ELLER.

Did you have any idy I was goin' ter let you slide that garter up my limb? (*She stoops over and starts to pull the garter up.*) Grab onto my petticoats, Laurey.

(*Noticing the* PEDDLER *looking at her, she turns her back on him pointedly and goes on with the operation. The* PEDDLER *turns to* ADO ANNIE.)

PEDDLER.

Funny woman. Would be much worse if I tried to take your garters off.

ADO ANNIE.

Yeh, cuz that ud make her stockin's fall down, wouldn't it?

AUNT ELLER.

Now give me the other one.

PEDDLER.

Which one? (*Picking it out of his case.*) Oh, you want to buy this one to match?

AUNT ELLER.

Whut do you mean do I want to *buy* it?

PEDDLER.

I can let you have it for fifty cents —four bits.

AUNT ELLER.

Do you want me to get that egg-beater and ram it down yer wind-pipe!

(*She snatches the second one away.*)

PEDDLER.

All right—all right. Don't anybody want to buy something? How about you, Miss Laurey? Must be wanting something—a pretty young girl like you.

LAUREY.

Me? Course I want sumpin. (*Working up to a kind of abstracted ecstasy.*) Want a buckle made outa shiny silver to fasten onto my shoes! Want a dress with lace. Want per-fume, wanta be purty, wanta smell like a honeysuckle vine!

AUNT ELLER.

Give her a cake of soap.

LAUREY.

Want things I've heared of and never had before—a rubber-t'ard buggy, a cut-glass sugar bowl. Want things I cain't tell you about—not only things to look at and hold in yer hands. Things to happen to you. Things so nice, if they ever did hap-pen to you, yer heart ud quit beatin'. You'd fall down dead!

PEDDLER.

I've got just the thing for you! (*He fishes into his satchel and pulls out a bottle.*) The Elixir of Egypt!

(*He holds the bottle high.*)

LAUREY.

What's 'at?

PEDDLER.

It's a secret formula, belonged to Pharaoh's daughter!

AUNT ELLER (*leaning over and putting her nose to it*).

Smellin' salts!

PEDDLER (*snatching it away*).

But a special kind of smelling salts. Read what it says on the label: "Take a deep breath and you see everything clear." That's what Phar-aoh's daughter used to do. When she had a hard problem to decide, like what prince she ought to marry, or what dress to wear to a party, or whether she ought to cut off some-body's head—she'd take a whiff of this.

LAUREY (*excited*).

I'll take a bottle of that, Mr. Ped-dler.

PEDDLER.

Precious stuff.

LAUREY.

How much?

PEDDLER.

Two bits.

(*She pays him and takes the bottle.*)

AUNT ELLER.

Throwin' away yer money!

LAUREY (*holding the bottle close to her, thinking aloud*).

Helps you decide what to do!

PEDDLER.

Now don't you want me to show you some pretty dewdads? You know, with lace around the bottom, and ribbons running in and out?

AUNT ELLER.

You mean fancy drawers?

PEDDLER (*taking a pair out of pack*).

All made in Paris.

AUNT ELLER.

Well, I never wear that kind myself, but I shore do like to look at 'em.

(PEDDLER *takes out a pair of red flannel drawers.*)

ADO ANNIE (*dubiously*).

Y-yeah, they's all right—if you ain't goin' no place.

AUNT ELLER.

Bring yer trappin's inside and mebbe I c'n find you sumpin to eat and drink.

(AUNT ELLER *exits.* PEDDLER *starts to repack. The two girls whisper for a moment.*)

LAUREY.

Well, ast him, why don't you?

(*She giggles and exits into house.*)

ADO ANNIE.

Ali, Laurey and me've been havin' a argument.

PEDDLER.

About what, Baby?

ADO ANNIE.

About what you meant when you said that about drivin' with me to the end of the world.

PEDDLER (*cagily*).

Well, I didn't mean really to the end of the world.

ADO ANNIE.

Then how fur did you want to go?

PEDDLER.

Oh, about as far as—say—Claremore—to the hotel.

ADO ANNIE.

Whut's at the hotel?

PEDDLER (*ready for the kill*).

In front of the hotel is a veranda—inside is a lobby—upstairs—upstairs might be Paradise.

ADO ANNIE.

I thought they was jist bedrooms.

PEDDLER.

For you and me, Baby—Paradise.

ADO ANNIE.

Y'see! I knew I was right and Laurey was wrong! You do want to marry me, don't you?

PEDDLER (*embracing her impulsively*).

Ah, Ado Annie! (*Pulling away.*) What did you say?

ADO ANNIE.

I said you do want to marry me, don't you? What did you say?

PEDDLER.

I didn't say nothing!

WILL (*off stage*).

Whoa, Suzanna! Yoohoo, Ado Annie, I'm back!

ALO ANNIE.

Oh, foot! Jist when—— 'Lo, Will! (WILL *lets out a whoop off stage.*) That's Will Parker. Promise me you won't fight him.

PEDDLER.

Why fight? I never saw the man before.

(WILL *enters.*)

WILL.

Ado Annie! How's my honey-bunch? How's the sweetest little hundred-and-ten pounds of sugar in the territory?

ADO ANNIE (*confused*).

Er—Will, this is Ali Hakim.

WILL

How are yuh, Hak? Don't mind the way I talk. 'S all right. I'm goin' to marry her.

PEDDLER (*delighted*).

Marry her? On purpose?

WILL

Well, sure.

ADO ANNIE.

No sich of a thing!

PEDDLER.

It's a wonderful thing to be married.

(*He starts off.*)

ADO ANNIE.

Ali!

PEDDLER.

I got a brother in Persia, got six wives.

ADO ANNIE.

Six wives? All at once?

WILL.

Shore. 'At's a way they do in them countries.

PEDDLER.

Not always. I got another brother in Persia only got one wife. He's a bachelor.

(*Exit.*)

ADO ANNIE.

Look, Will——

WILL.

Look, Will, nuthin'. Know whut I got fer first prize at the fair? Fifty dollars!

ADO ANNIE.

Well, that was good. . . . (*The significance suddenly dawning on her.*) Fifty dollars?

WILL.

Ketch on? Yer paw promised I cud marry you 'f I cud git fifty dollars.

ADO ANNIE.

'At's right, he did.

WILL.

Know whut I done with it? Spent it all on presents fer you!

ADO ANNIE.

But if you spent it you ain't got the cash.

WILL.

Whut I got is worth more'n the cash. Feller who sold me the stuff told me!

ADO ANNIE.

But, Will . . .

WILL.

Stop sayin' "But, Will—" When do I git a little kiss? . . . Oh, Ado Annie, honey, y'ain't been off my mind since I left. All the time at the fair grounds even, when I was chasin' steers. I'd rope one under the hoofs and pull him up sharp, and he'd land on his little rump . . . Nen I'd think of you.

ADO ANNIE.

Don't start talkin' purty, Will.

WILL.

See a lot of beautiful gals in Kansas City. Didn't give one a look.

ADO ANNIE.

How could you see 'em if you didn't give 'em a look?

WILL.

I mean I didn't look lovin' at 'em —like I look at you.

(*He turns her around and looks adoring and pathetic.*)

ADO ANNIE (*backing away*).

Oh, Will, please don't look like that! I cain't bear it.

WILL.

Won't stop lookin' like this till you give me a little ole kiss.

ADO ANNIE.

Oh, whut's a little ole kiss?

WILL.

Nothin'—less'n it comes from you.

(*Both stop.*)

ADO ANNIE (*sighing*).

You do talk purty! (WILL *steps up for his kiss. She nearly gives in, but with sudden and unaccounted-for strength of character she turns away.*) No, I won't!

WILL (*singing softly, seductively, "getting" her*).

S'posin' 'at I say 'at yer lips're like
cherries,
Er roses er berries?
Whut you gonna do?

(*Putting her hand on his heart.*)

Cain't you feel my heart palpatin' an'
bumpin',
A-waitin' fer sumpin,
Sumpin nice from you?
I gotta git a kiss an' it's gotta be
quick
Er I'll jump in a crick an' die!

ADO ANNIE (*overcome*).

Whut's a girl to say when you talk that-a-way?

(*And he gets his kiss. The boys and girls, and* CURLY *and* GERTIE *enter with lunch hampers, shouting and laughing.* WILL *and* ADO ANNIE *run off.* AUNT ELLER *and* LAUREY *come out of the house.* GERTIE *laughs musically.* LAUREY, *unmindful of the group of girls she has been speaking to, looks across at* CURLY *and* GERTIE *and boils over. All the couples and* CURLY *and* GERTIE *waltz easily, while they sing.*)

ALL.

Oh, what a beautiful mornin',

CURLY.

Oh, what a beautiful day.

ALL.

I got a beautiful feelin'

CURLY.

Ev'rythin's goin' my way. . . .

AUNT ELLER (*to the rescue*).

Hey, Curly! Better take the wagon down to the troft and give the team some water.

CURLY.

Right away, Aunt Eller.

(*He turns.*)

GERTIE.

C'n I come, too? Jist love to watch the way you handle horses.

CURLY (*looking across at* LAUREY).

'At's about all I *can* handle, I guess.

GERTIE.

Oh, I cain't believe that, Curly—not from whut I heared about you!

(*She takes his arm and walks him off, turning on more musical laughter. A girl imitates her laugh. Crowd laughs.* LAUREY *takes an involuntary step forward, then stops, frustrated, furious.*)

GIRL.

Looks like Curly's tuck up with that Cummin's girl.

LAUREY.

Whut'd I keer about that?

(*The girls and* LAUREY *chatter and argue, ad lib.*)

AUNT ELLER.

Come on, boys, better git these hampers out under the trees where it's cool.

(*Exit* AUNT ELLER *and boys. To show "how little she keers,"* LAUREY *sings the following song:*)

Why should a womern who is healthy and strong
Blubber like a baby if her man goes away?
A-weepin' and a-wailin' how he's done her wrong—
That's one thing you'll never hear me say!
Never gonna think that the man I lose
Is the only man among men.
I'll snap my fingers to show I don't care.
I'll buy me a brand-new dress to wear.
I'll scrub my neck and I'll bresh my hair,
And start all over again.

Many a new face will please my eye,
Many a new love will find me.
Never've I once looked back to sigh
Over the romance behind me.
Many a new day will dawn before I do!
Many a light lad may kiss and fly,
A kiss gone by is bygone,
Never've I asked an August sky,
"Where has last July gone?"
Never've I wandered through the rye,
Wonderin' where has some guy gone—
Many a new day will dawn before I do!

CHORUS.

Many a new face will please my eye,
Many a new love will find me.
Never've I once looked back to sigh
Over the romance behind me.
Many a new day will dawn before I do!

LAUREY.

Never've I chased the honey-bee
Who carelessly cajoled me.
Somebody else just as sweet as he
Cheered me and consoled me.
Never've I wept into my tea
Over the deal someone doled me.

CHORUS.

Many a new day will dawn,

LAUREY.

Many a red sun will set,
Many a blue moon will shine, before I do!

(*A dance follows.* LAUREY *and girls exit.* PEDDLER *enters from house,* ADO ANNIE *from the other side of the stage.*)

ADO ANNIE.

Ali Hakim——

PEDDLER.

Hello, kiddo.

ADO ANNIE.

I'm shore sorry to see you so happy, cuz whut I got to say will make you mis'able. . . . I got to marry Will.

PEDDLER.

That's sad news for me. Well, he is a fine fellow.

ADO ANNIE.

Don't hide your feelin's, Ali. I cain't stand it. I'd ruther have you come right out and say yer heart is busted in two.

PEDDLER.

Are you positive you got to marry Will?

ADO ANNIE.

Shore's shootin'.

PEDDLER.

And there is no chance for you to change your mind?

ADO ANNIE.

No chance.

PEDDLER (*as if granting a small favor*).

All right, then, my heart is busted in two.

ADO ANNIE.

Oh, Ali, you do make up purty things to say!

CARNES (*off stage*).

That you, Annie?

ADO ANNIE.

Hello, Paw. (CARNES *enters. He is a scrappy little man, carrying a shotgun.*) Whut you been shootin'?

CARNES.

Rabbits. That true whut I hear about Will Parker gittin' fifty dollars?

ADO ANNIE.

That's right, Paw. And he wants to hold you to yer promise.

CARNES.

Too bad. Still and all I cain't go back on my word.

ADO ANNIE.

See, Ali Hakim!

CARNES.

I advise you to git that money off'n him before he loses it all. Put it in yer stockin' er inside yer corset where he cain't git at it . . . or can he?

ADO ANNIE.

But, Paw—he ain't exackly kep' it. He spent it all on presents. . . .

(*The* PEDDLER *is in a panic.*)

CARNES.

See! Whut'd I tell you! Now he cain't have you. I said it had to be fifty dollars cash.

PEDDLER.

But, Mr. Carnes, is that fair?

CARNES.

Who the hell are you?

ADO ANNIE.

This is Ali Hakim.

CARNES.

Well, shet your face, er I'll fill yer behind so full of buckshot, you'll be walkin' around like a duck the rest of yer life.

ADO ANNIE.

Ali, if I don't have to marry Will, mebbe your heart don't have to be busted in two like you said.

PEDDLER.

I did not say that.

ADO ANNIE.

Oh, yes, you did.

PEDDLER.

No, I did not.

CARNES (*brandishing his gun*).

Are you tryin' to make out my daughter to be a liar?

PEDDLER.

No, I'm just making it clear what a liar I am if she's telling the truth.

CARNES.

Whut else you been sayin' to my daughter?

ADO ANNIE (*before the* PEDDLER *can open his mouth*).

Oh, a awful lot.

CARNES (*to* PEDDLER).

When?

ADO ANNIE.

Las' night, in the moonlight.

CARNES (*to* PEDDLER).

Where?

ADO ANNIE.

'Longside a haystack.

PEDDLER.

Listen, Mr. Carnes . . .

CARNES.

I'm lissening. Whut else did you say?

ADO ANNIE.

He called me his Persian kitten.

CARNES.

Why'd you call her that?

PEDDLER.

I don't remember.

ADO ANNIE.

I do. He said I was like a Persian kitten, cuz they was the cats with the soft round tails.

CARNES (*cocking his gun*).

That's enough. In this part of the country that better be a proposal of marriage.

ADO ANNIE.

That's whut I thought.

CARNES (*to* PEDDLER).

Is that whut you think?

PEDDLER.

Look, Mr. Carnes . . .

CARNES (*taking aim*).

I'm lookin'.

PEDDLER.

I'm no good. I'm a peddler. A peddler travels up and down and all around and you'd hardly ever see your daughter no more.

CARNES (*patting him on back*).

That'd be all right. Take keer of her, son. Take keer of my little rosebud.

ADO ANNIE.

Oh, Paw, that's purty. (CARNES *starts to exit into house.*) You shore fer sartin you can bear to let me go, Paw?

(CARNES *turns.*)

PEDDLER.

Are you *sure*, Mr. Carnes?

CARNES.

Jist try to change my mind and see whut happens to you.

(*He takes a firmer grip on his gun and exits into the house.*)

ADO ANNIE.

Oh, Ali Hakim, ain't it wonderful, Paw makin' up our mind fer us? He won't change neither. Onct he gives his word that you c'n have me, why, you *got* me.

PEDDLER.

I *know* I got you.

ADO ANNIE (*starry-eyed*).

Mrs. Ali Hakim . . . the Peddler's bride. Wait till I tell the girls.

(*She exits.* ALI *leans against the porch post as the music starts. Then he starts to pace up and down, thinking hard, his head bowed, his hands behind his back. The orchestra starts a vamp that continues under the melody. Some men enter and watch him curiously, but he is unmindful of them until they start to sing. Throughout this entire number, the* PEDDLER *must be burning, and he transmits his indignation to the men who sing in a spirit of angry protest, by the time the refrain is reached.*)

PEDDLER (*circling the stage*).

Trapped! . . .
Tricked! . . .
Hoodblinked! . . .
Hambushed! . . .

MEN.

Friend,
Whut's on yer mind?
Why do you walk
Around and around,
With yer hands
Folded behind,

And yer chin
Scrapin' the ground?

(*The* PEDDLER *walks away, then comes back to them and starts to pour out his heart.*)

PEDDLER.

Twenty minutes ago I am free like a breeze,
Free like a bird in the woodland wild,
Free like a gypsy, free like a child,
I'm unattached!
Twenty minutes ago I can do what I please,
Flick my cigar ashes on a rug,
Dunk with a doughnut, drink from a jug—
I'm a happy man!

(*Crescendo.*)

I'm minding my own business like I oughter,
Ain't meaning any harm to anyone.
I'm talking to a certain farmer's daughter—
Then I'm looking in the muzzle of a gun!

MEN.

It's gittin' so you cain't have any fun!
Ev'ry daughter has a father with a gun!

It's a scandal, it's a outrage!
How a gal gits a husband today!

PEDDLER.

If you make one mistake when the moon is bright,
Then they tie you to a contract, so you'll make it ev'ry night!

MEN.

It's a scandal, it's a outrage!
When her fambly surround you and say:
"You gotta take an' make a honest womern outa Nell!"

PEDDLER.

To make you make her honest, she will lie like hell!

MEN.

It's a scandal, it's a outrage!
On our manhood, it's a blot!
Where is the leader who will save us?
And be the first man to be shot?

PEDDLER (*spoken*).

Me?

MEN (*spoken*).

Yes, you!

(*Sing.*)

It's a scandal, it's a outrage!
Jist a wink and a kiss and you're through!

PEDDLER.

You're a mess, and in less than a year, by heck!
There's a baby on your shoulder making bubbles on your neck!

MEN.

It's a scandal, it's a outrage!
Any farmer will tell you it's true.

PEDDLER.

A rooster in a chickencoop is better off'n men.

He ain't the special property of just
one hen!

(ANNIE *and girls enter at side.*)

MEN.

It's a scandal, it's a outrage!
It's a problem we must solve!
We gotta start a revolution!

GIRLS.

All right, boys! Revolve!

(*The boys swing around, see the girls and are immediately cowed. The girls pick them off the line and walk off with them, to the music. All exit except one girl, who stalks around looking for a boy. Suddenly one appears, sees the girl and exits fast. She pursues him like mad.* GERTIE *enters through gate with* CURLY. LAUREY *enters on the porch and starts packing her lunch hamper.*)

GERTIE.

Hello, Laurey. Jist packin' yer hamper now?

LAUREY.

I been busy.

(GERTIE *looks in* LAUREY'S *hamper.* AUNT ELLER *enters.*)

GERTIE.

You got gooseberry tarts, too. Wonder if they is as light as mine. Mine'd like to float away if you blew on them.

LAUREY.

I did blow on one of mine and it broke up into a million pieces.

(GERTIE *laughs—that laugh again.*)

GERTIE.

Ain't she funny!

(*The girls step toward each other menacingly.*)

AUNT ELLER.

Gertie! Better come inside, and cool off.

GERTIE.

You comin' inside 'th me, Curly?

CURLY.

Not jist yet.

GERTIE.

Well, don't be too long. And don't fergit when the auction starts tonight, mine's the biggest hamper.

(*The laugh again, and she exits.*)

LAUREY (*going on with her packing*).

So that's the Cummin's girl I heared so much talk of.

CURLY.

You seen her before, ain't you?

LAUREY.

Yeow. But not since she got so old. Never did see anybody get so peaked-lookin' in sich a short time.

AUNT ELLER (*amused at* LAUREY).

Yeah, and she says she's only eighteen. I betcha she's nineteen.

(AUNT ELLER *exits.*)

CURLY.

What yer got in yer hamper?

LAUREY.

'At's jist some ole meat pies and apple jelly. Nothin' like whut Gertie Cummin's has in *her* basket.

(*She sits on the arm of a rocking chair.*)

CURLY.

You really goin' to drive to the Box Social with that Jud feller?

(*Pause.*)

LAUREY.

Reckon so. Why?

CURLY.

Nothin' . . . It's jist that ev'rybody seems to expec' *me* to take you.

(*He sits on the other arm of the rocker.*)

LAUREY.

Then, mebbe it's jist as well you ain't. We don't want people talkin' 'bout us, do we?

CURLY.

You think people *do* talk about us?

LAUREY.

Oh, you know how they air—like a swarm of mudwasps. Alw'ys gotta be buzzin' 'bout sumpin.

CURLY (*rocking the chair gaily*).

Well, whut're they sayin'? That you're stuck on me?

LAUREY.

Uh-uh. Most of the talk is that you're stuck on me.

CURLY.

Cain't imagine how these ugly rumors start.

LAUREY.

Me neither.

(*Sings.*)

Why do they think up stories that link my name with yours?

CURLY.

Why do the neighbors gossip all day behind their doors?

LAUREY.

I have a way to prove what they say
is quite untrue;
Here is the gist, a practical list of
"don'ts" for you:

Don't throw bouquets at me—
Don't please my folks too much,
Don't laugh at my jokes too much—
People will say we're in love!

CURLY (*leaving her*).

Who laughs at yer jokes?

LAUREY (*following him*).

Don't sigh and gaze at me,
Your sighs are so like mine,
(CURLY *turns to embrace her, she stops him.*)
Your eyes mustn't glow like mine—
People will say we're in love!
Don't start collecting things—

CURLY.

Like whut?

LAUREY.

Give me my rose and my glove.
(*He looks away, guiltily.*)

Sweetheart, they're suspecting things—
People will say we're in love!

CURLY.

Some people claim that you are to blame as much as I—
(*She is about to deny this.*)
Why do you take the trouble to bake my fav'rit pie?
(*Now she looks guilty.*)
Grantin' your wish, I carved our initials on that tree . . .
(*He points off at the tree.*)
Jist keep a slice of all the advice you give, so free!

Don't praise my charm too much,
Don't look so vain with me,
Don't stand in the rain with me,
People will say we're in love!
Don't take my arm too much,
Don't keep your hand in mine,
Your hand looks so grand in mine,
People will say we're in love!
Don't dance all night with me,
Till the stars fade from above.
They'll see it's all right with me,
People will say we're in love!

(*Music continues as* CURLY *speaks.*)

Don't you reckon y'could tell that Jud you'd ruther go with me tonight?

LAUREY.

Curly! I—no, I couldn't.

CURLY.

Oh, you couldn't? (*Frowning.*) Think I'll go down here to the smokehouse, where Jud's at. See whut's so elegant about him, makes girls wanta go to parties 'th him.

(*He starts off, angrily.*)

LAUREY.

Curly!

CURLY (*turning*).

Whut?

LAUREY.

Nothin'.

(*She watches* CURLY *as he exits, then sits on rocker crying softly and starts to sing:*)

Don't sigh and gaze at me,
Your sighs are so like mine,
Your eyes mustn't glow like mine—

(*Music continues. She chokes up, can't go on.* AUNT ELLER *has come out and looks with great understanding.*)

AUNT ELLER.

Got yer hamper packed?

LAUREY (*snapping out of it*).

Oh, Aunt Eller. . . . Yes, nearly.

AUNT ELLER.

Like a hanky?

LAUREY.

Whut'd I want with a ole hanky?

AUNT ELLER (*handing her hers*).

Y'got a smudge on yer cheek—jist under yer eye.

(LAUREY *dries her eyes, starts toward the house, thinks about the bottle of "Lixir of Egyp'," picks it up, looks at* AUNT ELLER, *and runs out through the gate and off stage.* AUNT ELLER *sits in the rocker and hums the refrain, happy and contented, as lights dim and the curtain falls.*)

SCENE II

SCENE: *The smokehouse.*
Immediately after Scene I.
It is a dark, dirty building where the meat was once kept. The rafters are smoky, covered with dust and cobwebs. On a low loft many things are stored —horse collars, plow-shares, a binder twine, a keg of nails. Under it, the bed is grimy and never made. On the walls, tobacco advertisements, and pink covers off Police Gazettes. *In a corner there are hoes, rakes and an axe. Two chairs, a table and a spittoon comprise the furniture. There is a mirror for shaving, several farm lanterns and a rope. A small window lets in a little light, but not much.*
JUD *enters and crosses to table. There is a knock on the door. He rises quickly and tiptoes to the window to peek outside. Then he glides swiftly back to the table. Takes out a pistol and starts to polish it. There is a second knock.*

JUD (*calling out sullenly*).

Well, open it, cain't you?

CURLY (*opening the door and strolling in*).

Howdy.

JUD.

Whut'd you want?

CURLY.

I done got th'ough my business up here at the house. Jist thought I'd pay a call. (*Pause.*) You got a gun, I see.

JUD.

Good un. Colt forty-five.

CURLY.

Whut do you do with it?

JUD.

Shoot things.

CURLY.

Oh. (*He moseys around the room casually.*) That there pink picture—now that's a naked womern, ain't it?

JUD.

Yer eyes don't lie to you.

CURLY.

Plumb stark naked as a jaybird. No. No, she ain't. Not quite. Got a couple of thingumbobs tied onto her.

JUD.

Shucks. That ain't a think to whut I got here. (*He shoves a pack of postcards across the table toward* CURLY.) Lookit that top one.

CURLY (*covering his eyes*).

I'll go blind! . . . (*Throwing it back on the table.*) That ud give me idys, that would.

JUD (*picking it up and looking at it*).

That's a dinger, that is.

CURLY (*gravely*).

Yeah, that shore is a dinger. . . . (*Taking down a rope.*) That's a good-lookin' rope you got there. (*He begins to spin it.*) Spins nice. You know Will Parker? He can shore spin a rope. (*He tosses one end of the rope over the rafter and pulls down on both ends, tentatively.*) 'S a good strong hook you got there. You could hang yerself on that, Jud.

JUD.

I could whut?

CURLY (*cheerfully*).

Hang yerself. It ud be as easy as fallin' off a log! Fact is, you could stand on a log—er a cheer if you'd rather—right about here—see? And put this here around yer neck. Tie that good up there first, of course. Then all you'd have to do would be to fall off the log—er the cheer, whichever you'd ruther fall off of. In five minutes, or less, with good luck, you'd be daid as a doornail.

JUD.

Whut'd you mean by that?

CURLY.

Nen folks ud come to yer funril and sing sad songs.

JUD (*disdainfully*).

Yamnh!

CURLY.

They would. You never know how many people like you till you're daid. Y'd prob'ly be laid out in the parlor. Y'd be all diked out in yer best suit with yer hair combed down slick, and a high starched collar.

JUD (*beginning to get interested*).

Would they be any flowers, d'you think?

CURLY.

Shore would, and palms, too—all around yer cawfin. Nen folks ud stand around you and the men ud bare their heads and the womern ud sniffle softly. Some'd prob'ly faint—ones that had tuck a shine to you when you wuz alive.

JUD.

Whut womern have tuck a shine to me?

CURLY.

Lots of womern. On'y they don't never come right out and show you how they feel less'n you die first.

JUD (*thoughtfully*).

I guess that's so.

CURLY.

They'd shore sing loud though when the singin' started—sing like their hearts ud break!

(*He starts to sing very earnestly and solemnly, improvising the sort of thing he thinks might be sung:*)

Pore Jud is daid,
Pore Jud Fry is daid!
All gether 'round his cawfin now and
  cry.
He had a heart of gold
And he wasn't very old—

Oh, why did sich a feller have to die?
Pore Jud is daid,
Pore Jud Fry is daid!
He's lookin', oh, so peaceful and serene.

JUD (*touched and suddenly carried away, he sings a soft response*).

And serene!

(*Takes off hat.*)

CURLY.

He's all laid out to rest
With his hands acrost his chest.
His fingernails have never b'en so clean!

(JUD *turns slowly to question the good taste of this last reference, but* CURLY *plunges straight into another item of the imagined wake.*)

Nen the preacher'd git up and he'd say: "Folks! We are gethered here to moan and groan over our brother Jud Fry who hung hisse'f up by a rope in the smokehouse." Nen there'd be weepin' and wailin' (*Significantly.*) from some of those womern.

(JUD *nods his head understandingly.*)

Nen he'd say, Jud was the most misunderstood man in the territory. People useter think he was a mean, ugly feller.

(JUD *looks up.*)

And they called him a dirty skunk and a ornery pig-stealer.

(CURLY *switches quickly.*)

But—the folks 'at really knowed him, knowed 'at beneath them two dirty shirts he alw'ys wore, there beat a heart as big as all outdoors.

JUD (*repeating reverently like a Negro at a revivalist meeting*).

As big as all outdoors.

CURLY.

Jud Fry loved his fellow man.

JUD.

He loved his fellow man.

CURLY

(CURLY *is warming up and speaks with the impassioned inflections of an evangelist.*)

He loved the birds of the forest and the beasts of the field. He loved the mice and the vermin in the barn, and he treated the rats like equals—which was right. And—he loved little children. He loved ev'body and ev'thin' in the world! . . . On'y he never let on, so nobody ever knowed it!

(*Returning to vigorous song:*)

Pore Jud is daid,
Pore Jud Fry is daid!
His friends'll weep and wail fer miles around.

JUD (*now right into it*).

Miles around.

CURLY.

The daisies in the dell
Will give out a diff'runt smell
Becuz pore Jud is underneath the ground.

(JUD *is too emotionally exalted by the spirit of* CURLY'S *singing to be analytical. He now takes up a refrain of his own.*)

JUD.

Pore Jud is daid,
A candle lights his haid,
He's layin' in a cawfin made of wood.

CURLY.

Wood.

JUD.

And folks are feelin' sad
Cuz they useter treat him bad,
And now they know their friend has gone fer good.

CURLY (*softly*).

Good.

JUD AND CURLY.

Pore Jud is daid,
A candle lights his haid!

CURLY.

He's lookin', oh, so purty and so nice.
He looks like he's asleep.
It's a shame that he won't keep,
But it's summer and we're runnin' out of ice . . .
Pore Jud—Pore Jud!

(JUD *breaks down, weeps, and sits at the table, burying his head in his arms.*)

Yes, sir. That's the way it ud be. Shore be a interestin' funril. Wouldn't like to miss it.

JUD (*his eyes narrowing*).

Wouldn't like to miss it, eh? Well, mebbe you will. (*He resumes polishing the gun.*) Mebbe you'll go first.

CURLY (*sitting down*).

Mebbe. . . . Le's see now, whur did you work at before you come here? Up by Quapaw, wasn't it?

JUD.

Yes, and before that over by Tulsa. Lousy they was to me. Both of 'em. Always makin' out they was better. Treatin' me like dirt.

CURLY.

And whut'd you do—git even?

JUD.

Who said anythin' about gittin' even?

CURLY.

No one, that I recollect. It jist come into my head.

JUD.

If it ever come to gittin' even with anybody, I'd know how to do it.

CURLY.

That?

(*Looking down at gun and pointing.*)

JUD.

Nanh! They's safer ways then that, if you use yer brains. . . . 'Member that f'ar on the Bartlett farm over by Sweet-water?

CURLY.

Shore do. 'Bout five years ago. Turrible accident. Burned up the father and mother and daughter.

JUD.

That warn't no accident. A feller told me—the h'ard hand was stuck on the Bartlett girl, and he found her in the hayloft with another feller.

CURLY.

And it was him that burned the place?

JUD (*nodding*).

It tuck him weeks to git all the kerosene—buying it at different times —feller who told me made out it happened in Missouri, but I knowed all the time it was the Bartlett farm. Whut a liar he was!

CURLY.

And a kind of a—a kind of a murderer, too. Wasn't he? (CURLY *rises, goes over to the door and opens it.*) Git a little air in here.

JUD.

You ain't told me yet whut business you had here. We got no cattle to sell ner no cow ponies. The oat crop is done spoke fer.

CURLY.

You shore relieved my mind consid'able.

JUD (*tensely*).

They's on'y one other thing on this farm you could want—and it better not be that!

CURLY (*closing the door deliberately and turning slowly, to face* JUD).

But that's jist whut it is.

JUD.

Better not be! You keep away from her, you hear?

CURLY (*coolly*).

You know somebody orta tell Laurey whut kind of a man you air. And fer that matter, somebody orta tell *you* onct about yerself.

JUD.

You better git outa here, Curly.

CURLY.

A feller wouldn't feel very safe in here with you . . . 'f he didn't know you. (*Acidly.*) But I know you, Jud. (CURLY *looks him straight in the eye.*) In this country, they's two things you c'n do if you're a man. Live out of doors is one. Live in a hole is the other. I've set by my horse in the bresh som'eres and heared a rattlesnake many a time. Rattle, rattle, rattle!—he'd go, skeered to death. Somebody comin' close to his hole! Somebody gonna step on him! Git his old fangs ready, full of pizen! Curl up and wait!—Long's you live in a hole, you're skeered, you got to have pertection. You c'n have muscles, oh, like arn—and still be as weak as a empty bladder—less'n you got things to barb yer hide with. (*Suddenly, harshly, directly to* JUD.) How'd you git to be the way you air, anyway—settin' here in this filthy hole—and thinkin' the way you're thinkin'? Why don't you do sumpin healthy onct in a while, 'stid of stayin' shet up here—a-crawlin' and festerin'!

JUD.

Anh!

(*He seizes a gun in a kind of reflex, a kind of desperate frenzy, and pulls the trigger. Luckily the gun is pointed toward the ceiling.*)

CURLY (*actually in a state of high excitement, but outwardly cool and calm, he draws his own gun*).

You orta feel better now. Hard on the roof, though. I wisht you'd let me show you sumpin. (JUD *doesn't move, but stands staring into* CURLY'S *eyes.*) They's a knot-hole over there about as big as a dime. See it a-winkin'? I jist want to see if I c'n hit it. (*Unhurriedly, with cat-like tension, he turns and fires at the wall high up.*) Bullet right through the knot-hole, 'thout tetchin', slick as a whistle, didn't I? I knowed I could do it. You saw it, too, didn't you? (*Ad lib off stage.*) Somebody's a-comin', I 'spect.

(*He listens.* JUD *looks at the floor.* AUNT ELLER, *the* PEDDLER *and several others come running in.*)

AUNT ELLER (*gasping for breath*).

Who f'ard off a gun? Was that you, Curly? Don't set there, you lummy, answer when you're spoke to?

CURLY.

Well, I shot onct.

AUNT ELLER.

What was you shootin' at?

CURLY (*rises*).

See that knot-hole over there?

AUNT ELLER.

I see lots of knot-holes.

CURLY.

Well, it was one of them.

AUNT ELLER (*exasperated*).

Well, ain't you a pair of purty nuthin's, a-pickin' away at knot-holes and skeerin' everybody to death! Orta give you a good Dutch rub and arn some of the craziness out of you! (*Calling off to people in doorway.*) 'S all right! Nobody hurt. Jist a pair of fools swappin 'noises.

(*She exits.*)

PEDDLER.

Mind if I visit with you, gents? It's good to get away from the women for a while. Now then, we're all by ourselves. I got a few purties, private knickknacks for to show you. Special for the menfolks.

(*Starts to get them out.*)

CURLY.

See you gentlemen later. I gotta git a surrey I h'ard fer tonight.

(*He starts to go.*)

PEDDLER (*shoving cards under* JUD'S *nose*).

Art postcards.

JUD.

Who you think yer takin' in that surrey?

CURLY.

Aunt Eller—and Laurey, if she'll come with me.

JUD.

She won't.

CURLY.

Mebbe she will.

(*Exits.*)

JUD (*raising his voice after* CURLY).

She promised to go with me, and she better not change her mind. She better not!

PEDDLER.

Now, I want ye to look at these straight from Paris.

JUD.

I don't want none o' them things now. Got any frog-stickers?

PEDDLER.

You mean one of them long knives? What would you want with a thing like that?

JUD.

I dunno. Kill a hog—er a skunk. It's all the same, ain't it? I tell you whut I'd like better'n a frog-sticker, if you got one. Ever hear of one of them things you call "The Little Wonder"? It's a thing you hold up to your eyes to see pitchers, only that ain't all they is to it . . . not quite. Y'see it's got a little jigger onto it, and you tetch it and out springs a sharp blade.

PEDDLER.

On a spring, eh?

JUD.

Y'say to a feller, "Look through this." Nen when he's lookin' you snap out the blade. It's jist above his chest and, bang! Down you come.

(*Slaps the* PEDDLER *on the chest, knocking the wind from him.*)

PEDDLER (*after recovering from blow*).

A good joke to play on a friend . . . I—er—don't handle things like that. Too dangerous. What I'd like to show you is my new stock of post-cards.

JUD.

Don't want none. Sick of them things. I'm going to get me a real womern.

PEDDLER.

What would you want with a woman? Why, I'm having trouble right now, all on account of a woman. They always make trouble. And you say you *want* one. Why? Look at you. You're a man what is free to come and go as you please. You got a nice cozy little place. (*Looking place over.*) Private. Nobody to bother you. Artistic pictures. They don't talk back to you. . . .

JUD.

I'm t'ard of all these *pitchers* of women!

PEDDLER.

All right. You're tired of them. So throw 'em away and buy some new ones. (*Showing him cards again.*) You get tired of a woman and what can you do? Nothing! Just keep getting tireder and tireder!

JUD.

I made up my mind.

PEDDLER (*packing his bag and starting off*).

So you want a real woman. . . . Say, do you happen to know a girl named Ado Annie?

JUD.

I don't want her.

PEDDLER.

I don't want her either. But I got her!

(*Exit.*)

JUD.

Don't want nuthin' from no peddler. Want real things! Whut am I doin' shet up here—like that feller says—a-crawlin' and a-festerin'? Whut am I doin' in this lousy smokehouse?

(*He looks about the room, scowling. Then he starts to sing, half talking at first, then singing in full voice:*)

The floor creaks,
The door squeaks,
There's a fieldmouse a-nibblin' on a broom,
And I set by myself
Like a cobweb on a shelf,
By myself in a lonely room.
But when there's a moon in my winder
And it slants down a beam 'crost my bed,
Then the shadder of a tree starts a dancin' on the wall
And a dream starts a-dancin' in my head.
And all the things that I wish fer
Turn out like I want them to be,
And I'm better'n that Smart Aleck cowhand
Who thinks he is better'n me!
And the girl that I want
Ain't afraid of my arms,
And her own soft arms keep me warm.

And her long, yeller hair
Falls acrost my face
Jist like the rain in a storm!

The floor creaks,
The door squeaks,
And the mouse starts a-nibblin' on the broom.
And the sun flicks my eyes—
It was all a pack o' lies!
I'm awake in a lonely room. . . .

I ain't gonna dream 'bout her arms no more!
I ain't gonna leave her alone!
Goin' outside,
Git myself a bride,
Git me a womern to call my own.

END OF SCENE II

SCENE III

AT RISE: *A grove on* LAUREY'S *farm. Singing girls and* GERTIE *seated under tree. A girl,* VIVIAN, *is telling* GERTIE'S *fortune.*

VIVIAN.

And to yer house a dark clubman!

(*Laughter from girls.* LAUREY *enters.*)

LAUREY.

Girls, could you—could you go som'eres else and tell fortunes? I gotta be here by myself.

GERTIE (*pointing to bottle*).

Look! She bought 'at ole smellin' salts the peddler tried to sell us!

LAUREY.

It ain't smellin' salts. It's goin' to make up my mind fer me. Lookit me take a good whiff now!

(*She chokes on it.*)

GERTIE.

That's the camphor.

LAUREY.

Please, girls, go away.

(GERTIE *laughs and exits.* LAUREY *closes her eyes tight.*)

ELLEN.

Hey, Laurey, is it true you're lettin' Jud take you tonight 'stid of Curly?

LAUREY.

Tell you better when I think ever'thin' out clear. Beginnin' to see things clear a'ready.

KATE.

I c'n tell you whut you want . . .

(*Singing.*)

Out of your dreams and into his arms
you long to fly.

ELLEN.

You don't need Egyptian smellin'
salts to tell you why!

KATE.

Out of your dreams and into the
hush of falling shadows.

VIRGINIA.

When the mist is low, and stars are
breaking through,

VIVIAN.

Then out of your dreams you'll go.

ALL THE GIRLS.

Into a dream come true.
Make up your mind, make up your
mind, Laurey, Laurey dear.
Make up your own, make up your
own story, Laurey dear.

Ol' Pharaoh's daughter won't tell you
what to do.
Ask your heart—whatever it tells you
will be true.

(*They drift off as* LAUREY *sings.*)

LAUREY.

Out of my dreams and into your arms
I long to fly.
I will come as evening comes to woo
a waiting sky.
Out of my dreams and into the hush
of falling shadows,
When the mist is low, and stars are
breaking through,
Then out of my dreams I'll go,
Into a dream with you.

BALLET

(*The things* LAUREY *sees in her dream that help her "make up her mind."*)

(*During the above refrain the lights dim to a spot on* LAUREY. CURLY *enters in another spot, walking slowly and standing perfectly still. Then his ballet counterpart enters and stands behind him.* LAUREY'S *ballet counterpart enters and stands behind her. These are figures fading into her dream. The real* CURLY *and the real* LAUREY *back off slowly, and leave the stage to their counterparts who move toward the center and into an embrace. The downstage drop is lifted and they are in another scene, full stage.*

These dream figures of LAUREY *and* CURLY *dance ecstatically. A young girl enters, sees them and bounds off to break the news and soon others dance on and off gaily. Two of* CURLY'S *cowboy friends stroll by and wave their greeting. "Curly" kisses "Laurey" again and walks away, happy and smug.*

A little girl runs on, presents "Laurey" with a nosegay and then bursts into tears. More girl friends dance on and embrace her. A bridal veil floats down from the skies and they place it on her head. "Curly" and the boys enter, in the manner of cowboys astride their horses. Following a gay dance, the music slows to wedding-march tempo. "Curly," a serious expression on his face, awaits his bride who walks down an aisle formed by the girls.

Now the ballet counterpart of JUD *walks slowly forward and takes off "Laurey's" veil. Expecting to see her lover,* CURLY, *she looks up and finds "Jud." Horrified, she backs away. Her friends, with stony faces, look straight ahead of them. "Curly," too, is stern and austere and when she appeals to him, he backs away from her. All of them leave her. She is alone with "Jud."*

"Jud" starts to dance with her but he is soon diverted by the entrance of three dance-hall girls who look very much like the Police Gazette *pictures* LAUREY *has seen tacked on to his walls in the smokehouse. Some of the cowboys follow the girls on, and whistle at them. But that is as far as they go. The cowboys are timid and inexpert in handling these sophisticated women. The women do an amusing, satirically bawdy dance. Then "Jud" and the boys dance with them.*

After the girls dance off, "Laurey" and "Jud" are again alone. "Curly" enters, and the long-awaited conflict with "Jud" is now unavoidable. "Curly," his hand holding an im-

uginary pistol, fires at "Jud" again and again, but "Jud" keeps slowly advancing on him, immune to bullets. He lifts "Curly" in the air and throws him to the ground. A fierce fight ensues. The friends of LAUREY *and* CURLY *run helplessly from one side to the other. Just when the tables seem to have turned in "Curly's" favor, "Jud" gets a death grip on his throat. He is killing "Curly." "Laurey" runs up to him and begs him to release her lover. It is clear by her pantomime that she will give herself to* JUD *to save* CURLY. *"Jud" drops "Curly's" limp body, picks up "Laurey" and carries her away. Over "Jud's" shoulder she blows a feeble, heart-broken kiss to "Curly's" prostrate form on the ground. The crowd surround him and carry him off in the dark as a spot comes up revealing the real* LAUREY *being shaken out of her dream by the real* JUD.)

JUD.

Wake up, Laurey. It's time to start fer the party.

(*As she awakens and starts mechanically to go with* JUD, *the* real CURLY *enters expectantly. She hesitates.* JUD *holds out his arm and scowls. Remembering the disaster of her recent dream, she avoids its reality by taking* JUD'S *arm and going with him, looking wistfully back at* CURLY *with the same sad eyes that her ballet counterpart had on her exit.* CURLY *stands alone, puzzled, dejected and defeated, as the curtain falls.*)

ACT TWO

SCENE I

SCENE: *The* SKIDMORE *ranch.*

SKIDMORE'S *guests dancing a "set." Soon after the curtain rises, the melody settles into a "vamp" and* CARNES *holds up his hand as a signal that he wants to sing. The dancing couples retire and listen to him.*

CARNES.

The farmer and the cowman should
be friends,
Oh, the farmer and the cowman
should be friends.
One man likes to push a plow,
The other likes to chase a cow,
But that's no reason why they cain't
be friends.

Territory folks should stick together,
Territory folks should all be pals.
Cowboys, dance with the farmers'
daughters!
Farmers, dance with the ranchers'
gals!

(*The chorus repeats this last quatrain.*)

(*They dance with gusto—sixteen measures—then the vamp is resumed and* CARNES *starts to sing again.*)

I'd like to say a word fer the farmer.

AUNT ELLER (*spoken*).

Well, say it.

CARNES.

He come out west and made a lot of changes.

WILL (*scornfully; singing*).

He come out west and built a lot of fences!

CURLY.

And built 'em right acrost our cattle ranges!

CORD ELAM (*a cowman; spoken*).

Whyn't those dirtscratchers stay in Missouri where they belong?

FARMER (*spoken*).

We got as much right here—

CARNES (*shouting*).

Gentlemen—shut up!

(*Quiet restored, he resumes singing.*)

The farmer is a good and thrifty citizen.

FRED (*spoken*).

He's thrifty, all right.

CARNES (*glaring at* FRED, *he continues with song*).

No matter whut the cowman says or thinks,
You seldom see him drinkin' in a barroom—

CURLY.

Unless somebody else is buyin' drinks!

CARNES (*barging in quickly to save the party's respectability*).

The farmer and the cowman should be friends,
Oh, the farmer and the cowman should be friends.
The cowman ropes a cow with ease,
The farmer steals her butter and cheese,
But that's no reason why they cain't be friends!

ALL.

Territory folks should stick together,
Territory folks should all be pals.
Cowboys, dance with the farmers' daughters!
Farmers, dance with the ranchers' gals!

(*Dance, as before. Then back to vamp.*)

AUNT ELLER (*singing*).

I'd like to say a word fer the cowboy . . .

FARMER (*anxious to get back at the cowmen; spoken*).

Oh, you would!

AUNT ELLER

The road he treads is difficult and stony.
He rides fer days on end
With jist a pony fer a friend. . . .

ADO ANNIE.

I shore am feelin' sorry fer the pony.

AUNT ELLER.

The farmer should be sociable with the cowboy,

If he rides by and asks fer food and water.
Don't treat him like a louse,
Make him welcome in yer house . . .

CARNES.

But be shore that you lock up yer wife and daughter!

(*Laughs, jibes, protests.*)

CORD ELAM (*spoken from here on*).

Who wants a ole farm womern anyway?

ADO ANNIE.

Notice you married one, so's you c'd git a square meal!

MAN (*to* CORD ELAM).

You cain't talk that-a-way 'bout our womern folks!

WILL.

He can say whut he wants.

(WILL *hauls off on him and a free-for-all fight ensues, all the men mixing with one another, the women striving vainly to keep peace by singing "The farmer and the cowman should be friends!"*)

(AUNT ELLER *grabs a gun from some man's holster and fires it. This freezes the picture. A still, startled crowd stops and looks to see who's been shot.* AUNT ELLER *strides forward, separating the fighters, pulling them away from one another, and none too gently.*)

AUNT ELLER.

They ain't nobody goin' to slug out anythin'—this here's a party! (*Pointing the gun at* CARNES.) Sing it, Andrew! Dum tiddy um tum tum—

CARNES (*frightened, obeys*).

The farmer and the cowman should be friends . . .

(AUNT ELLER *points her gun at a group, and conducts them. They join in quickly.*)

RIGHT GROUP.

Oh, the farmer and the cowman should be friends.

(*She turns her gun on the left group and now they all sing.*)

ALL.

One man likes to push a plow,
The other likes to chase a cow,
But that's no reason why they cain't be friends!

(IKE *comes down and joins* AUNT ELLER *and* CARNES.)

IKE.

And when this territory is a state,
And jines the union jist like all the others,
The farmer and the cowman and the merchant
Must all behave theirsel's and act like brothers.

AUNT ELLER.

I'd like to teach you all a little sayin'—
And learn these words by heart the way you should:
"I don't say I'm no better than anybody else,

But I'll be damned if I ain't jist as good!"

(*They cheer the sentiment, and repeat lustily:*)

ALL.

I don't say I'm no better than anybody else,
But I'll be damned if I ain't jist as good!
Territory folks should stick together,
Territory folks should all be pals.
Cowboys, dance with the farmers' daughters!
Farmers, dance with the ranchers' gals!

(*Now they go into a gay, unrestrained dance.*)

IKE (*after number is over*).

C'mon, everybody! Time to start the Box Social.

CORD ELAM.

I'm so hungry I c'd eat a gatepost.

DOROTHY.

Who's goin' to be the auctioneer?

TOM.

Aunt Eller!

(*Shouts of approval from the entire crowd.*)

AUNT ELLER (*playing coy*).

Let one of the men be the auctioneer.

CROWD.

"No, Aunt Eller, yore the best." "Ain't any ole men auctioneers as good as you."

AUNT ELLER.

All right then. Now you know the rules, gentlemen. Y'got to bid blind. Y'ain't s'posed to know what girl goes with whut hamper. Of course, if yer sweetheart has told you that hers'll be done up in a certain kind of way with a certain color ribbon, that ain't my fault. Now we'll auction all the hampers on t'other side of the house and work around back here. Follow me.

(AUNT ELLER *starts off, followed by the crowd. As the crowd exits, the* PEDDLER *strolls on, meeting* WILL *ambling along with his bag.*)

PEDDLER.

Hello, young fellow.

WILL.

Oh, it's you!

PEDDLER.

I was just hoping to meet up with you. It seems like you and me ought to have a little talk.

WILL.

We only got one thing to talk about. Well, Mr. Hakim, I hear you got yerself engaged to Ado Annie.

PEDDLER.

Well . . .

WILL.

Well, nothin'. I don't know what to call you. You ain't purty enough fer a skunk. You ain't skinny enough fer a snake. You're too little to be a man, and too big to be a mouse. I reckon you're a rat.

PEDDLER.

That's logical.

WILL.

Answer me one question. Do you really love her?

PEDDLER.

Well . . .

WILL.

'Cuz if I thought you didn't I'd tie you up in this bag and drop you in the river. Are you serious about her?

PEDDLER.

Yes, I'm serious.

WILL.

And do you worship the ground she walks on, like I do? You better say yes!

PEDDLER.

Yes—yes—yes.

WILL.

The hell you do!

PEDDLER.

Yes.

WILL.

Would you spend every cent you had fer her? That's whut I did. See that bag? Full of presents. Cost fifty bucks. All I had in the world.

PEDDLER.

If you had that fifty dollars cash . . .

WILL.

I'd have Ado Annie, and you'd lose her.

PEDDLER (*thoughtfully*).

Yes. I'd lose her. Let's see what you got in here. Might want to buy something.

WILL.

What would you want with them?

PEDDLER.

I'm a peddler, ain't I? I buy and sell. Maybe pay you real money. . . . (*Significantly.*) Maybe as much as—well, a lot. (WILL *becomes thoughtful. The* PEDDLER *fishes in bag and pulls out an item.*) Ah, what a beautiful hot-water bag. It looks French. Must have cost plenty. I'll give you eight dollars for it.

WILL.

Eight dollars? That wouldn't be honest. I only paid three-fifty.

PEDDLER.

All right. I said I'd give you eight and I will. . . . (*The* PEDDLER *pulls a nightgown out of the bag. It is made of white lawn and is notable for a profusion of ribbons and bows on the neckline.*) Say! That's a cracker-jake!

WILL.

Take your hands off that! (*Grabbing it and holding it in front of him.*) That wuz fer our weddin' night!

PEDDLER.

It don't fit you so good. I'll pay you twenty-two dollars.

WILL.

But that's——

PEDDLER.

All right then—twenty-two-fifty! (*Stuffing it into his coat with the hot-water bag.*) Not a cent more.

(WILL *smiles craftily and starts to count on his fingers. The* PEDDLER *now pulls out a pair of corsets.*)

WILL.

Them—those—that was fer her to wear.

PEDDLER.

I didn't hardly think they was for you. (*Looking at them.*) Mighty dainty. (*Putting them aside.*) Fifteen dollars. Le's see, eight and twenty-two makes thirty and fifteen is forty-five and fifty cents is forty-five-fifty.

(*He looks craftily at* WILL *out of the corner of his eye and watches the idea percolate through* WILL'S *thick head.*)

WILL.

Forty-five-fifty? Say, that's almos' —that's . . . (*Turning anxiously.*) Want to buy some more?

PEDDLER.

Might.

WILL (*taking "The Little Wonder" out of his pocket*).

D'you ever see one of these?

PEDDLER (*frightened*).

What made you buy this? Got it *in* for somebody?

WILL.

How d'you mean? It's jist funny pitchers.

PEDDLER (*examining it carefully*).

That all you think it is? Well, it's more'n that! It's . . .

(*He breaks off as* LAUREY *runs on, a frightened look on her face.*)

LAUREY.

Whur is ev'ybody? Whur's Aunt Eller?

WILL.

On t'other side of the house, Laurey.

JUD (*off stage*).

Laurey! Whur'd you run to?

(LAUREY *runs off, around the end of the house, putting hamper on porch.*)

WILL.

How much'll you give me fer that thing?

PEDDLER.

I don't like to handle things like this. I guess you don't know what it really is.

WILL.

Shore do. It's jist a girl in pink tights.

JUD (*entering, carrying* LAUREY'S *basket*).

Either of you two see Laurey?

WILL.

Jist went to th' other side of the house. Auction's goin' on there.

(JUD *grunts and starts upstage.*)

PEDDLER (*calling to him*).

Hey, Jud! Here's one of them things you was looking for. "The Little Wonder."

(JUD *comes back and examines it.*)

JUD (*to* WILL).

How much?

WILL (*closing his eyes to struggle with a mathematical problem*).

Three dollars and fifty cents.

JUD (*digging in his pocket*).

Lotta money but I got an idy it might be worth it.

(JUD *goes upstage to look it over, then exits.*)

WILL.

Let's see, three-fifty from him and forty-five-fifty from you. 'At makes fifty dollars, don't it?

PEDDLER.

No. One dollar short.

WILL.

Darn it. I musta figgered wrong. (*Impulsively.*) How much fer all the resta the stuff in this bag?

PEDDLER (*having the cash all ready*).

One dollar!

WILL.

Done! Now I got fifty dollars, ain't I? Know whut that means? Means I'm goin' to take Ado Annie back from you!

PEDDLER.

You wouldn't do a thing like that to me!

WILL.

Oh, wouldn't I? And when I tell her paw who I got mosta the money offa, mebbe he'll change his mind 'bout who's smart and who's dumb!

PEDDLER.

Say, young feller, you certainly bunkoed me!

(*Off right, there is a hum of voices and the crowd starts to drift on.* AUNT ELLER *enters, followed by the balance of the party.* JUD *eyes* LAUREY *throughout the ensuing dialogue.* CURLY *stands apart and pays little attention to anybody or anything.*)

AUNT ELLER.

Now, here's the last two hampers. Whose they are I ain't got no idy!

ADO ANNIE (*in a loud voice*).

The little un's mine! And the one next to it is Laurey's!

(*General laughter.*)

AUNT ELLER.

Well, that's the end of *that* secret. Now whut am I bid then fer Ado Annie's hamper?

SLIM.

Two bits.

CORD ELAM.

Four.

AUNT ELLER.

Who says six? You, Slim? (SLIM *shakes his head.*) Ain't nobody hungry no more?—Whut about you, Peddler-man? Six bits?

(*Pause.*)

PEDDLER

Naw!

(CARNES *takes a gun from his pocket and prods the* PEDDLER *in the back.*)

CARNES.

Come on.

PEDDLER.

Six bits!

AUNT ELLER.

Six bits ain't enough fer a lunch like Ado Annie c'n make. Le's hear a dollar. How about you, Mike? You won her last year.

MIKE.

Yeah. That's right. Hey, Ado Annie, y'got that same sweet-pertater pie like last year?

ADO ANNIE.

You bet.

AUNT ELLER.

Same old sweet-pertater pie, Mike. Whut d'you say?

MIKE.

I say it give me a three-day bellyache!

AUNT ELLER.

Never mind about that. Who bids a dollar?

CARNES (*whispering to* PEDDLER).

Bid!

PEDDLER (*whispering back*).

Mine's the last bid. I got her fer six bits.

CARNES.

Bid a dollar.

(*The* PEDDLER *looks doubtful.* CARNES *prods him with his gun.*)

PEDDLER.

Ninety cents.

AUNT ELLER.

Ninety cents, we're gittin' rich. 'Nother desk fer th' schoolhouse. Do I hear more?

WILL (*dramatically, his chin thrust forward*).

You hear fifty dollars!

PEDDLER (*immediately alarmed*).

Hey!

AUNT ELLER.

Fifty dollars! Nobody ever bid fifty dollars for a lunch! Nobody ever bid ten.

CARNES.

He ain't got fifty dollars.

WILL.

Oh, yes, I have. (*Producing the money.*) And 'f yer a man of honor y'gotta say Ado Annie b'longs to me, like y'said she would!

CARNES.

But where's yer money?

WILL (*shoving out his hand*).

Right here in my hand.

CARNES.

'At ain't yours! Y'jist bid it, didn't you? Jist give it to th' schoolhouse. (*To* PEDDLER, *chuckling. Back to* WILL.) Got to say the Peddler still gits my daughter's hand.

WILL.

Now wait a minute. That ain't fair!

AUNT ELLER.

Goin' fer fifty dollars! Goin' . . .

PEDDLER (*gulping*).

Fifty-one dollars!

(*A sensation, all turn to* PEDDLER.)

CARNES.

You crazy?

WILL (*mechanically*).

Fif— (*Prompted by frantic signs from the* PEDDLER, *he stops and suddenly realizes the significance of the* PEDDLER'S *bid.*) Wait a minute. Wait! 'F I don't bid any more I c'n keep my money, cain't I?

AUNT ELLER (*grinning*).

Shore can.

WILL.

Nen I still got fifty dollars. (*Waving it in front of* CARNES.) This is mine!

CARNES (*to* PEDDLER).

You feeble-minded shike-poke!

AUNT ELLER.

Goin', goin', gone fer fifty-one dollars and 'at means Ado Annie'll git the prize, I guess.

WILL.

And I git Ado Annie!

CARNES (*to* PEDDLER).

And whut're you gittin' fer yer fifty-one dollars?

PEDDLER (*shrugging his shoulders*).

A three-day bellyache!

(PEDDLER *and* ADO ANNIE *pick up her basket and leave* AUNT ELLER.)

AUNT ELLER.

Now here's my niece's hamper. (*General murmur of excitement runs through the crowd.*) I took a peek inside a while ago and I must say it looks mighty tasty. Whut do I hear, gents?

SLIM.

Two bits!

FRED.

Four bits!

AUNT ELLER.

Whut d'you say, Slim? Six?

(SLIM *shakes his head.*)

CARNES.

I bid one dollar.

AUNT ELLER.

More like it! Do I hear two?

JUD.

A dollar and a quarter.

(LAUREY *gets a start from his voice.*)

CORD ELAM.

Two dollars.

JOE.

Two-fifty.

CARNES.

Three dollars!

JUD.

And two bits.

CORD ELAM.

Three dollars and four bits!

JOE.

Four dollars.

JUD (*doggedly*).

And two bits.

(LAUREY *looks straight ahead of her, grimly.* AUNT ELLER *catches this look and a deep worry comes into her eyes.*)

AUNT ELLER.

Four dollars and a quarter. (*Looking at* CURLY, *an appeal in her voice.*) Ain't I goin' to hear any more? (CURLY *turns and walks off, cool and deliberate.* LAUREY *bites her lip.* AUNT ELLER'*s voice has panic in it.*) I got a bid of four and a quarter —from Jud Fry. You goin' to let him have it?

CARNES.

Four and a half.

AUNT ELLER (*shouting, as if she were cheering*).

Four and a half! Goin' fer four and a half! Goin' . . .

JUD.

Four-seventy-five.

AUNT ELLER (*deflated*).

Four-seventy-five, come on, gentlemen. Schoolhouse ain't built yet. Got to git a nice chimbley.

CORD ELAM.

Five dollars.

AUNT ELLER.

Goin' fer five dollars! Goin' . . .

JUD.

And two bits.

CORD ELAM.

Too rich for my blood! Cain't afford no more.

AUNT ELLER (*worried*).

Five and a quarter! Ain't got nearly enough yet. (*Looking at* CARNES.) Not fer cold duck with stuffin' and that lemon-meringue pie.

CARNES.

Six dollars.

AUNT ELLER.

Six dollars! Goin' . . .

JUD.

And two bits.

AUNT ELLER.

My, you're stubborn, Jud. Mr. Carnes is a richer man'n you. (*Looking at* CARNES.) And I know he likes custard with raspberry syrup. (*Pause. No one bids.*) Anybody goin' to bid any more?

JUD.

No. They all dropped out. Cain't you see?

FRED.

You got enough, Aunt Eller.

CARNES.

Let's git on.

JUD.

Here's the money.

AUNT ELLER (*looking off*).

Hold on, you! I ain't said "Goin', goin', gone" yet!

JUD.

Well, say it!

AUNT ELLER (*speaking slowly*).

Goin' to Jud fer six dollars and two bits! Goin' . . .

(CURLY *enters, a saddle over his arm.*)

CURLY.

Who'd you say was gittin' Laurey?

AUNT ELLER.

Jud Fry.

CURLY.

And fer how much?

AUNT ELLER.

Six and a quarter.

CURLY.

I don't figger 'at's quite enough, do you?

JUD.

It's more'n *you* got.

CURLY.

Got a saddle here cost me thirty dollars.

JUD.

Yo' cain't bid saddles. Got to be cash.

CURLY (*looking around*).

Thirty-dollar saddle must be worth sumpin to somebody.

TOM.

I'll give you ten.

SKIDMORE (*to* CURLY).

Don't be a fool, boy. Y'cain't earn a livin' 'thout a saddle.

CURLY (*to* TOM).

Got cash?

TOM.

Right in my pocket.

(CURLY *gives him the saddle.*)

CURLY (*turning to* JUD).

Don't let's waste time. How high you goin'?

JUD.

Higher'n you—no matter whut!

CURLY (*to* AUNT ELLER).

Aunt Eller, I'm biddin' all of this ten dollars Tom jist give me.

AUNT ELLER.

Ten dollars—goin' . . .

(*Pause. General murmur of excited comments.* LAUREY'S *eyes are shining now and her shoulders are straighter.*)

JUD (*determinedly*).

Ten dollars *and* two bits.

AUNT ELLER.

Curly . . .

(*Pause.* CURLY *turns to a group of men.*)

CURLY.

Most of you boys know my horse, Dun. She's a—(*he swallows hard*)—a kinda nice horse—gentle and well broke.

LAUREY.

Don't sell Dun, Curly, it ain't worth it.

CORD ELAM.

I'll give you twenty-five fer her!

CURLY (*to* CORD ELAM).

I'll sell Dun to you. (*To* AUNT ELLER.) That makes the bid thirty-five, Aunt Eller.

AUNT ELLER (*tickled to death*).

Curly, yer crazy! But it's all fer the schoolhouse, ain't it? All fer educatin' and larnin'. Goin' fer thirty-five. Goin'—

JUD.

Hold on! I ain't finished biddin'! (*He grins fiercely at* CURLY.) You jist put up everythin' y'got in the world, didn't yer? Cain't bid the clothes off yer back, cuz they ain't worth nuthin'. Cain't bid yer gun cuz you need that. (*Slowly.*) Yes, sir. You need that bad. (*Looking at* AUNT ELLER.) So, Aunt Eller, I'm jist as reckless as Curly McLain, I guess. Jist as good at gittin' whut I want. Goin' to bid all I got in the world—all I saved fer two years, doin' farm work. All fer Laurey. Here it is! Forty-two dollars and thirty-one cents.

(*He pours the money out of his pocket onto* LAUREY'S *hamper.* CURLY *takes out his gun. The crowd gasps.* JUD *backs away.*)

CURLY.

Anybody want to buy a gun? You, Joe? Bought it brand new last Thanksgivin'. Worth a lot.

LAUREY.

Curly, please don't sell your gun.

(CURLY *looks at* JOE.)

JOE.

Give you eighteen dollars fer it.

CURLY.

Sold. (*They settle the deal.* CURLY *turns to* AUNT ELLER.) That makes my bid fifty-three dollars, Aunt Eller. Anybody going any higher?

AUNT ELLER (*very quickly*).

Goin'—goin'—gone! Whut's the matter with you folks? Ain't nobody gonna cheer er nuthin'?

(*Uncertainly they start to sing "The Farmer and the Cowman."* CURLY *and* LAUREY *carry their basket away.* JUD *moves slowly toward* CURLY. CURLY *sets the basket down and faces him. The singing stops.*)

SKIDMORE (*in his deep, booming voice*).

That's the idy! The cowman and the farmer shud be friends. (*His hand on* JUD'S *shoulder.*) You lost the bid, but the biddin' was fair. (*To* CURLY): C'mon, cowman—shake the farmer's hand!

(CURLY *doesn't move a muscle.*)

JUD.

Shore, I'll shake hands. No hard feelin's, Curly.

(*He goes to* CURLY, *his hand outstretched. After a pause,* CURLY *takes his hand, but never lets his eyes leave* JUD'S.)

SKIDMORE.

That's better.

(*The* PEDDLER *has come downstage and is watching* JUD *narrowly.*)

JUD (*with a badly assumed manner of camaraderie*).

Say, Curly, I want to show you sumpin. (*He grins.*) 'Scuse us, Laurey. (*Taking* CURLY'S *arm, he leads him aside.*) Ever see one of these things?

(*He takes out "The Little Wonder." The* PEDDLER *is in a panic.*)

CURLY.

Jist whut *is* that?

(*The* PEDDLER *rushes to* AUNT ELLER *and starts to whisper in her ear.*)

JUD.

Something special. You jist put this up to yer eye like this, see?

(CURLY *is about to look when* AUNT ELLER'S *voice rings out, sharp and shrill.*)

AUNT ELLER.

Curly! Curly, whut you doin'?

(CURLY *turns quickly. So does* JUD, *giving an involuntary grunt of disappointment.*)

CURLY.

Doin'? Nuthin' much. What you want to squeal at a man like 'at fer?

Skeer the liver and lights out of a feller.

AUNT ELLER.

Well then, stop lookin' at those ole French pitchers and ast me fer a dance. You brung me to the party, didn't you?

CURLY.

All right then, you silly ole woman, I'll dance 'th you. Dance you all over the meadow, you want!

AUNT ELLER.

Pick 'at banjo to pieces, Sam!

(*And the dance is on. Everyone is dancing now.* WILL *takes* ADO ANNIE *by the waist and swings her around.* JUD *finally snaps the blade of "The Little Wonder" back, slips it into his pocket, then goes up to* LAUREY, *who has started to dance with the* PEDDLER. *He pushes the* PEDDLER *away and dances* LAUREY *off.* WILL *and* ADO ANNIE *dance off. The curtains close. Immediately,* WILL *and* ADO ANNIE *dance on to center stage. He stops dancing. They're alone in a secluded spot now, and he wants to "settle things."*)

WILL.

Well, Ado Annie, I got the fifty dollars cash, now you name the day.

ADO ANNIE.

August fifteenth.

WILL.

Why August fifteenth?

ADO ANNIE (*tenderly*).

That was the first day I was kissed.

WILL (*his face lighting up*).

Was it? I didn't remember that.

ADO ANNIE.

You wasn't there.

WILL.

Now looka here, we gotta have a serious talk. Now that you're engaged to me, you gotta stop havin' fun! . . . I mean with other fellers.

(*Sings.*)

You'll have to be a little more standoffish
When fellers offer you a buggy ride.

ADO ANNIE.

I'll give a imitation of a crawfish
And dig myself a hole where I c'n hide.

WILL.

I heared how you was kickin' up some capers
When I was off in Kansas City, Mo.

(*More sternly.*)

I heared some things you couldn't print in papers
From fellers who been talkin' like they know!

ADO ANNIE.

Foot!
I only did the kind of things I orta —sorta
To you I was as faithful as c'n be— fer me.
Them stories 'bout the way I lost my bloomers—Rumors!
A lot o' tempest in a pot o' tea!

WILL.

The whole thing don't sound very good to me——

ADO ANNIE.

Well, y'see——

WILL (*breaking in and spurting out his pent-up resentment at a great injustice*).

I go and sow my last wild oat!
I cut out all shenanigans!
I save my money—don't gamble er drink
In the back room down at Flannigan's!
I give up lotsa other things
A gentleman never mentions—
But before I give up any more,
I wanta know your intentions!

With me it's all er nuthin'!
Is it all er nuthin' with you?
It cain't be "in between"
It cain't be "now and then"
No half-and-half romance will do!
I'm a one-woman man,
Home-lovin' type,
All complete with slippers and pipe.
Take me like I am er leave me be!
If you cain't give me all, give me nuthin'—
And nuthin's whut you'll git from me!
(*He struts away from her.*)

ADO ANNIE.

Not even sumpin?

WILL.

Nuthin's whut you'll git from me!

(*Second refrain. He starts to walk away, nonchalantly. She follows him.*)

ADO ANNIE.

It cain't be "in between"?

WILL.

Uh-uh.

ADO ANNIE.

It cain't be "now and then"?

WILL.

No half-and-half romance will do!

ADO ANNIE.

Would you build me a house,
All painted white,
Cute and clean and purty and bright?

WILL.

Big enough fer two but not fer three!

ADO ANNIE.

Supposin' 'at we should have a third one?

WILL (*barking at her*).

He better look a lot like me!

ADO ANNIE (*skeered*).

The spit an' image!

WILL.

He better look a lot like me!

(*Two girls come on and do a dance with* WILL *in which they lure him away from* ADO ANNIE. ADO ANNIE, *trying to get him back, does an oriental dance.* WILL, *accusing her, says: "That's Persian!" and returns to the girls. But* ADO ANNIE *yanks him back.*

The girls dance off. ADO ANNIE *sings.)*

ADO ANNIE.

With you it's all er nuthin'—
All fer you and nuthin' fer me!
But if a wife is wise
She's gotta realize
That men like you are wild and free.

(WILL *looks pleased.)*

So I ain't gonna fuss,
Ain't gonna frown,
Have your fun, go out on the town,
Stay up late and don't come home till three,
And go right off to sleep if you're sleepy—
There's no use waitin' up fer me!

WILL.

Oh, Ado Annie!

ADO ANNIE.

There's no use waitin' up fer me!

WILL.

Come on and kiss me!

(ADO ANNIE *comes dancing back to* WILL. *They kiss and dance off.)*

BLACKOUT

SCENE II

SCENE: *The kitchen porch of* SKIDMORE'S *ranch house. There are a few benches on the porch and a large coal stove.*

The music for the dance can still be heard off stage. Immediately after the curtain rises, JUD *dances on with* LAUREY, *then stops and holds her. She pulls away from him.*

LAUREY.

Why we stoppin'? Thought you wanted to dance?

JUD.

Want to talk to you. Whut made you slap that whip onto Old Eighty, and nearly make her run away? Whut was yer hurry?

LAUREY.

'Fraid we'd be late fer the party.

JUD.

You didn't want to be with me by yerself—not a minnit more'n you had to.

LAUREY.

Why, I don't know whut you're talking about! I'm with you by my self now, ain't I?

JUD.

You wouldn'ta been, you coulda got out of it. Mornin's you stay hid in yer room all the time. Nights you set in the front room, and won't git outa Aunt Eller's sight. . . . Last time I see you alone it was winter 'th the snow six inches deep in drifts when I was sick. You brung me that hot soup out to the smokehouse and give it to me, and me in bed. I hadn't shaved in two days. You ast me 'f I had any fever and you put your hand on my head to see.

LAUREY (*puzzled and frightened*).

I remember . . .

JUD.

Do you? Bet you don't remember as much as me. I remember eve'ything you ever done—every word you ever said. Cain't think of nuthin' else. . . . See? . . . See how it is? (*He attempts to hold her. She pushes him away.*) I ain't good enough, am I? I'm a h'ard hand, got dirt on my hands, pig-slop. Ain't fitten to tetch you. You're better, so much better. Yeah, we'll see who's better—Miss Laurey. Nen you'll wisht you wasn't so free 'th yer airs, you're sich a fine lady. . . .

LAUREY (*suddenly angry and losing her fear*).

Air you making threats to me? Air you standing there tryin' to tell me 'f I don't 'low you to slobber over me like a hog, why, you're gonna do sumpin 'bout it? Why, you're nothin' but a mangy dog and somebody orta shoot you. You think so much about being a h'ard hand. Well, I'll jist tell you sumpin that'll rest yer brain, Mr. Jud. You ain't a h'ard hand fer me no more. You c'n jist pack up yer duds and scoot. Oh, and I even got better idys'n that. You ain't to come on the place again, you hear me? I'll send yer stuff any place you say, but don't you's much 's set foot inside the pasture gate or I'll sic the dogs onto you!

JUD (*standing quite still, absorbed, dark, his voice low*).

Said yer say! Brought it on yerself. (*In a voice harsh with an inner frenzy.*) Cain't he'p it. Cain't never rest. Told you the way it was. You wouldn't listen——

(*He goes out, passes the corner of the house and disappears.* LAUREY *stands a moment, held by his strangeness, then she starts toward the house, changes her mind and sinks onto a bench, a frightened little girl again.*)

LAUREY (*there is a noise off stage.* LAUREY *turns, startled*).

Who's 'at?

WILL (*entering*).

It's me, Laurey. Hey, have you seen Ado Annie? She's gone agin.

(LAUREY *shakes her head.*)

LAUREY (*calling to him as he starts away*).

Will! . . . Will, could you do sumpin fer me? Go and find Curly and tell him I'm here. (CURLY *enters.*) I wanta see Curly awful bad. Got to see him.

CURLY.

Then whyn't you turn around and look, you crazy womern?

LAUREY (*with great relief*).

Curly!

WILL.

Well, you found yours. Now I gotta look fer mine.

(*He exits.*)

CURLY.

Now whut on earth is ailin' the belle of Claremore? By gum, if you ain't cryin'!

(LAUREY *leans against him.*)

LAUREY.

Curly—I'm afraid, 'fraid of my life!

CURLY (*in a flurry of surprise and delight*).

Jumpin' toadstools! (*He puts his arms around* LAUREY, *muttering under his breath.*) Great Lord!

LAUREY.

Don't you leave me. . . .

CURLY.

Great Godamighty!

LAUREY.

Don't mind me a-cryin', I cain't he'p it. . . .

CURLY.

Cry yer eyes out!

LAUREY.

Oh, I don't know whut to do!

CURLY.

Here. I'll show you. (*He lifts her face and kisses her. She puts her arms about his neck.*) My goodness! (*He shakes his head as if coming out of a daze, gives a low whistle, and backs away.*) Whew! 'Bout all a man c'n stand in public! Go 'way from me, *you!*

LAUREY.

Oh, you don't like me, Curly——

CURLY.

Like you? My God! Git away from me, I tell you, plumb away from me! (*He backs away and sits on the stove.*)

LAUREY.

Curly! You're settin' on the stove!

CURLY (*leaping up*).

Godamighty! (*He turns around, puts his hand down gingerly on the lid.*) Aw! 'S cold's a hunk of ice!

LAUREY.

Wisht it ud burnt a hole in yer pants.

CURLY (*grinning at her, understandingly*).

You do, do you?

LAUREY (*turning away to hide her smile*).

You heared me.

CURLY.

Laurey, now looky here, you stand over there right whur you air, and I'll set over here—and you tell me whut you wanted with me.

LAUREY (*grave again*).

Well—Jud was here. (*She shudders.*) He skeered me . . . he's crazy. I never saw nobody like him. He talked wild and he threatened me. So I—I f'ard him! I wisht I hadn'ta! They ain't no tellin' whut he'll do now!

CURLY.

You f'ard him? Well then! That's all they is to it! Tomorrow, I'll get you a new h'ard hand. I'll stay on the place myself tonight, 'f you're nervous about that hound-dog. Now quit yer worryin' about it, er I'll spank you. (*His manner changes. He becomes shy. He turns away, unable to meet her eyes as he asks the question.*) Hey, while I think of it—how —how 'bout marryin' me?

(LAUREY, *confused, turns too. They are back to back.*)

LAUREY.

Gracious, whut'd I wanta marry you fer?

CURLY.

Well, couldn't you mebbe think of some reason why you might?

LAUREY.

I cain't think of none right now, hardly.

CURLY (*following her*).

Laurey, please, ma'am—marry me. I—don't know whut I'm gonna do if you—if you don't.

LAUREY (*touched*).

Curly—why, I'll marry you—'f you want me to. . . .

(*They kiss.*)

CURLY.

I'll be the happiest man alive soon as we're married. Oh, I got to learn to be a farmer, I see that! Quit a-thinkin' about th'owin' the rope, and start in to git my hands blistered a new way! Oh, things is changin' right and left! Buy up mowin' machines, cut down the prairies! Shoe yer horses, drag them plows under the sod! They gonna make a state outa this, they gonna put it in the Union! Country a-changin', got to change with it! Bring up a pair of boys, new stock, to keep up 'th the way things is goin' in this here crazy country! Now I got you to he'p me—I'll 'mount to sumpin yit! Oh, I 'member the first time I ever seen you. It was at the fair. You was a-ridin' that gray filly of Blue Starr's, and I says to someone—"Who's that skinny little thing with a bang down on her forehead?"

LAUREY.

Yeow, I 'member. You was riding broncs that day.

CURLY.

That's right.

LAUREY.

And one of 'em th'owed you.

CURLY.

That's—Did not th'ow me!

LAUREY.

Guess you jumped off, then.

CURLY.

Shore I jumped off.

LAUREY.

Yeow, you shore did.

(*He kisses her.*)

CURLY (*shouting over music*).

Hey! 'F there's anybody out around this yard 'at c'n hear my voice, I'd like fer you to know that Laurey Williams is my girl.

LAUREY.

Curly!

CURLY.

And she's went and got me to ast her to marry me!

LAUREY.

They'll hear you all the way to Catoosie!

CURLY.

Let 'em! (*Singing.*) Let people say we're in love! (*Making a gesture with his arm.*) Who keers whut happens now!

LAUREY (*reaching out, grabbing his hand and putting it back in hers*).

Jist keep your hand in mine.
Your hand feels so grand in mine——

BOTH.

Let people say we're in love!
Starlight looks well on us,
Let the stars beam from above,
Who cares if they tell on us?
Let people say we're in love!

(*The curtains close. In front of curtain, the* PEDDLER *walks on, with* ADO ANNIE.)

PEDDLER.

I'll say good-by here, Baby.

ADO ANNIE.

Cain't y'even stay to drink to Curly and Laurey?

PEDDLER (*shaking his head*).

Time for the lonely gypsy to go back to the open road.

ADO ANNIE.

Wisht I was goin'—nen you wouldn't be so lonely.

PEDDLER.

Look, Ado Annie, there is a man I know who loves you like nothing ever loved nobody.

ADO ANNIE.

Yes, Ali Hakim.

PEDDLER.

A man who will stick to you all your life and be a regular Darby and Jones. And that's the man for you—Will Parker.

ADO ANNIE (*recovering from surprise*).

Oh . . . yeh . . . well, I like Will a lot.

PEDDLER.

He is a fine fellow. Strong like an ox. Young and handsome.

ADO ANNIE.

I love him, all right, I guess.

PEDDLER.

Of course you do! And you love those clear blue eyes of his, and the way his mouth wrinkles up when he smiles——

ADO ANNIE.

Do you love him too?

PEDDLER.

I love him because he will make my Ado Annie happy. (*Taking her in his arms.*) Good-by, my baby. I will show you how we say good-by in Persia.

(*He draws her tenderly to him and plants a long kiss on her lips.*)

ADO ANNIE (*wistfully as he releases her*).

That was good-by?

PEDDLER (*his arms still around her*).

We have an old song in Persia. It says—(*singing*)—one good-by—(*speaking*)—is never enough. (*He kisses her again.* WILL *enters and stands still and stunned. He slowly awakes to action and starts moving toward them, but then the* PEDDLER *starts to talk and* WILL *stops again, surprised even more by what he hears than by what he saw.*) I am glad you will marry such a wonderful man as this Will Parker. You deserve a fine man and you got one.

(WILL *is almost ashamed of his resentment.*)

ADO ANNIE (*seeing* WILL *for the first time*).

Hello, Will. Ali Hakim is sayin' good-by.

PEDDLER.

Ah, Will! I want to say good-by to you, too.

(*Starting to embrace him.*)

WILL.

No, you don't. I just saw the last one.

PEDDLER (*patting* WILL *on the cheek*).

Ah, you were made for each other! (*He pulls* ADO ANNIE *close to him with one arm, and puts the other hand affectionately on* WILL*'s shoulder.*) Be good to her, Will. (*Giving* ADO ANNIE *a squeeze.*) And you be good to him! (*Smiling disarmingly at* WILL.) You don't mind? I am a friend of the family now?

(*He gives* ADO ANNIE *a little kiss.*)

WILL.

Did you say you was goin'?

PEDDLER.

Yes. I must. Back to the open road. A poor gypsy. Good-by, my baby——(*Smiling back at* WILL *before he kisses* ADO ANNIE, *pointing to himself.*) Friend of the family. I show you how we say good-by in my country. (ADO ANNIE *gets set for that old Persian good-by again. The* PEDDLER *finally releases her and turns back to* WILL.) Persian good-by. Lucky fellow! I wish it was me she was marrying instead of you.

WILL.

It don't seem to make no difference hardly.

PEDDLER.

Well, back to the open road, the lonely gypsy.

(*He sings a snatch of the Persian song as he exits.*)

WILL.

You ain't goin' to think of that ole peddler any more, air you?

ADO ANNIE.

'Course not. Never think of no one less'n he's with me.

WILL.

Then I'm never goin' to leave yer side.

ADO ANNIE.

Even if you don't, even if you never go away on a trip er nuthin', cain't you—onct in a while—give me one of them Persian good-bys?

WILL.

Persian good-by? Why, that ain't nuthin' compared to a Oklahoma hello!

(*He wraps her up in his arms and gives her a long kiss. When he lets her go, she looks up, supreme contentment in her voice.*)

ADO ANNIE.

Hello, Will!

BLACKOUT

SCENE III

SCENE: *Back of* LAUREY'S *house. Shouts, cheers and laughter are heard behind the curtain, continuing as it rises.*

CARNES *and* IKE *walk down toward house.* CARNES *carries a lantern.*

IKE.

Well, Andrew, why ain't you back of the barn gettin' drunk with us? Never see you stay so sober at a weddin' party.

CARNES.

Been skeered all night. Skeered 'at Jud Fry ud come up and start for Curly.

IKE.

Why, Jud Fry's been out of the territory for three weeks.

CARNES.

He's back. See him at Claremore last night, drunk as a lord!

(*Crowd starts to pour in.* IKE *and* CARNES, *continuing their conversation, are drowned out by the shouts and laughter of the crowd as they fill the stage.* LAUREY *wears her mother's wedding dress. The following lines are sung.*)

AUNT ELLER.

They couldn't pick a better time to start in life!

IKE.

It ain't too early and it ain't too late.

CURLY.

Startin' as a farmer with a brand-new wife——

LAUREY.

Soon be livin' in a brand-new state!

ALL.

Brand-new state
Gonna treat you great!

FRED.

Gonna give you barley,
Carrots and pertaters——

CORD ELAM.

Pasture for the cattle—

CARNES.

Spinach and termayters!

AUNT ELLER.

Flowers on the prairie where the June bugs zoom——

IKE.

Plen'y of air and plen'y of room——

FRED.

Plen'y of room to swing a rope!

AUNT ELLER.

Plen'y of heart and plen'y of hope. . . .

CURLY.

Oklahoma,
Where the wind comes sweepin' down the plain,
And the wavin' wheat
Can sure smell sweet
When the wind comes right behind the rain.
Oklahoma,
Every night my honey lamb and I
Sit alone and talk
And watch a hawk
Makin' lazy circles in the sky.
We know we belong to the land,
And the land we belong to is grand!
And when we say:
Ee-ee-ow! A-yip-i-o-ee-ay!
We're only sayin',
"You're doin' fine, Oklahoma!
Oklahoma, O.K.!"

(*The full company now joins in a refrain immediately following this one, singing with infectious enthusiasm. A special and stirring vocal arrangement.*)

CURLY (*after number*).

Hey! Y'better hurry into that other dress! Gotta git goin' in a minnit!

AUNT ELLER.

You hurry and pack yer own duds! They're layin' all over my room.

CURLY.

Hey, Will! Would you hitch the team to the surrey fer me?

WILL.

Shore will! Have it up in a jiffy!

(WILL *runs off*. CURLY *exits into house*. CORD ELAM *runs over to door*.

The manner of the group of men that surrounds the door becomes mysterious. Their voices are low and their talk is punctuated with winks and nudges.)

IKE (*to* CORD ELAM).

He's gone upstairs.

CORD ELAM.

Yeah.

(*The girls cross to men, but are shooed away. The men whisper and slip quietly off, except for* CARNES.)

ADO ANNIE.

Whut you goin' to do, Paw? Give Laurey and Curly a shivoree? I wisht you wouldn't.

CARNES.

Aw, it's a good old custom. Never hurt anybody. You women jist keep outa the way. Vamoose!

ADO ANNIE.

It ain't goin' to be rough, is it?

CARNES.

Sh! Stop gabbin' about it!

(CARNES *exits, leaving only women on the stage.*)

ADO ANNIE.

Seems like they's times when men ain't got no need for womern.

SECOND GIRL.

Well, they's times when womern ain't got no need fer men.

ADO ANNIE.

Yeow, but who wants to be dead?

(GERTIE's *well-known laugh is heard off stage.*)

ELLEN.

Gertie!

(GERTIE *enters.*)

ADO ANNIE.

Thought you was in Bushyhead.

GERTIE (*obviously having swallowed a canary*).

Jist come from there.

ELLEN.

Too bad you missed Laurey's wedding.

GERTIE.

Been havin' one of my own.

ELLEN.

Lands! Who'd you marry? Where is he?

ADO ANNIE (*looking off stage*).

Is that him?

GERTIE (*triumphantly*).

That's him!

(*All look off right. The* PEDDLER *enters, dejected, sheepish, dispirited, a ghost of the man he was.*)

ADO ANNIE.

Ali Hakim!

PEDDLER (*in a weak voice*).

Hello. Hello, Ado Annie.

GERTIE.

Did you see my ring, girls?

(*The girls surround* GERTIE *to admire and exclaim. The* PEDDLER *and* ADO ANNIE *are left apart from the group.*)

ADO ANNIE.

How long you been married?

PEDDLER.

Four days. (GERTIE'S *laugh is heard from group. He winces.*) Four days with that laugh should count like a golden wedding.

ADO ANNIE.

But if you married her, you musta wanted to.

PEDDLER.

Sure I wanted to. I wanted to marry her when I saw the moonlight shining on the barrel of her father's shotgun! I thought it would be better to be alive. Now I ain't so sure.

GERTIE (*coming out of group*).

Ali ain't goin' to travel around the country no more. I decided he orta settle down in Bushyhead and run Papa's store.

(WILL *enters.*)

ADO ANNIE.

Hey, Will! D'you hear the news? Gertie married the peddler?

WILL (*to* PEDDLER).

Mighty glad to hear that, peddler man. (*Turning to* GERTIE, *and getting an idea.*) I think I orta kiss the bride. (*He goes toward* GERTIE, *then looks back at* PEDDLER.) Friend of the fambly . . . remember? (*He gives* GERTIE *a big kiss, not realizing that it is* ADO ANNIE *and not the* PEDDLER *he is burning.*) Hey, Gertie, have you ever had a Oklahoma hello?

(*He plants a long one on* GERTIE. ADO ANNIE *pulls her away and stands in her place.* ADO ANNIE *socks* WILL, *then* GERTIE. GERTIE *strikes back.* WILL *comes between them but is beaten off by both of them. Kicking and slugging, the women resume the fight until* GERTIE *retreats, with* ADO ANNIE *close on her heels. The other girls follow.* WILL, *too, is about to go after them when he is called back by the* PEDDLER.)

PEDDLER.

Hey! Where you goin'?

WILL.

I'm goin' to stop Ado Annie from killin' yer wife.

PEDDLER (*grabbing* WILL'S *arm*).

Mind yer own business!

(*He leads* WILL *off. The stage is empty and quiet. A man sneaks on, then another, then more. Cautiously they advance on the house. One of the more agile climbs up a trellis and looks in the window of the second floor. He suppresses a laugh, leans down and reports to the others. There are suppressed giggles and snorts. He takes another peek, then comes down and whispers to them. The joke is passed from one to the other; they are doubled up with laughter. At a signal from one, they all start to pound on tinpans with spoons and set up a terrific din.)*

AUNT ELLER *(coming to the window with a lamp in her hand).*

Whut you doin' down there, makin' all thet racket, you bunch o' pig-stealers?

FRED *(shouting up).*

Come on down peaceable, Laurey sugar!

IKE.

And you, too, you curly-headed cowboy.

CORD ELAM.

With the dimple on yer chin!

IKE.

Come on, fellers, let's git 'em down!

(Three of the men run into the house. Those outside toss up rag dolls.)

MEN.

Hey, Laurey! Here's a girl baby fer you!
And here's a baby boy!
Here's twins!

*(*CURLY *is pulled from the house and hoisted on the shoulders of his friends.* LAUREY *and* AUNT ELLER *come out of the house. All are in high spirits. It is a good-natured hazing. Now* JUD *enters. Everyone becomes quiet and still, sensing trouble.)*

JUD.

Weddin' party still goin' on? Glad I ain't too late. Got a present fer the groom. But first I wanta kiss the bride. *(He grabs* LAUREY. CURLY *pulls him off.)* An' here's my present fer you!

(He socks CURLY. *The fight starts, with the crowd moving around the two men.* JUD *pulls out a knife and goes for* CURLY. CURLY *grabs his arm and succeeds in throwing him.* JUD *falls on his knife, groans and lies still. The crowd surges toward his motionless body.)*

CURLY.

Look—Look at him! Fell on his own knife.

(He backs away, shaken, limp. Some of the men bend over the prostrate form.)

MEN.

Whut's the matter?
Don't you tetch it!
Turn him over—
He's breathin', ain't he?
Feel his heart.
How'd it happen?

FRED.

Whut'll we do? Ain't he all right?

SLIM.

'S he jist stunned?

CORD ELAM.

Git away, some of you. Let me look at him.

(He bends down, the men crowding around. The women, huddled to-

gether, look on, struck with horror. CURLY *has slumped back away from the crowd like a sick man.* LAUREY *looks at* CURLY, *dazed, a question in her eyes.)*

LAUREY.

Curly—is he——?

CURLY.

Don't say anythin'.

LAUREY.

It cain't be that-a-way.

CURLY.

I didn't *go* to.

LAUREY.

Cain't be! Like that—to happen to us.

CORD ELAM *(getting up)*.

Cain't do a thing now. Try to get him to a doctor, but I don't know——

MAN.

Here, some of you, carry him over to my rig. I'll drive him over to Doctor Tyler's.

CORD ELAM.

Quick! I'm 'fraid it's too late.

(The men lift JUD *up.)*

MEN.

Handle him easy!
Don't shake him!
Hold on to him, careful there!

(A woman points to JUD, *being carried off.* IKE *and his companions run up and exit with the other men.)*

CURLY *(to* LAUREY *and* AUNT ELLER*)*.

I got to go see if there's anythin' c'n be done fer him. *(He kisses* LAUREY.*)* Take keer of her, Aunt Eller.

(He exits.)

AUNT ELLER.

Mebbe it's better fer you and Curly not to go 'way tonight.

(She breaks off, realizing how feeble this must sound.)

LAUREY *(as if she hadn't heard* AUNT ELLER*)*.

I don't see why this had to happen, when everythin' was so fine.

AUNT ELLER.

Don't let yer mind run on it.

LAUREY.

Cain't fergit, I tell you. Never will!

AUNT ELLER.

'At's all right, Laurey baby. If you cain't fergit, jist don't try to, honey. Oh, lots of things happens to folks. Sickness, er bein' pore and hungry even—bein' old and afeared to die. That's the way it is—cradle to grave. And you can stand it. They's one way. You gotta be hearty, you got to be. You cain't deserve the sweet and tender things in life less'n you're tough.

LAUREY.

I—I wisht I was the way you are.

AUNT ELLER.

Fiddlesticks! Scrawny and old? You couldn't h'ar me to be the way I am!

(LAUREY *laughs through her tears.*)

LAUREY.

Oh, whut ud I do 'thout you, you're sich a crazy!

AUNT ELLER (*hugging* LAUREY).

Shore's you're borned!

(*She breaks off as* CURLY *enters with* CORD ELAM, CARNES *and a few others. Their manner is sober. Some of the women come out of the house to hear what the men have to say.*)

CORD ELAM.

They're takin' Jud over to Dave Tyler's till the mornin'.

AUNT ELLER.

Is he—alive?

(CORD ELAM *shakes his head.*)

CURLY.

Laurey honey, Cord Elam here, he's a Fed'ral Marshal, y'know. And he thinks I orta give myself up—Tonight, he thinks.

LAUREY.

Tonight!

AUNT ELLER.

Why, yer train leaves Claremore in twenty minutes.

CORD ELAM.

Best thing is fer Curly to go of his own accord and tell the Judge.

AUNT ELLER (*to* CARNES).

Why, you're the Judge, ain't you, Andrew?

CARNES.

Yes, but——

LAUREY (*urging* CURLY *forward*).

Well, tell him now and git it over with.

CORD ELAM.

'T wouldn't be proper. You have to do it in court.

AUNT ELLER.

Oh, fiddlesticks. Le's do it here and say we did it in court.

CORD ELAM.

We can't do that. That's breaking the law.

AUNT ELLER.

Well, le's not break the law. Le's just bend it a little. C'mon, Andrew, and start the trial. We ain't got but a few minnits.

CORD ELAM.

Andrew—I got to protest.

CARNES.

Oh, shet yer trap. We can give the boy a fair trial without lockin' him up on his weddin' night! Here's the long and short of it. First I got to ask you: Whut's your plea? (CURLY *doesn't answer.* CARNES *prompts him.*) 'At means why did you do it?

CURLY.

Why'd I do it? Cuz he'd been pesterin' Laurey and I always said some day I'd——

CARNES.

Jist a minnit! Jist a minnit! Don't let yer tongue wobble around in yer mouth like 'at. Listen to my question. Whut happened tonight 'at made you kill him?

CURLY.

Why, he come at me with a knife and—and——

CARNES.

And you had to defend yerself, didn't you?

CURLY.

Why, yes—and furthermore . . .

CARNES.

Never mind the furthermores—the plea is self-defense—(*The women start to chatter.*) Quiet! . . . Now is there a witness who saw this happen?

MEN (*all at once*).

I seen it.
Shore did.
Self-defense all right.
Tried to stab him 'th a frog-sticker.

CORD ELAM (*shaking his head*).

Feel funny about it. Feel funny.

AUNT ELLER.

And you'll feel funny when I tell yer wife you're carryin' on 'th another womern, won't you?

CORD ELAM.

I ain't carryin' on 'th no one.

AUNT ELLER.

Mebbe not, but you'll shore feel funny when I tell yer *wife* you air.

(*Boisterous laughter.*)

CORD ELAM.

Laugh all you like, but as a Fed'ral Marshal——

SKIDMORE.

Oh, shet up about bein' a marshal! We ain't goin' to let you send the boy to jail on his weddin' night. We just ain't goin' to *let* you. So shet up!

(*This firm and conclusive statement is cheered and applauded.*)

SLIM.

C'mon, fellers! Let's pull them to their train in Curly's surrey! We'll be the horses.

CARNES.

Hey, wait! I ain't even told the verdick yet!

(*Everything stops still at this unpleasant reminder.*)

CURLY.

Well—the verdick's not guilty, ain't it?

CARNES.

'Course, but . . .

LAUREY.

Well, then *say* it!

(CARNES *starts, but the crowd drowns him out.*)

ALL.

Not guilty!

(CURLY *and* LAUREY *run into the house. The rest run out toward the stable.* CARNES *is left downstage without a court.*)

CARNES.

Court's adjourned!

(CARNES *joins* AUNT ELLER, *who has sat down to rest, after all this excitement.* ADO ANNIE *and* WILL *enter, holding hands soulfully.* ADO ANNIE'S *hair is mussed, and a contented look graces her face.*)

AUNT ELLER.

Why, Ado Annie, where on earth you been?

ADO ANNIE.

Will and me had a misunderstandin'. But he explained it fine.

(ADO ANNIE *and* WILL *go upstage and now tell-tale wisps of straw are seen clinging to* ADO ANNIE'S *back. Amid shouts and laughter, the surrey is pulled on.*)

IKE.

Hey, there, bride and groom, y'ready?

CURLY (*running out of the house with* LAUREY).

Here we come!

(*The crowd starts to sing lustily, "Oh, What a Beautiful Mornin'."* LAUREY *runs over and kisses* AUNT ELLER. *Then she is lifted up alongside* CURLY. AUNT ELLER *and three girls start to cry. Everyone else sings gaily and loudly.*)

ALL.

Oh, what a beautiful day!

(*The men start to pull off the surrey. Everybody waves and shouts.* CURLY *and* LAUREY *wave back.*)

CURTAIN

BIOGRAPHICAL NOTES

FRANK BACON (coauthor of *Lightnin'*), was born in Marysville, California, January 16, 1864. He had an eventful career from the time of leaving school at the age of fourteen, being a sheepherder, photographer, newspaper writer, and a candidate for the California Legislature. In 1890 he joined a California stock company and during the next few years acted in more than six hundred roles. After a short experience in a stock company in Oregon, he reached New York via the vaudeville route. He was tremendously popular among the stage folk and when he got the opportunity of collaborating with Winchell Smith in the play *Lightnin'* in 1918, which was to prove his starring vehicle for the few remaining years of his life, his success was hailed throughout the profession. After four years of almost constant playing of the famous role of Bill Jones, he died in harness in Chicago on November 19, 1922.

DION BOUCICAULT, author of *Rip Van Winkle,* is really the adapter rather than the author, who of course must be considered to have been Washington Irving. There were numerous adaptations of the story, but the one that Joe Jefferson made his starring vehicle was fashioned expressly for Jefferson by Boucicault. He was born in Dublin on December 26, 1822, the son of a French refugee and Irish mother. He is particularly famous for his play *London Assurance.* He toured America from 1863 to 1869, and was extremely popular in various roles. His greatest reputation as an actor, however, was probably achieved some years later, in 1875, when he played the leading role in *The Shaughraum.* The feeling that this country had for him he must have reciprocated, as after many visits here he finally made New York his permanent home and died there in September 1890.

ERSKINE CALDWELL, author of *Tobacco Road,* was born in White Oak, Georgia, December 21, 1902. After a public-school education he attended Erskine College, South Carolina University, and the University of Pennsylvania. Upon graduation he became a stagehand, a professional football player, a newspaper writer, a lecturer, and an editor. In the field of writing he introduced an original and forceful style of his own, and in 1933 received the recognition of the Yale Review Award for fiction. His second wife was Margaret Bourke-White, the famous photographer, and he wrote several books in collaboration with her. *Tobacco Road* (the dramatization by Jack Kirkland of one of his stories), when it was first produced, received but slight critical acclaim. It proved, however, to have been precisely what the public wanted, for it had a record stretch of seven and a half unbroken years on Broadway.

RUSSEL CROUSE, coauthor of *Life with Father,* was born in Findlay, Ohio, February 20, 1893. He left school to become a newspaper reporter on Cincinnati and Kansas City papers, and was still a journalist upon his arrival in New York some years later. He was conducting a column in the *Evening Post* when he wrote his first play. He has always proved a most successful collaborator and has tried his hand at various types of drama, including musical comedy. Crouse and Corey Ford wrote several successes together, but nothing to equal the fabulous products of Crouse and Lindsay, Inc. The two are virtually inseparable today, equally beloved by everybody in show business.

ADOLPHE D'ENNERY, author of *The Two Orphans,* was born in 1811 in Paris, and achieved considerable fame as a prominent French dramatist during the eighty-eight years of his life. In addition to numerous novels he authored some two hundred plays, the first, *Emile,* being produced when he was twenty years old. He was a frequent collaborator, and in the case of his most famous play his fellow worker was Eugene Cormon about whom little record survives. Although *The Two Orphans* is chiefly responsible for his fame in this country, he is probably better known abroad for his libretto for Massenet's *Le Cid,* and possibly better known than *Les Deux Orphelines* were two other of his plays, *Marie Jeanne,* produced in 1845, and *Michael Strogoff,* which first appeared in 1883.

OSCAR HAMMERSTEIN, II, coauthor of *Oklahoma!,* son of the late William Hammerstein and grandson of the famous opera impresario, was born in July 1895. He attended Columbia University and while there tested out his powers of versification and sense of the theater in numerous undergraduate shows. His real gift was immediately apparent and he became much in demand as the librettist for operettas and musical comedies. His name has been associated with an extraordinary number of outstanding successes; notably *Rose Marie, The Desert Song, Show Boat, New Moon,* and finally the miraculous success *Oklahoma!* For this last achievement, he and Richard Rodgers received a special award from the Pulitzer Prize committee in May of this year. His versatility is indicated not only by the extraordinary range of his dramatic instinct, but also by the fact that each of these outstanding productions was written in collaboration with a different composer. He is very rightly considered today one of the foremost librettists of all time.

AVERY HOPWOOD, coauthor of *The Bat,* was born in Cleveland, Ohio, in 1882. He graduated from the University of Michigan in 1905 and, like so many other playwrights, got his writing experience as a newspaperman with the Cleveland *Leader*. A year later he sold his first play, *Clothes,* which was written in collaboration with Channing Pollock. He was a prolific writer and adapted many of his farces in which he specialized from French prototypes. Probably the most successful of these were *Fair and Warmer* and *The Gold-Diggers.* His plays had universal appeal and were staged all over the world. He traveled extensively abroad, and it was at Nice, France, in 1928, that his life came to an untimely end by drowning.

JOSEPH KESSELRING, author of *Arsenic and Old Lace,* was born in New York in 1902. He seemed to have been destined for the opera rather than the dramatic stage, for he started out as a choirboy at the age of seven and became famous as a boy soprano; he once appeared in a joint recital with Madame Schumann-Heink. Apparently with the change of his voice his ambition to go into opera unfortunately seems to have been thwarted. He had not, however, given up his musical career entirely, for after a brief period of teaching at Bethel College in Newton, Kansas, he became a teacher of music at Lake Placid. A short career as an actor interested him in becoming a playwright. His first two attempts, *There's Wisdom in Women* in 1935 and *Cross Town* in 1937, were not successful, but with *Arsenic and Old Lace*—which, incidentally, first had the far inferior title *Bodies in Our Cellar*—he insured the perpetuation of his name in the annals of the stage.

HOWARD LINDSAY, coauthor of *Life with Father,* was born in Waterford, New York, March 29, 1889. He was educated at Boston Latin School and Harvard University, and almost immediately turned his attention to things dramatic. He appeared in the early silent pictures, vaudeville, and burlesque. He joined the company of Margaret Anglin in 1913 and stayed with her for over five years, when he joined the Army during World War I. At the close of the war he returned to the drama, supplementing his experience in stage managing and acting with writing and producing. All his work proved enormously successful, but in no case have his talents been so happily expressed as in his performance in *Life with Father,* in which his acting perfectly expresses what he himself has brilliantly written. The costar of *Life with Father,* incidentally, Miss Dorothy Stickney, in private life is Mrs. Howard Lindsay.

J. HARTLEY MANNERS, author of *Peg o' My Heart,* was born in London of Irish parentage August 10, 1870. He began his acting career in Australia in 1898. He was successful in many roles, and ultimately became a member of Sir Johnston Forbes-Robertson's company at the Imperial Theatre in London. He subsequently came to this country, and in 1912 he married Laurette (Cooney) Taylor and immediately brought her prominence with the writing of *Peg o' My Heart* in which she starred during that same year. The play was phenomenally successful and lasted for six hundred consecutive performances in New York, and served as a breadwinner for five road companies that toured for several seasons throughout the country. Although this was by far the most famous of his plays, he wrote many others, including *The Crossways* written for Mrs. Langtry, *The Girl in Waiting, Happiness,* and finally *The National Anthem,* his last production before his death in 1928.

ANNE NICHOLS, author of *Abie's Irish Rose,* is a native of Georgia. At sixteen she went to New York filled with ambition to become an actress. She got a few small parts and did some work in vaudeville, but soon found her talent lay in writing for the theater rather than in acting. She was successful as a collaborator and an individual playwright. *Heart's Desire, Linger Longer Letty,* and *Just Married* were among the hits that bore her name. When *Abie's Irish Rose* was first produced she was already represented on Broadway with other plays. Her record with her greatest success, however, so far outshadowed any other that these are likely to be forgotten. After a very slow start, in which the play was nearly taken off the boards, *Abie* picked up public following and was sent off for its record-breaking run of 2,532 performances. It has been played in practically every country in the world and in many languages. To this day it is one of the most popular radio programs from coast to coast.

MARY ROBERTS RINEHART, coauthor of *The Bat,* one of America's best-known women writers, was born in Pittsburgh August 12, 1876. Her entire life has been devoted to writing and travel, and the scope of her literary activities has been astonishing. Although she has probably achieved her highest degree of fame through her books—the better known of which perhaps are in the field of detective fiction—she has been a prolific playwright. One of her first great successes was the farce *Seven Days,* which she also wrote in collaboration with Avery Hopwood. Mrs. Rinehart has received public recognition of her genius in the field of letters by the bestowal of the degree of Litt.D. from the George Washington University in 1923. She makes her home in Washington and remains active in the publishing field in which she has particular interest through her son, who is president of the successful house of Farrar & Rinehart.

RICHARD RODGERS, coauthor of *Oklahoma!,* was born in New York in 1902 and attended Columbia University. His interest has always been in music, which he studied at the Institute of Musical Arts, principally concerning himself with theory and harmony. His name first became famous on Broadway through his collaboration with Lorenz Hart in creating *The Garrick Gaieties,* which in 1925 set a new standard for intelligent musical comedy. Since then he has become an increasingly successful composer of popular music, having written *A Connecticut Yankee* in 1927, *Heads Up* in 1929, *On Your Toes* in 1936, and *I Married an Angel* and *The Boys from Syracuse* in 1938. For a time he composed music for the films, and he has experimented in many other branches of his profession. Recently he wrote the ballet *Ghost Town* which was successfully performed by the Ballet Russe de Monte Carlo. His collaboration with Hammerstein in the production of *Oklahoma!* has resulted in what many believe to be the perfect American musical comedy. In place of their usual award for the best play of the year, the Pulitzer Prize committee made a special award to both collaborators for their work on *Oklahoma!*

BOOTH TARKINGTON, coauthor of *The Man from Home,* has been a popular figure in American letters for many years. He was born in Indianapolis July 29, 1869, and received his education at Phillips Exeter Academy, Purdue University, and Princeton. He has received honorary degrees from Princeton, De Pauw University, and Columbia. He has twice been awarded the Pulitzer Prize for literature, and in 1933 received the gold medal of the National Institute of Arts and Sciences. Although his chief fame undoubtedly rests with his novels, which include such diverse but equally famous characters as Monsieur Beaucaire and Penrod, he did considerable writing for the stage—chiefly the dramatization of some of his own stories. At seventy-five he is still an active writer. For many years he has made his home in Kennebunkport, Maine, and, aided in recent years by Kenneth Roberts, has brought literary distinction to that agreeable hamlet.

DENMAN THOMPSON, author of *The Old Homestead,* was born October 15, 1833, near Girard, Pennsylvania. He moved to Boston when he was seventeen years old, and immediately sought employment in the theater. He was never particularly prominent in his early years and played very minor roles with a number of traveling groups. He received a considerable portion of his experience with the Royal Lyceum Company in Toronto, but never proved particularly successful until he began writing his own material. In 1875 he put together a loosely-knit sketch of rural Yankee types with whom he had become familiar during his road-show travels, and finally expanded the idea into a full-length comedy called *Joshua Whitcomb.* This he subsequently developed into a four-act play with the now familiar title of *The Old Homestead.* In acting the principal part of this extremely homespun drama Thompson achieved immediate success. His gratification was such that he never experimented further, but acted exclusively in this vehicle almost to the time of his death at the ripe age of seventy-eight on April 14, 1911.

WINCHELL SMITH, coauthor of *Lightnin',* was born April 5, 1871, and was educated in the Hartford public schools. His interest in the theater began early in life, and he studied acting at the Lyceum Theatre school. He was connected with Arnold Daly in producing for the first time in this country the plays of George Bernard Shaw, and his activities and enthusiasm contributed largely toward starting the Shaw vogue in America. He soon gave up acting and confined his work to that of dramatics and director. He was very successful as a collaborator, and was much in demand as a "play doctor." He was particularly adept in the field of comedy, and for many years was identified one way or another with an astonishing number of Broadway successes. He died on June 10, 1933.

HARRIET BEECHER STOWE, author of *Uncle Tom's Cabin,* was the daughter of Lyman Beecher, the most distinguished Congregational minister of his time. She was born June 14, 1811, and received her education at the Hartford Female Seminary. When her father became head of Lane Seminary in Cincinnati, she moved to that city. There she met and married C. E. Stowe, one of her father's assistants. She was always greatly concerned with sociological topics, and *Uncle Tom's Cabin* first appeared in the anti-slavery paper *National Era* in 1851, almost a decade prior to the Civil War with which her famous book has always been so closely identified. So great was the success of this unique novel that it not only created a profound impression throughout this nation but was immediately taken up in foreign countries as well. It was translated into more than twenty languages and is still recognized as one of the most famous books of the century. Mrs. Stowe herself apparently had little to do with the dramatization of her novel and there have been many versions since it was first produced in 1853, and many liberties have been taken with her story. Probably one of its most successful adaptations was that made by A. E. Thomas and based on an earlier version by George L. Aiken which the Players' Club used for a brilliant revival in 1933, and is the text which appears in this volume. Mrs. Stowe was greatly affected by the death of her husband in 1886 and her brother Henry Ward Beecher who died soon after. Her health was severely undermined, and it was in a state of almost complete seclusion that she died ten years later, on July 1, 1896.

ELLEN (MRS. HENRY) WOOD, author of *East Lynne,* was born in Worcester, England, January 17, 1813. She suffered all her life from curvature of the spine and most of her novels were written in a wheel chair. Her earlier writings were almost all magazine articles, but shortly after her marriage, in 1856, she began writing more lengthy fiction. Her first novel, *Danesbury House,* was written in 1860. The following year *East Lynne* was published by Bentley. Several publishers had previously rejected it, and it had a very indifferent reception. It was not until an enthusiastic review appeared in the *Times* in 1862 that it attained any popularity, but its fame grew rapidly thereafter. It was translated into most of the European languages and several oriental, and undoubtedly was the most prominent novel of its time. Mrs. Wood wrote a great many other novels, mostly about the lower middle class of England, but none of them have left any very great mark on literature. The first dramatization of her most famous book was produced in 1864 under the title of *The Marriage Bells, or The Cottage on the Cliff,* and the book has been dramatized and adapted by various writers under various titles. The records show a performance in this country as early as 1863 which seems to antedate what is usually thought to be the initial production in England. Mrs. Wood died at the age of seventy-three in England, September 10, 1887.

These biographical notes were written in the summer of 1944. As revisions become necessary, they will be made in future editions.

THE EDITORS